The Big Book of Superfast Matchbox® Toys: 1969-2004

I0817487

Volume 1: Basic Models and Variation Lists

Charlie Mack

4880 Lower Valley Road, Atglen, PA 19310 USA

Acknowledgments

Special thanks to Christian Falkensteiner for his dedication to the hobby. His grateful assistance is much appreciated for his proofreading skills and additional material added to this massive volume of information including his frame number additions and cross reference charts. Thanks again to Frank Veres for his wonderful photography and to Bob Parker for his assistance during many hours of photography. Some models on loan from the collection of Tom Wiczkowicz.

Dedication

This book is dedicated to the memories of three great collectors who have helped me immensely over the years with my collection- Harley Flaws, Pasquale "Pat" Lamagna and Neil Waldmann.

Copyright © 2005 by Charlie Mack
Library of Congress Control Number: 2005925873

All rights reserved. No part of this work may be reproduced or used in any form or by any means—graphic, electronic, or mechanical, including photocopying or information storage and retrieval systems—without written permission from the publisher.

The scanning, uploading and distribution of this book or any part thereof via the Internet or via any other means without the permission of the publisher is illegal and punishable by law. Please purchase only authorized editions and do not participate in or encourage the electronic piracy of copyrighted materials.

"Schiffer," "Schiffer Publishing Ltd. & Design," and the "Design of pen and ink well" are registered trademarks of Schiffer Publishing Ltd.

Designed by Joseph M. Riggio Jr.
Type set in Zurich BT

ISBN: 0-7643-2321-0
Printed in China

Published by Schiffer Publishing Ltd.
4880 Lower Valley Road
Atglen, PA 19310
Phone: (610) 593-1777; Fax: (610) 593-2002
E-mail: Info@schifferbooks.com

For the largest selection of fine reference books on this and related subjects, please visit our web site at
www.schifferbooks.com
We are always looking for people to write books on new and related subjects. If you have an idea for a book please contact us at the above address.

This book may be purchased from the publisher.
Include $3.95 for shipping.
Please try your bookstore first.
You may write for a free catalog.

In Europe, Schiffer books are distributed by
Bushwood Books
6 Marksbury Ave.
Kew Gardens
Surrey TW9 4JF England
Phone: 44 (0) 20 8392-8585; Fax: 44 (0) 20 8392-9876
E-mail: info@bushwoodbooks.co.uk
Free postage in the U.K., Europe; air mail at cost.

Contents

Volume 1

Volume 2

Superfast/Miniatures

When Mattel introduced their Hot Wheels series, Lesney Products had to revamp their entire 1-75 line to have frictionless wheels. These models were introduced in mid-1969 as the "Superfast" series. The name "Superfast" was used to describe the 1-75 series until 1980, when the 1-75 line was simply termed "Miniatures." Early models were denoted as SF and later MB, but for the sake of conformity, all 1-75 models made from mid-1969 onwards will be denoted with the "MB" designation. The sequencing of models will begin again with the letter "A," rather than to continue with the lettering sequence from the Regular Wheels.

Many miniatures in post-1969 were not available as single releases or were issued as limited editions or in special sets. By 1982, the miniature range began to diversify in such a manner that models in the standard range were modified or issued in specialized miniature categories. These special ranges are denoted with prefixes and are based on the charting below. Certain models were only sold in certain countries and a special notation also notes these.

This two volume set adds frame numbers, also known as manufacturing (MAN) numbers to all post 1982 castings. These are three digit numbers cast inside a model casting to identify any given model at the factory. This will appear as an "MB" number in the heading of the given model. Certain models that were never introduced into the standard line only exist with these MAN numbers for identification and are listed after the standard models past #99.

Promotionals

AU–Australia
AS–Austria
BE–Belgium
BR–Brazil (Manaus)
CHI–China
CN–Canada
CZ–Czech Republic
DK–Denmark
DU–Dutch (Holland)
FR–French
GK–Greece
GR–Germany
HK–Hong Kong
HU–Hungary
IR–Ireland
IT–Italy
JP–Japan
MX–Mexico
SA–South Africa
SC–Scotland
SD–Sweden
SK–Slovakia
SP–Spain
SU–Saudi Arabia
SW–Switzerland
UK–United Kingdom
US–United States
WL–Wales

Sub–Category Listings

AM–Across America
AP–Action Pack/ Adventure Pack
AS–Action System Pack
ASAP–Short Run Premiums
AV–Adventure 2000
AW–Around the World
BS–Brroomstick
C2–Code 2
CA–cartoon series
CC–Collectors Choice
CCI–Color Comp
CG–Car Go Set
CH–75 Challenge
CK–Coke singles
CL–Collectibles
CM–Commando
CR–Code Red
CRO–Crocodile Hunter
CP–Corvette Premieres
CT–Caterpillar
CY–Convoy
DM–Dream Machines
DR–DARE series
DT–Days of Thunder
DY–Dinky
EG–Target Eggmobiles 3 pack
EL–Elvis Presley Collection
EM–Emergency Packs
FE–First Edition
F1–Formula 1
FA–Fisher Art set
FC–Feature Car
FM–Farming Series
GC–Gold Collection
GS–Gift Set
GF–Graffic Traffic
GW–Gift Ware
HD–Harley–Davidson
HR–Heroes
HS–Hot Stocks
IC–Intercom City
IN–Indy 500
IG–Inaugural
JB–James Bond
JC–JC Penney
JL–Justice League
JR–Jurassic Park
KB–Kaybee Toys exclusive
KP–King–Size Special
KS–King–Size
LD–Limited Run
LE–Limited Edition
LL–Live N Learn (preschool)
LP–Launcher 5 pack
LS–Light & Sound
LT–Lightning Wheels
LW–Laser Wheels
MB–Micro Brewery (sets 4 on)
MB1–3–Micro Brewery
MC–Motor City
MCC–My Classic Car
MN–Nigel Mansell
MP–Multi Pack
MT–Matchcaps
MU–Masters of The Universe
MW–Mattel Wheels 1998 onward model no.
NBA–National Basketball League
NM–Nutmeg promotional
OP–On pack offer
OS–Osbournes
PB–Pleasant books
PC1–22–Premiere Collection
PL–Parlor City Collectibles
PS–Play set
PZ–puzzle models
RB–Road Blasters
RN–Roman Numeral
RT–Real Talkin'
SB–Skybuster
SC–Super Color Changer
SC1–5 Select Class
SoC–Stars of Cars
SH–Showcase
SF–Superfast
SG–Stars of Germany
SNL–Saturday Night Live

SP–Sports Pack
SR–Siren Force/Rescue 911
SS–Show Stoppers
ST–Super Trucks
STR–Star Car
TC–Team Convoy
TH–Triple Heat
TM–Team Matchbox
TN–Then & Now
TP–Two Pack
TRU–Toys R Us
UC–Ultra Class
VG–Vegas models
WB–Warner Bros.
WC–World Class
WP–Whales Project
WR–White Rose Collectibles
YST–Collectibles Train Set
5pk–Five Pack
20pk–Twenty Pack

The earliest subdivision of miniatures was from gift sets. This idea developed from the late 1950s and continues today. It took years for the miniatures to break into a new sub category. One of the first was the Brroomstick series issued in 1970. An orange plastic handle had string attached in which a sticker could be adhered to the front of the model, so as to "drive" the model by string power.

In 1978, Lesney Products took ten models from the standard range including discontinued molds and reissued them in new colors with new names with Roman numerals on the baseplates. Some tough-to-find variations include crossover baseplates from the standard range.

In 1981, Lesney Products received a television license for Code Red in which seven miniatures and one Skybuster were issued in special colors and packaging.

In 1983, Matchbox introduced two models at the Dodge Las Vegas convention. There were only five thousand models of the Dodge Caravan and Dodge Daytona made with sealed castings, therefore no opening parts. The models were retooled to have opening parts and put into the standard line. One thousand of the special Vegas models were put on a signed plinth. The remaining four thousand were placed in special boxes.

The name "Superfast" was originally introduced in 1969 by Lesney Products to counter the marketing of Mattel's Hot Wheels. By 1980, this name was gradually phased out. The Superfast name was reborn in 1986 with twenty-five selected miniatures with specially designed, low-friction wheels and new twenty-four spoke wheel hubs. These were for the United States market only. In 1987, a similar set of models was issued worldwide which was called "Laser Wheels". The wheel hubs featured an iridescent design.

Roadblasters were introduced in 1987. These miniatures featured clip-on armament to make them into battle machines. Some models even had the main casting modified including windows replaced by battle ornamentation. The series included twelve Turbo Force "good guys" and twelve Motor Lord "bad guys."

In 1988, Matchbox Toys acquired the Dinky trademark. As no new castings were made, six miniatures were re-colored and placed on Dinky blistercards so as not to lose the licensed trademark.

In 1989, Super Color Changers were introduced. These models changed color when exposed to changes in temperature, namely by dipping the model in water. The Skybuster series also included color changing.

Also in 1989, the World Class series debuted at more than twice the price of a standard miniature. The models featured gray wheels with rubber tires and chrome windows. The series was dropped in 1993 in favor of the Premiere Collection.

A series of army vehicles was introduced in 1989 in the United States called Commando. These include Strike Team "good guys" and Dagger Force "bad guys." Two Convoys were included in the series.

In 1990, Matchbox introduced a preschool range from the Live 'N Learn series. The models were done in primary colors with preschool decorations and wheels to match. Lasertronics, termed Siren Force in the United States, were also introduced in 1990. Twelve selected models (four castings in three liveries each) featured press-down front axles, which activated working lights and sirens. The series was resurrected in 1991 for the "Rescue 911" TV series and again in 1996 for the Action System Light & Sound series.

Car & Driver series was a flop in 1990 as twelve cars, although issued with trading cards, were never produced in special colors. To commemorate the release of the Paramount Pictures "Days of Thunder," Matchbox introduced miniatures, Convoys, and Team Matchbox in 1990.

The debut of Lightning Wheels was in 1991. These "fastest cars on the market" featured bright colors with specially designed axles to feature extra speed on the track. The wheel hubs even featured lightning bolts.

Also in 1991, a series of all-white models called Graffic Traffic was introduced. Each model came in two and three packs and was issued with sets of water resistant marking pens and label sheets, so children could make and decorate their own special model. Of course, decorating these yourself puts the value to "zero" on the collectors market! Action Packs also were introduced in 1991. The models included extra play accessories with a specially colored variation.

To commemorate the seventy-fifth anniversary of the Indianapolis 500, Matchbox introduced its Indy 500 in 1991. The seventy-sixth and seventy-seventh Indys also received special attention until the line ended for 1993.

Hot Stocks, similar to Action Packs, were released in 1992. The series included only six pieces–all Chevy Luminas. Triple Heat debuted in 1992. The set of six included a three pack of a miniature, a Superfast Mini and a World's Smallest.

The Harley-Davidson series included miniatures, Superking, Convoy, and large plastic motorcycles. The range, introduced in 1992, runs through 1996.

The final 1992 release was Intercom City. The highly revolutionary idea features electronic bar codes on the bases of the models. When the bar code runs over another bar code on the play environment, it sets up a play in which spoken messages are given and in turn further play is continued as suggested by the message.

Showstoppers were introduced in 1993. Called Motor Show in Europe, the series paired manufacturer models with a mirror display stand. Super Trucks also debuted. Like the Hot Stocks series, this time with six trucks. A farming series was issued in 1993, which included retooled models along with newly cast trailers.

Licenses for Formula 1 and Nigel Mansell race teams were introduced in 1994. Collector's Choice also debuted in which twenty-four vehicles were realistically painted for more "collectible" appeal.

In 1994, Matchbox in the United Kingdom decided to offer very short-run promotionals on a selected set of models. As few as three- to five-hundred models could be specially ordered using "blanks" sent from the Orient and these were tampo printed in England. A similar program was set up in the United States in 1996 with a private company called ASAP in which as few as one hundred and forty-four models could be ordered. These are Code 2 releases, and due to tight controls by Tyco, none have been released to the collectors market and no one knows what exists outside the company doing the printing. Twelve all-white models were used.

The year 1996 saw the release of the much-heralded Premiere Collection. Similar to World Class but better, the models still had rubber tires but featured chrome wheels and normal clear windows. This was extended upon in late 1996 with the Gold Collection, a five-thousand piece premiere edition issued with a gold coin.

Matchbox Collectibles, normally associated with the Yesteryear and Dinky range, issued special miniatures with two different train sets as well as a Micro Brewery set in 1996.

Although listed as a 1997 edition on the package, the 75 Challenge cars were released by November 1996. All seventy-five of the 1997 range were available as a ten-thousand-piece run in metallic gold and issued with a collector box. These were mixed in with standard release models.

By 1997, Mattel started into many licenses both in Collectible and five pack categories. These include issues from Barrett-Jackson, Coca Cola and My Classic Car and ventured into character themed series such as Spongebob Squarepants, Peanuts and Clifford the Big Red Dog amongst many others.

In 2000, Mattel started a logo hunt in which all 100 cars from that year also featured "Matchbox 2000" logos somewhere on the vehicle. In 2002, this was done again with "Matchbox 50th" anniversary logos. Very few collectors have completed this set of 75 models as a handful of models were dispersed in odd areas such as Chile and Mexico making it virtually impossible to finish the set. This continued into 2003 with Mattel offering "Hero City" logos in both the US and ROW ranges. Again, a small portion of these has been hard to find disappointing many collectors.

The reintroduction of Superfast to mark the 35th anniversary of the brand was issued in mid 2004. These models include four recreations of old 1970's Superfast models using current molds in both original and new color schemes. These are packaged with recreated boxes in unique blistercards. Most numbers were released in time to include in this book's written section but the last "wave" is not included in the photographic section. The series will be on-going through 2005.

Ultra Heroes, a series of imaginative "creature" vehicles made up 30 of the 75 models in 2004. This series of models were very poor sellers and the last round ended up sold only in a 20 pack exclusively to Toys R Us. The MW19 Go-Rolla seems unduly hard to find and only ended up in the

ROW market in very limited quantities. These models are discontinued for 2005 in favor of realistic models.

White Rose & Nutmeg Collectibles

White Rose Collectibles has become a driving force in the Matchbox Company since business began in 1989. As much as ten to fifteen percent or more of Matchbox's business comes by way of White Rose Collectibles. The original introductions by White Rose included four Nascar transporters, but it wasn't until 1990 that the market really began to take off on the Nascar scene. By 1995, however, with many competing companies in Nascar related items, White Rose has been branching out even further from its original ventures.

White Rose has produced Sports Collectibles since 1990 with the introduction of its Major League baseball sets which continue today. This was followed by successful licenses for the NFL, NHL, college teams, and, most recently, trucking companies.

White Rose has developed some of its own miniatures with Matchbox that are exclusive to White Rose and offered nowhere else. These include different racing vehicles as well as an F800 Ford Delivery Van. White Rose even makes its own die cast line. In fact, White Rose "married" some Matchbox to Ertl and Winross models in a special gift box promotion.

Nutmeg Collectibles, founded by Mark Daddio, covers the Sprint and Modified Racing licenses but this ended in 1994, when Nutmeg decided to deal exclusively with the Ertl toy company.

A new company, Parlor City Collectibles, tried to venture into the Modified and Sprint markets after Nutmeg left the scene but after only a few ventures, the company folded.

ASAP Promotionals

In September of 1996, Tyco Toys went into a contractual agreement with a company called Advertising Specialties and Premiums- ASAP for short. ASAP would be supplied blank models from Tyco and later Mattel Toys to produce short run production models from as few as 96 or 144 up to several thousand. These models would be produced as "authorized by Matchbox" and therefore fit into the category of code 2. Early on in the program, ASAP used existing stock models such as the red no. 4 1997 Corvette or the no. 25 red BMW amongst others if a company required other than the white colored blank supplied through ASAP as manufactured by Matchbox. These short runs are very rare as Matchbox and ASAP do not supply any reference lists to what has been made. There are models made early on that we as collectors may never know about! These items come in white generic boxes clearly marked "Special Limited Edition! Matchbox" on the sides. Many of these have turned up on the Internet, tag sales, toy shows or by someone who may have worked at the company that ordered the model.

Color Comp Promotionals

Another promotional company, much like ASAP, is the New Jersey based company Color Comp, Inc. This company started its promotional business by tampo printing on existing castings. They added their own line of eight blanks for promotional purposes with more to be added . Early models were of both code 2 and code 3, whereas newer versions are termed code 2–as the ASAP promotionals are. In late 2003, ASAP made an agreement that CCI would produce all ASAP promotionals and ship them in their white boxes. Originally ASAP models were farmed out to different companies, which attribute to various levels of quality.

On-Pack Models

As a category, on-pack offers are unusual. Many on-pack models overlap into the promotional category. The model's promotional offering was through a direct mail-in offer based on sending in tokens, proofs of purchase, and sometimes a sum of money. Most of the offers were from the United Kingdom., Australia, or the United States. Some models are actually in-pack and offered by buying a product, which includes the special model directly attached in some fashion to the package. These will be included in this category.

Miniatures 1-75 Basic Listing

NOTE: In 1998, Mattel restructured the entire Matchbox 75 line. When doing so, all but 3 models were renumbered according to "series" themes. This has made mass confusion for cataloging the Matchbox miniatures. To alleviate the problem, only new model castings will be designated with current original numbers. All older editions will be listed according to their model release number. Following the description, a "MW" (Mattel Wheel) number will be designated to indicate what that model was in the lineup. This system has continued through 2004.

MB 1-A Mercedes Truck	1970
MB 1-B Mod Rod	1971
MB 1-C Dodge Challenger	1976
MB 1-D Dodge Challenger	1982
MB 1-E Jaguar XJ6 (ROW)	1987
MB 1-F Jaguar XJ6 Police Car (ROW)	1991
MB 1-G Dodge Viper GTS Coupe (USA)	1997
MB 1-H Mercedes Benz CLK Convertible	2000
MB 1-I Highway Pumper	2003
MB 1-J Whistle Car (USA)	2003
MB 1- K Squawkie Talkie (ROW)	2004
MB 1-L Fire Ladder Truck	2004
MB 1-M 1957 Shelby Cobra 427 A/C (SF)	2004
MB 2-A Mercedes Trailer	1970
MB 2-B Jeep Hot Rod	1971
MB 2-C Hovercraft	1976
MB 2-D S.2 Jet	1981
MB 2-E Pontiac Fiero	1985
MB 2-F Rover Sterling (ROW)	1988
MB 2-G 1965 Corvette Grand Sport (USA)	1990
MB 2-H BMW 850I (ROW)	1993
MB 2-I '98 Chevrolet Camaro SS Convertible (USA)	2000
MB 2-J Badge Car	2003
MB 3-A Mercedes Ambulance	1970
MB 3-B Monteverdi Hai	1973
MB 3-C Porsche Turbo	1978
MB 3-D Hummer	1994
MB 3-E Alfa Romeo 155	1997
MB 3-F Street Cleaner (ROW)	2002
MB 3-G Squawkie Talkie (USA)	2004
MB 3-H Fire Extinguisher (ROW)	2004
MB 3-I 1956 Cadillac Eldorado (SF)	2001
MB 4-A Dodge Stake Truck	1970
MB 4-B Gruesome Twosome	1971
MB 4-C Pontiac Firebird	1975
MB 4-D '57 Chevy	1979
MB 4-E London Taxi (ROW)	1987
MB 4-F 1997 Corvette	1997
MB 4-G Audi TT Roadster	2001
MB 4-H Ford Falcon (USA)	2002
MB 4-I Fire Extinguisher (USA)	2003
MB 4-J Flame Chopper (ROW)	2004
MB 4-K 1970 Plymouth Cuda (SF)	2004
MB 5-A Lotus Europa	1969
MB 5-B Seafire	1975
MB 5-C U.S. Mail Truck	1978
MB 5-D 4 X 4 Jeep (USA)	1982
MB 5-E Peterbilt Tanker (ROW)	1982
MB 5-F Ford Expedition Police Car (ROW)	2003
MB 5-G Flame Chopper (USA)	2004
MB 5-H Pound Hound (ROW)	2004
MB 6-A Ford Pickup	1970
MB 6-B Mercedes Tourer	1976
MB 6-C I.M.S.A. Mazda (USA)	1983
MB 6-D F.1 Racer (ROW)	1984
MB 6-E Ford Supervan II (USA)	1986
MB 6-F Atlas Excavator (USA reintro)	1990
MB 6-G Alfa Romeo SZ (ROW)	1991
MB 6-H Plymouth Prowler (ROW)	1995
MB 6-I Arctic Track Truck	2001
MB 6-J Opel Speedster	2003
MB 6-K Max Tractor (USA)	2004
MB 6-L Dragonfly Helicopter (ROW)	2004
MB 6-M Ford Mustang GT Concept (SF)	2004
MB 7-A Ford Refuse Truck	1970
MB 7-B Hairy Hustler	1971
MB 7-C V.W. Golf	1976
MB 7-D Rompin Rabbit	1982
MB 7-E I.M.S.A. Mazda (ROW)	1983
MB 7-F Porsche 959	1986
MB 7-G Ford Thunderbird (USA)	1993
MB 7-H Scissors Truck	1999
MB 7-I Ferrari 360 Spyder (USA)	2003
MB 7-J Milk Moo-ver (USA)	2004
MB 7-K Bulldozer 04 (ROW)	2004
MB 7-L 1969 Chevrolet Camaro (SF)	2004
MB 8-A Ford Mustang	1970
MB 8-B Wildcat Dragster	1971
MB 8-C DeTomaso Pantera	1975
MB 8-D Rover 3500 (ROW)	1982
MB 8-E Greased Lightning (USA)	1983
MB 8-F Scania T142 (USA)	1985
MB 8-G Vauxhall Astra Police Car (ROW)	1987
MB 8-H Mack CH800 Aerodyne (USA)	1990
MB 8-I Airport Tender (USA)	1992
MB 8-J Mazda RX7 (USA)	1994
MB 8-K Q.B. Roller (USA)	2004
MB 8-L Mixopotamus (ROW)	2004
MB 8-M Lotus Elise (USA)	2005
MB 9-A Boat and Trailer	1970
MB 9-B AMX Javelin	1972
MB 9-C Ford Escort RS2000	1978
MB 9-D Fiat Abarth (USA)	1982
MB 9-E AMX Prostocker (ROW)	1983
MB 9-F Toyota MR2 (USA)	1986
MB 9-G Caterpillar Bulldozer (ROW reintro)	1986
MB 9-H Faun Dump Truck (USA)	1990
MB 9-I BMW Z8	2002
MB 9-J Porsche 911 Turbo (USA)	2003
MB 9-K Bass Bus (USA)	2004
MB 9-L Mush Puppy (ROW)	2004
MB 9-M 1971 Chevy Chevelle (SF)	2004
MB10-A Pipe Truck	1970
MB10-B Piston Popper	1973
MB10-C Plymouth Gran Fury Police Car	1979
MB10-D Buick Le Sabre	1987
MB10-E 4 X 4 Chevy Van (ROW reintro)	1993
MB10-F Dodge Viper (USA)	1994
MB10-G J.R. Bumper (USA)	2004
MB10-H Go-Rolla (ROW)	2004
MB11-A Scaffold Truck	1970
MB11-B Flying Bug	1972
MB11-C Car Transporter	1976
MB11-D Boss Mustang (USA)	1982
MB11-E I.M.S.A. Mustang (USA)	1983

Model	Year
MB11-F Lamborghini Countach (ROW)	1985
MB11-G Chrysler Atlantic (USA)	1997
MB11-H BMW 328i Police Car (ROW)	2000
MB11-I Wrecker Truck	2001
MB11-J Emergency Response 4X4	2003
MB11-K Dragonfly Helicopter (USA)	2003
MB11-L Police Hat (ROW)	2003
MB12-A Safari Land Rover	1970
MB12-B Setra Coach	1970
MB12-C Big Bull	1975
MB12-D Citroen CX	1979
MB12-E Pontiac Firebird SE (USA)	1982
MB12-F Pontiac Firebird Racer (ROW)	1986
MB12-G Modified Racer (ROW)	1988
MB12-H Mercedes 500SL Convertible (USA)	1990
MB12-I Cattle Truck (ROW reintro)	1992
MB12-J Dodge Viper (ROW)	1994
MB12-K Audi Avus Quattro (USA)	1995
MB12-L '99 Ford Mustang Convertible (ROW)	2002
MB12-M Grasshopper Tow Truck (USA)	2003
MB12-N Military Helmet (ROW)	2003
MB13-A Dodge Wreck Truck	1970
MB13-B Baja Buggy	1971
MB13-C Snorkel Fire Engine	1977
MB13-D 4 X 4 Open Back Truck (USA)	1982
MB13-E Snorkel (ROW)	1983
MB13-F The Buster (USA)	1996
MB13-G Kenworth T2000	1999
MB13-H Snail Truck (USA)	2004
MB13-I Hot Head (ROW)	2004
MB14-A Iso Grifo	1969
MB14-B Mini Ha Ha	1975
MB14-C Rallye Royale (USA)	1981
MB14-D Leyland Tanker (ROW)	1982
MB14-E 1983/84 Corvette (USA)	1983
MB14-F 4 X 4 Jeep (ROW)	1984
MB14-G 1987 Corvette (USA)	1987
MB14-H Grand Prix Racer (ROW)	1988
MB14-I Flatbed Truck (ROW)	2001
MB14-J Ford Transit Ambulance (USA)	2003
MB14-K Web Wheeler (USA)	2004
MB14-L Rig Digger (ROW)	2004
MB15-A Volkswagen 1500	1969
MB15-B Fork Lift Truck	1972
MB15-C Hi Ho Silver (USA)	1981
MB15-D Ford Sierra (USA)	1983
MB15-E Peugeot 205 Turbo (ROW)	1984
MB15-F Saab 9000 Turbo (USA)	1988
MB15-G 1965 Corvette Grand Sport (ROW)	1990
MB15-H Alfa Romeo SZ (USA)	1991
MB15-I Sunburner (USA)	1992
MB15-J Mustang Mach III (USA)	1994
MB15-K Ford Transit (ROW)	1996
MB15-L DAF 3300 Space Cab (ROW)	1999
MB15-M Litter Bug (USA)	2004
MB15-N Cap'n Cop (ROW)	2004
MB16-A Badger	1974
MB16-B Pontiac	1979
MB16-C Pontiac T-Roof (ROW)	1983
MB16-D F.1 Racer (USA)	1984
MB16-E Ford LTD Police Car (USA)	1987
MB16-F Land Rover Ninety (ROW)	1987
MB16-G School Bus (USA)	2001
MB16-H Car Carrier	2003
MB16-I Dump Truck 2004 (USA)	2003
MB16-J 1965 Shelby Cobra (SF)	2002
MB17-A Horse Box	1970
MB17-B The Londoner	1972
MB17-C London Bus	1982
MB17-D AMX Prostocker (USA)	1983
MB17-E Ford Escort Cabriolet (USA)	1985
MB17-F Dodge Dakota (USA)	1987
MB17-G Ferrari 456GT (USA)	1994
MB17-H Ford Ambulance (ROW)	1997
MB17-I '99 Mustang (USA)	1999
MB17-J Bulldozer 04 (USA)	2003
MB18-A Field Car	1970
MB18-B Hondarora	1975
MB18-C Fire Engine	1984
MB18-D Mixopotamus (USA)	2004
MB19-A Lotus Racer	1970
MB19-B Road Dragster	1970
MB19-C Cement Truck	1976
MB19-D Peterbilt Cement Truck	1982
MB19-E BMW 328i (ROW)	2001
MB19-F Go Rolla (USA)	2004
MB20-A Lamborghini Marzal	1969
MB20-B Police Patrol	1975
MB20-C 4 X 4 Jeep (USA)	1982
MB20-D Volvo Container Truck (ROW)	1985
MB20-E Volkswagen Transporter (ROW)	1988
MB20-F Pontiac Firebird Ram Air (USA)	1997
MB20-G 1968 Mustang Cobra Jet (ROW)	1997
MB20-H Jumbo Sweeper (USA)	2004
MB21-A Foden Concrete Truck	1970
MB21-B Rod Roller	1973
MB21-C Renault 5TL	1978
MB21-D Corvette Pace Car (USA)	1983
MB21-E Chevy Breakdown Van	1985
MB21-F GMC Wrecker (USA)	1987
MB21-G Nissan Prairie (ROW)	1991
MB21-H Ferrari F50 (ROW)	1996
MB21-I Ford Transit Ambulance (GR)	1999
MB21-J X-33 RLV (ROW)	2000
MB21-K Tower Boat	2001
MB21-L Cadillac Escalade	2003
MB21-M Mush Puppy (USA)	2004
MB22-A Pontiac Grand Prix Sports Coupe	1970
MB22-B Freeman Intercity Commuter	1970
MB22-C Blaze Buster	1975
MB22-D 4 X 4 Mini Pickup (USA)	1982
MB22-E Jaguar XK120 (ROW)	1984
MB22-F Saab 9000 Turbo (ROW)	1988
MB22-G Vectra Cavalier Gsi 2000 (USA)	1990
MB22-H Lamborghini Diablo (USA)	1992
MB22-I Pontiac Grand Prix (ROW)	1994
MB22-J Mitsubishi Spyder (ROW)	1995
MB22-K Pound Hound (USA)	2004
MB23-A Volkswagen Camper/ Dormobile	1970
MB23-B Atlas	1975
MB23-C GT350 (USA)	1981
MB23-D Audi Quattro (USA)	1982
MB23-E Peterbilt Quarry Truck (ROW)	1982
MB23-F Honda ATC (USA)	1985
MB23-G Volvo Container Truck (USA)	1987
MB23-H Ford Box Van	1999
MB23-I Ford Panel Van (ROW)	2000
MB23-J Ford Explorer Sport Trac	2001
MB23-K Lock Boxer (USA)	2004
MB24-A Rolls Royce Silver Shadow	1970
MB24-B Team Matchbox	1973
MB24-C Shunter	1978
MB24-D Datsun 280ZX (USA)	1981
MB24-E Datsun 280ZX	1983
MB24-F Nissan 300ZX	1986
MB24-G Lincoln Town Car (ROW)	1989
MB24-H Ferrari F40 (USA)	1989
MB24-I Airport Tender (ROW)	1992
MB24-J Rhino Rod (ROW)	1994
MB24-K Chevy Transport Bus	1999
MB24-L Huski-Patrol (USA)	2004
MB25-A Ford Cortina	1970

MB25-B Mod Tractor 1972
MB25-C Flat Car & Container 1978
MB25-D Celica GT (USA) 1981
MB25-E Ambulance (USA) 1984
MB25-E Ambulance (ROW) 1990
MB25-F Audi Quattro (ROW) 1983
MB25-G Peugeot 205 Turbo (ROW reintro) 1991
MB25-H Model A Ford (ROW reintro) 1993
MB25-I Jeep 4 X 4 (ROW) 1994
MB25-J BMW Z3 (USA) 1997
MB25-K 1998 Jeep Wrangler 2001
MB25-L Space Buggy (USA) 2004
MB25-M 1955 Cadillac Fleetwood (SF) 2004

MB26-A GMC Tipper 1970
MB26-B Big Banger 1972
MB26-C Site Dumper 1976
MB26-D Cosmic Blues (USA) 1981
MB26-E Cable Truck (ROW) 1982
MB26-F Volvo Tilt Truck (ROW) 1984
MB26-G BMW 5 Series (USA) 1989
MB26-H 4 X 4 Chevy Van (USA reintro) 1991
MB26-I Jaguar XJ220 (ROW) 1994
MB26-J Airport Fire Pumper 2001
MB26-K Sport SUV 2003
MB26-L Police Hat (USA) 2003
MB26-M GMC Bucket Truck (ROW) 2004

MB27-A Mercedes 230SL 1970
MB27-B Lamborghini Countach 1973
MB27-C Swept Wing Jet 1981
MB27-D Jeep Cherokee 1986
MB27-E Mercedes Tractor (ROW) 1990
MB27-F Tailgator 1994
MB27-G Ladder Truck 2001
MB27-H Ford Falcon Police Car (ROW) 2002
MB27-I Military Helmet (USA) 2003
MB27-J 1961 Dodge Dart Phoenix (SF) 2004

MB28-A Mack Dump Truck 1970
MB28-B Stoat 1974
MB28-C Lincoln Continental MK V 1979
MB28-D Formula 5000 1981
MB28-E Dodge Daytona 1984
MB28-F London Bus (USA reintro) 1990
MB28-G 1987 Corvette (ROW reintro) 1990
MB28-H Forklift Truck 1991
MB28-I BMW Cabriolet (ROW reintro) 1991
MB28-J T-Bird Turbo Coupe (ROW reintro) 1992
MB28-K Mustang Mach III (ROW) 1994
MB28-L Mitsubishi Spyder (USA) 1995
MB28-M The Buster (ROW) 1996
MB28-N Delivery Truck (ROW) 2000
MB28-O Hot Head (USA) 2004

MB29-A Fire Pumper 1970
MB29-B Racing Mini 1970
MB29-C Tractor Shovel 1976
MB29-D BMW 328i Police Car (USA) 2003
MB29-E Rig Digger (USA) 2004

MB30-A Eight Wheel Crane 1970
MB30-B Beach Buggy 1970
MB30-C Swamp Rat 1976
MB30-D Leyland Articulated Truck 1981
MB30-E Peterbilt Quarry Truck (USA) 1982
MB30-F Mercedes "G" Wagon (ROW) 1985
MB30-G Toyota Supra (USA) 1995
MB30-H Helicopter (ROW reintro) 1997
MB30-I Chevy Tahoe 1998
MB30-J Dennis Sabre Fire Engine (USA) 2001
MB30-K Cap'n Cop (USA) 2004

MB31-A Lincoln Continental 1970
MB31-B Volksdragon 1971
MB31-C Caravan 1977
MB31-D Mazda RX7 (USA) 1981
MB31-E Mazda RX7 1983
MB31-F Rolls Royce Silver Cloud (ROW) 1986
MB31-G Rover Sterling (USA) 1988
MB31-H BMW 5 Series (ROW) 1989
MB31-I Nissan Prairie (USA) 1991
MB31-J Jaguar XJ220 (USA) 1993
MB31-K Audi Avus Quattro (ROW) 1995
MB31-L 1957 Chevy Bel Air 1998
MB31-M Beetle 4X4 (USA) 2001
MB31-N Ford Transit Ambulance (ROW) 2001
MB31-O BMW X5 2002
MB31-P Volkswagen Beetle Taxi 2003
MB31-Q Airport Fire Tanker 2003

MB32-A Leyland Tanker 1970
MB32-B Maserati Bora 1972
MB32-C Field Gun 1978
MB32-D Atlas Excavator 1981
MB32-E Modified Racer (USA) 1988
MB32-F 1962 Corvette (USA reintro) 1994
MB32-G 1970 El Camino 1998
MB32-H Mercedes Benz S500 (ROW) 2000
MB32-I Nissan Xterra with kayaks (USA) 2001
MB32-J 4X4 Fire Truck 2003
MB32-K Lincoln Navigator (SF) 2004

MB33-A Lamborghini Miura 1969
MB33-B Datsun 126X 1973
MB33-C Police Motorcycle 1977
MB33-D Volkswagen Golf GTi (USA) 1985
MB33-E Renault 11 (ROW) 1986
MB33-F Mercury Sable Wagon (ROW) 1989
MB33-G Utility Truck (USA) 1989
MB33-H Mercedes 500SL Convertible (ROW) 1990
MB33-I Ford Mondeo (ROW) 1995
MB33-J Hummer Police (ROW) 2002
MB33-K Boom Fire Truck 2004

MB34-A Formula 1 1971
MB34-B Vantastic 1975
MB34-C Chevy Prostocker 1981
MB34-D Ford RS200 1987
MB34-E Sprint Racer (USA) 1990
MB34-F Dodge Challenger (ROW reintro) 1991
MB34-G Plymouth Prowler (USA) 1995
MB34-H Chrysler Atlantic (ROW) 1997
MB34-I 1933 Ford Street Rod 1998
MB34-J Chevy Impala Police Car (USA) 2000
MB34-K Mercedes Benz E430 Wagon Police (ROW) 2001

MB35-A Merryweather Fire Engine 1970
MB35-B Fandango 1975
MB35-C Pontiac T-Roof (USA) 1982
MB35-D Zoo Truck (ROW) 1982
MB35-E 4 X 4 Mini Pickup (ROW) 1986
MB35-F Land Rover Ninety (USA) 1987
MB35-G Ford Bronco II (ROW) 1988
MB35-H Pontiac Grand Prix (USA) 1992
MB35-I Pontiac Stock Car (USA) 1993
MB35-J AMG Mercedes C Class (USA) 1996
MB35-K Dodge Viper GTS (ROW) 1997
MB35-L Police Motorcycle (USA) 1999
MB35-M Holden Commodore Police Car (ROW) 2001
MB35-N Hovercraft (ROW) 2002
MB35-O TVR Tuscan S (SF) 2004

MB36-A Opel Diplomat 1970
MB36-B Hot Rod Draguar 1970
MB36-C Formula 5000 1975
MB36-D Refuse Truck 1980
MB36-E 1957 Chevy Bel Air Convertible 1998
MB36-F 1999 Mustang Convertible (USA) 1999
MB36-G Ski Boat (ROW) 1999
MB36-H X-33 RLV (USA) 2000
MB36-I Road Roller 2001
MB36-J Troop Carrier (ROW) 2002
MB36-K Taxi Cab 2003
MB36-L Honda Element 2004

MB37-A Cattle Truck 1970
MB37-B Soopa Coopa 1972
MB37-C Skip Truck 1976
MB37-D Sunburner (USA) 1981
MB37-E Matra Rancho (ROW) 1982
MB37-F Jeep 4 X 4 (USA) 1984
MB37-G Ford Escort Cabriolet (ROW) 1985
MB37-H Nissan 300ZX (ROW) 1990
MB37-I 1970 Boss Mustang 1998
MB37-J Sea Plane (ROW) 1999
MB37-K Audi TT Roadster (Germany) 2000
MB37-L Bulldozer 2001
MB37-M Robot Truck (ROW) 2002

MB38-A Honda Motorcycle & Trailer 1970
MB38-B Stingeroo 1972
MB38-C Jeep 1976
MB38-D Ford Camper 1980
MB38-E Model A Ford Van 1982
MB38-F Ford Courier (ROW) 1992
MB38-G Ford Courrier (ROW) 1992
MB38-H Mercedes 600 SEL (USA) 1992
MB38-I Corvette Stingray III 1994
MB38-J Crown Victoria Police Car (ROW) 1997
MB38-K Sea Rescue Boat (ROW) 1999
MB38-L Ford Panel Van (USA) 2000
MB38-M Demolition Machine 2001
MB38-N Rescue Boat (ROW) 2002
MB38-O 1957 Corvette (SF/CL) 1999

MB39-A Clipper 1973
MB39-B Rolls Royce Silver Shadow 1979
MB39-C Toyota Supra (USA) 1983
MB39-D BMW Cabriolet 1985
MB39-E Ford Bronco II (USA) 1987
MB39-F Mack CH600 Aerodyne (ROW) 1990
MB39-G Mercedes 600 SEL (ROW) 1992
MB39-H Ford Thunderbird (ROW) 1995
MB39-I 1971 Camaro Z-28 1998
MB39-J Hydroplane (ROW) 1999
MB39-K Armored Response Vehicle (ROW) 2002
MB39-L 1968 Mercury Cougar (SF) 2004

MB40-A Vauxhall Guildsman 1971
MB40-B Horse Box 1977
MB40-C Corvette T-Roof (USA) 1982
MB40-D Rocket Transporter (ROW) 1985
MB40-E Ford Sierra (USA reintro) 1990
MB40-F Road Roller (USA) 1991
MB40-G Ford Mondeo (USA) 1995
MB40-H 1969 Camaro Roadster 1997
MB40-I FJ Holden Van (ROW) 1995
MB40-J Submersible (ROW) 1999
MB40-K Dodge Concept Vehicle (USA) 1999
MB40-L Mercedes G Wagon (USA) 2000
MB40-M Cement Mixer 2001

MB41-A Ford GT 1970
MB41-B Siva Spyder 1972
MB41-C Ambulance 1977
MB41-D Kenworth Aerodyne (USA) 1982
MB41-E Racing Porsche (ROW) 1983
MB41-F Jaguar XJ6 (USA) 1987
MB41-G Vectra Cavalier Gsi 2000 (ROW) 1990
MB41-H Cosmic Blues (USA reintro) 1991
MB41-I Sunburner (ROW) 1992
MB41-J Ferrari 456GT (ROW) 1994
MB41-K Ski Boat (USA) 1999
MB41-L Flat Bed Truck (USA) 2000
MB41-M Radar Plane 2001
MB41-N Sea Rescue Helicopter 2003
MB41-O Checker Taxi 2004
MB41-P Ford GT (SF) 2004

MB42-A Iron Fairy Crane 1970
MB42-B Tyre Fryer 1972
MB42-C Mercedes Container Truck 1977
MB42-D 1957 Ford Thunderbird 1982
MB42-E Faun Crane Truck (ROW) 1984
MB42-E Faun Crane Truck (USA) 1987
MB42-F Sea Plane (USA) 1999
MB42-G Pop Up Camper (ROW) 2000
MB42-H Ambulance 2001
MB42-I Bus 2004

MB43-A Pony Trailer 1970
MB43-B Dragon Wheels 1972
MB43-C 0-4-0 Loco 1978
MB43-D Peterbilt Conventional (USA) 1982
MB43-E AMG Mercedes 500SEC 1984
MB43-F Renault 11 (USA) 1987
MB43-G Lincoln Town Car (USA) 1989
MB43-H '57 Chevy (ROW reintro) 1990
MB43-I Camaro Z28 (USA) 1994
MB43-J Mustang Cobra (ROW) 1995
MB43-K Sea Rescue Boat (USA) 1999
MB43-L Ford F Series Truck 2001

MB44-A Refrigerator Truck 1970
MB44-B Boss Mustang 1972
MB44-C Passenger Coach 1978
MB44-D 4 X 4 Chevy Van (USA) 1982
MB44-E Citroen 15CV (ROW) 1983
MB44-F Datsun 280ZX Police Car (Japan) 1987
MB44-G Skoda 130LR (ROW) 1987
MB44-H 1921 Model T Ford 1990
MB44-I Ford Probe 1994
MB44-J Hydroplane (USA) 1999
MB44-K Audi TT (USA) 2000
MB44-L Truck Camper with roof light 2001

MB45-A Ford Group 6 1970
MB45-B BMW 3.0 CSL 1976
MB45-C Kenworth Aerodyne 1982
MB45-D Ford Cargo Skip Truck (ROW) 1987
MB45-E Highway Maintenance Vehicle (USA) 1990
MB45-F Submersible (USA) 1999
MB45-G Jeep Grand Cherokee (ROW) 2000
MB45-H Beetle 4X4 (ROW) 2002

MB46-A Mercedes 300SE 1970
MB46-B Stretcha Fetcha 1972
MB46-C Ford Tractor 1978
MB46-D Hot Chocolate/ Beetle Streaker (USA) 1981
MB46-E Sauber Group C Racer (ROW) 1984
MB46-F Mission Helicopter (USA) 1985
MB46-G Opel Calibra (ROW) 1997
MB46-H Chevy Tahoe Police 1998
MB46-I Watercraft with Trailer (ROW) 1999
MB46-J 1955 Chevy Bel Air Convertible (USA) 1999
MB46-K 4X4 Buggy 2003
MB46-L Ambulance 2004

MB47-A DAF Tipper Truck 1970
MB47-B Beach Hopper 1974
MB47-C Pannier Loco 1979
MB47-D Jaguar SS 100 1982
MB47-E School Bus (USA) 1985
MB47-E School Bus (ROW) 1987
MB47-F Rotwheeler (ROW) 1995
MB47-G M2 Bradley Tank 1998
MB47-H Armored Response Vehicle (USA) 2001
MB47-I Nissan Xterra 2002

MB48-A Dodge Dump Truck 1970
MB48-B Pi-Eyed Piper 1972
MB48-C Sambron Jacklift 1977
MB48-D Red Rider (USA) 1981
MB48-E Unimog with plow (ROW) 1983
MB48-F Vauxhall Astra/ Opel Kadett (ROW) 1986
MB48-G Pontiac Firebird Racer (USA) 1993
MB48-G Pontiac Firebird Racer (ROW) 1994
MB48-H 1956 Ford Pickup 1997
MB48-I '62 VW Beetle (ROW) 1999
MB48-J Delivery Truck (USA) 2000
MB48-K Air Lift (ROW) 2000

MB48-L Hummer Police (USA) 2001

MB49-A Unimog 1970
MB49-B Chop Suey 1973
MB49-C Crane Truck 1976
MB49-D Sand Digger 1983
MB49-E Peugeot Quasar 1986
MB49-F Lamborghini Diablo (ROW) 1992
MB49-G Volvo Tilt Truck (USA) 1990
MB49-H BMW 850I (USA) 1993
MB49-I Volkswagen Concept 1 (USA) 1996
MB49-J Ford Falcon Police Car (USA) 2004

MB50-A Kennel Truck 1970
MB50-B Articulated Truck 1973
MB50-C Articulated Trailer (TP) 1980
MB50-D Harley-Davidson Motorcycle 1980
MB50-E Chevy Blazer 1984
MB50-F Dodge Dakota (ROW) 1990
MB50-G Auxiliary Power Truck (ROW) 1991
MB50-H Harley-Davidson Chopper (HD) 1994
MB50-I Harley-Davidson Electraglide (HD) 1994
MB50-J 1997 Ford F150 1998
MB50-K Porsche Boxster (ROW) 1999
MB50-L Ford Expedition Police (USA) 2001
MB50-M Porsche 911 Carrera Cabriolet (ROW) 2001
MB50-N Ford Transit (USA) 2002
MB50-O '57 Lincoln Premiere 2002

MB51-A Eight Wheel Tipper 1970
MB51-B Citroen S.M. 1972
MB51-C Combine Harvester 1978
MB51-D Midnight Magic (USA) 1981
MB51-E Pontiac Firebird SE (ROW) 1982
MB51-F London Bus (USA reintro) 1985
MB51-G Camaro IROC-Z (USA) 1986
MB51-H Ford LTD Police Car (ROW) 1987
MB51-I Porsche 959 (USA reintro) 1994
MB51-J Jeep Cherokee (ROW reintro) 1996
MB51-K Ford Ambulance (USA) 1997
MB51-L Watercraft with Trailer (USA) 1999
MB51-M Mercedes A Class (ROW) 1999
MB51-N Robot Truck (USA) 2001
MB51-O Ford Falcon Police Car (AU) 2001
MB51-P Pontiac Vibe 2003
MB51-Q Jeep Compass 2004

MB52-A Dodge Charger MKIII 1970
MB52-B Police Launch 1976
MB52-C BMW M1 1981
MB52-D BMW M1 1983
MB52-E Isuzu Amigo 1991
MB52-F Ford Escort Cosworth 1994
MB52-G Snow Groomer (ROW) 1999
MB52-H VW Delivery Van (ROW) 2000
MB52-I Troop Carrier (USA) 2001
MB52-J Land Rover SVX 2004

MB53-A Ford Zodiac 1970
MB53-B Tanzara 1972
MB53-C Jeep CJ6 1977
MB53-D Flareside Pickup 1982
MB53-E Faun Dump Truck (ROW) 1989
MB53-F Chevy Breakdown Van (USA reintro) 1990
MB53-G Ford LTD Taxi (USA) 1992
MB53-H Rhino Rod (USA) 1994
MB53-I '62 VW Beetle (USA) 1999
MB53-J Truck Camper (ROW) 1999
MB53-K Police Car 2002
MB53-L 1960 Jeep 2001

MB54-A S&S Cadillac Ambulance 1970
MB54-B Ford Capri 1971
MB54-C Personnel Carrier 1976
MB54-D Mobile Home 1980
MB54-E NASA Tracking Vehicle 1982
MB54-F Command Vehicle 1984
MB54-G Chevy Lumina (DT) 1989
MB54-H Chevy Lumina 1990
MB54-I Mazda RX7 (ROW) 1994
MB54-J Abrams Tank (USA) 1995
MB54-K Crown Victoria Police Car (USA) 1997
MB54-L Holden Commodore (AU) 1996
MB54-M Chevy K-1500 Pickup (ROW) 1998
MB54-N White Water Raft (ROW) 1999
MB54-O Tanker Truck 2002

MB55-A Mercury Police Car 1970
MB55-B Mercury Police Commuter 1971
MB55-C Hellraiser 1975
MB55-D Ford Cortina 1979
MB55-E Ford Sierra (ROW) 1983
MB55-F Racing Porsche (USA) 1983
MB55-G Mercury Sable Wagon (USA) 1987
MB55-H Rolls Royce Silver Spirit (USA) 1990
MB55-I Model A Ford (USA reintro) 1991
MB55-J Flareside Pickup (reintro) 1994
MB55-K Flareside with load (WR) 1994
MB55-L Porsche Boxster (USA) 1999
MB55-M Rescue Chopper (ROW) 1999
MB55-N Amphibious Personnel Carrier (USA) 2000
MB55-O Golf Cart (ROW) 2000
MB55-P Dump Truck 2002
MB55-Q Mercedes Benz E430 Wagon (ROW) 2003
MB55-R 1969 Chevy Camaro (SF) 2004

MB56-A BMC Pininfarina 1969
MB56-B Hi-Tailer 1974
MB56-C Mercedes 450SEL 1979
MB56-D Peterbilt Tanker (USA) 1982
MB56-E Volkswagen Golf GTi (ROW) 1985
MB56-F 4 X 4 Jeep (ROW reintro) 1990
MB56-G Ford LTD Taxi (ROW) 1992
MB56-H Camaro Z28 (ROW) 1994
MB56-I Isuzu Rodeo (USA) 1995
MB56-J Camaro Z28 Police Car (ROW) 1995
MB56-K Mercedes A Class (USA) 1999
MB56-L UFO (ROW) 1999
MB56-M Dodge Viper GTSR 2001
MB56-N Bucket Fire truck 2002
MB56-O Billboard Truck 2003

MB57-A Land Rover Fire Engine 1970
MB57-B Eccles Caravan 1970
MB57-C Wildlife Truck 1973
MB57-D 4 X 4 Mini Pickup (USA) 1982
MB57-E Carmichael Commando (ROW) 1982
MB57-F Mission Helicopter (ROW) 1985
MB57-G Ford Transit (USA) 1990
MB57-H Auxiliary Power Truck (USA) 1991
MB57-I Snow Groomer (USA) 1999
MB57-J Mercedes Benz ML430 (ROW) 2000
MB57-K 2000 Chevrolet Corvette Convertible 2001
MB57-L Trash Truck 2002
MB57-M Chevrolet SSR (ROW) 2003

MB58-A DAF Girder Truck 1970
MB58-B Woosh-N-Push 1972
MB58-C Faun Dump Truck 1976
MB58-D Ruff Trek 1983
MB58-E Mercedes 300E 1986
MB58-F Corvette T-Roof (USA reintro) 1991
MB58-G Volkswagen Concept 1 (ROW) 1996
MB58-H 1939 Chevy Sedan Delivery (AU) 1997
MB58-I Porsche 911 GT1 (ROW) 1998
MB58-J Truck Camper (USA) 1999
MB58-K International Armored Car (USA) 2000
MB58-L Chevrolet Avalanche 2002

MB59-A Ford Galaxie Fire Chief Car 1970
MB59-B Mercury Fire Chief Car 1971
MB59-C Planet Scout 1975
MB59-D Porsche 928 1980
MB59-E Porsche 944 (ROW) 1987
MB59-F T-Bird Turbo Coupe (USA) 1987
MB59-G Aston Martin DB-7 (USA) 1994

MB59-H Camaro Z28 Police Car (USA) 1995
MB59-I Vauxhall Frontera (ROW) 1995
MB59-J White Water Raft (USA) 1999
MB59-K VW Transporter (ROW) 1999
MB59-L Chrysler Panel Cruiser 2001
MB59-M Cycle with Sidecar 2002
MB59-N Pontiac Piranha (ROW) 2003

MB60-A Site Hut Truck 1970
MB60-B Lotus Super Seven 1971
MB60-C Holden Pickup 1977
MB60-D Piston Popper (USA) 1982
MB60-E Toyota Supra (ROW) 1983
MB60-F Pontiac Firebird Racer (USA) 1985
MB60-G Ford Transit (ROW) 1986
MB60-H Rocket Transporter (USA) 1990
MB60-I Toyota Supra (ROW) 1995
MB60-J Helicopter (USA reintro) 1997
MB60-K Rescue Chopper (USA) 1999
MB60-L Chevy Suburban (ROW) 2000
MB60-M Mobile Light Truck 2002
MB60-N Ice Cream Truck (ROW) 2003

MB61-A Blue Shark 1971
MB61-B Wreck Truck 1978
MB61-C Peterbilt Wreck Truck 1982
MB61-D T-Bird Turbo Coupe (ROW) 1987
MB61-E Nissan 300ZX (USA) 1990
MB61-F Forklift Truck (ROW) 1991
MB61-G Abrams M1 Tank (ROW) 1995
MB61-H BMW Z3 (ROW) 1997
MB61-I Formula One Racer (ROW) 1998
MB61-J Land Rover Freelander (ROW) 1999
MB61-K UFO (USA) 1999
MB61-L VW Concept 1 Convertible (ROW) 2000
MB61-M Rescue Boat (USA) 2001
MB61-N Ford Falcon (AU) 2001
MB61-O Ice Breaker 2002
MB61-P Dennis Sabre Fire Truck 2003
MB61-Q BMW Z4 2004

MB62-A Mercury Cougar 1970
MB62-B Mercury Cougar Dragster 1970
MB62-C Renault 17TL 1974
MB62-D Chevrolet Corvette 1979
MB62-E Corvette T-Roof (ROW) 1982
MB62-F Rolls Royce Silver Cloud (USA) 1986
MB62-G Volvo 760 (ROW) 1986
MB62-H Oldsmobile Aerotech (USA) 1989
MB62-I Volvo Container Truck (ROW reintro) 1991
MB62-J Street Streak (USA) 1996
MB62-K Ford Expedition (ROW) 1999
MB62-L Pop Up Camper (USA) 2000
MB62-M Hovercraft (USA) 2001
MB62-N GMC Terradyne 2002
MB62-O Nissan Z 2004
MB62-P 1968 Mercury Cougar (SF) 2004

MB63-A Dodge Crane Truck 1970
MB63-B Freeway Gas Tanker 1973
MB63-C Freeway Gas Trailer (TP) 1978
MB63-D Dodge Challenger (USA) 1981
MB63-E Snorkel (USA) 1982
MB63-F 4 X 4 Open Back Truck (ROW) 1982
MB63-G Volkswagen Golf GTi (ROW reintro) 1990
MB63-H 0-4-0 Loco (ROW reintro) 1991
MB63-I Aston Martin DB-7 (ROW) 1994
MB63-J Ford Falcon (AU) 1996
MB63-K '98 Jeep Wrangler (ROW) 1999
MB63-L Mercedes Benz ML430 (German) 1999
MB63-M BMW 3 Series Coupe (ROW) 2000
MB63-N Air Boat (USA) 2001
MB63-O Rescue Helicopter 2002
MB63-P 2005 Chevrolet Corvette C6 2004

MB64-A MG 1100 1970
MB64-B Slingshot Dragster 1971
MB64-C Fire Chief Car 1976
MB64-D Caterpillar Bulldozer 1979
MB64-E Dodge Caravan (ROW) 1984
MB64-F Oldsmobile Aerotech (ROW) 1989
MB64-G 1970 Pontiac GTO (ROW) 1996
MB64-H Holden Commodore (ROW) 1998
MB64-I VW Transporter (USA) 1999
MB64-J Mercedes Benz Actross 1857 (GR) 1999
MB64-K Ford Focus (ROW) 2000
MB64-L Fork Lift Truck 2002
MB64-M Pontiac Solstice 2004

MB65-A Saab Sonnet 1973
MB65-B Airport Coach 1977
MB65-C Bandag Bandit (USA) 1982
MB65-D F.1 Racer (USA) 1985
MB65-E Plane Transporter (ROW) 1985
MB65-F Cadillac Allante (ROW) 1987
MB65-G Ford F150 Pickup 1995
MB65-H Chevy Silverado 4X4 Pickup (ROW) 1999
MB65- I Jeep Grand Cherokee (USA) 2000
MB65-J Police Cycle (ROW) 2001
MB65-K Ice Cream Truck (USA) 2002
MB65-L Ferrari 360 Spider (ROW) 2002

MB66-A Greyhound Bus 1970
MB66-B Mazda RX500 1971
MB66-C Ford Transit 1977
MB66-D Super Boss 1982
MB66-E Sauber Group C Racer (USA) 1984
MB66-F Rolls Royce Silver Spirit (ROW) 1987
MB66-G Opel Calibra (USA) 1997
MB66-H Pontiac Firebird Ram Air (ROW) 1997
MB66-I 1997 MGF 1998
MB66-J Land Rover Freelander (USA) 1999
MB66-K International Fire Engine (ROW) 1999
MB66-L Mercedes Benz S500 (GR) 1999
MB66-M Radar Truck 2001
MB66-N Limousine 2002
MB66-O Dodge Ram SRT-10 2003
MB66-P City Police Car 2003

MB67-A Volkswagen 1600TL 1970
MB67-B Hot Rocker 1973
MB67-C Datsun 260Z 1978
MB67-D Flame Out (USA) 1983
MB67-E I.M.S.A. Mustang (ROW) 1983
MB67-F Lamborghini Countach (USA) 1985
MB67-G Ikarus Coach (ROW) 1986
MB67-H Ford Expedition (USA) 1999
MB67-I Audi TT (ROW) 2000
MB67-J Land Rover Discovery 2001
MB67-K Foam Fire Truck 2002

MB68-A Porsche 910 1970
MB68-B Cosmobile 1975
MB68-C Chevy Van 1979
MB68-D 4 X 4 Chevy Van (ROW) 1983
MB68-E Dodge Caravan (USA) 1984
MB68-F Camaro Z28 (ROW) 1987
MB68-G TV News Truck (USA) 1989
MB68-H Road Roller (ROW) 1991
MB68-I Stinger 1995
MB68-J Porsche 911 GT1 (USA) 1998
MB68-K Ford Falcon (ROW) 1998
MB68-L Dennis Sabre Fire Engine (ROW) 1999
MB68-M '98 Jeep Wrangler (USA) 1999
MB68-N Mercedes Benz 430 Wagon (GR) 1999
MB68-O Air Lift (USA) 2000
MB68-P '99 Mustang (ROW) 2000
MB68-Q Speedboat 2001

MB69-A Rolls Royce Silver Shadow Coupe 1969
MB69-B Turbo Fury 1973
MB69-C Armored Truck 1978
MB69-D '33 Willys Street Rod (USA) 1982
MB69-E 1983/84 Corvette (ROW) 1983
MB69-F Volvo 480ES (ROW) 1988
MB69-G Highway Maintenance Vehicle (ROW) 1990

MB69-H 1968 Mustang Cobra Jet (USA)	1997
MB69-I BMW328i (Germany)	1999
MB69-J Lotus Elise (ROW)	2000
MB69-K Humvee	2001
MB69-L Porsche 911 Turbo (ROW)	2002
MB70-A Grit Spreader	1970
MB70-B Dodge Dragster	1971
MB70-C Self Propelled Gun	1976
MB70-D Ferrari 308 GTB	1981
MB70-E Ford Cargo Skip Truck (USA)	1989
MB70-F Ferrari F40 (ROW)	1989
MB70-G Weasel (USA reintro)	1993
MB70-H 1970 Pontiac GTO (USA)	1996
MB70-I Mercedes E Class	1998
MB70-J Chevy Silverado 4X4 Pickup (USA)	1999
MB70-K Chevrolet SSR (USA)	2002
MB70-L VW W12 Concept (ROW)	2002
MB71-A Ford Heavy Wreck Truck	1970
MB71-B Jumbo Jet	1973
MB71-C Cattle Truck	1976
MB71-D 1962 Corvette (USA)	1982
MB71-E Scania T142 (ROW)	1985
MB71-F GMC Wrecker (ROW)	1988
MB71-G Porsche 944 (USA)	1989
MB71-H Mustang Cobra (USA)	1995
MB71-I 1997 Jaguar XK8	1998
MB71-J Mercedes Benz CLK Convertible (GR)	1999
MB71-K Four Wheeler (ROW)	1999
MB71-L Ford Dump/ Utility Truck (ROW)	2000
MB71-M Jeep Liberty	2001
MB71-N Jeep Willys Concept	2003
MB72-A Jeep	1970
MB72-B SRN6 Hovercraft	1972
MB72-C Bomag Road Roller	1979
MB72-D Maxi Taxi (USA)	1981
MB72-E Dodge Delivery Van (ROW)	1982
MB72-F Sand Racer (USA)	1984
MB72-G Plane Transporter (USA)	1985
MB72-H Ford Supervan II (ROW)	1986
MB72-I Cadillac Allante (USA)	1987
MB72-J Sprint Racer (ROW)	1990
MB72-K Dodge Zoo Truck (ROW)	1992
MB72-L 1962 Corvette (ROW)	1994
MB72-M Peugeot Quasar (USA reintro)	1995
MB72-N Street Streak (ROW)	1996
MB72-O Chevy K-1500 Pickup (USA)	1996
MB72-P 1965 Mustang (USA)	1999
MB72-Q Dune Buggy (ROW)	1999
MB72-R Porsche 911 Carrera Cabriolet (Germany)	1999
MB72-S VW Delivery Van (USA)	2000
MB72-T Rescue Crane	2001
MB72-U Volkswagen Microbus	2002
MB72-V Chrysler PT Cruiser Convertible	2003
MB72-W Bulldozer	2004
MB73-A Mercury Commuter	1970
MB73-B Weasel	1974
MB73-C Model A Ford	1979
MB73-D TV News Truck (ROW)	1989
MB73-E Mercedes Tractor (USA)	1990
MB73-F Jeep Cherokee (USA reintro)	1994
MB73-G Rolls Royce Silver Spirit (USA reintro)	1995
MB73-H Rotwheeler (USA)	1995
MB73-I Dirt Bike (ROW)	1999
MB73-J 1955 Chevy Bel Air (USA)	1999
MB73-K Concept 1 Convertible (Germany)	1999
MB73-L Pontiac Piranha (USA)	2002
MB73-M Smart Cabrio (ROW)	2002
MB73-N Hummer H2 SUV Concept	2003
MB74-A Daimler Bus	1970
MB74-B Toe Joe	1972
MB74-C Cougar Villager	1978
MB74-D Orange Peel (USA)	1981
MB74-E Fiat Abarth (ROW)	1982
MB74-F Mustang GT (USA)	1984
MB74-G Toyota MR2 (ROW)	1986
MB74-H Grand Prix Racer (USA)	1987
MB74-I Utility Truck (ROW)	1989
MB74-J Formula One Racer (USA)	1996
MB74-K Snowmobile (ROW)	1999
MB74-L Audi TT (Germany)	1999
MB74-M BMW Z3	2002
MB74-N Opel Frogster	2003
MB75-A Ferrari Berlinetta	1970
MB75-B Alfa Carabo	1971
MB75-C Seasprite Helicopter	1977
MB75-D Helicopter	1982
MB75-E Ferrari Testarossa	1986
MB75-F AMG C Class Mercedes (ROW)	1996
MB75-G Ferrari F50 (USA)	1996
MB75-H Aero Junior (ROW)	1999
MB75-I 1957 Corvette (USA)	1999
MB75-J Golf Cart (USA)	2000
MB75-K Water Pumper	2002
MB75-L Mini Cooper S	2003
MB76-A Savanna RX7 (AU/USA)	1981
MB76-B 4X4 Open Back Truck (USA)	1998
MB76-C Model A Ford Van (USA)	1998
MB76-D International Fire Engine (USA)	1999
MB77-A Toyota Celica (AU/USA)	1981
MB77-B Weasel (USA reintro)	1996
MB77-C Mercedes Benz ML430 (USA)	2000
MB78-A Datsun 260Z (AU/USA)	1981
MB78-B Ferrari Testarossa (USA reintro)	1996
MB79-A Galant Eterna (AU/USA)	1981
MB80-A Chevy Suburban (USA)	2000
MB81-A Concept 1 Convertible (USA)	2000
MB82-A Missile Launcher	2000
MB83-A BMW 3 Series coupe (USA)	2000
MB84-A Ford Focus (USA)	2000
MB85-A Sherman Tank (USA)	1999
MB86-A 1999 Chevy Silverado Pickup (USA)	1999
MB90-A Battering Ram (USA)	2000
MB91-A Four Wheeler (USA)	1999
MB91-B Ford Dump/ Utility Truck (USA)	2000
MB92-A Dune Buggy (USA)	1999
MB93-A Dirt Bike (USA)	1999
MB94-A Snowmobile (USA)	1999
MB95-A Aero Junior (USA)	1999
MB96-A Street Cleaner (USA)	2000
MB97-A Postal Service Delivery Truck (USA)	2000
MB99-A GMC Bucket Truck (USA)	2000
MB214 Ford Aeromax Cab (CY only)	1992
MB215 Chevy Panel Van	1995
MB217 DIRT Modified (WR)	1992
MB236 Ford Tractor (FM)	1993
MB237 Tractor Shovel (FM)	1993
MB262 Chrysler Voyager (BE)	1994
MB267 Chevy Lumina (WR)	1994
MB268 Ford Thunderbird (WR)	1994
MB269 Pontiac Grand Prix (WR)	1994
MB283 Chevy Monte Carlo (WR)	1995
MB284 Chevrolet Super Truck (WR)	1996
MB285 Ice Maker (WR)	1996
MB315 Volvo Truck (AP)	1998
MB317 Ford Cargo Skip Truck (JR/AP)	1997
MB319 Mercedes AAV (with bucket)(JR)	1997
MB337 Mercedes AAV (with roof load)(JR)	1997
MB338 1938 Dodge Airflow Van (CL)	1998
MB339 1937 Mack Junior Van (CL)	1998
MB343 Excavator (CT)	1998
MB344 Dump Truck (CT)	1998
MB345 Bulldozer (CT)	1998
MB346 Front Loader (CT)	1998
MB347 Road Roller (CT)	1998
MB348 Scraper (CT)	1998
MB350 Road Grader (CT)	1998

MB351 Caterpillar Challenger Tractor (CT)	1998
MB352 Caterpillar Trailer (CT)	1998
MB353 Caterpillar Backhoe/ Loader (CT)	1998
MB354 Caterpillar Soil Compactor (CT)	1998
MB374 '62 Chevrolet Corvette (Taco Bell)	1998
MB375 Humvee (Taco Bell)	1998
MB376 VW Concept (Taco Bell/PS)	1998
MB377 Pontiac Firebird Formula (Taco Bell)	1998
MB381 Caterpillar Material Handler (CT)	1999
MB382 Caterpillar Tool Carrier (CT)	1999
MB383 Caterpillar Tractor Shovel (CT)	1999
MB388 Peterbilt Dumper with plow (CT)	1998
MB389 Volvo Container Truck (AP)	1998
MB393 Harley Davidson Springer Softail (HD)	1995
MB394 1939 Harley Davidson H-D Knucklehead (HD)	1995
MB403 Caterpillar Articulated Dump Truck (CT)	1999
MB404 Caterpillar Skidder (CT)	1999
MB443 Caterpillar Flatbed Trailer (CT)	2000
MB455 Blimp	1999
MB456 Pontiac Firebird SE Police	2000
MB457 Camaro IROC-Z Police	2000
MB460 1999 Mustang Police	2000
MB461 Caterpillar D11 Bulldozer (CT)	1999
MB462 Caterpillar Dump Truck (CT)	2000
MB464 Corvette Police	2000
MB465 VW Concept 1 Police	2000
MB474 Ford Panel Van with roof light	2001
MB477 Chevrolet Suburban Police	2001
MB502 1960 MGA	2001
MB507 '55 Chevy Bel Air Police Car (CL)	2001
MB508 '33 Ford Coupe Police Car	2001
MB533 BMW Z3 (opening doors) (BMW)	2002
MB534 BMW 3 Series Cabrio (GR)	2002
MB535 BMW X5 (opening doors)(BMW)	2002
MB560 1956 Ford Fairlane Sunliner (CL)	2002
MB570 1960 Jeep (roll bar) (CL)	2003
MB596 BMW X5 Police Car (SG)	2003
MB710 Tipping Trailer (FM)	1993
MB711 Farm Trailer (FM)	1993
MB712 Seeder (FM)	1993
MB713 Rotovator (FM)	1993
MB720 Side Tipper (TP)	1977
MB724 Peterbilt Cab (CY only)	1984
MB791 Motorcycle Trailer (TP)	1979
MB792 Cattle Trailer (TP)	1979
MB793 Inflatable on Trailer (TP)	1984
MB794 Glider Transporter (TP)	1976

WR002 Ford F800 Delivery Van (WR)	1995
FS002 Ford F800 Delivery Van (WR)	1996
FST Ford Super Truck (WR)	1996
WRP01 1996 Pontiac Grand Prix (WR)	1996
WRP02 1996 Ford Thunderbird (WR)	1996
MB 2 Savanna RX7 (JP)	1979
MB 5 Datsun 280Z (JP)	1979
MB J-21 Toyota Celica XX (JP)	1979
MBJ-22 Galant Eterna (JP)	1979

NOTE: Numbers noted are for cataloging purposes only on models below.

BK-001 Beach	2002
BK-002 Desert	2002
BK-003 Jungle	2002
BK-004 Water Pumper	2003
BK-005 Rescue Helicopter	2003
BK-006 Troop Carrier	2003
MD-001 Snorkel Fire Truck	2002
MD-002 Dodge Dakota	2002
MD-003 Ford Crown Victoria	2002
MD-004 International Pumper	2002
MD-005 Wrecker Truck	2002
MD-006 Ambulance	2002
SW-001 Shovel Nose Tractor	2000
TB-005 '97 Chevy Tahoe	1999
TB-006 '97 Chevy Corvette	1999
TB-007 '80 Chevy K-1500 Pickup	1999
TB-008 '57 Chevrolet Bel Air Hardtop	1999
MB I Silver Streak (USA)	1978
MBII Sleet-N-Snow (USA)	1978
MBIII White Lightning (USA)	1978
MBIV Flying Beetle (USA)	1978
MB V Hot Smoker (USA)	1978
MBVI Lady Bug (USA)	1978
MBVII Brown Sugar (USA)	1978
MBVIII Black Widow (USA)	1978
MBIX Flamin Manta (USA)	1978
MBX Golden X (USA)	1978
LV-1 1983 Dodge Daytona Turbo Z (VG)	1983
LV-2 1983 Dodge Caravan (VG)	1983

Variations

MB 1-A MERCEDES TRUCK, issued 1970 (MB801)
NOTE: Versions 1-4 with black or red axle covers. All models with England casting.
1. gold body, orange canopy, light green windows, 5 spoke wheels, no labels ($18-25)
2. gold body, orange canopy, light green windows, 4 spoke wheels, no labels ($18-25)
3. gold body, yellow canopy, light green windows, 5 spoke wheels, no labels ($15-18)
4. gold body, yellow canopy, light green windows, 4 spoke wheels, no labels ($15-18)
5. red body, yellow canopy, blue windows, 4 spoke wheels, "Transcontinental Haulage" labels ($5-6)(TP)
6. red body, orange-yellow canopy, blue windows, 4 spoke wheels, "Transcontinental Haulage" labels ($5-6)(TP)
7. olive body, tan canopy, blue windows, 4 spoke wheels, "USA48350" labels ($8-12)(TP)
8. olive body, tan canopy, blue windows, 4 spoke wheels, "4TS 702K" labels ($6-8)(TP)
9. olive body, tan canopy, blue windows, 5 spoke wheels, "4TS 702K" labels ($6-8)(TP)
10. olive drab body, tan canopy, blue windows, 4 spoke wheels, "USA48350" labels ($65-80)(TP)
11. olive drab body, tan canopy, blue windows, 4 spoke wheels, "4TS 702K" labels ($65-80)(TP)
12. blue body, orange-yellow canopy, blue windows, 4 spoke wheels, "IMS" labels ($15-20)(TP)
13. blue body, orange-yellow canopy, purple windows, 4 spoke wheels, "IMS" labels ($50-75 (TP)

MB 1-B MOD ROD, issued 1971
NOTE: Below models with 5 spoke front & 4 spoke rear wheels & England casting. Other wheel permutations exist. Versions 1-9 with chrome engine although some examples may be found with black engine,
1. yellow body, orange interior, unpainted base, red wheels, wildcat head label ($25-40)
2. yellow body, orange interior, unpainted base, black wheels, wildcat head label ($15-18)
3. yellow body, orange interior, unpainted base, black wheels, flower label ($15-18)
4. yellow body, orange interior, unpainted base, black wheels, spotted cat label ($15-18)
5. yellow body, red interior, unpainted base, black wheels, spotted cat label ($15-18)
6. yellow body, red interior, silver-gray base, black wheels, spotted cat label ($18-25)
7. yellow body, orange interior, silver-gray base, black wheels, spotted cab label ($18-25)
8. yellow body, orange interior, unpainted base, black wheels, scorpion label ($25-40)
9. yellow body, orange interior, silver-gray base, black wheels, scorpion label ($25-40)
10. yellow body, orange interior, unpainted base, black wheels, cow label (from MB73-A) ($175-250)
11. yellow body, orange interior, unpainted base, black wheels, sunburst label (from MB47-B) ($175-250)
12. silver plated body, orange interior, unpainted base, black engine, black wheels, stripes tempa ($75-100) (RN)
13. yellow body, orange interior, unpainted base, black engine, "6" label (from MB62-C) ($175-250)

MB 1-C DODGE CHALLENGER, issued 1976
NOTE: Below models with unpainted base & England casting.
1. red body, chrome interior, clear windows, dot dash wheels ($5-7)
2. red body, chrome interior, clear windows, 5 arch wheels ($3-4)
3. red body, white interior, clear windows, 5 arch wheels ($4-6)
4. red body, red interior, clear windows, 5 arch wheels ($7-10)
5. blue body, red interior, clear windows, 5 arch wheels ($4-6)
6. dark blue body, red interior, clear windows, 5 arch wheels ($4-6)

MB 1-D DODGE CHALLENGER, issued 1982 (MB001)
MB34-F DODGE CHALLENGER, reissued 1991 (ROW)
NOTE: Below models with clear windows & dot dash rear wheels unless noted otherwise. Versions 1 to 4 with 5 arch front wheels.
1. orange body, unpainted base, blue roof, black interior, cast engine, "Revin Rebel" tempa, England casting ($4-6)
2. orange body, silver-gray base, blue roof, black interior, cast engine, "Revin Rebel" tempa, England casting ($4-6)
3. orange body, silver-gray base, white roof, black interior, cast engine, "Revin Rebel" tempa, England casting ($7-10)
4. orange body, silver-gray base, blue roof, black interior, cast engine, no tempa, England casting ($7-10)

NOTE: Below models with plastic engine cast through hood opening.

5. yellow body, pearly silver base, black roof, red interior, 5 arch front wheels, "Toyman" tempa, Macau casting ($2-3)
6. yellow body, pearly silver base, black roof, red interior, dot dash front wheels, "Toyman" tempa, Macau casting ($2-3)
7. yellow body, pearly silver base, black roof, red interior, dot dash front wheels, "Toyman" tempa, China casting ($1-2)
8. lemon body, pearly silver base, black roof, red interior, dot dash front wheels, "Toyman" tempa, China casting ($1-2)
9. orange-yellow body, pearly silver base, black roof, red interior, dot dash front wheels, "Toyman" tempa, China casting ($1-2)
10. white body, white base, white roof, blue interior, dot dash front wheels, blue windows, no tempa, China casting ($10-15)(GF)
11 powder blue body, silver-gray base, black roof, white interior, dot dash front wheels, "Challenger" tempa, China casting ($8-10)(AP)
12. yellow body, yellow base, black roof, red interior, dot dash front wheels, no tempa, China casting ($8-12)(GS)(GR)
13. white body, silver-gray base, black roof, red interior, dot dash front wheels, "Toyman" tempa, China casting ($8-12)(MP)
14. dark blue body, silver-gray metal base, white roof, black interior, dot dash front wheels, clear windows, "Hemi" & white stripes tempa, China casting ($1-2)
15.florescent yellow body, gray plastic base, black roof, pink interior, gold 6-spoke spiral front & rear wheels, clear windows, black squiggly lines tempa, Thailand casting ($1-2)
16. dark purple body, gray plastic base, black roof, neon yellow interior, silver 6-spoke spiral front & rear wheels, yellow zigzag tempa , Thailand casting ($1-2)(5pk)

17. fluorescent yellow body, gray plastic base, black roof, pink interior, silver 6-spoke spiral front & rear wheels, clear windows, black squiggly lines tempa, Thailand casting ($1-2)
18. florescent lime body, gray plastic base, black roof, black interior, silver 6-spoke spiral front & rear wheels, clear windows, black stripes tempa, China casting ($1-2)(5pk)
19. white body, gray plastic base, black roof, purple interior, silver 6-spoke spiral front & rear wheels, clear windows, purple squiggly lines tempa, China casting ($2-3)
20. white body, gray plastic base, black roof, purple interior, 5 spoke concave star front & rear wheels, clear windows, purple squiggly lines tempa, China casting ($3-5)(CY)
21. dark purple body, chrome plastic base, black roof, black & white interior, chrome disc wheels with rubber tires, clear windows, white stripes tempa, China casting ($3-5)(PC9)
22. dark purple body, gray plastic base, black roof, black & white interior, 5 spoke concave front & rear wheels, clear windows, white stripes tempa, China casting ($50+)(CHI)
23. orange body, chrome plastic base, black roof, black & white interior, chrome disc wheels with rubber tires, clear windows, white stripes tempa, China casting ($3-5)(PC17)
24. red body, chrome plastic base, black roof , black & white interior, chrome disc wheels with rubber tires, clear windows, yellow & orange flames tempa, China casting ($3-5)(PC11)
25. red body, gray plastic base, black roof, black interior, 5 spoke concave star front & rear wheels, yellow & orange flames tempa, China casting ($50+)(CHI)

MB 1-E JAGUAR XJ6 *see MB41-F*

MB1-F JAGUAR XJ6 POLICE CAR, issued 1991 (ROW)(MB231)

NOTE: Below models with black plastic base.

1. white body, tan interior, blue windows & dome lights, 8 dot wheels, "Police" with blue & yellow stripes tempa, Thailand casting ($3-5)
2. white body, tan interior, blue windows & dome lights, 8 dot wheels, "Police" with checkers & stripes tempa, Thailand casting ($3-5)

MB1-G DODGE VIPER GTS, issued 1997 (USA) (MB276)
MB35-K DODGE VIPER GTS, issued 1997 (ROW)

NOTE: Below models with clear windows & black plastic base unless otherwise noted.

1. metallic blue body, gray & black interior, chrome disc with rubber tires, dual white stripes tempa, Thailand casting ($4-6)(IG)
2. unpainted body, gray interior, chrome disc with rubber tires, no tempa, Thailand casting ($4-6)(IG)
3. metallic blue body, gray interior, 5 spoke concave star wheels, dual white stripes tempa, Thailand casting ($1-2)
4. black body, orange interior, chrome disc with rubber tires, orange stripes & "Matchbox Convention" tempa, Thailand casting ($12-15)(US)
5. red body, black interior, chrome disc with rubber tires, dual white stripes tempa, Thailand casting ($4-6)(PC14)
6. red body, black interior, 5 spoke concave star wheels, dual white stripes tempa, Thailand casting ($50+)(CHI)
7. white body, dark blue interior, 5 spoke concave star wheels, dual blue stripes tempa, Thailand casting ($1-2)(MW1/1998 US)
8. white body, dark blue interior, 5 spoke concave star wheels, dual blue stripes tempa, China casting ($1-2)(MW1/ 1998 US)
9. metallic gold body, black interior, 5 spoke concave star wheels, no tempa, China casting ($5-10)(CH)
10. bright blue body, white & gray interior, chrome disc with rubber tires, dual white stripes tempa, China casting ($3-5)(GS-Chrysler)
11. blue body, black interior, 5 spoke concave star wheels, white stripe & "New York Knicks" tempa, China casting ($4-6)(NBA)
12. powder blue body, white interior, 5 spoke concave star wheels, "Utah Jazz" tempa, China casting ($4-6)(NBA)
13. teal blue body, black interior, 5 spoke concave star wheels, black stripe & "Detroit Pistons" tempa, China casting ($4-6)(NBA)
14. lavender & white body, white interior, 5 spoke concave star wheels, "Los Angeles Lakers" tempa, China casting ($4-6)(NBA)
15. black body, gray interior, 5 spoke concave star wheels, "Orlando Magic" tempa, China casting ($4-6)(NBA)
16. black & white body, red interior, 5 spoke concave star wheels, "Chicago Bulls" tempa, China casting ($4-6)(NBA)
17. orange & black body, red-orange interior, 5 spoke concave star wheels, "Atlanta Hawks" tempa, China casting ($4-6)(NBA)
18. red body, white interior, 5 spoke concave star wheels, "Houston Rockets" tempa, China casting ($4-6)(NBA)
19. silver-gray body, black interior, chrome disc with rubber tires, dual white stripes tempa, China casting ($4-6)(PC)
20. dark purple & black body, orange interior, 5 spoke concave star wheels, "Phoenix Suns" tempa, China casting ($4-6)(NBA)
21. orange-yellow body, green interior, 5 spoke concave star wheels, "Seattle Sonics" tempa, China casting ($4-6) (NBA)
22. white body, purple interior, 5 spoke concave star wheels, "Charlotte Hornets" tempa, China casting ($4-6)(NBA)
23. yellow & red body, black interior, 5 spoke concave star wheels, "Miami Heat" tempa, China casting ($6-8)(NBA)
24. green & white body, black interior, 5 spoke concave star wheels, "Boston Celtics" tempa, China casting ($8-12)(NBA)
25. lemon body, black interior, 5 spoke concave star wheels, painted lights tempa, China casting ($1-2) (5pk)
26. red & black body, white interior, 5 spoke concave star wheels, "Blazers" tempa, China casting ($4-6)(NBA)
27. white body, dark blue interior, 5 spoke concave star wheels, "Warriors" tempa, China casting ($4-6)(NBA)
28. yellow & white body, dark blue interior, 5 spoke concave star wheels, "Indiana Pacers" tempa, China casting ($4-6)(NBA)
29. lavender & blue body, orange interior, 5 spoke concave star wheels, "Cavs" tempa, China casting ($4-6)(NBA)
30. black & green body, blue interior, 5 spoke concave star wheels, "Timberwolves" tempa, China casting ($4-6)(NBA)
31. silver-gray body, red interior, 5 spoke concave star wheels, "Nets" tempa, China casting ($4-6)(NBA)
32. brown-gold body, red interior, 5 spoke concave star wheels, "Denver Nuggets" tempa, China casting ($4-6)(NBA)
33. silver-gray body, tan interior, smoke windows, 5 spoke concave star wheels, red tail lights tempa, China casting ($1-2)(MW19/ 2000 US)
34. silver-gray body, tan interior, smoke windows, 5 spoke concave star wheels, red tail lights & "Matchbox 2000" on windows tempa, China casting ($2-4)(MW19/2000 US)
35. white body, black interior, smoke windows, 5 spoke concave star wheels, "Midwest Regional Matchbox Convention" (blue hood print) tempa, China casting ($25-30)(CCI)
36. white body, black interior, smoke windows, 5 spoke concave star wheels, "Midwest Regional Matchbox Convention" (red hood print) tempa, China casting ($25-30)(CCI)
37. white body, black interior, smoke windows, 5 spoke concave star wheels, none tempa, China casting ($25-40)(CCI blank)

38. metallic charcoal body, silver-gray interior, clear windows, 5 spoke concave star wheels, head & tail lights tempa, China casting ($1-2)(5pk)
39. bright blue body, silver-gray interior, smoke windows, 10 spoke flower wheels, dual yellow stripes & "Viper" 3X tempa, China casting ($1-2)(MW5)
40. bright blue body, silver-gray interior, smoke windows, 10 spoke flower wheels, dual yellow stripes & "Viper" 3X tempa, metal base, China casting ($1-2)(MW3/ 2001)
41. silver-gray body, tan interior, smoke windows, 5 spoke concave star wheels, "Celebrating Dr. Roy R. Gal Ph.D. Astrophysics/ California Institute of Technology" tempa, China casting ($35-50)(CCI)
42. metallic charcoal body, silver-gray interior, clear windows, 10 spoke flower wheels, head & tail lights tempa, metal base, China casting ($1-2)(5pk)

NOTE: Below models with black interior, smoke windows, 5 spoke concave star wheels, China casting unless otherwise noted

43. white body, "Savannah 2001" tempa ($20-25)(CCI)
44. white body, "Hope Spring 2000" tempa, China casting ($10-15)(CCI)
45. white body, "Hope Spring 2001" tempa, China casting ($10-15)(CCI)
46. white body, "Bloomsburg Fair Association 2001" tempa, China casting ($10-15)(CCI)
47. white body, "Nittany Lions/ Penn State" tempa, China casting ($10-15)(CCI)
48. metallic blue body, gray interior, clear windows, "1st Annual Open House Matchbox Road Museum" tempa, Thailand casting ($25-40)(CCI)
49. white body, "A Merry Mattelica Christmas 2001" & Santa tempa ($75-100)(CCI)
50. white body, "Smart Energy, Smart Solutions- Trigen" tempa ($10-15)(CCI)
51. white body, "Yard Right Select" tempa ($10-15)(CCI)
52. white body, "MRMC Oct. 6, 2002" (blue lettering) tempa ($15-25)(CCI)
53. white body, "MRMC Oct. 6, 2002" (red lettering) tempa ($15-25)(CCI)
54. white body, "Napps Conference" tempa ($10-15)(CCI)
55. white body, "Matchbox USA Convention & Toy Show/ CCI On Site Demo Model" tempa ($10-15)(CCI)
56. white body, "Adriel's 5th Birthday" tempa ($25-40)(CCI)
57. white body, "8.8/ Upgrade 2004" tempa ($15-20)(CCI)
58. white body, "Troop 1 Flea Market 2004" tempa ($18-25)(CCI)
59. yellow body, "Troop 1 Flea Market 2004" tempa ($18-25)(CCI)
60. silver-gray body, tan interior, "Troop 1 Flea Market 2004" tempa ($18-25)(CCI)
61. light blue & maroon body, blue interior, clear windows, chrome disc with rubber tires, "Superman" tempa, China casting ($3-5)(JL)
62. silver-gray body, red interior, clear windows, 10 spoke flower wheels, small "Matchbox" logo tempa ($1-2)(LP)
63. silver-gray, white interior, red windows, lace wheels, "Tom & Jerry" tempa, gray base ($1-2)(5pk)

MB 1-H MERCEDES BENZ CLK CONVERTIBLE, issued 2000 (MB400)

MB71-K MERCEDES BENZ CLK CONVERTIBLE, issued 1999 (GR)

NOTE: Below models with black base, China casting unless otherwise noted.

1. metallic green body, black interior , clear windshield, 5 spoke concave star wheels , painted tail lights tempa($3-5)(MW71/ 1999GR)
2. metallic blue-green body, tan interior, clear windshield, 5 spoke concave star wheels, painted tail lights tempa ($1-2)(MW1/ 2000)
3. metallic blue-green body, tan interior, clear windshield, 5 spoke concave star wheels, painted tail lights &"Matchbox 2000" on windshield tempa ($2-4)(MW1/ 2000 US)
4. metallic gold body, black interior, clear windshield, lace wheels, head & tail lights tempa ($2-4)(MW48/ 2001 ROW)
5. dark metallic blue body, gray interior, smoke windshield, lace wheels, none tempa ($3-4)(SG)
6. white body, orange interior, smoke windshield, 10 spoke flower wheels, "Hero City Sports" tempa ($1-2)(5pk)
7. unpainted body, gray interior, smoke windshield, lace wheels, pop art decals ($75+)(FA)
8. metallic green body, black interior, smoke windshield, 10 spoke flower wheels, "Leaning Tower of Pisa- Italy" tempa ($2-3)(AM)
9. metallic silver body, black interior, dark smoke windshield, lace wheels, no tempa ($2-3)(MW20/2004 ROW)
10. silver blue body, black interior, smoke windshield, lace wheels, head & tail lights tempa ($3-5)(SoC)

MB 1-I HIGHWAY RESCUE FIRE TRUCK, issued 2003 (MB566)

NOTE: Below models with blue windows, gray base & 4 spoke domed wheels, China casting unless otherwise noted.

1. metallic red body, white rear, stripes & "1" tempa ($1-2)(MW1/ 2003)
2. metallic red body, white rear, stripes, "1" & "Hero City" tempa ($2-3)(MW1/ 2003)
3. light metallic red body, gray rear, "Fire Dept. USA" with stars & stripes tempa ($1-2)(HR)
4. metallic red body, white rear, stripes & "1" tempa, gold wheels ($3-4)(20pk)
5. iridescent white body, red rear, "Unit One" & design tempa, black base ($1-2)(LP)
6. red body, white rear, "Alarm Unit" tempa, white base, 5 crown dot wheels ($5-8)(CG)

MB1-J WHISTLE CAR, issued 2003 (USA) (MB617)

NOTE: Below models with red windows, lace wheels & gray base unless otherwise noted.

1. chrome plated body, blue chassis, "Police" & shield tempa, gold hubs ($1-2)(MW1/ 2004 US)
2. gold plated body, blue chassis, "2004 Toy Fair- Matchbox Hero City" tempa, gold hubs, screwed inside plexibox ($35-50)(US)
3. chrome plated body, red chassis, white stripes & referee tempa, silver hubs, black base ($1-2)(5pk)

MB 1-K SQUAWKIE-TALKIE *see MB 3-G*

MB 1-L FIRE LADDER TRUCK, issued 2004 (MB660)

1. red body, white boom, blue windows, chrome chassis, white base, 5 arch dot wheels, "59 MBFD" & stripes tempa ($1-2)(MW1/2005)

MB 1-M 1965 SHELBY COBRA 427 A/C, issued 2004 (SF)(MB557)

MB557 1965 SHELBY COBRA 427 A/C, issued 2002 (CL)

NOTE: Below models with black interior, & China casting

1. white body, small windscreen, "11" in circle tempa, with diorama, chrome disc wheels with rubber tires, black plastic base ($10-15)(EL)

2. red body, small windscreen, "13" in circle tempa, chrome disc wheels with rubber tires, black plastic base ($3-5)(MCC)
3. red body, small windscreen, "65" in circle tempa, 5 spoke slotted wheels, gray plastic base ($1-2)(SF1/2004)

MB2-A MERCEDES TRAILER, issued 1970 (MB702/ 802)

1. gold body, orange canopy, 4 spoke wheels, no labels ($18-25)
2. gold body, yellow canopy, 4 spoke wheels, no labels ($15-18)
3. red body, yellow canopy, 4 spoke wheels, "Transcontinental Haulage" labels ($4-6)(TP)
4. red body, orange-yellow canopy, 4 spoke wheels, "Transcontinental Haulage" labels ($4-6)(TP)
5. olive body, tan canopy, 4 spoke wheels, "USA48350" labels ($8-12)(TP)
6. olive body, tan canopy, 4 spoke wheels, "4TS 702K" labels ($8-12)(TP)
7. olive body, tan canopy, 5 spoke wheels, "4TS 702K" labels ($8-12)(TP)
8. olive drab body, tan canopy, 5 spoke wheels, "USA48350" labels ($65-80)(TP)
9. olive drab body, tan canopy, 5 spoke wheels, "4TS 702K" labels ($65-80)(TP)
10. olive drab body, tan canopy, 4 spoke wheels, "USA48350" labels ($65-80)(TP)
11. olive drab body, tan canopy, 4 spoke wheels, "4TS 702K" labels ($65-80)(TP)
12 blue body, yellow-orange canopy, 5 spoke wheels, "IMS" labels ($15-18)(TP)
13 yellow body, white canopy, 5 crown wheels, "Alpine Rescue" labels ($3-5)(TP)
14 yellow body, no canopy, 5 crown wheels, no tempa ($5-7)

NOTE: Above models with England casting.

15. yellow body, white canopy, 5 crown wheels, "Alpine Rescue" tempa , Macau casting ($3-5)(TP)
16. yellow body, white canopy, 5 crown wheels, "Alpine Rescue" tempa, no origin cast ($3-5)(TP)
17. red body, white canopy, 5 crown wheels, "Unfall Rettung" tempa, no origin cast ($3-5)(TP)
18. white body, orange canopy, 5 crown wheels, "C & S" tempa, no origin cast ($3-5)(TP)
19. red body, white canopy, dot dash wheels, "Big Top Circus" tempa, no origin cast ($4-6)(TP)

MB 2-B JEEP HOT ROD, issued 1971

NOTE: Below models with England casting. Versions 1-13 with chrome engine & black exhausts.

1. pink body, light green base, cream interior, 4 spoke wheels, with engine ($15-18)
2. pink body, dark green base, cream interior, 4 spoke wheels, with engine ($15-18)
3. orchid body, light green base, cream interior, 4 spoke wheels, with engine ($18-25)
4. orchid body, dark green base, cream interior, 4 spoke wheels, with engine ($18-25)
5. pink body, dark green base, yellow interior, 4 spoke wheels, with engine ($15-18)
6. pink body, dark green base, white interior, 4 spoke wheels, with engine ($15-18)
7. pink body, dark green base, cream interior, 5 spoke wheels, with engine ($15-18)
8. pink body, white base, cream interior, 4 spoke wheels, with engine ($18-25)
9. red body, dark green base, cream interior, 4 spoke wheels, with engine ($18-25)
10. red body, dark green base, ivory interior, 4 spoke wheels, with engine ($18-25)
11. red body, white base, cream interior, 4 spoke wheels, with engine ($15-18)
12. red body, white base, cream interior, 5 spoke wheels, with engine ($15-18)
13. red body, white base, cream interior, maltese cross wheels, with engine ($18-25)
14. olive body, black base, black interior, 4 spoke wheels, hood label ($8-12)(TP)
15. olive drab body, black base, black interior, 4 spoke wheels, hood label ($65-80)(TP)
16. olive body, black base, black interior, 5 spoke wheels, hood label ($10-15)(TP)
17. orange body, black base with Manaus label, cream interior, 4 spoke wheels, with engine ($250+)(BR)

MB 2-C HOVERCRAFT, issued 1976

NOTE: Below models with solid black wheels & England casting unless otherwise noted.

1. light metallic green body, tan hull, chrome scoop, amber windows, "Rescue" labels ($4-6)
2. light metallic lime body, tan hull, chrome scoop, amber windows, "Rescue" labels ($4-6)
3. light metallic lime body, beige hull, chrome scoop, amber windows, "Rescue" labels ($4-6)
4. dark metallic lime body, tan hull, chrome scoop, amber windows, "Rescue" labels ($4-6)
5. light metallic lime body, tan hull, chrome scoop, red windows, "Rescue" labels ($4-6)
6. dark metallic lime body, tan hull, chrome scoop, red windows, "Rescue" labels ($4-6)
7. avocado body, tan hull, chrome scoop, amber windows, no labels ($7-10)(AV)
8. avocado body, tan hull, chrome scoop, amber windows, "Rescue" labels ($7-10)(AV)
9. avocado body, black hull, chrome scoop, purple windows, "Rescue" labels ($7-10)(AV)
10. avocado body, black hull, chrome scoop, purple windows, "2000" labels ($7-10)(AV)
11. avocado body, black hull, red scoop, purple windows, "2000" labels ($7-10)(AV)
12. avocado body, tan hull, red scoop, purple windows, "2000" labels ($7-10)(AV)
13. dark metallic lime body, tan hull, red scoop, amber windows, "Rescue" labels ($5-8)
14. dark metallic lime body, tan hull, red scoop, purple windows, "Rescue" labels ($5-8)
15. dark metallic lime body, tan hull, chrome scoop, purple windows, "Rescue" labels ($4-6)
16. dark metallic lime body, beige hull, chrome scoop, amber windows, "Rescue" labels ($4-6)
17. dark metallic lime body, black hull, chrome scoop, amber windows, "Rescue" labels ($4-6)
18. dark metallic lime body, beige hull, chrome scoop, amber windows, "Rescue" labels ($4-6)
19. light lime body, tan hull with Manaus tab, dark green scoop, amber windows, "Rescue" labels ($35-50)(BR)

MB 2-D S.2 JET, issued 1981

1. black body, yellow base, yellow wings, amber windows, no tempa, England casting ($3-5)
2. black body, yellow base, yellow wings, red windows, no tempa, England casting ($3-5)

3. light metallic blue body, white base, white wings, clear windows, no tempa, England casting ($2-4)
4. light metallic blue body, white base, white wings, clear windows, "Viper" tempa, England casting ($2-4)
5. light metallic blue body, white base, gray wings, clear windows, "Viper" tempa, England casting ($2-4)
6. light metallic blue body, white base, gray wings, clear windows, no tempa, England casting ($2-4)
7. dark metallic blue body, white base, white wings, clear windows, "Viper" tempa, Macau casting ($2-4)
8. dark metallic blue body, white base, white wings, clear windows, "Viper" tempa, Hong Kong casting ($20-25)
9. dark metallic blue body, white base, white wings, clear windows, "Viper" tempa, China casting ($2-4)
10. olive green body, black base, olive green wings, clear windows, "AC152" & tan camouflage tempa, Macau casting ($4-6)(CM)

MB 2-E PONTIAC FIERO, issued 1985 (MB158)

NOTE: Below models with clear windows, silver-gray interior & black plastic base insert.

1. white upper body, dark blue lower body, 8 dot silver wheels, "Goodyear 85" tempa, Macau casting ($2-4)
2. white upper body, dark blue lower body, 8 dot gold wheels, "Goodyear 85" tempa, Macau casting ($5-8)
3. white upper body, dark blue lower body, dot dash wheels, "Goodyear 85" tempa, Macau casting ($4-6)
4. yellow upper body, orange lower body, starburst wheels, "Protech 16" tempa, Macau casting ($3-5)(SF)
5. yellow upper body, orange lower body, 8 dot silver wheels, "Protech 16" tempa, Macau casting ($50-75)
6. white upper body, red lower body, 8 dot silver wheels, "GT Fiero" tempa, Macau casting ($2-4)
7. yellow upper body, metallic gold lower body, laser wheels, "Protech 16" tempa, Macau casting ($3-5)(LW)
8. black upper body, red lower body, 8 dot silver wheels, "2 Dog Racing Team" tempa, Macau casting ($8-12)(HK)
9. white body, red lower body, 8 dot silver wheels, "GT Fiero" tempa, China casting ($2-4)
10. fluorescent orange body, black lower body, starburst wheels, black flames, and "Turbo" tempa, China casting ($4-6)(PS)

MB 2-F STERLING *see MB31-G*

MB 2-G 1965 CORVETTE GRAND SPORT, issued 1990 (USA) (MB200)

MB15-G 1965 CORVETTE GRAND SPORT, issued 1990(ROW)

NOTE: Below models have 5 arch front & 5 crown rear wheels unless otherwise noted.

1. metallic blue body, clear windows, chrome interior, white stripes & small '15" on doors tempa, black base, Macau casting ($2-3)
2. metallic blue body, clear windows, chrome interior, white stripes & larger "15" on doors tempa, black base, Macau casting ($2-3)
3. metallic red body, chrome windows, black interior, white stripes & "63" tempa, black base, gray disc with rubber tires, Macau casting ($15-20)(WC)
4. metallic red body, chrome windows, black interior, white stripes & "63" tempa, chrome base, gray disc with rubber tires, Macau casting ($5-8)(WC)
5. metallic blue body, clear windows, chrome interior, white stripes & larger "15" on doors tempa, black base, Thailand casting ($2-3)
6. metallic blue body, clear windows, chrome interior, white stripes & larger "15" on doors tempa, black base, China casting ($2-3)
7. metallic blue body, clear windows, chrome interior, "Heinz 57" tempa, black base, China casting ($20-25)(US)
8. metallic blue body, clear windows, chrome interior, white stripes & "Corvette" on doors tempa, black base, Thailand casting ($2-3)
9. white & blue body, clear windows, black interior, "9" & red stripes tempa, white disc with rubber tires, white base, Thailand casting ($5-7)(WP)
10. white body, clear windows, chrome interior, red striping & "Corvette" on doors tempa, black base, Thailand casting ($1-2)
11. bright yellow body, clear windows, chrome interior, purple & black design tempa, dark gray base, Thailand casting ($1-2)(5pk)
12. metallic blue body, clear windows, black interior, white stripes & "2" tempa, chrome base, Thailand casting ($2-3)(GS)
13. dark orange body, clear windows, dark blue interior, black tire tread tempa, black base, gold 6 spoke spiral wheels, Thailand casting ($1-2)
14. chrome plated body, amber windows, white interior, no tempa, white base, gold 6 spoke spiral wheels, Thailand casting ($2-4)(GF)
15. metallic blue body, clear windows, chrome interior, green flames tempa, black base, silver 6 spoke spiral wheels, Thailand casting ($1-2)(5pk)
16. white body, pink windows, chrome interior, orange "The Widow" & web with spider tempa, silver 6-spoke spiral wheels, black base, Thailand casting ($1-2)
17. white body, pink windows, white interior, red outlined "The Widow" & web with spider tempa, silver 6-spoke spiral wheels, black base, Thailand casting ($2-3)
18. silver body, red windows, white interior, blue stripes tempa, silver 6-spoke spiral wheels, black base, Thailand casting ($4-5)(MT)
19. dark purple body, clear windows, chrome interior, orange flames tempa, silver 6-spoke spiral; wheels, black base, China casting ($1-2)(5pk)
20. light metallic blue body, clear windows, light gray/black interior, "50" & white stripes tempa, chrome disc with rubber tires, black base, China casting ($4-5)(PC3)
21. black body, red windows, white interior, red outlined "The Widow" & Web with spider tempa, silver 6-spoke spiral wheels, black base, China casting($2-4)
22. metallic gray body, clear windows, ivory/black interior, "50" & white stripes tempa, chrome disc with rubber tires, black base, China casting ($3-5)(PC6)
23. metallic gold body, clear windows, chrome interior, no tempa, silver 6 spoke spiral wheels, black base, China casting ($5-10)(CH)
24. white body, clear windows, dark blue & black interior, "4" with black stripes tempa, chrome disc with rubber tires, black base, China casting ($3-5)(SC3)
25. white body, red windows, white interior, red outlined "The Widow" & web with spider tempa, silver 6 spoke spiral wheels, black base, China casting ($2-4)(Corvette Cologne)
26. dark charcoal body, clear windows, gray & black interior, detailed trim tempa, chrome disc with rubber tires, black & white base, China casting ($3-5)(CP)
27. blue body, clear windows, gray interior, detailed trim tempa, chrome disc with rubber tires, black base, China casting ($3-5)(CP)

28. black body, red windows, white interior, red outlined "The Widow" & web with spider tempa, 5 spoke concave star wheels, black base, China casting ($2-4)
29. white body, clear windows, blue & gray interior, yellow & orange flames tempa, chrome disc with rubber tires, chrome base, China casting ($3-5)(PC11)
30. lemon body, clear windows, black & gray interior, detailed trim tempa, chrome disc with rubber tires, black & white base, China casting ($3-5)(CP)
31. gold body, clear windows, black & gray interior, detailed trim tempa, chrome disc with rubber tires, black & white base, China casting ($3-5)(CP)
32. metallic green body, clear windows, gray & black interior, detailed trim tempa, chrome disc with rubber tires, black & white base, China casting ($3-5)(CP)
33. black body, clear windows, gray & black interior, detailed trim tempa, chrome disc with rubber tires, black base, China casting ($3-5)(CP)
34. red body, clear windows, chrome interior, white band tempa, 5 spoke concave star wheels, black base, China casting ($2-4)
35. black body, clear windows, gray & black interior, detailed trim tempa, gold 6 spoke spiral wheels, black base, China casting ($50+)(CHI)
36. gold body, clear windows, gray & black interior, detailed trim tempa, gold 6 spoke spiral wheels, black base, China casting ($50+)(CHI)
37. blue body, clear windows, chrome interior, white band tempa, 5 spoke concave star wheels, black base, China casting ($1-2)(MW3/ 1998 US)
38. lemon body, clear windows, black & gray interior, blue pinstripes & detailed trim tempa, chrome disc wheels with rubber tires, black & white base, China casting ($3-5)(PC20)
39. gold body, clear windows, gray interior, detailed trim tempa, gold 6 spoke spiral wheels, black base, China casting ($50+)(CHI)
40. blue body, clear windows, black & gray interior, detailed trim tempa, gold 6 spoke spiral wheels, black base, China casting ($50+)(CHI)
41. lemon body, clear windows, gray interior, detailed trim tempa, gold 6 spoke spiral wheels, black base, China casting ($50+)(CHI)
42. black body, clear windows, gray interior, detailed trim tempa, gold 6 spoke spiral wheels, black base, China casting ($50+)(CHI)
43. metallic green body, clear windows, gray interior, detailed trim tempa, 6 spoke gold spiral wheels, black base, China casting ($50+)(CHI)
44. lemon body, clear windows, dark blue & black interior, detailed trim tempa, 6 spoke gold spiral wheels, black & white base, China casting ($50+)(CHI)
45. dark charcoal, clear windows, gray interior, detailed trim tempa, 6 spoke gold spiral wheels, black base, China casting ($50+)(CHI)

MB 2-H BMW 850i *see MB49-H*

MB 2-I '99 CAMARO SS CONVERTIBLE, issued 2000 (USA) (MB366)

NOTE: Below models with black base & 5 spoke concave star wheels, China casting unless otherwise noted.

1. dark red body, black interior, smoke windshield with "Matchbox 2000" logo & head lights tempa ($2-4)(MW2/ 2000 US)
2. dark red body, black interior, smoke windshield, head lights tempa ($1-2)(MW2/ 2000 US)
3. salmon body, orange-yellow interior, blue windshield, "Sydney 2000" tempa ($1-2)(5pk)
4. red body, white interior, clear windshield with black trim, "Coca Cola" tempa ($4-6)(Avon TP)
5. black body, dark gray interior, smoke windshield with black trim, "Coca Cola" & polar bears tempa, chrome disc with rubber tires ($4-6)(Coke PC)
6. black body, tan & black interior, clear windshield with black trim, detailed trim tempa, chrome disc wheels with rubber tires ($4-6)(FE)
7. unpainted body, tan interior, clear windshield, none tempa, chrome disc with rubber wheels ($4-6)(FE)
8. dark red body, black interior, smoke windshield with "Matchbox 2000" logo, "South Jersey Camaro Group Productions/ East Coast Camaro Gathering IV" tempa ($25-40)(CCI)
9. very dark metallic blue body, black & gray interior, clear windshield with black trim, chrome disc wheels with rubber tires, detailed trim tempa ($3-4)(TN)
10. white body, turquoise interior, smoke windshield lace wheels, "Orange Mobile 27, Sunshine State Florida" tempa ($1-2)(AM)
11. lime body, white interior, smoke windshield lace wheels, "Florida- Joe's Alligator Corral" tempa ($5-8)(AM)
12. light blue body, blue interior, smoke windshield, lace wheels, "Rocket Power" tempa ($1-2)(5pk)
13. black body, tan & black interior, clear windshield with black trim, chrome wheels disc with rubber tires, "East Coast Camaro Gathering VII" tempa ($10-15)(CCI)
14. unpainted body, tan interior, clear windshield, chrome disc wheels with rubber tires, "East Coast Camaro Gathering VII" tempa ($10-15)(CCI)
15. lemon body, green interior, smoke windshield, lace wheels, "The Carrot Show/ Back In Action" tempa ($1-2)(5pk)
16. metallic blue body, yellow interior, clear windshield, lace wheels, "Sandy" tempa ($1-2)(5pk)
17. metallic blue body, tan interior, clear windshield with blue trim, 5 spoke slotted wheels, detailed trim tempa ($2-4)(SF30/2004)

MB 2-J BADGE CAR, issued 2004 (MB618)

NOTE: Below models with gold 5 dot crown wheels & China casting.

1. chrome plated upper body, red lower body, blue windows, "Chief 420" tempa, black base ($1-2)(MW2/ 2003 US)
2. gold plated upper body, blue lower body, red windows, "Police/ M" with light blue design tempa, gray base ($1-2)(5pk)
3. gold plated upper body, blue lower body, red windows, "Police/ M" with dark blue design tempa, gray base ($1-2)(5pk)

MB 3-A MERCEDES BENZ "BINZ" AMBULANCE, issued 1970 (MB803)

NOTE: Below models with red cross labels. Versions 1-3 with white plastic man on stretcher. Base lettering reads front to rear or rear to front on all variations. Early models with narrow wheels, later issues with wide wheels. All models with unpainted metal base & England casting.

1. cream body, blue windows, rear door opens, 5 spoke wheels ($25-40)
2. off white body, blue windows, rear door opens, 5 spoke wheels ($25-40)
3. off white body, dark blue windows, rear door opens, 5 spoke wheels ($25-40)
4. off white body, dark blue windows, rear door cast shut, dot dash wheels ($7-10)(TP)
5. olive body, dark blue windows, rear door cast shut, dot dash wheels- silver hubs ($7-10)(TP)

6. olive body, dark blue windows, rear door cast shut, dot dash wheels- black hubs ($7-10)(TP)

MB3-B MONTEVERDI HAI, issued 1973

NOTE: Below models with England casting.

1. orange body, unpainted base, ivory interior, blue windows, "3" label ($10-15)
2. orange body, silver-gray base, ivory interior, blue windows, "3" label ($15-20)
3. orange body, unpainted base, light yellow interior, blue windows, "3" label ($10-15)
4. orange body, unpainted base, light yellow interior, blue windows, no label ($10-15)
5. orange body, unpainted base, ivory interior, blue windows, "3" label ($10-15)
6. orange body, unpainted base, ivory interior, blue windows, "16" label ($15-20)
7. orange body, unpainted base, ivory interior, dark blue windows, "3" label ($10-15)
8. orange body, black base, ivory interior, blue windows, "3" label ($10-15)
9. orange body, black base, ivory interior, blue windows, "6" label ($15-20)

MB 3-C PORSCHE TURBO, issued 1978 (MB003)

NOTE: Below models with England casting & 5 arch wheels unless otherwise noted.

1. brown body, cream interior, unpainted base, clear windows, no tempa ($35-50)
2. brown body, cream interior, black base, clear windows, no tempa ($7-10)
3. silver-gray body, cream interior, black base, clear windows, no tempa ($6-8)
4. silver-gray body, cream interior, charcoal base, clear windows, no tempa ($6-8)
5. silver-gray body, red interior, black base, clear windows, no tempa ($3-5)
6. silver-gray body, red interior, brown base, clear windows, no tempa ($7-10)
7. silver-gray body, red interior, charcoal base, clear windows, no tempa ($3-5)
8. silver-gray body, tan interior, brown base, clear windows, no tempa ($7-10)
9. silver-gray body, tan interior, black base, clear windows, no tempa ($4-8)
10. silver-gray body, tan interior, charcoal base, clear windows, no tempa ($4-8)
11. matt gray body, red interior, brown base, clear windows, no tempa ($7-10)
12. matt gray body, red interior, charcoal base, clear windows, no tempa ($7-10)
13. metallic green body, cream interior, charcoal base, clear windows, no tempa ($7-10)
14. metallic green body, red interior, charcoal base, clear windows, no tempa ($7-10)
15. metallic green body, red interior, black base, clear windows, no tempa ($7-10)
16. metallic green body, orange-yellow interior, charcoal base, clear windows, no tempa ($3-5)
17. metallic green body, orange-yellow interior, black base, clear windows, no tempa ($3-5)
18. metallic green body, orange-yellow interior, blue-gray base, clear windows, no tempa ($5-8)
19. metallic green body, orange-yellow interior, unpainted base, clear windows, no tempa ($5-8)
20. red body, tan interior, black base, clear windows, "Porsche 90 Turbo" tempa ($3-5)
21. red body, tan interior, blue-gray base, clear windows, "Porsche 90 Turbo" tempa ($3-5)
22. red body, tan interior, charcoal base, clear windows, "Porsche 90 Turbo" tempa ($3-5)
23. red body, white interior, charcoal base, clear windows, "Porsche 90 Turbo" tempa ($3-5)
24. red body, white interior, black base, clear windows, "Porsche 90 Turbo" tempa ($3-5)
25. orange-red body, white interior, black base, clear windows, "Porsche 90 Turbo" tempa ($5-8)
26. red body, tan interior, black base, opaque white windows, "Porsche 90 Turbo" tempa ($10-15) (PS)
27. red body, tan interior, black base, clear windows, no tempa ($3-5)

NOTE: Below models with Macau casting

28. red body, brown interior, black base, clear windows, "Porsche 90 Turbo" tempa ($2-4)
29. black body, tan interior, black base, amber windows, "Porsche 90 Turbo" tempa ($2-4)
30. red body, tan interior, black base, clear windows, black edged tempa ($8-12)(JP)
31. white body, tan interior, black base, clear windows, "Boss 14" tempa ($8-12)(JP)
32. dark blue body, white interior, black base, clear windows, "Wrangler 47" tempa ($8-12)(UK)
33. white body, tan interior, black base, clear windows "Porsche" & "3" tempa ($8-12)
34. black body, tan interior, black base, clear windows, "Porsche" without side design tempa ($8-12)
35. white body, tan interior, black base, clear windows, "Boss 14" with "14" inside square tempa ($3-5)
36. white body, blue interior, black base, clear windows, "Boss 14" with "14" inside square tempa ($3-5)
37. black body, black interior, black base, clear windows, "90 Porsche Turbo" & "BP" tempa ($8-12)(DU)
38. red body, blue interior, black base, clear windows, "8 Dragon Racing Team" tempa ($8-12)(HK)
39. robin egg blue body, blue interior, black base, clear windows, "Boss 14" with "14" in square tempa ($3-5)(MP)
40. dark blue body, tan interior, black base, clear windows, "Porsche" & yellow stripes tempa ($2-3)
41. red body, tan interior, black base, clear windows, "Porsche" & "Porsche 911" tempa ($1-2)
42. black body, tan interior, black base, clear windows, "Porsche" & "Porsche 911" tempa ($2-4)(MP)

NOTE: Below models with Thailand casting unless noted otherwise.

43. red body, tan interior, black base, clear windows, "Porsche" & "Porsche 911" tempa ($1-2)
44. dark blue body, tan interior, black base, clear windows, "Porsche" & yellow stripes tempa ($1-2)
45. yellow body, tan interior, black base, clear windows, "Porsche" logo tempa ($3-5)(GS)
46. black body, tan interior, black base, clear windows, "Porsche 90 Turbo" tempa, 4 arch wheels, Manaus casting ($20-35)(BR)
47. black body, tan interior, black base, clear windows, "Porsche 90 Turbo" tempa, 8 dot silver wheels, Manaus casting ($20-35)(BR)
48. lemon body, black interior, black base, clear windows, spatter design & "Porsche" tempa ($2-3)(TP)

49. black body, tan interior, black base, clear windows, "Porsche 90 Turbo" tempa, 8 dot gold wheels, Manaus casting ($20-35)(BR)
50. red body, tan interior, black base, clear windows, "Porsche 90 Turbo" tempa, 8 dot gold wheels, Manaus casting ($20-35)(BR)
51. white body, red interior, black base, clear windows, small "Porsche" logo tempa, Thailand casting ($2-3)(SS)
52. white body, lt. tan interior, black base, clear windows, "Matchbox Fun Club" tempa, Thailand casting ($8-12)(UK)
53. black body, peach interior, black base, clear windows, gold "Porsche" tempa, Thailand casting ($2-3)(SP)
54. white body, blue interior, black base, clear windows, "Boss 14" with "14" inside square tempa, Thailand casting ($2-3)(SP)
55. blue body, cream interior, black base, clear windows, orange & white with "Porsche" tempa, Thailand casting ($1-2)(5pk)

MB3-D HUMMER, issued 1994 (MB256/329)

NOTE: Below models with opaque black windows & 8 spoke wheels with black hubs unless otherwise noted.

1. khaki gray body, tan gun, brown & white camouflage & pink cross tempa, khaki gray base, China casting ($1-2)
2. pink-tan body, tan gun, green & brown camouflage tempa, pink-tan base, Thailand casting ($1-2)(5pk)
3. dark beige body, tan gun, brown & white camouflage & pink stripe tempa, beige base, Thailand casting ($1-2)
4. olive body, black gun, "A-4873-2" & star tempa, black base, Thailand casting ($1-2)
5. green body, black gun, brown & black camouflage tempa, green base, Thailand casting ($1-2)(5pk)
6. white body, black gun, blue with "Police Unit 7" tempa, black base, Thailand casting ($1-2)(5pk)
7. beige body, black gun, brown camouflage tempa, black base, Thailand casting ($1-2)(5pk)
8. white body, gray gun, gray & olive camouflage tempa, gray base, Thailand casting ($1-2)(5pk)
9. olive body, black gun,, "Gen IV", small "8" & "The Lost World" logo tempa, black base, Thailand casting ($3-5)(JR)(PS)
10. matt olive body, black gun, "Gen IV", small "17" & "The Lost World" logo tempa, black base, Thailand casting, gray armament attachment ($3-5)(JR)
11. khaki tan body, black gun, "A4873-2" & star tempa, black base, Thailand casting ($1-2)(MW48/1998)
12. black body, brown gun, green & brown camouflage tempa, brown base, Thailand casting ($1-2)(5pk)
13. black body, brown gun, green & brown camouflage tempa, brown base, China casting ($1-2)(5pk)
14. khaki tan body, black gun, "A4873-2" & star tempa, black base, China casting ($1-2)(MW48/1998)
15. beige body, black gun, brown camouflage tempa, black base, China casting ($1-2)(PS)
16. olive body, black gun, "Unit 5 Communications" tempa, black base, China casting ($1-2)(RT)
17. matt olive body, black gun, black & brown camouflage tempa, green wheels with rubber tires, black base, China casting ($4-6)(PC)
18. dark olive body, olive gun & base, "Convoy Follows/ Unit 61" tempa, black base, China casting ($1-2)(MW81/ 1999 US)
NOTE: Above model with Matchbox International or Mattel casting.
19. beige body, brown gun, "Alpha Co. 5" & mud spatter tempa, black base, China casting ($1-2)(MW53/ 2000 US)
20. beige body, brown gun, "Alpha Co. 5", mud spatter & "Matchbox 2000" tempa, black base, China casting ($2-4)(MW53/ 2000 US)
21. khaki tan body, black gun, "A4872-2" & "Certive" tempa, black base, China casting ($25-40)(CCI)
22. dark olive body, olive gun, "Convoy Follows/ Unit 61" & "Certive" tempa, olive base, China casting ($25-40)(CCI)
NOTE: Later models have "Humvee" base name.

MB 3-E ALFA ROMEO 155, issued 1997 (MB296)

NOTE: Below models with clear windows, black interior & black base unless otherwise noted.

1. red body, "7" with cross & snake design tempa, chrome disc with rubber tires, China casting ($4-6)(IG)
2. unpainted body, no tempa, chrome disc with rubber tires, China casting ($4-6)(IG)
3. red body, "8" with cross & snake design tempa, 5 spoke concave star wheels, China casting ($1-2)
4. red body, "7" with cross & snake design tempa, 5 spoke concave star wheels, China casting ($30+)(CHI)
5. white body, "8" with cross & snake design tempa, 5 spoke concave star wheels, China casting ($1-2)(MW62/ 1998)
6. metallic gold body, no tempa, 5 spoke concave star wheels, China casting ($5-10)(CH)
7. red body, "Coca Cola" & polar bear tempa, 5 spoke concave star wheels, China casting ($1-2)(5pk)(CK)

MB 3-F STREET CLEANER *see MB96-A*

MB 3-G SQUAWKIE-TALKIE, issued 2004 (USA)(641)
MB 1-K SQUAWKIE-TALKIE, issued 2004 (ROW)

1. black body, gray base, blue-green windows, chrome roof, "CH 9/ HQ" tempa, gold lace wheels, China casting ($1-2)(MW3/ 2004 US)(MW1/ 2004 ROW)

MB 3-H FIRE EXTINGUISHER *see MB 4-I*

MB 3-I 1956 CADILLAC ELDORADO, issued 2004 (SF) (MB501)
MB501 1956 CADILLAC ELDORADO, issued 2001 (CL)

NOTE: Below models with clear windshield, chrome plastic base & China casting.

1. metallic grape body, white interior, chrome disc wheels with rubber tires, detailed trim tempa, with diorama ($10-15)(EL)
2. pink body, white & black interior, chrome disc wheels with rubber tires, detailed trim tempa ($3-5)(BJ)
3. metallic grape body, white interior, lace wheels, trim tempa ($2-4)(MP)(Avon)
4. metallic purple body, orange interior, lace wheels blue windshield, yellow base, "Mermaidman & Barnacleboy" tempa ($1-2)(5pk)
5. pale yellow body, black interior, 5 spoke slotted wheels, smoke windshield, detailed trim tempa ($3-5)(SF3/2004)

MB 4-A DODGE STAKE TRUCK, issued 1970

NOTE: Below models with unpainted base & England casting.

1. orange-yellow body, green stakes, 4 spoke front & rear wheels ($20-25)
2. orange-yellow body, green stakes, spiro front & rear wheels ($20-25)
3. orange-yellow body, green stakes, spiro front & 4 spoke rear wheels ($20-25)
4. yellow body, green stakes, 4 spoke wheels ($100-125)
5. yellow body, green stakes, spiro front & 4 spoke rear wheels ($100-125)

MB 4-B GRUESOME TWOSOME, issued 1971

NOTE: Below models with chrome engine, 5 spoke wheels & England casting.

1. gold body, unpainted base, amber windows, cream interior ($125-175)
2. gold body, unpainted base, purple windows, cream interior ($12-15)
3. gold body, unpainted base, purple windows, yellow interior ($12-15)
4. gold 5body, silver-gray base, purple windows, yellow interior ($12-15)
5. gold body, unpainted base, purple windows, white interior ($12-15)
6. gold body, silver-gray base, purple windows, cream interior ($12-15)
7. gold body, silver-gray base, purple windows, white interior ($12-15)
8. red body, unpainted base, purple windows, cream interior ($15-18)
9. red body, unpainted base, purple windows, yellow interior ($15-18)
10. red body, silver-gray base, purple windows, yellow interior ($15-18)
11. orange-gold body, unpainted base, purple windows, cream interior ($12-15)

MB 4-C PONTIAC FIREBIRD issued 1975

NOTE: Below models with chrome engine & interior & England casting.

1. light metallic blue body, unpainted base, amber windows, dot dash wheels ($5-7)
2. light metallic blue body, unpainted base, amber windows, maltese cross wheels ($5-7)
3. light metallic blue body, unpainted base, amber windows, 5 arch wheels ($5-7)
4. dark metallic blue body, unpainted base, amber windows, dot dash wheels ($5-7)

MB 4-D '57 CHEVY, issued 1979 (MB004)
MB43-H '57 CHEVY, reissued 1990 (ROW)

NOTE: Below models with chrome interior, clear windows, 5 arch front & 5 crown rear wheels unless otherwise noted.

1. light metallic purple body & hood, unpainted base, no tempa, England casting ($5-7)
2. red body & hood, unpainted base, "Cherry Bomb" tempa with painted hood, England casting ($2-4)
3. red body & hood, silver-gray base, "Cherry Bomb" tempa with painted hood, England casting ($2-4)
4. red body & hood, silver-gray base, "Cherry Bomb" tempa with plain hood, England casting ($2-4)
5. red body & hood, black base, "Cherry Bomb" tempa with plain hood, England casting ($50-75)
6. black body, red hood, pearly silver base, flames tempa, Macau casting ($1-2)
7. black body, red hood, pearly silver base, flames tempa, China casting ($1-2)
8. pink body, red hood, pearly silver base, flames tempa, Macau casting ($3-4)(SC)
9. light pea green body, red hood, pearly silver base, flames tempa, Macau casting ($3-4)(SC)
10. light peach body, red hood, pearly silver base, flames tempa, Macau casting ($3-4)(SC)
11. rose red body, red hood, pearly silver base, flames tempa, Macau casting ($3-4)(SC)
12. dark purple body, red hood, pearly silver base, flames tempa, Macau casting ($3-4)(SC)
13. red body & hood, pearly silver base, "Heinz 57 Chevy" tempa, Macau casting ($15-20)(US)
14. bluish purple body & hood, pearly silver base, "Milky Way" tempa, Macau casting ($15-20)(UK)(OP)
15. bluish purple body & hood, pearly silver base, "Milky Way" tempa, China casting ($15-20)(UK)(OP)
16. black body, dark red hood, pearly silver base, flames tempa, Thailand casting ($1-2)
17. black body, dark red hood, pearly silver base, flames tempa, China casting ($1-2)
18. metallic red body & hood, pearly silver base, silver stripe & detailed trim tempa, chrome windows, gray disc with rubber tires, China casting ($5-8)(WC)
19. yellow body & hood, pearly silver base, blue & red stripes & "57" tempa, black windows, Thailand casting ($3-5)(TH)
20. black body, dark red hood, black base, flames tempa, Thailand casting ($1-2)
21. red body, red hood, silver-gray base, flames & silver flash tempa, Thailand casting ($1-2)
22. black body, black hood, silver-gray base, yellow tempa, Thailand casting ($1-2)(5pk)
23. metallic blue body, metallic blue hood, black base, silver sides tempa, Thailand casting ($2-3)(CC)
24. red body, red hood, silver-gray base, flames & silver flash & "Chubby's Diner" tempa, Thailand casting ($7-10)(US)
25. white body, pink hood, silver-gray base, pink flames tempa, Thailand casting ($1-2)(5pk)
26. black body, yellow hood, steel gray base, yellow flames tempa, China casting ($1-2)(5pk)
27. iridescent white body & hood, pearly silver base, pink & blue tempa, China casting ($1-2)

NOTE: All above models with chrome interior. PC, SC & YST models with chrome disc wheels & rubber tires.

28. gunmetal gray body & hood, red & white interior, black base, white roof ,silver flash & detailed trim tempa, China casting ($3-4)(PC3)
29. black body & hood, red & white interior, black base, white roof, silver flash & detailed trim tempa, China casting ($3-4)(PC6)
30. red body & hood, chrome interior, pearly silver base, yellow flames & silver side flash only tempa (plain hood), Thailand casting ($2-4)
31. red body & hood, red & white interior, black base, white roof , silver flash & detailed trim tempa, China casting ($10-15)(YST)
32. bright blue body, yellow hood, chrome interior, silver-gray base, yellow flames tempa, China casting ($1-2)(MP)
33. dark maroon body & hood, red & white interior, black base, white roof, silver flash & detailed trim tempa, China casting ($3-5)(SC3)
34. red body, yellow hood, black & chrome interior, black base, orange flames & detailed trim tempa, China casting ($3-5)(PC9)
35. black body & hood, chrome interior, pearly silver base, "Night Stalker" & flames tempa, China casting ($2-4)(AU)
36. black body, red hood, red & chrome interior, pearly silver base, yellow flames& detailed trim tempa, China casting ($3-5)(PC11)
37. red body & hood, black & chrome interior, black base, yellow flames & detailed trim tempa, chrome disc with rubber tires, China casting ($10-15)(US- Hot August Nights)
38. metallic gold body & hood, black & chrome interior, black base, silver flash & detailed trim tempa, chrome disc with rubber tires, China casting ($200-400)(CH- Winner car)
39. orange body & hood, chrome interior, pearly silver base, "Enjoy Fanta" tempa, China casting ($100+)(CHI)

40. iridescent white body & hood, pearly silver base, "American Wheels" tempa, China casting ($20-35)(CCI)
41. metallic gold with yellow hood, red & chrome interior, pearly silver base, silver flash & detailed trim tempa, 5 arch front & 5 crown rear wheels ($50+)(CHI)
42. gun metal gray body & hood, red & white interior, black base, white roof with silver flash & detailed trim tempa, 5 arch front & 5 crown rear wheels ($50+)(CHI)

MB 4-E TAXI FX4R, issued 1987 (MB174)

NOTE: Below models with clear windows, black wheels with silver hubs unless otherwise noted.

1. black body, unpainted base, gray interior, no tempa, Macau casting ($2-4)
2. black body, unpainted base, gray interior, "Great Taxi Ride London to Sydney" tempa, Macau casting ($5-7)(AU)
3. yellow body, unpainted base, blue interior, "ABC Taxi" tempa, red wheels with yellow hubs, Macau casting ($4-6)(LL)
4. black body, unpainted base, gray interior, no tempa, China casting ($2-4)
5. black body, silver-gray base, gray interior, no tempa, China casting ($2-4)
6. black body, unpainted base, gray interior, "London Taxi" & British flag tempa (left side only), China casting ($2-4)
7. yellow body, unpainted base, blue interior, "ABC Taxi" tempa, all red wheels, China casting ($4-6)(LL)
8. black body, unpainted base, gray interior, "Old Eight" & British flag tempa, China casting ($75-100)(BR)
9. black body, unpainted base, gray interior, "Taxi" tempa, China casting ($1-2)(MW9/ 1999 ROW)
10. black body, black base, red interior, British flag tempa, China casting ($2-4)(MW11/ 2000 ROW)
11. yellow body, charcoal base, black interior, "Matchbox 50" & birthday designs tempa, Mattel China casting ($3-5)(ROW)
12. white body, red base, black interior, "Coca Cola" tempa, Mattel China casting ($1-3) (CK)
13. yellow body, charcoal base, black interior, "Matchbox 50", birthday designs & "Christine & Craig" tempa, Mattel China casting ($18-25)(CCI)

MB 4-F 1997 CORVETTE, issued 1997 (MB295)

NOTE: Below models with clear windows & black plastic base, China casting unless otherwise noted.

1. red body, black interior, 5 spoke concave star wheels, "Launch Commemorative Jan. 6th, 1997" tempa ($150-200)(US)
2. metallic blue body, gray & black interior, chrome disc wheels with rubber tires, detailed trim tempa ($4-6)(IG)
3. unpainted body, gray interior, chrome disc wheels with rubber tires, no tempa ($4-6)(IG)
4. red body, black interior, 5 spoke concave star wheels, "Corvette" on windshield tempa ($1-2)
5. red body, gray & black interior, chrome disc wheels with rubber tires, detailed trim tempa ($3-5)(CP)
6. white body, red & black interior, chrome disc wheels with rubber wheels, detailed trim tempa ($3-5)(CP)
7. red body, black interior, 5 spoke concave star wheels, "Fiery Driven" tempa ($100+)(ASAP)
8. red body, black interior, chrome disc wheels with rubber tires, "Corvette Cologne" tempa ($25-40)(US)
9. black body, red & black interior, chrome disc wheels with rubber tires, detailed trim tempa ($3-5)(CP)
10. silver-gray body, gray & black interior, chrome disc wheels with rubber tires, detailed trim tempa ($3-5)(CP)
11. metallic red body, gray & black interior, chrome disc wheels with rubber tires, detailed trim tempa ($3-5)(CP)
12. dark metallic green body, gray & black interior, chrome disc wheels with rubber tires, detailed trim tempa ($3-5)(CP)
13. metallic blue body, gray interior, 5 spoke concave star wheels, "Corvette" on windshield tempa ($1-2)(MW58/1998 US)(MW69/1998 ROW)

NOTE: Below models with black interior, 5 spoke concave star wheels unless otherwise noted.

14. white body, "Lucent Technologies" with red "Gigaspeed" tempa ($100+)(ASAP)
15. white body, "Lucent Technologies" with black "Gigaspeed/ Optispeed" tempa ($20-40)(ASAP)
16. white body, "Route 66 Promotions" tempa ($20-40)(ASAP)
17. white body, "Progress Pit Crew" tempa ($100+)(ASAP)
18. white body, "Sandvik Coromant" tempa ($100+)(ASAP)
19. metallic gold body, no tempa ($5-10)(CH)
20. white body, , no tempa ($20-40)(ASAP blank)
21. white body, "Cisco Systems" tempa ($100+)(ASAP)
22. red body, "Mid Town Bank" tempa ($100+)(ASAP)
23. charcoal body with black roof, red & black interior, chrome disc wheels with rubber tires, detailed trim tempa ($3-5)(GS-TRU)
24. white body, "Colorado Auto Auctions" tempa ($25+)(ASAP)
25. white body, "White's Guide Car of the Month #7" (red print) tempa ($8-12)(ASAP)
26. white body, "White's Guide Car of The Month #7" (purple print) tempa ($8-12)(ASAP)
27. white body, "Datamax" tempa ($75+)(ASAP)
28. white body, "RCA" tempa ($20-40)(ASAP)
29. maroon body, silver-gray interior, smoke windows, silver design & "Corvette" tempa (MW38/1999 US)(MW33/ 1999 ROW)
30. maroon body, silver-gray interior, smoke windows, "Frohe Weihnachten" tempa ($15-25)(C2)(GR)
31. white body, "Progressive AE" tempa ($75+)(ASAP)
32. white body, "Kitchen Aid" tempa ($100+)(ASAP)
33. white body, "IBM" (left only) tempa ($100+)(ASAP)
34. white body, "Pras" tempa ($15-25)(ASAP)
35. white body, "ND Go Irish" tempa ($15-25)(ASAP)
36. white body, "Consumer Finance Services" ($100+)(ASAP)
37. lavender body, lime interior, 5 spoke concave star wheels, "Scooby-Doo!/ Like Who?/ Daphne" tempa ($5-7)(WB)
38. red body, smoke windows, small logos tempa ($1-2)(MW85/ 2000 US)(MW65/ 2000 ROW)
39. red body, smoke windows, small logos & "Matchbox 2000" tempa ($2-4)(MW85/ 2000 US))
40. white body, "Serena" tempa ($100+)(ASAP)
41. black body, red interior, chrome disc wheels with rubber tires, "Coca Cola" & stars tempa ($4-6)(Coke PC)
42. yellow body, "Corvette" with white & black checkers tempa ($5-7)(PS)
43. white body, Alabama Crimson Tide" tempa ($75+)(ASAP)
44. white body, "Huskers" tempa ($12-15)(ASAP)
45. red body, smoke windows, small logo tempa, metal base, Mattel casting ($1-2)(MW85/2000 US)(MW65/ 2000 ROW)
46. white body, "Novell 6" tempa ($18-25)(ASAP)
47. red body, "Corvette Expo" tempa ($50+)(ASAP)
48. white body, "EDS/ eds.com" tempa ($35-50)(ASAP)
49. red body, smoke windows, "Matchbox USA Hershey 2001" tempa ($20-30)(CCI)
50. red body, smoke windows, "8th Toy Show Demo Model-Hershey" ($20-30)(CCI)
51. white body, "Buds Cruise-In" tempa ($50+)(ASAP)
52. white body, "Philips/ Sy's Samson" tempa ($50+)(ASAP)

53. red body, smoke windows, "All Chevy Show 2001- Steeltown Corvettes" tempa ($5-75)(CCI)
54. blue body, "All Chevys Show 2001- Steeltown Corvettes" tempa ($75+)(CCI)
55. white body, "BC" & eagles logo ($10-15)(ASAP)
56. yellow body, lace wheels, black & white checkers & "Corvette" tempa, metal base, Mattel casting ($2-4)(MW53/2001 ROW)(MW51/ 2001 UK)
57. white body, green "S" tempa ($10-15)(ASAP)
58. red body, smoke windows, "Vettes in Glasstown XXII" tempa ($50-75)(CCI)
59. white body, "R" in circular design tempa ($15-20)(ASAP)
60. light metallic lavender body, black & gray interior, chrome disc wheels with rubber tires, detailed trim tempa, metal base ($3-4)(TH)
61. maroon body, silver-gray interior, smoke windows, "20th annual Vettes in Glasstown XX" tempa ($25-40)(CCI)
62. white body, red "G" tempa ($12-15)(ASAP)
63. red body, smoke windows, "Bloomsburg Fair 2002" tempa ($25-40)(ASAP)
64. white body, "Web Application Publishing/ Nfuse Citrix" labels ($100+)(ASAP)
65. white body, "BS Auto Seaside Oregon" tempa ($15-20)(ASAP)
66. white body, "ISO Thermal Telecom" tempa ($100+)(ASAP)
67. white body, "MasterCard/ GM Card" tempa ($10-15)(ASAP)
68. orange-yellow body, gold lace wheels, metal base, "Hoosier- Indiana 19" tempa, Mattel casting ($1-2)(AM)
69. red body, smoke windows, "Matchbox Collectors Community Hall/ Matchbox Treasure Hunt" tempa ($20-25)(CCI)
70. red body, smoke windows, "Marvin & Ferro Attorneys at Law" tempa ($25-40)(CCI)
71. red body, smoke windows, metal base, "Bye Bye German Mark We Miss You" tempa, Mattel casting ($15-20)(CCI)
72. white body with clear roof, metal base, lace wheels, "Buds Cruise In" with plain roof tempa, Mattel casting ($50+)(ASAP)
73. white body with clear roof, metal base, lace wheels, "MSU" with plain roof tempa, Mattel casting ($15-20)(ASAP)
74. white body, "VT Hokies" tempa ($15-20)(ASAP)
75. white body, "ISR Global Telecom/ Perot Systems" tempa ($100+)(ASAP)
76. maroon body, silver-gray interior, smoke windows, "Kiddie Kar Kollectibles 20th Anniversary Birthday" tempa ($15-25)(CCI)
77. red body, "Kiddie Kar Kollectibles 20th Anniversary Birthday" tempa ($15-25)(CCI)
78. white body, metal base, lace wheels, "Cruise In/ 20th Anniversary Bud's" tempa ($50+)(ASAP)
79. yellow body, metal base, lace wheels, "Congratulations * Happy Birthday/ Corvette" & checkers tempa ($25-40)(CCI)
80. red body, "Congratulations & Happy Birthday" tempa ($25-40)(CCI)
81. charcoal body with black roof, red & black interior, chrome disc wheels with rubber tires, "Matchbox Toy Show 2003/ On Site Demonstration Model" tempa ($15-20)(CCI)
82. charcoal body with black roof, red & black interior, chrome disc wheels with rubber tires, "Millville Airshow 2004" tempa ($415-25)
83. red body with white roof, black interior, gold 6 spoke spiral wheels, detailed trim tempa ($50+)(CHI)
84. white body, black interior, gold 6 spoke spiral wheels, detailed trim tempa ($50+)
85. black body with silver-gray roof, gray interior, gold 6 spoke spiral wheels, detailed trim tempa ($50+)(CHI)
86. silver-gray body with red roof, red interior, gold 6 spoke spiral wheels, detailed trim tempa ($50+)(CHI)
87. dark metallic green body with black roof, red interior, gold 6 spoke spiral wheels, detailed trim ($50+)(CHI)
88. black body & roof, gray interior, gold 6 spoke spiral wheels, detailed trim tempa ($50+)(CHI)
89. white body, "abc" tempa ($50+)(ASAP)
90. white body, "Action" tempa ($50+)(ASAP)
91. white body, "manugistics" tempa ($50+)(ASAP)
92. white body, "msdn" tempa ($50+)(ASAP)
93. white body, "Broncos" tempa ($50+)(ASAP)
94. white body, "Test Drive" tempa ($50+)(ASAP)
95. metallic blue body, "Guld" tempa ($50+)(ASAP)
96. white body, "Serena" tempa ($50+)(ASAP)
97. white body, Arkansas Razorback" tempa ($50+)(ASAP)
98. white body, "G/ Georgia" tempa ($50+)(ASAP)
99. white body, "Greenberg Traurig" tempa ($50+)(ASAP)
100. white body with clear roof, metal base, Mattel casting, lace wheels, no tempa ($25-40)(ASAP blank)
101. white body with clear roof, metal base, Mattel casting, lace wheels, "USS" tempa ($50+)(ASAP)
102. white body with clear roof, metal base, Mattel casting, lace wheels, "Huskers" tempa ($50+)(ASAP)
103. white body, "Hilton" tempa ($50+)(ASAP)
104. maroon body, silver-gray interior, smoke windows, silver design with "Midwest Regional Convention" tempa ($18-25)(C2)
105. maroon body, silver-gray interior, smoke windows, silver design with "Midwest Regional Convention/ Special Dealer" tempa ($50-75)(C2)
106. white body with clear roof, metal base, Mattel casting, lace wheels, "Tella Tools & Mfg." Tempa ($20-25)

MB 4-G AUDI TT ROADSTER, issued 2001 (MB441)
MB37-K AUDI TT ROADSTER, issued 2000 (GR)

NOTE: Below models with clear windows, black plastic base & China casting.

1. light metallic green body, light tan interior, head & tail lights tempa, 5 spoke concave star wheels ($3-5)(MW37/2000GR)
2. metallic blue body, dark gray interior, head & tail lights tempa, 10 spoke flower wheels ($1-2)(MW4/ 2001)
3. metallic blue body, dark gray interior, head & tail lights tempa, 5 spoke concave star wheels ($1-2)(MW4/2001)
4. white body, red interior, "The Real Coca cola" tempa, chrome disc wheels with rubber tires ($3-4)(Coke PC)
5. red body, white interior, smoke windows, "Hero City Sports" tempa , lace wheels ($1-2)(5pk)
6. lemon body, red interior, smoke windows, "The Flash" tempa, lace wheels ($1-2)(5pk)
7. red body, white interior, lace wheels, "FC Bayern Munchen" tempa ($7-10)(GR)
8. metallic silver body, red interior, lace wheels, "FC Bayern Munchen" tempa ($7-10)(GR)
9. silver-gray body, black interior, lace wheels, red tail lights tempa ($2-4) (SG)

MB 4-H FORD FALCON *see MB63-J*

MB 4-I FIRE EXTINGUISHER, issued 2003 (USA)(MB619)
MB 3-H FIRE EXTINGUISHER, issued 2004 (ROW)

NOTE: Below models with gray base, 10 spoke flower wheels & China casting.

1. red body, dark gray extinguisher, chrome chassis, amber windows, extinguisher tempa, gold hubs($1-2)(MW4/ 2004)(MW3/ 2004 ROW)
2. metallic red body, dirty gray fire extinguisher, chrome chassis, black windows, "Force" tempa, silver hubs ($1-2)(5pk)

3. metallic red body, gray fire extinguisher, chrome chassis, amber windows, "Matchbox Hero City" & stars tempa, gold hubs ($8-12)(AW- Bonus car)
4. light metallic red body, dirty gray fire extinguisher, chrome chassis, black windows, "Force" tempa, silver hubs ($1-2)(5pk)

MB 4-J FLAME CHOPPER *see MB 5-G*

MB 4-K 1970 PLYMOUTH CUDA (SF)(MB616)
1. metallic silver body, clear windows, black interior, slotted 5 spoke wheels, detailed trim tempa, chrome base, China casting ($3-5)(SF4/2004)

MB 5-A LOTUS EUROPA, issued 1969
NOTE: Earliest versions with narrow wheels, later versions with wide wheels. Below models with clear windows & England casting.
1. blue body, unpainted base (NO "Superfast" cast), ivory interior, no labels, 5 spoke wheels ($75-90)
2. blue body, unpainted base, ivory interior, no labels, 5 spoke wheels ($10-15)
3. blue body, unpainted base, ivory interior, "20" labels, 5 spoke wheels ($15-18)(GS)
4. metallic pink body, unpainted base, ivory interior, no labels, 5 spoke wheels ($10-15)
5. metallic pink body, unpainted base, ivory interior, "20" labels, 5 spoke wheels ($15-18)(GS)
6. metallic pink body, silver-gray base, ivory interior, no labels, 5 spoke wheels ($10-15)
7. black body, unpainted base, ivory interior, "JPS" tempa, 5 spoke wheels ($18-25)(JP)(UK)
8. black body, unpainted base, ivory interior, no labels, 5 spoke wheels ($15-20)(TP)
9. black body, unpainted base, ivory interior, no labels, dot dash wheels ($15-20)(TP)

NOTE: Available as a Bulgarian casting- assorted colors available ($35-50 each)

MB 5-B SEAFIRE, issued 1975 (MB705)
NOTE: Below models with "Seafire" labels and England casting unless otherwise noted.
1. white deck, blue hull, black exhausts, blue driver, no trailer ($10-15)
2. white deck, blue hull, red exhausts, blue driver, no trailer ($10-15)
3. white deck, blue hull, red exhausts, orange-yellow driver, no trailer ($10-15)
4. white deck, blue hull, black exhausts, orange-yellow driver, no trailer ($10-15)
5. white deck, blue hull, red exhausts, lemon driver, no trailer ($10-15)
6. white deck, blue hull, red exhausts, orange-yellow driver, black trailer ($10-15)(TP)
7. red deck, white hull, red exhausts, orange-yellow driver, black trailer ($8-12)(TP)
8. red deck, white hull, red exhausts, lemon driver, black trailer ($8-12)
9. red deck, white hull, red exhausts, white driver, black trailer ($8-12)(TP)
10. red deck, blue hull, red exhausts, lemon driver, no trailer ($25-40)
11. white deck, brown hull, red exhausts, orange-yellow driver, no trailer ($85-110)
12. white deck, brown hull, red exhausts, orange-yellow driver, black trailer ($85-110)(TP)
13. white deck, brown hull, red exhausts, lemon driver, no trailer ($85-110)
14. white deck, brown hull, red exhausts, lemon driver, black trailer ($85-110)(TP)
15. red deck, yellow hull, red exhausts, red driver, black trailer ($35-50)(TP)
16. black deck, yellow hull, red exhausts, red driver, black trailer ($8-12)(TP)
17. white deck, white hull, white exhausts, no driver cast, white metal trailer (from MB9-A), "Bacardi" tempa , no origin cast ($10-15)(TP)(OP)
18. red deck, white hull, black exhausts, no driver cast, white plastic trailer, "Surf Rider" & silver stripes tempa , no origin cast ($2-3)(TP)
19. yellow deck, blue hull, no driver cast, black plastic trailer, "460" tempa, no origin cast ($3-5)(TP)
20. white deck, red hull, no driver cast, black plastic trailer, red & black design tempa , no origin cast($3-5)(TP)
21. white deck, florescent orange hull, no driver cast, black plastic trailer, blue splash tempa, no origin cast ($1-2)(5pk)
22. white deck, florescent orange hull, no driver cast, black plastic trailer (China), blue splash tempa, no origin cast ($1-2)(5pk)
23. navy blue body, green hull, no driver cast, black plastic trailer (China), green splash tempa, no origin cast ($1-2)(5pk)
24. white deck, blue hull with Manaus label, red exhausts, orange-yellow driver, no trailer ($35-50)(BR)
25. white deck, blue hull with Manaus label, red exhausts, orange-yellow driver, no trailer ($35-50)(BR)

MB 5-C U.S. MAIL TRUCK, issued 1978
NOTE: Below models with black interior & England casting. All models listed have "No. 5 U.S. Mail Truck" cast on base.
1. blue body, white base, white roof with small window, silver hubs, "U.S. Mail" tempa ($4-6)
2. blue body, white base, white roof with small window, black hubs, "U.S. Mail" tempa ($5-7)
3. yellow body, black base, no roof, silver hubs, "Gliding Club" labels ($8-12)(TP)
4. yellow body, black base, no roof, black hubs, "Gliding Club" labels ($8-12)(TP)
5. yellow body, blue-gray base, no roof, silver hubs, "Gliding Club" labels ($8-12)(TP)
6. yellow body, white base, no roof, silver hubs, "Gliding Club" labels ($8-12)(TP)
7. blue body, white base, white roof with large window, silver hubs, "U.S. Mail" tempa ($5-8)
8. blue body, black base, white roof with large window, silver hubs, "U.S. Mail" tempa ($5-8)
9. blue body, cream base, white roof with small windows, silver hubs, "U.S. Mail" tempa ($8-12)
10. olive body, charcoal base, gun cast, black hubs, "21 * 11" labels ($15-20)
11. olive body, charcoal base, gun cast, black hubs, no labels ($15-20)
12. red body, black base, "Gliding Club" labels, no gun or roof cast, silver hubs ($500-750)(TP)

MB 5-D 4 X 4 JEEP, issued 1982 (USA)(MB005)
MB56-F 4 X 4 JEEP, issued 1990 (ROW)
NOTE: Below models with black- right drive interior & maltese cross wheels unless noted otherwise
1. light metallic tan body, black metal base, "Golden Eagle" tempa, England casting ($3-5)

2. dark metallic tan body, black metal base, "Golden Eagle" tempa, England casting ($3-5)
3. metallic brown body, black metal base, "Golden Eagle" tempa, Macau casting ($2-4)
4. red body, black metal base, "Golden Eagle" tempa, Macau casting ($2-4)
5. olive body, black metal base, red, yellow & blue tempa, Macau casting, includes plastic armament ($6-8)(RB)
6. red body, black plastic base, "Golden Eagle" tempa, Macau casting ($1-2)
7. red body, black plastic base, "Golden Eagle" tempa, Thailand casting ($1-2)
8. yellow body, black plastic base, "50th Anniversary Jeep" tempa, Thailand casting ($12-18)(PS)
9. hot pink body, black plastic base, white bolt tempa, white interior, Thailand casting ($2-4)(DM)

NOTE: All previous models cast with right hand drive.

10. dark met. blue body, black plastic base, pink/white/yellow tempa, right hand drive, Thailand casting ($1-2)(5pk)
11. black body, black plastic base, "Laredo" tempa, right hand drive, Thailand casting ($50-75)
12. dark met. blue body, black plastic base, pink/white/yellow tempa, left hand drive, Thailand casting ($1-2)(5pk)
13. turquoise body, black plastic base, "Jeep" tempa, left hand drive, Thailand casting ($2-3)(CC)
14. red body, black plastic base, white headlamp tempa, left hand drive, Thailand casting ($15-18)(BE)
15. red body, black plastic base, "Golden Eagle" tempa, left hand drive, Thailand casting ($1-2)
16. red body, black plastic base, "Wolff Systems" tempa, left hand drive, Thailand casting ($15-25)(US)
17. white body, black plastic base, black cow patches tempa, left hand drive, Thailand casting ($1-2)(5pk)

NOTE: All above models with black interior.

18. dark purple body, turquoise interior, black plastic base, "Bad To The Bone" on hood with side tempa, left hand drive, Thailand casting ($1-2)
19. dark purple body, turquoise interior, black plastic base, "Bad To The Bone" on hood without side tempa, left hand drive, Thailand casting ($1-2)
20. charcoal body, black interior, black plastic base, "Bad To The Bone" on hood without side tempa. left hand drive, Thailand casting ($2-4)
21. metallic gold body, black interior, black plastic base, no tempa, left hand drive, Thailand casting ($10-15)(CH)
22. metallic blue body, yellow interior, black plastic base, pink & yellow hood design tempa, left hand drive, Thailand casting ($2-4)
23. red body, black interior, black plastic base, "4 X 4 Jeep" tempa, left hand drive, Thailand casting ($1-2)(5pk)
24. red body, black interior, black plastic base, "4 X 4 Jeep" tempa, left hand drive, China casting ($1-2)(5pk)
25. blue body, black interior, black plastic base, "Mork & Mindy" tempa, left hand drive, China casting ($5-8)(STR)

MB 5-E PETERBILT TANKER *see MB56-D*

MB 5-F FORD EXPEDITION POLICE *see MB50-L*

MB 5-G FLAME CHOPPER, issued 2004 (USA)(MB644)
MB 4-J FLAME CHOPPER, issued 2004 (ROW)

1. metallic red body, yellow boom with chrome hatchet, blue windows, gold 5 arch dot wheels, gray base, "Chopper" tempa, China casting ($1-2) (MB5-G/2004 US)(MB4-J/2004 ROW)

MB 5-H POUND HOUND *see MB22-K*

MB 6-A FORD PICKUP, issued 1970

NOTE: Below models with ivory interior, clear windows, 5 spoke wheels & England casting. Earliest versions with narrow wheels & later issues with wide wheels.

1. red body, white canopy, unpainted base, chrome grille ($85-110)
2. red body, white canopy, black base, chrome grille ($35-50)
3. red body, white canopy, green base, chrome grille ($35-50)
4. red body, white canopy, metallic green base, chrome grille ($35-50)
5. red body, white canopy, charcoal base, chrome grille ($35-50)
6. red body, white canopy, gray base, chrome grille ($35-50)
7. red body, white canopy, green base, white grille ($35-50)
8. red body, white canopy, charcoal base, white grille ($35-50)
9. red body, white canopy, gray base, white grille ($35-50)
10. red body, white canopy, black base, white grille ($35-50)
11. red body, white canopy, unpainted base, white grille ($35-50)

MB 6-B MERCEDES TOURER, issued 1973 (MB006)

NOTE: Below models with England casting unless otherwise noted.

1. orange body, black roof, unpainted base, clear windows, light yellow interior, 5 arch wheels ($7-10)
2. orange body, black roof, unpainted base, amber windows, light yellow interior, 5 arch wheels ($7-10)
3. orange body, black roof, unpainted base, amber windows, light yellow interior, 5 spoke wheels ($7-10)
4. orange body, black roof, unpainted base, amber windows, ivory interior, 5 arch wheels ($7-10)
5. orange body, black roof, unpainted base, clear windows, light yellow interior, 5 spoke wheels ($7-10)
6. yellow body, black roof, unpainted base, amber windows, light yellow interior, 5 arch wheels ($6-8)
7. yellow body, black roof, unpainted base, clear windows, light yellow interior, 5 arch wheels ($6-8)
8. silver-gray body, black roof, unpainted base, amber windows, light yellow interior, 5 arch wheels ($25-40)
9. silver-gray body, black roof, unpainted base, amber windows, light yellow interior, 5 arch wheels, "Rennservice" labels ($35-45)(GR)
10. bronze body, black roof, unpainted base, amber windows, light yellow interior, 5 arch wheels ($8-12)
11. bronze body, white roof, unpainted base, amber windows, light yellow interior, 5 arch wheels ($5-8)
12. bronze body, white roof, unpainted base, amber windows, cream interior, 5 arch wheels ($5-8)
13. maroon body, white roof, unpainted base, amber windows, light yellow interior, 5 arch wheels ($7-10)
14. cherry body, white roof, unpainted base, clear windows, light yellow interior, 5 arch wheels ($5-8)
15. cherry body, white roof, unpainted base, amber windows, light yellow interior, 5 arch wheels ($5-8)
16. bronze body, black roof, unpainted with Manaus tab, amber windows, light yellow interior, 5 arch wheels ($35-50)(BR)
17. blue body, no roof, unpainted base, clear windshield, white interior, 5 arch wheels ($5-8)
18. blue body, no roof, unpainted base, clear windshield, white interior, 5 arch wheels, silver stripe tempa ($5-8)
19. blue body, no roof, silver-gray base, clear windshield, white interior, 5 arch wheels, silver stripe tempa ($5-8)
20. blue body, no roof, silver-gray base, clear windshield, white interior, maltese cross wheels, silver stripe tempa ($5-8)

21. plum body, no roof, silver-gray base, clear windshield, white interior, 5 arch wheels ($7-10)
22. plum body, no roof, black base, clear windshield, white interior, 5 arch wheels ($7-10)
23. plum body, no roof, black base, clear windshield, white interior, dot dash wheels ($7-10)
24. plum body, no roof, unpainted base, clear windshield, white interior, dot dash wheels ($7-10)
25. plum body, no roof, unpainted base, clear windshield, white interior, 5 arch wheels ($7-10)
26. white body, no roof, silver-gray base, clear windshield, translucent red interior, 5 arch wheels, China casting ($8-12)(MP)
27. pale gray body, no roof, black plastic base, clear windshield, translucent white interior, 4 arch wheels, Manaus casting ($35-50)(BR)
28. beige body, no roof, black plastic base, clear windshield, translucent white interior, 4 arch wheels, Manaus casting ($35-50)(BR)
29. red body, no roof, black plastic base, clear windshield, translucent white interior, 4 arch wheels, Manaus casting ($35-50)(BR)
30. black body, no roof, black plastic base, clear windshield, white interior, 8 dot wheels, Manaus casting ($35-50)(BR)
31. rust red body, no roof, black plastic base, clear windshield, translucent white interior, 8 dot wheels, Manaus casting ($35-50)(BR)

NOTE: Available as a Bulgarian casting with "Dinky" cast on base. Assorted colors available ($5-25 each)

MB 6-C I.M.S.A. MAZDA, issued 1983 (USA)(MB116)
MB 7-E I.M.S.A. MAZDA, issued 1983 (ROW)

NOTE: Below models with clear windows & black metal base.

1. dark blue body, red interior, 5 arch wheels, white & orange tempa, Macau casting ($2-4)
2. dark blue body, red interior, dot dash wheels, white & orange tempa, Macau casting ($2-4)
3. dark blue body, red interior, 8 dot wheels, white stripes tempa, Manaus casting ($35-50)(BR)
4. dark blue body, red interior, 4 arch wheels, white stripes tempa, Manaus casting ($35-50)(BR)

MB 6-D F. 1 RACER *see MB16-D*

MB 6-E FORD SUPERVAN II, issued 1986 (USA)(MB166)
MB72-H FORD SUPERVAN II, issued 1986 (ROW)

NOTE: Below models with 8 dot wheels. Versions 1 & 2 cast with or without holes in front spoiler.

1. white body, black metal base, dark gray windows, no dome lights, dark blue "Ford Supervan" tempa, Macau casting ($2-4)
2. white body, black metal base, dark gray windows, no dome lights, light blue "Ford Supervan" tempa, Macau casting ($2-4)
3. dark blue body, black metal base, dark gray windows, no dome lights, "Duckhams QXR Engine Oils" tempa, Macau casting ($4-6)(TC)
4. dark gray body, black metal base, dark gray windows, no dome lights, "Danger High Explosive/ Heavy Load" tempa, Macau casting, includes plastic armament ($6-8)(RB)
5. white body, black metal base, dark gray windows, no dome lights, "Starfire" tempa, Macau casting ($3-5)
6. white body, black metal base, dark gray windows, no dome lights, "Fuji Racing Team" tempa, Macau casting ($3-5)(TC)
7. bright yellow body, black metal base, dark gray windows, no dome lights, "Service Car BP Oil" tempa, Macau casting ($10-15)(DU)
8. red body, black metal base, dark gray windows, no dome lights, "Tizer Flavoured Soft Drink" tempa, Macau casting ($3-5)(TC)
9. yellow body, black metal base, dark gray windows, no dome lights, "Goodyear Pit Stop" tempa, Macau casting ($3-5)(GS)
10. white body, black plastic base, dark gray windows, no dome lights, light blue "Ford Supervan" tempa, Macau casting ($2-4)
11. white body, black plastic base, dark gray windows, no dome lights, "Fuji Racing Team" tempa, Macau casting ($3-5)(TC)
12. red body, black plastic base, dark gray windows, no dome lights, "Tizer Flavoured Soft Drink" tempa, Macau casting ($3-5)(TC)
13. dark blue body, black plastic base, dark gray windows, no dome lights, "Duckhams QXR Engine Oils" tempa, Macau casting ($3-5)(TC)
14. red body, black plastic base, black windows, amber dome lights, "Fire Observer" tempa, Macau casting ($12-15)(SR)
15. red body, black plastic base, black windows, greenish yellow dome lights, "Fire Observer" tempa, Macau casting ($12-15)(SR)
16. white body, black plastic base, black windows, red dome lights, "Ambulance" tempa, Macau casting ($12-15)(SR)
17. dark blue body, black plastic base, black windows, red dome lights, "Police Control Unit" tempa, Macau casting ($12-15)(SR)
18. white body, black plastic base, dark gray windows, no dome lights, "Starfire" tempa, Macau casting ($3-5)
19. yellow body, black plastic base, dark gray windows, no dome lights, "Goodyear Pit Stop" tempa, Thailand casting ($3-5)(GS)
20. red body, black plastic base, black windows, amber dome lights, "Fire Observer/ Rescue 911" tempa, China casting ($12-15)(SR)
21. white body, black plastic base, black windows, red dome lights, "Ambulance/ Rescue 911" tempa, China casting ($12-15)(SR)
22. dark blue body, black plastic base, black windows, red dome lights, "Police Control Unit/ Rescue 911" tempa, China casting ($12-15)(SR)
23. white body, black plastic base, black windows, no dome lights, no tempa, China casting ($10-15)(GF)
24. white body, black plastic base, dark gray windows, no dome lights, light blue "Ford Supervan" tempa, Thailand casting ($3-5)
25. light gray body, black plastic base, dark gray windows, no dome lights, "Danger High Explosive/ Heavy Load" tempa, China casting ($15-20)(JP- Tomy box)
26. white body, black plastic base, black windows, red dome lights, "EMS" & orange band tempa, China casting ($3-5)(LS)
27. dark blue body, black plastic base, black windows, red dome lights, "S.W.A.T. Police Emergency" tempa, China casting ($3-5)(LS)
28. black body, black plastic base, black windows, red dome lights, "S.W.A.T. Police Emergency" tempa, China casting ($3-5)(LS)
29. bright yellow body, black plastic base, black windows, amber dome lights, "EMS" & orange band tempa, China casting ($3-5)(LS)
30. silver-gray body, black plastic base, black windows, red dome lights, "Flight Team" with purple & dark pink flames tempa, China casting ($4-6)(LS)(Avon)

MB 6-F ATLAS EXCAVATOR *see MB32-D*

MB 6-G ALFA ROMEO SZ *see MB15-H*

MB 6-H PLYMOUTH PROWLER *see MB34-G*

MB 6-I ARCTIC TRACK TRUCK, issued 2001 (MB480)

NOTE: Below models with smoke cab & container windows, 4 spoke domed wheels, black rollers & treads, China casting. Early base castings read "Artic Track Truck" on base. Later issues read "Snow Tracker" on base.

1. metallic blue body, pearly white plastic container, "Ambulance" & EMS symbol tempa, gray base ($1-2)(MW6/2001)
2. silver-gray body, amber windows, light blue container, "MTN 01" & snowflakes tempa, gray base ($1-2)(5pk)
3. iridescent white body, red-brown container, "49 Alaska Snow Tracker" tempa, gray base ($4-6)(AM)
4. metallic bronze body, blue container, chevron design tempa, black base ($1-2)(MW68/2002)
5. metallic bronze body, blue container, chevron design & "Matchbox 50" tempa, black base ($2-3)(MW68/2002)
6. metallic bronze body, blue container, chevron design, black base, lace wheels ($1-2)(MW68/2002)
7. metallic bronze body, blue container, chevron design, black base, 10 spoke flower wheels ($35-50)(MW68/2002)
8. silver-gray body, amber windows, light blue container, "MTN01" & snowflakes tempa, gray base, lace wheels ($1-2)(5pk)
9. orange-yellow body, white container, "Alarm" & snowflake tempa, black base ($1-2)(5pk)
10. orange-yellow body, white container, "Alarm" & snowflake tempa, black base, lace wheels ($1-2)(5pk)
11. red body, pearly white container, "Alarm" & snowflake tempa, black base ($1-2)(5pk)
12. dark blue body, light blue container, "Antarctica" tempa, gray rollers & base, 7 spoke sawblade wheels ($1-2)(AW)
13. orange body, black cab windows, light blue container, snowman & snowflakes tempa, gray rollers & base, 5 crown dot wheels ($2-4)(MP)
14. iridescent white body, brown container, "Alaska Snow Tracker" tempa ($10-15)(AM)

MB 6-J OPEL SPEEDSTER, issued 2003 (MB565)

NOTE: Below models with black plastic base, lace wheels & China casting.

1. metallic silver body, red interior, smoke windows, "6" & black louvers tempa ($1-2)(MW6/2003)
2. metallic silver body, red interior, smoke windows, "6", black louvers & "Hero City" tempa ($2-4) (MW6/ 2003)
3. orange body, black interior, smoke windows, black louvers tempa ($-6) (SG)
4. lime body, black interior, dark smoke windows, black side panel & praying mantis tempa ($1-2)(5pk)

MB 6-K MAX TRACTOR, issued 2004 (USA)(MB653)

1. metallic green body, brown hat, amber windows, gold 5 crown dot front wheels, gold 5 spoke oval rear wheels, "Max Tractor" tempa, China casting ($1-2)(MW6/ 2004 US)

MB 6-L DRAGONFLY HELICOPTER *see MB11-K*

MB 6-M FORD MUSTANG CONCEPT, issued 2004 (SF)(MB609)
MB609 FORD MUSTANG CONCEPT, issued 2004 (CL)

NOTE: Below models with black base & China casting.

1. silver-gray body, red & black interior, smoke windows, detailed trim tempa, chrome disc wheels with rubber tires ($3-5)(SHO)
2. metallic green body, black interior, smoke windows, head & tail lights tempa, slotted 5 spoke wheels ($3-5)(SF6/2004)
3. metallic silver body, orange-yellow interior, blue windows, "Spongebob & Patrick" tempa, lace wheels ($1-2)(5pk)
4. dark metallic blue body, black interior, smoke windows, detailed trim tempa, slotted 5 spoke wheels ($8-12)(SF6/US promo)
5. dark metallic blue body, black interior, smoke windows, "Matchbox Toy Show Hershey, PA 2004" tempa, slotted 5 spoke wheels ($8-12)(SF6/CCI)
6. red body, brown interior, smoke windows, white stripe & "Mustang" tempa, lace wheels ($1-2)(MW6/2005)
7. silver-gray body, black interior, smoke windows, black stripe & "Mustang" centered with black hood print tempa, 10 spoke flower wheels ($5-8)(CN)(OP)
8. silver-gray body, black interior, smoke windows, black stripe & "Mustang" toward front with black hood print tempa, 10 spoke flower wheels ($5-8)(CN)(OP)

MB 7-A FORD REFUSE TRUCK, issued 1970

NOTE: Below models with green windows, 4 spoke wheels, unpainted metal base & England casting. Earliest versions with narrow wheels, later versions with wide wheels.

1. red-orange cab & chassis, black axle covers ($20-35)
2. orange cab & chassis, black axle covers ($20-35)
3. orange cab & chassis, red axle covers ($20-35)

MB 7-B HAIRY HUSTLER, issued 1971

NOTE: Below models with chrome interior, 5 spoke front & maltese cross rear wheels. Some versions may have the wheel combination reversed.

1. bronze body, black base, purple windows, "5" yellow side labels, square "5" hood label ($125-175)
2. bronze body, light gray base, purple windows, "5" yellow side labels, square "5" hood label ($125-175)
3. bronze body, black base, amber windows, "5" yellow side labels, square "5" hood label ($15-20)
4. bronze body, light gray base, amber windows, "5" yellow side labels, square "5" hood label ($15-20)
5. bronze body, gray base, amber windows, "5" yellow side labels, square "5" hood label ($15-20)
6. bronze body, black base, amber windows, "5" blue side labels, square "5" hood label ($15-20)
7. bronze body, unpainted base, amber windows, "5" blue side labels, square "5" hood label ($15-20)
8. bronze body, black base, amber windows, square "5" side labels (from MB52-A), scorpion hood label ($25-40)
9. bronze body, green base, amber windows, "5" blue side labels, square "5" hood label ($15-20)
10. bronze body, green base, amber windows, no side labels, square "5" hood label ($15-20)
11. bronze body, black base, amber windows, round "3" side labels (from MB19-A), scorpion hood label ($40-60)
12. bronze body, green base, amber windows, round "3" side labels (from MB19-A), scorpion hood label ($40-60)
13. bronze body, black base, amber windows, square "137" side labels (from MB15-A), scorpion hood label ($25-40)
14. bronze body, black base, amber windows, no side labels, square "5" hood label ($15-20)
15. bronze body, green base, amber windows, round "3" side labels (from MB19-A), square "5" hood label ($15-20)
16. bronze body, green base, amber windows, square "137" side labels (from MB15-A), scorpion hood label ($40-60)
17. bronze body, green base, amber windows, square "5" side labels (from MB19-A), scorpion hood label ($25-40)
18. white body, charcoal base, amber windows, no labels ($50-75)

19. white body, black base, amber windows, checkers & stripes tempa ($15-18)
20. yellow body, black base (cast #7), amber windows, flames tempa ($100-150)(RN)

MB 7-C V.W. GOLF, issued 1976 (MB007)

NOTE: Below models with England casting unless otherwise noted.

1. metallic lime body, black base, yellow interior, amber windows, roof rack, no labels ($5-7)
2. metallic green body, black base, yellow interior, amber windows, roof rack, no labels ($5-7)
3. yellow body, black base, yellow interior, amber windows, antennae cast, "ADAC" labels ($35-35)(GR)(JP)
4. dark metallic green body, black base, yellow interior, amber windows, roof rack, no labels ($5-7)
5. dark metallic green body, charcoal base, yellow interior, amber windows, roof rack, no labels ($5-7)
6. dark metallic green body, charcoal base, lemon interior, amber windows, roof rack, no labels ($5-7)
7. dark metallic green body, charcoal base, lemon interior, orange windows, roof rack, no labels ($5-7)
8. dark metallic green body, charcoal base, red interior, amber windows, roof rack, no labels ($8-12)
9. dark metallic green body, black base, yellow interior, orange windows, roof rack, no labels ($5-7)
10. dark metallic green body, black base, yellow interior, clear windows, roof rack, no labels ($5-7)
11. mustard body, charcoal base, red interior, clear windows, roof rack, no labels ($5-7)
12. mustard body, black base, red interior, clear windows, roof rack, no labels ($5-7)
13. mustard body, blue- gray base, red interior, clear windows, roof rack, no labels ($5-7)
14. mustard body, gray- brown base, red interior, clear windows, roof rack, no labels ($5-7)
15. red body, black base, yellow interior, amber windows, roof rack, no labels ($5-7)
16. red body, black base, yellow interior, clear windows, roof rack, no labels ($5-7)
17. red body, black base, red interior, clear windows, roof rack, no labels ($10-15)
18. red body, black base, lemon interior, amber windows, roof rack, no labels ($5-7)
19. red body, black base, lemon interior, clear windows, roof rack, no labels ($5-7)
20. silver-gray body, black base, red interior, clear windows, no roof rack, green side tempa ($4-6)
21. silver-gray body, charcoal base, red interior, clear windows, no roof rack, green side tempa ($4-6)
22. silver-gray body, black base, tan interior, clear windows, no roof rack, green side tempa ($25-35)
23. silver-gray body, black base, blue interior, clear windows, no roof rack, green stripe tempa ($250-400)
24. black body, black base, red interior, clear windows, no roof rack, red stripe tempa, without tow hook cast, Macau casting ($5-7)(JP)
25. black body, black base, red interior, clear windows, no roof rack, red stripe tempa, Macau casting ($3-5)(TP)
26. black body, black base, red interior, clear windows, no roof rack, red & orange stripes with "9" tempa, Macau casting ($8-12)(DY)

NOTE: Available as a Bulgarian casting with "Universal Associated Co." cast on base. Assorted colors available ($5-25)

MB 7-D ROMPIN RABBIT, issued 1982 (MB099)

NOTE: Below models with clear windows, maltese cross wheels & black metal base.

1. white body, red interior, "Rompin Rabbit" with brown stripe tempa, England casting ($5-7)
2. white body, red interior, "Rompin Rabbit" without brown stripe tempa, England casting ($5-7)
3. white body, tan interior, "Rompin Rabbit" with brown stripe tempa, England casting ($5-7)
4. white body, tan interior, "Rompin Rabbit" without brown stripe tempa, England casting ($5-7)

NOTE: On below variations, rabbit on hood can face left or right.

5. yellow body, blue interior, "Ruff Rabbit" tempa, with tow hook, Macau casting ($3-5)
6. yellow body, blue interior, "Ruff Rabbit" tempa, with tow hook, Hong Kong casting ($3-5)
7. yellow body, blue interior, "Ruff Rabbit" tempa, without tow hook, Hong Kong casting ($3-5)
8. yellow body, blue interior, "Ruff Rabbit" tempa, without tow hook, Macau casting ($3-5)
9. yellow body, red interior, "Ruff Rabbit" tempa, without tow hook, Macau casting ($3-5)
10. yellow body, red interior, "Ruff Rabbit" tempa, with tow hook, Macau casting ($3-5)

MB 7-E I.M.S.A. MAZDA *see MB6-C*

MB 7-F PORSCHE 959, issued 1986 (MB173)
MB51-I PORSCHE 959, reissued 1994 (USA)

NOTE: Below models with red interior, clear windows and black plastic base unless otherwise noted.

1. pearly silver body, 5 arch silver wheels, "Porsche" on doors tempa, Macau casting ($2-3)
2. pearly gray body, 5 arch silver wheels, "Porsche" on doors tempa, Macau casting ($2-3)
3. pearly silver body, 8 dot silver wheels, "Porsche" on doors tempa, Macau casting ($2-3)
4. white body, 5 arch white wheels, "Porsche" on doors tempa, Macau casting ($3-5)
5. white body, 8 dot silver wheels, "Porsche" on doors tempa, Macau casting ($2-4)
6. white body, 5 arch silver wheels, "Porsche" on doors tempa, Macau casting ($2-4)
7. white body, 8 dot white wheels, "Porsche" on doors tempa, Macau casting ($3-5)
8. white body, 8 dot silver wheels, "Porsche" on doors tempa, China casting ($2-4)
9. white body, 5 arch silver wheels, "Porsche" on doors tempa, China casting ($2-4)
10. charcoal gray body, 5 arch silver wheels, "Porsche 959" tempa, Macau casting ($2-4)
11. white body, 5 arch silver wheels, "Porsche 959" with red/ yellow/black stripes tempa, Macau casting ($6-8)(KS)
12. pink body, 5 arch silver wheels, "Porsche 959" tempa, Macau casting ($3-4)(SC)
13. dark purple body, 5 arch silver wheels, "Porsche 959" tempa, Macau casting ($3-4)(SC)
14. white body, 5 arch silver wheels, "Redoxon" tempa, Macau casting ($20-35)(HK)
15. white body, 5 arch silver wheels, "Pace Car/ Shell" tempa, Macau casting ($3-5)(GS)
16. white body, 5 arch silver wheels, "313 Pirelli Gripping Stuff" tempa, Macau casting ($3-5)(TC)

17. silver-gray body, gray disc with rubber tires, chrome windows, "Porsche" & detailed trim tempa, Macau casting ($5-8)(WC)
18. black body, 5 arch silver wheels, "Porsche" logo tempa, Macau casting ($4-6)(MP)
19. white body, 5 arch silver wheels, "Pace Car/ Shell" tempa, Thailand casting ($3-5)(GS)
20. charcoal gray body, 5 arch silver wheels, "Porsche 959" tempa, Thailand casting ($2-3)
21. chrome plated body, 5 arch silver wheels, no tempa, Macau casting ($12-18)(C2)
22. white body, 5 arch silver wheels, "Porsche" logo tempa, Thailand casting ($3-5)(GS)
23. silver-gray body, gray disc with rubber tires, chrome windows, "Porsche" & detailed trim tempa, Thailand casting ($5-8)(WC)
24. white body, 5 arch silver wheels, red windows, no tempa, Thailand casting ($10-15)(GF)
25. silver-gray body, 5 arch silver wheels, black windows, checkers & red stripes with "959" tempa, Thailand casting ($3-5)(TH)
26. white body, 5 arch silver wheels, "Lloyds" tempa, Thailand casting ($8-12)(UK)
27. charcoal gray body, 5 arch silver wheels, "Porsche 959" (all red) tempa, Thailand casting ($1-2)
28. dark blue body, white interior, 5 arch silver wheels, small "Porsche" logo tempa, Thailand casting ($2-3)(SS)
29 silver-gray body, red interior, 5 arch silver wheels, "Porsche 959" (red only) tempa, base with bar code, Thailand casting ($75+)(IC)
30. white body, 5 arch silver wheels, "Porsche" on doors tempa, Thailand casting ($1-2)(MP)
31. white body, 5 arch silver wheels, "Porsche 959" with red/ yellow/ black stripes tempa, Thailand casting ($15-25)(CHI)(HU)
32. white body, 5 arch silver wheels, "313 Pirelli Gripping Stuff" tempa, Thailand casting ($1-2)(TC)
33. silver-gray body, red interior, gold 6-spoke spiral wheels, "Porsche 959" (red only) tempa, Thailand casting ($2-3)
34. dark florescent pink body, black interior, gold 6-spoke spiral wheels, black design & "Rage" tempa, Thailand casting ($1-2)
35. chrome plated body, white interior, gold 6-spoke spiral wheels, no tempa, white base, Thailand casting ($2-4)(GF)
36. white body, red interior, gold 6-spoke spiral wheels, "Pace Car" & checkers tempa, Thailand casting ($3-5)(FI)
37. dark florescent pink body, black interior, silver 6-spoke spiral wheels, black design with "Rage" on sides tempa, Thailand casting ($1-2)
38. dark florescent pink body, black interior, silver 6-spoke spiral wheels, black design without "Rage" on sides tempa, Thailand casting ($2-4)
39. silver body, red interior, silver 6-spoke spiral wheels, yellow & orange stripe design tempa, Thailand casting ($2-4)(MT)
40. florescent lime body, black interior, silver 6-spoke spiral wheels, black design without "Rage" on sides tempa, Thailand casting ($1-2)
41. florescent lime body, black interior, silver 6 spoke spiral wheels, black design without "Rage" on sides tempa, China casting ($1-2)
42. white body, red interior, silver 6 spoke spiral wheels, black checkers & "Pace Car" tempa, China casting ($1-2)(F1)
43. bright blue body, gray interior, 5 spoke concave star wheels, "Go Roos! 1997" tempa, China casting ($3-5)(AU)
44. dark blue body, gray & black, chrome disc with rubber wheels, detailed trim tempa, China casting ($8-12)(UC)
45. dark blue body, red interior, gold 6 spoke spiral wheels, detailed trim tempa, China casting ($100+)(CHI)
46. white body, dark red interior, 5 spoke concave star wheels, "Porsche" logo tempa, China casting ($1-2)
47. red body, tan interior, 5 spoke concave star wheels, "Porsche" and small logo tempa, China casting ($1-2)(MW56/ 1998ROW)
48. red body, black & red interior, chrome disc wheels with rubber tires, detailed trim tempa, China casting ($50+)(GC)(CHI)
NOTE: Above model was intended for the gold coin series but was issued separately in China.
49. metallic light bronze body, black interior, 5 spoke concave star wheels, black stripe with "359" & "Porsche" tempa, China casting ($1-2)(MW17/1999)
50. dark metallic charcoal body, black interior, smoke green windows, small logo tempa, China casting ($3-4)(MW17/ 1999 GR)
51. metallic red body, black interior, smoke windows, 5 spoke concave star wheels, small logo tempa, China casting ($2-4)(MW33/2000 ROW)
52. silver body, black interior, clear windows, lace wheels, "Porsche" & Porsche logo tempa, China casting ($2-4)(MW54/ 2001 UK)
53. white body, white interior, blue windows, lace wheels, "Porsche" & "Matchbox" logo tempa, China casting ($2-4)(MW51/ 2001 ROW)(MW55/ 2001 GR)
54. bright blue body, gray & black interior, gold 6 spoke spiral wheels, "Go Roos! 1997" tempa, China casting ($50+)(CHI)
55. blue body, red interior, gold 6 spoke spiral wheels, "P & L CO" tempa, China casting ($75+)(CHI)

MB 7-G FORD THUNDERBIRD, issued 1994 (USA) (MB212)
MB39-H FORD THUNDERBIRD, issued 1995 (ROW)

NOTE: Below models with clear windows, black plastic base & Goodyear slicks - white lettered unless noted. Versions 1 to 18 with China casting.

1. red body, red interior, "Motorcraft Quality Parts 15" tempa ($3-5)(WR)
2. black body, silver-gray interior, "Havoline/ Texaco 28" tempa ($3-5)(WR)
3. yellow body, red interior, "Matchbox 92" with assorted logos tempa ($20-25)(US)
4. white & orange-red body, black interior, "Hooters 7" tempa ($5-8)(WR)
5. dark red body, black interior, "Philips 66/ Trop Artic" tempa ($3-5)(WR)
6. bright red body, black interior, "Phillips 66/ Trop Artic" tempa ($3-5)(WR)
7. metallic blue body, black interior, "Maxwell House 22" tempa ($3-5)(WR)
8. bright red body, black interior, "White Rose Collectibles 92" tempa ($15-25)(WR)
9. red body, black interior, "Motorcraft Quality Parts" without Morgan Shephard tempa ($3-5)(WR)
10. black body, silver-gray interior, "Havoline/ Texaco 28" without "MAC" tempa ($3-5)(WR)
11. black body, gray interior, "Phillips 66/ Trop Artic" tempa ($3-5)(WR)
12. red body, red interior, "Bill Elliot 11" tempa ($3-5)(WR)
13. white body, silver-gray interior, "Baby Ruth 1" (orange) tempa ($4-6)(WR)
14. white body, silver-gray interior, "Baby Ruth 1" (red) tempa ($4-6)(WR)
15. white body, black interior, "Hooters 7" without "Classic/Naturally Fresh" tempa ($7-10)(WR)

16. brown & red body, silver-gray interior, "Snickers 8" tempa ($3-5)(WR)
17. red body, red interior, black disc with rubber tires, "Bill Elliot 11" tempa (WR)(TC)($4-6)
18. red & white body, black interior, "Melling 9" tempa ($3-5)(WR)
19. green body, black interior, "Quaker State 26" tempa, Thailand casting ($3-5)(WR)
20. white & orange body, black interior, "Hooters 7" tempa, black disc with rubber tires, Thailand casting ($12-15)(WR)(TC)
21.gray body, black interior, "Hooters 7" tempa, Thailand casting ($7-10)(WR)(TC)
22. black body, red interior, "Texaco/Havoline 28" (bright orange) tempa, Thailand casting ($8-12)(WR)
23.black body, red interior, "Texaco/Havoline 28" (bright orange) tempa, black disc with rubber tires, Thailand casting ($8-12)(WR)(TC)
24.matt black body, red interior, "Texaco 28" tempa, Thailand casting ($7-10)(WR)(TC)
25.white body, black interior, "Maui 17" tempa, Thailand casting ($3-5)
26. white body, black interior, "Ford 1" & checkered flag tempa, Thailand casting ($2-4) (SS)
27. dark blue body, gray interior, "Racetech Radios" tempa, Thailand casting ($1-2)(5pk)

NOTE: Following models with Goodyear slicks- yellow lettered unless noted.

28. bright blue body, red interior, "Purex 83" tempa, China casting ($3-5)(WR)
29. white & red body, red interior, "Citgo 21" tempa, China casting ($3-5)(WR)
30. white body, red interior, "Baby Ruth 8" tempa, China casting ($3-5)(WR)
31. metallic blue body, dark gray interior, "Maxwell House 22" tempa, China casting ($3-5)(WR)
32. metallic blue body, red interior, "Raybestos 8" tempa, China casting ($3-5)(WR)
33. white body, black interior, "Bojangles/Easter Seals 7" tempa, China casting ($18-25) (WR)
34. white body, black interior, "Hanes 7" tempa, China casting ($18-25)(WR)
35. white body, black interior, "Matchbox/White Rose 7" tempa, China casting ($10-15)(WR)
36. black body, silver-gray interior, "Cappio 48" tempa, China casting ($3-5)(WR)
37. fluorescent yellow body, black interior, "Country Time 68" tempa, Thailand casting ($3-5)(WR)(TC)
38. fluorescent pink body, black interior, "Country Time 68" tempa, Thailand casting ($3-5)(WR)(TC)
39. white body, red interior, "Matchbox/White Rose 1" tempa, China casting ($3-5)(WR)
40. black body, red interior, "Meineke 12" tempa, China casting ($3-5)(WR)
41. yellow body, gray interior, "Bojangles 98" tempa, China casting ($3-5)(WR)
42. white body, red interior, "Luxaire 1" tempa, plain black slicks, China casting ($12-15)(WR)
43. white body, gray interior, "Family Channel 7" tempa, China casting ($12-15)(WR)
44. white body, gray interior, "Matchbox/USA Bobsled 7" tempa, Thailand casting ($12-15)(WR)
45. red body, red interior, "Budweiser 11" tempa, black disc wheels rubber tires, Thailand casting ($25-35)(WR)(Ertl set)
46. flat black body, red interior, "Bud 11" tempa, black disc wheels rubber tires, Thailand casting ($25-35)(WR)(Ertl set)
47. white, red & dark blue body, gray interior, "Valvoline 6" tempa, China casting ($3-5)(WR)
48. white body, gray interior, "USA Bobsled Project 7" tempa, China casting ($12-15)(WR)
49. yellow body, gray interior, "Bojangles 98" tempa, black disc wheels rubber tires, China casting ($4-6)(WR)(TC)
50. black body, gray interior, "Bojangles 98" tempa, black disc wheels rubber tires, China casting ($4-6)(WR)(TC)
51. bright blue & white body, red interior, "Naturally Fresh 37" tempa, China casting ($5-8)(WR)
52. black body, black interior, "TIC Financial 0" tempa, China casting ($5-8)(WR)
53. black & red body, silver-gray interior, "Cellular One 7" tempa, China casting ($5-8)(WR)
54. blue body, gray interior, yellow lettered "Racetech Radios 16" tempa, gold 6-spoke spiral wheels, Thailand casting ($1-2)
55. white body, lime interior, no tempa, white base, gold 6-spoke spiral wheels, Thailand casting ($2-4)(GF)
56. yellow body, gray interior, "Nationwise Auto Parts" tempa, Thailand casting ($20-35) (US)
57. blue body, gray interior, white lettered "Racetech Radios 16" tempa, gold 6-spoke spiral wheels, Thailand casting ($4-6) (Aquafresh promo)
58. pink body, black interior, "Radical Cams 10" tempa, silver 6-spoke spiral wheels, Thailand casting ($1-2)
59. pink body, black interior, "Radical Cams 10" tempa, silver 6-spoke spiral wheels, China casting ($1-2)
60. blue body, black interior, "Mitre 10/ Stanley" tempa, silver 6-spoke spiral wheels, China casting ($5-7)(AU)
61. black body, lime interior, "12 Joltage Batteries" tempa, silver 6-spoke spiral wheels, China casting ($1-2)(5pk)
62. dark blue body, black interior, "Wieder Racing 11" tempa, silver 6-spoke spiral wheels, China casting ($1-2)
63. black body, red interior, "Carr Auto Care 4" tempa, 5 spoke concave star wheels, China casting ($1-2)
64. red body, gray interior, "Peterson Pistons 17" tempa, 5 spoke concave star wheels, China casting ($1-2)(5pk)
65. metallic gold body, black interior, no tempa, silver 6 spoke spiral wheels, China casting ($5-10)(CH)
66. dark blue body, black interior, "Wieder Racing 11" tempa, 5 spoke concave star wheels, China casting ($2-4)
67. blue body, red interior, "Carr Auto Care 4" tempa, 5 spoke concave star wheels, China casting ($3-5)(PS)
68. green body, black interior, "BP Car Care 25" tempa, 5 spoke concave star wheels, China casting ($20-25)(AU)
69. blue body, black interior, "Peterson Pistons 17" tempa, 5 spoke concave star wheels, China casting ($1-2)(MW64/1998 US)

MB 7-H SCISSORS TRUCK, issued 1999 (MB401)

NOTE: Below models with blue windows, 8 spoke wheels, black plastic base & China casting unless otherwise noted.

1. white body, white container & lifts, "World Jets" labels ($1-2)(MW7/1999)
2. white body, white container & lifts, "World Airways" labels ($1-2)(5pk)
3. white body, white container & lifts, "LSG Sky Chefs" labels ($3-5)(MW12/1999 GR)
4. white body, white container & lifts, blue & green design labels ($1-2)(5pk)
5. red body, white container & lifts, gray base, crate & ship design labels ($1-2)(5pk)
6. red body, gray container & lifts, jet & globe design labels ($3-5)(AS)

7. light gray body, smoke windows, white container & lifts, "Venture Star" labels ($1-2)(MW37/2000 US)(MW22/ 2000 ROW)
8. light gray body, smoke windows, white container & lifts, "Venture Star" labels & "Matchbox 2000" tempa ($2-4)(MW37/ 2000 US)
9. white body, smoke windows, white container & lifts, no labels ($25-40)(ASAP blank)

MB 7-I FERRARI 360 SPIDER *see MB65-L*

MB 7-J MILK MOO-VER, issued 2004 (USA)(MB656)
1. white body, gray tank, black patches tempa, orange plastic base, gold 10 spoke flower wheels, China casting ($1-2)(MW7/ 2004 US)

MB 7-K BULLDOZER 04 *see MB17-J*

MB 7-L 1969 CHEVROLET CAMARO (SF) (MB608)
1. metallic blue body, black interior, clear windows, dual white stripes & detailed trim tempa, slotted 5 spoke wheels, chrome base, China casting ($3-5)(SF9/2004)

MB 8-A FORD MUSTANG FASTBACK, issued 1970
NOTE: Below models with clear windows, 5 spoke wheels, black metal base & England casting.
1. white body, red interior ($50-75)
2. red body, red interior ($350-400)
3. red-orange body, red interior ($250-350)
4. red body, ivory interior ($35-50)
5. red-orange body, ivory interior ($35-50)

MB 8-B WILDCAT DRAGSTER, issued 1971
NOTE: Body colors range in shades of light to dark pinkish orange on all versions. All models with green windows & orange-yellow interior.
1. unpainted base, black & orange "Wildcat" labels ($18-25)
2. black base, black & orange "Wildcat" labels ($18-25)
3. dark yellow base, black & orange "Wildcat" labels ($18-25)
4. light yellow base, black & orange "Wildcat" labels ($18-25)
5. orange base, black & orange "Wildcat" labels ($18-25)
6. charcoal base, black & orange "Wildcat" labels ($18-25)
7. charcoal base, yellow & orange "Wildcat" labels ($18-25)
8. dark gray base, yellow & orange "Wildcat" labels ($18-25)
9. light gray base, yellow & orange "Wildcat" labels ($18-25)
10. black base, yellow & orange "Wildcat" labels ($18-25)
11. unpainted base, yellow & orange "Wildcat" labels ($18-25)
12. green base, yellow & orange "Wildcat" labels ($18-25)
13. black base, "Rat Rod" labels (from MB62-C) ($25-40)
14. black base, sailboat labels (from MB23-A) ($25-40)
15. black base, no labels ($18-25)
16. white body, unpainted base, no labels, origin ground off casting ($250+)(BR)

MB 8-C DE TOMASO PANTERA, issued 1975
NOTE: Versions 1 to 10 with England casting. Versions 12 & 13 with Hong Kong casting.
1. white body, blue base, "8" hood label, with side labels, light orange interior ($7-10)
2. white body, unpainted base, "8" hood label, with side labels, light orange interior ($7-10)
3. white body, blue base, "8" hood label, with side labels, dark orange interior ($7-10)
4. white body, blue base, "8" hood label, no side labels, dark orange interior ($7-10)
5. white body, blue base, "8" hood label, no side labels, light orange interior ($7-10)
6. white body, unpainted base, "8" hood label, no side labels, light orange interior ($7-10)
7. white body, blue base, "8" hood label, no side labels, red interior ($7-10)
8. white body, blue base, "9" hood label (from MB62-C), no side labels, light orange interior ($12-18)
9. white body, blue base, sunburst hood label (from MB47-C), no side labels, light orange interior ($18-25)
10. white body, blue base, sunburst hood label (from MB47-C), no side labels, dark orange interior ($18-25)
11. white body, lavender base, "8" hood label, with side labels, light orange interior ($50-75)(BR)
12. blue body, black base, tempa without "Pantera" on hood, black interior ($3-5)
13. blue body, black base, tempa with "Pantera" on hood, black interior ($3-5)

NOTE: Many versions have intermixing of front and rear wheels.

MB 8-D ROVER 3500, issued 1982 (ROW)(MB008)
NOTE: Below models with dot dash wheels & black plastic base unless otherwise noted. Versions without dome light come with black or gray sun roof.
1. bronze body, light tan interior, clear windows, no dome lights, England casting ($2-4)
2. bronze body, dark tan interior, clear windows, no dome lights, England casting ($2-4)
3. bronze body, white interior, clear windows, no dome lights, England casting ($2-4)
4. bronze body, white interior, clear windows, no dome lights, small maltese cross wheels, England casting ($5-8)
5. bronze body, light tan interior, clear windows, no dome lights, small maltese cross wheels, England casting ($5-8)
6. white body, white interior, blue windows & dome lights, black beacon, no tempa, England casting ($15-20)
7. white body, light tan interior, blue windows & dome lights, chrome beacon, blue & yellow "Police" tempa, England casting ($2-4)
8. white body, light tan interior, clear windows & dome lights, chrome beacon, blue & yellow "Police" tempa, England casting ($2-4)
9. white body, light tan interior, blue windows & dome lights, chrome beacon, no tempa, England casting ($2-4)
10. white body, black interior, blue windows & dome lights, chrome beacon, no tempa, England casting ($2-4)
11. white body, black interior, blue windows & dome lights, chrome beacon, blue & yellow "Police" tempa, England casting ($2-4)
12. white body, black interior, blue windows & dome lights, black beacon, black & yellow "Police" tempa, England casting ($2-4)
13. white body, light tan interior, blue windows & dome lights, black beacon, black & yellow "Police" tempa, England casting ($2-4)
14. white body, light tan interior, blue windows & dome lights, black beacon, black & yellow "Police" tempa, Macau casting ($2-4)
15. white body, light tan interior, blue windows & dome lights, black beacon, blue & red "Police" tempa, Macau casting ($2-4)
16. white body, light tan interior, blue windows & dome lights, black beacon, blue & red "Police" tempa, China casting ($3-5)
17. white body, translucent tan interior, blue windows & dome lights, black beacon, blue & red "Police" tempa, China casting ($3-5)(MP)

18. white body, orange-yellow interior, blue windows & dome lights, black beacon, black& yellow "Police" tempa, 4 arch wheels Manaus casting ($25-40)(BR)

MB 8-E GREASED LIGHTNING, issued 1983 (USA) (MB079)

NOTE: Below models with maltese cross front & five spoke rear wheels but other combinations can occur.

1. red body, white base, black interior, Macau casting ($5-8)
2. red body, white base, black interior, Hong Kong casting ($5-8)

MB 8-F SCANIA T142, issued 1985 (USA)(MB147/341)
MB71-E SCANIA T142, issued 1985 (ROW)

NOTE: This model was used as a component for Convoy models. Only models released as single issues will be cataloged. Below models with clear windows & 8 spoke wheels unless otherwise noted.

1. white body, red chassis, chrome base, red/orange/yellow stripes tempa, Macau casting ($2-4)
2. blue body, white chassis, chrome base, red/orange/yellow stripes tempa, Macau casting ($2-4)
3. blue body, white chassis, black base, red/orange/yellow stripes tempa, Macau casting ($2-4)
4. silver-gray body, silver-gray chassis, black base, "Scania" with black & orange stripes tempa, Mattel China casting (MW11/1999 ROW)(MW61/ 1999 GR)
5. red body, yellow chassis, gray base, "Coca-Cola" tempa, 7 spoke sawblade wheels, Mattel China casting ($2-4)(CK)

MB 8-G VAUXHALL ASTRA POLICE CAR, issued 1987 (ROW)(MB179)

NOTE: Below models listed have white interior, blue windows & dome lights unless otherwise noted.

1. white body, black base, 8 dot white wheels, "Police" with red & blue stripes tempa, Macau casting ($3-5)
2. white & dark green body, black base, 8 dot white wheels, "Polizei" tempa, Macau casting ($3-5)
3. white & dark green body, black base, 8 dot silver wheels, "Polizei" tempa, Macau casting ($3-5)
4. white body, black base, 8 dot silver wheels, "Police" with red & blue stripes tempa, Macau casting ($2-4)
5. white body, black base, 8 dot silver wheels, "Police" with red & blue stripes tempa, China casting ($2-4)
6. white & dark green body, black base, 8 dot silver wheels, "Polizei" tempa, China casting ($3-5)
7. white body, white base, blue 8 dot wheels with yellow hubs, "Police" with orange & blue stripes & face on hood tempa, China casting ($3-5)(LL)
8. white body, white base, blue 8 dot wheels (plain hubs), "Police" with orange & blue stripes & face on hood tempa, China casting ($3-5)(LL)
9. white body, white base, 8 dot silver wheels, no tempa, China casting ($10-15)(GF)
10. white body, white base, 8 dot silver wheels, "Police" with orange & yellow stripes & orange dot on roof tempa, China casting ($1-2)
11. white body, white base, 8 dot silver wheels, "Police" with orange & yellow stripes without dot on roof tempa, China casting ($1-2)
12. white body, white base, 8 dot silver wheels, "Police" with peach & yellow stripes without dot on roof tempa, China casting ($1-2)
13. white body, white base, 8 dot silver wheels, yellow & black checkers & "59" in shield tempa, China casting ($1-2)(5pk)
14. white body, white base, 8 dot silver wheels, "Police/Hertfordshire" tempa, China casting ($1-2)
15. black body, black base, gray interior, 8 dot silver wheels, "Police" & Commando emblem tempa, China casting ($15-20)(CM)(CHI)(MP)
16. black body, black base, white interior, 5 arch black wheels, "Police" & Commando emblem tempa, China casting ($15-20)(CM)(CHI)(MP)
17. white body, white base, red windows, 8 dot silver wheels, "World Cup Security/ France 98" tempa, China casting ($1-2)(5pk)
18. silver-gray body, black base, 8 dot silver wheels, "Police" with red & blue stripes tempa ($1-2)(MW24/ 1998ROW)

MB 8-H MACK CH600 AERODYNE, issued 1990 (USA)(MB202/311)
MB39-F MACK CH600 AERODYNE, issued 1990 (ROW)

NOTE: This model was used as a component for Convoy models. Only models released as singles will be listed here. Below models with clear windows.

1. white body, black chassis, gray base, black & red stripes tempa, 8 spoke wheels, Macau casting ($1-2)
2. white body, black chassis, gray base, black & red stripes tempa, 8 spoke wheels, Thailand casting ($1-2)
3. red & white body, black chassis, black base, "Coke" tempa, chrome disc wheels with rubber tires, Mattel China casting ($4-6)(PC)

MB 8-I AIRPORT TENDER, issued 1992 (USA)(MB233)
MB24-I AIRPORT TENDER, issued 1992 (ROW)

NOTE: Below models with dark blue windows, black base & China casting unless otherwise noted.

1. fluorescent orange body, white ladder, silver-gray interior, 8 dot wheels, "Fire Airport Fire Rescue" tempa, Thailand casting ($1-2)
2. fluorescent orange body, white ladder, silver-gray interior, 8 dot wheels, "Fire Airport Fire Rescue" & "IC" logo tempa, base with bar code ($35-50)(IC)
3. white & red body, silver-gray ladder, black interior, 8 dot wheels, "Fire Dept." with gold crest & star tempa ($1-2)(5pk)
4. red body, white ladder, silver-gray interior, 8 dot wheels, "Matchbox Fire Dept." & white band tempa ($1-2)(5pk)
5. florescent yellow body, silver-gray ladder, chrome disc wheels with rubber wheels, black interior, "Westford Airport Fire Rescue" tempa ($3-5)(PC7)
6. yellow body, gray ladder, 8 dot wheels, black interior, "Matchbox Fire Dept." & red band tempa ($1-2)(5pk)
7. lemon body, red ladder, 8 dot wheels, red interior, "Airways Fire & Rescue" tempa ($1-2)(5pk)
8. yellow body, white ladder, chrome disc with rubber tires, "Newfield Airport Fire Rescue" tempa ($3-5)(PC21)
9. bright blue body, amber windows, silver-gray ladder, 8 dot wheels, "Runway Rescue" & yellow stripe tempa ($1-2)(MW8/1999 US)
10. bright blue body, amber windows, silver-gray ladder, 8 dot wheels, yellow stripe tempa ($2-3)(MW8/1999 ROW)
11. red body, white ladder & base, 8 dot wheels, "Feuerwehr" tempa ($3-5)(MW13/1999 GR)(MW14/2000 GR)
12. florescent yellow body, silver-gray ladder, yellow disc wheels with rubber tires, "DIA 2" tempa ($12-15)(PC)
13. florescent yellow body, silver-gray ladder, 8 dot wheels, white band with "34" & hash marks tempa ($1-2)(5pk)
14. white body, red windows, black ladder, 8 dot wheels, "Runway Rescue" tempa ($1-2)(MW29/2000 US)

15. white body, red windows, black ladder, 8 dot wheels, "Runway Rescue" & "Matchbox 2000" tempa ($2-4)(MW29)
16. lemon body, red windows, white ladder, silver-gray base, 8 dot wheels, "5 Alarm" & red stripes tempa ($1-2)(LP)
17. red body, blue windows, white ladder, 10 spoke flower wheels, "5 Alarm" & yellow stripes tempa ($1-2)(LP)
18. lime green body, blue windows, silver-gray ladder, white base, 8 dot wheels, "Metro 24" & blue stripe tempa ($3-5)(ROW 3pk)
19. yellow body, red windows, silver-gray ladder, 10 spoke flower wheels, "Metro Alarm" & red bands tempa ($1-2)(5pk)
20. black body, blue windows, red ladder, gold base, 10 spoke flower wheels, "76ers" logo & basketball players tempa ($10-15)(US)

NOTE: Below model with Matchbox International or Mattel China casting.

21. orange body, blue windows, silver-gray ladder, 10 spoke flower wheels, "Alarm" tempa ($1-2)(MW41/2002)
22. orange body, blue windows, silver-gray ladder, 10 spoke flower wheels, "Alarm" & "Matchbox 50" tempa ($5-8)(MW41/2002)
23. lemon body, red windows, black ladder, 10 spoke flower wheels, "Matchbox FDMB 14" & dual flames tempa, Mattel casting ($1-2)(LP)
24. red body, amber windows, gray ladder, yellow base, 10 spoke flower wheels, "Metro Alarm" tempa, Mattel casting ($1-2)(5pk)

MB 8-J MAZDA RX7, issued 1994(USA)(MB251)
MB54-I MAZDA RX7, issued 1994 (ROW)

NOTE: Below models with black plastic base unless otherwise noted.

1. fluorescent orange body, black interior, clear windows, gold 6-spoke spiral wheels, "Matchbox Get In The Fast Lane- Toy Fair 1994" tempa, Thailand casting ($35-50)(US/GR)
2. yellow-orange body, gray interior, smoke windows, gold 6-spoke spiral wheels, black & pink hood & sides design tempa, Thailand casting ($1-2)
3. black body, orange interior, chrome windows, gray disc wheels with rubber tires, detailed trim tempa, Thailand casting ($2-4)(WC)
4. yellow-orange body, gray interior, smoke windows, gold 6-spoke spiral wheels, black & pink design tempa & "Nationwise Auto Parts" roof label, Thailand casting ($20-35)(US)
5. yellow-orange body, gray interior, smoke windows, gold 6-spoke spiral wheels, black & pink side design only tempa, Thailand casting ($4-6)(Aquafresh promo)
6. red body, gray interior, smoke windows, silver 6-spoke spiral wheels, black & yellow hood & side tempa, Thailand casting ($1-2)
7. silver body, white interior, blue windows, silver 6-spoke spiral wheels, red blotches tempa, Thailand casting ($3-4)(MT)
8. red body, gray interior, smoke windows, silver 6-spoke spiral wheels, yellow side design tempa, Thailand casting ($2-4)
9. gold & metallic red body, gray interior, smoke windows, silver 6-spoke spiral wheels, no tempa, Thailand casting ($1-2)
10. red body, clear windows, chrome disc wheels with rubber tires, detailed trim tempa, Thailand casting ($3-4)(PC1)
11. silver-gray body, clear windows, chrome disc wheels with rubber tires, detailed trim tempa, Thailand casting ($3-4)(SC1)
12. metallic green body, clear windows, chrome disc wheels with rubber tires, detailed trim tempa, Thailand casting ($3-5)(PC1-JC)
13. lemon body, clear windows, chrome disc wheels with rubber tires, detailed trim tempa, Thailand casting ($3-5)(PC4)

NOTE: Premiere & select editions have 2 tone interiors

14. metallic gold body, black interior, clear windows, silver 6-spoke spiral wheels, no tempa, Thailand casting ($10-15)(CH)
15. lavender chrome body, white interior, blue windows, 5 spoke concave star wheels, yellow & blue tempa, Thailand casting ($1-2)(5pk)
16. blue body, tan & black interior, clear windows, chrome disc wheels with rubber tires, detailed trim tempa, Thailand casting ($15-20)(GC)
17. gold & metallic red body, gray interior, smoke windows, 5 spoke concave star wheels, no tempa, Thailand casting ($2-4)
18. red body, gray interior, smoke windows, 5 spoke concave star wheels, "Go Bombers! 1997" tempa, Thailand casting ($3-5)(AU)
19. red body, black & brown interior, clear windows, chrome disc wheels with rubber tires, detailed trim with additional brown stripe at rear tempa, Thailand casting ($4-6)(PC1)
20. metallic green & black body, gray interior, clear windows, 5 spoke concave star wheels, no tempa, Thailand casting ($1-2)
21. dark lavender chrome body, white interior, blue windows, 5 spoke concave star wheels, yellow & blue tempa, Thailand casting ($1-2)(5pk)
22. purple chrome body, white interior, blue windows, 5 spoke concave star wheels, yellow & orange tempa, Thailand casting ($1-2)(5pk)
23. dark purple chrome body, white interior, blue windows, 5 spoke concave star wheels, yellow & orange tempa, Thailand casting ($1-2)(5pk)
24. metallic bronze & black body, gray interior, smoke windows, 5 spoke concave star wheels, no tempa, Thailand casting ($1-2)(MW67/ 1998 US)(MW41/ 1998 ROW))

NOTE: Version 24 comes in various shades of metallic gold

25. metallic orange & black body, gray interior, smoke windows, 5 spoke concave star wheels, no tempa, China casting ($1-2)(MW67/ 1998 US)(MW41/ 1998 ROW)
26. dark purple chrome body, white interior, blue windows, 5 spoke concave star wheels, yellow & orange tempa, China casting ($1-2)(5pk)
27. bronze & black body, gray interior, smoke windows, 5 spoke concave star wheels, none tempa, China casting ($1-2)(MW67/ 1998 US)(MW41/ 1998 ROW)
28. black body, silver-gray base, black interior, dark smoke windows, 5 spoke concave star wheels, silver stripes with "Mazda" tempa ($1-2)(MW20/1999)
29. red body, white interior, clear windows, chrome disc wheels with rubber tires, "Coca-Cola" tempa, Mattel China casting ($3-5)(Coke PC)

MB 8-K Q.B. ROLLER, issued 2004 (USA)(MB658)

1. brown upper body, metallic green lower body, blue-green windows, neon orange plastic base, gold 7 spoke sawblade wheels, "Hero City" tempa, China casting ($1-2)(MW8/ 2004 US)

MB 8-L MIXOPOTAMUS *see MB18-D*

MB 8-M LOTUS ELISE, *see MB69-J*

MB 9-A BOAT AND TRAILER, issued 1970 (MB709/ 809)

NOTE: Below models with clear windows, white interior & England casting unless otherwise noted.

1. blue deck, white hull, light blue trailer, no label, 5 spoke wheels ($18-25)
2. blue deck, white hull, dark blue trailer, no label, 5 spoke wheels ($18-25)

3. blue deck, white hull, dark blue trailer, no label, 5 spoke center cut wheels ($3-5)(TP)
4. black deck, white hull, dark blue trailer, no label, 5 spoke center cut wheels ($65-80)(TP)
5. blue deck, white hull, dark blue trailer, "8" label, dot dash wheels ($12-15)(TP)
6. white deck, blue hull, dark blue trailer, "8" label, dot dash wheels ($12-15)(TP)
7. blue deck, white hull, dark blue trailer, no label, dot dash wheels ($3-5)(TP)
8. white deck, blue hull, orange trailer, "8" label, dot dash wheels ($5-8)(TP)
9. white deck, white hull, orange trailer, "8" label, dot dash wheels ($7-10)(TP)
10. blue deck, white hull, orange trailer, no label, dot dash wheels ($5-8)(TP)
11. milk white deck, blue hull, white interior, orange trailer, "8" tempa, dot dash wheels, no origin cast($3-5)(TP)
12. white deck, white hull, gray interior, black trailer, "Seaspray" tempa, dot dash wheels, no origin cast ($3-5)(TP)
13. white deck, white hull, gray interior, dark metallic blue trailer, yellow dashes tempa, dot dash wheels, no origin cast ($3-5)(TP)
14. blue deck, blue hull, gray interior, black trailer, white & orange spatter tempa, dot dash wheels, no origin cast ($3-5)(TP)

MB 9-B AMX JAVELIN, issued 1972

NOTE: Below models listed with black air scoop & England casting unless noted. Versions 18 & 19 in USA as Limited Edition "Cam Cracker".

1. metallic lime body, lemon interior, unpainted base, doors open, 5 spoke wheels, chrome scoop ($10-15)
2. metallic lime body, lemon interior, unpainted base, doors open, 5 spoke wheels ($5-8)
3. metallic lime body, lemon interior, silver-gray base, doors open, 5 spoke wheels ($5-8)
4. metallic lime body, orange interior, unpainted base, doors open, 5 spoke wheels ($12-15)
5. metallic lime body, orange interior, silver-gray base, doors open, 5 spoke wheels ($12-15)
6. metallic lime body, orange interior, unpainted base, doors open, maltese cross wheels ($12-15)
7. metallic lime body, lemon interior, unpainted base, doors open, maltese cross wheels ($5-8)
8. metallic lime body, white interior, unpainted base, doors open, 5 spoke wheels ($50-75)
9. metallic lime body, blue interior, unpainted base, doors open, 5 arch wheels ($100-150)
10. metallic lime body, yellow-orange interior, unpainted base, doors open, 5 arch wheels ($5-8)
11. metallic lime body, yellow-orange interior, silver-gray base, doors open, 5 arch wheels ($5-8)
12. metallic blue body, lemon interior, unpainted base, doors open, 5 spoke wheels ($5-8)(TP)
13. metallic blue body, yellow-orange interior, unpainted base, doors open, 5 arch wheels ($5-8)(TP)
14. metallic blue body, yellow-orange interior, silver-gray base, doors open, 5 arch wheels ($5-8)(TP)
15. metallic blue body, yellow-orange interior, unpainted base, doors cast, 5 arch wheels ($5-8)(TP)
16. metallic blue body, yellow-orange interior, silver-gray base, doors cast, 5 arch wheels ($5-8)(TP)
17. metallic green body, yellow-orange interior, silver-gray base, doors open, 5 arch wheels ($5-8)(TP)
18. blue body, yellow-orange interior, silver-gray base, doors cast, 5 arch wheels, white tempa ($5-8)(LE)
19. blue body, yellow-orange interior, unpainted base, doors cast, 5 arch wheels, white tempa ($5-8)(LE)
20. blue body, yellow-orange interior, unpainted base, doors cast, 5 arch wheels ($20-30)(TP)
21. metallic green body, yellow-orange interior, unpainted base, doors cast, 5 arch wheels ($5-8)(TP)
22. metallic green body, yellow-orange interior, silver-gray base, doors cast, 5 arch wheels ($5-8)(TP)
23. red body, yellow-orange interior, unpainted base, doors cast, 5 arch wheels ($35-50)(TP)
24. red body, yellow-orange interior, silver-gray base, doors cast, 5 arch wheels ($35-50)(TP)
25. red-orange body, yellow-orange interior, unpainted base, doors cast, 5 arch wheels ($35-50)(TP)

MB 9-C FORD ESCORT RS2000, issued 1978 (MB009)

NOTE: All models with dot dash wheels & England casting.

1. white body, black base, tan interior, clear windows, "Dunlop" labels ($3-5)
2. white body, black base, tan interior, amber windows, "Dunlop" labels ($3-5)
3. white body, charcoal base, tan interior, clear windows, "Dunlop" labels ($3-5)
4. white body, charcoal base, tan interior, amber windows, "Dunlop" labels ($3-5)
5. white body, black base, tan interior, clear windows, "Phantom" labels ($7-10)(TP)
6. blue body, black base, tan interior, clear windows, "Phantom" labels ($3-5)(TP)
7. blue body, charcoal base, tan interior, clear windows, "Phantom" labels ($3-5)(TP)
8. blue body, blue-gray base, tan interior, clear windows, "Phantom" labels ($3-5)(TP)
9. white body, black base, red interior, clear windows, "Dunlop" labels ($150-175)

NOTE: Versions 10-13 are also available as single releases.

10. metallic green body, charcoal base, tan interior, clear windows, "Seagull" labels ($3-5)(TP)
11. metallic green body, black base, tan interior, clear windows, "Seagull" labels ($3-5)(TP)
12. metallic green body, black base, white interior, clear windows, "Seagull" labels ($3-5)(TP)
13. metallic green body, black base, red interior, clear windows, "Seagull" labels ($150-175)(TP)
14. white body, gray base, pink-tan interior, clear windows, "Dunlop" labels ($3-5)
15. white body, gray-brown base, tan interior, clear windows, "Dunlop" labels ($3-5)
16. dark green body, black base, tan interior, clear windows, "Seagull" labels ($3-5)(TP)

MB 9-D FIAT ABARTH, issued 1982 (USA)(MB074)
MB74-E FIAT ABARTH, issued 1982 (ROW)

NOTE: Below models with clear windows, 5 arch wheels & black plastic base unless otherwise noted.

1. white body, red interior, brown & orange "Matchbox" tempa, England casting ($2-4)
2. white body, red interior, red & orange "Matchbox" tempa, charcoal base, England casting ($2-4)
3. white body, red interior, maroon & orange "Matchbox" tempa, England casting ($2-4)

4. white body, red interior, red & orange "Matchbox" tempa, England casting ($2-4)
5. white body, black interior, red & orange "Matchbox" tempa, England casting ($150-200)
6. white body, red interior, red & orange "Matchbox" tempa, Macau casting ($2-4)
7. white body, red interior, red & orange "Matchbox" tempa, very light amber windows, Macau casting ($2-4)
8. white body, red interior, purple & orange "Matchbox" tempa, Macau casting ($2-4)
9. white body, red interior, purple & orange "Matchbox" tempa, amber windows, Macau casting ($2-4)
10. white body, red interior, green & red "Alitalia" tempa, Macau casting ($3-5)
11. white body, red interior, dark green & red "Alitalia" tempa, charcoal base, amber windows, Macau casting ($3-5)
12. white body, red interior, green & red "Alitalia" tempa, amber windows, Macau casting ($3-5)
13. white body, red interior, dark green & red "Alitalia" tempa, amber windows, Macau casting ($3-5)
14. white body, red interior, red/orange/yellow stripes tempa, Macau casting ($8-12)(DY)
15. white body, red interior, "Matchbox 11" tempa, 4 arch wheels, Manaus casting ($35-50)(BR)
16. white body, red interior, "Matchbox 11" tempa, 8 spoke wheels, Manaus casting ($35-50)(BR)
17. blue body, black base, red interior, clear windows, "Matchbox 16/ Superfast MB" & yellow spatter tempa, 8 spoke wheels, Manaus casting ($35-50)(BR)

NOTE: Available as a Bulgarian casting. Assorted colors available ($5-25)

MB 9-E AMX PROSTOCKER *see MB17-D*

MB 9-F TOYOTA MR2, issued 1986 (USA)(MB163)
MB74-G TOYOTA MR2, issued 1986 (ROW)

NOTE: Below models with white lower body, white plastic base insert, black interior, clear windows & Macau casting

1. white body, 8 dot wheels, "MR2 Pace Car" tempa ($2-4)
2. dark blue body, starburst wheels, "MR2" & pink stripe tempa ($3-5)(SF)
3. metallic dark blue body, laser wheels, "MR2" & pink stripe tempa ($3-5)(LW)
4. light green body, 8 dot wheels, "7 Snake Racing Team" tempa ($8-12)(HK)

MB 9-G CATERPILLAR BULLDOZER *see MB64-D*

MB 9-H FAUN DUMP TRUCK, issued 1990 (USA)(MB209)
MB53-E FAUN DUMP TRUCK, issued 1990 (ROW)

NOTE: Below models with maltese cross wheel and black plastic base unless noted.

1. yellow body, pearly silver dump, orange stripes tempa, Macau casting ($2-3)
2. yellow body, pearly silver dump, orange stripes tempa, China casting ($2-3)
3. blue body, yellow dump, red maltese cross wheels with yellow hubs, orange stripes & tools tempa, red base, China casting ($3-5)(LL)
4. orange-yellow body, orange-yellow dump, orange stripes tempa, China casting ($2-3)(AP)
5. orange-yellow body, red dump, no tempa, China casting ($1-2)

NOTE: Above model with or without black grille tempa.

6. blue body, yellow dump, red maltese cross wheels (plain hubs), orange stripes & tools tempa, red base, China casting ($3-5)(LL)
7. florescent orange body, silver- gray dump, no tempa, China casting ($1-2)(5pk)
8. florescent orange body, black dump, no tempa, China casting ($1-2)
9. met. gold body & dump, no tempa, China casting ($10-15)(CH)
10. light orange body, red dump, black grille tempa, China casting ($1-2)(AS)
11. light red body, silver-gray dump, no tempa, China casting ($1-2)
12. red body, silver-gray dump, no tempa, China casting ($1-2)
13. red body, black dump, no tempa, China casting ($1-2)(AS)
14. white body, green dump, dirt tempa, China casting ($1-2)(MW27/ 1999)
15. matt grape body, silver-gray dump, black & brown rust tempa, China casting ($1-2)(5pk)
16. light florescent orange body, black dump, none tempa, China casting ($2-4)(MW7/1999 GR)
17. blue body, gray dump, dirt tempa, China casting ($1-2)(MW95/ 2000 US)(MB75/1999 ROW)
18. blue body, gray dump, "Matchbox 2000" tempa, China casting ($2-4)(MW95/2000 USA)
19. blue body, gray dump, dirt tempa, China casting, 5 spoke oval wheels, China casting ($2-3)(MW95/ 2000 US)(MW75 1999 ROW)
20. white body, yellow dump, "MC18", "Matchbox" & rhino head tempa, gray base, 5 spoke oval wheels, China casting ($1-2)(5pk)

NOTE: Versions 21 & 22 come with Matchbox International or Mattel casting.

21. metallic green body, yellow dump, "Matchbox" & black bands tempa, black base, 5 spoke oval wheels, China casting ($1-2)(MW18/2002)
22. metallic green body, yellow dump, "Matchbox", black bands & "Matchbox 50" tempa, black base, 5 spoke oval wheels, China casting ($2-4)(MW18/ 2002)
23. orange body, silver-gray dump, "MC18/ Matchbox" & rhino head tempa, gray base, 5 spoke oval wheels, Mattel China casting ($1-2)(5pk)

MB9-I BMW Z8, issued 2002 (MB532)

NOTE: Below models with lace wheels, black base & China casting unless otherwise noted.

1. black body, black interior, smoke windshield, red stripes tempa ($1-2)(MW9/2002)
2. black body, black interior, smoke windshield, red stripes & "Matchbox 50" tempa ($4-6)(MW9/2002)
3. black body, black interior, smoke windshield, red stripes & "1997-2002 Mattel Mt. Laurel" tempa ($75-100)(CCI)
4. silver-gray body, red interior, clear windshield, detailed trim tempa ($3-5)(ROW BMW promo)
5. bright blue body, dark gray interior, smoke windshield, head lights & small logo tempa ($1-2)(LP)
6. silver blue body, gray interior, smoke green windshield, tail lights tempa ($3-5)(SG)
7. unpainted body, gray interior, smoke green windows, pop art decals ($75+)(FA)
8. light metallic blue body, tan interior, smoke windshield, design tempa ($1-2)(MW10/2003)
9. light metallic blue body, tan interior, smoke windshield, design & Hero City" tempa ($2-3)(MW10/2003)
10. silver-gray body, red interior, clear windshield, "Harro Fabbinder" tempa ($25-40)(C2)(GR)

11. metallic mustard body, gray interior, smoke windshield, small "Matchbox" logo tempa ($1-2)(LP)
12. silver blue body, gray interior, smoke windshield, "8. Treffen MCCD 2004" tempa ($18-25)(C2)(GR)
13. metallic green body, red-brown interior, smoke windshield, small "BMW" logos tempa, lace wheels ($2-3)(MW23/2004 ROW)
14. charcoal body, tan interior, smoke windshield, detailed trim tempa, 5 spoke slotted wheels ($1-2)(SF59/2004)

MB 9-J PORSCHE 911 TURBO *see MB69-L*

MB 9-K BASS BUS, issued 2004 (USA)9MB649)

1. yellow body, blue windows, "Hero City School" tempa, gold lace wheels, black plastic base, China casting ($1-2)(MW9/2004 USA)

MB 9-L MUSH PUPPY *see MB21-M*

MB 9-M '71 CHEVY CHEVELLE (SF)(MB610)

1. metallic green body, smoke windows, black interior, dual white stripes & detailed trim tempa, slotted 5 spoke wheels, chrome base, China casting ($3-5)(SF9/2004)

MB10-A PIPE TRUCK, issued 1970

NOTE: Below models with blue windows, 5 spoke wheels, six plastic pipes, plastic base & England casting.

1. red body, chrome base, gray pipes($35-50)
2. orange body, chrome base, yellow pipes ($18-25)
3. orange body, chrome base, gray pipes ($18-25)
4. orange body, gray base, gray pipes ($18-25)
5. orange body, gray base, yellow pipes ($18-25)

MB10-B PISTON POPPER, issued 1973

NOTE: Below models with white interior, amber windows, 5 spoke front & maltese cross rear wheels & England casting. Versions 2-6 with "Rola-Matics" cast on base.

1. blue body, unpainted base, no tempa, "Superfast" cast on base ($75-100)
2. blue body, unpainted base, no tempa($7-10)
3. blue body, silver-gray base, no tempa ($8-12)
4. blue body, unpainted base, "sunburst" label on roof (from MB47-B) ($175-250)
5. white body, unpainted base, no tempa ($275-400)(MP)
6. yellow body, unpainted base, flames tempa ($5-7)(LE) (issued in USA as "Hot Popper")

MB10-C GRAN FURY POLICE CAR, issued 1979 (MB010)

NOTE: Below models with white interior and dot dash wheels unless otherwise noted.

1. white body, unpainted base, amber windows, opaque blue dome lights, "Police" with shield tempa, England casting ($2-4)
2. white body, unpainted base, amber windows, blue dome lights, "Police" with shield tempa, England casting ($2-4)
3. white body, unpainted base, blue windows & dome lights, "Police" with shield tempa, England casting ($2-4)
4. white body, unpainted base, blue windows & dome lights, "Metro" tempa, England casting ($2-4)
5. white body, silver-gray base, blue windows & dome lights, "Metro" tempa, England casting ($2-4)
6. white body, silver-gray base, dark gray windows & dome lights, "Metro" tempa, England casting ($3-5)
7. white body, unpainted base, dark gray windows & dome lights, "Metro" tempa, England casting ($3-5)
8. white body, unpainted base, blue windows & dome lights, "Metro" on roof & hood with "Police" shield on sides tempa, England casting ($8-12)
9. white body, pearly silver base, dark blue windows & dome lights, "Metro" tempa, Macau casting ($3-5)
10. white body, light gray base, blue windows & dome lights, blue "Police" tempa, Macau casting ($2-4)
11. white body, pearly silver base, blue windows & dome lights, blue "Police" tempa, Macau casting ($2-4)
12. white body, pearly silver base, blue windows & dome lights, blue "Police" tempa, 8 dot wheels, Macau casting ($3-5)
13. white body, pearly silver base, dark blue windows & dome lights, "Police SFPD" tempa, Macau casting ($2-4)
14. white body, pearly silver base, dark blue windows & dome lights, "Sheriff SP-5" tempa, Macau casting ($2-4)(MP)
15. white body, pearly silver base, green windows & dome lights, "Police SFPD" tempa, Macau casting ($75-100)
16. white body, pearly silver base, dark blue windows & dome lights, "Police SFPD" tempa, Thailand casting ($2-4) (MC)
17. black & white body, pearly silver base, clear windows, opaque red dome lights, "Adam-12/ Police" tempa, China casting ($4-6)(STR)
18. black & white body, pearly silver base, clear windows, opaque red dome lights, "New Jersey Local 72 PBA/ Car 3" & crest tempa, China casting ($25-40)(CCI)

MB10-D BUICK LE SABRE, issued 1987 (MB185)

NOTE: Below models with clear windows & plastic base.

1. black body, white base, red interior, 8 dot wheels, "4" & "355 CID" tempa, Macau casting ($2-4)
2. grape & white body, white base, gray interior, laser wheels, "Ken Wells/ Quicksilver" tempa, white airscoop cast on hood, Macau casting ($5-8)(LW)
3. light pea green body, white base, red interior, 8 dot wheels, "4" & "355 CID" tempa, Macau casting ($3-4)(SC)
4. light brown body, white base, red interior, 8 dot wheels, "4" & "355 CID" tempa, Macau casting ($3-4)(SC)
5. orange body, white base, red interior, 8 dot wheels, "4" & "355 CID" tempa, Macau casting ($3-4)(SC)
6. rose red body, white base, red interior, 8 dot wheels, "4" & "355 CID" tempa, Macau casting ($3-4)(SC)
7. yellow body, red base, gray interior, 8 dot wheels, "10 Shell/ Marshall" tempa, Macau casting (2-3)
8. bright yellow body, red base, gray interior, 8 dot wheels "10 Shell/ Marshall" tempa, Thailand casting ($2-3)
9. bright yellow body, red base, gray interior, 8 dot wheels, "10 Shell/ Marshall" tempa, Thailand casting, large rear side window casting ($25-40)
10. white body, red base, gray interior, 8 dot wheels, "10 Shell/ Marshall" tempa, Thailand casting ($3-5)
11. red body, white base, silver-gray interior, 8 dot wheels, "Total Racing 07 " tempa, Thailand casting ($1-2)(5pk)

MB10-E 4X4 CHEVY VAN *see MB44-D*

MB10-F DODGE VIPER, issued 1994 (USA)(MB260)
MB12-J DODGE VIPER, issued 1994 (ROW)

1. red body, black interior, clear windshield, black headlights tempa, gold 6-spoke spiral wheels, Thailand casting ($1-2)
2. red body, black interior, chrome windshield, detailed trim tempa, gray disc rubber tires, Thailand casting ($2-4)(WC)
3. black body, gray interior, chrome windshield, "Matchbox 1995 Line Preview" tempa, gray disc with rubber tires, Thailand casting ($250-350)(US)

4. red body, black interior, clear windshield, black headlights tempa, silver 6-spoke spiral wheels, Thailand casting ($1-2)
5. red body, black interior, smoke windshield, black headlights tempa, silver 6-spoke spiral wheels, Thailand casting ($1-2)
6. black body, tan interior, clear windshield, black headlights tempa, silver 6-spoke spiral wheels, Thailand casting ($1-2)(5pk)
7. yellow body, black/gray interior, clear windshield, detailed trim tempa, chrome disc wheels with rubber tires , Thailand casting ($7-10)(PC1)
8. yellow body, black interior, chrome windshield, "California Viper's Club" tempa, gray disc wheels with rubber tires, Thailand casting ($12-18)(US)
9. white body, black interior, clear windshield, "69th Shenandoah Apple Blossom Festival 1996" tempa, silver 6-spoke spiral wheels, Thailand casting ($10-12)(US)
10. metallic green body, black & gray interior, clear windshield, detailed trim tempa, chrome disc wheels with rubber tires, Thailand casting ($8-12)(SC1)
11. red body, black& brown interior, clear windshield, detailed trim tempa, chrome disc wheels with rubber tires, Thailand casting ($3-5)(PC4)
12. charcoal body, black & gray interior, clear windshield, detailed trim tempa, chrome disc wheels with rubber tires, Thailand casting ($7-10)(PC1)(AU)
13. metallic gold body, black interior, clear windshield, black headlights tempa, silver 6-spoke spiral wheels, Thailand casting ($10-15)(CH)
14. red body, black & gray interior, clear windshield, dual yellow stripes tempa, chrome disc wheels with rubber tires wheels, Thailand casting ($25-50)(GC)
15. red body, black interior, smoke windshield, black headlights tempa, 5 spoke concave star wheels with yellow hubs, Thailand casting ($1-2)(5pk)
16. red body, black interior, clear windshield, "16th Annual Matchbox USA Convention 1997" decals, silver 6 spoke spiral wheels, Thailand casting ($10-15)(C2)
17. red body, black interior, clear windshield, black headlights tempa, 5 spoke concave star wheels, Thailand casting ($15-20)
18. green body, tan interior, smoke windshield, black headlights tempa, 5 spoke concave star wheels, Thailand casting ($2-3)
19. green body, gray & black interior, clear windshield, dual white stripes & detailed trim tempa, chrome disc with rubber tires, Thailand casting ($3-5)(PC12)
20. metallic blue body, black & gray interior, clear windshield, dual white stripes & detailed trim tempa, chrome disc with rubber tires, Thailand casting ($3-5)(PC14)
21. black body, black & gray interior, clear windshield, dual silver stripes tempa, chrome disc wheels with rubber tires, Thailand casting ($3-5)(SC4)
22. red body, black interior, smoke windshield, "Hope Spring Cancer Support Center 1997" tempa, silver 6 spoke wheels, Thailand casting ($15-20)(C2)
23. green body, tan interior, smoke windshield, "Hope Spring Cancer Support Center 1997" tempa, 5 spoke concave star wheels, Thailand casting ($85-110)(C2)
24. white body, black interior, clear windshield, "Merry Christmas Ad-Ventures" tempa, silver 6 spoke spiral wheels, Thailand casting ($20-25)(C2)
25. yellow body, black interior, smoke windshield, black headlights tempa, 5 spoke concave star wheels, Thailand casting ($1-2)(MW56/1998 US)(MB67/1998 ROW)
26. white body, black & gray interior, clear windshield, dual red stripes & detailed trim tempa, chrome disc wheels with rubber tires, Thailand casting ($3-5)(SC5)
27. red body, black interior, clear windshield, "Lucent Technologies" tempa, 5 spoke concave star wheels, China casting ($20-40)(ASAP)
28. red body, black interior, smoke windshield, black headlights tempa, 5 spoke concave star wheels with yellow hubs, China casting ($1-2)(5pk)
29. red body, black interior, clear windshield, "A-Pix Entertainment" & "Drive" tempa, 5 spoke concave star wheels, China casting ($100+)(ASAP)
30. yellow body, black interior, smoke windshield, black headlights tempa, 5 spoke concave star wheels, China casting ($1-2)(MW56/1998 US)((MB67/1998 ROW)
31. yellow body, black interior, smoke windshield, "Matchbox Forum 1998/ First Shot" tempa, 5 spoke concave star wheels, Thailand casting ($20-25)(C2)
32. white body, black interior, clear windshield, "98 White's Guide" tempa, silver 6 spoke spiral wheels, Thailand casting ($25-35)(C2)
33. red body, black interior, smoke windshield, "Fiery Driven" & black headlights tempa, silver 6 spoke spiral wheels, Thailand casting ($100+)(ASAP)
34. red body, black interior, clear windshield, no tempa, 5 spoke concave star wheels, China casting ($20-35)(ASAP-blank)
35. red body, black interior, clear windshield, "1998 Sales Meeting" tempa, 5 spoke concave star wheels, China casting ($100+)(ASAP)
36. white body, brown interior, clear windshield, blue stripes & "Viper" tempa, 5 spoke concave star wheels, China casting ($1-2)(5pk)
37. red body, black interior, clear windshield, "Concept 4/ Interact" tempa, 5 spoke concave star wheels, China casting ($15-25)(ASAP)
38. red body, black interior, clear windshield, "Mom, Me & Matchbox" tempa, gold 6 spoke spiral wheels, Thailand casting ($15-25)(CCI)
39. yellow body, black interior, clear windshield, "Mom, Me & Matchbox" tempa, 5 spoke concave star wheels, China casting ($15-25)(CCI)
40. green body, tan interior, clear windshield, "Mom Me & Matchbox" tempa, 5 spoke concave star wheels, Thailand casting ($75-100)(CCI)
41. yellow body, black interior, clear windshield, "Praktiker" tempa, 5 spoke concave star wheels, China casting ($40-65)(C2)(GR)
42. red body, black interior, clear windshield, "White's Guide Car of The Month #8 July 1999" (yellow print) tempa, 5 spoke concave star wheels, China casting ($8-12)(ASAP)
43. red body, black interior, clear windshield, "White's Guide Car of The month #8 July 1999" (white print) tempa, 5 spoke concave star wheels, China casting ($8-12)(ASAP)
44. white body, black interior, clear windshield, "1st Annual Golf Outing- Mattel" tempa, gold 6 spoke spiral wheels, Thailand casting ($300+)(CCI)
45. red body, black interior, clear windshield, "Yasnac PCNC/ Yaskawa Can Fly!" tempa, 5 spoke concave star wheels, China casting ($50+)(ASAP)
46. red body, black interior, clear windshield, "Moore" tempa, 5 spoke concave star wheels, China casting ($100+)(ASAP)
47. red body, black interior, clear windshield, "Nebraska" tempa, 5 spoke concave star wheels, China casting ($10-15)(ASAP)
48. red body, black interior, clear windshield, "Huffhines Dodge" tempa, 5 spoke concave star wheels, China casting ($100+)(ASAP)

49. red body, black interior, clear windshield, "Oberon Software" tempa, 5 spoke concave star wheels, China casting ($75+)(ASAP)
50. red body, black interior, clear windshield, "X" tempa, 5 spoke concave star wheels, China casting ($75+)(ASAP)
51. red body, black interior, clear windshield, "RCA" tempa, 5 spoke concave star wheels, China casting ($18-25)(ASAP)
52. white body, black interior, clear windshield, "Season's Greetings Color Comp Inc./ Christmas 1998" tempa, silver 6 spoke spiral wheels, Thailand casting ($250+)(CCI)
53. white body, black, blue & gray interior, clear windshield dual blue stripes tempa, chrome disc wheels with rubber tires, China casting ($4-6)(PC)
54. red body, black interior, clear windshield, "Marathon Ashland" tempa, 5 spoke concave star wheels, China casting ($75+)(ASAP)
55. yellow body, black interior, smoke windshield, "PMCC Happy Holidays" tempa, 5 spoke concave star wheels, China casting ($25-40)(CCI)
56. red body, black interior, clear windshield, "Faith/ Sunday School Evangelism Strategy" tempa, 5 spoke concave star wheels, China casting ($100+)(ASAP)
57. red body, silver-gray interior & base, clear windshield, dual white stripes tempa, 5 spoke concave star wheels, China casting ($2-3)(MW37/1999 US)(MW32/ 1999 ROW)
58. red body, black interior, smoke windshield, gray base, silver headlights &"Matchbox 2000" tempa, 5 spoke concave star wheels, China casting ($2-4)(MW43/2000 US)
59. red body, black interior, smoke windshield, gray base, silver headlights tempa, 5 spoke concave star wheels, China casting ($1-2)(MW43/2000 US)
60. blue body, gray interior, smoke windshield, gray base, dual white stripes tempa, 5 spoke concave star wheels, China casting (MW66/2000 ROW)
61. yellow body, black interior, smoke windshield, "Color Comp Demo Model 2000" tempa, 5 spoke concave star wheels, China casting ($18-25)(CCI)
62. yellow body, black interior, smoke windshield, "NJ Diecast Collectors Club" labels, 5 spoke concave star wheels, China casting ($25-40)(C2)
63. yellow body, black interior, smoke windshield, "Matchbox Forum International Matchbox Collectors Club Deutschland" tempa, 5 spoke concave star wheels, China casting ($25-40)(C2)
64. yellow body, black interior, smoke windshield, "Keystone Kollectible Kars" tempa, 5 spoke concave star wheels, China casting ($15-25)(CCI)
65. blue body, silver-gray interior & base, clear windshield, "Keystone Kollectible Kars" tempa, 5 spoke concave star wheels, China casting ($15-25)(CCI)
66. red body, black interior, clear windshield, "Keystone Kollectible Kars" tempa, silver 6 spoke spiral wheels, Thailand casting ($15-25)(CCI)
67. red body, black interior, clear windshield, "Fiery Driven" tempa, 5 spoke concave star wheels, China casting ($100+)(ASAP)
68. red body, black interior, silver-gray base, smoke windshield, "Matchbox Collectors/ Color Comp Inc. Conference", 5 spoke concave star wheels, China casting ($25-40)(CCI)
69. white body, tan interior, clear windshield, "District 16B Lion's Club New Jersey" & blue stripes tempa, 5 spoke concave star wheels, China casting ($20-35)(CCI)
70. yellow body, black interior, smoke windshield, "Matchbox Convoys Collectors Club/ M3CG" tempa, 5 spoke concave star wheels, China casting ($25-40)(CCI)

NOTE: Below models with black interior, clear windshield, 5 spoke concave star wheels, China casting unless otherwise noted.

71. red body, "Project Vertigo/ Citrix Developer Network" labels, ($75+)(ASAP)
72. red body, "Citrix Vertigo" labels ($75+)(ASAP)
73. red body, smoke windows, silver painted lights & small logo tempa, ($1-2)(MW66/2000 ROW)
74. red body, "Compaq" tempa, 5 spoke concave star wheels ($50+)(ASAP)
75. red body "NCR" & logo tempa ($50+)(ASAP)
76. red body, small "R" tempa ($25-40)(ASAP)
77. red body, "G" in circle tempa, ($15-25)(ASAP)
78. red body, "Mahle" tempa ($25-40)(ASAP)
79. red body, "Rensselaer Polytechnic" tempa ($15-25)(ASAP)
80. red body, "Microsoft" tempa ($75+)(ASAP)
81. red body, "Citrix Silver" tempa ($75+)(ASAP)
82. red body, "Intel PIII Pushing The Limits" tempa ($75+)(ASAP)
83. red body, "Skip Barber Driving School" tempa ($50+)(ASAP)
84. red body, "Huskers" (left side only) tempa ($12-15)(ASAP)
85. red body, "Novell 6" tempa ($18-25)(ASAP)
86. blue body, silver-gray interior & base, dual white stripes & "Praktiker" tempa ($15-20)(C2)(GR)
87. black body, black & gray interior, clear windshield, detailed trim tempa, chrome disc wheels with rubber tires ($3-5)(PC1-JC)
88. red body, yellow interior, gray base, , dual yellow stripes tempa, gold lace wheels ($2-4)(MW55/2001 ROW)(MB53/2001 UK)

NOTE: Above model with Matchbox International or Mattel casting.

89. red body, "NCR/ Teradata" tempa ($50+)(ASAP)
90. red body, smoke windshield, gray base, "Hope Spring 2001" tempa ($12-18)(CCI)
91. yellow body, smoke windshield, "Hope Spring 2001" tempa ($12-18)(CCI)
92. yellow body, smoke windshield, "Raytheon" tempa ($50+)(ASAP)
93. red body, no tempa ($5-8)(ASAP blank)
93. green body, brown interior, smoke windshield, "1st Annual Open House Matchbox Road Museum" tempa, Thailand casting ($75+)(CCI)
94. silver-gray body, purple interior, lace wheels, tail lights tempa ($2-4)(MB53/2001 GR)

NOTE: Above model with Matchbox International or Mattel casting.

95. black body, red interior, chrome disc wheels with rubber tires, "Coca Cola/ Coke Adds Life? The Real Thing" tempa ($3-4)(Coke PC)
96. red body, smoke windows, 10 spoke flower wheels, no tempa ($8-12)(ASAP Blank)

NOTE: Above model with Matchbox International or Mattel casting.

97. red body, "Huskers" (hood only) tempa ($8-12)(ASAP)
98. red body, "VT Hokies" tempa ($8-12)(ASAP)
99. red body, gray base, "Christmas Greetings/ Ad Ventures Inc. 2002" tempa ($25-35)(CCI)
100. red body, "Hewlett Packard/ Mentor Graphics" tempa ($75+)(ASAP)
101. yellow body, smoke windshield, "Robert was born/ Britta & Steffen" tempa ($25-40)(CCI)
102. red body, smoke windshield, no tempa ($5-8)(ASAP blank)
103. red body, "Wood Associates" tempa ($50+)(ASAP)
104. red body, "Compuware/ Driver Studio" tempa ($50+)(ASAP)

105. red body, "USS" tempa ($50+)(ASAP)
106. red body, "Bloomfield Acceptance Company" tempa ($50+)(ASAP)
107. red body, "Best Chairs, Inc." tempa ($50+)(ASAP)
108. red body, "Cannon" tempa ($50+)(ASAP)
109. red body, "Wells Fargo/ Convertible Equity Line" tempa ($50+)(ASAP)
110. white body, "Troop 1 Flea Market 2004" tempa ($25-40)(CCI)
111. red body, smoke windshield, 10 spoke flower wheels, "Huskers" (on sides) tempa ($15-20)(ASAP)
112. red body, smoke windshield, 10 spoke flower wheels, "Kronos" tempa ($50+)(ASAP)
113. red body, smoke windshield, 5 spoke concave star wheels, "Metra Tech" tempa ($50+)(ASAP)
114. white body, clear windshield, silver 6 spoke spiral wheels, "Troop 1 Flea Market 2004" ($18-25)(CCI)

MB10-G J.R. BUMPER, issued 2004 (USA)
1. red body, yellow cap, gold 10 spoke flower wheels, black base, China casting ($1-2)(MW10/ 2004 US)

MB10-H GO-ROLLA *see MB19-F*

MB11-A SCAFFOLD TRUCK, issued 1970
NOTE: Below model with 5 spoke wheels, "Builder's" labels, five yellow plastic scaffolds with 1 platform & England casting.
1. silver-gray body, red base, green windows, yellow scaffolding ($25-40)

MB11-B FLYING BUG, issued 1972
NOTE: Below models with flesh colored driver with chrome helmet, 5 spoke rear wheels & England casting.
1. metallic red body, unpainted base, gray windows, squared hood label, 5 spoke front wheels ($15-20)
2. metallic red body, unpainted base, gray windows, heart-shaped hood label, 5 spoke front wheels ($15-20)
3. metallic red body, silver-gray base, gray windows, heart-shaped hood label, 5 spoke front wheels ($18-25)
4. metallic red body, unpainted base, gray windows, heart-shaped hood label, 4 spoke front wheels ($50-75)
5. metallic red body, unpainted base, blue windows, heart-shaped hood label, 5 spoke front wheels ($50-75)

MB11-C CAR TRANSPORTER, issued 1976 (MB011)
NOTE: Cars are listed as front top car, rear top car, bottom car. Below models with England casting unless otherwise noted.
1. orange body, beige carrier, black base, red/yellow/blue cars, blue windows ($4-6)
2. orange body, beige carrier, black base, red/yellow/dark blue cars, blue windows ($4-6)
3. orange body, beige carrier, black base, yellow/red/blue cars, blue windows ($4-6)
4. orange body, bone white carrier, black base, red/blue/blue cars, blue windows ($7-10)
5. orange body, bone white carrier, black base, red/yellow/blue cars, blue windows ($4-6)
6. orange body, beige carrier, black base, red/yellow/blue cars, blue windows, black hubs ($4-6)
7. orange body, beige carrier, black base, red/yellow/blue cars, green windows ($4-6)
8. orange body, bone white carrier, black base, yellow/yellow/red cars, blue windows ($7-10)
9. orange body, bone white carrier, black base, yellow/yellow/blue cars, blue windows ($7-10)
10. orange body, beige carrier, black base, red/blue/blue cars, blue windows ($7-10)
11. orange body, beige carrier, charcoal base, red/orange-yellow/blue cars, blue windows ($4-6)
12. orange body, beige carrier, charcoal base, red/yellow/blue cars, green windows ($4-6)
13. orange body, beige carrier, black base, red/orange-yellow/blue cars, purple windows ($4-6)
14. orange body, beige carrier, unpainted base, red/orange-yellow/blue cars, purple windows ($4-6)
15. orange body, beige carrier, black base, red/orange-yellow/blue cars, blue-green windows ($4-6)
16. orange body, beige carrier, black base, blue/blue/blue cars, blue windows ($10-15)
17. orange body, beige carrier, black base, yellow/yellow/yellow cars, blue windows ($10-15)
18. orange body, beige carrier, black base, all yellow-orange cars, blue windows ($10-15)
19. orange body, beige carrier, black base, red/red/red cars, blue windows ($10-15)
20. red body, beige carrier, unpainted base, red/orange-yellow/blue cars, blue windows ($4-6)
21. red body, beige carrier, unpainted base, red/orange/blue cars, blue windows ($4-6)
22. red body, beige carrier, unpainted base, red/yellow/dark blue cars, blue windows ($4-6)
23. red body, beige carrier, silver-gray base, red/orange/blue cars, blue windows ($4-6)
24. red body, beige carrier, unpainted base, red/orange/blue cars, purple windows ($4-6)
25. red body, beige carrier, silver-gray base, red/yellow/blue cars, purple windows ($4-6)
26. red body, beige carrier, silver-gray base, red/yellow/blue cars, blue windows ($4-6)
27. red body, beige carrier, silver-gray base, red/yellow/dark blue cars, blue windows ($4-6)
28. red body, beige carrier, black base, red/yellow/dark blue cars, blue windows ($4-6)
29. red body, beige carrier, black base, red/orange-yellow/red cars, blue windows ($7-10)
30. red body, beige carrier, unpainted base, red/yellow/blue cars, purple windows ($4-6)
31. red body, gray carrier, black base, orange-yellow/red/blue cars, blue windows ($4-6)
32. red body, gray carrier, unpainted base, red/red/red cars, blue windows ($10-15)
33. red-orange body, gray carrier, black base, yellow/blue/blue cars, blue windows ($7-10)
34. red-orange body, gray carrier, black base, yellow/red/blue cars, blue windows ($4-6)
35. red-orange body, gray carrier, black base, red/yellow/blue cars, blue windows ($4-6)
36. red-orange body, gray carrier, black base, yellow/red/red cars, blue windows ($7-10)
37. red-orange body, gray carrier, black base, red/yellow/red cars, blue windows ($7-10)
38. red-orange body, gray carrier, black base, red/yellow/dark blue cars, blue windows ($4-6)
39. red-orange body, gray carrier, black base, yellow/red/dark blue cars, blue windows ($4-6)
40. red-orange body, gray carrier, black base, blue/yellow/dark blue cars, blue windows ($7-10)
41. red-orange body, gray carrier, black base, blue/blue/red cars, blue windows ($7-10)

42. orange body, gray carrier, pearly silver base, yellow/red/blue cars, blue windows, Macau casting ($7-10)
43. orange body, beige carrier, black base with Manaus tab, blue/yellow/red cars, blue windows ($35-50)
44. tan body, beige carrier, black base, red/blue/yellow cars, clear windows, Manaus casting ($35-50)(BR)
45. orange body, beige carrier, black base, red/yellow/blue cars, blue windows, 4 arch wheels, Manaus casting ($35-50)(BR)
46. orange body, beige carrier, black base, red/yellow/blue cars, blue windows, dot dash wheels, Manaus casting ($35-50)(BR)

MB11-D BOSS MUSTANG, issued 1982 (USA)

NOTE: Below models with chrome interior, amber windows, maltese cross wheels, unpainted metal base & England casting unless otherwise noted.

1. orange body, outlined "Boss" side tempa ($6-8)
2. orange body, black "Boss" side tempa ($6-8)
3. orange body, white "Boss" side tempa ($6-8)
4. orange body, no side tempa ($6-8)
5. dark orange body, white "Boss" tempa ($6-8)
6. dark orange body, white "Boss" tempa, 5 spoke front & maltese cross rear wheels ($6-8)

MB11-E I.M.S.A. MUSTANG, issued 1983 (USA)(MB122)
MB67-E I.M.S.A. MUSTANG, issued 1983 (ROW)

NOTE: Below models with amber windows, chrome interior & engine & dot dash rear wheels unless otherwise noted.

1. black body, black metal base, 5 spoke front wheels, red/white stripes & "Mustang Ford" tempa, Macau casting ($2-3)
2. black body, black metal base, 5 arch front wheels, red/white stripes & "Mustang Ford" tempa, Macau casting ($2-3)
3. black body, black metal base, 5 arch front wheels, yellow & green flames tempa, Macau casting ($1-2)
4. black body, black metal base, 5 spoke front wheels, yellow & green flames tempa, Macau casting ($1-2)
5. black body, black metal base, 5 arch front wheels, yellow & green flames tempa, China casting ($1-2)
6. yellow body, black metal base, 5 arch front wheels, black/red stripes & "47" tempa, China casting ($3-5)(AP)
7. red body, red metal base, 5 arch front wheels, no tempa, China casting ($8-12)(GR)(GS)
8. black body, greenish black metal base, 5 arch front wheels, yellow & green stripes tempa, China casting ($1-2)
9. dark orange body, black metal base, 5 arch front wheels, yellow & blue flames tempa, China casting ($1-2)
10. dark florescent orange body, black plastic base, gold 6-spoke spiral front & rear wheels, black squiggly lines tempa, China casting ($1-2)
11. dark florescent orange body, black plastic base, silver 6-spoke spiral front & rear wheels, black squiggly lines tempa , China casting ($1-2)
12. dark florescent orange body, black metal base, 5 arch front & dot dash rear wheels, black squiggly lines tempa, China casting ($15-25)(HU)

MB11-F LAMBORGHINI COUNTACH *see MB67-F*

MB11-G CHRYSLER ATLANTIC, issued 1997 (USA)(MB306)
MB34-H CHRYSLER ATLANTIC, issued 1997 (ROW)

NOTE: Below models with clear windows & black plastic base unless otherwise noted.

1. metallic tan body, tan interior, 5 spoke concave star wheels, black grille & red tail lights tempa, Thailand casting ($2-3)
2. metallic tan body, brown interior, 5 spoke concave star wheels, black grille, silver head lights & red tail lights tempa, Thailand casting ($1-2)(MW19/1998)
3. metallic tan body, brown interior, chrome disc wheels with rubber tires, "Matchbox" and "www.matchboxtoys.com" tempa, Thailand casting ($8-12)
4. metallic tan body, brown & tan interior, chrome disc wheels with rubber tires, detailed trim tempa, China casting ($3-5)(GS-Chrysler)
5. metallic tan body, brown interior, 5 spoke concave star wheels, black grille, silver head lights & red tail lights tempa, China casting ($1-2)(MW19/1998)
6. metallic gold body, black interior, 5 spoke concave star wheels, no tempa, China casting ($5-10)(CH)
7. metallic gold body, black interior, 5 spoke concave star wheels with black hubs, no tempa, China casting ($25-40)(CH)
8. metallic tan body, light tan interior, 5 spoke concave star wheels, silver grille & headlights & red tail lights tempa, China casting ($1-2)(MW39/1999 US)
9. metallic tan body, tan interior, 5 spoke concave star wheels, "Merry Christmas 1997 Seasons Greetings From Color Comp", Thailand casting ($100+)(CCI)
10. dark yellow body, black interior, chrome disc wheels with rubber tires, "Martian Manhunter" tempa, Mattel China casting ($3-4)(JL)

MB11-H BMW 328I POLICE CAR, issued 2000 (ROW)(MB439)
MB29-D BMW 328i POLICE CAR, issued 2003 (USA)

NOTE: Below models with black plastic base, China casting unless otherwise noted.

1. white & green body, blue & green bar light, smoke green windows, black interior, "Polizei" tempa , 5 spoke concave star wheels ($2-4)(MW11/2000 GR)
2. white body, blue & white bar light, smoke green windows, black interior, red band, blue stripes, crest & "35-1" tempa, 5 spoke concave star wheels ($2-4)(MW11/2000 ROW)
3. metallic silver body, blue bar light, smoke windows, dark blue interior, "Police" with orange band & checkers tempa, lace wheels ($1-2)(MW33/2001 ROW)
4. metallic silver body, blue bar light, smoke windows, dark blue interior, "Police" with orange band & checkers tempa, lace wheels, metal base ($3-5)(MW33/ 2001 ROW)
5. silver-gray body, amber bar light, clear windows, gray interior, "Metro 7" tempa, lace wheels ($1-2)(LP)
6. bright blue body, red bar light, smoke windows, gray interior, "Metro Police 3" tempa, lace wheels ($1-2)(5pk)
7. metallic blue body, amber bar light, smoke windows, gray interior, Mission H2O" tempa, lace wheels ($1-2)(LP)
8. dark green body, amber bar light, smoke windows, gray interior, "Polizei" & white bands tempa, lace wheels ($2-4)(MW28/2002 ROW)
9. dark green body, amber bar light, smoke windows, gray interior, "Polizei", white bands & "Matchbox 50" tempa, lace wheels ($2-4)(MW28/2002 ROW)
10. metallic red body, blue bar light, black windows, white interior, ."Mission H2O" tempa, lace wheels ($1-2)(LP)
11. bright blue body, red bar light, amber windows, white interior, "Accident Investigation" tempa, lace wheels ($1-2)(MW29/2003 US)
12. bright blue body, red bar light, amber windows, white interior, "Accident Investigation" & "Hero City" tempa, lace wheels ($1-2) (MW29/2003 US)

13. white & green body, blue & green bar light, smoke windows, black interior, "Polizei" & detailed trim tempa, lace wheels ($4-6)(ROW BMW promo)
14. silver-gray body, blue bar light, clear windows, black interior, blue band, hood & trunk with "Polizei" tempa, 10 spoke flower wheels ($3-5)(SoC)

M11-I WRECKER TRUCK, issued 2001 (MB481)

NOTE: Below models with 7 spoke sawblade wheels & China casting

1. black body, gray boom, hook & rear, dark smoke windows, chrome plastic base, "Auto Max Crash 00-207-600" tempa ($1-2)(MW11/2001)
2. black body, black boom & hook, chrome rear & windows, chrome plastic base, "Matchbox Mattel Toy Fair 2001" tempa, chrome disc wheels with rubber tires ($25-35)(US)
3. white body, blue boom & hook, blue rear & windows, chrome plastic base, "Metro Police 3" tempa ($1-2)(5pk)
4. bright blue body, red boom & hook, red rear, smoke windows, chrome plastic base, "All Star Towing" tempa ($1-2)(MW1/2002)
5. bright blue body, red boom & hook, red rear, smoke windows, chrome plastic base, "All Star Towing" & "Matchbox 50" tempa ($2-4)(MW1/2002)
6. white body, dark blue boom & hook, dark blue rear, dark smoke windows, "New York 11/ 24 Hour Towing" tempa ($3-5)(AM)
7. red body, blue boom & hook, blue rear, dark smoke windows, monkey & wrench tempa ($1-2)(5pk)
8. charcoal body, maroon boom & hook, maroon rear, black windows, chevrons & dog tempa ($1-2)(MW17/2003)
9. charcoal body, maroon boom & hook, maroon rear, dark smoke windows, chevron, dog & "Hero City" tempa ($2-4)(MW17/2003)
10. white body, gray boom & hook, gray rear, black windows, "Metro 1/45" tempa ($2-4)(PS)

MB11-J EMERGENCY RESPONSE 4X4, issued 2003 (MB572)

NOTE: Below models with 7 spoke sawblade wheels, red base & China casting.

1. metallic silver body, blue windows, black interior, red bed insert, "Unit #11" tempa ($1-2)(MW11/2003)
2. metallic silver body, blue windows, black interior, red bed insert, "Unit #11" & "Hero City" tempa ($2-4)(MW11/2003)
3. metallic silver body, blue windows, black interior, red bed insert, "Unit #11" tempa, gold hubs ($6-8)(20pk)
4. metallic silver body, amber windows, dark gray interior & bed insert, "Hangar Team 54" tempa ($1-2)(5pk)
5. iridescent white body, blue-green windows, blue-green interior & bed insert, snowflakes & snowman tempa, blue base ($2-4)(MP)

MB11-K DRAGONFLY HELICOPTER, issued 2003 (USA)(MB621)
MB 6-L DRAGONFLY HELICOPTER, issued 2003 (ROW)

1. metallic lime body, gray blades, blue windows, blue tail, turquoise base, "Hero City News" tempa, China casting ($1-2)(MW11)

MB11-L POLICE HAT *see MB26-L*

MB12-A LAND ROVER SAFARI, issued 1970

NOTE: Below models with white interior, clear windows, 5 spoke wheels & England casting.

1. bright blue body, red-brown roof luggage ($1,000+)
2. gold body, red-brown roof luggage ($20-35)

MB12-B SETRA COACH, issued 1970

NOTE: Below models with white interior, 5 spoke wheels & England casting.

1. gold body, pale tan roof, clear windows ($18-25)
2. gold body, white roof, clear windows ($15-18)
3. yellow body, white roof, clear windows ($12-15)
4. metallic burgundy body, white roof, clear windows ($12-15)
5. metallic burgundy body, white roof, green windows ($12-15)
6. metallic purple body, white roof, green windows ($12-15)
7. yellow body, white roof, green windows ($50-75)

NOTE: Version 7 was originally thought to be a 'fake variation' until a small quantity were found in sealed blisterpacks. As this variation can be faked, the price is considered "low" although a hard to find variation.

MB12-C BIG BULL, issued 1975

NOTE: Below models with chrome seat & engine, black treads & England casting unless otherwise noted.

1. orange body, green blade & base,, orange rollers ($4-6)
2. orange body, green blade & base, yellow rollers ($25-40)
3. orange body, green blade & base, black rollers ($75-100)
4. dark orange body, green blade & base with Manaus tab, orange rollers ($45-50)(BR)

MB12-D CITROEN CX, issued 1979 (MB012)

NOTE: Below models below with England casting unless otherwise noted.

1. light metallic blue body, cream interior, silver-gray base, blue windows, no tempa ($12-15)
2. light metallic blue body, cream interior, silver-gray base, clear windows, no tempa ($5-8)
3. light metallic blue body, light yellow interior, silver-gray base, clear windows, no tempa ($5-8)
4. light metallic blue body, ivory interior, silver-gray base, clear windows, no tempa ($5-8)
5. light metallic blue body, cream interior, unpainted base, clear windows, no tempa ($5-8)
6. light metallic blue body, cream interior, black base, clear windows, no tempa ($5-8)
7. light metallic blue body, cream interior, charcoal base, clear windows, no tempa ($5-8)
8. light metallic blue body, tan interior, silver-gray base, clear windows, no tempa ($5-8)
9. dark metallic blue body, cream interior, silver-gray base, clear windows, no tempa ($5-8)
10. dark metallic blue body, light yellow interior, silver-gray base, clear windows, no tempa ($5-8)
11. dark metallic blue body, dark yellow interior, silver-gray base, clear windows, no tempa ($5-8)
12. dark metallic blue body, red interior, silver-gray base, clear windows, no tempa ($250-400)
13. metallic blue body, yellow interior, silver-gray base, blue windows, no tempa ($8-12)
14. light metallic blue body, cream interior, silver-gray base, clear windows, "Climat" label ($125-175)(FR)
15. yellow body, red interior, black base, clear windows, no tempa ($5-8)
16. yellow body, red interior, charcoal base, clear windows, no tempa ($ 5-8)
17. yellow body, red interior, silver-gray base, clear windows, blue "Team" tempa ($4-6)((TP)
18. yellow body, red interior, black base, clear windows, blue "Team" tempa ($4-6)(TP)

19. yellow body, red interior, black base, clear windows, black "Team" tempa ($4-6)(TP)
20. yellow body, red interior, charcoal base, clear windows, blue "Team" tempa ($4-6)
21. yellow body, red interior, black base, blue windows, black "Team" tempa ($4-6)(TP)
22. yellow body, red interior, black base, blue windows, no tempa ($5-8)(TP)
23. yellow body, red interior, silver-gray base, clear windows, no tempa ($5-8)(TP)

NOTE: The models below have the rear side windows deleted from the casting.

24. white body, red interior, silver-gray base, blue windows, "Ambulance" tempa ($2-4)
25. white body, red interior, black base, blue windows, "Ambulance" tempa ($2-4)
26. white body, red interior, unpainted base, blue windows, "Ambulance" tempa ($2-4)
27. white body, red interior, silver-gray base, blue windows, "Marine Division" tempa ($2-4)(TP)
28. white body, red interior, unpainted base, blue windows, "Marine Division" tempa ($2-4)(TP)
29. white body, red interior, pearly silver base, blue windows, "Marine Division" tempa, Macau casting ($4-6)(TP)

MB12-E PONTIAC FIREBIRD SE, issued 1982 (USA)(MB051)
MB51-E PONTIAC FIREBIRD SE, issued 1982 (ROW)

NOTE: Below models with metal base unless otherwise noted.

1. dark red body, tan interior, clear windows, 5 arch silver wheels, no tempa, silver-gray base, England casting ($3-5)
2. dark red body, tan interior, amber windows, 5 arch silver wheels, no tempa, silver-gray base, England casting ($4-6)
3. dark red body, yellow interior, clear windows, 5 arch silver wheels, no tempa, silver-gray base, England casting ($3-5)
4. dark red body, yellow interior, amber windows, 5 arch silver wheels, no tempa, silver-gray base, England casting ($4-6)
5. dark red body, tan interior, clear windows, dot dash wheels, no tempa, silver-gray base, England casting ($4-6)
6. rose red body, tan interior, clear windows, 5 arch silver wheels, "Firebird" tempa, pearly silver base, Macau casting ($4-6)
7. dark red body, tan interior, clear windows, 5 arch silver wheels, no tempa, pearly silver base, Macau casting ($3-5)
8. black body, tan interior, clear windows, 5 arch silver wheels, "Firebird" tempa, pearly silver base, Macau casting ($3-5)
9. black body, red interior, clear windows, 5 arch silver wheels, "Firebird" tempa, pearly silver base, Macau casting ($2-4)
10. black body, gray interior, clear windows, starburst wheels, "Haley's Comet" tempa, black base, Macau casting ($8-10)(MP)(US)
11. black body, red interior, opaque white windows, 5 arch gold wheels, "Firebird" tempa, pearly silver base, Macau casting ($10-15)(PS)
12. black body, red interior, clear windows, 5 arch gold wheels, "Firebird" tempa, pearly silver base, Macau casting ($5-8)
13. black body, red interior, opaque white windows, 5 arch silver wheels, "Firebird" tempa, pearly silver base, Macau casting ($10-15)(PS)
14. blue body, white interior, blue windows, starburst wheels, red/orange/yellow stripes tempa, black base, Macau casting ($8-12)(SF)
15. blue body, white interior, blue windows, starburst wheels, red/orange/yellow stripes tempa, white base, Macau casting ($3-5)(SF)
16. red body, red interior, clear windows, 5 arch silver wheels, "Maaco" labels, pearly silver base, Macau casting ($7-10)(US)
17. metallic blue body, white interior, blue windows, laser wheels, red/orange/yellow stripes tempa, white base, Macau casting ($3-5)(LW)
18. powder blue body, red interior, clear windows, 5 arch silver wheels, green/yellow/white stripes tempa, pearly silver base, Macau casting ($10-15)(DY)
19. purple body, red interior, clear windows, 5 arch silver wheels, "Firebird" tempa, pearly silver base, Macau casting ($3-4)(SC)
20. black body, red interior, clear windows, 5 arch silver wheels, "Firebird" tempa, dark gray plastic base, Macau casting ($3-4)
21. blue body, white interior, blue windows, starburst wheels, red/orange/yellow stripes tempa, white plastic base, Macau casting ($4-6)(SF)
22. black body, dark red interior, clear windows, dot dash wheels, "Firebird" tempa, dark gray plastic base, China casting ($3-5)(MP)
23. black body, dark red interior, clear windows, starburst wheels, "Firebird" tempa, dark gray plastic base, China casting ($3-5)(MP)
24. black body, tan interior, clear windows, 8 dot wheels, "Knight Rider" tempa, black plastic base, China casting ($7-10)(STR)

MB12-F PONTIAC FIREBIRD RACER *see MB60-F*

MB12-G MODIFIED RACER *see MB32-E*

MB12-H MERCEDES 500SL CONVERTIBLE, issued 1990 (USA)(MB220)
MB33-H MERCEDES 500SL CONVERTIBLE, issued 1990 (ROW)

1. silver-gray body, gray base, clear windshield, dark blue interior/ tonneau, no tempa, 8 dot wheels, Macau casting ($1-2)
2. silver-gray body, gray base, clear windshield, dark blue interior/ tonneau, no tempa, 8 dot wheels, China casting ($1-2)
3. black body, metallic charcoal base, chrome windshield, dark gray interior/tonneau, detailed trim tempa, gray disc wheels with rubber tires, China casting ($5-8)(WC)
4. white body, gray base, clear windshield, brown interior/tonneau, "500SL" tempa, 8 dot wheels, China casting ($1-2)
5. silver-gray body, gray base, chrome windshield, maroon interior/tonneau, detailed trim tempa, gray disc wheels with rubber tires, China casting ($5-8)(WC)
6. silver/gray body, gray base, clear windshield, dark blue interior/tonneau, none tempa, 8 dot wheels, Thailand casting ($1-2)(SP)
7. white body, gray base, clear windshield, brown interior/tonneau, "500SL" tempa, 8 dot wheels, Thailand casting ($1-2)
8. red body, gray base, clear windshield, white interior/tonneau, none tempa, 8 dot wheels, Thailand casting ($2-3)(SS)
9. black body, white base, clear windshield, gray interior/ tonneau, pink & white tempa, 8 dot wheels, Thailand casting ($1-2)(5pk)
10. white body, white base, clear windshield, maroon & black interior, black tonneau, detailed trim tempa, chrome disc wheels with rubber tires, China casting ($12-18)(GC)
11. red body, red base, clear windshield, gray & black interior, black tonneau, detailed trim tempa, chrome disc wheels with rubber tires, Thailand casting ($3-5)(PC10)
12. black body, black painted base, clear windshield, brown & black interior, black tonneau, detailed trim tempa, chrome disc wheels with rubber wheels, Thailand casting ($3-5)(PC12)
13. dark blue body, dark blue painted base, clear windshield, light & dark gray interior, gray tonneau, detailed trim tempa,

chrome disc wheels with rubber tires, Thailand casting ($3-5)(PC16)
14. black body, white base, clear windshield, gray interior/ tonneau , pink & white tempa, 8 dot wheels, China casting ($1-2)(5pk)
NOTE: Below models with clear windshield.
15. bright green body, dark green base, red-brown interior & tonneau, no tempa, 5 spoke concave star wheels, China casting ($1-2)(5pk)(MW40/1999 GR)
16. bright green body, dark green base, red-brown interior & tonneau, "Merry Christmas/ Ad-Ventures 1999" tempa, 5 spoke concave star wheels, China casting ($18-25)(CCI)
17. metallic silver body, black base, black interior & tonneau, "Personal Lines 25 Years!" tempa, 8 dot wheels, China casting ($50+)(ASAP)
18. metallic silver body, black base, black interior & tonneau, "Citrix Technology Directions 2000" tempa, 8 dot wheels, China casting ($75+)(ASAP)
19. metallic silver body, black base, black interior & tonneau, no tempa, 8 dot wheels, China casting ($25-40)(ASAP blank)
20. metallic silver body, black base, black interior & tonneau, "Classic Collision" tempa, 8 dot wheels China casting ($75+)(ASAP)
21. metallic silver body, black base, black interior & tonneau, "Thunder Machines AMG Line" tempa, 8 dot wheels China casting ($75+)(ASAP)
22. metallic silver body, black base, black interior & tonneau, green "S" tempa, 8 dot wheels, China casting ($12-18)(ASAP)
23. metallic silver body, black base, black interior & tonneau, gold "WMU" tempa, 8 dot wheels, China casting ($18-25)(ASAP)
24. metallic silver body, black base, black interior & tonneau, "AFLAC" tempa, 8 dot wheels ($50+)(ASAP)
25. metallic silver body, black base, black interior & tonneau, black "G" tempa, 8 dot wheels ($50+)(ASAP)

MB12-I CATTLE TRUCK *see MB71-C*

MB12-J DODGE VIPER RT/10 *see MB10-F*

MB12-K AUDI AVUS QUATTRO, issued 1995 (USA)(MB279)
MB31-K AUDI AVUS QUATTRO, issued 1995 (ROW)
NOTE: Below models with black plastic base.
1. silver body, red interior, clear windows, silver 6-spoke spiral wheels, no tempa, Thailand casting ($1-2)
2. silver body, red/black interior, clear windows, chrome disc wheels with rubber tires, "Audi Avus" tempa, Thailand casting ($3-4)(PC1)
NOTE: Above model can be found with several wheel patterns including mixed.
3. iridescent white body, red interior, smoke windows, silver 6-spoke spiral wheels, "Avus Quattro" tempa, Thailand casting ($1-2)(5pk)
4. iridescent white body, red/black interior, clear windows, chrome disc wheels with rubber tires, "Audi Avus" tempa, Thailand casting ($3-4)(PC4)
5. red body, red/black interior, clear windows, chrome disc wheels with rubber tires, "Audi Avus" tempa, Thailand casting ($3-4)(SC1)
6. copper body, red/black interior, clear windows, chrome disc wheels with rubber tires, "Audi Avus" tempa, Thailand casting ($3-4)(PC1)(ROW)
7. red chrome body, black interior, smoke windows, 5 spoke concave star wheels, "OOOO Avus" tempa, Thailand casting ($1-2)
8. purple-red chrome body, black interior, smoke windows, 5 spoke concave star wheels, "OOOO Avus" tempa, Thailand casting ($1-2)
9. gold chrome body, black interior, smoke windows, 5 spoke concave star wheels, "OOOO Avus" tempa, Thailand casting ($1-2)(5pk)
10. metallic gold body, black interior, clear windows, silver 6 spoke spiral wheels, no tempa, Thailand casting ($5-10)(CH)
11. green chrome body, black interior, smoke windows, 5 spoke concave star wheels, "OOOO Avus" tempa, Thailand casting ($1-2)(MW18/1998 ROW)
12. green chrome body, black interior, smoke windows, 5 spoke concave star wheels, "OOOO Avus" tempa, China casting ($1-2)(MW18/1998 ROW)
13. white body, gray interior, green windows, 5 spoke concave star wheels, black with "Quattro" tempa, China casting ($1-2)(MW34/1999 ROW)
14. metallic green body, black interior, light smoke windows, 5 spoke concave star wheels, "OOOO" tempa, China casting ($1-2)(MW19/1999 ROW)
15. silver-gray body, black interior, clear windows, 5 spoke concave star wheels, no tempa, China casting ($25-40)(ASAP blank)
16. silver-gray body, black interior, clear windows, 5 spoke concave star wheels, "Iscar" tempa, China casting ($50+)(ASAP)
17. silver-gray body, black interior, clear windows, 5 spoke concave star wheels, "Motorola Intelligence Everywhere" tempa, China casting ($50+)

MB12-L '99 MUSTANG CONVERTIBLE *see MB36-F*

MB12-M GRASSHOPPER TOW TRUCK, issued 2003 (USA)(MB622)
NOTE: Below models with gold 5 dot crown wheels & China casting.
1. lime body, yellow boom, amber windows, green plastic base, "Hopper Towing" tempa ($1-2)(MW12/2004 USA)
2. dark metallic green body, lime boom, red windows, red plastic base, grasshopper tempa ($1-2)(5pk)

MB12-N MILITARY HELMET *see MB27-I*

MB13-A DODGE WRECK TRUCK, issued 1970
NOTE: Below models with green windows & England casting. Axle covers can exist in black or red on all versions. Earliest versions have narrow wheels with later versions having wide wheels.
1. pale yellow cab, green rear body, red hook, "BP" labels ($75-90
2. bright yellow cab, green rear body, red hook, "BP" labels ($75-90)
3. bright yellow cab, green rear body, red hook, "Esso" labels (from MB71-A)($250-500)

MB13-B BAJA BUGGY, issued 1971
NOTE: Below models with spiro wheels, unpainted metal base & England casting unless otherwise noted.
1. pale metallic green body, orange interior, black exhausts, red flower label ($10-15)
2. pale metallic green body, orange interior, red exhausts, red flower label ($10-15)
3. pale metallic green body, orange interior, black exhausts, orange flower label ($10-15)
4. pale metallic green body, light orange interior, black exhausts, orange flower label ($10-15)

5. pale metallic green body, orange interior, red exhausts, orange flower label ($10-15)
6. pale metallic green body, orange interior, red exhausts, police shield label (from MB55-A)($25-40)
7. pale metallic green body, red interior, red exhausts, police shield label (from MB55-A)($25-40)
8. pale metallic green body, red interior, red exhausts, orange flower label ($10-15)
9. pale metallic green body, orange interior (from MB47B), red exhausts, orange flower label ($25-40)
10. pale metallic green body, orange interior, red exhausts, no label ($10-15)
11. dark metallic green body, orange interior, red exhausts, orange flower label ($10-15)
12. dark metallic green body, light orange interior, red exhausts, orange flower label ($10-15)
13. dark metallic green body, orange interior, red exhausts, sunburst label (from MB47-B)($20-35)
14. lime green body, orange interior, red exhausts, orange flower label , base with Manaus label ($350-500)(BR)

MB13-C SNORKEL, issued 1977(MB013)

NOTE: Below models with 5 arch wheels, metal base & England casting.

1. red body, unpainted base, blue windows, yellow boom & bucket ($5-8)
2. red body, silver-gray base, blue windows, yellow boom & bucket ($5-8)
3. red body, unpainted base, amber windows, yellow boom & bucket ($10-15)
4. dark red body, unpainted base, blue windows, yellow boom & bucket ($5-8)
5. dark red body, silver-gray base, blue windows, yellow boom & bucket ($5-8)
6. dark red body, unpainted base, blue windows, white boom & bucket ($5-8)
7. dark red body, unpainted base, blue windows, white boom, yellow bucket ($8-10)
8. dark red body, unpainted base, blue windows, yellow boom, white bucket ($8-10)
9. dark red body, silver-gray base, blue windows, white boom & bucket ($5-8)
10. dark red body, silver-gray base, blue windows, yellow boom, white bucket ($8-10)
11. dark red body, gray base with Manaus label, blue windows, yellow boom & bucket ($50-75)(BR)
12. red body, unpainted gray base with Manaus tab, blue windows, yellow boom & bucket ($35-50)(BR)

MB13-D 4 X 4 OPEN BACK TRUCK, issued 1982 (USA)(MB063)
MB63-F 4 X 4 OPEN BACK TRUCK, issued 1982 (ROW)
MB76-B 4 X 4 OPEN BACK TRUCK, reissued 1996 (USA)

NOTE: Below models with maltese cross wheels & spare tire unless noted.

1. orange body, unpainted metal base, light purple windows, "FWD" tempa, England casting ($3-5)
2. orange body, unpainted metal base, orange windows, "FWD" tempa, England casting ($3-5)
3. orange body, unpainted metal base, red windows, "FWD" tempa, England casting ($3-5)
4. orange body, unpainted metal base, red windows, "4X4" tempa, England casting ($3-5)
5. yellow body, unpainted metal base, red windows, "4X4" tempa, England casting ($3-5)
6. yellow body, silver-gray metal base, red windows, "4X4" tempa, England casting ($3-5)
7. yellow body, pearly silver metal base, red windows, "4X4 Goodyear" tempa, Macau casting ($2-4)
8. yellow body, pearly silver metal base, red windows, "4X4 Goodrich" tempa, Macau casting ($2-4)
9. white body, pearly silver metal base, red windows, "Bob Jane T-Mart" tempa, Macau casting ($10-15)(AU)
10. white body, black metal base, red windows, "63" & stripes tempa, Macau casting (1-2)
11. white body, black plastic base, red windows, "63" & stripes tempa, Macau casting ($1-2)
12. white body, black plastic base, red windows, "63" & stripes tempa, Thailand casting ($1-2)
13. red body, chrome plastic base, chrome windows, black roll bar, white & black splash & yellow zigzag tempa, Thailand casting ($2-4)(ST)
14. white body, chrome plastic base, chrome windows, pink roll bar, blue & pink design tempa, Thailand casting ($2-4)(ST)
15. metallic blue body, black plastic base, red windows, pink roll bar, pink design tempa, Thailand casting ($1-2)(5pk)
16. white body, red plastic base, red windows, red roll bar, bat design & dripping blood tempa, Thailand casting ($1-2)
NOTE: Some versions issued in #76 Blisterpack as an error ($1-2)
17. metallic purple body, black plastic base, red windows, orange roll bar, skeleton & "Triceratops" tempa, Thailand casting ($1-2)(5pk)
18. metallic purple body, black plastic base, red windows, orange roll bar, skeleton & "Triceratops" tempa, China casting ($1-2)(5pk)
19. metallic pea green body, black plastic base, red windows, black roll bar, mud & steer skull tempa, China casting ($1-2)(5pk)
20. dark blue body, chrome plastic base, clear windows, green roll bar, "MTN" & mountains tempa, 5 spoke oval wheels, China casting ($1-2)(5pk)
21. dark blue body, chrome plastic base, clear windows, green roll bar, "MTN" & mountains tempa, 5 spoke oval wheels & spare tire, China casting ($1-2)(5pk)

MB13-E SNORKEL *see MB63-E*

MB13-F THE BUSTER, issued 1996 (USA)(MB286)
MB28-M THE BUSTER, issued 1996 (ROW)

NOTE: Below models with black windows &plastic base unless otherwise noted.

1. metallic blue body, 6-spoke spiral wheels, yellow design tempa, China casting ($1-2)
2. metallic gold body, 6-spoke spiral wheels, no tempa, China casting ($10-15)(CH)
3. purple-maroon body, 5 spoke concave star wheels, yellow & white design tempa, China casting ($1-2)
4. metallic blue body, 6 spoke spiral wheels, yellow design & "American Iron Cruise 97" tempa, China casting ($15-20)(C2)
5. raspberry body, 5 spoke concave star wheels, yellow & white design tempa, China casting ($1-2)
6. metallic green body, 5 spoke concave star wheels, yellow & white design tempa, China casting ($1-2)(MW20/1998)
7. light metallic green body, 5 spoke concave star wheels, yellow & white design tempa, China casting ($1-2)(MW20/1998)

MB13-G KENWORTH T2000, issued 1998 (MB318/432)

NOTE: Below models with clear windows, China casting unless otherwise noted. Models issued exclusively as part of a

Convoy/ Rig model are not listed. Versions 1 & 2 with Matchbox International or Mattel casting. All others are Mattel casting.

1. metallic red body, chrome interior & base, chrome disc wheels with rubber tires, detailed trim tempa ($5-8)(FE)
2. unpainted body, chrome interior & base, chrome disc wheels with rubber tires, no tempa ($5-8)(FE)
3. bright blue body, silver-gray interior & base, 8 spoke wheels, "Eagle Express" with stripes tempa ($1-2)(MW13/1999 US)
4. bright blue body, silver-gray interior & base, 8 spoke wheels, "Express" without "Eagle" with stripes tempa ($1-2)(MW13/ 199 ROW)
5. charcoal body, chrome interior & base, chrome disc wheels with rubber tires, "Matchbox Toyshow 2000" tempa ($6-8)(US promo)
6. metallic dark green body, chrome interior & base, chrome disc wheels with rubber tires, silver & green stripes tempa ($3-4)(TN)

MB13-H SNAIL TRUCK, issued 2004 (USA)(MB633)

NOTE: Below models with 10 spoke flower wheels & China casting.

1. bright blue body, iridescent white shell, opaque red windows, gold hubs, "S Cargo- Hero City Delivers" tempa, gray base ($1-2)(MW13/2004 US)
2. lime body, iridescent white shell, opaque yellow windows, silver hubs, "Gary" tempa, blue base ($1-2)(5pk)

MB13-I HOT HEAD *see MB28-O*

MB14-A ISO GRIFO, issued 1969

NOTE: Below models with clear windows, metal base & England casting unless otherwise noted. Earliest versions with narrow wheels with later versions having wide wheels.

1. dark blue body, light blue interior, 5 spoke wheels, unpainted base ($18-25)
2. dark blue body, dark blue interior, 5 spoke wheels, unpainted base ($18-25)
3. dark blue body, white interior, 5 spoke wheels, unpainted base ($18-25)
4. metallic dark blue body, white interior, 5 spoke wheels, unpainted base ($18-25)
5. light blue body, white interior, 5 spoke wheels, unpainted base ($18-25)
6. medium blue body, white interior, 5 spoke wheels, unpainted base ($18-25)
7. medium blue body, white interior, 5 spoke wheels, silver-gray base ($18-25)
8. powder blue body, white interior, 5 spoke wheels, unpainted base ($18-25)(JP)
9. powder blue body, white interior, dot dash wheels, unpainted base ($18-25)(JP)
10. red body, white interior, 5 spoke wheels, unpainted base with Manaus label "8" hood label ($250+)(BR)
11. metallic red body with black doors, white interior, 5 spoke wheels, unpainted base with Manaus label ($250+)(BR)

MB14-B MINI HA HA, issued 1975

NOTE: Below models with red body, large 5 spoke rear wheels, unpainted base & England casting unless otherwise noted.

1. light blue windows, flesh driver, brown helmet, 4 color labels, maltese cross front wheels ($15-18)
2. light blue windows, flesh driver, brown helmet, 2 color labels, maltese cross front wheels ($15-18)
3. light blue windows, pink driver, brown helmet, 2 color labels, maltese cross front wheels ($15-18)
4. light blue windows, pink driver, brown helmet, 4 color labels, maltese cross front wheels ($15-18)
5. light blue windows, flesh driver, brown helmet, 2 color labels, dot dash front wheels ($15-18)
6. light blue windows, flesh driver, brown helmet, 4 color labels, dot dash front wheels ($15-18)
7. light blue windows, purple driver, brown helmet, 4 color labels, maltese cross front wheels ($15-18)
8. light blue windows, purple driver, chocolate helmet, 4 color labels, maltese cross front wheels ($15-18)
9. light blue windows, flesh driver, chocolate helmet, 4 color labels, maltese cross front wheels ($15-18)
10. dark blue windows, purple driver, brown helmet, 4 color labels, maltese cross front wheels ($15-18)
11. dark blue windows, flesh driver, brown helmet, 4 color labels, maltese cross front wheels ($15-18)
12. dark blue windows, flesh driver, chocolate helmet, 4 color labels, maltese cross front wheels ($15-18)
13. light blue windows, flesh driver, brown helmet, 4 color labels, maltese cross front wheels, Manaus tab on base ($35-50)(BR)
14 dark green body, light blue windows, flesh driver, brown helmet, 3 color labels, dot dash front wheels, black base, origin ground off ($250+)(BR)

MB14-C RALLYE ROYALE, issued 1981 (USA)(MB080)

NOTE: Below models with black interior, 5 spoke wheels & black metal base.

1. pearly silver body, blue "14" tempa , Hong Kong casting ($7-10)
2. white body, blue & orange "8" tempa, Hong Kong casting ($7-10)

MB14-D LEYLAND TANKER, issued 1982 (ROW)(MB014)

NOTE: Versions 1 to 4 & 6 with white plastic cab base & red windows. Version 5 & 7 with black cab base & amber windows.

1. red cab & tank base, white tank, "Elf" labels, England casting ($2-4)
2. red cab & tank base, white tank, "Elf" tempa with red stripe, England casting ($2-4)
3. red cab & tank base, white tank, "Elf" tempa with maroon stripe, England casting ($2-4)
4. red cab & tank base, white tank, "Elf" tempa with brown stripe, England casting ($2-4)
5. yellow cab & tank base, white tank, "Shell" tempa, England casting ($7-10)(JP)
6. red cab & tank base, white tank, "Shell" tempa, England casting ($60-85)
7. black cab & tank, gray tank base, "Gas" tempa, Macau casting ($4-5)(CM)

MB14-E 1983/84 CORVETTE, issued 1983 (USA)(MB123)
MB69-E 1983/84 CORVETTE, issued 1983 (ROW)

NOTE: Early models cast "1983 Corvette" with later models cast "1984 Corvette". All models with black plastic base insert.

1. pearly silver upper & lower body, red interior, dot dash wheels, "83 Vette" tempa, Macau casting ($3-5)
2. pearly silver upper & lower body, red interior, 8 dot wheels, "83 Vette" tempa, Macau casting ($3-5)
3. red upper body, light gray lower body, black interior, dot dash wheels, "Vette" & silver/ black stripes tempa, Macau casting ($2-4)

4. red upper body, light gray lower body, black interior, 8 dot wheels, "Vette" & silver/ black stripes tempa, Macau casting ($2-4)
5. red upper body, light gray lower body, black interior, 5 arch wheels, "Vette" & silver/ black stripes tempa, Macau casting ($2-4)
6. red & white upper body, red lower body, black interior, starburst wheels, "350 CID" tempa, Macau casting ($2-4)(SF)
7. red & white upper body, red lower body, black interior, starburst wheels, "350 CID" tempa with "Chef Boyardee" label, Macau casting ($12-18)(US)(OP)
8. red & white upper body, red lower body, black interior, laser wheels, "350 CID" tempa with "Chef Boyardee" label, Macau casting ($75-90)(US)(OP)
9. red & white upper body, red lower body, black interior, laser wheels, "350 CID" tempa, Macau casting ($3-5)(LW)
10. gray upper body, bluish purple lower body, no interior- replaced with light gold plated window armament, starburst wheels, stripes & stars tempa, Macau casting, includes plastic armament ($6-8)(RB)
11. gray upper body, bluish purple lower body, no interior- replaced with dark gold plated window armament, starburst wheels, stripes & stars tempa, Macau casting, includes plastic armament ($6-8)(RB)
12. red upper body, pearly silver lower body, black interior, 8 dot wheels, blue & silver tempa , Macau casting ($8-12)(DY)

MB14-G 1987 CORVETTE, issued 1987 (USA)(204)
MB28-G 1987 CORVETTE, issued 1990 (ROW)

NOTE: Below models with clear windows & black plastic base insert unless otherwise noted.

1. yellow upper & lower body, black interior, clear windshield, 8 dot wheels, "Corvette" & logo tempa, Macau casting ($2-3)
2. white & red upper body, red lower body, black interior, clear windshield, laser wheels, "350 CID" tempa, Macau casting ($3-5)(LW)
3. white & red upper body, red lower body, black interior, clear windshield, starburst wheels, "350 CID" tempa, Macau casting ($3-5)(SF)
4. rose red upper & silver-gray lower body, black interior, clear windshield, 8 dot wheels, "Corvette" & logo tempa, Macau casting ($3-4)(SC)
5. orange upper & silver-gray lower body, black interior, clear windshield, 8 dot wheels, "Corvette" & logo tempa, Macau casting ($3-4)(SC)
6. lemon upper & lower body, black interior, clear windshield, 8 dot wheels, "Corvette" & logo tempa, Macau casting ($1-2)
7. metallic blue upper & lower body, black & gray interior, chrome windshield, gray disc with rubber tires, "Corvette" & detailed trim tempa, Macau casting ($5-8)(WC)
8. red upper & lower body, black interior, clear windshield, 8 dot wheels, flames tempa, Thailand casting ($7-10)(US)(OP)
9. orange-yellow upper & lower body, black interior, clear windshield, 8 dot wheels, "Corvette" & logo tempa, Thailand casting ($1-2)
   NOTE: Chevy logo on this version can appear forward or towards back on sides.
10. orange-yellow upper & lower body, black interior, clear windshield, 6-spoke ringed wheels, "Corvette" & logo tempa, Thailand casting ($60-85)
11. white upper & lower body, dark pink interior, clear windshield, 8 dot wheels, stripes & zigzags tempa, Thailand casting ($2-4)(DM)
12. lime upper & lower body, black interior, clear windshield, gray disc with rubber tires, "Rally Official- Joe Bulgin" tempa, Thailand casting ($6-8)(WP)
13. red upper & lower body, black interior, clear windshield, 8 dot wheels, "Corvette" & Chevy logo tempa, Thailand casting ($1-2)
14. blue-green upper & lower body, black interior, clear windshield, 8 dot wheels, "Corvette" tempa, Thailand casting ($2-4)(SS)
15. white upper & lower body, maroon interior, chrome windshield, gray disc rubber tires, detailed trim tempa, Thailand casting ($2-4)(WC)
16. purplish upper & lower body, black interior, clear windshield, 8 dot wheels, "Corvette" tempa, Thailand casting ($2-4)(GS)
17. black upper & lower body, neon yellow interior, clear windshield, gold 6-spoke spiral wheels, pink & yellow design tempa, Thailand casting ($1-2)
18. black upper & lower body, red interior & base insert , clear windshield, silver 6-spoke spiral wheels, detailed trim tempa, Thailand casting ($2-4)(CC)
19. red upper & lower body, black interior, clear windshield, 8 dot wheels, "Corvette" & "Matchbox Line Preview 1994" tempa, Thailand casting ($250-350)(US)
20. black upper & lower body, neon yellow interior, clear windshield, silver 6-spoke spiral wheels, pink & yellow design tempa, China casting ($1-2)
21. white upper & lower body, blue interior, clear windshield, silver 6-spoke spiral wheels, orange & blue design tempa, China casting ($1-2)
22. metallic lavender upper & lower body, orange interior, clear windshield, 5 spoke concave star wheels, white design tempa, China casting ($1-2)
23. red upper & lower body, black & red interior, clear windshield, chrome disc wheels with rubber tires, detailed trim tempa, China casting ($8-12)(UC)
24. bright green upper & lower body, white interior with pink side molding, clear windshield, 5 spoke concave star wheels, "70th Shenandoah Apple Blossom Festival 1997" tempa, China casting ($12-15)(US)
25. black upper & lower body, red & black interior, clear windshield, chrome disc wheels with rubber tires, "Corvette Cologne" tempa, China casting ($10-15)(US)
26. black upper & lower body, red & black interior, clear windshield, chrome disc wheels with rubber wheels, detailed trim tempa, China casting ($3-5)(CP)
27. yellow upper & lower body, black & gray interior, clear windshield, chrome disc wheels with rubber wheels, detailed trim tempa, China casting ($3-5)(CP)
28. metallic gold upper & lower body, black interior, clear windshield, 5 spoke concave star wheels, no tempa, China casting ($5-10)(CH)
29. dark green upper & lower body, black & gray interior, clear windshield, chrome disc wheels with rubber tires, detailed trim tempa, China casting ($8-12)(GC)
30. green-gold upper & lower body, gray & black interior, clear windshield, chrome disc wheels with rubber tires, detailed trim tempa, China casting ($3-5)(CP)
31. dark purple upper & lower body, gray & black interior, clear windshield, chrome disc wheels with rubber tires, detailed trim tempa, China casting ($3-5)(CP)
32. metallic light bronze upper & lower body, gray & black interior, clear windshield, chrome disc wheels with rubber tires, detailed trim tempa, China casting ($3-5)(CP)
33. metallic red upper & lower body, gray & black interior, clear windshield, chrome disc wheels with rubber tires, detailed trim tempa, China casting ($3-5)(CP)
34. bright blue upper & lower body, black & red interior, clear windshield, black disc wheels with rubber tires, white stripes tempa, China casting ($3-5)(PC15)

35. black upper body, green-gold lower body, gray & black interior, clear windshield, gold 6 spoke spiral wheels, no tempa, China casting ($50+)(CHI)
36. metallic light bronze upper & lower body, neon yellow interior, clear windshield, gold 6 spoke spiral wheels, no tempa, China casting ($50+)(CHI)
37. green-gold upper body, metallic red lower body, neon yellow interior, clear windshield, gold 6 spoke spiral wheels, detailed trim tempa, China casting ($50+)(CHI)
38. dark green upper body, black lower body, neon yellow interior, clear windshield, gold 6 spoke spiral wheels, detailed trim tempa, China casting ($50+)(CHI)
39. yellow upper body, dark purple lower body, black & red interior, clear windshield, gold 6 spoke spiral wheels, detailed trim tempa, China casting ($50+)(CHI)
40. metallic red upper body, black lower body, neon yellow interior, clear windshield, gold 6 spoke spiral wheels, detailed trim tempa, China casting ($50+)(CHI)
41. white upper & lower body, blue interior, clear windshield, gold 6 spoke spiral wheels, detailed trim tempa, China casting ($50+)(CHI)
42. dark purple upper body, green-gold lower body, black & gray interior, clear windshield, gold 6 spoke spiral wheels, detailed trim tempa, China casting ($50+)(CHI)
43. dark purple upper body, black lower body, neon yellow interior, clear windshield, gold 6 spoke spiral wheels, detailed trim tempa, China casting ($50+)(CHI)
43. dark purple upper body, metallic red lower body, neon yellow interior, clear windshield, gold 6 spoke spiral wheels, detailed trim tempa, China casting ($50+)(CHI)
44. dark purple upper & lower body, neon yellow interior, clear windshield, gold 6 spoke spiral wheels, detailed trim tempa, China casting ($50+)(CHI)
45. black upper & lower body, neon yellow interior, clear windshield, gold 6 spoke spiral wheels, detailed trim tempa, China casting ($50+)(CHI)
46. metallic red upper body, dark green lower body, neon yellow interior, clear windshield, gold 6 spoke spiral wheels, detailed trim tempa, China casting ($50+)(CHI)
47. black upper body, metallic red lower body, neon yellow interior, clear windshield, gold 6 spoke spiral wheels, "Corvette Cologne" & detailed trim tempa, China casting ($50+)(CHI)
48. bright green upper & lower body, white interior with pink side molding, clear windshield, 5 spoke concave star wheels, "White's Guide Car of the Month- December 1998" tempa, China casting ($12-15)(CCI)

MB14-H GRAND PRIX RACING CAR *see MB74-H*

MB14-I FLATBED TRUCK *see MB41-L*

MB14-J FORD TRANSIT AMBULANCE *see MB21-I*

MB14-K WEB WHEELER, issued 2004 (USA)(MB650)

1. metallic purple body, red plastic spider , yellow handlebars, gold 5 spoke oval wheels, chrome plastic base, China casting ($1-2)(MW14/2004 US)

MB14-L RIG DIGGER *see MB29-E*

MB15-A VOLKSWAGEN 1500, issued 1969

NOTE: Below models with ivory interior, clear windows, 5 spoke wheels, unpainted metal base & England casting.

1. cream body, "137" decals on sides, front bumper with decal ($18-25)
2. cream body, "137" labels on sides, front bumper with decal ($18-25)
3. off white body, "137" decals on sides, front bumper with decal ($18-25)
4. off white body, "137" labels on sides, front bumper with decal ($18-25)
5. metallic red body, "137" labels on sides, front bumper with decals ($20-35)
6. metallic red body, "137" labels on sides, front bumper with cast design ($20-35)
7. off white body, "137" labels on sides, front bumper with cast design ($7-10)(JP)

MB15-B FORK LIFT TRUCK, issued 1972 (MB015)

NOTE: Casting A with plastic steering wheel, Casting B with steering wheel cast to body, Casting C with roof cast. Below models with metal base & England casting unless otherwise noted.

1. red body, casting A, black base, gray forks, yellow hoist, "Lansing" labels ($10-15)
2. red body, casting A, unpainted base, gray forks, yellow hoist, "Lansing" labels ($10-15)
3. red body, casting A, green base, gray forks, yellow hoist, "Lansing" labels ($10-15)
4. red body, casting A, charcoal base, gray forks, yellow hoist, "Lansing" labels ($10-15)
5. red body, casting A, unpainted base with Manaus label, gray forks, yellow hoist, "T6AD" labels ($250+)(BR)

NOTE: Above models with spiro front wheels and five spoke rear wheels. All others except version 6 with dot dash front and rear wheels.

6. red body, casting A, black base, gray forks, yellow hoist, "Lansing" labels, spiro front wheels, dot dash rear wheels ($10-15)
7. red body, casting A, black base, gray forks, yellow hoist, "Lansing" labels ($10-15)
8. red body, casting A, unpainted base, gray forks, yellow hoist, "Lansing" labels ($10-15)
9. red body, casting A, charcoal base, yellow forks, unpainted hoist, "Lansing" labels ($10-15)
10. red body, casting A, black base, yellow forks, unpainted hoist, "Lansing" labels ($10-15)
11. red body, casting B, black base, yellow forks, unpainted hoist, "Lansing" labels ($10-15)
12. red body, casting B, black base, gray forks, unpainted hoist, "Lansing" labels ($10-15)
13. red body, casting B, black base, red long forks, unpainted hoist, "Lansing" labels ($18-25)(KS)
14. red body, casting B, unpainted base, red long forks, unpainted hoist, "Lansing" labels ($18-25)(KS)
15. red body, casting B, unpainted base, black forks, unpainted hoist, "Lansing" labels ($10-15)
16. red body, casting B, black base with Manaus tab, yellow forks, yellow hoist, "Lansing" labels ($35-50)(BR)
17. red body, casting C, black base, black forks, unpainted hoist, "Hi Lift" labels, black roof ($10-15)
18. orange body, casting C, unpainted base, black forks, unpainted hoist,, "Hi Lift" labels, black roof ($10-15)
19. orange body, casting C, (roof omitted), silver-gray base, black long forks, unpainted hoist, "Hi Lift" labels ($18-25)(KS)
20. orange body, casting C black base, black forks, unpainted hoist,, "Hi Lift" labels, black roof ($10-15)
21. orange body, casting C, silver-gray base, black forks, unpainted hoist, "Hi Lift" labels, black roof ($10-15)

22. pink-orange body, casting C, black base, black forks, unpainted hoist,, "Hi Lift" labels, black roof ($10-15)

NOTE: Below versions with 5 crown front wheels.

23. orange body, casting C, (roof omitted), silver-gray base, black long forks, unpainted hoist, "Hi Lift" labels ($18-25)(KS)
24. orange body, casting C, (roof omitted),charcoal base, black long fork, unpainted hoist, "Hi Lift" labels ($18-25)(KS)

MB15-C HI HO SILVER, issued 1981 (USA)(MB081)

NOTE: Below model with clear windows, 5 spoke wheels & black metal base.

1. pearly silver body, red interior, "Hi Ho Silver" tempa, Hong Kong casting ($7-10)

MB15-D FORD SIERRA, issued 1983 (USA)(MB120)
MB55-E FORD SIERRA, issued 1983 (ROW)
MB40-E FORD SIERRA, reissued 1990 (USA)

1. white body, dark gray lower body, clear windows, gray metal base, white interior, gray hatch, black door posts, 8 dot silver wheels, England casting ($85-100)
2. white body, dark gray lower body, clear windows, gray metal base, red interior, gray hatch, black door posts, 8 dot silver wheels, England casting ($3-5)
3. white body, dark gray lower body, clear windows, gray metal base, red interior, gray hatch, plain door posts, 8 dot silver wheels, England casting ($3-5)
4. white body, dark gray lower body, clear windows, gray metal base, red interior, white hatch, black door posts, 8 dot silver wheels, England casting ($3-5)
5. white body, dark gray lower body, clear windows, gray metal base, red interior, white hatch, plain door posts, 8 dot silver wheels, England casting ($3-5)
6. silver-gray body, dark gray lower body, clear windows, gray metal base, red interior, gray hatch, "Ford XR4i Sport" tempa, 8 dot silver wheels, England casting ($3-5)
7. silver-gray body, dark gray lower body, clear windows, gray metal base, red interior, gray hatch, "Ford XR4i Sport" tempa, 5 crown wheels, Macau casting ($2-3)
8. pearly silver body, dark gray lower body, amber windows, gray metal base, red interior, gray hatch, "Ford XR4i Sport" tempa, dot dash wheels, Macau casting ($2-3)
9. black body, dark gray lower body, clear windows, gray metal base, black interior, black hatch, white & green stripes with "85" tempa, starburst wheels, Macau casting ($3-4)(SF)
10. black body, dark gray lower body, amber windows, gray metal base, black interior, black hatch, white & green stripes with "85" tempa, starburst wheels, Macau casting ($2-4)(SF)
11. yellow body, black lower body, clear windows, black metal base, black interior, black hatch, "XR 4X4" tempa, 8 dot gold wheels, Macau casting ($5-8)
12. yellow body, black lower body, clear windows, black metal base, black interior, black hatch, "XR 4X4" tempa, 8 dot silver wheels, Macau casting ($5-8)
13. yellow body, dark gray lower body, clear windows, black metal base, red interior, gray hatch, "XR 4X4" tempa, 8 dot gold wheels, Macau casting ($35-50)
14. yellow body, dark gray lower body, clear windows, dark gray metal base, red interior, gray hatch, "XR 4X4" tempa, 8 dot silver wheels, Macau casting ($35-50)
15. yellow body, dark gray lower body, clear windows, dark gray metal base, red interior, gray hatch, "XR 4X4" tempa, 8 dot gold wheels, Macau casting ($35-50)
16. yellow body, dark gray lower body, clear windows, dark gray metal base, red interior, gray hatch, "XR 4X4" tempa, dot dash wheels, Macau casting ($35-50)
17. cream body, dark gray lower body, clear windows, dark gray metal base, black interior, black hatch, "55" & black band tempa, 8 dot silver wheels, Macau casting ($8-12)
18. metallic green body, dark gray lower body, clear windows, dark gray metal base, black interior, black hatch, white & gold stripe tempa, laser wheels, Macau casting ($3-4)(LW)
19. dark blue body, black lower body, clear windows, black metal base, black interior, black hatch, "Duckhams Race Team" tempa, 8 dot silver wheels, Macau casting ($3-5)(TC)
20. dark blue body, black lower body, clear windows, black plastic base, black interior, black hatch, "Duckhams Race Team" tempa, 8 dot silver wheels, Macau casting ($3-5)(TC)
21. white body, red lower body, clear windows, red metal base, black interior, red hatch, "Virgin Atlantic" tempa, 8 dot silver wheels, Macau casting ($3-5)(GS)
22. yellow body, dark gray lower body, amber windows, gray metal base, gray hatch, "XR 4X4" tempa, 8 dot silver wheels, Macau casting ($35-50)
23. black body, black lower body, clear windows, black metal base, red interior, black hatch, "Texaco 6/ Pirelli" tempa, 8 dot silver wheels, Macau casting ($2-3)
24. red body, black lower body, clear windows, black metal base, black interior, black hatch, "Tizer The Appetizer" tempa, 8 dot silver wheels, Macau casting ($3-5)(TC)
25. red body, black lower body, clear windows, black plastic base, black interior, black hatch, "Tizer The Appetizer" tempa, 8 dot silver wheels, Macau casting ($3-5)(TC)
26. red body, black lower body, black windows, black plastic base, no interior, black hatch, "Fire Dept." tempa, 8 dot silver wheels, amber dome lights, Macau casting ($8-12)(SR)
27. red body, black lower body, black windows, black plastic base, no interior, black hatch, "Fire Dept." tempa, 8 dot silver wheels, greenish yellow dome lights, Macau casting ($8-12)(SR)
28. yellow-orange body, black lower body, black windows, black plastic base, no interior, black hatch, "Airport Security" tempa, 8 dot silver wheels, red dome lights, Macau casting ($8-12)(SR)
29. yellow-orange body, black lower body, black windows, black plastic base, no interior, black hatch, "Airport Security" tempa, 8 dot silver wheels, green dome lights, Macau casting ($18-25)(SR)
30. white body, white lower body, black windows, black plastic base, no interior, white hatch, "Sheriff" tempa, 8 dot silver wheels, red dome lights, Macau casting ($8-12)(SR)
31. black body, black lower body, clear windows, black plastic base, red interior, black hatch, "Texaco 6/ Pirelli" tempa, 8 dot silver wheels, Macau casting ($2-3)
32. white body, red lower body, clear windows, red plastic base, black interior, red hatch, "Virgin Atlantic" tempa, 8 dot silver wheels, Macau casting ($3-5)
33. metallic green body, dark gray lower body, clear windows, black plastic base, black interior, black hatch, white & gold stripes tempa, laser wheels, Macau casting ($3-5)(LW)
34. metallic green body, dark gray lower body, clear windows, black plastic base, black interior, black hatch, white & gold stripes tempa, starburst wheels, Macau casting ($8-12)(SF)
35. black body, black lower body, clear windows, red interior, black plastic base, black hatch, "Texaco 6/ Pirelli" tempa, 8 dot silver wheels, Thailand casting ($1-2)
36. red body, yellow lower body, clear windows, blue interior, black plastic base, blue hatch, 3 faces & lion head tempa, 8 dot red wheels, Thailand casting ($15-18)(LL)

37. white body, red lower body, clear windows, red plastic base, black interior, red hatch, "Virgin Atlantic" tempa, 8 dot silver wheels, Thailand casting ($2-3)
38. black body, dark gray lower body, clear windows, gray plastic base, black interior, black hatch, white & green stripes with "85" tempa, starburst wheels, Macau casting ($3-4)(SF)
39. black body, dark gray lower body, amber windows, gray plastic base, black interior, black hatch, white & green stripes with "85" tempa, starburst wheels, Macau casting ($3-4)(SF)
40. white body, black lower body, clear window, black plastic base, red interior, black hatch, "Gemini/ N. Cooper/ 1" tempa, 8 dot silver wheels, Thailand casting ($2-3)
41. white body, red lower body, red plastic base, red interior, clear windows, red hatch, 8 dot silver wheels, "Virgin Atlantic" tempa, Thailand casting ($12-15)
42. white body, black lower body, black plastic base, no interior, black windows, black hatch, 8 dot silver wheels, red dome lights, black "Police" tempa, China casting ($1-2)(LS)
43. yellow body, black lower body, black plastic base, no interior, black windows, black hatch, 8 dot silver wheels, greenish yellow dome lights, "Matchbox Taxi Co. 555-7800" tempa, China casting ($3-5)(LS)
43. white body, black lower body, black plastic base, no interior, black windows, black hatch, 8 dot silver wheels, greenish yellow dome lights, "Matchbox Taxi Co. 555-7800" tempa, China casting ($3-5)(LS)
44. white body, black lower body, black plastic base, no interior, black windows, black hatch, 8 dot silver wheels, red dome lights, blue "Police" tempa, China casting ($3-5)(LS)

MB15-E PEUGEOT 205 TURBO, issued 1984 (ROW)(MB142)
MB25-G PEUGEOT 205 TURBO, reissued 1991 (ROW)

NOTE: Below models with clear windows, silver-gray interior, 8 spoke wheels & plastic base unless noted otherwise.

1. white body, white base, red "205" with stripes tempa, Macau casting ($2-4)
2. white body, white base, black "205" with stripes tempa, Macau casting ($2-4)
3. white body, white base, dark purple "205" with stripes tempa, Macau casting ($2-4)
4. white body, white base, purple "205" with stripes tempa, China casting ($2-4)
5. white body, white base, black "205" & "Matchbox 11" tempa, Manaus casting ($35-40)(BR)
6. white body, white base, black "205" tempa, Manaus casting ($25-40)(BR)
7. orange-red body, dark gray base, "48 Michelin/ Bilstein" tempa, China casting ($2-4)
8. green body, dark gray base, no tempa, China casting ($8-12)(GR)(GS)
9. yellow body, dark gray base, "Peugeot 205/ 48 Bilstein" tempa, China casting ($2-4)
10. dark gray body, dark gray base, "Shell 37" pink & yellow design tempa, Manaus casting ($35-45)(BR)

MB15-F SAAB 9000 TURBO, issued 1988 (USA)(MB190)
MB22-F SAAB 9000 TURBO, issued 1988 (ROW)

NOTE: Below models with clear windows & metal base.

1. metallic red body, brown interior, black base, 8 dot wheels, no tempa, Macau casting ($1-2)
2. metallic blue body, gray interior, black base, laser wheels, "Saab Turbo" & stripes tempa, Macau casting ($7-10)(LW)
3. metallic red body, brown interior, black base, 8 dot wheels, no tempa, China casting ($1-2)
4. metallic pink-red body, brown interior, black base, 8 dot wheels, no tempa, China casting ($1-2)
5. white body, brown interior, white base, 8 dot wheels, "Saab 22" & stripes tempa, China casting ($2-4)
6. dark blue body, brown interior, dark blue base, 8 dot wheels, no tempa, China casting ($8-12)(GR)(GS)
7. silver-gray body, brown interior, white base, 8 dot wheels, "Saab 22" & stripes tempa, China casting ($8-10)(GS)
8. dark cream body, yellow & brown interior, black base, chrome disc wheels with rubber tires, detailed trim tempa, China casting ($8-12)(UC)
9. dark cream body, brown interior, black base, gold 6 spoke spiral wheels, detailed trim tempa, China casting ($50+)(CHI)

MB15-G 1965 CORVETTE GRAND SPORT *see MB2-G*

MB15-H ALFA ROMEO SZ, issued 1991 (USA)(MB225)
MB 6-G ALFA ROMEO SZ, issued 1991 (ROW)

NOTE: Below models with black plastic base, tan interior, smoke gray windows & 8 dot wheel unless otherwise noted.

1. red body, black painted roof, China casting ($2-3)
2. dull red body, black painted roof, China casting ($2-3)
3. red body, plain roof, China casting ($8-12)(GR)(GS)
4. red body, black painted roof, "Alfa Romeo" tempa, China casting ($1-2)
5. red body, plain roof, "Alfa Romeo" tempa, China casting ($1-2)
6. lime body, plain roof, "Alfa Romeo" tempa, China casting ($8-10)(GS)
7. blue body & roof, black interior, clear windows, "Go Eagles! 1997" tempa, China casting ($3-5)(AU)

MB15-I SUNBURNER, issued 1992 (USA)(MB227)
MB41-I SUNBURNER, issued 1992 (ROW)

NOTE: Below models with smoke windshield, Goodyear slicks & black plastic base.

1. florescent yellow body, black interior, sun & flames tempa, China casting ($2-4)
2. white body, black interior, sun & flames tempa, China casting ($8-10)(GS)
3. blue body, black interior, white stripes tempa, China casting ($2-4)

MB15-J MUSTANG MACH III, issued 1994 (USA)(MB257)
MB28-K MUSTANG MACH III, issued 1994 (ROW)

NOTE: Below models with black painted windshield & black plastic base unless otherwise noted.

1. red body, red hood, black interior, gold 6-spoke spiral wheels, dark blue/white/black design tempa, Thailand casting ($1-2)
2. red body, red hood, black interior, gold 6-spoke spiral wheels, light blue/white/ black design tempa, Thailand casting ($1-2)
3. red body, red hood, black interior, gray disc wheels with rubber tires, detailed trim tempa, Thailand casting ($2-4)(WC)
4. yellow body, yellow hood, black interior, gold 6-spoke spiral wheels, "Nationwise Auto Parts" tempa, Thailand casting ($15-25)(US)
5. iridescent white body & hood, black interior, silver 6-spoke spiral wheels, "Ice Crusher" tempa, Thailand casting ($7-10)(PS)
6. red body & hood, black interior, silver 6-spoke spiral wheels, light blue/ white & black design tempa, Thailand casting ($1-2)
7. metallic red body & hood, black interior, silver 6-spoke spiral wheels, "Mach III" tempa, Thailand casting ($1-2)(5pk)
8. dark purple body & hood, orange interior, silver 6-spoke spiral wheels, green stripes & silver windshield tempa, gray base, Thailand casting ($1-2)(5pk)

9. black body & hood, red interior, silver 6-spoke spiral wheels, dark blue/ white & black design tempa, Thailand casting ($1-2)
10. white body, blue hood, black interior,, 5 spoke concave star wheels, red stripes & blue stars tempa, Thailand casting ($1-2)

11. metallic gold body & hood, black interior, silver 6 spoke spiral wheels, no tempa, Thailand casting ($5-10)(CH)
12. powder blue body & hood, black interior, 5 spoke concave star wheels, dark orange stripe tempa, Thailand casting ($1-2)(5pk)
13. metallic green body & hood, light tan & brown interior, chrome disc wheels with rubber tires, silver-gray windshield, detailed trim & "Mach III" tempa, Thailand casting ($3-5)(PC2-ROW)
14. metallic blue body & hood, ivory & blue interior, chrome disc wheels with rubber tires, silver-gray windshield, detailed trim & "Mach III" tempa, Thailand casting ($3-5)(PC12)
15. yellow body & hood, black & blue interior, chrome disc wheels with rubber tires, detailed trim tempa, Thailand casting ($15-20)(GC)
16. white body, red hood, red interior, 5 spoke concave star wheels, blue stripes & white stars tempa, Thailand casting ($1-2)(MW4/1998 US)
17. white body, red hood, red interior, 5 spoke concave star wheels, blue stripes & white stars tempa, China casting ($1-2)(MW4/1998 US)
18. candy apple red body & hood, black & gray interior, chrome disc wheels with rubber tires, "Mach III" & detailed trim tempa, China casting ($3-5)(PC)

MB15-K FORD TRANSIT VAN, issued 1995 (ROW)(MB281)
MB50-N FORD TRANSIT VAN, issued 2002 (USA)

NOTE: All models listed with gray interior, clear windows, 8 dot wheels, plastic base & China casting unless noted.

1. white body, gray base, "Fastway Couriers" tempa ($5-7)(AU)
2. light blue body, blue base, surfing scene tempa ($2-3)
3. white body, gray base, "Parcel Post" tempa ($4-6)(AU)
4. white body, black base, "SLP Engineering Ltd." (both sides) tempa ($12-18)(LD)(UK)
5. white body, black base, "SLP Engineering Ltd./ Lowestoft" tempa ($12-18)(LD)(UK)
6. white body, black base, "Evening Gazette" tempa ($12-18)(LD)(UK)
7. white & orange body, black base, "Grafi Press" tempa ($15-18)(DU)
8. white body, black base, "Scooter's Snowboard Shoppe" tempa ($12-18)(LD)(US)
9. black body with red roof, red base, "North Sydney Bears" tempa ($10-15)(AU)
10. black body with red roof, red base, "Balmain Tigers" tempa ($10-15)(AU)
11. black body with red roof, red base, "Gold Coast Seagulls" tempa ($10-15)(AU)
12. black body with dark blue roof, dark blue base, "Canterbury-Bankstown Bulldogs" tempa ($10-15)(AU)
13. black body with light blue roof, light blue base, "Cronulla Sharks" tempa ($10-15)(AU)
14. bright blue body with red roof, red base, "Eastern Suburbs Roosters" tempa ($10-15)(AU)
15. bright blue body with yellow roof, yellow base, "Parramatta Eels" tempa ($10-15)(AU)
16. dark gray body with white roof, dark blue base, "North Queensland Cowboys" tempa ($10-15)(AU)
17. green body with red roof, red base, "South Sydney Rabbitohs" tempa ($10-15)(AU)
18. green body with blue roof, blue base, "Auckland Warriors" tempa ($10-15)(AU)
19. lime body with yellow roof, yellow base, "Canberra Raiders" tempa ($10-15)(AU)
20. lemon body with red roof, red base, "Penrith Panthers" tempa ($10-15)(AU)
21. light yellow body with purple roof, purple base, "Brisbane Broncos" tempa ($10-15)(AU)
22. red body with yellow roof, yellow base, "Western Reds" tempa ($10-15)(AU)
23. red body with gold roof, gold base, "South Queensland Crushers" tempa ($10-15)(AU)
24. plum body with white roof, white base, "Manly Sea Eagles" tempa ($10-15)(AU)
25. white body, black base, "Western Suburbs Magpies" tempa ($10-15)(AU)
26. white body with orange roof, orange base, "Illawarra Steelers" tempa ($10-15)(AU)
27. white body with red roof, black base, "St. George Dragons" tempa ($10-15)(AU)
28. white body with bright blue roof, black base, "Newcastle Knights" tempa ($10-15)(AU)
29. white body, black base, "Rentokil Initial" tempa ($12-15)(UK)(LD)
30. white body, black base, "Hannant's" tempa ($12-15)(UK)(LD)
31. white body, black base, "Coldseal" tempa ($12-15)(UK)(LD)
32. white body, black base, "NSVA Van Nationals Billing Northampton" tempa ($15-20)(UK)(LD)
33. white body, black base, "NSVA Van 23 Years on the Road Members Van" tempa ($25-40)(UK)(LD)
34. white body, black base, "NSVA Van 23 Years on the Road Committee Van" tempa ($100-150)(UK)(LD)
35. white body, black base, "NGK- The World's Only" tempa ($50-75)(UK)(LD)
36. white body, black base, "Phoenix Natural Gas" tempa ($12-15)(UK)(LD)
37. white body, black base, "Starlec" tempa ($12-15)(UK)(LD)
38. white body, black base, "Ultra Link" tempa ($125-175)(UK)(LD)
39. white body, black base, "Euro Dollar" tempa ($12-15)(UK)(LD)
40. white body, black base, "EFI Disc Brakes" tempa ($12-15)(UK)(LD)
41. white body, black base, "Morgan Lovell" tempa ($12-15)(UK)(LD)
42. white body, black base, "Standish Van Hire" tempa ($12-15)(UK)(LD)
43. white body, black base, "Windscreen Auto" tempa ($100-150)(UK)(LD)
44. white body, black base, "Abbey Stainless" tempa ($12-15)(UK)(LD)
45. white body, white interior, black base, no tempa ($20-25)(ASAP-blank)
46. white body, black base, "Rotamole/ Pitmole" tempa ($100-175)(UK)(LD)
47. white body, black base, "Envelopes UK" tempa ($12-15)(UK)(LD)
48. white body, black base, "NSVA 25th Anniversary- Committee Van" tempa ($100-150)(UK)(LD)
49. white body, black base, "NSVA- 25 Years of Vanning" tempa ($15-20)(UK)(LD)
50. white body, black base, "National Windscreens" tempa ($12-15)(UK)(LD)
51. white body, black base, "Poltransplant Navartis" tempa ($85-110)(Poland)(LD)

52. white body, black base, "Panasonic Colin Smith" tempa ($12-15)(UK)(LD)
53. white body, blue base, surfing scene tempa ($1-2)(MW5/1998 ROW)
54. white body, black base, "Hankook Tyres" with black roof logo tempa ($15-20)(Malta)(LD)
55. white body, black base, "Hankook Tyres" with blue roof logo tempa ($15-20)(Malta)(LD)
56. white body, black base, "Hankook Tyres" with red roof logo tempa ($100-150)(Malta)(LD)
57. white body, black base, "Hankook Tyres" with orange roof logo tempa ($100-150)(Malta)(LD)
58. white body, white interior, black base, "Smith Kline Beecham" tempa ($50+)(ASAP)
59. white body, white interior, black base, "American International Recovery" tempa ($100+)(ASAP)
60. black body, white interior, silver-gray base, blue windows, "Stegosaurus" & skeleton tempa ($1-2)(5pk)
61. white body, black base, "Eurolines" tempa ($12-15)(UK)(LD)
62. white body, white interior, black base, "Lincare" tempa ($100+)(ASAP)
63. red body, gray interior, black base, "Vinnie's" tempa ($2-3)(MW25/1999 ROW)
64. white body, gray interior, black base, "AC Auto Clenz" tempa ($50+)(UK)(LD)
65. white body, gray interior, black base, "Van Club- 26 Years of Vanning" ($12-15)(UK)(LD)
66. white body, gray interior, black base, "Van Club- 25th Van Nationals- England" tempa ($12-15)(UK)(LD)
67. white body, gray interior, black base, "Long Time Vanners 1983-1999" tempa ($15-20)(UK)(LD)
68. white body, gray interior, black base, "Long Time Vanners Yet Another Millennium" tempa ($15-20)(UK)(LD)
69. silver-gray body, gray interior, black base, "Long Time Vanners Club Member" tempa ($25-40)(UK)(LD)
70. silver-gray body, gray interior, black base, "Upright" tempa ($25-40)(UK)(LD)
71. white body, white interior, black base, "Lufthansa 88-786" tempa ($2-4)(MW14/1999 GR)
72. white & yellow body, black interior, black base, "Coca Cola" tempa, chrome disc with rubber tires ($4-6)(Coke PC)(MP)
73. white body, gray interior, black base, "Transit" (red & black print) tempa ($35-50)(UK)(LD)
74. white body, gray interior, black base, "Transit" (red & blue print) tempa ($35-50)(UK)(LD)
75. silver-gray body, gray interior, black base, "Transit" (red & black print) tempa ($75+)(UK)(LD)
76. silver-gray body, gray interior, black base, "Transit" (red & blue print) tempa ($75+)(UK)(LD)
77. white body, gray interior, black base, "Delta Precision Ltd." Tempa ($12-15)(UK)(LD)
78. white body, white interior, black base, "Bell South Americast" tempa ($100+)(ASAP)
79. white body, gray interior, black base, "Trophy Gold Pet Foods" tempa ($12-15)(UK)(LD)
80. white body, gray interior, black base, "Disaster Care" tempa ($12-15)(UK)(LD)
81. white body, gray interior, black base, "Grime Busters" tempa ($12-15)(UK)(LD)
82. white body, gray interior,, black base, "www rent-a-van" tempa ($12-15)(UK)(LD)
83. white body, gray interior, black base, "Siemen's" tempa ($12-15)(UK)(LD)
84. white body, gray interior, black base, "The Sunrise Coast" tempa ($12-15)(UK)(LD)
85. silver-gray body, gray interior, black base, "The Sunrise Coast" tempa ($15-20)(UK)(LD)
86. silver-gray body, gray interior, black base, "Daybreak at Lowestoft/ The Sunrise Coast" tempa ($15-20)(UK)(LD)
87. white body, gray interior, black base, "Daybreak at Lowestoft/ The Sunrise Coast" tempa ($12-15)(UK)(LD)
88. white body, gray interior, black base, "Kingston Communications" tempa ($12-15)(UK)(LD)
89. white body, gray interior, black base, "Welcoming the New Millennium" (red print) tempa ($15-20)(UK)(LD)
90. white body, gray interior, black base, "Welcoming the New Millennium" (black print) tempa ($15-20)(UK)(LD)
91. white body, gray interior, black base, "Transit Ford/ NSVA/ Show & Shine" tempa ($15-20)(UK)(LD)
92. silver-gray body, gray interior, black base, "Transit Van/ NSVA Van/ Show & Shine" tempa ($50+)(UK)(LD)
93. white body, gray interior, black base, "Transit Ford/ C of C Ford/ Transit Plant Trip 2000" tempa ($15-20)(UK)(LD)
94. silver-gray body, gray interior, black base, "Transit Ford/ C of C Ford/ Transit Plant Trip 2000" tempa ($50+)(UK)(LD)
95. white body, gray interior, black base, "Council of Councils/ C of C The Old Ship" tempa ($15-20)(UK)(LD)
96. silver-gray body, gray interior, black base, "Council of Councils/ C of C The Old Ship" tempa ($50+) (UK)(LD)
97. white body, gray interior, black base, "Council of Councils/ I Did The Pub Crawl" tempa ($15-20)(UK)(LD)
98. silver-gray body, gray interior, black base, "Council of Councils/ I Did The Pub Crawl" tempa ($50+)(UK)(LD)
99. white body, gray interior, black base, "Councils of Councils/ France-Windsor-London-Stonehenge" tempa ($15-20)(UK)(LD)
100. silver-gray body, gray interior, black base, "Council of Councils/ France-Windsor-London-Stonehenge" tempa ($50+)(UK)(LD)
101. yellow body, black interior, yellow base, British flag with blue & red stripes tempa ($2-3)(MW13/2000 UK)
102. white body, gray interior, black base, "Web Force" tempa ($12-15)(UK)(LD)
103. white body, white interior, black base, "Citizens Communications" tempa ($25-40)(ASAP)
104. red & white body, black interior, white base, "Coca Cola" with hockey player bear tempa ($3-5)(FAO MP)(CK)
105. red & white body, black interior, white base, "Coca Cola" with 2 polar bears tempa ($15-20)(MW40/2000 GR)(CK)
106. white body, gray interior, black base, "Anglian Self Drive/ Norflex" tempa ($100+)(UK)(LD)
107. white body, gray interior, black base, "GCS Service Inc. Communications Food Service Equipment" tempa ($50+)(UK)(LD)
108. bright blue body, gray interior, black base, "SWAT/ Police 3" tempa, 10 spoke flower wheels ($1-2)(5pk)
109. white (repainted) body, cream interior, black base, "Pilsner-Urquell" tempa ($25-40)(C2)
110. silver-gray body, red interior, black base, "Coca Cola" tempa, lace wheels, Mattel casting ($1-3)(CK)
111. white body, white interior, black base, "Animal Control" tempa ($75+)(ASAP)
112. bright blue body, black interior, black base, "24 Hour Roofing 555-ROOF" tempa, 10 spoke flower wheels ($1-2)(MW50/2002 US)
NOTE: Above model with Matchbox International or Mattel casting.
113. bright blue body, black interior, black base, "24 Hour Roofing 555-ROOF" & "Matchbox 50" tempa, 10 spoke flower wheels ($10-15)(MW50/2002 US)

114. white body, white interior, black base, "Comcast" tempa ($75+)(ASAP)
115. cream (repainted) body, red interior, black base, "Staropramen" tempa ($25-40)(C2)(CZ)
116. cream (repainted) body, red interior, black base, lace wheels, "Staropramen" tempa ($25-40)(C2)(CZ)
117. cream (repainted) body, black interior, black base, "Staropramen" tempa ($25-40)(C2)(CZ)
118. cream (repainted) body, black interior, black base, lace wheels, "Staropramen" tempa ($25-40)(C2)(CZ)
119. metallic purple body, orange interior, amber windows, orange base, "Nickelodeon" tempa, 10 spoke flower wheels, Mattel casting ($1-2)(5pk)
120. light blue body, red interior, smoke windows, black base, paint bucket & roller design tempa, 10 spoke flower wheels, Mattel casting ($1-2)(MW29/2004 ROW)
121. white body, gray interior, black base, no tempa ($12-15)(LD blank)
122. white body, gray interior, black base, "Apetito Chefmobil" ($50+)(GR)(LD)
123. white body, gray interior, black base, "Lausitzer Rundschau" tempa ($50+)(GR)(LD)
124. white body, gray interior, black base, "Norgren" tempa ($50+)(GR)(LD)
125. white body, white interior, black base, "Nationwide Floor & Window" tempa ($50+)(ASAP)
126. white body, white interior, black base, "Ermco" tempa ($50+)(ASAP)
127. white body, white interior, black base, "Yankee Security Convention" tempa ($50+)(ASAP)
128. white body, white interior, black base, "Ridge Heating" tempa ($50+)(ASAP)
129. white body, white interior, black base, "Precision Air Cargo" tempa ($50+)(ASAP)
130. white body, gray interior, black base, "Hankook No. 1 Tyres" tempa ($15-20)(LD)(UK)
131. white body, white interior, black base, "I Climb the Tree-Bellsouth Americast" tempa ($50+)(ASAP)

MB15-L DAF 3300 SPACE CAB, issued 1999 (MB183/340)
NOTE: Issued in 1999 as a single release for the first time when normally associated with Convoy models which are not included in this list. Below model with black plastic base, blue windows, China casting.
1. orange body, black chassis, "DAF 3300 SC56" tempa ($2-3)(MW15/1999 ROW)(MW65/1999 GR)

MB15-M LITTER BUG, issued 2004 (USA)(MB651)
1. dark metallic maroon body, smoke windows, gold lace wheels, "Litter Bug" tempa, lime green plastic base, China casting ($1-2)(MW15/2004 US)

MB16-A BADGER, issued 1974
NOTE: Below models with maltese cross wheels, unpainted meta base & England casting.
1. bronze body, silver-gray base insert, green windows, chrome antennae ($8-10)
2. bronze body, light gray base insert, green windows, cream antennae ($4-6)
3. olive drab body, light gray base insert, green windows, cream antennae ($65-80)(TP)
4. olive body, light gray base insert, green windows, cream antennae ($5-7)(TP)
5. bronze body, dark gray base insert, green windows, cream antennae ($4-6)
6. bronze body, dark gray base insert, blue-green windows, cream antennae ($4-6)
7. bronze body, black base insert, blue-green windows, cream antennae ($4-6)
8. bronze body, black base insert, green windows, cream antennae ($4-6)
9. bronze body, black base insert, green windows, ivory antennae ($4-6)
10. bronze body, dark gray base insert, green windows, ivory antennae ($4-6)
11. bronze body, dark gray base insert, blue-green windows, black antennae ($4-6)
12. bronze body, dark gray base insert, green windows, black antennae ($4-6)
13. bronze body, black base insert, green windows, black antennae ($4-6)
14. bronze body, black base insert, purple windows, black antennae ($5-8)
15. bronze body, black base insert, blue-green windows, black antennae ($5-8)

MB16-B PONTIAC, issued 1979 (MB016)
NOTE: Below models with red interior, clear windows, metal base & England casting unless otherwise noted.
1. metallic tan body, unpainted base, dark tan hood label, dot dash wheels ($5-8)
2. metallic tan body, unpainted base, brown hood label, dot dash wheels ($5-8)
3. metallic light tan body, unpainted base, olive hood label, dot dash wheels ($5-8)
4. metallic tan body. unpainted base, chocolate hood label, dot dash wheels ($5-8)
5. green-gold body, unpainted base, olive hood label, dot dash wheels ($5-8)
6. green-gold body, unpainted base, olive hood label, 5 crown wheels ($5-8)
7. green-gold body, unpainted base, olive hood label, 5 arch wheels ($5-8)
8. green-gold body, unpainted base, no hood label, dot dash wheels ($5-8)
9. green-gold body, unpainted base, chocolate hood label, dot dash wheels ($5-8)
10. green-gold body, unpainted base, brown hood label, dot dash wheels ($5-8)
11. dark gold body, unpainted base, chocolate hood label, dot dash wheels ($5-8)
12 dark gold body, unpainted base, chocolate hood label, 5 arch wheels ($5-8)
13. dark gold body, unpainted base, olive hood label, 5 arch wheels ($5-8)
14. dark gold body, unpainted base, brown hood label, dot dash wheels ($5-8)
15. dark gold body, unpainted base, olive hood tempa, dot dash wheels ($5-8)
16. white body, unpainted base, blue hood tempa, dot dash wheels ($4-6)
17. white body, unpainted base, purple hood tempa, dot dash wheels ($4-6)
18. white body, unpainted base, no hood tempa, dot dash wheels ($4-6)
19. white body, silver-gray base, blue hood tempa, dot dash wheels ($4-6)
20. white body, silver-gray base, blue hood tempa, 5 crown wheels ($4-6)

21. white body, unpainted base, blue hood tempa, 5 arch wheels ($-6)
22. white body, pearly silver base, blue hood tempa, dot dash wheels, Macau casting ($4-6)
23. dark blue body, silver-gray base, no tempa, dot dash wheels, Manaus casting ($50-75)(BR)

NOTE: Available as a Bulgarian casting with "Universal Associated Co." cast on base. Assorted colors available ($5-25)

MB16-C PONTIAC T-ROOF *see MB35-C*

MB16-D F.1 RACER, issued 1984 (USA)(MB137)
MB 6-D F.1 RACER, issued 1984 (ROW)

NOTE: in 1985 an identical casting to MB 16-D was released in the USA only as MB65-D. Both models ran concurrently in the US range. Only certain variations appear on either model and are listed accordingly. ROW release models are listed here. Chrome and unchromed wheels refers to the lettering on the wheel sides. Versions 1-6 with chrome exhausts with all other versions having black exhausts.

1. red body, black metal base, black driver, black "Pirelli" airfoil, 5 arch front wheels, 8 dot chromed rear wheels, chrome exhausts, "Fiat 3" tempa, Macau casting ($2-4)
2. red body, black metal base, black driver, black "Pirelli" airfoil, 8 dot front wheels, racing special unchromed rear wheels, "Fiat 3" tempa, Macau casting ($2-4)
3. white/ orange/ green body, black metal base, yellow driver, yellow "Watson's" airfoil, 8 dot front wheels, racing special chromed rear wheels, "Mr. Juicy/ Sunkist" tempa, Macau casting ($20-25)(HK)
4. yellow body, black metal base, dark red driver, dark red "Goodyear" airfoil, 8 dot front wheels, racing special chromed rear wheels, "Matchbox Racing Team" tempa, Macau casting ($2-4)
5. white body, blue metal base, blue driver, blue "Shell" airfoil, 8 dot front wheels, racing special chromed rear wheels, "Matchbox/ Goodyear" tempa, Macau casting ($5-8)(KS)(GS)
6. white body, blue metal base, blue driver, blue "Shell" airfoil, 8 dot front wheels, racing special unchromed rear wheels, "Matchbox/ Goodyear" tempa, Macau casting ($5-8)(KS)(GS)
7. red body, black plastic base, black driver, black "Pirelli" airfoil, 8 dot front wheels, racing special unchromed rear wheels, "Fiat 3" tempa, Macau casting ($2-4)(KS)
8. white body, blue plastic base, blue driver, blue "Shell" airfoil, 8 dot front wheels, racing special unchromed rear wheels, "Matchbox/ Goodyear" tempa, Macau casting ($2-4)(GS)
9. white body, blue plastic base, blue driver, blue "Shell" airfoil, 8 dot front wheels, racing special unchromed rear wheels, "Matchbox/ Goodyear" tempa, Thailand casting ($2-4)(GS)
10. red body, black metal base, black driver, black "Pirelli" airfoil, 8 dot front wheels, racing special unchromed rear wheels, "Fiat 3" tempa, Macau casting ($2-4)(KS)
11. red body, black plastic base, black driver, black "Pirelli" airfoil, 8 dot front wheels, racing special unchromed rear wheels, "Fiat 3" tempa, China casting ($2-4)(KS)
12. white body, blue metal base, blue driver, blue "Shell" airfoil, 8 dot front wheels, racing special unchromed rear wheels, "Matchbox/ Goodyear" tempa, Macau casting ($2-4)(GS)(KS)

MB16-E FORD LTD POLICE CAR, issued 1987 (USA)(MB184)
MB51-H FORD LTD POLICE CAR, issued 1987 (ROW)

NOTE: Below models with white interior, blue windows, red/ blue dome lights, plastic base & 8 dot wheels unless otherwise noted.

1. white body, chrome base, "Police PD-21" tempa, Macau casting ($1-2)
2. dark purple body, chrome base, "Police PD-21" tempa, Macau casting ($3-4)(SC)
3. raspberry red body, chrome base, "Police PD-21" tempa, Macau casting ($3-4)(SC)
4. red body, chrome base, "Fire Dept. Fire Chief" tempa, Macau casting ($2-4)(MC)
5. red body, chrome base, "Fire Dept. Fire Chief" tempa, Thailand casting ($2-4)(MC)
6. white body, chrome base, "Police PD-21" tempa, Thailand casting ($1-2)
7. white body, chrome base, no tempa, Thailand casting ($10-15)(GF)
8. white body, blue base, Police face & cartoon figures tempa, 8 dot red wheels, Thailand casting ($6-8)(LL)
9. dark blue body, chrome base, "Police R-25" tempa, Thailand casting ($3-5)(TH)
10. white body, chrome base, "Police PD-21" without silver tempa on door shield, Thailand casting ($1-2)
11. white body, black base with bar code, "Police PD-21" & "Intercom City" tempa, Thailand casting ($10-15)(IC)
12. white body, chrome base, "Police PD-21" & "Intercom City" tempa, Thailand casting ($10-15)
13. white body, chrome base, "17 Police" tempa, Thailand casting ($1-2)(5pk)
14. white body, blue base, Police face & cartoon figures tempa, 8 dot yellow wheels, Thailand casting ($12-15)(LL)
15. blue body, chrome base, "Police 16" & white band tempa, Thailand casting ($2-4)(CC)
16. black body, chrome base, "Police Unit 3" & gold star tempa, Thailand casting ($1-2)(5pk)
17. red body, chrome base, "Fire Chief" & "FD No. 1" in gold crest, Thailand casting ($1-2)(5pk)
18. white body, chrome base, "Police PD-21" with blue background tempa, Thailand casting ($4-6)
19. white body, chrome base, blue "Police" & star logo tempa, Thailand casting ($1-2)(5pk)
20. metallic blue body, chrome base, "State Police SP16" tempa, Thailand casting ($1-2)
21. metallic gold body, chrome base, no tempa, Thailand casting ($10-15)(CH)

NOTE: Versions 22& 23 with all blue dome lights and chrome disc wheels with rubber tires.

22. black & tan body, white & black interior, chrome base, "Florida State Trooper" tempa, Thailand casting ($3-5)(PC8)
23. dark blue & gray body, white & black interior, chrome base, "State Police Virginia" tempa, Thailand casting ($3-5)(PC8)
24. white body, clear windows, gray & black interior, red dome lights, chrome base, "State Police New Jersey" tempa, chrome disc wheels with rubber tires, Thailand casting ($3-5)(PC8)
25. blue body, clear windows, chrome base, "Unit 22 Police" with white band tempa, Thailand casting ($1-2)(5pk)
26. metallic brown-gold body, chrome base, "Sheriff S-27" tempa, Thailand casting ($1-2)
27. white body, chrome base, "Sheriff S-27" tempa, Thailand casting ($1-2)(MW24/1998 US)
28. white body, chrome base, "Sheriff S-27" tempa, China casting ($1-2)(MW24/1998 US)
29. white body, chrome base, "Sheriff S-27" tempa, 5 spoke concave star wheels, China casting ($15-20)(MW24/1998 US)
30. blue body, clear windows, chrome base, "Unit 22 Police" & white band tempa, China casting ($1-2)(5pk)

31. silver-gray body, silver-gray interior, chrome base, "Police" with shield & red design tempa, China casting ($1-2)(5pk)
32. silver-gray body, white interior, chrome base., "Police" with shield & red design tempa, China casting ($1-2)(5pk)
33. white body, white interior, chrome base, "Corvettes Unlimited Salutes/ Vineland Police NJ" tempa, China casting ($75+)(CCI)
34. black & white body, white interior, chrome base, "42" in crest tempa, China casting ($5-8)(MW24/1999 GR)(MW15/2000 GR)
35. white body, silver-gray interior, chrome base, "Ridge NY Police" tempa, China casting ($1-2)(MW2/1999 US)

MB16-F LAND ROVER NINETY *see MB35-F*

MB16-G SCHOOL BUS, issued 2001 (USA)(MB482)

NOTE: Below models with clear windows, 4 spoke domed wheels, black plastic base, China casting.

1.orange-yellow body, dark red interior, "Burton Hill Elementary Buffalos" with black grille tempa ($1-2)(MW16/2001 US))
2. orange-yellow body, dark red interior, "Burton Hill Elementary Buffalos" with plain grille tempa ($1-2)(MW16/2001 US)
3. orange-yellow body, dark green interior, "History" & small emblems tempa ($1-2)(5pk)
4. orange-yellow body, red interior, "Bulldogs Football State Champs 2002" tempa ($1-2)(MW69/2002 US)
5. orange-yellow body, red interior, "Bulldogs Football State Champs 2002" & "Matchbox 50" tempa ($3-5)(MW69/2002 US)
6. orange-yellow body, green interior, "East Lake High School Spartans Cheerleading Squad" tempa ($3-5)(SNL)
7. orange-yellow body, red interior, "Hero City Elementary Bears 52" tempa ($1-2)(MW52/2003 US)
8. orange-yellow body, red interior, "Hero City Elementary Bears 52" & "Hero City" tempa ($75+)(MW52/2003 US)
9. orange-yellow body, green interior, none tempa, chrome disc wheels with rubber tires ($3-5)(CCI blank)
10. orange-yellow body, green interior,, "Camp Sunshine" tempa, chrome disc wheels with rubber tires $12-18)(CCI)
11. orange-yellow body, green interior, "York Fair 2003" tempa, chrome disc with rubber tires ($6-8)(US)
12. iridescent white body, red interior, "Hero City Elementary Metro Alarm" tempa, gold 4 spoke domed wheels ($3-4)(20pk)

MB16-H CAR CARRIER, issued 2003 (MB576)

NOTE: Below models with plastic base & China casting unless otherwise noted.

1. orange body, dark gray ramp, blue windows, truck design & "16" tempa, 4 spoke domed wheels, black base ($1-2)(MW16/2003)
2. orange body, dark gray ramp, blue windows, truck design, "16" & "Hero City" tempa, 4 spoke domed wheels, black base ($2-4)(MW16/2003)
3. dull green cab, black ramp, black windows, smashing cars & chain link tempa, 5 crown dot wheels, dirty gray base ($1-2)(MW60/2004)
4. bright blue body, yellow ramp, red windows, "Police" tempa, 5 crown dot wheels, black base ($1-2)(5pk)

MB16-I DUMP TRUCK 2004, issued 2003 (USA)(MB623)

NOTE: Below models with chrome windows, 5 spoke oval wheels & China casting.

1. lemon body, black dump, gold hubs, nondescript design with wrecking ball tempa, gray base ($1-2)
2. orange-yellow body, dark blue dump, chrome hubs, blue & white design with red dots tempa, black base ($1-2)(5pk)

MB16-J 1965 SHELBY COBRA 427 A/C, issued 2004 (SF) (MB587)

NOTE: Below models with black interior & black plastic base unless otherwise noted.

1. blue body, full windscreen, dual white stripes tempa, chrome disc wheels with rubber tires ($3-5)(BJ)
2. red body, full windscreen, white stripes tempa, chrome disc wheels with rubber tires ($3-5)(BJ)
3. pearl white body, full windscreen, blue stripes tempa, 5 spoke slotted wheels ($3-5)(SF16/2004)

MB17-A HORSE BOX, issued 1970

NOTE: Below models with two white plastic horses, blue windows, chrome plastic cab base, 5 spoke wheels & England casting.

1. red body, green box, gray door ($25-40)
2. red-orange body, green box, gray door ($25-40)
3. mustard body, green box, gray door ($20-35)
4. red-orange body, light gray box, light brown door ($20-35)
5. light orange body, light gray box, light brown door ($20-35)
6. red-orange body, light gray box, gray door ($20-25)

MB17-B THE LONDONER, issued 1972

NOTE: Following models with 5 spoke wheel, white interior & England casting unless otherwise noted. Type 1 labels have the "A" in" Carnaby" differently configured than in type 2. Type 1= α Type 2= a

1. red body, black metal base, "Swinging London" (type 1) labels ($8-12)
2. red body, black metal base, "Swinging London" (type 2) labels ($8-12)
3. red body, charcoal metal base, "Swinging London" (type 2) labels ($8-12)
4. red body, unpainted metal base with screw mounts cast, "Swinging London" (type 1) labels ($18-25)(GW)
5. gold plated body, unpainted metal base with screw mounts cast, "Swinging London" (type 1) labels ($750-1000)(GW)
6. gold plated body, unpainted metal base with screw mounts cast, "Berger Paints" labels ($750-1000)(GW)
7. silver plated body, unpainted metal base with screw mounts cast, "Swinging London" (type 1) labels ($750-1000)(GW)
8. silver plated body, unpainted metal base with screw mounts cast, "Berger Paints" labels ($750-1000)(GW)
9. red body, black metal base, "Preston Guild Merchant 1972" labels ($150-200)(UK)(LE)
10. red body, black metal base, "London/ Kensington Hilton" labels ($150-200)(UK)(LE)
11. red body, unpainted metal base, "London/ Kensington Hilton" labels ($150-200)(UK)(LE)
12. red body, black metal base, "Barclays Bank" labels ($125-175)(UK)(LE)
13. red body, black metal base, "Charbonnier Wine" labels ($75-100)(C2)(UK)
14. red body, black metal base, "Typhoo Tea" labels ($250-350)(CN)
15. red body, black metal base, "Impel 73" labels ($50-75)(UK)(LE)
16. red body, unpainted metal base, "Impel 73" labels ($50-75)(UK)(LE)
17. red body, black metal base, "Neil's Wheels" labels ($75-100)(C2)
18. red body, black metal base, "Berger Paints" labels ($8-12)
19. red body, unpainted metal base, "Berger Paints" labels ($8-12)
20. red body, black metal base "ICP Interchemicals & Plastics" labels ($750+)(LE)

21. red body, black metal base, "Borregaard Paper" labels ($750+)(LE)
22. red body, black metal base, "Sellotape Selbstklebebander" labels ($750+)(AS)(LE)
23. red body, black metal base, "Sellotape Packaging Systems/ 01-952-2345"" labels ($150-200)(UK)(LE)
24. red body, black metal base, "Sellotape Electrical Tapes/ 01-952-2345"" labels ($750+)(UK)(LE)
25. red body, black metal base, "Sellotape International Operations" labels ($750+)(UK)(LE)
26. red body, black metal base, "Sellotape Packaging Systems/ 611089-9" ($150-200)(IR)
27. red body, black metal base, "Chambourcy Yogurt" labels ($85-110)(FR)(OP)
28. red body, black metal base, "Esso Extra Petrol" labels ($35-50)
29. coffee & cream body, black metal base, "Berger Paints" labels ($175-250)
30. coffee & cream body, black metal base, "Impel 76" labels ($85-110)(UK)(LE)
31. red body, black metal base, "Impel 76" labels ($175-250)(UK)(LE)
32. red body, black metal base, "Selfridges" labels ($60-75)(UK)
33. red body, unpainted metal base, "Selfridges" labels ($60-75)(UK)(LE)
34. red body, black metal base, "Aviemore Centre/ Santa Claus Land" labels ($65-80)(UK)(LE)
35. red body, black metal base, "C Amcel" labels ($175-225)(UK)(LE)
36. red body, black metal base, "Baron of Beef" labels ($175-225)(UK)(LE)
37. lemon & red body, black metal base with or without Manaus tab, "Swinging London" (type 2) labels ($350-500)(BR)
38. red body, black metal base, "A.I.M. Building Fund 1976" labels ($40-60)(US)(LE)

NOTE: The following models are with dot dash wheels.

39. red body, black metal base, "A.I.M. Building Fund 1976" labels ($40-60)(US)(LE)
40. red body, charcoal metal base, "Berger Paints" labels ($6-8)
41. red body, black metal base, "Berger Paints" labels ($6-8)
42. red body, unpainted metal base, "Berger Paints" labels ($6-8)
43. red body, black metal base, no labels ($6-8)

NOTE: Versions 44-48 with Manaus tab on base

44. white & red body, unpainted metal base, "Berger Paints" labels ($350-500)(BR)
45. yellow & red body, unpainted metal base, "Berger Paints" labels ($350-500)(BR)
46. white & blue body, unpainted metal base, "Berger Paints" labels ($500-750)(BR)
47. yellow & blue body, unpainted metal base, "Berger Paints" labels ($500-750)(BR)
48. metallic red body, unpainted metal base, "Lufthansa" labels ($500-750)(BR)
49. red body, black metal base, "Army & Navy" labels ($50-65)(UK)
50. red body, charcoal metal base, "Army & Navy" labels ($60-65)(UK)
51. red body, black metal base, "Eduscho Kaffee" labels ($500-750)(GR)
52. orange body, black metal base, "Berger Paints" labels ($125-175)
53. orange body, black metal base, "Jacob's- The Biscuit Makers" labels ($25-40)(IR)
54. orange body, charcoal metal base, "Jacob's- The Biscuit Makers" labels ($25-40)(IR)
55. red body, charcoal metal base, "Jacob's- The Biscuit Makers" labels ($65-80)(IR)
56. red body, black metal base, "Jacob's- The Biscuit Makers" labels ($65-80)(IR)
57. red body, black metal base, "Ilford Hp5 Film" labels ($350-500)(LE)
58. red body, black metal base, "Museum of London" labels ($50-65)(UK)
59. red body, unpainted metal base, "Museum of London" labels ($50-65)(UK)
60. red body, charcoal metal base, "Museum of London" labels ($50-65)(UK)
61. red body, black metal base, "Silver Jubilee" labels ($175-225)(UK)

NOTE: Versions 62-66 with red interiors.

62. silver-gray body, charcoal metal base, "Silver Jubilee" labels ($10-15)(UK)
63. silver-gray body, unpainted metal base, "Silver Jubilee" labels ($10-15)(UK)
64. silver-gray body, charcoal metal base, "Berger Paints" labels ($75-100)
65. silver-gray body, unpainted metal base, "Berger Paints" labels ($75-100)
66. silver-gray body, charcoal metal base, "Matchbox 1953-1978" labels ($250-300)
67. blue body, charcoal metal base, "Deutschlands Autopartner" labels ($35-50)(GR)
68. blue body, black metal base, "Deutschlands Autopartner" labels ($35-50)(GR)
69. blue body, black metal base, "Matchbox 1953- 1978" labels ($35-50)
70. blue body, charcoal metal base, "Matchbox 1953- 1978" labels ($35-50)
71. orange body, charcoal metal base, "Matchbox 1953- 1978" labels ($75-100)
72. red body, black metal base, "Matchbox 1953- 1978" labels ($6-8)
73. red body, black metal base, "Busch Gardens" labels ($40-65)(US)
74. red body, brown metal base, "Berger Paints" labels ($7-10)
75. red body, charcoal metal base, "Berger Paints" labels ($6-8)
76. red body, gray metal base, "Berger Paints" labels ($6-8)
77. red body, black metal base, "The Bisto Bus" labels ($8-12)(UK)(OP)
78. red body, black plastic base, "The Bisto Bus" labels ($8-12)(UK)(OP)
79. red body, black plastic base, "Berger Paints" labels ($6-8)
80. red body, black metal base, "3rd A.I.M. Inc. Convention & Toy Show 1979" labels ($25-40)(C2)
81. red body, brown metal base, "The Bisto Bus" labels ($8-12)(UK)(OP)
82. red body, charcoal metal base, "Aviemore Centre/ Santa Claus Land" tempa ($65-80)(UK)
83. red body, "Matchbox Collectors Club 1997- Hershey 1997" labels ($15-25)(CCI)

NOTE: The above model has been recorded with at least nine (9) different base variations.

84. red body, black metal base, "Old Country Bush Gardens" labels ($18-25)(US)
85. red body, black metal base, "Deutschlands Autopartner" labels ($85-110)(GR)

MB17-C LONDON BUS, issued 1982 ()!&)
MB51-F LONDON BUS, reissued 1985 (USA)
MB28-F LONDON BUS, reissued 1990 (USA)

NOTE: Below models listed with white interior, dot dash wheels & black plastic base unless otherwise noted.

1. red upper & lower body, "Berger Paints" labels, England casting ($10-15)
2. red upper & lower body, "Laker Skytrain" labels, England casting ($7-10)
3. white upper body & powder blue lower body, "Matchbox London Bus" labels, England casting ($175-250)(UK)
4. white upper body, powder blue lower body, "Matchbox No. 1/ Montepna" labels, England casting ($25-40)(GK)
5. red upper & lower body, "Matchbox No. 1/ Montepna" labels, England casting ($175-250)(GK)
6. red upper & lower body, "Chesterfield Centenary" labels, England casting ($175-250)(UK)
7. dark green upper & lower body, "Chesterfield Centenary" labels, England casting ($10-15)(UK)
8. red upper & lower body, "Matchbox London Bus" labels, England casting ($3-5)
9. red upper & lower body, "Matchbox London Bus" labels, brown base, England casting ($10-15)

10 red upper & lower body, "Nice To Meet You! Japan 1984" labels, England casting ($15-20)(JP)

11 red upper & lower body, " 世界のダブルデッカー展 ㊋横浜松坂屋 2階バス運行記念 1984 " labels, England casting ($15-20)(JP)

12 red upper & lower body, "York Festival & Mystery Plays" labels, England casting ($10-15)(UK)

13. dark blue upper & lower body, "Nestles Milkybar" labels, England casting ($10-15)(UK)
14. dark green upper & lower body, "Rowntrees Fruit Gums" labels, England casting ($10-15)(UK)
15. dark blue upper & lower body, "Keddies No. 1 in Essex" labels, England casting ($40-65)(UK)
16. maroon upper & lower body, "Rapport" labels, England casting ($8-12)(UK)
17. white upper body, black lower body, "Torvale Fisher Engineering Co." labels, England casting ($8-12)(UK)
18. white upper body, orange lower body, "WH Smith Travel" labels, England casting ($10-15)(UK)
19. red upper & lower body, "Matchbox London Bus" labels, Macau casting ($3-4)
20. red upper & lower body, "Nestles Milkybar" labels, Macau casting ($10-15)
21. red upper & lower body, "Rowntrees Fruit Gums" labels, Macau casting ($10-15)
22. red upper & lower body, You'll ♥ New York" labels, Macau casting ($2-4)
23. blue upper body, white lower body, "Space for Youth 1985/ Staffordshire Police" labels, Macau casting ($8-12)(UK)
24. blue upper & lower body, "Sightseeing- Cityrama" labels, Macau casting ($8-12)
25. red upper & lower body, no labels, England casting ($3-5)
26. red upper & lower body, "You'll ♥ New York" labels, China casting ($2-4)
27. red upper & lower body, "Nuremberg 1986" labels, Macau casting ($100-150)(GR)
28. red upper & lower body, "1st M.I.C.A. Convention" labels, Macau casting ($250-300)(UK)
29. red upper & lower body, "1st M.I.C.A. Convention" labels, England casting ($250-300)(UK)
30. red upper & lower body, "1st M.I.C.A. Convention" labels, China casting ($250-300)(UK)
31. red upper & lower body, "Around London Tour Bus" labels, China casting ($2-3)
32. blue upper & lower body, "National Tramway Museum" labels, China casting ($8-12)(UK)
33. white upper body, dull red lower body, "Midland Bus Transport Museum" labels, China casting ($8-12)(UK)
34. dull red upper & lower body, "Band-Aid Plasters Playbus" labels, China casting ($8-12)(UK)(OP)
35. blue upper & lower body, "National Girobank" labels, China casting ($8-12)(UK)
36. red upper & lower body, "Matchbox- Niagara Falls" labels, China casting ($6-8)(CN)
37. red upper & lower body, "Feria Del Juguete Valencia, 12 Febrero 1987" labels, China casting ($175-225)(SP)
38. beige upper body, blue lower body, tan interior, "West Midlands Travel" labels, China casting ($8-12)(UK)
39. white upper & lower body, red interior, "M.I.C.A. Matchbox International Collectors Association" labels, China casting ($8-12)(UK)
40. white upper body, white & dark blue lower body, "Denny-Happy 1000th Birthday, Dublin" labels, China casting ($8-12)(IR)
41. red upper & lower body, orange-yellow interior, orange-yellow wheels with blue hubs, "123 abc" sides tempa & "My First Matchbox Nuremberg 1990" roof tempa, China casting ($10-15)(GR)
42. red upper & lower body, orange-yellow interior, orange-yellow wheels with blue hubs, "123 abc" sides tempa & teddy bear with "abc" roof tempa, China casting ($6-8)(LL)
43. red upper & lower body, no labels, China casting ($4-6)
44. yellow upper & lower body, "It's The Real Thing- Coke" labels, China casting ($12-18)(CN)
45. maroon upper & lower body, "Corning Glass Center" labels, China casting ($8-12)(US)
46. chrome plated upper & lower body, "Celebrating A Decade of Matchbox Conventions" labels, China casting ($25-40)(C2)
47. red upper & lower body, "Markfield Project Support Appeal 92" labels, China casting ($15-20)(UK)
48. red upper & lower body, "London Wide Tour Bus" labels, China casting ($1-2)
49. white upper & lower body, white base, no labels, China casting ($10-15)(GF)
50. red upper & lower body, orange-yellow interior & wheels (plain hubs), "123 abc" sides tempa & teddy bear with "abc" roof tempa, China casting ($6-8)(LL)
51. red upper & lower body, white interior, "Takashimaya" labels, China casting ($100-125) (JP)
52. red upper & lower body, white interior, "35/ ГОДИНИ РАЗНОИЗНОС Matchbox London Bus" labels, China casting ($175-250)(Bulgaria)
53. white upper & lower body, white interior, no labels, China casting ($20-25)(ASAP-blank)
54. white upper & lower body, white interior, "American International Recovery" (on roof) tempa, China casting ($100+)(ASAP)
55. white upper & lower body, white interior, "RCA" (on roof) tempa , China casting ($20-30)(ASAP)
56. orange upper & lower body, white interior, "Fanta" labels (sides) & "Enjoy Fanta" (roof) tempa, China casting ($100+)(CHI)
57. red upper & lower body, white interior, black & white stripes & scenic design tempa, Mattel China casting ($1-2)(MW74)
58. red upper & lower body, white interior, black & white stripes & scenic design tempa & "Matchbox 2000" tempa, Mattel China casting ($2-4)(MW74)
59. red upper & lower body, white interior, "Scansource & Symbol" (roof) tempa, China casting ($50+)(ASAP)

60. red upper & lower body, white interior, "www.citrix.com/cdn" (sides) & "Citrix Meta Frame For Unix Operating Systems" (roof) tempa, Mattel China casting ($50+)(ASAP)
61. red upper & lower body, white interior , www.mbxroad.com (sides) & "Matchbox Road Museum" (roof) tempa, England casting ($15-25)(CCI)
62. red upper & lower body, white interior, black & white stripes & scenic design tempa, China casting ($1-2)
63. red upper & lower body, very pale gray interior , "Union Jack Tours" tempa, dark blue base, China (Mattel) casting ($1-2)
64. red upper & lower body, very pale gray interior, "Union Jack Tours" & "Matchbox 50" tempa, dark blue base, Mattel China casting ($2-4)
65. red upper & lower body, white interior, "Tour New York- Matchbox USA" labels, Macau casting ($18-25)(CCI)
66. chrome plated upper & lower body, white interior, "Tour New York- Matchbox USA" labels ($50-75)(CCI)
67. red upper & lower body, white interior, black & white stripes & scenic design/ Kiddie Kar Kollectibles Take A Ride To Reading, PA" tempa, China (Mattel) casting ($10-15)(CCI)
68. red upper & lower body, very pale gray interior, "Union Jack Tours/ Kiddie Kar Kollectibles Take A Ride to Reading, PA" tempa, Mattel China casting ($10-15)(CCI)
69. red upper & lower body, white interior, no tempa, Mattel China casting ($8-12)(ASAP blank)

MB17-D AMX PROSTOCKER, issued 1983 (USA)(MB117)
MB 9-E AMX PROSTOCKER, issued 1983 (ROW)

NOTE: Below models with clear windows.

1. pearly silver body, black metal base, 5 arch wheels, red interior, red & black stripes with "AMX" tempa, Macau casting ($2-4)
2. pearly silver body, black metal base, dot dash wheels, red interior, red & black stripes with "AMX" tempa, Macau casting ($2-4)
3. maroon body, black metal base, dot dash wheels, black interior, "Dr. Pepper" tempa, Macau casting ($5-8)
4. maroon body, black plastic base, dot dash wheels, black interior, "Dr. Pepper" tempa, Macau casting ($5-8)
5. silver-gray body, black plastic base, dot dash wheels, black interior, red & black stripes with "AMX" tempa, China casting ($8-10)(MP)

NOTE: Available as a Hungarian and Bulgarian casting. Assorted colors available ($5-20).

MB17-E FORD ESCORT CABRIOLET, issued 1985 (USA)(MB156)
MB37-G FORD ESCORT CABRIOLET, issued 1985 (ROW)

NOTE: Below models with clear windows, gray interior, black tonneau & bumpers

1. white body & base, 8 dot silver wheels, no tow hook, "XR3i" tempa, Macau casting ($2-4)
2. white body & base, 8 dot gold wheels, no tow hook, "XR3i" tempa, Macau casting ($4-6)
3. white body & base, starburst wheels, no tow hook, "3" with stripes tempa, Macau casting ($3-5)(SF)
4. white body & base, 5 arch wheels, no tow hook, "XR3i" tempa, Macau casting ($2-4)
5. red body & base, 8 dot silver wheels, no tow hook, "XR3i" & "Ford" tempa, Macau casting ($8-12)
6. white body & base, 8 dot silver wheels, with tow hook, "XR3i" tempa, Macau casting ($2-4)(TP)
7. white body & base, 8 dot white wheels, with tow hook, "XR3i" tempa, Macau casting ($3-5)
8. metallic blue body & base, laser wheels, with tow hook, "3" with stripes tempa, Macau casting ($3-5)(LW)
9. white body & base, starburst wheels, with tow hook, "3" with stripes tempa, Macau casting ($3-5)(SF)
10. dark blue body & base, 8 dot silver wheels, with tow hook, "XR3i" tempa, Macau casting ($2-3)(TP)
11. white body & base, 8 dot silver wheels, with tow hook, "XR3i" tempa, Thailand casting ($2-3)(TP)
12. dark blue body & base, 8 dot silver wheels, with tow hook, "XR3i" tempa, Thailand casting ($2-3)(TP)
13. metallic blue body & base, 8 dot silver wheels, with tow hook, white & orange spatter tempa, Thailand casting ($2-3)(TP)
14. white body & base, 8 dot silver wheels, with tow hook, "XR3i " tempa, China casting ($2-4)
15. white body & base, red interior, 8 dot silver wheels, with tow hook, "Ocean Explorer" tempa ($1-2)(5pk)

MB17-F DODGE DAKOTA, issued 1987 (USA)(MB186)
MB50-F DODGE DAKOTA, issued 1990 (ROW)

NOTE: Below models with 8 spoke wheels & plastic base unless otherwise noted.

1. bright red body, chrome base, chrome rollbar, black interior, clear windows, black & white stripes (plain sides) tempa, Macau casting ($3-5)
2. bright red body, chrome base, chrome rollbar, black interior, clear windows, black & white stripes & "Dakota ST" tempa, Macau casting ($1-2)
3. dark red body, chrome base, black rollbar, black interior, clear windows, black & white stripes & "Dakota ST" tempa, China casting ($1-2)
4. metallic green body, chrome base, black rollbar, black interior, clear windows, "MB Construction" & stripes tempa, China casting ($3-5)(AP)
5. white body, chrome base, white rollbar, white interior, blue windows, no tempa, China casting ($10-15)(GF)
6. blue body, chrome base, black rollbar, black interior, clear windows, black & white stripes & "Dakota ST" tempa, China casting ($8-12)(GS)
7. florescent orange body, black base with bar code, white rollbar, white interior, clear windows, "Fire Chief 1- Intercom City" tempa, China casting ($10-15)(IC)
8. fluorescent orange body, chrome base, white rollbar, white interior, clear windows, "Fire Chief 1- Intercom City" tempa, China casting ($12-15)
9. purple body, chrome base, chrome rollbar, gray interior, clear windows, neon yellow & pink stripes tempa, China casting ($1-2)(5pk)
10. olive body, black base, black rollbar, black interior, blue windows, white bands tempa, 5 crown wheels with black hubs, China casting ($25-35)(CHI)(MP)
11. olive body, chrome base, chrome rollbar, gray interior, clear windows, white bands tempa, 5 crown wheels, China casting ($35-50)(CHI)(MP)
12. lemon body, chrome base, black rollbar, black interior, clear windows, "Highway Crew- Crew Chief" tempa ($1-2)(5pk)
13. black & gray body, gray base, black rollbar, black interior, clear windows, door logo & gray spots tempa, China casting ($1-2)(5pk)
14. black & gray body, gray base, black rollbar, black interior, clear windows, "Hershey 99" (silver print) tempa, China casting ($8-12)(CCI)
15. black & gray body, gray base, black rollbar, black interior, clear windows, "Hershey 99" (gold print) tempa, China casting ($8-12)(CCI)

NOTE: Below models with 7 spoke sawblade wheels & Mattel China casting.

16. metallic bronze body, gray base, silver-gray rollbar, gray interior, smoke windows, "Lonestar Texas" tempa ($5-8)(AM)
17. red body, gray base, blue rollbar, blue interior, smoke windows, "Marshall 28 Texas" tempa ($1-2)(AM)
18. metallic blue body, red interior, gray base, red rollbar, smoke windows, monkey & wrench tempa ($1-2)(5pk)
19. pink body, white interior, purple base, red rollbar, amber windows, "Sandy" tempa ($1-2)(5pk)
20. red body, white interior, orange base, blue rollbar, amber windows, "Sandy" tempa ($1-2)(5pk)

MB17-G FERRARI 456GT, issued 1994 (USA)(MB263)
MB41-J FERRARI 456GT, issued 1994 (ROW)

NOTE: Below models with black plastic base.

1. blue body, tan interior, clear windows, "456GT" tempa, gold 6-spoke spiral wheels, China casting ($1-2)
2. dark purple body, neon yellow interior, clear windows, white design on hood, roof, trunk & sides tempa, silver 6-spoke spiral wheels, China casting ($1-2)
3. dark purple body, neon yellow interior, clear windows, white design on sides only tempa, silver 6-spoke spiral wheels, China casting ($1-2)
4. metallic red body, brown interior, clear windows, no tempa, silver 6 spoke spiral wheels China casting ($2-4)
5. metallic gold body, black interior, clear windows, no tempa, silver 6 spoke spiral wheels, China casting ($10-15)(CH)
6. metallic red body, brown interior, clear windows, no tempa, 5 spoke concave star wheels, China casting ($1-2)
7. dark purple body, gray interior, clear windows, "Matchbox Racing Rush 11" tempa, 5 spoke concave star wheels, China casting ($1-2)
8. red body, black & brown interior, clear windows, small "Ferrari" logo & detailed trim tempa, chrome disc with rubber tires, Thailand casting ($3-5)(PC2-JC)
9. dark metallic red body, black interior, clear windows, "Ferrari" logo tempa, 5 spoke concave star wheels, China casting ($1-2)
10. black body, black & tan interior, clear windows, detailed trim tempa, chrome disc wheels with rubber tires, China casting ($3-5)(PC15)
11. red body, black interior, clear windows, small hood logo tempa, 5 spoke concave star wheels, China casting ($2-3)(MW29/1999 GR)
12. metallic sand body, brown interior, smoke windows, small hood logo tempa, 5 spoke concave star wheels, China casting ($1-2)(MW82/2000 US)(MW62/2000 ROW)
13. metallic sand body, brown interior, smoke windows, small hood logo & "Matchbox 2000" tempa, 5 spoke concave star wheels, China casting ($2-4)(MW82/2000 US)
14. metallic sand body, brown interior, smoke windows, small logo tempa, 10 spoke flower wheels, China casting ($10-15)(MW82/2000 US)((MW62/2000 ROW))
15. lemon body, black interior, smoke windows, small "Matchbox" logo tempa, lace wheels, China casting ($2-3)(MW18/2001 ROW)
16. metallic red body, black interior, clear windows, no tempa, gold 6 spoke spiral wheels, China casting ($50+)(CHI)
17. metallic red body, gray interior, clear windows, no tempa, gold 6 spoke spiral wheels, China casting ($50+)(CHI)

MB17-H FORD AMBULANCE *see MB51-K*

MB17-I '99 FORD MUSTANG, issued 1999 (USA)(MB367)
MB68-P '99 FORD MUSTANG, issued 2000 (ROW)

NOTE: Below models with clear windows, black plastic base & China casting unless otherwise noted.

1. red body & roof, tan interior, chrome disc wheels with rubber tires, detailed trim tempa ($5-8)(FE)
2. unpainted body & roof, tan interior, chrome disc wheels with rubber tires, no tempa ($5-8)(FE)
3. orange & white body, orange roof, black interior, 5 spoke concave star wheels (black hubs), "Matchbox 2/ Mattel Wheels" tempa ($12-18)(MW8 MX)
4. black body & roof, black interior, 5 spoke concave star wheels, dual white stripes tempa ($1-2)(5pk)
5. metallic green body & roof, tan interior, 5 spoke concave star wheels, painted lights & "Matchbox 2000" tempa ($2-4)(MW17/2000 US)
6. metallic green body & roof, tan interior, 5 spoke concave star wheels, painted lights tempa ($1-2)(MW17/2000 US)
7. metallic green body & roof, tan interior, star with 5 spokes wheels, painted lights tempa ($1-2)(MW17/2000 US)
8. red body & roof, tan interior, chrome disc wheels with rubber tires, "MDM Online/ Matchbox" tempa ($18-25)(C2)
9. unpainted body & roof, tan interior, chrome disc wheels with rubber tires, "MDM Online/ Matchbox" tempa ($18-25)(C2)
10. red body & roof, black interior, 5 spoke concave star wheels, "Coca Cola" & polar bears tempa ($4-6)(TP-Avon)
11. red body & roof, black interior, 5 spoke concave star wheels (black hubs), "Coca Cola" & polar bears tempa ($8-12)(TP-Avon)
12. cream body & roof, blue interior, 5 spoke concave star wheels, "Scooby-Doo!/ Like Wow!/ Fred" tempa ($5-7)(WB)
13. red body & roof, black interior, chrome disc wheels with rubber tires, "Coca Cola", black hood & polar bears tempa ($6-8)(PC)
14. white body, clear windows, black interior, 5 spoke concave star wheels, "DARE/ West Feliciana" tempa ($3-5)(DR)
15. white body, unpainted roof, smoke windows, black interior, 5 spoke concave star wheels, red striping & "Mustang" tempa ($2-4)(MW68/2000 ROW)
16. black body & roof, black interior, star with 5 spokes wheels, dual white stripes tempa ($1-2)(5pk)
17. white body & roof, black interior, 10 spoke flower wheels, red & blue stripes, "Thirty-Fifth Anniversary" & "Mustang" tempa ($1-2)(MW3/2001)
18. white body, unpainted roof, smoke windows, black interior, 10 spoke flower wheels, red striping & "Mustang" tempa ($8-10)(MW68/2000 ROW)
19. white body & roof, black interior, gold lace wheels, red & blue stripes, "Thirty-fifth Anniversary" & "Mustang" (plain roof) tempa ($10-15)(EG)
20. white body & roof, black interior, star with 5 spokes wheels, red & blue stripes, "Thirty –fifth Anniversary" & "Mustang" (plain roof) tempa ($10-15)(EG)
21. white body & roof, black interior, 10 spoke flower wheels, red & blue stripes, "Thirty-fifth Anniversary" & "Mustang" (plain roof) tempa ($2-3)(EG)
22. black body, clear windows, gray interior, 10 spoke flower wheels, none tempa ($5-8)(ASAP/CCI blank)
23. black body, clear windows, gray interior, 10 spoke flower wheels, "Color Comp Demo Model Matchbox USA" (white print) tempa ($8-12)(CCI)
24. black body, clear windows, gray interior, 10 spoke flower wheels, "Color Comp Demo Model Matchbox USA" (yellow print) tempa ($8-12)(CCI)

25. black body, clear windows, gray interior, 10 spoke flower wheels, "Color Comp Demo Model Matchbox USA" (lime print) tempa ($8-12)(CCI)
26. white body & roof, clear windows, black interior, 10 spoke flower wheels, "Ceal & Charlie/ Mustang" tempa ($25-40)(CCI)
27. black body, clear windows, gray interior, 10 spoke flower wheels, "96.5 TIC FM" tempa ($12-18)(CCI)
28. black body, clear windows, gray interior, 10 spoke flower wheels, "RLOL/ Pacifico Auto Group 75th Anniversary/ Ford 100/75" tempa ($25-40)(CCI)
29. black body, clear windows, gray interior, 10 spoke flower wheels, "Matchbox New York 2002/ On Location" (blue print) tempa ($15-20)(CCI)
30. black body, clear windows, gray interior, 10 spoke flower wheels, "Matchbox New York 2002/ On Location" (pink print) tempa ($15-20)(CCI)
31. black body, clear windows, gray interior, 10 spoke flower wheels, "USS" tempa ($50+)(ASAP)
32. black body, clear windows, gray interior, 10 spoke flower wheels, "DARE/ Covington Police" tempa ($50+)(ASAP)
33. metallic orange body, clear windows, black interior, lace wheels, "Mustang 53" tempa ($2-4)(MW53/2003 ROW)
34. metallic orange body, clear windows, black interior, lace wheels, "Mustang 53" & "Hero City" tempa ($4-6)(MW53/2003 ROW)
35. metallic red body, smoke windows, light tan interior, gold 10 spoke flower wheels, gold stripe and hood tempa ($5-8)(CN)(OP)

MB17-J BULLDOZER 04, issued 2003 (USA)(MB624)
MB 7-K BULLDOZER 04, issued 2003 (ROW)

NOTE: Below models with black horns, black wheels, chrome plastic base & China casting.

1. orange body, red blade, bull bursting through wall tempa ($1-2)(MW17-J/2004 US)(MW7-K 2004 ROW)
2. dark metallic maroon body, orange blade, bull design & "Team" tempa ($1-2)(5pk)

MB18-A FIELD CAR, issued 1970 (MB818)

NOTE: Below models with metal base & England casting. Earliest versions of 1-3 with thin wheels with later versions have wide wheels. All other versions with wide wheels.

1. yellow body, red-brown roof, unpainted base, ivory interior, no labels, 5 spoke wheels ($20-30)
2. yellow body, red-brown roof, unpainted base, ivory interior, no labels, 4 spoke wheels ($20-30)
3. yellow body, red-brown roof, silver-gray base, ivory interior, no labels, 4 spoke wheels ($25-35)

NOTE: All olive body models have black hubs, all others with silver hubs unless noted.

4. olive body, tan roof, black base, black interior, "A" label, 4 spoke wheels ($5-7)(TP)
5. olive body, tan roof, black base, black interior, "RA391" labels, 4 spoke wheels ($5-7)(TP)
6. olive body, tan roof, black base, black interior, "A" label, 5 spoke wheels ($5-7)(TP)
7. olive body, tan roof, black base, black interior, "RA391" label, 5 spoke wheels ($5-7)(TP)
8. olive body, tan roof, black base, black interior, star label, 5 spoke wheels ($25-40)(TP)
9. olive drab body, tan roof, black base, black interior, "A" label, 4 spoke wheels ($65-80)(TP)
10. olive drab body, tan roof, black base, black interior, "A" label, 5 spoke wheels ($65-80)(TP)
11. olive drab body, tan roof, black base, black interior, "A" label, 4 spoke wheels (silver hubs) ($65-80)(TP)
12. olive body, tan roof, black base, black interior, "RA391" labels, 4 spoke wheels (silver hubs) ($8-12)(TP)
13. white body, black roof, black base, black interior, checker label, 4 spoke (silver hubs) wheels ($300-450)(TP)
14. white body, black roof, black base, black interior, checker label, 4 spoke (black hubs) wheels ($300-450)(TP)
15. dull orange body, black roof, black base, black interior, checker label, 5 spoke wheels ($4-6)(TP)
16. dull orange body, black roof, black base, black interior, checker label, 4 spoke wheels ($4-6)(TP)
17. dull orange body, black roof, black base, black interior, checker label, 4 spoke (black hubs) wheels ($4-6)(TP)
18. dull orange body, black roof, silver-gray base, black interior, checker label, 4 spoke wheels ($4-6)(TP)
19. metallic red body, tan roof, black base, black interior, "44" label, 4 spoke wheels ($4-6)(TP)
20. metallic red body, tan roof, black base, black interior, "44" label, 4 spoke (black hubs) wheels ($4-6)(TP)
21. metallic red body, tan roof, silver-gray base, black interior, "44" label, 4 spoke wheels ($4-6)(TP)
22. metallic red body, tan roof, silver-gray base, black interior, checker label, 4 spoke (black hubs) wheels ($4-6)(TP)
23. metallic red body, tan roof, black base, black interior, checker label, 4 spoke wheels ($4-6)(TP)
24. dark orange body, black roof, black base, black interior, no label, 4 spoke wheels ($4-6)(TP)
25. dark orange body, black roof, black base, black interior, "179" tempa, 4 spoke wheels ($5-7)(LE)
26. dark orange body, black roof, silver-gray base, black interior, "179" tempa, 4 spoke wheels ($5-7)(TP)
27. dark orange body, tan roof, silver-gray base, black interior, "179" tempa, 4 spoke wheels ($5-7)(LE)
28. dark orange body, black roof, black base, black interior, "179" tempa, 5 spoke wheels ($5-7)(LE)
29. dark orange body, black roof, black base, white interior, "179" tempa, 4 spoke wheels ($8-10)(LE)
30. dark yellow body, tan roof, black base, black interior, checker label, 4 spoke wheels ($4-6)(TP)
31. dark yellow body, black roof, black base, black interior, checker label, 4 spoke wheels ($4-6)(TP)
32. dark yellow body, black roof, black base, black interior, checker label, 5 spoke wheels ($4-6)(TP)
33. orange body, black roof, black base, white interior, "179" tempa, 4 spoke wheels ($6-8)(TP)
34. orange body, tan roof, black base, black interior, "179" tempa, 4 spoke wheels ($6-8)(TP)
35. orange body, tan roof, black base, black interior, "179" tempa, 4 spoke wheels ($6-8)(TP)
36. orange body, black roof, black base, black interior, checker label, 4 spoke wheels ($4-6)(TP)
37. orange body, tan roof, black base, white interior, "44" label, 4 spoke wheels ($6-8)(TP)
38. orange body, black roof, silver-gray base, black interior, "179" tempa, 4 spoke wheels (black hubs) ($25-40)(TP)
39. metallic red body, tan roof, silver-gray base, black interior, checker label, 4 spoke wheels (black hubs) ($50-75)(TP)
40. orange body, black roof, black base, black interior, "179/ Matchbox USA Road Race Participant" tempa, 4 spoke wheels ($75+)(CCI)

NOTE: Models listed as (LE) were issued as limited edition "Bushwacker".

MB18-B HONDARORA, issued 1975

1. red body, chrome handlebars, no rider , chrome engine, with label, black seat, wire wheels ($10-15)

2. red body, black handlebars, no rider, chrome engine, with label, black seat, wire wheels ($5-7)
3. red body, black handlebars, no rider, chrome engine, no label, black seat, wire wheels ($5-7)
4. red body, black handlebars, no rider, chrome engine, with label, white seat, wire wheels ($95-125)
5. orange body, black handlebars, no rider, chrome engine, with label, black seat, wire wheels ($8-12)(KS)
6. olive drab body, black handlebars, no rider, black engine, no label, black seat, wire wheels ($50-75)(TP)
7. olive body, black handlebars, no rider, black engine, no label, black seat, wire wheels ($7-10)(TP)
8. red body, black handlebars, no rider, black engine, no label, black seat, wire wheels ($5-7)
9. red body, black handlebars, no rider, chrome engine, no label, black seat, mag wheels ($5-7)
10. red body, black handlebars, no rider, black engine, no label, black seat, mag wheels ($5-7)
11. metallic red body, black handlebars, no rider, chrome engine, no label, black seat, wire wheels ($75-100)(BR)
12. green body, black handlebars, no rider, chrome engine, no label, black seat, mag wheels ($5-7)
13. green body, black handlebars, no rider, black engine, no label, black seat, mag wheels ($5-7)
14. yellow body, black handlebars, no rider, chrome engine, no label, black seat, mag wheels ($4-6)
15. yellow body, black handlebars, tan rider, chrome engine, no label, black seat, mag wheels ($4-6)
16. yellow body, black handlebars, brown rider, chrome engine, no label, black seat, mag wheels ($4-6)
17. yellow body, black handlebars, green rider, chrome engine, no label, black seat, mag wheels ($50-75)(GR)

NOTE: Above models all with England casting.

18. yellow body, black handlebars, tan rider, chrome engine, no label, black seat, mag wheels, Macau casting ($3-5)
19. pearly silver body, black handlebars, red rider, black engine, with tempa, black seat, mag wheels, Macau casting ($8-12)(JP)
20. pearly silver body, black handlebars, red rider, black engine, with tempa, charcoal seat, mag wheels, Macau casting ($8-12)(JP)
21. orange body, black handlebars, tan rider, chrome engine, no label, black seat, mag wheels, Macau casting ($3-5)

MB18-C FIRE ENGINE, issued 1984(MB134/313)

NOTE: Below models with blue windows & plastic base unless otherwise noted.

1. red body, chrome base, white ladder, black turret, 5 arch wheels, no tempa, Macau casting ($1-2)
2. red body, chrome base, white ladder, black turret, 8 dot wheels, no tempa, Macau casting ($1-2)
3. red body, chrome base, white ladder, black turret, 5 arch wheels, no tempa, China casting ($1-2)
4. red body, chrome base, white ladder, black turret, 5 arch wheels, "Fire Dept." & shield tempa, China casting ($1-2)
5. lemon body, chrome base, white ladder, black turret, 8 dot wheels, no tempa, Macau casting ($2-4)(MP)
6. red body, chrome base, white ladder, black turret, 5 arch wheels, Japanese lettered tempa, Macau casting ($8-12)(JP)(GS)
7. red body, chrome base, white ladder, black turret, 8 dot wheels, "Fire Dept." & shield tempa, Macau casting ($1-2)
8. red body, chrome base, yellow ladder, black turret, 8 dot blue wheels (yellow hubs), fireman head tempa, Macau casting ($6-8)(LL)
9. red body, chrome base, white ladder, black turret, 8 dot wheels, "3" & crest tempa, Macau casting ($3-5)(GS)
10. red body, chrome base, white ladder, black turret, 8 dot wheels, "Fire Dept." & shield tempa, Thailand casting ($1-2)
11. red body, chrome base, white ladder, black turret, 5 arch wheels, "Fire Dept." & shield tempa, no origin cast ($8-12)(MP)
12. red body, chrome base, white ladder, black turret, 8 dot wheels, "3" & crest tempa, Thailand casting ($1-2)(GS)
13. lemon body, chrome base, white ladder, black turret, 8 dot wheels, no tempa, Thailand casting ($3-5)(MP)
14. red body, blue base, green & blue ladder, yellow turret, 8 dot yellow wheel s with blue hubs, fireman head tempa, Macau casting ($6-8)(LL)
15. red body, blue base, green & blue ladder, yellow turret, 8 dot yellow wheels with blue hubs , fireman head tempa, Thailand casting ($6-8)(LL)
16. red body, blue base, green & blue ladder, yellow turret, 8 dot yellow wheels with plain hubs, fireman head tempa, Thailand casting ($6-8)(LL)
17. florescent orange body, chrome base, white ladder, black turret, 8 dot wheels, "4" & checkers tempa, Thailand casting ($1-2)
18. white body, white base, white ladder, white turret, 8 dot wheels, no tempa, Thailand casting ($10-15)(GF)
19. florescent orange body, black base with bar code, white ladder, black turret, 8 dot wheels, "5" & "Intercom City" tempa, China casting ($10-15)(IC)
20. fluorescent orange body, chrome base, white ladder, black turret, 8 dot wheels, "5" & "Intercom City" tempa, China casting ($7-10)
21. fluorescent orange body, chrome base, white ladder, black turret, 8 dot wheels, "Metro Fire Dept." tempa, Thailand casting ($1-2)(5pk)
22. red body, chrome base, white ladder, black turret, 8 dot wheels, "Metro Fire Dept." & detailed trim tempa, Thailand casting ($2-4)(CC)
23. white & red body, chrome base, silver-gray ladder, 8 dot wheels, gold crest & pinstriping tempa, Thailand casting ($1-2)(5pk)
24. red body, black base, white ladder, black turret, 8 dot wheels, "4" & checkers tempa, Thailand casting ($7-10)
25. red body, black base, white ladder, black turret, 8 dot wheels, "FD No. 1" tempa, China casting ($1-2)(5pk)
26. white body, chrome base, orange ladder, black turret,, 8 dot wheels, "Metro" tempa, China casting ($1-2)
27. yellow body, chrome base, gray ladder, black turret,, 8 dot wheels, "Matchbox Fire Dept." & red stripe tempa, China casting ($1-2)(5pk)
28. yellow body, chrome base, gray ladder, black turret, chrome disc wheels with rubber tires, "Ladder 3 Bay District" & detailed trim tempa, China casting ($3-5)(PC7)
29. white & red body, chrome base, white ladder, black turret, chrome disc wheels with rubber tires, "Springfield Fire Dept." tempa, China casting ($3-5)(PC7)
30. red body, chrome base, white ladder with lever, black turret, 8 dot wheels, "FD" tempa, China casting ($1-2)(AS)(AP)
31. metallic green-gold body, black base, white ladder, black turret, 8 dot wheels, no tempa, China casting ($5-10)(CH)
32. red body, chrome base, white ladder, black turret, 8 dot wheels, "Matchbox Fire Dept." & white stripe tempa, China casting ($1-2)
33. red body, chrome base, gray ladder, black turret, 8 dot wheels, "Matchbox Fire Dept." & gold stripe tempa, China casting ($1-2)(5pk)(MW22/1999 GR)
34. white body, chrome base, translucent red ladder, black turret, 8 dot wheels, red band tempa, China casting ($1-2)(MW23/1999 GR)
35. lemon & white body, chrome base, gray ladder, black turret, chrome disc wheels with rubber wheels, "Park Ridge Fire Dept." & detailed trim tempa , China casting ($3-5)(PC21)

36. red & white body, chrome base, white ladder, black turret, chrome disc wheels with rubber tires, "Laurel Springs Fire Rescue" & detailed trim tempa, China casting ($3-5)(PC21)
37. red & white body, chrome base, white ladder, light gray turret, chrome disc with rubber tires, "City of Miami" & detailed trim tempa, China casting ($3-5)(PC)
38. lemon body, chrome base, gray ladder, black turret,, 8 dot wheels, "21" & crest tempa, China casting ($1-2)(MW69/1999 ROW)
39. lemon body, chrome base, gray ladder, black turret, 8 dot wheels, "21 Laurel Ladder" tempa, China casting ($1-2)(MW79/1999 US)
40. red body, amber windows, dark charcoal base, gray ladder & turret, 8 dot wheels, white bands "54" & "Matchbox" in circle logo tempa, China casting ($1-2)(5pk)
41. red & white body, black base, white ladder, black turret, 8 dot wheels, "Cleveland Fire Div." Tempa, China casting ($1-2)(MW32/2000 US)
42. red & white body, black base, white ladder, black turret, 8 dot wheels, "Cleveland Fire Div." & "Matchbox 2000" tempa, China casting ($2-4)(MW32/2000 US)
43. white body, black base, red ladder, black turret, 8 dot wheels, red bands & yellow hash marks on ladder tempa, China casting ($1-2)(5pk)
44. metallic maroon body, amber windows, chrome base, gray ladder & turret, 8 dot wheels, gold design, "14" & "Matchbox" logo tempa, China casting ($4-6)(PB)
45. red body, chrome base, gray ladder with black turret, "FDMB-E64" & "Ladder 3 Fire Rescue" with yellow & white stripes tempa, chrome disc with rubber tires, China casting ($5-8)(FC/KB)
46. white body, black base, gray ladder with black turret, "Metro Alarm" with orange & red stripe tempa, 10 spoke flower wheels, China casting ($1-2)(5pk)
47. white body, silver-gray metal base, gray ladder with black turret, "Metro Alarm" with orange & red tempa, 10 spoke flower wheels, Mattel China casting ($1-2)(5pk)
48. white body, silver-gray metal base, gray ladder with black turret, "Westworth Fire Dept. 8" tempa, 10 spoke flower wheels, Mattel China casting ($1-2)(MW29/2001)
49. white body, gray plastic base, gray ladder with black turret, "Westworth Fire Dept. 8" tempa, 10 spoke flower wheels, Mattel China casting ($1-2)(MW29/2001)
50. white & red body, pearly silver metal base, red ladder with black turret, "Emergency Patrol" tempa, 10 spoke flower wheels, Mattel China casting ($1-2)(5pk)
51. metallic maroon body, amber windows, chrome plastic base, white ladder & turret, gold design with "14" & "Matchbox" tempa, 10 spoke flower wheels, China casting ($3-5)(PB)
52. red body, amber windows, gray plastic base, white ladder & turret, "FD USA" & white band & flag tempa, 10 spoke flower wheels, China casting ($1-2)(HR)
53. red body, amber windows, dark blue metal base, white ladder with blue turret, "Delta Unit 20/ Mississippi" tempa, 10 spoke flower wheels, Mattel China casting ($1-2)(AM)
54. yellow body, red windows, silver-gray metal base, gray ladder & turret, "Super Peak 49" & stripes tempa, 10 spoke flower wheels, Mattel China casting ($1-2)(5pk)
55. metallic maroon body, amber windows, gray metal base, gray ladder & turret, gold design with "14" & "Matchbox" tempa, 10 spoke flower wheels, Mattel China casting ($3-5)(PB)
56. red body, charcoal metal base, yellow ladder with gray turret, stripes & "4" tempa, 10 spoke flower wheels, Mattel China casting ($1-2)(MW4/2003)
57. red body, charcoal metal base, yellow ladder with gray turret, stripes, "4" & "Hero City" tempa, 10 spoke flower wheels, Mattel China casting ($2-4)(MW4/2003)
58. red body, black plastic base, yellow ladder with gray turret, stripes & "4" tempa, 10 spoke flower wheels, Mattel China casting ($1-2)(MW4/2003)
59. red body, amber windows, gray plastic base, white ladder with gray turret, "Metro Alarm" & stripes tempa, 10 spoke flower wheels, Mattel China casting ($1-2)(5pk)
60. red body, amber windows, silver-gray metal base, white ladder with gray turret, "Metro Alarm" & stripes tempa, 10 spoke flower wheels, Mattel China casting ($1-2)(5pk)
61. metallic red body, black plastic base, yellow ladder with gray turret, "4" & stripes tempa, gold 10 spoke flower wheels, Mattel China casting ($3-4)(20pk)
62. metallic maroon body, gray plastic base, gray ladder with gray turret, stripes & "14" with new "Matchbox" logo tempa, 10 spoke flower wheels, Mattel China casting ($2-4)(PB)
63. white & yellow body, chrome plastic base, gray ladder with black turret, "Bay District" & detailed trim tempa, 8 dot wheels, China casting ($50+)(CHI)
64. white & red body, chrome plastic base, gray ladder with black turret, "Ladder 3/ Bay District" & detailed trim tempa, 8 dot wheels, China casting ($50+)(CHI)
65. white & red body, silver-gray metal base, white ladder & turret, "Emergency Patrol" & "Matchbox" tempa, 10 spoke flower wheels, China casting ($18-25)(CD Rom game)

MB18-D MIXOPOTAMUS, issued 2004 (USA)(MB638)
MB 8-L MIXOPOTAMUS, issued 2004 (ROW)

1. gray body, yellow barrel, red windows, gold 5 crown dot wheels, hippo design on barrel tempa, black plastic base, China casting ($1-3)(MW18-D/2004 US)(MB8-L/2004 ROW)

MB19-A LOTUS RACER, issued 1970

1. dark purple body, white driver, spiro wheels, unpainted metal base, round "3" labels & England casting ($35-50)

MB19-B ROAD DRAGSTER, issued 1970

NOTE: Below models with 5 spoke front & spiro rear wheels, chrome engine & England casting unless otherwise noted.

1. red body, unpainted base, ivory interior, "8" labels ($15-20)
2. red-orange body, unpainted base, ivory interior, "8" labels ($15-20)
3. red-orange body, silver-gray base, ivory interior, "8" labels ($15-20)
4. red-orange body, unpainted base, ivory interior, no labels ($15-20)
5. red-orange body, unpainted base, ivory interior, scorpion labels ($35-50)
6. red-orange body, silver-gray base, ivory interior, scorpion labels ($35-50)
7. red-orange body, unpainted base, white interior, "8" labels ($15-20)
8. pinkish red body, unpainted base, ivory interior, small "Wynn's" labels ($85-125)(LE)
9. pinkish red body, unpainted base, ivory interior, large "Wynn's" labels ($85-125)(LE)
10. pinkish red body, unpainted base, ivory interior, "8" labels ($15-20)
11. purple body, unpainted base, ivory interior, "8" labels ($18-25)
12. purple body, unpainted base, ivory interior, scorpion labels ($35-50)

13. metallic red body, unpainted base, ivory interior, "8" labels ($250-400)
14. dark orchid body, unpainted base with Manaus label, ivory interior, "8" labels ($250+)(BR)

MB19-C CEMENT TRUCK, issued 1976

NOTE: Red barrel stripes are normally shaped as slashes but can be found shaped as backslashes. Below models with 5 crown wheels, metal base & England casting.

1. red body, orange-yellow barrel, red stripes, green windows, unpainted base ($5-8)
2. red body, orange-yellow barrel, black stripes, green windows, unpainted base ($5-8)
3. red body, orange-yellow barrel, red stripes, blue-green windows, unpainted base ($5-8)
4. red body, orange-yellow barrel, no stripes, blue-green windows, unpainted base ($5-8)
5. red body, orange-yellow barrel, no stripes, green windows, unpainted base ($5-8)
6. red body, orange-yellow barrel, red stripes, no windows, unpainted base ($5-8)
7. red body, gray barrel, red stripes, no windows, unpainted base ($5-8)
8. red body, gray barrel, red stripes, green windows, unpainted base ($5-8)
9. red body, gray barrel, red stripes, purple windows, unpainted base ($5-8)
10. red body, orange barrel, red stripes, purple windows, unpainted base ($5-8)
11. red body, orange barrel, red stripes, green windows, unpainted base ($5-8)
12. red body, lemon barrel, red stripes, green windows, unpainted base ($5-8)
13. red body, lemon barrel, red stripes, purple windows, unpainted base ($5-8)
14. red body, orange-yellow barrel, red stripes, green windows, silver-gray base ($5-8)
15. red body, lemon barrel, no stripes, green windows, unpainted base ($5-8)

MB19-D PETERBILT CEMENT TRUCK, issued 1982 (MB019)

NOTE: Below models with 8 spoke wheels & plastic base unless otherwise noted.

1. emerald green body, orange barrel, chrome exhausts, yellow "Big Pete" tempa, amber windows, black mounts, chrome base, England casting ($2-4)
2. emerald green body, orange barrel, chrome exhausts, white "Big Pete" tempa, amber windows, black mounts, chrome base, England casting ($2-4)
3. pale green body, orange barrel, chrome exhausts, yellow/white "Big Pete" tempa, amber windows, black mounts, chrome base, Macau casting ($2-4)
4. dark green body, orange barrel, chrome exhausts, yellow/white "Big Pete" tempa, amber windows, black mounts, chrome base, Macau casting ($2-4)
5. dark green body, orange barrel, chrome exhausts, yellow/white "Big Pete" tempa, amber windows, charcoal mounts, chrome base, Macau casting ($2-4)
6. dark green body, orange barrel, chrome exhausts, yellow/white "Big Pete" tempa, clear windows, black mounts, chrome base, Macau casting ($2-4)
7. blue body, lemon barrel, chrome exhausts, "Kwik Set Cement" tempa, clear windows, black mounts, chrome base, Macau casting ($1-2)
8. blue body, orange barrel, chrome exhausts, "Kwik Set Cement" (roof only) tempa, clear windows, black mounts, chrome base, Macau casting ($8-12)
9. yellow body, orange barrel, chrome exhausts, "Dirty Dumper" tempa, clear windows, black mounts, chrome base, Macau casting ($60-80)
10. yellow body, gray barrel, chrome exhausts, "Pace Construction" tempa, clear windows, black mounts, chrome base, Macau casting ($2-3)(MP)
11. blue body, lemon barrel, gray exhausts, "Kwik Set Cement" tempa, clear windows, black mounts, chrome base, Macau casting ($1-2)
12. yellow body, gray barrel, gray exhausts, "Pace Construction" tempa, clear windows, black mounts, chrome base, Macau casting ($2-3)(MP)
13. red body, lime barrel, lime exhausts, face & stripe tempa, clear windows, yellow mounts, blue base, yellow wheels with blue hubs, Macau casting ($6-8)(LL)
14. light pink body, white barrel, gray exhausts, "Readymix" tempa, clear windows, light pink mounts, black base, Thailand casting ($8-12)(AU)
15. blue body, lemon barrel, gray exhausts, "Kwik Set Cement" tempa, clear windows, black mounts, chrome base, Thailand casting ($1-2)
16. yellow body, dark gray barrel, gray exhausts, "Pace Construction" tempa, clear windows, black mounts, Thailand casting ($3-4)(MC)
17. red body, lime barrel, lime exhausts, face & stripe tempa, clear windows, yellow mounts, blue base, yellow wheels with blue hubs, Thailand casting ($6-8)(LL)
18. red body, lime barrel, lime exhausts, face & stripes tempa, clear windows, yellow mounts, blue base, yellow wheels with plain hubs, Thailand casting ($6-8)(LL)
19. orange-yellow body, red barrel, gray exhausts, "Pace Construction" tempa, clear windows, black mounts, chrome base, Thailand casting ($1-2)
20. red body, orange barrel, gray exhausts, man tempa, clear windows, black mounts, gray base, Manaus casting ($35-50)(BR)
21. red body, orange barrel, gray exhausts, man tempa, clear windows, dark gray mounts, gray base, Manaus casting ($35-50)(BR)
22. white body, orange barrel, gray exhausts, "Cement Company" tempa, black mounts, gray base, Manaus casting ($30-45)(BR)
23. florescent orange body, black barrel, dark gray exhausts, no tempa, silver-gray mounts, Thailand casting ($1-2)(5pk)
24. florescent orange body, gray barrel, gray exhausts, no tempa, black mounts, chrome base, Thailand casting ($1-2)(5pk)
25. orange-yellow body, orange barrel, gray exhausts, "Pace Construction" tempa, black mounts, black base, Thailand casting ($4-5)
26. red body, black barrel, gray exhausts, white stripes tempa, gray mounts, black base, China casting ($1-2)
27. pumpkin body, gray barrel, gray exhausts, "Matchbox" tempa, black mounts, chrome base, China casting ($1-2)(5pk)
28. metallic gold body, white barrel, black exhausts, no tempa, black mounts, chrome base, China casting ($5-10)(CH)
29. powder blue body, black barrel, chrome exhausts, white stripes tempa, gray mounts, chrome base, China casting ($2-3)
30. metallic red body, black barrel, chrome exhausts, white stripes tempa, gray mounts, chrome base, China casting ($1-2)(MW8/1998)

31. lemon body, green barrel, chrome exhausts, "Highway Crew" tempa, black mounts, chrome base, China casting ($1-2)(5pk)
32. red body, white barrel, chrome exhausts, white stripes tempa, black mounts, chrome base, China casting ($45-60)(MW10/1998)
NOTE: Above model packaged as #10 Peterbilt Quarry Truck in 1998.
33. matt pink body, cream barrel, gray exhausts, red stripes on barrel & dirt tempa, gray mounts, translucent gray base, China casting ($1-2)(MW26/1999)
34. orange body, cream barrel, gray exhausts, small logo tempa, gray mounts, gray mounts, translucent gray base, China casting ($3-5)(MW6/1999 GR)
35. matt white body, red barrel, gray exhausts, white stripes on barrel with "Bilt" & dirt & "Matchbox 2000" tempa, gray mounts, translucent gray base, China casting ($5-8)(MW93/2000 US)
36. matt white body, red barrel, gray exhausts, white stripes on barrel with "Bilt" & dirt & "Matchbox 2000" tempa, gray mounts, translucent gray base, 7 spoke sawblade wheels, China casting ($3-4)(MW93/2000 US)
37. matt white body, red barrel, gray exhausts, white stripes on barrel with "Bilt" & dirt tempa, gray mounts, translucent gray base, China casting ($1-2)(MW93/2000 US)(MW73/2000 ROW)
38. white body, gray barrel & exhausts, none tempa, gray mounts, chrome base, China casting ($25-40)(ASAP blank)
39. white body, gray barrel & exhausts, "Hemler Bros." tempa, gray mounts, chrome base, China casting ($50+)(ASAP)
40. white body, gray barrel & exhausts, "CAT Service Co." tempa, gray mounts, chrome base, China casting ($50+)(ASAP)
41. white body, gray barrel & exhausts, "Redi-Way, Inc." tempa, gray mounts, chrome base, China casting ($50+)(ASAP)
42. white body, gray barrel & exhausts, "Blue Ridge Construction" tempa, gray mounts, chrome base, China casting ($50+)(ASAP)
43. matt white body, red barrel, gray exhausts, white stripes on barrel with "Bilt" & dirt tempa, 7 spoke sawblade wheels, gray mounts, translucent gray base, China casting ($2-3)(MW93/2000 US)
44. bright green body, white barrel, blue exhausts & mounts, "Matchbox/MC05" tempa, 7 spoke sawblade wheels, black base, China casting ($1-2)(5pk)
45 white body, gray barrel, exhausts & mounts, "HBE" tempa, 8 spoke wheels, gray mounts, chrome base, China casting ($50+)(ASAP)
46. white body, gray barrel, exhausts& mounts, no tempa, 7 spoke sawblade wheels, gray mounts, chrome base, China casting ($25-40)(ASAP blank)
47. dark blue body, gray barrel, neon orange exhausts & mounts, "MC05 Matchbox" tempa, 7 spoke sawblade wheels, black base, China casting ($1-2)(5pk)
48. dark blue body, gray barrel, neon orange exhausts & mounts, "MC05 Matchbox" tempa, 7 spoke sawblade wheels, black base, Mattel China casting ($1-2)(5pk)
49. white body, gray barrel, exhausts & mounts, no tempa, 8 spoke wheels, gray mounts, gray base, China casting ($25-40)(ASAP blank)
50. pumpkin body, gray barrel, exhausts & mounts, no tempa, 8 spoke wheels, black mounts, chrome base, China casting ($25-40)(ASAP blank)
51. red body, orange barrel, chrome exhausts, man tempa, 8 spoke wheels, black mounts, chrome base, Manaus casting ($35-50)(BR)

MB19-E BMW 328i *see MB69-I*

MB19-F GO-ROLLA, issued 2004 (USA)(MB640)
MB10-H GO-ROLLA, issued 2004 (ROW)

NOTE: This model had not been released in the USA and it appears to be very limited in ROW markets. No model was available at publication time to include for photography.

1. orange body, dark gray rollers, black & yellow stripes tempa, China casting ($8-12)(MW19/2004 US)(MW10-H/2004 ROW)

MB20-A LAMBORGHINI MARZAL, issued 1969

NOTE: Below models with ivory interior, amber windows, 5 spoke wheels, metal base & England casting.

1. metallic red body, unpainted base, no labels ($18-25)
2. metallic red body, unpainted base, with labels ($18-25)(GS)
3. salmon body, unpainted base, no labels ($15-20)
4. salmon body, unpainted base, with labels ($18-25)(GS)
5. salmon body, silver-gray base, no labels ($15-20)
6. yellow body, unpainted base, no labels ($35-50)(BS)
7. hot pink body, unpainted base, no labels ($15-20)
8. hot pink body, unpainted base, with labels ($18-25)(GS)
9. orange-pink body, unpainted base, no labels ($15-20)
10. yellow body, unpainted base, cow label (from MB73-A)($175-250)
11. metallic blue body, unpainted base, unpainted base with Manaus label, no labels ($250+)(BR)

MB20-B POLICE PATROL, issued 1975 (MB020)

NOTE: Below models with silver hubs and Lesney, England casting unless otherwise noted.

1. white body, unpainted base, frosted windows, orange dome/ spinner, 3/16" wide "Police" labels, maltese cross wheels ($8-12)
2. white body, unpainted base, blue frosted windows, orange dome/ spinner, 3/16" wide "Police" labels, maltese cross wheels ($8-12)
3. white body, unpainted base, frosted windows, orange dome/ spinner, 1/8" wide "Police" labels, maltese cross wheels ($8-12)
4. white body, unpainted base, frosted windows, orange dome/ spinner, 1/8" wide "Police" labels, 5 spoke wheels ($8-12)
5. white body, unpainted base, blue frosted windows, orange dome/ spinner, 1/8" wide "Police" labels, maltese cross wheels ($8-12)
6. white body, unpainted base, yellow frosted windows, orange dome/ spinner, 1/8" wide "Police" labels, maltese cross wheels ($8-12)
7. olive drab body, unpainted base, frosted windows, orange dome/ spinner, "Ambulance" labels, 5 spoke wheels, black hubs ($65-80)(TP)
8. olive drab body, unpainted base, frosted windows, orange dome/ spinner, "Ambulance" labels, maltese cross wheels, black hubs ($65-80)(TP)
9. olive drab body, unpainted base, frosted windows, orange dome/ spinner, "Ambulance" labels, maltese cross wheels, silver hubs ($65-80)(TP)
10. olive drab body, unpainted base, frosted windows, orange dome/ spinner, red & yellow "Police" labels, maltese cross wheels, black hubs ($65-80)(TP)
11. olive drab body, unpainted base, frosted windows, orange dome/ spinner, red & yellow "Police" labels, maltese cross labels, silver hubs ($65-80)(TP)
12. olive body, unpainted base, frosted windows, orange dome/ spinner, red & yellow "Police" labels, maltese cross wheels, black hubs ($6-8)(TP)
13. olive body, unpainted base, frosted windows, orange dome/ spinner, red & yellow "Police" labels, maltese cross wheels, silver hubs ($7-10)(TP)

14. olive body, unpainted base, frosted windows, orange dome/ spinner, "Ambulance" labels, 5 spoke wheels, black hubs ($6-8)(TP)
15. olive body, unpainted base, frosted windows, orange dome/ spinner, 1/8" wide "Police" labels, 5 spoke wheels, black hubs ($15-20)(TP)
16. olive body, unpainted base, frosted windows, orange dome/ spinner, "Ambulance" labels, maltese cross wheels, black hubs ($6-8)(TP)
17. olive body, unpainted base, frosted windows, orange dome/ spinner, 1/8" wide "Police" labels, maltese cross wheels, black hubs ($6-8)(TP)
18. olive body, unpainted base, frosted windows, orange dome/ spinner, red & yellow "Police" labels, 5 spoke wheels, black hubs ($6-8)(TP)
19 orange body, unpainted base, frosted windows, orange dome/ spinner, "Site Engineer" labels, maltese cross wheels ($15-20)(GS)
20. orange body, unpainted base, frosted windows, orange dome/ spinner, "Site Engineer" labels, 5 spoke wheels, black hubs ($15-20)(GS)
21. orange body, unpainted base, blue frosted windows, orange dome/ spinner, "Site Engineer" labels, maltese cross wheels ($15-20)(GS)
22. orange body, unpainted base, frosted windows, orange dome/ spinner, 1/8" wide "Police" labels, maltese cross wheels ($18-25)(GS)
23. orange body, unpainted base, frosted windows, orange dome/ spinner, "Ambulance" labels, maltese cross wheels ($20-25)(GS)
24. white body, unpainted base, frosted windows, orange dome/ spinner, "Ambulance" labels, maltese cross wheels ($20-25)(TP)
25. white body, unpainted base, frosted windows, orange dome/ spinner, "Site Engineer" labels, maltese cross wheels ($18-25)
26. white body, unpainted base, frosted windows, orange dome/ spinner, 1/8" wide "Police" labels, maltese cross wheels, black hubs ($8-12)
27. white body, unpainted base, amber frosted windows, orange dome/ spinner, 1/8" wide "Police" labels, maltese cross wheels ($8-12)
28. white body, unpainted base, frosted windows, blue dome, orange spinner, 1/8" wide "Police" labels, maltese cross wheels ($6-8)
29. white body, unpainted base, frosted windows, yellow dome, blue spinner, 1/8" wide "Police" labels, maltese cross wheels ($6-8)
30. white body, unpainted base, frosted windows, blue dome/ spinner, 1/8" wide "Police" labels, maltese cross wheels ($6-8)
31. white body, black base, frosted windows, blue dome/ spinner, 1/8" wide "Police" labels, maltese cross wheels ($8-12)
32. white body, unpainted base, frosted windows, blue dome, orange spinner, small "Police" labels, maltese cross wheels ($18-25)
33. white body, unpainted base, frosted windows, yellow dome, blue spinner, small "Police" labels, maltese cross wheels ($18-25)
34. white body, unpainted base, frosted windows, yellow dome, orange spinner, small "Police" labels, maltese cross wheels ($18-25)
35. white body, black base, frosted windows, blue dome, orange spinner, 1/8" wide "Police" labels, maltese cross wheels ($8-12)
36. white body, unpainted base, frosted windows, yellow dome, orange spinner, 1/8" wide "Police" labels, maltese cross wheels ($6-8)
37. blue body, unpainted base, frosted windows, orange dome/ spinner, "Paris Dakar 81" labels, maltese cross wheels ($35-50)(FR)
38. blue body, unpainted base, frosted windows, yellow dome/ spinner, "Paris Dakar 81" labels, maltese cross wheels ($35-50)(FR)
39. blue body, unpainted base, frosted windows, yellow dome, orange spinner, "Paris Dakar 81" labels, maltese cross wheels ($35-50)(FR)
40. white body, unpainted base, frosted windows, blue dome/ spinner, checkered "Police" labels, maltese cross wheels ($8-12)
41. white body, black base, frosted windows, blue dome/ spinner, checkered "Police:" labels, maltese cross wheels ($8-12)
42. white body, charcoal base, frosted windows, blue dome/ spinner, checkered "Police" labels, maltese cross wheels ($8-12)
43. white body, black base, frosted windows, blue dome/ spinner, "County Sheriff" labels, maltese cross wheels ($8-12)
44. white body, unpainted base, frosted windows, blue dome/ spinner, "County Sheriff" labels & blue roof tempa, maltese cross wheels ($8-12)
45. white body, black base, frosted windows, blue dome/ spinner, "County Sheriff" labels & blue roof tempa, maltese cross wheels($8-12)
46. white body, unpainted base with Manaus label, frosted windows, orange dome/ spinner, 3/16" wide "Police" labels, maltese cross wheels ($35-50)(BR)
47. metallic sand body, black base, frosted windows, red dome/ spinner, "Paris Dakar 83" labels, maltese cross wheels ($6-8)
48. beige body, black base, frosted windows, red dome/ spinner, "Paris Dakar 83" labels, maltese cross wheels ($6-8)

NOTE: Following models with "Matchbox International, England" base.

49. beige body, black base, frosted windows, red dome/ spinner, "Paris Dakar 83" tempa, maltese cross wheels ($4-6)
50. beige body, unpainted base, frosted windows, red dome/ spinner, "Paris Dakar 83" tempa, maltese cross wheels ($6-8)
51. white & black body, black base, frosted windows, red dome/ spinner, Japanese lettered tempa, maltese cross wheels ($8-12)(JP)

NOTE: Available as an Hungarian casting. Assorted colors available ($15-25)

MB20-C 4 X 4 JEEP, issued 1982 (USA)(MB095)
MB14-F 4 X 4 JEEP, issued 1984 (ROW)

NOTE: Below models with maltese cross wheels.

1. white body, black metal base, black interior, red canopy, "Desert Dawg" tempa, England casting ($3-5)
2. black body, black metal base, red interior, white canopy, "Laredo" tempa, Macau casting ($1-2)
3. black body, black metal base, red interior, white canopy, "Laredo" tempa, Hong Kong casting ($18-25)
4. dark metallic tan body, black metal base, black interior, red canopy, "Golden Eagle" tempa, England casting ($18-25)
5. red body, black metal base, gray interior, white canopy, "Golden Eagle" tempa, Macau casting ($7-10)
6. olive body, black metal base, black interior, tan canopy, black & tan camouflage tempa, Macau casting ($4-6)(CM)
7. olive body, black plastic base, black interior, tan canopy, black & tan camouflage tempa, Macau casting ($4-6)(CM)
8. black body, black plastic base, red interior, white canopy, "Laredo" tempa, Macau casting ($1-2)
9. yellow body, black plastic base, blue interior, lime canopy, caricature tempa, red wheels with green hubs, Macau casting ($6-8)(LL)

10. black body, black plastic base, red interior, white canopy, "Laredo" tempa, Thailand casting ($1-2)
11. red body, greenish black metal base, gray interior, white canopy, "Golden Eagle" tempa, Macau casting ($7-10)
12. yellow body, black plastic base, blue interior, lime canopy, caricature tempa, red wheels with plain hubs, Thailand casting ($6-8)(LL)
13. black body, black plastic base, red interior, red canopy, "Laredo" tempa, Macau casting ($12-18)
14. yellow body, black plastic base, black interior, black canopy, geometric hood design tempa, Thailand casting ($1-2)(5pk)

NOTE: Above models with right hand drive. Below models with left hand drive unless otherwise noted.

15. yellow body, black plastic base, black interior, black canopy, geometric hood design tempa, Thailand casting ($1-2)(5pk)
16. beige body, black plastic base, black interior, beige canopy, right hand drive, camouflage tempa, Thailand casting ($1-2)
17. beige body, black plastic base, black interior, beige canopy, camouflage tempa, Thailand casting ($1-2)
18. pink-tan body, black plastic base, black interior, tan canopy, green & brown camouflage tempa, Thailand casting ($1-2)(5pk)
19. olive body, black plastic base, black interior, black canopy, star & "V-9872-3" tempa, Thailand casting ($1-2)
20. beige body, black plastic base, black interior, black canopy, brown camouflage tempa, Thailand casting ($1-2)(5pk)
21. dark sand body, black plastic base, black interior, dark sand canopy, star & "V-9873-3" tempa, Thailand casting ($1-2)(GS)
22. olive body, black plastic base, black interior, black canopy, red cross & "RB104" tempa, Thailand casting ($1-2)(PS)
23. pale olive body, black plastic base, black interior, pale olive canopy, white cross & "RB104" tempa, Thailand casting ($1-2)(PS)
24. light olive body, black plastic base, black interior, olive canopy, red cross & "M*A*S*H" tempa, China casting ($4-6)(STR)
25. pale olive body, black plastic base, black interior, pale olive canopy, white cross & "RB104" tempa, China casting ($1-2)(PS)

MB20-D VOLVO CONTAINER TRUCK, issued 1985 (ROW)(MB148)
MB23-G VOLVO CONTAINER TRUCK, issued 1987 (USA)
MB62-I VOLVO CONTAINER TRUCK, reissued 1990 (ROW)

NOTE: Below models with black plastic base, amber windows, 5 arch wheels with silver hubs unless otherwise noted.

1. blue body, white container, "Coldfresh" labels, Macau casting ($3-5)
2. white body, white container, "Scotch Corner" labels, Macau casting ($8-12)(SC)
3. gray body, gray container, "Supersave Drugstores" labels, Macau casting ($8-12)(UK)
4. blue body, white container, "MB1-75 #1 in Volume Sales" labels, Macau casting ($35-50)(UK)
5. blue body, white container, "MB1-75 #1 in Volume Sales" labels, China casting ($35-50)(UK)
6. blue body, white container, "Coldfresh" labels, China casting ($3-5)
7. white body, white container, "Federal Express" labels, China casting ($3-5)
8. blue body, white container, "Unic" (towards front or rear) labels, China casting ($8-12)(BE)
9. blue body, blue container, "Crooke's Healthcare" labels, China casting ($6-8)(UK)
10. white body, white container, "Kellogg's/ Milch-Lait-Latte" labels, China casting ($35-50)(SW)(GR)
11. white body, white container, "TNT Ipec" labels, China casting ($4-6)(TC)
12. green body, gray container, "Hikkoshi Semmon Center" (in Japanese) labels, China casting ($10-15)(JP)
13. blue body, blue container, "Allders" labels, China casting ($6-8)(UK)
14. white body, white container, "XP Parcels" labels, China casting ($4-6)(MP)
15. blue body, blue container, "Comma Performance Motor Oils" labels, China casting ($8-12)(UK)(OP)
16. blue body, white container, "Kellogg's/ Milch-Lait-Latte" labels, China casting ($35-50)(GR)(SW)
17. white body, white container, "Federal Express" (container) labels & "XP Parcels" doors tempa, China casting ($15-20)
18. red body, brown container, "Merkur Kaffee" labels, China casting ($8-12)(SW)
19. green body, white container, "M" & green stripe labels, China casting ($8-12)(SW)
20. red body, white container, "Denner" labels, China casting ($8-12)(SW)
21. white body, white container, "Family Trust" labels, China casting ($8-12)(CN)
22. blue body, red container, "Christiaensen" labels, China casting ($8-12)(BE)
23. white body, dark cream container, "Federal Express" labels, China casting ($2-3)
24. white body, white container, "Kit Kat" labels, China casting ($25-40)(UK)
25. white body, white container, "Yorkie" labels, China casting ($25-40)(UK)
26. red body, white container, "Big Top Circus" labels, China casting ($1-2)
27. white body, powder blue container, "Co Op- People Who Care" labels, China casting ($6-8)(UK)
28. blue body, white container, "Big Top Circus" labels, China casting ($8-12)(GS)
29. white body, powder blue container, "99 Tea" labels, China casting ($7-10)(UK)(OP)
30. black body, black container, "Cool Paint Co." labels, dark gray base, China casting ($1-2)
31. orange body, orange container, "Polar Power" labels, gray base, blue windows, China casting ($3-5)(WR)(GS)
32. white & red body, white container, "Auto Palace" labels, black base, China casting ($5-7)(US)
33. florescent orange body, yellow container, "Matchbox Get In The Fast Lane" labels with cab tempa, black windows, black base, China casting ($1-2)
34. florescent orange body, yellow container, "Matchbox Get In The Fast Lane" labels without cab tempa, black windows, black base, China casting ($1-2)
35. purple body, purple container, "Continental Aero" labels, gray base, China casting ($8-12)(US)
36. yellow body, yellow container, black windows, "Action System" labels, dark gray base, China casting ($8-12)(OP)
37. black body, yellow container, "Matchbox Auto Products" labels, dark gray base, China casting ($1-2)
38. turquoise body, black container, smoke windows, "Matchbox Auto Products" labels, dark gray base, China casting ($1-2)(5pk)
39. dark turquoise body, white container, smoke windows, "Sagamore Insurance" tempa, dark gray base, China casting ($85-110)(US)
40. metallic gold body, black container, black windows, no labels, China casting ($5-10)(CH)
41. white body, white container, "Matchbox ASI 33000" tempa, China casting ($75+)(ASAP)
42. white body, white container, "PC Van Go" (left side only) tempa, China casting ($50+)(ASAP)

43. white body, white container, "Du Pont Answers" labels, China casting ($50+)(ASAP)
44. white body, white container, "Du Pont Floor Covering" labels, China casting ($50+)(ASAP)
45. white body, white container, "CFU" in red (right side only) tempa, China casting ($25+)(ASAP)
46. white body, white container, "CFU" in blue (right side only) tempa, China casting ($50+)(ASAP)
47. red body, yellow container, black windows, "Matchbox Animals" labels, China casting ($1-2)(MW44/1998 US))
48. red body, blue container, smoke windows, "Matchbox" with red arrow labels ($1-2)(MW1/1998 ROW)
49. white body, white container, "Two Men and A Truck" tempa, China casting ($10-15)(ASAP)
50. white body, white container, "Harty Press" labels, China casting ($100+)(ASAP)
51. blue body, yellow container, "Airways Air Cargo" labels, China casting ($1-2)(5pk)
52. white body, white container, "Bill Cairns- Let Bill Move you" tempa, China casting ($20+)(ASAP)
53. white body, blue container, blue windows, "The Matchbox Times" labels, China casting ($1-2)(5pk)
54. white body, white container, no labels, China casting ($15-25)(ASAP blank)
55. white body, white container, "Du Pont Floor Finishes" labels, China casting ($45+)(ASAP)
56. white body, white container, "RCA" tempa, China casting ($18-25)(ASAP)
57. orange body, orange container, blue-green windows, "Allied Van Lines" labels, gray base, China casting ($1-2)(MW22/1999 US)
58. orange body, orange container, blue-green windows, "Allied/ Pickfords" labels, gray base, China casting ($2-3)(MW22/1999 ROW)
59. white body, white container, "Hi-Speed/ Garvens" tempa, China casting ($25-50)(ASAP)
60. white body, white container, "Bulldog Caster Co." tempa, China casting ($25-40)(ASAP)
61. white body, white container, "Cookman Accounting Services" tempa, China casting ($15-30)(ASAP)
62. white body, white container, "Kuthasta Investment Supplies Group" tempa, China casting ($15-25)(ASAP)
63. white body, white container, "Certainteed/ Synergy" tempa, China casting ($35-70)(ASAP)
64. white body, white container, "Certainteed HVAC Insulation Products" tempa, China casting ($75+)(ASAP)
65. white body, white container, "Federated Realty Group Inc." labels, China casting ($35-60)(ASAP)
66. white body, white container, "Office Depot" tempa, China casting ($25-40)(ASAP)
67. orange body, orange container, smoke windows, "Enjoy Fanta" labels (2 different sided label), England casting ($75+)(CHI)
68. red body, red container, smoke windows, "Coca Cola" with polar bears labels, China casting ($10-15)(MW62/1999 GR)
69. red body, red container, blue windows, "Coca Cola" with polar bears labels, China casting ($25-40)(MW62/1999 GR)
70. red body, red container, amber windows, "Coca Cola" with polar bear labels, China casting ($25-40)(MW62/1999 GR)
71. red body, orange container, smoke windows, "Coca Cola" with polar bear labels, China casting ($75+)(MW62/1999 GR)
72. white body, white container, "Transply, Inc." tempa, China casting ($50+)(ASAP)
73. white body, white container, "Automotive Distributing Company" tempa, China casting ($50+)(ASAP)
74. white body, white container, "e-cycled.com" tempa, China casting ($50+)(ASAP)
75. white body, white container, "Cendant Mobility/ We treat each move like it's our own" tempa, China casting ($50+)(ASAP)
76. white body, white container, "Nestle" tempa, China casting ($25-40)(ASAP)

NOTE: Below models with China casting.

77. white body, white container, "Smartpages.com" tempa ($75+)(ASAP)
78. white body, white container, "Special People..." (left side only) tempa ($50+)(ASAP)
79. white body, white container, "City Drayage On The Road Again" tempa ($50+)(ASAP)
80. white body, white container, "Media Vehicles" labels ($50+)(ASAP)
81. white body, white container, "BTX Air Express" tempa ($50+)(ASAP)
82. white body, white container, "Stroehmann Pennsylvania Dutch Bakers" tempa ($50+)(ASAP)
83. white body, white container, "CJ Martin & Co., Est. 1833" (left side only) tempa ($50+)(ASAP)
84. black body, dark gray container, blue windows, black hubs, green & yellow cross tempa ($50+)(CM)(CHI)(MP)
85. white body, white container, "Movequest" labels ($50+)(ASAP)
86. white body, white container, "Resin Tech, Inc." labels ($50+)(ASAP)
87. white body, white container, "Simonton Windows/ Eastern Aluminum Supply" labels ($50+)(ASAP)
88. white body, white container, "CAM2" labels ($50+)(ASAP)
89. white body, white container, Capitol Building Supply" labels ($50+)(ASAP)
90. white body, white container, "Matco" labels ($50+)(ASAP)
91. white body, white container, "Steve Shannon" labels ($50+)(ASAP)
92. white body, white container, "Sprint/ Sprint PCS" labels ($50+)(ASAP)
93. white body, white container, "Hood" labels ($50+)(ASAP)
94. white body, white container, "Promotions East" labels ($50+)(ASAP)
95. white body, white container, "MSC Industrial Supply Co." labels ($50+)(ASAP)
96. white body, white container, "Ameritech Movers Voice Mail" labels ($50+)(ASAP)
97. white body, white container, "Price Costco" labels ($50+)(ASAP)
98. white body, white container, "Geiger 125" labels ($50+)(ASAP)
99. white body, white container, "Pegasus Trans Air" labels ($50+)(ASAP)

MB20-E VOLKSWAGEN TRANSPORTER, issued 1988 (ROW)(182)

NOTE: Below models with blue windows & dome lights, gray interior & black plastic base unless otherwise noted...

1. white body, 8 dot silver wheels, orange stripe & cross tempa, Macau casting ($2-4)
2. black body, 8 dot black wheels, green cross & "LS2081" tempa, Macau casting ($4-6)(CM)
3. white body, 8 dot silver wheels, red stripe & cross tempa, Macau casting ($2-4)
4. white body, 8 dot silver wheels, red stripe & cross tempa, China casting ($2-4)

5. black body, 8 dot black wheels, green cross & "LS2081" tempa, China casting ($4-6)(CM)
6. white body, white base, 8 dot silver wheels, no tempa, China casting ($10-15)(GF)
7. white body, 8 dot silver wheels, red stripe/ cross & "Ambulance" tempa, China casting ($1-2)
8. white body, 8 dot silver wheels, green "Ambulance" with orange dashes & "Paramedic" logo tempa, China casting ($2-3)
9. black body, black base, tannish cream interior, 8 dot silver wheels, green cross & "LS2081" tempa, China casting ($20-25)(CM)(CHI(MP)
10. black body, black base, tannish cream interior, 5 arch black wheels, green cross & "LS2081" tempa, China casting ($20-25)(CM)(CHI)(MP)

MB20-F PONTIAC FIREBIRD RAM AIR, issued 1997 (USA)(MB303)
MB66-H PONTIAC FIREBIRD RAM AIR, issued 1997 (ROW)
NOTE: Below models listed with clear windows & black base.
1. lemon body, black interior, 5 spoke concave star wheels, "Formula V-8/ Ram Air" tempa, Thailand casting ($1-2)
2. silver-gray body, black & maroon interior, chrome disc with rubber tires, detailed trim tempa, Thailand casting ($3-5)(PC14)
3. black body, tan interior, 5 spoke concave star wheels, "Formula V-8/ Ram Air" tempa, Thailand casting ($1-2)(MW72/1998 US)
4. black body, tan interior, 5 spoke concave star wheels, "Formula V-8/ Ram Air" tempa, China casting ($1-2)(MW72/1998 US)
5. metallic gold body, black interior, 5 spoke concave star wheels, no tempa, Thailand casting ($8-12)(CH)
6. metallic gold body, black interior, 5 spoke concave star wheels, no tempa, China casting ($5-10)(CH)
7. red body, black & tan interior, chrome disc wheels with rubber tires, detailed trim & "Trans Am" tempa, China casting ($5-8)(PC)
8. lemon body, black interior, chrome disc wheels with rubber tires, "Coca Cola Play Refreshed" tempa, China casting ($3-5)(Coke PC)

MB20-G 1968 FORD MUSTANG COBRA JET *see MB69-H*

MB20-H JUMBO SWEEPER, issued 2004 (USA)(MB659)
1. silver blue body, chrome eyes, orange chassis, red plastic base, gold 10 spoke flower wheels, garbage can tempa, China casting ($1-2)(MW20/2004 US)

MB21-A FODEN CEMENT TRUCK, issued 1970
NOTE: Below models with green windows, 5 spoke wheels, plastic base & England casting.
1. yellow body, yellow barrel, green base ($20-35)
2. bright yellow body, yellow barrel, green base ($20-35)
3. bright yellow body, yellow barrel, dark green base ($20-35)

MB21-B ROD ROLLER, issued 1973
NOTE: Below models with red seat, plastic base & England casting unless otherwise noted.
1. yellow body, green base, hood label, metallic red rear wheels ($18-25)
2. yellow body, green base, hood label, red rear wheels ($15-18)
3. yellow body, green base, hood label, black rear wheels ($12-15)
4. yellow body, black base, hood label, black rear wheels ($15-18)
5. yellow body, green base, no label, black rear wheels ($12-15)
6. orange-yellow body, black base, hood label, black rear wheels ($15-18)
7. orange-yellow body, green base, hood label, black rear wheels ($12-15)
8. orange body, green base with Manaus tab, hood label, black rear wheels ($250+)(BR)

MB21-C RENAULT 5TL, issued 1978 (MB021)
NOTE: Below models with dot dash silver wheels, metal base and England casting unless otherwise noted. Tailgate color matches body color.
1. yellow body, tan interior, silver-gray base, clear windows, "Le Car" tempa ($4-6)
2. yellow body, tan interior, black base, clear windows, "Le Car" tempa ($4-6)
3. yellow body, tan interior, silver-gray base, amber windows, "Le Car" tempa ($4-6)
4. yellow body, tan interior, black base, amber windows, Le Car" tempa ($4-6)
5. yellow body, red interior, black base, clear windows, "Le Car" tempa ($8-12)
6. yellow body, red interior, silver-gray base, clear windows, "Le Car" tempa ($8-12)
7. yellow body, tan interior, charcoal base, clear windows, "Le Car" tempa ($4-6)
8. yellow body, tan interior, charcoal base, amber windows, "Le Car" tempa ($4-6)
9. yellow body, gray-yellow interior, charcoal base, clear windows, "Le Car" tempa ($4-6)
10. metallic blue body, tan interior, silver-gray base, clear windows, no tempa, black hubs ($4-6)
11. metallic blue body, tan interior, silver-gray base, clear windows, no tempa ($4-6)
12. metallic blue body, tan interior, black base, clear windows, no tempa ($4-6)
13. metallic blue body, tan interior, silver-gray base, amber windows, no tempa ($4-6)
14. metallic blue body, tan interior, black base, amber windows, no tempa ($4-6)
15. metallic blue body, tan interior, charcoal base, clear windows, no tempa, ($4-6)
16. metallic blue body, red interior, silver-gray base, clear windows, no tempa ($8-12)
17. metallic blue body, red interior, black base, clear windows, no tempa ($8-12)
18. silver-gray body, tan interior, silver-gray base, clear windows, no tempa ($18-25)
19. silver-gray body, tan interior, black base, clear windows, no tempa ($18-25)
20. silver-gray body, red interior, black base, clear windows, "A5" tempa ($15-20)
21. silver-gray body, red interior, silver-gray base, clear windows, "A5" tempa ($15-20)
22. silver-gray body, red interior, silver-gray base, clear windows, no tempa ($4-6)
23. silver-gray body, red interior, black base, clear windows, "Le Car" tempa ($4-6)
24. silver-gray body, red interior, charcoal base, clear windows, "Le Car" tempa ($4-6)
25. silver-gray body, red interior, black base, amber windows, "Le Car" tempa ($4-6)
26. silver-gray body, red interior, charcoal base, amber windows, "Le Car" tempa ($4-6)

27. silver-gray body, red interior, charcoal base, clear windows, "Le Car" tempa, black hubs ($4-6)
28. silver-gray body, red interior, blue-gray base, orange windows, "Le Car" tempa ($4-6)
29. silver-gray body, red interior, gray-brown base, clear windows, "Le Car" tempa ($4-6)
30. silver-gray body, red interior, gray-brown base, amber windows, "Le Car" tempa ($4-6)
31. silver-gray body, red interior, black base, clear windows, "A5" tempa with "Climat" label on hood ($125-175)(FR)
32. silver-gray body, red interior, black base, clear windows, "Le Car" tempa with "Climat" label on hood ($125-175)(FR)
33. white body, tan interior, black base, clear windows, "Renault" tempa ($3-5)
34. white body, tan interior, charcoal base, clear windows, "Renault" tempa ($3-5)
35. white body, light yellow interior, black base, clear windows, "Renault" tempa($3-5)
36. white body, light yellow interior, charcoal base, clear windows, "Renault" tempa ($4-6)
37. white body, white interior, black base, clear windows, "Renault" tempa ($4-6)
38. white body, tan interior, black base, clear windows, "Renault" tempa (plain roof) ($4-6)
39. white body, tan interior, black base, clear windows, "Renault" tempa (plain sides) ($8-12)
40. white body, tan interior, black base, clear windows, "Roloil" tempa ($3-5)
41. white body, dark yellow interior, black base, clear windows, "Roloil" tempa ($3-5)
42. white body, white interior, black base, clear windows, "Roloil" tempa ($3-5)
43. white body, tan interior, orange base, clear windows, "Roloil" tempa ($15-20)
44. red body, orange interior, orange base, clear windows, "Turbo" tempa ($15-20)(JP)
45. red body, tan interior, black base, clear windows, "Turbo" tempa ($18-25)
46. white body, tan interior, black base, clear windows, "Roloil" tempa, Macau casting ($3-4)(TP)
47. pearly silver body, black interior, black base, clear windows, "Scrambler" tempa, Macau casting ($4-6)(TP)
48. white body, tan interior, charcoal base, clear windows, "Renault" tempa with plain roof ($4-6)
49. powder blue body, tan interior, black base, clear windows, no tempa, Manaus casting ($75-100)(BR)
50. white body, orange interior, cream plastic base, clear windows, "Roloil" tempa, Manaus casting ($35-50)(BR)
51. white body, tan interior, black base, clear windows, "Roloil" tempa, 8 dot wheels, Manaus casting ($35-50)(BR)
52. white body, orange interior, cream plastic base, clear windows, "Roloil" tempa, 8 dot wheels, Manaus casting ($35-50)(BR)
53. yellow body, tan interior, black base, clear windows, "Le Toy Show/ Matchbox Road Museum" tempa, England casting ($25-35)(CCI)
54. yellow body, tan interior, black base, amber windows, "Le Toy Show/ Matchbox Road Museum" tempa, England casting ($25-35)(CCI)
55. yellow body, tan interior, silver-gray base, clear windows, "Le Toy Show/ Matchbox Road Museum" tempa, England casting ($25-35)(CCI)
56. yellow body, red interior, black base, clear windows, "Le Toy Show/ Matchbox Road Museum" tempa, England casting ($25-35)(CCI)
57. brown body, yellow interior, black base & tailgate, clear windows, "Sofia 92" & Olympic rings tempa, Bulgaria casting ($50-75)(Bulgaria promo)

NOTE: Available as a Bulgarian casting ($5-25)

MB21-D CORVETTE PACE CAR, issued 1983 (USA)(MB115)

NOTE: Below models with 5 arch front & 5 crown rear wheels but other wheel combinations exist. All models with clear windows & metal base.

1. pearly silver body, red interior & base, without "Pace" on trunk, Macau casting ($5-8)
2. pearly silver body, red interior & base, with "Pace" on trunk, Macau casting ($5-8)

MB21-E CHEVY BREAKDOWN VAN, issued 1985 (MB150/316)
MB53-F CHEVY BREAKDOWN VAN, reissued 1990 (USA)

NOTE: Below models with blue windows, black tow hook, 8 spoke silver wheels unless otherwise noted.

1. red body, pearly silver base, silver-gray interior, white boom, "24 Hour Service" tempa, Macau casting ($1-2)
2. red body, pearly gray base, silver-gray interior, white boom, "24 Hour Service" tempa, China casting ($1-2)
3. red body, pearly gray base, silver-gray interior, white boom, "24 Hours" with white stripes tempa, China casting ($2-3)(MP)
4. yellow body, black base, black interior, black boom, "Auto Relay 24 Hr. Tow" tempa, China casting ($1-2)
5. black body, gray base, gray interior, gray boom, yellow stripes tempa, black hubs, China casting ($4-6)(CM)
6. black body, gray base, gray interior, gray boom, yellow stripes tempa, silver hubs, China casting ($5-7)(CM)
7. red body, yellow base, silver-gray interior, lime boom, cartoon towed car tempa, blue wheels with yellow hubs, China casting ($6-8)(LL)
8. dark orange body, black base, orange-yellow interior, orange-yellow boom, "Auto Relay 24 Hr. Tow" tempa, China casting ($3-5)(AP)
9. white body, black base, black interior, black boom, "Auto Rescue" tempa, China casting ($2-4)(EM)
10. white body, white base, red interior, white boom, no tempa, red windows, China casting ($10-15)(GF)
11. orange-yellow body, greenish black base, black interior, black boom, "Auto Relay 24 Hr. Tow" tempa, China casting ($1-2)
12. red body, yellow base, silver-gray interior, green boom, cartoon towed car tempa, all blue wheels, China casting ($6-8)(LL)
13. florescent orange body, black base with bar code, black interior, black boom, "Intercom City Auto Service 7" tempa, China casting ($10-15)(IC)
14. black body, black base, black interior, red boom & hook, "24" with hand & car logo tempa, China casting ($1-2)(5pk)
15. lemon body, black base, red windows, black interior, black boom, sling hook, "Rob's Towing 24 Hours" tempa, China casting ($1-2)(AS)
16. matt olive body, silver-gray base, smoke windows, pearly silver boom & sling hook, "Gen IV" & "The Lost World" tempa, China casting ($5-8)(JR)
17. silver-gray body, black base, red windows, black boom & sling hook, "Rob's Towing 24 Hours" tempa, China casting ($1-2)(AP)
18. black body, gray base, gray boom, 5 crown wheels with black hubs, yellow stripes & Commando logo tempa, China casting ($20-25)(CHI)(MP)
19. blue body, gray base, gray boom & sling, "MB" logo & dirt tempa, China casting ($1-2)(5pk)
20. white & purple body, silver-gray base, purple boom & sling, "Metro Alarm MA-BU1" tempa, China casting ($10-15)(5pk)

21. white & purple body, silver-gray base, purple boom & sling, "Metro Alarm MA-BU1" tempa, 7 spoke sawblade wheels, China casting ($1-2)(5pk)

MB21-F GMC WRECKER, issued 1987 (USA)(MB188)
MB71-F GMC WRECKER, issued 1987 (ROW)

NOTE: Below models with white rear bed, white boom, black hook, cloudy amber windows, 8 spoke wheels & chrome plastic base unless otherwise noted.

1. white body, unpainted metal base, "Frank's Getty" with phone no. tempa, Macau casting ($1-2)
2. white body, unpainted metal base, "Accessory Wholesalers Inc." tempa, Macau casting ($18-25)(US)
3. white body, "Frank's Getty" with phone no. tempa, Macau casting ($1-2)
4. white body, "Frank's Getty" with phone no. tempa, China casting ($1-2)
5. white body, "Frank's Getty" with phone no. tempa, Thailand casting ($1-2)
6. white body, "Frank's Getty" with phone no. tempa, no origin cast ($3-5)
7. white body, "Frank's Getty" tempa without phone no. tempa, China casting ($1-2)
8. white body, "Frank's Getty" tempa without phone no. (solid color tempa), Thailand casting ($1-2)
9. black body, "Official Wrecker Indy 500" tempa, Thailand casting ($5-8)(IN)
10. white body, "Police/Metro Emergency" tempa, Thailand casting ($1-2)(5pk)
11. white body, "Polioe/Metro Emergency" tempa, Thailand casting ($1-2)(5pk) *NOTE: Misspelled Police (POLIOE).*
12. red body, black boom, "Ron's Towing" tempa, Thailand casting ($2-4)(CC)
13. white body, florescent orange boom, "3 Rescue", checkers & wrench design tempa, Thailand casting ($2-4)(FI)
14. black body, white boom, "Police Emergency Unit 4" & gold star tempa, Thailand casting ($1-2)(5pk)
15. dark purple body, neon yellow boom, "Park Hill Towing" with hood design tempa, Thailand casting ($1-2)
16. dark purple body, neon yellow boom, "Park Hill Towing" without hood design tempa, Thailand casting ($1-2)
17. dark purple body, neon yellow boom, "Park Hill Towing" without hood design tempa, China casting ($1-2)
18. metallic gold body, black boom, no tempa, China casting ($5-10)(CH)
19. white body, florescent orange boom, "3 Rescue", checkers & wrench design tempa, China casting ($1-2)(F1)
20. dark purple body, neon yellow boom, "Park Hill Towing" without hood design tempa, China casting ($2-4)
21. orange body, black boom, "Park Hill Towing" without hood design tempa, orange hook, China casting ($5-8)(ROW)
22. white body, cloudy clear windows, black boom, "Matchbox 24 Hr. Towing" tempa, black plastic base, China casting ($2-4)(5pk)
23. white body, red windows, blue boom, "CAA Member Service" tempa, China casting ($100-150)(CN)
24. white body, amber windows, blue boom, "CAA Member Service" tempa, China casting ($10-15)(CN)
25. white body, white boom, "Matchbox ASI 33000" tempa, China casting ($50+)(ASAP)
26. white body, white boom, "Phil's Body Works" tempa, China casting ($100+)(ASAP)
27. black body, white boom, "Matchbox" with yellow & white design tempa, China casting ($1-2)(MW63/1998)
28. red body, white boom, "Matchbox" with yellow & white design tempa, China casting ($1-2)(MW63/1998)
29. white body, white boom, "PTROI" tempa, China casting ($20-35)(ASAP)
30. white body, white boom, no tempa, China casting ($20-25)(ASAP blank)
31. white body, white boom, "American International Recovery" tempa, China casting ($100+)(ASAP)
32. red body, black boom, "Ron's" with yellow & white markings tempa, China casting ($1-2)(MW14/1999 US)
33. red body, black boom, "Service GMC" with yellow & white markings tempa, China casting ($1-2)(MW14/1999 ROW)
34. black body, silver-gray boom, "Service GMC" with white & yellow markings, "Matchbox" logo tempa, China casting ($3-5)(PB)
35. metallic green body, silver-gray boom, "Ron's" with white & yellow markings, "Matchbox 2000" tempa, China casting ($2-4)(MW88/2000 US)
36. metallic green body, silver-gray boom, "Ron's" with white & yellow markings tempa, China casting ($1-2)(MW88/2000 US)
37. white body, white boom, "Riehl's Towing" tempa, China casting ($75+)(CCI)
38. white body, white boom, "Helmrich Towing & Recovery" tempa, China casting ($75+)(CCI)
39. white body, white boom, "Alenco Service" tempa, China casting ($75+)(ASAP)
40. black & silver-gray body, black boom, "Texaco 24 Hour Towing" tempa, chrome disc wheels with rubber tires, China casting ($3-5)(Texaco PC)
41. black & silver-gray body, black boom, "Texaco 24 Hour Towing" tempa, black disc wheels with rubber tires , China casting ($3-5)(Texaco PC)
42. yellow body, cloudy red windows, black plastic base, blue boom with chrome rear, "Rapid Rescue" tempa, 7 spoke sawblade wheels, China casting ($3-5)(PS)
43. metallic green body, silver-gray boom, "Ron's with yellow & orange markings tempa, 7 spoke sawblade wheels, China castings ($2-4)(MW88/2000)
44. black body, silver-gray boom, "Service GMC" tempa, 7 spoke sawblade wheels, China casting ($3-5)(PB)

MB21-G NISSAN PRAIRIE *see MB31-I*

MB21-H FERRARI F50 *see MB75-G*

MB21-I FORD TRANSIT AMBULANCE , issued 1999 (GR)(MB431/472/554)
MB14-J FORD TRANSIT AMBULANCE , issued 2003 (USA)
MB31-N FORD TRANSIT AMBULANCE, issued 2001 (ROW)

NOTE: Below models with 10 spoke flower wheel, plastic base & China casting unless otherwise noted.

1. red body, black base, white interior, clear windows, blue bar dome light, "112 Feuerwehr" tempa, 8 dot wheels ($4-6)(MW21/1999 GR)(MW12/2000 GR)
2. red body, white base, black interior, smoke windows, blue triangular dome light, "London Fire Brigade" & yellow stripes tempa, 8 dot wheels ($3-5)(MW40/2000 UK)
3. lemon body, black base, black interior, clear windows, blue bar dome light, "Medic" & blue stripes tempa ($2-3)(MW31/2001 ROW)
4. white body, chrome base, dark green interior, smoke windows, amber bar dome light, "K-9 Patrol" tempa ($1-2)(5pk)
5. bright blue body, black base, black interior, clear windows, red bar dome light, helmet & hose design tempa ($1-2)(LP)

6. metallic blue body, black base, black interior, smoke windows, amber bar dome light, "S.O.S." & dolphins design tempa ($1-2)(5pk)
7. white body, black base, blue interior, clear windows, blue bar dome light, "Polis" tempa ($2-4)(MW16/2002 ROW)
8. white body, black base, blue interior, clear windows, blue bar dome light, "Polis" & "Matchbox 50" tempa ($2-4) (MW16/2002 ROW)

NOTE: Below models with Mattel China casting.

9. white body, black base, blue interior, clear windows, blue bar dome light, medical design tempa ($1-2)(MW14/2003)
10. white body, black base, blue interior, clear windows, blue bar dome light, medical design & "Hero City" tempa ($2-4)(MW14/2003)

MB21-J X-33 RLV *see MB36-H*

MB21-K TOWER BOAT, issued 2001 (MB484)

1. red deck, white hull, red spoiler, smoke windshield, white wheels, "Unit 26" tempa, China casting ($1-2)(MW21/2001)
2. cream body, metallic red hull, dark red spoiler, red windshield, white wheels, helmet & hose design tempa, China casting (LP)
3. red body, white hull, yellow spoiler, amber windshield, white wheels, checkers & "120 120" design tempa, China casting ($2-4)(MW52/2002 ROW)
4. red body, white hull, yellow spoiler, amber windshield, white wheels, checkers & "120 120" & Matchbox 50" tempa, China casting ($3-5)(MW52/2002 ROW)
5. white body, black hull, black spoiler, black windshield, black wheels, "05 Police" tempa, China casting ($1-2)(5pk)

MB21-L CADILLAC ESCALADE, issued 2003 (MB567)

NOTE: Below models with 7 spoke sawblade wheels, black plastic base & China casting unless otherwise noted.

1. black body, gray interior, clear windows, gears & stripes design tempa ($1-2)(MW21/2003)
2. black body, gray interior, clear windows, gears & stripes design & "Hero City" tempa ($2-3)(MW21/2003)
3. black body, gray interior, clear windows, gears & stripes design/ "Mom Me & Matchbox/ Matchbox Chelsea Piers" tempa ($20-35)(CCI)
4. white body, orange interior, amber windows, "Nickelodeon" tempa ($1-2)(CA)
5. metallic green body, black interior, smoke windows, "Green Lantern" tempa ($1-2)(5pk)
6. metallic green body, orange interior, amber windows, "Nickelodeon" tempa ($1-2)(CA)
7. lime body, black interior, smoke windows, "Green Lantern" tempa ($1-2)(CA)
8. black body, tan interior, smoke windows, head & tail lights tempa, slotted 5 spoke wheels ($3-5)(SF11/2004)
9. white body, black interior, clear windows, "Coca-Cola Football Town/ Total Tailgate" tempa, 7 spoke sawblade wheels ($2-4)(CK)
10. green body, red interior, amber windows, "King Neptune-The Spongebob Squarepants Movie" tempa, lace wheels ($1-2)(5pk)

MB21-M MUSH PUPPY, issued 2004 (USA)(MB642)
MB 9-L MUSH PUPPY, issued 2004 (ROW)

NOTE: Below models with brown ears, red windows, brown barrel, black wheels, red-brown base, China casting unless otherwise noted.

1. white body, "24 7" & red grille tempa ($1-2)

MB22-A PONTIAC GRAND PRIX, issued 1970

NOTE: Below models with clear windows, plain grille, black metal base & England casting.

1. red body, doors open, gray interior ($2000+)
2. dark metallic purple body, doors cast shut, gray interior ($75-150)
3. light metallic purple body, doors cast shut, gray interior ($75-150)
4. metallic purple, doors cast shut, gray interior ($75-100)
5. metallic purple, doors cast shut, gray interior, silver grille ($100-150)

MB22-B FREEMAN INTERCITY COMMUTER, issued 1970

NOTE: Below models with, unpainted base & England casting unless otherwise noted.

1. metallic purple body, unpainted base, ivory interior, no labels ($15-18)
2. metallic purple body, unpainted base, ivory interior, with labels ($15-18)
3. gold body, unpainted base, ivory interior, with labels ($15-18)
4. metallic magenta body, unpainted base, ivory interior, no labels ($15-18)
5. metallic magenta body, unpainted base, ivory interior, with labels ($15-18)
6. metallic magenta body, silver-gray base, ivory interior, no labels ($15-18)
7. metallic magenta body, silver-gray base, ivory interior, with labels ($15-18)
8. metallic magenta body, unpainted base, white interior, no labels ($15-18)
9. cherry red body, unpainted base with Manaus label, ivory interior, no labels ($250+)(BR)
10. pink body, unpainted base with Manaus tab, ivory interior, with labels ($250+)(BR)

MB22-C BLAZE BUSTER, issued 1975 (MB022)

NOTE: Below models with amber windows, metal base & England casting unless otherwise noted.

1. red body, white ladder, unpainted base, chrome interior, 5 spoke wheels "Fire" labels ($300-450)
2. red body, black ladder, unpainted base, chrome interior, 5 spoke wheels, "Fire" labels ($20-35)
3. red body, yellow ladder, unpainted base, chrome interior, 5 spoke wheels, "Fire" labels ($5-8)
4. red body, yellow ladder, unpainted base with Manaus label, chrome interior, 5 spoke wheels, "Fire" labels ($35-50)(BR)
5. red body, yellow ladder, gray base with Manaus label, chrome interior, 5 spoke wheels, "Fire" label s ($65-85)(BR)
6. red body, yellow ladder, black base, chrome interior, 4 spoke wheels, "Fire" labels ($20-35)
7. red body, yellow ladder, black base, chrome interior, 5 spoke wheels, "Fire" labels ($5-8)
8. red body, yellow ladder, black base, white interior, 5 spoke wheels, "Fire" labels ($5-8)
9. red body, yellow ladder, black base, white interior, 4 spoke wheels, "Fire" labels ($15-20)
10. red body, yellow ladder, charcoal base, white interior, 5 spoke wheels, "Fire" labels ($5-8)
11. red body, yellow ladder, charcoal base, white interior, 4 spoke wheels, "Fire" labels ($15-20)
12. dark red body, yellow ladder, black base, white interior, 4 spoke wheels, "Fire" labels ($15-20)
13. dark red body, yellow ladder, charcoal base, white interior, 5 spoke wheels, "Fire" labels ($5-8)

14. dark red body, yellow ladder, gray-brown base, white interior, 5 spoke wheels, "Fire" labels ($5-8)
15. dull red body, orange-yellow ladder, black base, white interior, 5 spoke wheels, "Fire" labels ($5-8)
16. dull red body, orange-yellow ladder, black base, white interior, 5 spoke wheels, "No. 32" labels ($8-12)
17. red body, yellow ladder, black base with Manaus label, chrome interior, 5 spoke wheels, "Fire" labels ($35-50)(BR)
18. red body, yellow ladder, gray base with Manaus tab, chrome interior, 5 spoke wheels, "Fire" labels (BR)

NOTE: Available as a Bulgarian casting. Assorted variations available ($8-15)

MB22-D 4 X 4 MINI PICKUP, issued 1982 (USA)(MB098)
MB35-E 4 X 4 MINI PICKUP, issued 1986 (ROW)

NOTE: Below models with blue windows & maltese cross wheels.

1. silver-gray body, unpainted metal base, white stepped roof, "Big Foot" tempa, England casting ($4-6)
2. silver-gray body, unpainted metal base, white stepped roof, "Big Foot" tempa (plain sides), England casting ($5-8)
3. silver-gray body, unpainted metal base, white flat roof, "Big Foot" tempa, England casting ($4-6)
4. silver-gray body, silver-gray metal base, white flat roof, "Big Foot" tempa, England casting ($4-6)
5. silver-gray body, silver-gray metal base, white flat roof, "Big Foot" tempa (plain sides) tempa, England casting ($5-8)
6. pearly silver body, black metal base, white flat roof, "Big Foot" tempa, Hong Kong casting ($5-8)
7. pearly silver body, black metal base, white flat roof, "Big Foot" tempa, Macau casting ($4-6)
8. red body, black metal base, white flat roof, "Aspen Ski Holidays" tempa, Macau casting ($2-4)
9. white body, black metal base, white flat roof, "SLD Pump Service" tempa, Macau casting ($10-15)(UK)
10. red body, black plastic base, white flat roof, "Aspen Ski Holidays" tempa, Macau casting ($2-3)
11. red body, black plastic base, white flat roof, "Aspen Ski Holidays" tempa, Thailand casting ($2-3)

MB22-E JAGUAR XK120, issued 1984 (ROW) (MB138)

NOTE: Below models with 5 crown wheels & metal base unless otherwise noted.

1. dark green body, red interior, silver-gray base, clear windshield, no tempa, England casting ($2-4)
2. dark green body, red interior, unpainted base, clear windshield, no tempa, England casting ($2-4)
3. dark green body, red interior, pearly silver base, clear windshield, no tempa, Macau casting ($2-4)
4. dark green body, red interior, pearly silver base, amber windshield, no tempa, Macau casting ($2-4)
5. cream body, red interior, pearly silver base, clear windshield, "414" tempa, Macau casting ($1-2)
6. white body, dark maroon interior, pearly silver base, chrome windshield, detailed trim tempa, gray disc with rubber tires, Macau casting ($5-8)(WC)
7. dark cream body, dark red interior, pearly silver base, clear windshield, "414" tempa, Macau casting ($1-2)
8. cream body, red interior, pearly silver base, clear windshield, "414" tempa, Thailand casting ($1-2)
9. white body, purplish black interior, pearly silver base, chrome windshield, detailed trim tempa, gray disc with rubber tires, Thailand casting ($5-8)(WC)
10. white body, orange interior, pearly silver base, amber windshield, blue & orange flash tempa, Thailand casting ($3-5)(DM)
11. red body, white interior, pearly silver base, clear windshield, 5 crown wheels, silver head lights & rear trim tempa, Thailand casting ($2-4)(GS)
12. black body, orange interior, pearly silver base, clear windshield, 5 crown wheels, detailed trim tempa, Thailand casting ($2-4)(CC)
13. dark green body, tan/brown interior, black base, clear windshield, chrome disc wheels with rubber tires, detailed trim tempa, China casting ($3-5)(PC3)
14. red body, mustard/brown interior, black base, clear windshield, chrome disc wheels with rubber tires, detailed trim tempa, China casting ($3-5)(PC6)
15. black body, mustard & brown interior, black base, clear windshield, chrome wheels disc with rubber tires, detailed trim tempa, China casting ($3-5)(SC3)
16. pale olive body, maroon interior, black base, clear windshield, detailed trim tempa, 5 arch wheels, China casting ($2-4)(AU)
17. dark green body, tan interior, black base, clear windshield, detailed trim tempa, gold 6 spoke spiral wheels, China casting ($50+)(CHI)
18. red body, tan interior, black base, clear windshield,, detailed trim tempa, gold 6 spoke spiral wheels, China casting ($50+)(CHI)
19. black body, tan interior, black base, clear windshield, detailed trim tempa, gold 6 spoke spiral wheels, China casting ($50+)(CHI)
20. dark green body, mustard & brown interior, black base, clear windshield, detailed trim tempa, gold 6 spoke spiral wheels, China casting ($50+)(CHI)
21. red body, white interior, black base, clear windshield, "Coca Cola" tempa, chrome disc wheels with rubber tires, white walls, China casting ($3-5)(Coke PC)(MP)
22. red body, white interior, black base, clear windshield, "Coca Cola" tempa, chrome disc wheels with rubber tires, black walls, China casting ($3-5)(Coke PC)(MP)
23. black body, tan interior, black base, clear windshield, detailed trim tempa, gold 6 spoke spiral wheels, China casting ($50+)(CHI)
24. dark green body, mustard & brown interior, black base, clear windshield, detailed trim tempa, gold 6 spoke spiral wheels, China casting ($50+)(CHI)
25. dark cream body, brown & black interior, black base, clear windshield, detailed trim tempa, chrome disc wheels with rubber tires, China casting ($50+)(GC)(CHI)

NOTE: Above model was intended for the gold coin series but ended up for sale separately in China.

MB22-F SAAB 9000 TURBO *see MB15-F*

MB22-G VECTRA CAVALIER Gsi 2000, issued 1990 (USA)(MB201)
MB41-G VECTRA CAVALIER GSi 2000, issued 1990 (ROW)

NOTE: Below models with black plastic base, clear windows, gray interior & 8 dot wheels,.

1. metallic red body, silver headlights tempa, Macau casting ($1-2)
2. metallic pink-red body, silver headlights tempa, Macau casting ($1-2)
3. metallic pink-red body, silver headlights tempa, China casting ($1-2)
4. metallic pink-red body, no tempa, China casting ($1-2)
5. green body, no tempa, China casting ($8-12)(GR)(GS)

MB22-H LAMBORGHINI DIABLO, issued 1992 (USA)(MB232)
MB49-F LAMBORGHINI DIABLO, issued 1992 (ROW)

NOTE: Below models with plastic base.

1. yellow body, yellow base, black interior, clear windows, 8 dot wheels, "Diablo" tempa, China casting ($1-2)
2. red body, red base, black interior, chrome windows, gray disc wheels with rubber tires, detailed trim tempa, China casting ($5-8)(WC)
3. fluorescent yellow body, fluorescent yellow base, clear windows, black interior, 8 dot wheels, small "Lamborghini" logo tempa, China casting ($2-4)(SS)
4. red body, red base, black interior, clear windows, black interior, 8 dot wheels, "Diablo" tempa, Thailand casting ($50-75)(SP)(UK)
5. black body, black base, chrome windows, black interior, gray disc wheels with rubber tires, detailed trim tempa, Thailand casting ($2-4)(WC)
6. yellow body, yellow base, clear windows, black interior, 8 dot wheels, "Diablo" tempa, Thailand casting ($1-2)
7. yellow body, yellow base, clear windows, black interior, gold 6 spoke gold spiral wheels, "Diablo" tempa, Thailand casting ($2-3)
8. metallic blue & black body, black base, clear windows, orange interior, gold 6 spoke spiral wheels, orange & white flash tempa, Thailand casting ($1-2)
9. hot pink body, black base, clear windows, black interior, silver 6-spoke spiral wheels, black blotches tempa, Thailand casting ($1-2)(5pk)
10. florescent yellow body, black base, clear windows, pink interior, silver 6-spoke spiral wheels, black blotches tempa, Thailand casting ($1-2)
11. silver body, black base, amber windows, white interior, silver 6-spoke spiral wheels, orange & yellow flames tempa, Thailand casting ($3-5)(MT)
12. dark purple body, black base, clear windows, orange interior, silver 6-spoke spiral wheels, white blotches tempa, Thailand casting ($1-2)(5pk)
13. metallic mauve body, mauve base, clear windows, blue & black interior, chrome disc with rubber tires, detailed trim tempa, Thailand casting ($3-5)(PC2)
14. red body, black base, clear windows, yellow interior, silver 6-spoke spiral wheels, black blotches tempa, Thailand casting ($3-5)
15. silver-gray body, gray base, clear windows, blue/black interior, chrome disc wheels with rubber tires, detailed trim tempa, Thailand casting ($3-5)(PC5)
16. yellow body, yellow base, clear windows, gray/black interior, chrome disc wheels with rubber tires, detailed trim tempa, Thailand casting ($3-5)(PC1)(AU)
17. blue body, blue base, clear windows, blue/ gray interior, chrome disc wheels with rubber tires, detailed trim tempa, Thailand casting ($3-5)(SC2)
18. blue body, black base, clear windows, brown interior, 5 spoke concave star wheels, white "Diablo" with white & black design tempa, Thailand casting ($1-2)
19. metallic gold body, black base, clear windows, black interior, silver 6 spoke spiral wheels, no tempa, Thailand casting ($5-10)(CH)
20. white body, black base, clear windows, blue & gray interior, chrome disc wheels with rubber tires, detailed trim tempa, Thailand casting ($15-20)(GC)
21. metallic gold body, black base, clear windows, black interior, 5 spoke concave star wheels, no tempa, Thailand casting ($10-15)(CH)
22. blue body, black painted base, clear windows, brown interior, 5 spoke concave star wheels, white "Diablo" with black & white design tempa, Thailand casting ($2-4)(5pk)
23. black body, black base, clear windows, red interior, 5 spoke concave star wheels, "Lamborghini" tempa, Thailand casting ($1-2)(ROW)
24. metallic turquoise body, black base, clear windows, black & gray interior, chrome disc wheels with rubber tires, detailed trim tempa, Thailand casting ($3-5)(JC-PC)
25. red body, black base, clear windows, black & red interior, chrome disc wheels with rubber tires, detailed trim tempa, Thailand casting ($3-5)(SC4)
26. yellow chrome body, black base, black interior, 5 spoke concave star wheels, orange/white/dark pink tempa, Thailand casting ($1-2)(5pk)
27. metallic purple body, purple base, black & gray interior, chrome disc wheels with rubber tires, detailed trim tempa, Thailand casting ($3-5)(SC5)
28. gold body, gold base, gray & black interior, chrome disc wheels with rubber tires, detailed trim tempa, Thailand casting ($3-5)(PC19)
29. yellow chrome body, black base, black interior, 5 spoke concave star wheels, orange/white/dark pink tempa, China casting ($1-2)(5pk)
30. dark purple body, dark purple base, gray interior, 5 spoke concave star wheels, no tempa, China casting ($3-5)(MW28/1999 GR)
31. bright blue body, blue base, gray interior, 5 spoke concave star wheels, "Matchbox 2000" tempa, China casting ($2-4)(MW22/2000 US)
32. bright blue body, blue base, gray interior, 5 spoke concave star wheels, no tempa China casting ($1-2)(MW22/2000 US)(MW17/2000 ROW)
33. bright blue body, blue base, gray interior, small 5 spoke concave star wheels, no tempa , China casting($2-4)(MW22/2000 US)(MW17/2000 ROW)

34.metallic blue body, blue base, gray interior, 10 spoke flower wheels, "Lamborghini" & crest tempa, China casting ($2-4)(MW55/2001 UK)

35. metallic orange body, orange base, black interior, smoke windows, 10 spoke flower wheels, "Lamborghini" & crest tempa, China casting ($2-4)(MW54/2001 GR)
36. red body, red base, gray interior, 10 spoke flower wheels, "Lamborghini" & crest tempa, Mattel China casting ($2-4)(MW23/2002 ROW)
37. red body, red base, gray interior, 10 spoke flower wheels, "Lamborghini" & crest with "Matchbox 50" tempa, Mattel China casting ($3-5)(MW23/2003 ROW)

28\. red body, red base, black interior, 5 spoke concave star wheels, no tempa, China casting ($25-40)(ASAP blank)

29\. red body, red base, black interior, 5 spoke concave star wheels, "Zurich Small Business Rally 2002" tempa, China casting ($50+)(ASAP)

30\. red body, red base, black interior, 5 spoke concave star wheels, "Huskers" tempa, China casting ($18-25)(ASAP)

MB22-I PONTIAC GRAND PRIX *see MB35-H*

MB22-J MITSUBISHI SPYDER *see MB28-L*

MB22-K POUND HOUND, issued 2004 (USA)(MB643)
MB 5-H POUND HOUND, issued 2004 (ROW)

1. metallic gold body, chrome collar & eyes, yellow boom, white teeth, light brown base, gold 7 spoke sawblade wheels, China casting ($1-2)(MW22/2004 US)(MW5/2004 ROW)
2. metallic gold body, chrome collar & eyes, yellow boom, white teeth, dark brown base, gold 7 spoke sawblade wheels, China casting ($1-2) (MW22/2004 US)(MW5/2004 ROW)

MB23-A VOLKSWAGEN CAMPER/ DORMOBILE, issued 1970

NOTE: Below models with metal base & England casting.

1. blue body, unpainted base, orange interior, clear windows, no labels, 5 spoke wheels, orange roof cast, gas tank cast on left side ($50-75)
2. blue body, unpainted base, orange interior, clear windows, no labels, 5 spoke wheels, orange roof cast ($15-18)
3. blue body, unpainted base, orange interior, clear windows, sailboat labels, 5 spoke wheels, orange roof cast ($15-18)
4. blue body, unpainted base, white interior, clear windows, sailboat labels, 5 spoke wheels, orange roof cast ($175-250)
5. orange body, unpainted base, orange interior, clear windows, sailboat labels, 5 spoke wheels, orange roof cast ($17-250)
6. orange body, unpainted base, white interior, clear windows, sailboat labels, 5 spoke wheels, orange roof cast ($12-15)
7. orange body, unpainted base, white interior, clear windows, no labels, 5 spoke wheels, orange roof cast ($12-15)
8. olive body, black base, no interior, blue windows, cross labels, dot dash wheels with silver hubs ($6-8)(TP)
9. olive body, black base, no interior, blue windows, cross labels, dot dash wheels with black hubs ($6-8)(TP)
10. white body, black base, no interior, green windows, "Pizza Van" tempa, dot dash wheels with black hubs ($8-12)(LE)
11. white body, black base, no interior, green windows, "Pizza Van" tempa, dot dash wheels with silver hubs ($8-12)(LE)
12. white body, black base, no interior, green windows, "Pizza Van" tempa, 5 arch wheels ($8-12)(LE)

NOTE: Available as an Hungarian casting. Assorted colors available. Casting has the opening roof with various "Pizza Van" color variations ($15-35)

MB23-B ATLAS, issued 1975 (MB023)

NOTE: Below models with metal base & England casting unless otherwise noted.

1. blue body, orange dump, unpainted base, amber windows, chrome interior, spiro wheels, with labels ($8-12)

NOTE: Below models with no labels applied.

2. blue body, orange dump, unpainted base, amber windows, chrome interior, spiro wheels ($8-12)
3. blue body, orange dump, unpainted base, amber windows, chrome interior, dot dash wheels ($8-12)
4. blue body, orange dump, unpainted base, amber windows, gray interior, dot dash wheels ($8-12)
5. blue body, orange dump, silver-gray base, amber windows, gray interior, dot dash wheels ($8-12)
6. blue body, orange dump, unpainted base, clear windows, gray interior, dot dash wheels ($8-12)
7. blue body, orange dump, silver-gray base, clear windows, gray interior, dot dash wheels ($8-12)
8. blue body, orange dump, silver-gray base, clear windows, orange interior, dot dash wheels ($8-12)
9. blue body, silver-gray dump, silver-gray base, clear windows, gray interior, dot dash wheels ($10-15)
10. red body, silver-gray dump, silver-gray base, clear windows, gray interior, dot dash wheels ($7-10)
11. red body, silver-gray dump, silver-gray base, clear windows, black interior, dot dash wheels ($7-10)
12. mid blue body, yellow dump, black plastic base, clear windows, gray interior, maltese cross wheels, China casting ($7-10)(MP)

MB23-C GT350 MUSTANG, issued 1981 (USA)

1. white body, clear windows, blue interior, 5 arch wheels, black metal base, blue stripes tempa, Hong Kong casting ($8-12)

MB23-D AUDI QUATTRO, issued 1982 (USA)(MB025)
MB25-F AUDI QUATTRO, issued 1982 (ROW)

NOTE: Below models with black interior & metal base.

1. white body, charcoal base, clear windows, 5 arch wheels, "Audi 20" tempa, England casting ($2-4)
2. white body, black base, clear windows, 5 arch wheels, "Audi 20" tempa, England casting ($2-4)
3. white body, black base, clear windows, 5 arch wheels, "Audi 20" (plain sides) tempa, England casting ($2-4)
4. white body, black base, clear windows, 5 arch wheels, "Audi 20" tempa, Macau casting ($2-4)
5. white body, black base, light amber windows, 5 arch wheels, "Audi 20" tempa, Macau casting ($2-4)
6. white body, black base, clear windows, 5 arch wheels, "Duckhams/ Pirelli" tempa, Macau casting ($3-5)
7. white body, black base, clear windows, 5 arch wheels, "Duckhams/ Pirelli" (plain hood) tempa, Macau casting ($3-5)
8. white body, black base, clear windows, 5 arch wheels, "Duckhams" (without "Pirelli") tempa, Macau casting ($3-5)
9. white body, black base, amber windows, 5 arch wheels, "Duckhams/ Pirelli" tempa, Macau casting ($3-5)
10. plum body, black base, clear windows, 5 arch wheels, "Quattro 0000" tempa, Macau casting ($2-4)
11. plum body, black base, clear windows, 8 dot wheels, "Quattro 0000" tempa, Macau casting ($2-4)
12. dark blue body, black base, clear windows, 8 dot wheels, "Quattro 0000" & "Audi" tempa, Macau casting ($8-12)
13. dark blue body, black base, amber windows, 8 dot wheels, "Quattro 0000" & "Audi" tempa, Macau casting ($8-12)
14. dark plum body, black base, clear windows, 5 arch wheels, "Quattro 0000" tempa, China casting ($2-4)
15. dark gray body, black base, clear windows, 5 arch wheels, "0000 Quattro" & "Audi" tempa, China casting ($2-4)
16. dark blue body, black base, clear windows, 5 arch wheels, "上海友谊汽车联营公司" & "Audi 2584584" & "FT" tempa, China casting ($35-50)(CHI)
17. white body, black base, clear windows, 8 dot wheels, "Audi 20" tempa, Manaus casting ($35-50)(BR)
18. green body, black base, clear windows, 8 dot wheels, two-tone green band & silver "Audi" tempa, Manaus casting ($35-50)(BR)
19. dark cream body, black base, clear windows, 8 dot wheels, "Audi 20" tempa, Manaus casting ($35-50)(BR)
20. maroon body, black base, clear windows, 4 arch wheels, "Audi 20" tempa, Manaus casting ($35-50)(BR)
21. white body, black base, clear windows, 4 arch wheels, "Audi 20" tempa, Manaus casting ($35-50)(BR)

MB23-E PETERBILT QUARRY TRUCK *see MB30-E*

MB23-F HONDA ATC, issued 1985 (USA)(MB159)

NOTE: Below models with black engine & black rubber tires.

1. red body with blue painted seat, red handlebars, yellow wheels, Macau casting ($8-10)
2. red body with blue painted seat, red handlebars, yellow wheels, China casting ($8-10)
3. fluorescent green body with black painted seat, florescent orange handlebars, white wheels, China casting ($4-6)(KS)
4. fluorescent green body with black painted seat, fluorescent orange handlebars, white wheels, Macau casting ($3-5)(KS)

MB23-G VOLVO CONTAINER TRUCK *see MB20-D*

MB23-H FORD BOX VAN, issued 1999 (MB371)

NOTE: Below models with chrome plastic base, 5 spoke concave star wheels, China casting unless otherwise noted.

1. white body, black interior, clear windows, "Fed Ex" tempa ($1-2)(MW23/1999)
2. white body, black interior, clear windows, "Merry Christmas 1999/ Last Delivery- Matchbox Forum" decals ($20-30)(C2)
3. blue-green body, white interior, blue windows, silver-gray base, fish logo tempa ($1-2)(5pk)
4. white body, black interior, amber windows, red & black bands, "8845", "54" & "Matchbox" circle logo tempa ($1-2)(5pk)
5. white body, white interior, blue windows, "Fed Ex" tempa ($1-2)(MW59/2000 US)
6. white body, white interior, blue windows, "Fed Ex' & "Matchbox 2000" tempa ($2-4)(MW59/2000 US)
7. lemon body, red interior, clear windows, chrome disc wheels with rubber tires, "Coca Cola" tempa ($4-6)(Coke PC)
8. white body, black interior, clear windows, no tempa ($25-40)(ASAP blank)
9. white body, white interior, clear windows, no tempa ($25-40)(ASAP blank)
10. white body, white interior, clear windows, "County Line" tempa ($75+)(ASAP)
11. white body, white interior, clear windows, "Flowers Make It Special Roques" tempa ($75+)(ASAP)
12. white body, gray interior, clear windows, chrome disc wheels with rubber tires, "Matchbox Collectibles Toy Deliveries" tempa ($3-4)(TN)
13. red body, white interior, amber windows, "ABC XYZ" & stacked books tempa ($1-2)(5pk)
14. white body, white interior, blue windows, "The Spirit of Christmas/ Merry Christmas & A Happy New Year From Ad-Ventures Inc." tempa ($15-25)(CCI)
15. red body, red interior, gray base, clear windows, lace wheels, "Coca Cola The Real Thing" ($2-3)(CK)
16. white body, white interior, clear windows, 10 spoke flower wheels, no tempa ($10-15)(ASAP blank)
17. white body, white interior, clear windows, "Konematic/ 514-705-3954" tempa ($50+)(ASAP)
18. white body, white interior, clear windows, "Time Warner Communications/ Road Runner" tempa ($50+)(ASAP)
19. black body, dark gray interior, clear windows, chrome disc wheels with rubber tires, "Texaco" tempa ($3-5)(Texaco PC)
20. dark green body, white interior, amber windows, 10 spoke flower wheels, "Hey Arnold!" tempa ($1-2)(5pk)
21. red body, red interior, gray base, clear windows, lace wheels, "Budejovicky Budvar/ Matchbox Collectors Club Czechoslovakia MCCCS 2002" tempa ($15-20)(C2)(CZ)
22. white body, white interior, clear windows, "Stroehman's" tempa ($50+)(ASAP)
23. blue & white body, brown interior, clear windows, chrome disc wheels with rubber tires, "Little Chocolate Donuts" tempa ($3-5)(SNL)
24. red & white body, brown interior, clear windows, chrome disc wheels with rubber tires, "Coca Cola" tempa ($3-5)(Coke Diorama)
25. white body, white interior, clear windows, 10 spoke flower wheels, "New Home For the Holidays CCI" ($15-25)(CCI)
26. light blue body, blue interior, amber windows, 10 spoke flower wheels, "Spongebob" tempa, blue base ($1-2)(5pk)
27. white body, blue interior, amber windows, 10 spoke flower wheels, "Spongebob" tempa, blue base ($1-2)(CA)
28. white body, white interior, clear windows, 10 spoke flower wheels, Snow White Grill Hamburgers" ($18-25)(CCI)
29. white body, white interior, clear windows, 10 spoke flower wheels, "American Red Cross" tempa ($50+)(ASAP)
30. white body, white interior, clear windows, 10 spoke flower wheels, "Rubbermaid Commercial Products 2004- United Way" tempa ($18-25)(CCI)

MB23-I FORD PANEL VAN *see MB38-L*

MB23-J FORD EXPLORER SPORT TRAC, issued 2001 (MB485/605)

NOTE: Below models with opening tailgate, 7 spoke sawblade wheels, plastic base & China casting. unless otherwise noted.

1. red body, light gray interior, clear windows, black & white tempa, dark gray base, gray netting,($1-2)(MW23/2001)
2. orange-red body, chrome interior & windows, "2001 Matchbox Toy Show/ Hershey Matchbox Pennsylvania" tempa, chrome base, gray netting, chrome disc with rubber tires ($8-10)(US)
3. red body, light gray interior, clear windows, "3rd Annual Mt. Laurel Open" tempa, dark gray base, gray netting & golf clubs ($75-100)(CCI)
4. white body, blue interior, smoke windows, "Utah 45 Elk Mountain Ski Patrol" tempa, orange base, orange netting ($1-2)(AM)
5. black body, white interior, clear windows, "Coca Cola" & white splash tempa, chrome base, red netting ($3-5)(Coke PC)
6. white body, light blue interior, smoke windows, "Huskies Dog Sled Team tempa, gray base, red netting ($1-2)(MW24/2002 US)
7. white body, light blue interior, smoke windows, "Huskies Dog Sled Team" & "Matchbox 50" tempa, gray base, red netting ($2-4)(MW24/ 2002 US)
8. metallic blue body, gray interior, smoke windows, small "Matchbox" & "Ford" logos tempa, dark gray base, gray netting ($1-2)(5pk)
9. lemon body, orange-yellow interior, light purple windows, "Rescue Heroes" tempa, lime base, lime netting ($1-2)(5pk)
10. black body, dark red interior, clear windows, "Tune Up Auto Parts" tempa, purple base, dark red netting ($1-2)(MW40/2003 US)
11. black body, dark red interior, clear windows, "Tune Up Auto Parts" & "Hero City" tempa, purple base, dark red netting ($2-4)(MW40/2002 US)
12. silver blue body, white interior, red windows, nondescript design & "Hero City" tempa, dark red base, no netting, tail gate cast shut ($1-2)(MW47/2004)
13. silver blue body, white interior, red windows, nondescript design & "Hero City" tempa, bright red base, no netting, tail gate cast shut ($1-2)(MW47/2004)
14 metallic orange body, yellow interior, smoke windows, "The Alamo Texas" tempa, brown base, no netting, tail gate cast shut ($1-2)(AW)
15. brick red body, black windows, clear windows, "Coca-Cola Football Town/ Total Tailgate" tempa, gray base, no netting, tailgate cast shut ($2-4)(CK)

MB23-K LOCK BOXER, issued 2004 (USA)(MB646)

1. white cab, metallic gold body, dark green plastic chassis, gold 5 dot arch wheels, "Hero City" tempa, black base, China casting ($1-2)(MW23/2004 US)

MB24-A ROLLS ROYCE SILVER SHADOW, issued 1970

NOTE: Below models with ivory interior, clear windows, 5 spoke wheels, metal base & England casting. Earliest versions with thin wheels with later versions having wide wheels.

1. light metallic red body, black base ($12-15)
2. dark metallic red body, black base ($12-15)
3. dark metallic red body, gray base ($12-15)
4. dark metallic red body, charcoal base ($12-15)
5. dark metallic red body, silver-gray base ($12-15)
6. dark metallic red body, metallic green base ($15-18)
7. dark metallic red body, pink base ($15-18)
8. metallic gold body, black base ($15-18)(JP)
9. metallic gold body, unpainted base ($15-18)(JP)
10. metallic gold body, black base, dot dash wheels ($15-18)(MP)

NOTE: Available as a Bulgarian casting ($15-35)

MB24-B TEAM MATCHBOX, issued 1973

NOTE: Below models with unpainted metal base & England casting unless otherwise noted.

1. yellow body, white driver, "8" label, maltese cross front & rear wheels, no trailer ($225-275)
2. yellow body, white driver, "4" label, maltese cross front & rear wheels, no trailer ($300-375)(GS)
3. metallic blue body, white driver, "1" label, maltese cross front & rear wheels, no trailer ($300-375)(GS)
4. metallic blue body, white driver, "5" label, maltese cross front & rear wheels, no trailer ($300-375)(GS)
5. metallic green body, white driver, "5" label, maltese cross front & rear wheels, no trailer ($45-60)(GS)
6. metallic green body, white driver, "5" label, maltese cross front & 5 arch rear wheels, no trailer ($45-60)(GS)
7. metallic green body, white driver, "8" label, maltese cross front & rear wheels, no trailer ($45-60)(GS)
8. metallic red body, white driver, "8" label, maltese cross front & 5 arch rear wheels, no trailer ($6-8)
9. metallic red body, white driver, "8" label, maltese cross front & rear wheels, no trailer ($6-8)
10. metallic red body, white driver, "8" label, 5 spoke front & maltese cross rear wheels, no trailer ($6-8)
11. metallic red body, white driver, "8" label, maltese cross front & large 5 spoke rear wheels, no trailer ($8-12)
12. metallic red body, white driver, "8" label, maltese cross front & rear wheels, no trailer, Manaus label on base ($50-65)(BR)
13. metallic red body, white driver, "44" label, maltese cross front & rear wheels, no trailer ($5-7)(GS)
14. metallic red body, white driver, "44" label, maltese cross front & rear wheels, with trailer ($5-7)(TP)
15. metallic ed body, lemon driver, "44" label, maltese cross front & rear wheels, no trailer ($18-25)(GS)
16. non-metallic red body, white driver, "44" label, maltese cross & rear wheels, no trailer ($50-75)
17. orange body, tan driver, "44" label, maltese cross front & rear wheels, no trailer ($50-75)(GS)
18. orange body, tan driver, "44" label, maltese cross front & rear wheels, with trailer ($50-75)(TP)
19. orange body, lemon driver, "44" label, maltese cross front & rear wheels, no trailer ($50-75)(GS)
20. orange body, lemon driver, "44" label, 5 spoke front wheels & maltese cross rear wheels, with trailer ($50-75)(TP)

MB24-C SHUNTER, issued 1978 (MB024)

NOTE: Below models with black train wheels & plastic base.

1. dark green body, red metal undercarriage, red base, tan panel, "Rail Freight" labels, England casting ($7-10)
2. dark green body, red metal undercarriage, red base, tan panel, "D1496-RF" labels, England casting ($7-10)
3. light yellow body, red metal undercarriage, red base, tan panel, "D1496-RF" labels, England casting ($4-6)
4. light yellow body, red metal undercarriage, red base, brown panel, "D1496-RF" labels, England casting ($4-6)
5. light yellow body, red metal undercarriage, red base, no panel, "D1496-RF" labels, England casting ($4-6)
6. dark yellow body, red metal undercarriage, red base, tan panel, "D1496-RF" labels, England casting ($4-6)
7. dark yellow body, red metal undercarriage, red base, brown panel, "D1496-RF" labels, England casting ($4-6)
8. dark yellow body, red metal undercarriage, red base, no panel, "D1496-RF" labels, England casting ($4-6)
9. dark yellow body, metallic red undercarriage, red base, tan panel, "D1496-RF" labels, no origin casting ($75-100)(BR)
10. dark yellow body, red plastic undercarriage, red base, no panel, "D1496-RF" labels, England casting ($4-6)
11. dark yellow body, red plastic undercarriage, black base, no panel, "D1496-RF" labels, England casting ($5-8)
12. dark yellow body, yellow plastic undercarriage, black base, no panel, "D1496-RF" labels, England casting ($75-100)
13. dark yellow body, red plastic undercarriage, black base, no panel, "D1496-RF" tempa, Macau casting ($2-4)(MC)
14. dark yellow body, red plastic undercarriage, black base, no panel, "D1496-RF" tempa, China casting ($2-4)(MC)
15. orange-yellow body, red plastic undercarriage, black base, no panel, "D1496-RF" tempa, China casting ($2-4)(TP)
16. light yellow body, red plastic undercarriage, black base, no panel, "D1496-RF" tempa, China casting ($2-4)(TP)

MB24-D DATSUN 280ZX, issued 1981 (USA)(MB093)

NOTE: Below models with clear windows, black metal base & Hong Kong casting.

1. black body, white interior, red hood tempa, maltese cross wheels ($2-4)
2. black body, white interior, red hood tempa, 5 spoke star wheels ($2-4)
3. black body, dull red interior, red hood tempa, 5 spoke wheels ($3-5)
4. black body, dull red interior, no tempa, 5 spoke wheels ($3-5)

MB24-E DATSUN 280ZX, issued 1983(MB077)

NOTE: Below models with black metal base, tan interior & clear windows unless otherwise noted.

1. black body, 5 arch silver wheels, gold pin stripe tempa, Macau casting ($2-4)
2. black body, 5 arch silver wheels, "Turbo ZX" tempa, Macau casting ($2-4)
3. white body, 5 arch silver wheels, red & blue "Turbo 33" tempa, Macau casting ($8-12)(JP)
4. black body, small starburst wheels, orange/yellow/white "Turbo" tempa, Macau casting ($3-5)(SF)
5. black body, large starburst wheels, orange/yellow/white "Turbo" tempa, Macau casting ($3-5)(SF)
6. black body, 5 arch gold wheels, "Turbo ZX" tempa, Macau casting ($7-10)
7. black body, 8 dot gold wheels, "Turbo ZX" tempa, Macau casting ($10-15)
8. black body, laser wheels, orange/yellow/white tempa, Macau casting ($3-5)(LW)
9. charcoal gray body, laser wheels, orange/yellow/white tempa, Macau casting ($6-8)(LW)
10. red body, large starburst wheels, black interior, black modified windows & doors, black & orange tempa, Macau casting, includes plastic armament ($6-8)(RB)
11. metallic red body, gray interior, dot dash wheels, black base, no tempa, China casting ($50-75)(CHI)

MB24-F NISSAN 300ZX, issued 1986 (MB167)

NOTE: Below models with clear windows & metal base.

1. pearly silver body, light brown interior, 8 dot wheels, black base, gold stripe with "Turbo" tempa, Macau casting ($2-4)
2. pearly silver body, light brown interior, 5 arch wheels, black base, gold stripe with "Turbo" tempa, Macau casting ($2-4)
3. white body, red interior, 8 dot wheels, green base, "Fujicolor" tempa, Macau casting ($2-4)
4. red body, light brown interior, starburst wheels, black base, red & orange stripes tempa, Macau casting ($3-5)(SF)
5. metallic red body, light brown interior, laser wheels, black base, red & orange stripes tempa, Macau casting ($3-5)(LW)
6. white body, red interior, 8 dot wheels, black base "96 BP Racing Team" tempa, Macau casting ($8-12)(DU)
7. yellow body, red interior, 8 dot wheels, green base, "4 Monkey Racing Team" tempa, Macau casting ($8-12)(HK)

MB24-G LINCOLN TOWN CAR *see MB43-G*

MB24-H FERRARI F40, issued 1989 (USA)(MB207)
MB70-F FERRARI F40, issued 1989 (ROW)

NOTE: Below models with black plastic base unless otherwise noted.

1. red body, clear windows, black interior, 8 dot wheels, "Ferrari" logo tempa, Macau casting ($1-2)
2. red body, chrome windows, black interior, gray disc wheels with rubber tires, "Ferrari" logo& detailed trim tempa, Macau casting ($5-8)(WC)
3. chrome plated body, clear windows, black interior, 8 dot wheels, no tempa, Macau casting ($12-18)(C2)
4. dull red body, clear windows, black interior, 8 dot wheels, "Ferrari" logo tempa, Macau casting ($1-2)
5. red body, clear windows, black interior, 8 dot wheels, "Ferrari" logo tempa, Thailand casting ($1-2)
6. dull red body, clear windows, black interior, 8 dot wheels, "Ferrari" logo tempa, China casting ($1-2)
7. red body, chrome/black windows, no interior, silver & yellow lightning wheels, lemon stripe & "40" tempa, China casting ($2-4)(LT)
8. lemon body, blue-chrome/black windows, no interior, pink & yellow lightning wheels, blue with "F40" tempa, China casting ($2-4)(LT)
9. lemon body, blue-chrome/black windows, no interior, peach & yellow lightning wheels, blue with "F40" tempa, China casting ($2-4)(LT)
10. lemon body, blue-chrome/black windows, no interior, silver & red lightning wheels, blue with "F40" tempa, China casting ($2-4)(LT)
11. white body, blue-chrome/black windows, no interior, peach& silver lightning wheels, peach stripe & "F40" tempa, China casting ($3-5)(LT)
12. black body, black/chrome windows, no interior, pink& silver lightning wheels, pink stripe with "F40" tempa, China casting ($3-5)(LT)
13. red body, black windows, black interior, 8 dot wheels, yellow & white "F40" tempa, Thailand casting ($3-5)(TH)
14. yellow body, chrome windows, black interior, gray disc wheels with rubber tires, detailed trim tempa, China casting ($5-8)(WC)
15. red body, clear windows, black interior, 8 dot wheels, all yellow "Ferrari" logo tempa, Thailand casting ($1-2)
16. black body, clear windows, black interior, 8 dot wheels, "It's Matchbox '93- Tyco" tempa, Thailand casting ($30-45)(US)
17. red body, clear windows, black interior, 8 dot wheels, small "Ferrari" logo & painted tail lights tempa, Thailand casting ($2-3)(SS)
18. red body, clear windows, black interior, 8 dot wheels, yellow & black "Ferrari" logo tempa, base with bar code, Thailand casting ($75+)(IC)
19. red body, clear windows, black interior, gold 6-spoke spiral wheels, yellow & black "Ferrari" logo tempa, Thailand casting ($2-3)
20. orange body, opaque yellow windows, no interior, gold 6-spoke spiral wheels, black blotches tempa, Thailand casting ($1-2)
21. chrome plated body, pink windows, white interior & base, gold 6-spoke spiral wheels, no tempa, Thailand casting ($2-4)(GF)
22. iridescent white body, clear windows, blue interior, silver 6-spoke spiral wheels, small "Ferrari" logo & detailed trim tempa, Thailand casting ($2-4)(CC)
23. metallic red & black body, clear windows, black interior, silver 6-spoke spiral wheels, no tempa ($1-2)(5pk)
24. orange body, opaque yellow windows, no interior, silver 6-spoke spiral wheels, black blotches tempa, Thailand casting ($1-2)
25. red body, clear windows, black interior, silver 6-spoke spiral wheels, "Ferrari" logo tempa, Thailand casting ($2-4)
26. silver body, pink windows, white interior, silver 6-spoke spiral wheels, yellow & pink stripes tempa, Thailand casting ($3-5)(MT)
27. metallic red & purple body, clear windows, black interior, silver 6-spoke spiral wheels, no tempa, Thailand casting ($1-2)
28. white & orange body, clear windows, black interior, silver 6-spoke spiral wheels, no tempa, Thailand casting ($1-2)(5pk)
29. dark purple body, orange windows, white interior, 5 spoke concave star wheels, orange & white design tempa, Thailand casting ($1-2)(5pk)
30. light blue chrome body, red windows, white interior, 5 spoke concave star wheels, purple & yellow tempa, Thailand casting ($1-2)(5pk)
31. black body, clear windows, tan & black interior, chrome disc wheels with rubber tires, small "Ferrari" logo & detailed trim tempa, Thailand casting ($3-5)(PC2-ROW)
32. lemon body, clear windows, black & red interior, chrome disc wheels with rubber tires, detailed trim tempa, Thailand casting ($3-5)(PC10)
33. red body, clear windows, black interior, silver 6 spoke spiral wheels, "Old Eight" tempa, Thailand casting ($75-100)(BR)
34. metallic purple-red & dark purple body, clear windows, black interior, 5 spoke concave star wheels, no tempa, Thailand casting ($1-2)
35. lemon body, clear windows, black interior, 5 spoke concave star wheels, red stripe & black horse on hood tempa, Thailand casting ($1-2)
36. metallic gold body, clear windows, black interior, no tempa, silver 6 spoke spiral wheels, Thailand casting ($5-10)(CH)
37. metallic gold body, clear windows, black interior, no tempa, 5 spoke concave star wheels, Thailand casting ($25-40)(CH)
38. red body, clear windows, black & red interior, detailed trim & small logo tempa, 5 spoke concave star wheels, Thailand casting ($15-20)(GC)
39. iridescent white body, clear windows, red interior, red stripe & black horse on hood tempa, 5 spoke concave star wheels, Thailand casting ($1-2)(MW57/1998)
40. red chrome body, clear windows, white interior, light blue & yellow tempa, 5 spoke concave star wheels, Thailand casting ($1-2)(5pk)

41. metallic burgundy body, clear windows, white interior, light blue & yellow tempa, 5 spoke concave star wheels, Thailand casting ($1-2)(5pk)
42. silver-gray body, clear windows, red & black interior, detailed trim tempa, chrome mags with rubber tires, Thailand casting ($3-5)(PC19)
43. red chrome body, clear windows, white interior, light blue & yellow tempa, 5 spoke concave star wheels, China casting ($1-2)(5pk)
44. iridescent white body, clear windows, red interior, red stripe & black horse on hood tempa, 5 spoke concave star wheels, China casting ($1-2)(MW57/1998)
45. red body, clear windows, black interior, "Ferrari/ Pinifarina" tempa, 5 spoke concave star wheels, China casting ($1-2)(MW19/1999)
46. red body, clear windows, black interior, "Ferrari" without "Pininfarina" tempa, 5 spoke concave star wheels, China casting ($1-2)(MW19/1999)(MW19/199 GR)
47. red body, smoke windows, brown interior, small "Ferrari" logo & "Matchbox 2000" tempa, 5 spoke concave star wheels, China casting ($2-4)(MW232000 US))
48. red body, smoke windows, brown interior, small "Ferrari" logo tempa, 5 spoke concave star wheels, China casting ($1-2)(MW23/2000 US)(MW18/2000 ROW))
49. lemon body, smoke windows, black interior, small "Ferrari" logos tempa, lace wheels, China casting ($2-4)(MW62/2001 GR)

MB24-I AIRPORT TENDER *see MB8-I*

MB24-J RHINO ROD *see MB53-H*

MB24-K CHEVY TRANSPORT BUS, issued 1999(MB372)

NOTE: Below models with chrome base, 5 spoke concave star wheels & China casting unless otherwise noted.

1. green body, gray interior, smoke windows, "National" tempa ($1-2)(MW24/1999)
2. blue body, orange-yellow interior, amber windows, red & yellow design tempa ($1-2)(5pk)
3. dark green body, gray interior, smoke windows, "National" tempa ($12-18)(MW24/1999)(CN)
4. white body, black interior, clear windows, none tempa ($25-40)(ASAP blank)
5. dark cream body, dark blue interior, smoke windows, "Metro Motel Shuttle" & globe tempa ($1-2)(MW73/2000 US)(MW53/2000 ROW)
6. dark cream body, dark blue interior, smoke windows, "Metro Motel Shuttle" & globe & "Matchbox 2000" tempa ($2-4)(MW73/2000 US)
7. red body, dark gray interior, smoke windows, "Coca Cola" with polar bears tempa, chrome disc with rubber tires ($4-6)(Coke PC)
8. white body, black interior, clear windows, "Serving Meridian Since 1927" tempa ($75+)(ASAP)
9. white body, black interior, clear windows, "Happy Birthday Michelle" tempa ($75+)(ASAP)
10. apple green body, white interior, blue windows, "Science 1st" & chemistry logos tempa, 10 spoke flower wheels ($1-2)(5pk)
11. red body, dark gray interior, clear windows, "Coca Cola" tempa, lace wheels ($2-4)(CK)
12. lemon body, red interior, red windows, "Peanuts" with Linus & Lucy tempa, 10 spoke flower wheels ($1-2)(5pk)
13. dark blue body, yellow interior, amber windows, "Niagara Falls Canada" tempa, 10 spoke flower wheels ($1-2)(AW)

MB24-L HUSKI-PATROL, issued 2004 (USA)(MB657)

1. red body, chrome front section, yellow base & skis, black seat, black nose tempa, China casting ($1-2)(MW24/ 2004 US)

MB25-A FORD CORTINA, issued 1970

NOTE: Below models with ivory interior, clear windows, unpainted metal base, 5 spoke wheels & England casting.

1. light metallic brown body ($60-80)
2. light metallic blue body($18-25)
3. dark metallic blue body ($18-25)

NOTE: Available as a Hungarian & Bulgarian casting. Assorted colors available. ($15-25)

MB25-B MOD TRACTOR, issued 1972

NOTE: Below models with metal base, large maltese cross rear wheels & England casting.

1. metallic purple body, black base, yellow seat, maltese cross front wheels, headlights cast on fenders ($12-15)

NOTE: Below models with "V" cast on fenders.

2. metallic purple body, black base, yellow seat, maltese cross front wheels ($10-15)
3. metallic purple body, unpainted base, yellow seat, maltese cross front wheels ($10-15)
4. metallic purple body, black base, red seat, maltese cross front wheels ($35-50)
5. metallic purple body, black base, yellow seat, 4 spoke front wheels ($10-15)
6. metallic purple body, black base, yellow seat, 5 crown front wheels ($10-15)
7. metallic purple body, black base, yellow seat, 5 spoke front wheels ($10-15)
8. red body, black base, yellow seat, maltese cross front wheels ($7-10)(TP)
9. red body, black base, yellow seat, 5 crown front wheels ($7-10)(TP)
10. red body, black base, yellow seat, 5 spoke front wheels ($7-10)(TP)
11. dark green body, black base with Manaus tab, yellow seat, maltese cross front wheels ($250+)(BR)

MB25-C FLAT CAR & CONTAINER, issued 1979 (MB725)

NOTE: Below models with black train wheels & black plastic base. Base lettering can read front to rear or rear to front on all variations.

1. black flatbed, dark tan container, opening doors, "NYK" labels, England casting ($6-8)
2. black flatbed, dark tan container, opening doors, "United States Lines" labels, England casting ($8-12)
3. black flatbed, dark tan container, opening doors, "Sealand" labels, England casting ($6-8)
4. black flatbed, dark tan container, opening doors, "OCL" labels, England casting ($10-15)
5. black flatbed, chocolate container, opening doors, "NYK" labels, England casting ($15-20)
6. black flatbed, light tan container, opening doors, "NYK' labels, England casting ($6-8)
7. charcoal flatbed, light tan container, opening doors, "NYK" labels, England casting ($6-8)
8. charcoal flatbed, dark tan container, opening doors, "NYK" labels, England casting ($6-8)
9. black flatbed, beige container, opening doors, "NYK" labels, England casting ($10-15)
10. black flatbed, coffee container, opening doors, "NYK" labels, England casting ($6-8)
11. charcoal flatbed, yellow-tan container, opening doors, "NYK" labels, England casting ($6-8)

12. black flatbed, blue container, cast doors, "United States Lines" labels, England casting ($40-60)(PS)
13. black flatbed, blue container, cast doors, "Sealand" labels, England casting ($40-60)(PS)
14. black flatbed, dark blue container, cast doors, "Sealand" labels, England casting ($40-60)(PS)
15. black flatbed, orange container, cast doors, "NYK" labels, England casting ($40-60)(PS)
16. black flatbed, orange container, cast doors, "OCL" labels, England casting ($40-60)(PS)
17. black flatbed, red container, cast doors, "NYK" labels, England casting ($40-60)(PS)
18. black flatbed, light blue container, cast doors, no labels, England casting ($40-60)(PS)
19. black flatbed, white container, cast doors, no labels, China casting ($10-15)(PS)
20. black flatbed, yellow container, cast doors, no labels, China casting ($10-15)(PS)
NOTE: Ffor versions 18 & 19, the playset these come in has a separate label sheet for application to the containers.
21. dark cream flatbed, dark tan container, opening doors, "NYK" labels, Manaus casting (label)($150+)(BR)

MB25-D TOYOTA CELICA GT, issued 1981 (USA)(MB092)
NOTE: Below models with clear windows, black metal base & Hong Kong casting.
1. blue body, white interior, "78" tempa, maltese cross wheels, flat base ($4-6)
2. blue body, ivory interior, "78" tempa, maltese cross wheels, flat base ($4-6)
3. blue body, ivory interior, "78" tempa, 5 spoke star wheels, flat base ($4-6)
4. blue body, blue interior, "78" tempa, 5 spoke wheels, flat base ($4-6)
5. yellow body, blue interior, "Yellow Fever" tempa, 5 spoke wheels- all small size, raised rear base ($35-50)
6. yellow body, blue interior, "Yellow Fever" tempa, 5 spoke small front & 5 spoke large rear wheels, raised rear base ($4-6)
7. dark maroon body, blue interior, 5 spoke wheels, "NW Matchbox Collectors Club/ 50 Years" tempa ($12-18)(CCI)
8. dark maroon body, blue interior, 5 spoke wheels, "NW Matchbox Collectors Club/ MBNW" tempa ($12-18)(CCI)

MB25-E AMBULANCE, issued 1983 (USA)(MB041)
MB25-E AMBULANCE, issued 1990 (ROW)
NOTE: Below models with cream interior, blue windows, white rear doors & dot dash wheels unless otherwise noted.
1. white body, pearly silver base, "Pacific Ambulance" tempa, Macau casting ($4-6)
2. white body, unpainted base, "Pacific Ambulance" tempa, Hong Kong casting ($4-6)
3. white body, pearly silver base, "Paramedics E11" with orange band tempa, Macau casting ($1-2)
4. white body, dark gray base, "Paramedics E11" with orange band tempa, Macau casting ($1-2)
5. white body, pearly silver base, "Paramedics E11" with orange band tempa, China casting ($1-2)
6. white body, pearly silver base, "Paramedics E11" with orange band tempa, green windows, China casting ($50-75)
7. white body, pearly silver base, "EMT Ambulance" tempa, China casting ($3-4)(AP)
8. white body, white base, no tempa, China casting ($10-15)(GF)
9. yellow body, pearly silver base, "Paramedics E11" with orange band tempa, China casting ($8-12)(GS)
10. florescent orange body, black base with bar code, "Ambulance 7/ Intercom City" tempa, China casting ($10-15)(IC)
11. fluorescent orange body, black base (without barcode), "Ambulance 7/Intercom City" tempa, China casting ($8-12)
12. fluorescent yellow body & rear doors, silver-gray base, "Emergency Unit 3/ 3 EMT" tempa, China casting ($2-4)(CC)
13. white body, pearly silver base, "Paramedics/ Dial 911" with dark orange band without roof tempa, China casting ($2-3)
14. white body, pearly silver base, "Paramedics/ Dial 911" with neon orange band without roof tempa, China casting ($2-3)
15. red body & rear doors, black base, "Fire Rescue" tempa, China casting ($1-2)(5pk)
16. white body, pearly silver base, "Ambulance" with red & blue design tempa, China casting ($1-2)
17. white body, pearly silver base, "Action System" tempa, China casting ($7-10)(OP)
18. white body, pearly gray base, "Matchbox Ambulance Dial 911" tempa, China casting ($1-2)
19. white body, pearly gray base, orange band on sides tempa, China casting ($25-40)(ASAP blank)
20. white body, pearly silver base, orange band on side with "Manhattan National Life" on hood tempa, China casting ($100+)(ASAP)
21. black body, pearly gray base, "SWAT/ MB County Sheriff" tempa, black rear doors, China casting ($1-2)(MW)
22. white body, pearly gray base, "Methodist LeBonheur Healthcare" & orange band tempa, China casting ($25-50)(ASAP)
23. white body, pearly gray base, "Methodist Healthcare" & orange band tempa, China casting ($25-50)(ASAP)
24. white body, pearly gray base, "LeBonheur Children's Medical Center" & orange band tempa, China casting ($25-50)(ASAP)
25. white body, pearly gray base, "Compuware- We're Here To Help" & orange band tempa, China casting ($50+)(ASAP)
26. white body, pearly gray base, "Matchbox ASI# 33000" & orange band tempa, China casting ($50+)(ASAP)
27. white body, pearly gray base, "Frye Regional Medical Center" & orange band tempa, China casting ($50+)(ASAP)
28. white body, pearly gray base, "Commack Volunteer Ambulance Corps" & orange band tempa, China casting ($50+)(ASAP)
29. white body, pearly gray base, "nym" & orange band tempa, China casting ($50+)(ASAP)
30. white body, pearly gray base, "Orlando Research" tempa & orange band, China casting ($50+)(ASAP)

MB25-F AUDI QUATTRO *see MB23-D*

MB25-G PEUGEOT 205 TURBO *see MB15-E*

MB25-H MODEL A FORD *see MB73-C*

MB25-I JEEP 4X4 *see MB37-F*

MB25-J BMW Z3 ROADSTER, issued 1997 (USA) (MB297)
MB61-H BMW Z3 ROADSTER, issued 1997 (ROW)
NOTE: Below models with clear windows & black plastic base unless otherwise noted.
1. metallic blue body, tan & black interior, chrome disc with rubber tires, detailed trim tempa, Thailand casting ($4-6)(IG)
2. unpainted body, tan interior, chrome disc wheels with rubber tires, no tempa, Thailand casting ($4-6)(IG)

3. red body, black interior, 5 spoke concave star wheels, white splash & "Z3" tempa, Thailand casting ($1-2)
4. red body, black interior, 5 spoke concave star wheels, white splash, "Z3" & "Fiery Driven" tempa, Thailand casting ($100+)(ASAP)
5. red body, black interior, 5 spoke concave star wheels, silver tail lights tempa, Thailand casting ($2-4)(ROW)
6. silver-gray body, maroon & black interior, chrome disc wheels with rubber tires, detailed trim tempa, Thailand casting ($3-5)(PC12)
7. red body, gray & black interior, chrome disc wheels with rubber tires, detailed trim tempa, Thailand casting ($3-5)(PC16)
8. blue body, gray interior, 5 spoke concave star wheels, white splash & "Z3" tempa, Thailand casting ($1-2)(MW5/1998 US)(MB72/1998 ROW)
9. blue body, gray interior, 5 spoke concave star wheels, white splash & "Z3" tempa, China casting ($1-2)(MW5/1998 US)(MB72/1998 ROW)
10. metallic gold body, black interior, 5 spoke concave star wheels, no tempa, China casting ($5-10)(CH)
11. red body, black interior, 5 spoke concave star wheels, white splash, "Z3" & "Espe" tempa, Thailand casting ($100+)(ASAP)
12. metallic red body, black interior, 5 spoke concave star wheels, silver "Z3" tempa, China casting ($1-2)(MW50/1999 US)(MW45/1999 ROW)
13. metallic charcoal body, gray interior, 5 spoke concave star wheels, painted lights tempa, China casting ($3-5)(MW20/ 1999 GR)
14. white body, dark red interior, chrome disc wheels with rubber tires, "Coca Cola" tempa, China casting ($5-8)(Coke PC)(MP)
15. metallic red body, black interior, 5 spoke concave star wheels, silver "Z3" & "007" tempa, China casting ($75+)(ASAP)
16. metallic red body, black interior, star with 5 spokes wheels, silver "Z3" tempa, China casting ($1-2)(MW45/1999 ROW)
17. black body, dark red interior, 5 spoke concave star wheels, painted lights tempa, China casting ($1-2)(MW3/ 2000 ROW)
18. red body, black interior, 5 spoke concave star wheels, "3 Com" tempa, China casting ($75+)(ASAP)
19. green body, light tan interior, 5 spoke concave star wheels, painted lights tempa, China casting ($2-4)(LP)
20. red body, black interior, 5 spoke concave star wheels, "Compaq" tempa , China casting ($50+)(ASAP)
21. red body, black interior, 5 spoke concave star wheels, "Rigid Keenserts" tempa, China casting ($75+)(ASAP)
22. red body, black interior, 5 spoke concave star wheels, "Macola Software" tempa, China casting ($75+)(ASAP)
23. red body, black interior, 5 spoke concave star wheels, "Retek Broadvision" tempa, China casting ($75+)(ASAP)
24. black body, dark red interior, star with 5 spokes wheels, painted lights tempa, China casting ($2-4)(EG)
25. black body, dark red interior, star with 5 spokes wheels, painted lights tempa, metal base, Mattel China casting ($8-12)(EG)
26. black body, dark red interior, 5 spoke concave star wheels, "Millions of Reasons To Celebrate! Compaq" tempa, China casting ($50+)(ASAP)
27. red body, black interior, 5 spoke concave star wheels, "Millions of Reasons to Celebrate! Compaq" tempa, China casting ($50+)(ASAP)
28. light metallic green body, black interior, lace wheels, painted lights tempa, Mattel China casting ($2-4)(MW46/2001 ROW)
29. red body, black interior, 5 spoke concave star wheels, "Q" tempa, China casting ($50+)(ASAP)
30. red body, black interior, 5 spoke concave star wheels, "PFPC" tempa, China casting ($50+)(ASAP)
31. red body, black interior, 5 spoke concave star wheels, "Share Drivers Wanted", China casting ($50+)(ASAP)
32. red body, black interior, chrome disc wheels with rubber tires, "Enjoy the Real Thing- Coke" tempa, Mattel China casting ($3-5)(Coke PC)
33. black body, red interior, 5 spoke concave star wheels, "AflAC" tempa , China casting ($50+)(ASAP)
34. red body, black interior, 5 spoke concave star wheels, no tempa, China casting ($8-12)(ASAP blank)
35. red body, black interior, 5 spoke concave star wheels, "30-60" tempa, China casting ($50+)(ASAP)
36. red body, black interior, 5 spoke concave star wheels, "VH1 Music First" tempa, China casting ($50+)(ASAP)
37. red body, black interior, 5 spoke concave star wheels, "Strike" tempa, China casting ($50+)(ASAP)
38. red body, black interior, 5 spoke concave star wheels, "procarenet" tempa, China casting ($50+)(ASAP)
39. metallic charcoal body, gray interior, 5 spoke concave star wheels, "MCCC/01-01-2000" tempa, China casting (C2)(CZ)

MB25-K '98 JEEP WRANGLER, issued 2001 (MB486)

NOTE: Below models with smoke windshield, 7 spoke sawblade wheels, China casting unless otherwise noted. Spare tire is color of interior.

1. bronze body, mustard roof & base, dark green interior, "Tours" with lizard tempa, 5 spoke concave star wheels ($25-40)(MW25/2001)
2. bronze body, mustard roof & base, dark green interior, "Tours" with lizard tempa ($1-2)(MW25/2001)
3. metallic green body, gray roof & base, light gray interior, "South Dakota Rushmore Tours" tempa ($1-2)(AM)
4. black body, yellow roof, black base, blue interior, "Jeep" & stripes tempa ($2-4)(MW49/2002 ROW)
5. black body, yellow roof, black base, blue interior, "Jeep", stripes & "Matchbox 50" tempa ($3-5)(MW49/2002 ROW)
6. metallic blue body, neon yellow roof, blue-green base, red interior, multi-color design tempa ($1-2)(MP)

MB25-L SPACE BUGGY, issued 2004 (USA) (MB674)

1. dark metallic blue body, white helmet , amber windows, yellow plastic radar, interior & base, gold 5 spoke oval wheels, rocket & planet design tempa, China casting ($1-2)(MW25/2004 US)

MB25-M 1955 CADILLAC FLEETWOOD, issued 2004 (SF) (MB500)

MB500 1955 CADILLAC FLEETWOD, issued 2001 (EL)

NOTE: Below models with clear windows, chrome plastic base & China casting unless otherwise noted.

1. pink body, white roof, white interior, chrome disc with rubber tires, detailed trim tempa ($10-15)(EL)
2. metallic burgundy body, cream roof, cream interior, chrome disc with rubber tires, detailed trim & "50" logo tempa ($3-5)(CL)
3. pink body, white roof, white interior, lace wheels, head lights tempa ($2-4)(MP)(Avon)
4. black body & roof, cream interior, 5 spoke slotted wheels, smoke windows, silver pinstripe & detailed trim tempa ($2-4)(SF25/2004)

MB26-A GMC TIPPER, issued 1970

NOTE: Below models with black plastic base & England casting.

1. red cab, silver-gray dump, green chassis, green windows, 4 spoke wheels ($25-40)

2. red cab, silver-gray dump, green chassis, green windows, spiro wheels ($25-40)
3. red cab, silver-gray dump, green chassis, no windows, 4 spoke wheels ($25-40)

MB26-B BIG BANGER, issued 1972

NOTE: Below models with chrome engine, maltese cross wheels, metal base & England casting.

1. red body, blue windows, unpainted base, "Big Banger" labels ($15-18)
2. red body, amber windows, unpainted base, "Big Banger" labels ($15-18)
3. light blue body, blue windows, unpainted base with Manaus label, "Big Banger" labels ($250+)(BR)

MB26-C SITE DUMPER, issued 1976

NOTE: The front wheels are considered the large wheels on this model! All wheels are silver hubs unless noted otherwise. All models with metal base. Versions 1-9 with black plastic base insert. All with England casting.

1. yellow body & dump, black base, black interior, 5 spoke front & dot dash rear wheels ($4-6)
2. yellow body & dump, black base, black interior, 5 spoke front & 5 crown rear wheels ($4-6)
3. yellow body, red dump, black base, black interior, 5 spoke front & 5 arch rear wheels ($4-6)
4. yellow body, red dump, black base, black interior, 5 arch front & 5 crown rear wheels ($4-6)
5. yellow body, red dump, brown base, black interior, 5 arch front & 5 crown rear wheels ($7-10)
6. yellow body, red dump, brown base, black interior, 5 spoke front & 5 arch rear wheels ($4-6)
7. yellow body, red dump, charcoal base, black interior, 5 arch front & 5 crown rear wheels ($4-6)
8. yellow body, red dump, black base, black interior, 5 spoke front & 5 crown rear wheels ($4-6)
9. yellow body, red dump, black base, black interior, 5 spoke (black hubs) front & 5 crown rear wheels ($4-6)
10. orange-red body, red dump, black base, white interior, 5 arch front & 5 crown rear wheels ($150-250)
11. orange-red body, silver-gray dump, charcoal base, white interior, 5 arch front & 5 crown rear wheels ($4-6)
12. orange-red body, silver-gray dump, black base, white interior, 5 arch front & 5 crown rear wheels ($4-6)
13. orange-red body, silver-gray dump, black base, white interior, 5 arch front & 5 crown rear wheels, yellow hubs ($6-8)
14. orange-red body, silver-gray dump, charcoal base, white interior, 5 arch front & 5 crown rear wheels, yellow hubs ($6-8)
15. red body, silver-gray dump, silver-gray base, white interior, 5 arch front & 5 crown rear wheels, yellow hubs ($10-15)
16. yellow body & dump, unpainted base with Manaus label, black interior, 5 spoke front & 5 crown rear wheels ($35-50)(BR)
17. white body, brown dump, green base, black interior, 5 spoke front & 5 crown rear wheels, origin ground off base ($250+)(BR)

MB26-D COSMIC BLUES, issued 1982 (USA)(MB082)
MB41-H COSMIC BLUES, reissued 1991 (USA)

NOTE: Below models with chrome engine, blue windows & black metal base unless otherwise noted.

1. white body, clear windows, maltese cross front & maltese cross rear wheels, chrome exhausts, "Cosmic Blues" tempa, Hong Kong casting ($35-50)
2. white body, maltese cross front & maltese cross rear wheels, chrome exhausts, "Cosmic Blues" tempa, Hong Kong casting ($3-5)
3. white body, maltese cross front & 5 crown rear cross rear wheels, chrome exhausts, "Cosmic Blues" tempa, Macau casting ($1-2)
4. white body, maltese cross front & rear wheels, chrome exhausts, "Cosmic Blues" tempa, Macau casting ($1-2)
5. white body, 5 arch front & 5 crown rear wheels, chrome exhausts, "Cosmic Blues" tempa, China casting ($1-2)
6. blue body, 5 arch front & 5 crown rear wheels, chrome exhausts, "Cosmic Blues" tempa, China casting ($1-2)
7. blue body, 5 arch front & 5 crown rear wheels, black exhausts, "Cosmic Blues" tempa, China casting ($1-2)
8. orange body, maltese cross front & 5 crown rear wheels, black exhausts, "Hemi" & stripes tempa, China casting ($1-2)
9. orange body, 5 arch front & 5 crown rear wheels, black exhausts, "Hemi" & stripes tempa, Thailand casting ($1-2)
10. black body, 5 arch front & 5 crown rear wheels, gray exhausts, white & orange flames tempa, pearly silver base, Thailand casting ($1-2)
11. orange-red body, 5 arch front & 5 crown rear wheels, gray exhausts, "Dandelion/ Dsylexicon" tempa, Thailand casting ($7-10)(US)
12. black body, 5 arch front & 5 crown rear wheels, gray exhausts, orange & white flames tempa, Thailand casting ($1-2)
13. metallic green body, 5 arch front & 5 crown rear wheels, black exhausts, orange & white flames tempa, Thailand casting ($1-2)
14. metallic gold body, 5 arch front & 5 crown rear wheels, black exhausts, no tempa, Thailand casting ($5-10)(CH26)
15. red body, chrome base, 5 arch front & 5 crown rear wheels, chrome exhausts, "Big Banger" tempa, Thailand casting ($3-5)(PC13)

MB26-E VOLVO CABLE TRUCK, issued 1982 (ROW)(MB026)

NOTE: Below models with plastic base & England casting.

1. orange body, red base, gray cable, green windows, 5 arch wheels ($18-25)
2. orange body, red base, gray cable, blue windows, 5 arch wheels ($18-25)
3. orange body, red base, gray cable, blue windows, maltese cross wheels ($18-25)
4. orange body, red base, gray cable, blue windows, 5 spoke wheels ($18-25)
5. orange body, red base, gray cable, blue windows, 5 crown wheels ($18-25)
6. orange body, black base, gray cable, blue windows, maltese cross wheels ($18-25)
7. orange body, black base, gray cable, blue windows, 5 spoke wheels ($18-25)
8. orange body, black base, gray cable, blue windows, 5 arch wheels ($18-25)
9. orange body, black base, gray cable, blue windows, 5 crown wheels ($18-25)
10. orange body, black base, dark gray cable, blue windows, 5 crown wheels ($18-25)
11. orange body, charcoal base, dark gray cable, blue windows, 5 arch wheels ($18-25)
12. yellow body, black base, dark gray cable, blue windows, 5 arch wheels ($20-30)
13. yellow body, black base, dark gray cable, blue windows, 5 crown wheels ($20-30)
14. red body, black base, dark gray cable, blue windows, 5 arch wheels ($25-40)

MB26-F VOLVO TILT TRUCK, issued 1984 (ROW)(MB139)
MB49-G VOLVO TILT TRUCK, issued 1990 (USA)

NOTE: Below models with blue windows,5 arch wheels with silver hubs, black plastic base unless otherwise noted.

1. metallic blue body, yellow canopy, no tempa, England casting ($25-35)
2. metallic blue body, yellow canopy, "Fresh Fruit Co." tempa, England casting ($3-5)
3. metallic blue body, yellow canopy, "Fresh Fruit Co." tempa, Macau casting ($2-4)
4. yellow body, yellow canopy, "Ferrymasters Groupage" tempa, Macau casting ($2-4)
5. yellow body, yellow canopy, "Ferrymasters Groupage" tempa, China casting ($2-4)
6. white body, white canopy, "Federal Express" tempa, China casting ($2-4)
7. dark blue body, yellow canopy, "Michelin" tempa, dark gray base, China casting ($1-2)
8. olive body, tan canopy, "LS2020" tempa, black hubs, China casting ($15-20)(CM)
9. black body, dark gray canopy, "LS1509" tempa, black hubs, China casting ($15-20)(CM)
10. blue body, blue canopy, "Henniez" tempa, China casting ($8-12)(SW)
11. red body, green canopy, cartoon face & forklift tempa, yellow wheels, red hubs, blue base, China casting ($6-8)(LL)
12. red body, no canopy, "123" on doors tempa, yellow wheels, blue hubs, blue base, China casting ($6-8)(LL)
13. red body, green canopy, cartoon face & forklift tempa, yellow wheels, blue hubs, blue base, China casting ($6-8)(LL)
14. white body, white canopy, "Pirelli Gripping Stuff" & gray tread pattern tempa, China casting ($1-2)
15. white body, white canopy, "Pirelli Gripping Stuff" & black tread pattern tempa, China casting ($1-2)
16. red body, green canopy, cartoon face & forklift tempa, yellow wheels, plain hubs, blue base, China casting ($6-8)(LL)
17. red body, white canopy, "Big Top Circus" tempa, silver-gray base, China casting ($2-4)(AV)
18. pumpkin body, turquoise canopy, apple design tempa, China casting ($2-3)(MW4/1999 ROW)
19. pumpkin body, no canopy, www.matchboxclub.de tempa, China casting ($25-40)(C2)(GR)

MB26-G BMW 5 SERIES, issued 1989 (USA)(MB206)
MB31-H BMW 5 SERIES, issued 1989 (ROW)

NOTE: Below models with clear windows, 8 dot wheels & metal base unless otherwise noted.

1. dark charcoal body, black base, silver headlights tempa, Macau casting ($2-4)
2. dark charcoal body, black base, silver headlights tempa, Thailand casting ($2-4)
3. white body, white base, "Fina 31/ BMW Team/ Sachs/ Bilstein" tempa, Thailand casting ($2-4)
4. white body, white base, "Fina 31/ BMW Team" without "Sachs/ Bilstein" tempa, Thailand casting ($2-4)
5. red body, red base, no tempa, Thailand casting ($3-5)(SS)
6. white body, white base, "31 BMW Team" without "Fina" & "Michelin" tempa, Thailand casting ($2-3)
7. white body, white base, "Fina 31/ BMW Team" without "Sachs/ Bilstein" with blue "Michelin" tempa, Thailand casting ($1-2)
8. black body, black base, black & tan interior, detailed trim tempa, chrome disc wheels with rubber tires, Thailand casting ($3-5)(PC19)

MB26-H 4X4 CHEVY VAN *see MB44-D*

MB26-I JAGAUR XJ220 *see MB31-J*

MB26-J AIRPORT FIRE TENDER, issued 2001 (MB487)

NOTE: Below models with blue windows, blue rear canopy, black base, 7 spoke sawblade wheels, China casting unless otherwise noted.

1. florescent yellow body, gray boom, "MFD7/ Action" with large orange "7" & orange checkers tempa (MW26/2001)
2. lemon body, gray boom, "Birthday Party" tempa ($25-40)(US)
3. red body, yellow boom, "Alarm" with hose tempa ($1-2)(5pk)
4. blue body, amber windows & rear canopy, white boom, "Alabama 22 Rocket Recovery" tempa ($1-2)(AM)
5. silver-gray body, red boom, "71" & design tempa ($1-2)(MW71/2002)
6. silver-gray body, red boom, "71", design & "Matchbox 50" tempa ($8-12)(MW71/2002)
7. red body, orange boom & base, "Hangar 33" & design tempa ($1-2)(MW33/2003)
8. red body, orange boom & base, "Hangar 33", design & "Hero City" tempa ($8-12)(MW33/2003)
9. metallic red body, orange boom & base, gold hubs, "Hangar 33" & design tempa ($3-4)(20pk)

MB26-K SPORT SUV, issued 2003 (MB568)

NOTE: Below models with gray interior, blue windows, 7 spoke sawblade wheels, China casting unless otherwise noted.

1. silver-gray body, dark blue base, "Police 26" & stripe tempa ($1-2)(MW26/2003)
2. silver-gray body, dark blue base, "Police 26/ Hero City" & stripes tempa ($2-4)(MW26/2003)
3. iridescent white body, gray base, "365/ 555-3214/ Hero City" with blue front lights tempa ($1-2)(5pk)
4. iridescent white body, gray base, "365/ 555-3214/ Hero City" without painted front lights tempa ($1-2)(5pk)
5. silver-gray body, dark blue base, "Police 26" & stripes/ Mom Me & Matchbox/ Matchbox Chelsea Piers" tempa ($20-25)(CCI)
6. dark metallic blue body, yellow base, Marvin the Martian tempa ($1-2)(5pk)
7. dark green body, pea green base, red interior, "Giant Redwood Forest" tempa ($8-12)(AW-Bonus)
8. silver-gray body, blue base, red interior & windows, "Police" with shield & design tempa ($1-2)(5pk)
9. metallic green body, black base, red interior & windows, snowflakes & snowman tempa ($2-4)(MP)

MB26-L POLICE HAT, issued 2003 (USA)(MB625)
MB11-L POLICE HAT, issued 2003 (ROW)

NOTE: Below models with red windows, dark blue hat, gold 5 crown dot wheels, dark blue base, China casting.

1. iridescent white body, "MB Metro Police" tempa ($1-2)(MW26/2004 US)(MW11/2004 ROW)
2. white body, "Hero City Metro Police/ Police" tempa ($1-2)(5pk)

MB26-M GMC BUCKET , issued 2004 (ROW)(MB470)

NOTE: Although this model has the same frame number as MB99, the model is cast considerably different to warrant a new listing.,

1. black body, yellow boom & turret, frosted amber windows, neon orange base, 7 spoke sawblade wheels, "24/7" & tools design tempa, China casting ($1-2)(MW26/2004 ROW)

MB27-A MERCEDES 230SL, issued 1970

NOTE: Below models with clear windshield, 5 spoke wheels & England casting.

1. cream body, red interior, unpainted base ($25-40)
2. off white body, red interior, unpainted base ($25-40)
3. yellow body, red interior, unpainted base ($20-25)
4. yellow body, black interior, unpainted base ($15-20)

NOTE: Available as an Hungarian and Bulgarian casting. Assorted colors available ($15-25)

MB27-B LAMBORGHINI COUNTACH, issued 1973

NOTE: Below models with 5 spoke wheels, metal base & England casting unless otherwise noted.

1. yellow body, unpainted base, chrome interior, purple windows, "3" label ($10-15)
2. yellow body, black base, chrome interior, purple windows, "3" label ($10-15)
3. yellow body, unpainted base, chrome interior, red windows, "3" label ($10-15)
4. yellow body, black base, chrome interior, red windows, "3" label ($10-15)
5. yellow body, silver gray base, chrome interior, purple windows, "3" label ($10-15)
6. yellow body, black base, chrome interior, amber windows, "3" label ($10-15)
7. red body, black base, chrome interior, amber windows, "3" label ($10-15)
8. red body, black base, chrome interior, red windows, "3" label ($10-15)
9. red body, unpainted base, chrome interior, amber windows, lime tempa ($7-10)
10. red body, black base, chrome interior, amber windows, lime tempa ($7-10)
11. red body, black base, chrome interior, red windows, lime tempa ($7-10)
12. red body, unpainted base, chrome interior, blue-green windows, lime tempa ($7-10)
13. red body, black base, chrome interior, blue-green windows, lime tempa ($7-10)
14. red body, black base, light gray interior, blue-green windows, lime tempa ($7-10)
15. red body, unpainted base, light gray interior, blue-green windows, lime tempa ($7-10)
16. red body, black base, light gray interior, blue-green windows, green tempa ($7-10)
17. red body, black base, light gray interior, green windows, lime tempa ($7-10)
18. red body, black base, light gray interior, green windows, green tempa ($7-10)
19. red body, brown base, light gray interior, blue-green windows, lime tempa ($7-10)
20. red body, brown base, dark gray interior, blue-green windows, lime tempa ($7-10)
21. red body, charcoal base, light gray interior, blue-green windows, lime tempa ($7-10)
22. red body, charcoal base, dark gray interior, blue-green windows, lime tempa ($7-10)
23. red body, charcoal base, yellow interior, blue-green windows, lime tempa ($7-10)
24. red body, charcoal base, yellow interior, smoke windows, lime tempa ($7-10)
25. red body, gray-brown base, yellow interior, smoke windows, lime tempa ($7-10)
26. red body, charcoal base, white interior, smoke windows, lime tempa ($7-10)
27. red body, charcoal base, white interior, blue-green windows, lime tempa ($7-10)
28. red body, black base, white interior, clear windows, lime tempa ($7-10)
29. red body, gray-brown base, white interior, clear windows, lime tempa ($7-10)
30. red body, charcoal base, tan interior, blue-green windows, lime tempa ($7-10)
31. red body, charcoal base, tan interior, clear windows, lime tempa ($7-10)
32. red body, black base, tan interior, clear windows, lime tempa ($7-10)
33. red body, black base, tan interior, blue-green windows, lime tempa ($7-10)
34. red body, unpainted base, tan interior, blue-green windows, lime tempa ($7-10)
35. red body, charcoal base, tan interior, purple windows, lime tempa ($7-10)
36. red body, gray-brown base, tan interior, purple windows, lime tempa ($7-10)
37. red body, unpainted base, light gray interior, green windows, lime tempa ($7-10)
38. red body, charcoal base, light gray interior, purple windows, lime tempa ($7-10)
39. red body, black base, dark gray interior, purple windows, lime tempa ($7-10)
40. red body, blue-gray base, dark gray interior, purple windows, lime tempa ($7-10)
41. red body, charcoal base, dark gray interior, smoke windows, lime tempa ($7-10)
42. red body, black base, yellow interior, blue-green windows, lime tempa ($7-10)
43. yellow body, pearly silver base with Manaus label, light gray interior, blue-green windows, no labels ($150-200)(BR)
44. dark green body, pearly silver base with Manaus label, light gray interior, blue-green windows, "Shell" labels ($250+)(BR)
45. metallic red body with black tailgate, unpainted base with Manaus label, chrome interior, amber windows, "3" label ($250+)(BR)

MB27-C SWEPT WING JET, issued 1981 (MB027)

NOTE: Below models with metal base & solid black wheels.

1. dark red body, white wings & base, amber-red windows, no tempa, England casting ($2-4)
2. dark red body, white wings & base, red windows, no tempa, England casting ($2-4)
3. dark red body, white wings & base, pink windows, no tempa, England casting ($2-4)
4. dark red body, white wings & base, red windows, black & red tempa, England casting ($2-4)
5. dark red body, white wings & base, red windows, red only tempa, England casting ($2-4)
6. dark red body, white wings & base, red windows, black & red tempa, Macau casting ($2-4)
7. rose red body, white wings & base, red windows, black & red tempa, Macau casting ($2-4)
8. dark red body, light gray wings, white base, red windows, black & red tempa, Macau casting ($4-6)
9. dark red body, white wings & base, red windows, black & red tempa, China casting ($2-4)
10. black body, dark gray wings, gray base, red windows, yellow & black camouflage tempa, Macau casting ($3-5)(CM)
11. gray body, gray wings, gray base, clear windows, "Top Gun/ Navy" tempa, China casting ($5-8)(STR)

MB27-D JEEP CHEROKEE, issued 1986 (MB168/574)
MB73-F JEEP CHEROKEE, reissued 1994 (USA)
MB51-J JEEP CHEROKEE, reissued 1996 (ROW)

NOTE: Below models with clear windows & 8 spoke wheels unless otherwise noted. When interior is noted, this includes the color of the side molding.

1. white body, black interior, black metal base, "Quadtrak" tempa, Macau casting ($3-5)
2. beige body, black interior, black metal base, "Holiday Club" tempa, Macau casting ($2-4)(TP)
3. yellow body, dark gray interior, black metal base, "Forest Ranger County Park" tempa, Macau casting ($7-10)
4. yellow body, dark gray interior, black metal base, "Mr. Fixer" tempa, Macau casting ($1-2)
5. bright yellow body, dark gray interior, black metal base, "BP Chief" & green/ red stripes tempa, Macau casting ($8-12)(DU)
6. orange-yellow body, dark gray interior, black metal base, "Mr. Fixer" tempa, Macau casting ($1-2)
7. light pea green body, dark gray interior, black metal base, "Mr. Fixer" tempa, Macau casting ($3-4)(SC)
8. light brown body, dark gray interior, black metal base, "Mr. Fixer" tempa, Macau casting ($3-4)(SC)
9. dark brown body, dark gray interior, black metal base, "Mr. Fixer" tempa, Macau casting ($3-4)(SC)
10. beige body, dark gray interior, black metal base, "Holiday Club" tempa, Macau casting ($2-4)(TP)
11. yellow body, dark gray interior, black plastic base, "Mr. Fixer" tempa, Macau casting ($1-2)
12. reddish brown body, dark gray interior, black plastic base, "Mr. Fixer" tempa, Macau casting ($2-3)(SC)
13. dark brown body, dark gray interior, black plastic base, "Mr. Fixer" tempa, Macau casting ($2-3)(SC)
14. white body, dark gray interior, dark gray plastic base, "National Ski Patrol" tempa, Thailand casting ($8-12)
15. beige body, dark gray interior, black plastic base, "Holiday Club" tempa, Thailand casting ($2-4)(MP)
16. orange-yellow body, dark gray interior, black plastic base, "Mr. Fixer" tempa, Thailand casting ($2-4)
17. silver-gray body, black interior, black plastic base, "Sport" & "Jeep" tempa, Thailand casting ($2-4)
18. dark purple body, dark orange interior, black plastic base, white & orange flames tempa, Thailand casting ($1-2)
19. dark purple body, dark orange interior, black plastic base, white & orange flames tempa, China casting ($1-2)
20. medium green body, black interior, black plastic base, no tempa, Thailand casting ($18-25)(BE)
21. blue body, dark gray interior, gray plastic base, "Hellmann's/ Best Foods" tempa, China casting ($75-100)(US)
22. red body, black interior, black plastic base, "Fire Chief/ FD No. 1" tempa, blue dome lights cast, China casting ($1-2)(5pk)
23. red body, black & gray interior, black plastic base, "Fire Chief" tempa, blue dome lights cast, chrome disc with rubber tires, China casting ($3-5)(PC7)
24. dark green body, beige interior, black plastic base, no tempa, China casting ($1-2)(5pk)
25. dark purple body, red-orange interior, black plastic base, white & orange flames tempa, China casting ($1-2)
26. black body, red interior, black plastic base, pink-red & white flames tempa, China casting ($1-2)
27. white body, dark blue interior, black plastic base, "Rescue EMT" tempa, blue dome light cast, China casting ($1-2)(5pk)
28. white body, dark red interior, black plastic base, no tempa, China casting ($25-40)(ASAP blank)
29. black body, dark red interior, black plastic base, no tempa, China casting ($25-40)(ASAP blank)
30. black body, dark red interior, black plastic base, "American International Recovery" tempa, China casting ($100+)(ASAP)
31. red body, blue interior, blue plastic base, winged logo tempa, blue dome lights cast, China casting ($1-2)(5pk)(MW23/1999 GR)
32. white body, amber windows, blue interior, blue plastic base, "Water Works City Division" tempa, amber dome light cast, China casting ($1-2)(MW97/ 1999 US)
33. white body, dark red interior, white plastic base, "AT&T Network Management Services" tempa, China casting ($75+)(ASAP)
34. turquoise body, blue interior, black plastic base, smoke windows, "Animal Rescue" tempa, amber dome lights cast, China casting ($2-3)(M36/2000 AU)
35. white body, dark red interior, white plastic base, "V8 Splash" tempa, China casting ($100+)(ASAP)
36. dark blue body, black interior, black plastic base, smoke windows, "Camp Jeep 2000" & design tempa,, red dome lights cast, China casting ($1-2)(5pk)
37. white body, blue interior, blue plastic base, smoke windows, black & orange hash marks & polar bear logo tempa, blue dome lights cast, China casting ($1-2)(LP)
38. black body, dark red interior, black plastic base, "Linux Solutions" tempa, China casting ($75+)(ASAP)
39. white body, dark red interior, black plastic base, "Linux Solutions" tempa, China casting ($75+)(ASAP)
40. white body, dark red interior, black plastic base, "Microsoft" tempa, China casting ($75+)(ASAP)
41. black body, dark red interior, black plastic base, "Microsoft" tempa, China casting ($75+)(ASAP)
42. white body, dark red interior, black plastic base, "Unix User Conference Jan Jose" tempa, clear dome light cast, China casting ($75+)(ASAP)
43. white body, dark red interior, black plastic base, "Giant" tempa, clear dome light cast, China casting ($75+)(ASAP)
44. orange-red body, smoke windows, red interior, black plastic base, "Hilti expertise in every case" tempa, China casting ($10-15)(US)
45. white body, blue windows, orange interior, orange plastic base, "H042076" & storm logo tempa, 7 spoke sawblade wheels, China casting ($1-2)(LP)
46. black body, clear windows, black interior, black plastic base, none tempa, China casting ($15-20)(ASAP blank)
47. white body, smoke windows, red interior, red plastic base, "Chief HQ" & flames tempa, 7 spoke sawblade wheels, China casting ($1-2)(5pk)
48. white body, clear windows, red interior, white plastic base, "MRMC 2003/ MRMC " shield tempa, China casting ($15-25)(ASAP)
49. white body, clear windows, red interior, white plastic base, "MRMC 2003/ Police" tempa, China casting ($15-25)(ASAP)
50. red body, amber windows, orange interior, orange plastic base, "Chief HQ" & flames tempa, China casting ($1-2)(5pk)
51. red body, black interior, black plastic base, "Matchbox Fire Chief" with white stripe tempa, blue dome light cast, China casting ($1-2)(5pk)

    NOTE: Above model found with or without silver trim on the dome light.
52. white body, dark red interior, black plastic base, no tempa, clear dome light cast, China casting ($25-40)(ASAP blank)
53. white body, dark red interior, white plastic base, no tempa, China casting ($25-40)(ASAP blank)

54. white body, dark red interior, white plastic base, no tempa, clear dome light cast, China casting ($25-40)(ASAP blank)
55. black body, dark red interior, black plastic base, "Norvasc/ Road Rally" tempa, China casting ($25-40)(ASAP)
56. white body, dark red interior, black plastic base, "Alliance" tempa, clear dome light cast, China casting ($25-40)(ASAP)
57. white body, dark red interior, black plastic base, green "e" tempa, clear dome light cast, China casting ($50+)(ASAP)
58. orange body, orange interior, black metal base, "Enjoy Fanta" tempa, China casting ($75+)(CHI)
59. white body, red interior, white plastic base "Dillards/Jeep" tempa, China casting ($50+)(ASAP)

MB27-E MERCEDES TRACTOR *see MB73-E*

MB27-F TAILGATOR, issued 1994 (MB259)

NOTE: Below models with opaque black windows & painted eyes & teeth tempa & plastic base.

1. lime body, lime base, gold 6-spoke spiral wheels, China casting ($1-2)
2. lime body, lime base, silver 6-spoke spiral wheels, China casting ($1-2)
3. dark green body, dark green base, silver 6-spoke spiral wheels, China casting ($2-3)
4. metallic gold body, orange-gold base, silver 6-spoke spiral wheels, China casting ($10-15)(CH)
5. dark green body, dark green base, 5 spoke concave star wheels, China casting ($2-4)
6. dark purple body, dark purple base, 5 spoke concave star wheels, China casting ($1-2)
7. black body, black base, 5 spoke concave star wheels, China casting ($1-2)(MW45/1998US)
8. metallic gold body, yellow base, gold 6 spoke spiral wheels, China casting ($75+)(CHI)
9. dark green body & base, gold 6 spoke spiral wheels, China casting ($50+)(CHI)

MB27-G LADDER TRUCK, issued 2001 (MB488)

NOTE: Below models with 4 spoke domed wheels, plastic base & China casting. Turret color matches ladder color.

1. metallic red body, amber windows, white interior, white ladder, gray base, "5 Alarm Force/ Base 525" tempa ($1-2)(MW27/2001)
2. white body, blue windows, red interior, red ladder, red base, "50" with balloons design tempa ($3-5)(ROW)
3. metallic bronze body, smoke windows, red ladder, gray base, "Fire Rescue Super Splash" tempa ($1-2)(MW25/2002 US)
4. metallic bronze body, smoke windows, red ladder, gray base, "Fire Rescue Supersplash" & "Matchbox 50" tempa ($2-4)(MW25/2002 US)
5. red body, blue windows, gray interior, gray ladder, black base, "Alarm" & ladders tempa ($1-2)(5pk)
6. metallic red body, amber windows, white interior, white ladder, gray base, "Matchbox/ Alarm" tempa ($2-3)(PZ)
7. white body, blue windows, red interior, red ladder, gray base, stripes design tempa ($1-2)(MW3/2003)
8. white body, blue windows, red interior, red ladder, gray base, stripes design & "Hero City" tempa ($2-3)(MW3)
9. white body, red windows, red interior, red ladder, red base, "USA Fire Dept." & flag design tempa ($30-45)(HR)
10. iridescent white body, red windows, red interior, red ladder, red base, "USA Fire Dept." & flag design tempa ($1-2)(HR)
11. white body, blue windows, red interior, red ladder, gray base, gold hubs, stripes tempa ($3-4)(20pk)

MB27-H FORD FALCON POLICE CAR, issued 2002 (ROW)(MB545/553/635)
MB49-J FORD FALCON POLICE CAR, issued 2004 (USA)

NOTE: Below models with lace wheels, black plastic bases & China casting unless otherwise noted.

1. white body, blue interior, smoke windows, red dome light, yellow, blue & silver "Police" with badge tempa ($2-4)(PS)
2. white body, blue interior, clear windows, amber dome light, light yellow & blue checkers with "Police" tempa ($2-4)(MW27/2002 ROW)
3. white body, blue interior, clear windows, amber dome light, light yellow & blue checkers with "Police" & "Matchbox 50" tempa ($2-4)(MW27/2002 ROW)
4. white body, black interior, dark smoke windows, blue dome light, "Polizei 27" & "Hero City" tempa ($2-4)(MW27/2003 ROW)
5. white body, black interior, dark smoke windows, blue dome light, "Polizei 27" tempa ($2-4)(MW27/2003 ROW)
6. white body, white interior, red windows, red dome light, "Hero City" & nondescript design tempa ($1-2)(MW49/2004)
7. dark blue body, silver-gray interior, clear windows, red dome light, airplanes & orange design tempa ($1-2)(LP)
8. black body, white interior, red windows, red dome light, white painted doors & "Police" crest tempa ($1-2)(LP)

MB27-I MILITARY HELMET, issued 2003 (USA) (MB626)
MB12-N MILITARY HELMET, issued 2003 (ROW)

1. beige body, brown helmet, opaque green goggles, gold 5 crown dot wheels, black base, "004X1" with camouflage tempa, China casting ($1-2)(MW27-I/2003 US)(MW12-N/2003 ROW)
2. metallic gold body, blue helmet, amber goggles, gold 5 crown dot wheels, red base, "Police" with shield & design with tiny black "Matchbox" logo tempa, China casting ($1-2)(5pk)
3. metallic gold body, blue helmet, amber goggles, gold 5 crown dot wheels, red base, "Police" with shield & design with tiny blue "Matchbox" logo tempa, China casting ($1-2)(5pk)

MB27-J '61 DODGE DART PHOENIX, issued 2004 (SF)(MB558)
MB558 '61 DODGE DART PHOENIX, issued 2002

NOTE: Below models with chrome plastic base & China casting.

1. pale blue body, clear windshield, blue interior, "Hawaii Island Tours" tempa, chrome disc wheels with rubber tires ($10-15)(EL)
2. white & blue-green body, clear windshield, red interior, "Things Go Better With Coke- Ice Cold" tempa, chrome disc with rubber tires ($3-5)(Coke PC)
3. dark red body, smoke windshield, tan interior, silver pinstriping & detailed trim tempa, 5 spoke slotted wheels ($2-4)(SF27/2004)
4. silver blue body, amber windshield, purple interior, "Goddard" tempa, 10 spoke flower wheels, purple base ($1-2)(5pk)

MB28-A MACK DUMP TRUCK, issued 1970

NOTE: Below models with metal base & England casting.

1. pea green body, green windows, unpainted base, spiro wheels, black axle covers clip on ($20–35)
2. pea green body, green windows, unpainted base, spiro wheels, red axle covers clip on($20-35)
3. olive drab body, no windows, black base, dot dash wheels, black axle covers riveted ($65-80)(TP)
4. olive body, no windows, black base, dot dash wheels,. Black axle covers riveted ($6-8)(TP)

MB28-B STOAT, issued 1974

NOTE: Below models with metal base with black plastic base insert, brown soldier, 5 spoke wheels & England casting.

1. gold body, unpainted base, silver hubs ($8-12)
2. gold body, black base, silver hubs ($8-12)
3. olive drab body, black base, black hubs ($65-80)(TP)
4. olive body, black base, silver hubs ($7-10)(TP)
5. olive body, black base, black hubs ($6-8)(TP)

MB28-C LINCOLN CONTINENTAL MK V, issued 1979

NOTE: Below models with clear windshield, dot dash wheels, unpainted metal base & England casting.

1. pinkish-red body, tan interior, white roof ($3-5)
2. dark red body, tan interior, white roof ($3-5)
3. dark red body, gray interior, white roof ($4-6)
4. dark red body, brown interior, white roof ($4-6)
5. dark red body, chocolate interior, white roof ($5-7)

NOTE: Available as a Bulgarian casting. Assorted colors available ($15-25)

MB28-D FORMULA 5000, issued 1982 (MB028)

1. tan body, unpainted metal base, white driver, chrome engine, 5 arch front & maltese cross rear wheels, England casting ($3-5)
2. tan body, black metal base, white driver, chrome engine, 5 arch front & maltese cross rear wheels, England casting ($3-5)
3. tan body, black metal base, white driver, chrome engine, 5 arch front & 5 spoke rear wheels, England casting ($3-5)
4. tan body, black metal base, white driver, chrome engine, dot dash front & dot dash rear wheels, England casting ($3-5)
5. tan body, black metal base, white driver, chrome engine, 5 arch front & dot dash rear wheels, Macau casting ($3-5)
6. tan body, black metal base, white driver, chrome engine, dot dash front & dot dash rear wheels, Macau casting ($3-5)
7. tan body, black plastic base, white driver, chrome engine, 4 spoke front & maltese cross rear wheels, Manaus casting ($35-50)(BR)
8. rust red body, black plastic base, cream driver, gray engine, 8 dot front & 8 spoke rear wheels, Manaus casting ($35-50)(BR)
9. rust red body, black plastic base, white driver, chrome engine, 4 spoke front & maltese cross rear wheels, Manaus casting ($35-50)(BR)
10. dark green body, charcoal plastic base, white driver, 8 dot front & 8 spoke rear wheels, gray engine, Manaus casting ($30-45)(BR)
11. powder blue body, black plastic base, white driver, 8 dot front & 8 spoke rear wheels, gray engine, Manaus casting ($35-50)(BR)
12. powder blue body, black plastic base, white driver, chrome engine, 4 spoke front & maltese cross rear wheels, Manaus casting ($35-50)(BR)

MB28-E DODGE DAYTONA, issued 1984 (MB127)

NOTE: Below models with clear windows & black interior. All bases are metal. "Las Vegas" model is a different casting and is listed separately at the end of this section.

1. maroon body, silver-gray base with black insert, 8 dot silver wheels, no tempa, England casting ($3-5)
2. maroon body, silver-gray base with dark gray insert, 5 arch wheels, no tempa, England casting ($3-5)
3. maroon body, silver-gray base with dark gray insert, 8 dot silver wheels, no tempa, England casting ($3-5)
4. maroon body, silver-gray base with no insert, 8 dot silver wheels, no tempa, Macau casting ($50-75)
5. pearly silver body, black base, 8 dot silver wheels, red & black stripes tempa, Macau casting ($2-4)
6. pearly silver body, black base, large 5 crown wheels, red & black stripes tempa, Macau casting ($5-8)
7. pearly silver body, black base, dot dash wheels, red & black stripes tempa, Macau casting ($5-8)
8. pearly silver body, black base, 8 dot gold wheels, red & black stripes tempa, Macau casting ($4-6)
9. white body, blue base, starburst wheels, red & blue stripes with "8" tempa, Macau casting ($3-5)(SF)
10. white body, blue base, laser wheels, red & blue stripes with "8" tempa, Macau casting ($3-5)(LW)
11. plum body, gold base, starburst wheels, red/yellow/dark blue tempa, gray redesigned windows, Macau casting, includes plastic armament ($6-8)(RB)
12. dark blue body, black base, 8 dot silver wheels, "5 Goat Racing Team" tempa, Macau casting ($8-12)(HK)
13. red body, red base, 8 dot silver wheels, yellow & blue "Turbo Z" tempa, Macau casting ($2-3)
14. red body, red base, 8 dot silver wheels, yellow & blue "Turbo Z" tempa, hood cast shut, Macau casting ($2-3)
15. red body, red base, starburst wheels, yellow & blue "Turbo Z" tempa, hood cast shut, China casting ($5-7)(MP)

MB28-F LONDON BUS *see MB17-C*

MB28-G 1987 CORVETTE *see MB14-G*

MB28-H FORKLIFT TRUCK, issued 1991 (USA) (MB048)
MB61-F FORKLIFT TRUCK, issued 1991 (ROW)

NOTE: Below models with black forks & arms, black metal base with black plastic insert & 4 spoke wheels unless otherwise noted.

1. lime green body, red & white stripes tempa, Thailand casting ($1-2)
2. white body, red stripes tempa, Thailand casting ($2-4)(TC)
3. florescent green body, red & white stripes tempa, Thailand casting ($1-2)
4. orange-yellow body, orange-yellow forks, red & white stripes tempa, Thailand casting ($2-4)(GS)
5. bright lime body, red & white stripes tempa, Thailand casting ($1-2)

MB28-I BMW CABRIOLET *see MB39-D*

MB28-J T-BIRD COUPE *see MB59-F*

MB28-K MUSTANG MACH III *see MB15-J*

MB28-L MITSUBISHI SPYDER, issued 1995 (USA)(MB270)
MB22-J MITSUBISHI SPYDER, issued 1995 (ROW)

NOTE: Below models with clear windshield & black plastic base.

1. metallic blue body, green interior, white & green hood & side splash tempa, 6-spoke spiral wheels, Thailand casting ($1-2)
2. metallic blue body, green interior, no tempa, 6-spoke spiral wheels, Thailand casting ($2-4)
3. metallic blue body, white interior, no tempa, 6-spoke spiral wheels, Thailand casting ($1-2)
4. red body, dark gray interior, 6-spoke spiral wheels, no tempa, Thailand casting ($1-2)(5pk)
5. red body, dark gray & black interior, chrome disc wheels with rubber tires, detailed trim tempa, Thailand casting ($3-5)(PC1)
6. black body, dark gray & black interior, chrome disc wheels with rubber tires, detailed trim tempa, Thailand casting ($3-5)(SC1)

7. silver-gray body, red & black interior, chrome disc wheels with rubber tires, detailed trim tempa, Thailand casting ($3-5)(PC-JC)
8. metallic green body, gray & black interior, chrome disc wheels with rubber tires, detailed trim tempa, Thailand casting ($3-5)(PC4)
9. metallic gold body, black interior, 6 spoke spiral wheels, no tempa., Thailand casting ($5-10)(CH)
10. lemon body, gray interior, 5 spoke concave star wheels, "Spyder" tempa, Thailand casting ($1-2)
11. black body, red interior, 5 spoke concave star wheels, "Spyder" tempa, Thailand casting ($1-2)(5pk)
12. metallic blue body, gray & black interior, chrome disc wheels with rubber tires, detailed tempa, Thailand casting ($15-20)(GC)
13. black body, red interior, 5 spoke concave star wheels, "The Red Back" with spider & web tempa, Thailand casting ($3-5)(AU)
14. metallic gold body, black interior, 5 spoke concave star wheels, no tempa, Thailand casting ($10-15)(CH)
15. lemon body, gray & black interior, chrome disc wheels with detailed trim tempa, Thailand casting ($3-5)(PC12)
16. red body, gray interior, 5 spoke concave star wheels, skeleton & "Raptor" tempa, Thailand casting ($1-2)(5pk)
17. iridescent white body, maroon & black interior, chrome disc wheels with rubber tires, detailed trim tempa, Thailand casting ($3-5)(PC16)
18. dark green body, tan interior, 5 spoke concave star wheels, "Spyder" tempa , Thailand casting ($1-2)(MW69/1998 US)(MW42/1998 ROW)
19. dark green body, tan interior, 5 spoke concave star wheels, "Spyder" tempa, China casting ($1-2)(MW69/1998)(MW42/1998 ROW)
20. red body, gray interior, 5 spoke concave star wheels, skeleton & "Raptor" tempa, China casting ($1-2)(5pk)
21. black body, red interior, 5 spoke concave star wheels, "Spyder" tempa, China casting ($1-2)(5pk)
22. metallic gold body, black interior, 6 spoke spiral wheels, no tempa, China casting ($5-10)(CH)
23. blue body, gray interior, 5 spoke concave star wheels, "Spyder" tempa, China casting ($1-2)(MW49/1999 US)(MW44/1999 ROW)
24. blue body, gray interior, star with 5 spokes wheels, "Spyder" tempa, China casting ($2-3)(MW49/1999 US)(MW44/ 1999 ROW)
25. dark green body, tan interior, 5 spoke concave star wheels, "Fujihara Tuning Pros" tempa, China casting ($75+)(ASAP)
26. dark green body, tan interior, 5 spoke concave star wheels, "Yamaha Mufflers" tempa, China casting ($75+)(ASAP)
27. dark green body, tan interior, 5 spoke concave star wheels, "Mattel Mt. Laurel Closure/ Matchbox/ Spyder" tempa ($50+)(CCI)

MB28-M THE BUSTER *see MB13-F*

MB28-N DELIVERY TRUCK *see MB48-J*

MB28-O HOT HEAD, issued 2004 (USA)(MB639)
MB13-I HOT HEAD, issued 2004 (ROW)

1. red body, chrome helmet, "Hero City" helmet tempa, blue windows, gray plastic base, gold 5 crown dot wheels, "Force" logo & stripes tempa, China casting ($1-2)(MW28/2004 US)(MW13/2004 ROW)

MB29-A FIRE PUMPER, issued 1970

NOTE: Below models with blue windows & dome light, unpainted metal base & England base.

1. red body, no water gun cast, no labels, 5 spoke wheels ($50-75)
2. red body, water gun cast, "P1" tempa, dot dash wheels ($7-10)(CR)
3. red body, water gun cast, "P1" tempa, 5 spoke wheels ($25-40)(CR)

MB29-B RACING MINI, issued 1970

NOTE: Below models with clear windows, metal base & England casting unless otherwise noted.

1. bronze body, unpainted base, ivory interior, "29" orange outline labels, 5 spoke wheels ($15-20)
2. orange body, unpainted base, ivory interior, "29" orange outline labels, 5 spoke wheels ($10-15)
3. orange body, unpainted base, cream interior, "29" orange outline labels, 5 spoke wheels ($10-15)
4. orange body, silver-gray base, cream interior, "29" orange outline labels, 5 spoke wheels ($10-15)
5. orange body, unpainted base, ivory interior, "29" green outline labels, 5 spoke wheels ($10-15)
6. orange body, unpainted base, cream interior, "29" green outline labels, 5 spoke wheels ($10-15)
7. orange body, silver-gray base, cream interior, "29" green outline labels, 5 spoke wheels ($10-15)
8. orange body, silver-gray base, ivory interior, "29" green outline labels, 5 spoke wheels ($10-15)
9. red-orange body, unpainted base, ivory interior, "29" green outline labels, 5 spoke wheels ($10-15)
10. red body, unpainted base, ivory interior, "29" green outline labels, 5 spoke wheels ($10-15)
11. red body, unpainted base, cream interior, "29" green outline labels, 5 spoke wheels ($10-15)
12. red body, unpainted base, ivory interior, "29" green outline labels, 5 spoke center cut wheels ($5-7)(TP)
13. red body, unpainted base, ivory interior, "3" labels, 5 spoke center cut wheels ($15-18)(TP)
14. red body, unpainted base, ivory interior, no labels, 5 spoke center cut wheels ($5-7)(TP)
15. red body, unpainted base, ivory interior, "29" green outline labels, dot dash wheels ($5-7)(TP)
16. metallic blue body, unpainted base with Manaus tab, ivory interior, no labels, 5 spoke wheels ($250+)(BR)

MB29-C TRACTOR SHOVEL, issued 1976 (MB029)

NOTE: Below models listed with maltese cross wheels with silver hubs & plastic base unless otherwise noted.

1. light yellow body, red shovel, yellow base, chrome motor, no tempa, England casting ($8-12)
2. light yellow body, red shovel, yellow base, chrome motor, no tempa, black hubs, England casting ($10-15)
3. lime body, lemon shovel, lemon base, chrome motor, no tempa, England casting ($100-175)(GR)
4. dark yellow body, red shovel, yellow base, chrome motor, no tempa, England casting ($4-6)
5. dark yellow body, red shovel, yellow base, black motor, no tempa, England casting ($4-6)
6. dark yellow body, red shovel, pale tan base, black motor, no tempa, England casting ($4-6)
7. dark yellow body, red shovel, pale tan base, black motor, no tempa, yellow hubs, England casting ($6-8)
8. dark yellow body, maroon shovel, pale tan base, black motor, no tempa, yellow hubs, England casting ($6-8)
9. dark yellow body, maroon shovel, yellow base, black motor, no tempa, yellow hubs, England casting ($6-8)
10. dark yellow body, maroon shovel, lemon base, black motor, no tempa, England casting ($4-6)

11. dark yellow body, red shovel, lemon base, black motor, no tempa, England casting ($4-6)
12. dark yellow body, red shovel, black base, black motor, no tempa, England casting ($4-6)
13. dark yellow body, black shovel, yellow base, black motor, no tempa, England casting ($4-6)
14. dark yellow body, black shovel, lemon base, black motor, no tempa, England casting ($4-6)
15. dark yellow body, black shovel, pale tan base, black motor, no tempa, England casting ($4-6)
16. dark orange body, red shovel, black base, gray motor, no tempa, England casting ($50-75)
17. dark orange body, black shovel, black base, gray motor, no tempa, England casting ($8-10)
18. light orange body, black shovel, black base, gray motor, no tempa, England casting ($8-10)
19. dark yellow body, black shovel, black base, black motor, black stripes with "C" tempa, England casting ($2-4)
20. dark yellow body, black shovel, black base, black stripes tempa,, England casting ($2-4)
21. dark yellow body, black shovel, black base, gray motor, black stripes tempa, England casting ($2-4)
22. dark yellow body, black shovel, black base, gray motor, no tempa, England casting ($2-4)
23. purple body, black shovel, black base, black motor, lime & orange tempa, Macau casting, includes plastic armament ($6-8)(RB)
24. dark yellow body, red shovel, black base, black motor, black stripes tempa, Macau casting ($2-3)(TC)
25. dark yellow body, black shovel, black base, black motor, "Thomae Mucosolvan" tempa, Macau casting ($15-25)(GR)
26. light orange body, black shovel, black base, black motor, "Thomae Mucosolvan" tempa, Macau casting ($20-30)(GR)
27. blue body, red shovel, black base, red motor, yellow wheels with orange hubs, green stripes tempa, Macau casting ($6-8)(LL)
28. light yellow body, black shovel, black base, black motor, "Thomae Mucosolvan" tempa, Macau casting ($18-25)(GR)
29. light yellow body, black shovel, black base, black motor, "Thomae Mucosolvan" tempa, Thailand casting ($18-25)(GR)
30. dark yellow body, black shovel, black base, black motor, black stripes tempa, Thailand casting ($1-2)
31. dark yellow body, red shovel, black base, black motor, red stripes tempa, Thailand casting ($1-2)
32. light yellow body, black shovel, black base, black motor, "Thomae MucosolvanS" tempa, Thailand casting ($20-25)(GR)
33. light yellow body, black shovel, black base with tow hook, black motor, "Thomae MucosolvanS, Thailand casting ($20-25)(GR)
34. blue body, black shovel, black base, black motor, "Spasmo Mucosolvan" tempa, Thailand casting ($10-15)(GR)

NOTE: Below models with tow hook cast unless otherwise noted.

35. light yellow body, black shovel, black base, black motor, "Thomae Mucosolvan" on roof tempa, Thailand casting ($18-25)(GR)
36. blue body, black shovel, black base, black motor, "Spasmo Mucosolvan" on roof tempa, Thailand casting ($12-15)(GR)
37. dark yellow body, red shovel, black base, black motor, red stripes tempa, Thailand casting ($1-2)
38. fluorescent orange body, black shovel, black base, black motor, no tempa, Thailand casting ($1-2)(5pk)
39. orange body, silver-gray shovel, black base, black motor, black stripes tempa, Thailand casting ($1-2)
40. orange body, silver-gray shovel, black base, black motor, black stripes tempa, China casting ($1-2)
41. orange body, silver-gray shovel, black base, black motor, black stripes tempa, Thailand casting ($1-2)
42. florescent orange body, silver-gray shovel, black base, black motor, no tempa, China casting ($1-2)(5pk)
43. orange body, silver-gray shovel, black base, black motor, no tempa, Thailand casting ($1-2)(5pk)
44. pumpkin body, gray shovel, black base, black motor, no tempa, China casting ($1-2)(5pk)
45. light orange body, red shovel with lever, black base, black motor, red stripes tempa, China casting ($1-2)(AS)(AP)
46. metallic gold body, black shovel, black base, black motor, no tempa, China casting ($5-10)(CH)
47. light red body, silver-gray shovel, black base, black motor, no tempa, China casting ($1-2)
48. pink-red body, silver-gray shovel, black base, black motor, "Thomae MucosolvanS" tempa, China casting ($25-40)(GR)
49. blue body, black shovel, black base, black motor, "Thomae Mucosolvan" tempa, China casting ($25-40)(GR)
50. red body, black shovel with lever, black base, black motor, no tempa, China casting ($1-2)(AP)
51. white body, silver-gray shovel, black base, silver-gray motor, no tempa, China casting ($1-2)(MW13/1998)
52. beige body, silver-gray shovel, silver-gray base & motor, "3-MB34" & dirt tempa, China casting ($1-2)(MW28/1999)
53. orange body, black shovel, black base & motor, white roof tempa, China casting ($3-5)(MW7/ 1999GR)
54. yellow body, black shovel, black base & motor, "Thomae MucosolvanS tempa, China casting ($25-40)(GR)
55. green body, black shovel, black base & motor, "Thomae MucosolvanS" tempa, China casting ($35-50)(GR)
56. dull gold body, black shovel, black base & motor, none tempa, China casting ($75-100)(GR)
57. matt green body, gray shovel, gray base & motor, "#-MB34", dirt & silver-gray roof tempa, China casting ($1-2)(MW94/2000 US)(MW74/2000 ROW)
58. matt green body, gray shovel, gray base & motor, "3-MB34", dirt, silver-gray roof & "Matchbox 2000" tempa, China casting ($2-4)(MW94/2000 US)
59. pumpkin body, gray shovel, base & motor, "Hemler Bros." Tempa, China casting ($75+)(ASAP)
60. pumpkin body, gray shovel, base & motor, "CAT Service Co." tempa, China casting ($75+)(ASAP)
61. pumpkin body, gray shovel, base & motor, "Redi-Way Inc." tempa, China casting ($75+)(ASAP)
62. pumpkin body, gray shovel, base & motor, "Blue Ridge Construction" tempa, China casting ($75+)(ASAP)
63. matt green body, gray shovel, base & motor, "3-MB34", dirt & silver-gray roof tempa, Mattel/ China casting ($1-2)(MW94/2000 US)(MW74/2000 ROW)
64. matt green body, gray shovel , base & motor, "3-MB34", dirt & silver-gray roof tempa, Mattel/ China casting, 5 spoke oval wheels ($1-2)(MW94/2000 US)
65. blue body, white shovel, black base, gray motor, "Matchbox 24" tempa, Mattel/ China casting, 5 spoke oval wheels ($1-2)(MW39/2001)
66. tan body, black shovel, black base, black motor, no tempa, gold hubs, China casting ($75-100)(GR)
67. pumpkin body, black shovel, black base, black motor, no tempa, China casting ($10-15)(ASAP blank)

MB29-D BMW 328i POLICE CAR *see MB11-H*

MB29-E RIG DIGGER, issued 2004 (USA)(MB647)
MB14-L RIG DIGGER, issued 2004 (ROW)

1. orange platform, arm & shovel, yellow helmet, metallic silver plastic base, black wheels, "Hero City" tempa, China casting ($1-2)(MW29/ 2004 US)(MB14/2004 ROW)

MB30-A EIGHT WHEEL CRANE, issued 1970

1. red body, orange crane boom, unpainted base, yellow hook ($500-750)
2. red body, gold crane boom, unpainted base, yellow hook ($35-50)

MB30-B BEACH BUGGY, issued 1970

NOTE: Below models with spiro wheels, metal base & England casting unless otherwise noted.

1. metallic pink body, yellow spatter, white interior, unpainted base ($20-25)
2. metallic pink body, yellow spatter, yellow interior, unpainted base ($12-15)
3. metallic lavender body, yellow spatter, yellow interior, unpainted base ($15-20)
4. dark orchid body, no spatter, flame label (from MB40 A), orange-yellow interior, unpainted base with origin ground off ($250+)(BR)
5. red body, no spatter, yellow interior, unpainted base with Manaus label ($250+)(BR)

MB30-C SWAMP RAT, issued 1976 (MB730)

NOTE: Below models with black engine, propeller & solid wheels.

1. olive deck, light tan hull, tan man, "Swamp Rats" labels, England casting ($5-8)
2. olive deck, dark tan hull, tan man, "Swamp Rats" labels, England casting ($5-8)
3. olive deck, pinkish-tan hull, tan man, "Swamp Rats" labels, England casting ($5-8)
4. olive deck, dark tan hull, tan man, no labels, England casting ($5-8)
5. olive deck, tan hull, tan man, tan & black camouflage tempa, Macau casting ($4-6)(CM)
6. olive deck, tan hull, black man, tan & black camouflage tempa, China casting ($12-15)(CM)
7. olive deck, tan hull, black man, tan & black camouflage tempa (no side stripes), China casting ($12-15)(CM)(CHI)(MP)
8. dull olive deck, tan hull with Manaus tab, tan man, "Swamp Rat" labels ($35-50)(BR)

MB30-D LEYLAND ARTICULATED TRUCK, issued 1982 (ROW)(MB030)

NOTE: Below models with plastic cab base, red windows, England casting unless otherwise noted.

1. blue cab without "Leyland" cast on front, white cab base, silver-gray dump, no panel cast, no tempa ($15-20)
2. blue cab, white cab base, silver-gray dump, no panel cast, no tempa ($2-4)
3. blue cab, yellow cab base, silver-gray dump, no panel cast, no tempa ($2-4)
4. bright blue cab, yellow cab base, silver-gray dump, no panel cast, no tempa ($2-4)
5. bright blue cab, yellow cab base, yellow dump, cast panel, "International" tempa ($3-5)
6. red cab, yellow cab base, silver-gray dump, no panel cast, no tempa ($7-10)
7. red cab, yellow cab base, yellow dump, cast panel, "International" tempa ($6-8)
8. blue cab, yellow cab base, yellow dump, cast panel, "International" tempa ($6-8)
9. bright blue cab, lemon cab base, yellow dump, cast panel, "International" tempa ($3-5)
10. bright blue cab, white cab base, yellow dump, cast panel, "International" tempa ($3-5)
11. bright blue cab, yellow cab base, bright blue dump, cast panel, "Pauls" tempa ($25-40)(UK)
12. bright blue cab, lemon cab base, bright blue dump, cast panel, "Pauls" tempa ($25-40)(UK)
13. bright blue cab, white cab base, bright blue dump, cast panel, "Pauls" tempa ($25-40)(UK)
14. bright blue cab, lemon cab base, yellow dump, cast panel, amber windows, "International" tempa, Macau casting ($3-5)

MB30-E PETERBILT QUARRY TRUCK, issued 1982 (USA)(MB096)
MB23-E PETERBILT QUARRY TRUCK, issued 1982 (ROW)

NOTE: Below models with plastic base & 8 spoke wheels unless otherwise noted.

1. yellow body, light gray dump, amber windows, chrome exhausts & base, "Dirty Dumper" tempa, England casting ($2-4)
2. yellow body, dark gray dump, amber windows, chrome exhausts & base, "Dirty Dumper" tempa, England casting ($2-4)
3. yellow body, silver-gray dump, amber windows, chrome exhausts & base, "Dirty Dumper" tempa, England casting ($2-4)
4. yellow body, silver-gray dump, clear windows, chrome exhausts & base, "Dirty Dumper" tempa, England casting ($2-4)
5. yellow body, dark gray dump, amber windows, chrome exhausts & base, "Dirty Dumper" tempa, Macau casting ($1-2)
6. yellow-orange body, dark gray dump, amber windows, chrome exhausts & base, "Dirty Dumper" tempa, Macau casting ($1-2)
7. yellow-orange body, dark gray dump, clear windows, chrome exhausts & base, "Dirty Dumper" tempa, Macau casting ($1-2)
8. light yellow body, dark gray dump, clear windows, chrome exhausts & base, "Pace" tempa, Macau casting ($1-2)
9. dark yellow body, dark gray dump, clear windows, chrome exhausts & base, "Pace" tempa, Macau casting ($1-2)
10. dark yellow body, dark gray dump, clear windows, gray exhausts, chrome base, "Pace" tempa, Macau casting ($1-2)
11. orange body, dark gray dump, clear windows, chrome exhausts & base, "Losinger" tempa, Macau casting ($8-12)(SW)
12. dark yellow body, dark gray dump, clear windows, gray exhausts, chrome base, "Pace" tempa, Thailand casting ($1-2)
13. dark yellow body, red dump, clear windows, gray exhausts, chrome base, "Pace" tempa, Thailand casting ($1-2)
14. white body, silver-gray dump, clear windows, gray exhausts & base, "Cement Company" tempa, Manaus casting ($35-50)(BR)
15. orange-yellow body, red dump, clear windows, gray exhausts, black base with bar code, "Pace" & "Intercom City" tempa, China casting ($10-15)(IC)
16. red body, gray dump, gray base, gray exhausts, "530SP" & stripes tempa, Manaus casting ($30-45)(BR)
17. white body, silver-gray dump, gray base, gray exhausts, "Construction" tempa, Manaus casting ($35-50)(BR)
18. fluorescent orange body, black dump, chrome base, black exhausts, no tempa, Thailand casting ($1-2)(5pk)
19. red body, red dump, gray base, gray exhausts, "530SP" tempa, Manaus casting ($30-45)(BR)
20. orange-yellow body, red dump, chrome base, gray exhausts, "Pace" tempa, China casting ($2-4)

21. pumpkin body, gray dump, chrome base, dark gray exhausts, "Matchbox" tempa, China casting ($1-2)(5pk)
22. orange-yellow body, red dump, chrome base, gray exhausts, no tempa, China casting ($1-2)
23. white body, dark turquoise dump, chrome base, gray exhausts, "Sagamore Insurance" tempa, China casting ($85-110)(US)
24. dark yellow body, yellow dump, chrome base, chrome exhausts, "CAT" tempa, China casting ($2-3)(CT)
25. red body, dark gray dump, chrome base, chrome exhausts, white stripes tempa, China casting ($1-2)(MW10/1998)
26. pumpkin body, gray dump, chrome base, dark gray exhausts, no tempa, China casting ($15-25)(ASAP blank)
27. metallic gold body, gray dump, chrome base, dark gray exhausts, no tempa, China casting ($75-100)(CH- found as #19)
28. white body, gray dump, chrome base, silver-gray exhausts, no tempa, China casting ($25-40)(ASAP blank)
29. white body, gray dump, chrome base, silver-gray exhausts, "Coast To Coast Hydraulics" tempa, China casting ($20-30)(ASAP)
30. white body, gray dump, chrome base, silver gray exhausts, "Hemler Bros." Tempa, China casting ($75+)(ASAP)
31. white body, gray dump, chrome base, silver gray exhausts, "CAT Service Co." tempa, China casting ($75+)(ASAP)
32. white body, gray dump, chrome base, silver gray exhausts, "Redi-Way Inc." tempa, China casting ($75+)(ASAP)
33. white body, gray dump, chrome base, silver gray exhausts, "Blue Ridge Construction" tempa, China casting ($75+)(ASAP)
34. rose red body, yellow dump, chrome base, gray exhaust, "Joe Diesel", face & yellow design tempa, China casting ($4-6)(PS)
35. rose red body, yellow dump, chrome base, gray exhaust, "Joe Diesel", face & yellow design tempa, 7 spoke sawblade wheels, China casting ($4-6)(PS)
36. pumpkin body, gray dump, chrome base, gray exhaust, "United States Postal Service" tempa, China casting ($50+)(ASAP)
27. pumpkin body, gray dump, chrome base, gray exhaust, circular logo with blue design tempa, China casting ($18-25)(ASAP)
38. pumpkin body, gray dump, chrome base, gray exhausts, "Penn DOT" tempa, China casting ($50+)(ASAP)
39. white body, gray dump, chrome base, silver-gray exhausts, "HBE" tempa, China casting ($50+)(ASAP)
40. white body, gray dump, chrome base, silver-gray exhausts, "Expressway Authority" tempa, China casting ($50+)(ASAP)

MB30-F MERCEDES 'G' WAGON, issued 1985 (ROW)(MB149)
MB40-L MERCEDES 'G' WAGON, issued 2000 (USA)

NOTE: Below models with silver-gray interior unless otherwise noted. Lasertronic models have no interior fitted. All models with 8 spoke wheel & plastic base unless otherwise noted.

1. red body, white roof, black base, blue windows & dome lights, white "Rescue Unit" & checkers tempa, Macau casting ($2-3)
2. orange body, white roof, black base, blue windows & dome lights, "Lufthansa" tempa, Macau casting ($3-5)(GS)
3. white body, white roof, black base, blue windows & dome lights, "Polizei" & checkers tempa, Macau casting ($2-4)(TP)
4. white body, white roof, black base, blue windows & dome lights, "Polizei" with green doors & hood tempa, Macau casting ($2-4)
5. red body, white roof, black base, blue windows & dome lights, yellow "Rescue Unit" & checkers tempa, Macau casting ($2-3)(MC)
6. olive body, tan roof, black base, blue windows & dome lights, red cross in circle & "LS 2014" tempa, black hubs, Macau casting ($4-6)(CM)
7. white body, orange roof, orange base, blue windows & dome lights, "Ambulance" & checkers tempa, Macau casting ($3-5)(MC)
8. white body, white roof, black base, black windows, green dome lights, "Auto Rescue 24 Hrs. Towing" tempa, Macau casting ($8-12)(SR)
9. red body, red roof, black base, black windows, red dome lights, "Fire Metro Airport" tempa, Macau casting ($8-12)(SR)
10. navy blue body, navy blue roof, black base, black windows, red dome lights, "Swat Unit Team Support" tempa, Macau casting ($8-12)(SR)
11. red body, white roof, black base, blue windows & dome lights, yellow "Rescue Unit" & checkers, Thailand casting ($2-3)(MC)
12. white body, white roof, black base, blue windows & dome lights, "Polizei" with green hood & doors tempa, Thailand casting ($1-2)
13. white body, dark orange roof, orange base, blue windows & dome lights, "Ambulance" & checkers tempa, Thailand casting ($2-3)(MC)
14. white body, white roof, black base, blue windows & dome lights, "Lufthansa" tempa, Thailand casting ($1-2)(MP)
15. florescent orange body, white roof, black base, blue windows & dome lights, "Auto Rescue 24 Hrs. Towing", Thailand casting ($1-2)
16. white body, florescent orange roof & base, blue windows & dome lights, "Marine Rescue" & checkers tempa, Thailand casting ($2-3)(EM)
17. florescent orange body, white roof, black base with bar code, blue windows & dome lights, "Police 8" & "Intercom City" tempa, Thailand casting ($10-15)(IC)
18. florescent orange body, white roof, black base, blue windows & dome lights, white hood with "Rescue" & checker design on sides tempa, Thailand casting ($1-2)(EM)
19. red body, white roof, black base, black windows, red dome lights, "Matchbox Rescue Unit/ Fire Dept." tempa, China casting ($3-5)(LS)
20. lemon body, white roof, black base, black windows, greenish yellow dome lights, "Beach Patrol Unit 2" tempa, China casting ($3-5)(LS)
21. yellow body, black roof, black base, black windows, greenish-yellow dome lights, "Tough Construction- Construction Foreman" tempa, China casting ($3-5)(LS)
22. red body, gray roof, black base, black windows, red dome lights, "Matchbox Rescue Unit" tempa, China casting ($3-5)(LS)
23. beige body, dark green roof, black base, black windows, greenish yellow dome lights, green stripes tempa, China casting ($4-6)(LS)(Avon)
24. dark red body, white roof, black base, black windows, red dome lights, "Matchbox Fire Rescue Dept." tempa, China casting ($4-6)(LS)(Avon)
25. white body, green roof, green base, blue windows, white interior, blue dome lights, "Polizei" tempa, China casting ($3-5)(MW25/1999GR)
26. silver-gray body, black roof, black base, blue windows, black interior, blue dome lights, red stripe & fish logo tempa, China casting ($2-4)(5pk)
27. silver-gray body, black roof, black base, blue windows, black interior, blue dome lights, red stripes & "Marine Research" tempa, China casting ($1-2)(5pk)
28. red body, black roof, black base, amber windows, black interior, amber dome lights, "Mission Satellite Top Secret" & "Matchbox 2000" tempa, China casting ($2-4)(MW40/2000 US)

29. red body, black roof, black base, amber windows, black interior, amber dome lights, "Mission Satellite Top Secret" tempa, China casting ($1-2)(MW40/2000 US)(MW25/2000 ROW)
30. white body, blue roof, black base, blue windows, blue dome lights, "Test Centre" & blue hood tempa, China casting ($1-2)(LP)
NOTE: Below models with 7 spoke sawblade wheels.
31. metallic silver body, red roof, black base, blue windows, black interior, blue dome lights, "S.O.S." & design tempa, China casting ($1-2)(5pk)
32. white body, light blue roof, light blue base, amber windows, black interior, amber dome lights, "Police 82167" with stripes tempa, China casting ($10-15)(PS)
33. white body, blue roof, blue base, amber windows, blue interior, amber dome lights, "Metro 7" tempa, China casting ($1-2)(LP)
34. metallic red body, black roof, black base, blue windows, black interior, amber dome lights, "MTN Rescue" & mountains tempa, China casting ($1-2)(MW63/2001 UK)
35. dark yellow body, blue roof, black base, blue windows, black interior, blue dome lights, "Beach Patrol/ S.C.U.B.A." tempa, China casting ($1-2)(5pk)
36. white body, light blue roof, blue base, blue windows, black interior, blue dome lights, "Beach Patrol/ S.C.U.B.A." tempa, China casting ($1-2)(5pk)
37. blue body, light blue roof, red base, amber windows, white interior, amber dome lights, "Ha Ha Ha Ha/ Peanuts" tempa, China casting ($1-2)(5pk)
38. red body, black roof, gray base, amber windows, white interior, amber dome lights, blue & yellow bug & swatter design tempa, Mattel China casting ($2-3)(MW27/2004 ROW)

MB30-G TOYOTA SUPRA, issued 1995 (USA)(MB221)
MB60-I TOYOTA SUPRA, issued 1995 (ROW)

NOTE: Below models with gloss black metal base & Thailand casting unless otherwise noted.
1. white body, gray interior, smoke windows, red & yellow hood & sides design tempa, 6-spoke spiral wheels ($1-2)
2. white body, red interior, smoke windows, red & yellow side tempa, 6-spoke spiral wheels ($1-2)
3. florescent orange body, black interior, clear windows, "Matchbox Get In The Fast Lane/ Toy Fair 1996" tempa, chrome disc with rubber tires ($18-25)(US)
4. florescent yellow body, black interior, clear windows, "Matchbox Get In The Fast Lane/ Toy Fair 1996" tempa, chrome disc with rubber tires ($18-25)(UK)(GR)
5. iridescent white body, red & black interior, clear windows, detailed trim tempa, chrome disc wheels with rubber tires ($3-5)(PC1)
6. copper body, red & black interior, clear windows, detailed trim tempa, chrome disc wheels with rubber tires ($3-5)(SC1)
7. yellow body, gray & black interior, clear windows, detailed trim tempa, chrome disc wheels with rubber tires ($3-5)(PC1-JC)
8. charcoal body, red & black interior, clear windows, detailed trim tempa, chrome disc wheels with rubber tires ($3-5)(PC4)
9. red body, yellow interior, smoke windows, orange & white side tempa, 6-spoke spiral wheels ($2-4)
10. red body, silver-gray interior, smoke windows, white & black design tempa, 5 spoke concave star wheels ($1-2)(5pk)
11. chrome body, purple interior, clear windows, purple & pink design tempa, 5 spoke concave star wheels ($1-2)
12. red body, yellow interior, smoke windows, orange and white side tempa, 5 spoke concave star wheels ($2-4)
13. black body, tan & black interior, clear windows, detailed trim tempa, chrome disc wheels with rubber tires ($15-20)(GC)
14. metallic gold body, black interior, clear windows, no tempa, 5 spoke concave star wheels ($5-10)(CH)
15. greenish gold body, black interior, clear windows, no tempa, 5 spoke concave star wheels ($5-10)(CH)
NOTE: Versions 16, 17 & 19 can be found in multiple shades of blue.
16. blue chrome body, white interior, clear windows, pink/orange/white tempa, 5 spoke concave star wheels ($1-2)(5pk)
17. non-chrome blue body, white interior, clear windows, pink/orange/white tempa, 5 spoke concave star wheels ($1-2)(5pk)
18. black body, tan interior, clear windows, gold "Supra" tempa, 5 spoke concave star wheels ($1-2)(MW44/ 1998 ROW)
19. pale blue chrome body, white interior, clear windows, pink/orange/white tempa, 5 spoke concave star wheels ($1-2)(5pk)
20. pale blue chrome body, white interior, clear windows, pink/orange/white tempa, 5 spoke concave star wheels, China casting ($1-2)(5pk)
21. black body, tan interior, clear windows, gold "Supra" tempa, 5 spoke concave star wheels, China casting ($1-2)(MW44/1998 ROW)
22. dark blue body, black interior, smoke green windows, "Lucent Design & Engineering" tempa, 5 spoke concave star wheels, China casting ($75+)(ASAP)
23. dark blue body, black interior, smoke green windows, no tempa, 5 spoke concave star wheels, China casting ($25-40)(ASAP blank)
24. metallic black body, black interior, smoke windows, red stripe, painted lights & "Matchbox" tempa, 5 spoke concave star wheels, China casting ($2-3)(MW70/2000 ROW
25. dark blue body, black interior, smoke green windows, "HEDIS Group" tempa, 5 spoke concave star wheels, China casting ($75+)(ASAP)
26. dark blue body, black interior, smoke green windows, "Mas 90 User Conference Lexington" tempa, 5 spoke concave star wheels, China casting ($75+)(ASAP)
27. dark blue body, black interior, smoke green windows, "Wenchy's Antiques & Collectibles" tempa, 5 spoke concave star wheels, China casting ($15-20)(ASAP)
28. metallic black body, black interior, smoke windows, red stripe & painted lights with "Matchbox" & "Estadidad 2004" tempa, 5 spoke concave star wheels ($50+)(ASAP)

MB30-H HELICOPTER *see MB75-D*

MB30-I CHEVY TAHOE POLICE, issued 1998

NOTE: Below models with clear windows, chrome plastic base & China casting unless otherwise noted.
1. white body, red dome light, gray interior, "Police Unit 4" tempa, 5 spoke concave star wheels ($1-2)(MW30/1998)
2. black body, red dome light, red interior, "Official Matchbox Collectors Club" tempa , 5 spoke concave star wheels ($5-8)(US)
3. green & yellow body, red dome light, tan interior, "York Fair Police 1998" tempa , 5 spoke concave star wheels ($7-10)(US)
4. white body, gray interior, red & blue dome light, "Salt Lake City Police" tempa , chrome disc wheels with rubber tires ($15-25)(PC23)
5. red body, gray & black interior, blue dome light, "City of Seattle" tempa, chrome disc wheels with rubber tires ($5-8)(PC)
6. dark blue body, blue interior, red & blue dome light, "Wisconsin State Police" tempa, chrome disc wheels with rubber tires ($10-15)(PC)
7. olive body, dark gray interior, red dome light, "Military Police" tempa, green disc with rubber tires ($10-15)(PC)
8. white body, red interior, red dome light, yellow windows, "Fire Chief" with bands tempa, 5 spoke concave star wheels ($1-2)(MW78/1999 US)

9. red body, black interior, amber windows & dome light,, "Fire 3 Dept./ Dial 911" tempa, 5 spoke with concave star wheels ($2-4)(MW28/2000 US)
10. red body, black interior, amber windows & dome light, "Fire 3 Dept./ Dial 911" & "Matchbox 2000" tempa, 5 spoke concave star wheels ($8-12)(MW28/2000 US)
11. white body, blue interior, blue dome light, 2 tone blue stripes, "Police" & "Matchbox" tempa, 5 spoke concave star wheels ($3-5)(PB)
12. white body, white interior, red dome light, "Nassau County Police" & stripes tempa, 5 spoke concave star wheels ($20-25)(CCI)
13. white body, white interior, red dome light, no tempa, 5 spoke concave star wheels ($25-40)(ASAP blank)
14. black body, red interior, red dome light, "Official Matchbox Collectors Club/ Matchbox USA Membership Drive 2001" tempa, 5 spoke concave star wheels ($15-25)(CCI)
15. white body, white interior, red dome light, "Open Space Officer" tempa", 5 spoke concave star wheels ($75+)(ASAP)
16. white body, white interior, red dome light, "Thomas Hines Retired Finally" tempa, 5 spoke concave star wheels ($75+)(ASAP)
17. red body, black interior, blue dome light, "5 Alarm/ 67/ Hangar 34" tempa, lace wheels ($1-2)(LP)
18. black body, red interior, red dome light, "Official Matchbox Collectors Club/ Penn. Matchbox Collectors Club 2001" tempa, 5 spoke concave star wheels ($15-25)(CCI)
19. white body, black interior, amber dome light, "H2O Force" with red, orange & black stripes & extinguisher tempa, 10 spoke flower wheels ($1-2)(MW28/2001)
20. black body, red interior, red dome light, "Official Matchbox Collectors Club/ 5 Jahre MCCD 2001" tempa, 5 spoke concave star wheels ($20-25)(C2)
21. white & bright blue body, dark blue interior, amber dome light, dark blue interior, "Metro 7" tempa, lace wheels ($1-2)(LP)
22. black body, red interior, red dome light, "Official Matchbox Collectors Club/ Illinois Matchbox Collectors Club 2002" tempa, 5 spoke concave star wheels ($15-20)(CCI)
23. metallic blue body, black interior, amber dome light, "Pennsylvania 2/ Benjamin Electric" tempa, 10 spoke flower wheels ($1-2)(AM)
24. iridescent white body, blue interior, blue dome light, "Police TK-1072" tempa, silver-gray metal base, 7 spoke sawblade wheels, Mattel China casting ($1-2)(5pk)
25. yellow body, gray interior, red dome light, blue windows, "MB Radio" tempa, black plastic base, 7 spoke sawblade wheels ($3-5)(PS)
26. white body, white interior, red dome light, clear windows, "National Law Enforcement Officers Memorial" tempa, 5 spoke concave star wheels ($15-20)(ASAP)
27. red body, light gray interior, clear windows, red dome light, "Napanee Fire rescue/ Fire Dept. 11" tempa, 5 spoke concave star wheels ($15-20)(CCI)
28. white body, light gray interior, clear windows, red dome light, "Sheriff 122" tempa, 5 spoke concave star wheels ($15-20)(CCI)
29. silver-gray body, red interior, clear windows, red dome light, flame design, "14" & "Matchbox FDMB" tempa, 10 spoke flower wheels ($1-2)(LP)
NOTE: Above model with Matchbox International or Mattel casting.
30. black body, red interior, clear windows, red dome light, "Official Matchbox Collectors Club/ Matchbox Northwest Collectors Club" tempa, 5 spoke concave star wheels ($15-20)(CCI)
31. bright blue body, gray interior, clear windows, red dome light, "Police" & winged logo tempa, 7 spoke sawblade wheels ($1-2)(5pk)
32. bright blue body, gray interior, clear windows, red dome light, "Police" & winged logo tempa, 7 spoke sawblade wheels, base casting from MB46-H ($2-4)(5pk)
33. black body, red interior, clear windows, red dome light, "Official Matchbox Collectors Club" tempa & "NJ Diecast Collectors Club" label, 5 spoke concave star wheels ($15-20)(C2)
34. metallic blue body, gray interior, red windows, amber dome light, "Hero City Metro Police" tempa, 10 spoke flower wheels ($1-2)(5pk)

MB30-J DENNIS SABRE FIRE ENGINE *see MB68-L*

MB30-K CAP'N COP, issued 2004 (USA) (MB648)
MB15-N CAP'N COP, issued 2004 (ROW)
1. silver-gray body & engine, dark blue helmet, yellow headlights & saddlebags, gold spoked wheels, "Hero City Police" tempa, China casting ($1-2)(MW30/2004/ US)(MW15/2004 ROW)

MB31-A LINCOLN CONTINENTAL, issued 1970
NOTE: Below models with ivory interior, clear windows, 5 spoke wheels, unpainted metal base & England casting. Earliest versions have thin wheels with later versions having wide wheels.
1. mint green body, ($2000+)
2. metallic green-gold body ($45-60)

MB31-B VOLKSDRAGON, issued 1971
NOTE: Below models with 5 spoke wheels, metal base & England casting unless otherwise noted.
1. red body, unpainted base, purple windows, cream interior, eyes label ($12-15)
2. red body, unpainted base, purple windows, yellow interior, eyes label ($12-15)
3. red body, unpainted base, clear windows, yellow interior, eyes label ($12-15)
4. red body, silver-gray base, clear windows, yellow interior, eyes label ($12-15)
5. red body, silver-gray base, purple windows, yellow interior, eyes label ($12-15)
6. red body, unpainted base, purple windows, yellow interior, flower label ($15-20)
7. red body, silver-gray base, purple windows, yellow interior, flower label ($15-20)
8. red body, unpainted base, purple windows, yellow interior, no label ($12-15)
9. red body, silver-gray base, purple windows, yellow interior, no label ($12-15)
10. red body, unpainted base, purple windows, white interior, eyes label ($12-15)
11. metallic blue body, unpainted base with Manaus tab, purple windows, yellow interior, no labels ($250+)(BR)

MB31-C CARAVAN, issued 1977 (MB031)
NOTE: Below models with clear windows & metal base unless otherwise noted.
1. white body, unpainted base, orange door, ivory interior, orange labels, England casting ($3-5)
2. white body, unpainted base, orange door, light yellow interior, orange labels, England casting ($3-5)
3. white body, unpainted base, yellow door, light yellow interior, orange labels, England casting ($3-5)
4. white body, unpainted base, yellow door, ivory interior, orange labels, England casting ($3-5)
5. white body, unpainted base, orange door, tan interior, orange labels, England casting ($3-5)

6. white body, unpainted base, light blue door, tan interior, orange labels, England casting ($3-5)
7. white body, unpainted base, light blue door, light yellow interior, orange labels, England casting ($3-5)
8. white body, unpainted base, light blue door, light brown interior, orange labels, England casting ($3-5)
9. white body, unpainted base, light blue door, light yellow interior, blue labels, England casting ($3-5)
10. white body, silver-gray base, light blue door, light yellow interior, blue labels, England casting ($25-40)
11. white body, unpainted base, dark blue door, light yellow interior, blue labels, England casting ($3-5)
12. white body, unpainted base, light blue door, light yellow interior, no labels, England casting ($3-5)
13. white body, unpainted base, dark blue door, light yellow interior, no labels, England casting ($3-5)
14. white body, silver-gray base, dark blue door, light yellow interior, blue labels, England casting ($3-5)
15. white body, unpainted base, dark blue door, orange-yellow interior, blue labels, England casting ($3-5)
16. white body, black base, chocolate door, yellow interior, "Mobile 500" tempa, England casting ($2-4)(TP)
17. white body, black base, chocolate door, orange-yellow interior, "Mobile 500" tempa, England casting ($2-4)(TP)
18. white body, pearly silver base, chocolate door, lemon interior, amber windows, "Mobile 500" tempa, Macau casting ($2-4)(TP)
19. white body, black base, chocolate door, cream interior, amber windows, "Mobile 500" tempa, no origin cast ($2-4)(TP)
20. beige body, black base, chocolate door, cream interior, amber windows, "Mobile 500" tempa, no origin cast ($2-4)(TP)
21. gray body, black base, gray door, cream interior, amber windows, blue & red stripes tempa, no origin cast ($1-2)(TP)
22. white body, black base, red door, cream interior, yellow/orange/red stripes tempa, no origin cast ($2-3)(MC)
23. white body, black base, white door, cream interior, blue windows, blue/maroon/orange design tempa, no origin cast ($1-2)(TP)
24. white body, black base, white door, silver-gray interior, amber windows, "Caravan 2000" tempa, no origin cast ($1-2)(5pk)
25. white body, black base, white door, silver-gray interior, amber windows, "Caravan 2000" tempa, China casting ($1-2)(5pk)
26. white body, black base, white door, silver-gray interior, clear windows, turquoise & blue tempa, China casting ($1-2)(MW47/1999 ROW)
27. white body, black base, white door, silver-gray interior, clear windows, turquoise & blue tempa with "Sand Dollar" tempa, China casting ($1-2)(MW52/1999 US)

NOTE: Available as a Bulgarian casting. Bases are cast blank. Assorted colors available ($5-25)

MB31-D MAZDA RX7, issued 1982 (USA)(MB091)

NOTE: Below models with clear windows, black base & Hong Kong casting.

1. white body, ivory interior, wide maroon side stripe tempa, maltese cross wheels ($3-5)
2. white body, ivory interior, wide maroon side stripe tempa, 5 spoke star wheels ($3-5)
3. white body, ivory interior, thin maroon side stripe tempa, maltese cross wheels ($3-5)
4. white body, tan interior, wide maroon side stripe tempa, 5 spoke wheels ($3-5)
5. white body, tan interior, thin maroon side stripe tempa, 5 spoke wheels ($3-5)
6. black body, tan interior, wide gold side stripe tempa, 5 spoke wheels ($3-5)

MB31-E MAZDA RX7, issued 1983 (MB076)

NOTE: Below models with clear windows &, black metal base unless otherwise noted. Bulgarian issues with black plastic bases.

1. black body, red interior, 5 arch wheels, gold side stripe tempa , Macau casting ($2-4)
2. white body, red interior, 5 arch wheels, "7" with stripes tempa, Macau casting ($2-4)
3. black body, red interior, 5 arch wheels, "RX7" & "Mazda" tempa, Manaus casting ($35-50)(BR)
4. black body, red interior, dot dash wheels, "RX7" & "Mazda" tempa, Manaus casting ($35-50)(BR)
5. blue body, gray interior, dot dash wheels with black hubs, no tempa, black plastic base, China casting ($150-175)(CHI)

NOTE: Available as a Bulgarian casting. Assorted colors available ($5-25)

MB31-F ROLLS ROYCE SILVER CLOUD *see MB62-F*

MB31-G STERLING, issued 1988 (USA)(M192)
MB 2-F STERLING, Issued 1988 (ROW)

NOTE: Below models with smoke gray windows, tan interior, metal base & 8 dot wheels unless otherwise noted.

1. metallic red body, charcoal base, silver headlights & black door post tempa, Macau casting ($1-2)
2. pearly silver body, metallic blue base, laser wheels, blue/white/red stripes tempa, Macau casting ($4-6)(LW)
3. metallic red body, charcoal base, silver headlights & black door post tempa, China casting ($1-2)
4. blue body, yellow base, blue wheels with yellow hubs, exposed engine & tools design tempa, China casting ($6-8)(LL)
5. blue body, orange-yellow base, blue wheels with yellow hubs, exposed engine & tools design tempa, China casting ($6-8)(LL)
6. silver-gray body, metallic blue base, black door posts tempa, China casting ($1-2)
7. yellow body, yellow base, no tempa, China casting ($8-12)(GR)(GS)
8. silver-gray body, metallic blue base, black doors posts & "Rover Sterling" tempa, China casting ($1-2)
9. silver-gray body, metallic blue base, "Rover Sterling" tempa, China casting ($1-2)
10. white body, white base, white interior, no tempa, China casting ($10-15)(GF)
11. blue body, orange-yellow base, red interior, all blue wheels, exposed engine design & tools design tempa, China casting ($6-8)(LL)

MB31-H BMW 5 SERIES *see MB26-G*

MB31-I NISSAN PRAIRIE, issued 1991 (USA)(MB226)
MB21-G NISSAN PRAIRIE, issued 1991 (ROW)

NOTE: Below models with plastic base & 8 dot wheels.

1. metallic blue body, black base, clear windows, blue interior, silver sides tempa, China casting ($5-7)
2. silver-gray body, black base, clear windows, blue interior, black "Nissan" tempa, China casting ($2-3)
3. white body, white base, green windows, white interior, no tempa, China casting ($10-15)(GF)
4. red body, black base, clear windows, blue interior, black "Nissan" tempa, China casting ($8-12)(GS)
5. white body, black base, clear windows, blue interior, "Paramedic PS" tempa, China casting ($2-3)
6. dark green body, black base, clear windows, tan interior, gold "Nissan" tempa, China casting ($1-2)(MW45-ROW)

7. yellow body, black base, clear windows, black interior, "Citywide Taxi Service" tempa, China casting ($1-2)(5pk)
8. white body, black base, clear windows, blue interior, "Aqua" with diver tempa, China casting ($1-2)(5pk)

MB31-J JAGUAR XJ220, issued 1993 (USA)(MB239)
MB26-I JAGUAR XJ220, issued 1993 (ROW)

NOTE: Below models with black plastic base.

1. silver-gray body, red interior, clear windows, 8 dot wheels, no tempa, Thailand casting ($2-3)(SS)
2. dark blue body, ivory interior, clear windows, 8 dot wheels, no tempa, Thailand casting ($1-2)
3. purple body, ivory interior, chrome windows, gray disc wheels with rubber tires, detailed trim tempa, Thailand casting ($2-4)(WC)
4. fluorescent yellow (left side) & fluorescent orange (right side) body, blue interior, smoke windows, 6-spoke gold spiral wheels, geometric design tempa, Thailand casting ($1-2)
5. dark blue body, ivory interior, clear windows, gold 6-spoke spiral wheels, "Jaguar" logo tempa, Thailand casting ($2-3)
6. dark blue body, white interior, smoke windows, gold 6-spoke spiral wheels, "50" & "XJ220" tempa, Thailand casting ($2-3)(GS)
7. chrome plated body, white interior & base, amber windows, gold 6-spoke spiral wheels, no tempa, Thailand casting ($2-4)(GF)
8. silver-gray body, blue interior, smoke windows, silver 6-spoke spiral wheels, blue & yellow design tempa, Thailand casting ($1-2)(5pk)
9. florescent yellow (left side) & florescent orange (right side) body, blue interior, smoke windows, silver 6-spoke spiral wheels, geometric design tempa, Thailand casting ($1-2)
10. florescent orange body, blue interior, smoke windows, silver 6-spoke spiral wheels, geometric design tempa, Thailand casting ($1-2)
11. metallic red & black body, yellow interior, clear windows, silver 6-spoke spiral wheels, no tempa, Thailand casting ($1-2)(5pk)
12. dark blue body, ivory interior, clear windows, silver 6-spoke spiral wheels, gold "Jaguar" logo tempa, Thailand casting ($3-5)
13. dark blue body, ivory interior, smoke windows, silver 6-spoke spiral wheels, "50" & "XJ220" tempa, Thailand casting ($3-5)(GS)
14. dark green body, ivory interior, smoke windows, silver 6 spoke spiral wheels, white & lime flames tempa, Thailand casting ($1-2)(5pk)
15. metallic turquoise body, yellow interior, smoke windows, 5 spoke concave star wheels, yellow & white flames, Thailand casting ($1-2)
16. metallic gold body, black interior, clear windows, silver 6 spoke spiral wheels, no tempa, Thailand casting ($5-10)(CH)
17. metallic blue body, gray & black interior, clear windows, chrome disc wheels with rubber tires, detailed trim tempa, Thailand casting ($3-5)(PC2-ROW)
18. metallic maroon, gray & black interior, clear windows, chrome disc wheels with rubber tires, detailed trim tempa, Thailand casting ($3-5)(PC10)
19. dark blue body, white interior, clear windows, silver 6 spoke spiral wheels, "Old Eight" tempa, Thailand casting ($75-100)(BR)
20. dark green body, tan interior, clear windows, 5 spoke concave star wheels, "Jaguar" tempa, Thailand casting ($1-2)(MW75/1998 ROW)
21. dark green body, tan interior, smoke windows, 5 spoke concave star wheels, "Jaguar" tempa, China casting ($1-2)(MW75/1998 ROW)
22. dark green body, gray & black interior, clear windows, chrome disc wheels with rubber tires, detailed trim tempa, Thailand casting ($3-5)(PC19)
23. dark green body, tan interior, clear windows, 5 spoke concave star wheels, "Jaguar" tempa, China casting ($1-2)(MW75/1998 ROW)
24. red body, black interior, blue windows, 5 spoke concave star wheels, British flag & white band tempa, China casting ($2-3)(MW12/2000 ROW)
25. silver-steel blue body, chrome interior, clear windows, 10 spoke flower wheels, tiny logo tempa, China casting ($2-3)(MW16/2001 ROW)
26. metallic green body, black interior, clear windows, 10 spoke flower wheels, tiny logo tempa, China casting ($2-3)(MW21/2002 ROW)
27. metallic green body, black interior, clear windows, 10 spoke flower wheels, tiny logo & "Matchbox 50" tempa, China casting ($2-4)(MW21/2002 ROW)

MB31-K AUDI AVUS QUATTRO *see MB12-K*

MB31-L 1957 CHEVY BEL AIR, issued 1998 (MB321)

NOTE: Below models with clear windows, chrome plastic base and China casting.

1. bright blue body & roof, blue & white interior, silver flash & detailed trim tempa, chrome disc with rubber tires ($4-6)(FE)
2. unpainted body, gray roof, white interior, no tempa, chrome disc wheels with rubber tires ($4-6)(FE)
3. black body & roof, white interior, green & white design tempa, 5 spoke concave star wheels ($1-2)(MW31/1998)
4. maroonish purple body, beige roof, beige & maroon interior, silver flash & "Matchbox Premiere Collectors Club" tempa, chrome mag wheels with rubber tires ($10-15)(PC Club)
5. red body, red roof, white interior, silver flash tempa, 5 spoke concave star wheels ($1-2)(5pk)
6. black body & roof, white interior, green & white design tempa, large 5 spoke concave star wheels ($12-15)(MW31/1998)
7. red body & roof, white interior, silver flash & "Nostalgia" with dice tempa, 5 spoke concave star wheels ($50+)(CCI)
8. light blue body & roof, black interior, "Carhenge- Alliance,NE" tempa, 10 spoke flower wheels, Mattel casting ($8-12)(AW-Bonus)
9. light blue body, white roof, smoke windows, red interior, red & yellow checker design & "Burger Zone" tempa, lace wheels, Mattel casting ($3-5)(PS)
10. black body, white roof, smoke windows, red interior, silver flash & detailed trim tempa, 5 spoke slotted wheels (SF37/2004)

MB31-M BEETLE 4X4, issued 2001 (USA)(MB491/582)
MB45-H BEETLE 4X4, issued 2002 (ROW)

NOTE: Below models with black interior & plastic base, 5 spoke oval wheels, China casting unless otherwise noted.

1. lemon body, smoke windows, painted red & gray bar light, gray engine, cast open hood, "Desert Rescue" tempa ($1-2)(MW31/2001 US)
2. red body, smoke windows, opaque yellow bar light, chrome engine, cast open hood, "4X4 Off Road Rally" tempa ($2-4)(MW62/2001 UK)
3. white body, orange interior, smoke windows, opaque blue bar light, chrome engine, cast open hood, "Mission H2O" tempa ($1-2)(LP)
4. orange-yellow body, red windows, red bar light, red engine, cast open hood, palm trees, stripes & cross tempa ($1-2)(MW45/2002)

5. orange-yellow body, red windows, red bar light, red engine, cast open hood, palm trees, stripes & cross with "Matchbox 50" tempa ($18-25)(MW45/2002)
6. lemon body, blue interior, blue windows & bar light, blue engine, cast open hood, "Chief HQ" tempa ($1-2)(5pk)
7. lemon body, red windows, red bar light, black engine, cast shut hood, "Beach Patrol MHC" tempa ($1-2)(MW45)
8. lemon body, red windows, red bar light, black engine, cast shut hood, "Beach Patrol MHC" & "Hero City" tempa ($5-8)(MW45)
9. metallic silver body, white interior, blue windows & bar light, red engine, cast shut hood, "Mission H2O" tempa ($1-2)(LP)
10. white body, white interior, red windows & bar light, turquoise engine, cast shut hood, "Chief HQ" tempa ($1-2)(5pk)
11. metallic green body, red interior, red windows & bar light, gray engine, cast shut hood, "Matchbox" logo tempa ($1-2)(MW54/2004)

MB31-N FORD TRANSIT AMBULANCE *see MB21-I*

MB31-O BMW X5, issued 2002 (ROW)(MB539)

NOTE: Below models with gray interior, clear windows, lace wheels, black plastic base & China casting unless otherwise noted.

1. blue body, small "Matchbox" logo on side tempa ($1-2)(MW31/2002)
2. blue body, larger "Matchbox" logo on side tempa ($1-2)(MW31/2002)

   NOTE: To identify size of above- small logo has batch # on base, large logo has no batch # on base)
3. blue body, small "Matchbox" logo on side & "Matchbox 50" tempa ($2-4)(MW31/2002)
4. metallic red body, headlights tempa ($3-5)(SG)
5. blue body, "PMCC December 7, 2002" tempa ($15-20)(CCI)
6. unpainted body, pop art decals ($75+)(FA)
7. metallic gold body, black interior, smoke windows, red & black band tempa ($2-4)(5pk)
8. metallic red body, brown interior, smoke windows, silver stripe & "54" tempa ($2-4)(MW54/2003 ROW)
9. metallic red body, brown interior, smoke windows, silver stripe & "54" with "Hero City" tempa ($4-6)(MW54/2003 ROW)
10. green gold body, white interior, blue windows, "Gateway Arch" tempa ($1-2)(AW)
11. metallic green body, gray interior, clear windows, no tempa ($1-2)(LP)
12. dark metallic green body, tan interior, clear windows, head & tail lights tempa, slotted 5 spoke wheels, gray base ($3-5)(SF14/2004)

MB31-P VOLKSWAGEN BEETLE TAXI, issued 2003 (MB578)

1. white upper & green lower body, black interior, smoke windows, lace wheels, "31 Taxi 042076" tempa, green base, China casting ($1-2)(MW31/2003)
2. white upper & green lower body, black interior, smoke windows, lace wheels, "31 Taxi 042076" & "Hero City" tempa, green base, China casting ($2-4)(MW31/2003)
3. metallic red body, white interior, amber windows, lace wheels, "Hero City Taxi" tempa, gray base, China casting ($1-2)(MW44/2004)

MB31-Q AIRPORT FIRE TANKER, issued 2003 (MB594)

NOTE: Below models with 7 spoke sawblade wheels plastic base, China casting unless otherwise noted.

1. metallic bronze body, blue turret, blue windows, "Alarm" tempa, black base ($1-2)(MW31/2004)
2. lime body, neon orange turret, amber windows, blue stripes & "Police" crest tempa, bright blue base ($1-2)(LP)

MB32-A LEYLAND TANKER, issued 1970

NOTE: Below models with blue windows, 5 spoke wheels, plastic base & England casting. "Aral" & "BP" labels can be fitted towards the front or in the center of the tank.

1. blue cab & chassis, white tank, chrome base, "Aral" labels ($50-75)
2. green cab & chassis, white tank, chrome base, "BP" labels ($15-20)
3. green cab & chassis, white tank, gray base, "BP" labels ($18-25)
4. red cab, white tank, chrome base, "N.A.M.C./ The Miniature Vehicle" labels ($400-600)(LE)
5. metallic purple cab & chassis, silver-gray tank, chrome base, "National Association of Matchbox Collectors" labels ($75-100)(C2)
6. metallic purple cab & chassis, silver-gray tank, chrome base, no labels ($125-150)

   NOTE: Although issued back in 1972 with "National Association of Matchbox" labels, unlabelled versions were not offered for sale until 1994. Less than 300 probably exist this way.
7. green cab & chassis, white tank, chrome base, "Burmah" labels (from MB63-B) ($175-250)

MB32-B MASERATI BORA, issued 1972

NOTE: Below models with light yellow interior, clear windows, metal base & England casting unless otherwise noted. Most models with wide wheels although some exist with narrow wheels.

1. burgundy body, unpainted base, "8" label, no tow hook, 5 spoke wheels ($125-175)
2. burgundy body, light green base, "8" label, no tow hook, 5 spoke wheels ($8-12)
3. burgundy body, dark green base, "8" label, no tow hook, 5 spoke wheels ($8-12)
4. burgundy body, dark green base, no label, no tow hook, 5 spoke wheels ($8-12)
5. burgundy body, dark green base, "8" label, no tow hook, 5 arch wheels ($8-12)
6. burgundy body, dark green base, "3" label, no tow hook, 5 arch wheels ($10-15)
7. burgundy body, metallic green base, "8" label, no tow hook, 5 arch wheels ($8-12)
8. metallic burgundy body, dark green base "6" label (from MB41-A), no tow hook, 5 spoke wheels ($175-250)
9. gold body, silver-gray base, no label, with tow hook, 5 arch wheels ($15-20)(TP)
10. gold body, silver-gray base, orange-yellow interior, no label, with tow hook, 5 arch wheels ($15-20)(TP)
11. lime body with black doors, black base with Manaus label, no label, no tow hook, 5 spoke wheels ($250+)(BR)
12. metallic blue body, black base with Manaus tab, "8" label, no tow hook, 5 arch wheels ($250+)(BR)

MB32-C FIELD GUN, issued 1978

NOTE: Below models with plastic diorama base with two figures & England casting unless otherwise noted.

1. olive body, olive guard, no plastic diorama, 5 arch black wheels ($5-7)(TP)
2. olive body, olive guard, 5 arch black wheels ($5-7)
3. olive body, olive guard, dot dash silver wheels ($75-100)
4. olive body, black guard, plastic diorama with Manaus tab, 5 arch black wheels ($65-80)(BR)

5. green body, green guard, plastic diorama with Manaus tab, 5 arch black wheels ($75-100)(BR)

MB32-D ATLAS EXCAVATOR, issued 1981 (MB032)
MB 6-F ATLAS EXCAVATOR, reissued 1990 (USA)

NOTE: Below models with solid black wheels & plastic base.

1. dark orange body, black scoop, black platform, gray base, no tempa, England casting ($6-8)
2. dark orange body, black scoop, charcoal platform, gray base, no tempa, England casting ($6-8)
3. light orange body, black scoop, black platform, gray base, no tempa, England casting ($6-8)
4. light orange body, black scoop, charcoal platform, gray base, no tempa, England casting ($6-8)
5. yellow body, black scoop, black platform, gray base, black stripes with "C" tempa, England casting ($2-4)
6. yellow body, black scoop, black platform, black base, black stripes with "C" tempa, England casting ($2-4)
7. yellow body, black scoop, black platform, black base, black stripes tempa, England casting ($2-4)
8. yellow body, black scoop, black platform, black base, black stripes tempa, Macau casting ($1-2)
9. yellow-orange body, black scoop, black platform, black base, black stripes tempa, Macau casting ($1-2)
10. light yellow body, yellow scoop, light yellow platform & base, "JCB" label, Macau casting ($7-10)(GS)
11. yellow body, black scoop, black platform, black base, black stripes tempa, Thailand casting ($1-2)
12. yellow body, red scoop, black platform, black base, red stripes tempa, Thailand casting ($1-2)
13. florescent orange body, black scoop, black platform, black base, no tempa, Thailand casting ($1-2)(5pk)
14. red body, red scoop, black platform, black base, black & white stripes tempa, Thailand casting ($1-2)
15. red body, red scoop, black platform, black base, white stripes tempa, Thailand casting ($1-2)
16. metallic gold body, black scoop, black platform, black base, no tempa, Thailand casting ($5-10)(CH6)
17. dull orange body, orange scoop, black platform, black base, black & white stripes tempa, Thailand casting ($1-2)
18. bright orange body, orange scoop, black platform, black base, black & white stripes tempa, Thailand casting ($1-2)
19. bright lime body, lime scoop, black platform, black base, black & white stripes tempa, Thailand casting ($1-2)(MW6/1998)
20. bright lime body, lime scoop, black platform, black base, black & white stripes tempa, China casting ($1-2)(MW6/1998)
21. white body, black scoop with silver-gray arm, charcoal platform, black base, "X-4970" & dirt tempa, China casting ($1-2)(MW30/1999)
22. orange body, orange scoop, orange platform, black base, none tempa, China casting ($3-5)(MW10GR)
23. matt yellow body, silver-gray scoop, black platform, black base, "X-4970" & dirt tempa, China casting ($1-2)(MW92/2000 US)(MW2/2000 ROW)
24. matt yellow body, silver-gray scoop, black platform, black base, "X-4970", dirt & "Matchbox 2000" tempa, China casting ($2-4)(MW92/2000 US)
25. pumpkin body, black scoop, black platform, black base, "Hemler Bros." tempa, China casting ($75+)(ASAP)
26. pumpkin body, black scoop, black platform, black base, "CAT Service Co." tempa, China casting ($75+)(ASAP)
27. pumpkin body, black scoop, black platform, black base, "Redi-Way, Inc." tempa, China casting ($75+)(ASAP)
28. pumpkin body, black scoop, black platform, black base, "Blue Ridge Construction" tempa, China casting ($75+)(ASAP)
29. matt yellow body, black scoop, black platform, black base, "X-4970" & dirt tempa, China casting ($1-2)(5pk)
30. silver-gray body, orange arm with gray scoop, gray platform, orange base, "MC21/ Matchbox" tempa, China casting ($1-2)(5pk)
31. silver-gray body, orange arm with gray scoop, gray platform, gray base with orange painted rollers, "MC21/Matchbox" tempa, China casting ($1-2)(5pk)
32. red body, black arm with red scoop, black platform, black base, white stripes & "NNC/ Northwest Nazarene College" tempa, Thailand casting ($50+)(ASAP)
33. dark blue body, blue arm with neon yellow scoop, dark blue platform, blue base, "Matchbox MC21" & rhino head tempa, China casting ($1-2)(5pk)
34. orange body, orange scoop, orange platform, black base, "4th Lane Opening" tempa, China casting ($50+)(ASAP)
35. pumpkin body, black scoop, black platform, black base, no tempa, China casting ($15-20)(ASAP blank)

MB32-E MODIFIED RACER, issued 1988 (USA)(MB194)
MB12-G MODIFIED RACER, issued 1988 (ROW)

NOTE: Below models with chrome plastic base, & racing special slicks

1. orange body, black interior, chrome exhausts, "12" tempa, Macau casting ($1-2)
2. rose red body, black interior, chrome exhausts, "12" tempa, Macau casting ($3-4)(SC)
3. pale orange body, black interior, chrome exhausts, "12" tempa, Macau casting ($3-4)(SC)
4. orange body, black interior, black exhausts, "12" tempa, Macau casting ($1-2)
5. red body, black interior, black exhausts, "12" tempa, Macau casting ($3-4)(SC)
6. pale orange body, black interior, black exhausts, "12" tempa, Macau casting ($3-4)(SC)
7. orange body, black interior, black exhausts, "12" tempa, China casting ($1-2)
8. red body, black interior, chrome exhausts, "Mike 15" tempa, China casting ($4-6)(NM)
9. yellow body, green interior, chrome exhausts, "44 Reggie/ Magnum Oils" tempa, China casting ($4-6)(NM)
10. white body, red interior, chrome exhausts, "U2 Jamie" tempa, China casting ($4-6)(NM)
11. white body, black interior, chrome exhausts, "1 Tony/ Universal Joint Sales" tempa, China casting ($4-6)(NM)
12. dark purple body, black interior, black exhausts, "12" tempa, China casting ($3-4)(AP)
13. chrome plated body, black interior, black exhausts, no tempa, China casting ($12-18)(C2)
14. red body, red interior, black exhausts, "36" & Stripes tempa, China casting ($4-6)(NM)
15. red body, orange-yellow interior, black exhausts, "12" & stripes tempa, China casting ($4-6)(NM)
16. white & blue body, blue interior, black exhausts, "ADAP 15" tempa, China casting ($4-6)(NM)
17. white body, translucent blue interior, black exhausts, "41" & stripes tempa, China casting ($4-6)(NM)
18. white body, lavender interior, white exhausts, no tempa, China casting ($10-15)(GF)
19. red body, red interior, chrome exhausts, "38 Jerry Cook" tempa, China casting ($4-6)(NM)
20. white body, orange interior, chrome exhausts, "Maynard Troyer" tempa, China casting ($4-6)(NM)

21. dark blue body, black interior, chrome exhausts, "3 Ron Bouchard" tempa, China casting ($4-6)(NM)
22. orange-yellow body, red interior, chrome exhausts, "4 Bugs" tempa, China casting ($4-6)(NM)
23. red body, red interior, chrome exhausts, "U2 Jamie Tomaino" tempa, China casting ($4-6)(NM)
24. orange-yellow body, red interior, chrome exhausts, "4 Satch Wirley" tempa, China casting ($4-6)(NM)
25. dark blue body, blue interior, chrome interior, "3 Doug Heveron" tempa, China casting ($4-6)(NM)
26. black body, black interior, chrome exhausts, "21 George Kent" tempa, China casting ($4-6)(NM)
27. dark blue body, black interior, black exhausts, "12" tempa, China casting ($8-12)(GS)
28. blue body, black interior, chrome exhausts, "3 Mike McLaughlin" tempa, China casting ($4-6)(NM)
29. black body, red interior, chrome exhausts, "44 Rick Fuller" tempa, China casting ($4-6)(NM)
30. black body, red interior, chrome exhausts, "7 NY" tempa, China casting ($4-6)(NM)
31. red body, red interior, chrome exhausts, "25 Jan Leaty" tempa, China casting ($4-6) (NM)
32. red body, red interior, chrome exhausts, "69 Parts Peddler" tempa, China casting ($4-6)(NM)
33. red body, white interior, chrome exhausts, "12 Sherri Cup" tempa, China casting ($4-6)(NM)
34. orange body, orange interior, chrome exhausts, "61 BR DeWitt" tempa, China casting ($4-6)(NM)
35. blue body, yellow interior, chrome exhausts, "24 Jimmy Spencer" tempa, China casting ($4-6)(NM)
36. white body, red interior, chrome exhausts, "99 Phil's Chevrolet" tempa, China casting ($4-6)(NM)
37. white body, green interior, chrome exhausts, "Polar 77" tempa, China casting ($4-6) (NM)
38. red body, red interior, chrome exhausts, "2X" tempa, China casting ($4-6)(NM)
39. dark blue body, white interior, chrome exhausts, "11 Hummels" tempa, China casting ($4-6) (NM)
40. powder blue body, powder blue interior, chrome exhausts, "5" tempa, China casting ($4-6)(NM)
41. red body, red interior, chrome exhausts, "15 Wayne Anderson" tempa, China casting ($4-6)(NM)
42. yellow body, dark blue interior, chrome exhausts, "56 Miller Brick Co." tempa, China casting ($4-6)(NM)
43. white & powder blue body, powder blue interior, chrome exhausts, "31 Tony Ferrante" tempa, China casting ($4-6)(NM)
44. metallic blue body, black interior, chrome exhausts, "JVB27-Jan Leaty" tempa, China casting ($4-6)(NM)
45. orange body, black interior, chrome exhausts, "73" tempa, China casting ($4-6)(NM)
46. white body, red interior, chrome exhausts, "1" tempa, China casting ($4-6)(NM)
47. red body, red interior, chrome exhausts, "37" tempa, China casting ($4-6)(NM)
48. red body, red interior, chrome exhausts, "Craz 8" tempa, China casting ($4-6)(NM)
49. red body, red interior, chrome exhausts, "21 Spearpoint Auto" tempa, China casting ($4-6)(NM)
50. white & orange body, orange interior, chrome exhausts, "17 Perth Amboy Spring" tempa, China casting ($4-6)(NM)
51. black body, pale orange interior, chrome exhausts, "39 Fyne Lyne" tempa, China casting ($4-6)(NM)
52. black & gold body, red interior, chrome exhausts, "0" tempa, China casting ($4-6)(NM)
53. black body, white interior, chrome exhausts, "1" with pink & white stripes tempa, Thailand casting ($1-2)(5pk)
54. blue & silver- gray body, silver-gray interior, chrome exhausts, "Collector's Toys 95/ Gary's" tempa, Thailand casting ($5-8)(TC)(PL)

MB32-F 1962 CORVETTE *see MB71-D*

MB32-G 1970 EL CAMINO, issued 1998 (MB328)

NOTE: Below models with clear windows, chrome plastic base & China casting unless otherwise noted.

1. red body, black & white interior, 2 white hood stripes tempa, chrome base, chrome disc wheels with rubber tires ($4-6)(FE)
2. unpainted body, black interior, no tempa, chrome base, chrome disc wheels with rubber tires ($4-6)(FE)
3. metallic gold body, black interior, 2 black hood stripes tempa, chrome base, 5 spoke concave star wheels ($1-2)(MW32/1998)
NOTE: Above model found in various shades of gold from light to dark.
4. metallic gold body, black interior, 2 black hood stripes tempa, translucent white base, 5 spoke concave star wheels ($50-75)(MW32/1998)
5. red & white body, black interior, "Coca Cola" tempa, chrome base, chrome disc wheels with rubber tires ($4-6)(Coke PC)
6. light yellow body, blue interior, dark brown & blue tempa, chrome base, 5 spoke concave star wheels ($1-2)(MW74/1999 US)
7. maroon body, black interior, smoke windows, "Canyon Base" tempa, chrome base, 5 spoke concave star wheels ($1-2)(5pk)
8. metallic blue body, white interior, yellow windows, "Freestyle", skateboarder & "Matchbox 2000" tempa, 5 spoke concave star wheels ($2-4)(MW60/2000 US)
9. metallic blue body, white interior, yellow windows, "Freestyle" & skateboarder tempa, 5 spoke concave star wheels ($1-2)(MW60/2000 US)
10. metallic blue body, white interior, yellow windows, "Freestyle" & skateboarder tempa, 10 spoke flower wheels ($1-2)(MW60/2000 US)
11. maroon body, black interior, smoke windows, "Canyon Base" tempa, 10 spoke flower wheels ($1-2)(5pk)
NOTE: Below models with Mattel China casting.
12. maroon body, black interior, smoke windows, "Canyon Base" tempa, 10 spoke flower wheels, silver-gray metal base ($8-12)(EG)
13. maroon body, black interior, smoke windows, "Canyon Base" tempa, 5 spoke concave star wheels, silver-gray metal base ($8-12)(EG)
14. red body, black interior, clear windows, "Coca Cola It's the Real Thing" tempa, lace wheels, silver-gray metal base ($4-5)(Avon)(TP)
15. black body, black & white interior, clear windows, white bands & detailed trim tempa, dark gray disc wheels with rubber tires, silver-gray metal base ($3-5)(TN)
16. red body, black interior, clear windows, "Texaco" tempa, dark gray disc with rubber tires, silver-gray metal base ($4-5)(Texaco PC)
17. metallic orange body, yellow interior, clear windows, "Rocket Power" tempa, lace wheels, silver-gray metal base ($1-2)(5pk)
18. metallic olive body, red interior, light amber windows, "Back In Action- Looney Tunes Ranch" tempa, lace wheels, red plastic base ($1-2)(5pk)
19. metallic tan body, black interior, clear windows, black stripes tempa, 5 spoke slotted wheels, chrome plastic base ($2-4)(SF29/2004)

MB32-H MERCEDES BENZ S500 *see MB66-L*

MB32-I NISSAN XTERRA , issued 2001 (USA) (MB490)

NOTE: Below models with smoke windows, black plastic base, 7 spoke sawblade wheels, China casting

1. silver-gray body, blue interior, yellow with red print kayaks, "Xterra" & kayaking design tempa ($1-2)(MW32/2001 US)
2. blue body, blue interior, yellow kayaks, "Kayaking Adventures" & wavy design tempa ($1-2)(MW65/2001 AU)
3. white body, blue interior, pea green kayaks, "The Crocodile Hunter" & mud spatter tempa, chrome disc with rubber tires ($3-5)(CRO)
4. bright blue body, red interior, smoke windows, red kayaks, "MHC Outfitters 39" tempa ($1-2)(MW39/2003 US)
5. bright blue body, red interior, smoke windows, red kayaks, "MHC Outfitters" & "Hero City" tempa ($2-4)(MW39/2003 US)
6. red body, lime interior, smoke windows, blue kayaks, "Amazon Rain Forest" tempa ($1-2)(AW)

MB32-J 4X4 FIRE TRUCK, issued 2003 (MB593)

NOTE: Below models with 5 spoke oval wheels, plastic base & China casting.

1. metallic red body, pearly white cap , blue windows, "Alarm Unit Hero City" tempa, black base ($1-2)(MW32/2004)
2. dark olive body, green cap, amber windows, "Force Canyon 98' tempa, brown base ($1-2)(5pk)

MB32-K LINCOLN NAVIGATOR, issued 2004 (SF)(MB645)

1. pearly white body, clear windows, black interior, detailed trim tempa, gray plastic base, 5 spoke slotted wheels, China casting ($2-4)(SF32/2004)

MB33-A LAMBORGHINI MIURA, issued 1969

NOTE: Below models with 5 spoke wheels, clear windows, metal base & England casting unless otherwise noted

1. yellow body, ivory interior, unpainted base ($175-250)
2. yellow body, red interior, unpainted base ($90-110)
3. dark bronze body, red interior, unpainted base ($35-50)
4. light bronze body, red interior, unpainted base ($18-25)
5. dark gold body, red interior, unpainted base ($18-25)
6. dark gold body, ivory interior, unpainted base ($15-20)
7. light gold body, ivory interior, unpainted base ($15-20)
8. light gold body, ivory interior, dark red base ($15-20)
9. light gold body, ivory interior, florescent red base ($15-20)
10. light gold body, ivory interior, bright florescent red base ($15-20)
11. light gold body, ivory interior, black base ($15-20)
12. light gold body, ivory interior, black base, dot dash wheels ($15-20)
13. lime body, ivory interior, unpainted base with Manaus tab ($250+)

NOTE: Available as a Bulgarian casting. Assorted colors available ($65-90)

MB33-B DATSUN 126X, issued 1973

NOTE: Below models with chrome interior, amber windows, 5 spoke wheels, metal base & England casting.

1. yellow body, orange base, no tempa ($10-15)
2. yellow body, unpainted base, no tempa ($25-40)
3. yellow body, orange base, orange & red flames tempa ($15-18)
4. yellow body, orange base, black & red flames tempa ($15-18)

MB33-C POLICE MOTORCYCLE, issued 1977 (MB033)

NOTE: Below models with England casting unless otherwise noted.

1. white body, "Police" labels, white seat, dark blue rider, chrome motor, wire wheels ($5-7)
2. white body, "Police" labels, white seat, dark blue- painted rider, chrome motor, wire wheels ($5-7)(KS)
3. white body, "Police" labels, white seat, navy blue rider, chrome motor, wire wheels ($5-7)
4. white body, "Police" labels, white seat, light blue rider, chrome motor, wire wheels ($5-7)
5. white body, "Police" labels, white seat, gray-blue rider, chrome motor, wire wheels ($5-7)
6. cream body, "Polizei" labels, green seat, green rider, chrome motor, wire wheels ($25-40)(GR)
7. cream body, "Polizei" labels, green seat, green rider, black motor, wire wheels ($25-40)(GR)
8. white body, "Polizei" labels, green seat, green rider, chrome motor, wire wheels ($20-35)(KS)
9. white body, "Polizei" labels, green seat, green rider, black motor, wire wheels ($20-35)(KS)
10. white body, "Polizei" labels, green seat, green rider- painted, black motor, wire wheels ($20-35)(GR)
11. white body, "Police" labels, white seat, navy blue rider, black motor, wire wheels ($5-7)
12. white body, "Police" labels, white seat, navy blue- painted rider, black motor, wire wheels ($5-7)
13. white body, "Police" labels, white seat, blue rider, black motor, wire wheels ($5-7)
14. white body, "Police" labels, white seat, navy blue- painted rider, black motor, mag wheels ($5-7)
15. white body, "Police" labels, white seat, light blue- painted rider, black motor, mag wheels ($5-7)
16. white body, "Polizei" labels, green seat, green- painted rider, black motor, mag wheels ($20-35)(GR)
17. white body, "Police" labels, green seat, dark blue rider, black motor, mag wheels ($15-20)
18. black body, "L.A.P.D." labels, white seat, light blue rider, chrome motor, mag wheels ($6-8)(CR)
19. white body, "Police" labels, black seat, dark blue rider, chrome motor, mag wheels ($5-7)
20. white body, "4" labels, red seat & air dam, no rider, chrome motor, mag wheels ($12-15)(KS)
21. white body, "Police" labels, black seat, shiny blue rider, chrome motor, mag wheels, Macau casting ($2-4)
22. white body, "Honda" & "Police" labels, white seat, bright blue rider, chrome motor, mag wheels, Macau casting ($2-4)
23. black body, "Police" labels, white seat, dark blue- painted rider, chrome motor, mag wheels, Macau casting ($2-4)
24. white body, Japanese lettered tempa, white seat, dark blue rider, chrome motor, mag wheels, Macau casting ($8-12)(JP)

MB33-D VOLKSWAGEN GOLF GTi, issued 1985 (USA)(MB152)
MB56-E VOLKSWAGEN GOLF GTi, issued 1985 (ROW)
MB63-G VOLKSWAGEN GOLF GTi, reissued 1991 (ROW)

NOTE: Below models with black interior, grille & bumpers, clear windows & metal base.

1. red body & base, 8 dot silver wheels, black & silver "Golf GTi" tempa, Macau casting ($2-4)
2. red body & base, 8 dot silver wheels, white "GTi" tempa, Macau casting ($2-4)
3. red body & base, 8 dot gold wheels, white "GTi" tempa, Macau casting ($3-5)
4. red body & base, dot dash wheels, white "GTi" tempa, Macau casting ($3-5)
5. white body & base, 8 dot silver wheels, "Federal Express" tempa, Macau casting ($3-5)(GS)
6. white body & base, 8 dot silver wheels, "Quantum" tempa, Macau casting ($6-8)(UK)

NOTE: Versions 7 & 8 found as singles or as a Two Pack model.

7. dark gray body & base, 8 dot silver wheels, silver sides tempa, Macau casting ($2-4)
8. yellow body & base, 8 dot silver wheels, "PTT" tempa, Macau casting ($8-12)(SW)
9. dark gray body & base, 8 dot silver wheels, silver sides with "GTI" tempa, Thailand casting ($2-4)
10. white body & base, 8 dot silver wheels, "Abstract" tempa, Thailand casting ($3-5)(UK)
11. white body & base, 8 dot silver wheels, "Lippische Landes-Zeitung" tempa, Thailand casting ($15-20)(GR)

MB33-E RENAULT 11, issued 1986 (ROW) (MB161)
MB43-F RENAULT 11, issued 1986 (USA)

NOTE: Below models with gray plastic base and clear windows.

1. metallic blue body, gray interior, 8 dot wheels, gray side tempa, "Taxi Parisien" roof sign, England casting ($10-15)(JB)
2. black body, gray interior, dot dash wheels, "Turbo" & silver stripes tempa, England casting ($2-4)
3. black body, gray interior, 8 dot wheels, no tempa, England casting ($2-4)
4. black body, gray interior, 8 dot wheels, "Turbo" & silver stripes tempa, England casting ($2-4)
5. black body, tan interior, dot dash wheels, "Turbo" & silver stripes tempa, England casting ($2-4)
6. black body, tan interior, dot dash wheels, "Turbo" & silver stripes tempa, Macau casting ($2-4)
7. black body, tan interior, 8 dot wheels, "Turbo" & silver stripes tempa, Macau casting ($2-4)
8. black body, tan interior, dot dash wheels, "Turbo" & silver stripes tempa, China casting ($2-4)
9. black body, tan interior, 8 dot wheels, "Turbo" & silver stripes tempa, China casting ($2-4)

NOTE: Available as a Bulgarian casting. Assorted colors available ($5-25)

MB33-F MERCURY SABLE WAGON *see MB55-G*

MB33-G UTILITY TRUCK, issued 1989 (USA) (MB211)
MB74-I UTILITY TRUCK, issued 1989 (ROW)

NOTE: Below models with blue windows, 8 spoke wheels & plastic base.

1. gray body, black base, white boom, turret & bucket, "Energy Inc." tempa, Macau casting ($1-2)
2. red body, yellow base, blue turret, no boom or bucket, "53"/circle/bolt tempa, blue wheels with yellow hubs, China casting ($6-8)(LL)
3. red body, yellow base, yellow turret, no boom or bucket, "53"/circle/bolt tempa, blue wheels with yellow hubs, China casting ($6-8)(LL)
4. red body, yellow base, blue & yellow boom, blue turret, lime bucket, "53"/circle/bolt tempa, blue wheels with yellow hubs, China casting ($6-8)(LL)
5. red body, yellow base, blue & lime boom, yellow turret, blue bucket, "53"/circle/bolt tempa, blue wheels with yellow hubs, China casting ($6-8)(LL)
6. gray body, black base, white boom, turret & bucket, "Energy Inc." tempa, China casting ($1-2)
7. orange-yellow body, black base, white boom, turret & bucket, "Energy Inc." with red cab front tempa, China casting ($3-4)(AP)
8. dark yellow body, black base, white boom, turret & bucket, "Telephone Co. Unit 4" & checkers tempa, Thailand casting ($1-2)
9. green body, black base with bar code, white boom, turret & bucket, "Intercom City"/"Service" & checkers tempa, Thailand casting ($7-10)(IC)
10. cream body, green base, green boom, turret & bucket, "Tree Care 14" (light green) tempa, China casting ($1-2)
11. cream body, green base, green boom, turret & bucket, "Tree Care 14" (dark green) tempa, China casting ($1-2)
12. dark yellow body, black base, white boom, turret & bucket, "Telephone Co. Unit 4" & black checkers tempa, China casting ($1-2)
13. metallic green body, gray base, white boom, turret & bucket, "Tree Care 14" tempa, China casting ($1-2)
14. metallic gold body, black base, black boom, turret & bucket, no tempa, China casting ($10-15)(CH)
15. silver-gray body, black base, red boom, turret & bucket, "Global Electric" tempa, China casting ($1-2)(5pk)
16. silver-gray body, black base, dark red boom, turret & bucket, "Global Electric" tempa, China casting ($1-2)(5pk)
17. silver-gray body, black base, maroon boom, turret & bucket, "Global Electric" tempa, China casting ($1-2)(5pk)
18. blue body, chrome base, yellow boom, turret & bucket, "P & L Co. Response Unit 20" tempa, China casting ($1-2)
19. red body, chrome base, white boom, turret & bucket, "Matchbox Fire Dept." tempa, China casting ($1-2)(5pk)
20. orange body, chrome base, white boom, turret & bucket, "P & L Response Unit 20" tempa, China casting ($1-2)(MW9/1998)
21. black body, gray base, green boom, turret & bucket, "Highway Crew- Caution High Voltage Unit #45" tempa, China casting ($1-2)(5pk)

NOTE: Below models with chrome base, white boom, turret & bucket, China casting unless otherwise noted.

22. white body, no tempa, ($25-40)(ASAP blank)
23. white body, "American International Recovery" tempa ($100+)(ASAP)
24. white body, "GI" temps, ($50+)(ASAP)
25. silver-gray body, black base, yellow boom, turret & bucket, Ideal Power/ Clean Safe power" tempa,($1-2)(MW15/1999 US)
26. white body, "MTI" (left side only) tempa ($50+)(ASAP)
27. white body, "Bell Atlantic" tempa, (50+)(ASAP)
28. white body, "LCEC" tempa ($35+)(ASAP)
29. white body, yellow sun & green lined logo tempa ($50+)(ASAP)
30. white body, "Gulf Power" tempa ($50+)(ASAP)
31. white body, "RMLD" tempa ($25-40)(ASAP)
32. white body, "Pac. Tel" tempa, ($50+)(ASAP)
33. white body, "Western States Co-Op" tempa ($50+)(ASAP)
34. white body, "Xcel Energy" tempa ($50+)(ASAP)
35. white body, "Verizon" tempa ($50+)(ASAP)
36. white body, "Georgia Power Co." tempa ($50+)(ASAP)
37. white body, "Graphic Installatioons Services GIS" tempa ($50+)(ASAP)
38. white body, "KPL" tempa ($50+)(ASAP)
39. white body, "Intergraph" tempa ($50+)(ASAP)
40. white body, "First Energy" tempa ($50+)(ASAP)
41. white body, yellow circle logo tempa ($50+)(ASAP)
42. white body, "Florida Power" tempa ($50+)(ASAP)
43. white body, "Touchstone Energy" tempa ($50+)
44. white body, no tempa, 7 spoke sawblade wheels ($25-40)(ASAP blank)
45. white body, "Edison" tempa, 7 spoke sawblade wheels ($50+)(ASAP)
46. white body, "First Energy" tempa, 7 spoke sawblade wheels ($50+)(ASAP)

47. white body, "Xcel Energy" tempa, 7 spoke sawblade wheels ($50+)(ASAP)
48. white body, yellow sun & green lined logo tempa, 7 spoke sawblade wheels ($50+)(ASAP)
49. white body, "Westar" tempa, 7 spoke sawblade wheels ($50+)(ASAP)
50. white body, gold design tempa ($50+)(ASAP)
51. white body, "Cipco" tempa ($50+)(ASAP)
52. white body, "Cox Communications", 7 spoke sawblade wheels ($50+)(ASAP)
53. lemon body, green base, green boom, turret & bucket, "York Fair Power" tempa, 7 spoke sawblade wheels ($8-12)(US)

MB33-H MERCEDES 500SL CONVERTIBLE *see MB12-H*

MB33-I FORD MONDEO *see MB40-G*

MB33-J HUMMER POLICE *see MB48-L*

MB33-K BOOM FIRE TRUCK, issued 2004 (MB613)

NOTE: Below models with blue windows, gray base & China casting.

1. black body, red nozzle, 5 crown dot wheels, "H2O" & design tempa ($1-2)(MW33/2004)
2. red body, yellow nozzle, 7 spoke sawblade wheels, "Force 76" tempa ($1-2)(5pk)
3. dark red body, yellow nozzle, 5 crown dot wheels, "E-331" & yellow stripes tempa ($1-2)(MW33/2004)

MB34-A FORMULA 1, issued 1971

NOTE: Below models with clear windshield, white driver, unpainted base & England casting unless otherwise noted.

1. metallic pink body, "16" yellow label, 4 spoke front & rear wheels ($15-20)
2. metallic pink body, "16" yellow label, spiro front & rear wheels ($15-20)
3. metallic pink body, "16" yellow & "Wynn's" labels 4 spoke front & rear wheels ($75-125)(UK)
4. metallic blue body, "15" label, 4 spoke front & rear wheels ($40-65)(GS)
5. metallic blue body, "15" label, 4 spoke front & 5 spoke rear wheels ($40-65)(GS)
6. metallic blue body, "16" blue label, 4 spoke front & 5 spoke rear wheels, amber windshield ($40-65)(GS)
7. metallic blue body, "15" label, maltese cross front & 5 spoke rear wheels ($40-65(GS)
8. metallic blue body, "15" label, maltese cross front & 5 spoke rear wheels, amber windshield ($40-65)(GS)
9. orange body, "16" blue label, 4 spoke front & rear wheels ($12-15)
10. orange body, "16" blue label, maltese cross front & 5 spoke rear wheels ($12-15)
11. orange body, "16" blue label, maltese cross front & 5 spoke rear wheels, amber windshield ($12-15)
12. orange body, "16" yellow label, 4 spoke front & rear wheels ($12-15)
13. orange body, "16" yellow label, maltese cross front & 5 spoke rear wheels ($12-15)
14. orange-yellow body, "16" blue label, 4 spoke front & 5 spoke rear wheels ($12-15)
15. yellow body, "16" blue label, 4 spoke front & rear wheels ($12-15)
16. yellow body, "16" blue label, maltese cross front & 5 spoke rear wheels ($12-15)
17. yellow body, "16" blue label, maltese cross front & 5 spoke rear wheels, amber windshield ($12-15)
18. yellow body, "16" yellow label, maltese cross front & 5 spoke rear wheels ($12-15)
19. yellow body, "16" blue label, maltese cross front & 5 spoke rear wheels, silver-gray base ($12-15)
20. yellow body, "16" blue label, 4 spoke front & 5 spoke rear wheels ($12-15)
21. yellow body, "16" blue label, 4 spoke front & maltese cross rear wheels ($12-15)
22. yellow body, "15" label, maltese cross front & 5 spoke rear wheels ($12-15)
23. yellow body, "16" yellow label, maltese cross front & 5 spoke rear wheels, amber windshield ($12-15)
24. white body, "16" yellow label, maltese cross front & 5 spoke rear wheels ($250+)(BR)
25. red body, "16" blue label, maltese cross front & 5 spoke rear wheels, base with Manaus label ($250+)(BR)

MB34-B VANTASTIC, issued 1975

NOTE: Below models with 5 arch front & dot dash rear wheels, white interior & England casting unless otherwise noted.

1. orange body, unpainted base, blue-green windows, with motor, fish-like side label ($125-175)
2. orange body, white base, blue-green windows, with motor, fish-like side labels ($10-15)
3. orange body, white base, blue-green windows, with motor, stripes side label s($10-15)
4. orange body, white base, blue-green windows, no motor, "34" hood & stripes side labels ($8-12)
5. orange body, white base, blue-green windows, no motor, "34" hood & no side labels ($8-12)
6. orange body, white base, clear windows, no motor, "34" hood & no side labels ($8-12)
7. orange body, white base, blue-green windows, no motor, "34" hood & no side labels, 5 arch rear wheels ($8-12)
8. orange body, white base, blue-green windows, no motor, "34" hood & no side labels, dot dash front wheels ($8-12)
9. orange body, white base, blue-green windows, no motor, sunburst hood (from MB47-B) & no side labels ($15-20)
10. orange body, white base, blue-green windows, no motor, "Jaffa Mobile" hood & no side labels ($375-450)
11. orange body, white base with Manaus tab, blue-green windows, no motor, "34" hood & no side labels ($65-80)(BR)
12. orange body, white base with Manaus tab, blue-green windows, no motor, "3" hood (from MB19-A) & no side labels ($75-100)(BR)
13. orange body, white base, blue-green windows, no motor, "34" hood & no side labels, 5 crown rear wheels ($8-12)

MB34-C CHEVY PROSTOCKER, issued 1981 (MB034)

NOTE: Below models with metal base.

1. white body, red interior, clear windows, unpainted base, no tempa, 5 arch front & 5 crown rear wheels, England casting ($15-20)
2. white body, red interior, clear windows, unpainted base, "34" (plain sides) tempa, 5 arch front & 5 crown rear wheels, England casting ($5-8)
3. white body, red interior, clear windows, unpainted base, "34" tempa, 5 arch front & rear wheels, England casting ($5-8)
4. white body, red interior, clear windows, unpainted base, "34" tempa, 5 arch front & 5 crown rear wheels, England casting ($5-8)
5. white body, red interior, clear windows, unpainted base, "34" tempa, 5 crown front & rear wheels, England casting ($5-8)

6. white body, red interior, clear windows, unpainted base, "34" tempa, 5 crown front & 5 arch rear wheels, England casting ($5-8)
7. white body, red interior, clear windows, silver-gray base, "34" tempa, dot dash front & 5 crown rear wheels, England casting ($5-8)
8. white body, red interior, clear windows, silver-gray base, "34" tempa, 5 arch front & 5 crown rear wheels, England casting ($5-8)
9. white body, red interior, clear windows, silver-gray base, "34" tempa, 5 arch front & rear wheels, England casting ($5-8)
10. white body, red interior, clear windows, silver-gray base, "34" tempa, 5 crown front & rear wheels, England casting ($5-8)
11. white body, red interior, clear windows, silver-gray base, "34" tempa, 5 crown front & 5 arch rear wheels, England casting ($5-8)
12. white body, red interior, clear windows, red base, "34" tempa, 5 arch front & 5 crown rear wheels, England casting ($15-20)
NOTE: Versions 12 onwards with revised headlight grille that incorporates an airfoil below the headlights.
13. yellow-orange body, black interior, clear windows, black base, "4" & stripes tempa, 5 arch front & 5 crown rear wheels, Macau casting ($2-4)
14. yellow-orange body, black interior, clear windows, black base, "4" & stripes tempa, 5 spoke front & 5 crown rear wheels, Macau casting ($2-4)
15. yellow-orange body, black interior, clear windows, black base, "4" & stripes tempa, 5 spoke front & rear wheels, Macau casting ($2-4)
16. yellow-orange body, black interior, clear windows, black base, "4" & stripes tempa, 5 arch front & rear wheels, Macau casting ($2-4)
17. white body, red interior, amber windows, black base, "Pepsi 14" tempa, 5 spoke front & 5 crown rear wheels, Macau casting ($2-4)
18. white body, red interior, amber windows, black base, "Pepsi 14" tempa, 5 arch front & 5 crown rear wheels, Macau casting ($2-4)
19. white body, black interior, clear windows, black base, "Pepsi 14" tempa, 5 arch front & 5 crown rear wheels, Macau casting ($65-90)(TM)
20. white body, black interior, clear windows, black base, "Pepsi 14" tempa, 5 spoke front & 5 crown rear wheels, Macau casting ($65-90)(TM)
21. white body, red interior, clear windows, black base, "Super Star 217" tempa, 5 arch front & 5 crown rear wheels, Macau casting ($3-5)(TM)
22. black body, red interior, clear windows, black base, "Haley's Comet" tempa, starburst wheels, Macau casting ($8-12)(MP)
23. white & orange body, red interior, clear windows, black base, "21 355CID" tempa, starburst wheels, Macau casting ($4-6)(SF)
24. white & orange body, red interior, clear windows, black base, "21 355CID" tempa, laser wheels, Macau casting ($4-6)(LW)
25. white body, red interior, clear windows, black base, "7 Up" tempa, 5 arch front & 5 crown rear wheels, Macau casting ($3-5)(TM)
26. white body, black interior, clear windows, black base, "7 Up" tempa, 5 spoke front & 5 crown rear wheels, Macau casting ($75-100)(TM)
27. white body, black interior, clear windows, black base, "7 Up" tempa, 5 spoke front & rear wheels, Macau casting ($75-100)(TM)
28. white body, red interior, clear windows, black base, "Pepsi 14" tempa, 5 arch front & 5 crown rear wheels, Macau casting ($3-5)
29. white body, red interior, clear windows, black base, "Pepsi 14" tempa, 5 arch front & 5 crown rear wheels, Thailand casting ($3-5)(GS)
30. blue & white body, black interior, clear windows, silver-gray base, "70 Bailey Excavating" tempa, Goodyear slicks, Thailand casting ($4-6)(WR)(TC)

MB34-D FORD RS200, issued 1987 (MB175)

NOTE: Below models with 8 spoke wheels & metal base.

1. white body, black base, clear windows, silver-gray interior, blue with "7" tempa, Macau casting ($1-2)
2. white body, black base, clear windows, silver-gray interior, blue with "7" tempa, China casting ($1-2)
3. blue body, black base, clear windows, silver-gray interior, white with "2" tempa, China casting ($1-2)
4. mid blue body, black base, clear windows, silver-gray interior, white with "2" tempa, China casting ($1-2)
5. white body, black base, clear windows, silver-gray interior, red with "7" tempa, China casting ($1-2)
6. white body, white base, red windows, white interior, no tempa, China casting ($10-15)(GF)
7. dark blue body, dark blue base, clear windows, silver-gray interior, no tempa, China casting ($8-12)(GR)(GS)
8. white body, black base, clear windows, silver-gray interior, red & blue with "7" tempa, China casting ($1-2)
9. white body, greenish black base, clear windows, silver-gray interior, red & blue with "7" tempa, China casting ($1-2)
10. orange body, black base, clear windows, silver-gray interior, white with "12" & "Enjoy Fanta" tempa, China casting ($75+)(CHI)

MB34-E SPRINT RACER, issued 1990 (USA) (MB208)
MB72-J SPRINT RACER, issued 1990 (ROW)

NOTE: Below models with plastic black base, chrome airfoils, Goodyear front slicks, racing special rear slicks.

1. red body, white driver, "2 Rollin Thunder" (yellow & red "2") tempa, China casting ($1-2)
2. red body, white driver, "Williams 5M" (blue letters) tempa, China casting ($4-6)(NM)
3. red body, white driver, "Williams 5M" (white letters) tempa, China casting ($75-100)(NM)
4. black body, white driver, "TMC 1" tempa, China casting ($4-6)(NM)
5. white body, red driver, "Maxim 11" tempa, China casting ($4-6)(NM)
6. white body, red driver, "Schnee 8D" tempa, China casting ($4-6)(NM)
7. yellow body, white driver, "Ben Cook & Sons 33x" tempa, China casting ($4-6)(NM)
8. blue body, white driver, "Ben Allen 1a" tempa, China casting ($4-6)(NM)
9. metallic blue body, white driver, "Lucky 7" tempa, China casting ($3-5)(AP)
10. red body, white driver, "7 Joe Gaerte" tempa, China casting ($4-6)(NM)
11. red body, white driver, "4 Gambler" tempa, China casting ($4-6)(NM)
12. yellow body, white driver, "17 F&G Classics Eash" tempa, China casting ($4-6)(NM)
13. yellow body, white driver, "7c Vivarin- D. Blaney" (purple background) tempa, China casting ($4-6)(NM)
14. powder blue body, white driver, "69 Schnee- D. Krietz" tempa, China casting ($4-6)(NM)
15. black body, white driver, "49 Doug Wolfgang" tempa, China casting ($4-6)(NM)

16. metallic blue body, white driver, "2 Rollin Thunder" tempa, China casting ($8-12)(GS)
17. black body, white driver, "TMC 1" tempa, China casting ($4-6)(NM)
18. black body, white driver, "JW Hunt 69" tempa, China casting ($4-6)(NM)
19. orange body, white driver, "Williams Payless 5m" tempa, China casting ($4-6)(NM)
20. white body, red driver, "Alvis O Rock 69" tempa, China casting ($4-6)(NM)
21. yellow body, white driver, "Vivarin" (blue background) tempa, China casting ($7-10) (NM)
22. red body, white driver, "Rollin' Thunder 2" (all red "2") tempa, China casting ($1-2)
23. red body, white driver, "Allweld 14" tempa, China casting ($4-6)(NM)
24. red body, white driver, "IW Lew" tempa, China casting ($4-6)(NM)
25. white & dark blue body, white driver, "Valvoline 11" tempa, China casting ($4-6)(NM)
26. white/red & dark blue body, white driver, "Casey Luna 10" tempa, China casting ($4-6) (NM)
27. white body, blue driver, "Weitkerk's Livestock 29" tempa, China casting ($4-6)(NM)
28. gold body, red driver, "Vandermark & Wahlie lm" tempa, China casting ($4-6)(NM)
29. red body, white driver, "Shoff 23s" tempa, China casting ($4-6)(NM)
30. black body, black driver, "Gebhart's 4j" tempa, China casting ($4-6)(NM)
31. purple body, yellow driver, "Hot Shot 34" tempa, Thailand casting ($1-2)(5pk)

MB34-F DODGE CHALLENGER *see MB1-D*

MB34-G PLYMOUTH PROWLER, issued 1995 (USA) (MB280)
MB 6-H PLYMOUTH PROWLER, issued 1995 (ROW)

1. plum body, gray base, clear windshield, gray interior, 6 spoke spiral wheels, silver grille tempa, Thailand casting ($1-2)
   NOTE: Version 1 appears in multiple shade variations from light to dark.
2. yellow body, gray base, smoke windshield, gray interior, chrome disc wheels with rubber tires, "Matchbox 1996 Line Preview" tempa, Thailand casting ($275-350)(US)
3. plum body, gray base, clear windshield, gray interior, 6-spoke spiral wheels, no tempa (plain grille), Thailand casting ($1-2)
4. plum body, gray base with painted detail, clear windshield, gray & purple interior, chrome disc with rubber tires, detailed trim tempa, Thailand casting ($100-150)(PC1)
5. plum body, gray base, clear windshield, gray & purple interior, chrome disc wheels with rubber tires, detailed trim tempa, Thailand casting ($7-10)(PC1)
6. red body, black base, smoke windshield, black interior, 6-spoke spiral wheels, "Prowler" tempa, Thailand casting ($1-2)(5pk)
7. black body, gray base, smoke windshield, purple interior, 6-spoke spiral wheels, "Prowler" tempa, Thailand casting ($1-2)(5pk)
8. white body, blue base, clear windshield, blue interior, 6-spoke spiral wheels, "Tyco Playtime Toy Fair 96" tempa, Thailand casting ($35-50)(US)
9. white body, blue base, clear windshield, blue interior, 6-spoke spiral wheels, "Tyco Playtime Dallas 96" tempa, Thailand casting ($35-50)(US)
10. white body, blue base, clear windshield, blue interior, 6-spoke spiral wheels, "Tyco Playtime Hong Kong 96" tempa, Thailand casting ($35-50)(US)(HK)
11. charcoal body, gray base, clear windshield, gray & purple interior, chrome disc wheels with rubber tires, detailed trim tempa, Thailand casting ($7-10)(SC1)
12. red body, gray base, clear windshield, gray & red interior, chrome disc wheels with rubber tires, detailed trim tempa, Thailand casting ($3-5)(PC)(JC)
13. silver-gray body, gray base, clear windshield, gray & purple interior, chrome disc wheels with rubber tires, detailed trim tempa, Thailand casting ($3-5)(PC4)
14. dark metallic blue body, gray base, clear windshield, black interior, chrome disc wheels with rubber tires, detailed trim tempa, Thailand casting ($7-10)(PC1-ROW)
15. metallic gold body, black base, clear windshield, black interior, 6 spoke spiral wheels, no tempa, Thailand casting ($5-10)(CH)
16. blue body, black base, clear windshield, green interior, 5 spoke concave star wheels, green & white design tempa, Thailand casting ($1-2)(5pk)
17. black body, black base, clear windshield, orange interior, chrome disc wheels with rubber tires, "Toy Fair 97- Matchbox" tempa, Thailand casting ($75-100)(US)
18. black body, black base, clear windshield, yellow interior, chrome disc wheels with rubber tires, "Toy Fair- 97- Matchbox" tempa, Thailand casting ($15-25)(UK)(GR)
19. iridescent white body, silver-gray base, clear windshield, purple interior, 5 spoke concave star wheels, "Prowler" tempa, Thailand casting ($1-2)(5pk)
20. plum body, gray base, smoke windshield, gray interior, 5 spoke concave star wheels, no tempa, Thailand casting ($2-4)
21. black body, gray base, clear windshield, red interior, chrome disc wheels with rubber tires, detailed trim tempa, Thailand casting ($15-20)(GC)
22. plum body, gray base, smoke windshield, gray interior, 6 spoke spiral wheels, "16th Annual Matchbox USA Convention 1997" decals, Thailand casting ($10-15)(C2)
23. metallic gold body, black base, clear windshield, black interior, 5 spoke concave star wheels, no tempa, Thailand casting ($15-25)(CH)
24. plum body, gray base, smoke windshield, gray interior, silver 6 spoke spiral wheels, "Mattel Wheels- Driving To Win" tempa, Thailand casting ($250-400)(C2)
25. plum body, gray base, smoke windshield, gray interior, 5 spoke concave star wheels, "Mattel Wheels- Driving To Win" tempa, Thailand casting ($250-400)(C2)
26. metallic purple body, gray base, clear windshield, gray & black interior, chrome disc wheels with rubber tires, detailed trim tempa, Thailand casting ($3-5)(PC14)
27. metallic red body, gray base, smoke windshield, black interior, 5 spoke concave star wheels, silver grille tempa, Thailand casting ($2-3)
28. metallic red body, gray base, clear windshield, gray & black interior, chrome disc wheels with rubber tires, detailed trim tempa, Thailand casting ($3-5)(SC4)
29. dark orange body, gray base, clear windshield, gray & black interior, chrome disc wheels with rubber tires, detailed trim tempa, Thailand casting ($3-5)(PC16)
30. yellow body, gray base, clear windshield, gray & black interior, chrome disc wheels with rubber tires, detailed trim tempa, Thailand casting ($3-5)(SC5)
31. metallic tan body, black base, clear windshield, black interior, 5 spoke concave star wheels, no tempa, Thailand casting ($1-2)(MW18/1998 US)

32. metallic tan body, black base, clear windshield, black interior, 5 spoke concave star wheels, no tempa, China casting ($1-2)(MW18/1998 US)
33. blue body, black base, clear windshield, green interior, 5 spoke concave star wheels, green & white flames tempa, China casting ($1-2)(5pk)
34. metallic gold body, black base, clear windshield, black interior, 6 spoke spiral wheels, no tempa, China casting ($8-12)(CH)
35. plum body, gray base, clear windshield, white & gray interior, chrome disc wheels with rubber tires, detailed trim tempa, China casting ($3-5)(GS-Chrysler)
36. metallic orange body, gray base, clear windshield, gray interior, chrome disc wheels with rubber tires, detailed trim tempa, China casting ($4-6)(PC)
37. lemon body, gray base, clear windshield, black interior, 5 spoke concave star wheels, blue & red stripe tempa, China casting ($1-2)(5pk)
38. white body, blue base, clear windshield, blue interior, silver 6 spoke spiral wheels, "Beep Beep the Clown" tempa, Thailand casting ($35-50)(CCI)
39. black body, gray base, smoke windshield, red interior, 5 spoke concave star wheels, no tempa, China casting ($1-2)(MW4/2000 US)
40. black body, gray base, smoke windshield, red interior, 5 spoke concave star wheels, "Matchbox 2000" tempa, China casting ($2-4)(MW4/2000 US)
41. metallic tan body, black base, clear windshield, black interior, 5 spoke concave star wheels, "White's Guide Movie #1" tempa, China casting ($50-75)(ASAP)
42. yellow body, gray base, clear windshield, black interior, 5 spoke concave star wheels, "Convention 2000 Lion's Club-Honolulu Hawaii" tempa, China casting ($25-40)(CCI)
NOTE: Below castings with smoke windows, black interior, 5 spoke concave wheels, black base, China casting unless otherwise noted.
43. yellow body, no tempa, ($25-40)(CCI blank)
44. grape body, no tempa,($25-40)(CCI blank)
45. tan body, black base (textured or smooth), black interior, lace wheels, "Prowler" tempa, China casting ($1-2)(MW58/2001)
46. tan body, black base, black interior, lace wheels, "Prowler" tempa, Mattel China casting ($1-2)(MW58/2001)
47. yellow body, "Tyler Elliot Memorial Model/ 10" tempa ($20-30)(CCI)
48. grape body, "Thank You For Buying from the Chris Getz Collection" tempa ($20-25)(CCI)
49. grape body, "Great Strides/ Cystic Fibrosis Foundation" tempa ($15-25)(CCI)
50. yellow body, "Happy Birthday- Miko Marie is 3" tempa ($10-15)(CCI)
51. yellow body, "Midwest Diecast Miniatures- 2001 Customer Appreciation" tempa ($25-40)(CCI)
52. tan body, black base, smoke windows, black interior, lace wheels, "Prowler/ Reading PA The Pretzel City" tempa ($25-40)(CCI)
53. metallic red body, gray base, clear windows, gray interior, 5 spoke concave star wheels, "Reading PA The Pretzel City" tempa, Thailand casting ($25-40)(CCI)
54. grape body, "Daddy's Girl is 6/ Kerry Kiko Ozima" tempa,($10-15)(CCI)
55. yellow body, "Artcraft & Foremost/ Give Us A Test Drive" tempa ($10-15)(CCI)
56. grape body, "Artcraft & Foremost/ Give Us A Test Drive" tempa,($10-15)(CCI)
57. grape body, "Matchbox International Toy Show" tempa ($8-12)(CCI)
58. yellow body, "MRMC 2002 Toy Show/ Vendor Appreciation" tempa ($25-40)(CCI)
59. yellow body, "Happy Harvest 2002" tempa ($10-15)(CCI)
60. yellow body, "Auto Magic/ Accessories & Detailing" tempa($10-15)(CCI)
61. plum body, "Auto Magic/ Accessories & Detailing" tempa ($10-15)(CCI)
62. plum body, "Happy 2003 Valentine's" tempa, Mattel casting ($10-15)(CCI)
63. yellow body, "Welcome Matchbox 2003 Line Review Visitor " tempa ($15-25)(CCI)
64. black & red body, gray interior, clear with black trim windows, chrome disc with rubber tires, detailed trim tempa ($3-5)(BJ)
65. yellow body, "Helen Peirce School Alumni 77/ Classmates of 1977 Turn 40" tempa ($10-15)(CCI)
66. plum body, "The Purple Penguin" tempa ($10-15)(CCI)
67. yellow body, "CCI On Site Demo Model" tempa ($8-12)(CCI)
68. metallic blue body, orange interior, lace wheels, orange base, "Nickelodeon" tempa ($1-2)(5pk)
69. yellow body, "Just For Me/ CCI" tempa, Mattel casting ($8-12)(CCI)
70. black body, purple interior, clear windows, chrome disc wheels with rubber tires, gray base, "Batman" tempa, Mattel casting ($3-5)(JL)
71. black body, orange interior, smoke windows, lace wheels, orange base, "Nickelodeon" tempa, Mattel casting ($1-2)(CA)
72. black & silver-gray body, gray interior, smoke windows, chrome disc wheels with rubber tires, detailed trim tempa, Mattel casting ($3-5)(BJ)
73. yellow body, black interior, gray base, "Jamaica Jam 2000-Freeman PR" tempa ($75+)(CCI)
74. yellow body, "Troop 11 Flea Market" tempa ($15-20)(CCI)
75. yellow body, "Give Us A Test Drive/ Artcraft" (black print) tempa ($15-25)(CCI)
76. plum body, "Give Us A Test Drive/ Artcraft" (bright lime print) tempa ($15-25)(CCI)
77. black body, green base, blue windshield, lime interior, lace wheels, "Green Lantern" tempa ($1-2)(5pk)
78. plum body, "It's A Boy/ Jason S. Fuller" tempa ($18-25)(CCI)
79. yellow body, "Matchbox USA Toy Show 2004" tempa ($10-15)(CCI)
80. yellow body, "Matchbox Toy Show Kids Demo Model Hershey, PA 2004" tempa ($10-15)(CCI)
81. yellow body, "Ad Ventures 2nd Annual Picnic 2004" ($18-25)(CCI)
82. metallic blue & black body, head & tail lights tempa, 5 spoke slotted wheels (SF58/2004)
NOTE: For the baseball series see MLB97 Plymouth Prowler at the end of the Miniatures list.

MB34-H CHRYSLER ATLANTIC *see MB11-E*

MB34-I '33 FORD COUPE, issued 1998 (MB327)

NOTE: Below models with clear windows, chrome engine, black grille, black plastic base & China casting unless otherwise noted
1. unpainted body, Goodyear rubber tires, no tempa ($4-6)(FE)
2. black body, Goodyear rubber tires, red stripe tempa ($4-6)(FE)
3. maroon body, Goodyear slicks wheels, black & yellow design tempa ($1-2)(MW34/1998)
4. maroon body, Goodyear slicks wheels, "IMCC Est. 1998/ Join Today" tempa ($20-30)(C2)
5. black body, Goodyear rubber tires, "IMCC Est. 1998/ Join Today" tempa ($25-40)(C2)

6. unpainted body, Goodyear rubber tires, "IMCC Est. 1998/ Join Today" tempa ($25-40)(C2)
7. matt gray body, black grille, Goodyear slicks wheels, purple door, brown dirt & door logo tempa ($1-2)(5pk)
8. lemon body, yellow & black grille, Goodyear rubber tires with gray rims, "American Graffiti" tempa ($10-15)(STR)
9. matt gray, black grille, Goodyear slicks wheels, purple door, brown dirt & "American Iron Cruise Night" tempa ($12-15)(CCI)
10. red & white body, Goodyear rubber tires, "Coca Cola" tempa ($4-6)(Coke PC)
11. maroon body, Goodyear slicks, black & yellow design with "1999 Ballarat" tempa ($18-25)(C2)(AU)
12. metallic grape body, Goodyear slicks wheels, light smoke windows, none tempa ($1-2)(MW20/2000 US)
13. metallic grape body, Goodyear slicks wheels, light smoke windows, "Matchbox 2000" tempa ($2-4)(MW20/2000 US)
14. lemon body, Goodyear slicks wheels, black roof tempa ($2-4)(MW13/ AU)
15. lemon body, Goodyear slicks wheels, black roof & "Matchbox 2000 Demo Model- Color Comp Inc." tempa ($25-30)(CCI)
16. lemon body, Goodyear slicks wheels, black roof & "Glenside Motor Vehicle Show 2000" tempa ($15-25)(CCI)
17. lemon body, Goodyear slicks wheels, black roof & "Midwest Regional Convention" tempa ($20-25)(C2)
18. metallic grape body, Goodyear slicks wheels, "Midwest Regional Convention/ MRMC 2000" tempa ($20-25)(C2)
19. metallic grape body, Goodyear slicks wheels, "Midwest Regional Convention/ MRMC 2000 Vendor" tempa ($25-40)(C2)
20. purple body, Goodyear rubber tires with gold rims, blue flames & "Hot August Nights 2000" tempa ($15-20)(US)
21. lemon body, Goodyear slicks wheels, "2001 Ballarat 12th Super Southern Swapmeet" tempa ($10-15)(C2)(AU)
22. lemon body, Goodyear slicks wheels, "Cruise Down Memory Lane/ Corvettes Unlimited" tempa ($15-20)(CCI)
23. lemon body, Goodyear slicks wheels, "Cruisin New England Magazine All Wheels Festival 2001" tempa ($45-60)(CCI)
24. lemon body, Goodyear slicks wheels, "Western Wayne Junior Wildcats/ Car Show July 15, 2001" tempa ($15-20)(CCI)
25. metallic burgundy body, chrome & black grille, chrome disc wheels with rubber tires, silver stripe & "50" logo tempa ($3-5)(CL)
26. lemon body, Goodyear slicks wheels, "Matchbox/ 2001 Bendigo National Swap Meet" tempa($15-20)(C2)
27. lemon body, Goodyear slicks wheels, "Buggies-N-Blues" tempa ($10-15)(CCI)
28. lemon body, Goodyear slicks wheels, "Midwest Regional Convention & Toy Show Model" tempa ($10-15)(CCI)

NOTE: Below models with Mattel China casting.

29. metallic blue body, chrome disc with rubber tires, "100" with flames tempa ($3-5)(CL)
30 metallic burgundy body, lace wheels, "Wooa" & vampire tempa ($1-2)(5pk)
31. metallic orange-gold body, 5 spoke slotted wheels, blue & white flames tempa, gray base ($3-5)(SF13/2004)
32.black body, gold lace wheels, "Dennis- The Spongebob Squarepants Movie" tempa, gray engine, black base ($1-2)(5pk)

MB34-J CHEVROLET IMPALA POLICE CAR, issued 2000 (USA)(MB420)

NOTE: Below models with 5 spoke concave star wheels, black plastic base & China casting unless otherwise noted

1. white body, dark blue interior, clear windows, red dome light, "Cleveland Police" tempa ($1-2)(MW34/2000 US)
2. white body, dark blue interior, clear windows, red dome light, "Cleveland Police" & "Matchbox 2000" tempa ($2-4)(MW34/2000 US)
3. white body, dark navy blue interior, clear windows, red dome light, "Cleveland Police" tempa ($1-2)(MW34/2000 US)
4. orange-yellow & blue body, blue interior, blue windows, red dome light, "Sydney 2000" tempa ($1-2)(5pk)
5. black body, gray interior, clear windows, red dome light, "Test Mission" & red dashes tempa ($1-2)(5pk)
6. black body, gray interior, clear windows, red dome light, "Test Mission" & red dashes tempa, 10 spoke flower wheels ($2-4)(5pk)
7. white & blue body, dark blue interior, smoke windows, red dome light, "Metro Alarm/ Police" tempa, 10 spoke flower wheels ($1-2)(5pk)

NOTE: Below models with lace wheels unless otherwise noted.

8. white body, blue interior, clear windows, red dome light, "Westworth Village" tempa ($1-2)(MW53/2001 US)
9. white body, blue interior, clear windows, amber dome light, "Metro 7" tempa ($1-2)(LP)
10. white body, gray interior, blue windows, red dome light, "DARE" tempa ($1-2)(MW5/2002 US)
11. white body, gray interior, blue windows, red dome light, "DARE" & "Matchbox 50" tempa ($2-4)(MW6)
12. dark red body, black interior, smoke windows, blue dome light, "Chief PFD11-5" with crest tempa ($3-5)(PS)
13. metallic blue body, dark gray interior, smoke windows, amber dome light, "Police XL-023" & winged logo tempa ($1-2)(5pk)

NOTE: Numerous shades from light to dark metallic blue exist on the above model.

14. white body, blue interior, clear windows, amber dome light, "Virginia Blue Ridge Police 10" tempa ($1-2)(AM)
15. white body, gray interior, blue windows, red dome light, "Nassau County Police" tempa ($15-25)(CCI)
16. white body, gray interior, blue windows, red dome light, "Nassau County Police" tempa ($15-25)(CCI)
17. blue body, black interior, smoke windows, red dome light, "Police 02" & design tempa ($1-2)(5pk)
18. white body, gray interior, amber windows, blue dome light, "Police XL-023" & winged logo tempa ($1-2)(5pk)
19. blue body, gray interior, smoke windows, red dome light, "Crossing Guard 53" tempa ($1-2)(MW53/2003 US)
20. blue body, gray interior, smoke windows, red dome light, "Crossing Guard 53" & "Hero City" tempa ($20-35)(MW53/2003)
21. white body, dark blue interior, clear windows, red dome light, "Police" with USAF logo decals ($50+)(ASAP)
22. dark blue body, black interior, smoke windows, red dome light, white doors with "Police Unit 704" tempa ($1-2)(MW3/2005)

MB34-K MERCEDES BENZ E430 WAGON POLICE, issued 2001 (ROW) (MB476)

NOTE: Below models with clear windows, black metal base, 10 spoke flower wheels, China casting

1. metallic green body, white interior, amber bar light, checkers & "Polizei/ K-9" tempa ($2-4)(MW34/2001 ROW)
2. silver-gray body, blue interior, blue bar light, "Police" tempa ($2-4)(MW26/2002 ROW)
3. silver-gray body, blue interior, blue bar light, "Police" & "Matchbox 50" tempa ($2-4)(MW26/2002 ROW)
4. silver-gray body, black interior, blue & green bar light, "Polizei" & green doors tempa ($3-5)(SG)
5. white body, black interior, blue bar light, "Notarzt" with orange side band & hood tempa ($3-5)(SoC)

MB35-A MERRYWEATHER FIRE ENGINE, issued 1970

NOTE: Below models with blue windows & dome lights, plastic base, "London Fire Service" labels, white ladder & England casting. Earliest models with narrow wheels with later models having wide wheels. Some examples exist with missing labels.

1. metallic red body, light gray base, 2 clips on base, 5 spoke wheels ($15-18)
2. bright red body, light gray base, 2 clips on base, 5 spoke wheels ($12-15)
3. bright red body, tan base, 2 clips on base, 5 spoke wheels ($18-25)
4. bright red body, light gray base, 4 rivets on base, 5 spoke wheels ($12-15)
5. bright red body, black base, 4 rivets on base, 5 spoke wheels ($18-25)
6. bright red body, light gray base, 4 rivets on base, 5 arch wheels ($12-15)
7. bright red body, light gray base, 4 rivets on base, dot dash wheels ($5-8)(TP)
8. bright red body, gray-brown base, 4 rivets on base, 5 arch wheels ($5-8)(TP)

MB35-B FANDANGO, issued 1975

NOTE: Below models with 5 spoke wheels, metal base & England casting unless otherwise noted.

1. white body, red base, clear windows, red interior, silver prop, "6" label (from MB41-A) ($15-20)
2. white body, red base, clear windows, red interior, red prop, "35" label ($8-12)
3. white body, red base, clear windows, red interior, silver prop, "35" label ($8-12)
4. white body, unpainted base, clear windows, red interior, silver prop, "35" label ($8-12)
5. red body, red base, clear windows, ivory interior, silver prop, "35" label ($10-15)
6. red body, unpainted base, clear windows, ivory interior, silver prop, "35" label ($8-12)
7. red body, white base, clear windows, ivory interior, silver prop, "35" label ($8-12)
8. red body, white base, clear windows, ivory interior, red prop, "35" label ($8-12)
9. red body, white base, clear windows, ivory interior, light blue prop, "35" label ($8-12)
10. red body, unpainted base, clear windows, ivory interior, light blue prop, "35" label ($8-12)
11. red body, unpainted base, clear windows, cream interior, mid blue prop, "35" label ($8-12)
12. red body, unpainted base, clear windows, white interior, dark blue prop, "35" label ($8-12)
13. red body, unpainted base, purple windows, cream interior, dark blue prop, "35" label ($8-12)
14. red body, unpainted base, clear windows, white interior, light blue prop, "35" label ($8-12)
15. purple body, charcoal base, clear windows, white interior, light blue prop, "35" label ($500-750)(BR)
16. red body, black base with Manaus tab, clear windows, white interior, light blue prop, "35" label ($60-85)(BR)
17. red body, red base, clear windows, red interior, silver prop, "35" label ($500-750)
18. red body, unpainted base, clear windows, white interior, dark blue prop, sunburst label (from MB47-B) ($15-20)
19. red body, unpainted base, purple windows, ivory interior, dark blue prop, "35" label ($8-12)

MB35-C PONTIAC T-ROOF, issued 1982 (USA) (MB101)
MB16-C PONTIAC T-ROOF, issued 1983 (ROW)

NOTE: Below models with clear windows, dot dash wheels & metal base.

1. black body, unpainted base, red interior, green eagle & "Turbo" tempa, England casting ($2-4)
2. black body, silver-gray base, red interior, green eagle & "Turbo" tempa, England casting ($2-4)
3. black body, pearly silver base, red interior, white eagle & "Trans Am" tempa, Macau casting ($2-4)
4. black body, pearly silver base, red interior, yellow eagle & "Trans Am" tempa, Macau casting ($2-4)
5. black body, pearly silver base, red interior, orange tiger stripes tempa, Macau casting ($12-15)(UK)(OP)
6. pearly silver body, black base, red interior, red/orange/yellow eagle & red/orange stripes tempa, Macau casting ($2-3)
7. red body, black base, red interior, "3 Rooster Racing Tram" tempa, Macau casting ($8-12)(HK)
8. black body, silver-gray base, black interior, "Smokey & The Bandit" tempa, China casting ($5-7)(STR)

NOTE: Available as a Bulgarian casting with "Universal Associated Co." cast on base. Assorted colors available ($5-25)

MB35-D ZOO TRUCK, issued 1982 (ROW) (MB035)

NOTE: Below models with blue windows, plastic base & England casting unless otherwise noted.

1. red body, red base, blue cage, orange-yellow lions, 5 arch wheels ($18-25)
2. red body, black base, blue cage, orange-yellow lions, 5 arch wheels ($18-25)
3. red body, black base, blue cage, lemon lions, 5 arch wheels ($18-25)
4. red body, black base, blue cage, orange-yellow lions, 5 spoke wheels ($18-25)
5. red body, charcoal base, blue cage, orange-yellow lions, 5 arch wheels ($18-25)
6. red body, black base, blue cage, orange-yellow lions, maltese cross wheels ($18-25)
7. red body, black base, gray cage, brown lions, 5 arch wheels ($18-25)
8. red body, black base, gray cage, tan lions, 5 arch wheels ($18-25)
9. red body, black base, gray cage, light tan lions, 5 arch wheels ($18-25)
10. red body, black base, gray cage, white lions, 5 arch wheels ($25-40)
11. red body, black base, gray cage, orange-yellow lions, 5 arch wheels ($18-25)
12. red body, black base, blue cage, orange-yellow lions, dot dash wheels ($18-25)
13. orange body, black base, blue cage, orange-yellow lions, maltese cross wheels ($18-25)
14. orange body, black base, gray cage, dark tan lions, 5 arch wheels ($18-25)
15. red body, black base, blue cage, white lions, 5 arch wheels ($50-75)
16. red body, black base, gray cage, tan lions, 5 arch wheels, Macau casting ($18-25)

MB35-E 4X4 MINI PICKUP *see MB22-D*

MB35-F LAND ROVER NINETY, issued 1987 (USA) (MB180)
MB16-F LAND ROVER NINETY, issued 1987 (ROW)

NOTE: Below models with clear windows, black interior/ grille and silver dot dash wheels unless otherwise noted.

1. blue body, pearly gray base, white roof, yellow & orange stripes tempa, Macau casting ($2-3)

2. green body, pearly gray base, white roof, yellow & orange stripes tempa, Macau casting ($1-2)(MC)
3. dark blue body, pearly gray base, white roof, "RN Royal Navy" tempa, Macau casting ($2-3)(GS)
4. red body, pearly gray base, white roof, blue & gray stripes with "County" tempa, Macau casting ($1-2)
5. black body, dark gray base, dark gray roof & interior, gray & yellow camouflage tempa, black hubs, Macau casting ($4-5)(CM)
6. white body, pearly gray base, white roof, black & red stripes with "County" tempa, Macau casting ($1-2)(TP)
7. white body, pearly gray base, white roof, black & red stripes with "County" tempa, Thailand casting ($1-2)(TP)
8. green body, pearly gray base, white roof, yellow & orange stripes tempa, Thailand casting ($1-2)(MC)(TP)
9. red body, pearly gray base, white roof, blue & gray stripes with "County" tempa, Thailand casting ($1-2)
10. dark blue body, pearly gray base, white roof, "RN Royal Navy" tempa, Thailand casting ($2-3)(GS)
11. light gray & dark navy body, dark navy base, light gray roof, red stripe tempa, Thailand casting ($3-4)(MC)
12. yellow body, pearly silver base, white roof, large "Park Ranger" tempa, Thailand casting ($1-2)
13. white body, white base, blue roof, "KLM" tempa, Thailand casting ($3-5)(MP)
14. white body, white base, blue roof, "SAS" tempa, Thailand casting ($3-5)(MP)
15. white body, white base, green roof, "Alitalia" tempa, Thailand casting ($3-5)(MP)
16. white body, pearly silver base, white roof, "Bacardi Rum" tempa, Thailand casting ($25-40)(TP)(OP)
17. yellow body, yellow base, white roof, small "Park Ranger" tempa, Thailand casting ($1-2)
18. red body, black base, white roof, "Red Arrows/ Royal Air Force" tempa, Thailand casting ($3-5)(MC)
19. white body, white base, white roof, pink windows, neon red interior, no tempa, Thailand casting ($10-15)(GF)
20. white body, pearly silver base, white roof, "Rescue Police" & checkers tempa, Thailand casting ($1-2)(EM)
21. white body, red base, white roof, red interior, "Circus Circus" tempa, Thailand casting ($2-4)(MC)
22. white body, pearly silver base, green roof, "Garden Festival Wales" tempa, Thailand casting ($6-8)(WL)(GS)
23. yellow body, pearly silver base, white roof, small "Park Ranger" tempa, Thailand casting ($1-2)
24. orange body, pearly silver base, black roof, "Safari Park" & black stripes tempa, Thailand casting ($1-2)(5pk)
25. white body, pearly silver base, white roof, "55 Rijkspolitie" tempa, Thailand casting ($3-5)(GS)(DU)
26. white body, dark blue base, white roof, pink interior, smoke windows, neon pink/ neon yellow & blue side splash tempa, Thailand casting ($2-5)
27. red body, black base, white roof, yellow interior, clear windows, "Red Valley Camp" tempa, Thailand casting ($1-2)(5pk)
28. lemon body, black base, black roof, black interior, clear windows, "Mountain Trails" tempa, Thailand casting ($1-2)(5pk)
29. dark green body, pearly silver base, white roof, black interior, clear windows, small "Land Rover" tempa, Thailand casting ($1-2)
30. white body, black base, black roof, red interior, clear windows, black design & "Land Rover" tempa, China casting ($1-2)(MW53/1998 ROW)
31. lemon body, black base, black roof, black interior, clear windows, "Mountain Trails" tempa, China casting ($1-2)(5pk)
32. red body, black base, white roof, yellow interior, clear windows, "Red Valley Camp" tempa, China casting ($1-2)(5pk)
33. dark green body, black base, black roof, black interior, clear windows, "0321" & tree tempa, China casting ($3-5)(MW41/1999GR)
34. yellow body, black base, black roof, black interior, clear windows, "Canyon", crest & dashes tempa, China casting ($2-3)(MW12/2000 ROW)
35. white body, black base, black roof, black interior, clear windows, "Metropolitan Police" & stripes tempa, China casting ($2-3)(MW36/2000UK)
36. black body, charcoal base, green roof, gray interior, clear windows, "Land Rover" with stripes tempa, 7 spoke sawblade wheels, China casting ($2-4)(MW61/2001 ROW/UK)
37. blue body, black base, dark blue roof, black interior, amber windows, "K-9 Patrol" tempa, 7 spoke sawblade wheels, China casting ($1-2)(5pk)

NOTE: Version 38 with Matchbox International or Mattel casting.

38. orange-yellow body, silver blue base, brown roof, brown interior, smoke windows, "Mexico- Walking Tours" tempa, 7 spoke sawblade wheels, China casting ($1-2)(AM)(MP)
39. white body, black base, black roof, black interior, clear windows, "The Crocodile Hunter" & mud spatter tempa, chrome disc wheels with rubber tires, China casting ($3-5)(CRO)
40. red body, black base, black roof, red interior, red windows, Clifford the Big Red Dog depiction tempa, 7 spoke sawblade wheels, China casting ($1-2)(5pk)
41. red body, black base, lime roof, black interior, smoke windows, "555-1212" & pizza design tempa, 7 spoke sawblade wheels, China casting ($1-2)(MW58/2004)

MB35-G FORD BRONCO II *see MB39-E*

MB35-H PONTIAC GRAND PRIX, issued 1992 (USA) (MB216)
MB22-I PONTIAC GRAND PRIX, issued 1993 (ROW)

NOTE: Below models with clear windows & black plastic base unless otherwise noted.

1. bright yellow body, black interior, Goodyear slicks, "Pennzoil 30" tempa, China casting ($3-5)(WR)
2. bright yellow body, black interior, gray disc with rubber tires, "Pennzoil 30" tempa, China casting ($4-6)(WR)(TC)
3. blue body, black interior, Goodyear slicks, "STP 43" tempa, China casting ($3-5)(WR)
4. blue body, black interior, blue disc wheels with rubber tires, "STP 43" tempa, China casting ($4-6)(WR)(TC)
5. blue body, black interior, black disc wheels with rubber tires, "Rumple 70/ Son's" tempa, China casting ($4-6)(WR)(TC)
6. yellow body, gray interior, Goodyear slicks, "White House Apple Juice 4" tempa, China casting ($4-6)(WR)(OP)
7. yellow body, gray interior, 9 spoke Goodyear slicks, "White House Apple Juice 4" tempa, China casting ($4-6)(WR)(OP)
8. black body, black interior, Goodyear slicks, "Pontiac Excitement 2" tempa, China casting ($3-5)(WR)
9. black body, black interior, black disc wheels with rubber tires, "Pontiac Excitement 2" tempa, China casting ($4-6)(WR)(TC)
10. black & green body, black interior, Goodyear slicks, "Mello Yello 42" tempa, China casting ($3-4)(WR)
11. black & green body, black interior, black disc with rubber tires, "Mello Yello 42" tempa, China casting ($4-6)(WR)(TC)
12. blue & white body, gray interior, Goodyear slicks, "Evinrude 89" tempa, China casting ($4-6)(WR)
13. matt yellow body, black interior, Goodyear slicks, "Country Time 68" tempa, China casting ($3-5)(WR)
14. white & yellow body, red interior, Goodyear slicks, "Medford Speed Shop/ Valtrol 48" tempa, China casting ($4-6)(WR)

NOTE: Previously listed as MB216. All below with Goodyear slicks unless noted.

15. white & red body, blue interior, "Nastrak 1" tempa, China casting ($3-5)(GS)(WR)
16. red body, gray interior, "Nastrak 2" tempa, China casting ($3-5)(GS)(WR)
17. red & yellow body, gray interior, "Nastrak 3" tempa, China casting ($3-5)(GS)(WR)
18. red-brown body, gray interior, "Nastrak 4" tempa, China casting ($3-5)(GS)(WR)
19. red & yellow body, red interior, "Nastrak 5" tempa, China casting ($3-5)(GS)(WR)
20. blue & white body, blue interior, "Nastrak 6" tempa, China casting ($3-5)(GS)(WR)
21. white & black body, black interior, "White Rose Collectibles 93" tempa, China casting ($25-30)(WR)
22. fluorescent yellow body, black interior, gold 6-spoke spiral wheels, "Pro Auto 10" tempa, Thailand casting ($1-2)
23. black body, blue interior, silver 6-spoke spiral wheels, "Outlaw Auto 7" tempa, Thailand casting ($2-3)
24. orange-yellow body, black interior, Goodyear slicks wheels, "Pennzoil 30" tempa, China casting ($12-18)(WR)
25. blue body, black interior, Goodyear slicks, "Rumple 70/ Son's" tempa, China casting ($3-5)(WR)

MB35-I PONTIAC STOCK CAR, issued 1993 (USA) (MB238)

NOTE: Below models with clear windows & black plastic base.

1. yellow body, black interior, white lettered Goodyear slicks, "Pro Auto 10" tempa, Thailand casting ($1-2)(5pk)
2. fluorescent yellow body, black interior, white lettered Goodyear slicks, "Seaside 15" tempa, Thailand casting ($3-5)
3. black body, silver-gray interior, yellow lettered Goodyear slicks, "Dirt Devil 40" (white print), Thailand casting ($3-5)(WR)
4. black body, silver-gray interior, yellow lettered Goodyear slicks, "Dirt Devil 40" (orange print), Thailand casting ($3-5)(WR)(TC)
5. black body, silver-gray interior, black disc wheels with rubber tires, "Dirt Devil 40" (white print) tempa, Thailand casting ($3-5)(WR)(TC)
6. black body, silver-gray interior, yellow lettered Goodyear slicks, "Duron 66" tempa, Thailand casting ($7-10)(WR)
7. orange body, red interior, yellow lettered Goodyear slicks, "Burn Foundation/Motorsports 94" tempa, Thailand casting ($15-18)(US)
8. purple body, translucent red interior, white lettered Goodyear slicks, "JD Graphics 17" tempa, Thailand casting ($1-2)(5pk)

MB35-J AMG MERCEDES C CLASS, issued 1996 (USA) (MB288)
MB75-F AMG MERCEDES C CLASS, issued 1996 (ROW)

NOTE: Below models with black plastic base.

1. metallic blue body, gray interior, clear windows, silver 6-spoke spiral wheels, "25 Camsport" tempa, China casting ($1-2)
2. silver-gray body, yellow interior, clear windows, 5 spoke concave star wheels, "25 Camsport" tempa, China casting ($1-2)(5pk)
3. metallic gold body, black interior, clear windows, silver 6 spoke spiral wheels, no tempa, China casting ($5-10)(CH)
4. metallic blue body, gray interior, clear windows, 5 spoke concave star wheels, "25 Camsport" tempa, China casting ($3-5)
5. lemon body, red interior, clear windows, 5 spoke concave star wheels, "25 Camsport" tempa, China casting ($1-2)
6. silver-gray & florescent orange body, black/gray/white interior, clear windows, chrome disc wheels with rubber tires, "Team Matchbox 1" tempa, China casting ($3-5)(PC15)

MB35-K DODGE VIPER GTS *see MB1-G*

MB35-L POLICE MOTORCYCLE, issued 1999 (USA) (MB412)
MB65-J POLICE MOTORCYCLE, issued 2002 (ROW)

NOTE: Below models with China casting

1. black body, gray handlebars, gray saddlebags, chrome spoked wheels, chrome engine, "Police" tempa ($1-2)(MW35/1999 US)
2. blue body, black handlebars, black saddlebags, gray spoked wheels, gray engine, "Radio" tempa ($1-2)(5pk)
3. black body, black & gray handlebars, black saddlebags, gray spoked wheels, gray engine, "MBI" tempa ($1-2)(MW46/2001 US)(MW65/2001 ROW)
4. light blue body, blue handlebars, blue saddlebags, gray spoked wheels, gray engine, "Polittie 29" tempa ($1-2)(MW29/2003 ROW
5. light blue body, blue handlebars, blue saddlebags, gray spoked wheels, gray engine, "Polittie 29" & "Hero City" tempa ($2-4)(MW29/2003 ROW)
6. metallic blue body, black handlebars, black saddlebags, gray spoked wheels, gray engine, "Police" star & small "Matchbox" tempa ($3-5)(PB)

MB35-M HOLDEN COMMODORE POLICE CAR, issued 2001 (ROW) (MB475)

NOTE: Below models with gray interior, smoke windows, amber bar light, black plastic base, lace wheels, China casting

1. blue body, "Police" with crest & blue sides tempa ($2-3)

MB35-N HOVERCRAFT *see MB62-M*

MB35-O TVR TUSCAN S, issued 2004 (SF)(MB595)
MB595 TVR TUSCAN S, issued 2003

NOTE: Below models with China casting.

1. silver-gray body, smoke windows, red interior, "Looney Tunes Back in Action" tempa, black base, lace wheels ($1-2)(5pk)
2. metallic gold body, red windows, red interior, "Flash" tempa, black base, lace wheels ($1-2)(5pk)
3. dark blue body, dark smoke windows, red interior, "London" tempa, blue base, lace wheels ($1-2)(AW)
4. metallic green body, smoke windows, tan interior, detailed trim tempa, metallic green base, 5 spoke slotted wheels ($2-4)(SF35/2004)
5. silver-gray body, red windows, red interior, The Flash tempa, red base, lace wheels ($1-2)(CA)

MB36-A OPEL DIPLOMAT, issued 1970

NOTE: Below models with white interior, clear windows, chrome engine, metal base & England casting.

1. green-gold body, black base, plain grille ($25-40)
2. dark gold body, black base, plain grille ($25-40)
3. dark gold body, black base, silver grille ($25-40)
4. light gold body, black base, silver grille ($25-40)

MB36-B HOT ROD DRAGUAR, issued 1970

NOTE: Below models with 5 spoke wheels, unpainted metal base & England casting.

1. metallic red body, orange interior, clear windows, with label ($15-20)
2. metallic red body, orange interior, clear windows, no label ($15-20)
3. metallic red body, ivory interior, clear windows, with label ($15-20)
4. metallic red body, light yellow interior, clear windows, with label ($15-20)
5. metallic red body, light yellow interior, clear windows, no label ($15-20)
6. metallic pink body, light yellow interior, clear windows, with label ($15-20)

7. metallic pink body, light yellow interior, amber windows, with label ($15-20)
8. metallic pink body, white interior, clear windows, with label ($15-20)
9. metallic pink body, light yellow interior, yellow windows, with label ($15-20)
10. metallic pink body, yellow interior, amber windows, with label ($15-20)
11. metallic pink body, dark yellow interior, yellow windows, with label ($15-20)
12. metallic pink body, white interior, amber windows, with label ($15-20)
13. metallic pink body, light yellow interior, amber windows, with label ($15-20)
14. metallic pink body, light yellow interior, clear windows, no label ($15-20)
15. metallic pink body, light yellow interior, amber windows, no label ($15-20)

MB36-C FORMULA 5000, issued 1975

NOTE: Below models with unpainted metal base,5 spoke front wheels & England casting unless otherwise noted.

1. orange body, blue driver, "5000" hood & spoiler label, 5 arch rear wheels ($8-12)
2. orange body, blue driver, "5000" hood & spoiler label, maltese cross rear wheels ($8-12)
3. orange body, yellow-orange driver, "5000" hood & spoiler label, maltese cross rear wheels ($8-12)
4. red body, yellow-orange driver, "5000" hood & spoiler label, maltese cross rear wheels ($7-10)
5. red body, yellow-orange driver, "Texaco" hood label, "Marlboro" spoiler label, maltese cross rear wheels ($7-10)
6. red body, yellow-orange driver, "Texaco" hood label, no spoiler label , maltese cross rear wheels ($7-10)
7. red body, yellow-orange driver, "Texaco" hood label, "Champion" spoiler label, maltese cross rear wheels ($7-10)
8. red body, lemon driver, "Texaco" hood label, "Champion" spoiler label, maltese cross rear wheels ($7-10)
9. red body, yellow-orange driver, "Texaco" hood label, "Champion" spoiler label, maltese cross rear wheels, Manaus tab on base ($45-60)(BR)
10. white body, yellow-orange driver, "Texaco" hood label, "Champion" spoiler label, maltese cross rear wheels, Manaus tab on base ($350+)(BR)
11. red body, yellow-orange driver, "Texaco" hood label, "Champion" spoiler label, dot dash rear wheels ($7-10)
12. white body, yellow-orange driver, "5000" hood & spoiler labels, maltese cross rear wheels, Manaus tab on base ($250+)(BR)
13. red body, yellow-orange driver, "Monsieur Meuble" hood & spoiler labels, maltese cross rear wheels ($500+)(FR)

MB36-D REFUSE TRUCK, issued 1980 (MB036)

NOTE: Below models with red windows, metal base & 5 arch wheels unless otherwise noted. Version 2 with red or orange windows.

1. metallic red body, orange-yellow dump & hatch, silver-gray base, no label, red trigger, without "Colectomatic" cast on front of dump, England casting ($18-25)
2. metallic red body, orange-yellow dump & hatch, silver-gray base, no label, red trigger, England casting ($2-4)
3. metallic red body, orange-yellow dump & hatch, unpainted base, no label, red trigger, England casting ($2-4)
4. metallic red body, orange-yellow dump & hatch, silver-gray base, no label, red trigger, dot dash wheels, England casting ($8-12)
5. metallic magenta body, orange-yellow dump & hatch, silver-gray base, no label, red trigger, England casting ($2-4)
6. blue body, yellow dump & hatch, silver-gray base, "Metro" label, red trigger, England casting ($3-5)
7. blue body, yellow dump & hatch, silver-gray base, "Metro" label, black trigger, England casting ($3-5)
8. blue body, orange dump & hatch, silver-gray base, "Metro" label, red trigger , England casting ($2-4)
9. blue body, orange dump & hatch, silver-gray base, "Metro" label, black trigger, England casting ($2-4)
10. blue body, orange dump, yellow hatch, silver-gray base, "Metro" label, red trigger, England casting ($5-7)
11. blue body, dull orange dump, yellow hatch, silver-gray base, no label, red trigger, England casting ($5-7)
12. blue body, orange dump & hatch, pearly silver base, "Metro" label, red trigger, Macau casting ($2-4)
13. white body, blue dump & hatch, light metallic gray base, "Metro" label, blue trigger, Macau casting ($2-3)
14. white body, blue dump & hatch, pearly silver base, Japanese lettered tempa, blue trigger, Macau casting ($8-12)(JP)
15. white body, blue dump & hatch, light metallic gray base, no label, blue trigger, Macau casting ($2-3)
16. white body, blue dump & hatch, pearly silver base, "Metro" label, red trigger, purple windows, China casting ($2-3)
17. green body, yellow dump & hatch, pearly gray base, "State City" tempa, red trigger, China casting ($1-2)
18. green body, lemon dump & hatch, pearly gray base, "State City" tempa, red trigger, China casting ($1-2)
19. orange body, gray dump & hatch, black base, "Refuse Disposal" tempa, red trigger, China casting ($1-2)
20. green body, light yellow dump & hatch, black base, "Refuse Disposal" tempa, red trigger, China casting ($1-2)
21. red body, light yellow dump & hatch, black base, "Refuse Disposal" tempa, red trigger, China casting ($8-12)(GS)
22. orange body, white dump & hatch, black base, orange trigger, "Refuse Disposal" tempa, China casting ($1-2)
23. pale orange body, white dump & hatch, black base, orange trigger, "Refusal Disposal" without dump tempa, China casting ($1-2)
24. red body, silver-gray dump & hatch, black base, red trigger, smoke windows, caricature tempa, China casting ($1-2)
25. white body, blue dump & hatch, black base, red trigger, red arrows & caricature tempa, China casting ($3-5)(5pk)
26. metallic gold body, white dump & hatch, black base, black trigger, no tempa, China casting ($5-10)(CH)
27. orange-yellow body, dark blue dump & hatch, black base, orange-yellow trigger, "Metro DPW Unit 17" tempa ($1-2)
28. white body, white dump & hatch, black base, white trigger, no tempa, China casting ($25-40)(ASAP blank)
29. white body, white dump & hatch, black base, white trigger, "Bulldog Castor Co." tempa, China casting ($75+)(ASAP)
30 white body, white dump & hatch, black base, white trigger, maroon design tempa, China casting ($75+)(ASAP)
31. white body, white dump & hatch, black base, white trigger, "Waste Industries" tempa, China casting ($75+)(ASAP)
32. orange body, orange dump & hatch, black base, black trigger, "Metro DPW Unit 17" tempa, China casting ($1-2)(MW7/1998 US)(MW4/1998 ROW))
33. dark green body, clear windows, silver-gray dump & hatch, black base, red trigger, "Recycle" tempa, China casting ($1-2)(5pk)
34. dark green body, clear windows, silver-gray dump & hatch, black base, black trigger, "Recycle" tempa, China casting ($1-2)(5pk)
35. white body, white dump & hatch, black base, black trigger, "Metro DPW" tempa, China casting ($2-4)(MP)

36. light orange body, silver-gray dump & hatch, yellow trigger, "Ridge, NY Recycles" tempa, China casting ($1-2)(MW3/1999 US))
37. white body, white dump & hatch, white trigger, "Vince Coleen" & heart tempa, China casting ($100+)(ASAP)
38. white body, smoke windows, dark blue dump & hatch, red trigger, "Mill Run" & flag tempa, charcoal base, China casting ($1-2)(5pk)
39. white body, smoke windows, dark blue dump & hatch, red trigger, globe without "Mill Run" tempa, charcoal base, China casting ($2-4)(5pk)
40. blue body, amber windows, white dump & hatch, blue trigger, "City of Cleveland Ohio" tempa, China casting ($1-2)(MW35/2000 US)
41. blue body, amber windows, white dump & hatch, blue trigger, "City of Cleveland Ohio" & "Matchbox 2000" tempa, China casting ($2-4)(MW35/2000 US)
42. white body, white dump & hatch, white trigger, "Renfro Cartage" tempa, China casting ($50+)(ASAP)
43. bright blue body, white dump & hatch, blue trigger, "Fort Worth" red stripes & Texas outline tempa, charcoal base, lace wheels, China casting ($1-2)(MW19/2001 US)
44. white body, white dump & hatch, white trigger, no tempa, black base, lace wheels, China casting ($20-35)(ASAP blank)
45. dark green body, white dump & hatch, white trigger, charcoal base, "Trash Dept. 12" tempa, lace wheels, Mattel China casting ($1-2)(PB)
46. white body, white dump & hatch, white trigger, black base, "CID" tempa, China casting ($50+)(ASAP)
47. white body, white dump & hatch, white trigger, black base, "EFI" tempa, China casting ($50+)(ASAP)
48. white body, white dump & hatch, white trigger, black base, "Wastec" tempa, China casting ($50+)(ASAP)

MB36-E 1957 CHEVY BEL AIR CONVERTIBLE, issued 1998 (MB320)

NOTE: Below models with clear windshield, chrome plastic base & China casting unless otherwise noted.

1. black body, white interior, chrome disc wheels with rubber tires, "Toy Fair 98- Matchbox" tempa ($85-110)(US)
2. red body, red & white interior, chrome disc with rubber tires, silver flash & detailed trim tempa ($4-6)(FE)
3. unpainted body, white interior, chrome disc wheels with rubber tires, no tempa ($4-6)(FE)
4. turquoise body, white interior, 5 spoke concave star wheels, silver flash with purple & white design tempa ($1-2)(MW36/1998)
5. turquoise body, white interior, chrome disc wheels with rubber tires, silver flash with purple & white design tempa ($100+)
   NOTE: The above model was found packaged as a First Edition but is probably done so as a manufacturing error.
6. turquoise body, white & turquoise interior, chrome disc wheels with rubber tires, silver flash tempa ($4-6)(PC)
7. pale yellow body, red interior, smoke windows, 5 spoke concave star wheels, red & black tempa ($1-2)(MW47/1999 US)(MW42/1999 ROW)
8. pale yellow body, red interior, smoke windows, 5 spoke concave star wheels, red & black with "American Wheels Show" tempa ($20-25)(CCI)
9. pale yellow body, red interior, smoke windows, 5 spoke concave star wheels, red & black with "Parsippany Demo Model/ Matchbox USA Toy Show & Convention" tempa ($18-25)(CCI)
10. turquoise body, white interior, 5 spoke concave star wheels, "Matchbox 2000 Convention- Hershey, PA- Color Comp Inc. Demo Model" tempa ($18-25)(CCI)
11. turquoise body, white interior, 5 spoke concave star wheels, "Cruisin New England Magazine Elite Dream Machines/ Mohegan Sun" tempa ($35-50)(CCI)
   NOTE: Below models with Mattel China casting.
12. silver blue body, red interior, smoke windshield, lace wheels, "Coke Brightens Every Bite" tempa, silver-gray metal base ($5-6)(Avon)(TP)
13. lavender body, neon yellow interior, clear windshield, 10 spoke flower wheels, "Snap Crackle Pop/ Kellogg's Rice Krispies" tempa, silver- gray metal base ($5-6)(Avon TP)(5pk)
14. turquoise body, white interior, clear windshield, 5 spoke concave star wheels, "Nostalgia" with dice tempa ($50+)(CCI)
15. black body, purple interior, smoke windshield, 10 spoke flower wheels, "Hero City Sports" tempa, gray plastic base ($1-2)(5pk)
16. canary yellow body, blue interior, smoke windshield, 10 spoke flower wheels, Easter egg design tempa, red plastic base ($1-2)(MP)

MB36-F '99 MUSTANG CONVERTIBLE, issued 1999 (USA) (MB368)

MB12-L '99 MUSTANG CONVERTIBLE, issued 2002 (ROW)

NOTE: Below models with clear windshield, black plastic base & China casting unless otherwise noted.

1. black body, gray interior, chrome disc wheels with rubber tires, "Toy Fair 2000 Matchbox" tempa ($50-75)(US)
2. white body, tan interior, 5 spoke concave star wheels, "Mustang" & black stripes tempa ($1-2)(MW36/1999 US)
3. black body, tan interior, chrome disc wheels with rubber tires, detailed trim tempa ($5-8)(PC)
4. red body, black interior, 5 spoke concave star wheels, white band & stripes tempa ($1-2)(5pk)
5. yellow body, black interior, 5 spoke concave star wheels, "Mustang", black stripes & "Matchbox 2000" tempa ($2-4)(MW3/2000 US)
6. yellow body, black interior, 5 spoke concave star wheels, "Mustang" & black stripes tempa ($1-2)(MW3/2000 US)
7. yellow body, black interior, star with 5 spokes wheels, "Mustang" & black stripes tempa ($1-2)(MW3/2000 US)
8. light red body, tan interior, 5 spoke concave star wheels, "Subway" tempa ($3-5)(US)
   NOTE: Above model has "Subway Mfg. By b. little" cast on the base.
9. red body, white interior, smoke windshield, 5 spoke concave star wheels, "Coca Cola" tempa ($1-2)(5pk)
10. red body, white interior, smoke windshield, star with 5 spokes wheels, "Coca Cola" tempa ($1-2)(5pk)
11. blue body, white interior, 5 spoke concave star wheels, white stripes tempa ($1-2)(5pk)
12. blue body, white interior, star with 5 spokes wheels, white stripes tempa ($1-2)(5pk)
13. blue body, white interior, 10 spoke flower wheels, white stripes tempa ($1-2)(5pk)
14. bronze body, black interior, smoke windshield, 10 spoke flower wheels, blue & silver stripes & horse logo with "Mustang" tempa ($1-2)(5pk)
15. dark yellow body, black interior, clear windshield, 5 spoke concave star wheels, "Mustang" & black stripes tempa ($2-4)(MP)
16. bronze body, black interior, smoke windshield, gold lace wheels, blue & silver stripes & horse logo with "Mustang" tempa ($10-15)(EG)
17. metallic red body, purple interior, smoke windshield, lace wheels, "Mustang" & purple design tempa ($1-2)(MW12/2002)
18. metallic red body, purple interior, smoke windshield, lace wheels, "Mustang", purple design & "Matchbox 50" tempa ($5-8)(MW12/2002)

19. red body, white interior, smoke windshield, 5 spoke concave star wheels, "Coca Cola" tempa ($2-3)(CK)
20. bronze body, black interior, smoke windshield, star with 5 spokes wheels, blue & silver stripes, horse logo & "Mustang" tempa ($10-15)(EG)
21. red body, white interior, clear windshield, chrome disc wheels with rubber tires, "The Real Thing- Ice Cold" tempa ($3-5)(Coke PC)
22. white body, red interior, smoke windshield, 10 spoke flower wheels, "Coca Cola" tempa ($2-3)(CK)
23. red body, black interior, clear windshield, 10 spoke flower wheels, "100" tempa ($2-4)(TP)(Avon)
24. black body, tan-gray interior, black trim on clear windshield, chrome disc wheels with rubber tires, "100" tempa ($3-5)(MP)
25. white body, light tan interior, smoke windshield, 5 spoke slotted wheels, gold stripes tempa, gray base ($1-2)(SF47/2004)

MB36-G SKI BOAT *see MB41-K*

MB36-H X-33 RLV, issued 2000 (USA) (MB452)
MB21-J X-33 RLV, issued 2000 (ROW)

NOTE: Below models with black plastic base, black wheel, China casting.

1. white body, "Venture Star/ USA" tempa, "X-33 RLV" base name ($1-2)(MW362000 US)(MW21/2000 ROW))
2. white body, "Venture Star/ USA/ Matchbox 2000" tempa, "X-33 RLV" base name ($2-4)(MW36/2000 US))
3. white body, "Venture Star/ USA" tempa, "X-33 Lockheed Martin" base name ($1-2)(5pk)
4. white body, "Citrix MetaFrame XP" tempa, "X-33 Lockheed Martin" base name ($25+)(CCI)
5. white body, "Citrix MetaFrame XP" tempa, "X-33 RLV" base name ($25+)(CCI)

MB36-I ROAD ROLLER, issued 2001 (MB492)

NOTE: Below models with plastic base & China casting.

1. orange body, gray interior, blue roll cage, black rollers, gray roller swivel, blue swivel base, gray stationary base, "36 Matchbox" tempa ($1-2)(MW36/2001)
2. red body, gray interior, black roll cage, black rollers, gray roller swivel, black swivel base, gray stationary base, "36 Matchbox" tempa ($1-2)(MW320/2002)
3. red body, gray interior, black roll cage, black rollers, gray roller swivel, black swivel base, gray stationary base, "36 Matchbox" & "Matchbox 50" tempa ($10-15)(MW20/2002
4. green body, dark gray interior, yellow roll cage, gray rollers, dark gray roller swivel, yellow swivel base, black stationary base, "42" & steer head tempa ($1-2)(5pk)
5. green body, dark gray interior, orange-yellow roll cage, gray rollers, dark gray roller swivel, orange-yellow swivel base, black stationary base, "42" & steer head tempa ($1-2)(5pk)
6. red body, yellow interior, gray roll cage, black rollers, yellow roller swivel, gray swivel base, yellow stationary base, "23" & design tempa ($1-2)(MW23)
7. red body, orange-yellow interior, gray roll cage, black rollers, orange-yellow roller swivel, gray swivel base, orange-yellow stationary base, "23" & design tempa ($5-8)(MW23/2003)
8. red body, orange-yellow interior, gray roll cage, black rollers, orange-yellow roller swivel, gray swivel base, orange-yellow stationary base, "23", design & "Hero City" tempa ($10-15)(MW23/2003)
9. lime body, orange interior, red roll cage, gray rollers, orange roller swivel, red swivel base, orange stationary base, "Hero City" & roller design tempa ($1-2)(5pk)
10. canary yellow body, blue interior & roll cage, light gray rollers, blue roller swivel & swivel base, blue stationary base, "Matchbox" with blue & red stripes tempa ($3-5)(PB)
11. orange body, red interior, black roll cage, dark gray rollers, red roller swivel, black swivel base, red stationary base, "Hero City" tempa ($1-2)(MW71/2004)

MB36-J TROOP CARRIER issued MB52-I

MB36-K TAXI CAB, issued 2003 (MB577)

1. lemon body, blue windows, black interior, lace wheels, "Taxi 36" with checkers, dark gray base, China casting ($1-2)(MW36/2003)
2. lemon body, blue windows, black interior, lace wheels, "Taxi 36", checkers & "Hero City" tempa, dark gray base, China casting ($2-4)(MW36/2003)
3. yellow body, smoke windows, black interior, chrome disc wheels with rubber tires, "2003 Matchbox Hero City Toy Show/ Taxi" tempa, China casting ($5-8)(US)
4. iridescent white body, blue windows, gray interior, lace wheels, "Hero City Taxi" & design tempa, black base, China casting ($2-3)(MW43/2004)
5. iridescent white body, blue windows, gray interior, 10 spoke flower wheels, "Hero City Taxi" & design tempa, black base, China casting ($1-2)(MW43/2004)
6. orange-yellow body, blue windows, light bluish interior, lace wheels, "Statue of Liberty" tempa, black base, China casting ($1-2)(AW)
7. yellow body, smoke windows, black interior, lace wheels, "Taxi Little Bill" & checkers tempa, yellow base, China casting ($1-2)(5pk)

MB36-L HONDA ELEMENT, issued 2004 (MB632)

1. metallic orange body, dark gray fenders, very dark smoke windows, black interior, 7 spoke sawblade wheels, painted lights & detailed trim tempa, gray plastic base, China casting ($1-2)(MW36/2004)
2. metallic orange body, dark gray fenders, dark smoke windows, black interior, 7 spoke sawblade wheels, painted lights & detailed trim tempa, gray plastic base, China casting ($1-2)(MW36)
3. metallic green body, tan fenders, smoke windows, tan interior, 5 spoke slotted wheels, painted lights & detailed trim tempa, gray plastic base, China casting ($8-12)(SF44/2004)

MB37-A CATTLE TRUCK, issued 1970

NOTE: Below models green windows, 5 spoke wheels, two white plastic cows, unpainted metal base & England casting.

1. light yellow body, gray box ($25-40)
2. orange-yellow body, gray box ($25-40)
3. orange body, gray box ($25-40)
4. orange body, silver-gray box ($65-80)

MB37-B SOOPA COOPA, issued 1972

NOTE: Below models with yellow interior, amber windshield, metal base & England casting.

1. light metallic blue body, unpainted base, no labels, maltese cross wheels ($15-20)
2. mid metallic blue body, unpainted base, no labels, maltese cross wheels ($15-20)
3. mid metallic blue body, silver-gray base, no labels, maltese cross wheels ($15-20)
4. mid metallic blue body, unpainted base, no labels, 4 spoke wheels ($35-50)
5. dark metallic blue body, unpainted base, no labels, maltese cross wheels ($15-20)
6. dark metallic blue body, unpainted base, no labels, 5 spoke wheels ($15-20)

7. metallic pink body, unpainted base, flower label, maltese cross wheels ($18-25)
8. metallic pink body, red base, flower label, maltese cross wheels ($50-75)
9. orange body, unpainted base, "Jaffa Mobile" labels, maltese cross wheels ($100-150)(OP)
10. lime body, unpainted base with Manaus label, star label, maltese cross wheels ($250+)(BR)

MB37-C SKIP TRUCK, issued 1976

NOTE: Below models with dot dash wheels, unpainted metal arms, metal base & England casting unless otherwise noted.

1. red body, yellow skip, black base, amber windows, chrome interior ($5-7)
2. red body, yellow skip, black base, amber windows, gray interior ($4-6)
3. red body, yellow skip, black base, clear windows, gray interior ($4-6)
4. red body, yellow skip, unpainted base, clear windows, gray interior ($4-6)
5. red body, yellow skip, black base, light blue windows, gray interior ($4-6)
6. red body, yellow skip, black base, smoke windows, gray interior ($4-6)
7. red body, yellow skip, brown base, clear windows, gray interior ($7-10)
8. red body, yellow skip, brown base, smoke windows, gray interior ($7-10)
9. red body, yellow skip, charcoal base, clear windows, gray interior ($4-6)
10. red body, blue skip, black base, clear windows, gray interior ($90-125)
11. red body, yellow skip, black base, clear windows, orange interior ($4-6)
12. red body, yellow skip, charcoal base, clear windows, orange interior ($4-6)
13. orange-red body, yellow skip, black base, clear windows, gray interior ($4-6)
14. orange-red body, yellow skip, black base, smoke windows, gray interior ($4-6)
15. orange body, red skip, black base, clear windows, gray interior ($85-110)(GR)
16. orange body, yellow skip, black base, clear windows, gray interior ($85-110)(GR)
17. metallic blue body, yellow skip, charcoal base, clear windows, gray interior ($3-5)
18. metallic blue body, yellow skip, silver-gray base, clear windows, gray interior ($3-5)
19. metallic blue body, yellow skip, black base, clear windows, gray interior ($3-5)
20. metallic blue body, yellow skip, black base, clear windows, black interior ($35-50)
21. metallic blue body, yellow skip, charcoal base, clear windows, black interior ($35-50)
22. red body, yellow skip, black base with Manaus tab, clear windows, gray interior ($35-50)(BR)
23. dark metallic blue body, yellow skip, charcoal base, clear windows, gray interior ($200-300)(BR)

MB37-D SUNBURNER, issued 1981 (USA) (MB083)

NOTE: Versions 1, 2 & 4 have "Lesney" cast bases. Version 3 has Matchbox International" bases, noting that version 3 has both. Below models with clear window & 5 spoke wheels.

1. black body, black base, red interior, yellow & red flames tempa, England casting ($3-5)
2. black body, black base, red interior, green & red flames tempa, England casting ($3-5)
3. black body, black base, red interior, yellow & red flames tempa, Macau casting ($3-5)
4. black body, black base, red interior, yellow & red flames tempa, Hong Kong casting ($3-5)

MB37-E MATRA RANCHO, issued 1982 (ROW) (MB037)

NOTE: Below models with black interior & clear windows.

1. turquoise body & base, no tempa, blue tailgate, 5 arch silver wheels, England casting ($8-12)
2. light blue body & base, no tempa, blue tailgate, 5 arch silver wheels, England casting ($8-12)
3. light blue body & base, no tempa, blue tailgate, dot dash wheels, England casting ($8-12)
4. yellow body & base, red stripe tempa, yellow tailgate, 5 arch silver wheels, England casting ($7-10)
5. navy blue body, white base, "Surf Rescue" tempa, blue tailgate, 5 arch silver wheels, England casting ($4-6)(TP)
6. dark blue body, black base, no tempa, blue tailgate, 5 arch silver wheels, England casting ($7-10)
7. dark blue body, black base, no tempa, blue tailgate, 5 arch gold wheels, England casting ($15-18)
8. dark blue body, yellow base, no tempa, yellow tailgate, 5 arch gold wheels, England casting ($18-25)(TP)
9. dark blue body, yellow base, no tempa, yellow tailgate, 5 arch silver wheels, England casting ($15-18)(TP)
10. dark blue body & base, no tempa, blue tailgate, 5 arch gold wheels, England casting ($15-18)
11. yellow body & base, no tempa, yellow tailgate, 5 arch silver wheels, England casting ($6-8)
12. yellow body & base, red stripe tempa, yellow tailgate, 5 arch gold wheels, England casting ($15-18)
13. navy blue body, white base, "Surf Rescue" tempa, blue tailgate, 5 arch silver wheels, England casting ($3-5)(TP)
14. navy blue body, white base, "Surf Rescue" tempa, black tailgate, 5 arch silver wheels, England casting ($4-6)
15. navy blue body, yellow base, "Surf Rescue" tempa, black tailgate, 5 arch silver wheels, England casting ($12-15)(TP)
16. black body, white base, "Surf Rescue" tempa, black tailgate, 5 arch silver wheels, Macau casting ($3-5)(TP)
17. orange body, black base, "Surf 2" tempa, orange tailgate, 5 arch silver wheels, Macau casting ($2-4)(TP)
18. florescent yellow body, yellow base, "Marine Rescue" tempa, florescent yellow tailgate, 5 arch silver wheels, China casting ($1-2)(EM)
19. white body, white base, white interior & tailgate, amber windows, no tempa, 5 arch silver wheels, China casting ($10-15)(GF)
20. blue body, yellow base, "Marine Rescue" (gold) tempa, blue tailgate, clear windows, 5 arch silver wheels, China casting ($3-5)(MP)

NOTE: Available as a Bulgarian casting. Assorted colors available ($5-25)

MB37-F JEEP 4 X 4, issued 1984 (USA) (MB131)
MB25-I JEEP 4 X 4, issued 1994 (ROW)

NOTE: Below models with black rollcage & white antenna unless otherwise noted.

1. black body, pearly silver metal base, black interior, red/orange/yellow tempa, Macau casting ($2-3)
2. black body, pearly silver metal base, black interior, red/orange/yellow tempa, China casting ($2-3)
3. white body, pearly silver metal base, black interior, orange/red/blue tempa, Macau casting ($1-2)

4. white body, pearly silver metal base, black interior, orange/red/blue tempa, China casting ($1-2)
5. white body, gray plastic base, black interior, orange/red/blue tempa, Macau casting ($1-2)
6. white body, gray plastic base, black interior, orange/red/blue tempa, Thailand casting ($1-2)
7. white body, gray plastic base, black interior, orange/red/blue tempa, China casting ($1-2)
8. dark florescent orange body, gray plastic base, black interior, "Cool Mud" with hood tempa, China casting ($1-2)
9. dark florescent orange body, gray plastic base, black interior, "Cool Mud" without hood tempa, China casting ($1-2)
10. metallic red body, gray plastic base, black interior, no tempa, China casting ($1-2)(5pk)
11. pink body, gray plastic base, black interior, "Cool Mud" without hood tempa, China casting ($2-4)
12. metallic gold body, black plastic base, black interior, no tempa, China casting ($10-15)(CH)
13. beige body, dark gray plastic base, black interior, green stripes tempa, black antenna, China casting ($1-2)(AS)(AP)
14. metallic blue body, dark gray plastic base, black interior, orange flames tempa, China casting ($1-2)(5pk)
15. silver-gray body, black plastic base, black interior & antenna, purple & pink flames tempa, black antenna, China casting ($1-2)(AS)
16. powder blue body, dark gray plastic base, black interior, "Cool Mud" & black design tempa, China casting ($2-4)
17. yellow body, dark gray plastic base, black interior, red flames tempa, China casting ($1-2)(5pk)
18. bright blue body, dark gray plastic base, black interior, white splash tempa, China casting ($1-2)(MW52/1998)
19. metallic red body, black plastic base, silver-gray interior & roll cage, no tempa, China casting ($4-5)(MW57/1999GR)
20. orange-yellow body, gray plastic base, blue roll cage & black interior, "Wilderness Tours" tempa, China casting ($1-2)(5pk)
21. orange-yellow body, gray plastic base, blue roll cage & black interior, blue & red circle design tempa, China casting ($2-4)(5pk)
22. lime body, brown plastic base, chartreuse roll cage, black interior, & antenna, "Jeep" & mud tempa, brown wheels, China casting ($1-2)(5pk)

MB37-G FORD ESCORT CABRIOLET *see MB17-E*

MB37-H NISSAN 300ZX *see MB61-E*

MB37-I 1970 BOSS MUSTANG, issued 1998 (MB322)

NOTE: Below models with clear windows.

1. lemon body, white & black interior, chrome disc wheels with rubber tires, black stripe tempa, lemon plastic base, China casting ($4-6)(FE)
2. unpainted body, white interior, chrome disc wheels with rubber tires, no tempa, chrome plastic base, China casting ($4-6)(FE)
3. purple body, yellow interior, 5 spoke concave star wheels, "Boss" with stripes tempa, chrome plastic base, China casting ($1-2)(MW37/1998
4. purple body, yellow interior, 5 spoke concave star wheels, "Boss" with stripes tempa, translucent white plastic base, China casting ($50-75)(MW37/1998)
5. black body, light gray interior, 5 spoke concave star wheels, silver design tempa, chrome plastic base, China casting ($2-4)(RT)
6. black body, light gray interior, 5 spoke concave star wheels, silver design tempa, translucent white plastic base, China casting ($50-75)
7. powder blue body, white & black interior, chrome disc wheels with rubber tires, black stripes tempa, powder blue plastic base, China casting ($3-5)(MP)
8. purple body, yellow interior, 5 spoke concave star wheels, "Boss" with stripes & "South Jersey Mustang" tempa, chrome plastic base, China casting ($20-35)(CCI)

NOTE: Below models with Mattel China casting.

9. lemon body, black interior, 10 spoke flower wheels, "Coca Cola" tempa, silver-gray metal base, China casting ($5-6)(Avon)(TP)
10. metallic lime body, white & black interior, chrome disc wheels with rubber tires, black design tempa, metallic lime plastic base, China casting ($3-5)(TN)
11. blue-green body, white & black interior, chrome disc wheels with rubber tires, black design tempa, painted blue-green plastic base, China casting ($3-5)(BJ)
12. metallic blue body, white & black interior, chrome disc wheels with rubber tires, black stripes tempa, painted metallic blue plastic base, China casting ($3-5)(BJ)
13. white body, red interior, 5 spoke slotted wheels, black stripes tempa, chrome plastic base, China casting ($2-4)(SF28/2004)
14. metallic green body, black interior, 10 spoke flower wheels, black stripes tempa, chrome plastic base, China casting ($5-8)(CN)(OP)

MB37-L BULLDOZER, issued 2001 (MB493)

NOTE: Below models with gray engine & rollers, black treads, China casting unless otherwise noted.

1. red body, yellow plastic blade, maroon base, "Matchbox 48" tempa ($1-2)(MW37/2001)
2. bright blue body, yellow plastic blade, blue base, "Matchbox 48" tempa ($1-2)(MW19/2002)
3. bright blue body, yellow plastic base, blue base, "Matchbox 40" & "Matchbox 50" tempa ($2-4)(MW19/2002)
4. white body, white plastic blade, white motor, black rollers, gray base, no tempa ($25-40)(ASAP blank)
5. pumpkin body, red plastic shovel, lemon base, "42" & steer head tempa ($1-2)(5pk)
6. orange-yellow body, black plastic blade, neon orange motor & wheels, yellow base, "MHC67" tempa ($1-2)(MW67/2003 US)
7. orange-yellow body, black plastic blade, neon orange motor & rollers, yellow base, "MHC67" & "Hero City" tempa ($2-4)(MW67/2003 US)

MB37-J SEAPLANE *see MB42-F*

MB37-K AUDI TT ROADSTER *see MB 4-G*

MB38-A HONDA MOTORCYCLE & TRAILER, issued 1970 (MB838)

NOTE: Below models with wire wheels on motorcycle, black kickstand & England casting.

1. metallic blue cycle, light yellow trailer, "Honda" labels, 5 spoke wheels ($15-18)
2. metallic purple cycle, light yellow trailer, "Honda" labels, 5 spoke wheels ($20-30)
3. pink cycle, light yellow trailer, "Honda" labels, 5 spoke wheels ($20-30)
4. metallic blue-green cycle, orange trailer, no labels, 5 spoke center cut wheels ($5-7)(TP)
5. metallic blue-green cycle, orange trailer, "Honda" labels, 5 spoke center cut wheels ($5-7)(TP)
6. metallic blue-green cycle, dark yellow trailer, no labels, 5 spoke center cut wheels ($5-7)(TP)
7. metallic blue-green cycle, dark yellow trailer, "Honda" labels, 5 spoke center cut wheels ($5-7)(TP)

MB38-B STINGEROO, issued 1973

NOTE: Below models with chrome plastic engine & plastic base, white horse head, 5 spoke rear wheels & solid black front wheels & England casting unless otherwise noted.

1. purple body, chrome handlebars ($350-400)
2. purple body, purple handlebars ($15-18)
3. purple body, blue-gray handlebars ($18-25)
4. metallic magenta body, purple handlebars, Manaus label on base ($250+)(BR)

MB38-C JEEP, issued 1976

NOTE: Below models with black interior, 5 crown wheels, metal base & England casting unless otherwise noted.

1. olive body, black base, star label, no gun or roof cast, black hubs ($18-25)(TP)
2. olive drab body, black base, "21 * 11" label, no gun or roof cast, black hubs ($65-80)(TP)
3. olive body, black base, "21 * 11" label, no gun or roof cast, black hubs ($8-12)(TP)
4. olive body, black base, star label gun cast, black hubs ($8-12)
5. olive body, black base, "21 * 11" label, gun cast, silver hubs ($8-12)
6. olive body, black base, "21 * 11" label, gun cast, black hubs ($5-7)
7. green body, black base, no label, gun cast, silver hubs ($150-225)(BR)
8. green body, charcoal base with Manaus tab "21* 11" label, gun cast, silver hubs ($150-225)(BR)
9. yellow body, black base, "Gliding Club" label, no gun or roof cast, silver hubs ($8-12)(TP)
10. yellow body, black base, "Gliding Club" label, no gun or roof cast, black hubs ($8-12)(TP)
11. red body, black base, "Gliding Club" label, no gun or roof cast, silver hubs ($500-750)(TP)
12. blue body, white base, "U.S. Mail" tempa, white roof, silver hubs ($6-8)
13. powder blue body, white base, "U.S. Mail" tempa, white roof, silver hubs ($8-12)

NOTE: All models have "No. 38 Jeep" cast on base.

MB38-D FORD CAMPER, issued 1980

NOTE: Below models with dot dash wheels, unpainted metal base & England casting. All versions except #1 with "No. 38" cast on base.

1. orange-red body, green cab windows, beige camper, amber camper windows, "No. 35" cast on base ($50-75)
2. orange-red body, green cab windows, beige camper, amber camper windows ($50-75)
3. orange-red body, green cab windows, beige camper, no camper windows ($4-6)
4. orange-red body, blue-green cab windows, beige camper, no camper windows ($4-6)
5. red body, blue-green cab windows, beige camper, no camper windows ($4-6)
6. red body, green cab windows, beige camper, no camper windows ($4-6)

MB38-E MODEL A FORD VAN, issued 1982 (MB038)
MB76-C MODEL A FORD VAN, reissued 1998 (USA)

NOTE: Below models with clear windows, black sub base,, chrome grille & 5 crown front & dot dash rear wheels unless otherwise noted.

1. blue body, black chassis, white roof, amber windows, "Champion" labels, England casting ($5-7)
2. blue body, black chassis, white roof, "Champion" labels, England casting ($5-7)

NOTE: Below models below with Macau base unless otherwise noted.

3. blue body, black chassis, white roof, "Champion" labels ($4-6)
4. blue body, black chassis, white roof, "Kellogg's" labels ($7-10)(UK)(OP)
5. blue body, black chassis, white roof, "Matchbox On The Move in 84" labels ($20-40)(US)
6. blue body, black chassis, white roof, "Matchbox On The Move in 84" labels with "Toy Fair 84" roof label ($20-40)(US)
7. white body, blue chassis, red roof, "Pepsi" with "Come Alive" tempa ($7-10)
8. white body, blue chassis, red roof, "Pepsi" without "Come Alive" tempa ($4-6)
9. white body, blue chassis, red roof, "Matchbox USA" labels ($20-35)(US)
10. white body, blue chassis, red roof, "Ben Franklin" labels ($500-700)(US)
11. red body, black chassis, black roof, "Arnotts Biscuits" tempa ($7-10)(AU)
12. gray body, red chassis, red roof, "Tittensor First School" tempa ($5-8)(UK)
13. beige body, brown chassis, brown roof, "Larklane Motor Museum" tempa ($5-8)(UK)
14. dark blue body, black chassis, red roof, "Bass Museum" tempa ($5-8)(UK)
15. yellow body, green chassis, green roof, "Toy Collectors Pocket Guide" tempa ($6-8)(UK)
16. white body, black chassis, black roof, "The Australian" tempa ($6-8)(AU)
17. olive body, black chassis, black roof, "BBC 1925" tempa ($6-8)(UK)
18. dark blue body, black chassis, black roof, "Matchbox Speedshop" with yellow pinstriping tempa, 5 arch front & chromed racing special rear wheels ($75-100)
19. dark blue body, black chassis, black roof, "Matchbox Speedshop" with yellow pinstriping tempa, 5 arch front & unchromed racing special rear wheels ($1-2)
20. dark blue body, black chassis, black roof, "Matchbox Speedshop" with orange pinstriping tempa, 5 arch front & unchromed racing special rear wheels ($1-2)
21. cream body, black chassis, green roof, "H.H. Brain" tempa ($18-25)(UK)(OP)
22. powder blue body, dark blue chassis, red roof, "Isle of Man TT86" tempa ($5-7)(UK)
23. dark green body, black chassis, dark green roof, "Weetabix/Sanitarium Food" tempa ($7-10)(AU)(OP)
24. dark blue body, red chassis, white roof, "Smiths Potato Crisps" tempa ($7-10)(AU)(OP)
25. black body, red chassis, red roof, "Isle of Man TT87" tempa ($5-7)(UK)
26. dark yellow body, blue chassis, blue roof, "Junior Matchbox Club" tempa ($6-8)(CN)
27. black body, black chassis, black roof, "2nd M.I.C.A. Convention" decals ($375-450)(UK)
28. white body, black chassis, black roof, "Chesty Bonds" tempa ($5-7)(AU)
29. red body, black chassis, black roof, "I.O.M. Post Office" tempa ($6-8)(UK)
30. blue body, black chassis, black roof, "Silvo" tempa ($7-10)(UK)
31. red body, black chassis, black roof, "W.H. Smith & Sons" tempa ($18-25)(UK)(OP)

32. red body, black chassis, black roof, "Dewhurst Master Butcher" tempa ($8-12)(UK)
33. dark olive body, red chassis, red roof, "John West Salmon" tempa ($8-12)(AU)(OP)
34. light blue body, black chassis, white roof, "Kellogg's Rice Krispies" labels ($8-12)(UK)(OP)
35. dark blue body, black chassis, red roof, "Matchbox- This Van Delivers" with phone # on doors tempa ($12-18)(UK)
36. dark blue body, black chassis, red roof, "Matchbox- This Van Delivers" without phone # on doors tempa ($60-75)(HK)
37. red body, black chassis, black roof, gold grille, "Royal Mail" tempa ($6-8)(UK)(MP)
38. orange body, black chassis, black roof, "North America M.I.C.A. Convention 1988" tempa ($6-8)(US)
39. yellow body, black chassis, red roof, "Isle of Man TT88" tempa ($5-7)(UK)
40. yellow body, yellow chassis, red roof, "3rd M.I.C.A. Convention" tempa ($8-12)(UK)
41. yellow body, dark blue chassis, white roof, "James Neale & Sons" tempa ($8-12)(UK)
42. red body, black chassis, black roof, "I.O.M. Post Office" with phone # on rear doors tempa ($6-8)(UK)
43. red body, black chassis, black roof, "Manx Cattery" labels ($12-15)(UK)
44. red body, black chassis, black roof, "Mervyn Wynne" labels ($12-15)(UK)
45. dark orange body, black chassis, black roof, "P.M.G." tempa ($7-10)(AU)
46. red body, black chassis, black roof, "Alex Munro Master Butcher" tempa ($8-12)(UK)
47. red body, black chassis, black roof, "Rayner's Crusha" tempa ($8-12)(UK)(OP)
48. red body, greenish black chassis, black roof, "Rayner's Crusha" tempa ($8-12)(UK)(OP)
49. powder blue body, dark gray chassis, dark gray roof, "Chester Heraldry Centre" tempa ($6-8)(UK)
50. yellow body, black chassis, red roof, "Barratt's Sherbet" tempa ($10-15)(UK)(OP)
51. blue body, black chassis, blue roof, "Guernsey Post" tempa ($5-7)(UK)
52. dark green body, black chassis, black roof, "Historical Collection/ Powerhouse" tempa ($6-8)(AU)
53. dark green body, greenish black chassis, black roof, "Historical Collection/ Powerhouse" tempa ($6-8)(AU)
54. brown body, black chassis, black roof, "Cobb of Knightsbridge" tempa ($7-10)(UK)
55. red body, black chassis, black roof, "Big Sister" tempa ($6-8)(AU)(OP)
56. powder blue body dark gray roof & chassis, "Chester Toy Museum" labels ($6-8)(UK)
57. green body, black chassis, yellow roof, "Rowntree's Table Jelly" tempa ($8-12)(UK)(OP)
58. blue body, silver-gray chassis, gray roof, "Nat West Action Bank" tempa ($6-8)(UK)
59. black body, light maroon chassis, red roof, "Uniroyal Royal Care" tempa ($18-25)(CN)
60. yellow body, black chassis, black roof, "Matchbox Series Model A Ford Van" tempa ($2-3)
61. yellow body, black chassis, black roof, 5 arch front wheels, "Matchbox Series Model A Ford Van" tempa ($2-3)
62. light yellow body, black chassis, black roof, "W.H. Smith & Sons" tempa ($12-15)(UK)
63. dark green body, dark green chassis & roof, "Green's Sponge Mixture" tempa ($8-12)(UK)(OP)
64. olive green body, red-brown chassis & roof, black grille & hubs, "Aldershot- 4th M.I.C.A. Convention" tempa ($8-10)(UK)
65. black body, orange chassis, orange roof, "2nd M.I.C.A. NA Convention 1989" tempa ($6-8)(US)
66. yellow body, blue chassis, blue roof, "Welcome Ye To Chester" labels ($15-20)(UK)(C2)
67. dark blue body, black chassis, black roof, "Cheeses of England & Wales" tempa ($10-15)(UK)(OP)
68. cream body, red chassis, red roof, "Isle of Man TT89" tempa ($5-7)(UK)
69. cream body, black chassis, black roof, "Jordan's" tempa ($10-15)(UK)(OP)
70. dark blue body, black chassis, black roof, "Ribena" tempa ($8-12)(UK)
71. yellow body, red chassis, red roof, "Barratt's Sherbet" tempa ($8-12)(UK)
72. yellow body, black chassis, black roof, "Barratt's Sherbet" tempa ($8-12)(UK)
73. light blue body, blue chassis, blue roof, "Junior Matchbox Club- The Gang" tempa ($6-8)(CN)
74. dark blue body, cream chassis & roof , "Lightwater Theme Park Valley" tempa ($6-8)(UK)
75. red body, blue chassis, blue roof, "Tandy Electronics" tempa ($12-15)(AU)
76. light gray body, dark gray chassis, dark gray roof, "Moorland Centre" tempa ($6-8)(UK)
77. black body, orange chassis, orange roof, "Baltimore Orioles 1989" tempa ($6-8)(WR)
78. yellow body, dark green chassis & roof, "York Fair 1989" tempa ($6-8)(WR)
79. silver body, silver chassis, black roof, "Matchbox Collectors Club 1989" labels ($125-150)(C2)
80. white body, red chassis, blue roof, "Ten Years Lion" tempa ($7-10)(UK)
81. white body, black chassis, black roof, "Jacky Maeder" tempa ($8-12)(SW)
82. cream body, brown chassis, brown roof, "Johnson's Seeds" tempa ($8-12)(UK)(OP)
83. red body, red chassis, red roof, "Asda Baked Beans" tempa ($7-10)(UK)(OP)
84. dark blue body, dark blue chassis & roof, "Matchbox 40th Anniversary 1990" ($7-10)(US)
85. white body, blue chassis, white roof, "New York Yankees 1990" tempa ($3-5)(WR)
86. white body, blue chassis, white roof, "Los Angeles Dodgers 1990" tempa ($3-5)(WR)
87. white body, blue chassis, white roof, "Texas Rangers 1990" tempa ($3-5)(WR)
88. white body, blue chassis, white roof, "Chicago White Sox 1990" tempa ($3-5)(WR)
89. white body, blue chassis, white roof, "Houston Astros 1990" tempa ($3-5)(WR)
90. white body, blue chassis, white roof, "Atlanta Braves 1990" tempa ($3-5)(WR)
91. white body, blue chassis, white roof, "Cleveland Indians 1990" tempa ($3-5)(WR)
92. white body, blue chassis, white roof, "New York Mets 1990" tempa ($3-5)(WR)
93. white body, blue chassis, white roof, "Minnesota Twins 1990" tempa ($3-5)(WR)
94. white body, blue chassis, white roof, "Toronto Blue Jays 1990" tempa ($3-5)(WR)
95. white body, mid blue base, white roof, "Milwaukee Brewers 1990" tempa ($3-5)(WR)

96. white body, mid blue base, red roof, "Chicago Cubs 1990" tempa ($3-5)(WR)
97. white body, blue chassis, orange roof, "Detroit Tigers 1990" tempa ($3-5)(WR)
98. white body, blue chassis, yellow roof, "Mariners 1990" tempa ($3-5)(WR)
99. white body, red chassis, white roof, "Boston Red Sox 1990" tempa ($3-5)(WR)
100. white body, red chassis, white roof, "Cincinnati Reds 1990" tempa ($3-5)(WR)
101. white body, red chassis, white roof, "St. Louis Cardinals 1990" tempa ($3-5)(WR)
102. white body, red chassis, white roof, "Montreal Expos 1990" tempa ($3-5)(WR)
103. white body, red chassis, yellow roof, "California Angels 1990" tempa ($3-5)(WR)
104. white body, maroon chassis, white roof, "Philadelphia Phillies 1990" tempa ($3-5)(WR)
105. white body, black chassis, white roof, "San Francisco Giants 1990" tempa ($3-5)(WR)
106. white body, black chassis & roof, "Pittsburgh Pirates 1990" tempa ($3-5)(WR)
107. white body, brown chassis, orange roof, "San Diego Padres 1990" tempa ($3-5)(WR)
108. powder blue body, blue chassis, white roof, "Kansas City Royals 1990" tempa ($3-5)(WR)
109. black body, orange chassis, black roof, "Baltimore Orioles 1990" tempa ($3-5)(WR)
110. yellow body, green chassis, white roof, "Oakland A's 1990" tempa ($3-5)(WR)
111. yellow body, red chassis, red roof, "Pava" tempa ($8-12)(DK)
112. dark blue body, black chassis, black roof, "Swarfega" tempa ($18-25)(UK)(OP)
113. dark blue body, black chassis, black roof, "Kellogg's Rice Krispies" tempa ($4-6)(US)(OP)
114. dark green body, dark green chassis & roof, "Carmelle" tempa ($15-20)(SU)
115. dark blue body, black chassis, black roof, "Lyceum Theatre" tempa ($6-8)(UK)
116. light blue body, black chassis, white roof, "Fresh Dairy Cream" tempa ($8-12)(UK)(OP)
117. yellow body, red chassis, red roof, "Drink Coca Cola" with brown bottles tempa ($7-10)(CN)
118. yellow body, red chassis, red roof, "Drink Coca Cola" with red bottles tempa ($8-12)(SW)
119. yellow body, dark green chassis & roof, "Drink Coca Cola" tempa ($7-10)(CN)
120. white body, maroon chassis, white roof, "Matchbox USA 9th Annual Convention 1990" tempa ($8-10)
121. blue body, red chassis, yellow roof, "Isle of Man TT90" tempa ($5-7)(UK)
122. florescent green body, florescent orange chassis, black roof, "Matchbox Collectors Club 1990" labels ($85-110)(C2)
123. dark blue body, white chassis, white roof, "Penn State 1990" tempa ($6-8)(WR)
124. white body, dark blue chassis, dark blue roof, "Penn State 1990" tempa ($6-8)(WR)
125. cream body, red chassis, red roof, "York Fair 1990- 225 Years" tempa ($5-7)(WR)
126. white body, navy blue chassis, orange roof, "Bears 1990" tempa ($3-5)(WR)
127. white body, blue chassis, blue roof, "Colts 1990" tempa ($3-5)(WR)
128. white body, green chassis, green roof, "Jets 1990" tempa ($3-5)(WR)
129. white body, red-brown chassis, maroon roof, "Cardinals 1990" tempa ($3-5)(WR)
130. white body, red chassis, lemon roof, "KC Chiefs 1990" tempa ($3-5)(WR)
131. navy blue body, yellow chassis, white roof, "Chargers 1990" tempa ($3-5)(WR)
132. blue body, white chassis, white roof, "Giants 1990" tempa ($3-5)(WR)
133. blue body, red chassis, white roof, "Bills 1990" tempa ($3-5)(WR)
134. bright blue body, red chassis, bright blue roof, "Oilers 1990" tempa ($3-5)(WR)
135. silver-gray body, blue chassis, white roof, "Seahawks 1990" tempa ($3-5)(WR)
136. silver-gray body, light blue chassis, white roof, "Lions 1990" tempa ($3-5)(WR)
137. silver-gray body, navy blue chassis, & roof, "Cowboys 1990" tempa ($3-5)(WR)
138. silver-gray body, black chassis, black roof, "Raiders 1990" tempa ($3-5)(WR)
139. silver-gray body, green chassis, white roof, "Eagles 1990" tempa ($3-5)(WR)
140. green-gold body, black chassis, white roof, "Saints 1990" tempa ($3-5)(WR)
141. gold body, red chassis, white roof, "49ers 1990" tempa ($3-5)(WR)
142. red body, black chassis, light gray roof, "Falcons 1990" tempa ($3-5)(WR)
143. red body, white chassis, blue roof, "Patriots 1990" tempa ($3-5)(WR)
144. red-brown body, lemon chassis, white roof, "Redskins 1990" tempa ($3-5)(WR)
145. dark orange body, brown chassis, white roof, "Browns 1990" tempa ($3-5)(WR)
146. dark orange body, blue chassis, orange roof, "Broncos 1990" tempa ($3-5)(WR)
147. light orange body, black chassis, black roof, "Buccaneers 1990" tempa ($3-5)(WR)
148. blue-green body, orange chassis, white roof, "Dolphins 1990" tempa ($3-5)(WR)
149. olive body, lemon chassis, white roof, "Packers 1990" tempa ($3-5)(WR)
150. yellow body, blue chassis, yellow roof, "Rams 1990" tempa ($3-5)(WR)
151. yellow body, black chassis, yellow roof, "Steelers 1990" tempa ($3-5)(WR)
152. black body, dark orange chassis, white roof, "Bengals 1990" tempa ($3-5)(WR)
153. purple body, purple chassis, yellow roof, "Vikings 1990" tempa, ($3-5)(WR)
154. metallic green body & chassis, green roof, "Canada Dry" tempa ($8-12)(CN)
155. dark blue body, black chassis, black roof, "Kellogg's Rice Krispies" tempa, Thailand casting ($4-6)(US)(OP)
156. cream body, green chassis, green roof, "William Lusty" tempa ($6-8)(UK)
157. dark plum body, black chassis, black roof, "Johnnie Walker" tempa ($18-25)(UK)(OP)
158. blue body, black chassis, blue roof, "Mitre 10" tempa ($7-10)(AU)
159. orange-red body, black chassis, black roof, "Tyne Brand" tempa ($12-15)(UK)(OP)
160. dark blue body, black chassis, black roof, "Tyne Brand" tempa ($12-15)(UK)(OP)

161. cream body, green chassis, red roof, "PG Tips" tempa ($12-15)(UK)(OP)
162. powder blue body, dark gray chassis & roof, "Open Every Day" tempa on doors, plain main panel ($12-15)(MP)
163. dark blue body, black chassis, black roof, "Kellogg's Rice Krispies" tempa, China casting ($4-6)(US)(OP)
164. white body, black chassis, black roof, "Rutter Bros. Dairy" tempa ($6-8)(WR)
165. dark blue body, black chassis, white roof, "Lyons Tea" tempa ($6-8)(UK)

NOTE: Below models with China casting unless otherwise noted.

166. yellow body, black chassis, black roof, black grille, "Matchbox Dinky Toy Convention 1991" ($8-12)(UK)
167. white body, red chassis, dark blue roof, "Indians 1991" tempa ($3-5)(WR)
168. white body, red chassis, dark blue roof, "Yankees 1991" tempa ($3-5)(WR)
169. white body, red chassis, white roof, "Cardinals 1991" tempa ($3-5)(WR)
170. white body, yellow chassis, white roof, "Brewers 1991" tempa ($3-5)(WR)
171. white body, black chassis, dark gray roof, "White Sox 1991" tempa ($3-5)(WR)
172. lemon body, blue chassis, mid blue roof, "Mariners 1991" tempa ($3-5)(WR)
173. orange-yellow body, red chassis, dark blue roof, "Angels 1991" tempa ($3-5)(WR)
174. orange body, black chassis, white roof, "Orioles 1991" tempa ($3-5)(WR)
175. orange body, blue chassis, white roof, "Mets 1991" tempa ($3-5)(WR)
176. orange body, dark blue chassis, orange-yellow roof, "Astros 1991" tempa ($3-5)(WR)
177. red body, blue chassis, white roof, "Rangers 1991" tempa ($3-5)(WR)
178. red body, white chassis, white roof, "Cubs 1991" tempa ($3-5)(WR)
179. red body, red chassis, white roof, "Reds 1991" tempa ($3-5)(WR)
180. dark maroon body & chassis, white roof, "Phillies 1991" tempa ($3-5)(WR)
181. dark blue body, red chassis, white roof, "Red Sox 1991" tempa ($3-5)(WR)
182. dark blue body, red chassis, white roof, "Twins 1991" tempa ($3-5)(WR)
183. blue body, red chassis, white roof, "Braves 1991" tempa ($3-5)(WR)
184. blue body, baby blue chassis, white roof, "Royals 1991" tempa ($3-5)(WR)
185. medium blue body, blue chassis, white roof, "Blue Jays 1991" tempa ($3-5)(WR)
186. baby blue body, red chassis, white roof, "Expos 1991" tempa ($3-5)(WR)
187. pearly silver body, blue chassis, orange roof, "Dodgers 1991" tempa ($3-5)(WR)
188. pearly silver body, dark blue chassis, orange roof, "Padres 1991" tempa ($3-5)(WR)
189. silver-gray body, dark blue chassis, orange roof, "Tigers 1991" tempa ($3-5)(WR)
190. lavender gray body, black chassis, orange roof, "Giants 1991" tempa ($3-5)(WR)
191. black body, yellow chassis, white roof, "Pirates 1991" tempa ($3-5)(WR)
192. green body, yellow chassis, white roof, "Athletics 1991" tempa ($3-5)(WR)
193. powder blue body, blue chassis, red roof, gold grille, "Isle of Man TT91" tempa ($5-7)(UK)
194. orange-yellow body, black chassis, black roof, "Celebrating A Decade of Matchbox Conventions 1991" tempa ($8-10)(US)
195. white body, dark pink chassis, black roof, "Matchbox Collectors Club 1991" labels, Macau casting ($60-75)(C2)
196. chrome plated body, red chassis, red roof, "15th Anniversary Matchbox USA 1991" tempa, Macau casting ($35-50)(C2)
197. light yellow body, light blue chassis & roof, "Dairylea" tempa ($15-20)(UK)(OP)
198. white body, white chassis & sub-base, white roof & grille, no tempa ($10-15)(GF)
199. yellow body, green chassis, white roof, "Notre Dame 1991" tempa ($5-7)(WR)
200. silver-gray body, red chassis, white roof, "UNLV 1991" tempa ($5-7)(WR)
201. white body, blue chassis, blue roof, "Rugby Child Development Centre" tempa ($7-10)(UK)
202. dark plum body, black chassis, black roof, "Johnnie Walker" tempa, Thailand casting ($18-25)(UK)
203. red body, black chassis, black roof, "Mervyn Wynne" with black island on doors tempa, Macau casting ($18-25)(UK)
204. silver-gray body, turquoise chassis & roof, "York Fair 1991" tempa ($6-8)(WR)

NOTE: Football set models for 1991 have roof blades cast with labels applied.

205. lemon body, maroon chassis, maroon roof, "Redskins 1991" tempa ($3-5)(WR)
206. lemon body, red chassis, white roof, "Chiefs 1991" tempa ($3-5)(WR)
207. yellow body, navy blue chassis, navy blue roof, "Chargers 1991" tempa ($3-5)(WR)
208. yellow body, black chassis, black roof, "Steelers 1991" ($3-5)(WR)
209. yellow body, dark blue chassis, dark blue roof, "Rams 1991" tempa ($3-5)(WR)
210. lemon body, purple chassis, purple roof, "Vikings 1991" tempa ($3-5)(WR)
211. orange body, blue-green chassis & roof, "Dolphins 1991" tempa ($3-5)(WR)
212. dark orange body, dark blue chassis & roof, "Broncos 1991" tempa ($3-5)(WR)
213. dark orange body, black chassis, black roof, "Bengals 1991" tempa ($3-5)(WR)
214. light orange body, red chassis, white roof, "Buccaneers 1991" tempa ($3-5)(WR)
215. white body, dark orange chassis, navy blue roof, "Bears 1991" tempa ($3-5)(WR)
216. white body, dull green chassis & roof, "Jets 1991" tempa ($3-5)(WR)
217. white body, dark blue chassis, red roof, "Bills 1991" tempa ($3-5)(WR)
218. white body, dark blue chassis & roof, "Giants 1991" tempa ($3-5)(WR)
219. white body, green-gold chassis, black roof, "Saints 1991" tempa ($3-5)(WR)
220. blue body, silver-gray chassis, white roof, "Lions 1991" tempa ($3-5)(WR)
221. bright blue body, red chassis, white roof, "Oilers 1991" tempa ($3-5)(WR)
222. red body, black chassis, black roof, "Falcons 1991" tempa ($3-5)(WR)
223. red body, gold chassis, gold roof, "49ers 1991" tempa ($3-5)(WR)
224. maroon body, white chassis, white roof, "Cardinals 1991" tempa ($3-5)(WR)

225. brown body, brown chassis, orange roof, "Browns 1991" tempa ($3-5)(WR)
226. black body, silver-gray chassis, white roof, "Raiders 1991" tempa ($3-5)(WR)
227. dark blue body, green chassis, white roof, "Seahawks 1991" tempa ($3-5)(WR)
228. dark blue body, white chassis, white roof, "Colts 1991" tempa ($3-5)(WR)
229. dark blue body, red chassis, red roof, "Patriots 1991" tempa ($3-5)(WR)
230. navy blue body, silver-gray chassis, purple-blue roof, "Cowboys 1991" tempa ($3-5)(WR)
231. olive body, yellow chassis, yellow roof, "Packers 1991" tempa ($3-5)(WR)
232. silver-gray body, green chassis, green roof, "Eagles 1991" tempa ($3-5)(WR)
233. orange-yellow body, purple chassis, white roof, "University of Washington 1992" tempa ($4-6)(WR)
234. dark yellow body, black chassis, white roof, "University of Colorado 1992" tempa ($4-6)(WR)
235. yellow body, navy blue chassis, yellow roof, "University of Michigan 1992" tempa ($4-6)(WR)
236. dark orange body, blue chassis, white roof, "Clemson University 1992" tempa ($4-6)(WR)
237. dark orange body, blue chassis, white roof, "Syracuse University 1992" tempa ($4-6)(WR)
238. white body, dark blue chassis, dark blue roof, "Penn State 1991" tempa ($6-8)(WR)

NOTE: Following models with Thailand casting unless otherwise noted. The 1992 hockey set models is only available as paired editions. ($10-15) per pair (WR)

239. red body, blue chassis, white roof, "Canadiennes (logo) 1917" tempa
240. white body, red chassis, white roof, "Canadiennes (logo) 1992" tempa
241. black body, red chassis, white roof, "Chicago Black Hawks 1917" tempa
242. white body, black chassis, white roof, Indian's head (Black Hawk logo) "1992" tempa
243. tan body, brown chassis, white roof, "Boston Bruins 1917" tempa
244. black body, yellow chassis, white roof, Bruin's logo & "1992" tempa
245. red body, white chassis, white roof, Redwings logo & "1917" tempa
246. white body, red chassis, white roof, Redwings logo & "1992" tempa
247. bright red body, red chassis, white roof, "Rangers 1917" tempa
248. white body, bright blue chassis, white roof, "New York Rangers 1992" tempa
249. navy blue body, white chassis, white roof, "Toronto Maple Leafs 1917" tempa
250. white body, blue chassis, white roof, "Toronto Maple Leafs 1992" tempa

NOTE: Following models with China casting unless otherwise noted. #251- 256 sold only as a set ($30-40)(AU)

251. lime body, black chassis, black roof, "Milo" tempa
252. red body, black chassis, black roof, "Uncle Toby's" tempa
253. dark blue body, black chassis, black roof, "IXL" tempa
254. orange body, black chassis, black roof, "Billy Tea" tempa
255. beige body, black chassis, black roof, "Aeroplane Jelly" tempa
256. dark purple body, black chassis, black roof, "Violet Crumble" tempa
257. powder blue body & chassis, white roof, "North Carolina 1992" tempa ($4-6)(WR)
258. white body, orange chassis, white roof, "Tennessee Vol. 1992" tempa ($4-6)(WR)
259. white body, blue chassis, blue roof, "Camperdown Cumberland" tempa ($10-15)(AU)
260. white body, white chassis, white roof, amber windows, no tempa, Thailand casting ($10-15)(GF)
261. brown body, black chassis, black roof, "Cobb of Knightsbridge" tempa, Thailand casting ($8-12)(UK)
262. white body, black chassis, red roof, "Big Ben" tempa ($6-8)(AU)
263. white body, white chassis, white roof, "Matthew Walker" tempa ($8-12)(UK)
264. red body, black chassis, black roof, "McVities Digestive" tempa ($12-15)(UK)(OP)
265. orange-yellow body, green chassis, green roof, "1st M.I.C.A. Australia Convention 1992" tempa ($8-12)(AU)
266. red body, black chassis, black roof, "Pritt Stick" tempa ($7-10)(UK)(OP)
267. black body, black chassis, black roof, "City Ford" tempa, China casting ($7-10)(AU)
268. orange body, black chassis, black roof, "P.M.G." tempa ($8-12)(AU)
269. brass plated body, black chassis, black roof, "Matchbox Collectors Club 1992" tempa ($40-65)(C2)
270. pale gray body, brown chassis, brown roof, "Yardley" tempa ($8-12)(UK)
271. white body, white chassis, white roof, no tempa ($10-15)(GF)

NOTE: Following models with Thailand casting unless otherwise noted.

272. orange body, black chassis, black roof, "Philadelphia Flyers 1993" tempa ($6-8)(WR)
273. black body, silver-gray chassis & roof, "LA Kings 1993" tempa ($6-8)(WR)
274. white body, red chassis, blue roof, "Washington Capitals 1993" tempa ($6-8)(WR)
275. white body, metallic turquoise chassis, black roof, "San Jose Sharks 1993" tempa ($6-8)(WR)

NOTE: Versions #276-281 sold only as a set ($35-40)(AU)

276. purple body, black chassis, black roof, "Tyrrells Dry Red" tempa
277. red body, black chassis, black roof, "McWilliams Cream Sherry" tempa
278. brown body, black chassis, black roof, "Yalumba Port" tempa
279. blue body, black chassis, black roof, "Houghton White Burgundy" tempa
280. green body, black chassis, black roof, "Penfold's" tempa
281. black body, black chassis, black roof, "Hardy's Black Bottle" tempa
282. dark green body, dark green chassis, black roof, "Selfridge & Co." tempa, China casting ($5-7)(UK)
283. green body, green chassis, green roof, "William Lusty" tempa, China casting ($6-8)(UK)
284. yellow body, greenish black chassis, black roof, "Matchbox Series Model A Ford Van" tempa ($2-3)
285. yellow body, black chassis, black roof, "Matchbox Series Model A Ford Van" tempa ($2-3)
286. red body, white chassis, white roof, "Vileda" tempa, China casting ($8-12)(UK)(OP)
287. dark blue body, white chassis, red roof, "Dale Farms" tempa, China casting ($6-8)(UK)
288. cream body, red chassis, red roof, "Indiana Hoosiers 1993" tempa, China casting ($4-6)(WR)
289. red body, yellow chassis, dark blue roof, "8th MICA Event" tempa, China casting ($10-15)(UK)

290. red body, yellow chassis, black roof, "1st MICA European Convention", China casting ($12-18)(GR)
291. black body, black chassis, black roof, "Gowings" tempa, China casting ($8-12)(AU)
292. white body, red chassis, black roof, "Georgia" tempa, China casting ($4-6)(WR)
293. black body, green chassis, green roof, "Matchbox Collectors Club 1993" labels, China casting ($15-25)(C2)
294. green body, red chassis, red roof, "Merry Christmas 1993" labels, China casting ($25-45)(C2)
295. cream body, blue chassis, green roof with blade, "York Fair 1993" tempa, China casting ($4-6)(WR)
296. dark cream body, blue chassis, cream roof, "Pure Cod Liver Oil" tempa, Thailand casting ($4-6)(GS)
297. green body, blue chassis, green roof, "Vicks" tempa, Thailand casting ($4-6)(GS)
298. blue body, dark blue chassis, blue roof, "Milk of Magnesia" tempa, Thailand casting ($4-6)(GS)
299. red body, dark blue chassis, red roof, "Tiger Balm" tempa, Thailand casting ($4-6)(GS)
300. dark blue body, dark blue chassis, dark blue roof, "Alka-Seltzer" tempa, Thailand casting ($4-6)(GS)
301. tan body, brown chassis, tan roof, "Bayer Aspirin" tempa, Thailand casting ($4-6)(GS)
302. yellow body, red chassis, yellow roof, "Vegemite" tempa, Thailand casting ($7-10) (AU)
303. lime body, orange chassis, orange roof, "True Value Hardware" tempa, Thailand casting ($7-10)(AU)
304. maroon body, beige chassis, beige roof, "Automodel Exchange" tempa, Thailand casting ($7-10)(AU)
305. maroon body, maroon chassis, white roof, "Matchbox 1991" labels, China casting ($50-75)(CHI)
306. blue body, light blue chassis, white roof, "Matchbox 1991" labels, China casting ($50-75)(CHI)
307. orange body, black chassis, white roof, "Matchbox 1991" labels, China casting ($50-75)(CHI)
308. white body, red chassis, blue roof, "Matchbox 1991" labels, China casting ($50-75)(CHI)
309. green body, yellow chassis, white roof, "Matchbox 1991" labels, China casting ($50-75)(CHI)
310. silver-gray body, black chassis, orange roof, "Matchbox 1991" labels, China casting ($50-75)(CHI)

NOTE: 305-310 are relabeled at the Chinese factory over baseball vans and issued on the Chinese market. These 6 are confirmed with 22 more possible versions!

311. white body, red chassis, powder blue roof, "Ironbridge Telford 1994- MICA 9" tempa, Thailand casting ($12-15)(UK)
312. white body, red chassis, lime roof, "Dusseldorf Deutschland 94" tempa, Thailand casting ($12-15)(GR)
313. fluorescent orange & yellow body, yellow chassis, orange roof, "Get In The Fast Lane Matchbox" tempa, Thailand casting ($7-10)(US)
314. black body, maroon chassis, maroon roof, "Hershey, Penn.- MICA 7" labels, Macau casting ($12-15)(C2)
315. green body, green chassis, green roof, "Young's Sheep Dips" tempa, Thailand casting ($7-10)(AU)
316. beige body, blue chassis, blue roof, kangaroo & MICA logo tempa, Macau casting (base secured by screws) ($90-125)(AU)(C2)
317. tan body, blue chassis, blue roof, kangaroo & MICA logo tempa, Thailand casting ($7-10)(AU)

NOTE: Versions 318-323 only available as a set ($25-35)

318. cream body, red chassis, red roof, "Gerry Cottle's Circus" tempa, Thailand casting
319. white body, red chassis, blue roof, "Circus Barum" tempa, Thailand casting
320. yellow body, red chassis, red roof, "Circus Oz" tempa, Thailand casting
321. red body, black chassis, red roof, "Circus Krone" tempa, Thailand casting
322. red body, black chassis, black roof, "Chipperfield's Circus" tempa, Thailand casting
323. blue body, blue chassis, blue roof, "Big Apple Circus" tempa, Thailand casting
324. metallic gold body, green chassis, green roof, "Matchbox Collectors Club Christmas 1994", Thailand casting ($5-7)(US)
325. white body, red chassis, white roof, "Hansell's" tempa, Thailand casting($7-10)(AU)(OP)
326. white body, black chassis, red roof, "Matchbox" tempa , Thailand casting ($20-30)(AU)
327. gold body, black chassis, black roof, "Memories 1993" tempa, Macau casting ($400-600)(C2)

NOTE: Below models below with Thailand casting unless noted.

328. brown body, cocoa brown chassis, white roof, "Matchbox & Lesney Toy Museum" tempa, 5 crown rear wheels ($8-12)(US)
329. cocoa brown body, black chassis, cocoa brown roof, "Beechworth Bakery" tempa, ($5-7)(AU)
330. cocoa brown body, black chassis, yellow roof, "Beechworth Bakery" ($15-25)(AU)
331. silver-gray body, black chassis, black roof, "10th MICA Convention" tempa ($8-12)(UK)
332. brown body, cocoa brown chassis, white roof, "Matchbox & Lesney Toy Museum" tempa ($5-7)(US)
333. red body, black chassis, black roof, "Postes Canada Post" tempa ($5-7)(GS)
334. red body, black chassis, black roof, "De Post" tempa ($5-7)(GS)
335. orange-red body, black chassis, black roof, "Australia Post" tempa ($5-7)(GS)
336. yellow body, black chassis, white roof, "Reichspost" tempa ($5-7)(GS)
337. blue body, blue chassis, white roof, "Guernsey Post Office" tempa ($5-7)(GS)
338. white body, white chassis, white roof, "U.S. Mail" tempa ($5-7)(GS)
339. white body, red chassis, red roof, "Sydney Swans" tempa ($7-10)(AU)
340. white body, white chassis, red roof, "St. Kilda Saints" tempa ($7-10)(AU)
341. white body, blue chassis, white roof, "No. Melbourne Kangaroos" tempa ($7-10)(AU)
342. blue body, yellow chassis, blue roof, "West Coast Eagles" tempa ($7-10)(AU)
343. blue body, red chassis, blue roof, "Fitzroy Lions" tempa ($7-10)(AU)
344. blue body, red chassis, red roof, "Footscray Bulldogs" tempa ($7-10)(AU)
345. dark blue body, chassis & roof, "Carlton Blues" tempa ($7-10)(AU)
346. dark blue body, white chassis, dark blue roof, "Geelong Cats" tempa ($7-10)(AU)
347. dark blue body, red chassis, dark blue roof, "Melbourne Demons" tempa ($7-10)(AU)
348. dark blue body, red chassis, yellow roof, "Adelaide Crows" tempa ($7-10)((AU)
349. purple body, red chassis, purple roof, "Fremantle Dockers" tempa ($7-10)(AU)
350. black body, yellow chassis, black roof, "Richmond Tigers" tempa ($7-10)(AU)

351. black body, white chassis, black roof, "Collingwood Magpies" tempa ($7-10)(AU)
352. black body, red chassis, black roof, "Essendon Bombers" tempa ($7-10)(AU)
353. brown body, yellow chassis, brown roof, "Hawthorn Hawks" tempa ($7-10)(AU)
354. rose body, yellow chassis, rose roof, "Brisbane Bears" tempa ($7-10)(AU)
355. blue body, red chassis & roof, "Eastern Suburbs" tempa ($7-10)(AU)
356. blue body, red chassis & roof, "Newcastle Knights" tempa ($7-10)(AU)
357. blue body, yellow chassis, blue roof, "Parramatta Eels" tempa ($7-10)(AU)
358. dark blue body, red chassis & roof, So. Queensland Crushers" tempa ($7-10)(AU)
359. dark blue body, gray chassis & roof, "No. Queensland Cowboys" tempa ($7-10)(AU)
360. light blue body, black chassis, bright blue roof, "Cronulla Sharks" tempa ($7-10)(AU)
361. black body, red chassis, black roof, "Penrith Panthers" tempa ($7-10)(AU)
362. black body, white chassis, black roof, "Western Suburbs" tempa ($7-10(AU)
363. black body, white chassis, red roof, "No. Sydney Bears" tempa ($7-10)(AU)
364. orange body, white chassis, black roof, "Balmain Tigers" tempa ($7-10)(AU)
365. red body, white chassis & roof, "Western Reds" tempa ($7-10)(AU)
366. red body, white chassis, red roof, "Illawarra Steelers" tempa ($7-10)(AU)
367. dark red body, white chassis, dark red roof, "Sea Eagles" tempa ($7-10)(AU)
368. light plum body, white chassis, yellow roof, "Brisbane Broncos" tempa ($7-10)(AU)
369. white body, blue chassis, white roof, "C-B Bulldogs" tempa ($7-10)(AU)
370. white body, black chassis, white roof, "Gold Coast Seagulls" tempa ($7-10)(AU)
371. white body, red chassis, white roof, "St. George" tempa ($7-10)(AU)
372. green body, blue chassis & roof, "Auckland Warriors" tempa ($7-10)(AU)
373. bright green body, red chassis, bright green roof, "So. Sydney Rabbitohs" tempa ($7-10)(AU)
374. bright lime body, white chassis, blue roof, "Canberra Raiders" tempa ($7-10)(AU)
375. white body, green chassis, turquoise roof, "Gold Coast Rollers" tempa ($7-10)(AU)
376. white body, yellow chassis, white roof, "Perth Wildcats" tempa ($7-10)(AU)
377. purple body, orange-yellow chassis, white roof, "Sydney Kings" tempa ($7-10)(AU)
378. turquoise body, purple chassis, white roof, "No. Melbourne Giants" tempa ($7-10)(AU)
379. dark blue body, red chassis & roof, "Adelaide Super Sixers" tempa ($7-10)(AU)
380. dark blue & white body, red chassis & roof, "Geelong Supercats" tempa ($7-10)(AU)
381. dark blue body, red chassis & roof, "Newcastle Falcons" tempa ($7-10)(AU)
382. black body, red chassis, blue roof, "Magic" tempa ($7-10)(AU)
383. red body, yellow chassis, red roof, "Melbourne Tigers" tempa ($7-10)(AU)
384. red body, blue chassis, red roof, "Canberra Cannons" tempa ($7-10)(AU)
385. red & white body, red chassis & roof, "Illawarra Hawks" tempa ($7-10)(AU)
386. yellow body, salmon chassis, red roof, "Townsville Suns" tempa ($7-10)(AU)
387. orange-yellow body, red chassis & roof, "Tassie Devils" tempa ($7-10)(AU)
388. orange-yellow body, blue chassis, orange-yellow roof, "Brisbane Bullets" tempa ($7-10)(AU)
389. yellow body & chassis, black roof, "Matchbox For Serious Collectors" tempa ($8-12)(GR)
390. yellow body, bright blue chassis, blue roof, "RACQ 90" tempa ($10-15)(AU)
391. dark blue body, black chassis, white roof, "Kellogg's" tempa ($40-55)(SD)(OP)
392. bright orchid body, black roof & chassis, "Kellogg's Raisin Bran" tempa ($8-12)(US)(OP)
393. dark orchid body, black roof & chassis, "Kellogg's Raisin Bran" tempa ($8-12)(US)(OP)
394. orange body, black chassis & roof, "Kellogg's Frosted Mini Wheats" tempa ($8-12)(US)(OP)

NOTE: Below models with China casting, unless noted

395. red-brown body, dark cream chassis, cream roof, "XITH MICA Convention" tempa ($10-15)(UK)
396. fawn body, red chassis & roof, "Street's Ice Cream" tempa ($15-20)(AU)
397. dark blue body, red chassis, yellow roof, "Smith's Crisps" tempa ($15-20)(AU)
398. yellow body, red chassis, yellow roof, "Shell Motor Oil" tempa ($15-20)(AU)
399. cream body & chassis, red roof, "Coca Cola" tempa ($15-20)(AU)
400. violet body, dark gold chassis, violet roof, "Cadbury's Chocolate" tempa ($15-20)(AU)
401. dark orchid body, black roof & chassis, "Kellogg's Raisin Bran" tempa ($8-12)(US)(OP)
402. pale orange body, black roof & chassis, "Kellogg's Frosted Mini Wheats" tempa ($8-12)(US)(OP)
403. brown body, cocoa brown chassis, white roof, "Greater Pennsylvania Toy Show" decals, Thailand casting ($8-12)(C2)
404. brown body, cocoa brown chassis, white roof, "LaRue Bros. Auto Inc." decals, Thailand casting ($8-12)(C2)
405. white body, blue chassis & roof, "Shipyard Brewing Co.- Export Ale" tempa, rubber tires ($8-12)(MB1)(CL)
406. cream body, green chassis, dark green roof & base, "Kentucky Pride- Dixie Lexington Brewery" tempa , rubber tires($8-12)(MB2)(CL)
407. blue body, black chassis & roof, "Left Hand Brewing Co." tempa, rubber tires ($8-12)(MB3)(CL)
408. yellow body, black chassis & red roof, "Kellogg's Eggo" tempa ($10-15)(US)(OP)
409. purple body, black chassis & roof, "Continental Aero" tempa ($8-12)(US)
410. florescent orange body, blue chassis & roof, "3rd MICA Australia Convention 1996" labels, base screws ($85-110)(C2)
411. dark blue body, black chassis, yellow roof, "Sammler Treffen 1988" tempa, 5 arch front & racing special rear wheels, Macau casting ($150-250)(C2)

NOTE: This model was only just documented as a German code 2 in early 1997.

412. green body, metallic gold chassis & roof, "Fish Tales Ales" tempa, rubber tires ($8-12)(MB4)(CL)
413. blue body, blue chassis & roof, "Big Apple Circus" tempa ($5-8)(US)

414. white body, blue chassis, red roof, "Auto 1" tempa ($5-8)(AU)
415. white body, black chassis & roof, "TMLP" tempa ($30-40)(ASAP)
416. white body, black chassis & roof, "Brew Works" tempa ($100+)(ASAP)
417. red body, black chassis & roof, "Canadian Tire" tempa, rubber tires ($4-6)(CN)(GS)
418. red body, black chassis & roof, "Canadian Tire Corp'n" tempa, rubber tires ($4-6)(CN)(GS)
419. red body, black chassis & roof, "Canadian Tire Associate Store" tempa, rubber tires ($4-6)(CN)(GS)
420. black body, red chassis & roof, "Moto Master" tempa, rubber tires ($4-6)(CN)(GS)
421. white body, blue chassis, red roof, "Bendigo National Swapmeet" tempa ($10-15)(AU)(C2)
422. white body, black chassis & roof, "Dutchway Farm Market" tempa ($10-15)(ASAP)
423. white body, black chassis & roof, "Matchbox 33000" tempa ($75+)(ASAP)
424. white body, black chassis & roof, "Smith Kline Beecham" tempa ($100+)(ASAP)
425. white body, black chassis & roof, "Farmers Auto Loans/ Farmers Insurance Group" tempa ($100+)(ASAP)
426. bright blue body, yellow chassis & roof, "Hudson Lager" tempa, rubber tires ($8-12)(MB)(CL)
427. red body, blue chassis, white roof, "Big Apple Circus" tempa ($50-75)(US)
428. red body, black chassis & roof, "Beechworth Bakery" tempa ($3-5)(AU)
429. white body, black chassis & roof, "Melcer Tile 30 Years" tempa ($100+)(ASAP)
430. white body, black chassis & roof, "Carroll County Fair" tempa ($50+)(ASAP)
431. white body, black chassis & roof, "Two Men and A Truck" tempa ($10-15)(ASAP)
432. white body, black chassis & roof, "Corning Building Co." tempa ($75+)(ASAP)
433. white body, black chassis & roof, no tempa ($25-40)(ASAP blank)
434. light neon orange body, black chassis & roof, "Cave Creek Chili Beer" tempa, rubber tires ($8-12)(MB)(CL)
435. green body, yellow chassis & roof, "River-Horse Lager" tempa, rubber tires ($8-12)(MB)(CL)
436. red body, black chassis & roof, "Coca Cola Quality Assurance" tempa, rubber tires ($4-6)(Coke PC)
437. white body, black windows, blue chassis & roof, "Special Edition 76" labels ($1-2)(MW76/1998 US)
NOTE: Above model with Matchbox International or Mattel casting.
438. white body, black chassis & roof, "Avant Garde Drum & Bugle Corps" tempa ($10-15)(ASAP)
439. yellow-orange body, green roof & chassis, "3rd MICA Australia Convention" with koala in tree on sides tempa ($8-12)(AU)
440. green body, black roof & chassis, "Fred Meyer 75th Anniversary" tempa ($8-12)(US)
441. white body, black chassis & roof, "Bakker Bros. Seeds" tempa ($35-50)(ASAP)
442. white body, black chassis & roof, "Tom's Antiques Art & Collectibles" tempa ($35-50)(ASAP)
443. white body, black chassis & roof, "RCA" tempa ($20-35)(ASAP)
444. white body, black chassis & roof, black windows, Mattel casting,, "72nd Shenandoah Apple Blossom Festival" tempa($8-12)(US)
445. white body, black chassis & roof, "Pepsi Cola" tempa ($50+)(ASAP)
446. white body, black chassis & roof, "Ritz Carlton Hotel & Casino" tempa($300+)(ASAP)
447. white body, black chassis & roof, black windows, Mattel casting, "Roosevelt For President 1932 White's Guide" tempa ($15-20)(CCI)
448. white body, black chassis & roof, "Ritz Carlton Hotel, Spa & Casino" tempa ($200+)(ASAP)
449. white body, black chassis & roof, "Unionville Community Fair" tempa($20-45)(ASAP)
450. white body, black chassis & roof, "Transply, Inc." tempa ($50+)
451. white body, black chassis & roof, black windows, "Route 11 Potato Chips" tempa, Mattel casting ($15-20)(CCI)
452. blue body, black chassis & roof, "75th Anniversary Borough of Newfield" tempa, Macau casting ($12-15)(CCI)
453. white body, red chassis, green roof, "Season's Greetings From Color Comp Inc." & snowman tempa, Macau casting ($100+)(CCI)
454. white body, black chassis & roof, "Ship McQuaide" tempa ($25-40)(ASAP)
455. white body, black chassis & roof, Mattel casting, "Ship McQuaide" tempa ($25-40)(ASAP)
456. white body, black chassis & roof, "Krispy Kreme Doughnuts" tempa ($100+)(ASAP)
457. white body, black chassis & roof, "Celebrate Michigan's Greatness/ Governor John Engler 1999 Inauguration" tempa ($75+)(ASAP)
458. brown body, cocoa brown chassis, white roof, "Matchbox Convention 2000- Hershey Demo Model" tempa, Thailand casting ($35-50)(CCI)
459. white body, black chassis & roof, black windows, Mattel casting, "Lion's Club Fund Raising Activity" tempa ($25-40)(CCI)
460. white body, black chassis & roof, "Unionville Community Fair 2000" tempa ($20-35)(ASAP)
461. white body, black chassis & roof, "New England Ice cream 508-580-6100" tempa ($100+)(ASAP)
462. white body, black chassis & roof, "Tyco- Portland, Oregon" tempa ($100+)(ASAP)
463. white body, black chassis & roof, "2000 Southern California Rod Run Sept. 4th 2000" tempa ($75+)(ASAP)
464. white body, black chassis & roof, "Old Tymers Model A Club Rod Run" tempa ($75+)(ASAP)
465. white body, black roof & chassis, "Cooter's Garage/ Christmas 2000" tempa ($25-40)(CCI)
466. white body, black roof & chassis, "Acco Chain & Lifting Products" (left side only) tempa ($25+)(ASAP)
467. black body, dull green roof & chassis, "Texaco Petroleum Products" tempa, chrome disc wheels with rubber tires ($4-6)(PC)
468. white body, black roof & chassis, "The New Crawford" tempa ($75+)(ASAP)
469. white body, black roof & chassis, "Delacre World's Finest Belgian Chocolate Biscuits" tempa ($150+)(CCI)
470. white body, black windows, roof & chassis, "Kathy's Tortuga" tempa, Mattel casting ($15-20)(CCI)
471. white body, black chassis & roof, "Matchbox Convention 2001 Hershey/ Demo Model" tempa ($15-20)(CCI)
472. white body, black chassis & roof, "South Jersey Ghost Research" tempa ($15-25)(CCI)
473. white body, black chassis & roof, "Bosal/ Western Automotive Systems" tempa ($15-25)(CCI)
474. white body, black chassis & roof, "Jacqueline Eileen/ Additions by Amy & Mark McPeak" tempa($25-40)(CCI)
475. white body, black chassis & roof, "Cooter's Garage/ "01" tempa ($15-20)(CCI)
476. brown body, cocoa brown chassis, white roof, "Matchbox & Lesney Toy Museum/ 10th Anniversary Since 1992" tempa ($25-40)(CCI)

477. white body, blue chassis & roof, chrome disc with rubber tires, "Toys R Us" tempa ($3-5)(TN)
478. white body, black chassis & roof, "47th West Virginia Black Walnut Festival" tempa ($10-15)(CCI)
479. white body, black chassis & roof, "Daytona Turkey Run" tempa ($10-15)(CCI)
480. white body, black chassis & roof, "40th Anniversary 2001 Wayside" tempa ($10-15)(CCI)
481. white body, black chassis & roof, "Lukas Michael Mullaney" tempa ($20-35)(CCI)
482. white body, black chassis & roof, "Australian Matchbox & Hot Wheels Collectors Club" tempa ($10-15)(CCI)
483 white body, black chassis & roof, "Daytona Farmers Market" tempa ($10-15)(CCI)
484. white body, black chassis & roof, "Mountain State Forest Festival" tempa ($10-15)(CCI)
485. white body, bright blue chassis, red roof, gray grille, lace wheels, "Matchbox 50" tempa ($4-6)(ROW)
486. white body, black chassis & roof, "Pappy's Aircraft Parts Co." tempa ($10-15)(CCI)
487. white body, black chassis & roof, "Richard's Jewelry" tempa ($10-15)(CCI)
488. white body, black chassis & roof, "20th Annual Fayetteville Dogwood Festival" tempa ($10-15)(CCI)
489. white body, black chassis & roof, "Susan & Brian- Just Married" tempa ($25-40)(CCI)
490. white body, black chassis & roof, "Buggies-N-Blues" tempa ($18-25)(CCI)
491. white body, bright blue chassis, red roof, gray grille, lace wheels, "Matchbox 50/ NYTF 2002" tempa ($75-100)(CCI)
492. white body, black chassis & roof, "GTA 2002 Crawler Tractors" tempa ($10-15)(CCI)
493. chrome body, black chassis, red roof, 8 spoke wheels, "25th Anniversary Matchbox USA" decals, Macau casting ($25-40)(CCI)
494. chrome body, black chassis, black roof, 8 spoke wheels, "25th Anniversary Matchbox USA" decals, Macau casting ($40-60)(CCI)
495. white body, black chassis & roof, "Unionville Community Fair 2002" tempa ($12-18)(ASAP)
496. white body, black chassis & roof, "An Aussie in New York" tempa ($10-15)(CCI)
497. white body, black chassis & roof, "Town of Woodstock, VA 250th Anniversary" tempa ($10-15)(CCI)
498. white body, black chassis & roof, black windows, "Rich's 25th Anniversary 1974-1999" tempa, Mattel casting ($100+)(CCI)
499. pearly white body, metallic red chassis, bright blue roof, screws in base, "Color Comp Salutes 50 Years of Matchbox" tempa ($25-40)(CCI)
500. metallic gold body, black chassis & roof , screws in base, "Matchbox 50th Birthday Party- New York" tempa, mounted to wood plinth ($50-75)(CCI)
501. white body, black chassis & roof, "Midwest Regional Matchbox Convention" tempa ($12-18)(CCI)
502. white body, black chassis & roof, "Creanies Ice Cream" tempa ($12-18)(CCI)
503. white body, black chassis & roof, "Generations Furniture" tempa ($12-18)(CCI)
504. white body, black chassis & roof, "Jake's 3rd Birthday/ Farm Party" & barnyard scene tempa ($15-20)(CCI)
505. white body, black chassis & roof, "Happy New Year 2003/ CCI" tempa ($10-15)(CCI)
506. white body, black chassis & roof, "Daily Grind Fresh Roasted Coffee" (black print) tempa ($12-18)(CCI)
507. white body, black chassis & roof, "Credit Union Direct Lending" tempa ($12-18)(CCI)
508. white body, blue chassis & roof, "Shipyard Brewing Co." with circle design at rear tempa ($6-8)(MB1)(CL)
509. cream body, green chassis, red roof, very dark green base, "Dixie- Kentucky Pride" tempa ($6-8)(MB2)(CL)
510. metallic blue body, black chassis, white roof, gray grille, lace wheels, "Ford Motor Company 100 Years" tempa ($6-8)(TP)(Avon)
511. white body, black chassis & roof, "Kaitlyn Marie/ Amy & Mark McPeak" tempa ($25-40)(CCI)
512. white body, black chassis & roof, "Great Strides 2003" tempa ($10-15)(CCI)
513. white body, black chassis & roof, "MB38BBBerlinaol.com/ 2003" tempa ($75+)(CCI)
514. white body, black chassis & roof, "10th Annual Dusty Lobb Memorial Golf Tournament" tempa ($10-15)(CCI)
515. white body, black chassis & roof, "4th Annual Salmon River Festival" tempa ($10-15)(CCI)
516. white body, black chassis & roof, "Granite Threshing Bee 2003/ o6 Series" tempa ($12-18)(CCI)
517. white body, black chassis & roof, "Georgia-Pacific" tempa ($75+)(CCI)
518. white body, black chassis & roof, "Gregory P. Davis- Preventive Family Dentistry" tempa ($12-18)(CCI)
519. white body, black chassis & roof, black windows, "40th Annual Barnesville Pumpkin Festival" tempa ($10-15)(CCI)
520. white body, black chassis & roof, "Rubbermaid- United Way" tempa ($10-15)(CCI)
521. white body, black chassis & roof, "Coca-Cola- United Way" tempa ($10-15)(CCI)
522. white body, black chassis & roof, "Carrier Rude" with oval rear logos tempa ($12-18)(CCI)
523. white body, black chassis & roof, "Carrier Rude" with lined rear logo tempa ($12-18)(CCI)
524. white body, black chassis & roof, "17th Annual First Night-2004" tempa ($10-15)(CCI)
525. white body, black chassis & roof, "Holiday Greeting 2003/ Happy New Year 2004/ Mom Me & Matchbox" tempa ($25-40)(CCI)
526. white body, black chassis & roof, "Mill Stores Discount Factory Outlets" tempa ($100+)(CCI)
527. white body, black chassis & roof, "Blue Ridge Power Association" tempa ($12-18)(CCI)
528. white body, black chassis & roof "Daily Grind Fresh Roasted Coffee" (brown print) tempa ($12-18)(CCI)
529. white body, black chassis & roof , "Daily Grind Fresh Roasted Coffee/ Winchester Medical Center Locations" tempa ($12-18)(CCI)
530. white body, black chassis & roof, "Daily Grind Fresh Roasted Coffee/ Daily Grind Old Town Walking Mall" tempa ($12-18)(CCI)
531. white body, black chassis & roof, "Stroehmann Pennsylvania Dutch Bakers" tempa ($50+)(ASAP)
532. black body, dark gray roof, silver-gray chassis, "Detroit Michigan" tempa, lace wheels ($8-12)(AW-Bonus)
533. white body, black chassis & roof, "Strasburg Mayfest 2004/ 150 Years of Railroads" tempa ($12-18)(CCI)
534. white body, black chassis & roof, "Newtown Heritage Festival" tempa ($12-18)(CCI)
535. white body, black chassis & roof, "Cousin Boogy's" tempa ($12-18)(CCI)
536. white body, black windows, black chassis & roof, "Cousin Boogy's" tempa, Mattel casting ($18-25)(CCI)
537. white body, black chassis & roof, "Columbia University" tempa ($12-18)(CCI)

NOTE: Above model can be found with Matchbox International or Mattel casting.

538. white body, black chassis & roof, "Happy Father's Day" tempa ($12-18)(CCI)
539. white body, black chassis & roof, "20th Anniversary Granite Thresher Bee" tempa ($12-18)(CCI)
540. white body, purple-maroon chassis, white roof, "Christmas Greetings 2003" tempa ($25-40)(CCI)
541. white body, bright blue chassis, yellow roof, "Independence Hall" tempa, blue windows, gray grille, lace wheels, Mattel casting ($2-4)(AW)(MP)
542 white body, black chassis & roof, "Coastal Engraving" tempa, Mattel casting ($18-25)(CCI)
543. white body, black chassis & roof, "Marshall County Blueberry Festival" tempa, Mattel casting ($15-20)(CCI)
544. white body, black chassis & roof, "Mom Me & Matchbox/ Farewell to Mt. Laurel/ Happy Return to Hershey" ($18-25)(CCI)
545. white body, black chassis & roof, "NAIA" tempa ($50+)(ASAP)
546. white body, black chassis & roof, "Amtrak 1979-1999" tempa ($50+)(ASAP)
547. white body, black chassis & roof, "Amtrak Mail & Express" tempa ($50+)(ASAP)
548. white body, black chassis & roof, "Eyman Fence Company" tempa ($50+)(ASAP)
549. white body, black chassis & roof, "The Quaker Oats Company" tempa, Mattel casting ($50+)(ASAP)
550. white body, black chassis & roof, "Heinz" tempa, Mattel casting ($50+)(ASAP)
551. white body, black chassis & roof, "Amtrak Crescent" tempa, Mattel casting ($50+)(ASAP)
552. white body, black chassis & roof, "Cleburne Cafeteria", Mattel casting ($50+)(ASAP)
553. white body, black chassis & roof, "Les Kuba" tempa, Mattel casting ($50+)(ASAP)
554. white body, black chassis & roof, "Phillips" tempa, Mattel casting ($50+)(ASAP)
555. white body, black chassis & roof, black windows, "Troop 1 Flea Market" tempa, Mattel casting ($15-20)(CCI)
556. white body, black chassis & roof, black windows, "Cooter's Garage 1999" tempa, Mattel casting ($15-20)(CCI)
557. white body, black chassis & roof, black windows, "Cooter's Garage/ Christmas 1999", Mattel casting ($15-20)(CCI)
558. white body, black chassis & roof, "Cooter's Garage 2000" tempa ($15-20)(CCI)
559. white body, black chassis & roof, "Savannah 2001" tempa ($15-25)(CCI)
560. white body, black chassis & roof, "Church on the Rock" tempa ($18-25)(CCI)
561. white body, black chassis & roof , "Hot Air Balloon & Wines Festival 2004" ($18-25)(CCI)
562. white body, black chassis & roof, "16th Annual Alabama Pecan Festival 2004" ($18-25)(CCI)
563. white body, black chassis & roof , "Page County Heritage Festival 35th Anniversary" ($18-25)(CCI)
564. white body, black chassis & roof, "Crossroad Car Show & Quilt Auction for the Kids!" ($18-25)(CCI)
565. white body, black chassis & roof, "31st Annual Apple Butter Festival 2004" ($18-25)(CCI)
566. white body, blue chassis & roof, blue base, no tempa, lace wheels ($18-25)(CCI blank)

NOTE: A series of models with NBA liveries using this casting are not listed here as they are classified as "Models of Yesteryear" on the base.

MB38-F FORD COURIER, issued 1992 (ROW) (MB198)

NOTE: Below clear windows, 8 dot wheels & plastic base unless otherwise noted.

1. white body, white metal base, gray interior, "Courier" & painted lights tempa, China casting ($12-15)(UK)(LE)
2. white body, white metal base, gray interior, painted lights only tempa, China casting ($35-50)(FR)(LE)
3. lilac body, lilac plastic base, gray interior, "Milka" tempa, China casting ($2-3)
4. dark blue body, black plastic base, gray interior, "Matchbox-The Ideal Premium" tempa , China casting ($20-25)(GR)
5. dark lilac body, dark lilac plastic base, "Milka" tempa, Thailand casting ($1-3)
6. red body, red base, "Axa Insurance?" tempa, Thailand casting ($75-100)(LD)(UK)
7. red body, red base, "Ford County Emergency Services" tempa, Thailand casting ($12-18)(LD)(UK)
8. red body, red base, "Australian Matchbox News" with "Club Member" on roof tempa, Thailand casting ($75-100)(LD)(AU)
9. red body, red base, "Australian Matchbox News" tempa, Thailand casting ($15-20)(LD)(AU)
10. red body, red base, no tempa, Thailand casting ($25-40)(LD blank)
11. dark blue body, dark blue base, "Australian Matchbox News" tempa, Thailand casting ($15-20)(LD)(AU)
12. dark blue body, dark blue base, no tempa, Thailand casting ($25-40)(LD blank)
13. white body, white base, no tempa, Thailand casting ($25-40)(LD blank)
13. white body, white base, "Dent Magician" tempa, Thailand casting ($45-60)(LD)(UK)
14. dark blue body, dark blue base, "Axa" tempa, Thailand casting ($18-25)(LD)(UK)
15. dark blue body, dark blue base, "Benedick's Coffee Service", Thailand casting ($12-18)(LD)(UK)
16. dark blue body, dark blue base, "County Police", Thailand casting ($12-18)(LD)(UK)
17. dark blue body, dark blue base, "Community Service Officer", Thailand casting ($12-18)(LD)(UK)
18. dark blue body, dark blue base, "Hampshire Police" tempa, Thailand casting ($12-18)(LD)(UK)

MB38-G FORD COURIER, issued 1992 (UK)(MB199)

NOTE: Below models with clear windows * 8 dot wheels.

1. red body, red metal base, gray interior, no tempa, China casting ($12-15)(LE)

NOTE: MB38-G features side cast windows, whereas MB38-F features no side windows.

MB38-H MERCEDES 600SEL, issued 1992 (USA)(MB234)
MB39-G MERCEDES 600SEL, issued 1992 (ROW)

1. silver-gray body, gray base, clear windows, light gray interior, 8 dot wheels, gray sides tempa, China casting ($1-2)
2. silver-gray body, gray base, clear windows, light gray interior, 8 dot wheels, gray sides tempa, Thailand casting ($1-2)
3. metallic brown body, brown base, clear windows, light gray interior, 8 dot wheels, brown sides tempa, Thailand casting ($2-3)(SS)
4. black body, charcoal base, clear windows, lt./dk. gray interior, chrome disc wheels with rubber tires, detailed trim tempa, Thailand casting ($3-5)(PC2)

5. blue body, charcoal base, clear windows, lt./dk. gray interior, chrome disc wheels with rubber tires, detailed trim & charcoal sides tempa, Thailand casting ($3-5)(PC5)
6. dark green body, charcoal base, clear windows, lt./dk gray interior, chrome disc wheels with rubber tires, detailed trim & charcoal sides tempa, Thailand casting ($3-5)(PC1)(ROW)
7. white body, charcoal base, clear windows, lt./dk. gray interior, chrome disc wheels with rubber tires, detailed trim & charcoal sides tempa, Thailand casting ($3-5)(SC2)
8. metallic red body, charcoal base, clear windows, gray & black interior, chrome disc wheels with rubber tires, charcoal sides tempa, Thailand casting ($8-12)(UC)
9. silver blue body, silver-gray base, clear windows, lt./dk. gray interior, chrome disc wheels with rubber tires, silver-gray sides tempa, Thailand casting ($3-5)(PC2-JC)

MB38-I CORVETTE STINGRAY III, issued 1994 (MB255)

NOTE: Below models with black plastic base unless otherwise noted.

1. dark purple body, clear windshield, dark gray interior, gold 6-spoke spiral wheels, pink & white tempa, Thailand casting ($1-2)
2. dark purple body, purple base, chrome windshield, dark gray interior, gray disc wheels with rubber tires, detailed trim tempa, Thailand casting ($2-4)(WC)
3. red body, clear windshield, black interior, gold 6-spoke spiral wheels, "7-Eleven" tempa, Thailand casting ($4-6)(US)
4. florescent yellow body, smoke windshield, gray interior, silver 6-spoke spiral wheels, "Ice Breaker" tempa, Thailand casting ($7-10)(PS)
5. florescent orange body, smoke windshield, gray interior, silver 6-spoke spiral wheels, "Ice Breaker" tempa, Thailand casting ($7-10)(PS)
6. florescent orange & yellow body, smoke windshield, black interior, silver 6-spoke spiral wheels, "Matchbox Get In The Fast Lane/ Toy Fair 1995" tempa, Thailand casting ($18-25)(US)
7. yellow & florescent orange body, smoke windshield, black interior, silver 6-spoke spiral wheels, "Matchbox Get In The Fast Lane/ Toy Fair 1995" tempa, Thailand casting ($85-100)(UK)(GR)
8. dark purple body, smoke windshield, gray interior, silver 6-spoke spiral wheels, pink & white hood & side design tempa, Thailand casting ($1-2)
9. dark purple body, smoke windshield, light gray interior, silver 6-spoke spiral wheels, pink & white side design tempa, Thailand casting ($1-2)
10. red body, chrome windshield, black interior, chrome disc wheels with rubber tires, detailed trim tempa, Thailand casting ($20-35)(US)(OP)
11. silver body, amber windshield, white interior, silver 6-spoke spiral wheels, peach & white design tempa, Thailand casting ($3-5)(MT)
12. dark purple & metallic blue body, smoke windshield, white interior, silver 6-spoke spiral wheels, no tempa, Thailand casting ($1-2)(5pk)
13. black & florescent orange body, smoke windshield, white interior, silver 6-spoke spiral wheels, no tempa, Thailand casting ($2-4)(5pk)
14. white body, smoke windshield, blue interior, silver 6-spoke spiral wheels, blue & black spray design tempa, Thailand casting ($1-2)(5pk)
15. metallic blue body, clear windshield, lt./dk. gray interior, chrome disc wheels with rubber tires, detailed trim tempa, Thailand casting ($3-5)(PC2)
16. white body, smoke windshield, red interior, silver 6-spoke spiral wheels, red & yellow design tempa, Thailand casting ($2-4)
17. lemon body, clear windshield, lt./dk. gray interior, chrome disc wheels with rubber tires, detailed trim tempa, Thailand casting ($3-5)(PC5)
18. metallic gold body, clear windshield, black interior, silver 6-spoke spiral wheels, no tempa, Thailand casting ($10-15)(CH)
19. silver-gray body, clear windshield, black & 2 tone gray interior, chrome disc wheels with rubber tires, detailed trim tempa, Thailand casting ($3-5)(SC2)
20. red body, chrome windshield, black interior, chrome disc wheels with rubber tires, "Matchbox USA 97" tempa, Thailand casting ($100-150)(C2)
21. black body, clear windshield, red & gray interior, chrome disc wheels with rubber tires, detailed trim tempa, Thailand casting ($15-20)(GC)
22. blue chrome body, clear windshield, gray interior, 5 spoke concave star wheels, pink & orange tempa, Thailand casting ($1-2)(5pk)
23. white body, smoke windshield, red interior, 5 spoke concave star wheels, red & yellow side design tempa, Thailand casting ($2-4)
24. blue body, clear windshield, gray interior, 5 spoke concave star wheels, orange & white stripes with "Corvette" tempa, Thailand casting ($1-2)
25. red body, clear windshield, brown & black interior, chrome disc wheels with rubber tires, detailed trim tempa, Thailand casting ($3-5)(PC12)
26. iridescent white body, clear windshield, brown & black interior, chrome disc wheels with rubber tires, detailed trim tempa, Thailand casting ($3-5)(SC4)
27. crimson body, clear windshield, dark & light gray interior, chrome disc wheels with rubber tires, detailed trim tempa, Thailand casting ($3-5)(PC16)
28. crimson body, clear windshield, dark & light gray interior, 5 spoke concave star wheels, detailed trim tempa, Thailand casting ($50+)(found as PC16)
29. red body, clear windshield, gray interior, 5 spoke concave star wheels, blue & white stripes with "Corvette" tempa, Thailand casting ($1-2)(MW2/1998 US
30. red body, clear windshield, gray interior, 5 spoke concave star wheels, blue & white stripes with "Corvette" tempa, China casting ($1-2)(MW2/1998 US)

MB38-J FORD CROWN VICTORIA POLICE CAR *see MB54-K*

MB38-K SEA RESCUE BOAT *see MB43-K*

MB38-L FORD PANEL VAN, issued 2000 (USA) (MB444/479)
MB23-I FORD PANEL VAN, issued 2000 (ROW)

NOTE: Below models with frosted smoke windows, gray ladder, 5 spoke concave star wheels, China casting unless otherwise noted.

1. white body, gray base, "Mission 1 Base Shuttle" & world map tempa ($1-2)(MW38/2000 US)(MW23/2000 ROW)
2. white body, gray base, "Mission 1 Base Shuttle", world map design & "Matchbox 2000" ($2-4)(MW38/2000 US)
3. white body, gray base, "MICA Hershey 2000" tempa ($15-20)(CCI)
4. white body, black base, no tempa ($25-40)(CCI blank)
5. white body, black base, "Camp Sunshine" tempa ($18-25)(CCI)
6. white body, black base, "Virtek" tempa ($18-25)(CCI)
7. white body, black base, "M.J. Engineering & Land Surveying, P.C." tempa ($18-25)(CCI)
8. white body, black base, "Kendall Windows & Doors" tempa ($50+)(CCI)
9. white body, black base, "Firehouse Electric" tempa ($18-25)(CCI)

10. white body, black base, "Oil Heat Association of South Jersey Associates Night" tempa ($18-25)(CCI)
11. white body, black base, "Michael Heim Co., Inc" tempa ($18-25)(CCI)
12. white body, black base, "RCH Cable Contractors" tempa ($18-25)(CCI)
13. white body, black base, "Runnemeade" tempa ($18-25)(CCI)
14. white body, black base, "Bellsouth" tempa ($50+)(ASAP)
15. white body, black base, "Nassau County Police" tempa ($10-15)(CCI)
16,. white body, black base, "Austermuhl & Ward/ Puron, Bryant" tempa ($12-18)(CCI)
17. white body, black base, "Kerry Pacifico Ford" tempa ($18-25)(CCI)
18. white body, black base, "Troop 1 Flea Market" ($10-15)(CCI)
19. metallic red body, gray base, no ladder, lace wheels, "Rugrats" tempa ($1-2)(5pk)
20. silver-gray body, black base, blue ladder, 10 spoke flower wheels, "H&N Emergency Service" tempa ($1-2)(MW52/2002 US)
21. silver-gray body, black base, blue ladder, 10 spoke flower wheels, "H&N Emergency Service" & Matchbox 50" tempa ($20-30)(MW52/2002 UK)
22. white body, black base, "Alison Plumbing & Heating" tempa ($12-18)(CCI)
23. white body, black base, "Monroe Heating & Chimney" tempa ($12-18)(CCI)
24. white body, black base, "10th Van Toy Convention" tempa & purple roof label ($15-25)(CCI)
25. white body, black base, "10th Van Toy Convention" tempa & green roof label ($15-25)(CCI)
26. blue body, gray base, no ladder, 10 spoke flower wheels, "24/7" rushing worker & "555-2134" tempa ($1-2)(5pk)
27. blue body, gray base, no ladder, 10 spoke flower wheels, "24/7", rushing worker & "555-2134 Hero City" tempa ($1-2)(5pk)
28. lime body, blue base, amber windows, no ladder, 10 spoke flower wheels, "Peanuts/ Aaugh!" tempa ($1-2)(5pk)
29. red body, green base, amber windows, no ladder, 10 spoke flower wheels, "Hong Kong New Year" tempa ($1-2)(AW)
30. white body, black base, smoke windows, 10 spoke flower wheels, "Comcast" tempa ($12-18)(CCI)
31. white body, chrome base, smoke windows ,no ladder, lace wheels, "11th Toy Van Convention" (red background) tempa ($12-18)(CCI)
32. white body, chrome base, smoke windows, no ladder, lace wheels, "11th Toy Van Convention" (blue background)/ "Race Winner" tempa ($75+)(CCI)
33. white body, black base, smoke windows, 10 spoke flower wheels, no tempa ($15-20)(CCI blank)
34. white body, chrome base, smoke windows, lace wheels, no tempa ($15-20)(CCI blank)
35. white body, black base, smoke windows, 5 spoke concave star wheels, "Intergraph" tempa ($50+)(ASAP)
36. white body, black base, smoke windows, 10 spoke flower wheels, "Carrier" tempa ($50+)(ASAP)
37. white body, chrome base, smoke windows, lace wheels, "Charlie's 23rd Matchbox Show/ Demo Model" tempa ($12-18)(CCI)
38. white body, chrome base, smoke windows, lace wheels, "RCH Cable Outsourcing Services" tempa ($12-18)(CCI)
39. white body, chrome base, smoke windows, lace wheels, "DiPietro Concrete" tempa ($12-18)(CCI)

MB38-M DEMOLITION MACHINE, issued 2001 (MB494)

NOTE: Below models with black wheels, China casting

1. white body, white plastic platform, blue arm, dark blue base, "Matchbox 43" tempa ($1-2)(MW38/2001)
2. dark orange body, orange plastic platform, blue arm, blue base, "42" & steer head tempa ($1-2)(5pk)
3. bright blue body, bright blue plastic platform, orange arm, black base, "25" & brick design tempa ($1-2)(MW25/2003)
4. bright blue body, bright blue plastic platform, orange arm, black base, "25", brick design & "Hero City" tempa ($8-12)(MW25/2003)
5. metallic blue body, bright blue plastic platform, orange arm, black base, "25" & brick design tempa ($3-4)(20pk)
6. orange-yellow body, orange plastic platform, red arm, orange base, red dashes & design tempa ($1-2)(5pk)
7. orange body, orange plastic platform, neon yellow arm, dark green base, "Hero City TNT" tempa (MW73/2004)

MB38-O 1957 CORVETTE CONVERTIBLE, issued 2004 (SF) (MB362)

MB362 1957 CORVETTE CONVERTIBLE, issued 1999

NOTE: Below models with clear windshield, black base & China casting unless otherwise noted.

1. red body, red interior, chrome disc wheels with rubber tires, detailed trim tempa ($5-8)(FE)
2. unpainted body, white interior, chrome disc wheels with rubber tires, none tempa ($5-8)(FE)
3. red body, white interior, chrome wire disc wheels with rubber tires, white flash, Santa & "Coca Cola" tempa ($6-8)(Coke PC)
4. red body, white interior, chrome mag disc wheels with rubber tires, white flash, Santa & "Coca Cola" tempa ($6-8)(Coke PC)
5. lemon body, black interior, 5 spoke concave star wheels, "Coke" with white flash tempa, chrome base ($3-5)(5pk)
6. red body, red interior, chrome disc wheels with rubber tires, detailed trim with "FTD" rear license plate tempa ($18-25)(US)
NOTE: Above model was sold with a ceramic planter in the shape of a 1950's diner exclusively through FTD florists.
7. white body, red interior, chrome disc wheels with rubber tires, silver flash & detailed trim tempa ($3-5)(TN)
8. metallic gold body, cream interior, chrome disc wheels with rubber tires, cream flash & detailed trim tempa ($3-5)(BJ)
9. red body, red interior, chrome disc wheels with rubber tires, "Matchbox People Make a Difference/ Together for Tyler Sponsor" tempa ($75+)(CCI)
10. cherry red body, yellow interior, lace wheels, "Booo!" & skeleton tempa ($1-2)(5pk)
11. bright blue body, red interior, 10 spoke flower wheels, "Washington's Crossing" tempa, gray base ($2-4)(AW)(MP)
12. silver blue body, white interior, 5 spoke slotted wheels, white flash & detailed trim tempa, gray base ($1-2)(SF38/2004)

MB39-A CLIPPER, issued 1973

NOTE: Below with maltese cross front & 5 spoke rear wheels, metal base & England casting unless otherwise noted.

1. metallic magenta body, unpainted base, yellow interior, amber windows, chrome tailpipes ($10-15)
2. metallic magenta body, green base, yellow interior, amber windows, chrome tailpipes ($10-15)
3. metallic magenta body, green base, yellow interior, clear windows, chrome tailpipes ($10-15)
4. metallic magenta body, unpainted base, yellow interior, amber windows, white tailpipes ($10-15)
5. metallic magenta body, green base, yellow interior, amber windows, white tailpipes ($10-15)
6. metallic magenta body, green base, yellow interior, clear windows, white tailpipes ($10-15)
7. hot pink body, green base, yellow interior, amber windows, chrome tailpipes ($250+)

8. cherry red body, unpainted base with Manaus tab, yellow interior, amber windows, white tailpipes ($250+)(BR)
NOTE: Available as a Bulgarian casting. Assorted colors available ($60-85)

MB39-B ROLLS ROYCE SILVER SHADOW, issued 1979 (MB039)
NOTE: Below models with England casting unless otherwise noted.
1. silver-gray body, unpainted base, red interior, clear windows, dot dash wheels ($4-6)
2. silver-gray base, unpainted base, red interior, clear windows, dot dash wheels, "Climat" label ($125-175)(FR)
3. matt gray body, unpainted base, red interior, clear windows, dot dash wheels ($4-6)
4. metallic red body, unpainted base, ivory interior, clear windows, dot dash wheels ($4-6)
5. metallic red body, unpainted base, light yellow interior, clear windows, dot dash wheels ($3-5)
6. metallic red body, unpainted base, brown interior, clear windows, dot dash wheels ($4-6)
7. metallic red body, unpainted base, ivory interior, clear windows, dot dash wheels, "Climat" label ($125-175)(FR)
8. dark metallic tan body, unpainted base, white interior, clear windows, dot dash wheels ($2-4)
9. light metallic tan body, unpainted base, white interior, clear windows, dot dash wheels ($2-4)
10. light metallic tan body, silver-gray base, white interior, clear windows, dot dash wheels ($2-4)
11. light metallic tan body, silver-gray base, white interior, clear windows, 5 arch wheels ($2-4)
12. light metallic tan body, unpainted base, white interior, smoke windows, dot dash wheels ($2-4)
13. light metallic tan body, unpainted base, white interior, amber windows, dot dash wheels ($3-5)
14. light metallic tan body, silver-gray base, white interior, amber windows, dot dash wheels ($3-5)
15. plum body, unpainted base, white interior, clear windows, dot dash wheels ($4-6)
16. plum body, silver-gray base, white interior, clear windows, dot dash wheels ($4-6)
17. plum body, black base, white interior, clear windows, dot dash wheels ($4-6)
18. black body, black base, gray interior, clear windows, dot dash wheels, China casting ($50-75)(CHI)
19. maroon body, pearly silver base, white interior, clear windows, dot dash wheels, Macau casting ($4-6)
NOTE: Available as an Hungarian casting with "Universal Associated Co." cast on base. Assorted colors available ($15-25)

MB39-C TOYOTA SUPRA, issued 1983 (USA) (MB078)
MB60-E TOYOTA SUPRA, issued 1983 (ROW)
NOTE: Below models feature red interior & black hatch unless otherwise noted.
1. white body, black base, clear windows, 5 arch wheels, "41" tempa, Macau casting ($2-4)
2. white body, black base, light amber windows, 5 arch wheels, "41" tempa, Macau casting ($2-4)
3. white body, charcoal base, light amber windows, 5 arch wheels, "41" tempa, Macau casting ($2-4)
4. red body, black base, clear windows, 5 arch wheels, "Twin Cam 24" tempa, Macau casting ($7-10) (JP)
5. red body, black base, amber windows, 5 arch wheels, "Twin Cam 24" tempa, Macau casting ($7-10)(JP)
6. dark red body, black base, clear windows, 8 dot wheels, "Twin Cam 24" tempa, Macau casting ($7-10)(JP)
7. white body, black base, clear windows, 5 arch wheels, "Supra" & pinstripes tempa, Macau casting ($2-4)
8. white body, black base, amber windows, 5 arch wheels, "Supra" & pinstripes tempa, Macau casting ($2-4)
9. white body, black base, clear windows, 8 dot wheels, "Supra" & pinstripes tempa, Macau casting ($2-4)
10. white body, black base, clear windows, 8 dot wheels, red/blue/yellow design tempa, Macau casting ($8-12)(DY)
NOTE: Available as a Bulgarian casting. Assorted colors available ($5-25)

MB39-D BMW CABRIOLET, issued 1985 (MB151)
MB28-I BMW CABRIOLET, reissued 1991 (ROW)
NOTE: Below models with clear windshield.
1. metallic silver blue body & base, red-brown interior, 8 dot silver wheels, no tow hook, "323i" tempa, Macau casting ($2-3)
2. metallic silver blue body & base, red-brown interior, dot dash wheels, no tow hook, "323i " tempa, Macau casting ($2-3)
3. red body & base, red-brown interior, 8 dot gold wheels, no tow hook, "323i" tempa, Macau casting ($1-2)
4. red body & base, red-brown interior, 8 dot silver wheels, no tow hook, "323i" tempa, Macau casting ($1-2)
5. red body & base, red-brown interior, 5 arch wheels, no tow hook, "323i" tempa, Macau casting ($2-3)
6. white body & base, red-brown interior, starburst wheels, no tow hook, "Alpina" tempa, Macau casting ($3-5)(SF)
7. white body & base, red-brown interior, 8 dot silver wheels, no tow hook, "BMW" & "323i" tempa, Macau casting ($8-12)
8. white body & base, red-brown interior, 8 dot silver wheels, with tow hook, "BMW" & "323i" tempa, Macau casting ($8-12)
9. red body & base, red-brown interior, 8 dot silver wheels, with tow hook, "Gliding Club" tempa, Macau casting ($3-4)(TP)
10. white body & base, red-brown interior, starburst wheels, with tow hook, "Alpina" tempa, Macau casting ($3-5)(SF)
11. white body & base, red-brown interior, laser wheels, with tow hook, "Alpina" tempa, Macau casting ($3-5)(LW)
12. dark blue body, black base, black interior, 8 dot silver wheels, with tow hook, "323i" & "BP" tempa, Macau casting ($8-12)(DU)
13. silver-blue body & base, gray interior, 8 dot silver wheels, with tow hook, dark blue stripe tempa, Macau casting ($2-4)(TP)
14. light silver-blue body & base, gray interior, 8 dot silver wheels, with tow hook, dark blue stripe tempa, Thailand casting ($2-4)(TP)
15. red body & base, red-brown interior, 8 dot silver wheels, with tow hook, "323i" tempa, Thailand casting ($1-2)
16. white body & base, gray interior, 8 dot silver wheels, with tow hook, blue & red with "323i" tempa, Thailand casting ($2-3)(TP)
17. white body & base, maroon interior, 8 dot silver wheels, with tow hook, purple/orange/blue tempa, Thailand casting ($1-2)(TP)
18. metallic silver blue body & base, red-brown interior, 8 dot silver wheels, with tow hook, "323i" tempa, Thailand casting ($1-2)(SP)

MB39-E FORD BRONCO II, issued 1987 (USA) (MB187)
MB35-G FORD BRONCO II, issued 1988 (ROW)
NOTE: Below models with clear windows, black tire carrier, maltese cross wheels unless otherwise noted.
1. white body, chrome base, red interior, "Bronco" & stripes tempa, Macau casting ($1-2)
2. dark brown body, chrome base, red interior, "Bronco" & stripes tempa, Macau casting ($3-4)(SC)
3. orange body, chrome base, red interior, "Bronco" & stripes tempa, Macau casting ($3-4)(SC)

4. white body, chrome base, red interior, "Coast Guard Beach Patrol" tempa, Macau casting ($1-2)
5. white body, chrome base, red interior, "Coast Guard Beach Patrol" tempa, Thailand casting ($1-2)
6. bright yellow body, chrome base, red interior, flames & "4X4" tempa, Thailand casting ($6-8)(US)(OP)
7. red body, blue base, orange-yellow interior, map & compass tempa, all yellow wheels, no spare tire carrier, Thailand casting ($6-8)(LL)
8. metallic blue body, chrome base, silver-gray interior, white splash marks & orange "4X4 Bronco" tempa, with window tempa, Thailand casting ($1-2)
9. metallic blue body, chrome base, silver-gray interior, white splash marks & orange "4X4 Bronco" tempa, with plain window, Thailand casting ($1-2)
10. white body, chrome base, red interior, "Police PD-22" tempa, Thailand casting ($1-3)(EM)
11. red body, chrome base, silver- gray interior, "4X4 Bronco" & splash marks tempa, Thailand casting ($1-2)(5pk)
12. metallic green body, chrome base, tan interior, tan fenders tempa, Thailand casting ($2-4)(CC)
13. fluorescent orange body, chrome base, black interior, black zebra stripes tempa, Thailand casting ($1-2)(5pk)
14. black body, chrome base, red interior, "Piranha" & fish design tempa, Thailand casting ($1-2)
15. black body, chrome base, red interior, fish design only tempa, Thailand casting ($1-2)
16. yellow body, chrome base, blue interior, "World 4 Kids" tempa, Thailand casting ($18-25)(AU)
17. white body, chrome base, black interior, black zebra stripes tempa, Thailand casting ($1-2)(5pk)
18. black body, chrome base, red interior, fish design only tempa, China casting ($1-2)
19. silver-gray body, chrome base, blue interior, fish design only tempa, China casting ($2-3)
20. white body, chrome base, red interior, "Luigi's Pizza" tempa, China casting ($1-2)
21. metallic gold body, chrome base, black interior, no tempa, China casting ($5-10)(CH)
22. purple body, chrome base, gray interior, white stripes tempa, China casting ($1-2)(5pk)
23. black body, chrome base, black interior, "Kidz 1.75FM" with pink & yellow stripes tempa, China casting ($4-6)(AU)
24. red body, chrome base, black interior, "Luigi's Pizza" tempa, China casting ($1-2)(MW51/1998)
25. orange-red body, chrome base, gray interior, "Vinnie's" tempa, China casting ($1-2)(MW25/1999 US)

NOTE: Below model base is modified. Interior is redesigned to eliminate gun & load in rear section.

26. purple body, chrome base (modified casting), gray interior, white stripes tempa, China casting ($3-5)(PS)
27. white body, gray base (Mattel), "Montana Glacier- Grizzly Research 41" tempa, 5 spoke oval wheels, Mattel China casting ($1-2)(AM)

MB39-F MACK CH600 AERODYNE *see MB8-H*

MB39-G MERCEDES 600SEL *see MB38-H*

MB39-H FORD T-BIRD *see MB7-G*

MB39-I 1971 CAMARO Z-28, issued 1998 (MB336)

NOTE: Below models with clear windows, black interior, black plastic base, China casting unless otherwise noted.

1. green body, dual white stripes tempa, 5 spoke concave star wheels ($1-2)(MW39/1998)

NOTE: Above model in various shades from light to dark.

2. light metallic blue body, dual black stripes tempa, black disc wheels with rubber tires ($20-35)(PC)
3. tan body, dual black stripes & "Matchbox 2000" tempa, 5 spoke concave star wheels ($2-4)(MW18/2000 US)
4. tan body, dual black stripes tempa, 5 spoke concave star wheels ($1-2)(MW18/2000 US)
5. dark green body, dual white stripes & "Great Camaro Gathering 1999" tempa ($25-40)(CCI)
6. green body, dual white stripes & "Cruisin New England Magazine 2002" tempa, 5 spoke concave star wheels ($50+)(CCI)
7. tan body, dual white stripes & "Cruisin New England Magazine 2002" tempa, 5 spoke concave star wheels ($50+)(CCI)
8. red body, chrome base, tire marks & "Coca Cola Play Refreshed" tempa, chrome disc wheels with rubber tires ($3-5)(Coke PC)
9. red body, black base, dual black stripes tempa, gray disc wheels with rubber tires ($3-5)(TN)
10. blue body, black base, dual white stripes tempa, gray disc wheels with rubber tires ($3-5)(BJ)
11. light slate blue & yellow body, "Coca Cola- Thirst Knows No Season" tempa, chrome disc wheels with rubber tires ($3-5)(Coke PC)
12. metallic pea green body, smoke windows, dual stripes with head & tail light tempa, slotted 5 spoke wheels, gray base ($3-5)(SF19/2004)

MB39-J HYDROPLANE *see MB44-J*

MB39-K ARMORED RESPONSE VEHICLE *see MB47-H*

MB39-L 1968 MERCURY COUGAR, issued 2004 (SF)(MB636)

1. yellow body, smoke windows, black interior, black hood design & detailed trim tempa, chrome plastic base, 5 spoke slotted wheels ($1-2)(SF39)

MB40-A VAUXHALL GUILDSMAN, issued 1971

NOTE: Below models with ivory interior & metal base. Version 1 label has star with black or blue background.

1. pink body, unpainted base, green windows, flames label, 5 spoke wheels ($12-15)
2. pink body, silver-gray base, green windows, flames label, 5 spoke wheels ($12-15)
3. pink body, unpainted base, green windows, "40" tempa, 5 spoke wheels ($15-20)
4. pink body, unpainted base, green windows, sunburst label (from MB47-B), 5 spoke wheels ($175-250)
5. red body, silver-gray base, amber windows, flames label, dot dash wheels ($10-15)
6. red body, unpainted base, green windows, flames label, 5 spoke wheels ($10-15)
7. red body, unpainted base, amber windows, flames label, 5 spoke wheels ($10-15)
8. red body, unpainted base, amber windows, flames label, dot dash wheels ($10-15)
9. red body, unpainted base, green windows, "40" tempa, 5 spoke wheels ($10-15)
10. red body, unpainted base, amber windows, "40" tempa, 5 spoke wheels ($10-15)
11. red body, unpainted base, amber windows, "40" tempa, dot dash wheels ($10-15)
12. red body, silver-gray base, amber windows, "40" tempa, dot dash wheels ($10-15)

13. cherry red body, unpainted base, amber windows, "40" tempa, 5 spoke wheels ($10-15)
NOTE: Available as a Bulgarian casting. Assorted colors available ($15-25)

MB40-B HORSE BOX, issued 1977 (MB040)
NOTE: Below models with dot dash wheels, two white plastic horses & England casting unless noted otherwise.
1. red body, beige box, light brown door, black base, green windows ($45-60)
2. orange body, beige box, light brown door, black base, green windows ($4-6)
3. orange body, bone white box, light brown door, black base, green windows (4-6)
4. orange body, beige box, light brown door, silver-gray base, green windows ($4-6)
5. orange body, beige box, dark brown door, black base, green windows ($4-6)
6. orange body, beige box, dark brown door, charcoal base, green windows ($4-6)
7. orange body, beige box, dark brown door, charcoal base, clear windows ($8-10)
8. orange body, beige box, dark brown door, black base, clear windows ($8-10)
9. orange body, beige box, dark brown door, charcoal base, purple windows ($5-8)
10. orange body, beige box, dark brown door, unpainted base, green windows ($4-6)
11. light metallic green body, beige box, dark brown door, unpainted base, green windows ($5-8)
12. light metallic green body, beige box, white door, unpainted base, green windows ($5-8)
13. dark metallic green body, beige box, dark brown door, black base, green windows ($5-8)
14. dark metallic green body, beige box, dark brown door, unpainted base, green windows ($5-8)
15. dark metallic green body, beige box, gray-brown door, unpainted base, green windows ($5-8)
16. dark metallic green body, beige box, dark brown door, charcoal base, green windows ($5-8)
17. dark metallic green body, beige box, dark brown door, silver-gray base, green windows ($5-8)
18. dark metallic green body, beige box, lime door, black base, green windows ($7-10)
19. dark metallic green body, beige box, lime door, silver-gray base, green windows ($7-10)
20. dark metallic green body, translucent bone box, dark brown door, unpainted base, green windows ($7-10)
21. dark metallic green body, chocolate box, white door, unpainted base, green windows ($10-15)
22. dark metallic green body, beige box, dark brown door, black base, clear windows ($10-15)
23. red body, chocolate box, white door, silver-gray base, green windows ($10-15)
24. red body, chocolate box, white door, black base, green windows ($10-15)
25. orange body, chocolate box, dark brown door, unpainted base, green windows ($10-15)
26. orange body, cream box, lime door, black base, green windows ($10-15)
27. orange body, chocolate box, white door, black base, green windows ($6-8)
28. orange body, chocolate box, white door, unpainted base, green windows ($6-8)
29. orange body, chocolate box, white door, silver-gray base, green windows ($6-8)
30. orange body, chocolate box, lime door, black base, green windows ($6-8)
31. yellow body, chocolate box, white door, black base, green windows ($6-8)
32. yellow body, chocolate box, lime door, black base, green windows ($6-8)
33. dark orange body, beige box, gray-brown door, charcoal base, green windows ($6-8)
34. dark orange body, chocolate box, lime door, black base, green windows ($4-6)
35. dark orange body, chocolate box, lime door, unpainted base, green windows ($4-6)
36. dark orange body, chocolate box, lime door, unpainted base, green windows, black hubs ($5-8)
37. dark orange body, chocolate box, lime door, black base, green windows, black hubs ($5-8)
38. dark orange body, chocolate box, white door, black base, green windows ($4-6)
39. orange body, chocolate box, white door, black base, green windows, Macau casting ($4-6)
40. blue body, yellow box, lime door, red base, green windows, caricature tempa, lime wheels with red hubs, no horses, Macau casting ($6-8)(LL)
41. blue body, yellow box, lime door, red base, green windows, caricature tempa, lime wheels with blue hubs, no horses, Thailand casting ($15-20)(LL)
NOTE: Versions 42 to 44 with 8 dot wheels.
42. red body, dark tan box, dark brown door, black base, green windows, Manaus casting ($35-50)(BR)
43. red body, dark tan box, light brown door, black base, green windows, Manaus casting ($35-50)(BR)
44. red body, dark tan box, chocolate door, black base, green windows, Manaus casting ($35-50)(BR)
45. white body, white box, white door, red base, blue windows, "Circus Circus" tempa, Thailand casting ($3-5)(MC)
46. yellow body, chocolate box, white door, black base, amber windows, black horses, Thailand casting ($2-4)(FM)(GS)
47. blue body, yellow box, lime door, red base, green windows, caricature tempa, all lime wheels, no horses, Thailand casting ($15-20)(LL)
NOTE: Below models with two black plastic horses.
48. metallic turquoise body, translucent gray box, black door, smoke windows, "Express" tempa, large white horses, China casting ($1-2)(MW2/1999 ROW)
49. metallic turquoise body, translucent gray box, black door, smoke windows, "Kentucky Stables" tempa, large white horses, China casting ($2-3)(MW87/1999 US)
50. charcoal body, mustard box, light brown door, smoke windows, "Express" tempa, large black horses, China casting ($1-2)(MW49/2000 US)(MW29/2000 ROW)
51. charcoal body, mustard box, light brown door, smoke windows, "Express" & "Matchbox 2000" tempa, large black horses, China casting ($2-4)(MW49/2000 US)
52. blue body, beige box, brown door, green windows, black base, 8 dot wheels, white plastic horses, Manaus casting ($35-50)(BR)

MB40-C CORVETTE T-ROOF, issued 1982 (USA) (MB097)
MB62-E CORVETTE T-ROOF, issued 1982 (ROW)
MB58-F CORVETTE T-ROOF, reissued 1991 (USA)
NOTE: Below models with clear windows unless otherwise noted.
1. white body, gray interior, unpainted metal base, stripes tempa, 5 arch front & 5 crown rear wheels, England casting ($4-6)

2. white body, gray interior, unpainted metal base, stripes tempa, 5 arch front & rear wheels, England casting ($4-6)
3. white body, gray interior, unpainted metal base, stripes tempa, 5 crown front & rear wheels, England casting ($4-6)
4. white body, gray interior, unpainted metal base, stripes tempa, 5 crown front & 5 arch rear wheels, England casting ($4-6)
5. white body, gray interior, silver-gray metal base, stripes tempa, 5 arch front & 5 crown rear wheels, England casting ($4-6)
6. white body, red interior, red metal base, stripes tempa, 5 arch front & 5 crown rear wheels, Macau casting ($2-3)
7. white body, red interior, red metal base, stripes tempa, 5 crown front & 5 arch rear wheels, Macau casting ($2-3)
8. white body, red interior, red metal base, stripes tempa, 5 crown front & rear wheels, Macau casting ($2-3)
9. dark blue body, red interior, pearly silver metal base, flames tempa, 5 arch front & 5 crown rear wheels, Macau casting ($2-3)
10. dark blue body, red interior, pearly silver metal base, flames tempa, 5 arch front & 5 crown rear gold wheels, Macau casting ($3-5)
11. dark blue body, red interior, pearly silver metal base, flames tempa, starburst wheels, Macau casting ($75-100)
12. yellow body, silver-gray interior, black metal base, "Corvette" tempa, 5 arch front & 5 crown rear wheels, Macau casting ($1-2)
13. yellow body, silver-gray interior, black plastic base, "Corvette" tempa, 5 arch front & 5 crown rear wheels, Macau casting ($1-2)
14. yellow body, silver-gray interior, black plastic base, "Corvette" tempa, 5 arch front & 5 crown rear wheels, China casting ($1-2)
15. dark blue body, red interior, black plastic base, yellow & red stripes tempa, 4 arch wheels, Manaus casting ($35-50)(BR)
16. dark blue body, red interior, black plastic base, yellow & red stripes tempa, 8 dot wheels, Manaus casting ($35-50)(BR)
17. dark orange body, black interior, gray plastic base, detailed trim tempa, gray disc with rubber tires, chrome windshield, China casting ($5-8)(WC)
18. red body, white interior, gray plastic base, "Vette" & Chevy logo tempa, 5 arch front & 5 crown rear wheels, China casting ($1-2)
19. metallic blue body, dark gray interior, silver-gray plastic base, detailed trim tempa, gray disc wheels with rubber tires, chrome windshield, China casting ($5-8)(WC)
20. black body, black interior, silver-gray plastic base, "22" & stripes tempa, black disc wheels with rubber tires, China casting ($5-7)(WP)
21. dark cream body, red interior, silver/gray plastic base, red & gray stripes tempa, 8 dot wheels, Manaus casting ($30-45)(BR)
22. dark gray body, white interior, gray plastic base, white stripes & "Corvette" tempa, 5 arch front & 5 crown rear wheels, Thailand casting ($2-4)(GS)
23. red body, white interior, gray plastic base, "Vette" & white design tempa, 5 arch front & 5 crown rear wheels, Thailand casting ($1-2)
24. dark teal blue body, pink interior, gray plastic base, white & pink grid tempa, gold 6 spoke spiral wheels, Thailand casting ($1-2)
25. dark green body, orange interior, chrome base, detailed trim tempa, silver 6 spoke spiral wheels, Thailand casting ($2-4)(CC)
26. red body, white interior, gray plastic base, "Vette" & white design tempa, silver 6 spoke spiral wheels, Thailand casting ($1-2)
27. white & black body, pink interior, gray plastic base, pink design tempa, silver 6 spoke spiral wheels, Thailand casting ($1-2)
28. white & black body, pink interior, gray plastic base, pink design tempa, silver 6 spoke spiral wheels, China casting ($1-2)
29. white body, black interior, gray plastic base, pink design tempa, silver 6 spoke spiral wheels, China casting ($1-2)
30. silver-gray body, purple interior, gray plastic base, white & purple design tempa, silver 6 spoke spiral wheels, China casting ($1-2)
31. silver-gray body, purple interior, gray plastic base, white & purple design tempa, 5 spoke concave star wheels, China casting ($2-4)
32. candy apple red body, black & white interior, chrome plastic base, black & white design tempa, chrome disc with rubber tires, China casting ($3-5)(PC9)
33. yellow body, black & white interior, chrome plastic base, detailed trim tempa, chrome disc wheels with rubber tires, China casting ($3-5)(CP)
34. red body, black & red interior, chrome plastic base, detailed trim tempa, chrome disc wheels with rubber tires, China casting ($3-5)(CP)
35. green body, black interior, gray plastic base, white & purple design tempa, 5 spoke concave star wheels, China casting ($1-2)
36. dark green body, chrome plastic base, white & black interior, detailed trim tempa, chrome disc wheels with rubber tires, China casting ($3-5)(CP)
37. black body, chrome plastic base, red & black interior, detailed trim tempa, chrome disc wheels with rubber tires, China casting ($3-5)(CP)
38. bright blue body, chrome plastic base, black & white interior, detailed trim tempa, chrome disc wheels with rubber tires, China casting ($3-5)(CP)
39. white body, chrome plastic base, red & black interior, detailed trim tempa, chrome disc wheels with rubber tires, China casting ($3-5)(CP)
40. salmon pink body, chrome plastic base, black & white interior, detailed trim tempa, chrome disc wheels with rubber tires, China casting ($15-20)(GC)
41. metallic red body, gray plastic base, black interior, white & purple design tempa, 5 spoke concave star wheels, China casting ($1-2)(MW74/1998)
42. metallic gold body, chrome plastic base, black interior, no tempa, 5 spoke concave star wheels, China casting ($50+)(CHI)(MW20-Canada)
43. candy apple red body, purple interior, black plastic base, black & white design tempa, gold 6 spoke spiral wheels, China casting ($50+) (CHI)(MW20-Canada)
44. yellow body, black interior, black plastic base, detailed trim tempa, gold 6 spoke spiral wheels, China casting ($50+)(CHI)(MW20-Canada)
45. red body, black interior, black plastic base, detailed trim tempa, gold 6 spoke spiral wheels, China casting ($50+) (CHI)(MW20-Canada)
46. red body, purple interior, black plastic base, detailed trim tempa, gold 6 spoke spiral wheels, China casting ($50+) (CHI)(MW20-Canada)
47. maroon body, purple interior, black plastic base, detailed trim tempa, gold 6 spoke spiral wheels, China casting ($50+) (CHI)(MW20-Canada)
48. dark green body, black interior, black plastic base, detailed trim tempa, gold 6 spoke spiral wheels, China casting ($50+)(CHI)(MW20-Canada)
49. black body, black interior, black plastic base, detailed trim tempa, gold 6 spoke spiral wheels, China casting ($50+) (CHI)(MW20-Canada)
50. dark green body, white & black interior, black plastic base, detailed trim tempa, gold 6 spoke spiral wheels, China casting ($50+)(CHI)

51. metallic gold body, black interior, black plastic base, no tempa, gold 6 spoke spiral wheels, China casting ($50+)(CHI)
52. dark cream body, red interior, red plastic base, red & gray stripes tempa, 4 arch wheels, Manaus casting ($35-50)(BR)
53. white body, red interior, black plastic base, "Wonder Woman" tempa, chrome disc wheels with rubber tires, Mattel China casting ($3-5)(JL)
54. yellow body, red & black interior, black plastic base, detailed trim tempa, gold 6 spoke spiral wheels, China casting ($50+)(CHI)
55. yellow body, white & black interior, black plastic base, detailed trim tempa, gold 6 spoke spiral wheels, China casting ($50+)(CHI)
56. rose red body, black interior, black plastic base, detailed trim tempa, gold 6 spoke spiral wheels, China casting ($50+)(CHI)

MB40-D ROCKET TRANSPORTER, issued 1985 (ROW) (MB145)
MB60-H ROCKET TRANSPORTER, issued 1990 (USA)

NOTE: Below models with 8 spoke wheels & black plastic base unless otherwise noted.

1. white body, blue windows, white rocket, "NASA" with US flag tempa, silver hubs, Macau casting ($1-2)
2. white body, blue windows, white rocket, "NASA" with US flag tempa, silver hubs, China casting ($1-2)
3. black body, blue windows, dark gray rocket, yellow & gray camouflage tempa, black hubs, China casting ($25-35)(CM)
4. white body, blue windows, white rocket, "NASA" with checkers tempa, silver hubs, China casting ($1-2)
5. pink-tan body, smoke windows, pink-tan rocket, green & brown camouflage tempa, black hubs, Thailand casting ($1-2)(5pk)
6. white body, blue windows, white rocket, "NASA" with checkers tempa, silver hubs, Thailand casting ($1-2)
7. white body, blue windows, white rocket (rocket has print on 1 side only), "NASA" with checkers tempa, silver hubs, Thailand casting ($1-2)
8. green body, smoke green windows, green rocket, black hubs, black & brown camouflage tempa, Thailand casting ($1-2)(5pk)
9. olive body, smoke green windows, olive rocket, black hubs, "T-7871-6" tempa, Thailand casting ($1-2)
10. beige body, smoke windows, black rocket, black hubs, brown camouflage tempa, Thailand casting ($1-2)(PS)
11. white body, smoke green windows, gray rocket, black hubs, gray & olive camouflage tempa, gray base, Thailand casting ($1-2)(5pk)
12. dark sand body, smoke windows, dark sand rocket, black hubs, "T-7871-6" & star tempa, Thailand casting ($1-2)(5pk)
13. black body, blue windows, red rocket, black hubs, skull & crossbones tempa, Thailand casting ($3-5)(AU)
14. white body, smoke windows, olive rocket, black hubs, gray & olive camouflage tempa, gray base, Thailand casting ($1-2)(PS)
15. black body, smoke green windows, black rocket, black hubs, green & brown camouflage tempa, brown base, Thailand casting ($1-2)(5pk)
16. black body, smoke green windows, black rocket, black hubs, green & brown camouflage tempa, brown base, China casting ($1-2)(5pk)
17. lime body, smoke windows, black rocket, "Intergalactic Defence" tempa, China casting ($1-2)(MW58/1999 ROW)
18. lime body, smoke windows, black rocket, "Intergalactic Defense" tempa, China casting ($1-2)(MW63/1999 ROW)
19. white body, smoke windows, olive rocket, chrome hubs, gray & olive camouflage tempa, China casting ($8-12)(PS)
20. lemon body, red windows, silver-gray rocket, "Mission1 Missiles" tempa, China casting ($1-2)(MW39/2000 US)(MW24/2000 ROW)
21. lemon body, red windows, silver-gray rocket, "Mission 1 Missiles/ Matchbox 2000" tempa, China casting ($2-4)(MW39/2000 US)
22. brick red body, amber windows, orange-yellow rocket, "Test Mission" & yellow stripes tempa, China casting ($1-2)(5pk)
23. black body, blue windows, dark gray rocket, yellow & gray camouflage tempa, 5 crown wheels with black hubs, China casting ($25-40)(CM)(CHI)(MP)
24. dark blue body, amber windows, yellow rocket, "Jimmy Neutron Boy Genius" tempa, 7 spoke sawblade wheels, China casting ($1-2)(5pk)
25. metallic blue body, blue windows, orange rocket, "Cape Canaveral" tempa, 7 spoke sawblade wheels, China casting ($1-2)(AW)

MB40-E FORD SIERRA *see MB15-D*

MB40-F ROAD ROLLER, issued 1991 (USA) (MB772)
MB68-H ROAD ROLLER, issued 1991 (ROW)

NOTE: Below models with black plastic front roller & 5 crown rear wheels.

1. dark orange body, & base, dark gray interior, 5 crown rear wheels, blue stripes tempa, Thailand casting ($1-2)
2. orange-yellow body & base, dark gray interior, 5 crown rear wheels, red stripes & design tempa, Thailand casting ($1-2)
3. orange body & base, dark gray interior, 5 crown rear wheels, black stripes & design tempa, Thailand casting ($1-2)(5pk)
4. blue body & base, silver-gray interior, 5 crown rear wheels, white stripes & "PR-510" & dots tempa, China casting ($1-2)(MW29/1999)
5. orange body & base, black interior, 5 crown rear wheels, white roof & black dashes & "R75" tempa, China casting ($3-5)(MW9/1999GR)

MB40-G FORD MONDEO, issued 1995 (USA) (MB272)
MB33-I FORD MONDEO, issued 1995 (ROW)

NOTE: Below models with clear windows & black plastic base.

1. blue body, tan interior, 6-spoke spiral wheels, "15ICS" with blue "Mondeo" tempa, Thailand casting ($1-2)
2. blue body, tan interior, 6-spoke spiral wheels, "15ICS" with red "Mondeo" tempa, Thailand casting ($1-2)
3. blue body, tan interior, 5 spoke concave star wheels, "Ford" logo tempa, Thailand casting ($1-2)
4. white body, dark blue interior, 5 spoke concave star wheels, "Airport Security" tempa, China casting ($10-15)(PS)(AS)

MB40-H 1969 CAMARO SS-396, issued 1997 (MB302)

NOTE: Below models with clear windshield, black plastic base & China casting unless otherwise noted

1. metallic blue body, black interior, 5 spoke concave star wheels, "Camaro SS" & dual white stripes tempa ($1-2)
2. red body, black interior, 5 spoke concave star wheels, dual white stripes tempa ($1-2)(AP)
3. dark green body, white & black interior, white side stripes tempa, chrome disc wheels with rubber tires ($3-5)(PC17)
4. metallic blue body, black interior, 5 spoke concave star wheels, dual white stripes & "Great Camaro Gathering 1997" tempa ($35-50)(C2)
5. white body, bright red interior, 5 spoke concave star wheels, dual black stripes tempa ($1-2)(MW33/1998)
6. white body, dark red interior, 5 spoke concave star wheels, dual black stripes tempa ($1-2)(MW33/1998)
7. orange body, white & black interior, chrome disc wheels with rubber wheels, white & black stripes tempa ($3-5)(PC20)

8. metallic gold body, black interior, 5 spoke concave star wheels, no tempa ($5-10)(CH)
9. orange body, black interior, 5 spoke concave star wheels, black stripes tempa ($1-2)(5pk)
10. white body, red & black interior, chrome disc wheels with rubber tires, red bands & "Coca Cola" tempa ($4-6)(Coke PC)
11. white body, red & black interior, chrome disc wheels with rubber tires, red bands, "Coca Cola" & www.cocacolastore.com tempa ($50+)(CCI)
12. white body, red interior, 5 spoke concave star wheels, "East Coast Camaro Gathering IV" tempa ($20-30)(CCI)

NOTE: Below models with Mattel China casting.

13.red body, smoke windows, orange interior, lace wheels, "Nickelodeon" tempa, lime base ($1-2)(CA)
14. light blue body, smoke windows, orange interior, lace wheels, "Nickelodeon" tempa, lime base ($1-2)(CA)
15. black body, amber windows, purple interior, lace wheels, "Oooo! & ghosts tempa, gray base ($1-2)(5pk)
16. blue-green body, light smoke windows, yellow interior, lace wheels, "Wile E." with Wile E. Coyote tempa, blue base ($1-2)(5pk)
17. metallic lime body, light smoke windows, yellow interior, lace wheels, "Wile E." with Wile E. Coyote tempa, blue base ($1-2)(CA)
18. metallic pea green body, clear windshield, black interior, 5 spoke slotted wheels, black pinstripe & detailed trim tempa, gray base ($1-2)(SF40/2004)

MB40-I FJ HOLDEN VAN , issued 1998 (ROW) (MB282)
MB282 FJ HOLDEN VAN, issued 1995 (AU)

NOTE: Below models listed with clear windows, black interior, black plastic base, solid disc wheels &Thailand casting unless otherwise note. This model was never given a series number until 1998 when it was introduced in the ROW line.

1. white body, "Kids World" & blue oblong tempa ($4-6)(AU)
2. orange-red body, "Royal Mail" tempa ($4-6)(AU)
3. white body, "Auto One" tempa ($4-6)(AU)
4. black body, no tempa ($4-6)(AU)
5. black body, "Sunday Age/ View" tempa ($25-35)(LD)(AU)
6. black body, "Automodels for Model Cars 1995" tempa ($25-35)(LD)(AU)
7. baby blue body, "Your Own Promotional Van/ Matchbox- Your Logo Here" tempa ($20-25)(AU)
8. black body, "Automodels For Model Cars 1996" tempa ($25-35)(LD)(AU)
9. white & dark blue body, "Premiers 1995/ Blues" tempa ($3-5)(AU)
10. dark blue & black body, "Premiers 1995/ Bulldogs" tempa ($3-5)(AU)
11. white & black body, "Magpies" tempa ($3-5)(AU)
12. white & dark blue body, "Cats" tempa ($3-5)(AU)
13. white & dark blue body, "Blues" tempa ($3-5)(AU)
14. white & blue body, "Kangaroos" tempa ($3-5)(AU)
15. red & white body, "Sydney" tempa ($3-5)(AU)
16. red & green body, "Dockers" tempa ($3-5)(AU)
17. red & blue body, "Bulldogs" tempa ($3-5)(AU)
18. red & dark blue body, "Demons" tempa ($3-5)(AU)
19. red & black body, "Bombers" tempa ($3-5)(AU)
20. light red & black body, "Saints" tempa ($3-5)(AU)
21. burgundy & yellow body, "Bears" tempa ($3-5)(AU)
22. brown & yellow body, "Hawks" tempa ($3-5)(AU)
23. yellow & blue body, "West Coast" tempa ($3-5)(AU)
24. yellow & dark blue body, "Crows" tempa ($3-5)(AU)
25. yellow & black body, "Tigers" tempa ($3-5)(AU)
26. red & blue body, "Lions" tempa ($3-5)(AU)
27. baby blue body, "Bevic" tempa ($18-25)(AU)
28. blue body, "True Blue" tempa ($3-5)(AU)
29. red body, "Matchbox" tempa, China casting ($1-2) (MW40/1998 ROW)
30. white body, "Laverne & Shirley/ Shotz" tempa, China casting ($4-6)(STR)
31. green body, fruit design tempa, China casting ($2-3) (MW21/1999 ROW)
32. beige body, chrome interior, surfer design tempa, China casting ($2-3) (MW14/2000AU)
33. green body, chrome interior, "Coca Cola Good with Food" tempa, China casting ($5-6)(Avon)(TP)
34. black body, gray interior, orange & red design tempa, China casting ($2-4)(MW63/2001 AU)

NOTE: Below models with Mattel China casting.

35. brown body, black interior, "Cocoa Puffs" tempa, dot dash wheels, gray base, China casting ($1-2)(5pk)
36. slate blue & white body, blue interior, "Coca Cola Sign of Good Taste" tempa ($3-5)(Coke PC)
37. metallic pea green, amber windows, black interior, "Tweety" & Tweety Bird tempa, dark blue base ($1-2)(5pk)
38. red body, black interior, amber windows, "Tweety" & Tweety Bird tempa, black base ($1-2)(CA)
39. white body, orange-yellow interior & grille, clear windows, "Nickelodeon" tempa, blue base ($1-2)(5pk)
40. black body, "Omps Funeral Home" ($18-25)(CCI)
41. black body, "MICA Australian Convention 2003" ($20-25)(C2)(AU)
42. beige body, chrome interior, "Bendigo/ Celebrating 50 Years" ($25-40)(C2)(AU)
43. baby blue body, "Super Southern Swap Meet 2004 Ballarat" tempa ($18-25)(C2)(AU)
44. lemon body, orange-yellow interior & grille, amber windows, "Nickelodeon" tempa, blue base ($1-2)(CA)
45. white & blue body, "Thrifty Hardware- Your Handy Hardware Store", black base ($8-12)(AU)
46. blue & black body, "Gowing Bros- Pioneer Distributors of Australian Goods", black base ($12-18)(AU)
47. red & black body, "Gowing Bros- Pioneer Distributors of Australian Goods", black base ($12-18)(AU)

MB40-J SUBMERSIBLE *see MB45-F*

MB40-K DODGE CONCEPT CAR, issued 1999 (USA) (MB357

NOTE: Below models with clear windows, black plastic base & China casting.

1. unpainted body, black interior, no tempa, chrome disc wheels with rubber tires ($4-6)(FE)
2. bronze body, black interior, detailed trim tempa, chrome disc wheels with rubber tires ($4-6)(FE)
3. bronze body, black interior, no tempa, 5 spoke concave star wheels ($1-2)(MW40/1999 US)
4. black & gray-green body, white interior, "Green Lantern" tempa, chrome disc wheels with rubber tires ($3-5)(JL)
5. green body, blue windows, red interior, "Martian Manhunter" tempa, 10 spoke flower wheels ($1-2)(5pk)
6. lemon body, blue windows, red interior, "Martian Manhunter" tempa, 10 spoke flower wheels ($1-2)(CA)

MB40-L MERCEDES "G" WAGON *see MB30-F*

MB40-M CEMENT MIXER, issued 2001 (MB495)

NOTE: Below models with 4 spoke domed wheels, ,black base & China casting unless otherwise noted.

1. white body, smoke windows, red barrel, "Matchbox 27" tempa ($1-2)(MW40/2001)

2. orange-yellow body, blue windows, blue barrel, "Matchbox 27" tempa ($1-2)(MW17/2002)
3. orange-yellow body, blue windows, blue barrel, "Matchbox 27" & "Matchbox 50" tempa ($2-4)(MW17/2002)
4. metallic red body, dark smoke windows, gray barrel, "Matchbox" on barrel tempa ($3-5)(PS)
5. dark blue body, amber windows, white barrel, large steer head barrel tempa, "42" & small "Matchbox" on door tempa ($1-2)(5pk)
6. dark blue body, amber windows, white barrel, small steer head on barrel tempa, "42" & small "Matchbox" behind rear wheel tempa ($1-2)(5pk)
7. white body, dark smoke windows, orange-yellow barrel, "22" stripes & dashes tempa with "E22" barrel tempa ($1-2)MW22/2003)
8. white body, dark smoke windows, orange-yellow barrel, "23", stripes & dashes & "Hero City" tempa with "E22" barrel tempa ($2-4)(MW22/2003)
9. orange body, red windows, yellow barrel, "Team" tempa with mixer design barrel tempa, 5 crown dot wheels ($1-2)(5pk)

MB41-A FORD GT, issued 1970

NOTE: Below models with clear windows, red interior & England casting. Earliest versions with narrow wheels with later versions with wide wheels.

1. white body, black base, "6" label, 5 spoke wheels ($12-15)
2. white body, light green base, "6" label, 5 spoke wheels ($12-15)
3. white body, dark green base, "6" label, 5 spoke wheels ($12-15)
4. bronze body, black base, "6" label, 5 spoke wheels ($12-15)
5. bronze body, light yellow base, "6" label, 5 spoke wheels ($12-15)
6. bronze body, dark yellow base, "6" label, 5 spoke wheels ($12-15)
7. bronze body, green base, "6" label, 5 spoke wheels ($12-15)
8. bronze body, charcoal base, "6" label, 5 spoke wheels ($12-15)
9. bronze body, light gray base, "6" label, 5 spoke wheels ($12-15)
10. bronze body, dark gray base, "6" label, 5 spoke wheels ($12-15)
11. white body, black base, cat head label (from MB1-B), 5 spoke wheels ($15-20)
12. white body, black base, "6" label (from MB62-C), 5 spoke wheels ($18-25)
13. white body, black base, "6" label (from MB62-C), dot dash wheels ($18-25)
14. yellow body, black base, no label, dot dash wheels ($1500+)(MP)(IT)

NOTE: Available as an Hungarian and Bulgarian casting. Assorted colors available. ($5-25)

MB41-B SIVA SPYDER, issued 1972

NOTE: Below models with clear windows, unpainted metal base & England casting unless otherwise noted.

1. metallic red body, no tempa, cream interior, chrome body strap, 5 spoke wheels ($15-20)
2. metallic red body, no tempa, cream interior, black body strap, 5 spoke wheels ($12-15)
3. metallic red body, no tempa, white interior, black body strap, 5 spoke wheels ($12-15)
4. metallic red body, no tempa, ivory interior, black body strap, 5 spoke wheels ($12-15)
5. metallic red body, no tempa, ivory interior, black body strap, 4 spoke wheels ($12-15)
6. dark blue body, stripes tempa, ivory interior, black body strap, 5 spoke wheels ($15-18)
7. dark blue body, stripes tempa, white interior, black body strap, 5 spoke wheels ($15-18)
8. dark blue body, stripes tempa, cream interior, black body strap, 5 spoke wheels ($15-18)
9. powder blue body, spider & web tempa, ivory interior, black body strap, 5 spoke wheels ($15-18)(LE)
10. powder blue body, spider & web tempa, ivory interior, black body strap, 5 spoke wheels, black windows ($15-18)(LE)
11. dark blue body, no tempa, cream interior, black body strap, 5 spoke wheels, Manaus tab on base ($50-75)(BR)
12. blue body, stripes tempa, cream interior, black body strap, 5 spoke wheels, Manaus tab on base ($35-50)

MB41-C AMBULANCE, issued 1977 (MB041)

NOTE: Below models with blue windows, white rear doors, dot dash wheels & England casting unless otherwise noted. Versions with Macau, Hong Kong or China castings see MB25E.

1. white body, unpainted base, gray interior, "Ambulance" & cross labels ($5-8)
2. white body, unpainted base, light yellow interior, "Ambulance" & cross labels ($5-8)
3. white body, unpainted base, orange interior, "Ambulance" & cross labels ($7-10)
4. white body, unpainted base with Manaus tab, gray interior, "Ambulance" & cross labels ($35-50)(BR)
5. white body, white base with Manaus tab, gray interior, "Ambulance" & cross labels ($35-50)(BR)
6. white body, clear windows, unpainted base, gray interior, "Emergency Medical Service" labels ($10-15)
7. white body, unpainted base, gray interior, "Emergency Medical Service" labels ($5-8)
8. white body, unpainted base, light yellow interior, "Emergency Medical Service" labels ($5-8)
9. white body, unpainted base, orange interior, "Emergency Medical Service" labels ($7-10)
10. white body, unpainted base, dark tan interior, "Emergency Medical Service" labels ($5-8)
11. white body, silver-gray base, light yellow interior, "Emergency Medical Service" labels ($5-8)
12. white body, unpainted base, gray interior, "Ambulance" & EMS logo labels ($5-8)
13. white body, silver-gray base, gray interior, "Ambulance" & EMS logo labels ($5-8)
14. white body, unpainted base, gray interior, 5 arch wheels, "Ambulance" & EMS logo labels ($10-15)
15. white body, unpainted base, gray interior, small "Ambulance" labels ($15-18)
16. silver-gray body, unpainted base, gray interior, "Paris Dakar 81" labels ($25-30)(FR)
17. silver-gray body & rear doors, unpainted base, gray interior, "Paris Dakar 81" labels ($25-30)(FR)
18. red body, unpainted base, gray interior, "Notarzt" tempa ($25-40)(GR)
19. red body, unpainted base, orange interior, "Notarzt" labels ($50-75)(GR)
20. white body, unpainted base, gray interior, maroon "Pacific Ambulance" tempa ($6-8)(CR)
21. white body, unpainted base, gray interior, red "Pacific Ambulance" tempa ($6-8)(CR)
22. white body, silver-gray base, gray interior, red "Pacific Ambulance" tempa ($6-8)(CR)

MB41-D KENWORTH AERODYNE, issued 1982 (USA) (MB103/310)

NOTE: Other variations on this model exist as cabs to Convoy models but these are not listed as singles. England base models 1-3 have "Lesney" cast. Version 4 onwards with England base have "Matchbox International" cast. All models with chrome plastic base & 8 spoke wheels.

1. red body, amber windows, black & white flared stripes tempa, England casting ($3-5)
2. red body, clear windows, black & white flared stripes tempa, England casting ($3-5)
3. red body, amber windows, black & white straight stripes tempa, England casting ($3-5)
4. red body, clear windows, black & white straight stripes tempa, England casting ($3-5)
5. red body, clear windows, black & white curved stripes tempa, England casting ($3-5)
6. black body, clear windows, orange/yellow/white stripes tempa, Macau casting ($4-6)
7. pearly silver body, clear windows, red & blue stripes tempa, Macau casting ($3-5)
8. blue body, clear windows, no tempa, Macau casting ($4-6)(MP)
   NOTE: Above model normally associated with CY-9A Mitre 10 Convoy but found as a release in multipacks
9. black body, clear windows, "1928 Kenworth 1998" tempa, China casting ($35-50)(US)
10. white body, clear windows, two-tone blue stripes & black rear section tempa, China casting, chrome disc wheels with rubber tires, antennas cast ($3-4)(TN)

MB41-E RACING PORSCHE *see MB55-F*

MB41-F JAGUAR XJ6, issued 1987 (USA) (MB141/244)
MB 1-E JAGUAR XJ6, issued 1987 (ROW)

NOTE: Below models with black base, clear windows and 8 dot wheels unless otherwise noted. Version 1 with 1984 or 1986 date on base.

1. metallic red body, tan interior, no tempa, doors open, metal base, Macau casting ($1-2)
2. black body, maroon interior, "W&M" & crest tempa, doors open, metal base, Macau casting ($25-40)(UK)(OP)
3. green body, maroon interior, "Redoxon/ Jaguar" tempa, doors open, metal base, Macau casting ($18-25)(HK)
4. white body, black interior, no tempa, doors open, metal base, Macau casting($7-10)(KS)(UK)
5. metallic red body, tan interior, no tempa, doors open, metal base, Thailand casting ($1-2)
   NOTE: Versions 1-5 with doors cast open & metal bases. Below versions doors cast shut & plastic bases.
6. blue body, black base, tan interior, clear windows, 8 dot wheels, no tempa, Thailand casting ($2-3)(SS)
7. white body, black base, tan interior, clear windows, 8 dot wheels, "Police" with shield & checkers tempa, Thailand casting ($2-4)
8. metallic blue body, blue base, tan interior, chrome windows, gray disc wheels with rubber tires, detailed trim tempa, Thailand casting ($2-4)(WC)
9. met. silver blue body, black base, white interior, blue windows, 8 dot wheels, painted lights & bumpers tempa, Thailand casting ($2-4)(GS)
10. dark green body, black base, black & tan interior, clear windows, chrome disc wheels with rubber tires, detailed trim tempa, Thailand casting ($8-12)(UC)
11. charcoal body, charcoal base, black & red interior, clear windows, chrome disc wheels with rubber tires, detailed trim tempa, Thailand casting ($3-5)(JC)(PC)
12. white body, gray base, blue interior, clear windows, 8 dot wheels, "Police" with shield & checkers tempa , Thailand casting($1-2)(MW27/1998 ROW)
13. white body, gray base, blue interior, clear windows, 8 dot wheels, "Police" with shield & checkers tempa , China casting($1-2)(MW27/1998 ROW)
14. blue body, black base, gray interior, smoke windows, 8 dot wheels, British flag tempa, China casting ($2-4)(MW14/2000 UK)
15. dark green body, black base, black interior, smoke windows, 10 spoke flower wheels, light green stripe & Jaguar design tempa, China casting ($2-4)(MW52/2001 ROW)(MW51/2001 GR)

MB41-G VECTRA CAVALIER GSi 2000 *see MB22-G*

MB41-H COSMIC BLUES *see MB26-D*

MB41-I SUNBURNER *see MB15-I*

MB41-J FERRARI 456GT *see MB17-G*

MB41-K SKI BOAT, issued 1999 (USA) (MB411/453)
MB36-G SKI BOAT, issued 1999 (ROW)

NOTE: Below models with smoke windshield & China casting.

1. yellow deck, white hull, blue driver, blue skier, two tone blue tempa, white wheels ($1-2)(MW41/1999 US/MW36/1999 ROW)(MW31/1999 GR)
2. blue-gray deck, black hull, yellow driver, no skier, maroon & white tempa, black wheels ($1-2)(5pk)
3. blue & orange deck, white hull, orange driver, orange skier, purple/orange/blue tempa, white wheels ($1-2)(MW24/2001)
4. light blue & brown deck, yellow hull, yellow driver, amber windshield, no skier, "Nickelodeon" tempa, black wheels ($1-2)(5pk)
5. light blue & brown deck, red hull, yellow driver, amber windshield, no skier, "Nickelodeon" tempa, black wheels ($1-2)(CA)

MB41-L FLATBED TRUCK, issued 2000 (USA) (MB443B)
MB14-I FLATBED TRUCK, issued 1001 (ROW)

NOTE: Below models with pale blue windows, blue dome lights, China casting.

1. lemon body, gray flat bed, silver-gray base, "HB Show Cars" tempa , 8 spoke wheels ($1-2)(MW41/2000 US)
2. lemon body, gray flat bed, silver-gray base, "HB Show Cars" & "Matchbox 2000" tempa, 8 spoke wheels ($2-4)(MW41/2000 US)
3. orange body, black flatbed, silver-gray base, "Auto Club" tempa, 8 spoke wheels ($2-4)(MW14/2001)
4. orange body, black flatbed, silver-gray base, "Auto Club" tempa, 7 spoke sawblade wheels ($1-2)(MW14/2001)
5. metallic blue body, black flatbed, silver-gray base, monkey & wrench tempa, 7 spoke sawblade wheels ($1-2)(5pk)
6. metallic green body, gray flatbed, charcoal base, "Matchbox Towing" & stripes tempa, 7 spoke sawblade wheels ($3-5)(PB)
7. white body, gray flatbed, black base, no tempa, 8 spoke wheels ($25-40)(ASAP)

MB41-M RADAR PLANE, issued 2001 (MB497)

NOTE: Below models with black wheels & China casting unless otherwise noted.

1. blue body, yellow wings & radar, gray base, "439" & medic cross tempa ($1-2) (MW41/2001)
2. blue body, yellow wings & radar, gray base, "429" without medic cross tempa ($1-2)(MW41/2001)

3. orange-yellow body, red wings & radar, checkers & globe tempa ($1-2)(5pk)
4. dark metallic green body, glow lime wings & radar, globe design tempa ($1-2)(MW40/2002)
5. dark metallic green body, glow lime wings & radar, globe design & "Matchbox 50" tempa ($3-5)(MW40/2002)
6. black body, blue wings & radar, globe design tempa ($1-2)(5pk)
7. light orange-yellow body, orange wings & radar, design & "34" tempa ($1-2)(MW342003)
8. light orange-yellow body, orange wings & radar, design, "34" & "Hero City" tempa ($3-5)(MW34/2003)
9. metallic gold body, orange wings & radar, design & "34" tempa ($3-4)(20pk)
10. dark metallic blue body, orange wings & radar, "Jet" & eagle head tempa ($1-2)(5pk)

MB41-N SEA RESCUE HELICOPTER, issued 2003 (MB571)

NOTE: Below models with blue windows, red blades, red tail, red base, black wheels, China casting unless otherwise noted.

1. white body, nondescript design tempa ($1-2)(MW41/2003)
2. white body, nondescript design & "Hero City" tempa ($2-4)(MW41/2003)
3. light metallic blue body, nondescript design tempa ($3-4)(20pk)
4. dark metallic blue body, amber windows, gray blades, blue tail & base, multi-color & design & "Police Force" tempa (MW70/2004)

MB41-O CHECKER CAB, issued 2004 (MB600)

NOTE: Below models with clear windows, black interior, gray plastic base & China casting.

1. orange-yellow body, lace wheels, "Checker Special", checkers & sign board design tempa ($1-2)(MW41/2004)
2. light orange-yellow body, 10 spoke flower wheels, "Checker Special", checkers & sign board design tempa ($1-2)(MW4/2005)

MB41-P FORD GT, issued 2004 (SF)(MB634)

NOTE: Below models with clear windows, red interior, 5 spoke wheels, black base & China casting.

1. white body, blue stripe with "6" & head & tail light tempa ($3-5)(SF41/2004)
2. silver-gray body, blue stripe with "6" & head & tail lights tempa ($40-60) (SF41/US promo)

MB42-A IRON FAIRY CRANE, issued 1970

NOTE: Below models with yellow plastic base, yellow interior, 4 spoke wheels & yellow hook & England casting. Earliest versions with narrow wheels with later versions having wide wheels.

1. red body, yellow boom ($65-80)
2. red body, lime boom ($250-350)
3. dark orange-red body, yellow boom ($40-55)
4. dark orange-red body, lime boom ($40-55)
5. light orange-red body, lime boom ($40-55)

MB42-B TYRE FRYER, issued 1972

NOTE: Below models with 5 spoke rear wheels, metal base & England casting.

1. light metallic blue body, black base, yellow interior, no labels, 5 spoke front wheels ($12-15)
2. mid metallic blue body, unpainted base, yellow interior, no labels, 5 spoke front wheels ($12-15)
3. mid metallic blue body, black base, yellow interior, no labels, 5 spoke front wheels ($12-15)
4. mid metallic blue body, black base, yellow interior, no labels, maltese cross front wheels ($12-15)
5. mid metallic blue body, black base, orange-yellow interior, no labels, 5 spoke front wheels ($12-15)
6. dark metallic blue body, black base, yellow interior, no labels, 5 spoke front wheels ($12-15)
7. orange body, black base, yellow interior, "Jaffa Mobile" labels, 5 spoke front wheels ($85-110)(UK)(OP)

MB42-C MERCEDES CONTAINER TRUCK, issued 1977

NOTE: Below models with dot dash wheels, metal base & England casting.

1. red body, beige container, red roof & doors, black base, blue windows, "Sealand" labels ($5-7)
2. red body, beige container, red roof & doors, unpainted base, blue windows, "Sealand" labels ($5-7)
3. red body, beige container, red roof & doors, unpainted base, blue windows, "N.Y.K." labels ($5-7)
4. red body, beige container, red roof & doors, black base, blue windows, "N.Y.K." labels ($5-7)
5. red body, beige container, red roof & doors, unpainted base, blue windows, "N.Y.K." labels, black hubs ($5-7)
6. red body, beige container, red roof & doors, unpainted base, blue windows, "Sealand" labels, black hubs ($5-7)
7. red body, beige container, red roof & doors, unpainted base, blue windows, "O.C.L." labels ($10-15)
8. yellow body, yellow container, roof & doors, black base, blue windows, "Deutsche Bundespost" labels ($25-40)(GR)
9. red body, beige container, red roof & doors, unpainted base, blue windows, "Confern" labels ($35-45)(GR)
10. red body, yellow-tan container, red roof & doors, unpainted base, blue windows, "Sealand" labels ($5-7)
11. red body, white container, red roof & doors, unpainted base, blue windows, "Matchbox" labels ($8-12)
12. red body, white container, red roof & doors, unpainted base, purple windows, "Matchbox" labels ($8-12)
13. red body, white container, red roof & doors, unpainted base, red windows, "Mayflower" labels ($8-12)
14. red body, white container, red roof & doors, unpainted base, blue windows, "Mayflower" labels ($8-12)
15. red body, white container, red roof & doors, unpainted base, blue windows, "Confern" applied over "Mayflower" labels ($45-60)
16. green body, green container, yellow roof & doors, unpainted base, blue windows, "Confern" applied over "Mayflower" labels ($100-150)
17. green body, green container, yellow roof & doors, unpainted base, purple windows, "Confern" applied over "Mayflower" labels ($100-150)
18. green body, green container, yellow roof & doors, unpainted base, purple windows, "Mayflower" labels ($6-8)
19. green body, green container, yellow roof & doors, unpainted base, red windows, "Mayflower" labels ($6-8)
20. green body, green container, orange roof & doors, unpainted base, red windows, "Mayflower" labels ($6-8)
21. green body, green container, orange roof & doors, unpainted base, purple windows, "Mayflower" labels ($6-8)
22. green body, green container, orange roof & doors, unpainted base, blue windows, "Mayflower" labels ($6-8)
23. blue body, blue container, roof & doors, unpainted base, blue windows, "Karstadt" labels ($35-50)(GR)
24. red body, gray plastic dump, unpainted base, blue windows , white label with stripes ($50-75)(PS)
25. red body, beige container, red roof & doors, black base with Manaus tab, blue windows, "Sealand" labels ($35-50)(BR)

26. red body, white container, red doors & roof, unpainted base, blue windows, "Stenval" over "Matchbox" labels on left side only ($150-175)(FR)
27. red body, white container, red doors & roof, unpainted base, blue windows, "Uniroyal" labels (from Convoy CY-3A) ($150-175)

MB42-D 1957 FORD THUNDERBIRD, issued 1982 (MB042)

1. red body, unpainted metal base, white interior, clear windshield, no tempa, dot dash wheels, England casting ($3-5)
2. red body, unpainted metal base, white interior, clear windshield, no tempa, 5 arch wheels, England casting ($3-5)
3. red body, silver-gray base, white interior, clear windshield, 5 arch wheels, no tempa, England casting ($3-5)
4. red body, silver-gray base, white interior, clear windows, 5 arch front & dot dash wheels, no tempa, England casting ($4-6)
5. cream & red body, pearly silver metal base, clear windshield, red interior, with tempa, Macau casting ($3-5)
6. cream & red body, pearly silver metal base, light amber windshield, with tempa, 5 arch wheels, Macau casting ($3-5)
7. cream & red body, pearly silver metal base, clear windshield, with tempa, 5 arch wheels, China casting ($3-5)
8. black body, pearly silver metal base, red interior, amber windshield, no tempa, 5 arch wheels, China casting ($3-5)
9. black body, pearly silver metal base, red interior, amber windshield, dot dash front & 5 arch rear wheels, China casting ($3-5)
10. turquoise body, pearly silver metal base, white interior, clear windshield, 5 arch wheels, , "Chubby's" tempa, China casting ($8-12)(US)
11. black body, chrome plastic base, red & white interior, clear windshield, chrome disc wheels with rubber tires, detailed trim tempa, China casting ($3-5)(PC3)
12. red body, chrome plastic base, white interior, clear windshield, 5 arch wheels, "Celebrating Patsy" tempa, China casting ($12-15)(US)
13. met. candy red body, chrome plastic base, white & red interior, clear windshield, chrome disc wheels with rubber tires, detailed trim tempa, China casting ($3-5)(PC6)
14. turquoise body, chrome plastic base, white & turquoise interior, clear windshield, chrome disc wheels with rubber tires, detailed trim tempa, China casting ($10-15)(YST)
15. iridescent white body, chrome plastic base, red interior, clear windshield, 5 arch wheels, no tempa, China casting ($1-2)(5pk)
16. red body, chrome plastic base, white & red interior, clear windshield, chrome disc wheels with rubber tires, detailed trim tempa, China casting ($3-5)(SC3)
17. blue body, chrome plastic base, white & red interior, clear windshield, chrome disc wheels with rubber tires, yellow & orange flames tempa, China casting ($3-5)(PC11)
18. white body, chrome plastic base, red & pink interior, clear windshield, chrome disc wheels with rubber tires, detailed trim tempa, China casting ($15-20)(GC)
19. blue body, chrome plastic base, white interior, clear windshield, 5 arch wheels, yellow & orange flames tempa, China casting ($50+)(CHI)
20. lemon body, chrome plastic base, black & white interior, clear windshield, chrome disc wheels with rubber tires, detailed trim tempa, China casting ($3-5)(PC17)
21. metallic silver body, chrome plastic base, blue & white interior, clear windshield, chrome disc wheels with rubber tires, T-Bird design tempa, China casting ($3-5)(PC20)
22. pink body, unpainted metal base, white & pink interior, clear windshield, 5 arch wheels, "Pinky/Happy Days" tempa, China casting ($8-12)(STR-Avon)
23. pale yellow body, gray plastic base, light gray interior, smoke windshield, 5 arch wheels, "Matchbox 2000" tempa, China casting ($2-4)(MW16/2000 US)
24. pale yellow body, gray plastic base, light gray interior, smoke windshield, 5 arch wheels, no tempa, China casting ($1-2)(MW16/2000 US)
25. pale yellow body, chrome plastic base, black & white interior, clear windshield, chrome disc wheels with rubber white wall tires, yellow painted spare tempa, China casting ($10-15)(EL)

    NOTE: Above issued with Graceland diorama & plexiglass cover.
26. red body, chrome plastic base, white interior, clear windshield, 5 arch wheels, "Always Patsy/ Crazy For The Bloom" tempa, China casting ($10-15)(CCI)
27. red body, chrome plastic base, white interior, clear windshield, 5 arch wheels, "April 28, 2001/ Joy & Michael" tempa, China casting ($50+)(CCI)
28. red body, chrome plastic base, white interior, clear windshield, 5 arch wheels, "Always Patsy" with her pic on trunk and "2001" tempa, China casting ($10-15)(CCI)
29. white body, gray plastic base, red interior, blue windshield, 10 spoke flower wheels, "United States of America" tempa, Mattel China casting ($1-2)(AM)(MP)
30. red body, chrome plastic base, white interior, clear windshield, 5 arch wheels, "3rd Annual Salmon River Festival" tempa, China casting ($10-15)(CCI)
31. pale yellow body, gray plastic base, light gray interior, smoke windshield, 5 arch wheels, "Cruisin New England Magazine 2002" tempa, China casting ($50+)(CCI)
32. red body, chrome plastic base, tan interior, clear windshield with trim, chrome disc wheels with rubber tires, detailed trim tempa, Mattel China casting ($3-5)(MCC)
33. light blue body, gray plastic base, red interior, smoke windshield, 10 spoke flower wheels, "Hero City Sports" tempa, Mattel China casting ($1-2)(5pk)
34. orange body, neon pink plastic base, neon pink interior, amber windshield, lace wheels, "Magenta" tempa, Mattel China casting ($1-2)(5pk)
35. metallic purple body, neon pink plastic base, neon pink interior, amber windshield, lace wheels, "Magenta" tempa, Mattel China casting ($1-2)(CA)
36. yellow body, turquoise plastic base, red interior, dark smoke windshield, 10 spoke flower wheels, "Las Vegas Nevada" tempa, Mattel casting ($1-2)(AW)

MB42-E FAUN CRANE TRUCK, issued 1984 (ROW) (MB140/314)

MB42-E FAUN CRANE TRUCK, issued 1987 (USA)

NOTE: Below models with black plastic base & maltese cross wheels.

1. yellow body, yellow metal crane cab, black boom, red hook, "Reynolds Crane Hire" tempa, England casting ($2-3)
2. yellow body, yellow metal crane cab, black boom, red hook, "Reynolds Crane Hire" tempa, Macau casting ($1-2)
3. yellow body, yellow metal crane cab, black boom, red hook, "Reynolds Crane Hire" tempa, China casting ($1-2)
4. yellow body, yellow metal crane cab, black boom, red hook, no tempa, Macau casting ($2-3)(MC)
5. yellow body, yellow plastic crane cab, black boom, red hook, "Reynolds Crane Hire" tempa, Thailand casting ($1-2)
6. yellow body, yellow plastic crane cab, black boom, red hook, no tempa, Thailand casting ($2-3)(MC)
7. yellow body, red plastic cane cab, black boom, red hook, bridge & road design tempa, Thailand casting ($1-2)

8. yellow body, florescent orange plastic crane cab, black boom, red hook, checkers & "IC" logo tempa, bar code on base, China casting ($10-15)(IC)
9. yellow body, florescent orange plastic crane cab, black boom, red hook, checkers & "IC" logo tempa, (base without bar code), China casting ($12-15)
10. orange body, gray plastic crane cab, black boom, gray hook, bridge & road design tempa, Thailand casting ($1-2)(MP)
11. florescent orange body, black plastic crane cab, silver-gray boom, black hook, no tempa, Thailand casting ($1-2)
12. florescent orange body, gray plastic crane cab, black boom, gray hook, no tempa, China casting ($1-2)(5pk)
13. pale florescent orange body, black plastic crane cab, silver-gray boom, black hook, no tempa, Thailand casting ($1-2)
14. dark orange body, black plastic crane cab, black boom, black hook, no tempa, China casting ($1-2)
15. light orange body, black plastic crane cab, yellow & lemon boom with lever, black hook, road design tempa, China casting ($1-2)(AS)
16. metallic gold body, black plastic crane cab, black boom, black hook, no tempa, China casting ($5-10)(CH)
17. powder blue body, black plastic crane cab, silver-gray boom, black hook, no tempa, China casting ($1-2)
18. red body, black plastic crane cab, silver-gray boom, black hook, no tempa, China casting ($1-2)(MW15/1998)
19. blue-green body, black plastic cab, silver-gray boom with lever, black hook, dolphin & waves tempa, China casting ($2-4)(AP)
20. matt blue body, plum plastic cab, gray & brown boom, gray hook, dirt & cab logo tempa, China casting ($1-2)(5pk)
21. matt blue body, plum plastic cab, gray & brown boom, gray hook, dirt, cab logo & "Hershey 99" tempa, China casting ($10-15)(CCI)
22. matt blue body, plum plastic cab, gray & brown boom, gray hook, dirt, cab logo & "Up, Up & Away SWFIA!" tempa, China casting ($10-15)(CCI)

MB42-F SEAPLANE, issued 1999 (USA) (MB408)
MB37-J SEAPLANE, issued 1999 (ROW)

NOTE: Below models with China casting.

1. yellow body, yellow wings, silver-gray base, yellow propeller, blue windows, "NJ328" wing tempa, blue stripes body tempa ($1-2)(MW42/1999 US)(MW37/1999 ROW)(MW32/1999 GR)
2. dark blue body, dark blue wings, white base, silver propeller, clear windows, none wing tempa, "90-276/EB32" & red stripes body tempa ($1-2)(5pk)
3. dark cream body, dark blue wings, dark blue base, dark blue propeller, smoke green windows, cream stripes wing tempa, blue stripes & "N165LA" body tempa ($1-2)(5pk)
4. white body, gray wings, red base, gray propeller, clear windows, "Coca Cola" wings tempa, reclining woman & "Coca Cola" body tempa ($4-6)(Coke PC)
5. white body, gray wings, red base, gray propeller, clear windows, "Coca Cola" wings tempa, reclining woman & "Coca Cola" body tempa, www.cocacolastores.com float tempa ($50+)(CCI)
6. red body, red wings, white base, red propeller, smoke windows, none wings tempa, "EB32" with red & black stripes tempa ($1-2)(MW67/ 2000 US)(MW47/2000)
7. red body, red wings, white base, red propeller, smoke windows, none wing tempa, "EB32" with red & black stripes & "Matchbox 2000" tempa ($2-4)(MW67/ 2000 US)
8. white body, white wings & base, white propeller, smoke windows, no tempa ($25-40)(ASAP blank)
9. white body, white wings & base, white propeller, smoke windows, "The Perfect Storm" tempa ($75+)(ASAP)
10. white body, red wings & base, red propeller, amber windows, "Hangar 34 Beach Patrol" tempa ($1-2)(5pk)
11. orange body, white wings, gray base, white propeller, dark smoke windows, "Mountain Base" tempa ($1-2)(5pk)
12. white body, light blue wings & base, light blue propeller, blue windows, "Hangar 14 Beach Patrol" tempa ($1-2)(5pk)
13. light blue body, lime wings, dark blue base, lime propeller, blue windows, "Galapagos" with tortoise tempa ($1-2)(AW)
14. white body, red wings, dark blue base, red propeller, black windows, "H2O Alarm" tempa ($1-2)(5pk)

MB42-G POP-UP CAMPER *see MB62-L*

MB42-H AMBULANCE, issued 2001 (MB498)

NOTE: Below models with China casting.

1. white body, green chassis, blue windows, 4 spoke domed wheels, black base, "Medic M3" tempa ($1-2)(MW42/2001)
2. red body, black chassis, blue windows, 4 spoke domed wheels, chrome base, helmet & hose design tempa ($1-2)(LP)
3. white body, red chassis, blue windows, 4 spoke domed wheels, red base, "USA Ambulance" with star & flag tempa ($1-2)(HR)
4. silver-gray body, green chassis, amber windows, 4 spoke domed wheels, black base, "Ambulance" with yellow & green stripes tempa ($2-4)(MW13/2002 ROW)
5. silver-gray body, green chassis, amber windows, 4 spoke domed wheels, black base, "Ambulance" with yellow & green stripes & "Matchbox 50" tempa ($3-5)(MW13/2002 ROW)
6. metallic gold body, gray chassis, blue windows, 4 spoke domed wheels, red base, "Ultra Med Alarm" tempa ($1-2)(MW26/2002 US)
7. metallic gold body, gray chassis, blue windows, 4 spoke domed wheels, red base, "Ultra Med Alarm" & "Matchbox 50" tempa ($2-4)(MW26/2002 US)
8. white body, blue chassis, red windows, 4 spoke domed wheels, black base, "Super Peak Ambulance" tempa ($1-2)(5pk)
9. white body, blue chassis, red windows, lace wheels, black base, "Super Peak Ambulance" tempa ($1-2)(5pk)
10. white body, blue chassis, amber windows, 4 spoke domed wheels, "Matchbox Ambulance" tempa ($2-4)(PZ)
11. metallic gold body, gray chassis, blue windows, lace wheels, red base, "Ultra Med Alarm" tempa ($1-2)(MW26/2002 US)
12. silver-gray body, red chassis, blue windows, 4 spoke domed wheels, "Apple County Rescue Washington 42" tempa ($1-2)(AM)
13. silver-gray body, red chassis, blue windows, lace wheels, "Apple County Rescue Washington 42" tempa ($5-8)(AM)
14. blue body, gray chassis, amber windows, 4 spoke domed wheels, "Ambulance 12" & "Hero City" tempa ($2-4)(MW12/2003)
15. blue body, gray chassis, amber windows, 4 spoke domed wheels, "Ambulance 12" tempa ($1-2)(MW12/2003)
16. blue body, gray chassis, amber windows, lace wheels, "Ambulance 12" tempa ($1-2)(MW12/2003)

MB42-I 2004 SCHOOL BUS, issued 2004 (MB614)

1. yellow body, clear windows, blue interior, gold 5 crown dot wheels, "Hero City School" tempa, gray base & China casting ($1-2)(MW42/2004)

MB43-A PONY TRAILER, issued 1970 (MB743/843)

NOTE: Versions 1 to 14, & 21 with two white plastic horses. Versions 15 to 20 with two black plastic horses. All versions with clear windows.

1. yellow body, light green base, no label, gray tailgate, 5 spoke wheels, England casting ($18-25)

2. yellow body, dark green base, no label, gray tailgate, 5 spoke wheels, England casting ($18-25)
3. orange body, black base, horse head label, brown tailgate, 5 spoke center cut wheels, England casting ($4-6)(TP)
4. orange body, charcoal base, horse head label, brown tailgate, 5 spoke center cut wheels, England casting ($4-6)(TP)
5. orange body, black base, no label, brown tailgate, 5 spoke center cut wheels, England casting ($4-6)(TP)
6. beige body, black base, horse head label, brown tailgate, 5 spoke center cut wheels, England casting ($4-6)(TP)
7. beige body, charcoal base, horse head label, brown tailgate, 5 spoke center cut wheels, England casting ($4-6)(TP)
8. beige body, black base, no label, brown tailgate, 5 spoke center cut wheels, England casting ($4-6)(TP)
9. beige body, silver-gray base, no label, lime tailgate, dot dash wheels, England casting ($7-10)(TP)
10. beige body, unpainted base, no label, lime tailgate, dot dash wheels, England casting ($7-10)(TP)
11. beige body, black base, horse head label, brown tailgate, dot dash wheels, England casting ($3-5)(TP)
12. beige body, black base, "Silver Shoes" tempa, brown tailgate, dot dash wheels, England casting ($4-6)
13. beige body, black base, "Silver Shoes" tempa, white tailgate, dot dash wheels, Macau casting ($2-3)(TP)
14. beige body, black base, "Silver Shoes" tempa, white tailgate, dot dash wheels, no origin cast ($2-3)(TP)
15. white body, black base, "Polizei" & checkers tempa, blue-gray tailgate, dot dash wheels, no origin cast ($2-3)(TP)
16. white body, black base, horse silhouette tempa, lime tailgate, dot dash wheels, no origin cast ($1-2)(TP)
17. green body with white roof, black base, "Polizei" tempa, green tailgate, dot dash wheels, no origin cast ($1-2)(TP)
18. white body with red roof, black base, black & red dashed stripes tempa, white tailgate, dot dash wheels, no origin cast ($1-2)(TP)
19. blue body, black base, "Kentucky 15" tempa, white tailgate, dot dash wheels, no origin cast ($1-2)(AM)
20. blue body, black base, "Kentucky 15" tempa, white tailgate, dot dash wheels, China imprinted casting ($2-3)(AM)
21. beige body, black base, horse silhouette & mud tempa, black tailgate, dot dash wheels, no origin cast ($1-2)(5pk)

MB43-B DRAGON WHEELS, issued 1972

NOTE: Below models with chrome interior, amber window, "Dragon Wheels" labels, maltese cross rear wheels & England casting unless otherwise noted.

1. light green body, black base, 5 spoke front wheels ($15-18)
2. dark green body, black base, 5 spoke front wheels ($15-18)
3. dark green body, unpainted base, 5 spoke front wheels ($15-18)
4. dark green body, blue-gray base, 5 spoke front wheels ($15-18)
5. dark green body, gray base, 5 spoke front wheels ($15-18)
6. dark green body, black base, dot dash front wheels ($15-18)
7. dark green body, black base, dot dash front & rear wheels ($15-18)
8. lime body, black base with origin ground off, 5 spoke front wheels ($250+)(BR)
9. lime body, unpainted base with Manaus label, "7" with black dot labels, 5 spoke front wheels ($50-75)(BR)
10. metallic red body, black base with Manaus label, 5 spoke front wheels ($250+)(BR)

MB43-C 0-4-0 STEAM LOCO, issued 1978 (MB043)
MB63-H 0-4-0 STEAM LOCO, reissued 1991 (ROW)

NOTE: Below models with black train wheels unless otherwise noted.

1. red body, black boiler, black base, "4345" labels, England casting ($4-6)
2. red body, black boiler, black base, "NP" labels, England casting ($8-12)
3. red body, charcoal boiler, black base, "4345" labels, England casting ($4-6)
4. cherry red body, black boiler, black base, "4345" labels, England casting ($4-6)
5. metallic red body, black boiler, black base, "4345" labels, no origin cast ($150-200)(BR)
6. green body, black boiler, black base, "4345" labels, England casting ($8-12)
7. green body, black boiler, black base, "NP" labels, England casting ($5-8)(TP)
8. green body, black boiler, black base, "British Railways" tempa, Macau casting ($6-8)(UK)
9. red body, black boiler, black base, "4345" tempa, Macau casting ($2-4)(MC)
10. green body, black boiler, black base, "4345" tempa, Macau casting ($2-4)(MC)
11. green body, black boiler, black base, "West Somerset Railway" tempa, Macau casting ($6-8)(UK)
12. red body, black boiler, black base, "North Yorkshire Moors" (all white) tempa, Macau casting ($6-8)(UK)
13. red body, black boiler, black base, "North Yorkshire Moors Railway" (white & black) tempa, Macau casting ($15-20)(SW)
14. yellow body, red boiler, blue base & wheels, "123/efg" tempa, Macau casting ($6-8)(LL)
15. blue body, black boiler, black base, "Hutchinson" tempa, Macau casting ($6-8)(UK)
16. green body, black boiler, black base, white emblem tempa, Macau casting ($15-20)(UK)(OP)
17. matt olive body, black boiler, black base, "GWR" tempa, Macau casting ($6-8)(UK)
18. matt black body, black boiler, black base, "British Railways" tempa, Macau casting ($6-8)(UK)
19. yellow body, lime boiler, blue base & wheels, "123/ 456" tempa, Macau casting ($6-8)(LL)
20. blue body, black boiler, black base, red coach line tempa, Macau casting ($6-8)(UK)
21. yellow body, lime boiler, blue base & wheels, "123/ 456" tempa, China casting ($6-8)(LL)
22. green body, black boiler, black base, "British Railways" (red, black & white) tempa, China casting ($1-2)
23. red body, black boiler, black base, "4345" tempa, China casting ($2-3)(MP)
24. green body, black boiler, black base, white Kellogg's rooster head tempa, China casting ($75-100)(FR)(DU)(OP)
25. white body, white boiler, white base, no tempa, China casting ($10-15)(GF)
26. green body, black boiler, black base, "British Railways" (red & white) tempa, China casting ($1-2)
27. red-brown body, black boiler, black base, "Gold Rush Australia" tempa, China casting ($4-6)(AU)

MB43-D PETERBILT CONVENTIONAL, issued 1982 (USA)(MB106/307)

NOTE: Other variations exist as components to Convoy models. Only single releases are listed here. England bases are

either (L) Lesney or (M) Matchbox International. All models with chrome exhausts & plastic base & 8 spoke wheels unless otherwise noted.
1. black body, amber windows, white & red design tempa, England (L) casting ($4-6)
2. black body, clear windows, white & red design tempa, England (L) casting ($4-6)
3. black body, amber windows, white & red "Ace" tempa, England (L) casting ($4-6)
4. black body, clear windows, white & red "Ace" tempa, England (L) tempa ($4-6)
5. black body, clear windows, white & brown "Ace" tempa, England (L) tempa ($4-6)
6. black body, amber windows, white & black design tempa, England (L) casting ($4-6)
7. black body, clear windows, white & red "Super" tempa, England (L) casting ($4-6)
8. black body, clear windows, white & red "Super" tempa, England (M) casting ($4-6)
9. black body, amber windows, white & red "Ace" tempa, England (M) casting ($2-4)
10 black body, clear windows, white & red "Ace" tempa, England (M) casting ($2-4)
11. black body, clear windows, white & red "Z" pattern tempa, England (M) casting ($3-5)
12. black body, amber windows, white & red "Z" pattern tempa, England (M) casting ($3-5)
13. black body, amber windows, white & red "Z" pattern tempa, Macau casting ($2-4)
14. white body, clear windows, gray exhausts, "NASA" & rocket tempa, Macau casting ($3-5)(MP)

MB43-E MERCEDES 500 SEC, issued 1984 (MB135)
1. white body, black metal base, clear windows, blue interior, 8 dot silver wheels, "AMG" tempa, Macau casting ($2-4)
2. red body, black metal base, clear windows, black interior, 8 dot silver wheels, "AMG" tempa, Macau casting ($2-3)
3. red body, black metal base, clear windows, black interior, starburst wheels, "AMG" with stripes tempa, Macau casting ($3-5)(SF)
4. white body, black metal base, clear windows, black interior, 8 dot gold wheels, red & blue with "7" tempa, Macau casting ($2-4)
5. white body, black metal base, clear windows, black interior, 8 dot silver wheels, red & blue with "7" tempa, Macau casting ($2-4)
6. white body, black metal base, clear windows, black interior, starburst wheels, red & blue with "7" tempa, Macau casting ($75-100)
7. white body, black metal base, clear windows, black interior, 8 dot silver wheels, "AMG" on hood & sides tempa, Macau casting ($6-8)
8. black body, black metal base, clear windows, brown interior, 8 dot silver wheels, "500SEC" tempa, Macau casting ($2-3)
9. metallic red body, black metal base, clear windows, black interior, laser wheels, "AMG" & stripes tempa, Macau casting ($3-5)(LW)
10. red body, pearly silver metal base, clear windows, brown interior, 8 dot silver wheels, green & yellow stripes tempa, Macau casting ($8-12)(DU)
11. white body, pearly silver metal base, clear windows, brown interior, 8 dot silver wheels, "1 Pig Racing Team" tempa, Macau casting ($8-12)(HK)
12. black body, pearly silver metal base, clear windows, brown interior, 8 dot silver wheels, "500SEC" & stripe tempa, Macau casting ($2-3)
13. metallic red body, pearly silver metal base, clear windows, black interior, laser wheels, "AMG" & stripes tempa, Macau casting ($3-5)(LW)
14. white body, pearly silver metal base, clear windows, brown interior, 8 dot silver wheels, "500SEC" & silver stripe tempa, Macau casting ($18-25)(SU)
15. black body, black metal base, clear windows, brown interior, 8 dot silver wheels, "Redoxon/ 500SEC AMG" tempa, Macau casting ($18-25)(HK)
16. white body, black metal base, chrome windows, no interior, gray disc wheels with rubber tires, detailed trim tempa, Macau casting ($5-8)(WC)
17. black body, black metal base, navy blue windows, no interior, 8 dot silver wheels, "Pace Car Heuer" tempa, amber dome lights, Macau casting ($7-10)(SR)
18. black body, black plastic base, navy blue windows, no interior, 8 dot silver wheels, "Pace Car Heuer" tempa, amber dome lights, Macau casting ($7-10)(SR)
19. white body, black metal base, black windows, no interior, 8 dot silver wheels, "Police" tempa, red dome lights, Macau casting ($7-10)(SR)
20. white body, black plastic base, black windows, no interior, 8 dot silver wheels, "Police" tempa, red dome lights, Macau casting ($7-10)(SR)
21. cream body, black metal base, black windows, no interior, 8 dot silver wheels, "Emergency Doctor" tempa, green dome lights, Macau casting ($7-10)(SR)
22. cream body, black plastic base, black windows, no interior, 8 dot silver wheels, "Emergency Doctor" tempa, green dome lights, Macau casting ($7-10)(SR)
23. cream body, black metal base, black windows, no interior, 8 dot silver wheels, "Emergency Doctor/ Rescue 911" tempa, green dome lights, China casting ($7-10)(SR)
24. white body, black metal base, black windows, no interior, 8 dot silver wheels, "Police/ Rescue 911" tempa, red dome lights, China casting ($7-10)(SR)
25. black body, black metal base, black windows, no interior, 8 dot silver wheels, "Pace Car Heuer/ Rescue 911" tempa, green dome lights, China casting ($7-10)(SR)
26. red body, silver-gray metal base, clear windows, brown interior, starburst wheels, "AMG" with stripes tempa, Macau casting ($3-5)(SF)
27. white body, black plastic base, black windows, no interior, 8 dot silver wheels, "Police 17" & blue stripe tempa, red dome lights, China casting ($3-5)(LS)
28. olive body, black plastic base, black windows, no interior, 8 dot silver wheels, "Matchbox Military Police MP-090196" tempa, green–yellow dome lights, China casting ($3-5)(LS)
29. dull olive body, black plastic base, black windows, no interior, 8 dot silver wheels, "Matchbox Military Police MP-090196" tempa, amber dome lights, China casting ($3-5)(LS)
30. silver-gray body, black plastic base, black windows, no interior, 8 dot silver wheels, "Police 17" & blue stripe tempa, red dome lights, China casting ($3-5)(LS)

MB43-F RENAULT 11 *see MB33-E*

MB43-G LINCOLN TOWN CAR, issued 1989 (USA) (MB197)
MB24-G LINCOLN TOWN CAR, issued 1989 (ROW)

NOTE: Below models with red interior, smoke windows & black base unless otherwise noted.
1. white body, metal base, dot dash wheels, no tempa, Macau casting ($1-2)

2. black body, plastic base, gray disc with rubber tires, detailed trim tempa, chrome windows, Macau casting ($5-8)(WC)
3. white body, plastic base, dot dash wheels, no tempa, Thailand casting ($1-2)
4. silver-gray body, plastic base, dot dash wheels, pink & yellow design tempa, Thailand casting ($2-3)(DM)
5. orange-yellow body, plastic base, dot dash (blue) wheels, face on hood tempa, Thailand casting ($10-15)(LL)
6. metallic maroon body, plastic base, dot dash wheels, brown rear half of roof tempa, Thailand casting ($2-4)
7. metallic maroon body, plastic base, dot dash wheels, no tempa, Thailand casting ($1-2)
8. charcoal body, clear windows, plastic base, chrome disc wheels with rubber tires, purple rear half of roof & detailed trim tempa, China casting ($8-12)(UC)
9. silver-gray body, clear windows, plastic base, chrome disc wheels with rubber tires, detailed trim tempa, China casting ($50+)(GC)(CHI)

NOTE: Above model was intended to be released with the gold coin series but ended up for sale separately in China.

MB43-H '57 CHEVY *see MB4-D*

MB43-I CAMARO Z28, issued 1994 (USA) (MB254)
MB56-H CAMARO Z28, issued 1994 (ROW)

NOTE: Below models with plastic black base.

1. black body, gray interior, clear windows, gold 6-spoke spiral wheels, purple/blue/white tempa, Thailand casting ($1-2)
2. white body, no interior, chrome windows, gray disc wheels with rubber tires, black roof & detailed trim tempa, Thailand casting ($2-4)(WC)
3. metallic light gold body, black interior, clear windows, chrome disc wheels with rubber tires, "Matchbox Collectors Club" tempa, Thailand casting ($10-15)(US)
4. florescent orange body, black interior, smoke windows, silver 6-spoke spiral wheels, "Matchbox Get In The Fast Lane- 95 Premium Show" tempa, Thailand casting ($25-45)(US)
5. silver body, white interior, amber windows, silver 6-spoke spiral wheels, lavender/ purple & blue tempa, Thailand casting ($3-5)(MT)
6. black body, gray interior, smoke windows, silver 6-spoke spiral wheels, purple/ blue & white hood & side design tempa, Thailand casting ($1-2)
7. black body, white interior, clear windows, silver 6-spoke spiral wheels, purple/ blue & white side design only tempa, Thailand casting ($1-2)
8. florescent orange body, black interior, smoke windows, silver 6-spoke spiral wheels, "Matchbox Get In The Fast Lane- Melbourne Motor Show 96" tempa, Thailand casting ($25-45)(AU)
9. dark green body, dk. tan/ black interior, clear windows, chrome disc wheels with rubber tires, black roof & detailed trim tempa, Thailand casting ($3-5)(PC2)
10. metallic blue body, gray/ black interior, clear windows, chrome disc wheels with rubber tires, black roof & detailed trim tempa, Thailand casting ($3-5)(PC)(JC)
11. metallic charcoal body, blue interior, clear windows, silver 6-spoke spiral wheels, purple/ blue & white side design only tempa, Thailand casting ($1-2)
12. red body, black/ brown interior, clear windows, chrome disc wheels with rubber tires, black roof & detailed trim tempa, Thailand casting ($3-5)(PC5)
13. dark purple body, black/ gray interior, clear windows, chrome disc wheels with rubber tires, black roof & detailed trim tempa, Thailand casting ($3-5)(SC2)
14. purple chrome body, white interior, yellow windows, 5 spoke concave star wheels, orange & yellow tempa, Thailand casting ($1-2)(5pk)
15. metallic charcoal body, blue interior, clear windows, 5 spoke concave star wheels, purple/blue & white design tempa, Thailand casting ($1-2)
16. candy apple red body, black & gray interior, clear windows, chrome disc wheels with rubber tires, black roof tempa, Thailand casting ($15-20)(GC)
17. orange body, dark gray & white interior, clear windows, chrome disc wheels with rubber tires, dual white stripes tempa, Thailand casting ($3-5)(PC14)
18. metallic gold body, black interior, clear windows, 5 spoke concave star wheels, no tempa, Thailand casting ($5-10)(CH)
19. silver-gray body, blue interior, smoke windows, 5 spoke concave star wheels, blue/ red & white design tempa, Thailand casting ($1-2)
20. florescent orange body, black interior, smoke windows, silver 6 spoke spiral wheels, "Matchbox Get in The Fast Lane/ Sydney Motor Show" tempa, Thailand casting ($15-25)(C2)(AU)
21. lemon body, gray & black interior, clear windows, chrome disc wheels with rubber tires, black roof tempa, Thailand casting ($3-5)(SC4)
22. metallic turquoise body, black & gray interior, clear windows, chrome disc wheels with rubber tires, black roof tempa, Thailand casting ($3-5)(SC5)
23. metallic purple body, silver-gray interior, clear windows, 5 spoke concave star wheels, checkers & salmon flash tempa, Thailand casting ($1-2)(MW75/1998 US)
24. metallic light gold body, black interior, clear windows, chrome disc wheels with rubber tires, "Great Camaro Gathering II 1998" tempa, Thailand casting ($35-50)(C2)
25. dark gold chrome body, white interior, yellow windows, 5 spoke concave star wheels, blue & yellow tempa, China casting ($1-2)(5pk)
26. metallic purple body, silver-gray interior, clear windows, 5 spoke concave star wheels, checkers & salmon flash tempa, China casting ($1-2)(MW75/1998 US)
27. black body, white interior, clear windows, 5 spoke concave star wheels, no tempa, China casting ($25-40)(ASAP blank)
28. black body, white interior, clear windows, 5 spoke concave star wheels, "DDCM DuPage Diecast Collectors Meet" tempa, China casting ($15-25)(ASAP)
29. black body, white interior, clear windows, 5 spoke concave star wheels, "Speed Equipment World" tempa, China casting ($75+)(ASAP)
30. black body, white interior, clear windows, 5 spoke concave star wheels, "Real Cars Wear Bow Ties" tempa, China casting ($75+)(ASAP)
31. black body, white interior, clear windows, 5 spoke concave star wheels, "RCA" tempa, China casting ($15-25)(ASAP)
32. black body, white interior, clear windows, 5 spoke concave star wheels, "Novell 6" tempa, China casting ($18-25)(ASAP)
33. blue body, white interior, clear windows, 5 spoke concave star wheels, "AAL Racing 02" tempa, China casting ($15-20)(US)
34 black body, white interior, clear windows, 5 spoke concave star wheels, "Progressive AE" tempa, China casting ($20-40)(ASAP)
35. red body, black interior, clear windows, 5 spoke concave star wheels, "Rush Hour 2" tempa, China casting ($50+)(ASAP)
36. black body, white interior, clear windows, 5 spoke concave star wheels, "DMSI" tempa, China casting ($50+)(ASAP)
37. red body, black interior, clear windows, 5 spoke concave star wheels, no tempa, China casting ($25-40)(ASAP blank)

38. black body, white interior, clear windows, lace wheels, no tempa, China casting ($18-25)(ASAP blank)
39. black body, white interior, clear windows, 5 spoke concave star wheels, "Zurich Small Business Rally 2002" tempa, China casting ($50+)(ASAP)
40. black body, white interior, clear windows, 5 spoke concave star wheels, "Alliance" tempa, China casting ($50+)(ASAP)
41. black body, white interior, clear windows, 5 spoke concave star wheels, white soccer player logo tempa, China casting ($50+)(ASAP)

MB43-J MUSTANG COBRA *see MB71-H*

MB43-K SEA RESCUE BOAT, issued 1999 (USA) (MB407)
MB38-K SEA RESCUE BOAT, issued 1999 (ROW)

NOTE: Below models with China casting.

1. white deck, black hull, black windows, silver-gray railings, black rear insert, red & silver stripes tempa, black wheels ($1-2)(MW38/1999 ROW)(MW33/1999 GR)
2. white deck, black hull, black windows, silver-gray railings, black rear insert,, red & silver stripes & "World Ocean Exploration" tempa, black wheels ($1-2)(MW43/1999 US)
3. red deck, white hull, dark blue windows, dark blue railings, dark blue rear insert, blue stripe & "489-4" tempa, black wheels ($1-2)(5pk)
4. red deck, white hull, dark blue windows, dark blue railings, dark blue rear insert, blue stripes & "489-4" tempa, white wheels ($2-4)(5pk)
5. blue deck, white hull, opaque yellow windows, white railings, yellow rear insert, "Base 2000" & yellow & black stripes tempa, white wheels ($1-2)(LP)
6. white deck, metallic gold hull, opaque red windows, black railings, red rear insert, red & black stripe & "Matchbox 2000" tempa, black wheels ($2-4)(MW26/2000 US)
7. white deck, metallic gold hull, opaque red windows, black railings, red rear insert, red & black stripes tempa, black wheels ($1-2)(MW26/2000 US)
8. white deck, white hull, black windows, white railings, white rear insert, no tempa, black wheels ($25-40)(ASAP blank)
9. white deck, white hull, black windows, white railings, white rear insert, "The Perfect Storm" tempa, black wheels ($75+)(ASAP)
10. dark blue deck, orange hull, powder blue windows, red railings, powder blue rear insert, "042076" & storm logo tempa, black wheels ($1-2)(LP)
11. orange-yellow deck, dark blue hull, opaque dark blue windows, red railings, dark blue rear insert, "S.O.S." & design tempa, blue wheels($1-2)(5pk)
12. red deck, white hull, opaque orange-yellow windows, black railings, orange-yellow rear insert, "Marine Rescue" & stripes tempa, black wheels ($2-4)(PB)
13. blue deck, white hull, opaque gray windows, purple railings, gray rear insert, "X-Treme Force" tempa, black wheels ($1-2)(MW75/2001)
14. red deck, white hull, white windows, white railings, white rear insert, "7 Maryland Blue Point Crab" tempa, black wheels ($1-2)(AM)
15. white & brown deck, black hull, black windows, gray railings, black rear insert, "Texaco" tempa, black wheels ($3-5)(Texaco PC)
16. dark blue deck, white hull, opaque red windows, yellow railings, red rear insert, "Hydro Police" & designs tempa, black wheels ($1-2)(5pk)

MB43-L FORD F SERIES FIRE TRUCK, issued 2001 (MB499/581)

NOTE: Below models with 7 spoke sawblade wheels & China casting unless otherwise noted.

1. red body, white rear ramp, yellow raft, clear windows, black interior, gray base, "MBFD" tempa ($1-2)(MW43/2001)
2. orange-yellow body, dark blue ramp, blue raft, smoke windows, dark blue interior, "North Star Rescue- Minnesota" with blue "32" tempa ($1-2)(AM)
3. orange-yellow body, dark blue ramp, blue raft, smoke windows, dark blue interior, "North Star Rescue- Minnesota" with black "32" tempa ($1-2)(AM)
4. metallic silver body, black ramp, blue raft, smoke windows, black interior, "Police Lake Patrol" tempa ($1-2)(MW16/2002 US)
5. metallic silver body, black ramp, blue raft, smoke windows, black interior, "Police Lake Patrol" & "Matchbox 50" tempa ($2-4)(MW16/2002 US)
6. charcoal body, yellow ramp, blue raft, blue windows, black interior, "Spider Peak" tempa ($1-2)(5pk)
7. charcoal body, light yellow ramp, blue raft, blue windows, black interior, "Spider Peak" tempa ($1-2)(5pk)
8. maroon body, gray ramp, yellow raft, amber windows, white interior, flames "H20, 14" & "Matchbox FDMB" tempa ($1-2)(LP)
9. beige body, black ramp, pea green raft, clear windows, black interior, "The Crocodile Hunter" tempa, chrome disc with rubber tires ($3-5)(CRO)
10. white body, yellow ramp, yellow raft, blue windows, no interior, "MHC Beach Patrol 42" tempa ($1-2)(MW42/2003)
11. white body, yellow ramp, yellow raft, blue windows, no interior, "MHC Beach Patrol 42" & "Hero City" tempa ($2-4)(MW42/2003)

MB44-A GMC REFRIGERATOR TRUCK, issued 1970

NOTE: Below models with gray plastic cab base & rear door, green windows, 4 spoke wheels & England casting. Earliest versions with narrow wheels with later versions having wide wheels.

1. red body, turquoise container, black axle covers ($45-60)
2. yellow body, red container, black axle covers ($20-30)
3. yellow body, red container, red axle covers ($20-30)
4. yellow body, turquoise container, black axle covers ($2000+)

MB44-B BOSS MUSTANG, issued 1972

NOTE: Below models with chrome interior & engine, amber windows, metal base & England casting.

1. lemon body, unpainted hood, unpainted base, no tempa, maltese cross wheels ($75-100)
2. lemon body, black hood, unpainted base, no tempa, maltese cross wheels ($6-8)
3. lemon body, black hood, silver-gray base, no tempa, maltese cross wheels ($6-8)
4. lemon body, black hood, unpainted base, no tempa, 5 spoke front & maltese cross rear wheels ($6-8)
5. lemon body, black hood, unpainted base, no tempa, maltese cross wheels ($6-8)
6. dark green body & hood, unpainted base, with tempa, maltese cross wheels ($8-12)(LE)

NOTE: Above model issued as Limited Edition "Cobra Mustang"

MB44-C PASSENGER COACH, issued 1978 (MB044)

NOTE: Below models with black plastic base & black train wheels unless otherwise noted.

1. red body, flat beige roof, light green windows, train wheels, red "431 432" labels, England casting ($4-6)
2. red body, flat bone roof, light green windows, train wheels, red "431 432" labels, England casting ($4-6)
3. red body, flat beige roof, dark green windows, train wheels, red "431 432" labels, England casting ($4-6)
4. red body, flat beige roof, dark green windows, dot dash wheels,, red "431 432" labels, England casting ($6-8)\
5. red body, flat beige roof, green windows, train wheels, "NYK" labels (from MB25-C), no origin cast ($100-150)(BR)

6. red body, flat beige roof, clear windows, train wheels, red "431 432" labels, England casting ($4-6)
7. red body, flat bone roof, clear windows, train wheels, red "431 432" labels, England casting ($4-6)
8. red body, flat beige roof, no windows, train wheels, red "431 432" labels, England casting ($4-6)
9. red body, flat bone roof, no windows, train wheels, red "431 432" labels, England casting ($4-6)
10. red body, flat cream roof, no windows, train wheels, "GWR" labels (from MB47-C), England casting ($8-12)
11 red body, flat beige roof, no windows, train wheels, "GWR" labels (from MB47-C), England casting ($8-12)
12. red body, flat beige roof, no windows, train wheels, "5810-6102" labels, England casting ($8-12)
13. red body, flat cream roof, no windows, train wheels, "5810-6102" labels, England casting ($8-12)
14. red body, flat beige roof, no windows, dot dash wheels, "5810-6102" labels, England casting ($8-12)
15. red body, flat tan roof, no windows, dot dash wheels, "5810-6102" labels, England casting ($8-12)
16. red body, flat beige roof, no windows, dot dash wheels, red "431 432" labels, England casting ($4-6)
17. red body, flat tan roof, no windows, dot dash wheels, red "431 432" labels, England casting ($4-6)
18. red body, flat tan roof, no windows, dot dash wheels, green "431 432" labels, England casting ($4-6)
19. red body, flat beige roof, no windows, dot dash wheels, green "431 432" labels, England casting ($4-6)
20. green body, flat beige roof, no windows, train wheels, red "431 432" labels, England casting ($8-12)(TP)
21. green body, raised beige roof, no windows, train wheels, "5810-6102" labels, England casting ($6-8)(TP)
22. red body, raised beige roof, no windows, dot dash wheels, "5810-6102" labels, England casting ($8-12)
23. red body, raised beige roof, no windows, train wheels, red "431 432" labels, England casting ($7-10)
24. red body, flat cream roof, no windows, train wheels, "431 432" tempa, Macau casting ($2-3)
25. lime & yellow body, flat red roof, blue base, no windows, blue train wheels, 2 figures with clock tempa, Macau casting ($6-8)(LL)
26. lime & yellow body, flat red roof, blue base, no windows, blue train wheels, 2 figures with clock tempa, China casting ($6-8)(LL)
27. green body, flat beige roof, no windows, train wheels, "British Railways" tempa, China casting ($2-3)(TP)
28. red body, flat cream roof, no windows, train wheels, "431 432" tempa, China casting ($1-2)(MP)
29. red body, flat cream roof, no windows, train wheels, "431 432" tempa, very small "Kellogg's" label on base, China casting ($18-25)(DU)(OP)
30. white body, flat white roof, white base, no windows, no tempa, China casting ($10-15)(GF)
31. white body, flat cream roof, white base, no windows, no tempa, China casting ($10-15)(GF)(CHI)

MB44-D 4 X 4 CHEVY VAN, issued 1982 (USA) (MB102)
MB68-D 4 X 4 CHEVY VAN, issued 1983 (ROW)
MB26-H 4 X 4 CHEVY VAN, reissued 1991 (USA)
MB10-E 4 X 4 CHEVY VAN, reissued 1993 (ROW)

NOTE: Below models with blue windows & maltese cross wheels unless otherwise noted.

1. light metallic green body, black metal base, "Ridin High" tempa with plain hood, England casting ($3-5)
2. light metallic green body, black metal base, "Ridin High" tempa with black horseshoes on hood, England casting ($3-5)
3. dark metallic green body, black metal base, "Ridin High" tempa with black horseshoes on hood, England casting ($3-5)
4. dark metallic green body, black metal base, "Ridin High" tempa with white horseshoes on hood, England casting ($7-10)
5. dark emerald green body, black metal base, "Ridin High" tempa with black horseshoes on hood, England casting ($15-18)
6. white body, black metal base, "Matchbox Racing" tempa, Macau casting ($2-3)
7. white body, black metal base, "Tokyo Giants/ Matsumoto 2" labels, Macau casting ($8-12)(JP)
8. white body, black metal base, "Tokyo Giants/ Shinozuka 6" labels, Macau casting ($8-12)(JP)
9. white body, black metal base, "Tokyo Giants/ Hara 8" labels, Macau casting ($8-12)(JP)
10. white body, black metal base, "Tokyo Giants/ Yamakura 15" labels, Macau casting ($8-12)(JP)
11. white body, black metal base, "Tokyo Giants/ Sadaoka 20" labels, Macau casting ($8-12)(JP)
12. white body, black metal base, "Tokyo Giants/ Nakahata 24" labels, Macau casting ($8-12)(JP)
13. white body, black metal base, "Tokyo Giants/ Nishimoto 26" labels, Macau casting ($8-12)(JP)
14. white body, black metal base, "Tokyo Giants/ Egawa 30" labels, Macau casting ($8-12)(JP)
15. white body, black metal base, "Castrol Racing Team" tempa, Macau casting ($7-10)(AU)
16. white body, silver-gray metal base, "Matchbox Motorsports" tempa, Macau casting ($1-2)
17. white body, gray plastic base, "Matchbox Motorsports" tempa , Macau casting ($1-2)
18. white body, gray plastic base, "Matchbox Motorsports" tempa, Thailand casting ($1-2)
19. white body, black plastic base, no tempa, Thailand casting ($10-15)(GF)
20. fluorescent yellow body, gray plastic base, blue & pink design tempa, Thailand casting ($1-2)
21. black body, gray plastic base, pink & green design tempa, Thailand casting ($1-2)(5pk)
22. white body, gray plastic base, "Surf's Up" with wave design tempa, Thailand casting ($1-2)(5pk)
23. black body, gray plastic base, "S.W.A.T. Unit 5" & gold star tempa, Thailand casting ($1-2)(5pk)
24. green & purple body, gray plastic base, "23rd National Truck-In" tempa, Thailand casting ($8-12)(US)
25. white body, gray plastic base, purple & green design tempa, Thailand casting ($1-2)
26. red body, gray plastic base, "Claws" tempa, Thailand casting ($1-2)
27. metallic gold body, black plastic base, no tempa, Thailand casting ($5-10)(CH26)
28. black body, gray plastic base, skeleton & "Stegosaurus" tempa, Thailand casting ($1-2)(5pk)
29. black body, gray plastic base, skeleton & "Stegosaurus" tempa, China casting ($1-2)(5pk)
30. white body, gray plastic base, "Matchbox Motorsports/ PA Matchbox Collectors Club 20th Anniversary" tempa, Thailand casting ($10-15)(ASAP)
31. red body, gray plastic base, "Coca Cola" & polar bears at pool table tempa, China casting ($1-2)(5pk)
32. white body, amber windows, gray plastic base, "100 Amazing Flavors" tempa, China casting ($1-2)(MW96/1999 US)

NOTE: Below models with 5 spoke oval wheels.

33. metallic blue body, smoke windows, black plastic base, "S.O.S." with dolphins tempa, China casting ($1-2)(5pk)
34. red body, gray plastic base, "Coca Cola" & polar bears at pool table tempa, China casting ($3-5)(CK)
35. light metallic blue body, black plastic base, "Alarm" & snowflake tempa, China casting ($1-2)(5pk)
36. lime body, black plastic base, "Alarm" & snowflake tempa, China casting ($1-2)(5pk)
37. white body, gray plastic base, no tempa, 8 spoke wheels, Mattel China casting ($25-40)(ASAP blank)
38. white body, gray plastic base, "Federal Express" tempa, 8 spoke wheels, Mattel China casting ($50+)(ASAP)
39. red body, gray plastic base, "Coca Cola" & polar bears at pool table tempa, 5 spoke oval wheels, Mattel China casting ($1-2)(CK)
40. silver-gray body, black plastic base, "Coca-Cola Football Town/ Total Tailgate" tempa, 5 spoke oval wheels, Mattel China casting ($2-4)(CK)

MB44-E CITROEN 15CV, issued 1983 (ROW) (MB124)

NOTE: Below models with clear windows & 5 crown wheels unless otherwise noted.

1. black body, chrome base, light gray interior, England casting ($2-3)
2. black body, chrome base, silver-gray interior, England casting ($2-3)
3. black body, chrome base, beige interior, England casting ($2-3)
4. black body, chrome base, white interior, England casting ($2-3)
5. black body, chrome base, silver-gray interior, Macau casting ($2-3)
6. dark blue body, chrome base, silver-gray interior, Macau casting ($2-3)
7. dark blue body, chrome base, red interior, Macau casting ($2-3)
8. dark green body, chrome base, red interior, Macau casting ($8-12)(DY)
9. black body, gray base, cream interior, 5 arch wheels, China casting ($4-6)(MP)

MB44-F DATSUN 280ZX POLICE CAR, issued 1987 (JP) (MB144)

1. white & black body, clear windows, opaque red dome lights, tan interior, black metal base, Japanese lettered tempa, 5 arch wheels, Macau casting ($8-12)(JP)

MB44-G SKODA 130LR, issued 1987 (ROW) (MB176)

NOTE: Below models with powder blue plastic base, red trunk, black interior, clear windows and 8 dot wheels.

1. white body, "Skoda 44" with "Duckhams" on sides tempa, Macau casting ($2-4)
2. white body, "Skoda 44" without "Duckhams" on sides tempa, Macau casting ($2-4)
3. white body, "Skoda 44" with "Duckhams" on sides tempa, China casting ($2-4)

MB44-H 1921 MODEL T FORD VAN, issued 1990 (MB213/293)

NOTE: Below models with clear windshield, chrome grille, plastic chassis & black plastic spoked wheels unless otherwise noted.

1. yellow body, red roof, blue chassis, "Bird's Custard Powder" tempa, Macau casting ($1-2)
2. cream body, dark blue roof, dark blue chassis, "5th MICA Convention 1990" tempa, Macau casting ($8-10)(UK)
3. cream body, dark blue roof, dark blue chassis, "3rd MICA NA Convention 1990" tempa, Macau casting ($8-10)(US)
4. red body with black hood, black roof, black chassis, "Royal Mail GR" tempa, Macau casting ($7-10)(UK)
5. white body, powder blue roof & chassis, "Para 90" tempa, Macau casting ($8-10)(UK)
6. white body, powder blue roof & chassis, "Chester Doll Hospital/ World's Largest Matchbox Display" tempa, Macau casting ($8-10)(UK)
7. dark green body, black roof, dark charcoal chassis, "Swarfega" tempa, Macau casting ($35-50)(UK)(OP)
8. black body, black roof & chassis, "Mars" tempa, Macau casting ($10-15)(UK)
9. cream body, red roof, green chassis, "PG Tips" tempa, Macau casting ($15-20)(UK)(OP)
10. cream body, red roof, green chassis, "PG Tips" tempa, China casting ($15-20)(UK)(OP)
11. yellow body, red roof, blue chassis, "Bird's Custard Powder" tempa, China casting ($2-3)
12. black body, black roof & chassis, "4th M.I.C.A. NA Convention/ Detroit Motor City" tempa, China casting ($8-12)(US)
13. red body, red roof, black chassis, "Mars" tempa, China casting ($15-20)(UK)
14. white body, powder blue roof & chassis, "M.I.C.A. 7- I Could Have Danced All Night" labels, Macau casting ($10-15)(UK)(C2)
15. cream body, dark blue roof & chassis, "Greetings From Philadelphia 1992/ MICA NA" labels, Macau casting ($10-15)(US)(C2)
16. white body, red roof, dark blue chassis, "Lloyds" tempa, China casting ($10-15)(UK)
17. black body, black roof & chassis, "William Lusty" tempa, China casting ($6-8)(UK)
18. white body, red roof, dark blue chassis, "Dale Farm" tempa, China casting ($7-10)(UK)
19. powder blue body, black roof, dark blue chassis, "Goodyear Tyres" tempa, China casting ($1-2)
20. dark blue body, black roof & chassis, "Kellogg's Corn Flakes" tempa, China casting ($15-20)(AU)(OP)
21. black body, black roof & chassis, "Philadelphia MICA NA" labels, China casting ($10-15)(C2)
22. white body, black roof & chassis, "Financial Times" tempa, China casting ($8-12)(UK)
23. red body, black roof & chassis, "Matchbox Toy Delivery" tempa, China casting ($2-4) (CC)
24. yellow body, red roof & chassis, "Vegemite" tempa, China casting ($7-10)(AU)(OP)
25. yellow body, blue roof & chassis, "Chesdale" tempa, China casting ($7-10)(AU)(OP)
26. blue body, yellow roof & chassis, "Kraft" tempa, China casting ($7-10)(AU)(OP)
27. blue body, red roof & chassis, "Craig's" tempa, China casting ($7-10)(AU)(OP)
28. orange-red body, black roof & chassis, "P.M.G." tempa, China casting ($7-10)(AU)

NOTE: Below models with China casting unless otherwise noted.

29. dark blue body & roof, black plastic chassis, "Matchbox USA 95" tempa ($15-25)(LD)(US)
30. white body, blue roof, black plastic chassis, "Lowestoft Town Football Club/ Blues of Crown Meadow" tempa ($25-40)(LD)(UK)
31. white body, white roof, black plastic chassis, "Lowestoft Town Football Club/ John Grose Ford" tempa ($25-40)(LD)(UK)
32. white body, white roof, black plastic chassis, "Lowestoft Town Football Club/ Blues of Crown Meadow" with "John Grose Ford" on roof tempa ($175-250)(LD)(UK)
33. white body, white roof, black plastic chassis, "Freihofer's" tempa ($12-15)(LD)(US)
34. white body, white roof, black plastic chassis, "Matchbox Drive Your Name Home" tempa ($18-25)(LD)(UK)

35. dark blue body & roof, black plastic chassis, "Matchbox Drive Your Name Home" tempa ($18-25)(LD)(UK)
36. red body, red roof, black plastic chassis, "Matchbox Drive Your Name Home" tempa ($18-25)(LD)(UK)
37. red body, red roof, black plastic chassis, "Matchbox Official Visitor" tempa ($50-75)(LD)(UK)
38. white body & roof, black plastic chassis, "50 Years Liberation/ War & Occupation Museum" tempa ($18-25)(LD)(DU)
39. white body & roof, black plastic chassis, "1939 1945/ War & Occupation Museum" tempa ($18-25)(LD)(DU)
40. orange body & roof, black plastic chassis, "Jacob's" tempa ($18-25)(IR)(OP)
41. white body & roof, black plastic chassis, "The Royal Tournament" labels ($18-25)(LD)(UK)
42. white body & roof, black plastic chassis, "The Royal Tournament" with "Earl's Court" rear labels ($125-175)(LD)(UK)
43. dark blue body & roof, black plastic chassis, "BASC/ Beccles Amateur Sailing Club" tempa ($35-50)(LD)(UK)
44. dark blue body & roof, black plastic chassis, "TTK" tempa ($35-50)(LD)(UK)
45. green body, red roof, green metal chassis, "Matchbox Collectibles" tempa ($35-50)(YST)
46. red body, green roof, red metal chassis, "Klaus Toys" tempa ($35-50)(YST)

NOTE: Above two models issued only with Holiday Express Train.

47. white body & roof, black plastic chassis, "7th Jan 1996- Farnham Maltings 1" tempa ($15-25)(LD)(UK)
48. white body & roof, black plastic chassis, "Matchbox USA 96" tempa (base secured with screws) ($18-25)(LD)(US)
49. red body & roof, black plastic chassis, "Matchbox USA 96" tempa ($18-25)(LD)(US)
50. red body & roof, black plastic chassis, "Bradford AFC" tempa ($18-25)(LD)(UK)
51. yellow body, red roof, blue plastic chassis, "Kellogg's Corn Pops" tempa ($8-12)(US)(OP)
52. florescent lime body, black roof & plastic chassis, "Kellogg's Apple Jacks" tempa ($8-12)(US)(OP)
53. yellow body, red roof, black plastic chassis, "Kellogg's Eggo" tempa ($18-25)(US)(OP)
54. white body & roof, black plastic chassis, "10th March 1996- Farnham Maltings 2" tempa ($15-25)(LD)(UK)
55. purple body & roof, black plastic chassis, "Continental Aero" tempa ($12-15)(US)
56. dark blue body & roof, black plastic chassis, "Ford On Show" tempa ($75-100)(LD)(UK)
57. black body & roof, black metal chassis, "Your Own Promotional Vehicle/ Matchbox- Put Your Logo Here" tempa ($18-25)(AU) Special edition in gift box ($75-125)(AU)
58. dark blue body & roof, black plastic chassis, "Matchbox USA 15th Annual Toy Show" tempa ($18-25)(LD)(US)
59. red body & roof, black plastic chassis, "Matchbox USA 15th Annual Toy Show" tempa ($18-25)(LD)(US)
60. yellow body & roof, black plastic chassis, "Matchbox USA 15th Annual Toy show" tempa (base secured by screws) ($75-125)(LD)(US)
61. cream body , white roof, blue plastic chassis, Macau casting, "26th May 1996- Farnham Maltings 3" tempa (base secured by screws) ($18-25)(LD)(UK)
62. white body & roof, black metal chassis, "26th May 1996- Farnham Maltings 3" tempa ($18-25)(LD)(UK)
63. black body & roof, black metal chassis, "SAE International" tempa ($35-50)(US)
64. red body & roof, black plastic chassis, "1896 1996" tempa ($15-20)(LD)(UK)
65. dark blue body & roof, black plastic chassis, "Stirling Old Town Jail" tempa ($50-75)(LD)(UK)
66. white body & roof, black metal chassis, "North Walsham Carnival 1996" tempa ($18-25)(LD)(UK)

NOTE: Models listed below with same team names are packaged only as two packs with a special pewter medallion. Each set of two is ($40-60) each pair

67. white body, tan-beige roof & metal chassis, "St. Kilda Saints 1897" tempa(AU)
68. white body, red roof & metal chassis, "St. Kilda Saints 1996" tempa(AU)
69. black body, tan-beige roof & metal chassis, "Essendon Bombers 1897" tempa(AU)
70. black body, black roof & metal chassis, "Essendon Bombers 1996" tempa(AU)
71. dark blue body, tan-beige roof & metal chassis, "Fitzroy Lions 1897" tempa(AU)
72. pink-red body, dark blue roof & metal chassis, "Fitzroy Lions 1996" tempa(AU)
73. dark blue body, tan-beige roof & metal chassis, "Carlton Blues 1897" tempa(AU)
74. dark blue body & roof, black metal chassis, "Carlton Blues 1996" tempa(AU)
75. dark blue body, tan-beige roof & metal chassis, "Melbourne Demons 1897" tempa(AU)
76. dark blue body & roof, pink-red metal chassis, "Melbourne Demons 1996" tempa(AU)
77. white body, tan-beige roof & metal chassis, "Collingwood Magpies 1897" tempa(AU)
78. white body, black roof & metal chassis, "Collingwood Magpies 1996" tempa(AU)
79. white body, tan-beige roof & metal chassis, "South Melbourne 1897" tempa(AU)
80. white body, red roof & metal chassis, "South Melbourne 1996" tempa(AU)
81. dark blue body, tan-beige roof & metal chassis, "Geelong Cats 1897" tempa(AU)
82. dark blue body & roof, dark blue metal chassis, "Geelong Cats 1996" tempa(AU)
83. blue body, red roof & metal chassis, "North Coast Brewing Company- Scrimshaw" tempa, gold wire wheels with rubber tires, gold grille ($8-12)(MB1)(CL)
84. black body, red roof & metal chassis, "Firehouse Brewing Co." tempa, chrome wire wheels with rubber tires ($8-12)(MB2)(CL)
85. green body, black roof, red metal chassis, "Holy Cow/ Ambler Gambler" tempa, gold wire wheels with rubber tires, gold grille ($8-12)(MB3)(CL)
86. dark blue body & roof, black plastic chassis, "DM David Meek" tempa ($50-75)(LD)(UK)
87. white body & roof, black metal chassis, "8th Sep 1996- Farnham Maltings 4" tempa ($18-25)(LD)(UK)
88. white body & roof, black metal chassis, "Cromer Carnival 1996" tempa($18-25)(LD)(UK)
89. white body & roof, black metal chassis, "Springfest Extravaganza 1996" tempa ($18-25)(LD)AU)
90. red body & roof, black plastic chassis, "Springfest Extravaganza 1996" tempa ($18-25)(LD)(AU)
91. red body & roof, black plastic chassis, "Bendigo National Swapmeet 1996" tempa ($18-25)(LD)(AU)
92. white body & roof, black metal chassis, "Bendigo National Swapmeet 1996" tempa ($18-25)(LD)(AU)

93. red body & roof, black plastic chassis, "Merry Christmas/Best Wishes from Carr Collectables" tempa ($35-50)(LD)(UK)
94. red body & roof, black plastic chassis, "8th Super Southern Swapmeet" tempa ($8-12)(LD)(AU)
95. yellow & roof , black plastic chassis, "8th Super Southern Swapmeet" tempa ($8-12)(LD)(AU)
96. white body & roof, black plastic chassis, "Runnymeade Meccano Guild" tempa ($10-15)(LD)(UK)
97. red body, green roof, black plastic chassis, "Runnymeade Meccano Guild" tempa ($10-15)(LD)(UK)
98. gold body, green roof & metal chassis, "Anderson Valley" tempa, rubber tires, gold wire wheels with rubber tires, gold grille ($8-12)(MB5)(CL)
99. red body, blue roof, gold metal chassis, "Red Tail Ale" tempa, gold wire wheels with rubber tires, gold grille ($8-12)(MB6)(CL)
100. white body & roof, black metal chassis, "Farnham 6 16th March 1997" tempa ($10-15)(LD)(UK)
101. yellow body & roof, black plastic chassis, "Adtrucks" tempa ($10-15)(LD)(UK)
102. light beige body & roof, dark rose metal chassis, "Haigh's Chocolates" tempa, dark rose spoked wheels, gold grille ($10-15)(AU)
103. white body & roof, black plastic chassis, "Farnham 6 16th March 1997" tempa ($10-15)(LD)(UK)
104. yellow body & roof, blue metal chassis, "Weidman's Brewery/ Naked Brown Nut Ale" tempa, gold wire wheels with rubber tires, gold grille ($81-12)(MB4)(CL)
105. yellow body & roof, black plastic chassis, "Great Yarmouth/ Wellesley Main Grandstand" tempa ($10-15)(LD)(UK)
106. yellow body & roof, black plastic chassis, "Great Yarmouth/ The Bloaters" tempa ($10-15)(LD)(UK)
107. yellow body & roof, black plastic chassis, "15 Jaar Model Auto 97" tempa ($10-15)(LD)(DU)
108. yellow body & roof, black plastic chassis, "Bishop's Move" tempa ($10-15)(LD)(UK)
109. yellow body & roof, black plastic chassis, "16th Matchbox USA Toy Show" tempa ($10-15)(LD)(US)
110. white body & roof, black plastic chassis, "16th Matchbox USA Toy Show" tempa ($10-15)(LD)(US)
111. white body & roof, black metal chassis, "16th Matchbox USA Toy Show" tempa ($10-15)(LD)(US)
112. white body & roof, black metal chassis, "Farnham 7 - May 1997" tempa ($10-15)(LD)(UK)
113. white body & roof, black plastic chassis., "Farnham 7- May 1997" tempa ($10-15)(LD)(UK)
114. white body & roof, black plastic chassis, "Dyspraxia Foundation" tempa ($10-15)(LD)(UK)
115. white body & roof, black plastic chassis, "NGK- The Heartbeat of Your Engine" tempa ($50-75)(LD)(UK)
116. white body & roof, black plastic chassis, "Starlec" tempa ($10-15)(LD)(UK)
117. yellow body & roof, black plastic chassis, "Kia-Ora" tempa ($10-15)(LD)(UK)
118. yellow body & roof, black plastic chassis, "Bala Lake Railway" tempa ($10-15)(LD)(UK)
119. red body & roof, black plastic chassis, "Cromer Carnival 1997" tempa ($10-15)(LD)(UK)
120. red body & roof, black plastic chassis, "Encyclopedia of Matchbox Toys" tempa ($10-15)(LD)(UK)
121. yellow body & roof, black plastic chassis, "Encyclopedia of Matchbox Toys" (blue letters) tempa ($15-25)(LD)(US)
122. yellow body & roof, black plastic chassis, "Encyclopedia of Matchbox Toys" (black letters) tempa ($15-25)(LD)(US)
123. white body & roof, black plastic chassis, "40th Anniversary Spar" tempa ($100-150)(LD)(UK)
124. white body & roof, black plastic chassis, "Finlaystone" tempa ($10-15)(LD)(UK)
125. yellow body & roof, black plastic chassis, "Finlaystone" tempa ($10-15)(LD)(UK)
126. yellow body & roof, black plastic chassis, "St. Marien Sandersleben" tempa ($15-20)(LD)(GR)
127. red body & roof, black plastic chassis, "St. Marien Sandersleben" tempa ($20-40)(LD)(GR)
128. white body & roof, black plastic chassis, "St. Marien Sandersleben" tempa ($35-50)(LD)(GR)
129. white body & roof, black plastic chassis, "Farnham 8- 11th Sept 1997" tempa ($10-15)(LD)(UK)
130. blue body, red roof & chassis, "Mastercraft" tempa, gold wire wheels with rubber tires, gold grille ($4-6)(CN)(GS)
131. pink-red body, dark blue roof & chassis, "Crazy Clown" tempa ($8-12)(AU)
132. red body & roof, black plastic chassis, "Merry Christmas Australian Matchbox" tempa ($15-20)(C2)
133. white body & roof, black plastic chassis, "5th Anniversary Australian Matchbox News" tempa ($15-20)(C2)
134. white body & roof, black plastic chassis, "Mundesley Inshore Lifeboat" tempa ($10-15)(LD)(UK)
135. yellow body & roof, black plastic chassis, "Evening Gazette Car Awards 1997" tempa ($10-15)(LD)(UK)
136. beige body & roof, black plastic chassis, "Encyclopedia of Matchbox Toys" tempa ($35-50)(LD)(US)
137. beige body & roof, black plastic chassis, "Catalogue of Matchbox Toys" tempa ($15-18)(LD)(US)
138. yellow body & roof, black plastic chassis, "Catalogue of Matchbox Toys" tempa ($50-75)(LD)(US)
139. white body & roof, black plastic chassis, "Ferne Animal Sanctuary" tempa ($10-15)(LD)(UK)
140. white body & roof, black plastic chassis, "MD" tempa ($10-15)(LD)(UK)
141. yellow body & roof, black plastic chassis, "QATC & EMC Projects/ QA Testing Centre" tempa ($20-30)(LD)(UK)
142. beige body & roof, black plastic chassis, "Bostik" tempa ($10-15)(LD)(UK)
143. beige body & roof, black plastic chassis, "The Story of Mann" tempa ($10-15)(LD)(UK)
144. yellow body & roof, black plastic chassis, "Ford Motor Co." tempa ($20-30)(LD)(UK)
145. blue body, red roof & metal chassis, "Sea Dog Brewing Co." tempa , gold wire wheels with rubber tires, gold grille ($8-12)(MB)(CL)
146. yellow body & roof, black plastic chassis, "MCCD 1998" tempa ($50-75)(LD)(GR)
147. white body & roof, black plastic chassis, "MCCD 1998" tempa ($15-20)(LD)(GR)
148. red body & roof, black plastic chassis, "MCCD 1998" tempa ($15-20)(LD)(GR)
149. beige body & roof, black plastic chassis, "MCCD 1998" tempa ($40-60)(LD)(GR)
150. beige body & roof, black plastic chassis, "Norwich Citadel-Salvation Army" tempa ($10-15)(LD)(UK)
151. yellow body & roof, black plastic chassis, "Norwich Citadel-Salvation Army" tempa ($10-15)(LD)(UK)
152. white body & roof, black plastic chassis, "NGK- The UK's No. 1 Professional Plug" tempa ($65-80)(LD)(UK)
153. pink-beige body, dark green roof & metal chassis, "Mt. Wilson Wheat Beer" tempa, gold wire wheels with rubber tires, gold grille ($8-12)(MB)(CL)
154. pale orange body, orange-red roof & metal chassis, "Zonker Stout" tempa, gold wire wheels with rubber tires, gold grille ($8-12)(MB)(CL)

155. beige body & roof, blue plastic chassis, "Barrettine The Independent Choice" tempa ($12-15)(LD)(UK)
156. white body & roof, black plastic chassis, "Biddestone Village" tempa ($12-15)(LD)(UK)
157. bright blue body, red roof, red plastic chassis, no tempa ($25-40)(ASAP blank)
158. white body & roof, black plastic chassis, "Glenturret" tempa ($12-15)(LD)(UK)
159. white body & roof, black plastic chassis, "CE Engineering Europe Ltd." Tempa ($12-15)(LD)(UK)
160. red body & roof, white plastic chassis, "Coca Cola" tempa, chrome wire wheels with rubber tires ($4-6)(Coke PC)
161. dark blue body, red roof, red plastic chassis, "Ritz Carlton Hotel, Spa & Casino" tempa ($200+)(ASAP)
162. white body & roof, black plastic chassis, "Open Business Solutions" tempa ($15-20)(LD)(UK)
163. white body & roof, black plastic chassis, "The Sunrise Coast" tempa ($12-15)(LD)(UK)
164. white body & roof, black plastic chassis, "Daybreak at Lowestoft/ The Sunrise Coast/The Dawn of A New Millennium" tempa ($12-15)(LD)(UK)
165. beige body & roof, blue plastic chassis, "Daybreak at Lowestoft/ The Sunrise Coast/ The Dawn of A New Millennium" tempa ($12-15)(LD)(UK)
166. beige body & roof, blue plastic chassis, "The Sunrise Coast" tempa ($12-15)(LD)(UK)
167. beige body & roof, blue plastic chassis, "Welcoming The New Millennium" tempa ($18-25)(LD)(UK)
168. red body & roof, black plastic chassis, "Welcoming The New Millennium" tempa ($18-25)(LD)(UK)
169. white body & roof, black chassis, "Garde D'Or" tempa ($12-15)(LD)(UK)
170. dark blue body, red roof, red plastic chassis, "Pool's Plus, Inc." tempa ($12-18)(ASAP)
171. white body & roof, black plastic chassis, "Ad Trucks 2001" tempa ($12-15)(LD)(UK)
172. beige body & roof, blue plastic chassis, "Ad Trucks 2001" tempa ($12-15)(LD)(UK)
173. white body & roof black plastic chassis, "Dunaskin" tempa ($12-15)(LD)(UK)
174. white body & roof, black plastic chassis, "The Arndale" tempa ($12-15)(LD)(UK)
175. white body & roof, black plastic chassis, "The Quote Engine" tempa ($12-15)(LD)(UK)
176. brown body, black roof, black plastic chassis, "Michigan Auto Works Plant 26" tempa ($1-2)(AM)
NOTE: Above model with Matchbox International or Mattel casting.
177. white body & roof, black plastic chassis, "Durham Cathedral" tempa ($12-15)(LD)(UK)
178. white body & roof, black plastic chassis, "Mentecaptos, Ltd." Tempa ($12-15)(LD)(UK)
179. white body & roof, black plastic chassis, "The Ironbridge Gorge Museum" tempa ($12-15)(LD)(UK)
180. beige body & roof, blue plastic chassis, "The Ironbridge Gorge Museum" tempa ($12-15)(LD)(UK)
181. beige body & roof, black plastic chassis, "Whalley Abbey" tempa ($12-15)(LD)(UK)
182. white body & roof, black plastic chassis, "Whalley Abbey" tempa ($12-15)(LD)(UK)
183. white body & roof, black plastic chassis, no tempa ($12-15)(LD blank)
184. white body & roof, black metal chassis, no tempa ($12-15)(LD blank)
185. red body & roof, black plastic chassis, no tempa ($12-15)(LD blank)
186. dark blue body & roof, black plastic chassis, no tempa ($12-15)(LD blank)
187. yellow body & roof, black plastic chassis, no tempa ($12-18)(LD blank)
188. beige body & roof, blue plastic chassis, no tempa ($12-18)(LD blank)
189. gold body, green roof & metal chassis, "Bendigo National Swap Meet 2003" tempa, gold wire wheels with rubber tires, gold grille ($18-25)(C2)(AU)
190. pink-beige body, dark green roof & metal chassis, "Bendidgo National Swap Meet 2003", gold wire wheels with rubber tires, gold grille ($18-25)(C2)(AU)
191. red body, black roof, black metal chassis, "Texaco Petroleum Products" tempa, Mattel casting ($3-5)(Texaco PC)
192. lemon body, bright blue roof, pale orange plastic chassis, gray grille, "Squidward" tempa, Mattel casting ($1-2)(5pk)
193. white body, silver blue roof, blue plastic chassis, gray grille, "Squidward" tempa, Mattel casting ($1-2)(5pk)
194. metallic blue body, white roof, black metal chassis, "Ford Motor Company 100 Years" tempa, Mattel casting ($3-5)(CL)
195. white body & roof, black plastic chassis, "Ladies Circle Great Britain & Ireland" tempa ($100+)(LD)(UK)
196. white body & roof, black plastic chassis, "Esso Lubricants Europe" tempa ($100+)(LD)(UK)
197. dark yellow body, red roof, blue plastic chassis, smoke windows, gray grille, "Hot Dog Cart" & Clifford tempa, Mattel casting ($1-2)(5pk)
198. bright blue body, red roof, red plastic chassis, "Bosal/ Bosal 80- 1923-2003" tempa ($18-25)(CCI)
199. salmon body, orange-yellow roof, gray plastic chassis, "Ghost Town- Bodie CA" tempa, Mattel casting ($1-2)(AW)
200. white body, black roof, black plastic base, "Evening Gazette Car Awards 1996" tempa ($12-15)(LD)(UK)
201. yellow body & roof, black plastic base, "Bishop's Move" tempa ($12-15)(LD)(UK)

MB44-I FORD PROBE, issued 1994 (MB250)

NOTE: Below models with clear windows & black plastic base.

1. black body, blue interior, gold 6-spoke spiral wheels, blue & red tempa, Thailand casting ($1-2)
2. black body, blue interior, gold 6-spoke spiral wheels, blue & red tempa, China casting ($1-2)
3. metallic red body, black interior, silver 6-spoke spiral wheels, orange & yellow design tempa , China casting ($1-2)
4. metallic red body, black interior, silver 6-spoke spiral wheels, peach & white design tempa, China casting ($1-2)
5. dark purple body, black interior, silver 6-spoke spiral wheels, green & white design tempa, China casting ($2-3)
6. metallic red body, black interior, silver 6-spoke spiral wheels, yellow & peach design with "Princeton Nassau-Conover" on hood tempa, China casting ($15-20)(C2)(CCI)
7. metallic gold body, black interior, silver 6-spoke spiral wheels, no tempa, China casting ($10-15)(CH)
8. dark purple body, black interior, 5 spoke concave star wheels, green & white design tempa , China casting ($2-4)
9. metallic blue body, gray & black interior, chrome disc wheels with rubber tires, gray flames tempa, engine cast , China casting ($3-5)(PC9)
10. metallic bronze body, black interior, 5 spoke concave star wheels, blue & white design tempa, China casting ($1-2)
11. metallic blue body, gray & black interior, gold 6 spoke spiral wheels, gray flames tempa, engine cast, China casting ($50+)(CHI)

MB44-J HYDROPLANE, issued 1999 (USA) (MB409)
MB39-J HYDROPLANE, issued 1999 (ROW)

NOTE: Below models with clear windows, China casting unless otherwise noted.

1. red body, white base, black interior, black airfoil, turquoise, white & purple tempa, black wheels ($1-2)(MW441999 US)(MW39/1998 ROW)(MW34/1999 GR))
2. dark blue body, red base, silver-gray interior, silver-gray airfoil, red & white with "492" tempa, black wheels ($1-2)(5pk)
3. dark blue body, red base, silver-gray interior, silver-gray airfoil, red & white with "492" tempa, white wheels ($2-4)(5pk)
4. bright blue body, orange base, amber windows, silver-gray interior, silver-gray airfoil, orange & white with "492" & "Matchbox 2000" tempa, orange wheels ($1-2)(MW10/2000 US)
5. bright blue body, orange base, amber windows, silver-gray interior, silver-gray airfoil, orange & white with "492" tempa, orange wheels ($1-2)(MW10/2000 US)
6. red body, gray base, gray interior, gray airfoil, "Coca Cola" & polar bears tempa, black wheels ($4-6)(Coke PC)
7. red body, gray base, gray interior, gray airfoil, "Coca Cola", polar bears & "www..cocacolastore.com" tempa, black wheels ($50+)(CCI)
8. metallic green body, black interior, blue airfoil, "H495" with multi-color design tempa, white wheels ($1-2)(5pk)

MB44-K AUDI TT, issued 2000 (USA) (MB433)
MB74-K AUDI TT, issued 1999 (GR)
MB67-I AUDI TT, issued 2000 (ROW)

NOTE: Below models with black plastic base & China casting.

1. silver-gray body, smoke windows, black interior, grille & headlights tempa, 5 spoke concave star wheels ($3-5)(MW74/1999GR)
2. metallic blue body, smoke windows, gray interior, "OOOO" with head & tail lights tempa , 5 spoke concave star wheels ($2-4)(MW67/2000 ROW)
3. metallic blue body, smoke windows, gray interior, "OOOO/ TT Coupe" with head & tail lights tempa, 5 spoke concave star wheels ($1-2)(MW44/2000 US)
4. metallic blue body, smoke windows, gray interior, "OOOO" with head & tail lights tempa, large 5 spoke concave star wheels ($2-4)(MW67/2000 ROW)
5. metallic blue body, smoke windows, gray interior, "OOOO/TT Coupe" with head & tail lights tempa & "Matchbox 2000" tempa, 5 spoke concave star wheels ($2-4)(MW44/2000)
6. dark green body, clear windows, black interior, head & tail lights tempa, 5 spoke concave star wheels ($1-2)(5pk)
7. dark green body, clear windows, black interior, head & tail lights tempa, 10 spoke flower wheels ($1-2)(5pk)
8. black body, clear windows, dark gray interior, head & tail lights tempa, 5 spoke concave star wheels ($1-2)(LP)
9. metallic blue body, smoke windows, gray interior, "OOOO/TT Coupe" with head & tail lights tempa, 10 spoke flower wheels ($8-12)(EG)
10. metallic blue body, smoke windows, gray interior, "OOOO" with head & tail lights tempa, 10 spoke flower wheels ($8-12)(EG)
11. metallic blue body, smoke windows, gray interior, head & tail lights with "MB38BBBerlinaol.com" tempa, 5 spoke concave star wheels ($18-25)(C2)(GR)
12. red body, smoke windows, gray interior, head & tail lights tempa, 10 spoke flower wheels ($2-3)(MW17/2001 ROW)

NOTE: Below models with metal base unless otherwise noted.

13. red body, smoke windows, gray interior, head & tail lights tempa, 10 spoke flower wheels ($2-3)(MW17/2001 ROW)
14. dark green body, clear windows, black interior, head & tail lights tempa, 10 spoke flower wheels ($1-2)(5pk)
15. white body, clear windows, dark red interior, "Coca Cola" tempa, chrome disc with rubber tires ($3-5)(Coke PC)
16. metallic maroon body, clear windows, brown interior, yellow band with "37" & "OOOO" tempa, 10 spoke flower wheels, plastic base ($2-4)(MW37/2003 ROW)
17. metallic maroon body, clear windows, brown interior, yellow band with "37", "OOOO" & "Hero City" tempa, 10 spoke flower wheels, plastic base ($4-6)(MW37/2003 ROW)
18. red body, amber windows, orange interior, bee & honeycomb design tempa, 10 spoke flower wheels, plastic base ($1-2)(5pk)

MB44-L TRUCK CAMPER POLICE, issued 2001 (MB503/591)

NOTE: Below models with 4 spoke domed wheels, gray plastic base, China casting unless otherwise noted.

1. iridescent white body, blue door & interior, clear windows, red triangular dome light, "Police HO32" tempa, ($1-2)(MW44/2001)
2. white body, red door & interior, blue windows, blue triangular dome light, "Metro Base 15" tempa ($1-2))MW15/2003)
3. white body, red door & interior, blue windows, blue triangular dome light, "Metro Base 15" & "Hero City" tempa ($2-4)(MW15/2003)
4. white body, white door & interior, blue windows, blue bar dome light, "Hero City First Aid Squad" tempa ($3-5)(PB)

MB45-A FORD GROUP 6, issued 1970

NOTE: Below models with 5 spoke wheels, ivory interior, metal base & England casting unless otherwise noted..

1. non-metallic green body, unpainted base, clear windows, chrome motor, round "7" label ($1500+)
2. metallic green body, unpainted base, clear windows, chrome motor, round "7" label ($12-15)
3. metallic green body, black base, clear windows, chrome motor, round "7" label ($12-15)
4. metallic green body, black base, clear windows, chrome motor, round "7" & "Burmah" label ($12-15)(GS)
5. metallic green body, black base, clear windows, chrome motor, square "7" label ($12-15)
6. metallic green body, unpainted base, clear windows, chrome motor, square "7" & "Burmah" label ($12-15)(GS)
7. metallic green body, black base, clear windows, chrome motor, square "7" & "Burmah" label ($12-15)(GS)
8. metallic green body, pink base, clear windows, chrome motor, "45" & "Burmah" label ($12-15)(GS)
9. metallic green body, black base, clear windows, chrome motor, "45" & "Burmah" label ($12-15)(GS)
10. metallic green body, yellow base, clear windows, chrome motor, "45" & "Burmah" label ($12-15)(GS)
11. metallic green body, charcoal base, clear windows, chrome motor, "45" & "Burmah" label ($12-15)(GS)
12. metallic green body, black base, clear windows, chrome motor, "45" label ($12-15)
13. metallic green body, gray base, clear windows, chrome motor, "45" label ($12-15)
14. metallic green body, yellow base, clear windows, chrome motor, "45" label ($12-15)
15. metallic green body, pink base, clear windows, chrome motor, "45" label ($12-15)
16. metallic green body, pink base, amber windows, chrome motor, "45" label ($12-15)

17. metallic lime body, black base, amber windows, chrome motor, "45" label ($12-15)
18. metallic lime body, charcoal base, amber windows, chrome motor, "45" label ($12-15)
19. metallic lime body, gray base, amber windows, chrome motor, "45" label ($12-15)
20. metallic lime body, light gray base, amber windows, chrome motor, "45" label ($12-15)
21. metallic lime body, pink base, amber windows, chrome motor, "45" label ($12-15)
22. metallic lime body, yellow base, amber windows, chrome motor, "45" label ($12-15)
23. metallic lime body, gray base, amber windows, chrome motor, "45" & "Burmah" label ($12-15)(GS)
24. metallic lime body, black base, amber windows, gray motor, "45" label ($12-15)
25. metallic lime body, charcoal base, amber windows, gray motor, "45" label ($12-15)
26. metallic lime body, gray base, amber windows, gray motor, "45" label ($12-15)
27. metallic lime body, pink base, amber windows, chrome engine, "45" & "Burmah" labels ($12-15)(GS)
28. metallic purple body, gray base, amber windows, chrome motor, "45" label ($12-15)
29. metallic purple body, black base, amber windows, gray motor, "45" label ($12-15)
30. metallic purple body, black base, amber windows, chrome motor, "45" label ($12-15)
31. metallic purple body, green base, amber windows, chrome motor, "45" label ($12-15)
32. metallic purple body, black base, amber windows, chrome motor, eyes label ($12-15)
33. metallic purple body, green base, amber windows, chrome motor, eyes label ($12-15)
34. purple body, black base, amber windows, chrome motor, eyes label, white interior ($12-15)
35. purple body, green base, amber windows, chrome motor, eyes label, white interior ($12-15)
36. purple body, green base, amber windows, chrome motor, no label, white interior ($12-15)

MB45-B BMW 3.0 CSL, issued 1976

NOTE: Below models with 5 arch wheels, unpainted metal base & England casting unless otherwise noted.

1. orange body, light yellow interior, green windows, "BMW" hood label ($6-8)
2. orange body, light yellow interior, green windows, no hood label ($6-8)
3. white body, light yellow interior, green windows, green hood & trunk with "Polizei" labels, amber dome light ($35-45)(GR)(JP)
4. white body, light yellow interior, green windows, green hood & trunk with "Polizei" labels, blue dome light ($35-45)(GR)(JP)
5. white body, light yellow interior, green windows, green hood & trunk tempa ($85-110)(GR)
6. white body, light yellow interior, green windows, "BMW" & "Manhalter" label ($50-65)(AS)
7. orange body, ivory interior, green windows, "BMW" hood label ($6-8)
8. orange body, light yellow interior, clear windows, "BMW" hood label ($7-10)
9. orange body, ivory interior, clear windows, "BMW" hood label ($7-10)
10. orange body, light yellow interior, dark green windows, "BMW" hood label ($7-10)
11. orange body, ivory interior, dark green windows, "BMW" hood label ($7-10)
12. orange body, light yellow interior, green windows, "BMW" hood label, dot dash wheels ($8-12)
13. red body, light yellow interior, green windows, no hood label ($65-80)(GS)
14. orange body, light yellow interior, green windows, no hood label, base with Manaus tab ($35-50)(BR)

NOTE: Available as a Hungarian & Bulgarian casting. Assorted colors available ($15-35)

MB45-C KENWORTH AERODYNE, issued 1982 (MB045/309)

NOTE: Other versions exist as components to Convoy models. Only models issued as single releases are listed here. Below models with chrome plastic base & 8 spoke wheels.

1. white body, amber windows, chrome exhausts, brown & blue stripes tempa, England casting ($3-5)
2. white body, amber windows, chrome exhausts, brown & blue stripes tempa, Macau casting ($2-4)
3. pearly silver body, amber windows, chrome exhausts, purple & orange tempa, Macau casting ($2-4)
4. white body, amber windows, chrome exhausts, "Chef Boyardee" label, Macau casting ($35-50)(US)(OP)
5. red body, amber windows, chrome exhausts, yellow/orange/white stripes tempa, Macau casting ($1-2)
6. red body, amber windows, chrome exhausts, orange/yellow/white stripes tempa, Macau casting ($1-2)
7. red body, amber windows, gray exhausts, yellow/orange/white stripes tempa, Macau casting ($1-2)
8. red body, amber windows, gray exhausts, yellow/orange/white stripes tempa, Thailand casting ($1-2)(MP)

MB45-D FORD CARGO SKIP TRUCK *see MB70-E*

MB45-E HIGHWAY MAINTENANCE VEHICLE, issued 1990 (USA) (M222)

MB69-G HIGHWAY MAINTENANCE VEHICLE, issued 1990 (ROW)

NOTE: Below models with black plastic base, amber windows & 8 spoke wheels, China casting unless otherwise noted.

1. pale lemon body, pale lemon dump & plow, "Int'l Airport Authority 45" tempa ($1-2)
2. red body, gray dump & plow, "Aspen Snow Removal" tempa ($2-4)(AP)
3. pale lemon body, red dump & plow, "Int'l Airport Authority 45" tempa ($1-2)
4. dark orange body, red dump & plow, "Int'l Airport Authority 45" tempa ($8-12)(GS)
5. green body, yellow dump & plow, "Intercom City" tempa, base with bar code, Thailand casting ($7-10)(IC)
6. pale lemon body, red dump & plow, "Int'l Airport Authority 45" tempa, Thailand casting ($1-2)
7. orange body, gray dump & plow, "Highway Maintenance 45" tempa, Thailand casting ($2-4)(CC)
8. white body, blue dump & plow, ""Highway Dept." with hood design tempa ($1-2)
9. white body, blue dump & plow, "Highway Dept." without hood design tempa ($1-2)
10. pumpkin body, gray dump & plow, "Matchbox" tempa ($1-2)(5pk)
11. orange body, black dump & plow, "Road Crew" tempa ($1-2)
12. metallic gold body, black dump & plow, none tempa ($5-10)(CH)
13. red body, black dump & plow, "Matchbox Road Crew" tempa ($1-2)(MW11/1998)

14. florescent green body, black dump, yellow plow, "Highway Crew" tempa ($1-2)(5pk)
15. dark orange body, black dump, black plow, "DOT 13" tempa ($1-2)(MW11/1999 US)
16. orange body, dark gray dump, gray plow & base, "Test Centre" & polar bear logo tempa ($1-2)(LP)
17. florescent yellow body, gray dump, gray plow & base, "DOT 13" & "Matchbox 2000" tempa ($1-2)(MW79/2000 US)
18. florescent yellow body, gray dump, gray plow & base, "DOT 13" tempa ($1-2)(MW79/2000 US/ MW59/2000 ROW)
19. pumpkin body, gray dump, gray plow, black base, "Minnesota Guidestar" tempa ($75+)(ASAP)
20. pumpkin body, gray dump, gray plow, black base, "Hemler Bros." Tempa ($75+)(ASAP)
21. pumpkin body, gray dump, gray plow, black base, "CAT Service Co." tempa ($75+)(ASAP)
22. pumpkin body, gray dump, gray plow, black base, "Redi-Way Inc." tempa ($75+)(ASAP)
23. pumpkin body, gray dump, gray plow, black base, Blue Ridge Construction" tempa ($75+)(ASAP)

NOTE: Below models with 7 spoke sawblade wheels unless otherwise noted.

24. orange-yellow body, orange-yellow dump, red plow, chrome base, "17 Airport Plow" tempa ($3-5)(PB)
25. dark blue body, orange dump, orange plow, gray base, "North Dakota Roughrider Snow Removal ND39" tempa, Mattel casting ($1-2)(AM)
26. metallic green body, orange dump, orange plow, gray base, ram with "20" tempa, Mattel casting ($1-2)(MW20/2003)
27. metallic green body, orange dump, orange plow, gray base, ram with "20" & "Hero City" tempa, Mattel casting ($2-4)(MW20/2003)
28. orange body, yellow dump, yellow plow, gray base, "263" with worker tempa, Mattel casting ($1-2)(5pk)
29. orange body, yellow dump, yellow plow, gray base, "263" with worker & "Hero City" tempa, Mattel casting ($1-2)(5pk)
30. pumpkin body, gray dump, gray plow, black base, circular logo with blue arrow tempa, 8 spoke wheels ($25-40)(ASAP)
31. pumpkin body, gray dump, gray plow, black base, no tempa, 8 spoke wheels ($8-12)(ASAP blank)
32. orange body, dark blue dump, yellow plow, black base, "Centre Action" tempa, 7 spoke sawblade wheels ($1-2)(5pk)(PB)
33. white body, blue dump, blue plow, black base, "Airways Plow" tempa ($1-2)(5pk)
34. lemon body, orange dump, no plow cast, black base, "Matchbox Dot#042076" tempa, 7 spoke sawblade wheels ($5-8)(CG)

MB45-F SUBMERSIBLE, issued 1999 (USA) (MB410)
MB40-J SUBMERSIBLE, issued 1999 (ROW)

NOTE: Below models with China casting.

1. orange-yellow body, blue cab & hatch, blue base & wheels, purple windows, globe design & white & blue design tempa ($1-2)(MW40/1999 ROW) (MW35/1999 GR)
2. orange-yellow body, blue cab & hatch, blue base & wheels, purple windows, globe design & "World Ocean Exploration" tempa ($1-2)(MW45/1999US)
3. lime body, blue cab & hatch, blue base & wheels, amber windows, globe design & white & blue design tempa ($1-2)(MW6/2000)
4. lime body, blue cab & hatch, blue base & wheels, amber windows, globe design & white & blue design with "Matchbox 2000" tempa ($1-2)(MW6)/2000 US
5. lemon body, blue cab & hatch, blue base & wheels, amber windows, "Base 2000/ BX-22775" tempa ($1-2)(LP)
6. metallic blue body, lemon cab & hatch, lemon base & wheels, blue windows, globe design & yellow & red design & "Matchbox" tempa ($3-5)(PB)
7. red body, blue cab & hatch, blue base, black wheels, amber windows, "#042076" & storm logo tempa ($1-2)(LP)
8. white body, white cab, black hatch, black base & wheels, amber windows, "Rescue 4/ Sub Nautical Rescue" tempa ($1-2)(MW64/2001 US)
9. metallic blue body, yellow cab & hatch, yellow base & wheels, amber windows, "Spongebob Squarepants" tempa ($1-2)(5pk)
10. blue-green body, blue cab, orange hatch, blue base, black wheels, amber windows, "Great Barrier Reef" tempa ($1-2)(AW)

MB46-A MERCEDES 300 SE, issued 1970 (MB846)

NOTE: Below models with clear windows, ivory interior, silver hubs, metal base & England casting unless otherwise noted.

1. blue body, unpainted base, opening doors & trunk, no labels, 5 spoke wheels ($75-90)
2. dark gold body, unpainted base, opening doors & trunk, no labels, 5 spoke wheels ($20-25)
3. light gold body, unpainted base, opening doors & trunk, no labels, 5 spoke wheels ($20-25)
4. light gold body, unpainted base, cast doors, opening trunk, no labels, 5 spoke wheels ($20-25)
5. olive body, unpainted base, cast doors & trunk, "Staff" labels, 5 arch wheels with black hubs ($7-10)(TP)
6. olive body, unpainted base, cast doors & trunk, "Staff" labels, dot dash wheels with black hubs ($7-10)(TP)
7. silver-gray body, unpainted base, cast doors & trunk, no labels, dot dash wheels ($85-110)(MP)
8. silver-gray body, unpainted base, cast doors & trunk, no labels, dot dash wheels with black hubs ($85-110)(MP)

NOTE: Available as a Bulgarian casting. Assorted colors available. ($20-30)

MB46-B STRETCHA FETCHA, issued 1972

NOTE: Below models with white plastic tailgate & England casting unless otherwise noted.

1. white body, unpainted base, blue windows, "Ambulance" labels, light yellow interior, maltese cross wheels ($12-15)
2. white body, red base, blue windows, "Ambulance" labels, light yellow interior, maltese cross wheels ($12-15)
3. white body, red base, blue windows, "Ambulance" labels, cream interior, maltese cross wheels ($12-15)
4. white body, red base, blue windows, cross labels (from MB3-A), light yellow interior, maltese cross wheels ($12-15)
5. white body, red base, blue windows, "Ambulance" labels, light yellow interior, 5 spoke wheels ($20-25)
6. white body, red base, blue windows, "Ambulance" labels, light yellow interior, 4 spoke wheels ($20-25)
7. red body & tailgate, red base, blue windows, "Unfall Rettung" labels, light yellow interior, maltese cross wheels ($35-45)(GR)
8. white body, red base, blue windows, no labels, light yellow interior, maltese cross wheels ($12-15)
9. white body, red base, amber windows, "Ambulance" labels, light yellow interior, maltese cross wheels ($15-18)
10. white body, red base, amber windows, cross labels (from MB3-A), light yellow interior, maltese cross wheels ($15-18)
11. lime body, black base, amber windows, "Viper Van" tempa, light yellow interior, maltese cross wheels ($12-15)(LE)
12. lime body, white base, amber windows, "Viper Van" tempa, light yellow interior, maltese cross wheels ($12-15)(LE)
13. lime body, white base, amber windows, "Viper Van" tempa, cream interior, maltese cross wheels ($12-15)(LE)

14. lime body, unpainted base, amber windows, "Viper Van" tempa, light yellow interior, maltese cross wheels ($12-15)(LE)
15. white body, red base with Manaus tab, blue windows, "Ambulance" labels, light yellow interior, maltese cross wheels ($35-50)(BR)

NOTE: Versions 11-14 issued as a limited edition in US as "Viper Van".

MB46-C FORD TRACTOR, issued 1978 (MB046)

NOTE: Below models without tempa unless otherwise noted.

1. blue body, unpainted base, light yellow interior, yellow harrow, black front & rear hubs, England casting ($3-5)
2. blue body, unpainted base, light yellow interior, orange harrow, black front & rear hubs, England casting ($3-5)
3. blue body, unpainted base, light yellow interior, no harrow, black front & rear hubs, England casting ($3-5)(TP)
4. blue body, unpainted base, light yellow interior, yellow harrow, yellow front & rear hubs, England casting ($3-5)
5. blue body, unpainted base, dark yellow interior, yellow harrow, black front & rear hubs, England casting ($3-5)
6. blue body, unpainted base, white interior, yellow harrow, yellow rear hubs only, England casting ($3-5)
7. blue body, unpainted base, white interior, yellow harrow, yellow front & rear hubs, England casting ($3-5)
8. metallic lime body, unpainted base, light yellow interior, yellow harrow, yellow front & rear hubs, England casting ($5-7)
9. metallic green body, unpainted base, light yellow interior, yellow harrow, yellow front & rear hubs, England casting ($5-7)
10. mid blue body, unpainted base with Manaus tab, light yellow interior, yellow harrow, yellow front & rear hubs, no origin cast ($65-80)(BR)
11. blue body, pearly silver base, white interior, no harrow, gold front & rear hubs, Macau casting ($2-3)(TP)
12. yellow body, pearly silver base, black interior, no harrow, orange front & rear hubs, orange stripe tempa, Macau casting ($1-2)(TP)
13. yellow body, pearly silver base, black interior, red harrow, orange front & rear hubs, orange stripe tempa, Macau casting ($1-2)(GS)
14. green body, pearly silver base, white interior, red harrow, orange front & rear hubs, no tempa, Macau casting ($1-2)(MC)
15. green body, pearly silver base, black interior, no harrow, orange front & rear hubs, Macau casting ($1-2)(MP)
16. green body, pearly silver base, black interior, no harrow, orange front & rear hubs, Thailand casting ($1-2)(TP)
17. green body, pearly silver base, black interior, yellow harrow, orange front & rear hubs, Thailand casting ($1-2)(MC)

MB46-D HOT CHOCOLATE/ BEETLE STREAKER, issued 1981 (USA) (MB085)

NOTE: Versions 1 & 2 cast with "Hot Chocolate" as base name. Versions 3 onward cast with "Beetle Streaker" as base name. All models with chrome interior, amber windows & 5 arch front & 5 spoke rear wheels unless otherwise noted.

1. black body, black base, white roof stripes with brown sides tempa , Hong Kong casting ($4-6)
2. black body, black base, no roof stripes with brown sides tempa, Hong Kong casting ($35-50)
3. silver blue body, pearly silver base, "Big Blue" tempa, Macau casting ($3-5)
4. silver blue body, pearly silver base, "Big Blue" tempa, Hong Kong casting ($3-5)
5. blue body, pearly silver base, "Big Blue" tempa, Hong Kong casting ($3-5)
6. blue body, light gray base, "Big Blue" tempa, Hong Kong casting ($3-5)
7. silver blue body, light gray base, "Big Blue" tempa, Hong Kong casting ($3-5)
8. dark blue body, pearly silver base, "Big Blue" tempa, Macau casting ($3-5)
9. blue body, light gray base, "Big Blue" tempa, 5 spoke front wheels, Hong Kong casting ($3-5)
10. green body, black base, "Dragon Wheels" tempa, dot dash rear wheels, China casting ($4-6)(PC13)

MB46-E SAUBER GROUP C RACER *see MB66-E*

MB46-F MISSION HELICOPTER, issued 1985 (USA) (MB153/330)

MB57-F MISSION HELICOPTER, issued 1985 (ROW)

NOTE: Below versions with blue windows except 18 & 24 with smoke windows.

1. dark blue body, silver-gray base & skis, white tail & blades, orange tempa, Macau casting ($1-2)
2. red body, white base & skis, white tail & blades, "Sheriff Air 1" tempa, Macau casting ($1-2)
3. olive green body, tan base & skis, tan tail & blades, star & emblem tempa, Macau casting ($2-3)(SB)
4. red body, white base & skis, white tail & blades, "Rebels/ Rescue/ Air 1" tempa, Macau casting ($1-2)(MC)
5. dark blue body, silver-gray base & skis, white tail & blades, bullseye tempa, Macau casting ($2-3)(GS)
6. olive green body, black base & skis, black tail & blades, "AC15" & logo tempa, Macau casting ($4-5)(CM)
7. black body, dark gray base & skis, dark gray tail, yellow blades, "AC99" & logo tempa, Macau casting ($4-5)(CM)
8. red body, white base & skis, white tail & blades, "Sheriff Air 1" tempa, Thailand casting ($1-2)
9. dark blue body, silver-gray base & skis, white tail & blades, bullseye tempa, Thailand casting ($2-3)
10. red body, white base & skis, white tail & blades, "Rebels/ Rescue/ Air 1" tempa, Thailand casting ($1-2)(MC)
11. olive green body, bright tan base & skis, bright tan tail & blades, star & emblem tempa, Thailand casting ($2-3)(SB)
12. olive green body, pink-tan base & skis, pink-tan tail & blades, star & emblem tempa, Thailand casting ($2-3)(SB)
13. white body, dark blue base & skis, white tail & blades, "Police" & crest tempa, Thailand casting ($1-2)
14. green body, white base & skis, white tail & blades, "Polizei" tempa, Thailand casting ($2-3)(CY)
15. black body, white base & skis, white tail & blades, "Police" tempa, Thailand casting ($2-3)(CY)
16. white body, fluorescent orange base/skis, white tail & blades, "Metro Swat 7" tempa, Thailand casting ($1-2)(5pk)
17. beige body, yellow-tan base/skis, yellow-tan tail & blades, camouflage tempa, Thailand casting ($1-2)
18. white body, fluorescent orange base/skis, white tail & blades, "Politie 06-11" tempa, Thailand casting ($3-4)(DU)(CY)
19. white body, blue base/skis, white tail & blades, "Intercom City/Police" tempa, Thailand casting ($7-10)(IC)
20. white body, red base/skis, white tail & blades, "Sky" tempa, Thailand casting ($2-3) (NM)
21. yellow body, blue base/skis, white tail & blades, "Canon" tempa, Thailand casting ($2-3)(NM)
22. white body, blue base/skis, white tail & blades, green crest & "Rescue" tempa, Thailand casting ($3-4)(5pk)
23. black body, white base & skis, white tail & blades, "Police Unit 2" & gold star tempa, Thailand casting ($1-2)(5pk)

24. pink-tan body, tan base & skis, tan tail & blades, green & brown camouflage tempa, Thailand casting ($1-2)(5pk)
NOTE: Following models with blue windows unless noted.
25. white body, tan base & skis, tan tail & blades, "Rescue" & green logo tempa, Thailand casting ($2-4)(5pk)
26. white body, red base & skis, red tail, white blades, "Aces" & ace logo tempa, Thailand casting ($2-3)(CY)
27. olive body, black base & skis, olive tail, black blades, star & "T-7521-6" tempa, Thailand casting ($1-2)
28. green body, green base & skis, green tail, black blades, green smoke windows, black & brown camouflage tempa, Thailand casting ($1-2)(5pk)
29. white body, black base & skis, black tail & blades, "Police Unit 3" tempa, Thailand casting ($1-2)(5pk)
30. florescent lime body, black base & skis, neon blue tail, black blades, "12 Air Patrol" tempa, Thailand casting ($1-2)(5pk)

31. blue body, white base & skis, blue tail, silver-gray blades, "Police Air Rescue" tempa, Thailand casting ($1-2)
32. beige body, smoke windows, black base & skis, beige tail, black blades, brown camouflage tempa ($1-2)(5pk)
33. white body, black base & skis, white tail & blades, "Police"" tempa, Thailand casting ($1-2)
34. white body, smoke windows, gray base & skis, white tail & blades, gray & olive camouflage tempa, Thailand casting ($1-2)(5pk)
35. black body, amber windows, black base & skis, black tail & blades, "INGEN" & "Lost World" tempa, gray armament attached, Thailand casting ($5-8)(JR)
36. white body, red windows, black base & skis, black & tail blades, black camouflage tempa, Thailand casting ($1-2)(PS)
37. pale gray body, red windows, black base & skis, black tail & blades, black camouflage tempa, Thailand casting ($1-2)(PS)
38. metallic gold body, smoke windows, black base & skis, black tail & blades, no tempa, Thailand casting ($5-10)(CH)
39. khaki tan body, dark smoke windows, black base & skis, black tail & blades, "AT-7521" & star tempa, Thailand casting ($1-2)(MW49/1998)
40. black body, smoke green windows, brown base & skis, brown tail & blades, green & brown camouflage tempa, Thailand casting ($1-2)(5pk)
41. black body, smoke green windows, brown base & skis, brown tail & blades, green & brown camouflage tempa, China casting ($1-2)(5pk)
42. blue body, white base & skis, blue tail, silver-gray blades, "Police Air Rescue" tempa, China casting ($1-2)(5pk)
43. florescent lime body, blue base & skis, neon blue tail, black blades, "12 Air Patrol" tempa, China casting ($1-2)(5pk)
44. pale gray body, smoke windows, black base & skis, black tail & blades, black camouflage tempa, China casting ($1-2)(5pk)
45. khaki tan body, dark smoke windows, black base & skis, black tail & blades, "AT-7521" & star tempa, China casting ($1-2)(MW49/1998)
46. black body, blue base & skis, blue tail & blades, "SWAT Stand Clear 000256" tempa, China casting ($1-2)(5pk)
47. white body, gray base & skis, blue tail & blades, "Police Air Search" tempa, China casting ($1-2)(MW31/1999 US)
48. purple body, turquoise base & skis, smoke windows, yellow tail & blades, "Hanger 12" tempa , China casting ($1-2)(MW66/2000 US)(MW46/2000 ROW)
49. purple body, turquoise base & skis, smoke windows, yellow tail & blades, "Hanger 12" & "Matchbox 2000" tempa, China casting ($2-4)(MW66/2000 US)
50. white body, white base & skis, smoke windows, white tail & blades, none tempa, China casting ($25-40)(ASAP blank)
51. white body, white base & skis, smoke windows, white tail & blades, "Storm Troopers Reunion at the Mark 2000" tempa, China casting ($75+)(ASAP)
52. black body, blue base & skis, smoke windows, dark blue tail & wings, "Police A1" & logo tempa, China casting ($1-2)(5pk)
53. black body, blue bases & skis, smoke windows, dark blue tail & wings, "Police A1" & logo tempa, Mattel China ($1-2)(5pk)
54. dark green body, gray base & skis, blue windows, red tail & blades, teeth design tempa, Mattel China casting ($1-2)(5pk)
55. silver-gray body, blue base & skis, amber windows, red tail & blades, "Police" & winged logo tempa, Mattel China casting ($1-2)(5pk)
56. white body, gray base & skis, red windows, dark blue tail & blades, "Police" & winged logo tempa, Mattel China casting ($1-2)(5pk)
NOTE: Available as a Bulgarian casting. Models have skis or wheels fitted. Bases are cast blank. Assorted colors available ($15-25)

MB46-G OPEL CALIBRA *see MB66-G*

MB46-H CHEVY TAHOE, issued 1998 (MB324)
NOTE: Below models with clear windows, chromo plastic base & China casting unless otherwise noted.
1. dark metallic green body, tan & black interior, chrome disc with rubber tires, silver band & detailed trim tempa ($4-6)(FE)
2. unpainted body, tan interior, chrome disc with rubber tires, no tempa ($4-6)(FE)
3. metallic red body, tan interior, 5 spoke concave star wheels, "454" & white & yellow design tempa ($1-2)(MW46/1998)
4. dark metallic red body, tan interior, 5 spoke concave star wheels, "454" & white & yellow design tempa ($1-2)(MW46/1998)
5. silver-gray body, red interior, 5 spoke concave star wheels, "Coca Cola" & logo tempa ($1-2)(5pk)(CK)
6. black body, white interior, 5 spoke concave star wheels, "Chicago Bulls 23/ Michael Jordan" tempa ($5-8)(MP)
7. white body, black interior, 5 spoke concave star wheels, "Chicago Bulls 23/ Michael Jordan" tempa ($5-8)(MP)
NOTE: Versions 6 & 7 were sold together as an exclusive for Target stores.
8. bright blue body, red interior, amber windows, 5 spoke concave star wheels, "Sydney 2000" tempa ($1-2)(5pk)
9. silver-gray body, blue interior, 5 spoke concave star wheels, "Clogs" tempa ($10-15)(MW99/1999 US)
NOTE: This was the only 1999 model never issued in the USA. It showed up only in Canada & Mexico.
10. blue body, red interior, smoke windows, 5 spoke concave star wheels, "City of Cleveland Ohio" tempa ($1-2)(MW33/2000 US)
11. blue body, red interior, smoke windows, 5 spoke concave star wheels, "City of Cleveland Ohio" & "Matchbox 2000" tempa ($2-4)(MW33/2000 US)
12. red body, gray interior, 5 spoke concave star wheels, black flare & mud spatter tempa ($10-15)(PS)
13. metallic red body, tan interior, 5 spoke concave star wheels, "454" & white & yellow design tempa & "Matchbox Madness" decal ($75+)(CCI)
14. white body, red interior, 5 spoke concave star wheels, "Rough Riders" tempa ($75+)(ASAP)
15. white body, red interior, 5 spoke concave star wheels, "Ford Tough Mud Run" tempa ($75+)(ASAP)
16. blue body, red interior, 5 spoke concave star wheels, "City of Cleveland Ohio" & "Matchbox 2000" tempa ($25-40)(MW33/2000 US)
NOTE: Above model has base casting from MB30-I.. Below models with Mattel China casting unless otherwise noted.
17. lemon body, red interior & windows, 10 spoke flower wheels, "Coca Cola" tempa, pearly silver metal base ($2-4)(CK)

18. red body, gray interior, 5 spoke concave star wheels, black flare & mud spatter tempa, pearly silver metal base ($8-12)(PS)
19. black body, black interior, 10 spoke flower wheels, "Hammer Demolition 24 Hour" tempa, pearly silver metal base ($1-2)(MW51/2002 US)
20. black body, black interior, 10 spoke flower wheels, "Hammer Demolition 24 Hour" tempa, gray plastic base ($1-2)(MW51/2002 US)
21. black body, black interior, 10 spoke flower wheels, "Hammer Demolition 24 Hour" & "Matchbox 50" tempa, gray plastic base ($75+)(MW51/2002 US)
22. lemon body, red interior & windows, 10 spoke flower wheels, "Coca Cola" tempa, gray plastic base ($2-4)(CK)
23. silver-gray body, red interior, 5 spoke concave star wheels, "Coca Cola" & logo tempa, silver-gray metal base, Mattel casting ($2-4)(CK)
24. blue body, orange interior, amber windows, 10 spoke flower wheels, "Bugs" tempa, dark blue plastic base ($1-2)(5pk)
25. blue body, orange interior, amber windows, 10 spoke flower wheels, "Blue" tempa, light blue plastic base ($1-2)(5pk)
26. yellow body, orange interior, amber windows, 10 spoke flower wheels, "Blue" tempa, light blue plastic base ($1-2)(CA)
27. white body, red interior, 5 spoke concave star wheels, no tempa, chrome plastic base, Matchbox International casting ($25-40)(ASAP blank)
28. black body, gray interior, blue windows, 10 spoke flower wheels, "Washington DC" tempa, gray plastic base ($1-2)(AW)

MB46-I WATERCRAFT WITH TRAILER *see MB51-L*

MB46-J 1955 CHEVROLET BEL AIR CONVERTIBLE, issued 1999 (MB359)

NOTE: Below models with clear windshield, chrome plastic base & China casting unless otherwise noted.

1. black body, white & black interior, 5 spoke concave star wheels, "The Brady Bunch" & white stripe tempa ($10-15)(STR-Avon)
2. powder blue body, gray interior, 5 spoke concave star wheels, "1999 Matchbox Official Parade Car" tempa ($1-2)(MW46/1999 US)
3. powder blue body, gray interior, large 5 spoke concave star wheels, "1999 Matchbox Official Parade Car" tempa ($3-5)(MW46/1999 US)
4. red & cream body, red & cream interior, chrome disc wheels with rubber tires, detailed trim tempa, black painted base ($8-12)(PC)
5. white body, red interior, smoke windshield, 5 spoke concave star wheels, "Coca Cola" tempa ($1-2)(5pk)
6. pale yellow body, white interior, smoke windshield, lace wheels, "California Dreamin' Surf Shop 31" tempa ($1-2)(AM)
7. metallic burgundy & cream body, cream & black interior, clear windshield, chrome disc wheels with rubber tires, "50" logo tempa ($3-5)(CL)
8. turquoise body, orange interior, smoke windshield, lace wheels, "California Legend Tours" tempa ($5-8)(AM)
9. pale yellow body, white interior, smoke windshield, lace wheels, "California Dreamin' Surf Shop 31/ Pi Kappa Alpha 2002" tempa ($15-20)(CCI)
10. bright blue body, green interior, smoke windshield, 10 spoke flower wheels, "Patrick" tempa, blue base ($1-2)(5pk)
11. purple body, turquoise interior, smoke windshield, 10 spoke flower wheels, "Patrick" tempa, pink base ($1-2)(5pk)
12. pale yellow body, white interior, smoke windshield, lace wheels, "California Dreamin' Surf Shop 31/ Kiddie Kar 2003/ Got Lemons?" tempa ($12-15)(CCI)
13. pale yellow body, white interior, smoke windshield, lace wheels, "California Dreamin' Surf Shop 31/ Kiddie Kar 2003/ Make Lemonade!" tempa ($12-15)(CCI)
14. metallic gold body, white interior, smoke windshield, lace wheels, "White River Hornets/ Class of 1953- 50 Year Reunion" tempa ($50+)(CCI)
15. metallic burgundy, white interior, smoke windshield, lace wheels, "White River Hornets/ Class of 1953- 50 Year Reunion" tempa ($50+)(CCI)
16. lime body, yellow interior, smoke windshield, lace wheels, "Hero City Sports" tempa, black base ($1-2)(5pk)
17. dark blue body, light blue interior, smoke windshield, 10 spoke flower wheels, "Patrick" tempa ($1-2)(CA)
18. plum body, dark blue interior, clear windshield, 10 spoke flower wheels, "Squidward" tempa, blue base ($1-2)(5pk)
19. silver blue body, dark blue interior, clear windshield, 10 spoke flower wheels, "Squidward" tempa, blue base ($1-2)(CA)

MB46-K 4 X 4 BUGGY, issued 2003 (MB569)

NOTE: Below models with 5 spoke oval wheels, black base, China casting.

1. metallic green body, yellow interior, stripes, design & "46" tempa ($1-2)(MW46/2003)
2. metallic green body, yellow interior, stripes, design, "46" & "Hero City" tempa ($2-4)(MW46/2003)
3. dark green body, red interior, "The Great Wall of China" tempa ($1-2)(AW)
4. metallic gold body, maroon interior, small "Matchbox" logo tempa ($1-2)(MW55/2004)
5. black body, yellow interior, "Jimmy" tempa, 5 dot crown wheels, red base ($1-2)(5pk)

MB46-L AMBULANCE, issued 2004 (MB598)

1. red body, white roof, blue windows, 4 spoke domed wheels, "Ambulance" & design tempa, black plastic base, China casting ($1-2)(MW46/2004)
2. white body, light blue roof, amber windows, 5 arch dot wheels, red stripes, blue swirl & "Police" crest tempa, dark blue plastic base, China casting ($1-2)(LP)

MB47-A DAF TIPPER TRUCK, issued 1970

NOTE: Below models with green windows, 5 spoke wheels & England casting.

1. silver-gray body, yellow container, gray roof, red base ($25-35)
2. silver-gray body, dark yellow container, gray roof, red base ($25-35)

MB47-B BEACH HOPPER, issued 1974

NOTE: Below models with pink spatter tempa, 5 spoke wheels, sunburst label & England casting unless otherwise noted.

1. dark blue body, windshield cast, silver-gray base, orange interior, tan driver ($90-110)
2. dark blue body, windshield cast, pink base, orange interior, tan driver ($12-15)
3. dark blue body, windscreen cast, pink base, orange interior, tan driver ($12-15)
4. dark blue body, windscreen cast, pink base, orange interior, pink-tan driver ($12-15)
5. dark blue body, windscreen cast, pink base, yellow interior, pink-tan driver ($15-18)
6. dark blue body, windscreen cast, pink base, yellow interior, tan driver ($15-18)
7. dark blue body, windscreen cast, salmon base, orange interior, tan driver ($12-15)

8. dark blue body, windscreen cast, lavender base, orange interior, tan driver ($12-15)
9. dark blue body, windscreen cast, unpainted base, orange interior, tan driver ($12-15)
10. dark blue body, windscreen cast, unpainted base, light orange interior, tan driver ($12-15)
11. metallic blue body without spatter tempa, windscreen cast, unpainted base with Manaus tab, orange interior, tan driver ($50-75)(BR)

MB47-C PANNIER LOCO, issued 1979

Below models with black train wheels, "GWR" labels & England casting.

1. dark green body, black frame, black base ($4-6)
2. light green body, black frame, black base ($4-6)
3. light green body, black frame, brown base ($7-10)
4. light green body, black frame, unpainted base ($4-6)
5. light green body, black frame, charcoal base ($4-6)
6. light green body, black frame, blue-gray base ($4-6)
7. light green body, black frame, charcoal brown base ($4-6)
8. light green body, charcoal frame, black base ($4-6)

MB47-D JAGUAR SS 100, issued 1982

NOTE: Below models with dot dash wheels & chrome windscreen frame & grille.

1. red body, partially painted hood, gray base, tan interior, England casting ($7-10)
2. red body, red hood, gray base, tan interior, England casting ($2-4)
3. red body, red hood, black base, tan interior, England casting ($2-4)
4. red body, red hood, gray base, tan interior, Macau casting ($2-3)
5. red body, red hood, black base, tan interior, Macau casting ($2-3)
6. dark blue body, pearly silver hood, black base, white interior, Macau casting ($4-6)
7. dark green body, red hood, black base, black interior, Thailand casting ($12-15)(UK)(OP) & (US)(GS)
8. silver-gray body with dark gray hood, black base, blue interior, Thailand casting ($3-5)(GS)

MB47-E SCHOOL BUS, issued 1985 (USA) (MB157)
MB47-E SCHOOL BUS, issued 1987 (ROW)

NOTE: Below models with black interior, black plastic base, clear windows & dot dash wheels unless otherwise noted. Early models cast with small window in two sizes in lower section of rear door. Later models cast solid with black painted tempa.

1. yellow body, "School District 2" tempa, Macau casting ($1-2)
2. yellow body, "School District 2" tempa, China casting ($1-2)
3. olive body, "06181988/ Govt Property" tempa, black hubs, China casting ($8-12)(US)
4. yellow body, "School District 2" tempa with "Chef Boyardee" hood label, China casting ($8-12)(US)(OP)
5. orange-yellow body, "School District 2" tempa with "Chef Boyardee" hood label, China casting ($8-12)(US)(OP)
6. orange-yellow body, "School District 2" tempa, China casting ($1-2)
7. orange-yellow body, "1 + 2 = 3 abc" tempa, red base, green wheels with red hubs, China casting ($6-8)(LL)
8. orange-yellow body, "1 + 2 = 3 abc" tempa, red base, green wheels with blue hubs, China casting ($6-8)(LL)
9. orange-yellow body, "School District 2" tempa, Thailand casting ($10-15)
10. orange-yellow body, "St. Paul Public Schools" tempa, China casting ($25-45)(US)
11. blue body, "Police 88" tempa, China casting ($2-4)(AP)
12. dark blue body, "Hofstra University" tempa, China casting ($7-10)(US)
13. yellow body, "Harvey World Travel" tempa, China casting ($7-10)(AU)
14. dark orange body, "School District 2" tempa, China casting ($8-12)(GS)
15. white & dark blue body, "Penn State- The Loop" tempa, China casting ($6-8)(WR)
16. orange-yellow body, red base, "1 + 2 = 3 abc" tempa, all green wheels, China casting ($4-6)(LL)
17. dark pink body, "Mt. Laurel Preschool" tempa, China casting ($2-4)(CC)
18. orange-yellow body, "School District 2" without rear tempa, China casting ($1-2)
19. orange-yellow body, "Carpenter High School" tempa, China casting ($1-2)
20. metallic gold body, no tempa, China casting ($10-15)(CH)
21. orange-yellow body, red interior, "Matchbox Elementary School" tempa, China casting ($1-2)(5pk)
22. olive body, blue windows, "08181988" with Commando hood logo tempa, black hubs, China casting ($25-40)(CHI)(MP)
23. orange-yellow body, "Cap'n Crunch- Quaker Oats" tempa, China casting ($100+)(ASAP)
24. orange-yellow body, "Go Team Go- Oaklyn Middle School PS33" tempa, China casting ($1-2)
25. orange-yellow body, "Montgomery High School" tempa, China casting ($15-20)(C2)
26. orange-yellow body, small "School Bus" at front & rear only tempa, China casting ($20-35)(ASAP blank)
27. orange-yellow body, "Vancom" tempa, China casting ($75-100)(US)
28. orange-yellow body, "Van Lear" tempa, China casting ($75+)(ASAP)
29. lemon body, dark green interior, "Go Team Go- Oaklyn Middle School PS33" tempa, China casting ($1-2)(MW12/1998)
30. orange-yellow body, "RCA" tempa, China casting ($20-30)(ASAP)
31. orange-yellow body, "Go Ridge Go! Ridge Elementary School" tempa, China casting ($1-2)(MW1/1999 US)
32. orange-yellow body, "Off To Northwestern" tempa, China casting ($25-40)(ASAP)
33. orange-yellow body, "White's Guide Car of The Month" (red print), China casting ($5-8)(ASAP)
34. orange-yellow body, "White's Guide Car of The Month" (black print) , China casting ($5-8)(ASAP)
35. orange-yellow body, "Downington Area School District" , China casting ($25-40)(ASAP)
36. orange-yellow body, "Durham" tempa, China casting ($50+)(ASAP)
37. orange-yellow body, "George Dapper, Inc- Iselin, NJ" tempa, China casting ($75+)(ASAP)
38. orange-yellow body, "On My Way To RPI" tempa, China casting ($15-20)(ASAP)
39. orange-yellow body, "On My Way to Bowdoin" tempa, China casting ($15-20)(ASAP)
40. orange-yellow body, "On My way to UCLA" tempa, China casting ($50+)(ASAP)
41. orange-yellow body, "Wolfington" tempa, China casting ($50+)(ASAP)
42. orange-yellow body, "St. Thomas Elementary School- Rocky River Ohio" & "Matchbox 2000" tempa , China casting ($2-4)(MW31/2000 US)

43. orange-yellow body, "St. Thomas Elementary School- Rocky River Ohio" tempa, China casting ($1-2)(MW31/2000 US)
44. orange body, "Matchbox Elementary School/ Enjoy Fanta" tempa,, China casting ($75+)(CHI)
45. orange-yellow body, "On My Way To Cal Poly" tempa, China casting ($15-20)(ASAP)
46. orange-yellow body, "ND Irish Mobile" tempa, China casting ($18-25)(ASAP)
47. orange-yellow body, "Sage" tempa, China casting ($75+)(ASAP)
48. orange-yellow body, green interior, "Matchbox Elementary" & "Matchbox" tempa , China casting ($3-5) (PB)
49. orange-yellow body, "JMOA Engineering PC- K-12 Specialists" tempa, China casting ($75+)(ASAP)
50. orange-yellow body, "Atlantic Coast Surety" tempa, China casting ($75+)(ASAP)
51. lemon body, "Horlicks School Bus" tempa, China casting ($20-25)(MW22)(HK)
52. orange-yellow body, "Storm Troopers Reunion at the Mark 2000" tempa, China casting ($75+)(ASAP)
53. orange-yellow body, "Martin Luther King Drug Free" tempa, China casting ($75+)(ASAP)
54. orange-yellow body, "Rutgers University" tempa, China casting ($20+)(ASAP)
55. orange-yellow body, "On My Way to UGI" tempa, China casting ($25+)(ASAP)
56. orange-yellow body, "On My Way to Maryland" tempa, China casting ($25+)(ASAP)
57. orange-yellow body, "Rosarita" tempa, China casting ($50+)(ASAP)
58. orange-yellow body, "Off to BJU/ Bob Jane University" tempa, China casting ($20-30)(ASAP)
59. orange-yellow body, "On My Way to UK" (left side only) tempa, China casting ($10-15)(ASAP)
60. orange-yellow body, "On My Way to BC" (left side only) tempa, China casting ($10-15)(ASAP)
61. orange-yellow body, "Michigan State Spartans" (left side only) tempa, China casting ($12-18)(ASAP)
62. yellow body, green interior, metal base, "Hey Arnold!" tempa, Mattel China casting ($1-2)(5pk)
63. orange-yellow body, "www.execsource.com/ ESQ" tempa, Mattel China casting ($50+)(ASAP)
64. red body, silver-gray metal base, "Police Transport" & barbed wire tempa, Mattel China casting ($1-2)(MW15/2002 US)
65. red body, silver-gray metal base, "Police Transport", barbed wire & "Matchbox 50" tempa, Mattel China casting ($8-12)(MW15/2002 US)
66. orange-yellow body, "Greenwich Nursery School 2000" tempa, China casting ($50+)(ASAP)
67. orange-yellow body, green interior, metal base, "Matchbox Elementary School" tempa, China casting ($2-4)(PB)
68. orange-yellow body, metal base, "Blue Bird" tempa, Mattel China casting ($25-40)(ASAP)
69. lemon body, green interior, "Matchbox" & book design tempa, Mattel China casting ($2-4)(PZ)
70. orange-yellow body, "On My Way To Delhi College" (left side only) tempa, China casting ($25-40)(ASAP)
71. orange-yellow body, metal base, "Bet-cha Transport, Inc." tempa, Mattel China casting ($50+)(ASAP)
72. orange-yellow body, "On My Way to VT" (left side only) tempa, China casting ($12-18)(ASAP)
73. orange-yellow body, "On My Way to UConn" (left side only) tempa, China casting ($12-18)(ASAP)
74. orange-yellow body, metal base, "On My Way to UConn" (left side only) tempa, Mattel China tempa ($12-18)(ASAP)
75. orange-yellow body, metal base, "On My Way to USC" (left side only) tempa, Mattel China casting ($12-18)(ASAP)
76. orange-yellow body, metal base, "On My Way to Nebraska" (left side only) tempa, Mattel China casting ($12-18) (ASAP)
77. orange-yellow body, "On My Way to UVM" tempa, China casting ($12-18)(ASAP)
78. orange-yellow body, "On My Way to UVM" tempa, Mattel China casting ($12-18)(ASAP)
79. orange-yellow body, "On My Way to Elmira College" tempa, China casting ($15-20)(ASAP)
80. orange-yellow body, "NAIA" tempa, China casting ($50+)(ASAP)
81. orange-yellow body, "Capacity Coverage Company", China casting ($50+)(ASAP)
82. orange-yellow body, "Washington Twp. Cons. School" tempa, China casting ($50+)(ASAP)
83. orange-yellow body, "Western Michigan Broncos" tempa, China casting ($50+)(ASAP)
84. orange-yellow body, "Orix/ www.orix-cac.com" tempa, China casting ($50+)(ASAP)
85. orange-yellow body, "Dattco" tempa, Mattel China casting ($50+)(ASAP)
86. orange-yellow body, metal base, "Downington Area School District 2003" tempa, Mattel China casting ($50+)(ASAP)
87. orange-yellow body, small "School Bus" at front & rear only tempa, Mattel China casting ($8-12)(ASAP blank)
88. orange-yellow body, metal base, small "School Bus" at front & rear only tempa, Mattel China casting ($8-12)($8-12)(ASAP blank)
89. red body, gray plastic base, "Police Transport" & barbed wire tempa, Mattel China casting ($2-4)(Ghost 2 pack)

MB47-G M2 BRADLEY TANK, issued 1998 (MB323)

NOTE: Below models with plastic base & black wheels unless otherwise noted.

1. beige body & turret, black gun, black base, star & "T-0927" tempa, China casting ($1-2)(MW47/ 1998)
2. olive body & turret, black gun, olive base, black & tan camouflage tempa, China casting ($3-5)(MW83/1999 US)
3. dark olive body & turret , dark olive gun, black base, "Mountain Tiger J020764" & "476" tempa, China casting ($3-5)(PC)
4. khaki tan body & turret, tan gun, tan base & wheels, small American flag tempa, China casting ($3-5)(CL)(MP)
5. black body, bright green turret, gray gun, gray base, tank design tempa, Mattel China casting ($1-2)(5pk)

NOTE: Above model with Matchbox International or Mattel casting.

MB47-H ARMORED RESPONSE VEHICLE, issued 2001 (USA) (MB510/606)

MB39-K ARMORED RESPONSE VEHICLE, issued 2002 (ROW)

NOTE: Below models with 5 spoke oval wheels & China casting unless otherwise noted

1. charcoal body, silver-gray canopy, blue windows, blue interior, black base, "Police/ ARV05" tempa ($1-2)(MW47/2001 US)
2. metallic maroon body, glow yellow canopy, amber windows, glow yellow interior, red base, skyline, bolt & green cross tempa ($1-2)(MW39/2002)
3. metallic maroon body, glow yellow canopy, amber windows, glow yellow interior, red base, skyline, bolt & green cross with "Matchbox 50" tempa ($2-4)(MW38/2002)

4. brown & matt blue body, gray canopy, black windows, brown interior, chrome disc wheels with rubber tires, blue base, "Stratos" tempa ($3-5)(MU)
5. red body, black canopy, amber windows, yellow interior, "45678 87654" & grid tempa ($1-2)(5pk)
6. dark gray body, olive canopy, black windows, black interior, avocado base, "Secret Force" tempa ($1-2)(HR)
NOTE: Background color of tempa on above model exists in shades of olive or tan.
7. orange body, light blue canopy, amber windows, light blue interior, black base, "Turbo Zap" tempa ($1-2)(5pk)
8. metallic blue body, dark blue canopy, red windows, yellow-orange interior, gray base, "Police" & star emblem casting ($1-2)(MW69/2004)

MB47-I NISSAN X-TERRA, issued 2002 (MB543)

NOTE: Below models with 7 spoke sawblade wheels, plastic base & China casting unless otherwise noted.
1. white body, amber windows, black interior, "Music" tempa, blue base ($1-2)(5pk)
2. metallic brown body, smoke windows, black interior, "16.0 FM Tennessee" tempa, black base ($1-2)(AM)
3. metallic brown body, smoke windows, black interior, "16.0 FM Tennessee" tempa, black base, 10 spoke flower wheels ($35-50)(AM)
4. white body, clear windows, red interior, "Patrol" tempa, gray base ($1-2)(MW47/2002)
5. white body, clear windows, red interior, "Patrol" & "Matchbox 50" tempa, gray base ($25-40)(MW47/2002)
6. silver blue body, smoke windows, yellow interior, "Taz Mania" tempa, red base ($1-2)(5pk)
7. lemon body, blue windows, black interior, oars & wave design tempa, black base ($1-2)(MW39/2004)

MB48-A DODGE DUMP TRUCK, issued 1970

NOTE: Below models green windows, chrome plastic base & England casting.
1. blue body, yellow dump, 5 spoke front & rear wheels ($250+)
2. metallic blue body, yellow dump, 5 spoke front & rear wheels ($25-40)
3. metallic blue body, yellow dump, 4 spoke front & spiro rear wheels ($25-40)
4. metallic blue body, yellow dump, 4 spoke front & rear wheels ($25-40)

MB48-B PI-EYED PIPER, issued 1972

NOTE: Below models with chrome engine, maltese cross wheels, unpainted metal base & England casting.
1. blue body, amber windows, 8 stacks engine, "8" roof label ($15-18)
2. blue body, blue windows, 8 stacks engine, "8" roof label ($15-18)
3. red body, blue windows, single engine (from MB26-B), "Big Banger" labels ($85-110)

MB48-C SAMBRON JACKLIFT, issued 1977 (MB048)

NOTE: Most versions can be found with combinations of yellow & yellow-orange forks & arms. The yellow-orange is only slightly darker on this particular model. Below models with metal base with black plastic base insert & England casting.
1. yellow body, yellow forks & arm, black base, 4 spoke wheels, silver hubs ($5-7)
2. yellow body, yellow forks & arm, black base, 5 arch wheels, silver hubs ($5-7)
3. yellow body, yellow forks & arm, brown base, 5 arch wheels, silver hubs ($7-10)
4. yellow body, yellow forks & arm, charcoal base, 5 arch wheels, silver hubs ($5-7)
5. yellow body, yellow forks & arm, black base, 5 arch wheels, silver hubs, "Sambron" tempa ($350-500)
6. yellow body, yellow forks & arm, charcoal base, 5 arch wheels, yellow hubs ($7-10)
7. yellow body, black forks, yellow arm, charcoal base, 5 arch wheels, silver hubs ($5-7)
8. yellow body, black forks & arm, black base, 5 arch wheels, silver hubs ($5-7)
9. yellow-orange body, yellow forks & arm, black base, 5 arch wheels, silver hubs ($5-7)

MB48-D RED RIDER, issued 1982 (USA) (MB086)

NOTE: Versions 1-8 with white flames tempa. Below models with black metal base & red windows.
1. red body, maltese cross front & rear wheels, Hong Kong casting ($4-6)
2. red body, maltese cross front & rear wheels, England casting ($4-6)
3. red body, maltese cross front & 5 crown rear wheels, England casting ($4-6)
4. red body, maltese cross front & rear wheels, Macau casting ($1-2)
5. red body, maltese cross front & 5 crown rear wheels, Macau casting ($1-2)
6. red body, 5 spoke front & 5 crown rear wheels, Macau casting ($1-2)
7. red body, 5 arch front & 5 crown rear wheels, China casting ($1-2)
8. dark red body, 5 arch front & 5 crown rear wheels, China casting ($1-2)
9. dark blue body, 5 arch front & 5 crown rear wheels, "8" tempa, China casting ($3-5)(PC13)

MB48-E UNIMOG WITH PLOW, issued 1983 (ROW) (MB125/331)

NOTE: Below models with dot dash wheels. Versions 1-3 with stripes on canopy can be towards the front or rear.
1. yellow body, white base & plow, black plow stripes, amber windows, white canopy, "Rescue" tempa, England casting ($8-10)
2. yellow body, yellow-orange base & plow, black plow stripes, amber windows, white canopy, "Rescue" tempa, England casting ($3-5)
3. yellow body, black base & plow, no plow stripes, amber windows, white canopy, "Rescue" tempa, England casting ($25-40)
4. yellow body, yellow-orange base & plow, black plow stripes, amber windows, no canopy, "Rescue" tempa, England casting ($3-5)
5. yellow body, lemon base & plow, black plow stripes, amber windows, white canopy, "Rescue" tempa, Macau casting ($2-4)
6. red body, red base & plow, white plow stripes, amber windows, white canopy, "UR83" tempa, Macau casting ($2-4)(TP)
7. white body, yellow base & plow, black plow stripes, red windows, no canopy, red & dark blue stripes tempa, Macau casting, includes plastic armament ($6-8)(RB)
8. white body, orange base & plow, black plow stripes, amber windows, orange canopy, "C&S" tempa, Macau casting ($2-4)(TP)
9. white body, orange base & plow, black plow stripes, amber windows, orange canopy, "C&S" tempa, Thailand casting ($2-4)(TP)

10. white body, yellow base & plow, black plow stripes, red windows, no canopy, red & dark blue stripes tempa, Thailand casting, includes plastic armament ($8-12)(JP) (Tomy box)
11. bright green body, silver-gray base & plow, no plow stripes, amber windows, black stake bed, "The Lost World" tempa, black hubs, Thailand casting includes metal dinosaur ($5-8)(JR)
12. white body, light olive base & plow, no plow stripes, amber windows, light olive canopy, gray & olive camouflage tempa, black hubs, Thailand casting ($2-4)(PS)
13. white body, light olive base & plow, no plow stripes, amber windows, light olive canopy, gray & olive camouflage tempa, black hubs, China casting ($2-4)(PS)

MB48-F VAUXHALL ASTRA/ OPEL KADETT, issued 1986 (ROW) (MB162)

NOTE: Early model bases cast "Vauxhall Astra" only. Later models cast "Vauxhall Astra/ Opel Kadett". All models with clear windows.

1. red body, black base, black interior, 8 dot silver wheels, "GTE" & stripe tempa, Macau casting ($2-4)
2. red body, black base, black interior, 5 arch wheels, "GTE" & stripe tempa, Macau casting ($2-4)
3. white body, black base, black interior, 8 dot silver wheels, "AC Delco 48" tempa, Macau casting ($1-2)
4. white body, black base, black interior, 8 dot white wheels, "AC Delco 48" tempa, Macau casting ($2-4)
5. yellow body, blue base, black interior, 8 dot silver wheels, "Mobile Phone/ Telecom" tempa, Macau casting ($3-5)(GS)
6. black body, black base, black interior, 8 dot silver wheels, "BP 52" & yellow band tempa, Macau casting ($8-12)(DU)
7. white body, black base, black interior, 8 dot silver wheels, "AC Delco 48" tempa, China casting ($1-2)
8. white body, black base, blue interior, 8 dot silver wheels, "STP 7/ Sphere Drake" tempa, China casting ($1-2)
9. yellow body, yellow base, blue interior, 8 dot silver wheels, no tempa, China casting ($8-12)(GR)(GS)
10. white body, black base, blue interior, 8 dot silver wheels, "STP/ Sphere" without "7" tempa, China casting ($1-2)

MB48-G PONTIAC FIREBIRD RACER *see MB60-F*

MB48-H 1956 FORD PICKUP, issued 1997 (MB300/437)

NOTE: Below models with clear windows ,chrome plastic base & China casting unless otherwise noted.

1. black body, red & white interior, chrome disc wheels with rubber tires, white roof tempa ($4-6)(IG)
2. unpainted body, red interior, chrome disc wheels with rubber tires, no tempa ($4-6)(IG)
3. dark purple body, gray interior, 5 spoke concave star wheels, white & peach flames tempa ($2-3)
4. metallic red body, tan interior, 5 spoke concave star wheels, "Happy Days" tempa ($4-6)(STR)
5. red body, white & red interior, chrome disc wheels with rubber tires, detailed trim tempa ($3-5)(PC17)
6. red body, white interior, 5 spoke concave star wheels, no tempa ($1-2)(MW35/1998)
7. metallic blue body, blue & gray interior, chrome disc wheels with rubber tires, white roof & "Matchbox Toy Show Hershey 98" tempa ($10-15)(US)
8. turquoise body, black & white interior, chrome disc wheels with rubber tires, pink & purple pinstriping tempa ($3-5)(PC20)
9. light pumpkin body, maroon & white interior, chrome disc wheels with rubber tires, maroon roof & "MBRR Service" tempa ($25-40)(CL)
10. metallic gold body, black interior, 5 spoke concave star wheels, no tempa ($5-10)(CH)
11. red body, white interior, 5 spoke concave star wheels, "Matchbox USA" logo & "www.matchbox-usa.com" decals ($10-15)(C2)
12. red body, black interior, chrome disc wheels with rubber tires, white roof & "Coca Cola in Bottles" tempa ($4-6)(Coke PC)
13. green body, light gray interior, 5 spoke concave star wheels, "Fresh Produce Delivery" tempa ($1-2)(MW21/1999 US)
14. yellow body, black interior, smoke windows, 5 spoke concave star wheels, mud spray tempa ($1-2)(5pk)
15. yellow body, black interior, smoke windows, star with 5 spokes wheels, mud spray tempa ($1-2)(5pk)
16. red body, white interior, 5 spoke concave star wheels, "Bendigo 1999 National Swap Meet" tempa ($15-20)(C2)(AU)
17. black body, black interior, 5 spoke concave star wheels, "Great White Adventures" tempa ($2-3)(MW15/2000 AU)
18. red body, light gray interior, 5 spoke concave star wheels, "2nd Annual Mattel Open" tempa ($100+)(CCI)
19. red body, black interior, smoke windows, 5 spoke concave star wheels, "Texaco" tempa ($1-2)(MW56/2000 US)
20. red body, black interior, smoke windows, star with 5 spokes wheels, "Texaco" tempa ($1-2)(MW56/2000 US)
21. red body, black interior, smoke windows, star with 5 spokes wheels, "Texaco" & "Matchbox 2000" tempa ($2-4)(MW56/2000 US)
22. red body black interior, smoke windows, 5 spoke concave star wheels, "Texaco" & "Matchbox 2000" tempa ($2-4)(MW56)
23. red & white body, white interior, smoke windows, 5 spoke concave star wheels, "Coca Cola" tempa ($3-5)(TP-Avon)
24. red body, light gray interior, 5 spoke concave star wheels, "Matchbox Madness" decal ($75+)(CCI)
25. black body, black interior, 5 spoke concave star wheels, "Great Connecticut Toy Show 2000" tempa ($10-15)(CCI)
26. dark red body, white interior, 5 spoke concave star wheels, "Mr. Timmerman's" tempa, silver-gray metal base ($2-4)(MW15/2001)
27. dark red body, white interior, 10 spoke flower wheels, "Mr. Timmerman's" tempa, silver-gray metal base, Mattel casting ($1-2)(MW15/2001)
28. dark red body, white interior, 10 spoke flower wheels, "Mr. Timmerman's" tempa ($3-5)(MW14)
29. dark red body, white interior, 5 spoke concave star wheels, "Mr. Timmerman's" tempa ($8-12)(MW14)
30. red body, gray interior, 5 spoke concave star wheels, "Cruisin New England Magazine Limited Edition" tempa ($50+)(CCI)
31. black body, black interior, 5 spoke concave star wheels, "American Wheels 2001" tempa ($25-40)(CCI)
32. light yellow body, black & gray interior, chrome disc wheels with rubber tires, silver-gray metal base, white roof with brown bed & detailed trim tempa, Mattel casting ($3-5)(TN)
33. black body, black interior, 5 spoke concave star wheels, "Ballarat 2002" tempa ($15-20)(C2)(AU)
34. dull green & black body, gray interior, chrome disc wheels with rubber tires, "Texaco", brown bed & detailed trim tempa, chrome plastic base ($3-5)(Texaco PC)
35. dull green & black body, gray interior, chrome disc wheels with rubber tires, "Texaco", brown bed & detailed trim tempa, silver-gray metal base ($8-12)((Texaco PC)
36. metallic pea green body, white interior, smoke windows, 10 spoke flower wheels, silver-gray metal base, "Al's Maine Lobster Shack" tempa, Mattel casting ($1-2)(AM)
37. metallic pea green body, white interior, smoke windows, 10 spoke flower wheels, gray plastic base, "Al's Maine Lobster Shack" tempa, Mattel casting ($2-4)(AM)

38. lime body, dark gray interior, 10 spoke flower wheels, silver-gray metal base, "Lucky Charms" tempa ($1-2)(5pk)
39. lime body, dark gray interior, 10 spoke flower wheels, gray plastic base, "Lucky Charms" tempa ($1-2)(5pk)
40. white body, red interior & windows, 10 spoke flower wheels, orange-yellow plastic base, monkey & wrench tempa ($1-2)(5pk)
41. metallic blue body, gray interior, chrome disc wheels with rubber tires, "100" & white roof tempa, Mattel casting ($3-5)(CL)
42. black body, black interior, 5 spoke concave star wheels, "25th/ 7th Anniversary/ 100" tempa ($25-40)(CCI)
43. metallic red body, tan interior, 5 spoke concave star wheels, "Happy Days/ James Wood H.S." tempa ($12-18)(CCI)
44. metallic pea green body, 10 spoke flower wheels, gray interior, smoke windows, "Matchbox Toy Show NYC 1953-2003-50" tempa , Mattel casting ($25-40)(CCI)

NOTE: Below models with Mattel China casting.

45. red body, red interior, chrome disc wheels with rubber tires, clear windows, white roof, brown bed & detailed trim tempa ($3-5)(BJ)
46. dark purple body, gray interior, chrome disc wheels with rubber tires, clear windows, no tempa ($45-50)(CCI blank)
47. dark purple body, gray interior, chrome disc wheels with rubber tires, clear windows, "Continental Aero" tempa ($25-40)(CCI)
48. metallic purple body, gray interior, chrome disc wheels with rubber tires, clear windows, "Continental Aero" tempa ($25-40)(CCI)
49. metallic purple body, gray interior, chrome disc wheels with rubber tires, clear windows, "Wheels & Wings/ Millville Airshow" tempa ($18-25)(CCI)
50. metallic purple body, gray interior, chrome disc wheels with rubber tires, clear windows, "Cystic Fibrosis Foundation/ Great Strides" tempa ($18-25)(CCI)
51. metallic purple body, gray interior, chrome disc wheels with rubber tires, clear windows, "F100 Super Nationals/ Chilowee Park 2004" tempa ($18-25)(CCI)
52. metallic purple body, gray interior, chrome disc wheels with rubber tires, clear windows, "Artcraft- We Deliver" tempa ($18-25)(CCI)
53. metallic purple body, gray interior, chrome disc wheels with rubber tires, clear windows, no tempa ($18-25)(CCI blank)
54. metallic purple body, gray interior, chrome disc wheels with rubber tires, clear windows, "2nd Annual MCCH Gathering/ Matchbox '04" tempa ($18-25)(CCI)

NOTE: Above model comes with three different style roof print patterns.

55. metallic purple body, gray interior, chrome disc wheels with rubber tires, clear windows, "Hershey 2004/ A Big Kiss for a Big Show/ Midwest Diecast Miniatures" tempa ($18-25)(CCI)
56. dark purple body, gray interior, chrome disc wheels with rubber tires, clear windows, "Heading West 2004/ Thanks Mt. Laurel" tempa ($75+)(CCI)
57. black body, red & white interior, silver 6 spoke spiral wheels, white roof & detailed trim ($50+)(CHI)
58, metallic purple body, gray interior, chrome disc wheels with rubber tires, clear windows, "Midwest Diecast Miniatures Customer Appreciation 2003" tempa ($18-25)(CCI)
59. metallic purple body, yellow interior, 10 spoke flower wheels, amber windows, "Huckleberry Hound" tempa, white plastic base ($1-2)(5pk)
60. dark blue body, gray interior, 5 spoke slotted wheels, smoke windows, detailed trim tempa, chrome plastic base ($2-4)(SF26/2004)
61. metallic purple body, gray interior, chrome disc wheels with rubber tires, clear windows, "The 1st Annual Winchester Holiday Toy Show 11-28-04" tempa ($18-25)(CCI)

MB48-I '62 VW BEETLE *see MB53-I*

MB48-J DELIVERY TRUCK, issued 2000 (USA)
(MB445)DELIVERY TRUCK, issued 2000 (ROW)

NOTE: Below models with 8 spoke wheels, silver-gray metal base & China casting.

1. red cab, white container & rear doors, blue windows & interior, barn & rooster labels ($1-2)(MW48/ 2000 US/MW28/ 2000 ROW)
2. red cab, white container & rear doors, blue windows & interior, barn & rooster labels with "Matchbox 2000" tempa ($2-4)(MW48/2000 US)

NOTE: Version #2 baseplate can read "Delivery Truck" or "Flatbed Truck" cast.

3. bronze cab, gray container & rear doors, clear windows & interior, black base, "Test Mission" labels ($1-2)(5pk)
4. dark orange body, bright blue container & rear doors, bright blue windows & interior, black base, "MC-09" & rhino head tempa ($8-12)(5pk)
5. dark orange body, bright blue container & rear doors, bright blue windows & interior, black base, "MC-09" & rhino head tempa , 7 spoke sawblade wheels ($1-2)(5pk)
6. metallic blue body, blue container & rear doors, blue windows & interior, gray base, lion with "MBOX AR001" tempa, 7 spoke sawblade wheels ($1-2)(LP)
7. neon yellow body, black container & rear doors, blue windows & interior, gray base, "MC09" & rhino head tempa, 7 spoke sawblade wheels ($1-2)(5pk)
8. red body, white container & rear doors, amber windows, orange-yellow base, "Times Square" tempa, 7 spoke sawblade wheels ($2-4)(MP)(AW)
9. bright blue body, yellow container & rear doors, amber windows, silver-gray base, "Hero City Matchbox" tempa, 7 spoke sawblade wheels ($1-2)(5pk)
10. red body, white container & rear doors, blue windows, silver-gray base, "Matchbox USA Now In Living Color" labels, 8 spoke wheels ($12-15)(CCI)
11. salmon body, gray container & rear doors, smoke windows, black base, "Duracell Coppertop Quality That Lasts" tempa, 7 spoke sawblade wheels ($1-2)(MW9/2005)

MB48-K AIR LIFT *see MB68-O*

MB48-L HUMMER POLICE, issued 2001 (USA)(MB506)
MB33-J HUMMER POLICE, issued 2002 (ROW)

NOTE: Below models with blue windows, 4 spoke domed wheels, China casting unless otherwise noted.

1. blue body, light blue hatch, neon orange interior, smoke windows, gray base, "Police/ PDH 15" tempa ($3-5)(MW48/2001 US
2. silver-gray body, blue hatch, orange-yellow interior, black base, "Police" & checkers tempa ($8-12)(MW64/2001 UK)
3. white body, red hatch, black interior, red base, "Base 33" tempa ($1-2)(MW33/2002)
4. white body, red hatch, black interior, red base, "Base 33" & "Matchbox 50" tempa ($2-4)(MW33/2002)
5. white body, light red hatch, black interior, light red base, "Base 33" tempa ($1-2)(MW33/2002)
6. maroon body, gray hatch, black interior, clear windows, black base, "14" with flames & "Matchbox MBFD" tempa ($1-2)(LP)
7. neon yellow body, white hatch, red interior & windows, gray base, "MHC65" tempa ($1-2)(MW65/2003)

8. neon yellow body, white hatch, red interior & windows, gray base, "MHC65" & "Hero City" tempa ($3-5)(MW65/2002)
9. white body, white hatch, black interior, red base, "Base 33" & "Matchbox 50" tempa ($100+)(MW33)
10. iridescent white body, orange hatch, red interior, black base, plane design tempa ($1-2)(LP)
11. dark metallic maroon body, dark smoke windows, blue hatch, blue interior, orange base, "Force 34" tempa, 7 spoke sawblade wheels ($1-2)(5pk)

MB49-A UNIMOG, issued 1970 (MB849)

NOTE: Below models with green windows & England casting. Versions 1-6 with black or red axle covers.

1. blue body, plain grille, red base, spiro wheels, no label, no shellbox ($18-25)
2. blue body, silver grille, red base, spiro wheels, no label, no shellbox ($18-25)
3. blue-green body, plain grille, red base, spiro wheels, no label, no shellbox ($18-25)
4. bright blue body, plain grille, red base, spiro wheels, no label, no shellbox ($18-25)
5. metallic blue body, plain grille, red base, spiro wheels, no label, no shellbox ($18-25)
6. metallic blue body, silver grille, red base, spiro wheels, no label, no shellbox ($18-25)
7. olive body, plain grille, olive base, dot dash wheels, star label, no shellbox ($75-100)(TP)
8. olive body, plain grille, olive base, dot dash wheels, star label, with shellbox ($75-100)(TP)
9. olive body, plain grille, olive base, dot dash wheels, "A" label, with shellbox ($7-10)(TP)

MB49-B CHOP SUEY, issued 1973

NOTE: Below models with chrome engine & plastic base, yellow cow head, solid black plastic wheels & England casting unless otherwise noted.

1. metallic magenta body, chrome handlebars ($450-525)
2. metallic magenta body, orange handlebars ($15-20)
3. metallic magenta body, red handlebars ($12-15)
4. metallic magenta body, black handlebars ($20-25)(MP)
5. metallic magenta body, dark red handlebars ($12-15)
6. lime body, Manaus label on base, dark red handlebars ($250+)(BR)

MB49-C CRANE TRUCK, issued 1976

NOTE: Below models with black plastic base & England casting unless otherwise noted.

1. yellow body, yellow boom, dark green windows, no labels, dot dash wheels ($4-6)
2. yellow body, yellow boom, dark green windows, no labels, 5 arch wheels ($4-6)
3. yellow body, yellow boom, light green windows, no labels, 5 arch wheels ($4-6)
4. dark red body, yellow boom, dark green windows, no labels, 5 arch wheels ($60-75)(GR)
5. bright red body, yellow boom, clear windows, no labels, 5 arch wheels ($60-75)(GR)
6. yellow body, black boom, dark green windows, no labels, 5 arch wheels ($4-6)
7. yellow body, black boom, red windows, no labels, 5 arch wheels ($4-6)
8. yellow body, black boom, purple windows, no labels, 5 arch wheels ($4-6)
9. yellow body, black boom, dark green windows, "A-1 Crane" labels with stripes & "C" tempa, 5 arch wheels ($3-5)
10. yellow body, black boom, dark green windows, "A-1 Crane" labels with stripes tempa, 5 arch wheels ($3-5)
11. yellow body, black boom, blue windows, stripes only tempa, 5 arch wheels ($50-75)
12. yellow body, yellow boom, dark green windows, no labels, 5 arch wheels, base with Manaus tab ($35-50)(BR)
13. red body, yellow boom, dark green windows, no labels, 5 arch wheels, base with Manaus tab ($50-75)(BR)

MB49-D SAND DIGGER, issued 1983 (MB119)

NOTE: Below models with maltese cross wheels.

1. emerald green body, black base, ivory interior, "Sand Digger" tempa, Macau casting ($2-3)
2. very dark metallic green body, black base, ivory interior, "Sand Digger" tempa, Macau casting ($2-3)
3. red body, black base, white interior, "Dune Man" tempa, Macau casting ($2-3)
4. red body, black base, rust red interior, "Dune Man" tempa, Macau casting ($2-3)
5. red body, black base, rust red interior, "Dune Man" tempa, China casting ($2-3)

NOTE: Available as a Bulgarian casting. Assorted colors available ($5-25)

MB49-E PEUGEOT QUASAR, issued 1986 (MB169)
MB72-M PEUGEOT QUASAR, reissued 1995 (USA)

1. white body & base, chrome interior, smoke gray windows, 8 dot silver wheels, "Quasar" tempa, Macau casting ($2-3)
2. dark blue body, black base, chrome interior, smoke gray windows, starburst wheels, "9" & pink stripes tempa, Macau casting ($3-5)(SF)
3. metallic blue body, black base, chrome interior, smoke gray windows, laser wheels, "9" & pink stripes tempa, Macau casting ($3-5)(LW)
4. white body & base, chrome interior, smoke gray windows, 8 dot white wheels, "Quasar" tempa, Macau casting ($2-4)
5. black body & base, no interior, red modified windows, starburst wheels, lime & orange stripes tempa, Macau casting, includes plastic armament ($5-8)(RB)
6. plum body & base, chrome interior, smoke gray windows with purple tempa, 8 dot silver wheels, "Quasar" tempa, Macau casting ($1-2)
7. plum body & base, chrome interior, smoke gray windows, 8 dot silver wheels, "Quasar" tempa, Macau casting ($1-2)
8. yellow body, lime base, red interior, smoke gray windows, 8 dot blue wheels with yellow hubs, "3" with stripes & flames tempa, Macau casting ($6-8)(LL)
9. yellow body, lime base, red interior, smoke gray windows, 8 dot blue wheels with yellow hubs, "3" with stripes & flames tempa, China casting ($6-8)(LL)
10. orange-yellow body, lime base, red interior, smoke gray windows, 8 dot blue wheels with yellow hubs, "3" with stripes & flames tempa, China casting ($6-8)(LL)
11. plum body & base, chrome interior, smoke gray windows, 8 dot silver wheels, "Quasar" tempa, China casting ($1-2)

NOTE: Version 11 was briefly reintroduced in the US as MB72 in 1995 ($1-2)

12. orange-yellow body, lime base, red interior, smoke gray windows, 8 dot all blue wheels, "3" with stripes & flames tempa, China casting ($6-8)(LL)
13. orange body & base, chrome interior, smoke gray windows, 8 dot silver wheels, "Fanta" tempa, China casting ($75+)(CHI)

MB49-F LAMBORGHINI DIABLO *see MB22-H*

MB49-G VOLVO TILT TRUCK *see MB26-F*

MB49-H BMW 850i, issued 1993 (USA) (MB240)
MB 2-H BMW 850i, issued 1993 (ROW)

NOTE: Below models with clear windows unless otherwise noted.

1. silver/gray body, silver-gray base, blue interior, 8 dot wheels, black grille & red tail lights tempa, Thailand casting ($2-3)
2. silver body, silver base, blue interior, 8 dot wheels, black grille & red tail lights tempa , Thailand casting ($2-4)
3. white body, white base, red interior, 8 dot wheels, black grille & red tail lights tempa, Thailand casting ($3-5)(SS)
4. metallic charcoal body, met. charcoal base, chrome windows, red interior, gray disc wheels with rubber tires, detailed trim tempa, Thailand casting ($2-4)(WC)
5. black body, black base, neon yellow interior, gold 6 spoke spiral wheels, yellow flash & "850i" tempa, Thailand casting ($1-2)
6. black body, black base, neon yellow interior, gold 6 spoke spiral wheels, yellow flash & "850i" tempa, China casting ($1-2)
7. silver-gray body, silver-gray base, blue interior, gold 6 spoke spiral wheels, black grille & red tail lights tempa, Thailand casting ($2-3)
8. black body, black base, florescent yellow interior, silver 6 spoke spiral wheels, yellow flash & "850i" tempa, China casting ($2-4)
9. red body, red base, white interior, silver 6-spoke spiral wheels, "Ripper" on sides with skull on hood tempa, China casting ($1-2)
10. red body, red base, white interior, silver 6-spoke spiral wheels, "Ripper" on sides only tempa, China casting ($1-2)
11. red body, red base, white interior, silver 6-spoke spiral wheels, no tempa, China casting ($25-50)(US) *(issued with Kentucky Fried Chicken Kids Meal)*
12. dark plum body, black base, tan & black interior, chrome disc wheels with rubber tires, detailed trim tempa , China casting ($8-12)(UC)
13. red body, red base, white interior, 5 spoke concave star wheels, "Ripper" on sides only tempa, China casting ($2-4)
14. black body, black base, black interior, 5 spoke concave star wheels, "Go Tigers! 1997" tempa, China casting ($3-5)(AU)
15. black body, black base, neon yellow interior, 5 spoke concave star wheels, yellow flash & "850i " tempa, China casting ($2-4)
16. dark blue body, dark blue base, tan interior, 8 dot wheels, no tempa, China casting ($1-2)
17. candy red body, black base, black & tan interior, chrome disc wheels with rubber tires, detailed trim tempa, Thailand casting ($3-5)(PC2-JC)
18. red body, black base, black & red interior, chrome disc wheels with rubber tires, detailed trim tempa, China casting ($3-5)(PC15)
19. metallic red body, metallic red base, tan interior, 5 spoke concave star wheels, no tempa, China casting ($1-2)(MW73-ROW)
20. lemon body, lemon base, red interior, 5 spoke concave star wheels, "Coca Cola" & polar bears tempa,. China casting ($1-2)(5pk)
21. metallic red body, metallic red base, tan interior, 5 spoke concave star wheels, black grille tempa, China casting ($3-4)(MW54/1999GR)
22. metallic red body, metallic red base, smoke windows, black interior, 10 spoke flower wheels, "BMW 850i" tempa, China casting ($1-2)(MW2/2001)
23. metallic red body, metallic red base, smoke windows, black interior, 5 spoke concave star wheels, "BMW 850i " tempa, China casting ($2-4)(MW2/2001)
24. lemon body, lemon base, clear windows, red interior, 10 spoke flower wheels, "Coca Cola" & polar bears tempa ($10-15)(CK)
25. dark green body, black base, clear windows, tan interior, lace wheels, small "BMW" logo & tail lights tempa ($2-4)(ROW BMW promo)
26. dark plum body, black base, clear windows, white interior, gold 6 spoke spiral wheels, detailed trim tempa ($50+)(CHI)

MB49-I VOLKSWAGEN CONCEPT 1, issued 1996 (USA) (MB287)
MB58-G VOLKSWAGEN CONCEPT 1, issued 1996 (ROW)

NOTE: Below models with clear windows & plastic base unless otherwise noted

1. red body, red base, gray interior, black roof tempa, 6-spoke spiral wheels, Thailand casting ($1-2)
   NOTE: Version 2 can also be found with inverted hood & trunk logos- found in New Zealand.
2. red body, red base, gray interior, black roof & "Mark I V.W.S." tempa, chrome disc wheels with rubber tires, Thailand casting ($8-12)(US)
3. metallic gold body, black base, black interior, no tempa, 6 spoke spiral wheels, Thailand casting ($5-10)(CH)
4. metallic purple body, black base, gray interior, black roof tempa, 5 spoke concave star wheels, Thailand casting ($1-2)(5pk)
   NOTE: Version 4 can also come with inverted hood logo.
5. red body, red base, black interior, black roof tempa, 5 spoke concave star wheels, Thailand casting ($3-5)
6. green body, red base, black interior, black roof tempa, 5 spoke concave star wheels, Thailand casting ($100+)
7. green body, green base, black interior, black roof tempa, 5 spoke concave star wheels, Thailand casting ($1-3)
   NOTE: Version 7 can come with inverted front & rear logos or with only one inverted or both correctly positioned.
8. orange body, orange base, black interior, black roof tempa, 5 spoke concave star wheels, Thailand casting ($1-2)(MW17/1998)
   NOTE: Version 8 can come with inverted or correctly positioned logos.
9. red body, red base, black interior, black roof tempa & "17th Annual Matchbox USA Convention 1998" decals, 6 spoke spiral wheels, Thailand casting ($12-18)(C2)
10. green body, green base, black interior, black roof tempa & "17th Annual Matchbox USA Convention 1998" decals, 5 spoke concave star wheels, Thailand casting ($12-18)(C2)
11. orange body, orange base, black interior, black roof tempa, 5 spoke concave star wheels, China casting ($1-2)(MW17/1998)
12. red body, black base, black interior, white roof , "Coca Cola" & "Always Coca Cola" logo tempa, chrome disc wheels with rubber tires, China casting ($4-6)(MP-Target)
13. orange body, orange base, black interior, black roof, "Matchbox World of Wheels" tempa, 5 spoke concave star wheels, China casting ($100+)(CCI)
14. orange body, orange base, black interior, black roof, "Hope Spring Cancer Support Centre 1998" tempa, 5 spoke concave star wheels, China casting ($15-25)(C2)
15. pumpkin body, orange base, black interior, black roof, "Hope Spring Cancer Support Centre 1998" tempa, 5 spoke concave star wheels, China casting ($100+)(C2)
16. brown body, orange base, black interior, black roof, "Hope Spring Cancer Support Centre 1998" tempa, 5 spoke concave star wheels, China casting ($100+)(C2)

17. maroon body, orange base, black interior, black roof, "Hope Spring Cancer Support Centre 1998" tempa, 5 spoke concave star wheels, China casting ($100+)(C2)

NOTE: Versions 14-16 are limited to only 25 pieces of each and were given out to persons directly involved with Hope Spring charities.

18. light lime body, black base, white interior, white flowers & globe design tempa, chrome disc wheels with rubber tires, China casting ($10-15)(US)
19. red body, red base, black interior, "Matchbox Collectors Club Deutschland" tempa, 6 spoke spiral wheels, China casting ($15-20)(C2)(GR)
20. yellow body, black base, black interior, painted lights tempa, 5 spoke concave star wheels, China casting ($3-5)(MW18/1999 GR)
21. iridescent white body, black base, turquoise interior, "VW" & stripes tempa, 5 spoke concave star wheels, China casting ($1-2)(MW18/1999)
22. red body, black base, black interior, white roof with "Coca Cola" & white wave tempa, chrome disc wheels with rubber tires, China casting ($4-6)(Coke PC)(Target MP)
23. orange body, orange base, black interior, "Matchbox Convention Hershey PA 1999 Demo Model" tempa, 5 spoke concave star wheels, China casting ($25-40)(CCI)
24. orange body, orange base, black interior, "MICA Hershey 1999" tempa, 5 spoke concave star wheels, China casting ($18-25)(CCI)
25. raspberry body, orange base, black interior, "MICA Hershey 1999" tempa, 5 spoke concave star wheels, China casting ($18-25)(CCI)
26. orange body, orange base, black interior, black roof & "RLI" tempa, 5 spoke concave star wheels, China casting ($75+)(ASAP)
27. yellow body, black base, black interior, "10 Jahre Mauerfall/ Berlin 1989 1999" tempa, 5 spoke concave star wheels, China casting ($25-40)(C2)(GR)
28. iridescent white body, black base, turquoise interior, "Blue Angels" tempa, 5 spoke concave star wheels, China casting ($15-20)(ASAP)
29. orange body, orange base, black interior, "Bill Cairns Realtor" tempa, 5 spoke concave star wheels, China casting ($25-40)(ASAP)
30. black body, black base, black interior, smoke windows, orange-yellow stripe & "Matchbox 2000" tempa, 5 spoke concave star wheels, China casting ($2-4)(MW42/2000 US)
31. black body, black base, black interior, smoke windows, orange-yellow stripes tempa, 5 spoke concave star wheels, China casting ($1-2)(MW42/2000 US)
32. orange body, orange base, black interior, www.sachs.com tempa, 5 spoke concave star wheels, China casting ($100+)(ASAP)
33. iridescent white body, black base, turquoise interior, "Happy New Millennium/ Y2K Bug" tempa, 5 spoke concave star wheels, China casting ($20-25)(C2)
34. yellow body, black base, black interior, "Happy New Millennium/ Y2K Bug" tempa, 5 spoke concave star wheels, China casting ($20-25)(C2)
35. metallic lime body, black base, black interior, painted lights tempa, 5 spoke concave star wheels, China casting ($3-5)(MW34/2000 ROW)
36. iridescent white body, black base, turquoise interior, "New Way Lunch" tempa, 5 spoke concave star wheels, China casting ($50+)(ASAP)
37. metallic lime body, black base, black interior, painted lights, small hood logo & "Matchbox" tempa, 5 spoke concave star wheels, China casting ($3-5)(PB)
38. silver-gray body, black base, black interior, smoke windows, painted lights tempa, chrome disc wheels with rubber tires, China casting ($5-8)(MP-FAO)
39. iridescent white body, black base, turquoise interior, "RCA" tempa, 5 spoke concave star wheels, China casting ($20-30)(ASAP)
40. dark red body, black base, white interior, gold glitter & "Matchbox" tempa, 5 spoke concave star wheels, China casting ($2-4)(Target)
41. dark red body, black base, white interior, gold glitter & "Matchbox" tempa, star with 5 spokes wheels, China casting ($2-4)(Target)
42. dark red body, black base, white interior, gold glitter & "20th Annual MBUSA Demo Model" tempa, 5 spoke concave star wheels, China casting ($15-20)(CCI)
43. dark red body, black base, white interior, gold glitter & "20th Annual MBUSA Demo Model" tempa, star with 5 spokes wheels, China casting ($15-20)(CCI)
44. dark red body, black base, white interior, gold glitter & "8th Toy Show Demo Model Hershey" tempa, 5 spoke concave star wheels, China casting ($15-20)(CCI)
45. dark red body, black base, white interior, gold glitter & "8th Toy Show Demo Model Hershey" tempa, star with 5 spokes wheels, China casting ($15-20)(CCI)
46. iridescent white body, black base, turquoise interior, "VW" & stripe with large "Y" on roof tempa, 5 spoke concave star wheels, China casting ($25-40)(ASAP)
47. dark red body, black base, white interior, "Suzanne & Corey Just Married" with glitter tempa, star with 5 spoke wheels, China casting ($20-35)(CCI)
48. black body, black metal base, black interior, smoke windows, gray "VW" logo tempa, 10 spoke flower wheels, China casting (MW60/2001)
49. orange body, orange base, black interior, "NIVA 2001" tempa, 5 spoke concave star wheels, China casting ($25-40)(ASAP)
50. metallic lime body, black base, black interior, painted lights & ""5. Club Treffen Speyer 2001" tempa, 5 spoke concave star wheels, China casting ($18-25)(C2)(GR)
51. iridescent white body, black base, turquoise interior, "N" & "Huskers" tempa, 5 spoke concave star wheels, China casting ($10-15)(ASAP)
52. black body, black base, black interior, smoke windows, gray "VW" logo tempa, 10 spoke flower wheels, China casting ($1-2)(MW60/2001)
53. black body, black base, black interior, smoke windows, gray "VW" logo tempa, lace wheels, China casting ($50+)(MW60/2001)
54. black body, black metal base, black interior, smoke windows, "www.kruizinwagon.com.au/ VW" & red logo tempa, 10 spoke flower wheels, China casting ($12-18)(CCI)
55. white body, orange metal base, white interior, amber windows, "Kellogg's Froot Loops/ Toucan Sam" tempa, 10 spoke flower wheels, China casting ($3-5)(TP)(Avon)
56. silver-gray body, black metal base, gray interior, dark smoke windows, hockey design tempa, 10 spoke flower wheels, China casting ($1-2)(5pk)
57. metallic lime body, black metal base, black interior, painted tail lights with small hood logo & "Matchbox" tempa, 10 spoke flower wheels, China casting ($3-5)(PB)
58. metallic lime body, black base, black interior, "21" with black stripes & "Matchbox USA Toy Show" tempa, 5 spoke concave star wheels, China casting ($12-18)(CCI)
59. black body, black metal base, black interior, smoke windows, "21" with white stripes & "Matchbox USA Toy Show" tempa, 10 spoke flower wheels, China casting ($25-40)(CCI)

60. red body, black base, white interior, "Midwest Regional Matchbox Convention 2002" & glitter tempa, star with 5 spokes tempa, China casting ($12-18)(CCI)
61. red body, black base, white interior, "Midwest Regional Matchbox Convention 2002" & glitter tempa, 5 spoke concave star wheels, China casting ($12-18)(CCI)
62. orange body, orange base, black interior, black roof & "Pearsol's" tempa, 5 spoke concave star wheels, China casting ($50+)(ASAP)
63. iridescent white body, turquoise interior, "Roswell 2K" tempa, 5 spoke concave star wheels, China casting ($18-25)(ASAP)
64. iridescent white body, turquoise interior, "VW" & stripe with blue "UK" on roof tempa, 5 spoke concave star wheels, China casting ($18-25)(ASAP)
65. iridescent white body, turquoise interior, "VW" & stripes with "Huskers" on roof tempa, 5 spoke concave star wheels, China casting ($12-18)(ASAP)
66. iridescent white body, turquoise interior, large "Huskers" on roof tempa, 5 spoke concave star wheels, China casting ($12-18)(ASAP)
67. iridescent white body, turquoise interior, small "Huskers" on roof tempa, 5 spoke concave star wheels, China casting ($12-18)(ASAP)
68. iridescent white body, turquoise interior, "VW" & stripe with green "S" on roof tempa, 5 spoke concave star wheels, China casting ($12-18)(ASAP)
69. iridescent white body, turquoise interior, "VW" & stripe with black "G" on roof tempa, 5 spoke concave star wheels, China casting ($12-18)(ASAP)
70. iridescent white body, turquoise interior, "Guaranty/ TASFAA 99" tempa, 5 spoke concave star wheels, China casting ($50+)(ASAP)
71. red body, black metal base, black interior, smoke windows, "Delaware 1- The Official State Bug" tempa, 10 spoke flower wheels, Mattel China casting ($4-6)(AM)
72. metallic lime body, black base, black interior, "Mom Me & Matchbox- Seasons Greetings 2002" tempa, 5 spoke concave star wheels, China casting ($25-40)(CCI)
73. blue body, blue metal base, black interior, "Spongebob Squarepants" tempa, 10 spoke flower wheels, Mattel China casting ($3-5)(TP- Blockbuster)
74. yellow body, black base, black interior, "Space Shuttle Columbia/ In Memory of the Crew" tempa, 5 spoke concave star wheels, China casting ($25-40)(CCI)
75. red body, black base, white interior, "Sabrina Corinne D'Angelo- What A Cutie!" & glitter tempa, 5 spoke concave star wheels, China casting ($25-40)(CCI)
76. red body, orange base, green interior, smoke windows, "Bugs" tempa, 10 spoke flower wheels, Mattel China casting ($1-2)(5pk)
77. light blue body, purple base, white interior, smoke windows, "Looney Tunes Paris" tempa, 10 spoke flower wheels, Mattel China casting ($1-2)(5pk)
78. bright blue body, blue base, black interior, "S04" & soccer ball design tempa, lace wheels, Mattel China casting ($6-8)(GR)
79. dark red body, gray base, black interior, head lights tempa, 10 spoke flower wheels, China casting ($1-2)(SG)
80. metallic lime body, black base, black interior, painted tail lights with small hood logo & "Matchbox" tempa, 10 spoke flower wheels, China casting ($3-5)(PB)
81. lime body, red windows, blue base, red interior, Easter eggs design tempa, lace wheels, China casting ($1-2)(MP)
82. orange body, red windows, blue base, red interior, Easter eggs design tempa, lace wheels, China casting ($18-25)(MP)
83. silver blue body, blue windows, black base, green interior, "Stonehenge" tempa, lace wheels, China casting ($1-2)(AW)
84. lemon body, blue windows, blue base, white interior, "Periwinkle" tempa, 10 spoke flower wheels, China casting ($1-2)(5pk)
85. orange body, blue windows, blue base, white interior, "Periwinkle" tempa, 10 spoke flower wheels, China casting ($1-2)(CA)
86. lemon body, clear windows, black base, black interior, "Happy Birthday Superfast/ Matchbox USA Toy Show" tempa, 5 spoke concave star wheels, China casting ($25+)(CCI)
87. metallic lime body, black base, black interior, "Millersville Area Meals on Wheels 16" tempa, 5 spoke concave star wheels, China casting ($50+)(CCI)
88. lemon body, purple base, red interior, amber windows, "Pearl" tempa, 10 spoke flower wheels, China casting ($1-2)(5pk)
89. dark red body, black base, black interior, glitter & "Judi & Joe/ Just Married" tempa, 5 spoke concave star wheels, China casting ($50+)(CCI)
90. orange body, orange base, black interior, black roof & "ASAP ASI 33000" tempa, 5 spoke concave star wheels, China casting ($50+)(ASAP)
91. black body, black base, red interior, tire tread, umbrellas with "550 Der Regenreifen- Uniroyal Funcup" tempa, 10 spoke flower wheels, China casting ($3-5)(SoC)
92. charcoal body, gray base, purple interior, black roof with detailed trim tempa, 5 spoke slotted wheels, China casting ($1-2)(SF48/2004)

MB49-J FORD FALCON POLICE CAR *see MB27-H*

MB50-A KENNEL TRUCK, issued 1970

NOTE: Below models with green windows, 5 spoke wheels, four white plastic dogs, clear canopy & England casting.

1. metallic green body, black base, chrome grille ($35-50)
2. metallic green body, light yellow base, chrome grille ($35-50)
3. metallic green body, dark yellow base, chrome grille ($35-50)
4. metallic green body, gray base, chrome grille ($35-50)
5. metallic green body, charcoal base, chrome grille ($35-50)
6. dark metallic green body, black base, chrome grille ($35-50)
7. apple green body, black base, chrome grille ($35-50)
8. apple green body, charcoal base, chrome grille ($35-50)
9. apple green body, gray base, chrome grille ($35-50)
10. apple green body, black base, white grille ($35-50)
11. apple green body, charcoal base, white grille ($35-50)
12. apple green body, gray base, white grille ($35-50)
13. apple green body, unpainted base, white grille ($35-50)
14. apple green body, unpainted base, chrome grille ($35-50)

MB50-B ARTICULATED DUMP TRUCK, issued 1973

NOTE: Below models with black plastic cab base, maltese cross front & 5 spoke rear wheels although other combinations exist. All models with England casting..

1. orange-yellow cab, purple windows, blue dump, orange-yellow trailer base, with labels ($6-8)
2. orange-yellow cab, purple windows, blue dump, orange-yellow trailer base ($3-5)
3. yellow cab, purple windows, blue dump, orange-yellow trailer base, with labels ($6-8)
4. orange-yellow cab, purple windows, blue dump, orange trailer base ($3-5)
5. orange-yellow cab, red windows, blue dump, orange-yellow trailer base ($3-5)

6. yellow cab, purple windows, blue dump, lemon trailer base ($3-5)
7. orange-yellow cab, purple windows, blue dump, lemon trailer base, with tow hook ($4-6)(TP)
8. yellow cab, purple windows, blue dump, lemon trailer base, with tow hook ($4-6)(TP)
9. yellow cab, red windows, blue dump, orange trailer base ($3-5)
10. yellow cab, red windows, blue dump, lemon trailer base ($3-5)
11. yellow cab, purple windows, dark blue dump, lemon trailer base, with tow hook ($85-110)(BR)
12. yellow cab, purple windows, very dark blue dump, orange-yellow trailer base ($175-200)(BR)
13. red cab, purple windows, blue dump, red trailer base ($35-45)
14. red cab, red windows, blue dump, red trailer base ($35-45)
15. red cab, red windows, silver-gray dump, red trailer base, with tow hook ($8-12)(TP)
16. red body, purple windows, silver-gray dump, red trailer base, with tow hook ($8-12)(TP)

MB50-C ARTICULATED TRAILER, issued 1980 (TP)

NOTE: Below models with 5 arch front & 5 spoke rear wheels. No origin cast.

1. blue dump, yellow coupling & trailer base ($4-6)(TP)
2. silver-gray dump, red coupling & trailer base ($6-8)(TP)

MB50-D HARLEY-DAVIDSON MOTORCYCLE, issued 1980 (MB050)

NOTE: Below models with black seat, wire wheels & no tempa unless otherwise noted.

1. light metallic tan body, black handlebars, no rider, England casting ($3-5)
2. dark metallic tan body, black handlebars, no rider, England casting ($3-5)
3. light copper body, black handlebars, tan rider, England casting ($3-5)
4. mid metallic tan body, black handlebars, tan rider, England casting ($3-5)
5. dark metallic tan body, black handlebars, tan rider, England casting ($3-5)
6. dark metallic tan body, black handlebars, brown rider, England casting ($3-5)
7. metallic brown body, black handlebars, tan rider, Macau casting ($2-3)
8. dark metallic tan body, black handlebars, brown rider, Macau casting ($2-3)

NOTE: Below models with no rider.

9. light blue body, chrome handlebars, orange on white tank tempa, Thailand casting ($2-3)(HD)
10. orange body, chrome handlebars, orange on white tank tempa, Thailand casting ($2-3)(HD)
11. silver-gray body, chrome handlebars, gold on black tank tempa, Thailand casting ($2-3)(HD)
12. metallic red body, chrome handlebars, black on silver tank tempa, Thailand casting ($2-3)(HD)
13. metallic blue body, chrome handlebars, orange on white tank tempa, Thailand casting ($2-3)(HD)
14. white body, chrome handlebars, blue on gold tank tempa, Thailand casting ($2-3)(HD)(PS)
15. orange-red body, chrome handlebars, Thailand casting ($2-3)(HD)(PS)
16. metallic charcoal body, chrome handlebars, black & gold logo tank tempa, Thailand casting ($2-3)(HD)
17. dark purple body, chrome handlebars, red on silver tank tempa, Thailand casting ($2-3)(HD)
18. fluorescent yellow body, chrome handlebars, blue on silver tank tempa, Thailand casting ($2-3)(HD)(GS)
19. dark orange body, chrome handlebars, black on white tank tempa, Thailand casting ($2-3)(HD)(GS)
20. metallic turquoise body, chrome handlebars, red on silver tank tempa, Thailand casting ($2-3)(HD)(GS)
21. yellow body, chrome handlebars, red on silver tank tempa, Thailand casting ($2-3)(HD)
22. gold plated body, chrome handlebars, white on black tank tempa, Thailand casting ($2-3)(HD)
23. florescent orange body, chrome handlebars, red on silver tank tempa, China casting ($7-10)(HD)
24. red body, chrome handlebars, black on white tank tempa, China casting ($2-3)(HD)

MB50-E CHEVY BLAZER, issued 1984 (MB129)

NOTE: Below models with white interior & antenna, blue windows & dome lights, maltese cross wheels unless otherwise noted.

1. white body, chrome base, "Sheriff 7" tempa, Macau casting ($1-2)
2. white body, black base, "Sheriff 7" tempa, Macau casting ($1-2)
3. grape body, black base, orange/red/black tempa, Macau casting, includes plastic armament ($5-8)(RB)
4. white body, black base, "Sheriff 7" tempa, Thailand casting ($1-2)
5. white body, black base, "Sheriff 7" (without red hood print) tempa, Manaus casting ($45-60)(BR)

NOTE: Version 1-5 dome lights cast with metal strip in center. Versions 6 onward cast with one piece plastic unit.

6. white body, black base, blue windows, "Metro EMS" tempa, Thailand casting ($1-2)(5pk)
7. white body, chrome base, chrome windows, blue/peach/magenta tempa, Thailand casting ($2-4)(ST)
8. black body, chrome base, chrome windows, pink & yellow tempa, Thailand casting ($2-4)(ST)
9. white body, black base, blue windows, "Sheriff 7" tempa, Thailand casting ($1-2)
10. white body, black base, blue windows, "7 Eleven" tempa, Thailand casting ($4-6)(US)
11. metallic red body, black base, blue windows, no tempa, Thailand casting ($1-2)(5pk)
12. black body, chrome base, blue windows, "Police Unit 3" & gold star tempa, Thailand casting ($1-2)(5pk)
13. blue body, chrome base, blue windows, "Police 50/ Police Dial 911" & star tempa, Thailand casting ($1-2)
14. blue body, chrome base, red windows, "Police 50/ Police Dial 911" & star tempa, Thailand casting ($1-2)
15. white body, chrome base, blue windows, "Police Unit 3" tempa, Thailand casting ($1-2)(5pk)
16. black & white body, chrome base, blue windows, "Emergency Unit 50/ Off Road Patrol" tempa, Thailand casting ($1-2)
17. blue & white body, chrome base, blue windows, "Police Unit 14" tempa, Thailand casting ($1-2)(5pk)
18. metallic gold body, chrome base, blue windows, no tempa, Thailand casting ($5-10)(CH)
19. white & black body, chrome base, blue windows, "Emergency Unit 50/ Off Road Patrol" tempa, Thailand casting ($1-2)(MW22/1998)
20. white & black body, chrome base, blue windows, "Emergency Unit 50/ Off Road Patrol" tempa, China casting ($1-2)(MW22/1998)
21. blue & white body, chrome base, blue windows, "Police 50/ Police Dial 911" tempa, China casting ($1-2)(5pk)

22. beige & green body, chrome base, blue windows, "Park Police" tempa, tan interior & antenna, China casting ($1-2)(5pk)
23. white body, chrome base, blue windows, "Police MB- To Protect & Serve" tempa, China casting ($1-2)(MW32/1999 US)
24. blue body, chrome base, blue windows, "Rocky Mountain Rescue MB County 682" tempa, China casting ($1-2)(5pk)
25. blue body, chrome base, blue windows, green stripes, logo & "682" tempa, China casting ($3-5)(5pk)
26. brown body, chrome base, amber windows, black interior & antenna, "Action Tours", vines & "Matchbox 2000" tempa, China casting ($2-4)(MW71/2000 US)
27. brown body, chrome base, amber windows, black interior & antenna, "Action Tours" & vines tempa, China casting ($1-2)(MW71/2000 US((MW51/2000 ROW)
28. red-brown body, chrome base, amber windows, black interior & antenna, "Action Tours" & vines tempa, China casting ($1-2)(MW71/2000 US)

NOTE: Below models with Mattel China casting.

29. black body, chrome base, amber windows, "Action Radar/ Xtreme Mission" tempa, China casting ($1-2)(5pk)
30. white & blue body, black base, red windows, black interior & antenna, "MB3 Metro Police 3" tempa, China casting ($1-2)(5pk)
31. white body, gray base, red windows, red interior & antenna, "Smokey Says Prevent Forest Fires" tempa, China casting ($1-2)(MW6/2002 US)
32. white body, gray base, red windows, red interior & antenna, "Smokey Says Prevent Forest Fires" & "Matchbox 50" tempa, China casting ($2-4)(MW6/2002 US)
33. pea green body, black base, amber windows, black interior & antenna, "Chief HQ" tempa, China casting ($1-2)(5pk)
34. lime body, gray base, amber windows, white interior, gray antenna. "Chief HQ" tempa, China casting ($1-2)(5pk)
35. metallic red body, white base, blue windows, white interior, white antenna, "Hero City Ambulance" tempa, China casting ($1-2)(MW50/2004)

MB50-F DODGE DAKOTA *see MB17-F*

MB50-G MACK AUXILIARY POWER TRUCK *see MB57-H*

MB50-H HARLEY-DAVIDSON CHOPPER, issued 1993 (HD) (MB391)

NOTE: Below models with black seat, chrome engine & wire wheels.

1. metallic maroon body, chrome handlebars, white on orange tank tempa, Thailand casting ($2-3)
2. yellow body, chrome handlebars, yellow on orange tank tempa, Thailand casting ($2-3)
3. dk. fluorescent orange body, chrome handlebars, black flames tempa, Thailand casting ($2-3)(GS)
4. silver-gray body, chrome handlebars, yellow on orange tank tempa, Thailand casting ($2-3)(GS)
5. red body, chrome handlebars, white on orange tank tempa, Thailand casting ($2-3)
6. gold plated body, chrome handlebars, white on orange tank tempa, Thailand casting ($2-3)
7. metallic blue body, chrome handlebars, Thailand casting ($2-3)
8. dark purple body, chrome handlebars, white on orange tank tempa, China casting ($7-10)
9. turquoise body, chrome handlebars, Thailand casting ($12-15)
10. pale florescent orange body, chrome handlebars, black flames tempa, China casting ($2-3)
11. black body, chrome handlebars, white on orange tank tempa, China casting ($2-3)
12. blue body, chrome handlebars, white on orange tank tempa, China casting ($2-3)

MB50-I HARLEY-DAVIDSON ELECTRAGLIDE, issued 1993 (HD) (MB392)

NOTE: Below models with black seat, chrome engine, clear windshield & wire wheels.

1. white body, chrome handlebars, blue saddlebags, "MBPD" blue on gold tank tempa with "Police" saddlebag tempa, Thailand casting ($2-3)
2. black body, chrome handlebars, black saddlebags, "MBPD" blue on white tank tempa" tempa with "Police" saddlebag tempa, Thailand casting ($2-3)
3. metallic blue body, chrome handlebars, black saddlebags, "MBPD" blue on white tank tempa with "Police" saddlebag tempa, Thailand casting ($2-3)(GS)
4. pale gray body, chrome handlebars, black saddlebags, "MBPD" blue on white tank tempa with "Police" saddlebag tempa, Thailand casting ($2-3)
5. gold plated body, chrome handlebars, black saddlebags, "Harley-Davidson" red on white tank tempa, Thailand casting ($2-3)
6. orange-red body, orange handlebars, orange saddlebags, "PMG" tank & saddlebag tempa, Thailand casting ($7-10)(AU)
7. orange-red body, orange handlebars, orange saddlebags, "PMG" tank & saddlebag tempa, China casting ($7-10)(AU)
8. metallic red body, chrome handlebars, black saddlebags, "Harley Davidson" black tank tempa China casting ($7-10)
9. dark blue body, chrome handlebars, black saddlebags, "Harley-Davidson" black tank tempa, China casting ($2-3)
10. red body, chrome handlebars, black saddlebags, "Harley-Davidson" black on white tank tempa, China casting ($2-3)
11. white body, chrome handlebars, white saddlebags, "MBPD" blue on gold tank tempa with "Police" saddlebag tempa, China casting ($2-3)
12. black body, chrome handlebars, black saddlebags, "Harley Davidson" black on white tank tempa, China casting ($2-3)

MB50-J 1997 FORD F150 PICKUP, issued 1998 (MB326)

NOTE: Below models with clear windows, chrome plastic base & China casting.

1. unpainted body, tan interior, Goodyear rubber tires, no tempa ($4-6)(FE)
2. black body, black & tan interior, Goodyear rubber tires beige band tempa ($4-6)(FE)
3. black body, black & tan interior, Goodyear rubber tires, pink-tan band tempa ($4-6)(FE)
4. red body, black interior, small 5 spoke concave star wheels, "4X4 Off Road" tempa ($1-2)(MW50/1998)
5. black body, black & tan interior, Goodyear rubber tires, pink-tan band with "Matchbox/MDM/630-681-2101" tempa ($35-50)(C2)
6. black body, black & tan interior, Goodyear rubber tires, beige band with "Matchbox/MDM/630-681-2101" tempa ($35-50)(C2)
7. unpainted body, tan interior, Goodyear rubber tires, "Matchbox/MDM/630-681-2101" tempa ($35-50)(C2)
8. red body, black interior, large 5 spoke concave star wheels, "4X4 Off Road" tempa ($1-2)(MW50/1998)
9. blue body, gray interior, large 5 spoke concave star wheels, orange & white with fish logo tempa ($1-2)(MW64/ROW)
10. blue body, gray interior, large 5 spoke concave star wheels, "Patrol Vehicle/ Catch & Release" with orange & white stripes tempa ($1-2)(MW69/1999 US)
11. white body, gray interior, large 5 spoke concave star wheels, "Action Radar/ Xtreme Mission" tempa ($1-2)(5pk)

12. white body, gray interior, chrome spiral disc wheels with rubber tires, "Texaco- A World of Energy" & black bed tempa , black base ($4-6)(Texaco-PC)
13. red body, black interior, lace wheels, "Miller's Auto Parts" & black bands tempa ($2-4)(MW64/2001 AU)
14. red body, black interior, large 5 spoke concave star wheels, "4X4 Off Road" tempa & "Matchbox Madness" decal ($50+)(CCI)
15. blue body, gray interior, 10 spoke flower wheels, "Kellogg's Frosted Flakes/ They're G-r-r-reat!" tempa ($1-2)(5pk)
16. blue body, gray interior, 10 spoke flower wheels, "Kellogg's Frosted Flakes/ They're G-r-r-reat!" with smaller "Kellogg's" tempa ($1-2)(TP)(Avon)
NOTE: Above model with Matchbox International or Mattel casting.
17. metallic turquoise, black & gray interior, chrome disc wheels with rubber tires, silver band & detailed trim tempa, black base ($3-5)(TN)
18. yellow body, brown interior, lace wheels, "K-9 Patrol" tempa, Mattel casting ($1-2)(5pk)
19. metallic pea green body, blue interior, lace wheels, "H2O Surfboards" tempa, black base, Mattel casting ($1-2)(MW21/2002 US)
20. metallic pea green body, blue interior, lace wheels, "H2O Surfboards" & "Matchbox 50" tempa, black base, Mattel casting ($1-2)(MW21/2002 US)
21. white body, gray interior, mag chrome disc wheels with rubber tires, "Texaco- A World of Energy" & black bed tempa, black base ($3-5)(Texaco PC)
22. white body, red interior, 10 spoke flower wheels, "555-1432" & worker tempa, black base, Mattel casting ($1-2)(5pk)
23. white body, red interior, 10 spoke flower wheels, "555-1432", worker & "Hero City" tempa, black base, Mattel casting ($1-2)(5pk)
24. black body, tan-gray interior, chrome disc wheels with rubber tires, "100" tempa, black base, Mattel casting ($3-5)(MP)(CL)
25. red body, black interior, chrome disc wheels with rubber tires, "Coca-Cola" tempa, black base ($3-5)(Coke PC)
26. red body, orange-yellow interior, 7 spoke sawblade wheels, "HCFD Alarm 04 Unit" tempa, gray base, Mattel casting ($1-2)(5pk)
27. metallic pea green body, black interior, dark smoke windows, 10 spoke flower wheels, "Easter Island" tempa, gray base, Mattel casting ($8-12)(PS)(AW)
28. dark orange body, black interior, dark smoke windows, 10 spoke flower wheels, "The Home Depot" tempa, black base, Mattel casting ($8-12)(US- in pack)

MB50-K PORSCHE BOXSTER *see MB55-L*

MB50-L FORD EXPEDITION POLICE, issued 2001 (USA) (MB489)
MB 5-F FORD EXPEDITION POLICE, issued 2003 (ROW)
NOTE: Below models with chrome plastic base & China casting unless otherwise noted.
1. white body, black interior, yellow windows, red dome lights, 5 spoke concave star wheels, red stripes , circular "Matchbox" logo & "54/3460" tempa ($1-2)(5pk)
2. white & metallic red body, gray interior, clear windows, red dome lights, chrome disc with rubber tires, "Fire Chief PTF01/ Matchbox PTF 2001" tempa ($40-60)(US)
3. metallic blue body, white interior, red windows, amber dome lights, lace wheels, "#042076" & storm logo tempa ($1-2)(LP)
4. blue body, blue interior, smoke windows, amber dome lights, 5 spoke concave star wheels, "State Patrol" & Texas map tempa ($1-2)(MW50/2001 US)
5. blue body, blue interior, smoke windows, amber dome light, 10 spoke flower wheels, "State Patrol" & Texas map tempa ($3-5)(MW50/2001 US)
6. blue body, blue interior, smoke windows, amber dome light, lace wheels, "State Patrol" & Texas map tempa ($25-40)(MW50/2001 US)
7. white & bright blue body, dark gray interior, clear windows, blue dome lights, 10 spoke flower wheels, "K-9 Patrol" tempa ($1-2)(5pk)
8. bright blue body, dark gray interior, clear windows, amber dome light, 10 spoke flower wheels, "K-9 Patrol" tempa ($2-4)(5pk)
9. light metallic blue body, dark gray interior, clear windows, amber dome light, 10 spoke flower wheels, "K-9 Patrol" tempa ($2-4)(5pk)
10. silver-gray body, red interior, smoke windows, red dome lights, lace wheels, "Spider Peak Shuttle" tempa, black base ($1-2)(5pk)
11. red & white body, gray interior, clear windows, red dome lights, chrome disc with rubber tires, "Fire MBFD/ Matchbox Toy Show 50th Birthday Party" tempa, black base ($4-6)(US)
12. white body, orange-yellow interior, amber windows, amber dome lights, lace wheels, "New Mexico Rio Grande Rescue" tempa, orange base ($1-2)(AM)
13. white body, orange-yellow interior, amber windows, amber dome lights, 7 spoke sawblade wheels, "New Mexico Rio Grand Rescue" tempa, orange base ($50-75)(EG)
14. white body, orange-yellow interior, blue windows, blue dome lights, 10 spoke flower wheels, "Metro Alarm" tempa, gray base ($1-2)(MW5/2003)
15. white body, orange-yellow interior, blue windows, blue dome lights, 10 spoke flower wheels, "Metro Alarm" & "Hero City" tempa, gray base ($2-4)(MW5/2003)
16. bright blue body, light gray interior, amber windows, amber dome lights, 10 spoke flower wheels, "USA Police" tempa ($1-2)(MP)(HR)
17. blue & white body, black interior, clear windows, amber dome light, 10 spoke flower wheels, "Metro 7" tempa ($1-2)(LP)

MB50-M PORSCHE 911 CARRERA CABRIOLET *see MB72-R*

MB50-N FORD TRANSIT VAN *see MB15-K*

MB50-O '57 LINCOLN PREMIERE, issued 2004 (SF)
MB559 LINCOLN PREMIERE, issued 2002 (MB559)
NOTE: Below models with clear windshield, chrome plastic base, detailed trim & China casting.
1. white body, cream interior, chrome disc wheels with rubber tires, with diorama ($10-15)(EL)
2. pink body, pink & black interior, chrome disc wheels with rubber tires ($3-5)(BJ)
3. mid blue body, light blue & black interior, chrome disc wheels with rubber tires ($3-5)(BJ)
4. metallic tan body, smoke windshield, black interior, silver pinstripe & detailed trim tempa, 5 spoke slotted wheels ($1-2)(SF50/2004)

MB51-A EIGHT WHEEL TIPPER, issued 1970
NOTE: Below models with blue windows, 5 spoke wheels, plastic base & England casting.
1. yellow cab, silver-gray dump, chrome base, "Pointer" labels ($25-40)
2. yellow cab, silver-gray dump, chrome base, no labels ($25-40)

3. yellow cab, silver-gray dump, gray base, "Pointer" labels ($25-40)
4. yellow cab, silver-gray dump, gray base, no labels ($25-40)

MB51-B CITROEN S.M., issued 1972

NOTE: Below models with clear windows & England casting.

1. bronze body, orange interior, unpainted base, no labels, 5 spoke wheels ($20-30)
2. bronze body, cream interior, unpainted base, no labels, 5 spoke wheels ($8-12)
3. bronze body, cream interior, silver-gray base, no labels, 5 spoke wheels ($8-12)
4. bronze body, light yellow interior, unpainted base, no labels, 5 spoke wheels ($8-12)
5. bronze body, dark yellow interior, unpainted base, no labels, 5 spoke wheels ($8-12)
6. bronze body, tan interior, unpainted base, no labels, 5 spoke wheels ($8-12)
7. metallic blue body, tan interior, unpainted base, no labels, 5 spoke wheels ($15-18)

NOTE: Version 8 exists with orange or red tempa; versions 9-14 with red only tempa.

8. metallic blue body, tan interior, unpainted base, "8" tempa, 5 spoke wheels ($8-12)
9. metallic blue body, dark yellow interior, unpainted base, "8" tempa, 5 spoke wheels ($8-12)
10. metallic blue body, ivory interior, unpainted base, "8" tempa, 5 spoke wheels ($8-12)
11. metallic blue body, lemon interior, unpainted base, "8" tempa, 5 spoke wheels ($8-12)
12. metallic blue body, lemon interior, unpainted base, "8" tempa, dot dash wheels ($8-12)
13. metallic blue body, yellow-orange interior, unpainted base, "8" tempa, dot dash wheels ($8-12)
14. metallic blue body, tan interior, unpainted base, "8" tempa, dot dash wheels ($8-12)
15. metallic blue body, yellow-orange interior, unpainted base, with label, dot dash wheels, roof rack ($5-8)(TP)
16. metallic blue body, red interior, unpainted base, with label, dot dash wheels, roof rack ($50-75)(TP)
17. white body with black doors, cream interior, unpainted base with Manaus tab, no labels, 5 spoke wheels ($250+)(BR)

NOTE: Available as an Hungarian & Bulgarian casting. Assorted colors available ($15-35)

MB51-C COMBINE HARVESTER, issued 1978

1. red body, black metal base, solid black wheels, no hubs, yellow rotor & chute, no tempa, England casting ($4-6)
2. red body, black metal base, black Superfast wheels, black hubs, yellow rotor & chute, no tempa, England casting ($4-6)
3. red body, black metal base, black Superfast wheels, yellow hubs, yellow rotor & chute, no tempa, England casting ($4-6)
4. red body, no base, black Superfast wheels, black hubs, yellow rotor & chute, no tempa, England casting ($4-6)
5. red body, no base, black Superfast wheels, yellow hubs, yellow rotor & chute, no tempa, England casting ($4-6)
6. orange body, black metal base with Manaus tab, solid black wheels, yellow rotor & chute, no tempa, no origin cast (tab) ($250+)(BR)
7. dark green body, black metal base with Manaus tab, solid black wheels, yellow rotor & chute, no tempa, no origin cast (tab) ($250+)(BR)
8. yellow body, no base, solid black wheels, red rotor & chute, "2" with stripes tempa, Macau casting ($1-2)(MC)
9. orange-yellow body, no base, solid black wheels, red rotor & chute, "2" with stripes tempa, Macau casting ($1-2)(MC)
10. lime & blue body, no base, solid red wheels, yellow rotor, lime chute, faces/gears/ haystack tempa, Macau casting ($6-8)(LL)
11. lime & blue body, no base, solid red wheels, yellow rotor, lime chute, faces/gears/ haystack tempa, Thailand casting ($6-8)(LL)
12. orange-yellow body, no base, solid black wheels, maroon rotor & chute, "2" with stripes tempa, Thailand casting ($1-2)(MC)
13. dark blue body, no base, solid black wheels, yellow rotor & chute, "Harvester 379a" tempa, China casting ($1-2)(MW89/ 1999 US)(MW3/ 1999 ROW)
14. green body, no base, solid black wheels, yellow rotor & chute, yellow stripe & design tempa, China casting ($3-5)(MW3/GR)
15. dark green body, no base, solid black wheels, yellow rotor & chute, "Harvester Model 379a" & "Matchbox 2000" tempa, China casting ($2-4)(MW47/2000 US)
16. dark green body, no base, solid black wheels, yellow rotor & chute, "Harvester Model 379a" tempa, China casting ($1-2)(MW47/2000 US)(MW27/2000 ROW)
17. red body, black metal base with Manaus tab, solid black wheels, yellow rotor & chute, no tempa, no origin cast ($35-50)(BR)

MB51-D MIDNIGHT MAGIC, issued 1981 (USA) (MB087)

NOTE: Versions 1-3 with "Lesney" base; versions 4-6 have "Matchbox Toys" base. Below models with chrome engine & interior.

1. black body, silver sides, pearly silver base, 5 spoke front & maltese cross rear wheels, Hong Kong casting ($3-5)
2. black body, silver sides, pearly silver base, maltese cross front & 5 spoke rear wheels, Hong Kong casting ($3-5)
3. black body, silver sides, pearly silver base, 5 spoke front & rear wheels, Hong Kong casting ($3-5)
4. black body, silver sides, pearly white base, 5 spoke front & maltese cross rear wheels, Macau casting ($2-3)
5. black body, silver sides, pearly silver base, 5 spoke front & maltese cross rear wheels, Macau casting ($2-3)
6. black body, silver sides, unpainted base, 5 spoke front & maltese cross rear wheels, Hong Kong casting ($2-3)
7. white body, red & blue tempa, chrome base, 5 spoke front & maltese cross rear wheels, China casting ($4-6)(PC13)

NOTE: Available as a Bulgarian casting. Assorted colors available ($5-25).

MB51-E PONTIAC FIEREBIRD SE *see MB12-E*

MB51-F LONDON BUS *see MB17-C*

MB51-G CAMARO IROC Z28, issued 1986 (USA) (MB164)
MB68-F CAMARO IROC Z28, issued 1986 (ROW)

NOTE: Below models with black base, silver-gray interior & clear windows unless otherwise noted.

1. apple green body, metal base, 8 dot wheels, "IROC Z" tempa, Macau casting ($4-6)
2. apple green body, metal base, 5 arch wheels, "IROC Z" tempa, Macau casting ($4-6)
3. blue body, metal base, 5 arch wheels, "IROC Z" on sides only tempa, Macau casting ($2-4)
4. blue body, metal base, 8 dot wheels, "IROC Z" on sides only tempa, Macau casting ($2-4)
5. red body, metal base, starburst wheels, "Carter/ Goodyear" tempa, Macau casting ($3-5)(SF)

6. metallic red body, metal base, laser wheels, "Carter/ Goodyear" tempa, Macau casting ($3-5)(LW)
7. blue body, metal base, 8 dot wheels, "IROC Z" hood & sides tempa without extra black line, Macau casting ($2-4)
8. blue body, metal base, 8 dot wheels, "IROC Z" hood & sides tempa with extra black line, Macau casting ($2-4)
9. lemon body, metal base, 8 dot wheels, "IROC Z" with stripes tempa, Macau casting ($1-2)
10. metallic copper body, metal base, laser wheels, "Carter/ Goodyear" tempa, Macau casting ($4-6)(LW)
11. blue-green body, black interior, metal base, 8 dot wheels, "BP Stunt Team" & stripes tempa, Macau casting ($8-12)(DU)
12. lemon body, plastic base, 8 dot wheels, "IROC Z" with stripes tempa, Macau casting ($1-2)
13. lemon body, plastic base, 8 dot wheels, "IROC Z" with stripes tempa, Thailand casting ($1-2)
14. metallic blue body, plastic base, 8 dot wheels, black windows, "350Z" with pink/ purple/ lime stripes tempa, Thailand casting ($3-5)(TH)
15. black body, plastic base, 8 dot wheels, "Z28" with orange bands & white stripes tempa, Thailand casting ($1-2)
16. red body, plastic base, 8 dot wheels, white stripes tempa, Thailand casting ($2-3)(SS)
17. dark purple body, plastic base, 8 dot wheels, silver band & "Z28" tempa, Thailand casting ($2-4)(CC)

MB51-K FORD AMBULANCE, issued 1997 (USA) (MB299)
MB17-H FORD AMBULANCE, issued 1997 (ROW)

NOTE: Below models listed with smoke windows, red dome lights & China casting.

1. white body, chrome base, chrome disc wheels with rubber tires, "Ambulance Dial 911" ($4-6)(IG)
2. unpainted body, chrome base, chrome disc wheels with rubber tires, no tempa ($4-6)(IG)
3. white body, chrome base, 8 dot wheels, "27 Matchbox Ambulance" with blue & silver tempa ($1-2)
4. yellow body, chrome base, 8 dot wheels, "York Fair Emergency 1997" tempa ($5-8)(WR)
5. yellow body, chrome base, 8 dot wheels, "27 Matchbox Ambulance" with red & white tempa ($1-2)(MW25/1998)
6. yellow body, translucent white base, 8 dot wheels, "27 Matchbox Ambulance" with red & white tempa ($50-75)(MW25/1998)
7. red body, chrome base, chrome disc wheels with rubber tires, "Fire Rescue" with white band tempa ($3-5)(PC21)
8. metallic gold body, chrome base, 8 dot wheels, no tempa ($5-10)(CH)
9. white body, chrome base, 8 dot wheels, maroon cab & "County EMS" tempa ($1-2)(5pk)
10. white body, chrome base, 8 dot wheels, no tempa ($25-40)(ASAP blank)
11. white body, chrome base, 8 dot wheels, "American International Recovery" tempa ($100+)(ASAP)
12. bright blue body, chrome base, 8 dot wheels, "Ambulance-Ridge, New York" tempa ($1-2)(MW5/1999 US)
13. white body, chrome base, 8 dot wheels, "Alice 106 FM" tempa ($100+)(ASAP)
14. white body, chrome base, 8 dot wheels, "Midwest Regional Matchbox Convention" (gold print) ($10-15)(ASAP)
15. white body, chrome base, 8 dot wheels, "Midwest Regional Matchbox Convention" (red print) ($25-40)(ASAP)
16. white body, chrome base, 8 dot wheels, "Midwest Regional Matchbox Convention" (green print) ($50-65)(ASAP)
17. white body, chrome base, 8 dot wheels, "Ambulance 3-1926" with olive & blue stripes tempa ($1-2)(5pk)
18. white body, chrome base, chrome disc wheels with rubber tires, "Las Vegas Fire Department" tempa, red & blue dome lights ($12-15)(PC)
19. dark blue body, chrome base, black disc wheels with rubber tires, "Flight Crew Transport" tempa, amber dome lights tempa ($20-35)(PC)
20. white body, chrome base, 8 dot wheels, "Windham Hospital EMS" (left side only) tempa ($12-15)(ASAP)
21. white body, chrome base, 8 dot wheels, "27 Matchbox Ambulance/ 48-91/ Newfield Ambulance Corps" tempa ($15-25)(CCI)
22. white body, chrome base, 8 dot wheels, "Windham Hospital EMS/ 2000" tempa ($12-15)(ASAP)
23. white body, chrome base, 8 dot wheels, "5 Alarm Ambulance" tempa ($1-2)(LP)
24. white body, chrome base, 8 dot wheels, "Police/ Metropolitan Police" with red, yellow & blue stripes tempa ($2-4)(MW38/2000)
25. white body, chrome base, 8 dot wheels, "Squantz Engine Co." tempa ($12-15)(ASAP)
26. white body, chrome base, 8 dot wheels, "Kimball Day Hospital" tempa ($12-15)(ASAP)
27. white body, chrome base, 8 dot wheels "NAEMT/MAEMT-25 Years of Service" tempa ($12-15)(ASAP)
28. silver-gray body, chrome base, 8 dot wheels, "EMT", red band, yellow design tempa ($1-2)(MW87/2000 US)
29. silver-gray body, chrome base, 8 dot wheels, "EMT", red band, yellow design & "Matchbox 2000" tempa ($2-4)(MW87/2000 US)
30. red body, chrome base, 8 dot wheels, yellow & red snake & rod tempa ($1-2)(5pk)
31. white body, chrome base, 8 dot wheels, "Bill Cairns Realtor" tempa ($12-15)(ASAP)
32. white body, chrome base, 8 dot wheels, "FSU" tempa ($12-15)(ASAP)
33. silver-gray body, chrome base, 10 spoke flower wheels, "EMT", red band & yellow design tempa ($2-4)(MW87/2000 US)
34. white body, red windows, chrome base, 10 spoke flower wheels, "5 Alarm Ambulance" tempa ($1-2)(LP)
35. orange & white body, chrome base, 10 spoke flower wheels, "Metro Alarm/ Ambulance" tempa ($1-2)(5pk)
36. silver-gray body, chrome base, 8 dot wheels, "Ambulance" with dark blue bands & EMS logo ($3-5)(ROW 3pk)
37. white body, chrome base, 8 dot wheels, "Sugar Grove Fire Department 2000" tempa ($15-20)(ASAP)
38. white body, chrome base, amber windows, 10 spoke flower wheels, "911 Emergency" with red & silver band tempa, Mattel casting ($3-5)(PB)
39. white body, chrome base, blue windows, 10 spoke flower wheels, "Ambulance" with red dashes, black hood tempa, Mattel casting ($2-4)(MW62/2001)(MW52/2001 AU)
40. white body, chrome base, 8 dot wheels, "9-1-1/ PSAP/ Nena 2001" tempa ($75+)(ASAP)
41. yellow body, chrome base, 8 dot wheels, "Thank You To Our Heroes" tempa ($50-75)(CCI)
42. white body, chrome base, chrome disc with rubber tires, "Rescue EMT" tempa ($3-5)(MP)(HR)
43. white body, chrome base, 8 dot wheels, "St. Vincent & Medical Mobile Life" tempa ($75+)(ASAP)
44. white body, chrome base, 8 dot wheels, "VT- Virginia Tech" (left side only) tempa ($25-40)(ASAP)
45. red body, chrome base, chrome disc wheels with rubber tires, "Fire Rescue" with "TTKA" tempa & decal logo ($25-40)(CCI)
46. white body, chrome base, 10 spoke flower wheels, "Kingston General Hospital Cardiac Care/ A112/ Thanks! From Bill Cairns" tempa, Mattel casting ($75+)(CCI)

47. white body, chrome base, 10 spoke flower wheels, "Napanee Fire Rescue/ A113" tempa, Mattel casting ($35-50)(CCI)
48. white body, chrome base, 10 spoke flower wheels, "Toronto Paramedic Association/ Paramedicine 2003" tempa, Mattel casting ($20-30)(CCI)
49. white body, chrome base, 10 spoke flower wheels, "Matchbox CCI Rescue Unit/ 10th Annual Toy Show" tempa, Mattel casting ($10-15)(CCI)
50. red body, chrome base, 10 spoke flower wheels, "Squantz Engine Co./ Ambulance" & gold stripe tempa, Mattel casting ($25-40)(CCI)
51. white body, chrome base, 8 dot wheels, "5 Alarm Ambulance" tempa ($1-2)(LP)
52. white body, chrome base, 8 dot wheels, "TapeWare" tempa ($50+)(ASAP)
53. white body, chrome base, 8 dot wheels, "The Tenet Rescue Unit" tempa ($50+)(ASAP)
54. white body, chrome base, 8 dot wheels, "County Line" tempa ($50+)(ASAP)
55. white body, chrome base, 8 dot wheels red "General Hospital Port Charles" tempa ($50+)(ASAP)
56. white body, chrome base, 8 dot wheels, blue "General Hospital Port Charles" tempa ($50+)(ASAP)
57. white body, chrome base, 8 dot wheels, "Lowe's Home Safety Council" tempa ($50+)(ASAP)
58. white body, chrome base, 8 dot wheels, "CHS/ Ambulance" & red cross tempa ($50+)(ASAP)
59. white body, chrome base, 8 dot wheels, "Eastern PA EMS Council" tempa ($50+)(ASAP)
60. white body, chrome base, 8 dot wheels, "West Virginia EMS" tempa ($50+)(ASAP)
61. white body, chrome base, 10 spoke flower wheels, no tempa, Mattel casting ($25-40)(ASAP blank)
62. white body, chrome base, 10 spoke flower wheels, "West Virginia EMS" tempa, Mattel casting ($50+)(ASAP)
63. white body, chrome base, 10 spoke flower wheels, "Eastern PA EMS Council" tempa, Mattel casting ($50+)(ASAP)
64. white body, chrome base, 10 spoke flower wheels, "Sheriff Ambulance" tempa, Mattel casting ($25-40)(CCI)
65. white body, chrome base, 10 spoke flower wheels, "Grosse Pointe Park/ Ambulance" tempa, Mattel casting ($50+)(CCI)
66. white body, chrome base, 10 spoke flower wheels, "Kansas EMT Association/ KEMTA 2004" tempa, Mattel casting ($25-40)(CCI)
67. white body, chrome base, 10 spoke flower wheels, "Skagit County Medic One- Emergency Medical Services" tempa, Mattel casting ($25-40)(ASAP)
68. white body, chrome base, 10 spoke flower wheels, "Patient Transfer Ambulance" tempa, Mattel casting ($25-40)(CCI)
69. white body, chrome base, 10 spoke flower wheels, "Police Emergency Services" tempa, Mattel casting ($25-40)(CCI)
70. white body, chrome base, 10 spoke flower wheels, "2nd Annual MCCH Gathering 2004" & large "Hot Wheels" logo ($50-75)(CCI)
71. white body, chrome base, 10 spoke flower wheels, "Ambulance- Nassau County Police" tempa ($18-25)(CCI)
72. white body, chrome base, 10 spoke flower wheels, "Advanced Medical Transport" & dark blue band tempa ($25-40)(CCI)

MB51-L WATERCRAFT WITH TRAILER, issued 1999 (USA) (MB373)
MB46-I WATERCRAFT WITH TRAILER, issued 1999 (ROW)

NOTE: Below models with white hull, 4 spoke wheels & China casting unless otherwise noted.

1. turquoise deck, purple seat & handlebars, turquoise & purple tempa, purple trailer, white hubs ($1-2)(MW51/ 1999 US/ GR)(MW46/1999 ROW)
2. orange deck, blue seat & handlebars, orange & blue with "Matchbox 2000" tempa, blue trailer, white hubs ($2-4)(MW8 US/2000)
3. orange deck, blue seat & handlebars, orange & blue tempa, blue trailer, white hubs ($1-2)(MW8/2000)
4. orange deck, blue seat & handlebars, orange & blue tempa, blue trailer, black hubs ($1-2)(MW8/2000)
5. orange deck, blue seat & handlebars, orange & blue tempa, blue trailer, silver hubs ($1-2)(MW8/2000)
6. red deck, black seats & handlebars, yellow & red tempa, black trailer, black hubs ($1-2)(5pk)
7. yellow deck, black seat & handlebars, black base, purple & blue octopuses tempa, gray trailer, black hubs ($1-2)(5pk)
8. purple deck, black seat & handlebars, white base, "R9-2" & bolts tempa, black trailer, black hubs ($2-4)(MW50/2002 ROW)
9. purple deck, black seat & handlebars, white base, "R9-2", bolts & "Matchbox 50" tempa, black trailer, black hubs ($3-5)(MW50/ 2002 ROW)
10. white body, red seat & handlebars, blue-green base, white squiggles tempa, yellow trailer, black hubs ($1-2)(5pk)
11. white body, blue seat & handlebars, unpainted base, no tempa, blue trailer, black hubs ($35-50)(MW8/2000) *(Found in USA-Kaybee)*

MB51-N ROBOT TRUCK, issued 2001 (USA) (MB512)
MB37-M ROBOT TRUCK, issued 2002 (ROW)

NOTE: Below models with 7 spoke sawblade wheels & China casting.

1. white body, red interior, black roof unit, smoke windows, black base, "Police Patrol Unit 12" tempa ($1-2)(MW51/2001 US)
2. dark blue body, orange-yellow interior, red roof unit, amber windows, red base, "Matchbox 50th Birthday Party- 2002 Toy Fair" tempa ($20-35)(US)
3. bright blue body, white interior, silver-gray roof unit, amber windows, gray base, "Police RB-07" & winged logo tempa ($1-2)(5pk)
4. black body, glow yellow interior, glow yellow roof unit, smoke windows, glow yellow base, skyline design tempa ($1-2)(MW37/2002)
5. black body, glow yellow interior, glow yellow roof unit, smoke windows, glow yellow base, skyline design & "Matchbox 50" tempa ($5-8)(MW37/2002)
6. black body, red interior, blue roof unit, light purple windows, blue base, "Jimmy Neutron" tempa ($1-2)(5pk)
7. silver-gray body, red interior, dark blue roof unit, amber windows, dark blue base, "Police RB-07" & winged logo tempa ($1-2)(5pk)
8. lime body, glow lime interior, glow lime roof unit, black windows, glow lime base, ghost & net tempa ($5-8)(PS)

MB51-O FORD FALCON POLICE CAR, issued 2001 (AU) (MB513)

1. white body, black interior, smoke windows, blue bar dome light, 10 spoke flower wheels, "Police" & checkers tempa, black base, China casting ($2-4)(MW51/2001 AU)

MB51-P PONTIAC VIBE, issued 2003 (MB585)

NOTE: Below models with smoke windows, black base & China casting unless otherwise noted.

1. metallic silver body, black interior, "51" & small logo tempa, lace wheels ($1-2)(MW51/2003)
2. metallic silver body, black interior, "51", small logo & "Hero City" tempa, lace wheels ($3-5)(MW51/2003)

3. silver-gray body, gray & black interior, detailed trim tempa, chrome disc with rubber tires ($4-5)(SH)
4. black body, silver-gray interior, detailed trim tempa, slotted 5 spoke wheels, dark gray base ($3-5)(SF23/2004)

MB51-Q JEEP COMPASS, issued 2004 (MB627)

1. green body, black windows, no interior, 5 spoke oval wheels, no tempa, silver-gray plastic base, China casting ($1-2)(MW51/2004)

MB52-A DODGE CHARGER, issued 1970

NOTE: Below models with clear windows, black interior, 5 spoke wheels & England casting.

1. pinkish metallic red body, green base, no labels ($10-15)
2. pale metallic red body, green base, no labels ($10-15)
3. pale metallic red body, green base, "5" on roof with side labels ($10-15)(GS)
4. dark metallic red body, green base, "5" on roof with side labels ($10-15)(GS)
5. dark metallic red body, green base, no labels ($10-15)
6. dark metallic red body, green base, yellow & black hood label ($10-15)
7. metallic magenta body, green base, no labels ($10-15)
8. metallic magenta body, green base, stripes & "STP" label ($10-15)(GS)
9. metallic purple body, green base, no labels ($15-20)
10. metallic purple body, green base, "5" on roof with side labels ($15-20)(GS)
11. metallic lime body, bright red base, no labels ($10-15)
12. metallic lime body, red base, no labels ($10-15)
13. metallic lime body, red base, "5" on roof with sides labels ($15-20)(GS)
14. metallic lime body, red base, "Castrol" hood label ($750+)
15. metallic lime body, unpainted base, no labels ($10-15)
16. metallic lime body, red base, cow label (from MB73-A) ($175-250)
17. metallic purple body, green base, scorpion hood label ($175-250)

MB52-B POLICE LAUNCH, issued 1976 (MB113)

NOTE: Below models with plastic hull, black wheels unless otherwise noted.

1. white deck, blue hull, light blue figures, dark blue windows, "Police" labels, horns cast, England casting ($5-7)
2. white deck, blue hull with Manaus tab, light blue figures, dark blue windows, "Police" labels, horns cast, no origin cast ($50-65)(BR)
3. white deck, blue hull, light blue figures, dark blue windows, "Police" labels, hatch cast, England casting ($4-6)
4. white deck, blue hull, light blue figures, opaque blue windows, "Police" labels, hatch cast, England casting ($4-6)
5. white deck,, dark blue hull, light blue figures, light blue windows, "Police" labels, hatch cast, England casting ($4-6)
6. white deck, dark blue hull, light blue figures, opaque blue windows, "Police" labels, hatch cast, England casting ($4-6)
7. white deck, red hull, orange-yellow figures, light blue windows, "LA Fire" labels, hatch cast, England casting ($6-8)(CR)
8. white deck, red hull, light blue figures, light blue windows, "LA Fire" labels, hatch cast, England casting ($10-15)(CR)
9. black deck, dark gray hull, dark gray figures, light blue windows, tan & gray camouflage tempa, hatch cast, Macau casting ($4-5)(CM)
10. white deck, blue hull, red figures & wheels, light blue windows, "123" & rope pattern tempa, hatch cast, Macau casting ($6-8)(LL)
11. white deck, blue hull, red figures & wheels, light blue windows, "123" & rope pattern tempa, hatch cast, Thailand casting ($6-8)(LL)
12. white deck ,white hull, white figures, light blue windows, no tempa, hatch cast, China casting ($10-15)(GF)
13. white deck, blue hull with brown painted base, blue figures, clear windows, "Amity Police/ Jaws" tempa, hatch cast, China casting ($5-8)(STR)
14. yellow deck, black hull, red figures, clear windows, "Rescue B-1" with red & white stripe tempa, horns cast, China casting ($2-4)(RT)
15. white deck, dark blue hull, dark blue figures, blue windows, "Police" & orange stripes tempa, horns cast, China casting ($2-4)(AP)
16. white deck, red hull, blue figures, blue windows, "UT-35-091m" & stripes tempa, hatch cast, China casting ($1-2)(MW80/1999 USA)(MW70/1999 ROW)
17. red deck, white hull, florescent yellow figures, blue windows, blue band & "2416/134" tempa, hatch cast, China casting ($1-2)(5pk)
18. dark blue deck, white hull, lemon figures, smoke windows, white hash marks & light blue bands, "OD-593" tempa, hatch cast, China casting ($1-2)(5pk)
19. lemon & black deck, white hull, blue figures, blue windows, "Base 2000" with blue & black stripes, hatch cast, China casting ($1-2)(LP)
20. white deck, red metal hull, blue figures, blue windows, "UT-35-091m" & stripes tempa, hatch cast, Mattel China casting ($5-8)(EG)
21. metallic blue deck, dark blue metal hull, blue figures, red windows, storm design tempa, hatch cast, Mattel China casting ($1-2)(LP)
22. blue deck, white metal hull, black figures, amber windows, "Mission H2O- Metro Police" tempa, hatch cast, white wheels, Mattel China casting ($1-2)(LP)
23. red deck, white metal hull, black figures, blue windows, "Coca Cola" tempa, hatch cast, Mattel China casting ($2-4)(CK)
24. silver blue deck, white hull, red figures, black windows, "Mission H2O" tempa, hatch cast, Mattel China casting ($1-2)(LP)

MB52-C BMW M1, issued 1981

NOTE: Below models with 5 arch wheels & England casting unless otherwise noted.

1. silver-gray body, black base, clear windows, red interior, "52" tempa ($2-4)
2. silver-gray body, blue-gray base, clear windows, red interior, "52" tempa ($2-4)
3. silver-gray body, blue-gray base, smoke windows, red interior, "52" tempa ($2-4)
4. silver-gray body, black base, amber windows, red interior, "52" tempa ($12-15)
5. silver-gray body, black base, green windows, red interior, "52" tempa ($60-75)
6. silver-gray body, black base, clear windows, pink-red interior, "52" tempa ($2-4)
7. silver-gray body, black base, amber windows, pink-red interior, "52" tempa ($12-15)
8. silver-gray body, black base, clear windows, red interior, "52" tempa, small dot dash wheels ($25-40)
9. silver-gray body, black base, clear windows, red interior, no tempa ($40-50)
10. silver-gray body, black base, clear windows, red interior, "52" tempa & "Climat" label ($125-175)(FR)

MB52-D BMW M1, issued 1983 (MB052)

NOTE: This is a highly modified version to MB52-C in which the hood has been cast closed with a spoiler added to the front & rear of the body. Below models with black plastic base, clear windows, 5 arch wheels unless otherwise noted.

1. white body, black interior, "BMW M1" tempa, Macau casting ($2-3)
2. black body, red interior, "Pirelli 59" tempa, Macau casting ($3-5)
3. yellow body, black interior, "11" with stripes tempa, Macau casting ($1-2)
4. yellow body, black interior, "11" with stripes tempa, China casting ($1-2)
5. yellow body, black interior, "11" with stripes tempa (all black "Bell" logo & all red "Champion" logo), China casting ($1-2)
6. bright red body, black interior, "1" with stripes tempa, Macau casting ($1-2)
7. red body, black interior, "1" with stripes tempa, China casting ($1-2)
8. dark yellow body, black interior, chrome windows, gray disc wheels with rubber tires, detailed trim tempa, Macau casting ($5-8)(WC)
9. chrome plated body, black interior, no tempa, Macau casting ($12-18)(C2)
10. chrome plated body, black interior, no tempa, China casting ($12-18)(C2)
11. bright red body, black interior, "1" with stripes tempa, Thailand casting ($1-2)
12. black body, red interior, "Pirelli 59" tempa, 4 arch wheels, Manaus casting ($35-50)(BR)
13. black body, red interior, "Pirelli 59" tempa, 8 dot wheels, Manaus casting ($35-50)(BR)
14. metallic blue body, black & gray interior, detailed trim tempa, chrome disc wheels with rubber tires, Thailand casting ($15-20)(GC)

MB52-E ISUZU AMIGO, issued 1991 (MB230)

NOTE: Below models with clear windows, chrome plastic base, & dot dash wheels unless otherwise noted.

1. metallic blue body, gray interior, "Isuzu Amigo" tempa, Thailand casting ($5-7)
2. lemon body, gray interior, pink stripes & design tempa, Thailand casting ($2-3)(DM)
3. red body, gray interior, "Amigo" with silver & orange stripes tempa, Thailand casting ($2-3)
4. white body, neon orange interior, blue splash tempa, Thailand casting ($1-2)(5pk)
5. purple body, black interior, skeleton & "Hadrosaur" tempa, Thailand casting ($1-2)(5pk)
6. purple body, black interior, skeleton & "Hadrosaur" tempa, China casting ($1-2)(5pk)
7. white body, neon orange interior, blue splash tempa, China casting ($1-2)(5pk)
8. navy blue body, gray interior, green splash tempa, China casting ($1-2)(5pk)
9. white body, black interior, "Surf Shop/ Surf's Up" tempa, China casting ($1-2)(MW54/1999 US)(MW49/1999 ROW)(MW52/1999 GR)
10. metallic red body, smoke windows, black interior, "S.O.S." & design tempa, 4 spoke domed wheels, China casting ($1-2)(5pk)
11. lime body, yellow interior & base, "Jungle Base" tempa, 4 spoke domed wheels, China casting ($1-2)(5pk)
12. metallic blue body, amber windows, cream interior, orange base, "Diego" tempa, 7 spoke sawblade wheels, China casting ($1-2)(5pk)

MB52-F FORD ESCORT COSWORTH, issued 1994 (MB252)

NOTE: Below models with clear windows & plastic base unless otherwise noted.

1. white body, white spoiler & base, blue interior, gold 6-spoke spiral wheels, "Mobil l/Michelin 5" tempa, Thailand casting ($1-2)
2. white body, white spoiler & base, blue interior, gold 6-spoke spiral wheels, "Mobil l/Michelin 5" tempa, China casting ($1-2)
3. white body, white spoiler & base, blue interior, silver 6-spoke spiral wheels, "Mobil 1/ Michelin 5" tempa, China casting ($1-2)
4. white body, white spoiler, blue base, white interior, silver 6-spoke spiral wheels, "Mobil 1/ Michelin 5" tempa, China casting ($2-4)
5. metallic red body, red spoiler & base, white interior, silver 6-spoke spiral wheels, lime & white design tempa, China casting ($1-2)
6. white body, white spoiler & base, blue interior, silver 6 spoke spiral wheels, "Ford 23" & black design tempa, China casting ($1-2)(5pk)
7. red body, black spoiler, red base, light gray interior, silver 6 spoke spiral wheels, "5" on yellow splash tempa, China casting ($3-5)(5pk)
8. white body, white spoiler & base, white interior, silver 6 spoke spiral wheels, "MOL" with orange & 2 tone green stripes tempa, China casting ($25-40)(HU)
9. metallic gold body, black spoiler & base, black interior, silver 6 spoke spiral wheels, no tempa , China casting ($5-10)(CH)
10. white body, dark blue spoiler, white base, dark blue interior, 5 spoke concave star wheels, "Matchbox 3" tempa, China casting ($1-2)(5pk)
11. metallic red body, red spoiler & base, white interior, 5 spoke concave star wheels, lime & white design tempa, China casting ($2-3)
12. red body, black spoiler, red base, light gray interior, 5 spoke concave star wheels, "5" on yellow splash tempa, China casting ($1-2)(5pk)
13. black body, black spoiler & base, light gray interior, 5 spoke concave star wheels, "1" with yellow & white design tempa, China casting ($1-2)
14. white body, red spoiler, white base, dark blue interior, smoke windows, 5 spoke concave star wheels, British flag tempa, China casting ($2-4)(MW15/2000 UK)

MB52-G SNOW GROOMER *see MB57-I*

MB52-H VW DELIVERY VAN *see MB72-S*

MB52-I TROOP CARRIER, issued 2001 (USA) (MB514/584)
MB36-J TROOP CARRIER, issued 2002 (ROW)

NOTE: Below models with 4 spoke domed wheels & China casting unless otherwise noted.

1. blue body, white interior, red windows, tan canopy, brown rear seats, gray base, "Police Carrier One" tempa ($1-2)(MW52/2001 US)
2. beige body, black interior, red windows, dark green canopy, black rear seats, black base, "Fire Rescue" tempa ($3-5)(PS)
3. silver-gray body, black interior, amber windows, orange canopy, purple rear seats, purple base, "Base 36" tempa ($1-2)(MW36/2002)
4. silver-gray body, black interior, amber windows, orange canopy, purple rear seats, purple base, "Base 36" & "Matchbox 50" tempa ($2-4)(MW36/2002)
5. silver-gray body, black interior, amber windows, orange canopy, purple rear seats, purple base, "Base 36" tempa, lace wheels ($1-2)(MW36/2002)

6. white body, black interior, red windows, black canopy, black rear seats, black base, "D4 Metro Police" tempa ($1-2)(5pk)
7. white body, black interior, amber windows, black canopy, black rear seats, black base, "D4 Metro Police" tempa ($20-35)(5pk)
8. olive body, dark tan interior, blue windows, none canopy, brown rear seats, gray base, "Bunyan's 555-1234" tempa ($1-2)(5pk)
9. olive body, dark tan interior, blue windows, none canopy, brown rear seats, gray base, "Bunyan's 555-1234" & "Hero City" tempa ($1-2)(5pk)
10. red body, gray interior, blue windows, bright yellow canopy, gray rear seats, gray base, cross design & ice chunks design tempa ($8-12)(PS)
11. blue body, gray interior, amber windows, no canopy, gray rear seats, silver-gray base, stripes & "Police" crest tempa ($1-2)(LP)

MB52-J LAND ROVER SVX, issued 2004 (MB628)

1. black body, black interior, gray roll bar, gray base, 5 spoke oval wheels, small "Matchbox" logo at rear tempa, China casting ($1-2)(MW52/2004)

MB53-A FORD ZODIAC MK IV, issued 1970

NOTE: Below models with clear windows, ivory interior, chrome engine, 5 spoke wheels & England casting.

1. light metallic blue body, unpainted base ($350-425)
2. light metallic green body, unpainted base ($15-20)
3. mid metallic green body, unpainted base ($15-20)
4. dark metallic green body, unpainted base, ($15-20)
5. emerald green body, unpainted base ($15-20)
6. apple green body, unpainted base ($25-30)
7. emerald green body, unpainted base, small 5 spoke wheels with black hubs ($75+)

MB53-B TANZARA, issued 1972

NOTE: Below models with maltese cross wheels & England casting.

1. orange body, unpainted base, chrome interior, blue-green windows, no tempa ($12-15)
2. orange body, unpainted base, chrome interior, amber windows, no tempa ($15-18)
3. white body, unpainted base, chrome interior, amber windows, no tempa ($18-25)
4. white body, unpainted base, chrome interior, amber windows, orange stripes tempa ($12-15)
5. white body, unpainted base, chrome interior, amber windows, red stripes tempa ($12-15)
6. white body, silver-gray base, chrome interior, amber windows, red stripes tempa ($12-15)
7. white body, unpainted base, chrome interior, blue-green windows, red stripes tempa ($15-20)
8. white body, unpainted base, red interior, amber windows, red stripes tempa ($25-40)

MB53-C JEEP CJ6, issued 1977

NOTE: Below models with 5 crown wheels & England casting.

1. red body, tan roof, orange-yellow interior, unpainted base, no tempa ($4-6)
2. red body, tan roof, orange-yellow interior, silver-gray base, no tempa ($4-6)
3. red body, tan roof, orange-yellow interior, unpainted base, no tempa, black hubs ($5-7)
4. red body, light tan roof, orange-yellow interior, unpainted base, no tempa ($4-6)
5. red body, tan roof, light orange interior, unpainted base, no tempa ($4-6)
6. red body, tan roof, black interior, unpainted base, no tempa ($5-8)
7. metallic green body, tan roof, orange-yellow interior, unpainted base, no tempa ($5-8)
8. metallic green body, tan roof, orange-yellow interior, silver-gray base, no tempa ($5-8)
9. metallic green body, tan roof, black interior, unpainted base, no tempa ($4-6)
10. metallic green body, brown roof, orange-yellow interior, unpainted base, no tempa ($4-6)
11. metallic green body, tan roof, orange-yellow interior, unpainted base, "Climat" label on hood ($125-175)(FR)
12. light metallic green body, pink-tan roof, black interior, unpainted base, no tempa ($4-6)
13. light yellow body, brown roof, black interior, black base, stripes tempa ($5-7)
14. yellow body, brown roof, black interior, black base, stripes tempa ($5-7)
15. yellow body, brown roof, black interior, charcoal base, stripes tempa ($4-6)
16. yellow body, brown roof, black interior, black base, no tempa ($25-40)
17. yellow body, brown roof, black interior, silver-gray base, stripes tempa ($4-6)

NOTE: Available as an Hungarian casting. Assorted colors available. ($15-25)

MB53-D FLARESIDE PICKUP, issued 1982 (MB053)
MB55-J FLARESIDE PICKUP, reissued 1994

1. blue body, charcoal base, white interior, clear windows, 8 spoke wheels, "326 Baja Bouncer" tempa, England casting ($2-4)
2. blue body, black base, white interior, clear windows, 8 spoke wheels, "326 Baja Bouncer" tempa, England casting ($2-4)
3. blue body, black base, white interior, clear windows, 8 spoke wheels, "326 Baja Bouncer" (plain sides) tempa, England casting ($4-6)
4. blue body, black base, white interior, clear windows, 8 spoke wheels, "326 Baja Bouncer" (plain hood) tempa, England casting ($4-6)
5. blue body, black base, white interior, blue windows, 8 spoke wheels, "326 Baja Bouncer" tempa, England casting ($45-60)
6. blue body, black base, white interior, clear windows, 8 spoke wheels, no tempa, England casting ($125-175)
7. orange body, black base, white interior, clear windows, 8 spoke wheels, "326 Baja Bouncer" tempa, Macau casting ($2-4)
8. yellow body, black base, white interior, clear windows, 8 spoke wheels, "Ford 460" tempa, Macau casting ($175-225)
9. yellow body, black base, black interior, clear windows, 8 spoke wheels, "Ford 460" tempa, Macau casting ($35-50)
10. yellow body, black base, black interior, clear windows, racing slicks (chromed letters) wheels, "Ford 460" tempa, Macau casting ($2-3)
11. yellow body, black base, black interior, clear windows, racing slicks (unchromed letters) wheels, "Ford 460" tempa, Macau casting ($1-2)
12. khaki green body, black base, black interior, opaque green windows, dark purple & blue design tempa, racing slicks wheels, Macau casting, includes plastic armament ($5-8)(RB)
13. white body, black base, black interior, clear windows, "Deb" tempa, racing slicks wheels, Macau casting ($35-50)(UK)(OP)
14. red body, black base, white interior, clear windows, "326 Baja Bouncer" tempa, 8 spoke wheels, Manaus casting ($75-100)(BR)
15. lime body, yellow base, red interior, clear windows, jack & wheel design tempa, red racing slicks, Thailand casting ($6-8)(LL)

16. red body, black base, black interior, clear windows, "Bill Elliot 11" tempa, racing slicks wheels, Thailand casting ($5-7)(WR)(TC)
17. fluorescent yellow body, chrome base, no interior, chrome windows, racing slicks (unchromed letters), pink/red/blue flash tempa, Thailand casting ($2-4)(ST)
18. metallic blue body, chrome base, no interior, chrome windows, racing slicks (unchromed letters), yellow with orange flames tempa, Thailand casting ($2-4)(ST)
19. red body, chrome base, black interior, clear windows, racing slicks (unchromed letters), orange & yellow flames tempa, Thailand casting ($1-2)
20. dark yellow body, black base, black interior, clear windows, racing slicks (unchromed letters), "Ford 460" tempa, Thailand casting ($2-4)(MP)
21. white body, chrome base, chrome interior, clear windows, racing slicks (gray insert), silver band & red stripe tempa, Thailand casting ($2-4)(CC)
22. dark blue body, black base, chrome interior, clear windows, racing slicks (unchromed letters), "QC Quality Care 15" tempa, Thailand casting ($3-5)(WR)(TC)
23. florescent orange body, chrome base, black interior, clear windows, racing slicks, black front design tempa, China casting ($1-2)
24. red body, chrome base, black interior, clear windows, racing slicks, orange & yellow flames tempa, China casting ($1-2)
25. silver-gray body, chrome base, purple interior, clear windows, racing slicks, purple & lavender flames tempa, China casting ($1-2)(5pk)
26. blue body, chrome base, pale orange interior, clear windows, racing slicks, white splash tempa, China casting ($1-2)
27. blue body, chrome base, dark orange interior, clear windows, racing slicks, white splash tempa, China casting ($1-2)
28. silver-gray body, black interior, clear windows, racing slicks, "Jay's Flight Team" tempa, China casting, includes black launcher & white glider ($2-4)(AS)
29. met. green-gold body, black interior, chrome base, clear windows, racing slicks, no tempa, China casting ($50-75)(CH)
30. black body, yellow interior, chrome base, clear windows, racing slicks, orange & yellow flames tempa, China casting ($1-2)(5pk)
31. dark purple body, gray interior, chrome base, clear windows, racing slicks, white splash tempa, China casting ($1-2)(MW55/1998)
32. silver-gray body, black interior, chrome base, clear windows, racing slicks, "Jay's Flight Team" tempa, China casting ($1-2)(LS)(Avon)

MB53-E FAUN DUMP TRUCK *see MB9-H*

MB53-F CHEVY BREAKDOWN VAN *see MB21-E*

MB53-G FORD LTD TAXI, issued 1992 (USA) (MB235)
MB56-G FORD LTD TAXI, issued 1992 (ROW)

NOTE: Below models with clear windows & chrome plastic base unless otherwise noted.

1. yellow body, blue interior, 8 dot wheels, "Radio XYZ Cab" & checkers tempa, Thailand casting ($3-5)
2. yellow body, white interior, clear windows, 8 dot wheels, checkers & "Taxi" tempa, Thailand casting ($4-6)(STR)
3. lemon body, dark blue interior, 8 dot wheels, black checkers with plane & taxi silhouette tempa, China casting ($1-2)(MW9/1999 US)
4. pumpkin body, silver-gray interior, 5 spoke concave star wheels, "Taxi" tempa, China casting ($1-2)(5pk)
5. pumpkin body, silver-gray interior, 5 spoke concave star wheels, "Cabbies For Life" tempa, China casting ($75+)(ASAP)
6. pumpkin body, silver-gray interior, 5 spoke concave star wheels, "Ronnie & Rene August 19, 2000" tempa, China casting ($75+)(ASAP)
7. pumpkin body, black interior, 5 spoke concave star wheels, "Convention Taxi/ Matchbox USA 2004" & checkers tempa, China casting ($12-18)(ASAP)
8. pumpkin body, black interior, 5 spoke concave star wheels, "Convention Taxi/ Matchbox" & checkers tempa, China casting ($25-40)(ASAP)
9. pumpkin body, black interior, 5 spoke concave star wheels, no tempa, China casting ($15-20)(ASAP blank)

MB53-H RHINO ROD, issued 1994 (USA) (MB258)
MB24-J RHINO ROD, issued 1994 (ROW)

NOTE: Below models with white horns, chrome engine & rear bumper.

1. dark gray body, gray base, red painted eyes tempa, gold 6-spoke spiral wheels, China casting ($1-2)
2. dark gray body, gray base, orange painted eyes tempa, silver 6-spoke spiral wheels, China casting ($1-2)
3. dark gray body, gray base, black painted eyes tempa, silver 6-spoke spiral wheels, China casting ($1-2)
4. black body, black base, white painted eyes tempa, silver 6-spoke spiral wheels, China casting ($1-2)
5. black body, black base, white painted eyes tempa, 5 spoke concave star wheels, China casting ($2-4)
6. pale gray body, light gray base , red painted eyes tempa, 5 spoke concave star wheels, China casting ($1-2)
7. metallic gold body, black base, black painted eyes tempa, 5 spoke concave star wheels, China casting ($5-10)(CH)
8. metallic dark gray body, dark charcoal base, yellow painted eyes, 5 spoke concave star wheels, China casting ($1-2)(MW43/1998)

MB53-I '62 VW BEETLE, issued 1999 (USA) (MB363)
MB48-I '62 VW BEETLE, issued 1999 (ROW)

NOTE: Below models with chrome plastic base, clear windows, China casting unless otherwise noted.

1. black body, turquoise interior, black roof, turquoise sides & "Matchbox" tempa, 5 spoke concave star wheels ($1-2)(MW53/1999 US)(MW48/1999 ROW)
2. white & red body, black interior, black roof & "Coca Cola" tempa, chrome disc wheels with rubber tires ($4-6)(Coke PC)
3. red & white body, black interior, black roof & "Things Go Better with Coke" tempa, chrome disc wheels with rubber tires ($4-6)(MP-Target)
4. dark powder blue body, gray interior, black roof & "Beetle" tempa, 5 spoke concave star wheels ($1-2)(5pk)
5. white body, black interior, black roof & turquoise sides tempa, 5 spoke concave star wheels ($1-2)(MW12/2000 US)
6. white body, black interior, black roof, turquoise sides & "Matchbox 2000" tempa, 5 spoke concave star wheels ($2-4)(MW12/2000 US)
7. orange body, black interior, black roof & "Xtreme Mission 33" tempa, 5 spoke concave star wheels ($1-2)(5pk)
8. pumpkin body, red interior, "Scooby-Doo!' Jinkies/Velma" tempa , 5 spoke concave star wheels ($5-7)(WB)
9. lemon body, brown interior, black roof tempa, chrome disc wheels with rubber tires ($6-8)(MP-FAO)
10. red body, black interior, black roof & silver pinstripes tempa, 5 spoke concave star wheels ($1-2)(5pk)
11. white body, black interior, black roof & turquoise sides with "Northern New Jersey Toy Show" tempa, 5 spoke concave star wheels ($15-20)(CCI)
12. metallic purple body, gray interior, black roof with black, blue & lavender fish design tempa, lace wheels ($1-2)(5pk)

13. red body, black interior, black roof with "Coca Cola" tempa, 10 spoke flower wheels ($5-6)(Avon)(TP)
14. baby blue body, black interior, detailed trim tempa, chrome disc wheels with rubber tires, black base ($3-5)(TN)
15. metallic burgundy body, gray interior, cream roof with detailed trim & "50" logo tempa, chrome disc wheels with rubber tires ($3-5)(CL)
16. lime body, gray interior, amber windows, "Matchbox 50" tempa, lace wheels ($3-5)(ROW)
17. steel blue body, blue interior, "Massachusetts 6 Patriot's Day" tempa, 10 spoke flower wheels ($1-2)(AM)
18. white body, blue interior, "Massachusetts Patriot's Day Official Parade Car" tempa, 10 spoke flower wheels ($5-8)(AM)
19. orange body, white interior, black roof tempa, lace wheels, gray base ($4-6)(SG)
20. red body, blue-green interior, smoke windows, burst design tempa, 10 spoke flower wheels, blue-green base ($1-2)(5pk)
21. unpainted body, white interior, pop art decals, lace wheels, gray base ($75+)(FA)
22. white body, gray interior, gray roof with detailed trim tempa, chrome disc with rubber tires, black base ($8-10)(MCC)
23. lime body, yellow interior, amber windows, "Nickelodeon" tempa, 10 spoke flower wheels, yellow base ($1-2)(CA)
24. white body, black interior, smoke windows, "Cruisin New England Magazine- All Wheels Festival 2001" tempa, 5 spoke concave star wheels ($75+)(CCI)
25. metallic blue body, yellow interior, amber windows, "Nickelodeon" tempa, 10 spoke flower wheels, yellow base ($1-2)(CA)
26. pumpkin body, black interior, flowers & peace sign tempa, 10 spoke flower wheels, gray base ($4-6)(SG)
27. light blue body, black interior, gray roof & detailed trim tempa, chrome disc wheels with rubber tires, black base ($3-5)(BJ)
28. orange body, white interior, black roof with "137" & small lettering tempa, lace wheels, gray base ($12-18)(CCI)
29. black body, black interior, white sides & detailed trim tempa, chrome disc wheels with rubber tires, black base ($3-5)(BJ)
30. turquoise body, white interior, "Lombard St.- San Francisco" tempa, 10 spoke flower wheels, purple base ($8-12)(AW-Bonus)
31. white body, cream interior, "137" with head & tail light tempa, 5 spoke wheels, chrome base ($3-5)(SF15/2004)
32. metallic lime body, cream interior, "137" with head & tail light tempa, 5 spoke wheels, chrome base ($40-60)(SF15/US promo)
33. black body, turquoise interior, blue side panel with "Camp Sunshine" & "In Memory of Neil Waldmann/ Neil's Wheels" tempa, 5 spoke concave star wheels, chrome base ($50-75)(CCI)
34. black body, gray interior, white sides with "16th Annual Bug Jam 2004" & "Dawn of a New Day" tempa, chrome disc wheels with rubber tires, black base ($25-40)(CCI)

MB53-J TRUCK CAMPER *see MB58-J*

MB53-K POLICE CAR, issued 2002 (MB528)

NOTE: Below models with 7 spoke sawblade wheels & China casting unless otherwise noted.

1. iridescent white body, white interior, blue windows, "Police Force/ MPF-2002" tempa, dark blue base ($1-2)(MW53/2002)
2. iridescent white body, white interior, blue windows, "Police Force/ MPF-2002" & "Matchbox 50" tempa, dark blue base ($2-4)(MW53/2002)
3. pumpkin body, white interior, blue windows, "Hollywood 2003 Pre-Toy Fair/ Studio Police" tempa, dark blue base, chrome disc wheels with rubber tires ($15-25)(US)
4. dark blue body, gray interior, amber windows, "Matchbox Police" tempa, gray base ($2-4)(PZ)
5. blue body, gray interior, amber windows, "Police Chief 452 HQ" tempa, white base ($1-2)(5pk)
6. silver-gray body, red interior, clear windows, "He-Man" tempa, brown base, chrome disc wheels with rubber tires ($3-5)(MU)
7. white body, blue interior, red windows, "Policia 30" tempa, blue base ($12-18)(MW30/2003 ROW)
8. white body, blue interior, red windows, "Policia 30" & "Hero City" tempa, blue base ($3-5)(MW30/2003 ROW)
9. black body, blue interior, red windows, "Highway Patrol 27" tempa, blue base ($1-2)(MW27/2003 US)
10. black body, blue interior, red windows, "Highway Patrol 27" & "Hero City" tempa, blue base ($2-4)(MW27/2003 US)
11. black body, black interior, blue windows, "Sheriff 102/ Police Rescue/2003 Limited Edition" tempa, light gray base ($2-4)(Duracell in pack)
12. black body, white interior, blue windows, "Police Chief 452 HQ" tempa, blue base ($1-2)(5pk)
13. black body, black interior, blue windows, "Police 102/ Police Rescue/ 2004 Limited Edition" tempa, light gray base ($8-10)(Duracell in pack)(CN)
14. dark blue body, gray interior, red windows, "Police Force" & star emblem tempa, gray base ($1-2)(MW68/2004)

MB53-L 1960 JEEP, issued 2004 (SF)
MB505 1960 JEEP, issued 2001 (EL)(MB505)

NOTE: Below models with China casting.

1. dark pink body, light pink windscreen, white roof with pink stripes, white & pink interior, chrome disc wheels with rubber tires, detailed trim tempa, black base, with diorama ($10-15)(EL)
2. dark pink body & windscreen, white roof with pink stripes, white interior, 7 spoke sawblade wheels, head lights tempa, gray base ($2-4)(MP)(Avon)
3. metallic maroon body & windscreen, black roof, black interior, 5 spoke slotted wheels, headlights & grille tempa, chrome base ($1-2)(SF53/2004)

MB54-A S&S CADILLAC AMBULANCE, issued 1970

NOTE: Below models with blue windows, white interior, red dome lights, 5 spoke wheels & England casting. All variations with either small or large red cross label (from MB-3A)

1. white body, black base, plain grille ($45-60)
2. white body, black base, silver grille ($45-60)
3. off white body, black base, plain grille ($45-60)

MB54-B FORD CAPRI, issued 1971

NOTE: Below models with clear windows, chrome engine & England casting. Earliest versions with narrow wheels although most versions exist with wide wheels.

1. light peach body, black hood, ivory interior, unpainted base, 5 spoke wheels ($12-15)
2. dark peach body, black hood, ivory interior, unpainted base, 5 spoke wheels ($12-15)
3. metallic purple body & hood, ivory interior, unpainted base, 5 spoke wheels ($10-15)
4. metallic purple body & hood, white interior, unpainted base, 5 spoke wheels ($10-15)
5. metallic purple body & hood, ivory interior, silver-gray base, 5 spoke wheels ($10-15)
6. metallic purple body & hood, ivory interior, unpainted base, maltese cross wheels ($10-15)
7. orange body & hood, ivory interior, unpainted base, 5 spoke wheels ($7-10)(TP)

MB54-C PERSONNEL CARRIER, issued 1976

NOTE: Below models with black metal base, dot dash wheels & England casting.

1. olive body, green windows, no rear seats, silver hubs ($4-6)
2. olive body, green windows, tan rear seats, silver hubs ($4-6)
3. olive body, green windows, tan rear seats, black hubs ($4-6)
4. olive body, blue-green windows, tan rear seats, black hubs ($4-6)
5. dull olive body, green windows, tan rear seats, Manaus tab on base, black hubs ($35-50)

MB54-D MOBILE HOME, issued 1980

NOTE: Below models with orange interior, clear windows, dot dash wheels & England casting.

1. ivory body, black base, dark brown door, no tempa ($3-5)
2. ivory body, charcoal base, dark brown door, no tempa ($3-5)
3. cream body, black base, dark brown door, no tempa ($3-5)
4. cream body, charcoal base, dark brown door, no tempa ($3-5)
5. cream body, black base, chocolate door, no tempa ($3-5)
6. cream body, charcoal base, chocolate door, no tempa ($3-5)
7. white body, charcoal base, light brown door, no tempa ($3-5)
8. white body, gray-brown base, light brown door, no tempa ($3-5)
9. white body, gray-brown base, dark brown door, no tempa ($3-5)
10. white body, black base, light brown door, no tempa ($3-5)
11. white body, black base, dark brown door, no tempa ($3-5)
12. white body, charcoal base, light brown door, stripes tempa ($4-6)
13. white body, charcoal base, dark brown door, stripes tempa ($4-6)

MB54-E NASA TRACKING VEHICLE, issued 1982 (MB054)

NOTE: Below models with red interior, "NASA" roof tempa either upright or reversed.

1. white body, black base, red door, clear windows, no side tempa, dot dash wheels, England casting ($4-6)
2. white body, black base, red door, clear windows, with side tempa, dot dash wheels, England casting ($3-5)
3. white body, charcoal base, red door, clear windows, with side tempa, dot dash wheels, England casting ($3-5)
4. white body, black base, red door, clear windows, with side tempa, dot dash wheels, Macau casting ($2-3)
5. white body, black base, maroon door, clear windows, with side tempa, dot dash wheels, Macau casting ($2-3)
6. white body, black base, red door, blue windows, with side tempa, dot dash wheels, Macau casting ($3-5)
7. white body, black base, red door, blue windows, with side tempa, 8 dot wheels, Macau casting ($3-5)
8. white body, black base, maroon door, blue windows, with side tempa, dot dash wheels, Macau casting ($3-5)

MB54-F COMMAND VEHICLE, issued 1984 (MB143)

NOTE: Below models with black base & blue windows unless otherwise noted.

1. red body with white painted roof, metal base, 8 dot silver wheels, chrome beacons, red pumper, "Foam Unit" & checkerboard tempa, Macau casting ($35-50)
2. yellow body, metal base, 8 dot silver wheels, chrome beacons, red pumper, "Foam Unit 3 Metro Airport" tempa, Macau casting ($2-4)
3. red body, metal base, 8 dot silver wheels, chrome beacons, red pumper, "Foam Unit 3 Metro Airport" tempa, Macau casting ($2-3)
4. red body, metal base, dot dash wheels, chrome beacons, red pumper, "Foam Unit 3 Metro Airport" tempa, Macau casting ($2-3)
5. red body, plastic base, dot dash wheels, chrome beacons, red pumper, "Foam Unit 3 Metro Airport" tempa, Macau casting ($2-3)
6. red body, plastic base, 8 dot silver wheels, chrome beacons, red pumper, "Foam Unit 3 Metro Airport" tempa, Macau casting ($2-3)
7. red body, plastic base, 8 dot gold wheels, chrome beacons, red pumper, "Foam Unit 3 Metro Airport" tempa, Macau casting ($18-25)
8. white body, plastic base, 8 dot silver wheels, chrome beacons & radar, "NASA Space Shuttle Command Center" tempa, Macau casting ($3-4)(TC)
9. yellow body, plastic base, 8 dot silver wheels, chrome beacons, red pumper, "Foam Unit 3 Metro Airport" tempa, Macau casting ($2-3)(MP)
10. red body, plastic base, 8 dot silver wheels, chrome beacons, red pumper, "3" & Japanese lettered tempa, Macau casting ($8-12)(JP)(GS)
11. olive body, plastic base, 8 dot black wheels, black beacons & radar, "9" & red/ white stripes tempa, Macau casting ($4-5)(CM)
12. olive body, plastic base, 8 dot silver wheels, black beacons & radar, "9" & red/ white stripes tempa, Macau casting ($18-25)(CM)
13. black body, plastic base, 8 dot black wheels, dark gray beacons & radar, "LS150" & yellow stripes tempa, Macau casting ($4-5)(CM)
14. yellow body, plastic base, 8 dot silver wheels, black beacons, red pumper, "Foam Unit 3 Metro Airport" tempa, Macau casting ($2-4)
15. red body, plastic base, 8 dot silver wheels, black beacons, red pumper, "Foam Unit 3 Metro Airport" tempa, Macau casting ($2-4)
16. white body, plastic base, 8 dot silver wheels, black beacons, chrome radar, "NASA Space Shuttle Command Center" tempa, Macau casting ($2-4)
17. red body, plastic base, 8 dot silver wheels, black beacons, red pumper, "Foam Unit 3 Metro Airport" tempa, Thailand casting ($1-2)
18. yellow body, plastic base, 8 dot silver wheels, black beacons, red pumper, "Foam Unit 3 Metro Airport" tempa, Thailand casting ($1-2)
19. white body, plastic base, 8 dot silver wheels, black beacons, chrome radar, "NASA Space Shuttle Command Center" tempa, Thailand casting ($1-2)
20. florescent orange body, plastic base, 8 dot silver wheels, chrome beacons & pumper, "Foam Unit/ City Airport/ Emergency Rescue" tempa, Thailand casting ($1-2)(EM)
21. red body, plastic base, 8 dot silver wheels, silver beacons, silver pumper, "Fire Rescue" with gold crest, white band & black & gold stripes tempa, Thailand casting ($1-2)(5pk)
22. black body, smoke windows, brown plastic base, 8 dot black wheels, brown beacons, brown pumper, brown & green camouflage tempa, Thailand casting ($1-2)(5pk)
23. blue body, plastic base, 8 dot silver wheels, silver beacons, silver pumper, "Command Center" tempa, Thailand casting ($1-2)(5pk)
24. blue body, plastic base, 8 dot silver wheels, silver beacons, silver pumper, "Command Center" tempa, China casting ($1-2)(5pk)
25. black body, smoke windows, brown plastic base, 8 dot black wheels, brown beacons, brown pumper, brown & green camouflage tempa, China casting ($1-2)(5pk)

MB54-G CHEVY LUMINA, issued 1989 (MB224)

NOTE: The body casting for MB54-G is based on a redesigned casting of the MB10-D Buick LeSabre with different size window and redesigned grille. Below models with clear windows & Goodyear slicks.

1. matt pink & white body, white base, black interior, "Superflo 46" tempa, Macau casting ($6-8)(DT)
2. dark pink & white body, white base, black interior, "Superflo 46" tempa, Macau casting ($6-8)(DT)

3. matt green & lime body, green base, black interior, "City Chevrolet 46" tempa, Macau casting ($4-6)(DT)
4. bright green & lime body, green base, black interior, "City Chevrolet 46" tempa, Macau casting ($4-6)(DT)
5. bright orange & blue body, orange base, black interior, "Hardees 18" tempa, Macau casting ($6-8)(DT)
6. black body, black base, red interior, "Exxon 51" without roof signature tempa, Macau casting ($6-8)(DT)
7. black body, black base, red interior, "Exxon 51" with roof signature tempa, Macau casting ($6-8)(DT)
8. black body, green base, gray interior, "Mello Yello 51" tempa, Macau casting ($6-8)(DT)
9. white body, white base, white interior, no tempa, Thailand casting ($10-15)(GF)

NOTE: Due to the demand of "Days of Thunder" at the time, Matchbox couldn't keep up supply. They asked the company that makes Racing Champions to supply their castings and place them in Matchbox blistercards. These are quickly identified as the base of the model faces down against the blistercard. ($8-12) each.

MB54-H CHEVY LUMINA, issued 1990 (MB221)

NOTE: Below models with black base unless otherwise noted.

1. dark pink & white body, clear windows, black interior, Goodyear slicks, "Superflo 46" tempa, Macau casting ($6-8)(DT)
2. green & lime body, clear windows, black interior, Goodyear slicks, "City Chevrolet 46" tempa, Macau casting ($6-8)(DT)
3. bright orange & blue body, clear windows, black interior, Goodyear slicks, "Hardees 18" tempa, Macau casting ($6-8)(DT)
4. black body, clear windows, red interior, Goodyear slicks, large "Exxon 51" (with signature) tempa, Macau casting ($6-8)(DT)
5. black body, clear windows, red interior, Goodyear slicks, small "Exxon 51" (without signature) tempa, Macau casting ($25-40)(DT)
6. black body, clear windows, gray interior, Goodyear slicks, "Mello Yello 51" tempa, Macau casting ($4-6)(DT)
7. black body, clear windows, red interior, Goodyear slicks, "Goodwrench 3/ GM" without "Western Steer" & plain trunk tempa, Macau casting ($12-15)(WR)
8. dark blue body, clear windows, gray interior, Goodyear slicks, "Matchbox Motorsports 35" tempa, Macau casting ($2-3)
9. dark blue body, clear windows, gray interior, Goodyear slicks, "Matchbox Motorsports 35" tempa, China casting ($2-3)
10. black body, clear windows, red interior, Goodyear slicks, "Goodwrench 3/ GM" without "Western Steer" with trunk tempa, China casting ($7-10)(WR)
11. white body, clear windows, black interior, Goodyear slicks, "PG Tags" tempa, Macau casting ($85-110)(UK)(OP)
12. chrome plated body, clear windows, gray interior, Goodyear slicks, no tempa, Macau casting ($15-18)(C2)
13. white & florescent yellow body, blue-chrome & black windows, no interior, lightning wheels, blue spatter & lightning bolts tempa, China casting ($7-10)(LT)(PS)
14. white & black body, chrome & black windows, no interior, lightning wheels, pink spatter & lightning bolts tempa, China casting ($7-10)(LT)(PS)
15. black body, clear windows, red interior, black disc wheels with rubber tires, "Goodwrench 3/GM" with "Western Steer" tempa, China casting ($5-7)(WR)(TC)
16. orange-yellow body, clear windows, black interior, black disc wheels with rubber tires, "Kodak Film 4 Racing" tempa, China casting ($5-7)(WR)(TC)
17. yellow body, clear windows, black interior, Goodyear slicks, "MAC Tool Distributors 10" tempa, China casting ($15-20)(WR)
18. red & yellow body, clear windows, black interior, Goodyear slicks, "Matchbox Racing 7" tempa, China casting ($2-3)(HS)
19. white & metallic blue body, clear windows, red interior, Goodyear slicks, "Matchbox Racing 1" tempa, China casting ($2-3)(HS)
20. white body, clear windows, gray interior, Goodyear slicks, "Team Goodyear 11" tempa, China casting ($2-3)(HS)
21. orange body, clear windows, black interior, Goodyear slicks, "Team Goodyear 22" tempa, China casting ($2-3)(HS)
22. black body, clear windows, red interior, Goodyear slicks , "Champion 4" tempa, China casting ($2-3)(HS)
23. yellow body, clear windows, gray interior, Goodyear slicks, "Champion 3" tempa, China casting ($2-3)(HS)
24. orange-yellow body, clear windows, black interior, Goodyear slicks, "Kodak Film 4 Racing" tempa, China casting ($3-4)(WR)
25. florescent orange & white body, clear windows, black interior, gray disc wheels with rubber tires, "Purolator 10" tempa, China casting ($4-5)(WR)(TC)
26. dark pink & white body, clear windows, black interior, Goodyear slicks, "Superflo 46" tempa, China casting ($3-5)(DT)
27. green & lime body, clear windows, black interior, Goodyear slicks, "City Chevrolet 46" tempa, China casting ($3-5)(DT)
28. bright orange & blue body, clear windows, black interior, Goodyear slicks, "Hardees 18" tempa, China casting ($3-5)(DT)
29. black body, clear windows, red interior, Goodyear slicks, "Exxon 51" tempa, China casting ($3-5)(DT)
30. black body, clear windows, gray interior, Goodyear slicks, "Mello Yello 51" tempa, China casting ($3-5)(DT)
31. black body, clear windows, red interior, gray disc wheels with rubber tires, "Goodwrench 3/ GM" with "Western Steer" tempa, China casting ($6-8)(WR)(TC)
32. black body, clear windows, red interior, gray disc wheels with rubber tires, "Goodwrench 3/ GM" without "Western Steer" tempa, China casting ($15-25)(WR)(Winross promo)
33. matt black body, clear windows, red interior, gray disc wheels with rubber tires, "3" & "GM Parts" tempa, China casting ($15-25)(WR)(Winross promo)
34. white & green body, clear windows, silver-gray interior, gold disc wheels with rubber tires, "Hendricks 25" tempa, China casting ($6-8)(WR)(TC)
35. florescent green body, clear windows, silver-gray interior, Goodyear slicks, "Matchbox Motorsports 35" with black grille tempa, China casting ($2-3)
36. black body, clear windows, red interior, Goodyear slicks, "Goodwrench/ GM/ Mom N Pops" with "Western Steer" tempa, China casting ($6-8)(WR)(OP)
37. white & orange body, clear windows, orange interior, Goodyear slicks, "Ferree Chevrolet 49" tempa, China casting ($3-5)(WR)
38. yellow & orange body, black & chrome windows, no interior, lightning wheels, red spatter & lightning bolts tempa, China casting ($3-4)(LT)(PS)
39. green & white body, black & chrome windows, no interior, lightning wheels, purple spatter & lightning bolts tempa, China casting ($3-4)(LT)(PS)
40. dark purple & white body, clear windows, silver-gray interior, Goodyear slicks, "Phil Parsons Racing 29/ Matchbox" tempa, China casting ($12-15)(WR)
41. dark purple & white body, clear windows, silver-gray interior, Goodyear slicks, "White Rose Collectibles 29/ Matchbox" tempa, China casting ($3-5)(WR)
42. maroon body, clear windows, silver-gray interior, Goodyear slicks, "Penrose 44/ Fire Cracker Sausage/ Big Mama" tempa, China casting ($6-8)(WR)

43. lime & black body, clear windows, silver-gray interior, Goodyear slicks, "Interstate Batteries 18" tempa, China casting ($3-5)(WR)
44. metallic blue & white body, clear windows, red interior, Goodyear slicks, "Raybestos 12" tempa, China casting ($3-5)(WR)
45. metallic blue & white body, clear windows, red interior, Goodyear slicks, "Raybestos 12" without "Tic Tac" logo tempa, China casting ($75-100)(WR)
46. florescent orange & white body, clear windows, black interior, 9 spoke Goodyear slicks, "Purolator 10" tempa, China casting ($3-5)(WR)
47. florescent orange & white body, clear windows, black interior, Goodyear slicks wheels, "Purolator 10" tempa, China casting ($3-5)(WR)
48. black body, clear windows, gray interior, Goodyear slicks, "Stanley Tools 92" tempa, China casting ($3-5)(WR)
49. black body, clear windows, gray interior, 9 spoke Goodyear slicks, "Stanley Tools 92" tempa, China casting ($3-5)(WR)
50. maroon body, clear windows, silver-gray interior, Goodyear slicks, "Slim Jim 44" tempa, China casting ($6-8)(WR)
51. florescent green body, clear windows, silver-gray interior, Goodyear slicks, "Matchbox Motorsports 35" (without black grille) tempa, China casting ($1-2)
52. yellow body, clear windows, silver-gray interior, Goodyear slicks, "MAC Tools 7" tempa, China casting ($7-10)(WR)
53. lemon & white body, clear windows, gray interior, yellow disc wheels with rubber tires, "Texas Pete/ Lozito's 87" tempa, Thailand casting ($4-6)(WR)
54. black body, clear windows, red interior, 9 spoke Goodyear slicks, "Goodwrench 3/ GM" with "Western Steer" tempa, China casting ($3-5)(WR)

NOTE: Below models with clear windows unless otherwise noted.

55. black body, gray interior, Goodyear slicks, "TIC Financial 8" tempa, Thailand casting ($3-5)(WR)
56. black body, gray interior, Goodyear slicks, "Moly Black Gold 98" tempa, Thailand casting ($3-5)(WR)
57. black body, red interior, Goodyear slicks, "Ireland 31" tempa, Thailand casting ($3-5)(WR)
58. dark blue body, gray interior, Goodyear slicks, "Sunoco Ultra 94" tempa, Thailand casting ($3-5)(WR)
59. white body, red interior, Goodyear slicks, "Freedom Village/ Jasper 55" tempa, Thailand casting ($3-5)(WR)
60. white body, red interior, Goodyear slicks, "Matchbox/White Rose 29" tempa, Thailand casting ($3-5)(WR)
61. red body, gray interior, Goodyear slicks, "Performance Parts 12" tempa, Thailand casting ($1-2)
62. white body, red interior, Goodyear slicks, "Matchbox/White Rose 29- Brad's Toys" tempa, Thailand casting ($6-8)(WR)
63. white body, red interior, Goodyear slicks, "Matchbox/White Rose 29- Matchbox Road Museum" tempa, Thailand casting ($6-8)(WR)
64. white body, red interior, Goodyear slicks, "Matchbox/White Rose 29- Diecast Toy Exchange" tempa, Thailand casting ($6-8)(WR)
65. white body, red interior, Goodyear slicks, "Matchbox/White Rose 29- Craig Hill" tempa, Thailand casting ($6-8)(WR)
66. white body, red interior, Goodyear slicks, "Matchbox/White Rose 29- Cars Plus" tempa, Thailand casting ($6-8)(WR)
67. white body, red interior, Goodyear slicks, "Matchbox/White Rose 29–Kiddie Kar Kollectibles" tempa, Thailand casting ($6-8)(WR)
68. baby blue body, gray interior, Goodyear slicks, "Performance Parts 12" tempa, Thailand casting ($1-2)(MP)
69. light blue body, gray interior, Goodyear slicks, "Performance Parts 12" tempa, Thailand casting ($1-2)(5pk)
70. yellow & red body, red interior, Goodyear slicks, "Matchbox USA 12" tempa, Thailand casting ($6-8)(US)

NOTE: Above models with white-lettered slicks, below with yellow-lettered slicks unless otherwise noted

71. red & white body, silver-gray interior, Goodyear slicks, "Dentyne 87" tempa, Thailand casting ($3-5)(WR)
72. metallic blue & neon orange body, red interior, Goodyear slicks, "Dupont 24" tempa, Thailand casting ($3-5)(WR)
73. red body, gray interior, Goodyear slicks, "Active 32" tempa, Thailand casting ($3-5)(WR)
74. black body, orange interior, Goodyear slicks, "WFE 69" tempa, Thailand casting ($15-18)(WR)
75. white body, red interior, Goodyear slicks, "MW Windows/ Freedom 14" tempa, China casting ($3-5)(WR)
76. fluorescent yellow & lime body, silver-gray interior, Goodyear slicks, "Manheim 41" tempa, China casting ($3-5)(WR)
77. black body, red interior, gray disc wheels with rubber tires, "Goodwrench 3" with large "Goodwrench" on sides & revised small logos tempa, China casting ($4-7)(WR)(TC)
78. flat black body, red interior, Goodyear slicks, "GM" & "Goodwrench" tempa, China casting ($4-7)(WR)(TC)
79. black body, red interior, Goodyear slicks, "Virginia is for Lovers 25" tempa, China casting ($3-5)(WR)
80. white & blue body, red interior, Goodyear slicks, "American Zoom 93" tempa, China casting ($10-15)(WR)
81. yellow body, gray interior, Goodyear slicks, "Pic N Pay Shoes/ Shoe City 32" tempa, China casting ($3-5)(WR)
82. metallic blue body, silver-gray interior, Goodyear slicks, "Du Pont 99" tempa, China casting ($3-5)(WR)
83. blue body, black interior, Goodyear slicks, "Enck's Custom Catering 71" tempa, China casting ($3-5)(WR)
84. metallic blue & neon orange body, silver-gray interior, black disc wheels with rubber tires, "Dupont 24" tempa, China casting ($4-6)(WR)(TC)
85. gold plated body, red interior, black disc wheels with rubber tires, "Rookie of The Year 1993" tempa, China casting ($7-10)(WR)(TC)
86. yellow body, gray interior, Goodyear slicks, "De Walt 08" (gray print) tempa, China casting ($3-5)(WR)
87. yellow body, gray interior, Goodyear slicks, "De Walt 08" (lavender print) tempa, China casting ($3-5)(WR)
88. metallic turquoise & pink body, gray interior, Goodyear slicks, "FDP Brakes 9" tempa, China casting ($3-5)(WR)
89. white body, gray interior, Goodyear slicks, "Cintas 87" tempa, China casting ($7-10) (WR)
90. yellow & red body, black interior, Goodyear slicks, "Matchbox USA 13" tempa, Thailand casting ($6-8)(US)
91. dark purple body, gray interior, Goodyear slicks, "Performance Parts 12" tempa, Thailand casting ($2-4)(CC)
92. yellow body, gray interior, Goodyear slicks, "Nationwise Auto Parts" tempa, Thailand casting ($20-35)(US)
93. red body, gray interior, Goodyear slicks, white lettered "Performance Parts 12" tempa, Thailand casting ($4-6)(Aquafresh)
94. white body, red interior, Goodyear slicks, white base, no tempa, Thailand casting ($5-8)(GF)
95. silver- gray body, red interior, Goodyear slicks, "Matchbox USA 14" tempa, Thailand casting ($6-10)(US)(PL)
96. black body, red interior, black disc wheels with rubber tires, "Goodwrench 3/ Sydney Motorshow 1997", China casting ($20-30)(C2)(AU)
97. black body, red interior, black disc wheels with rubber tires, "Goodwrench 3/ Melbourne Motor Show 1997" tempa, China casting ($20-30)(C2)(AU)
98. white body, white base, red interior, Goodyear slicks, "Avis" tempa, China casting ($50+)(ASAP)
99. white body, white base, red interior, Goodyear slicks, "Drive/ A-Pix Entertainment" tempa, China casting ($50+)(ASAP)

100. white body, white base, red interior, Goodyear slicks, no tempa, China casting ($15-25)(ASAP blank)
101. white body, white base, red interior, Goodyear slicks, "98 Cutler-Hammer" tempa, China casting ($50+)(ASAP)
102. white body, white base, red interior, Goodyear slicks, "Ithaca Finish First/ 607-257-8901" tempa, China casting ($50+)(ASAP)
103. white body, white base, red interior, Goodyear slicks, "Ideal" tempa, China casting ($75+)(ASAP)
104. white body, white base, red interior, Goodyear slicks, "US Transplant Olympics- Tyler Elliot" tempa, China casting ($25-40)(CCI)
105. white body, white base, red interior, Goodyear slicks, "Ica Citrix/ CDN" tempa, China casting ($50+)(ASAP)
106. white body, white base, red interior, Goodyear slicks, "Nopa 01" tempa, China casting ($50+)(ASAP)
107. white body, white base, red interior, Goodyear slicks, "Zurich Small Business/Rally 2002" (left side only) tempa ($50+)(ASAP)
108. white body, white base, red interior, Goodyear slicks, "MRO.Com" tempa, China casting ($50+)(ASAP)
109. white body, white base, red interior, Goodyear slicks, "Compaq UPS" tempa, China casting ($50+)(ASAP)
110. white body, white base, red interior, lace wheels, "Fose 1" tempa ($50+)(ASAP)
111. white body, white base, red interior, lace wheels, no tempa ($25-40)(ASAP blank)

MB54-I MAZDA RX7 *see MB8-J*

MB54-J ABRAMS TANK, issued 1995 (USA) (MB274)
MB61-G ABRAMS TANK, issued 1995 (ROW)

NOTE: Below models with solid black wheels.

1. beige body, turret & gun, beige base, brown & white camouflage tempa, Thailand casting ($1-2)
2. olive body, turret & gun, olive base, star & "T-7521-6" & star tempa, Thailand casting ($1-2)
3. green body, turret & gun, green base, black & brown camouflage tempa, Thailand casting ($1-2)(5pk)
4. beige body & turret, black gun, black base, brown camouflage tempa, Thailand casting ($1-2)(5pk)
5. white body & turret, gray gun, gray base, gray & olive camouflage tempa, Thailand casting ($1-2)(5pk)
6. dark sand body & turret, black gun, dark sand base, "T-7521-6" & star tempa, Thailand casting ($2-4)(MP)
7. olive body & turret, gray gun, black base, gray & brown camouflage tempa, Thailand casting ($1-2)(PS)
8. black body, turret & gun, black base, rose & white design tempa, Thailand casting ($3-5)(AU)
9. black body & turret , brown gun, brown base, green & brown camouflage tempa, Thailand casting ($1-2)(5pk)
10. black body & turret, brown gun, brown base, green & brown camouflage tempa, China casting ($1-2)(5pk)
11. matt olive body & turret, black gun & base, black & tan camouflage tempa, China casting ($4-6)(PC)
12. dark olive body & turret, black gun & base, "476 BD98675" tempa, China casting ($1-2)(MW84/1999 US)
13. beige body & turret, gray gun, black base, "Force" tempa, China casting ($1-2)(HR)

NOTE: Above model with Matchbox International or Mattel casting.

MB54-K FORD CROWN VICTORIA POLICE CAR, issued 1997 (USA) (MB304/459/466)
MB38-J FORD CROWN VICTORIA POLICE CAR, issued 1997 (ROW)

NOTE: Below models listed with clear windows & black plastic base, unless otherwise noted.

1. blue body, red dome lights, gray interior, 8 dot wheels, "D-22 Police" tempa, Thailand casting ($2-4)
2. black body, red dome lights, gray interior, 5 spoke concave star wheels, "D-22 Police" tempa, Thailand casting ($1-2)(MW28/1998)
3. dark burgundy body, red dome lights, black & gray interior, chrome disc wheels with rubber tires, "State Police "(Minnesota) tempa, Thailand casting ($3-5)(PC18)
4. white body, blue & red dome lights, black & gray interior, chrome disc wheels with rubber tires, "SD Highway Patrol" tempa, Thailand casting ($3-5)(PC18)
5. black body, blue dome lights, black & gray interior, chrome disc wheels with rubber tires, "Montana Highway Patrol" tempa, Thailand casting ($3-5)(PC18)
6. black body, red dome lights, gray interior, 5 spoke concave star wheels, "D-22 Police" tempa, China casting ($1-2)(MW28/1998)
7. white body, red dome lights, gray interior, 5 spoke concave star wheels, "Drive/ A-Pix Entertainment" tempa, China casting ($100+)(ASAP)
8. metallic gold body, red dome lights, black interior, 5 spoke concave star wheels, no tempa, China casting ($5-10)(CH)
9. white body, red dome lights, gray interior, 5 spoke concave star wheels, no tempa, China casting ($25-40)(ASAP blank)
10. blue body, red dome lights, gray interior, 5 spoke concave star wheels, "Police K-9 Canine Unit" tempa, China casting ($1-2)(MP)
11. white body, red dome light, black & blue interior, chrome disc wheels with rubber wheels, "North Dakota State Patrol" tempa, China casting ($4-6)(PC)
12. white body, red & blue dome light, black & blue interior, chrome disc wheels with rubber tires, "Missouri State" tempa, China casting ($4-6)(PC)
13. white body, red dome light, gray interior, 5 spoke concave star wheels, "IACP" tempa, China casting ($50+)(ASAP)
14. white body, red dome light, gray interior, 5 spoke concave star wheels, "Aegis NT New World Systems" tempa, China casting ($35-75)(ASAP)
15. white body, red & blue dome light, black & tan interior, chrome disc wheels with rubber tires, "Dallas Police" tempa , China casting ($250-400)(PC22)
16. white body, blue dome lights, black & blue interior, chrome disc wheels with rubber tires, "Atlanta Police" tempa, China casting ($200-250)(PC22)
17. white body, red dome lights, gray interior, 5 spoke concave star wheels, "Route 66 Promotions" tempa , China casting ($15-25)(ASAP)
18. white body, red & blue dome light, gray interior, 5 spoke concave star wheels, "Police" & blue checkers tempa , China casting ($15-20)(AU)
19. blue body, red dome lights, gray interior, 5 spoke concave star wheels, "Police" with red & white design tempa, China casting ($1-2)(MW33/1999 US)
20. white body, red dome lights, gray interior, 5 spoke concave star wheels, "Freeport Police" tempa, China casting ($20-35)(ASAP)
21. white body, red dome lights, gray interior, 5 spoke concave star wheels, "Nassau County Police" tempa, China casting ($20-35)(ASAP)
22. white body, red & blue dome light, gray interior, 5 spoke concave star wheels, "Police/ DARE" tempa, China casting ($3-5)(DR)
23. black body, red triangular dome lights, gray interior, 5 spoke concave star wheels, "Wanaque Police/ DARE" tempa, China casting ($3-5)(DR)

24. gray body, red dome lights, light blue interior, chrome disc wheels with rubber tires, "Rhode Island State Police" tempa, China casting ($5-8)(PC)
25. white body, red & blue dome lights, black interior, 5 spoke concave star wheels, "Police Landover Hills/ DARE" tempa, China casting ($3-5)(DR)
26. white body, red triangular dome lights, orange interior, smoke windows, 5 spoke concave star wheels, "Ocean City Police" with orange & blue stripes tempa, China casting ($1-2)(MW86/2000 US)
27. white body, red triangular dome lights, orange interior, smoke windows, 5 spoke concave star wheels, "Ocean City Police" with orange & blue stripes & "Matchbox 2000" tempa, China casting ($2-4)(MW86/2000 US)
28. white body, red triangular dome lights, orange interior, smoke windows, star with 5 spokes wheels, "Ocean City Police" with orange & blue stripes tempa, China casting ($1-2)(MW86/2000 US)
29. blue body, red dome lights, dark gray interior, clear windows, star with 5 spokes wheels, red & yellow stripes with crest tempa, China casting ($1-2)(5pk)
30. blue body, red dome lights, dark gray interior, clear windows, 5 spoke concave star wheels, red & yellow stripes with crest tempa, China casting ($3-5)(5pk)
31. white body, red triangular roof lights, black interior, smoke windows, 5 spoke concave star wheels, no tempa, China casting ($25-40)(CCI blank)
32. white body, red triangular dome lights, black interior, clear windows, 5 spoke concave star wheels, "DARE" & blue flames tempa, China casting ($3-5)(DR)
33. white body, red triangular dome lights, black interior, clear windows, star with 5 spokes wheels, "Justice for Police Officer Daniel Faulkner/ 4699/ Philadelphia Police" tempa, China casting ($25+)(CCI)
34. white body, red triangular dome lights, black interior, clear windows, star with 5 spokes wheels, "Verona Police/ Verona PBA" tempa, China casting ($20-30)(CCI)
35. white body, red triangular dome lights, black interior, clear windows, star with 5 spokes wheels, "Verona Police" tempa, China casting ($20-30)(CCI)
36. white body, red dome lights, gray interior, clear windows, 5 spoke concave star wheels, "Verona Police" tempa, China casting ($50+)(CCI)
37. black & white body, red dome lights, clear windows, gray interior, star with 5 spokes wheels, "Police D-19" tempa, China casting ($4-6)(PS)
38. white body, red triangular dome lights, clear windows, black interior, star with 5 spokes wheels, "Police/ To Serve & Protect Scotchguard" tempa, China casting ($25+)(CCI)
39. white body, red triangular dome lights, orange interior, smoke windows, star with 5 spokes wheels, "Ocean City police" with orange & blue stripes tempa, metal base, Mattel China casting ($2-3)(MW86/2000 US)
40. blue body, red dome lights, dark gray interior, clear windows, star with 5 spokes wheels, red & yellow stripes with crest tempa, metal base, Mattel China casting ($12-15)(EG)
41. white body, red triangular dome lights, dark blue interior, clear windows, 10 spoke flower wheels, "Police" with red & blue stripes tempa, metal base, Mattel China casting (MW32/ 2001 ROW)
42. white body, red bar dome lights, gray interior, clear windows, 5 spoke concave star wheels, "National Law Enforcement Officers Memorial 2001" tempa, China casting ($50+)(ASAP)
43. white body, red triangular dome lights, black interior, clear windows, star with 5 spokes wheels, "If You Don't Collect Matchbox... Get Out of the Way" tempa, China casting ($25-30)(CCI)
44. white body, red triangular dome lights, black interior, clear windows, star with 5 spokes wheels, "C.E.R.T./ Toy Show Police/ Color Comp Emergency Response Team/ Emergency Demo Model" tempa, China casting ($25-40)(CCI)
45. white body, red bar dome lights, gray interior, clear windows, 5 spoke concave star wheels, blue logo decal, China casting ($20-35)(ASAP)
46. black body, blue bar dome lights, black interior, smoke windows, lace wheels, "MBI Special Agents" & "X" tempa, metal base, China casting ($1-2)(MW49/2001 US)
47. white body, red triangular dome lights, black interior, clear windows, star with 5 spokes tempa, Franklin Township Police" tempa, China casting ($25-40)(CCI)
48. white body, red triangular dome lights, black interior, clear windows, star with 5 spokes tempa, "Support Your local Police/ Bill Cairns Realtor" tempa, China casting ($10-15)(CCI)
49. bright blue body, red bar dome lights, gray interior, amber windows, lace wheels, "Math", numbers, apples, balls & pears tempa, metal base, Mattel China casting ($1-2)(5pk)
50. white body, red bar dome lights, red interior, clear windows, lace wheels, "Police USA", flag & eagle tempa, metal base, China casting ($1-2)(HR)
51. white body, red bar dome lights, gray interior, clear windows, 5 spoke concave star wheels, "Open Sky" tempa, China casting ($50+)(ASAP)
52. white body, red triangular dome lights, black interior, smoke windows, star with 5 spokes wheels, "In Memory of Our Fallen Heroes" tempa, China casting ($25-40)(CCI)
53. white body, red triangular dome lights, black interior, smoke windows, star with 5 spokes wheels, "Jonelle's Crown Vic Page" tempa, China casting ($12-18)(CCI)
54. black body, blue bar dome lights, black interior, smoke windows, 10 spoke flower wheels, "Police 911" & yellow design tempa, metal base, Mattel China casting ($1-2)(MW13/2002 US)
55. black body, blue bar dome lights, black interior, smoke windows, 10 spoke flower wheels, "Police 911", yellow design & "Matchbox 50" tempa, metal base, China casting ($3-5)(MW13/2002 US)
56. white body, red triangular dome lights, black interior, smoke windows, star with 5 spokes wheels, "Police- Grosse Pointe Park" (plain roof) tempa, China casting ($18-25)(CCI)
57. white body, red triangular dome lights, black interior, smoke windows, star with 5 spokes wheels, "Police- Grosse Pointe Park" with "174" on roof tempa, China casting ($18-25)(CCI)
58. white body, blue bar dome lights, dark blue interior, amber windows, "Police" & orange stripes tempa, metal base, Mattel China casting ($2-4)(MW25/2002 ROW)
59. white body, blue bar dome lights, dark blue interior, amber windows, "Police", orange stripes & "Matchbox 50" tempa, metal base, Mattel China casting ($2-4)(MW25/2002 ROW)
60. blue body, amber bar dome lights, gray interior, clear windows, "Police USA", flag & eagle tempa, metal base, Mattel China casting ($1-2)(MP)(HR)
61. white body, red triangular dome lights, black interior, smoke windows, star with 5 spokes wheels, "Great Strides" tempa, China casting ($12-18)(CCI)
62. white body, red triangular dome lights, black interior, smoke windows, star with 5 spokes wheels, "Sheriff 280/ Patrol 8" tempa, China casting ($15-20)(CCI)
63. white body, red triangular dome lights, black interior, smoke windows, star with 5 spokes wheels, "Fire Marshall/ Inspector 7" tempa, China casting ($15-20)(CCI)
64. white body, red triangular dome lights, black interior, smoke windows, star with 5 spokes wheels, "Matchbox 50th Birthday Party/ Illinois Matchbox Club Security 2002", China casting ($12-18)(CCI)

65. black body, red bar dome lights, black interior, smoke windows, 10 spoke flower wheels, "17 Ohio Buckeye Police" tempa, China casting ($5-8)(AM)
66. white body, blue bar dome lights, black interior, smoke windows, star with 5 spokes wheels, "Sheriff's Office" tempa, China casting ($15-20)(CCI)
67. maroon body, red bar dome lights, white interior, smoke windows, lace wheels, "Station 02" tempa, metal base, China casting ($1-2)(5pk)
68. maroon body, red bar dome lights, white interior, smoke windows, lace wheels, "Station 02" tempa, China casting ($1-2)(5pk)
69. light maroon body, red bar dome lights, white interior, smoke windows, lace wheels, "Station 02" tempa, China casting ($1-2)(5pk)
70. white body, red bar dome lights, black interior, amber windows, lace wheels, "14/ Matchbox FDMB" & flames tempa, metal base, Mattel China casting ($1-2)(LP)
71. white body, blue bar dome lights, black interior, amber windows, lace wheels, "14/ Matchbox FDMB" & flames tempa, metal base, Mattel China casting ($1-2)(LP)
72. white body, blue bar & dome lights, black interior, amber windows, lace wheels, "14/ Matchbox FDMB" & flames tempa, Mattel China casting ($1-2)(LP)
73. white body, red bar dome lights, black interior, amber windows, lace wheels, "14/ Matchbox FDMB" & flames tempa, Mattel China casting ($1-2)(LP)
74. white body, red triangular dome lights, black interior, smoke windows, star with 5 spokes wheels, "Police/ Gerard Vincent 10-18-02" tempa, China casting ($12-18)(CCI)
75. white body, red triangular dome lights, black interior, smoke windows, star with 5 spokes wheels, "NYPD/ Chase-U Collectibles" tempa, China casting ($18-25)(CCI)
76. white body, red triangular dome lights, black interior, smoke windows, 5 spoke concave star wheels, "Illinois Matchbox Club Security 2003" tempa, China casting ($12-18)(CCI)
77. white body, red triangular dome lights, black interior, smoke windows, star with 5 spokes wheels, "Illinois Matchbox Club Security 2003" tempa, China casting ($12-18)(CCI)
78. white body, blue bar dome lights, black interior, smoke windows, 5 spoke concave star wheels, "Sheriff Frederick County" tempa, China casting ($12-18)(CCI)
79. white body, red triangular dome lights, black interior, smoke windows, 5 spoke concave star wheels, "MJ Employee Patrol 1533" tempa, China casting ($50+)(CCI)
80. light blue body, red bar dome lights, white interior, smoke windows, lace wheels, "Rescue Heroes" tempa, China casting ($1-2)(CA)
81. white body, red triangular dome lights, black interior, smoke windows, star with 5 spokes wheels, "Party Patrol- Happy Birthday" tempa, China casting ($12-18)(CCI)
82. white body, red triangular dome lights, black interior, smoke windows, star with 5 spokes wheels, "Matchbox Toy Show-On Site Demo/ Little Cars... Big City Police" (blue print) tempa, China casting ($12-18)(CCI)
83. white body, red triangular dome lights, black interior, smoke windows, star with 5 spokes wheels, "Matchbox Toy Show-On Site Demo/ Little Cars... Big City Police" (black print) tempa, China casting ($12-18)(CCI)
84. white body, red triangular dome lights, black interior, smoke windows, star with 5 spokes wheels, "Bowmac PD/ Police" tempa, China casting ($20-35)(CCI)
85. white body, blue bar dome lights, black interior, smoke windows, star with 5 spokes wheels, "Police Stephens City" tempa, China casting ($20-25)(CCI)
86. white body, red bar dome lights, gray interior, clear windows, 5 spoke concave star wheels, "University Park Police" tempa, China casting ($50+)(ASAP)
87. white body, red bar dome lights, gray interior, clear windows, 5 spoke concave star wheels, "Covington Police" tempa, China casting ($50+)(ASAP)
88. white body, red bar dome lights, gray interior, clear windows, 5 spoke concave star wheels, "Cherry Hill Police" tempa, China casting ($50+)(ASAP)
89. white body, red bar dome lights, gray interior, clear windows, 5 spoke concave star wheels, "Macom" tempa, China casting ($50+)(ASAP)
90. white body, red bar dome light, gray interior, clear windows, 5 spoke concave star wheels, "Alliance" tempa, China casting ($50+)(ASAP)
91. black body, red bar dome light, blue interior, clear windows, lace wheels, "Police" with crest & red stripes tempa, China casting ($1-2)

MB54-L HOLDEN COMMODORE, issued 1997 (AU) (MB294)
MB64-H HOLDEN COMMODORE, issued 1998 (ROW)

NOTE: Below models listed with clear windows, black plastic base & China casting unless otherwise noted.

1. white body, white interior, chrome disc wheels with rubber tires, Thailand casting, "Castrol 11" tempa ($15-20)(AU)
2. metallic silver body, black interior, chrome disc wheels with rubber tires, "Australia's First" tempa ($10-15)(IG)(AU)
3. unpainted body, black interior, chrome disc wheels with rubber tires, 5 spoke concave star wheels, no tempa ($10-15)(IG)(AU)
4. white body, white interior & base, 5 spoke concave star wheels, "Commodore Race Team 25" tempa ($3-5)(AU)
5. red & dark blue body, white interior, 5 spoke concave star wheels, "Bulldogs 1998" tempa ($3-5)(AU)
6. red & dark blue body, white interior, 5 spoke concave star wheels "Demons 1998" tempa ($3-5)(AU)
7. red & black body, white interior, 5 spoke concave star wheels, "Bombers 1998" tempa ($3-5)(AU)
8. red & green body, white interior, 5 spoke concave star wheels, "Fremantle 1998" tempa ($3-5)(AU)
9. white & red body, white interior, 5 spoke concave star wheels, "Saints 1998" tempa ($3-5)(AU)
10. white & black body, white interior, 5 spoke concave star wheels, "Magpies 1998" tempa ($3-5)(AU)
11. turquoise & black body, white interior, 5 spoke concave star wheels, "Power 1998" tempa ($3-5)(AU)
12. yellow & brown body, white interior, 5 spoke concave star wheels, "Hawks 1998" tempa ($3-5)(AU)
13. pumpkin body, blue interior, 5 spoke concave star wheels, white design with "99 Holden Commodore" tempa (MW64/ 1998 ROW)
14. white body, black interior, smoke windows, 5 spoke concave star wheels, "Holden" & red design tempa ($2-4)(MW11/2000 AU)
15. metallic silver body, black interior, chrome disc wheels with rubber tires, "50th Anniversary" tempa ($12-18)(C2)
16. unpainted body, black interior, chrome disc wheels with rubber tires, "50" tempa ($12-18)(C2)
17. silver-gray body, dark blue interior, smoke windows, 5 spoke concave star wheels, "Olympic Torch Relay" tempa ($8-12)(AU)

MB54-M CHEVY K-1500 PICKUP *see MB72-O*

MB54-N WHITE WATER RAFT BOAT *see MB59-J*

MB54-O TANKER TRUCK, issued 2002 (MB529/583)

NOTE: Below models with amber windows, stationary rear cast hose, gray plastic base & China casting unless otherwise noted.

1. metallic red body, transparent blue tank with silver-gray cap, amber windows, 4 spoke domed wheels, "H2O Patrol" tempa, rear hose pulls out ($1-2)(MW54/2002)
2. metallic red body, transparent blue tank with silver-gray cap, amber windows, 4 spoke domed wheels, "H2O Patrol" & "Matchbox 50" tempa, rear hose pulls out ($2-4)(MW54/2002)
3. metallic red body, transparent blue tank with silver-gray cap, amber windows, 4 spoke domed wheels, "H2O Patrol" tempa ($1-2)(EG)(PS)
4. metallic red body, transparent blue tank with silver-gray cap, amber windows, 7 spoke sawblade wheels, "H2O Patrol" tempa ($1-2)(EG)
5. maroon body, white tank with silver-gray cap, amber windows, 4 spoke domed wheels, "Station 02" tempa ($1-2)(5pk)
6. maroon body, white tank with silver-gray cap, amber windows, 7 spoke sawblade wheels, "Station 02" tempa ($1-2)(5pk)
7. white body, transparent blue tank with gray cap, blue-green windows, 7 spoke sawblade wheels, fish design & "48" tempa, light gray base ($1-2)(MW48/2003)
8. white body, transparent blue tank with gray cap, blue-green windows, 7 spoke sawblade wheels, fish design & "48" with "Hero City", light gray base ($2-4)(MW48/2003)
9. red body, yellow tank with gray cap, amber windows, 7 spoke sawblade wheels, "Rescue Heroes" tempa, black base ($1-2)(CA)
10. white body, transparent blue tank with silver-gray cap, blue-green windows, 7 spoke sawblade wheels, "H2O Patrol" tempa, light gray base ($75-100)(EG)
11. red body, transparent blue tank with red cap, amber windows, 7 spoke sawblade wheels, "HCFD Alarm 04 Unit" tempa ($1-2)(5pk)

MB55-A MERCURY POLICE CAR, issued 1970

NOTE: Below models with clear windows, ivory interior, shield hood & side labels, 5 spoke wheels & England casting.

1. white body, unpainted base, blue dome light ($15-20)
2. white body, unpainted base, red dome light ($15-20)

MB55-B MERCURY POLICE COMMUTER, issued 1971

NOTE: Below models with clear windows, clear windows, 5 spoke wheels & England.

1. white body, unpainted base, shield hood & side labels, red dome lights ($15-18)
2. white body, unpainted base, red & yellow "Police" hood & side labels, red dome lights ($15-18)
3. white body, silver-gray base, red & yellow "Police" hood & side labels, red dome lights ($15-18)
4. white body, unpainted base, red & yellow "Police" hood label only, red dome lights ($15-18)
5. white body, silver-gray base, red & yellow "Police" hood label only, red dome lights ($15-18)
6. white body, unpainted base, red & yellow "Police" hood & side labels, amber dome lights ($125-175)
7. white body, unpainted base with Manaus tab, red & yellow "Police" hood label only, red dome lights ($50-75)
8. metallic blue body, unpainted base with Manaus tab, stars & stripes side labels (cut from MB48-B), red dome lights ($250+)(BR)

MB55-C HELLRAISER, issued 1975

NOTE: Below models with 5 crown front & dot dash rear wheels, England casting unless otherwise noted.

1. white body, unpainted base, red interior, clear windshield, stars & stripes label ($15-18)
2. white body, unpainted base, red interior, clear windshield, stars & stripes label, dot dash front wheels ($15-18)
3. white body, unpainted base with Manaus label, red interior, clear windshield, stars & stripes label ($35-50)
4. white body, unpainted base with Manaus etched, red interior, clear windshield, stars & stripes label ($35-50)
5. metallic blue body, unpainted base, ivory interior, clear windshield, stars & stripes label ($12-15)
6. metallic blue body, silver-gray base, ivory interior, clear windshield, stars & stripes label ($12-15)
7. metallic blue body, silver-gray base, ivory interior, clear windshield, no label ($12-15)
8. metallic blue body, silver-gray base, red interior, clear windshield, stars & stripes label ($12-15)
9. metallic blue body, silver-gray base, red interior, amber windshield, stars & stripes label ($12-15)
10. metallic blue body, silver-gray base, red interior, clear windshield, "3" label ($12-15)
11. metallic blue body, silver-gray base, ivory interior, clear windshield, "3" label ($12-15)
12. metallic blue body, unpainted base, red interior, amber windshield, no label ($12-15)

MB55-D FORD CORTINA, issued 1979 (MB055)

1. green body, unpainted base, red interior, clear windows, no tempa, dot dash wheels, doors open, England casting ($4-6)
2. metallic green body, unpainted base, red interior, clear windows, no tempa, dot dash wheels, doors open, England casting ($4-6)
3. bright metallic green body, unpainted base, light yellow interior, clear windows, no tempa, dot dash wheels, doors open, England casting ($4-6)
4. metallic red body, unpainted base, light yellow interior, clear windows, no tempa, dot dash wheels, doors open, England casting ($4-6)
5. light metallic tan body, unpainted base, light yellow interior, clear windows, black stripe tempa, dot dash wheels, doors open, England casting ($3-5)
6. light metallic tan body, unpainted base, white interior, clear windows, black stripe tempa, dot dash wheels, doors open, England casting ($3-5)
7. light metallic tan body, unpainted base, white interior, clear windows, black stripe tempa, 5 arch wheels, doors open, England casting ($3-5)
8. light metallic tan body, silver-gray base, white interior, clear windows, black stripe tempa, dot dash wheels, doors open, England casting ($3-5)
9. light metallic tan body, unpainted base, white interior, clear windows,. no tempa, dot dash wheels, doors open, England casting ($3-5)
10. light metallic tan body, silver-gray base, white interior, opaque white windows, no tempa, dot dash wheels, doors open, England casting ($60-85)
11. red body, silver-gray base, white interior, opaque white windows, no tempa, dot dash wheels, doors cast, England casting ($12-15)(PS)
12. red body, unpainted base, white interior, opaque white windows, no tempa, dot dash wheels, doors cast, England casting ($12-15)(PS)
13. red body, silver-gray base, white interior, clear windows, no tempa, dot dash wheels, doors cast, England casting ($3-5)
14. red body, unpainted base, white interior, clear windows, no tempa, dot dash wheels, doors cast, England casting ($3-5)
15. red body, black base, white interior, clear windows, no tempa, dot dash wheels, doors cast, England casting ($3-5)
16. red body, silver-gray base, white interior, clear windows, black stripe tempa, dot dash wheels, doors cast, England casting ($3-5)(TP)

17. red body, unpainted base, white interior, clear windows, black stripe tempa, dot dash wheels, doors cast, England casting ($3-5)(TP)
18. red body, unpainted base, brown interior, clear windows, black stripe tempa, dot dash wheels, doors cast shut, England casting ($3-5)(TP)
19. red body, black base, white interior, opaque white windows, no tempa, dot dash wheels, doors cast shut, England casting ($12-15)(PS)
20. red body, silver-gray base, white interior, clear windows, white & orange flames tempa, dot dash wheels, doors cast, China casting ($150-200)(CHI)
21. orange-red body, black base, yellow interior, clear windows, "Nigel Cooper for Matchbox Toys/ Christmas 96" tempa, dot dash wheels, doors cast, Bulgaria casting ($35-50)(UK)
22. red body, silver-gray base, white interior, clear windows, no tempa, dot dash wheels, doors cast, China casting ($7-10)(MP)
NOTE: Available as a Bulgarian casting. Assorted colors available. ($5-25)

MB55-E FORD SIERRA *see MB15-D*

MB55-F PORSCHE, issued 1983 (USA) (MB118)
MB41-E RACING PORSCHE, issued 1983 (ROW)
NOTE: Below models with black plastic base & clear windows unless otherwise noted.
1. powder blue body, black interior, 8 dot silver wheels, "Elf 71 Sachs" tempa, Macau casting ($2-4)
2. baby blue body, black interior, 8 dot silver wheels, "Elf 71 Sachs" tempa, Macau casting ($2-4)
3. white body, black interior, 8 dot silver wheels, "Cadbury Buttons" tempa, Macau casting ($8-12)(UK)
4. red body, black interior, starburst wheels, "Autotech 35" tempa, Macau casting ($3-5)(SF)
5. metallic red body, black interior, laser wheels, "Autotech 35" tempa, Macau casting ($3-5)(LW)
6. white body, black interior, 8 dot gold wheels, "Porsche 10" tempa, Macau casting ($4-6)
7. white body, black interior, 8 dot silver wheels, "Porsche 10" tempa, Macau casting ($2-4)
8. baby blue body, black interior, 8 dot gold wheels, "Elf 71 Sachs" tempa, Macau casting ($40-65)
9. black body, black interior, 8 dot silver wheels, "11 Ox Racing Team" tempa, Macau casting ($8-12)(HK)
10. red body, tan interior, 8 dot silver wheels, "41 Porsche" tempa, Macau casting ($1-2)
11. red body, tan interior, 8 dot silver wheels, "Porsche" logo tempa, Thailand casting ($2-4)(MC)
12. yellow body, tan interior, 8 dot silver wheels, "Porsche 10" tempa, Macau casting ($2-4)(MP)
13. lemon body, no interior, gray disc wheels with rubber tires, chrome windows, detailed trim tempa, China casting ($5-8)(WC)
14. white body, no interior, lightning wheels, blue-chrome & black windows, orange stripes with "935" tempa, China casting ($2-4)(LT)
15. black body, no interior, lightning wheels, black & chrome windows, lime stripes with "935" tempa, China casting ($2-4)(LT)
16. iridescent cream body, gray interior, gray disc with rubber tires, chrome windows, detailed trim tempa, China casting ($5-8)(WC)
17. yellow body, black interior, 8 dot silver wheels, "Porsche 10" tempa, Thailand casting ($2-4)(MP)
18. powder blue body, black interior, dot dash wheels, "SAR Porsche 71 Sachs" tempa, silver-gray base, Manaus casting ($35-50)(BR)
19. powder blue body, black interior, 8 dot silver wheels, "SAR Porsche 71 Sachs" tempa, silver-gray base, Manaus casting ($35-50)(BR)
20. white body, black interior, 8 dot wheels, "Elf/ Porsche/71 Sachs" with green wavy line & lavender stripes tempa, silver-gray base, Manaus casting ($35-50)(BR)

MB55-G MERCURY SABLE WAGON, issued 1987 (USA) (MB193)
MB33-F MERCURY SABLE WAGON, issued 1989 (ROW)
1. white body, gray base, silver-gray interior, clear windows, 8 dot wheels, gray side stripe tempa, white painted hatch, Macau casting ($2-4)
2. white body, gray base, silver-gray interior, clear windows, 8 dot wheels, gray side stripe tempa, white painted hatch, China casting ($2-4)
3. white body, gray base, silver-gray interior, clear windows, 8 dot wheels, light gray side stripe tempa, clear hatch, China casting ($25-40)(CHI)
4. pea green body, tan interior, silver-gray base, clear windows, 8 dot wheels, woodgrain sides & "The Brady Bunch" tempa, lime painted hatch, China casting ($4-6)(STR)

MB55-H ROLLS ROYCE SILVER SPIRIT *see MB66-F*

MB55-I MODEL A FORD *see MB73-C*

MB55-J FLARESIDE PICKUP *see MB53-D*

MB55-K FLARESIDE PICKUP with LOAD, issued 1994 (WR) (MB266)
NOTE: Below models below with chrome base, black interior, white rear load, slicks with gray inserts wheels.
1. gold body, "Royals 94" tempa ($3-5)(WR)
2. gold body, "Astros 94" tempa ($3-5)(WR)
3. silver-gray body, "White Sox 94" tempa ($3-5)(WR)
4. black body, "Pirates 94" tempa ($3-5)(WR)
5. black body, "Orioles 94" tempa ($3-5)(WR)
6. black body, "Reds 94" tempa ($3-5)(WR)
7. red body, "Phillies 94" tempa ($3-5)(WR)
8. red body, "Yankees 94" tempa ($3-5)(WR)
9. red body, "Indians 94" tempa ($3-5)(WR)
10. red body, "Cubs 94" tempa ($3-5)(WR)
11. dark green body, "Athletics 94" tempa ($3-5)(WR)
12. dark green body, "Brewers 94-25th Anniversary" tempa ($3-5)(WR)
13. blue-green body, "Marlins 94" tempa ($3-5)(WR)
14. dark blue-green body, "Mariners 94" tempa ($3-5)(WR)
15. purple body, "Rockies 94" tempa ($3-5)(WR)
16. dark blue body, "Angels 94" tempa ($3-5)(WR)
17. blue body, "Mets 94" tempa ($3-5)(WR)
18. blue body, "Dodgers 94" tempa ($3-5)(WR)
19. blue body, "St. Louis Cardinals 94" tempa ($3-5)(WR)
20. blue body, "Expos 94" tempa ($3-5)(WR)
21. dull blue body, "Twins 94" tempa ($3-5)(WR)
22. metallic blue body, "Braves 94" tempa ($3-5)(WR)
23. light blue body, "Blue Jays 94" tempa ($3-5)(WR)
24. dark gray body, "Red Sox 94" tempa ($3-5)(WR)
25. khaki gray body, "Rangers 94" tempa ($3-5)(WR)
26. orange body, "Tigers 94" tempa ($3-5)(WR)
27. orange body, "Giants 94" tempa ($3-5)(WR)
28. orange body, "Padres 94" tempa ($3-5)(WR)
29. dark blue body, "Penn State Nittany Lions 94" tempa ($4-6)(WR)
30. white body, "Baltimore Football 1994" tempa ($4-6)(WR)

MB55-L PORSCHE BOXSTER, issued 1999 (USA) (MB356)
MB50-K PORSCHE BOXSTER, issued 1999 (ROW)

NOTE: Below models with clear windshield, black plastic base & China casting unless otherwise noted.

1. silver-gray body, red-brown interior, 5 spoke concave star wheels, no tempa ($1-2)(MW55/1999 US/GR)(MW50/1999 ROW)
2. candy apple red body, gray & black interior, chrome disc wheels with rubber tires, detailed trim tempa ($5-8)(FE)
3. unpainted body, gray interior, chrome disc wheels with rubber tires, no tempa ($5-8)(FE)
4. silver-gray body, red-brown interior, 5 spoke concave star wheels, "Grand Opening Mattel- Die-Cast Factory/ Matchbox" tempa ($200-300)(CCI)
5. silver-gray body, red-brown interior, 5 spoke concave star wheels, silver trim on windshield tempa ($3-5)(MW55/1999 US)
6. silver-gray body, black interior, 5 spoke concave star wheels, "Matchbox 2000" tempa ($2-4)(MW5/2000 US)
7. silver-gray body, black interior, 5 spoke concave star wheels, no tempa ($1-2)(MW5/2000)
8. silver-gray body, black interior, star with 5 spokes wheels, no tempa ($1-2)(MW5/2000)
9. silver-gray body, red-brown interior, star with 5 spokes wheels, none tempa ($2-4)(MW50/1999 ROW)
10. blue body, red-brown interior, blue windshield, 5 spoke concave star wheels, "Millennium Convention" tempa ($20-35)(CCI)
11. purple body, black interior, purple windshield, 5 spoke concave star wheels, "Millennium Toy Show" tempa ($7-10)(CCI)
12. light green body, light brown interior, light smoke windshield, 10 spoke flower wheels, gold stripe & "Porsche/ Boxster" tempa ($1-2)(5pk)
13. silver-gray body, black interior, clear windshield, star with 5 spokes wheels, "CFS Bowl 2000" tempa ($50+)(ASAP)
14. light metallic red body, dark gray interior, clear windshield with red trim, 10 spoke flower wheels, head lights tempa ($3-5)(MW64/2001 GR)
15. silver-gray body, black interior, clear windshield, star with 5 spokes wheels, inverted "V" tempa ($50+)(ASAP)
16. yellow body, black interior, clear windshield with yellow trim, lace wheels, small "Porsche" logo tempa ($2-4)(MW5/2002 ROW)
17. yellow body, black interior, clear windshield with yellow trim, lace wheels, small "Porsche" logo & "Matchbox 50" tempa ($3-5)(MW5)
18. yellow body, black interior, clear windshield with yellow trim, lace wheels, "49 During 50" tempa ($12-18)(CCI)
19. red body, gray interior, smoke windshield, 10 spoke flower wheels, no tempa ($4-6)(SG)
20. unpainted body, gray interior, smoke windshield, 10 spoke flower wheels, pop art decals ($75+)(FA)
21. silver-gray body, red-brown interior, clear windshield, 5 spoke concave star wheels, "Exclusive Bodywerks" tempa ($18-25)(CCI)
22. silver-gray body, red-brown interior, clear windshield, star with 5 spokes wheels, "Exclusive Bodywerks" tempa ($18-25)(CCI)
23. silver-gray body, black interior, clear windshield, star with 5 spokes wheels, "Exclusive Bodywerks" tempa ($18-25)(CCI)
24. silver-gray body, black interior, clear windshield, 5 spoke concave star wheels, "Exclusive Bodywerks" tempa ($18-25)(CCI)
25. white body, black interior, clear windshield, lace wheels, tail lights & small :Matchbox" logo tempa ($1-2)(5pk)
26. silver-gray body, red-brown interior, clear windshield, star with 5 spokes wheels, "MIS/ Medical Imaging Systems" tempa ($12-18)(CCI)
27. silver-gray body, red-brown interior, clear windshield, 5 spoke concave star wheels, "MIS/ Medical Imaging Systems" tempa ($12-18)(CCI)
28. silver-gray body, black interior, clear windshield, 5 spoke concave star wheels, "MIS/ Medical Imaging Systems" tempa ($12-18)(CCI)
29. silver-gray body, black interior, clear windshield, star with 5 spokes wheels, "MIS/ Medical Imaging Systems" tempa ($12-18)(CCI)
30. red body, gray interior, smoke windshield, 10 spoke flower wheels, "5.10.2003 Matchbox Hero City" tempa ($18-25)(C2)
31. metallic silver body, red interior, smoke windshield, lace wheels, small logo tempa ($1-2)(LP)
32. silver-gray body, black interior, clear windshield, 5 spoke concave star wheels, green lettered "Toy Show Demo Model/ CCI" tempa ($15-20)(CCI)
32. silver-gray body, black interior, clear windshield, 5 spoke concave star wheels, blue lettered "Toy Show Demo Model/ CCI" tempa ($15-20)(CCI)
34. silver-gray body, black interior, clear windshield, 5 spoke concave star wheels, yellow lettered "Toy Show Demo Model/ CCI" tempa ($15-20)(CCI)
35. yellow body, black interior, clear windshield with yellow trim, lace wheels, "MB38BBBerlinaol.com" & "Matchbox 50" tempa ($18-25)(C2)(GR)
36. yellow body, black interior, clear windshield, 5 spoke slotted wheels, head & tail lights tempa, gray base ($1-2)(SF56/2004)

MB55-M RESCUE CHOPPER *see MB60-K*

MB55-N AMPHIBIOUS PERSONNEL CARRIER, issued 2000 (USA) (MB413)

NOTE: Below models with olive turret & China casting unless otherwise noted. Mud spatter is in varying degrees.

1. olive body, "Bravo Co. 17" & mud spatter tempa, black base ($1-2)(MW55/2000 US)
2. olive body, "Bravo Co. 17", mud spatter & "Matchbox 2000" tempa, black base ($2-4)(MW55/2000 US)
3. khaki body, dark olive turret, "MB04XT" tempa, brown base ($1-2)(HR)

MB55-OGOLF CART *see MB75-J*

MB55-P DUMP TRUCK, issued 2002 (MB536)

NOTE: Below models with 5 spoke oval wheels, China casting unless otherwise noted.

1. metallic red body, gray dump, "Matchbox Demolition Force" tempa, black base ($1-2)(MW55/2002)
2. metallic red body, gray dump, "Matchbox Demolition Force" & "Matchbox 50" tempa, black base ($10-15)(MW55/2002)
3. orange-yellow body, red dump, :Matchbox DT5700" tempa, black base ($2-4)(PS)
4. orange body, black dump, "MHC69" tempa, gray base ($1-2)(MW69/2003 US)
5. orange body, black dump, "MHC69" & "Hero City" tempa, gray base ($2-4)(MW69/2003 US)
6. metallic orange body, black dump, "MHC69" tempa, gray base, gold hubs ($3-4)(20pk)
7. dark pea green body, dark yellow dump, "Hero City" & dump truck tempa, blue-gray base ($1-2)(MW75/2004)

MB55-Q MERCEDES BENZ E430 WAGON *see MB68-N*

MB55-R 1969 CHEVROLET CAMARO, issued 2004 (SF)(MB608)

1. salmon body, clear windows, black interior, white pinstripe & detailed trim tempa, 5 spoke slotted wheels, black plastic base, China casting ($1-2)(SF55/2004)

   NOTE: This model casting is different than MB7-M in that the head lights are now cast closed & both have different frame numbers, although identical frame numbers are cast on the base..

MB56-A BMC PININFARINA, issued 1969

NOTE: Below models with clear windows, ivory interior, 5 spoke wheels & England casting. Earliest versions with narrow wheels with later models having wide wheels.

1. gold body, unpainted base, no hood or side labels ($15-20)
2. gold body, unpainted base, hood label only ($15-20)(GS)
3. gold body, unpainted base, with hood & side labels ($15-20)(GS)
4. peach body, unpainted base, no labels ($20-25)
5. orange body, unpainted base, no labels ($15-20)
6. orange body, unpainted base, with hood & side labels ($15-20)(GS)
7. orange body, silver-gray base, no labels ($15-20)

MB56-B HI-TAILER, issued 1974

NOTE: Below models with England casting.

1. white body, unpainted base, blue driver, "MB5" labels, 5 spoke front & maltese cross rear wheels ($7-10)
2. white body, unpainted base, blue driver, "MB5" labels, maltese cross front & 5 spoke rear wheels ($7-10)
3. white body, unpainted base, yellow-orange driver, "MB5" labels, 5 spoke front & maltese cross rear wheels ($7-10)
4. white body, red base, yellow-orange driver, "MB5" labels, 5 spoke front & maltese cross rear wheels ($8-12)
5. white body, red base, yellow-orange driver, "MB5" labels, maltese cross front & 5 spoke rear wheels ($8-12)
6. white body, red base, yellow-orange driver, "Martini" labels, 5 spoke front & maltese cross rear wheels ($8-12)
7. white body, red base, lemon driver, "Martini" labels, 5 spoke front & maltese cross rear wheels ($8-12)
8. white body, red base, yellow-orange interior, "Martini" labels 5 spoke front & 5 spoke rear wheels ($8-12)
9. white body, unpainted base with Manaus tab, yellow-orange driver, "MB5" labels, 5 spoke front & maltese cross rear wheels ($8-12)

MB56-C MERCEDES 450SEL, issued 1979 (MB056)

NOTE: Below models with dot dash wheels.

1. metallic blue body, unpainted base, tan interior, clear windows, no tempa, England casting ($2-4)
2. metallic blue body, unpainted base, red interior, clear windows, no tempa, England casting ($6-8)
3. beige body, unpainted base, tan interior, clear windows, no tempa, red "Taxi" sign, England casting ($2-4)
4. beige body, unpainted base, dark tan interior, clear windows, no tempa, red "Taxi" sign, England casting ($2-4)
5. beige body, silver-gray base, dark tan interior, clear windows, no tempa, red "Taxi" sign, England casting ($2-4)
6. beige body, silver-gray base, chocolate interior, clear windows, no tempa, red "Taxi" sign, England casting ($3-5)
7. white body, silver-gray base, tan interior, blue windows & dome light, chrome beacon, no tempa, England casting ($7-10)
8. white & green body, silver-gray base, tan interior, blue windows & dome light, chrome beacon, "Polizei" tempa, England casting ($2-4)
9. white & dark green body, unpainted base, tan interior, blue windows & dome light, chrome beacon, "Polizei" tempa, England casting ($2-4)
10. white & dark green body, unpainted base, tan interior, blue windows & dome light, black beacon, "Polizei" tempa, England casting ($2-4)
11. white & dark green body, silver-gray base, tan interior, blue windows & dome light, black beacon, "Polizei" tempa, England casting ($2-4)
12. white & dark green body, unpainted base, tan interior, blue windows & dome light, black beacon, "Polizei" (plain sides) tempa, England casting ($2-4)
13. white & dark green body, silver-gray base, tan interior, blue windows & dome light, black beacon, "Polizei" tempa, England casting ($2-4)
14. white & light green body, pearly silver base, tan interior, blue windows & dome light, black beacon, "Polizei" tempa, Macau casting ($2-4)
15. cream body, black base, black interior, clear windows & dome light, black beacons, "Matchbox" logo/"Toy Show/23" & checkers tempa, Bulgaria casting ($12-18)(CCI)
16. cream body, black base, black interior, clear windows & dome light, black beacon, "Matchbox USA" logo/"Toy Show/23" & checkers tempa, Bulgaria casting ($25-40)(CCI)

NOTE: Available as a Bulgarian casting. Assorted colors available ($5-25)

MB56-D PETERBILT TANKER, issued 1982 (USA) (MB100)
MB 5-E PETERBILT TANKER, issued 1982 (ROW)

NOTE: Below models with 8 spoke wheels unless otherwise noted.

1. blue body, white tank, amber windows, chrome base & exhausts, "Milk" with red "Milk" door tempa, England casting ($4-6)
2. blue body, white tank, amber windows, chrome base & exhausts, "Milk" with white "Milk" door tempa, England casting ($3-5)
3. blue body, white tank, amber windows, chrome base & exhausts, "Milk" with no door tempa, England casting ($3-5)
4. blue body, white tank, clear windows, chrome base & exhausts, "Milk" with no door tempa, England casting ($3-5)
5. blue body, white tank, clear windows, chrome base & exhausts, "Milk" with white "Milk" door tempa, England casting ($3-5)
6. black body, yellow tank, amber windows, chrome base & exhausts, "Supergas" tempa, Macau casting ($2-4)
7. black body, orange-yellow tank, amber windows, chrome base & exhausts, "Supergas" tempa, Macau casting ($2-4)
8. white body, gray tank, amber windows, chrome base & exhausts, "Shell" tempa, Macau casting ($2-4)
9. red body, chrome tank, clear windows, chrome base & exhausts, "Getty" tempa, Macau casting ($2-4)
10. white body, yellow tank, amber windows, chrome base & exhausts, "Supergas" tempa, Macau casting ($25-40)
11. white body, gray tank, amber windows, chrome base & exhausts, "Ampol" tempa, Macau casting ($7-10)(AU)
12. white body, gray tank, clear windows, chrome base & exhausts, "Shell" tempa, Macau casting ($2-4)
13. black body, black tank, clear windows, chrome base & exhausts, "Amoco" tempa, Macau casting ($3-5)
14. black body, chrome tank, clear windows, chrome base & exhausts, "Amoco" tempa, Macau casting ($60-75)
15. black body, white tank, clear windows, chrome base & exhausts, "Amoco" tempa, Macau casting ($35-50)
16. white body, white tank, clear windows, chrome base & exhausts, "Amoco' tempa, Macau casting ($2-4)
17. red body, chrome tank, clear windows, chrome base & exhausts, "Amoco" on tank & "Getty" on doors tempa, Macau casting ($40-65)
18. white body, white tank, clear windows, chrome base & exhausts, no tempa, Macau casting ($40-55)
19. blue body, white tank, clear windows, chrome base & exhausts, no tempa, England casting ($5-8)
20. olive body, olive tank, clear windows, black base & exhausts, "Gas" tempa, Macau casting ($4-5)(CM)
21. white body, chrome tank, clear windows, chrome base, gray exhausts, "Shell" tempa, Macau casting ($1-2)

22. lime body, yellow tank, clear windows, blue base, red exhausts, gas pump & stripes tempa, red wheels with yellow hubs, Macau casting ($6-8)(LL)
23. lime body, yellow tank, clear windows, blue base, red exhausts, gas pump & stripes tempa, red wheels with yellow hubs, Thailand casting ($6-8)(LL)
24. lime body, yellow tank, clear windows, blue base, red exhausts, gas pump & stripes tempa, red wheels (plain hubs), Thailand casting ($6-8)(LL)
25. white body, chrome tank, clear windows, chrome base, gray exhausts, "Shell" tempa, Thailand casting ($1-2)
26. white body, white tank, blue windows, chrome base, gray exhausts, no tempa, Thailand casting ($10-15)(GF)
27. black body, black tank, clear windows, chrome base & exhausts, "Indy Racing Fuel" tempa, Thailand casting ($12-15)(IN)
28. black body, black tank, clear windows, gray base & exhausts, "Matchbox" & "Getty" tempa, gold hubs, Manaus casting ($35-50)(BR)
29. black body, black tank, clear windows, gray base & exhausts, "Matchbox" & "Getty" tempa, silver hubs, Manaus casting ($35-50)(BR)
30. white body, chrome tank, clear windows, chrome base & gray exhausts, "Shell" (without yellow on cab) tempa, Thailand casting ($1-2)
31. white body, chrome tank, clear windows, black base with bar code, gray exhausts, "Shell" with "IC" door logo tempa, China casting ($10-15)(IC)
32. white body, cream tank, clear windows, gray base, gray exhausts, "Esso" tempa, Manaus casting ($30-45)(BR)
33. black & white body, black tank, clear windows, chrome base & exhausts, chrome base, "Official Indy Fuel Truck" tempa, Thailand casting ($7-10)(IN)
34. white body, chrome tank, clear windows, gray exhausts, chrome base, "Shell" with "IC" logo on doors tempa, China casting ($12-15)
35. blue body, white tank, clear windows, gray exhausts, chrome base, "Fresh Milk" tempa, Thailand casting ($20-25) (FM)(GS)
36. white & red body, white tank, clear windows, gray exhausts, chrome base, "Avia" tempa, Thailand casting ($12-18)(BE)
37. white body, chrome tank, clear windows, gray exhausts, chrome base, "Shell" tank tempa, red line on cab tempa, China casting ($1-2)
38. white body, green tank, clear windows, gray exhausts, chrome base, "BP" tempa, China casting ($8-12)(MW7/1998 AU)
39. neon yellow body, chrome tank, clear windows, chrome exhausts, chrome base, "Airways Caution Jet Fuel" tempa, China casting ($1-2)(5pk)
40. white body, chrome tank, clear windows, chrome exhausts, chrome base, no tempa, China casting ($25-40)(ASAP blank)
41. white body, chrome tank, clear windows, chrome exhausts, chrome base, "American International Recovery" tempa, China casting ($100+)(ASAP)
42. white body, cream tank, clear windows, silver-gray exhausts, silver-gray base, "Dairy Line" with & black patches & cow tempa, China casting ($1-2)(MW12/1999 US)
43. white body, cream tank, clear windows, silver-gray exhausts, silver-gray base, black patches & cow tempa, China casting ($1-2)(MW12/1999 ROW)
44. white body, cream tank, clear windows, silver-gray exhausts, silver-gray base, black patches & cow with "Dairy Line" on cab only tempa, China casting ($8-12)(MW12/1999 ROW)
45. dark blue body, chrome tank, clear windows, chrome exhausts, chrome base, flammable insignia tempa, China casting ($1-2)(5pk)
46. white body, chrome tank, clear windows, gray exhausts, chrome base, "White's Guide Car of The Month #10" (left only) tempa, China casting ($8-12)(ASAP)
47. white body, chrome tank, clear windows, gray exhausts, chrome base, "Arco Lar 75" tempa, China casting ($75+)(ASAP)
48. slate blue body, gray tank, clear windows, silver-gray exhausts, silver-gray base, "Test Mission" tempa, China casting ($1-2)(5pk)
49. white body, chrome tank, clear windows, gray exhausts, chrome base, "Hemler Bros." tempa, China casting ($75+)(ASAP)
50. white body, chrome tank, clear windows, gray exhausts, chrome base, "Blue Ridge Construction" tempa, China casting ($75+)(ASAP)
51. white body, chrome tank, clear windows, gray exhausts, chrome base, "Giant Industries" tempa, China casting ($75+)(ASAP)
52. white body, chrome tank, clear windows, gray exhausts, chrome base, "Fullbright Oil Co." tempa, China casting ($75+)(ASAP)
53. white body, chrome tank, clear windows, gray exhausts, chrome base, "Systend Dairies" tempa, China casting ($75+)(ASAP)
54. white body, chrome tank, clear windows, gray exhausts, chrome base, "Maalcovich Pumping" tempa, China casting ($75+)(ASAP)
55. white body, chrome tank, clear windows, gray exhausts, chrome base, "Darry Brothers" tempa, China casting ($75+)(ASAP)
56. white body, chrome tank, clear windows, gray exhausts, chrome base, "100% Divine" tempa, China casting ($75+)(ASAP)
57. white body, chrome tank, clear windows, gray exhausts, chrome base, "BP Super" tempa, China casting ($75+)(ASAP)
58. white body, chrome tank, clear windows, gray exhausts, chrome base, "CT Tank Removal" tempa, China casting ($75+)(ASAP)
59. black body, chrome tank, clear windows, chrome exhausts, chrome base, "Texaco" tempa, China casting, chrome disc wheels with rubber tires ($3-5)(Texaco PC)
60. black body, chrome tank, clear windows, chrome exhausts, chrome base, "Texaco" tempa, China casting, black disc wheels with rubber tires ($3-5)(Texaco PC)
61. white body, white tank, clear windows, white exhausts, chrome base, "Lasser, Inc." tempa, China casting ($75+)(ASAP)
62. white body, white tank, clear windows, white exhausts, chrome base, no tempa, China casting ($25-40)(ASAP blank)
63. white body, chrome tank, clear windows, chrome exhausts & base, "Yeager's Fuel, Inc." tempa, China casting ($50+)(ASAP)
64. white body, white tank, amber windows, gray exhausts, chrome base, "Eagle River Dairy Farm Wisconsin" tempa, 7 spoke sawblade wheels, China casting ($1-2)(AM)
65. dark green body, white tank, clear windows, chrome exhausts, chrome base, "Swill" tempa, chrome disc wheels with rubber tires, China casting ($3-5)(SNL)

MB56-E VOLKSWAGEN GOLF GTi *see MB33-D*

MB56-F 4 X 4 JEEP *see MB5-D*

MB56-G FORD LTD TAXI *see MB53-G*

MB56-H CAMARO Z-28 *see MB43-I*

MB56-I ISUZU RODEO, issued 1995 (USA) (MB273)
MB59-I VAUXHALL FRONTERA, issued 1995 (ROW)

NOTE: Model has different names printed on the baseplate on U.S. vs. ROW issues. Below models with 8 spoke wheels, black spare tire cover & black roof luggage unless otherwise noted.

1. black body, white interior, blue windows, silver-gray "Rodeo" base, pink spatter on hood & sides tempa, Thailand casting ($1-2)

2. white body, white interior, blue windows, black "Frontera" base, brown spatter on sides only tempa, Thailand casting ($3-5)
3. white body, white interior, blue windows, black "Frontera" base, no tempa, Thailand casting ($12-15)
4. black body, white interior, blue windows, silver-gray "Rodeo" base, pink spatter on sides only tempa, Thailand casting ($1-2)
5. white body, white interior, blue windows, silver-gray "Rodeo" base, pink spatter on sides only tempa, Thailand casting ($2-4)
6. metallic gold body, white interior, blue windows, silver-gray "Rodeo" base, no tempa, Thailand casting ($5-10)(CH)
7. red body, white interior, blue windows, silver-gray "Rodeo" base, "Power Parts 21" tempa, Thailand casting ($2-3)
8. metallic red body, black interior, clear windows, black "Frontera" base, no tempa, Thailand casting ($2-3)
9. green body, white interior, blue windows, gray (no name) base, skeleton & "Brontosaurus" tempa , Thailand casting ($1-2)(5pk)
10. silver-gray body, maroon interior, clear windows, black "Frontera" base, no tempa, Thailand casting ($1-2)
11. black body, light gray interior, clear windows, silver-gray "Rodeo" base, red & white design tempa, Thailand casting ($1-2)(5pk)
12. black body, light gray interior, clear windows, silver-gray "Rodeo" base, red & white design tempa, China casting ($1-2)(5pk)
13. green body, white interior, blue windows, gray (no name) base, skeleton & " Brontosaurus" tempa, China casting ($1-2)(5pk)
14. black body, light gray interior, clear windows, silver-gray "Frontera" base, red & white design tempa, China casting ($1-2)(5pk)
15. blue body, black interior, clear windows, black "Opel Frontera" base, red tail lights tempa, China casting ($3-5)(MW59)(GR)
16. white body, yellow interior, blue windows, blue-green "Rodeo" base, "Wilderness Tours" tempa, dark green roof luggage, China casting ($1-2)(5pk)
17. white body, yellow interior, blue windows, blue-green "Frontera" base, design without "Wilderness Tours" tempa, China casting ($1-2)(5pk)
18. pink-beige body, olive interior, light smoke windows, black "Rodeo" base, "Operations Safari 1999/ Matchbox" & green camouflage tempa, China casting ($18-25)(US)
19. white body, black interior, light smoke windows, black "Frontera" base, orange & blue design tempa, China casting ($2-4) (MW40/2002 AU)
20. orange-yellow body, black interior, light smoke windows, black "Rodeo" base, "555-Res-Q" & "Roadside Rescue" tempa, China casting ($1-2)(MW100/2000 US)
21. orange-yellow body, black interior, light smoke windows, black "Rodeo" base, "555-Res-Q" , "Roadside Rescue" & "Matchbox 2000" tempa, China casting ($2-4)(MW100/2000 US)
22. metallic green body, dark blue interior, clear windows, black "Rodeo" base, "Rugrats" tempa, 7 spoke sawblade wheels, China casting ($1-2)(5pk)
23. bright blue body, dark gray interior, smoke windows, chrome "Frontera" base, "Vauxhall" & griffin crest tempa, 7 spoke sawblade wheels, China casting ($2-4)(MW65/2001 UK)
24. light pumpkin body, green interior, smoke windows, black "Rodeo" base, "Arizona Canyon Rescue 48" tempa, 10 spoke flower wheels, China casting ($1-2)(AM)
25. orange-yellow body, black interior, smoke windows, black "Rodeo" base, "555-RES-Q Roadside Rescue/ Matchbox USA Toy Show" & Matchbox 2000" tempa ($12-18)(CCI)

MB56-J CAMARO 28 POLICE CAR *see MB59-H*

MB56-K MERCEDES A CLASS, issued 1999 (USA) (MB380)
MB51-M MERCEDES A CLASS, issued 1999 (ROW)

NOTE: Below models with clear windows, 5 spoke concave star wheels, black base & China casting unless otherwise noted.

1. red body, purple interior, kayak & splash design tempa ($1-2)(MW56/1999 US)(MW51/1999 ROW)
2. red body, black interior, none tempa ($2-4)(MW75/1999 GR)
3. silver-gray body, black interior, smoke windows, no tempa ($2-4)(MW31/2000 ROW)
4. silver-gray body, black interior, smoke windows, "New Hope Auto Show 2000" tempa ($12-18)(CCI)
5. red body, purple interior, kayak & splash design with "New Hope Auto Show 2000" tempa ($12-18)(CCI)
6. green body, black interior, "Rugrats- Chuckie" tempa, 10 spoke flower wheels ($1-2)(5pk)
7. black body, gray interior, head & tail lights tempa, 10 spoke flower wheels ($2-4)(MW63/2001 GR)
8. metallic purple body, black interior, "Rugrats- Chuckie" tempa, 10 spoke flower wheels ($1-2)(5pk)
9. white body, gray interior, blue windows, "Alarm" & snowflake tempa, charcoal base ($1-2)(5pk)
10. lemon body, black interior, red tail lights tempa, lace wheels ($4-6)(SG)
11. unpainted body, black interior, pop art decals, lace wheels ($75+)(FA)
12. lemon body, black interior, "C.A.M.e.V. Rostock" label, lace wheels ($18-25)(C2)
13. lemon & white body, green interior, "Coca Cola- Pause Refresh Yourself" tempa, chrome disc wheels with rubber tires ($3-5)(Coke PC)
14. silver blue body, blue interior, blue windows, "Alarm" & snowflake tempa, 10 spoke flower wheels ($1-2)(5pk)
15. silver-gray body, black interior, smoke windows, "25th Anniversary PMCC/ Home For the Holidays" tempa, 5 spoke concave star wheels ($12-18)(CCI)
16. white body, red interior, red windows, "Parthenon Athens" tempa, lace wheels, green base ($1-2)(AW)
17. metallic lime body, turquoise interior, purple windows, "Plankton" tempa, lace wheels, black base ($1-2)(5pk)
18. lemon body, black interior, "Mattel" logo on roof tempa, lace wheels ($60-85)(C2)(GR)

MB56-L UFO *see MB61-K*

MB56-M DODGE VIPER GTSR, issued 2001 (MB517)

NOTE: Below models with smoke windows, black base & China casting unless otherwise noted.

1. red body, black interior, silver bands tempa, lace wheels ($1-2)(MW56/2001)
2. metallic blue body, gray interior, "Viper GTSR" tempa, lace wheels ($1-2)(MW10/2002)
3. metallic blue body, gray interior, "Viper GTSR" & "Matchbox 50" tempa, lace wheels ($5-8)(MW10/2002)
4. black body, dark gray interior, clear windows, "Dodge" tempa, gold lace wheels ($1-2)(5pk)
5. red body, gray interior, silver bands & detailed trim tempa, chrome disc wheels with rubber tires ($3-5)(SH)
6. lemon body, gray interior, black bands & detailed trim tempa, 5 spoke slotted wheels ($2-4)(SF33/2004)
7. orange body, gray interior, blue windows, tarantula design tempa, lace wheels, gray base ($1-2)(5pk)

MB56-N BUCKET FIRE TRUCK, issued 2002 (MB540/602)

NOTE: Below models with amber windows, 4 spoke domed wheels, gray plastic base, operating boom & China casting unless otherwise noted.

1. red body, black interior, gray boom, "Water Dragons" tempa ($1-2)(MW56/2002)
2. red body, black interior, gray boom, "Water Dragons" & "Matchbox 50" tempa ($2-4)(MW56/2002)
3. metallic red body, dark gray interior, black boom, gray base, "Metro Alarm" & stripes tempa ($1-2)(MW2/2003)
4. metallic red body, dark gray interior, black boom, gray base, "Metro Alarm", stripes & "Hero City" tempa ($2-4)(MW2/2003)
5. metallic red body, gray interior, white boom, gray base, "Liberty Squad Fire Company USA" tempa ($1-2)(MP)(HR)
6. bright blue body, red interior, black (fixed) boom, red windows, 7 spoke sawblade wheels, cream base, "Aqua Force" tempa ($1-2)(MW35/2004)
7. bronze body, black interior, gray (fixed) boom, purple windows, 5 crown dot wheels, gray base, "Alarm" & plane design tempa ($1-2)(LP)
8. red body, yellow interior, white (fixed) boom, blue windows, 5 crown dot wheels, chrome base, "MFD/ E-121" & white stripes tempa (MW35/2004)
9. red body, yellow interior, black (fixed) boom, blue windows, 5 crown dot wheels, chrome base, "MFD/E-121" & white stripes tempa ($8-12)(20pk/2004)

MB56-O BILLBOARD TRUCK, issued 2003 (MB586)

NOTE: Below models with amber windows, 7 spoke sawblade wheels, black plastic base & China casting unless otherwise noted.

1. metallic blue body, white billboard, "56 Matchbox Hero City Toy Store" tempa ($1-2)(MW56/2003)
2. metallic blue body, white billboard, "56 Matchbox Hero City Toy Store" & "Hero City" tempa ($4-6)(MW56/2003)
3. metallic blue body, white billboard, "Matchbox Hero City Police" tempa, gold hubs ($3-4)(20pk)
4. olive body, light blue billboard, "Roswell NM" tempa ($1-2)(AW)
5. metallic blue body, white billboard, "Matchbox USA Now in Living Color" labels ($12-18)(CCI)

MB57-A LAND ROVER FIRE ENGINE, issued 1970

1. red body, blue windows & dome light,, gray base, "Kent Fire Brigade" labels, white ladder, 5 spoke wheels, England casting ($45-60)

MB57-B ECCLES CARAVAN, issued 1970

NOTE: Below models with England casting. Base is part of body casting.

1. cream body, orange roof, green interior, brown stripe labels, black axle cover, 5 spoke wheels ($10-15)
2. cream body, orange roof, green interior, brown stripe & flower labels, black axle cover, 5 spoke wheels ($10-15)
3. cream body, orange roof, green interior, brown stripe & flower labels, red axle cover, 5 spoke wheels ($10-15)
4. cream body, orange roof, green interior, brown stripe labels, red axle cover, 5 spoke wheels ($10-15)
5. light yellow body, orange roof, green interior, brown stripe & flower label, black axle cover, 5 spoke wheels ($10-15)
6. dark yellow body, dark orange roof, white interior, black stripe & flower label, black axle cover, 5 spoke center cut wheels ($5-7)(TP)
7. dark yellow body, dark orange roof, white interior, dots label (from K-27-A), black axle cover, 5 spoke center cut wheels ($7-10)(TP)
8. dark yellow body, dark orange roof, white interior, brown stripe & flower labels, black axle cover, 5 spoke center cut wheels (&-10)(TP)
9. dark yellow body, dark orange roof, white interior, sailboat labels (from MB23-A), black axle cover, 5 spoke center cut wheels ($175-250)(TP)
10. beige body, dark orange roof, white interior, black stripe & flower label, black axle cover, 5 spoke center cut wheels ($5-7)(TP)
11. beige body, dark orange roof, white interior, stripe with seagull label (from MB31-B), black axle cover, 5 spoke center cut wheels ($7-10)(TP)
12. white body, dark orange roof, white interior, "Sun Set" tempa, black axle cover, 5 spoke center cut wheels ($8-12)(TP)

MB57-C WILDLIFE TRUCK, issued 1973

NOTE: Below models with 5 spoke wheels & England casting unless otherwise noted.

1. yellow body, unpainted base, red windows, amber canopy, orange lion, hood label ($5-7)
2. yellow body, unpainted base, red windows, light blue canopy, orange lion, hood label ($5-7)
3. yellow body, unpainted base, red windows, clear canopy, orange lion, hood label ($5-7)
4. yellow body, silver-gray base, red windows, amber canopy, orange lion, hood label ($5-7)
5. yellow body, unpainted base, red windows, amber canopy, orange lion, hood label ($5-7)
6. yellow body, unpainted base, red windows, smoke canopy, brown lion, hood label, ($5-7)
7. yellow body, unpainted base, red windows, light blue canopy, brown lion, hood label ($5-7)
8. yellow body, unpainted base, red windows, clear canopy, brown lion, hood label ($5-7)
9. yellow body, unpainted base, red windows, amber canopy, brown lion, hood label ($5-7)
10. yellow body, unpainted base, no windows, clear canopy, brown lion, hood label ($5-7)
11. yellow body, unpainted base, orange windows, smoke canopy, brown lion, hood label ($5-7)
12. white body, unpainted base, red windows, light blue canopy, brown lion, stripes tempa ($5-7)
13. white body, unpainted base, red windows, light blue canopy, red-brown lion, stripes tempa ($5-7)
14. white body, unpainted base, red windows, clear canopy, brown lion, stripes tempa ($5-7)
15. white body, unpainted base, red windows, clear canopy, red-brown lion, stripes tempa ($5-7)
16. white body, unpainted base, red windows, smoke canopy, brown lion, stripes tempa ($5-7)
17. white body, unpainted base, red windows, smoke canopy, red-brown lion, stripes tempa ($5-7)
18. white body, unpainted base, purple windows, clear canopy, brown lion, stripes tempa ($5-7)
19. white body, unpainted base, purple windows, clear canopy, red-brown lion, stripes tempa ($5-7)
20. white body, unpainted base, purple windows, smoke canopy, brown lion, stripes tempa ($5-7)
21. white body, unpainted base, purple windows, smoke canopy, red-brown lion, stripes tempa ($5-7)
22. white body, unpainted base, purple windows, light blue canopy, brown lion, stripes tempa ($5-7)
23. white body, unpainted base, purple windows, light blue canopy, red-brown lion, stripes tempa ($5-7)
24. white body, unpainted base, orange windows, clear canopy, brown lion, stripes tempa ($5-7)
25. white body, unpainted base, orange windows, clear canopy, red-brown lion, stripes tempa ($5-7)

26. white body, unpainted base, orange windows, smoke canopy, brown lion, stripes tempa ($5-7)
27. white body, unpainted base, orange windows, smoke canopy, red-brown lion, stripes tempa ($5-7)
28. white body, unpainted base, orange windows, light blue canopy, brown lion, stripes tempa ($5-7)
29. white body, unpainted base, orange windows, light blue canopy, red-brown lion, stripes tempa ($5-7)
30. white body, unpainted base, red windows, clear canopy, orange lion, stripes tempa with "Climat" hood label ($125-175)(FR)
31. lime body, unpainted base with Manaus label, red windows, clear canopy, brown lion, hood label ($250+)(BR)

MB57-D 4 X 4 MINI PICKUP, issued 1982 (USA) (MB107)

NOTE: Below models with maltese cross wheels & black roll bar.

1. orange-red body, unpainted metal base, blue windows, white/silver/black stripes tempa, England casting ($3-5)
2. dark red body, unpainted metal base, blue windows, white/silver/black stripes tempa, England casting ($3-5)
3. dark red body, silver-gray metal base, blue windows, white/silver/black stripes tempa, England casting ($3-5)
4. silver-gray body, unpainted metal base, blue windows, "Big Foot" tempa, England casting ($75-100)
5. dark powder blue body, black metal base, blue windows, "Mountain Man" tempa, Hong Kong casting ($2-3)
6. light powder blue body, black metal base, blue windows, "Mountain Man" tempa, Macau casting ($2-3)
7. baby blue body, black metal base, blue windows, "Mountain Man" tempa, Macau casting ($2-3)
8. baby blue body, black plastic base, blue windows, "Mountain Man" tempa, Macau casting ($1-2)
9. baby blue body, black plastic base, blue windows, "Mountain Man" tempa, Thailand casting ($1-2)(MP)

MB57-E CARMICHAEL COMMANDO, issued 1982 (ROW) (MB057)

NOTE: Below models with blue windows & 5 arch wheels unless otherwise noted.

1. white body, black base, gray interior, "Police Rescue" tempa, England casting ($18-25)
2. white body, charcoal base, gray interior, "Police Rescue" tempa England casting ($18-25)
3. red body, black base, gray interior, "Fire" tempa, England casting ($15-18)
4. red body, charcoal base, gray interior, "Fire" tempa, England casting ($15-18)
5. red body, black base, gray interior, "Fire" tempa (plain hood), England casting ($15-18)
6. red body, black base, gray interior, "Fire" tempa, Macau casting ($15-18)

NOTE: Below models with dot dash wheels.

7. white body, black base, gray interior, "Midwest Regional Matchbox Convention/ MRMC" tempa, Bulgaria casting ($25-40)(CCI)
8. cream body, black base, gray interior, "Lightning Rod Matchbox Forum 07" tempa , Bulgaria casting ($18-25)(CCI)
9. red body, black base, gray interior, "Lightning Rod Matchbox Forum 07" tempa, Bulgaria casting ($18-25)(CCI)

NOTE: Available as a Bulgarian casting. Assorted colors available. ($5-25)

MB57-F MISSION HELICOPTER *see MB46-F*

MB57-G FORD TRANSIT VAN *see MB60-G*

MB57-H MACK AUXILIARY POWER TRUCK, issued 1991 (USA) (MB229)

MB50-G MACK AUXILIARY POWER TRUCK, issued 1991 (ROW)

NOTE: Below models with chrome plastic base, white roof, red windows & 8 spoke wheels unless otherwise noted.

1. yellow body, chrome & yellow roof fixtures, "Floodlight Heavy Rescue" & door shield tempa, China casting ($2-3)
2. florescent orange body, chrome & yellow roof fixtures, "Fire Rescue Unit 2" & checkers with "Floodlight Heavy Rescue" tempa, China casting ($1-2)
3. white body, chrome & white roof fixtures, no roof or body tempa, China casting ($10-15)(GF)
4. red body, chrome & yellow roof fixtures, "Fire Rescue Unit 2" & "Floodlight Heavy Rescue" tempa, China casting ($8-12)(GS)
5. orange body, blue windows, chrome & yellow roof fixtures, "Reithoffer's" tempa, China casting ($4-6)(WR)(GS)
6. florescent orange body, black & yellow roof fixtures, black base, "Fire Rescue Unit 2" with blue & white checkers tempa, China casting ($4-6)
7. red body, chrome & yellow roof fixtures, chrome base, "Shrewsbury Fire Co." with white painted roof tempa, China casting ($10-15)(WR)
8. red body, blue windows, chrome & black roof fixtures, chrome base, "Floodlight Rescue Unit/ Fire Rescue" tempa, China casting ($1-2)(5pk)
9. white body, chrome & black roof fixtures, chrome base, "Bridge & Highway Dept. 57" tempa, China casting ($1-2)
10. orange-red body, chrome & yellow roof fixtures, chrome base, "Fire Rescue Unit 2/ Action System" tempa, China casting ($7-10)(OP)
11. metallic gold body, blue windows, chrome & yellow roof fixtures, chrome base, "Floodlight Rescue Unit" tempa, China casting ($10-15)(CH)
12. red body, blue windows, chrome & black roof fixtures, chrome base, "Matchbox Fire Rescue/ Fire Dept." tempa, China casting ($1-2)(5pk)
13. red & white body, chrome & black roof fixtures, chrome base, chrome disc with rubber tires, "Acorn Hill Fire Dept.", China casting ($3-5)(PC7)
14. yellow body, chrome & black roof fixtures, chrome base, "Bridge & Highway Dept. 57" tempa, China casting ($2-3)
15. red body, chrome & black roof fixtures, chrome base, "Clearbrook Fire & Rescue" tempa, China casting ($8-12)(US)
16. white body, blue windows, chrome & black roof fixtures, chrome base, "Matchbox Fire Rescue/ Fire Dept." tempa, China casting ($1-2)(5pk)
17. red body, chrome & black roof fixtures, chrome base, "Bridge & Highway Rescue Dept. 57" tempa, China casting ($1-2)(MW21/1998)
18. metallic red & white body, chrome & black roof fixtures, chrome base, chrome disc wheels with rubber tires, "Eagle Point Fire Rescue", China casting ($3-5)(PC21)
19. red body, chrome & black roof fixtures, chrome base, no tempa, China casting ($25-40)(ASAP blank)
20. red body, chrome & black roof fixtures, chrome base, "American International Recovery" tempa, China casting ($100+)(ASAP)

NOTE: Below models with China casting.

21. white & red body, black roof fixtures, chrome base, "Houston Dire Dept. 11/ Heavy Rescue" tempa ($4-6)(PC)
22. red body, black roof fixtures, chrome base, "Main Transit Fire Dept. Amherst NY" tempa ($15-20)(ASAP)

23. lime body, chrome & black roof fixtures, chrome base, "Action Metro Base 33" tempa ($1-2)(MW77/1999 US)(MW67/1999 ROW)
24. red body, blue windows, chrome & black roof fixtures, black base, "Emergency Power 77" tempa ($1-2)(5pk)
25. red body, blue windows, chrome & black roof fixtures, black base, "Emergency Power 34" tempa ($3-5)(5pk)
26. red body, lemon & black roof fixtures, silver-gray base, "Garage 33/ 5 Alarm" tempa ($1-2)(LP)
27. red body, chrome & black roof fixtures, chrome base, "Sugar Grove Fire Department" (left side only) tempa ($15-20)(ASAP)
28. lemon body, blue windows, blue & black roof fixtures, gray base, "Garage 33/ 5 Alarm" tempa , 7 spoke sawblade wheels ($1-2)(LP)
29. white & green body, black roof, chrome & gray roof fixtures, gray base, "Metro Alarm/ MA-RC1" tempa, 4 spoke domed wheels ($1-2)(5pk)
30. red body, white roof, chrome & black roof fixtures, chrome base, "Sugar Grove Fire Dept. 2000" tempa, 8 spoke wheels ($18-25)(ASAP)
31. white body, white roof, chrome & gray roof fixtures, gray base, "Universe Alarm Centre 4" tempa, 4 spoke domed wheels ($1-2)(MW45/2001)
32. white body, white roof, chrome & gray roof fixtures, gray base, "Universe Alarm Centre 4" with no cab print tempa, 4 spoke domed wheels ($1-2)(MW45/2001)
33. red body, white roof, chrome & black roof fixtures, chrome base, "Cetronia Fire Co. 1924-1999" tempa, 8 spoke wheels ($50+)(ASAP)
34. red body, white roof, chrome & black roof fixtures, chrome base, "Open Sky" tempa, 8 spoke wheels ($50+)(ASAP)
35. metallic blue body, blue roof, gray roof fixtures, gray base, "Arkansas 25- Ozark Fire Rescue" tempa, 4 spoke domed wheels ($1-2)(AM)

NOTE: Above model with Matchbox International or Mattel casting.

36. red body, white roof, chrome & black roof fixtures, chrome base, "Citrix Technical Support" tempa, 8 spoke wheels ($50+)(ASAP)
37. red body, white roof, chrome & black roof fixtures, chrome base, "MBFD Heavy Rescue" & white stripes tempa, chrome disc with rubber tires, Mattel casting ($3-5)(MP)(HR)
38. lemon body, red roof, black roof fixtures, black base, "42" & panel design tempa, 4 spoke domed wheels ($1-2)(MW42/2002)

NOTE: Above model with Matchbox International or Mattel casting.

39. lemon body, red roof, black roof fixtures, black base, "42" & panel design with "Matchbox 50" tempa, 4 spoke domed wheels, Mattel casting ($75+)(MW42/2002 US)
40. lemon body, red roof, black roof fixtures, black base, "42" & panel design tempa, 7 spoke sawblade wheels, Mattel casting ($1-2)(MW42/2002)
41. white body, white roof, chrome roof fixtures, gray base, "Police Emergency Service- NYPD" tempa, 4 spoke domed wheels ($18-25)(CCI)
42. red body, white roof, chrome & black roof fixtures, chrome base, "Scorex/ Supply Chain" tempa, 8 spoke wheels ($50+)(ASAP)

MB57-I SNOW GROOMER, issued 1999 (USA)(MB419)
MB52-G SNOW GROOMER, issued 1999 (ROW)

NOTE: Below models with China casting unless otherwise noted

1. orange body, black plow, blue dome lights & windows, black hatch, silver-gray base & wheels, "FF-525" & mountain scene tempa ($2-4)(MW52/1999 ROW)(MW42/1999 GR)
2. orange body, black plow, blue dome lights & windows, black hatch, silver-gray base & wheels, "Hilltop Unit 3 Resort" & mountain scene tempa ($1-2)(MW57/1999 US)
3. white body, black plow, red dome lights & windows, black hatch, silver-gray base & wheels, red band & yellow hash marks tempa ($1-2)(5pk)
4. blue body, silver-gray plow, red dome lights & windows, black base, silver-gray hatch, black wheels, "42-06", cross & white design tempa ($1-2)(5pk)
5. silver-gray body, blue plow, amber dome lights & windows, black base, blue hatch, black wheels, white & dark blue design tempa ($1-2)(MW78/2000 US)(MW58/2000 ROW)
6. silver-gray body, blue plow, amber dome lights & windows, black base, blue hatch, black wheels, white & blue design with "Matchbox 2000" tempa ($2-4)(MW78/ 2000 US)
7. white body, blue plow, blue dome lights & windows, silver-gray base, black hatch, silver-gray wheels, "Test Centre", polar bear logo & hash marks tempa ($1-2)(LP)
8. dark gray body, green plow, blue dome lights & windows, black base, green hatch, "Alarm" & snowflake tempa ($1-2)(5pk)
9. dark blue body, orange-yellow plow, amber dome lights & windows, orange-yellow base, orange-yellow hatch, "Alarm" & snowflake tempa ($1-2)(5pk)

MB57-J MERCEDES BENZ ML430 *see MB77-C*

MB57-K 2000 CORVETTE, issued 2001 (MB515)

NOTE: Below models with smoke windshield, lace wheels, black plastic base & China casting unless otherwise noted.

1. metallic dark maroon body, black interior, clear windshield, tiny "Corvette" logo tempa ($1-2)(MW57/2001)
2. metallic silver body, black interior, "Corvette" tempa ($1-2)(MW11/2002)
3. metallic silver body, black interior, "Corvette" & "Matchbox 50" tempa ($8-12)(MW11/2002)
4. dark green body, tan interior, nondescript design tempa ($1-2)(MW8/2003)
5. dark green body, tan interior, nondescript design & "Hero City" tempa ($2-4)(MW8/2003)
6. metallic red body, gray interior, "Corvette" with multi-color design tempa ($1-2)(5pk)
7. metallic green-gold body, black interior, dark smoke windshield, small "Matchbox" logo tempa ($1-2)(LP)
8. lime body, black interior, dark smoke windshield, soccer player design & "33" tempa ($1-2)(5pk)
9. metallic red body, light tan interior, smoke windshield, detailed trim tempa, 5 spoke slotted wheels ($1-2)(SF46/2004)
10. metallic silver body, turquoise interior, blue windshield, "Sheen" tempa, lace wheels ($1-2)(5pk)

MB57-L TRASH TRUCK, issued 2002 (MB542)

NOTE: Below models with 4 spoke domed wheels & China casting unless otherwise noted.

1. black body, black dump with gray insert, opaque gray windows, "Matchbox" & caricatures tempa, gray base ($1-2)(MW57/2002)
2. black body, black dump with gray insert, opaque gray windows, "Matchbox" & caricatures with "Matchbox 50" tempa, gray base ($2-4)(MW57/2002)
3. yellow body, blue-green dump with black insert, black windows, "Action BWS 19" tempa, black base ($1-2)(MW19/2003)
4. yellow body, blue-green dump with black insert, black windows, "Action BWS 19" & "Hero City" tempa, black base ($2-4)(MW19/2003)

5. dark green body, lime dump with red insert, opaque red windows, recycle bin & arrows design tempa, dark gray base, 5 crown dot wheels ($1-2)(MW56/2004)

MB57-M CHEVY SSR *see MB70-K*

MB58-A DAF GIRDER TRUCK, issued 1970

NOTE: Below models with green windows, 5 spoke wheels, red plastic base,12 red plastic girders & England casting.

1. cream body ($75-90)
2. metallic green-gold body ($25-30)

MB58-B WOOSH-N-PUSH, issued 1972

NOTE: Below models with unpainted metal base, maltese cross rear wheels & England casting unless otherwise noted.

1. yellow body, red interior, flower label (from MB13-B), maltese cross front wheels ($15-18)
2. yellow body, red interior, flower label (from MB13-B), 5 spoke front wheels ($15-18)
3. yellow body, red interior, "2" label, maltese cross front wheels ($15-18)
4. yellow body, red interior, "2" label, 5 spoke front wheels ($15-18)
5. yellow body, light yellow interior, "2" label, maltese cross front wheels ($15-18)
6. yellow body, red interior, sunburst label (from MB47-B), maltese cross front wheels ($175-250)
7. metallic red body, light yellow interior, "2" label, maltese cross front wheels ($15-18)
8. metallic magenta body, light yellow interior, "2" label, maltese cross front wheels ($15-18)
9. metallic magenta body, light yellow interior, "8" label (from MB48-B), maltese cross front wheels ($15-18)
10. white body, red interior, "8" label (from MB48-B), maltese cross front wheels, Manaus label on base ($250+)(BR)

MB58-C FAUN DUMP TRUCK, issued 1976

NOTE: Below models with maltese cross wheels, black plastic base & England casting.

1. orange-yellow body & dump, no tempa ($3-5)
2. yellow body & dump, no tempa ($3-5)
3. yellow body, red dump, no tempa ($20-35)
4. yellow body & dump, "CAT" tempa ($4-6)
5. yellow body & dump, "CAT" tempa without "C" on side ($4-6)

MB58-D RUFF TREK, issued 1983 (MB121)

NOTE: Below models with black metal base & 8 spoke wheels unless otherwise noted.

1. metallic tan body, red interior, amber windows, "Ruff Trek" tempa, black load, Macau casting ($2-4)
2. white body, red interior, amber windows, "Ruff Trek" tempa, black load, Macau casting ($7-10)(JP)
3. white body, red interior, amber windows, "217" tempa, black load, Macau casting ($3-4)(TM)
4. white body, red interior, clear windows, "217" tempa, black load, Macau casting ($3-4)(TM)
5. white body, black interior, clear windows, "Brut/ Faberge" tempa, black load, Macau casting ($3-4)(TM)
6. white body, red interior, clear windows, "Brut/ Faberge" tempa, black load, Macau casting ($75-100)(TM)
7. dark blue body, red interior, clear windows, "STP/ Goodyear" tempa, black load, Macau casting ($45-60)(TM)
8. white body, red interior, clear windows, "7 Up" tempa, black load, Macau casting ($3-4)(TM)
9. brown body, red interior, olive green windows, red/yellow/ blue tempa, green rear load, Macau casting, includes plastic armament ($5-8)(RB)
10. white body, black interior, clear windows, flames tempa, black load, Macau casting ($8-12)(GS)(JB)
11. yellow body, black interior, clear windows, "Matchbox Rescue Team Support" tempa, black load, Macau casting ($3-5)(MC)
12. yellow body, black interior, clear windows, black load, "Matchbox Rescue Team Support" tempa, Thailand casting ($3-5)(MC)
13. brown body, red interior, dark olive windows, red/yellow/ blue tempa, dark green load, Thailand casting, includes plastic armament ($10-15)(JP) (Tomy box)

MB58-E MERCEDES BENZ 300E, issued 1986 (MB181)

NOTE: Below models with black metal base, clear windows & 8 dot wheels. Version 1 with or without star emblem on grille.

1. silver blue body, dark blue interior, no tempa, Macau casting ($1-2)
2. silver blue body, dark blue interior, no tempa, Thailand casting ($1-2)
3. white body, tan interior, green stripe & silver star with "Polizei 5075" tempa, Thailand casting ($1-2)
4. white body, tan interior, green stripe (without star) & "Polizei 5075" tempa, Thailand casting ($1-2)
5. white body, dark blue interior, "61 Rijkspolitie" tempa, Thailand casting ($4-6)(GS)(DU)
6. white body, tan interior, green stripes & "Polizei 5075" tempa, China casting ($2-4)
7. blue-gray body, gray interior, "Go Blues! 1997" tempa, China casting ($3-5)(AU)

MB58-F CORVETTE T-ROOF *see MB40-C*

MB58-G VW CONCEPT I *see MB49-I*

MB58-H 1939 CHEVY SEDAN DELIVERY, issued 1997 (AU) (MB245)

MB245 1939 CHEVY SEDAN DELIVERY, issued 1992 (WR)

NOTE: This is a larger casting than the MB215 and has the rear bumper omitted. Below models with clear windows, silver 5 crown wheels, silver-gray plastic base & China casting unless otherwise noted.

1. white body, brown chassis, "Browns 1992" tempa ($3-5)(WR)
2. white body, red-brown chassis, "Redskins 1992" tempa ($3-5)(WR)
3. white body, orange chassis, "Buccaneers 1992" tempa ($3-5)(WR)
4. white body, red chassis, "Falcons 1992" tempa ($3-5)(WR)
5. white body, turquoise chassis, "Dolphins 1992" tempa ($3-5)(WR)
6. white body, dark blue chassis, "Patriots 1992" tempa ($3-5)(WR)
7. white body, dark blue chassis, "Bills 1992" tempa ($3-5)(WR)
8. white body, dark blue chassis, "Colts 1992" tempa ($3-5)(WR)
9. white body, bright blue chassis, "Oilers 1992" tempa ($3-5)(WR)
10. white body, green chassis, "Jets 1992" tempa ($3-5)(WR)
11. white body, green chassis, "Eagles 1992" tempa ($3-5)(WR)
12. yellow body, purple chassis, "Vikings 1992" tempa ($3-5)(WR)
13. yellow body, black chassis, "Steelers 1992" tempa ($3-5)(WR)
14. yellow body, dark blue chassis, "Chargers 1992" tempa ($3-5)(WR)
15. yellow body, mid blue chassis, "LA Rams 1992" tempa ($3-5)(WR)
16. bright yellow body, green chassis, "Packers 1992" tempa ($3-5)(WR)
17. bright yellow body, red chassis, "Chiefs 1992" tempa ($3-5)(WR)
18. bright yellow body, red-brown chassis, "Cardinals 1992" tempa($3-5)(WR)
19. orange body, black chassis, "Bengals 1992" tempa ($3-5)(WR)
20. orange body, dark blue chassis, "Bears 1992" tempa ($3-5)(WR)

21. orange body, mid blue chassis, "Broncos 1992" tempa ($3-5)(WR)
22. gold body, red chassis, "49ers 1992" tempa ($3-5)(WR)
23. green-gold body, black chassis, "Saints 1992" tempa ($3-5)(WR)
24. silver-gray body, black chassis, "Raiders 1992" tempa ($3-5)(WR)
25. silver-gray body, dark blue chassis, "Cowboys 1992" tempa ($3-5)(WR)
26. silver-gray body, mid blue chassis, "Seahawks 1992" tempa ($3-5)(WR)
27. silver-gray body, bright blue chassis, "Lions 1992" tempa ($3-5)(WR)
28. red body, dark blue chassis, "Giants 1992" tempa ($3-5)(WR)
29. florescent orange body, lavender chassis, "York Fair 1992" tempa ($6-8)(WR)
30. bright blue body, yellow chassis, "Brewers 1993" tempa ($5-7)(WR)
31. dark blue body, orange chassis, "Astros 1993" tempa ($5-7)(WR)
32. dark blue body, red chassis, "Red Sox 1993" tempa ($5-7)(WR)
33. dark blue body, red chassis, "Twins 1993" tempa ($5-7)(WR)
34. blue body, red chassis, "Expos 1993" tempa ($5-7)(WR)
35. blue body, bright blue chassis, "Toronto Blue Jays 1993" tempa ($5-7)(WR)
36. blue body, orange chassis, "NY Mets 1993" tempa ($5-7)(WR)
37. blue body, white chassis, "Dodgers 1993" tempa ($5-7)(WR)
38. gray body, black chassis, "Giants 1993" tempa ($5-7)(WR)
39. gray body, dark blue chassis, "Indians 1993" tempa ($5-7)(WR)
40. gray body, red chassis, "Chicago Cubs 1993" tempa ($5-7)(WR)
41. silver-gray body, black chassis, "White Sox 1993" tempa ($5-7)(WR)
42. silver-gray body, blue-green chassis, "Mariners 1993" tempa ($5-7)(WR)
43. orange-yellow body, green chassis, "Oakland A's 1993" tempa ($5-7)(WR)
44. black body, lemon chassis, "Pirates 1993" tempa ($5-7)(WR)
45. black body, purple chassis, "Rockies 1993" tempa ($5-7)(WR)
46. red body, black chassis, "Reds 1993" tempa ($5-7)(WR)
47. red body, dark blue chassis, "Cardinals 1993" tempa ($5-7)(WR)
48. red body, white chassis, "Phillies 1993" tempa ($5-7)(WR)
49. white body, orange chassis, "Padres 1993" tempa ($5-7)(WR)
50. white body, dark blue chassis, "Angels 1993" tempa ($5-7)(WR)
51. white body, light blue chassis, "Marlins 1993" tempa ($5-7)(WR)
52. white body, blue chassis, "Yankees 1993" tempa ($5-7)(WR)
53. white body, blue chassis, "Tigers 1993" tempa ($5-7)(WR)
54. white body, metallic blue chassis, "Braves 1993" tempa ($5-7)(WR)
55. white body, red chassis, "Rangers 1993" tempa ($5-7)(WR)
56. powder blue body, dark blue chassis, "Royals 1993" tempa ($5-7)(WR)
57. orange body, black chassis, "Orioles 1993" tempa ($5-7)(WR)
58. red-brown body, yellow chassis, "Redskins 1993" tempa ($5-7)(WR)
59. white body, orange chassis, "Reithoffer's-Tickets for All Attractions" tempa ($4-6) (WR)(GS)
60. white & blue body, blue chassis, gold grille & wheels, "Penn State 1993" tempa ($5-7)(WR)
61 white body, dark blue chassis, "Florida Panthers 1993" tempa ($5-7)(WR)
62. white body, grape chassis, "Mighty Ducks 1993" tempa ($5-7)(WR)
63 white body, blue chassis, "Washington Capitals 20th Anniversary 1974-1994" tempa ($5-7)(WR)
64. black body, gold chassis, "Dallas Stars 1993" tempa ($5-7)(WR)
65. light blue body, lavender chassis, gold grille & wheels, "York Fair 1994" tempa ($5-7)(WR)
66. red body, white chassis, "1995 Temecula Rod Run" tempa, China casting ($10-15)(WR)

NOTE: Below models with black plastic base unless otherwise noted.

67. yellow body, black chassis, "Pioneer Distributors-Gowings" tempa, China casting ($10-15)(AU)
68. florescent orange body & chassis, "Matchbox Get In The Fast Lane-Hershey 1995" tempa, China casting ($8-12)(US)
69. red body, purple chassis, "Raptors 1995" tempa ($8-12)(AU)
70. red body, blue chassis, "Detroit Pistons 1995" tempa ($8-12)(AU)
71. dark red body, dark blue chassis, "Denver Nuggets 1995" tempa ($8-12)(AU)
72. orange body, purple chassis, "Phoenix Suns 1995" tempa ($8-12)(AU)
73. orange-yellow body, dark blue chassis, "Pacers 1995" tempa ($8-12)(AU)
74. lavender body, orange-yellow chassis, "Los Angeles Lakers 1995" tempa ($8-12)(AU)
75. blue-green body, orange chassis, "Knicks 1995" tempa ($8-12)(AU)
76. blue body, white chassis, "Orlando Magic 1995" tempa ($8-12)(AU)
77. dark blue body, orange-yellow chassis, "Golden State Warriors 1995" tempa ($15-20)(AU)
78. dark blue body, orange chassis, "San Antonio Spurs 1995" tempa ($8-12)(AU)
79. dark blue body, red chassis, "Chicago Bulls 1995" tempa ($8-12)(AU)
80. dark blue body, red chassis, "Houston Rockets 1995" tempa ($8-12)(AU)
81. dark green body, orange-yellow chassis, "Seattle Sonics 1995" tempa ($8-12)(AU)
82. green body, orange-yellow chassis, "Utah Jazz 1995" tempa ($8-12)(AU)
83. green body, white chassis, "Boston Celtics 1995" tempa ($8-12)(AU)
84. green body, blue chassis, "Dallas Mavericks 1995" tempa ($8-12)(AU)
85. black body, turquoise chassis, "Vancouver Grizzlies 1995" tempa ($8-12)(AU)
86. turquoise body, blue chassis, "Charlotte Hornets 1995" tempa ($8-12)(AU)
87. dark purple & black body, blue-green chassis, chrome disc wheels with rubber tires, "San Andreas Brewing Co." ($8-12)(MB)(CL)
88. silver blue & black body, cream chassis, chrome disc wheels with rubber tires, "Blue Ridge Brewing Co./ Hawksbill Lager" tempa ($8-12)(MB)(CL)
89. red & black body, black chassis, chrome disc wheels with rubber tires, "Dubuque Red" tempa ($8-12)(MB)(CL)
90. white & black body, lavender chassis & base, chrome disc wheels with rubber tires, "Samuel Adams" tempa ($8-12)(MB)(CL)
91. yellow & black body, red chassis & base, chrome disc wheels with rubber tires, "Red Ale" tempa ($8-12)(MB)(CL)
92. yellow & black body, green chassis & base, chrome disc wheels with rubber tires, "Gator Lager Beer" tempa ($8-12)(MB)(CL)

93. black body, chassis & base, money bags & bullet marks tempa ($4-6)(AU)
94. black body, gold chassis & base, chrome disc wheels with rubber tires, "75 Years/ Annes" tempa ($3-5)(MP)(CN)

MB58-I PORSCHE 911 GTi *see MB68-J*

MB58-J TRUCK CAMPER, issued 1999 (USA) (MB417)
MB53-J TRUCK CAMPER, issued 1999 (ROW)

NOTE: Below models with white door, 8 spoke wheels & China casting unless otherwise noted.

1. white body, silver-gray base, white interior, yellow windows, blue & yellow design with USA map tempa ($1-2)(MW58/1999 US)
2. white body, silver-gray base, white interior, yellow windows, blue & yellow design tempa ($1-2)(MW53/1999 ROW)(MW43/ 1999 GR)
3. cream body, black base, cream interior, blue windows, blue & lavender tempa ($1-2)(5pk)
4. white body, black base, red interior, blue windows, red & black stripes tempa ($1-2)(5pk)
5. light gray body, black base, gray interior, blue windows, red & yellow stripes tempa ($1-2)(MW612000 US/MW41/2000 ROW)
6. light gray body, black base, gray interior, blue windows, red & yellow stripes & "Matchbox 2000" tempa ($2-4)(MW61/2000 US)
7. light gray body, black base, gray interior, blue windows, red & yellow stripes & "Candy Hill Campgrounds" tempa ($18-25)(CCI)
8. dull yellow, lavender & brown body, black base, light brown interior, light smoke windows, "Wild Thornberry's" tempa, 7 spoke sawblade wheels ($1-2)(5pk)
9. white body, white base, white interior, clear windows, no tempa ($25-40)(ASAP blank)
10. white body, gray base, white interior, amber windows, "September 11/ All the German People Are On Your Side" tempa ($25-40)(CCI)
11. light gray body, black base, white interior, smoke windows, "September 11/ All the German People Are On Your Side" tempa ($25-40)(CCI)
12. orange body, black base, white interior, smoke windows, "Wyoming- Buffalo Bill's Traveling Horse Show" tempa ($2-4)(AM)
13. metallic green body, gray base, white interior, blue windows, "AR003", elephant & paw prints tempa ($1-2)(LP)
14. metallic pea green body, gray base, lime interior, red windows, "Camp Clifford" tempa ($1-2)(5pk)
15. yellow body, brown base, yellow interior, pale green windows, "Yogi Bear" tempa ($1-2)(5pk)
16. white body, white base, white interior, clear windows, "Health Care" tempa ($50+)(ASAP)

MB58-K INTERNATIONAL ARMOURED CAR, issued 2000 (MB446)

NOTE: Below models with China casting.

1. light gray body, blue windows, blue base, "Matchbox Armored Car Service" tempa, 8 spoke wheels ($1-2)(MW58/2000 US)
2. light gray body, blue windows, blue base, "Matchbox Armored Car Service" & "Matchbox 2000" tempa, 8 spokes ($2-4)(MW58/ 2000 US)
3. pearly gray body, smoke windows, black base, red & yellow crest tempa, 8 spoke wheels ($1-2)(5pk)
4. white body, blue windows, black base, no tempa, 8 spoke wheels ($25-40)(ASAP blank)
5. white body, blue windows, black base, "Selmac Savings" tempa, 8 spoke wheels ($75+)(ASAP)
6. beige & brown body, blue windows, black base, "AMSA" tempa, 8 spoke wheels ($35-50)(CCI)

   NOTE: Model above was disassembled & repainted & refitted with glue to the rivets area
7. blue body, smoke windows, gray base, "$ Money Mobile" tempa, 8 spoke wheels ($1-2)(MW17/2001 US)
8. blue body, smoke windows, gray base, "$ Money Mobile" tempa, 7 spoke sawblade wheels ($1-2)(MW17/2001 US)
9. silver-gray body, smoke windows, black base, "Nevada- Diamond Armored Delivery" tempa, 7 spoke sawblade wheels ($2-4)(AM)
10. white body, blue windows, white base, "PSI Armored" tempa, 7 spoke sawblade wheels ($25-40)(CCI)
11. white body, blue windows, white base, no tempa, 7 spoke sawblade wheels ($25-40)(CCI blank)
12. metallic charcoal body, blue windows, black painted (screws) base, "Titan Armored" tempa, 7 spoke sawblade wheels ($25-40)(CCI)
13. metallic purple body, blue windows, blue-green base, "Mr. Krabs" tempa, 7 spoke sawblade wheels ($1-2)(5pk)
14. silver blue body, blue windows, yellow base, "Mr. Krabs" tempa, 7 spoke sawblade wheels ($1-2)(5pk)
15. blue body, smoke windows, gray base, "$ Money Mobile/ Boston Bancgroup Inc." tempa, 7 spoke sawblade wheels ($25-40)(CCI)
16. white body, blue windows, white base, "Get On Board Matchbox Message Board/ Matchbox 50th Birthday Party" tempa, 7 spoke sawblade wheels ($15-20)(CCI)
17. white body, blue windows, white base, "MJ" & small lettering tempa, 7 spoke sawblade wheels ($45-60)(CCI)
18. lime body, blue windows, gray base, "MHC Bank 38" & piggy bank tempa, 7 spoke sawblade wheels ($1-2)(MW38/2003 US)
19. lime body, blue windows, gray base, "MHC Bank 38" & piggy bank with "Hero City" tempa, 7 spoke sawblade wheels ($2-4)(MW38/2003 US)
20. white body, blue windows, white base, "Matchbox USA Toy Show Security" (blue-green print) tempa, 7 spoke sawblade wheels ($12-18)(CCI)
21. white body, blue windows, white base, "Matchbox USA Toy Show Security" (orange print) tempa, 7 spoke sawblade wheels ($12-18)(CCI)
22. metallic silver body, black windows, black base, "NSB Nevada State Bank" tempa, 7 spoke sawblade wheels ($25-40)(US)
23. red & black body, black windows, black base, "Dunbar Armored" tempa, 7 spoke sawblade wheels ($25-40)(US)
24. white body, blue windows, white base, "Mobile Equipment Maintenance & Repair" tempa, 7 spoke sawblade wheels ($25-40)(ASAP)
25. white body, blue windows, white base, "2nd Annual Mambo Memorial" with black roof print tempa, 7 spoke sawblade wheels ($18-25)(CCI)
26. white body, blue windows, white base, "2nd Annual Mambo Memorial" with green roof print tempa, 7 spoke sawblade wheels ($25-40)(CCI)
27. white body, blue windows, white base, "2nd Annual Mambo Memorial" with gold roof print tempa 7 spoke sawblade wheels ($50-75)(CCI)
28. white body, blue windows, white base, "Artcraft Promotional Concepts" tempa, 7 spoke sawblade wheels ($25-40)(CCI)
29. white body, blue windows, white base, "Loomis Fargo & Co." tempa, 7 spoke sawblade wheels ($50+)(ASAP)
30. white body, blue windows, white base, "Armor Clad Friendship MCCH Gathering/ We're With You in Spirit CCI 2004" tempa, 7 spoke sawblade wheels ($18-25)(CCI)

MB58-L CHEVY AVALANCHE, issued 2002 (MB546)

NOTE: Below models with gray interior, gray rear canopy, 7 spoke sawblade wheels & China casting unless otherwise noted.

1. metallic green body, clear windows, gray base, "Avalanche" tempa ($1-2)(MW58)
2. metallic green body, clear windows, gray base, "Avalanche" & "Matchbox 50" tempa ($2-4)(MW58)
3. metallic green body, clear windows, gray base, "Happy Holidays- Color Comp Inc." tempa ($25-40)(CCI)
4. metallic green body, clear windows, gray base, "Happy Holidays- Matchbox Road Museum" tempa ($25-40)(CCI)
5. metallic lime body, amber windows, dark gray base & rear canopy, "49 Pine Forest" tempa ($1-2)(MW49)
6. metallic lime body, amber windows, dark gray base & rear canopy, "49 Pine Forest" & "Hero City" tempa ($2-4)(MW49)
7. white body, red windows, gray base, "Ace the Helpful Place" tempa ($3-5)(US- in pack offer)
8. red body, amber windows, gray base, "Ace the Helpful Place" tempa ($3-5)(US- in pack offer)
9. white body, beige interior, clear windows, gray base, detailed trim tempa, chrome disc wheels with rubber tires ($3-5)(SH)
10. dark metallic blue body, gray interior, clear windows, gray base, head & tail lights tempa, slotted 5 spoke wheels ($3-5)(SF5/2004)
11. pale gold body, black interior, smoke windows, gray base, "Coca-Cola Football Town/ Total Tailgate", 7 spoke sawblade wheels ($2-4)(CK)
12. orange-yellow body, dark blue interior, purple windows, dark blue base, "Team Force" & design tempa, 7 spoke sawblade wheels ($1-2)(5pk)

MB59-A FORD GALAXIE FIRE CHIEF, issued 1970

NOTE: Below models with blue dome light, ivory interior, clear windows, 5 spoke wheels & England casting.

1. red body, decal on hood, labels on sides ($35-50)
2. red body, labels on hood & sides ($35-50)
3. red body, labels on sides only ($35-50)
4. red body, labels on hood & sides with "Lyons Tea" label on trunk ($175-250)(BE)

MB59-B MERCURY FIRE CHIEF, issued 1971 (MB112/114/859)

NOTE: Below models cast with driver & passenger in interior. All models with blue dome or bar light unless otherwise noted.

1. red body, unpainted base, clear windows, dome light, ivory interior, 5 spoke wheels, "Fire Chief" in square hood label, shield side label, England casting ($12-15)
2. red body, unpainted base, clear windows, dome light, ivory interior, 5 spoke wheels, helmet & axes hood label, shield side label, England casting ($12-15)
3. red body, unpainted base, clear windows, dome light, ivory interior, 5 spoke wheels, helmet & axes hood & side labels, England casting ($8-12)
4. red body, unpainted base, clear windows, dome light, ivory interior, 5 spoke wheels, helmet & axes hood label only, England casting ($8-12)
5. red body, silver-gray base, clear windows, dome light, ivory interior, 5 spoke wheels, helmet & axes hood label only, England casting ($8-12)
6. red body, unpainted base, clear windows, dome light, ivory interior, 5 spoke wheels, "Fire Chief" in square hood label, helmet & axes side labels, England casting ($12-15)
7. red body, unpainted base, clear windows, dome light, ivory interior, 5 spoke wheels, red & yellow "Fire Chief" hood label, helmet & axes side labels, England casting ($12-15)
8. red body, unpainted base, clear windows, dome light, ivory interior, dot dash wheels, helmet & axes hood & side labels, England casting ($8-12)

NOTE: Below models cast without driver & passenger in interior.

9. red body, unpainted base, clear windows, dome light, ivory interior, dot dash wheels, helmet & axes hood & side labels, England casting ($8-12)
10. red body, unpainted base, clear windows, bar light, ivory interior, dot dash wheels, no hood labels, "Fire" with shield (from MB64-C) side labels, England casting ($5-7)(TP)
11. red body, unpainted base, clear windows, bar light, ivory interior, dot dash wheels, red & yellow "Fire Chief" hood label, "Fire" with shield side labels, England casting ($5-7)(TP)
12. white body, unpainted base, purple windows, bar light, ivory interior, dot dash wheels, no hood label, "Police" with shield side labels, England casting ($30-45)(TP)
13. white body, unpainted base, blue windows, bar light, ivory interior, dot dash wheels, "Los Angeles Police" tempa, England casting ($6-8)(CR)
14. white body, unpainted base, clear windows, bar light, ivory interior, dot dash wheels, "Los Angeles Police" tempa, England casting ($6-8)(CR)
15. white body, unpainted base, blue windows, bar light, white interior, dot dash wheels, "Los Angeles Police" tempa, England casting ($15-20)(CR)
16. red body, unpainted base, clear windows, bar light, ivory interior, dot dash wheels, "Los Angeles Fire Dept." tempa, England casting ($6-8)(CR)
17. red body, unpainted base, blue windows, bar light, ivory interior, dot dash wheels, Los Angeles Fire Dept." tempa, England casting ($15-20)(CR)
18. red body, unpainted base, clear windows, yellow bar light, ivory interior, dot dash wheels, "Los Angeles Fire Dept." tempa, England casting ($20-25)(CR)
19. white body, unpainted base, clear windows, bar light, ivory interior, dot dash wheels, "Police" with shield & black fenders tempa, England casting ($8-12)
20. white body, unpainted base, clear windows, bar light, white interior, dot dash wheels, "Police" with shield & black fenders tempa, England casting ($8-12)
21. white body, unpainted base, blue windows, bar light, white interior, dot dash wheels, "Police" with shield & black fenders tempa, England casting ($8-12)
22. white body, unpainted base, purple windows, bar light, ivory interior, dot dash wheels, "Police" with shield & black fenders tempa, England casting ($35-50)
23. white body, unpainted base, purple windows, bar light, white interior, dot dash wheels, "Police" with shield & black fenders tempa, England casting ($35-50)
24. white body, unpainted base, clear windows, bar light, white interior, dot dash wheels, "Metro Police" (without black fenders) tempa, England casting ($10-15)
25. white body, unpainted base, blue windows, bar light, white interior, dot dash wheels, "Metro Police" tempa, England casting ($8-12)
26. white body, silver-gray base, blue windows, bar light, white interior, dot dash wheels, "Metro Police" tempa, England casting ($8-12)
27. white body, silver-gray base, blue windows, bar light, white interior, dot dash wheels, "Los Angeles Police" tempa, England casting ($6-8)(CR)
28. white body, silver-gray base, blue windows, bar light, white interior, dot dash wheels, "201" roof & hood tempa , "Metro Police" side tempa, England casting ($25-40)

29. white body, unpainted base, blue windows, bar light, white interior, dot dash wheels, "201" roof & hood tempa, no side tempa, England casting ($15-20)
30. white body, silver-gray base, blue windows, bar light, white interior, dot dash wheels, "Metro" on hood tempa, shield on sides tempa, England casting ($8-12)
31. white body, silver-gray base, blue windows, bar light, white interior, dot dash wheels, "Metro Police" without black fenders tempa, England casting ($8-12)
32. red body, unpainted base, purple windows, bar light, ivory interior, dot dash wheels, no hood label, "Fire' with shield (from MB64-C) side labels, England casting ($35-50)(TP)
33. red body, unpainted base, clear windows, yellow bar light, ivory interior, dot dash wheels, no hood label, "Fire" with shield (from MB64-C) side labels, England casting ($15-25)(TP)
34. white body, unpainted base, clear windows, bar light, white interior, dot dash wheels, "Metro Police" tempa, England casting ($8-12)
35. white body, silver-gray base, smoke windows, bar light, white interior, dot dash wheels, "Metro Police" tempa, England casting ($8-12)
36. white body, unpainted base, blue windows, bar light, white interior, dot dash wheels, no labels, England casting ($8-12)
37. white body, silver-gray base, blue windows, bar light, white interior, dot dash wheels, "201" on roof only tempa, "Metro" side tempa, England casting ($8-12)
38. white body, unpainted base, clear windows, bar light, white interior, dot dash wheels, no labels, England casting ($8-12)
39. white body, silver-gray base, clear windows, bar light, white interior, dot dash wheels, no labels, England casting ($8-12)
40. white body, unpainted base, clear windows, bar light, ivory interior, dot dash wheels, "Police" with shield tempa, England casting ($8-12)(TP)
41. white body, unpainted base, clear windows, bar light, ivory interior, dot dash wheels, no hood label, "Police" shield side labels, England casting ($8-12)(TP)
42. white body, unpainted base, clear windows, yellow bar light, ivory interior, dot dash wheels, no hood label, "Police" shield side labels, England casting ($8-12)(TP)
43. white body, unpainted base, blue windows, bar light, ivory interior, dot dash wheels, "Metro" on hood, shield on sides tempa, England casting ($8-12)
44. white body, unpainted base, clear windows, bar light, ivory interior, dot dash wheels, "Metro" on hood, shield on sides tempa, England casting ($8-12)
45. white body, unpainted base, smoke windows, bar light, ivory interior, dot dash wheels, "Metro" on hood, shield on sides tempa, England casting ($8-12)
46. white body, silver-gray base, clear windows, bar light, white interior, dot dash wheels, "Metro" with black fenders tempa, England casting ($8-12)
47. white body, pearly silver base, blue windows, bar light, gray interior, starburst wheels, "State Police" tempa, Macau casting ($3-5)(SF)
48. white body, black base, blue windows, bar light, gray interior, starburst wheels, "State Police" tempa, Macau casting ($7-10)(SF)
49. white body, pearly silver base, blue windows, bar light, gray interior, laser wheels, "State Police" tempa, Macau casting ($3-5)(LW)
50. black body, black base, blue windows, bar light, gray interior, "Haley's Comet" tempa, Macau casting ($7-10)(MP)
51. metallic blue body, pearly silver base, blue windows, bar light, gray interior, starburst wheels, yellow/blue/red tempa, Macau casting, includes plastic armament ($5-8)(RB)
52. white body, silver-gray base, blue windows, bar light, gray interior, 8 dot wheels, orange & blue "State Police" tempa, China casting ($75+)(CHI)(Zimbabwe, Africa)
53. white body, pearly silver base, blue windows, bar light, gray interior, 8 dot wheels, orange & blue "State Police" tempa, Macau casting ($75+)(HK)

MB59-C PLANET SCOUT, issued 1975

NOTE: Below models with 5 crown front & dot dash rear wheels but other combinations do exist. Below models with metal chassis with black plastic base insert, chrome interior & England casting.

1. metallic green upper body, lime chassis, amber windows ($12-15)
2. metallic green upper body, apple green chassis, amber windows ($12-15)
3. metallic red upper body, beige chassis, amber windows ($12-15)
4. avocado upper body, black chassis, amber windows ($25-35)(AV)
5. avocado upper body, black chassis, purple windows ($25-35)(AV)
6. metallic dark blue body, black chassis, purple windows ($40-55)(AV)

NOTE: Available as a Bulgarian casting. Assorted colors available ($5-25)

MB59-D PORSCHE 928, issued 1980 (MB059)

NOTE: Below models with 5 arch wheels unless otherwise noted. Numerous intermediate shades of tan exist; too many to properly identify.

1. light metallic tan body, black base, ivory interior, clear windows, no tempa, England casting ($4-6)
2. light metallic tan body, black base, cream interior, clear windows, no tempa, England casting ($4-6)
3. light metallic tan body, black base, brown interior, clear windows, no tempa, England casting ($4-6)
4. metallic gray-brown body, black base, brown interior, clear windows, no tempa, England casting ($4-6)
5. light metallic tan body, black base, milky tan interior, clear windows, no tempa, England casting ($4-6)
6. mid metallic tan body, black base, brown interior, clear windows, no tempa, England casting ($4-6)
7. mid metallic tan body, black base, brown interior, amber windows, no tempa, England casting ($4-6)
8. mid metallic tan body, black base, tan interior, amber windows, no tempa, England casting ($4-6)
9. mid metallic tan body, black base, brown interior, orange windows, no tempa, England casting ($4-6)
10. dark metallic tan body, black base, brown interior, clear windows, no tempa, England casting ($4-6)
11. dark metallic tan body, black base, brown interior, amber windows, no tempa, England casting ($4-6)
12. light metallic tan body, charcoal base, brown interior, orange windows, no tempa, England casting ($4-6)
13. mid metallic tan body, charcoal base, brown interior, clear windows, no tempa, England casting ($4-6)
14. dark metallic tan body, charcoal base, brown interior, clear windows, no tempa, England casting ($4-6)
15. dark metallic tan body, black base, brown interior, orange windows, no tempa, England casting ($4-6)
16. dark metallic tan body, charcoal base, tan interior, amber windows, no tempa, England casting ($4-6)
17. dark metallic tan body, brown base, brown interior, amber windows, no tempa, England casting ($7-10)
18. dark metallic tan body, brown base, tan interior, amber windows, no tempa, England casting ($7-10)
19. dark metallic tan body, brown base, tan interior, clear windows, no tempa, England casting ($7-10)

20. metallic blue body, unpainted base, brown interior, clear windows, no tempa, England casting ($4-6)
21. metallic blue body, black base, tan interior, clear windows, no tempa, England casting ($4-6)
22. metallic blue body, black base, brown interior, clear windows, no tempa, England casting ($4-6)
23. metallic blue body, charcoal base, brown interior, clear windows, no tempa, England casting ($4-6)
24. metallic blue body, silver-gray base, brown interior, clear windows, no tempa, England casting ($4-6)
25. metallic blue body, silver-gray base, tan interior, clear windows, no tempa, England casting ($4-6)
26. metallic blue body, black base, brown interior, clear windows, "Climat" label on hood, England casting ($125-175)(FR)
27. black body, silver-gray base, brown interior, clear windows, "Porsche" & stripes tempa, England casting ($8-12)
28. black body, silver-gray base, red interior, clear windows, "Porsche" & stripes tempa, England casting ($3-5)
29. black body, unpainted base red interior, clear windows, "Porsche" & stripes tempa, England casting ($3-5)
30. black body, pearly silver base, red interior, clear windows, "Porsche" & stripes tempa, Macau casting ($2-4)
31. black body, pearly silver base, red interior, light amber windows, "Porsche" & stripes tempa, Macau casting ($2-4)
32. light metallic gray body & base, red interior, clear windows, purple & blue tempa, Macau casting ($3-5)
33. pearly silver body, & base, red interior, clear windows, "Martini Racing Porsche" tempa, Macau casting ($7-10)(JP)
34. white & metallic blue body, white base, red interior, clear windows, "28" with "Cale Jenkins" tempa, starburst wheels, Macau casting ($3-5)(SF)
35. white & metallic blue body, white base, red interior, clear windows, "28" without "Cale Jenkins" tempa, starburst wheels, Macau casting ($3-5)(SF)
36. white & metallic blue body, white base, red interior, clear windows, "28" with "Cale Jenkins" tempa, laser wheels, Macau casting ($3-5)(LW)
37. white & metallic blue body, white base, red interior, clear windows, "28" without "Cale Jenkins" tempa, laser wheels, Macau casting ($3-5)(LW)
38. orange body, pearly silver base, red interior, clear windows, "Lufthansa" tempa, Macau casting ($4-6)(GS)
39. charcoal gray body & base, no interior, chrome windows, detailed trim tempa, gray disc wheels with rubber tires, doors cast shut, Macau casting ($5-8)(WC)
40. charcoal gray body & base, no interior, chrome windows, detailed trim tempa, gray disc wheels with rubber tires, doors cast shut, Thailand casting ($5-8)(WC)
41. white body, white base, red interior, clear windows, "56 Porsche" with red stripes tempa, starburst wheels, doors cast shut, China casting ($12-15)(PS)
42. yellow body, pearly silver base, red interior, clear windows, "Porsche 928" & logo tempa, starburst wheels, doors cast shut, China casting ($12-15)(PS)
43. silver-gray body, silver-gray base, purple & gray interior, clear windows, "928S" & detailed trim tempa, chrome disc wheels with rubber tires, Thailand casting ($3-5)(JC)(PC)

MB59-E PORSCHE 944 TURBO *see MB71-G*

MB59-F T-BIRD TURBO COUPE, issued 1987 (USA) (MB196)
MB61-D T-BIRD TURBO COUPE, issued 1987 (ROW)
MB28-J T-BIRD TURBO COUPE, reissued 1992 (ROW)

NOTE: Below models with metal base & black side stripe unless otherwise noted. Versions 1, 3-6, 9 & 10 with bird emblem towards front, towards rear or omitted.

1. plum body & base, clear windows, silver-gray interior, 8 dot wheels, "Turbo Coupe" tempa, Macau casting ($1-2)
2. metallic gold body & base, clear windows, silver-gray interior, laser wheels, "56 Motorcraft" tempa, Macau casting ($3-5)(LW)
3. light pea green body, silver-gray base, clear windows, silver-gray interior, 8 dot wheels, "Turbo Coupe" tempa, Macau casting ($3-4)(SC)
4. dark brown body, silver-gray base, clear windows, silver-gray interior, 8 dot wheels, "Turbo Coupe" tempa, Macau casting ($3-4)(SC)
5. pink body, silver-gray base, clear windows, silver-gray interior, 8 dot wheels, "Turbo Coupe" tempa, Macau casting ($3-4)(SC)
6. dark purple body, silver-gray base, clear windows, silver-gray interior, 8 dot wheels, "Turbo Coupe" tempa, Macau casting ($3-4)(SC)
7. silver-gray body & base, chrome windows, silver-gray interior with red side stripe, gray disc wheels with rubber tires, detailed trim tempa, Macau casting ($5-8)(WC)
8. silver-gray body & base, chrome windows, silver-gray interior with black side stripe, gray disc wheels with rubber tires, detailed trim tempa, Macau casting ($50-65)(WC)
9. plum body & base, clear windows, silver-gray interior, 8 dot wheels, "Turbo Coupe" tempa, Thailand casting ($1-2)
10. bright plum body & base, clear windows, silver-gray interior, 8 dot wheels, "Turbo Coupe" tempa, Thailand casting ($1-2)
11. metallic blue body, florescent pink base, clear windows, silver-gray interior, 8 dot wheels, stripes tempa, Thailand casting ($1-2)
12. metallic red body & base, clear windows, silver-gray interior, 8 dot wheels, small wing logos tempa, Thailand casting ($3-4)(SS)
13. gold body & base, clear windows, ivory & black interior, chrome disc wheels with rubber tires, detailed trim tempa, Thailand casting ($3-5)(PC1)
14. charcoal body & base, clear windows, red & black interior with dark red side stripe, chrome disc wheels with rubber tires, detailed trim tempa, Thailand casting ($3-5)(PC)(JC)
15. dark green body & base, clear windows, black & ivory interior, chrome disc wheels with rubber tires, detailed trim tempa, Thailand casting ($3-5)(PC5)
16. red body & base, clear windows, black & ivory interior, chrome disc wheels with rubber tires, detailed trim tempa, Thailand casting ($3-5)(SC2)
17. white body & base, clear windows, red & black interior with red side stripe, chrome disc wheels with rubber tires, detailed trim tempa, Thailand casting ($15-20)(GC)
18. black body, charcoal base, clear windows, black & gray interior with blue side stripe, chrome disc wheels with rubber tires, detailed trim & blue side stripe tempa, Thailand casting ($3-5)(SC5)

MB59-G ASTON MARTIN DB-7, issued 1994 (USA) (MB261)
MB63-I ASTON MARTIN DB-7, issued 1994 (ROW)

NOTE: Below models with black plastic base.

1. metallic green body, tan interior, clear windows, gold 6-spoke spiral wheels, "DB-7" & stripe tempa, Thailand casting ($1-2)
2. metallic green body, tan interior, clear windows, gold 6-spoke spiral wheels, small hood logo tempa, Thailand casting ($1-2)

NOTE: Above model with or without sun roof cast.

3. charcoal gray body, tan interior, chrome windows, gray disc wheels with rubber tires, detailed trim tempa, Thailand casting ($2-4)(WC)

NOTE: Above model with "007" or "DB7" license plate and with or without sun roof cast.

4. blue body, tan interior, clear windows, silver 6-spoke spiral wheels, no tempa, Thailand casting ($3-5)

5. silver-gray body, gray & black interior, clear windows, chrome disc wheels with rubber tires, detailed trim tempa, Thailand casting ($6-10)(PC1-ROW)
6. silver blue body, black interior, clear windows, chrome disc wheels with rubber tires, detailed trim tempa, Thailand casting ($8-12)(UC)
7. pearl white body, black & brown interior, clear windows, chrome disc wheels with rubber tires, detailed trim tempa, Thailand casting ($3-5)(PC10)
8. blue body, tan interior, clear windows, 5 spoke concave star wheels, small hood logo tempa, Thailand casting ($2-3)
9. candy red body, black & brown interior, clear windows, chrome disc wheels with rubber tires, detailed trim tempa, Thailand casting ($3-5)(PC2-JC)
10. metallic green body, black & brown interior, clear windows, chrome disc wheels with rubber tires, detailed trim tempa, Thailand casting ($50+)(GC)(CHI)

NOTE: Above model was intended to be sold in the gold coin series but was issued separately for sale in China.

MB59-H CAMARO Z-28 POLICE CAR, issued 1995 (USA) (MB254B/458/483)
MB56-J CAMARO Z-28 POLICE CAR, issued 1995 (ROW)

NOTE: Below models with black plastic base.

1. black body, white interior, smoke windows, 6 spoke spiral wheels, red bar light, "Police" with gold on white star on doors tempa, Thailand casting ($1-2)
2. black body, white interior, smoke windows, 6 spoke spiral wheels, red bar light, "Police" with black on white star on doors tempa, Thailand casting ($1-2)
3. white body, white interior, smoke windows, 6 spoke spiral wheels, red bar light, blue "Police" with star logo tempa, Thailand casting ($1-2)(5pk)
4. black & white body, black & gray interior, clear windows, chrome disc wheels with rubber tires, red bar light, "Highway Patrol" tempa, Thailand casting ($3-5)(PC8)
5. white & black body, black & gray interior, clear windows, chrome disc wheels with rubber tires, blue bar light, "Texas Dept. Public Safety Trooper" tempa, Thailand casting ($3-5)(PC8)
6. bright blue body, black & blue interior, clear windows, chrome disc wheels with rubber tires, red bar light, "NY State Police" tempa, Thailand casting ($3-5)(PC8)
7. blue body, white interior, blue windows, 5 spoke concave star wheels, red bar light, "Police Unit 4" tempa, Thailand casting ($1-2)(5pk)
8. white body, blue interior, clear windows, 5 spoke concave star wheels, blue bar light, "Matchbox Police" tempa, Thailand casting ($1-2)
9. metallic gold body, black interior, clear windows, 6 spoke spiral wheels, red bar light, no tempa, Thailand casting ($5-10)(CH)
10. black body, white interior, blue windows, 5 spoke concave star wheels, red bar light, "Matchbox Police 911" tempa, Thailand casting ($1-2)(MW27/1998 US)
11. black body, black & gray interior, clear windows, chrome disc wheels with rubber tires, red bar light, "Kansas Highway Patrol" tempa, Thailand casting ($3-5)(PC18)
12. metallic blue & silver-gray body, black & gray interior, clear windows, chrome disc wheels with rubber tires, red & blue bar light, "Nevada Highway Patrol" tempa, Thailand casting ($3-5)(PC18)
13. white body, black & gray interior, clear windows, red & blue bar light, chrome disc wheels with rubber tires, "Utah Highway Patrol" tempa, Thailand casting ($3-5)(PC18)
14. black body, white interior, blue windows, red bar light, 5 spoke concave star wheels, "Matchbox Police 911" tempa, China casting ($1-2)(MW27/1998 US)
15. blue body, white interior, blue windows, red bar light, 5 spoke concave star wheels, "Matchbox Police" tempa, China casting ($1-2)(5pk)
16. white body, black interior, clear windows, red bar light, 5 spoke concave star wheels, "Highway Patrol/ DWI Enforcement" tempa, China casting ($1-2)(5pk)
17. black & white body, black & blue interior, clear windows, red & blue bar light, chrome disc wheels with rubber tires, "Wyoming Highway Patrol" tempa, China casting ($4-6)(PC)
18. white body, black & blue interior, clear windows, red & blue bar light, chrome disc wheels with rubber wheels, "City of Miami 7630" tempa, China casting ($125-175)(PC22)
19. white body, black & red interior, red & blue bar light, clear windows, chrome disc wheels with rubber wheels, "State Patrol Nebraska" tempa, China casting ($4-6)(PC)
20. white body, black interior, amber bar light, amber windows, 5 spoke concave star wheels, "Dial 1-888-Road Rescue" with dashed road, "Dial" (slants left) tempa, China casting ($1-2)(MW98/1999 US)
21. white body, black interior, amber bar light, amber windows, star with 5 spokes wheels, "Dial 1-888-Road Rescue" with dashed road, "Dial" (slants left) tempa, China casting ($8-12)(MW98/1999 US)
22. white body, black interior, amber bar light, amber windows, 5 spoke concave star wheels, "Dial 1-888-Road Rescue" with dotted road, "Dial" (slants right) tempa, China casting ($25-50)(MW98/1999 US)
23. red body, black interior, red bar light, smoke windows, 5 spoke concave star wheels, "5", crest & white band tempa, China casting ($1-2)(LP)
24. white & powder blue body, gray interior, red bar light, clear windows, 5 spoke concave star wheels, "Police DARE/ New Rochelle" tempa, China casting ($3-5)(DR)
25. black body, black interior, red & blue bar light, clear windows, 5 spoke concave star wheels, "DARE/ Crime Stopper" with stripes & stars tempa, China casting ($3-5)(DR)
26. red body, black interior, amber bar light, smoke windows, 5 spoke concave star wheels, silver & blue stripes with crest tempa, China casting ($1-2)(5pk)
27. white body, gray interior, red bar light, smoke windows, 5 spoke concave star wheels, "DARE" with lion & flag tempa, China casting ($1-2)(MW89/2000 US)
28. white body, gray interior, red bar light, smoke windows, 5 spoke concave star wheels, "DARE" with lion & flag & "Matchbox 2000" tempa, China casting ($2-4)(MW89/2000 US)
29. white & black body, gray interior, triangular dome light, smoke windows, chrome disc wheels with rubber tires, "Dare America/ Matchbox" tempa, China casting ($8-12)(US)(DR)
30. white body, gray interior, red bar light, smoke windows, 10 spoke flower wheels, "DARE" with lion & flag tempa, China casting ($2-3)(MW89/2000 US)
31. blue body, black interior, red bar light, smoke windows, lace wheels, "5", crest & white band tempa, China casting ($1-2)(LP)
32. blue body, black interior, red bar light smoke windows, 5 spoke concave star wheels, "5", crest & white band tempa, China casting ($8-10)(LP)

NOTE: Below models with China casting.

33. orange-red body, black interior, blue bar light, smoke windows, lace wheels, "DARE" with white & blue design tempa ($1-2)(5pk)
34. silver-gray body, gray interior, red bar light, red windows, lace wheels, "Take a Bite Out of Crime" tempa ($1-2)(MW7/2002 US)

NOTE: Above model with Matchbox International or Mattel casting.

35. silver-gray body, gray interior, red bar light, red windows, lace wheels, "Take a Bite Out of Crime" & "Matchbox 50" tempa ($2-4)(MW7/2002 US)
36. white body, black interior, red bar light, smoke windows, lace wheels, "New Hampshire Presidential Primary Parade Security" tempa ($1-2)(AM)

NOTE: Above model with Matchbox International or Mattel casting.

37. white body, white interior, red bar light, smoke windows, lace wheels, "Police Emergency 911" tempa, Mattel casting ($1-2)(MW30/2003 US)
38. white body, white interior, red bar light, smoke windows, lace wheels, "Police Emergency 911" & "Hero City" tempa , Mattel casting ($2-4)(MW30/2003 US)
39. white body, black interior, red bar light, amber windows, lace wheels, "Police" with shield & design tempa, Mattel casting ($1-2)(5pk)

MB59-I VAUXHALL FRONTERA *see MB56-I*

MB59-J WHITE WATER RAFT BOAT, issued 1999 (USA) (MB422)
MB54-N WHITE WATER RAFT BOAT, issued 1999 (ROW)

NOTE: Below models with black motor, 5 spoke center cut wheels & China casting.

1. blue deck, white hull, "Action Canyon" boat tempa, blue trailer , "Raft" trailer tempa ($1-2)(MW59/1999 US)(MW54/1999 ROW)
2. yellow deck, turquoise hull, orange ropes boat tempa, black trailer, "Water Rescue" trailer tempa ($3-4)(MW37/2000 AU)
3. orange deck, orange hull, "RNLI Lifeboats" boat tempa, blue trailer "Lifeboats/ RNLI" trailer tempa ($3-4)(MW37/2000 UK)
4. red deck, yellow hull, "Base-1/ A1697-935L" boat tempa, black trailer, "Base-1" trailer tempa ($3-4)(MW14/2000 ROW)
5. yellow deck, metallic blue hull, lime motor, none boat tempa, lime trailer, "River Research" tempa, black hubs ($5-6)(PB)
6. dark blue deck, metallic silver hull, orange-yellow motor, none boat tempa, blue trailer, "S.O.S. & logo tempa, blue hubs ($1-2)(5pk)
7. yellow deck, red hull, black motor, "303 Surf Rescue" boat tempa, black trailer, none trailer tempa, black hubs ($2-4)(MW54/2001 AU)
8. turquoise deck, white hull, dark gray motor, none boat tempa, silver-gray trailer, "S.C.U.B.A. Rescue" trailer tempa, silver hubs ($1-2)(MW65/2001 US)
9. turquoise deck, white hull, silver-gray motor, none boat tempa, silver-gray trailer, "S.C.U.B.A. Rescue" trailer tempa, black hubs ($1-2) (MW65/2001 US)
10. red deck, white hull, dark blue motor, none boat tempa, yellow trailer, "Beach Patrol S.C.U.B.A." trailer tempa, black hubs ($1-2)(5pk)
11. white deck, yellow hull, red motor, "Louisiana" boat tempa, white trailer, "18 La Cajun Bayou" trailer tempa, silver hubs ($1-2)(AM)
12. red deck, orange hull, light blue motor, "Beach Patrol S.C.U.B.A." tempa, black hubs ($1-2)(5pk)

MB59-K VW TRANSPORTER *see MB64-J*

MB59-L CHRYSLER PANEL CRUISER, issued 2001 (MB516)

NOTE: Below models with 10 spoke flower wheels, black plastic base & China casting unless otherwise noted.

1. blue body, black interior, dark smoke windows, "Panel Cruiser" with black rear panel tempa ($1-2)(MW59/2001)
2. blue body, black interior, dark smoke windows, "Panel Cruiser" without rear panel tempa ($1-2)(MW59/2001)
3. blue body, black interior, dark smoke windows, "PMCC Holiday Dinner" tempa ($12-18)(CCI)
4. blue body, black interior, dark smoke windows, "2nd Northern New Jersey Toy Show 2002" tempa ($10-15)(CCI)
5. powder blue body, white interior, amber windows, "Matchbox Car Wash" tempa, gray base ($3-5)(PS)
6. metallic gold body, brown interior, clear windows, woodgrain sides tempa ($1-2)(MW30/2002)
7. metallic gold body, brown interior, clear windows, woodgrain sides & "Matchbox 50" tempa ($2-4)(MW30/2002)
8. black body, dark gray interior, smoke windows, basketball design tempa ($1-2)(5pk)
9. dark blue body, black interior, smoke windows, "NJDCC 2002" decals ($10-15)(C2)
10. blue body, black interior, smoke windows, "Discount Bestattangshaus Croellwitz" tempa ($12-18)(C2)(GR)
11. metallic gold body, brown interior, clear windows, "Discount Bestattangshaus Croellwitz" tempa & woodgrain sides tempa ($12-18)(C2)(GR)
12. black & butterscotch tempa, white interior, clear windows, "Coca Cola Here's Something Good" tempa, chrome disc wheels with rubber tires ($3-5)(Coke PC)
13. blue body, black interior, smoke windows, "One Vision One Voice" tempa ($1-15)(CCI)
14. white body, silver-gray interior, blue windows, "Richie's Burgerama 37" tempa, silver-gray base ($1-2)(MW37/2003 US)
15. white body, silver-gray interior, blue windows, "Richie's Burgerama" & "Hero City" tempa, silver-gray base ($2-4)(MW37/2003 US)
16. metallic gold body, brown interior, clear windows, "Matchbox Treffen Deutschland Leipzig- Mambo Lifestyle Service" tempa ($12-18)(C2)(GR)
17. metallic gold body, brown interior, clear windows, "Millersville Area Meals on Wheels" tempa ($12-18)(CCI)
18. red body, orange-yellow interior, blue windows, "Boston Tea Party" tempa, lace wheels ($2-4)(AW)(MP)
19. bright blue body, gray interior, smoke windows, detailed trim & black rear window tempa, 5 spoke slotted wheels, gray base ($1-2)(SF45/2004)

MB59-M CYCLE WITH SIDECAR, issued 2002 (MB547)

NOTE: Below models with black spoke wheels & China casting.

1. metallic blue body, white forks, white seats, white base, "Matchbox No. 420 Police" tempa ($1-2)(MW59/2002)
2. metallic blue body, white forks, white seats, white base, "Matchbox No. 420 Police" & "Matchbox 50" tempa ($2-4)(MW59/2002)
3. red body, blue & yellow forks, yellow seats, blue base, "Toy Fair Police/ Matchbox Hero City" tempa ($15-25)(US)
4. metallic blue body, white & yellow forks, yellow seats, white base, "Rescue Heroes" tempa ($1-2)(5pk)
5. lime body, blue & white forks, white seats, blue base, "Police 28" tempa ($2-4)(MW28/2003 ROW)
6. lime body, blue & white forks, white seats, blue base, "Police 28" & "Hero City" tempa ($2-4)(MW28/2003 ROW)
7. lime body, blue forks, white seats, blue base, "Police 28" & "Hero City" tempa ($50-75)(MW28/2003 ROW)
8. lime body, blue forks, white seats, blue base, "Police 28" tempa ($50-75)(MW28/2003 ROW)
9. yellow body, yellow & blue forks, blue seats, yellow base, "Police 28" & stripes tempa ($1-2)(MW28/2003 US)
10. yellow body, yellow & blue forks, blue seats, yellow base, "Police 28" & stripes with "Hero City" tempa ($2-4)(MW28/2003 US)

11. metallic yellow body, yellow & blue forks, blue seats, yellow base, "Police 28" & stripes tempa ($3-4)(20pk)
12. metallic maroon body, white forks, white seats, white base, "Matchbox Hero City" tempa ($1-2)(MW40/2004)

MB60-A SITE HUT TRUCK, issued 1970
1. blue body, blue windows, yellow plastic building with green roof , chrome base, 5 spoke wheels, England casting ($25-40)

MB60-B LOTUS SUPER SEVEN, issued 1971
NOTE: Below models with unpainted base, black interior, clear windshield, 4 spoke wheels & England casting unless otherwise noted.
1. orange body, flames label ($15-18)
2. yellow body, flames label ($150-175)
3. yellow body, checkers & "60" tempa ($18-25)
4. red body, flames label, base with Manaus label ($250+)(BR)

MB60-C HOLDEN PICK-UP, issued 1977 (MB060)
NOTE: Below models with dot dash wheels, unpainted metal base & England casting.
1. metallic maroon body, orange interior, amber windows, yellow cycles, "500" label ($12-15)
2. metallic maroon body, light yellow interior, amber windows, yellow cycles, "500" label ($12-15)
3. red body, light yellow interior, amber windows, yellow cycles, "500" label ($7-10)
4. red body, light yellow interior, orange windows, yellow cycles, "500" label ($7-10)
5. red body, light yellow interior, amber windows, lemon cycles, "500" label ($7-10)
6. red body, light yellow interior, clear windows, yellow cycles, "500" label ($7-10)
7. red body, light yellow interior, amber windows, yellow cycles, star label ($20-25)
8. red body, red interior, amber windows, yellow cycles, "500" label ($8-12)
9. red body, red interior, amber windows, olive cycles, "500" label ($10-15)
10. red body, red interior, orange windows, olive cycles, "500" label ($10-15)
11. red body, red interior, amber windows, olive cycles, sunburst (from MB47-B) label ($10-15)
12. red body, red interior, orange windows, olive cycles, sunburst label (from MB47-B) ($10-15)
13. cream body, red interior, amber windows, yellow cycles, "Superbike" labels ($8-12)
14. cream body, red interior, amber windows, red cycles, "Superbike" labels ($6-8)
15. cream body, red interior, orange windows, red cycles, "Superbike" labels ($6-8)
16. cream body, tan interior, amber windows, red cycles, "Superbike" labels ($6-8)
17. cream body, tan interior, amber windows, yellow cycles, "Superbike" labels ($6-8)
18. white body, red interior, amber windows, red cycles, "Superbike" labels ($12-15)
19. cream body, red interior, amber windows, red cycles, "Honda" labels ($15-20)
20. metallic blue body, light yellow interior, amber windows, yellow cycles, "Paris Dakar 81" label ($35-50)(FR)
21. metallic blue body, light yellow interior, amber windows, yellow cycles, "Paris Dakar 81" & "Climat" (on roof) label ($125-175)(FR)
22. tan body, yellow interior, amber windows, yellow cycles, "500" label, light gray base with Manaus label ($250+)(BR)

MB60-D PISTON POPPER, issued 1982 (USA) (MB104)
NOTE: Below models with unpainted metal base, amber windows & maltese cross rear wheels unless otherwise noted.
1. yellow body, red interior, maltese cross front wheels, no tempa, England casting ($7-10)
2. yellow body, red interior, 5 spoke front wheels, "60" towards front side tempa, no trunk tempa, England casting ($5-7)
3. yellow body, red interior, 5 spoke front wheels, "60" towards rear side tempa, no trunk tempa, England casting ($5-7)
4. yellow body, red interior, 5 spoke front wheels, "60" towards rear side tempa, with trunk tempa, England casting ($5-7)
5. yellow body, white interior, 5 spoke front wheels, "60" towards rear side tempa, with trunk tempa, England casting ($10-15)
6. yellow body, red interior, 5 spoke front wheels, no side tempa, with trunk tempa, England casting ($7-10)
7. yellow body, red interior, maltese cross front, "60" towards rear side tempa, no trunk tempa, England casting ($10-15)
8. orange body, red interior, 5 spoke front wheels, unpainted base, "Sunkist" tempa, Hong Kong casting ($4-6)
9. orange body, red interior, 5 spoke front wheels, black base, "Sunkist" tempa, Macau casting ($4-6)

MB60-F PONTIAC FIREBIRD RACER, issued 1985 (USA) (MB155)
MB12-F PONTIAC FIREBIRD RACER, issued 1985 (ROW)
MB48-G PONTIAC FIREBIRD RACER, reissued 1993 (USA)
MB48-G PONTIAC FIREBIRD RACER, reissued 1994 (ROW)
NOTE: Below models with clear windows unless otherwise noted.
1. yellow body, blue metal base, red interior, 8 dot silver wheels, "Son of A Gun 55" tempa, Macau casting ($4-6)
2. yellow body, blue metal base, red interior, 8 dot silver wheels, "Pirelli 56" tempa, Macau casting ($4-6)
3. yellow body, blue metal base, red interior, 8 dot gold wheels, "Son of A Gun 55" tempa, Macau casting ($4-6)
4. yellow body, blue metal base, red interior, 8 dot gold wheels, "Pirelli 56" tempa, Macau casting ($4-6)
5. yellow body, blue metal base, red interior, dot dash wheels, "Son of A Gun 55" tempa, Macau casting ($4-6)
6. yellow body, blue metal base, red interior, dot dash wheels, "Pirelli 56" tempa, Macau casting ($4-6)
7. yellow body, blue metal base, red interior, 5 arch wheels, "Pirelli 56" tempa, Macau casting ($4-6)
8. yellow body, blue metal base, red interior, 8 dot silver wheels, "Pirelli 56" (plain sides) tempa, Macau casting ($4-6)
9. powder blue body, blue metal base, gray interior, starburst wheels, "10" with blue & yellow tempa, Macau casting ($3-5)(SF)
10. metallic blue body, blue metal base, gray interior, laser wheels, "10" with blue & yellow tempa, Macau casting ($3-5)(LW)
11. white body, blue metal base, red interior, 5 arch wheels, "Fast Eddies 15" tempa, Macau casting ($2-4)
12. white body, blue metal base, red interior, 8 dot silver wheels, "Fast Eddies 15" tempa, Macau casting ($2-4)
13. white body, blue metal base, red interior, 8 dot silver wheels, "6 Horse Racing Team" tempa, Macau casting ($8-12)(HK)
14. dark brown body, blue metal base, red interior, 8 dot silver wheels, "Fast Eddies 15" tempa, Macau casting ($7-10)(SC)
15. light pea green body, blue metal base, red interior, 8 dot silver wheels, "Fast Eddies 15" tempa, Macau casting ($7-10)(SC)
16. white body, blue plastic base, red interior, 8 dot silver wheels, "Fast Eddies 15" tempa, Macau casting ($3-5)

17. powder blue body, blue plastic base, gray interior, starburst wheels, "10" with blue & yellow tempa, Macau casting ($7-10)(SF)
18. yellow body, red plastic base, red interior, starburst wheels, "10" with red & white stripes tempa, Macau casting ($15-20)(SF)
19. metallic blue body, blue plastic base, gray interior, laser wheels, "10" with yellow & blue stripes tempa, Macau casting ($7-10)(LW)
20. white body, blue plastic base, red interior, starburst wheels, "Fast Eddies 15" tempa, China casting ($6-8)(GS)
21. black body, pink plastic base, silver-gray interior, 8 dot wheels, blue & pink tempa, Thailand casting ($2-3)
22. fluorescent pink body, bright yellow plastic base, gold 6-spoke spiral wheels, yellow & white design tempa, Thailand casting ($1-2)
23. purple body, bright yellow plastic base, gold 6-spoke spiral wheels, yellow & white design tempa, Thailand casting ($6-8)(PS)
24. florescent pink body, bright yellow plastic base, silver 6-spoke spiral wheels, yellow & white hood & side design tempa, Thailand casting ($1-2)
25. dark florescent pink body, bright yellow plastic base, silver 6-spoke spiral wheels, yellow & white side design only tempa, China casting ($1-2)
26. metallic turquoise body, bright yellow plastic base, silver 6-spoke spiral wheels, yellow & white hood & sides design tempa, China casting ($2-4)
27. silver-gray body, dark gray plastic base, chrome disc wheels with rubber tires, two tone blue design tempa, China casting ($3-5)(PC9)
28. black body, black plastic base, 5 spoke concave star wheels, "Go Pies! 1997" tempa, China casting ($3-5)(AU)
29. florescent pink body, bright yellow plastic base, silver 6 spoke spiral wheels, yellow & white hood & sides design tempa, China casting ($1-2)

MB60-G FORD TRANSIT VAN, issued 1986 (USA) (MB165)
MB57-G FORD TRANSIT VAN, issued 1990 (USA)

NOTE: Below models with clear windows, dark gray plastic base, gray interior & 8 dot wheels unless otherwise noted.

1. red body, left hand drive, "Motorsport" tempa, Macau casting ($2-4)
2. red body, right hand drive, no tempa, Macau casting ($30-45)(UK)
3. red body, left hand drive, no tempa, Macau casting ($2-4)
4. red body, left hand drive, "Motorsport" tempa, dot dash wheels, Macau casting ($3-5)
5. white body, left hand drive, red cross & stripe with gray rectangle tempa, Macau casting ($2-3)
6. white body, left hand drive, "Federal Express" tempa, Macau casting ($2-3)
7. yellow body, left hand drive, "British Telecom" tempa, Macau casting ($4-6)(GS)
8. red body, left hand drive, "Australia Post" tempa, Macau casting ($6-8)(AU)
9. white body, left hand drive, red cross & stripe with gray rectangle tempa, China casting ($2-4)
10. white body, right hand drive, "Unichem" tempa, Macau casting ($7-10)(UK)
11. white body, right hand drive, "JCB Site Shop" tempa, Macau casting ($6-8)(GS)
12. white body, left hand drive, "Federal Express" tempa, China casting ($1-2)
13. white body, right hand drive, "XP Express Parcels" tempa, China casting ($6-8)(UK)
14. red body & base, right hand drive- black interior, "Royal Mail" tempa, Macau casting ($5-8)(UK)(MP)
15. orange-red body, left hand drive, "Australia Post- We Deliver" tempa, Chinas casting ($6-8)(AU)
16. white body, left hand drive, "Wigwam" tempa, China casting ($7-10)(DU)
17. lime green body, left hand drive, no tempa, China casting ($12-15)(DU)
18. white body, right hand drive, "Wishing Well Appeal", China casting ($6-8)(UK)
19. white body, left hand drive, "Wella" tempa, China casting ($6-8)(GR)
20. white body, right hand drive, "Australia Telecom" tempa, China casting ($6-8)(AU)
21. white body, left hand drive, "XP Express Parcels" tempa, China casting ($4-6)(UK)
22. white body, right hand drive, "Federal Express" tempa, China casting ($3-5)
23. white body, right hand drive, "Peter Cox Preservation" tempa, China casting ($7-10)(UK)
24. white body, left hand drive, "Kiosk" tempa, China casting ($8-12)(SW)
25. red body, left hand drive, "Blick" tempa, China casting ($8-12)(SW)
26. orange body, left hand drive, "Ovomaltine" tempa, China casting ($8-12)(SW)
27. silver-gray body, left hand drive, "Isostar/ Perform/ Powerplay" tempa, China casting ($8-12)(SW)
28. white body, left hand drive, "Kellogg's" tempa, China casting ($60-75)(SW)(AS)(OP)
29. white body, right hand drive, "Kellogg's" tempa, China casting ($60-75)(SW)(AS)(OP)
30. yellow body, left hand drive, "Ryder" tempa, China casting ($2-3)
31. white body, left hand drive, "DCS" tempa, China casting ($85-110)(SC)
32. white body, left hand drive, white interior & base, amber windows, no tempa, China casting ($10-15)(GF)
33. white body, left hand drive, "Supertoys" tempa, China casting ($20-25)(IR)
34. metallic green body, left hand drive, "Taronga Zoomobile" tempa, China casting ($6-8)(AU)
35. white body, left hand drive, "McKesson" tempa, China casting ($50-75)(US)
36. yellow body, left hand drive, "Cadbury's Flake" tempa, China casting ($1-2)

    NOTE: Above model found in China with "SUTC" logo cast on base.
37. white body, left hand drive, "Garden Festival Wales" tempa, China casting ($5-8)(WL)(GS)
38. powder blue & white body, left hand drive, "OCS" tempa, China casting ($15-18)(AU)
39. white body, left hand drive, "Matchbox" tempa, China casting ($2-3)
40. orange-red body with all white roof, left hand drive, "Australia Post- We Deliver" tempa, China casting ($3-5)(AU)(GS)
41. yellow body, right hand drive, "Express Post" tempa, China casting ($3-5)(AU)(GS)
42. red body, left hand drive, "14th Annual Toy Show- Ft. Washington, PA" tempa, China casting ($18-25)(US)(LD)
43. white body, left hand drive, "Hankook Tyres" tempa, China casting ($25-40)(US)(LD)
44. red body, left hand drive, "Brantho-Korrux" tempa, China casting ($25-40)(GR)(LD)
45. red body, left hand drive, "Viewmaster" tempa, China casting ($85-90)(US)(LD)

NOTE: Above model only available in wooden display box with viewer & special reel

46. white body, left hand drive, "Viewmaster" tempa, China casting ($18-25)(US)(LD)
47. white body, left hand drive, "Pickfords Record Management", China casting ($25-50)(UK)(LD)
48. red body, left hand drive, "Kit Kat" tempa, China casting ($20-30)(UK)(LD)
49. white & teal body, left hand drive, "Hilton" with red letters tempa, China casting ($18-25)(US)(LD)
50. white & teal body, left hand drive, "Hilton" with black letters tempa, China casting ($15-18)(US)(LD)
51. white body, left hand drive, "97.5 PST" tempa, China casting ($15-18)(US)(LD)
52. dark blue body, left hand drive, "97.5 PST" tempa, China casting ($18-25)(US)(LD)
53. dark blue body, left hand drive, "Midwest Diecast Miniatures" tempa, China casting ($12-15)(US)(LD)
54. white body, left hand drive, "24th National Truck In 1996" tempa, China casting ($12-15)(US)(LD)
55. red body, left hand drive, "24th National Truck In 1996" tempa, China casting ($18-25)(US)(LD)
56. red body, left hand drive, "Smoke Detectors Saves Lives" tempa, China casting ($15-18)(US)(LD)
57. dark blue body, left hand drive, "Scooter's Snowboard Shoppe" tempa, China casting ($18-25)(US)(LD)
58. red body, left hand drive, "Hankook" tempa, China casting ($12-15)(Malta)(LD)
59. red body, left hand drive, "Waterway Recovery Group" tempa, China casting ($12-15)(UK)(LD)
60. red body, left hand drive, "Manrose Extractor Fans" tempa, China casting ($12-15)(UK)(LD)
61. red body, left hand drive, "Magna" tempa, China casting ($100-150)(UK)(LD)
62. red body, left hand drive, "Belfast Evening Telegraph" tempa, China casting ($100-150)(IR)(LD)
63. dark blue body, left hand drive, "NSVA- 25th Anniversary Members Van" tempa, China casting($25-40)(UK)(LD)
64. dark blue body, left hand drive, "NSVA- 25th Anniversary Committee Van" tempa, China casting ($100-150)(UK)(LD)
65. dark blue body, left hand drive, "Long Time Vanners 1999- Club Member" tempa, China casting ($12-15)(UK)(LD)\
66. olive body, left hand drive, blue windows, 5 arch black wheels, "LS 2010" tempa with red cross tempa, China casting ($60-75)(CM)(CHI)(MP)
67. white body, left hand drive, no tempa, China casting ($8-12)(LD blank)
68. red body, left hand drive, no tempa, China casting ($8-12)(LD blank)
69. dark blue body, left hand drive, no tempa, China casting ($8-12)(LD blank)
70. dark blue body, left hand drive, "Dulux" tempa, China casting ($50+)(UK)(LD)
71. lime green body, left hand drive, "AutoRent" decals, China casting ($8-12)(C2)(DU)
72. white body, left hand drive, "Evening Gazette" tempa, China casting ($12-15)(UK)(LD)

MB60-H ROCKET TRANSPORTER *see MB40-D*

MB60-I TOYOTA SUPRA *see MB30-G*

MB60-J HELICOPTER *see MB75-D*

MB60-K RESCUE CHOPPER, issued 1999 (USA) (MB416)
MB55-M RESCUE CHOPPER, issued 1999 (ROW)

NOTE: Below models with China casting. Interior color is same as base color.

1. white body, blue base, clear windows, blue tail, silver-gray blades, yellow & red tempa ($1-2)(MW55/1999 ROW)(MW45/1999 GR)
2. white body, blue base, clear windows, blue tail, silver-gray blades, yellow & red with "Alpine Rescue" tempa ($1-2)(MW60/1999 US)
3. white body, red base, clear windows, red tail, black blades, "Med Air" with yellow & dark blue stripes tempa ($1-2)(5pk)
4. white body, red base, clear windows, red tail, black blades, yellow & dark blue stripes tempa ($2-3)(5pk)
5. white body, blue base, blue windows, blue tail, silver-gray blades, orange & lime stripes tempa ($1-2)(MW7/2000)
6. white body, blue base, blue windows, blue tail, silver-gray blades, orange & blue stripes & "Matchbox 2000" tempa ($2-4)(MW7/2000 US)
7. bright blue body, orange-yellow base, red windows, orange-yellow tail, orange-yellow blades, "Sydney 2000" tempa ($1-2)(5pk)
8. white body, dark blue base, clear windows, dark blue tail, silver-gray blades, "Alpine Rescue" & "Matchbox" tempa ($3-5)(PB)
9. baby blue body, dark blue base, clear windows, dark blue tail, dark blue blades, "Res-026" & "067/299" tempa ($1-2)(MW10/2001)
10. black body, bright neon orange base, amber windows, neon orange tail, blue blades, "Air Ambulance- Spider Peak 54" tempa ($1-2)(5pk)
11. white body, purple base, amber windows, purple tail, purple blades, "Rescue Heroes" tempa ($1-2)(5pk)
12. beige body, pea green base, clear windows, black tail, gray blades, "The Crocodile Hunter" & mud spatter tempa ($3-5)(CRO)
13. blue body, black base, smoke windows, black tail, black blades, "Police Mission Radar" tempa ($1-2)(5pk)
14. black body, yellow interior, black base, smoke windows, black tail, white blades, "Trump" & red stripes tempa ($20-35)(US)
15. white body, white interior, white base, blue windows, white tail, white blades, "Citrix Technical Support" tempa ($35-50)(ASAP)
16. white body, white interior, white base, blue windows, white tail, white blades, no tempa ($25-40)(ASAP blank)
17. orange-yellow body, blue interior, blue base, blue tail, red blades, "M" & design tempa ($1-2)(5pk)

MB60-M MOBILE LIGHT TRUCK, issued 2002 (MB548)

NOTE: Below models with 7 spoke sawblade wheels & China casting.

1. red body, white boom, black base, "Zap" tempa ($1-2)(MW60/2002)
2. red body, white boom, black base, "Zap" & "Matchbox 50" tempa ($2-4)(MW60/2002)
3. orange body, orange-yellow boom, gray base, "MHC68" tempa ($1-2)(MW68/2003 US)
4. orange body, orange-yellow boom, gray base, "MHC68" & "Hero City" tempa ($2-4)(MW68/2003 US)
5. metallic silver body, orange-yellow boom, gray base, "MHC68" tempa ($3-4)(20pk)
6. lime body, yellow boom, black base, "X Force" tempa ($1-2)(5pk)

7. blue body, light green boom, black base, yellow design tempa (MW30/2004 ROW)

MB60-N ICE CREAM TRUCK *see MB65-K*

MB61-A BLUE SHARK, issued 1971

NOTE: Below models with white driver, 4 spoke wheels & England casting.

1. dark blue body, clear windshield, unpainted base, "86" label ($15-18)
2. dark blue body, clear windshield, silver-gray base, "86" label ($15-18)
3. dark blue body, amber windshield, unpainted base, "86" label ($15-18)
4. dark blue body, amber windshield, silver-gray base, "86" label ($15-18)
5. dark blue body, clear windshield, unpainted base, "69" label (from MB69-B) ($15-18)
6. dark blue body, amber windshield, unpainted base, "69" label (from MB69-B) ($15-18)
7. dark blue body, clear windshield, silver-gray base, "69" label (from MB69-B) ($15-18)
8. dark blue body, amber windshield, silver-gray base, "69" label (from MB69-B) ($15-18)
9. dark blue body, clear windshield, unpainted base, scorpion label ($25-40)
10. dark blue body, amber windshield, unpainted base, scorpion label ($25-40)
11. metallic blue body, clear windshield, silver-gray with Manaus tab base, "86" label ($250+)(BR)

MB61-B WRECK TRUCK, issued 1978

NOTE: Below models with 5 crown wheels & England casting unless otherwise noted.

1. red body, black base, amber windows, white booms, red hooks, no tempa ($4-6)
2. red body, black base, blue windows, white booms, red hooks, no tempa ($8-12)
3. red body, charcoal base, amber windows, white booms, red hooks, no tempa ($4-6)
4. red body, black base, amber windows, white booms, black hooks, no tempa ($4-6)
5. red body, black base, amber windows, red booms, red hooks, no tempa ($6-8)
6. red body, charcoal base, amber windows, red booms, red hooks, no tempa ($6-8)
7. red body, black base, amber windows, red booms, black hooks, no tempa ($6-8)
8. bright yellow body, black base, amber windows, white booms, red hooks, no tempa ($4-6)
9. dull yellow body, black base, amber windows, white booms, red hooks, no tempa ($4-6)
10. bright yellow body, charcoal base, amber windows, green booms, red hooks, no tempa, ($5-7)
11. dull yellow body, charcoal base, amber windows, green booms, red hooks, no tempa ($5-7)
12. bright yellow body, black base, amber windows, green booms, black hooks, no tempa ($5-7)
13. dull yellow body, black base, amber windows, green booms, black hooks, no tempa ($5-7)
14. bright yellow body, charcoal base, amber windows, green booms, black hooks, no tempa ($5-7)
15. dull yellow body, charcoal base, amber windows, green booms, black hooks, no tempa ($5-7)
16. bright yellow body, black base, amber windows, red booms, red hooks, no tempa ($4-6)
17. dull yellow body, black base, amber windows, red booms, red hooks, no tempa ($4-6)
18. bright yellow body, charcoal base, amber windows, red booms, red hooks, no tempa ($4-6)
19. dull yellow body, charcoal base, amber windows, red booms, red hooks, no tempa ($4-6)
20. bright yellow body, blue-gray base, amber windows, red booms, red hooks, no tempa ($4-6)
21. dull yellow body, blue-gray base, amber windows, red booms, red hooks, no tempa ($4-6)
22. bright yellow body, unpainted base, amber windows, red booms, black hooks, no tempa ($4-6)
23. dull yellow body, unpainted base, amber windows, red booms, black hooks, no tempa ($4-6)
24. red body, black base, amber windows, white booms, red hooks, "24 Hour" tempa ($5-7)(TP)
25. white body, charcoal base with Manaus tab, amber windows, white booms, red hooks, red stripe label ($250+)(BR)
26. orange-red body, black base with Manaus tab, amber windows, white booms, red hooks, no tempa ($225-300)(BR)
27. bright yellow body, blue-gray base, amber windows, red booms, black hooks, no tempa ($4-6)
28. bright yellow body, blue-gray base, amber windows, white booms, red hooks, no tempa ($5-8)
29. bright yellow body, brown base, amber windows, red booms, black hooks, no tempa ($7-10)
30. dull yellow body, brown base, amber windows, red booms, black hooks, no tempa ($7-10)
31. lemon body, blue-gray base, amber windows, white booms, red hooks, no tempa ($10-15)
32. red body, black base, amber windows, green booms, black hooks, no tempa ($250-325)(TP)

MB61-C PETERBILT WRECKER, issued 1982 (MB061)

NOTE: Below models with 8 spoke wheels unless otherwise noted/

1. blue body, black booms, amber windows, chrome exhausts & base, no tempa, England casting ($150-200)(GS)
2. orange body, black booms, amber windows, chrome exhausts & base, black "Eddie's Wrecker" tempa, England casting ($4-6)
3. orange body, black booms, clear windows, chrome exhausts & base, black "Eddie's Wrecker" tempa, England casting ($4-6)
4. orange body, black booms, amber windows, chrome exhausts & base, white "Eddie's Wrecker" tempa, England casting ($4-6)
5. white body, black booms, amber windows, chrome exhausts & base, black "9" tempa, Macau casting ($2-3)
6. white body, black booms, clear windows, chrome exhausts & base, black "9" tempa, Macau casting ($2-3)
7. white body, black booms, amber windows, chrome exhausts & base, blue "9" tempa, Macau casting ($1-2)
8. white body, blue booms, amber windows, chrome exhausts & base, blue "9" tempa, Macau casting ($1-2)
9. white body, blue booms, clear windows, chrome exhausts & base, blue "911" tempa, Macau casting ($1-2)
10. white body, orange booms, clear windows, chrome exhausts & base, "SFPD" & star tempa, Macau casting ($1-2)
11. white body, dull orange booms, clear windows, chrome exhausts & base, "SFPD" & star tempa, Macau casting ($1-2)
12. orange body, dark green booms, dark green windows, gray exhausts & base, black stripes tempa, Macau casting includes plastic armament ($5-8)(RB)

13. olive body, black booms, clear windows, black exhausts & base, "8" with red/white stripes tempa, Macau casting ($4-5)(CM)
14. white body, orange booms, clear windows, gray exhausts, chrome base, "SFPD" & star tempa , Macau casting ($1-2)
15. white body, orange booms, clear windows, gray exhausts, chrome base, "SFPD" & star tempa, Thailand casting ($1-2)(MC)
16. orange body, dark green booms, dark green windows, gray exhausts & base, black stripes tempa, Thailand casting ($8-12)(JP) (Tomy box)
17. red body, black booms, clear windows, gray exhausts & base, "Police" tempa, Manaus casting ($35-50)(BR)
18. white body, black booms, clear windows, gray exhausts, chrome base, black "9" tempa, Manaus casting ($35-50)(BR)
19. blue body, black booms, clear windows, gray exhausts & base, "C.P. City Police" tempa, Manaus casting ($30-45)(BR)
20. red body, black booms, clear windows, gray exhausts, chrome base, "Police" tempa, Manaus casting ($30-45)(BR)
21. white body, black booms, clear windows, gray exhausts & base, "Esso" tempa, Manaus casting ($30-45)(BR)
22. red body, green booms (from MB74-B), clear windows, chrome exhausts & base, "Getty" tempa, Manaus casting ($75+)(BR)
23. white body, dull orange booms, clear windows, gray exhausts, black base with bar code, "Police M9" & "Intercom City" tempa, Thailand casting ($7-10)(IC)
24. white body, orange booms, clear windows, chrome exhausts & base, "Police PD-22" & checkers tempa, Thailand casting ($2-4)(TP)
25. lemon body, blue booms, amber windows, chrome exhausts & base, "Metro Recovery" tempa, China casting ($1-2)(5pk)
26. lemon body, blue booms, amber windows, chrome exhausts & base, car design tempa, China casting ($2-4)(5pk)
27. black body, chrome booms, clear windows, chrome exhausts & base, "Texaco" logo tempa, chrome disc wheels with rubber tires China casting ($3-5)(Texaco PC)

MB61-D T-BIRD TURBO COUPE *see MB59-F*

MB61-E NISSAN 300ZX, issued 1990 (USA) (MB219)
MB37-H NISSAN 300ZX, issued 1990 (ROW)

NOTE: Below models with black plastic base.

1. yellow body, smoke gray windows, white interior, 8 dot wheels, outlined "300ZX" tempa, Macau casting ($1-2)
2. chrome plated body, smoke gray windows, white interior, 8 dot wheels, no tempa, Macau casting ($12-18)(C2)
3. chrome plated body, smoke gray windows, white interior, 8 dot wheels, no tempa, Thailand casting ($12-18)(C2)
4. yellow body, smoke gray windows, white interior, 8 dot wheels, outlined "300ZX" tempa, Thailand casting ($1-2)
5. iridescent cream body, chrome windows, pink interior, gray disc wheels with rubber tires, detailed trim tempa, China casting ($5-8)(WC)
6. iridescent cream body, chrome windows, dark gray interior, gray disc wheels with rubber tires, detailed trim tempa, China casting ($5-8)(WC)
7. iridescent cream body, chrome windows, white interior, gray disc wheels with rubber tires, detailed trim tempa, China casting ($5-8)(WC)
8. iridescent pink-cream body, blue-chrome & black windows, no interior, peach & silver lightning wheels, "Turbo Z" tempa, China casting ($2-3)(LT)
9. iridescent pink-cream body, blue-chrome & black windows, no interior, pink & silver lightning wheels, "Turbo Z" tempa, China casting ($2-3)(LT)
10. metallic blue body, chrome & black windows, no interior, lightning wheels, "300ZX" tempa, China casting ($2-3)(LT)
11. bright orange body, blue-chrome & black windows, no interior, lightning wheels, "300ZX" tempa, China casting ($2-3)(LT)
12. lemon body, black & chrome windows, no interior, lightning wheels, "Turbo Z" tempa, China casting ($2-3)(LT)
13. yellow body, smoke gray windows, white interior, 8 dot wheels, outlined "300ZX" tempa, China casting ($1-2)
14. yellow body, smoke gray windows, white interior, 8 dot wheels, solid "300ZX" tempa, China casting ($1-2)
15. metallic red body, chrome windows, dark gray interior, gray disc wheels with rubber tires, detailed trim tempa, China casting ($5-8)(WC)
16. metallic red body, black & chrome windows, no interior, silver & yellow lightning wheels, "Turbo Z" tempa, China casting ($5-8)(LT)(US)(OP)
17. metallic red body, black & chrome windows, no interior, pink & red lightning wheels, "Turbo Z" tempa, China casting ($5-8)(LT)(US)(OP)
18. white, lime & pink body, black & chrome windows, no interior, lightning wheels, "Z" & "Turbo" tempa, China casting ($2-3)(LT)
19. white, orange & black body, black & chrome windows, no interior, lightning wheels, "Z" & "Turbo" tempa, China casting ($2-3)(LT)
20. dark teal blue body, clear windows, pink interior, gold 6-spoke spiral wheels, yellow & pink streaks tempa, Thailand casting ($1-2)
21. yellow body, smoke gray windows, gray interior, 8 dot wheels, "300ZX" tempa & "Nationwise Auto Parts" labels, Thailand casting ($20-35)(US)
22. silver-gray & metallic blue body, clear windows, florescent orange interior, silver 6-spoke spiral wheels, steel grid pattern tempa, China casting ($1-2)
23. flat black body, clear windows, florescent orange interior, silver 6-spoke spiral wheels, white lines on side with orange & white lines on hood tempa, China casting ($3-5)
24. black body, clear windows, pink interior, silver 6-spoke spiral wheels, white swirls tempa, China casting ($1-2)
25. metallic gold body, clear windows, black interior, silver 6-spoke spiral wheels, no tempa, China casting ($10-15)(CH)
26. yellow body, clear windows, white interior, 8 dot wheels, solid "300ZX" tempa, Thailand casting ($1-2)
27. silver-gray & metallic blue body, clear windows, florescent orange interior, steel grid pattern tempa, silver 6 spoke spiral wheels, Thailand casting ($1-2)
28. black body, clear windows, pink interior, 5 spoke concave star wheels, white swirls tempa, China casting ($1-2)
29. silver body, clear windows, orange interior, 5 spoke concave star wheels, yellow & orange design with "ZX" tempa, China casting ($1-2)
30. lemon body, clear windows, black & gray interior, chrome disc wheels with rubber tires, detailed trim tempa, China casting ($3-5)(PC15)
31. white body, clear windows, silver-gray interior, 5 spoke concave star wheels, orange & yellow design with "ZX" tempa, China casting ($1-2)(MW43-ROW)
32. orange-yellow body, dark smoke windows, black interior, 5 spoke concave star wheels, "DARE/ Sanibel Police" tempa, China casting ($3-5)(DR)
33. lemon body, clear windows, silver-gray interior, gold 6 spoke spiral wheels, detailed trim tempa, China casting ($50+)(CHI)

MB61-F FORK LIFT TRUCK *see MB28-H*

MB61-G ABRAMS TANK *see MB54-J*

MB61-H BMW Z3 ROADSTER *see MB25-J*

MB61-I FORMULA ONE RACER *see MB74-J*

MB61-J LAND ROVER FREELANDER *see MB66-J*

MB61-K UFO, issued 1999 (USA)
MB56-L UFO, issued 1999 (ROW)

1. lavender body & wings, blue-green windows, China casting ($1-2)(MW61/1999 US)(MW56/1999 ROW)

MB61-L VW CONCEPT I BEETLE CABRIOLET *see MB81-A*

MB61-M RESCUE BOAT, issued 2001 (USA)
MB38-N RESCUE BOAT, issued 2002 (ROW)

NOTE: Below models with black wheels & China casting.

1. white deck, purple hull, blue windows, orange rear insert, "Rescue R.1" tempa ($1-2)(MW61/2001 USA)
2. slate blue deck, white hull, smoke windows, gray rear insert, "Sea Base" tempa ($1-2)(5pk)
3. powder blue deck, bright blue base, smoke windows, glow yellow rear insert, light house design tempa ($1-2)(MW38/2002)
4. powder blue deck, bright blue base, smoke windows, glow yellow rear insert, light house design & "Matchbox 50" tempa ($3-5)(MW38/2002)
5. red deck, bright blue base, amber windows, silver-gray rear insert, "Matchbox Hero City Beach Patrol" tempa ($1-2)(MW43/2003)
6. red deck, bright blue base, amber windows, silver-gray rear insert, "Matchbox Hero City Beach Patrol" & "hero City" tempa ($2-4)(MW43/2003)
7. dark purple deck, orange hull, blue windows, lime rear insert, "Loch Ness Scotland" tempa ($1-2)(AW)

MB61-N FORD FALCON, issued 2001 (AU) (MB521)

NOTE: Below models with lace wheels, black base & China casting.

1. metallic blue body, gray interior, clear windows, painted lights tempa ($2-4)(MW61/2001 AU)
2. dark green body, red interior, smoke windows, "Coca Cola" tempa ($2-3)(CK)
3. orange body, white interior, clear windows, "Honey Nut Cheerios" tempa ($1-2)(5pk)
4. lemon body, yellow interior, blue windows, "Patrick" tempa ($1-2)(5pk)
5. dark metallic blue body, yellow interior, blue windows & base, "Patrick" tempa ($1-2)(CA)

MB61-O ICE BREAKER, issued 2002 (MB551)

NOTE: Below models with China casting.

1. dark blue deck, metallic red hull, white cab, blue windows, white wheels, cross & design tempa ($1-2)(MW61/2002)
2. dark blue deck, metallic red hull, white cab, blue windows, white wheels, cross & design with "Matchbox 50" tempa ($20-35)(MW61/2002)
3. light blue deck, dark blue hull, white cab, light blue windows, black wheels, "Spongebob Squarepants" tempa ($1-2)(5pk)
4. blue deck, metallic gold hull, red cab, opaque blue windows, red wheels, "AR0002" with rhino hoof prints tempa ($1-2)(LP)
5. red deck, blue hull, white cab, opaque red windows, black wheels, "Clifford" tempa ($1-2)(5pk)
6. red deck, bright blue hull, gray cab, opaque red windows, black wheels, "Hydro Unit Matchbox Hero City" tempa ($1-2)(MW38/2004)

MB61-P DENNIS SABRE, issued 2003 (MB588)

NOTE: Below models with blue windows, 7 spoke sawblade wheels & China casting.

1. red body, gray ladder, white turret, "Matchbox 61" tempa ($1-2)(MW61/2003)
2. red body, gray ladder, white turret, "Matchbox 61" & "Hero City" tempa ($3-5)(MW61/2003)
3. metallic silver body, red ladder & turret, "Metro Alarm" tempa ($1-2)(MW34/2004)

MB61-Q BMW Z4, issued 2004 (MB607)

1. metallic silver body, smoke windshield, black interior, small "BMW" logos & "Matchbox" logo tempa, lace wheels, black base, China casting ($1-2)(MW61/2004)

MB62-A MERCURY COUGAR, issued 1970

NOTE: Below models with clear windows, red interior, unpainted metal base & England casting.

1. metallic green body ($25-40)
2. metallic yellow-green body ($25-40)

MB62-B MERCURY COUGAR DRAGSTER, issued 1970

NOTE: Below models with red interior, clear windows, 5 spoke front wheels & England casting.

1. yellow-green body, unpainted base, 5 spoke rear wheels, "Rat Rod" labels ($15-20)
2. yellow-green body, unpainted base, 4 spoke rear wheels, "Rat Rod" labels ($15-20)
3. dark lime body, unpainted base, 4 spoke rear wheels, "Rat Rod" labels ($15-20)
4. dark lime body, silver-gray base, 4 spoke rear wheels, "Rat Rod" labels ($15-20)
5. dark lime body, unpainted base, 4 spoke rear wheels, "Wildcat" (from MB8-B) labels ($20-25)
6. blue body, unpainted base with Manaus label, 4 spoke rear wheels, no labels ($250+)(BR)

MB62-C RENAULT 17TL, issued 1974

NOTE: Below models with green windows, ivory interior, black metal base & England casting unless otherwise noted.

1. dark red body, "9" hood label, 5 spoke wheels ($7-10)
2. orange-red body, "9" hood label, 5 spoke wheels ($7-10)
3. orange-red body, "6" hood label, 5 spoke wheels ($7-10)
4. orange-red body, "Fire" side labels, 5 spoke wheels ($12-15)
5. orange-red body, "6" hood label, maltese cross wheels ($18-25)
6. orange body, "6" hood label, 5 spoke wheels ($7-10)
7. orange-red body, "3" hood label (from MB3-B), 5 spoke wheels ($50-75)
8. orange body, "9" hood label, 5 spoke wheels, base with Manaus tab ($35-50)(BR)

MB62-D CHEVROLET CORVETTE, issued 1979 (MB062)

NOTE: Most versions exist with combinations of all 5 arch wheels, all 5 crown wheels, 5 arch front & 5 crown rear wheels and vice versa, unless otherwise noted. Below models with metal base unless otherwise noted.

1. red body, unpainted base, gray interior, clear windows, white hood & side tempa, no "Corvette" cast at rear or front, England casting ($35-50)
2. red body, unpainted base, gray interior, clear windows, white hood & sides tempa, England casting ($4-6)
3. red body, unpainted base, gray interior, clear windows, white hood tempa only, England casting ($4-6)

4. red body, unpainted base, black interior, clear windows, white hood & sides tempa, England casting ($4-6)
5. red body, unpainted base, black interior, clear windows, white hood tempa only, England casting ($4-6)
6. red body, unpainted base, white interior, clear windows, white hood tempa only, England casting ($4-6)
7. black body, unpainted base, gray interior, clear windows, green & orange stripes hood tempa, England casting ($3-5)
8. black body, silver-gray base, gray interior, clear windows, green & orange stripes hood tempa, England casting ($3-5)
9. black body, unpainted base, gray interior, white windows, green & orange stripes hood tempa, England casting ($10-15)(PS)
10. black body, red base, gray interior, clear windows, yellow & orange stripes hood tempa, Macau casting ($2-4)
11. black body, silver-gray base, gray interior, clear windows, "The Force" tempa, Macau casting ($2-4)
12. black body, pearly silver base, gray interior, clear windows, "The Force" tempa, Macau casting ($2-4)
13. green body, pearly silver base, gray interior, clear windows, "Brut/ Faberge" tempa, Macau casting ($6-8)(TM)
14. black body, pearly silver base, red interior, clear windows, "Turbo Vette" tempa, starburst wheels, Macau casting ($3-5)(SF)
15. black body, pearly silver base, red interior, clear windows, "Turbo Vette" tempa, laser wheels, Macau casting ($3-5)(LW)
16. metallic red body, pearly silver base, red interior, clear windows, "Turbo Vette" tempa, laser wheels, Macau casting ($10-15)(LW)
17. black body, red plastic base, red interior, clear windows, "The Force" tempa, 8 dot wheels, Manaus casting ($35-50)(BR)

NOTE: Following models with plastic base, clear windows, gray disc wheels with rubber tires & China casting unless otherwise noted.

18. blue body, white base, dark blue interior, "Dodgers 1992" tempa ($3-5)(WR)
19. blue body, pumpkin orange base, dark blue interior, "Royals 1992" tempa ($3-5)(WR)
20. blue body, dark blue base, black interior, "Mariners 1992" tempa ($3-5)(WR)
21. blue body, dark silver-gray base, gray interior, "Rockies 1992" tempa ($3-5)(WR)
22. blue body, bright orange base, black interior, "Mets 1992" tempa ($3-5)(WR)
23. dark blue body, white base, red interior, "Red Sox 1992" tempa ($3-5)(WR)
24. dark blue body, gray base, black interior, "Twins 1992" tempa ($3-5)(WR)
25. metallic blue body, red base, black interior, "Braves 1992" tempa ($3-5)(WR)
26. bright blue body, dark blue base, black interior, "Blue Jays 1992" tempa ($3-5)(WR)
27. powder blue body, white base, dark blue interior, "Expos 1992" tempa ($3-5)(WR)
28. green body, dark yellow base, dark yellow interior, "Athletics 1992" tempa ($3-5)(WR)
29. yellow body, red base, red interior, "Angels 1992" tempa ($3-5)(WR)
30. orange body, silver-gray base, dark blue interior, "Tigers 1992" tempa ($3-5)(WR)
31. gray body, black base, red interior, "Giants 1992" tempa ($3-5)(WR)
32. white body, yellow base, dark blue interior, "Brewers 1992" tempa ($3-5)(WR)
33. white body, dark blue base, dark blue interior, "Indians 1992" tempa ($3-5)(WR)
34. white body, dark blue base, dark blue interior, "Padres 1992" tempa ($3-5)(WR)
35. white body, blue base, orange interior, "Astros 1992" tempa ($3-5)(WR)
36. white body, turquoise base, orange interior, "Marlins 1992" tempa ($3-5)(WR)
37. white body, red base, red interior, "Yankees 1992" tempa ($3-5)(WR)
38. red body, white base, black interior, "Reds 1992" tempa ($3-5)(WR)
39. red body, white base, dark blue interior, "Phillies 1992" tempa ($3-5)(WR)
40. red body, white base, dark blue interior, "Cubs 1992" tempa ($3-5)(WR)
41. red body, white base, red interior, "Cardinals 1992" tempa ($3-5)(WR)
42. red body, blue base, dark blue interior, "Rangers 1992" tempa ($3-5)(WR)
43. black body, white base, black interior, "Pirates 1992" tempa ($3-5)(WR)
44. black body, white base, orange interior, "Orioles 1992" tempa ($3-5)(WR)
45. black body, silver-gray base, red interior, "White Sox 1992" tempa ($3-5)(WR)
46. white body, red base, red interior, "Cooperstown 1993" tempa ($3-5)(WR)
47. white body, gray base, maroon interior, red stripes tempa, 5 arch front & 5 crown rear wheels, Thailand casting ($2-4)(GS)
48. black body, red plastic base, red interior, "The Force" tempa, 4 arch wheels, Manaus casting ($30-45)(BR)
49. black body, gray plastic base, red interior, "The Force" tempa, 8 dot wheels, Manaus casting ($30-45)(BR)
50. black body, red plastic base, red interior, "The Force" tempa, 8 dot wheels, Manaus casting ($30-45)(BR)
51. black body, silver-gray base, gray interior, opaque white windows, "The Force" tempa, 5 arch front & 5 crown rear wheels, Macau casting ($8-12)(PS)
52. silver-gray body, gray base, purple interior, clear windows, white & purple design tempa, 5 spoke concave star wheels, China casting ($8-12)(PS)
53. lemon body, chrome base, black interior, smoke windows, red band with "Coca Cola Play Refreshed" tempa, chrome disc wheels with rubber tires ($3-5)(Coke PC)

MB62-E CORVETTE T-ROOF *see MB40-C*

MB62-F ROLLS ROYCE SILVER CLOUD, issued 1986 (USA) (MB160)
MB31-F ROLLS ROYCE SILVER CLOUD, issued 1986 (ROW)

1. silver-gray body, chrome base, dark gray interior, clear windows, dot dash wheels, England casting ($8-10)(JB)
2. cream body, chrome base, dark gray interior, clear windows, dot dash wheels, England casting ($1-2)
3. cream body, chrome base, dark gray interior, clear windows, dot dash wheels, Macau casting ($1-2)
4. green-gold body, chrome base, black interior, chrome windows, detailed trim tempa, gray disc wheels with rubber tires, Macau casting ($5-8)(WC)
5. green-gold body, chrome base, black interior, chrome windows, detailed trim tempa, gray disc wheels with rubber tires, Thailand casting ($5-8)(WC)

6. cream body, chrome base, dark gray interior, clear windows, dot dash wheels, Thailand casting ($1-2)(MP)
7. plum body, chrome base, purple & gray interior, clear windows, chrome disc wheels with rubber tires, Thailand casting ($18-25)(GC)

MB62-G VOLVO 760, issued 1986 (ROW) (MB171)
NOTE: Below models with black metal base & 8 dot wheels unless otherwise noted.
1. pearly silver body, black interior, clear windows, Macau casting ($2-3)
2. dark silver-gray body, black interior, clear windows, China casting ($2-3)
3. plum body, black interior, clear windows, China casting ($2-3)
4. dark plum body, black interior, clear windows, China casting ($2-3)
5. white body & base, white interior, amber windows, China casting ($10-15)(GF)
6. silver-gray body, black base, gray & blue interior, clear windows, chrome disc wheels with rubber tires, detailed trim tempa, China casting ($8-12)(UC)

MB62-H OLDSMOBILE AEROTECH, issued 1989 (USA) (MB210)
MB64-F OLDSMOBILE AEROTECH, issued 1989 (ROW)
NOTE: Below models with gray plastic base & smoke windows unless otherwise noted.
1. silver-gray body, "Quad 4/ Aerotech/ Oldsmobile" tempa, 8 dot wheels, Macau casting ($1-2)
2. silver-gray body, "Quad 4/ Aerotech/ Oldsmobile" tempa, 8 dot wheels, Thailand casting ($1-2)
3. florescent orange body, "Aerotech" tempa, 8 dot wheels, Thailand casting ($1-2)
4. dark purple & white body, purple flash & "Aerotech" tempa, gold 6 spoke spiral wheels, Thailand casting ($1-2)
5. dark purple & white body, purple flash & "Aerotech" tempa, silver 6 spoke spiral wheels, Thailand casting ($1-2)
6. dark purple & white body, purple flash & "Aerotech" tempa, silver 6-spoke spiral wheels, China casting ($1-2)
7. dark purple & white body, purple flash without "Aerotech" tempa, silver 6-spoke spiral wheels, China casting ($1-2)

MB62-I VOLVO CONTAINER TRUCK *see MB20-D*

MB62-J STREET STREAK, issued 1996 (USA) (MB290)
MB72-N STREET STREAK, issued 1996 (ROW)
NOTE: Below models with black plastic base.
1. purple & white body, smoke windows, 6-spoke spiral wheels, Thailand casting ($3-5)
2. florescent orange & black body, black windows, 6-spoke spiral wheels, Thailand casting ($1-2)(5pk)
3. metallic dark red & silver-gray body, chrome windows, 5 spoke concave star wheels, Thailand casting ($1-2)
4. red & black body, chrome windows, 5 spoke concave star wheels, Thailand casting ($1-2)(5pk)
5. metallic gold body, smoke windows, 5 spoke concave star wheels, Thailand casting ($5-10)(CH)
6. metallic blue & silver-gray body , chrome windows, 5 spoke concave star wheels, Thailand casting ($1-2)(MW16/1998)
7. metallic blue & silver-gray body, chrome windows, 5 spoke concave star wheels, China casting ($1-2)(MW16/1998)

MB62-K FORD EXPEDITION *see MB67-H*

MB62-L POP-UP CAMPER, issued 2000 (USA) (MB447)
MB42-G POP-UP CAMPER, issued 2000 (ROW)
NOTE: Below models with dot dash wheels & China casting.
1. metallic pea body, blue roof, gray interior, green & blue tempa, black base ($1-2)(5pk)
2. red body, white roof, tan interior, white & black design tempa, black base ($1-2)(MW62/2000 US)(MW42/2000 ROW)
3. red body, white roof, tan interior, white & black design & "Matchbox 2000" tempa, black base ($2-4)(MW62/2000 US)
4. white body, red roof, blue interior, footprints & burst design tempa, blue-green base ($1-2)(5pk)
5. red body, neon yellow roof & interior, camper design tempa, gray base ($1-2)(MP)

MB62-M HOVERCRAFT, issued 2001 (USA) (MB519)
MB35-N HOVERCRAFT, issued 2002 (ROW)
NOTE: Below models with black wheels & China casting.
1. red deck, black hull, yellow airfoils, "Rescue" tempa ($1-2)(MW62/2001 US)
2. white deck, red hull, light blue airfoils, "H2O" tempa ($1-2)(MW35/2002)
3. white deck, red hull, light blue airfoils, "H2O" & "Matchbox 50" tempa ($2-4)(MW64/2003)
4. white deck, red hull, neon yellow airfoils, "Matchbox Hero City" tempa ($1-2)(MW64/2003)
5. white deck, red hull, neon yellow airfoils, "Matchbox Hero City" & "Hero City" tempa ($10-15)(MW)
6. white deck, red hull, dark yellow airfoils, "Alarm 04 Unit" tempa ($1-2)(5pk)
7. metallic red deck, white & black hull, lemon airfoils, "Unit 2" tempa ($1-2)(LP)

MB62-N GMC TERRADYNE, issued 2002 (MB555)
NOTE: Below models with smoke windows, 7 spoke sawblade wheels, black base, China casting unless otherwise noted.
1. silver-gray body, black interior, "Terradyne" tempa ($1-2)(MW62/2002)
2. silver-gray body, black interior, "Terradyne" & "Matchbox 50" tempa ($2-4)(MW62/2002)
3. dark metallic lime body, yellow interior, "X-Treme" tempa ($1-2)(MW58/2003)
4. dark metallic lime body, yellow interior, "X-Treme" & "Hero City" tempa ($2-4)(MW58/2003)
5. metallic maroon body, blue interior, blue windows, "Superman" tempa ($1-2)(5pk)
6. metallic silver body, blue interior, blue windows, "Superman" tempa ($1-2)(CA)
7. metallic blue body, orange-yellow interior, blue-green windows, green base, "Nickelodeon" tempa ($1-2)(5pk)
8. iridescent white body, orange-yellow interior, blue-green windows, green base, "Nickelodeon" tempa ($1-2)(CA)

MB62-O NISSAN Z, issued 2004 (MB611)
NOTE: Below models with clear windows, black interior & China casting.
1. red body, lace wheels, silver head lights tempa, black plastic base ($1-2)(MW62/2004)
2. metallic orange body, 5 spoke slotted wheels, detailed trim tempa, gray plastic base ($2-4)(SF34/2004)
3. bright blue body, lace wheels, silver head lights tempa, black plastic base ($1-2)(MW62/2004)

MB62-P 1968 MERCURY COUGAR, issued 2004 (SF)(MB636)

NOTE: Below models with clear windows, head & tail-lights tempa, chrome base & China casting.

1. metallic lime body, red interior, 5 spoke wheels ($3-5)(SF62/2004)
2. orange-red body, cream interior, 5 spoke wheels ($40-60)(SF62/US promo)

MB63-A DODGE CRANE TRUCK, issued 1970

NOTE: Below models with green windows, yellow hook, 4 spoke wheels & England casting.

1 yellow body, black axle covers ($25-40)
2. yellow body, red axle covers ($25-40)

MB63-B FREEWAY GAS TANKER, issued 1973

NOTE: Below models with white tank and maltese cross front & 5 spoke rear wheels unless otherwise noted. Other wheel combinations can exist.

1. "Castrol" labels (from A-1-C Car Ramp), red cab with black base, red trailer base, purple windows ($90-120)

   NOTE: Version #2 labels can have insignia blue over red or inverted red or blue.
2. "Burmah" labels, red cab with black base, red trailer base, purple windows ($6-8)
3. "Burmah" labels, red cab with black base, red trailer base, purple windows, with tow hook ($6-8)(TP)
4. "Octane" labels, olive cab with black base, black trailer base with olive tank, purple windows ($7-10)(TP)
5. "Octane" labels, olive drab cab, black base, black trailer base with olive drab tank, purple windows ($65-80)
6. French flag labels (from SB15-A Skybuster), olive drab cab with black base, black trailer base with olive drab tank, purple windows ($65-80)(TP)
7. Canadian flag labels (from SB15-A Skybuster), olive drab cab with black base, black trailer base with olive drab tank, purple windows ($250-300)(TP)
8. "Aral" labels, blue cab with black base, blue trailer base, purple windows ($25-40)(GR)
9. "Chevron" labels, red cab with black base, red trailer base, purple windows ($6-8)
10. "Chevron" labels, red cab with black base, red trailer base, purple windows, with tow hook ($6-8)(TP)
11. "Shell" labels, white cab with yellow base, yellow trailer base, purple windows ($6-8)
12. "Shell" labels, white cab with yellow base, dark yellow trailer base, purple windows ($6-8)
13. "Shell" labels, white cab with yellow base, yellow trailer base, purple windows, with tow hook ($6-8)(TP)
14. "Shell" labels, white cab with yellow base, yellow trailer base, red windows ($6-8)
15. "Shell" labels, white cab with yellow base, dark yellow trailer base, red windows ($6-8)
16. "Shell" labels, white cab with yellow base, yellow trailer base, amber windows ($6-8)
17. "Shell" labels, yellow cab with black base, yellow trailer base, purple windows ($8-12)
18. "Shell" labels, yellow cab with black base, dark yellow trailer base, purple windows ($8-12)
19. "Exxon" labels, white cab with black base, white trailer base, purple windows ($7-10)
20. "Exxon" labels, white cab with yellow base, yellow trailer base, purple windows ($20-25)
21. "Exxon" labels, white cab with yellow base, white trailer base, purple windows, with tow hook ($6-8)(TP)
22. "Exxon" labels, red cab with black base, white trailer base, purple windows, with tow hook ($50-75)(TP)
23. "BP" labels, white cab with black base, green trailer base, purple windows ($8-12)
24. "BP" labels, white cab with yellow base, yellow trailer base, purple windows, with tow hook ($50-75)(TP)
25. "Shell" labels, red cab with black base, red trailer base, purple windows, no tow hook ($125-150)

26 "Sellosign" labels, red cab with black base, red trailer base, purple windows, no tow hook ($250-400)(C2)(UK)

MB63-C FREEWAY GAS TRAILER, issued 1978 (TP)

NOTE: Below models with white tank & 5 arch front & 5 spoke rear wheels with no origin cast.

1. red coupling, red base, "Burmah" labels ($6-8)
2. red coupling, red base, "Chevron" labels ($6-8)
3. yellow coupling, yellow base, "Shell" labels ($6-8)
4. yellow coupling, dark yellow base, "Shell" labels ($6-8)
5. yellow coupling, white base, "Exxon" labels ($7-10)
6. red coupling, white base, "Exxon" labels ($55-65)
7. yellow coupling, yellow base, "BP" labels ($30-45)
8. yellow coupling, green base, "BP" labels ($6-8)

MB63-D DODGE CHALLENGER, issued 1981 (USA) (MB090)

NOTE: Below models with clear windows, black metal base & Hong Kong casting.

1. green body, dark green & white "2" tempa, ivory interior, 5 spoke star wheels ($10-15)
2. green body, dark green & white "2" tempa, ivory interior, 5 spoke wheels ($10-15)
3. green body, dark green & white "2" tempa, ivory interior, maltese cross wheels ($10-15)
4. green body, black "2" tempa, green interior, 5 spoke wheels ($10-15)

MB63-E SNORKEL, issued 1982 (USA) (MB111)
MB13-E SNORKEL, issued 1983 (ROW)

NOTE: Below models with black interior, white boom, 5 arch wheels & plastic base unless otherwise noted. Base inserts are metal.

1. red body, gray base, unpainted base insert, "Los Angeles" tempa, England casting ($6-8)(CR)
2. red body, gray base, silver-gray base insert, "Los Angeles" tempa, England casting ($6-8)(CR)
3. red body, black base, black metal base insert, "Metro Fire" tempa, Macau casting ($1-2)
4. red body, black base, black plastic base insert, "Metro Fire" tempa, Macau casting ($1-2)
5. red body, black base, black plastic base insert, "Metro Fire" tempa, China casting ($1-2)
6. dull red body, black base, black plastic base insert, "Fire Dept." & shield tempa, China casting ($1-2)
7. red body, black base, black plastic base insert, Japanese lettered tempa, China casting ($8-12)(JP)
8. greenish yellow body, black base, black plastic base insert, "Fire Dept." & shield tempa, China casting ($3-4)(AP)
9. florescent orange body, black base, black plastic base insert, "Rescue Unit 1 Fire" & checkers tempa, China casting ($1-2)
10. white body, white base, white plastic base insert, no tempa, China casting ($10-15)(GF)
11. red body, black base, black plastic base insert, "Rescue Unit 1 Fire" & checkers tempa, China casting ($8-12)(GS)
12. florescent orange body, black base, black plastic insert with bar code, "Rescue Unit 1 Fire", checkers & "IC" logo tempa, China casting ($10-15)(IC)

NOTE: Below versions with silver-gray boom & black base unless otherwise noted.
13. red body, blue interior, black plastic base insert, "12th Rescue Squad" with gold outline tempa, China casting ($1-2)
14. red body, blue interior, black plastic base insert, "12th Rescue Squad" with white outline tempa, China casting ($1-2)
15. white & red body, blue interior, black plastic base insert, "FD No. 1 Fire Dept." tempa, China casting ($1-2)(5pk)
16. white body, black interior, black plastic base insert, "Matchbox Fire Dept." & red stripes tempa, China casting ($1-2)(5pk)
17. dark purple body, black interior, black plastic base insert, "Matchbox Fire Dept." & white stripes tempa, China casting ($1-2)
18. metallic gold body, black interior, black boom, black plastic base insert, no tempa, China casting ($5-10)(CH)
19. red body, gray & black interior, black boom, black plastic base insert, "Richfield Co." tempa, chrome disc wheels with rubber tires, China casting ($3-5)(PC7)
20. red body, black interior, black plastic base insert, "Matchbox Fire Dept." & gold stripes tempa, China casting ($1-2)(MW26/1998)
21. red body, black interior, black plastic base insert, "Matchbox Fire Dept." & gold stripes tempa, 5 spoke concave star wheels, China casting ($18-25)(MW26/1998)
22. metallic red body, gray & black interior, white boom, black plastic base insert, "Seaside Fire Co./ Snorkel Unit 2" tempa, chrome disc wheels with rubber tires, China casting ($3-5)(PC21)
23. white body, black interior, white boom, black plastic base insert, no tempa, China casting ($25-40)(ASAP blank)
24. red body, black interior, white boom, black plastic base insert, "Ridge, NY Fire & Rescue" tempa, China casting ($1-2)(MW4/1999 US)
25. red body, gold interior, black boom, black plastic base insert, "J.D.F.D. Fire Rescue 25" tempa, China casting ($1-2)(MW27/2000 US)
26. red body, gold interior, black boom, black plastic base insert, "J.D.F.D. Fire Rescue 25" & "Matchbox 2000" tempa, China casting ($2-4)(MW27/2000 US)
27. white body, black interior, white boom, black plastic base insert, "Screamin' Red Fire Engines" (red print) tempa, China casting ($12-15)(ASAP)
28. white body, black interior, white boom, black plastic base insert, "Screamin' Red Fire Engines" (purple print) tempa, China casting ($12-15)(ASAP)
29. red body, black interior, gray boom, black plastic base insert, "Metro Alarm/ MA-ST1" tempa, China casting ($1-2)(5pk)
NOTE: Below models with 10 spoke flower wheels unless otherwise noted
30. red & white body, black interior, black boom, gray base & plastic base insert, "K-9 Patrol" tempa, amber windows, China casting ($1-2)(5pk)
31. neon yellow body, blue interior & base, white boom, black plastic base insert, "Metro Alarm" & checkers tempa, China casting ($2-4)(MW14/2002 ROW)(PS)
NOTE: Above model with Matchbox International or Mattel casting.
32. neon yellow body, blue interior, white boom, black plastic base insert, "Metro Alarm" & checkers with "Matchbox 50" tempa, China casting ($2-4)(MW14/2002 ROW)
33. white body, black interior, white boom, white base with black plastic base insert, none tempa, lace wheels, 10 spoke flower wheels, China casting ($25-40)(ASAP blank)
34. red body, black interior, gray boom, black plastic base insert, "Matchbox Fire Dept." & white stripes tempa, China casting ($1-2)(5pk)
35. bright blue body, brown interior, brown boom, black plastic base insert, "Blue Ridge 12/ North Carolina" tempa, Mattel China casting ($3-5)(AM)
36. metallic bronze body, black interior, black boom, black plastic base insert. "Unit 4" & white stripes tempa, Mattel China casting ($1-2)(LP)
37. white body, gray interior, yellow boom, black plastic base insert, city design & yellow stripes tempa, Mattel China casting ($4-6)(PS)

MB63-E 4 X 4 OPEN BACK TRUCK *see MB13-D*

MB63-G VOLKSWAGEN GTi *see MB33-D*

MB63-H 0-4- STEAM LOCO *see MB43-C*

MB63-I ASTON MARTIN DB-7 *see MB59-G*

MB63-J FORD FALCON, issued 1997 (AU) (MB292)
MB68-K FORD FALCON, issued 1998 (ROW)
MB 4-H FORD FALCON, issued 2002 (USA)

NOTE: Below models listed with clear windows & China casting
1. white body, white interior, white base, chrome disc wheels with rubber tires, "Australian Open 1997" tempa ($7-10)(AU)
2. white body, white interior, black base, chrome disc wheels with rubber tires, "Castrol 25" tempa ($15-20)(AU)
3. white body, gray interior, black base, 5 spoke concave star wheels, "Go Cats! 1997" tempa ($3-5)(AU)
4. gold body, black interior, black base, chrome disc wheels with rubber tires, "Australia's First" tempa ($10-15)(IG)(AU)
5. unpainted body, black interior, black base, chrome disc wheels with rubber tires, no tempa ($10-15)(IG)(AU)
6. white & dark blue body, gray interior, gray base, 5 spoke concave star wheels, "Ford 75" tempa ($2-4)(AU)
7. blue body, gray interior, gray base, yellow disc with rubber tires, "Mitre 10 Accent Paint Racing" tempa ($7-10)(AU)
8. white & mid blue body, white interior, black base, 5 spoke concave star wheels, "Kangaroos 1998" tempa ($3-5)(AU)
9. white & dark blue body, white interior, black base, 5 spoke concave star wheels, "Blues 1998" tempa ($3-5)(AU)
10. white & black body, white interior, black base, 5 spoke concave star wheels, "Cats 1998" tempa ($3-5)(AU)
11. white & red body, white interior, black base, 5 spoke concave star wheels, "Swans 1998" tempa ($3-5)(AU)
12. yellow & plum body, white interior, black base, 5 spoke concave star wheels, "Brisbane 1998" tempa ($3-5)(AU)
13. yellow & dark blue body, white interior, black base, 5 spoke concave star wheels, "Eagles 1998" tempa ($3-5)(AU)
14. yellow & black body, white interior, black base, 5 spoke concave star wheels, "Tigers 1998" tempa ($3-5)(AU)
15. red & dark blue body, white interior, black base, 5 spoke concave star wheels, "Crows 1998" tempa ($3-5)(AU)
16. metallic grape body, white interior, black base, 5 spoke concave star wheels, "Ford Falcon 4" tempa ($1-2)(MW68/1998 ROW)
17. maroon body, black interior, smoke windows, black base, 5 spoke concave star wheels, "Ford" & white stripes tempa ($2-3)(MW12/2000 AU)
18. white body, white interior, white base, chrome disc wheels with rubber tires, "Official Matchbox Collectors Club/ Australian Matchbox News" tempa ($15-20)(C2)
19. gold body, black interior, black base, chrome disc wheels with rubber tires, "Official Matchbox Collectors Club/ Australian Matchbox News" tempa ($15-20)(C2)

20. unpainted body, black interior, black base, chrome disc wheels with rubber tires, "Official Matchbox Collectors Club/ Australian Matchbox News" tempa ($15-20)(C2)
21. maroon body, black interior, smoke windows, black base, 5 spoke concave star wheels, "Ford" & white stripes & "Midwest Regional Matchbox Convention 2000/ Toy Show Demo Model" tempa ($10-15)(CCI)
22. maroon body, black interior , smoke windows, black base, 5 spoke concave star wheels, "Ford" & white stripes & "Special Edition Puerto Rico" & Puerto Rico flag tempa ($8-12)(CCI)
23. maroon body, black interior, smoke windows, black base, 5 spoke concave star wheels, "Ford" & white stripes & "Great Strides/ Cystic Fibrosis Foundation" tempa ($18-25)(CCI)
24. lemon body, blue-green interior, clear windows, 10 spoke flower wheels, "Taxi 2001" with checkers & emblem tempa, black base ($2-4)(MW62/2001 AU)
25. orange-yellow body, gray interior, clear windows, 10 spoke flower wheels, "Roy Roo's Taxi" & checkers tempa, dark blue base ($1-2)(MW4/2002)
26. orange-yellow body, gray interior, clear windows, 10 spoke flower wheels, "Roy Roo's Taxi", checkers & "Matchbox 50" tempa, dark blue base ($2-4)(MW4/2002)
27. white body, red interior, smoke windows, 10 spoke flower wheels, "Coca Cola" tempa, red base ($2-3)(CK)
28. white body, green interior, clear windows, 10 spoke flower wheels "Coca Cola" with yellow & green wave design tempa, Mattel casting ($2-3)(CK)

MB63-K '98 JEEP WRANGLER *see MB68-M*

MB63-L MERCEDES BENZ ML430 *see MB77-C*

MB63-M BMW 3 SERIES COUPE *see MB83-A*

MB63-N AIR BOAT, issued 2001 (USA) (MB520)

1. red deck, white base, silver-gray airfoil, black propeller, white wheels, "Rescue 2" & red dashes tempa ($1-2)(MW63/2001 US)

MB63-O RESCUE HELICOPTER, issued 2002 (MB541)

NOTE: Below models with clear windows & China casting unless otherwise noted.

1. white body, blue base, blue tail, silver-gray blades & interior, "Med Alarm" tempa ($1-2)(MW63/2002)
2. white body, blue base, blue tail, silver-gray blades & interior, "Med Alarm" & "Matchbox 50" tempa ($2-4)(MW63/2002)
3. black body, red base, red tail, silver-gray blades & interior, yellow design tempa ($1-2)(MW13/2003)
4. black body, red base, red tail, silver-gray blades & interior, yellow design & "Hero City" tempa ($2-4)(MW13/2003)
5. metallic blue body, gray base, gray tail, white blades & interior, "Police Dept. USA" tempa ($1-2)(MP)(HR)
6. metallic gold body, red base, red tail, silver-gray base & interior, yellow design tempa ($3-4)(20pk)
7. charcoal body, light blue base, light blue tail, red blades & interior, amber windows, "Hero City" & design tempa ($1-2)(MW48/2004)
8. light green body, dark blue base, light blue tail, silver-gray blades & interior, blue windows, "Mt. Everest/ Tibet" tempa ($1-2)(AW)
9. white body, yellow base, red tail, silver-gray blades & interior, red windows, "Hero City Metro Police" tempa ($1-2)(5pk)

MB63-P CHEVROLET CORVETTE C6 (MB630)

NOTE: Below models with black base & China casting.

1. maroon body, smoke windows, gray interior, head lights tempa without rear flag design, lace wheels ($3-5)(MW63/2004)
2. maroon body, smoke windows, gray interior, head lights tempa with rear flag design, lace wheels ($1-2)(MW63/2004)
3. black body, clear windows, tan interior, detailed trim tempa, chrome disc wheels with rubber tires ($8-12)(SF24/2004)
4. dark blue body, clear windows, tan interior, detailed trim tempa, chrome disc wheels with rubber tires ($8-12)(SF24/2004)
5. metallic maroon body, smoke windows, black interior, head & tail lights tempa, slotted 5 spoke wheels ($8-12)(SF24/ US promo)
6. metallic maroon body, smoke windows, black interior, "Matchbox Toy Show Hershey, PA 2004", slotted 5 spoke wheels (SF24/CCI)
7. light blue body, blue windows, yellow-orange interior, "Spongebob- The Spongebob Squarepants Movie" tempa, lace wheels ($1-2)(5pk)
8. metallic copper body, smoke windows, black interior, black, gray & orange flames tempa, lace wheels ($1-2)(MW5/2005)

MB64-A MG 1100, issued 1970

NOTE: All versions come with two different diameter wheels. Below models with clear windows, ivory interior, 5 spoke wheels, unpainted metal base & England casting.

1. green body ($175-250)
2. light metallic blue body ($30-45)
3. dark metallic blue body ($30-45)

MB64-B SLINGSHOT DRAGSTER, issued 1971

NOTE: Below models with white driver, 5 spoke front & spiro rear wheels & England casting. Earliest versions with narrow front wheels with later versions having wide front wheels.

1. pink body, black base, black pipes, "9" with flames label ($15-20)
2. orange body, black base, black pipes, "9" with flames label ($125-150)
3. orange body, unpainted base, red pipes, "9" with flames label ($175-225)
4. steel blue body, black base, black pipes, "9" with flames label ($15-18)
5. steel blue body, unpainted base, red pipes, "9" with flames label ($15-18)
6. steel blue body, black base, red pipes, "9" with flames label ($15-18)
7. steel blue body, black base, red pipes, star with flames label (from MB40-A) ($50-75)
8. steel blue body, black base, red pipes, "3" with yellow stripe label (from MB19-A) ($18-25)

MB64-C FIRE CHIEF CAR, issued 1976

NOTE: Below models with chrome interior, blue windows, unpainted metal base & England casting.

1. red body, plain shield labels, 5 arch front & 5 crown rear wheels ($8-12)
2. red body, outline shield labels, 5 arch front & 5 crown rear wheels ($8-12)
3. red body, outline shield labels, 5 arch front & rear wheels ($8-12)
4. red body, outline shield labels, 5 crown front & rear wheels ($8-12)
5. red body, outline shield labels, 5 arch front & 5 crown rear wheels, Manaus tab on base ($35-50)(BR)

MB64-D CATERPILLAR BULLDOZER, issued 1979 (MB064)
MB 9-G CATERPILLAR BULLDOZER, reissued 1986 (ROW)

NOTE: Below models with black treads unless otherwise noted.

1. yellow body, yellow blade, unpainted metal base, orange rollers, tan canopy, no tempa, England casting ($4-6)
2. yellow body, yellow blade, unpainted metal base, yellow-orange rollers, tan canopy, no tempa, England casting ($4-6)
3. yellow body, yellow blade, unpainted metal base, dark yellow rollers, tan canopy, no tempa, England casting ($4-6)
4. yellow body, yellow blade, unpainted metal base, lemon rollers, tan canopy, no tempa, England casting ($4-6)
5. yellow body, yellow blade, unpainted metal base, lemon rollers, black canopy, "C" tempa, England casting ($4-6)
6. yellow body, yellow blade, unpainted metal base, yellow-orange rollers, black canopy, "C" tempa, England casting ($4-6)
7. yellow body, yellow blade, unpainted metal base, dark yellow rollers, black canopy, "C" tempa, England casting ($4-6)
8. yellow body, black blade, unpainted metal base, lemon rollers, black canopy, "C" tempa, England casting ($4-6)
9. yellow body, black blade, unpainted metal base, lemon rollers, black canopy, "C Cat" tempa, England casting ($4-6)
10. yellow body, black blade, silver-gray metal base, lemon rollers, black canopy, "C" tempa, England casting ($4-6)
11. yellow body, yellow blade, silver-gray metal base, lemon rollers, black canopy, "C" tempa, England casting ($4-6)
12. yellow body, black blade, unpainted metal base, lemon rollers, tan canopy, "C Cat" tempa, England casting ($4-6)
13. yellow body, yellow blade, unpainted metal base, lemon rollers, tan canopy, "C Cat" tempa, England casting ($4-6)
14. yellow body, no blade, silver-gray base, lemon rollers, black canopy, "C Cat" tempa, England casting ($12-15)
15. yellow body, yellow blade, unpainted metal base, orange rollers, tan canopy, no tempa, black treads (from MB70-C), England casting ($18-25)
16. yellow body, yellow blade, pearly silver metal base, lemon rollers, black canopy, "C Cat" tempa, Macau casting ($1-2)
17. yellow body, yellow blade, pearly silver metal base, lemon rollers, black canopy, "C Cat" tempa, China casting ($1-2)
18. yellow body, yellow blade, pearly silver metal base, lemon rollers, black canopy, no tempa, Macau casting ($1-2)
19. yellow body, gray blade, pearly silver metal base, lemon rollers, black canopy, no tempa, Macau casting ($2-3)(5pk)
20. red body, yellow blade, blue metal base, blue rollers, yellow treads, blue canopy, yellow stripes tempa, Macau casting ($6-8)(LL)
21. orange body, orange blade, pearly silver metal base, orange rollers, black canopy, "Losinger" tempa, Macau casting ($8-12)(SW)
22. yellow body, yellow blade, light gray plastic base, yellow rollers, black canopy, no tempa, Thailand casting ($1-2)
23. yellow body, yellow blade, dark gray plastic base, yellow rollers, black canopy, no tempa, Thailand casting ($1-2)
24. yellow body, dark gray blade, light gray plastic base, yellow rollers, black canopy, no tempa, Thailand casting ($1-2)
25. red body, lime blade, yellow plastic base, lemon rollers, yellow treads, blue canopy, gravel design tempa, Thailand casting ($6-8)(LL)
26. orange-yellow body, yellow blade, light gray plastic base, yellow rollers, black canopy, no tempa, Thailand casting ($1-2)
27. orange-yellow body, yellow blade, light gray plastic base, yellow rollers, red canopy, red stripes (blade) tempa, Thailand casting ($1-2)
28. orange-yellow body, yellow blade, silver-gray plastic base, yellow rollers, red canopy, red stripes (blade) tempa, Thailand casting ($1-2)
29. orange body, orange blade, silver-gray plastic base, orange rollers, black canopy, black stripes (blade) tempa, Thailand casting ($1-2)(5pk)
30. dark orange body, silver-gray blade, silver-gray plastic base, dark orange rollers, black canopy, detailed trim tempa, Thailand casting ($2-4)(CC)
31. fluorescent orange body, black blade, silver-gray plastic base, orange rollers, black canopy, no tempa, Thailand casting ($1-2)(5pk)
32. orange-yellow body, yellow blade, silver-gray plastic base, yellow rollers, red canopy, no tempa (plain blade), Thailand casting ($1-2)
33. florescent orange body, gray blade, black plastic base, orange rollers, black canopy, no tempa, China casting ($1-2)(5pk)
34. red body, silver-gray blade, silver-gray plastic base, red rollers, black canopy, no tempa, China casting ($1-2)
35. pumpkin body, gray blade, black plastic base, yellow rollers, black canopy, no tempa, China casting ($1-2)(5pk)
36. neon yellow body, gray blade, gray plastic base, black rollers, black canopy, no tempa, China casting ($1-2)
37. orange-yellow body, black blade, gray plastic base, black rollers, yellow canopy, "Matchbox" & detailed trim tempa, China casting ($2-4)(PC-CY)
38. orange body, orange blade, silver-gray plastic base, orange rollers, orange canopy, "Metro DPW" (blade) tempa, China casting ($1-2)(MW14/1998)
39. yellow body, black blade, silver-gray plastic base, yellow rollers, yellow canopy, small "C" & detailed trim tempa, China casting ($2-4)(PC-CY)
40. florescent green body, yellow blade, black base, green rollers, black canopy, "Unit 3" tempa, China casting ($1-2)(5pk)
41. metallic gold body, black blade, black base, black rollers, black canopy, none tempa, China casting ($5-10)(CH)
42. orange-yellow body, orange-yellow blade, gray plastic base, black rollers, orange-yellow canopy, detailed trim tempa, China casting ($3-5)(PC)
43. pumpkin body, silver-gray blade, gray plastic base, black rollers, black canopy, "CT Tank Removal" tempa, China casting ($75+)(ASAP)
44. pumpkin body, silver-gray blade, gray plastic base, black rollers, black canopy, "Amavia" tempa, China casting ($50+)(ASAP)
45. pumpkin body, silver-gray blade, gray plastic base, black rollers, black canopy, "LCT" tempa, China casting ($50+)(ASAP)
46. pumpkin body, silver-gray blade, gray plastic base, black rollers, black canopy, "Hemler Bros." Tempa, China casting ($50+)(ASAP)
47. pumpkin body, silver-gray blade, gray plastic base, black rollers, black canopy, "CAT Service Co." tempa, China casting ($50+)(ASAP)
48. pumpkin body, silver-gray blade, gray plastic base, black rollers, black canopy, Blue Ridge construction Co." tempa, China casting ($50+)(ASAP)
49. pumpkin body, silver-gray blade, gray plastic base, black rollers, black canopy, "General Fill" tempa, China casting ($50+)(ASAP)
50. pumpkin body, silver-gray blade, gray plastic base, black rollers, black canopy, "Beers" tempa, China casting ($50+)(ASAP)
51. pumpkin body, silver-gray blade, gray plastic base, black rollers, black canopy, no tempa, China casting ($12-18)(ASAP blank)
52. pumpkin body, silver-gray blade, gray plastic base, black rollers, black canopy, "Happy 5th Birthday Jake" roof label ($50+)(CCI)

MB64-E DODGE CARAVAN *see MB68-E*

MB64-F OLDSMOBILE AEROTECH *see MB62-H*

MB64-G 1970 PONTIAC GTO *see MB70-H*

MB64-H HOLDEN COMMODORE *see MB54-L*

MB64-I VW TRANSPORTER, issued 1999 (USA) (MB390)
MB59-K VW TRANSPORTER, issued 1999 (ROW)

NOTE: Below models with 5 spoke concave star wheels & China casting unless otherwise noted.

1. white & red body, red interior, light smoke windows, space caricatures tempa, white base ($2-3)(MW59/1999 ROW)
2. white & red body, red interior, light smoke windows, "We Have Visitors/ They Are Here" tempa, white base ($1-2)(MW64/1999 US)
3. dark green body, white interior, blue windows with curtains, 4 bumper stickers tempa, gray base ($1-2)(5pk)
4. light sea green & white body, gray interior, clear windows, "Coca Cola" tempa, chrome disc with rubber tires, chrome base ($4-6)(Coke PC)
5. light sea green & white body, gray interior, clear windows, "Coca Cola" & "www.cocacolastore.com" tempa, chrome disc with rubber tires, chrome base ($50+)(CCI)
6. black body, gray interior, smoke windows, , "Action Radar/ Xtreme Mission" tempa, chrome base ($1-2)(5pk)
7. black body, red interior, smoke windows, "Richie's Pizzeria" tempa, light brown base, 10 spoke flower wheels ($1-2)(MW57/ 2000US)
8. black body, red interior, smoke windows, "Richie's Pizzeria" & "Matchbox 2000" tempa, light brown base, 10 spoke flower wheels ($2-4)(MW57/2000 US)
9. lime body, orange-yellow interior, clear windows, "Scooby-Doo!/ Zoinks!/ Shaggy" tempa, blue-gray base ($5-7)(WB)
10. white & turquoise body, turquoise interior, smoke windows, detailed trim tempa, chrome disc with rubber tires, chrome base ($4-6)(MP-FAO)
11. white ,turquoise & dark blue body, red interior, clear windows, "VW Transporter" & stripes tempa, chrome base ($20-35)(MW12/2001 US)
12. white, turquoise & dark blue body, orange interior, clear windows, "VW Transporter" & stripes tempa, 10 spoke flower wheels, chrome base ($1-2)(MW12/2001 US)
13. black body, gray interior, smoke windows, "Action Radar/ X-Treme Mission" tempa, star with 5 spokes wheels, chrome base ($1-2)(5pk)

NOTE: Below models with 10 spoke flower wheels unless otherwise noted.

14. metallic purple body, translucent pink interior, clear windows, "Angelica/ Rugrats" tempa, blue base ($1-2)(5pk)
15. yellow body, orange interior, clear windows, "Come Visit New York- Big Apple Taxi" tempa, chrome base ($25-40)(CCI)
16. silver-gray body, orange interior, clear windows, "Come Visit New York- Big Apple Tours" tempa , chrome base($25-40)(CCI)
17. white & orange body, gray interior, clear windows, detailed trim tempa, chrome disc wheels with rubber tires, black base ($3-5)(BJ)
18. white & red body, black interior, clear windows, "Coca Cola" & splash design tempa, chrome disc wheels with rubber tires, chrome base ($3-5)(Coke PC)
19. white, turquoise & dark blue body, orange interior, clear windows, "VW Transporter/ Reading, PA" & pagoda tempa, chrome base ($18-25)(CCI)
20. white & orange body, gray interior, clear windows, "Kyle James Dickinson" & toy design tempa, black base ($75+)(CCI)
21. lemon body, light blue interior, clear windows, "Angelica/ Rugrats" tempa , blue base($1-2)(5pk)
22. orange-yellow & green body, white interior, clear windows, "York Fair 2002" tempa, chrome disc wheels with rubber tires, chrome base ($6-8)(US)
23. orange-yellow & green body, white interior, clear windows, detailed trim tempa tempa, chrome disc wheels with rubber tires, chrome base ($6-8)(blank over-run of above issue)
24. orange-yellow & green body, white interior, clear windows, "Camp Sunshine" tempa, chrome disc wheels with rubber tires, chrome base ($18-25)(CCI)
25. orange-yellow & green body, white interior, clear windows, "2003 Gotham/ MICA Goes to Gotham" tempa, chrome disc wheels with rubber tires, chrome base ($18-25)(CCI)
26. white, turquoise & dark blue body, orange interior, clear windows, "Happy 70th Birthday/ VW Transporter/ Celebration!" tempa , white base ($15-20)(CCI)
27. white body, blue interior, amber windows, burst design tempa, blue-green base ($1-2)(5pk)
28. red & dark beige body, white interior, clear windows, "Drink Coca Cola" tempa, chrome disc with rubber tires, green base ($3-5)(Coke PC)
29. orange-yellow & green body, white interior, clear windows, "MRMC Matchbox/ 2003 Midwest Regional Matchbox Convention" tempa, chrome disc with rubber tires, chrome base ($18-25)(CCI)
30. red body, orange-yellow interior, amber windows, "Klunk! Peanuts" tempa, blue-green base ($1-2)(5pk)
31. orange-yellow & green body, white interior, clear windows, "D&S Racing Collectibles Happy Holidays 2003" tempa, chrome disc with rubber tires, chrome base ($18-25)(CCI)
32. metallic purple body, neon yellow interior, clear windows, "Hero City Shuttle", gray base ($1-2)(MW45/2004)
33. orange-yellow & green body, white interior, clear windows, "Happy Holidays 2003- Van Toy Collector" tempa, chrome disc with rubber tires, chrome base ($18-25)(CCI)
34. orange-yellow & green body, white interior, clear windows, "Vintage Volkswagen Club of America 2004" tempa, chrome disc with rubber tires, chrome base ($18-25)(CCI)
35. metallic blue body, gold interior, red windows, "76ers 40th Anniversary" tempa, lace wheels, gray base ($25-40)(US)
36. white body, red interior, blue windows, "Moscow" & blue sides tempa, lace wheels, red base ($1-2)(AW)
37. white & dark brick red body, black interior, smoke windows, detailed trim tempa, slotted 5 spoke wheels, white base ($3-5)(SF17/2004)
38. white, turquoise & blue body, orange interior, clear windows, "Cruisin' New England" tempa, 5 spoke concave star wheels, chrome base ($50+)(CCI)
39. orange-yellow & green body, white interior, clear windows, "Kerry is great... She turned 8! Happy Birthday" tempa, chrome disc wheels with rubber tires ($18-25)(CCI)

MB64-J MERCEDES BENZ ACTROS 1857, issued 1999 (GR) (MB425)

1. lemon body, smoke windows, black interior, 8 spoke wheels, silver headlights tempa, black base, China casting ($5-8)(MW64/1999GR)

MB64-L FORK LIFT, issued 2002 (MB562)

NOTE: Below models with black plastic base & China casting unless otherwise noted.

1. orange body, black boom & forks, 4 spoke domed wheels, stripes & design tempa ($1-2)(MW64/2002)

2. orange body, black boom & forks, 4 spoke domed wheels, stripes & design with :Matchbox 50" tempa ($2-4)(MW64/2002)
3. white body, neon orange boom & forks, 4 spoke domed wheels, "MHC70" tempa ($1-2)(MW70/2003 US)
4. white body, neon orange boom & forks, 4 spoke domed wheels, "MHC70" & "Hero City" tempa ($1-2)(MW70/2003 US)
5. iridescent white body, neon orange boom & forks, 4 spoke domed wheels with gold hubs, "MHC70" tempa ($3-4)(20pk)
6. orange-yellow body, red boom & forks, 7 spoke sawblade wheels, "Hero City" & design tempa ($1-2)(5pk)
7. orange-yellow body, red boom & forks, 5 crown dot wheels, "Hero City" & design tempa ($5-8)(5pk)
8. yellow body, black boom & forks, 5 crown dot wheels, red & purple stripes with gray cog design tempa, gray base ($1-2)(MW28/2004 ROW)
9. orange-yellow body, red boom & forks, lace wheels, "Hero City" & design tempa ($2-3)(5pk)

MB64-M PONTIAC SOLSTICE, issued 2004 (MB612)

1. silver blue body, clear windows, black interior, head & tail lights tempa, lace wheels, black base, China casting ($1-2)(MW64/2004)

MB65-A SAAB SONNET, issued 1973

NOTE: Below models with amber windows, yellow interior, blue hatch, unpainted metal base & England casting.

1. metallic blue body ($10-15)
2. white body ($275-400)(MP)

MB65-B AIRPORT COACH, issued 1977

NOTE: Below models with metal base & dot dash wheels unless otherwise noted.

1. blue body, "American Airlines" labels, amber windows, light yellow interior, unpainted base, England casting ($4-6)
2. blue body, "American Airlines" labels, clear windows, light yellow interior, unpainted base, England casting ($4-6)
3. blue body, "American Airlines" labels, amber windows, light yellow interior, unpainted (tab) base, no origin cast ($35-50)(BR)
4. blue body, "American Airlines" labels, clear windows, ivory interior, unpainted base, England casting ($4-6)
5. blue body, "American Airlines" labels, amber windows, ivory interior, unpainted base, England casting ($4-6)
6. blue body, "American Airlines" labels, clear windows, cream interior, unpainted base, England casting ($4-6)
7. blue body, "British Airways" labels, amber windows, light yellow interior, unpainted base, England casting ($4-6)
8. blue body, "British Airways" labels, clear windows, light yellow interior, unpainted base, England casting ($4-6)
9. blue body, "British Airways" labels, amber windows, light yellow interior, unpainted base (tab), no origin cast ($35-50)(BR)
10. blue body, "British Airways" labels, clear windows, ivory interior, unpainted base, England casting ($4-6)
11. blue body, "British Airways" labels, amber windows, ivory interior, unpainted base, England casting ($4-6)
12. blue body, "Lufthansa" labels, amber windows, light yellow interior, unpainted base, England casting ($4-6)
13. blue body, "Lufthansa" labels, clear windows, light yellow interior, unpainted base, England casting ($4-6)
14. blue body, "Lufthansa" labels, amber windows, light yellow interior, unpainted base (tab), no origin cast ($35-50)(BR)
15. blue body, "Lufthansa" labels, clear windows, ivory interior, unpainted base, England casting ($4-6)
16. blue body, "Lufthansa" labels, amber windows, ivory interior, unpainted base, England casting ($4-6)
17. red body, "Qantas" labels, amber windows, light yellow interior, unpainted base, England casting ($8-12)
18. red body, "Qantas" labels, amber windows, light yellow interior, silver-gray base, England casting ($8-12)
19. red body, "TWA" labels, amber windows, light yellow interior, unpainted base, England casting ($7-10)
20. red body, "TWA" labels, amber windows, light yellow interior, silver-gray base, England casting ($7-10)
21. red body, "Climat" over "TWA" labels, amber windows, light yellow interior, unpainted base, England casting ($125-175)(FR)
22. orange body, "Schulbus" labels, amber windows, light yellow interior, unpainted base, England casting ($35-45)(GR)
23. blue body, "British" labels, amber windows, light yellow interior, unpainted base, England casting ($7-10)
24. blue body, "British" labels, amber windows, light yellow interior, silver-gray base, England casting ($7-10)
25. white body, "Alitalia" labels, amber windows, light yellow interior, unpainted base, England casting ($7-10)
26. white body, "Alitalia" labels, amber windows, light yellow interior, silver-gray base, England casting ($7-10)
27. white body, "Lufthansa" labels, amber windows, light yellow interior, silver-gray base, England casting ($25-40)
28. white body, "Alitalia" tempa, amber windows, light yellow interior, pearly silver base, Macau casting ($3-5)
29. orange body, "Lufthansa" tempa, amber windows, light yellow interior, pearly silver base, Macau casting ($3-5)(GS)
30. white body, "Pan Am" tempa, amber windows, light yellow interior, pearly silver base, Macau casting ($3-5)(GS)
31. white body, "Stork SB" tempa, amber windows, light yellow interior, pearly silver base, Macau casting ($8-12)(AU)(OP)
32. red body, "Virgin Atlantic" tempa, amber windows, light yellow interior, pearly silver base, Macau casting ($3-5)(GS)
33. blue body, "Australian" tempa, amber windows, light yellow interior, pearly silver base, Macau casting ($7-10)(AU)
34. blue body, "Girobank" labels, blue windows, light yellow interior, pearly silver base, Macau casting ($7-10)(UK)

NOTE: Above models all with white plastic roof.

35. white body, green roof, "Alitalia" tempa, amber windows, white interior, white base, Thailand casting ($5-7)(MP)
36. white body, blue roof, "KLM" tempa, amber windows, white interior, white base, Thailand casting ($5-7)(MP)
37. white body, blue roof, "SAS" tempa, amber windows, white interior, white base, Thailand casting ($5-7)(MP)
38. white body & roof, "Lufthansa" tempa, amber windows, white interior, pearly silver base, Thailand casting ($5-7)(MP)
39. red body, white roof, "Virgin Atlantic" tempa, amber windows, white interior, pearly silver base, Thailand casting ($3-5)
40. red body, white roof, "TWA" tempa, amber windows, white interior, white plastic base, Manaus casting ($35-50)(BR)
41. green body, white roof, "TWA" tempa, amber windows, white interior, white plastic base, 8 dot wheels, Manaus casting ($45-60)(BR)

MB65-C BANDAG BANDIT, issued 1982 (USA)

NOTE: Below models with green windows & Chrome plastic base.

1. black body, green & white stripes tempa, "Tyrone" & 4 stripes on airfoil, 5 crown front & dot dash rear wheels, England casting ($3-5)
2. black body, green & white stripes tempa, "Tyrone" & 4 stripes on airfoil, dot dash front & rear wheels, England casting ($3-5)
3. black body, green & white stripes tempa, "Tyrone" & 2 stripes on airfoil, 5 crown front & dot dash wheels, England casting ($3-5)

4. black body, green & white stripes tempa, "Tyrone" & 2 stripes on airfoil, dot dash front & rear wheels, England casting ($3-5)
5. black body, green & white stripes tempa, plain airfoil, 5 crown front & dot dash rear wheels, England casting ($3-5)
6. black body, green & white stripes tempa, "Tyrone" & 4 stripes on airfoil, 5 crown front & rear wheels, England casting ($3-5)
7. black body, yellow & white stripes tempa, "Tyrone" & no stripes on airfoil, 5 crown front & dot dash rear wheels, Macau casting ($1-2)
8. black body, yellow & white stripes tempa, "Tyrone" & 4 stripes on airfoil, 5 crown front & dot dash rear wheels, Macau casting ($1-2)
9. black body, yellow & white stripes tempa, plain airfoil, maltese cross front wheels & dot dash rear wheels, China casting ($4-6)(MP)

MB65-D F.1 RACER, issued 1985 (USA) (MB137)

NOTE: Below models with 8 dot front & racing special rear wheels unless otherwise noted.

1. dark blue body, black metal base, red driver, red "Goodyear" airfoil, 5 arch front wheels, chrome lettered rear wheels, chrome exhausts, "20 Bosch STP" tempa, Macau casting ($4-6)
2. dark blue body, black metal base, red driver, red "Goodyear" airfoil, 5 arch front wheels, unchromed rear wheels, chrome exhausts, "20 Bosch STP" tempa, Macau casting ($4-6)
3. dark blue body, black metal base, red driver, red "Goodyear" airfoil, unchromed rear wheels, chrome exhausts, "20 Bosch STP" tempa, Macau casting ($4-6)
4. dark blue body, black metal base, red driver, red plain airfoil, unchromed rear wheels, chrome exhausts, "20 Bosch STP" tempa, Macau casting ($4-6)
5. yellow body, black metal base, red driver, red "Goodyear" airfoil, chrome exhausts, "Matchbox Racing Team" tempa, Macau casting ($2-3)
6. yellow body, black metal base, dark red driver, dark red "Goodyear" airfoil, chrome exhausts, "Matchbox Racing Team" tempa, Macau casting ($2-3)
7. yellow body, black metal base, red driver, red "Goodyear" airfoil, black exhausts, "Matchbox Racing Team" tempa, Macau casting ($2-3)
8. pink body, black metal base, red driver, red "Goodyear" airfoil, chrome exhausts, "Matchbox Racing Team" tempa, Macau casting ($3-4)(SC)
9. light pea green body, black metal base, red driver, red "Goodyear" airfoil, chrome exhausts, "Matchbox Racing Team" tempa, Macau casting ($3-4)(SC)
10. light peach body, black metal base, red driver, red "Goodyear" airfoil, chrome exhausts, "Matchbox Racing Team" tempa, Macau casting ($3-4)(SC)
11. red body, black plastic base, red driver, red "Goodyear" airfoil, black exhausts, "Matchbox Racing Team" tempa, Macau casting ($3-4)(SC)
12. orange body, black plastic base, red driver, red "Goodyear" airfoil, black exhausts, "Matchbox Racing Team" tempa, Macau casting ($3-4)(SC)
13. yellow body, black plastic base, red driver, red "Goodyear" airfoil, black exhausts, "Matchbox Racing Team" tempa, Macau casting ($1-2)
14. white body, red plastic base, red driver, red plain airfoil, blue wheels with yellow hubs, lime exhausts, "123456" & flames tempa, Macau casting ($6-8)(LL)
15. white body, red plastic base, red driver, red plain airfoil, blue wheels with yellow hubs, lime exhausts, "123456" & flames" tempa, Thailand casting ($6-8)(LL)
16. yellow body, black plastic base, red driver, red "Goodyear" airfoil, black exhausts, "Matchbox Racing Team" tempa, Thailand casting ($1-2)
17. white/hot pink/blue body, black plastic base, pink driver, pink "Rain-X" airfoil, black exhausts, "Amway/Speedway 22" tempa, China casting ($3-5)(IN)
18. dark blue & white body, black plastic base, dark blue driver, dark blue "Valvoline" airfoil, black exhausts, "Valvoline 5" tempa, China casting ($3-5)(IN)
19. orange-yellow & blue body, black plastic base, yellow driver, yellow "Kraco" airfoil, black exhausts, "Kraco/Otter Pops 18" tempa, China casting ($3-5)(IN)
20. lemon & black body, black plastic base, lemon driver, lemon "Goodyear" airfoil, black exhausts, "Indy 11" tempa, China casting ($3-5)(IN)
21. lemon & black body, black plastic base, lemon driver, lemon "Indy" airfoil, black exhausts, "Indy 11" tempa, China casting ($4-6)(IN)
22. black body, black plastic base, black driver, black "Havoline" airfoil, black exhausts, "Havoline 86" tempa, China casting ($3-5)(IN)
23. chrome plated body, black plastic base, red driver, red "Goodyear" airfoil, black exhausts, no tempa, Thailand casting ($12-18)(C2)
24. yellow body, black plastic base, red driver, red "Goodyear" airfoil, black exhausts, "Matchbox Racing Team" tempa, China casting ($1-2)
25. orange-yellow & blue body, black plastic base, orange-yellow driver, orange-yellow "Kraco" airfoil, black exhausts, "Kraco 18" tempa, Thailand casting ($3-5)(IN)
26. yellow body, black plastic base, maroon driver, maroon "Goodyear" airfoil, black exhausts, "Matchbox Racing Team" tempa, Thailand casting ($1-2)
27. white/hot pink/blue body, black plastic base, pink driver, pink "Rain-X" airfoil, black exhausts, "Amway/Speedway 22" tempa, Thailand casting ($3-5)(IN)
28. blue & white body, black plastic base, blue driver, blue "Mitre 10" airfoil, black exhausts, "Mitre 10/Larkham/Taubmans 3" tempa, Thailand casting ($6-8)(AU)(TC)
29. white body, black plastic base, plum driver, plum "Hyflo" airfoil, black exhausts, "Hyflo Exhausts 5" tempa, Thailand casting ($1-2)(5pk)
30. black body, black plastic base, black driver, black "Rad" airfoil, black exhausts, "Rad 5" with green & white stripes tempa, Thailand casting ($1-2)
31. blue body, black plastic base, blue driver, blue "Mitre 10" airfoil, black exhausts, "Mitre 10/2/M10" tempa, Thailand casting ($5-7)(AU)(CY)
32. white & dark orange body, black plastic base, orange driver, orange "AGFA" airfoil, black exhausts, "AGFA Film 29" tempa, Thailand casting ($7-10)(US)
33. white & red body, black plastic base, red driver, red "AGFA" airfoil, black exhausts, "AGFA Film 29" tempa, Thailand casting ($7-10)(US)
34. black body, black plastic base, black driver, black "Rad" airfoil, black exhausts, "Rad 5" with white stripes only tempa, Thailand casting ($4-6) (Aquafresh)
35. red body, black plastic base, black driver, black airfoil, black exhausts, "3 Tech Racing" tempa, Thailand casting ($1-2)(5pk)

MB65-E AIRPLANE TRANSPORTER *see MB72-G*

MB65-F CADILLAC ALLANTE *see MB72-I*

MB65-G FORD F150 PICKUP, issued 1995 (MB248)

NOTE: Below models with clear windows, maltese cross wheels & chrome plastic base unless otherwise noted.

1. red body, black interior, chrome rollbar, white band tempa, Thailand casting ($1-2)
2. red body, black interior, black rollbar, white band tempa, Thailand casting ($1-2)
3. purple body, black interior, chrome rollbar, greenish yellow design tempa, China casting ($1-2)(5pk)
4. red body, black interior, black rollbar, white band tempa, China casting ($1-2)
5. dark metallic blue, black interior, black rollbar, silver band tempa, China casting ($1-2)
6. red body, black interior, chrome rollbar, "Ford" with white & blue tempa, China casting ($1-2)(5pk)
7. black body, gray interior, chrome rollbar, red band tempa, China casting ($1-2)
8. metallic tan body, black interior, chrome rollbar, white & blue splash tempa, China casting ($1-2)(5pk)
9. metallic gold body, black interior, chrome rollbar, no tempa, China casting ($5-10)(CH)
10. iridescent white body, dark blue interior, dark blue rollbar, pink & blue with "Ford" tempa, China casting ($1-2)(MW53/1998 US))
11. dark metallic blue body, black interior, black rollbar, silver band & "Whirlpool" tempa, China casting ($100+)(ASAP)
12. black body, gray interior, green rollbar, "Black Star Ranch", mud & "Don't Mess with Texas" tempa, China casting ($1-2)(5pk)
13. black body, gray interior, green rollbar, "Black Star Ranch" & mud tempa, China casting ($1-2)(5pk)
14. red body, blue windows, black interior, black rollbar, "Beach Patrol Unit 44" tempa, China casting ($1-2)(MW14/2000 US)
15. red body, blue windows, black interior, black rollbar, "Beach Patrol Unit 44" & "Matchbox 2000" tempa, China casting ($2-4)(MW14/2000 US)
16. red body, blue windows, black interior, black roll bar, "Beach Patrol Unit 44" tempa with "Matchbox Madness" decal, China casting ($50+)(CCI)
17. black body, blue windows, black interior, dark green rollbar, "MC15" & rhino head tempa, China casting, China casting ($1-2)(5pk)
18. white body, clear windows, black interior, black rollbar, "Manheim Auto Auction" tempa, black base, China casting ($50+)(ASAP)
19. white body, clear windows, black interior, black roll bar, no tempa, black base, China casting ($25-40(ASAP blank)
20. white body, clear windows, black interior, black roll bar, "Field Direct" tempa, black base, China casting ($50+)(ASAP blank)
21. white body, clear windows, black interior, black roll bar, "Pearsol's" tempa, black base, China casting ($50+)
20. green-gold body, dark smoke windows, black interior, black rollbar, baseball design tempa, Mattel China casting ($1-2)(5pk)
21. neon yellow body, blue windows, black interior, black rollbar, rhino head tempa, 5 spoke oval wheels, Mattel China casting ($1-2)(5pk)

MB65-H CHEVY SILVERADO 4 X 4 PICKUP *see MB70-J*

MB65-I JEEP GRAND CHEROKEE, issued 2000 (USA) (MB442/471)
MB45-G JEEP GRAND CHEROKEE, issued 2000 (ROW)

NOTE: Below models with smoke windows, black plastic base & China casting unless otherwise noted.

1. silver-gray body, black interior, red roof raft, "Grand Cherokee" tempa, 5 spoke concave star wheels ($1-2)(MW65/2000 US)(MW45/2000 ROW)
2. silver-gray body, black interior, red roof raft, "Grand Cherokee" & "Matchbox 2000" tempa, 5 spoke concave star wheels ($2-4)(MW65/2000 US)
3. red body, brown interior, no roof raft, "Camp Jeep 2000" with black stripes & odd design tempa, 5 spoke concave star wheels ($1-2)(5pk)
4. blue body, white interior, yellow roof raft, "Action Canyon" tempa, 5 spoke concave star wheels ($1-2)(MW22/2001))
5. blue body, white interior, yellow roof raft, "Action Canyon" tempa, 7 spoke sawblade wheels ($1-2)(MW22/2001)
6. red body, white interior, clear windows, no roof raft, "Metro Alarm" & yellow band tempa, lace wheels ($1-2)(5pk)
7. silver-gray body, white interior, red roof raft, "Grand Cherokee" tempa, 10 spoke flower wheels ($10-15)(MW65/2000 US)
8. metallic blue body, red interior, none roof raft, football design tempa, 7 spoke sawblade wheels ($1-2)(5pk)
9. lemon body, white interior, blue roof raft, "Gauley Rivers Guides 33- West Virginia" tempa, 7 spoke sawblade wheels ($3-5)(AM)
10. metallic purple body, black interior, yellow roof raft, waves & raft tempa, 7 spoke sawblade wheels ($1-2)(MW48/2002)
11. metallic purple body, black interior, yellow roof raft, waves & raft with "Matchbox 50" tempa, 7 spoke sawblade wheels ($5-8)(MW48/2002)
12. light metallic purple body, black interior, yellow roof raft, waves & raft tempa, 7 spoke sawblade wheels ($1-2)(MW48/2002)
13. brick red body, orange-yellow interior, clear windows, no roof raft, "Coca Cola Hospitality" tempa, chrome disc wheels with rubber tires ($3-5)(Coke PC)
14. black body, silver-gray interior, red windows, no roof raft, "Metro Alarm" tempa, lace wheels ($1-2)(5pk)
15. bright blue body, black interior, orange roof raft, "Grand Canyon" tempa, 7 spoke sawblade wheels ($1-2)(AW)
16. lime body, lime interior, amber windows, purple roof raft & base, "Dora" tempa, 10 spoke flower wheels ($1-2)(5pk)

MB65-J POLICE MOTORCYCLE

MB65-K ICE CREAM TRUCK, issued 2002 (USA) (MB530)
MB60-N ICE CREAM TRUCK, issued 2003 (ROW)

NOTE: Below models with 7 spoke sawblade wheels & China casting.

1. white body, blue windows, blue-green interior, red door, yellow base, "Jimmies Ice Cream" tempa ($1-2)(MW65/2002 US))
2. white body, blue windows, blue-green interior, red door, yellow base, "Jimmies Ice cream" & "Matchbox 50" tempa ($2-4)(MW65/2002 US)
3. white body, red windows, red interior, blue door, purple base, ice cream cone cartoon design tempa ($1-2)(MW60/2003)
4. white body, red windows, red interior, blue door, purple base, ice cream cone cartoon design & "Hero City" tempa ($2-4)(MW60/2003)
5. white body, red windows, orange interior, light yellow door, light blue base, clown design tempa ($1-2)(MW59/2004)
6. white body, red windows, red interior, blue door, purple base, ice cream cone cartoon design with "Stop" on door tempa ($5-8)(Ghost 2 pack)

MB65-L FERRARI 360 SPIDER, issued 2002 (ROW) (MB531)
MB 7-I FERRARI 360 SPIDER, issued 2003 (USA)

NOTE: Below models with black interior, lace wheels, black base & China casting.

1. red body, clear windshield, tiny "Ferrari" logos tempa ($2-4)(MW65/2002 ROW)

2. red body, clear windshield, tiny "Ferrari" logos & "Matchbox 50" tempa ($3-5)(MW65/2002 ROW)
3. silver-gray body, smoke windshield, small "Ferrari" tempa ($1-2)(MW7/2003)
4. silver-gray body, smoke windshield, small "Ferrari" & "Hero City" tempa ($2-4)(MW7/2003)
5. yellow body, smoke windshield, small "Ferrari" logos tempa ($2-4)(MW22/2004 ROW)
6. red body, smoke windshield, small "Ferrari" logos tempa, 10 spoke flower wheels ($3-5)(SoC)

MB66-A GREYHOUND BUS, issued 1970

NOTE: Below models with amber windows, white interior, 5 spoke wheels, metal base & England casting.

1. silver-gray body, black base, black front axle cover & red rear axle cover ($35-50)
2. silver-gray body, black base, black front & rear axle cover ($25-40)
3. silver-gray body, pink base, black front & rear axle cover ($35-50)
4. silver-gray body, light yellow base, black front & rear axle cover ($35-50)
5. silver-gray body, dark yellow base, black front & rear axle cover ($35-50)
6. silver-gray body, black base, red front axle cover & black rear axle cover ($35-50)
7. silver-gray body, black base, red front & rear axle covers ($35-50)

MB66-B MAZDA RX500, issued 1971

NOTE: Versions 1 to 11 with England casting. Version 12 with Hong Kong casting.

1. orange body, unpainted base, amber windows, chrome interior, no tempa, 5 spoke wheels ($50-75)
2. orange body, unpainted base, purple windows, chrome interior, no tempa, 5 spoke wheels ($10-15)
3. orange body, white base, purple windows, chrome interior, no tempa, 5 spoke wheels ($10-15)
4. orange body, white base, amber windows, chrome interior, no tempa, 5 spoke wheels ($18-25)
5. red body, white base, purple windows, chrome interior, no tempa, 5 spoke wheels ($18-25)
6. red body, white base, purple windows, tan interior, no tempa, 5 spoke wheels ($18-25)
7. red body, white base, purple windows, chrome interior, "Castrol" label, 5 spoke wheels ($650-800)
8. red body, white base, purple windows, chrome interior, "77" tempa, 5 spoke wheels ($12-15)
9. red body, white base, amber windows, chrome interior, "77" tempa, 5 spoke wheels ($8-12)
10. red body, white base, amber windows, chrome interior, "77" tempa, 5 arch wheels ($8-12)
11. red body, unpainted base, amber windows, chrome interior, "77" tempa, 5 arch wheels ($8-12)
12. red body, white base, amber windows, tan interior, "77" tempa, 5 arch wheels ($8-12)
13. green body, pearly silver base, amber windows, chrome interior, "66" tempa, 5 arch wheels ($10-15)(US)

NOTE: Available as a Bulgarian casting. Assorted colors available. ($15-25)

MB66-C FORD TRANSIT, issued 1977

NOTE: Below models with dot dash wheels & England casting.

1. dark orange body, unpainted base, light yellow interior, blue-green windows, brown cargo ($6-8)
2. dark orange body, unpainted base, tan interior, blue-green windows, brown cargo ($6-8)
3. dark orange body, unpainted base, light yellow interior, blue-green windows, dark tan cargo ($6-8)
4. dark orange body, unpainted base, light yellow interior, dark green windows, dark tan cargo ($6-8)
5. dark orange body, unpainted base, tan interior, amber windows, light tan cargo ($6-8)
6. dark orange body, unpainted base, olive interior, amber windows, light tan cargo ($6-8)
7. dark orange body, unpainted base, light yellow interior, amber windows, light tan cargo ($6-8)
8. dark orange body, unpainted base, white interior, amber windows, light tan cargo ($6-8)
9. dark orange body, unpainted base, olive interior, amber windows, brown cargo ($6-8)
10. dark orange body, unpainted base, olive interior, dark green windows, light tan cargo ($6-8)
11. dark orange body, unpainted base, olive interior, blue-green windows, dark tan cargo ($6-8)
12. dark orange body, unpainted base, olive interior, amber windows, dark tan cargo ($6-8)
13. dark orange body, unpainted base with Manaus tab, cream interior, blue-green windows, light tan cargo ($35-50)(BR)
14. light orange body, unpainted base, cream interior, blue-green windows, light tan cargo ($6-8)
15. light orange body, black base, cream interior, blue-green windows, light tan cargo ($6-8)
16. light orange body, unpainted base, olive interior, blue-green windows, light tan cargo ($6-8)
17. light orange body, unpainted base, cream interior, blue-green windows, dark tan cargo ($6-8)
18. light orange body, black base, cream interior, blue-green windows, dark tan cargo ($6-8)
19. light orange body, charcoal base, lemon interior, green windows, dark tan cargo ($6-8)
20. light orange body, charcoal base, cream interior, blue-green windows, light tan cargo ($6-8)

MB66-D SUPER BOSS, issued 1982 (MB066)

NOTE: Below models with chrome plastic base & 5 crown front wheels unless otherwise noted.

1. white body, no "Detroit Diesel" on roof, green windows, dot dash rear wheels, tempa & 4 stripes on spoiler, England casting ($2-4)
2. white body, no "Detroit Diesel" on roof, green windows, dot dash rear wheels, no tempa on spoiler, England casting ($2-4)
3. white body, no "Detroit Diesel" on roof, green windows, dot dash rear wheels, tempa & 2 stripes on spoiler, England casting ($2-4)
4. white body, with "Detroit Diesel" on roof, green windows, dot dash rear wheels, no tempa on spoiler, England casting ($2-4)
5. white body, with "Detroit Diesel" on roof, green windows, 5 arch rear wheels, no tempa on spoiler, England casting ($2-4)
6. white body, with "Detroit Diesel" on roof, red windows, 5 arch rear wheels, no tempa on spoiler, England casting ($7-10)(CY)
7. white body, no "Detroit Diesel" on roof, green windows, dot dash front & rear wheels, tempa & 2 stripes on spoiler, England casting ($2-4)
8. white body, no "Detroit Diesel" on roof, dot dash rear wheels, tempa & 4 stripes on spoiler, Macau casting ($1-2)
9. white body, with "Detroit Diesel" on roof, dot dash rear wheels, decal & 4 stripes on spoiler, Macau casting ($1-2)
10. white body, with "Detroit Diesel" on roof, dot dash rear wheels, decal & no stripes on spoiler, Macau casting ($1-2)

11. white body no "Detroit Diesel" on roof, dot dash rear wheels, decal & 4 stripes on rear spoiler, Macau casting ($1-2)
12. white body, no "Detroit Diesel" on roof, dot dash rear wheels, tempa & 4 stripes on spoiler, China casting ($1-2)
13. white body, with "Detroit Diesel" on roof, maltese cross front & dot dash rear wheels, plain spoiler, China casting ($1-2)
14. tan body, orange/yellow/black stripes tempa, dot dash rear wheels, silver-gray armament replaces spoiler, Macau casting, includes plastic armament ($5-8)(RB)
15. white body, no "Detroit Diesel" on roof, dot dash rear wheels, plain spoiler, China casting ($2-3)
16 white body, no tempa, dot dash rear wheels, white base, China casting ($10-15)(GF)

MB66-E SAUBER GROUP C RACER, issued 1984 (USA) (MB130)
MB46-E SAUBER GROUP C RACER, issued 1984 (ROW)

NOTE: Below models with black plastic base.

1. red body, clear windows, ivory interior, black airfoil, 8 dot silver wheels, "BASF Cassettes" tempa, Macau casting ($3-5)
2. red body, clear windows, ivory interior, black airfoil, 8 dot gold wheels, "BASF Cassettes" tempa, Macau casting ($3-5)
3. white body, clear windows, ivory interior, black airfoil, 8 dot silver wheels, "Jr. Matchbox Collector's Club" tempa, Macau casting ($8-12)(AU)
4. white body, clear windows, ivory interior, black airfoil, 8 dot gold wheels, "61 Sauber Castrol" tempa, Macau casting ($2-3)
5. white body, clear windows, ivory interior, black airfoil, 8 dot silver wheels, "61 Sauber Castrol" tempa, Macau casting ($1-2)
6. yellow body, clear windows, ivory interior, blue airfoil, starburst wheels, orange & blue tempa, Macau casting ($3-5)(SF)
7. yellow body, clear windows, ivory interior, blue airfoil, laser wheels, orange & blue tempa, Macau casting ($3-5)(LW)
8. black body, black windows, ivory interior, black airfoil, starburst wheels, "Cargantua" tempa, Macau casting ($15-18)(PS)
9. pink-red body, dark blue windows, no interior or airfoil, starburst wheels, black/white/yellow tempa, Macau casting, includes plastic armament ($5-8)(RB)
10. white & orange body, clear windows, ivory interior, orange airfoil, 8 dot silver wheels, "Bisotherm/Baustein" tempa, Macau casting ($8-12)(SW)
11. red body, clear windows, black interior, red airfoil, 8 dot silver wheels, "Royal Mail Swiftair" tempa, Macau casting ($5-7)(UK)(MP)
12. robin egg blue body, clear windows, dark blue interior, black airfoil, 8 dot silver wheels, "Grand Prix 46" tempa, Macau casting ($4-6)(MP)
13. white body, clear windows, ivory interior, black airfoil, 8 dot silver wheels, "Grand Prix 46" tempa, Thailand casting ($1-2)
14. chrome plated body, clear windows, ivory interior, black airfoil, 8 dot silver wheels, no tempa, Macau casting ($12-18)(C2)
15. florescent pink & blue body, chrome & black windows, black interior, blue airfoil, lightning wheels, "Matchbox" & flames tempa, China casting ($3-4)(LT)
16. florescent orange & yellow body, blue-chrome & black windows, black interior, florescent yellow airfoil, lightning wheels, lightning bolts tempa, China casting ($3-4)(LT)
17. florescent yellow & orange body, blue-chrome & black windows, black interior, florescent yellow airfoil, lightning wheels, "Lightning" & flames tempa, China casting ($3-4)(LT)
18. blue & florescent pink body, chrome & black windows, black interior, blue airfoil, lightning wheels, "Lightning" & flames tempa, China casting ($3-4)(LT)
19. white body, clear windows, ivory interior, 8 dot silver wheels, black airfoil, "Grand Prix 46" tempa, China casting ($1-2)
20. yellow & red body, clear windows, red interior, 8 dot silver wheels, red airfoil, "Matchbox USA 11th Annual Convention & Toy Show 1992" tempa, China casting ($10-12)(US)
21. red & white body, clear windows, ivory interior, red airfoil, 8 dot silver wheels, "Champion 51" tempa, China casting ($1-2)
22. red & white body, clear windows, ivory interior, maroon airfoil, 8 dot silver wheels, "Champion 51" tempa, China casting ($1-2)
23. red & white body, clear windows, ivory interior, maroon airfoil, 8 dot silver wheels, "Champion 51" tempa, Thailand casting ($1-2)
24. white body, clear windows, pink interior, pink airfoil, gold 6 spoke spiral wheels, "50" & blue/pink design tempa, Thailand casting ($1-2)
25. white body, clear windows, ivory interior, black airfoil, gold 6 spoke spiral wheels, "Grand Prix 46" tempa, Thailand casting ($2-3)
26. white body & base, blue windows, white interior, white airfoil, gold 6 spoke spiral wheels, no tempa, Thailand casting ($7-10)(GF)
27. white body, clear windows, pink interior, pink airfoil, silver 6 spoke spiral wheels, "50" & blue/pink design tempa, Thailand casting ($1-2)
28. white body, blue windows, white interior, pink airfoil, silver 6 spoke spiral wheels, "50" & blue (sides only) & pink (hood only) tempa, Thailand casting ($1-2)
29. white body, blue windows, white interior, pink airfoil, silver 6 spoke spiral wheels, "50" & blue (sides only) & pink (hood only) tempa, China casting ($1-2)
30. white body, clear windows, ivory interior, black airfoil, silver 6 spoke spiral wheels, "Grand Prix 46" tempa, Thailand casting ($3-5)
31. white body, clear windows, red interior, blue airfoil, silver 6 spoke spiral wheels, "50" & red stripes tempa, China casting ($1-2)(5pk)
32. white body, clear windows, ivory interior, black airfoil, 8 dot silver wheels, "Grand Prix 46" tempa, Macau casting ($1-2)
33. white body, clear windows, ivory interior, black airfoil, silver 6 spoke spiral wheels, "Grand Prix 46" tempa, China casting ($1-2)

MB66-F ROLLS ROYCE SILVER SPIRIT, issued 1987 (ROW) (MB177)
MB55-H ROLLS ROYCE SILVER SPIRIT, issued 1990 (USA)
MB73-G ROLLS ROYCE SILVER SPIRIT, reissued 1995 (USA)

NOTE: Below models with black metal base, clear windows & 8 dot wheels.

1. tan body, tan interior, no tempa, Macau casting ($2-4)
2. green-gold body, tan interior, no tempa, Macau casting ($3-5)
3. metallic red body, tan interior, no tempa, Macau casting ($1-2)
4. metallic red body, tan interior, no tempa, Thailand casting ($1-2)
5. metallic red body, cream interior, crest tempa, Thailand casting ($1-2)
6. metallic red body, cream interior, no tempa, Thailand casting ($1-2)
7. metallic red body, tan interior, no tempa, China casting ($1-2)

MB66-G OPEL CALIBRA, issued 1997 (USA) (MB301)
MB46-G OPEL CALIBRA, issued 1997 (ROW)

NOTE: Below models with 5 spoke concave star wheels, black plastic base and China casting unless otherwise noted.

1. orange body, gray interior, smoke windows, "33 Opel Racing" & "Calibra" tempa ($1-2)

2. white body, red interior, clear windows, "World Cup/ France 98" tempa ($1-2)(5pk)
3. white body, yellow interior, clear windows, "World Cup/ France 98" tempa ($1-2)(MW65)
4. white body, blue interior, clear windows, "World Cup/ France 98" tempa ($1-2)(AP)
5. metallic gold body, black interior, clear windows, no tempa ($5-10)(CH)
6. white body, red interior, light smoke windows, "Coca Cola" & bear tempa ($1-2)(5pk)(CK)
7. orange-yellow body, orange-yellow interior, red windows, "Sydney 2000" tempa ($1-2)(5pk)
8. orange-yellow body, red interior, red windows, "Sydney 2000" tempa, small wheels ($3-5)(5pk)

MB66-H PONTIAC FIREBIRD RAM AIR *see MB20-G*

MB66-I MGF, issued 1998 (MB333)

NOTE: Below models with clear windshield, 5 spoke concave star wheels, black base & China casting unless otherwise noted.

1. yellow body, black interior, orange band & "MG" logo tempa, plastic base ($1-2) (MW66/1998)
2. white body, black interior, no tempa, plastic base ($2-4)(MW41/1999 ROW)(MW36/1999 GR)
3. red body, black interior, detailed trim tempa, plastic base ($2-4)(MW4/2000 ROW)
4. bright red body, black interior, "Coke/ Coca-Cola" tempa, plastic base ($1-2)(5pk)(CK)
5. bright red body, black interior, detailed trim tempa, plastic base ($2-4)(MW4/2000 ROW)
6. red body, black interior, detailed trim tempa, 10 spoke flower wheels, plastic base ($3-5)(EG)

NOTE: Below models with Mattel casting.

7. metallic green body, neon yellow interior, "Kellogg's Smacks/ Dig 'Em" tempa, 10 spoke flower wheels, metal base ($1-2)(5pk)
8. bright red body, gray interior, smoke windshield, "Coke/ Coca-Cola" tempa, 5 spoke concave star wheels, metal base ($2-4)(CK)
9. charcoal body, red interior, "Ice Cold/ The Real Thing Coca-Cola" tempa, chrome disc wheels with rubber tires, metal base ($3-5)(Coke PC)
10. red body, gray interior, smoke windshield, "Coke/ Coca Cola" tempa, lace wheels, metal base ($2-4)(CK)
11. black body, red interior, "Coca Cola" tempa, 10 spoke flower wheels, metal base ($2-4)(CK)

MB66-J LAND ROVER FREELANDER, issued 1999 (USA) (MB406)

MB61-J LAND ROVER FREELANDER, issued 1999 (ROW)

NOTE: Below models with smoke windows, plastic base, black spare tire & China casting unless otherwise noted.

1. silver-gray body, dark gray interior, dark gray base, 5 spoke concave star wheels, "Canyon Park", green band & door crest tempa ($1-2)(MW61/1999 ROW)(MW56/1999 GR)
2. silver-gray body, dark gray interior, dark gray base, 5 spoke concave star wheels, "Canyon Park", green band & "Ranger" tempa ($1-2)(MW66/1999 US)
3. silver-gray body, dark gray interior, dark gray base, small 5 spoke concave star wheels, "Canyon Park", green band & "Ranger" tempa ($5-8)(MW66/1999 US)
4. silver-gray body, dark gray interior, dark gray base, star with 5 spokes wheels, "Canyon Park", green band & door crest tempa ($1-2)(MW61/1999 ROW)
5. metallic pea green body, green interior, gray base, star with 5 spokes wheels, "Canyon Base" tempa ($1-2)(5pk)
6. metallic pea green body, green interior, gray base, 5 spoke concave star wheels, "Canyon Base" tempa ($1-2)(5pk)
7. metallic blue body, blue interior, black base, 5 spoke concave star wheels, "Canyon Park" tempa ($1-2)(MW64/2000 US/ MW44/2000 ROW)
8. metallic blue body, blue interior, black base, 5 spoke concave star wheels, "Canyon Park" & "Matchbox 2000" tempa ($5-8)(MW64/2000 US)
9. metallic blue body, blue interior, black base, star with 5 spokes wheels, "Canyon Park" & "Matchbox 2000" tempa ($2-4)(MW64/2000 US)
10. metallic blue body, blue interior, black base, star with 5 spokes wheels, "Canyon Park" tempa ($1-2)(MW64/2000 US)(MW44/2000 ROW)
11. metallic blue body, blue interior, black base, 10 spoke flower wheels, "Canyon Park" tempa ($1-2)(MW64/2000 US)
12. metallic blue body, blue interior, pearly silver metal base, 10 spoke flower wheels, "Canyon Park" tempa ($1-2)(MW64)
13. bright blue body, neon orange interior & spare tire, pearly silver metal base, 10 spoke flower wheels, "Powder" & "Turbo" tempa ($1-2)(MW9/2001)
14. plum body, orange-yellow interior & spare tire, clear windows, orange-yellow metal base, 10 spoke flower wheels, "Rugrats/ Tommy" tempa ($1-2)(5pk)
15. red body, blue interior & spare tire, clear windows, blue metal base, 10 spoke flower wheels, 13 Rhode Island Yacht Club/ RIYC" tempa ($1-2)(AM)
16. yellow body, green interior, black spare, green plastic base, 7 spoke sawblade wheels, "Rescue Heroes" tempa ($1-2)(CA)
17. metallic maroon body, gray interior & spare tire, pearly silver metal base, 7 spoke sawblade wheels, soccer design tempa ($1-2)(5pk)
18. bright blue body, yellow interior & spare tire, clear windows, orange-yellow metal base, 10 spoke flower wheels, "Rugrats/ Tommy" tempa ($1-2)(5pk)
19. orange-yellow body, gray interior, black spare tire, gray plastic base, 7 spoke sawblade wheels, "Station 05" tempa ($1-2)(5pk)
20. dark silver blue body, blue interior, black spare tire, blue plastic base, 7 spoke sawblade wheels, picture of Taz tempa ($1-2)(5pk)
21. pea green body, brown interior, black spare tire, brown plastic base, 7 spoke sawblade wheels, "Ayers Rock Australia" tempa ($1-2)(AW)
22. metallic lime body, light orange interior, light orange spare tire, orange plastic base, 7 spoke sawblade wheels, "Nickelodeon" tempa ($1-2)(5pk)

MB66-K INTERNATIONAL FIRE PUMPER *see MB76-D*

MB66-L MERCEDES BENZ S500, issued 1999 (GR) (MB434)

MB32-H MERCEDES BENZ S500, issued 2000 (ROW)

NOTE: Below models with smoke windows, black plastic base & China casting unless otherwise noted.

1. silver-gray body, black interior, no tempa, 5 spoke concave star wheels, gray base ($3-5)(MW66/1999 GR)
2. black body, black interior, no tempa, 5 spoke concave star wheels ($2-3)(MW32/2000 ROW)
3. dark yellow body, black interior, blue stripe tempa, 5 spoke concave star wheels ($2-3)(5pk)
4. dark yellow body, black interior, blue stripe tempa, 10 spoke flower wheels ($1-2)(5pk)
5. silver blue body, dark blue interior, taillights tempa, lace wheels ($2-4)(MW65/2001 GR)
6. maroon body, gray interior, no tempa, lace wheels ($3-5)(SG)

7. unpainted body, gray interior, pop art decals, lace wheels ($75+)(FA)
8. silver blue body, gray interior, "The Osbournes" tempa, chrome disc wheels with rubber tires tempa ($3-5)(OS)
9. lemon body, white interior, "Coca Cola" tempa, lace wheels ($2-4)(CK)
10. silver blue body, dark blue interior, taillights tempa, lace wheels ($2-3)(MW38/2004 ROW)
11. silver blue body, dark blue interior, taillights & "Hero City" tempa, lace wheels ($4-6)(MW38/2004 ROW)
NOTE: Versions 10 & 11 with Matchbox International or Mattel casting.
12. metallic maroon body, clear windows, dark gray interior, small "Matchbox" logo tempa, lace wheels, Mattel casting ($1-2)(LP)
13. black body, clear windows, black interior, "9th MICA European Convention" tempa, 5 spoke concave star wheels ($18-25)(C2)(GR)
14. pearly white body, clear windows, tan interior, detailed trim tempa, 5 spoke slotted wheels ($1-2)(SF60/2004)

MB66-M RADAR TRUCK, issued 2001 (MB523)
NOTE: Below models with 4 spoke domed wheels, black plastic base, China casting unless otherwise noted.
1. light maroon body, blue windows, black interior, gray radar, "Radar" & yellow design tempa ($1-2)(MW66/2001)
2. dark maroon body, blue windows, black interior, gray radar, "Radar" & yellow design tempa ($1-2)(MW66/2001)
3. metallic blue body, red windows, black interior, orange-yellow radar, "Kansas 34" tempa ($1-2)(AM)
4. silver-gray body, smoke windows, black interior, red radar, "Mission Radar" tempa ($1-2)(MW43/2002)
5. silver-gray body, smoke windows, black interior, red radar, "Mission Radar" & "Matchbox 50" tempa ($4-6)(MW43/2002)
6. red body, amber windows, gray interior, gray radar, "Storm School Radar 1" tempa ($2-4)(PB)
7. black body, blue windows, black interior, blue radar, "MHC Radar 35" tempa ($1-2)(MW35/2003)
8. black body, blue windows, black interior, blue radar, "MHC Radar 35" & "Hero City" tempa ($3-5)(MW35/2003)
9. light avocado body, dark smoke windows, black interior, avocado radar, "Satellite Radar" tempa ($1-2)(HR)
10. orange body, light smoke windows, gray interior, red radar, "Radar" tempa, 7 spoke sawblade wheels ($1-2)(5pk)
11. white body, blue windows, gray interior, red radar, "Police" & barbed wire with blue & yellow dashes, 5 crown dot wheels ($1-2)(MW67/2004)

MB66-N LIMOUSINE, issued 2002 (MB537)
NOTE: Below models with smoke windows, lace wheels & China casting unless otherwise noted.
1. black body, dark gray interior, small "Matchbox" logo tempa, chrome base ($1-2)(MW66/2002)
2. black body, dark gray interior, small "Matchbox" logo & "Matchbox 50" tempa, chrome base ($4-6)(MW66/2002)
3. black body, dark gray interior, "21st Matchbox USA Convention" tempa, chrome base ($10-15)(CCI)
4. black body, dark gray interior, "Julie & Greg- Just Married" tempa, chrome base ($50+)(CCI)
5. black body, dark gray interior, "ETS" tempa, chrome base ($18-25)(CCI)
6. white body, blue interior, "Washington DC" tempa, chrome base ($5-8)(AM)
7. charcoal body, blue interior, small "Matchbox" logo tempa, chrome base ($1-2)(LP)
8. metallic purple body, white interior, "Count Chocula" tempa, gray base ($1-2)(5pk)
9. metallic lavender body, pale blue interior, "Skeletor" tempa, chrome base, chrome disc wheels with rubber tires ($3-5)(MU)
10. black body, dark gray interior, clear windows, "The Osbournes" tempa, chrome base, chrome disc with rubber tires ($3-5)(OS)
11. silver-gray body, white interior, "VIP Shuttle" tempa, black base ($1-2)(MW32/2003)
12. silver-gray body, white interior, "VIP Shuttle" & "Hero City" tempa, black base ($4-6)(MW32/2003)
13. black body, black interior, "T" logo tempa, black base ($20-35)(US)
14. burgundy body, white interior, small "Matchbox" logo tempa, gray base ($1-2)(LP)
15. silver-gray body, white interior, "VIP Shuttle tempa, black base, gold hubs ($3-4)(20pk)
16. black body, red interior, "Hollywood" tempa, gray base ($1-2)(AW)
17. black body, black interior & windows, "Happy 80th Birthday/ Congratulations Kerry Pacifico" tempa, chrome base ($35-50)(CCI)

MB66-O DODGE RAM SRT-10, issued 2003 (MB589)
NOTE: Below models with 5 spoke oval wheels, black plastic base & China casting.
1. black body, red windows, "Dodge 66" & ram logo tempa ($1-2)(MW66/2003)
2. black body, red windows, "Dodge 66" & ram logo with "Hero City" tempa ($5-8)(MW66/2003)
3. charcoal body, amber windows, multi-colored design tempa ($1-2)(MW74/2004)
4. black body, black windows, "Coca Cola Football Town- You Make the Game" tempa ($2-4)(CK)

MB66-P CITY POLICE CAR, issued 2003 (MB592)
NOTE: Below models with blue windows, lace wheels & China casting.
1. iridescent white body, gray interior, "Matchbox Police Hero City" tempa, black plastic base ($1-2)(MW66/2004)
2. white body, lime interior, rockets & alien tempa, bright blue plastic base ($3-5)(PS)

MB67-A VOLKSWAGEN 1600TL, issued 1970
NOTE: Below models with clear windows, ivory interior, 5 spoke wheels, unpainted metal base & England casting. Earliest versions with narrow wheels with later issues with wide wheels.
1. red body ($85-110)
2. pale grape body ($20-30)
3. light purple body ($20-30)
4. dark purple body ($20-30)
5. metallic purple body, unpainted base, ($20-30)
6. metallic pink body, unpainted base ($18-25)

MB67-B HOT ROCKER, issued 1973
NOTE: Below models with clear windows, ivory interior & England casting.
1. metallic yellow-green body, unpainted base, 5 spoke wheels ($12-15)
2. metallic lime green body, unpainted base, 5 spoke wheels ($12-15)
3. metallic apple green body, unpainted base, 5 spoke wheels ($12-15)
4. metallic apple green body, silver-gray base, 5 spoke wheels ($12-15)

5. metallic apple green body, unpainted base, maltese cross wheels ($12-15)
6. orange-red body, unpainted base, 5 spoke wheels ($10-15)

MB67-C DATSUN 260Z, issued 1978

NOTE: Below models with dot dash wheels.

1. metallic burgundy body, doors open, black base, light yellow interior, clear windows, no tempa, England casting ($3-5)
2. metallic burgundy body, doors open, black base, dark yellow interior, clear windows, no tempa, England casting ($3-5)
3. metallic burgundy body, doors open, charcoal base, light yellow interior, clear windows, no tempa, England casting ($3-5)
4. metallic purple body, doors open, charcoal base, light yellow interior, clear windows, no tempa, England casting ($8-12)
5. metallic magenta body, doors open, black base, light yellow interior, clear windows, no tempa, England casting ($5-8)
6. metallic magenta body, doors open, black base, light yellow interior, smoke windows, no tempa, England casting ($5-8)
7. metallic blue body, doors open, black base, light yellow interior, clear windows, no tempa, England casting ($6-8)(TP)
8. metallic blue body, doors open, black base, red interior, clear windows, no tempa, England casting ($6-8)(TP)
9. metallic blue body, doors open, gray-brown base, red interior, clear windows, no tempa, England casting ($6-8)(TP)
10. silver-gray body, doors open, blue-gray base, red interior, clear windows, no tempa, England casting ($2-4)
11. silver-gray body, doors open, charcoal base, red interior, clear windows, no tempa, England casting ($2-4)
12. silver-gray body, doors open, charcoal base, red interior, smoke windows, no tempa, England casting ($2-4)
13. silver-gray body, doors open, gray-brown base, red interior, clear windows, no tempa, England casting ($2-4)
14. silver-gray body, doors open, gray-brown base, red interior, smoke windows, no tempa, England casting ($2-4)
15. silver-gray body, doors open, black base, red interior, clear windows, no tempa, England casting ($2-4)
16. silver-gray body, doors open, black base, red interior, smoke windows, no tempa, England casting ($2-4)
17. silver-gray body, doors open, blue-gray base, light yellow interior, clear windows, no tempa, England casting ($6-8)
18. silver-gray body, doors open, black base, white interior, clear windows, red & black tempa, England casting ($2-4)
19. silver-gray body, doors open, black base, white interior, smoke windows, red & black tempa, England casting ($2-4)
20. silver-gray body, doors open, charcoal base, white interior, clear windows, red & black tempa, England casting ($2-4)
21. black body, doors cast shut, black base, white interior, clear windows, no tempa, England casting ($4-6) (TP)(GS)
22. black body, doors cast shut, black base, black interior, opaque white windows, no tempa, England casting ($4-6)(PS)(TP)
23. black body, doors cast shut, black base, black interior, clear windows, no tempa, England casting ($4-6) (TP)(GS)
24. black body, doors cast shut, black base, white interior, opaque white windows, no tempa, England casting ($4-6)(PS)(TP)

    NOTE: Above England base models with "Lesney" casting. Below England models with Matchbox International casting.
25. black body, black base, white interior, clear windows, no tempa, England casting ($3-5)(TP)(GS)
26. black body, black base, black interior, opaque white windows, no tempa, England casting ($8-12)(PS)(TP)
27. silver-gray body, black base, black interior, clear windows, two tone blue tempa, England casting ($2-4)(TP)
28. black body, black base, black interior, opaque milky white windows, no tempa, England casting ($8-12)(PS)(TP)
29. silver-gray body, black base, black interior, clear windows, no tempa, England casting ($5-8)(TP)(GS)
30. silver-gray body, black base, black interior, opaque white windows, no tempa, England casting ($8-12)(PS)
31. silver-gray body, black base, black interior, clear windows, green & blue tempa, China casting ($125-175)(CHI)
32. silver-gray body, silver-gray base, black interior, clear windows, two-tone blue tempa, England casting ($4-6)(TP)
33. silver-gray body, silver-gray base, black interior, clear windows, no tempa, England casting ($3-5)(TP)(GS)
34. silver-gray body, black base, red interior, clear windows, no tempa, China casting ($8-12)(MP)
35. silver-gray body, black base, black interior, clear windows, no tempa, China casting ($12-15)(MP)
36. black body, black base, black interior, clear windows, no tempa, England casting ($4-6)(TP)(GS)
37. black body, black base, white interior, opaque windows, no tempa, England casting ($8-12)(PS)(TP)
38. silver-gray body, silver-gray base, black interior, clear windows, "Coca Cola/ 2003 Matchbox Takes Manhattan" tempa, Bulgaria casting ($18-25)(CCI)

    NOTE: Available as a Bulgarian casting. Assorted colors available ($5-25)

MB67-D FLAME OUT, issued 1983 (USA) (MB126)

NOTE: Below models with "Flame Out" tempa, black metal base & maltese cross front wheels. Name cast on base reads "Red Rider".

1. white body, red windows, maltese cross rear wheels, Macau casting ($4-6)
2. white body, red windows, 5 crown rear wheels, Macau casting ($4-6)

MB67-E I.M.S.A. MUSTANG *see MB11-E*

MB67-F LAMBORGHINI COUNTACH, issued 1985 (USA) (MB154)

MB11-F LAMBORGHINI COUNTACH, issued 1985 (ROW)

1. red body & metal base, tan interior, clear windows, 5 arch silver wheels, "Lamborghini" logo tempa, Macau casting ($2-3)
2. red body & metal base, tan interior, clear windows, 8 dot silver wheels, "Lamborghini" logo tempa, Macau casting ($2-3)
3. red body & metal base, tan interior, clear windows, 8 dot gold wheels, "Lamborghini" logo tempa, Macau casting ($8-12)
4. black body & metal base, tan interior, clear windows, 5 arch silver wheels, "5" with stripes tempa, Macau casting ($2-3)
5. black body & metal base, tan interior, clear windows, 8 dot gold wheels, "5" with stripes tempa, Macau casting ($3-5)
6. white body & metal base, dark blue interior, clear windows, starburst wheels, "LP500S" & stripes tempa, Macau casting ($3-5)(SF)
7. metallic pearly silver body & metal base, dark blue interior, clear windows, laser wheels, "LP500S" & stripes tempa, Macau casting ($3-5)(LW)
8. red body & metal base, tan interior, clear windows, 5 arch silver wheels, green "15" & "BP" tempa, Macau casting ($8-12)(DU)
9. yellow body & metal base, clear windows, 5 arch silver wheels, "10 Tiger Racing Team" tempa, Macau casting ($8-12)(HK)
10. yellow body & metal base, white interior, clear windows, 5 arch silver wheels, "Countach" & "Lamborghini" logo tempa, Macau casting ($2-3)
11. canary yellow body & metal base, white interior, chrome windows, gray disc wheels with rubber tires, "LP500" tempa, Macau casting ($5-8)(WC)

12. black body & metal base, white interior, clear windows, starburst wheels, "LP500" with stripes tempa, Macau casting ($12-15)(SF)
13. chrome plated body & metal base, white interior, clear windows, 5 arch wheels, no tempa, Macau casting ($12-18)(C2)
14. red body & metal base, white interior, clear windows, 5 arch wheels, "Countach" tempa, Thailand casting ($1-2)
15. red body & metal base, white interior, chrome windows, gray disc wheels with rubber tires, "Countach" & detailed trim tempa, China casting ($5-8)(WC)
16. red body & metal base, white interior, clear windows, 5 arch wheels, "Countach" tempa, China casting ($1-2)
17. white body & metal base, white interior, clear windows, 5 arch wheels, no tempa, China casting ($10-15)(GF)
18. iridescent cream & metal base, white interior, black windows, 5 arch wheels, "Countach" & logo tempa, Thailand casting ($3-5)(TH)
19. fluorescent green body, black plastic base, white interior, clear windows, 5 arch silver wheels, small logo tempa, Thailand casting ($2-3)(SS)
20. red body, black plastic (barcode) base, white interior, clear windows, 5 arch silver wheels, "Countach" & "Lamborghini" logos tempa, Thailand casting ($35-50)(IC)
21. fluorescent yellow & blue body, blue plastic base, pink interior, clear windows, gold 6 spoke spiral wheels, blue design on sides & hood tempa, Thailand casting ($1-2)
22. red body, red plastic base, white interior, clear windows, gold 6 spoke spiral wheels, "Countach" & "Lamborghini" logos tempa, Thailand casting ($2-3)
23. white body, white plastic base, white interior, pink windows, gold 6 spoke spiral wheels, no tempa, Thailand casting ($2-4)(GF)
24. silver-gray body, silver-gray plastic base, maroon interior, clear windows, silver 6 spoke spiral wheels, "Countach" & detailed trim tempa, Thailand casting ($2-4)(CC)
25. fluorescent yellow & blue body, blue plastic base, pink interior, clear windows, gold 6 spoke spiral wheels, blue design on sides only tempa, Thailand casting ($4-6)(Aquafresh)
26. metallic blue body, blue plastic base, white interior, pink windows, silver 6 spoke spiral wheels, no tempa, Thailand casting ($4-6)(5pk)
27. florescent yellow & blue body, blue plastic base, pink interior, clear windows, silver 6 spoke spiral wheels, blue design on sides & hood tempa, Thailand casting ($1-2)
28. silver body, black plastic base, white interior, red windows, silver 6 spoke spiral wheels, lavender/blue & white design tempa, Thailand casting ($3-5)(MT)
29. metallic red body, black plastic base, gray interior, clear windows, silver 6 spoke spiral wheels, "Lamborghini" tempa, Thailand casting ($1-2)
30. red body, black plastic base, black interior, clear windows, silver 6 spoke spiral wheels, "Lamborghini" tempa, Thailand casting ($1-2)(5pk)
31. red body, red plastic base, white interior, clear windows, silver 6 spoke spiral wheels, "Countach" tempa, Thailand casting ($3-5)
32. metallic gold body, black plastic base, black interior, clear windows, silver 6 spoke spiral wheels, no tempa, Thailand casting ($10-15)(CH)
33. red chrome body, black plastic base, white interior, yellow windows, 5 spoke concave star wheels, purple/ white/ yellow design tempa, Thailand casting ($1-2)(5pk)
34. red body, black plastic base, black interior, clear windows, chrome disc with rubber tires, detailed trim tempa, Thailand casting ($8-12)(UC)
35. metallic red body, black plastic base, gray interior, clear windows, 5 spoke concave star wheels, "Lamborghini" tempa, Thailand casting ($1-2)
36. white body, white plastic base, black & brown interior, clear windows, chrome disc with rubber tires, detailed trim tempa, Thailand casting ($3-5)(PC2-ROW)
37. metallic purple body, purple plastic base, gray & black interior, clear windows, chrome disc with rubber tires, detailed trim tempa, Thailand casting ($3-5)(PC10)
38. red body, red plastic base, white interior, clear windows, 5 spoke concave star wheels, "Countach" tempa, Thailand casting ($1-2)
39.black body, black plastic base, red interior, clear windows, 5 spoke concave star wheels, "Lamborghini" tempa, Thailand casting ($1-2)
40. dark green body, black plastic base, tan interior, clear windows, 5 spoke concave star wheels, "Lamborghini" tempa, Thailand casting ($1-2)(MW60/1998)
41. dark orange body, orange base, black & tan interior, clear windows, chrome disc wheels with rubber tires, detailed trim tempa, Thailand casting ($15-20)(GC)
42. dark green body, black plastic base, tan interior, clear windows, 5 spoke concave star wheels, "Lamborghini" tempa, China casting ($1-2)(MW60/1998)
43. silver-blue body, black plastic base, black interior, dark smoke green windows, 5 spoke concave star wheels, "Lamborghini" tempa, China casting ($1-2)(MW16/1999)(MW26/1999 GR)
44. light metallic red body, black plastic base, gray interior, clear windows, silver 6 spoke spiral wheels, "Lamborghini/ Bloomberg" tempa, Thailand casting ($100+)(ASAP)
45. lemon body, black plastic base, black interior, dark smoke windows, 5 spoke concave star wheels, "Lamborghini" & "Matchbox 2000" tempa, China casting ($2-4)(MW24/2000 US)
46. lemon body, black plastic base, black interior, dark smoke windows, 5 spoke concave star wheels, "Lamborghini" tempa, China casting ($1-2)(MW24/2000 US)(MW19/2000 ROW)
47. metallic red body, black plastic base, gray interior, clear windows, silver 6 spoke spiral wheels, "Lamborghini/ DOT/ 56" tempa, Thailand casting ($25-40)(ASAP)
48. white body, black plastic base, white interior, red windows, 5 spoke concave star wheels, "Lamborghini" tempa, Thailand casting ($1-2)(5pk)

MB67-G IKARUS COACH, issued 1986 (ROW) (MB170)

NOTE: Below models with black plastic base & dot dash wheels. The interior is part of the body casting.

1. white body, orange roof, smoke windows, "Voyager" tempa, Macau casting ($2-4)
2. white body, orange roof, clear windows, "Voyager" tempa, Macau casting ($2-4)
3. white body, orange roof, amber windows, "Voyager" tempa, Macau casting ($2-4)
4. cream body, cream roof, smoke windows, "Ikarus" tempa, Macau casting ($2-4)
5. white body, red roof, clear windows, "Gibraltar" tempa, Macau casting ($5-7)(SP)
6. white body, green roof, smoke windows, "City Line Tourist" tempa, China casting ($2-4)
7. white & orange body, white roof, smoke windows, "Airport Limousine 237" tempa, China casting ($8-12)(JP)(GS)
8. white body, orange roof, smoke windows, "Voyager" tempa, China casting ($2-3)
9. white body, white roof, smoke windows, "Canary Island" tempa, China casting ($7-10)(SP)

10. beige body, brown roof, smoke windows, "Marti" tempa, China casting ($8-12)(SW)
11. white body, red roof, smoke windows, "Gibraltar" tempa, China casting ($5-7)(SP)
12. white body,, green roof, smoke windows, " 上海交通汽车服务公司 /2384584" & "FT" tempa, China casting ($30-50)(CHI)
13. white body, white roof, smoke windows, "Espana" tempa, China casting ($1-2)
14. white body, red roof, smoke windows, smiling face tempa, China casting ($3-5)(5pk)
15. white body, red roof, blue windows, "World Cup Tour Bus" tempa, China casting ($1-2)(5pk)
16. yellow body, white roof, smoke windows, sunset scene tempa, China casting ($1-2)(MW2/1998 ROW)
17. white body, white roof, smoke windows, no tempa, China casting ($25-40)(ASAP blank)
18. grape body, grape roof, smoke windows, "Shuttle" tempa, China casting ($1-2)(5pk)
19. white body, white roof, smoke windows, "Wackenhut Corrections" tempa, China casting ($50+)(ASAP)
20. white body, white roof, smoke windows, "Court TV" tempa, China casting ($50+)(ASAP)

NOTE: Below models with Mattel China casting.

21. white body, white roof, smoke windows, no tempa, China casting ($18-25)(ASAP blank)
22. slate blue body, slate blue roof, light smoke windows, "Down the Shores Tours New Jersey 3" tempa, China casting ($1-2)(AM)
23. silver blue body, silver blue roof, blue windows, "Blue's Friends" tempa, China casting ($1-2)(5pk)
24. silver-gray body, silver-gray roof, smoke windows, "Coca-Cola Football Town/ Total Tailgate" tempa, China casting ($2-4)(CK)
25. white body, white roof, smoke windows, "Celebration on the Hill" tempa, Mattel China casting ($50+)(ASAP)
26. white body, white roof, smoke windows, small "Citrix" on roof tempa, China casting ($50+)(ASAP)

MB67-H FORD EXPEDITION, issued 1999 (USA) (MB360)
MB62-K FORD EXPEDITION, issued 1999 (ROW)

NOTE: Below models with chrome plastic base & China casting unless otherwise noted.

1. bright blue body, tan interior, clear windows, chrome disc with rubber tires, detailed trim tempa ($4-6)(FE)
2. unpainted body, tan interior, clear windows, chrome disc with rubber tires, no tempa ($4-6)(FE)
3. yellow body, red interior, clear windows, 5 spoke concave star wheels, red stripes & medical cross tempa ($2-3)(MW62/1999 ROW)
4. yellow body, red interior, clear windows, small 5 spoke concave star wheels, red stripes & medical cross tempa ($2-3)(MW62/1999 ROW)
5. yellow body, red interior, clear windows, 5 spoke concave star wheels, red stripes, "Rescue" & "Mountain Patrol" tempa ($1-2)(MW67/1999 US)
6. light yellow body, red interior, clear windows, 5 spoke concave star wheels, red stripes, "Rescue" & "Mountain Patrol" tempa ($1-2)(MW67/1999 US)
7. black body, gray interior, light smoke windows, 5 spoke concave star wheels, "09-99" & red & black design tempa ($1-2)(5pk)
8. lemon & white body, blue interior, blue windows, 5 spoke concave star wheels, "Base 2000" with red bands & "3456/54" tempa ($1-2)(LP)
9. olive body, black interior & base, smoke windows, 5 spoke concave star wheels, "Military Police/ Matchbox 2000" & mud spray tempa ($2-4)(MW54/2000 US)
10. olive body, black interior & base, smoke windows, 5 spoke concave star wheels, "Military Police" & mud spray tempa ($1-2)(MW54/2000 US)
11. olive body, black interior & base, smoke windows, 5 spoke concave star wheels, "Military Police" & mud spatter tempa ($1-2)(MW54/2000 US)
12. black body, brown interior, clear windows, 5 spoke concave star wheels, "Scooby-Doo!/ Iriuih-Irioih/ Scooby Dooby Doo!" tempa ($5-7)(WB)
13. lemon body, gray interior, clear windows, chrome disc with rubber tires, "Coca Cola", red band & polar bears tempa ($5-8)(Coke PC)
14. black body, gray interior, smoke windows, star with 5 spokes wheels, "09-99" with red & white design tempa ($2-4)(EG)
15. powder blue body, yellow interior, clear windows, lace wheels, "Rugrats/ Phil and Lil" tempa ($1-2)(5pk)
16. metallic purple body, orange-yellow interior, clear windows, lace wheels, "Catdog" tempa ($1-2)(5pk)
17. yellow body, red interior, clear windows, lace wheels, red stripes & medical cross tempa ($25-40)(MW62/ROW)
18. lemon body, red interior, blue windows, 10 spoke flower wheels, "Team Tony/ They're G-r-r-eat" tempa, gray base ($2-4)(TP)(Avon)
19. metallic silver body, black interior, red windows, lace wheels, "Road Rescue Fire Patrol" tempa, dark purple base ($1-2)(MW28/2002 US)
20. metallic silver body, black interior, red windows, lace wheels, "Road Rescue Fire Patrol" & "Matchbox 50" tempa, dark purple base ($2-4)(MW28/2002 US)
21. metallic silver body, black interior, red windows, lace wheels, "Road Rescue Fire Patrol" & "Matchbox 50" tempa, light purple base ($2-4)(MW28/2002 US)
22. metallic silver body, black interior, red windows, lace wheels, "Road Rescue Fire Patrol" tempa, light purple base ($1-2)(MW28/2002 US)
23. metallic green body, orange-yellow interior, clear windows, lace wheels, "Rugrats/ Phil and Lil" tempa, light gray base ($1-2)(5pk)
24. white body, blue interior, clear windows, lace wheels, "100" tempa ($4-5)(TP)(Avon)
25. metallic blue body, dark gray interior, clear windows, chrome disc wheels with rubber tires, "100" tempa, chrome base ($3-5)(CL)
26. black body, tan-gray interior, clear windows, chrome disc wheels with rubber tires, "100" tempa, chrome base ($3-5)(MP)(CL)
27. metallic gold body, red interior, red windows, lace wheels, "Hangar Team HT" tempa, gray base ($1-2)(5pk)
28. white body, white interior, clear windows, clear windows, 5 spoke concave star wheels, no tempa, white base ($25-40)(ASAP)

MB67-I AUDI TT *see MB44-K*

MB67-J LAND ROVER DISCOVERY, issued 2001 (MB524)

NOTE: Below models with black spare, 7 spoke sawblade wheels, black plastic base & China casting unless otherwise noted.

1. silver blue body, black interior, smoke windows, "Storm Watch" tempa ($1-2)(MW67/2001)
2. pea green body, tan interior, smoke windows, "Vermont/ 14 Forest Rescue" tempa, brown base ($2-4)(AM)

3. white body, black interior, smoke windows, "Artic Base" tempa ($1-2)(5pk)
4. metallic green body, yellow interior, clear windows, forest silhouette tempa ($2-4)(MW51/2002 ROW)
5. metallic green body, yellow interior, clear windows, forest silhouette & "Matchbox 50" tempa ($4-6)(MW51/2002 ROW)
6. metallic pea green body, black interior, red windows, "Bighorn Forest 50" tempa ($1-2)(MW50/2003)
7. metallic pea green body, black interior, red windows, "Bighorn Forest 50" & "Hero City" tempa ($2-4)(MW50/2003)
8. metallic green body, blue interior, blue windows, "Sphinx of Giza" tempa ($1-2)(AW)

MB67-K FOAM FIRE TRUCK, issued 2002 (MB564)

NOTE: Below models with 7 spoke sawblade wheels & China casting.

1. metallic red body, gray tank & interior, "Fire MB Dept. #67" tempa, black base with base name spelled "Turck" ($1-2)(MW67/2002)
2. metallic red body, gray tank & interior, "Fire MB Dept. #67" tempa, black base ($1-2)(MW67/2002)
3. metallic red body, gray tank & interior, "Fire MB Dept. #67" & "Matchbox 50" tempa, black base ($2-4)(MW67/2002)
4. dark maroon body, gray tank & interior, "MHC63" tempa, neon yellow base ($1-2)(MW63/2003)
5. dark maroon body, gray tank & interior, "MHC63" & "Hero City" tempa, neon yellow base ($2-4)(MW63/2003)
6. dark maroon body, gray tank & interior, "MHC63" tempa, neon yellow base, gold hubs ($3-4)(20pk)
7. metallic silver body, black tank & interior, "Hero City" & dolphin tempa, black base ($1-2)(MW37/2004)
8. metallic silver body, black tank & interior, "H2O" & plane design tempa, black base ($1-2)(LP)
9. white body, blue tank & interior, "Force" & design tempa, red base ($1-2)(5pk)

MB68-A PORSCHE 910, issued 1970

NOTE: Below models with ivory interior, 6 spoke wheels, unpainted metal base & England casting unless otherwise noted.

1. metallic red, amber windows, "68" hood label ($12-15)
2. metallic red body, amber windows, "68" hood & side labels ($12-15)(GS)
3. metallic red body, clear windows, "68" hood label ($12-15)
4. metallic red body, amber windows, "45" hood label ($15-18)
5. metallic red body, clear windows, "45" hood label ($15-18)
6. metallic red body, amber windows, scorpion hood label ($175-250)
7. metallic red body, amber windows, "137" hood label (from MB15-A)($175-250)
8. metallic red body, amber windows, "45" hood label (from MB45-A) & scorpion trunk label ($175-250)
9. white body, amber windows, no labels ($18-25)(BM)
10. white body, amber windows, "68" hood label ($35-50)(BM)
11. turquoise body, amber windows, "68" hood label, base with Manaus label ($250+)(BR)

MB68-B COSMOBILE, issued 1975

NOTE: Most variations appear with 5 arch front & 5 crown rear wheels both large 5 crown front & rear wheels or with front wheels on back and back wheels on front. Below models with metal base with black plastic base insert, chrome roof horns & England casting..

1. blue body, yellow base, chrome interior, amber windows ($12-15)
2. blue body, yellow base, white interior, amber windows ($12-15)
3. red body, beige base, chrome interior, amber windows ($15-18)
4. red body, beige base, white interior, amber windows ($15-18)
5. avocado body, black base, white interior, purple windows ($25-35)(AV)
6. avocado body, black base, chrome interior, purple windows ($25-35)(AV)
7. avocado body, black base, chrome interior, amber windows ($30-40)(AV)
8. avocado body, black base, white interior, amber windows ($30-40)(AV)
9. metallic dark blue body, black base, chrome interior, purple windows ($40-55)(AV)
10. blue body, white base with Manaus tab, chrome interior, amber windows ($50-75)(BR)
11. green body, white base with Manaus tab, chrome interior, amber windows ($250+)(BR)

MB68-C CHEVY VAN, issued 1979 (MB068)

NOTE: Most variations appear with both 5 crown front & rear wheels, dot dash front & rear wheels or with front wheels on back and back wheels on front.

1. orange body, unpainted base, clear windows, wide blue & narrow red stripes tempa, England casting ($30-40)
2. orange body, unpainted base, blue windows, wide blue & narrow red stripes tempa, England casting ($3-5)
3. orange body, unpainted base, blue windows, wide blue & white narrow stripes tempa, England casting ($4-6)
4. orange body, unpainted base, blue windows, wide red & black narrow stripes tempa, England casting ($4-6)
5. orange body, unpainted base, orange windows, wide red & narrow black stripes tempa, England casting ($4-6)
6. orange body, unpainted base, red windows, wide red & narrow black stripes tempa, England casting ($4-6)
7. orange body, unpainted base, green windows, wide red & black narrow stripes tempa, England casting ($6-8)
8. dark orange body, unpainted base, blue windows, wide blue & red narrow stripes tempa, England casting ($15-20)
9. orange body, unpainted base, blue windows, no tempa, England casting ($8-12)
10. orange body, unpainted base, blue windows, "Matchbox Collectors Club" labels, England casting ($20-25)(LE)
11. white body, unpainted base, blue windows, "USA 1" tempa, England casting ($8-12)
12. white body, unpainted base, blue windows, "Adidas" tempa, England casting ($35-45)(GR)
13. green body, unpainted base, blue windows, "Chevy" with brown stripes tempa, England casting ($8-12)
14. green body, unpainted base, blue windows, "Chevy" with yellow stripes tempa, England casting ($8-12)
15. metallic green body, unpainted base, blue windows, "Ridin High" tempa, England casting ($75-100)
16. silver-gray body, unpainted base, blue windows, "Vanpire" tempa, England casting ($3-5)
17. silver-gray body, silver-gray base, blue windows, "Vanpire" tempa, England casting ($3-5)
18. yellow body, unpainted base, blue windows, "Matchbox Collecting" with kangaroo tempa, England casting ($10-15)(AU)
19. pearly silver body, black base, blue windows, "Vanpire" tempa, Macau casting ($3-5)
20. yellow body, pearly silver base, blue windows, "Pepsi Challenge" tempa, Macau casting($4-6)(TM)

21. white & maroon tempa, pearly silver base, blue windows, "Dr. Pepper" tempa, Macau casting ($7-10)(TM)
22. bright yellow body, pearly silver base, blue windows, "STP Son of A Gun" tempa, Macau casting ($50-65)(TM)
23. black body, pearly silver base, blue windows, "Goodwrench Racing Team Pit Crew" tempa, Macau casting ($4-6)(WR)(TC)
24. black body, silver-gray base, blue windows, "Goodwrench Racing Team Pit Crew" tempa, Thailand casting ($4-6)(WR)(TC)
25. orange-yellow body, silver-gray base, blue windows, "Kodak Film 4 Racing" tempa, Thailand casting ($4-6)(WR)(TC)
26. white body, silver-gray base, blue windows, gold hubs, "25" & green design tempa, Thailand casting ($4-6)(WR)(TC)
27. black body, silver-gray base, blue windows, "Goodwrench 5 Time National Champion Dale Earnhardt" tempa, Thailand casting ($4-6)(WR)(TC)
28. bright yellow body, silver-gray base, blue windows, "Pennzoil 30" tempa, Thailand casting ($4-6)(WR)(TC)
29. blue & florescent orange body, silver-gray base, blue windows, "43 STP Oil Treatment" tempa, Thailand casting ($4-6)(WR)(TC)
30. black body, silver-gray base, blue windows, "Pontiac Excitement 2" tempa, Thailand casting ($4-6)(WR)(TC)
31. black & green body, silver-gray base, blue windows, "Mello Yello 42" tempa, Thailand casting ($4-6)(WR)(TC)
32. florescent orange & white body, silver-gray base, blue windows, "Purolator 10" tempa, Thailand casting ($4-6)(WR)(TC)
33. blue & dark orange body, silver-gray base, blue windows, "21st National Truckin' VAM" tempa, Thailand casting ($8-12)(US)
34. white & yellow body, yellow base, blue windows, "Renault Canon Williams" tempa, Thailand casting ($4-6)(MN)
35. orange-yellow body, silver-gray base, clear windows, "DeWalt 08" tempa, Thailand casting ($4-6)(WR)(TC)
36. powder blue body, silver-gray base, blue windows, "Bostongas" & white band tempa, Thailand casting ($75-100)(US)
37. orange body, chrome base, blue windows, blue & red stripes tempa, Thailand casting ($3-5)(PC13)
38. black body, silver-gray base, blue windows, "Automodels 98912244" & "Sydney Motorshow" tempa, Thailand casting ($15-20)(AU)(C2)
39. black body, silver-gray base, blue windows, "Automodels 98912244" & "Melbourne Motorshow" tempa, Thailand casting ($15-20)(AU)(C2)
40. white body, white base, blue windows, "Sears Home Central" tempa, Thailand casting ($20-35)(ASAP)
41. white body, white base, blue windows, "MCI Scholar Award" tempa, Thailand casting ($100+)(ASAP)
42. white body, white base, blue windows, "Consolidated Engineering" tempa, Thailand casting ($100+)(ASAP)
43. white body, white base, blue windows, "American International Recovery" (black lettering) tempa, Thailand casting ($100+)(ASAP)
44. white body, white base, blue windows, "American International Recovery" (blue lettering) tempa, Thailand casting ($100+)(ASAP)
45. white body, white base, blue windows, no tempa, Thailand casting ($25-40)(ASAP blank)
46. white body, white base, blue windows, "Sears May I Reward" tempa, Thailand casting ($20-35)(ASAP)
47. white body, white base, blue windows, "Huffman" tempa, China casting ($25-40)(ASAP)
48. white body, white base, blue windows, "RCA" tempa, China casting ($20-30)(ASAP)
49. white body, white base, blue windows, "Bulldog Castor Co." tempa, China casting ($18-25)(ASAP)
50. white body, white base, blue windows, "Servpro" tempa, Thailand casting ($50+)(ASAP)
51. white body, white base, blue windows, "Bell South" tempa, Thailand casting ($25-40)(ASAP)
52. white body, white base, blue windows, "Sonitrol" tempa, Thailand casting ($50+)(ASAP)
53. white body, white base, blue windows, "News ABC 7" tempa, Thailand casting ($50+)(ASAP)
54. white body, white base, blue windows, no tempa, Thailand casting ($25-40)(ASAP blank)
55. white body, white base, blue windows, "Sears Home Service" tempa, Thailand casting ($50+)(ASAP)
56. white body, white base, blue windows, "Bostongas" tempa, China casting ($50+)(ASAP)
57. white body, white base, blue windows, "Matco" tempa, China casting ($50+)(ASAP)
58. white body, white base, blue windows, "USS" tempa, China casting ($50+)(ASAP)
59. white body, white base, blue windows, "Comcast" tempa, China casting ($50+)(ASAP)
60. white & black body, silver-gray base, smoke windows, "Coca Cola Be Refreshed" tempa, Mattel China casting ($3-5)(Coke PC)
61. white body, white base, blue windows, "31st National Truck-In 2003" tempa, Thailand casting ($18-25)(CCI)
62. black & pink body, blue windows, "Fingerhut" tempa, Thailand casting ($4-6)(WR)(TC)
63. white body, white base, blue windows, "In Memory of Robert Sheppard 1950-2002" tempa, Thailand casting ($50+)(CCI)

MB68-D 4 X 4 CHEVY VAN *see MB44-D*

MB68-E DODGE CARAVAN, issued 1984 (USA) (MB128)
MB64-E DODGE CARAVAN, issued 1984 (ROW)

NOTE: Model with cast door and "Las Vegas" base listed at end of this guide. Early models cast "1983," later ones cast "1984." Below models with clear windows & chrome plastic base unless otherwise noted.

1. burgundy body, maroon door & interior, black side stripe tempa, England casting ($15-20)(US)
2. silver-gray body, gray door, maroon interior, black side stripe tempa, England casting ($6-8)
3. silver-gray body, gray door, brown-red interior, black side stripe tempa, England casting ($6-8)
4. black body, black door, maroon interior, no tempa, England casting ($5-8)
5. black body black door, maroon interior, silver side stripe tempa, England casting ($3-5)
6. black body, black door, maroon interior, silver side stripe tempa, Macau casting ($2-4)
7. black body, black door, maroon interior, silver & gold stripes tempa, Macau casting ($2-4)
8. white body, white door, maroon interior, "Pan Am" tempa, Macau casting ($3-5)(GS)
9. white body, white door, maroon interior, "Caravan" with stripes tempa, Macau casting ($2-4)
10. white body, white door, maroon interior, "Fly Virgin Atlantic" tempa, Macau casting ($3-5)(GS)
11. black body, black door, maroon interior, silver stripe tempa with "Adidas" hood label, England casting ($250-300)(US)

12. black body, black door, maroon interior, green & yellow stripes tempa, Macau casting ($8-12)(DU)
13. white body, white door, maroon interior, "NASA Shuttle Personnel" tempa, Macau casting ($3-5)(MP)
14. light gray & dark navy body, light gray door, red interior, "British Airways" tempa, Thailand casting ($3-5)(MC)
15. red body, red door, black interior & base, "Red Arrows/Royal Air Force" tempa, Thailand casting ($3-5)(MC)
16. black body, black door, red interior, gray base, silver & gold stripes tempa, Manaus casting ($35-50)(BR)
17. black body, black door, red interior, gray base, lemon & blue stripes tempa, Manaus casting ($35-50)(BR)
18. light gray & dark navy body, gray door, red interior, "British Airways" tempa, black base with bar code, Thailand casting ($75+)(IC)
19. black body, black door, maroon interior, silver & gold stripes tempa, China casting ($3-5)

MB68-F CAMARO IROC Z28 *see MB51-G*

MB68-G TV NEWS TRUCK, issued 1989 (USA) (MB205)
MB73-D TV NEWS TRUCK, issued 1989 (ROW)

NOTE: Below models with frosted windows & dot dash wheels unless otherwise noted. Later issues with non-frosted windows.

1. dark blue body, silver-gray roof, orange roof units, amber windows, black base, "75 News/MB TV Mobile One" tempa, Macau casting ($1-2)
2. dark blue body, silver-gray roof, orange roof units, amber windows, black base, "75 News/MB TV Mobile One" tempa, Thailand casting ($1-2)
3. dark blue body, silver-gray roof, pale orange roof units, amber windows, black base, "75 News/MB TV Mobile One" tempa, Thailand casting ($1-2)
4. white body, white roof, orange roof units, amber windows, white base, no tempa, Thailand casting ($10-15)(GF)
5. white body, white roof, brown roof units, amber windows, white base, no tempa, Thailand casting ($10-15)(GF)
6. white body, dark blue roof, white roof units, blue windows, black base, "Sky Satellite Television" tempa, Thailand casting ($1-2)
7. white body, blue roof, white roof units, blue windows, black base, "Rock TV" tempa, Thailand casting ($1-2)
8. white body, blue roof, white roof units, blue windows, black base with bar code, "Intercom City TV" tempa, Thailand casting ($7-10)(IC)
9. white body, blue roof, white roof units, blue windows, black base, "Sky Satellite TV" tempa, China casting ($2-3)
10. white body, blue roof, white roof units, amber windows, black base, "Sky Satellite TV" tempa, China casting ($18-25)
11. yellow body, red roof, black roof units, blue windows, red base, "Matchbox Cable TV" tempa, China casting ($1-2)(5pk)
12. white body, blue roof, dark red roof units, amber windows, red base, "World Cup Mobile Unit Television" tempa, China casting ($1-2)(5pk)
13. black body, dark gray roof, dark gray roof units, smoke windows, dark gray base, "Mission Impossible" tempa, China casting ($4-6)(STR)
14. blue body, yellow roof, lime roof units, smoke windows, dark gray base, "TV 6" tempa, China casting ($1-2)(MW3/ 1998 ROW)
15. white body, yellow roof, lime roof units, clear windows, silver-gray base, no tempa, China casting ($25-40)(ASAP blank)
16. white body, yellow roof, lime roof units, clear windows, silver-gray base, "American International Recovery" tempa, China casting ($100+)(ASAP)
17. white body, blue roof, white roof units, blue windows, blue base, "World Cup Mobile Unit Television" tempa, China casting ($1-2)(AP)
18. black body, red roof, yellow roof units, clear windows, red base, "Matchbox Channel 4" tempa, China casting ($1-2)(5pk)
19. white body, yellow roof, lime roof units, smoke windows, dark gray base, "RCA" tempa, China casting ($20-30)(ASAP)
20. bright blue body, red roof, light gray roof units, smoke windows, light gray base, "Super RTL Live!" tempa, China casting ($3-5)(MW62/1999) US)(MW57/1999 ROW)
21. maroon body, black roof, silver-gray roof units, smoke windows, black base, "Intergalactic Research" tempa, China casting ($1-2)(MW62/1999 US)(MW57/1999 ROW)
22. white body, yellow roof, lime roof units, smoke windows, black base, "Action News 6" tempa, China casting ($15-20)(ASAP)
23. black body, yellow roof, yellow roof units, smoke windows, black base, "Action TV" with football tempa, China casting ($1-2)(5pk)
24. black body, yellow roof, yellow roof units, smoke windows, black base, "Action TV" with soccer ball tempa, China casting ($2-4)(5pk)
25. lime body, silver-gray roof, silver-gray roof units, dark smoke windows, black base, "Action Radar/ Xtreme Mission" tempa, China casting ($1-2)(5pk)
26. white body, black roof, red roof units, smoke windows, black base, globe & satellite design tempa, China casting ($2-4)(MP)
27. silver-gray body, black roof, silver-gray roof units, smoke windows, black base, "Weather, News at Noon, Sports" tempa, China casting ($1-2)(MW98/2000 US)
28. silver-gray body, black roof, silver-gray roof units, smoke windows, black base, "Weather, News at Noon, Sports" & "Matchbox 2000" tempa, China casting ($2-4)(MW98/2000 US)
29. silver-gray body, black roof, silver-gray roof units, blue windows, black base, "Weather, News at Noon, Sports" tempa, China casting ($15-25)(MW98/US)
30. white body, yellow roof, lime roof units, smoke windows, black base, "Fox 8 WJW Cleveland" tempa, China casting ($15-20)(ASAP)
31. white body, black roof, white roof units, smoke windows, black base, "Fox 8 WJW Cleveland" tempa, China casting ($15-20)(ASAP)
32. white body, black roof, white roof units, blue windows, black base, none tempa, China casting ($25-40)(ASAP blank)
33. bright blue body, black roof, black roof units, smoke windows, black base, "Storm Watch", China casting ($1-2)(MW70/2001)

    NOTE: Above model with Matchbox International or Mattel casting.
34. bright blue body, black roof, black roof units, smoke windows, black base, "Storm Watch", China casting, 5 arch wheels ($1-2) (MW70/2001)
35. white body, black roof, silver-gray roof units, smoke windows, black base, "Today/ NBC-050/ Matchbox 50" tempa, China casting ($75+)(CCI)
36. lavender body, blue-gray roof, blue-gray roof units, smoke windows, black base, "Missouri 24 Channel Show Me News" tempa, China casting ($1-2)(AM)

    NOTE: Above model with Matchbox International or Mattel casting.
37. white body, black roof, chrome roof units, smoke windows, chrome base, "Weekend Update- Roseanne Roseannadanna" tempa, chrome disc wheels with rubber tires, Mattel China casting ($3-5)(SNL)

38. brown body, blue-green roof, gold roof units, smoke windows, blue-green base, "Sasquatch" tempa, 10 spoke flower wheels, Mattel China casting ($1-2)(AW)
39. white body, black roof, white roof units, blue windows, black base, "Thirteen" tempa, China casting ($50+)(ASAP)
40. white body, black roof, white roof units, blue windows, black base, "Sony" tempa, China casting ($50+)(ASAP)
41. white body, black roof, white roof units, blue windows, black base, "Cn8/ The Comcast Network" tempa, China casting ($50+)(ASAP)

MB68-H ROAD ROLLER *see MB40-F*

MB68-I STINGER, issued 1995 (MB278)

1. black & dark yellow upper & lower body, clear propeller wings, yellow mid & rear fins, black stand, Thailand casting ($1-2)
2. gold & black upper & lower body, clear propeller wings, gold mid & rear fins, black stand, Thailand casting ($5-10)(CH)
3. orange & black upper & lower body, clear propeller wings, orange mid & rear fins, black stand, Thailand casting ($1-2)
4. green & black upper & lower body, clear propeller wings, green mid & rear fins, black stand, Thailand casting ($1-2)(MW41/1998 US)
5. green & black upper & lower body, clear propeller wings, green mid & rear fins, black stand, China casting ($1-2)(MW41/1998 US)

MB68-J PORSCHE 911 GT1, issued 1998 (USA) (MB335)
MB58-I PORSCHE 911 GT1, issued 1998 (ROW)

NOTE: Below models with clear windows, black plastic base, "Matchbox International" & China casting unless otherwise noted.

1. white body & spoiler, black interior, 5 spoke concave star wheels, "911 GT1" tempa ($1-2)(MW68/1998US)(MW58/1998 ROW)
2. silver-gray body & spoiler, black interior, 5 spoke concave star wheels, black fenders & "Porsche" tempa, light smoke windows ($2-4)(MW31/1999 ROW)
3. metallic silver-gray body, gray spoiler, black interior, 5 spoke concave star wheels, "911 GT1" tempa ($2-3)(MW16/1999 GR)
4. lemon body & spoiler, black interior, 5 spoke concave star wheels, "911GT1" & "Matchbox 2000" tempa ($2-4)(MW45/2000 US)
5. lemon body & spoiler, black interior, 5 spoke concave star wheels, "911GT1" tempa ($1-2)(MW45/2000 US)
6. metallic blue body, blue spoiler, black interior, 5 spoke concave star wheels, "911GT1" tempa ($3-5)(MW35/2000 ROW)
7. white body & spoiler, white interior, 5 spoke concave star wheels, "Citrix Vertigo/Citrix.com/CDN" tempa ($75+)(ASAP)
8. white body & spoiler, white interior, 5 spoke concave star wheels, "Citrix Vertigo/CDN" tempa ($75+)(ASAP)
9. metallic red body, red spoiler, black interior, 5 spoke concave star wheels, headlights tempa, smoke windows ($1-2)(5pk)
10. metallic red body, red spoiler, black interior, 5 spoke concave star wheels, headlights tempa, smoke windows, "Mattel" casting ($1-2)(5pk)
11. metallic red body, red spoiler, black interior, 10 spoke flower wheels, headlights tempa, smoke wheels, Mattel casting ($1-2)(5pk)
12. white body, white spoiler, white interior, 5 spoke concave star wheels, upside down "V" with emitting lines tempa ($50+)(ASAP)
13. metallic blue body, blue spoiler, yellow interior, lace wheels, "Matchbox/ GT1" on yellow door tempa, Mattel casting ($2-3)(MW20/2001 ROW)
14. metallic red body, red spoiler, black interior, lace wheels, headlights tempa, Mattel casting ($2-4)(5pk)
15. white body, white spoiler, black interior, 10 spoke flower wheels, "Matchbox/ GT1 Porsche" tempa, Mattel casting ($2-4)(MW22/2002 ROW)
16. white body, white spoiler, black interior, 10 spoke flower wheels, "Matchbox/ GT1 Porsche" & "Matchbox 50" tempa, Mattel casting ($3-5)(MW22/2002 ROW)
17. silver-gray body, gray spoiler, black interior, lace wheels, none tempa, Mattel casting ($2-4)(MW22/2002 ROW)
18. metallic red body, gray spoiler, black interior, lace wheels, "GT1/ Porsche" tempa, Mattel casting ($2-4)(MW21/ROW2004)
19. white body, white spoiler, white interior, 5 spoke concave star wheels, no tempa ($18-25)(ASAP blank)
20. white body, white spoiler, white interior, lace wheels, no tempa, Mattel casting ($18-25)(ASAP blank)
21. white body, white spoiler, white interior, lace wheels, "axs" tempa, Mattel casting ($50+)(ASAP)
22. silver-gray body, light smoke windows, black spoiler, black interior, 5 spoke concave star wheels, black fenders & "LSI Logic" tempa, China casting ($50+)(ASAP)
23. bright blue body, blue spoiler, black interior, 10 spoke flower wheels, small "Matchbox" logo tempa ($1-2)(LP)
24. metallic silver body, gray spoiler, black interior, lace wheels, no tempa ($4-6)(SG)

MB68-K FORD FALCON MB63-J

MB68-L DENNIS SABRE FIRE ENGINE, issued 1999 (ROW) (MB402)
MB30-J DENNIS SABRE FIRE ENGINE, issued 2001 (USA)

NOTE: Below models with 8 spoke wheels, silver-gray plastic base & China casting unless otherwise noted. Dome lights are color of windows.

1. red body, blue windows, white ladder, yellow & silver panels tempa ($2-3)(MW68/1999 ROW)
2. red body, blue windows, white ladder, white stripes & panels with "4589/54" & "Matchbox" in circle logo tempa ($1-2)(5pk)
3. red body, blue windows, white ladder, white dashes & "35-3" tempa ($2-3)(MW15/2000 ROW)
4. red body, blue windows, white ladder, "London Fire Brigade" & silver panels tempa ($2-4)(MW39/2000 UK)
5. red body, blue windows, white ladder, "Metro Alarm/ WR-1168" & yellow bands tempa, 7 spoke sawblade wheels ($1-2)(5pk)
6. white body, blue windows, gray ladder, "Universe Action Base", red stripes & yellow panels tempa, 7 spoke sawblade wheels ($1-2)(MW30/2001)
7. red body, amber windows, gray ladder, "911 Emergency/ 911 Be Ready for an Emergency" & silver panels tempa, 7 spoke sawblade wheels ($2-4)(backpack)(US)
8. black body, red windows, gray ladder, "Oregon 33- Mount Hood Fires Rescue" tempa, 7 spoke sawblade wheels ($1-2)(AM)
9. metallic burgundy body, blue windows, gray ladder, silver panels & "50" logo tempa, chrome disc wheels with rubber tires ($3-5)(CL)
10. white body, red windows, yellow ladder, "Matchbox 5 Alarm" & stripes tempa, 7 spoke sawblade wheels ($1-2)(5pk)
11. red body, amber windows, gray ladder, "44", white panels & planes tempa, 7 spoke sawblade wheels ($1-2)(MW44/2002)
12. red body, amber windows, gray ladder, "44", white panels & planes with "Matchbox 50" tempa, 7 spoke sawblade wheels ($2-4)(MW44/2002)
13. dark yellow body, red windows, red ladder, "Metro Alarm" tempa, 7 spoke sawblade wheels ($1-2)(5pk)

14. orange-yellow body, red windows, white ladder, "Station 2" tempa, 7 spoke sawblade wheels ($1-2)(5pk)
15. white body, red windows, blue ladder, "HCFD" tempa, 7 spoke sawblade wheels ($1-2)(5pk)

MB68-M '98 JEEP WRANGLER, issued 1999 (USA) (MB369)
MB63-K '98 JEEP WRANGLER, issued 1999 (ROW)

NOTE: Below models with 8 spoke wheels & China casting unless otherwise noted.

1. green body, light smoke windshield, tan interior, black roll bar & base, yellow & white tempa ($2-3)(MW63/1999 ROW) (MW58/1999 GR)
2. green body, light smoke windshield, tan interior, black roll bar & base, yellow & white with "Forest Ranger" tempa ($1-2)(MW68/1999 US)
3. beige body, clear windshield, green interior, black roll bar & base, "Black Star Ranch" & mud tempa ($1-2)(5pk)
4. bright blue body, smoke windshield, silver-gray interior, silver-gray roll bar & base, "10-17 MB" with octopus tempa ($1-2)(MW9/2000)
5. bright blue body, smoke windshield, silver-gray interior, silver-gray roll bar & base, "10-17 MB" with octopus & "Matchbox 2000" tempa ($2-4)(MW9/2000 US)
6. bronze body, clear windshield, tan interior, tan roll bar, black base, "Matchbox New York Toy Fair 2000/ Matchbox 2000" tempa ($35-60)(US)

NOTE: Versions 7 & 8 with chrome disc with rubber tires.

7. lemon body, clear windshield, red interior, red roll bar, black base, "Coca Cola" tempa ($4-6)(Coke PC)
8. lemon body, clear windshield, red interior, red roll bar, black base, "Coca Cola" & "www.cocacolastores.com " tempa ($50+)(CCI)
9. white body, light smoke windows, red interior, red roll bar, black base, "Base 2000" tempa ($1-2)(LP)
10. silver-gray body, clear with mud tempa, gray interior, black roll bar & base, "Jeep" & mud design tempa ($1-2)(5pk)
11. dark green body, clear windows with mud design, gray interior, black roll bar & base, "Jeep", mud design & "Matchbox" tempa ($3-5)(PB)

NOTE: Below models with 7 spoke sawblade wheels unless otherwise noted.

12. white body, clear windows, orange-yellow interior, red roll bar, green base, "Kellogg's Corn Flakes/ Corny" tempa ($1-2)(5pk)
13. neon yellow body, smoke windows, gray interior, turquoise roll bar & base, "Hawaii 50th" tempa ($5-8)(AM)
14. white & silver-gray body, clear windows with white trim, red interior, black roll bar & base, "Coca Cola" tempa, chrome disc with rubber tires ($3-5)(Coke PC)
15. orange body, smoke windows, white interior, blue roll bar, black base, "Mission H2O" tempa ($1-2)(LP)
16. pea green body, smoke windows, black interior, black roll bar & base, "Desert Base" tempa ($1-2)(5pk)
17. white body, smoke windows, black interior, black roll bar & base, "Dana & Tom- Shore Love" tempa ($18-25)(CCI)
18. white body, smoke windows, black interior, black roll bar & base, "Troop 1 33rd Flea Market/ Winchester Virginia 2003" tempa ($10-15)(CCI)
19. black body, smoke windows, white interior, red roll bar, black base, "Mission H2O" tempa ($1-2)(LP)
20. white body, smoke windows, black interior, black roll bar, black base, no tempa ($18-25)(CCI blank)
21. black body, clear windows, tan interior, gray roll bar, gray base, detailed trim tempa ($1-2)(SF57/2004)

MB68-N MERCEDES BENZ E430 WAGON, issued 1999 (GR) (MB426)
MB55-Q MERCEDES BENZ E430 WAGON, issued 2003 (ROW)

NOTE: Below models with China casting.

1. metallic dark blue body, gray interior, clear windows, head & tail lights tempa, 5 spoke concave star wheels, black base ($2-4)(MW68/1999 GR)
2. white body, brown interior, clear windows, "Euro Taxi" & green band tempa, 5 spoke concave star wheels, black base ($2-4)(MW38/2000 GR)
3. metallic green body, black interior, clear windows, head & tail lights tempa, 10 spoke flower wheels, black base ($2-4)(MW61/2001 GR)
4. blue-green body, blue interior, amber windows, mountains & sunburst tempa, 10 spoke flower wheels, red base ($1-2)(5pk)
5. blue body, light gray interior, clear windows, detailed trim tempa, 10 spoke flower wheels tempa, black base ($2-4)(MW55/2003 ROW)
6. blue body, light gray interior, clear windows, detailed trim & "Hero City" tempa, 10 spoke flower wheels tempa, black base ($4-6)(MW55/2003 ROW)
7. blue body, light gray interior, clear windows, "Slovakia to Europe" tempa, 10 spoke flower wheels, black base ($50-75)(C2)(SK)

MB68-O AIR LIFT, issued 2000 (USA) (MB448)
MB48-K AIR LIFT, issued 2000 (ROW)

NOTE: Below models with black blades, black hook, smoke windows & China casting unless otherwise noted.

1. dark red body, gray base & skis, yellow & black design tempa ($1-2)(MW68/2000 USA/MW48/2000 ROW)
2. dark red body, gray base & skis, yellow & black design & "Matchbox 2000" tempa ($2-4)(MW68/2000 US)
3. dark green body, gray base & skis, "MTN" & snowflakes tempa, amber windows ($1-2)(5pk)
4. yellow body, gray base & skis, "Hangar 5" tempa ($1-2)(MW73/2001)
5. lime green body, black base & skis, cross & design tempa ($1-2)(MW34/2002)
6. lime green body, black base & skis, cross & design with "Matchbox 50" tempa ($2-4)(MW34/2002)
7. black body, blue base & skis, cross & globe tempa ($1-2)(5pk)
8. brown-gold body, blue-green base & skis, red windows, blades & hook, "Raccoon Forest 47" tempa ($1-2)(MW47/2003)
9. brown-gold body, blue-green base & skis, red windows, blades & hook, "Raccoon Forest 47" & "Hero City" tempa ($2-4)(MW47/2003)

MB68-P '99 FORD MUSTANG *see MB17-I*

MB68-Q SPEED BOAT, issued 2001 (MB525)

NOTE: Below models with gray radar & China casting unless otherwise noted.

1. white deck, yellow hull, red roof, blue radar, yellow wheels, "NJBP" with blue design & silver stripes tempa ($1-2)(MW68/2001)
2. silver-gray body, metallic blue body, red roof, black radar, blue wheels, "911 Sea Police" tempa ($1-2)(MW14/2002 US)
3. silver-gray body, metallic blue body, red roof, black radar, blue wheels, "911 Sea Rescue" & "Matchbox 50" tempa ($4-6)(MW14/2002 US)
4. red deck, black hull, red roof, red radar, black wheels, "Trump Racing Team" & flames tempa ($20-35)(US)
5. red deck, white hull, gray roof, red wheels, "MHC Beach Patrol" tempa ($1-2)(MW44/2003)

6. red deck, white hull, gray roof, red wheels, "MHC Beach Patrol" & "Hero City" tempa ($2-4)(MW44/2003)
7. red deck, white hull, gray roof, white wheels, "MHC Beach Patrol" & "Hero City" tempa ($2-4)(MW44/2003)
8. red deck, white hull, gray roof, white wheels, "MHC Beach Patrol" tempa ($1-2)(MW44/2003)
   NOTE: Versions 5 & 8 can have full red band or a notch in the band where the "Hero City" design is omitted.
9. red deck, light blue hull, gray roof, white wheels, "MHC Beach Patrol" tempa ($3-5)(20pk)
10. red deck, dark blue hull, turquoise roof, black wheels, "Venice" tempa ($1-2)(AW)

MB69-A ROLLS ROYCE SILVER SHADOW COUPE, issued 1969

NOTE: Below models with amber windshield, 5 spoke wheels & England casting. Earliest versions with narrow wheels with later versions having wide wheels.

1. metallic blue body, orange-brown interior, tan tonneau, black base ($20-25)
2. metallic blue body, orange-brown interior, tan tonneau, light yellow base ($20-25)
3. metallic blue body, orange-brown interior, tan tonneau, dark yellow base ($20-25)
4. metallic gold body, orange-brown interior, tan tonneau, tan base ($20-25)
5. metallic gold body, orange-brown interior, tan tonneau, light yellow base ($20-25)
6. metallic gold body, orange-brown interior, tan tonneau, dark yellow base ($20-25)
7. metallic gold body, orange-brown interior, tan tonneau, black base ($20-25)
8. metallic gold body, orange-brown interior, tan tonneau, silver base ($20-25)
9. metallic gold body, orange-brown interior, black tonneau, black base ($20-25)
10. metallic gold body, orange-brown interior, black tonneau, silver base ($20-25)
11. metallic gold body, orange-brown interior, black tonneau, charcoal base ($20-25)
12. metallic gold body, orange-brown interior, black tonneau, light yellow base ($20-25)
13. metallic gold body, ivory interior, black tonneau, black base ($20-25)
14. metallic gold body, ivory interior, black tonneau, gray base ($20-25)
15. dark gold body, orange-brown interior, black tonneau, black base ($20-25)
16. dark gold body, orange-brown interior, black tonneau, silver base ($20-25)
17. dark gold body, orange-brown interior, black tonneau, charcoal base ($20-25)
18. dark gold body, ivory interior, black tonneau, silver base($20-25)
19. lime gold body, orange-brown interior, black tonneau, charcoal base ($20-25)
20. lime gold body, ivory interior, black tonneau, charcoal base ($20-25)
21. lime gold body, ivory interior, black tonneau, black base ($20-25)
22. lime gold body, ivory interior, black tonneau, silver base ($20-25)

MB69-B TURBO FURY, issued 1973

NOTE: Below models with white driver, black metal base & England casting.

1. metallic red body, clear windshield, "69" label, 5 spoke wheels ($15-18)
2. metallic red body, amber windshield, "69" label, 5 spoke wheels ($15-18)
3. metallic red body, clear windshield, "86" label (from MB61-A), 5 spoke wheels ($15-18)
4. metallic red body, clear windshield, "86" label (from MB61-A), 4 spoke wheels ($15-18)
5. metallic red body, clear windshield, scorpion label, 4 spoke wheels ($25-40)
6. metallic red body, clear windshield, scorpion label, 5 spoke wheels ($25-40)
7. metallic red body, clear windshield, "69" label, 5 spoke wheels, charcoal base ($15-18)
8. metallic red body, clear windshield, spotted cat head label (from MB1-B), 5 spoke wheels ($175-250)
9. metallic red body, clear windshield, "69" label , 5 spoke wheels, black base with Manaus tab ($35-50)(BR)

MB69-C ARMORED TRUCK, issued 1978 (MB069)

1. red body, silver-gray base, clear windows, 5 crown wheels, "Wells Fargo/732-2031" tempa, England casting ($25-40)
2. red body, silver-gray base, blue windows, 5 crown wheels, no tempa, England casting ($20-35)
3. red body, silver-gray base, blue windows, 5 crown wheels, "Wells Fargo/732-2031" tempa, England casting ($4-6)
4. red body, silver-gray base, blue windows, 5 arch wheels, "Wells Fargo/732-2031" tempa, England casting ($4-6)
5. red body, unpainted base, blue windows, 5 crown wheels, "Wells Fargo/732-2031" tempa, England casting ($4-6)
6. red body, silver-gray base, blue windows, 5 crown wheels, "Wells Fargo/QZ-2031" tempa, England casting ($4-6)
7. green body, silver-gray base, blue windows, 5 crown wheels, "Dresdner Bank" tempa, England base ($35-45)(GR)
8. dark olive body, pearly silver base, blue windows, 5 crown wheels, "Dresdner Bank" tempa, Macau casting ($60-75)(GR)
9. green body, light gray base with Manaus label, blue windows, 8 spoke star (Majorette) wheels, no tempa ($50-75)(BR)

MB69-D '33 WILLYS STREET ROD, issued 1982 (USA) (MB108)

NOTE: Below models with chrome interior & engine.

1. white body, unpainted metal base, orange flames tempa, dot dash rear wheels, England casting ($3-5)
2. white body, unpainted metal base, red flames tempa, dot dash rear wheels, England casting ($3-5)
3. white body, silver-gray metal base, orange flames tempa, dot dash rear wheels, England casting ($3-5)
4. white body, silver-gray metal base, red flames tempa, dot dash rear wheels, England casting ($3-5)
5. dark blue body, pearly silver metal base, orange flames tempa, dot dash rear wheels, Macau casting ($1-2)
6. dark blue body, pearly silver metal base, red flames tempa, dot dash rear wheels, Macau casting ($1-2)
7. dark blue body, light gray metal base, red flames tempa, dot dash rear wheels, Hong Kong casting ($1-2)
8. dark blue body, light gray metal base, red flames tempa, 5 spoke rear wheels, Hong Kong casting ($1-2)
9. dark blue body, black plastic base, red flames tempa, dot dash rear wheels, Macau casting ($1-2)
10. dark blue body, black plastic base, red flames tempa, dot dash rear wheels, China casting ($1-2)
11. black body, black plastic base, red flames tempa, dot dash rear wheels, China casting ($7-10)(US)(OP)
12. iridescent cream body, black plastic base, pink & yellow flames & "Pro Street" tempa, dot dash rear wheels, China casting ($1-2)

13. iridescent cream body, black plastic base, pink & yellow flames without "Pro Street" tempa, dot dash rear wheels, China casting ($2-4)
14. metallic turquoise body, black plastic base, pink & white design tempa, dot dash rear wheels, China casting ($1-2)(5pk)
15. black body, black plastic base, pink & white tempa, dot dash rear wheels, China casting ($5-7)
16. turquoise body, black plastic base, pink/ purple/ white tempa, dot dash rear wheels, China casting ($1-2)(5pk)
17. grape body, black plastic base, "Bad To The Bone" & crossbones tempa, dot dash rear wheels, China casting ($3-5)(AU)
18. iridescent white body, black plastic base, "Grease" & silver flash tempa, dot dash rear wheels, China casting ($4-6)(STR)

MB69-E 1983/84 CORVETTE *see MB14-E*

MB69-F VOLVO 480ES, issued 1988 (ROW) (MB195)

NOTE: Below models with gray interior & smoke windows.

1. pearly silver body, gray metal base, laser wheels, "Volvo 480" with dual green stripes tempa, Macau casting ($3-5)(LW)
2. white body, gray metal base, 8 dot wheels, "Volvo" & "480ES" tempa, Macau casting ($2-3)
3. white body, gray metal base, 8 dot wheels, "480ES" tempa, Macau casting ($2-3)
4. white body, gray plastic base, 8 dot wheels, "480ES" tempa, Macau casting ($2-3)
5. white body, gray plastic base, 8 dot wheels, "Volvo" & "480ES" tempa, China casting ($5-7)
6. white body, gray plastic base, 8 dot wheels, "480ES" tempa with "Toys City" roof label, Macau casting ($75-100)(Malaysian)

MB69-G HIGHWAY MAINTENANCE VEHICLE issued MB69-G
MB69-H 1968 FORD MUSTANG COBRA JET, issued 1997 (USA) (MB298)
MB20-G 1968 FORD MUSTANG COBRA JET, issued 1997 (ROW)

NOTE: Below models with clear windows, black plastic base and China casting unless otherwise noted.

1. black body, red & black interior, chrome disc wheels with rubber tires, red pinstripe tempa ($4-6)(IG)
2. unpainted body, chrome interior, chrome disc wheels with rubber tires, no tempa ($4-6)(IG)
3. yellow body, chrome interior, 5 spoke concave star wheels, yellow base, purple & white tempa ($1-2)
4. silver blue body, black & blue interior, chrome disc wheels with rubber tires, black painted base, black stripes tempa ($12-18)(CL)
5. white body, black & red interior, chrome disc wheels with rubber tires, black on hood & red pinstripes tempa ($3-5)(PC17)
6. bright blue body, chrome interior, 5 spoke concave star wheels, orange & white tempa ($1-2)(MW40)
7. red body, tan & black interior, chrome disc wheels with rubber tires, white & black stripes tempa ($3-5)(PC20)
8. bright blue body, translucent white interior, 5 spoke concave star wheels with black hubs, orange & white tempa ($50-75)(MW40/1998 US)
9. medium blue body, chrome interior, 5 spoke concave star wheels, orange & white tempa ($1-2)(MW40/1998 US)
10. dark blue body, chrome interior, 5 spoke concave star wheels, orange & white tempa ($1-2)(MW40/1998 US)
11. maroon body, black & tan interior, chrome disc wheels with rubber tires, black & white stripes tempa ($3-5)(TRU-GS)
12. dark blue body, black & cream interior, chrome disc wheels with rubber tires, black & gold stripes tempa ($6-8)(PC)
13. lemon body, black interior, chrome disc wheels with rubber tires, "Coca Cola" tempa ($5-8)(Coke PC)
14. metallic gold body, chrome interior, 5 spoke concave star wheels, no tempa ($5-10)(CH)
15. green body, beige & black interior, chrome disc wheels with rubber tires, gold side stripes & black hood band tempa ($5-8)(PC)
16. green-gold body, black interior, 5 spoke concave star wheels, black stripes tempa ($1-2)(5pk)
17. green-gold body, painted black interior, 5 spoke concave star wheels, black stripes tempa ($1-2)(5pk)
18. green-gold body, painted black interior, star with 5 spokes wheels, black stripes tempa ($1-2)(5pk)
19. metallic light gold body, painted black interior, 5 spoke concave star wheels, black stripes tempa ($1-2)(5pk)
20. dark green body, painted white interior, dark green base, 5 spoke concave star wheels, "Ice Cold Coca Cola" tempa, dark green base ($3-5)(TP-Avon)
21. silver-blue body, black painted interior, 5 spoke concave star wheels, black band & stripes tempa ($1-2)(5pk)
22. silver-blue body, black painted interior, star with 5 spokes wheels, black band & stripes tempa ($1-2)(5pk)
23. silver-blue body, black painted interior, 10 spoke flower wheels, black band & stripes tempa ($25-40)(5pk)
24. black body, red & black interior, chrome disc wheels with rubber tires, "Bendigo Swap Meet 2000" tempa ($18-25)(C2)(AU)
25. unpainted body, chrome interior, chrome disc wheels with rubber tires, "Bendigo Swap Meet 2000" tempa ($18-25)(C2)(AU)
26. white body, red painted interior, chrome disc wheels with rubber tires, "Coca Cola Play Refreshed" tempa, chrome base ($3-5)(Coke PC)
27. dark blue body, chrome interior, 5 spoke concave star wheels, white band & "Cruisin New England Magazine All Wheels Festival 2001" tempa ($50+)(CCI)
28. metallic green body, black interior, chrome disc wheels with rubber tires, black band & pinstripe tempa ($3-5)(BJ)
29. maroon body, black & tan interior, chrome disc wheels with rubber tires, "S.E.R. Diecutting/ Satisfaction Efficiency Reliability" ($18-25)(CCI)
30. green-gold body, black interior, 5 spoke concave star wheels, black stripes & "Mustang Club 2003" tempa ($50+)(CCI)
31. metallic blue body, black interior, 10 spoke flower wheels, white striping & "100" tempa, blue base, Mattel casting ($3-5)(MP)(Avon)
32. metallic green body, lime interior, lace wheels, "Ughh!" & Frankenstein image tempa, purple base, Mattel casting ($1-2)(5pk)
33. red body, black interior, chrome disc wheels with rubber tires, black band & white pinstripes tempa, black base, Mattel casting ($3-5)(BJ)
34. black body, red & black interior, gold 6 spoke spiral wheels, red pinstriping tempa, black base ($50+)(CHI)
35. black body, red & black interior, gold 6 spoke spiral wheels, red pinstriping tempa, yellow base ($50+)(CHI)
36. lemon body, black interior, 10 spoke flower wheels, black pinstriping tempa, yellow base ($5-8)(CN)(OP)
37. dark green body, black interior, 5 spoke slotted wheels, detailed trim tempa, dark green base ($1-2)(SF52/2004)

MB69-I BMW 328i, issued 1999 (GR) (MB424)
MB19-E BMW 328i, issued 2001 (ROW)

NOTE: Below models with head & taillights tempa, black base & China casting unless otherwise noted.

1. metallic dark green body, clear windows, light tan interior, plastic base, 5 spoke concave star wheels ($3-5)(MW69/1999GR)

2. metallic blue body, smoke windows, light gray interior, plastic base, spoke concave star wheels ($1-2)(5pk)
3. dark metallic blue body, smoke windows, black interior, plastic base, 5 spoke concave star wheels ($1-2)(LP)
4. charcoal body, clear windows, light gray interior, lace wheels, plastic base, "BMW328i" & painted lights tempa ($2-4)(MW19/2001 ROW)
5. charcoal body, clear windows, light gray interior, lace wheels, metal base, "BMW328i" & painted lights tempa ($2-4)(MW19/2001 ROW)
6. red body, clear windows, black interior, lace wheels, metal base, head & tail lights tempa & small "BMW" logo tempa ($2-4)(ROW BMW promo)
7. dark green body, clear windows, gray interior, lace wheels, plastic base, no tempa ($3-5)(SG)
8. metallic gold body, smoke windows, black interior, lace wheels, plastic base, painted grille tempa ($2-4)(MW40/2003 ROW)
9. metallic gold body, smoke windows, black interior, lace wheels, plastic base, painted grille & "Hero City" tempa ($10-15)(MW40/2003 ROW)

MB69-J LOTUS ELISE, issued 2000 (ROW) (MB440)
MB 8-M LOTUS ELISE, issued 2005 (USA)

NOTE: Below models with smoke windshield, lace wheels, black metal base & China casting unless otherwise noted.
1. yellow body, black interior, 5 spoke concave star wheels, headlights & black louvers tempa ($2-4)(MW69/2000 ROW)
2. iridescent white body, black interior, small "Matchbox" logo & black louvers tempa ($2-4)(MW49/2001 ROW)
3. metallic blue body, black interior, small "Matchbox" logo & black louvers tempa ($2-4)(MW24/2002 ROW)
4. metallic blue body, black interior, small "Matchbox" logo, black louvers & "Matchbox 50" tempa ($4-6)(MW24/ROW)
5. metallic green body, black interior, small "Matchbox" logo tempa ($2-4)(5pk)
6. black body, red interior, small "Matchbox" logo tempa ($2-4)(MW67/2003 ROW)
7. black body, red interior, small "Matchbox" logo & "Hero City" tempa ($4-6)(MW67/2003 ROW)
8. dark green body, tan interior, small "Matchbox" logo tempa ($2-4)(MW18/ROW 2004)
9. silver-gray body, black interior, detailed trim tempa ($3-5)(SoC)
10. lemon body, black interior, "Lotus Elise" with black, green & silver stripes tempa ($1-2)(MW8/2005)
11. metallic orange body, black interior, detailed trim tempa, 5 spoke slotted wheels ($1-2)(SF42/2004)

MB69-K HUMVEE, issued 2001 (MB522)

NOTE: Below models with black windows, 4 spoke domed wheels, chrome hubs, black base & China casting unless otherwise noted.
1. white body, "Sky High Rescue Mission/ 51 Garage/ Matchbox" tempa, 8 spoke wheels, black hubs ($2-4)(PS)
2. red body, "Toys For Tots Lebanon, PA/ Marine Corp League/ Marines" tempa ($18-25)(CCI)
3. red body, no tempa ($50-75)(CCI blank)
4. lemon body, "Hummer" tempa, chrome base ($1-2)(MW69/2001)
5. metallic green body, "Matchbox" tempa ($1-2)(MW32/2002)
6. metallic green body, "Matchbox" & "Matchbox 50" tempa ($2-4)(MW32/2002)
7. metallic green body, "Happy Holidays 2002/ Matchbox Road Museum" tempa ($18-25)(CCI)
8. white body, "Sky High Rescue Mission/ 51 Garage/ Matchbox" tempa, black hubs ($8-12)(EG)
9. dark yellow body, "Rescue Hummer/ Limited Edition 2003" with cross tempa ($2-4)(Duracell In pack)
10. metallic green body, "www.convoys.de/ Merry Christmas & Happy New Year" tempa ($25-40)(CCI)
11. silver-gray body, "Kenya Safari 2004-05" tempa, green windows ($1-2)(AW)
12. dark yellow body, "Rescue Hummer/ Limited Edition 2004" with cross tempa ($8-10)(Duracell in pack)(CN)
13. flat black body, "Coca-Cola Football Town/ Total Tailgate" tempa, smoke windows ($2-4)(CK)
14. bright blue body, white doors & "Police" crest tempa, amber windows, 5 arch dot wheels ($1-2)(LP)

MB69-L PORSCHE 911 TURBO , issued 2002 (ROW) (MB544)
MB 9-J PORSCHE 911 TURBO, issued 2003 (USA)

NOTE: Below models with black interior, black plastic base & China casting.
1. yellow body, smoke windows, 10 spoke flower wheels, painted lights & small logo tempa ($2-4)(MW69/2002 ROW)
2. yellow body, smoke windows, 10 spoke flower wheels, painted lights & small logo with "Matchbox 50" tempa ($4-6)(MW69/2002 ROW)
3. metallic lime body, clear windows, lace wheels, painted headlights tempa ($3-5)(SG)
4. unpainted body, clear windows, lace wheels, pop art decals ($75+)(FA)
5. red body, smoke windows, 10 spoke flower wheels, "9 Porsche" tempa ($1-2)(MW9/2003)
6. red body, smoke windows, 10 spoke flower wheels, "9 Porsche" & "Hero City" tempa ($2-4)(MW9/2003)
7. metallic lime body, clear windows, lace wheels, "4.10.2003 Matchbox Hero City" tempa ($18-25)(C2)(GR)
8. metallic charcoal body, smoke windows, 5 spoke slotted wheels, head & tail lights tempa ($3-5)(SF20/2004)
9. bright blue body, dark smoke windows, 10 spoke flower wheels, small "Matchbox" logo tempa ($1-2)(LP)

MB70-A FORD GRIT SPREADER, issued 1970

NOTE: Below models with green windows, unpainted metal base & England casting.
1. red cab & chassis, yellow dump, 5 spoke wheels ($25-40)
2. red cab & chassis, yellow dump, 4 spoke wheels ($25-40)

MB70-B DODGE DRAGSTER, issued 1971

NOTE: Below models with chrome interior & grille, black roll bar & England casting.
1. hot pink body, black base, light green snake labels, 4 spoke rear wheels ($15-20)
2. dark pink body, black base, light green snake labels, 4 spoke rear wheels ($15-20)
3. dark pink body, unpainted base, light green snake labels, 4 spoke rear wheels ($15-20)
4. dark pink body, light green base, light green snake labels, 4 spoke rear wheels ($15-20)
5. dark pink body, light yellow base, light green snake labels, 4 spoke rear wheels ($15-20)
6. dark pink body, dark yellow base, light green snake labels, 4 spoke rear wheels ($15-20)
7. dark pink body, tan base, light green snake labels, 4 spoke rear wheels ($15-20)
8. dark pink body, lavender base, light green snake labels, 4 spoke rear wheels ($15-20)
9. dark pink body, charcoal base, light green snake labels, 4 spoke rear wheels ($15-20)

10. dark pink body, black base, light green snake labels, 5 spoke rear wheels ($15-20)
11. dark pink body, black base, dark green snake labels, 4 spoke rear wheels ($15-20)
12. dark pink body, black base, "Rat Rod" labels (from MB62-B), 4 spoke rear wheels ($25-35)
13. dark pink body, black base, "Wildcat" labels (from MB8-B), 4 spoke rear wheels ($25-35)
14. dark pink body, black base, star with flame labels (from MB40-A), 4 spoke rear wheels ($200-275)
15. dark pink body, black base, "Castrol" label, 4 spoke rear wheels ($750-1000)

MB70-C SELF PROPELLED GUN, issued 1976 (MB770)

NOTE: Below models with black rollers & black gun.

1. olive green body & base, black treads, no tempa, England casting ($2-4)
2. olive green body & base, tan treads, no tempa, England casting ($2-4)
3. matt olive green body & base, tan treads, no tempa, England casting ($2-4)
4. black body, dark gray base, tan treads, gray & yellow camouflage tempa, Macau casting ($4-5)(CM)
5. olive green body & base, tan treads, tan & black camouflage tempa, Macau casting ($4-5)(CM)
6. olive green body & base, tan treads, tan & black camouflage tempa, China casting ($6-8)(CM)

MB70-D FERRARI 308 GTB, issued 1981 (MB070)

NOTE: Below models with metal base unless otherwise noted.

1. red body & base, no tempa, 5 arch wheels, black interior, clear windows, England casting ($2-4)
2. red body, orange-red base, no tempa, 5 arch wheels, black interior, clear windows, England casting ($2-4)
3. orange-red body & base, no tempa, 5 arch wheels, black interior, clear windows, England casting ($2-4)
4. orange-red body & base, "Ferrari" tempa, 5 arch wheels, black interior, clear windows, England casting ($2-4)
5. orange-red body & base, "Ferrari" tempa, 5 arch wheels, black interior, amber windows, England casting ($2-4)
6. orange-red body, silver-gray base, "Ferrari" tempa, 5 arch wheels, black interior, clear windows, England casting ($8-12)
7. orange-red body, pearly silver base, "Ferrari" & logo tempa, 5 arch wheels, black interior, clear windows, Macau casting ($2-3)
8. orange-red body, pearly silver base, "Ferrari" & logo tempa, 5 spoke wheels, black interior, clear windows, Macau casting ($2-3)
9. dark red body, pearly silver base, "Ferrari" & logo tempa, 5 spoke wheels, black interior, clear windows, Macau casting ($2-3)
10. red body, blue base, "Pioneer 39" tempa, 5 arch wheels, white interior, clear windows, Macau casting ($2-3)
11. yellow body, red base, "Ferrari 308GTB" tempa, starburst wheels, black interior, clear windows, Macau casting ($3-5)(SF)
12. yellow body, red base, "Ferrari 308GTB" tempa, laser wheels, black interior, clear windows, Macau casting ($3-5)(LW)
13. orange body, blue base, "12 Rat Racing Team" tempa, 5 arch wheels, white interior, clear windows, Macau casting ($8-12)(HK)
14. red body & base, "Data East/Secret Service" tempa, 5 arch wheels, black interior, clear windows, Macau casting ($65-80)(CN)
15. red body & base, detailed trim tempa, gray disc wheels with rubber tires, black interior, chrome windows, Macau casting ($5-8)(WC)
16. red body & base, rectangular "Ferrari" logo on hood tempa, 5 arch wheels, black interior, clear windows, Macau casting ($2-3)(MP)
17. red body & base, rectangular "Ferrari" logo on hood tempa, 5 arch wheels, black interior, clear windows, Thailand casting ($2-3)(MC)
18. white body & base, no tempa, 5 arch wheels, black interior, green windows, Thailand casting ($10-15)(GF)
19. lemon body & base, geometric designs tempa, 5 arch wheels, black interior, clear windows, Thailand casting ($2-4)(DM)
20. red body, gray plastic base, 8 dot wheels, black interior, clear windows, "Ferrari" on sides tempa, Manaus casting ($8-25)(BR)
21. red body, gray plastic base, 4 arch wheels, black interior, clear windows, "Ferrari" on sides tempa, Manaus casting ($18-25)(BR)
22. red body & base, chrome disc wheels with rubber tires, black interior, clear windows, detailed trim tempa, Thailand casting ($50+)(GC)(CHI)

    NOTE: Above model was intended to be released with the gold coin series but was issued separately in China instead.
23. red body, red plastic base, 5 spoke concave star wheels, yellow-orange & black interior, clear windows, "Magnum P.I." & black roof tempa, China casting ($4-6)(STR)

MB70-E FORD CARGO SKIP TRUCK, issued 1989 (USA) (MB178)
MB45-D FORD CARGO SKIP TRUCK, issued 1987 (ROW)

NOTE: Below models with blue windows & 8 spoke wheels.

1. yellow body, pearly gray metal dump, black base & arms, orange stripe tempa, Macau casting ($1-2)
2. blue body, red metal dump, yellow base & arms, white stripe tempa, yellow wheels with orange hubs, Macau casting ($6-8)(LL)
3. yellow body, pearly gray metal dump, black base & arms, orange stripe tempa, Thailand casting ($1-2)
4. yellow body, gray plastic dump, black base & arms, orange stripe tempa, Macau casting ($1-2)
5. yellow body, gray plastic dump, black base & arms, orange stripe tempa, Thailand casting ($1-2)
6. yellow body, red plastic dump, black base & arms, no tempa, Thailand casting ($1-2)
7. orange-yellow body, red plastic dump, black base, yellow arms, no tempa, China casting ($2-3)

MB70-F FERRARI F40 *see MB24-H*

MB70-G WEASEL *see MB73-B*

MB70-H 1970 PONTIAC GTO, issued 1996 (USA) (MB289)
MB64-G 1970 PONTIAC GTO, issued 1996 (ROW)

NOTE: Below models with clear windows, black base & China casting unless otherwise noted.

1. orange body & spoiler, black interior, blue & yellow tempa, 6 spoke spiral wheels ($1-2)
2. silver-gray body, gray spoiler, blue & black interior, blue & yellow tempa, chrome disc wheels with rubber tires ($5-8)(PC3)
3. white body & spoiler, blue & black interior, blue & yellow tempa, chrome disc wheels with rubber tires ($5-8)(PC6)
4. dark purple body, white & purple interior, detailed trim tempa, chrome disc wheels with rubber tires ($12-18)(CL)
5. black body, gray interior, yellow & red tempa, 5 spoke concave star wheels ($1-2)(5pk)
6. dark green body, tan & black interior, orange & yellow tempa, chrome disc wheels with rubber tires ($3-5)(SC3)

7. yellow body, black & gray interior, green & blue flames tempa, chrome disc wheels with rubber tires ($3-5)(PC11)
8. orange body, black interior, blue & yellow tempa, 5 spoke concave star wheels ($100+)
9. red body, black interior, blue & yellow tempa, 6 spoke spiral wheels ($100+)
10. red body, black interior, blue & yellow tempa, 5 spoke concave star wheels ($2-3)
11. metallic blue body, black & gray interior, red & white tempa, chrome disc wheels with rubber tires ($15-20)(GC)
12. metallic gold body, black interior, no tempa, 5 spoke concave star wheels ($5-10)(CH)
13. lemon body, black interior, red & blue tempa, 5 spoke concave star wheels ($1-2)(MW38/1998)
14. dark green body, tan & black interior, orange & yellow tempa, 6 spoke spiral wheels ($75+)(CHI)
15. silver-gray body, dark blue & black interior, black & yellow tempa, 6 spoke spiral wheels ($75+)(CHI)
16. dark charcoal body, purplish & black interior, red & white tempa, chrome disc wheels with rubber tires ($3-5)(PC17)
17. dark blue body, gray & black interior, white/yellow/orange/red tempa, chrome disc wheels with rubber tires ($3-5)(PC20)
18. lemon body, black interior, purple & blue tempa, 5 spoke concave star wheels ($1-2)(MW38/1998)
19. light pumpkin body, black & gray interior, blue & red tempa, chrome disc wheels with rubber tires ($5-8)(PC)
20. black body, black interior, orange & white band & "GTO" tempa, 5 spoke concave star wheels ($1-2)(MW71/1999 US)
21. orange body, black interior, blue & yellow tempa with "Calvert Limited Term" roof label, 6 spoke spiral wheels ($50+)(ASAP)
22. lemon body, black interior, purple & blue with "Cruisin New England Magazine" tempa, 5 spoke concave star wheels ($50+)(CCI)
23. black body, black interior, orange & white band & "GTO" with "Cruisin New England Magazine" tempa, 5 spoke concave star wheels ($50+)(CCI)
24. white body, black interior, "Coca Cola Play Refreshed" tempa, chrome disc wheels with rubber tires, chrome base ($3-5)(Coke PC)
25. silver blue body, blue interior, detailed trim tempa, chrome disc wheels with rubber tires ($3-5)(BJ)
26. silver-gray body, tan & black interior, blue & yellow pinstripe with detailed trim tempa, gold 6 spoke spiral wheels ($50+)(CHI)

NOTE: Below models with Mattel China casting.

27. blue body, black interior, pink & yellow design tempa, chrome disc wheels with rubber tires ($3-5)(MCC)
28. metallic brown-gold, black interior, detailed trim tempa, chrome disc wheels with rubber tires ($3-5)(BJ)
29. metallic lime body, black interior, green & yellow pinstripes tempa, chrome disc with rubber tires ($3-5)(MCC)
30. silver blue body, black interior, "Ummm" & mummy tempa, lace wheels ($1-2)(5pk)
31. red body, black interior, smoke windows, blue & yellow pinstripes & headlights tempa, 5 spoke slotted wheels, gray base ($3-5)(SF18/2004)
32. dark purple body, white & purple interior, detailed trim tempa, gold 6 spoke spiral wheels ($50+)(CHI)

MB70-I MERCEDES E CLASS, issued 1998 (MB334)

NOTE: Below models with clear windows, black plastic base & China casting unless otherwise noted.

1. charcoal body, dark red interior, red pinstripe & " E Class" with head light trim tempa, 5 spoke concave star wheels ($1-2)(MW70/1998)
2. silver-gray body, dark red interior, "Intergalactic Research" tempa, 5 spoke concave star wheels ($1-2)(MW65/1999 US)(MW60/1999 ROW)
3. cream body, black interior, "Taxi 23000" tempa, 5 spoke concave star wheels ($3-5)(MW70/1999 GR)
4. metallic pink (various shades) body, dark red interior, "Matchbox USA 20th Anniversary Convention/ Color Comp Inc. Conference" tempa, 5 spoke concave star wheels ($25-30)(CCI)
5. metallic blue body, gray interior, "Mercedes-Benz" & 2 silver bands tempa, lace wheels ($2-4)(MW8/2002 ROW)
6. metallic blue body, gray interior, "Mercedes-Benz" & 2 silver bands with "Matchbox 50" tempa, lace wheels ($4-6)(MW8/2002 ROW)
7. cream body, black interior, "Taxi Kommt wie gerufen 230023" tempa, lace wheels, Mattel casting ($3-5)(SG)
8. light metallic blue body, gray interior, headlight trim tempa, lace wheels, silver-gray base ($2-3)(MW38/2003 ROW)

NOTE: Above model with Matchbox International or Mattel casting.

9. light metallic blue body, gray interior, headlight trim & "Hero City" tempa, lace wheels, silver-gray base ($10-15)(MW38/2003)

MB70-J CHEVY SILVERADO 4X4 PICKUP, issued 1999 (USA) (MB399)
MB65-H CHEVY SILVERADO 4X4 PICKUP, issued 1999 (USA)

NOTE: Below models with maltese cross wheels, chrome plastic base & China casting.

1. black body, turquoise interior, clear windows, "Canyon Mission" tempa ($2-3)(MW65/1999 ROW)((MW60/1999 GR))
2. black body, turquoise interior, clear windows, "Game Warden/ Protect Wild Life" tempa ($1-2)(MW70/US 1999)
3. purple body, orange interior, smoke windows, "Surf Shop-The Hottest Boards On The Beach" tempa ($1-2)(MW11/2000 US)
4. purple body, orange interior, smoke windows, "Surf Shop-The Hottest Boards On The Beach" & "Matchbox 2000" tempa ($2-4)(MW11/2000 US)
5. lemon body, black interior, clear windows, "Zero" & mountain design tempa ($1-2)(5pk)

NOTE: Below models with 5 spoke oval wheels.

6. white body, neon lime interior, clear windows, "Fast Ride Snowboards 22" tempa ($1-2)(MW7/2001)
7. metallic purple body, black interior, smoke windows, snowflake & skier tempa ($1-2)(MW22/2002 US)
8. metallic purple body, black interior, smoke windows, snowflake & skier with "Matchbox 50" tempa ($2-4)(MW22)
9. metallic red body, black interior, smoke windows, "Unit 5" & design tempa ($1-2)(LP)
10. dark metallic blue body, lime interior, amber windows, "Komodo Island" tempa, orange base ($1-2)(AW)
11. black body, gray interior, black windows, "Coca-Cola Football Town/ Total Tailgate" tempa, gray base ($2-4)(CK)
12. charcoal body, black interior, red windows, "Hero City" with screws & screwdriver design tempa, black base ($1-2)(MW74/2004)

MB70-K CHEVROLET SSR, issued 2002 (USA) (MB550)
MB57-M CHEVROLET SSR, issued 2003 (ROW)

NOTE: Below models with black interior, lace wheels, black plastic base & China casting unless otherwise noted.

1. bright blue body, clear windows, detailed trim tempa ($1-2)(MW70/2002 US)
2. bright blue body, clear windows, detailed trim & "Matchbox 50" tempa ($2-4)(MW70/2002 US)
3. bright blue body, clear windows, "3rd Northern New Jersey Toy Show" tempa ($10-15)(CCI)
4. bright blue body, clear windows, detailed trim tempa, chrome disc wheels with rubber tires ($3-5)(MCC)
5. lemon body, white interior, clear windows, "Tony's Pizza" tempa ($1-2)(MW57/2003)
6. lemon body, white interior, clear windows, "Tony's Pizza" & "Hero City" tempa ($4-6)(MW57/2003)
7. white body, red windows, "Ace the helpful place" & red stripes tempa ($3-5)(US in-pack)
8. red body, amber windows, "Ace the helpful place" & white stripes tempa ($3-5)(US in-pack)
9. orange body, smoke windows, green interior, "Team 35" & basketball design tempa ($1-2)(5pk)
10. dark metallic maroon body, blue windows, orange-yellow interior, "Superman" tempa ($1-2)(5pk)
11. bright blue body, clear windows, "Matchbox Toy Show 2004" with Ferris wheel & roller coaster design ($25-40)(CCI)
12. lemon body, smoke windows, gray interior, detailed trim tempa, 5 spoke slotted wheels ($3-5)(SF21/2004)
13. blue body, blue windows, orange-yellow interior, "Superman" tempa, blue base ($1-2)(CA)

MB70-L VW W12 CONCEPT, issued 2002 (ROW) (MB549)

NOTE: Below models with dark smoke windows & China casting.

1. orange-yellow body, black interior, headlights & small "Matchbox" tempa, orange-yellow base, lace wheels ($2-4)(MW70/2002 ROW)
2. orange-yellow body, black interior, headlights, small "Matchbox" & "Matchbox 50" tempa, orange-yellow base, lace wheels ($4-6)(MW70/2002 ROW)
3. red & yellow body, yellow interior, "The Flash" tempa, tan base, chrome disc wheels with rubber tires ($3-5)(JL)
4. red body, black interior, headlights tempa, lace wheels ($3-5)(SG)
5. salmon body, black interior, Daffy Duck tempa, lace wheels, salmon base ($1-2)(5pk)
6. red body, black interior, head lights & small "Matchbox" tempa, lace wheels ($2-4)(MW68/2003 ROW)
7. red body, black interior, head lights & small "Matchbox" with "Hero City" tempa, lace wheels ($4-6)(MW68/2003 ROW)
8. silver blue body, black interior, Daffy Duck tempa, lace wheels, slate blue base ($1-2)(CA)
9. iridescent white body, black interior, head & tail lights & small "Matchbox" tempa, lace wheels, pearl white base ($2-3)(MW24/2004 ROW)

MB71-A FORD HEAVY WRECK TRUCK, issued 1970

NOTE: Below models with green windows, 4 spoke wheels & England casting.

1. red cab, white body, red clip axle covers, silver hubs, red hook, "Esso" labels ($35-50)
2. red cab, white body, black clip axle covers, silver hubs, red hook, "Esso" labels ($35-50)
3. red cab, white body, black clip axle covers, silver hubs, yellow hook, "Esso" labels ($35-50)
4. olive green cab & body, riveted axle covers, black hubs, black hook, "3LGS64" labels ($8-12)(TP)
5. olive green cab & body, riveted axle covers, silver hubs, black hook, "3LGS64" labels ($8-12)(TP)
6. blue cab & body, riveted axle covers, silver hubs, black hook, no labels ($175-225)(MP)
7. blue cab & body, riveted axle covers, black hubs, black hook, no labels ($175-225)(MP)

MB71-B JUMBO JET, issued 1973

NOTE: Below models with chrome engine & plastic base, red elephant head, solid black wheels & England casting.

1. dark metallic blue body, light blue handlebars ($15-20)
2. dark metallic blue body, dark blue handlebars ($15-20)

MB71-C CATTLE TRUCK, issued 1976 (MB071)
MB12-I CATTLE TRUCK, reissued 1992 (ROW)

NOTE: Below models with 5 crown front & rear wheels & England casting unless otherwise noted. First 14 variations listed with two black cows.

1. bronze body, orange-yellow stakes, dark green windows, unpainted base, no tow hook ($3-5)
2. bronze body, orange-yellow stakes, dark green windows, silver-gray base, no tow hook ($3-5)
3. bronze body, orange yellow stakes, blue windows, unpainted base, no tow hook ($3-5)
4. bronze body, orange-yellow stakes, blue windows, silver-gray base, no tow hook ($3-5)
5. bronze body, light yellow stakes, blue windows, silver-gray base, no tow hook ($3-5)
6. bronze body, yellow stakes, blue windows, silver-gray base, no tow hook ($3-5)
7. bronze body, orange-yellow stakes, light green windows, silver-gray base, no tow hook ($3-5)
8. bronze body, orange-yellow stakes, purple windows, silver-gray base, no tow hook ($3-5)
9. bronze body, orange-yellow stakes, orange windows, silver-gray base, no tow hook ($3-5)
10. bronze body, orange-yellow stakes, blue windows, silver-gray base, black tow hook ($3-5)(TP)
11. dull red body, beige stakes, blue windows, silver-gray base, black tow hook ($3-5)(TP)
12. dull red body, cream stakes, blue windows, silver-gray base, black tow hook ($3-5)(TP)
13. dull red body, beige stakes, red windows, silver-gray base, black tow hook ($3-5)(TP)
14. dull red body, beige stakes, purple windows, silver-gray base, black tow hook ($3-5)(TP)
15. dull red body, beige stakes, blue windows, silver-gray base, black tow hook, brown cows ($3-5)(TP)
16. dull red, orange-yellow stakes, orange windows, silver-gray base, black tow hook ($3-5)(TP)
17. dull red body, orange-yellow stakes, purple windows, silver-gray base, no tow hook ($3-5)(TP)
18. dull red body, orange-yellow stakes, blue windows, unpainted base with Manaus tab, no tow hook ($35-50)(BR)

NOTE: Due to permutations of the cows, green bodied models can be found with brown, coffee, or white cows with earliest green versions having brown cows only.

19. light metallic green, orange-yellow stakes, blue windows, silver-gray base, no tow hook ($3-5)
20. light metallic green body, beige stakes, orange windows, silver-gray base, no tow hook ($6-8)
21. dark metallic green body, orange-yellow stakes, red windows, silver-gray base, no tow hook, 5 arch front & rear wheels ($6-8)
22. dark metallic green body, beige stakes, orange windows, silver-gray base, no tow hook ($6-8)

23. light metallic green body, orange-yellow stakes, orange windows, silver-gray base, no tow hook ($3-5)
24. light metallic green body, orange-yellow stakes, red windows, silver-gray base, no tow hook ($3-5)
25. dark metallic green body, orange-yellow stakes, orange windows, silver-gray base, no tow hook ($3-5)
26. dark metallic green body, orange-yellow stakes, red windows, silver-gray base, no tow hook ($3-5)
27. dark metallic green body, chocolate stakes, red windows, silver-gray base, no tow hook ($6-8)
28. dark metallic green body, chocolate stakes, amber windows, black base, no tow hook ($6-8)
29. dark metallic green body, chocolate stakes, amber windows, silver-gray base, no tow hook ($6-8)
30. dark metallic green body, chocolate stakes, amber windows, black base, no tow hook ($6-8)
31. dark metallic green body, chocolate stakes, clear windows, silver-gray base, no tow hook ($6-8)
32. dark metallic green body, chocolate stakes, clear windows, black base, no tow hook ($6-8)
33. metallic green body, chocolate stakes, red windows, silver-gray base, no tow hook ($6-8)
34. metallic green body, chocolate stakes, red windows, black base, no tow hook ($6-8)
35 metallic green body, chocolate stakes, amber windows, silver-gray base, no tow hook ($6-8)
36. metallic green body, chocolate stakes, amber windows, black base, no tow hook ($6-8)
37. metallic green body, chocolate stakes, clear windows, silver-gray base, no tow hook ($6-8)
38. metallic green body, chocolate stakes, clear windows, black base, no tow hook ($6-8)
39. dark metallic green body, brown stakes, red windows, silver-gray base, no tow hook ($6-8)
40. dark metallic green body, brown stakes, red windows, black base, no tow hook ($6-8)
41. dark metallic green body, brown stakes, amber windows, silver-gray base, no tow hook ($6-8)
42. dark metallic green body, brown stakes, amber windows, black base, no tow hook ($6-8)
43. dark metallic green body, brown stakes, clear windows, silver-gray base, no tow hook ($6-8)
44. dark metallic green body, brown stakes, clear windows, black base, no tow hook ($6-8)
45. metallic green body, brown stakes, red windows, silver-gray base, no tow hook ($6-8)
46. metallic green body, brown stakes, red windows, black base, no tow hook ($6-8)
47. metallic green body, brown stakes, amber windows, silver-gray base, no tow hook ($6-8)
48. metallic green body, brown stakes, amber windows, black base, no tow hook ($6-8)
49. metallic green body, brown stakes, clear windows, silver-gray base, no tow hook ($6-8)
50. metallic green body, brown stakes, clear windows, black base, no tow hook ($6-8)

NOTE: Due to permutations, yellow bodied models can be found with coffee or red-brown cows.

51. yellow body, chocolate stakes, red windows, unpainted base, no tow hook, 8 dot front wheels ($6-8)
52. yellow body, chocolate stakes, red windows, silver-gray base, no tow hook ($3-5)
53. yellow body, chocolate stakes, red windows, silver-gray base, black tow hook ($3-5)(TP)
54. yellow body, chocolate stakes, amber windows, silver-gray base, no tow hook ($3-5)
55. yellow body, chocolate stakes, amber windows, silver-gray base, black tow hook ($3-5)(TP)
56. yellow body, chocolate stakes, amber windows, black base, black tow hook ($3-5)(TP)
57. yellow body, chocolate stakes, clear windows, silver-gray base, no tow hook ($3-5)
58. yellow body, chocolate stakes, clear windows, silver-gray base, black tow hook ($3-5)(TP)
59. yellow body, chocolate stakes, red windows, black base, no tow hook ($3-5)
60. yellow body, chocolate stakes, red windows, black base, black tow hook ($3-5)(TP)
61. yellow body, chocolate stakes, red windows, unpainted base, no tow hook ($3-5)
62. yellow body, chocolate stakes, red windows, unpainted base, black tow hook ($3-5)(TP)
63. yellow body, chocolate stakes, red windows, silver-gray base, black tow hook ($3-5)(TP)
64. yellow body, chocolate stakes, red windows, black base, black tow hook ($3-5)(TP)
65. yellow body, chocolate stakes, red windows, black base, no tow hook, dot dash rear wheels ($7-10)
66. yellow body, chocolate stakes, amber windows, black base, no tow hook, dot dash rear wheels ($7-10)
67. yellow body, chocolate stakes, red windows, black base, no tow hook, 5 arch rear wheels ($7-10)
68. yellow body, chocolate stakes, red windows, black base, no tow hook, 5 arch front & rear wheels ($7-10)
69. yellow body, tan stakes, red windows, unpainted base, no tow hook ($4-6)
70. yellow body, tan stakes, red windows, black base, no tow hook ($4-6)
71. yellow body, tan stakes, amber windows, black base, no tow hook ($4-6)
72. dull red body, beige stakes, blue windows, silver-gray base, no tow hook, 5 arch front & rear wheels ($7-10)
73. powder blue body, chocolate stakes, red windows, black base, black cows, black tow hook, 5 crown wheels, Macau casting ($2-4)(TP)
74. red body, yellow stakes, red windows, yellow base, no cows, red tow hook, 5 crown blue wheels with yellow hubs, cow head tempa, Macau casting ($6-8)(LL)
75. green body, yellow stakes, red windows, black base, black cows, black tow hook, 5 crown wheels, Macau casting ($1-2)(TP)
76. green body, yellow stakes, red windows, black base, black cows, black tow hook, 5 crown wheels, Thailand casting ($1-2)(TP)
77. green body, yellow stakes, red windows, black base, black cows, no tow hook, 5 crown wheels, Thailand casting ($1-2)
78. yellow body, chocolate stakes, red windows, black base, black cows, black tow hook, 5 crown wheels, Macau casting ($1-2)
79. yellow body, red stakes, purple windows, black base, black cows, black tow hook, 5 crown wheels, China casting, cow head tempa ($1-2)(MW1/1999 ROW)
80. yellow body, red stakes, purple windows, black base, black cows, black tow hook, 5 crown wheels, China casting, "Target Beef" tempa ($1-2)(MW88/1999 US)
81. blue body, light brown stakes, amber windows, black base, coffee cows, black tow hook, 5 crown wheels, China casting, cow head tempa ($1-2)(MW502000 US/ MW30/2000 ROW)

82. blue body, light brown stakes, amber windows, black base, coffee cows, black tow hook, 5 crown wheels, China casting, cow head & "Matchbox 2000" tempa ($2-4)(MW50/2000 US)
83. orange body, light tan stakes, smoke windows, black base, black cows, black tow hook, 7 spoke sawblade wheels, China casting, "Oklahoma 46 Pride Farms" tempa ($1-2)(AM)

MB71-D 1962 CORVETTE, issued 1982 (USA) (MB094)
MB32-F 1962 CORVETTE, reissued 1994 (USA)
MB72-L 1962 CORVETTE, reissued 1994 (ROW)

NOTE: Below models with clear windows unless otherwise noted.

1. dark blue body & base, blue interior, white tempa, 5 arch silver wheels, England casting ($3-5)
2. dark blue body & base, blue interior, white tempa, maltese cross wheels, England casting ($3-5)
3. dark blue body & base, chrome interior, white tempa, 5 arch silver wheels, England casting ($3-5)
4. dark blue body & base, chrome interior, white tempa, maltese cross wheels, England casting ($3-5)
5. white body & base, blue interior, red tempa, 5 arch silver wheels, England casting ($7-10)
6. white body & base, chrome interior, red tempa, 5 arch silver wheels, England casting ($7-10)
7. white body, dark blue base, chrome interior, red tempa, 5 arch silver wheels, England casting ($7-10)

NOTE: Below models with chrome interior & clear windows unless otherwise noted.

8. white body & base, red flames & "Blue Flame 39" tempa, 5 arch silver wheels, Macau casting ($2-4)
9. white body & base, orange flames & "Blue Flame 39" tempa, 5 arch silver wheels, Macau casting ($2-4)
10. white body & base, red flames & "Blue Flame 39" tempa, 5 arch silver wheels, Hong Kong casting ($2-4)
11. white body & base, orange flames tempa, 5 arch silver wheels, Hong Kong casting ($2-4)
12. bright blue body & base, "Firestone" tempa, 5 arch silver wheels, Macau casting ($7-10)(JP)
13. orange body & base, "11" & white stripe tempa, small starburst wheels, Macau casting ($3-5)(SF)
14. orange body & base, "11" & white stripe tempa, large starburst wheels, Macau casting ($3-5)(SF)
15. red body & base, "454 Rat" tempa, 5 arch gold wheels, Macau casting ($2-3)
16. red body & base, "454 Rat" tempa, 5 arch silver wheels, Macau casting ($2-3)
17. metallic copper body & base, "11" & white stripe tempa, laser wheels, Macau casting ($3-5)(LW)
18. metallic green body & base, "11" & white stripe tempa, laser wheels, Macau casting ($3-5)(LW)
19. rose red body & base, "Heinz 57" tempa, 5 arch silver wheels, Macau casting ($25-35)(US)
20. turquoise body & base, white roof & detailed trim tempa, gray disc wheels with rubber tires, China casting ($3-4)(WC)
21. white body & base, no tempa, 5 arch silver wheels, China casting ($6-8)(GF)
22. red body & base, "454 Rat" tempa, 5 arch silver wheels, China casting ($1-2)
23. metallic copper body & base, "4" & black roof tempa, black disc wheels with rubber tires, China casting ($5-8)(WP)
24. red body & base, white roof & side flash tempa, 5 arch silver wheels, Thailand casting ($2-4)(GS)
25. metallic blue body & base, blue & red design tempa, gold 6 spoke spiral wheels, Thailand casting ($1-2)
26. black body & base, white roof & side flash tempa, silver 6 spoke spiral wheels, China casting ($2-4)(CC)
27. metallic red body & base, white roof with "Matchbox/DMB & B" tempa, chrome disc wheels with rubber tires, Thailand casting ($275-350)(US)
28. metallic red body & base, white roof with "Matchbox/DMB & B" tempa, gray disc wheels with rubber tires, Thailand casting ($275-350)(US)
29. metallic blue body & base, white & red design tempa, silver 6 spoke spiral wheels, Thailand casting ($1-2)
30. blue body & base, white & red design (sides only) tempa, silver 6 spoke spiral wheels, China casting ($1-2)
31. metallic red body & base, "Corvette 62" tempa, silver 6 spoke spiral wheels, China casting ($1-2)(5pk)
32. candy red body & base, red chrome & white interior, white roof & detailed trim tempa, chrome disc wheels with rubber tires, China casting ($3-5)(PC3)
33. gold body & base, gold & white interior, white roof & detailed trim tempa, chrome disc wheels with rubber tires, China casting ($3-5)(PC6)
34. metallic blue body & base, white & red design tempa, silver 6 spoke spiral wheels, China casting ($1-2)
35. white body & base, blue windows, orange flames tempa, silver 6 spoke spiral wheels, China casting ($2-4)
36. white body & base, blue windows, orange flames tempa, 5 spoke concave star wheels, China casting ($1-2)
37. dark purple body & base, yellow tiger stripes tempa, 5 spoke concave star wheels, China casting ($1-2)(5pk)
38. red body & base, "Chubby's/ Pepsi Cola" tempa, 5 spoke concave star wheels, China casting ($5-10)(US)
39. lemon body & base, yellow & black interior, white roof & detailed trim tempa, chrome disc wheels with rubber tires, China casting ($3-5)(SC3)
40. black body & base, white & black interior, silver/ blue/ purple tempa, chrome disc wheels with rubber tires, engine cast on hood, China casting ($3-5)(PC9)
41. silver-gray body & base, silver & black interior, white roof & side flash & detailed trim tempa, chrome disc wheels with rubber tires, China casting ($3-5)(CP)
42. blue body & base, blue & white interior, white roof & side flash tempa, chrome disc wheels with rubber tires, China casting ($3-5)(CP)
43. purple body & base, purple & white interior, orange & yellow flames tempa, chrome disc wheels with rubber tires, chrome engine cast on roof, China casting ($3-5)(PC11)
44. white body & base, red & black interior, white roof & side flash & detailed trim tempa, chrome disc wheels with rubber tires, China casting ($3-5)(CP)
45. red body & base, red & white interior, white roof & side flash & detailed trim tempa, chrome disc wheels with rubber tires, China casting ($3-5)(CP)
46. red body & base, white stripes & "62" on roof tempa, 5 spoke concave star wheels, China casting ($4-6)(AU)
47. lemon body & base, yellow & black interior, white roof & side flash & detailed trim tempa, gold 6 spoke spiral wheels, China casting ($75+)(CH)
48. metallic gold body & base, no tempa, 5 spoke concave star wheels, China casting ($5-10)(CH)
49. black body & base, black & white interior, white roof & side flash & detailed trim tempa, chrome disc wheels with rubber tires, China casting ($3-5)(CP)

50. metallic blue body & base, met. blue & white interior, white roof & side flash & detailed trim tempa, chrome disc wheels with rubber tires, China casting ($3-5)(CP)
51. purple body, red base, red & white interior, orange & yellow flames tempa, blue windows, 5 spoke concave star wheels, chrome engine cast on hood, China casting ($75+)(CHI)
52. purple body, red base, purple & white interior, orange & yellow flames tempa, blue windows, 5 spoke concave star wheels, chrome engine cast on hood, China casting ($75+)(CHI)
53. red body & base, white stripes & "62" tempa, 5 spoke concave star wheels, China casting ($4-6)(AU)
54. black body & base, pink roof & "Matchbox/ Hot August Nights 1998" tempa, chrome disc wheels with rubber tires, China casting ($12-18)(US)
55. red body & base, white roof & side flash with "Animal House" tempa, 5 spoke concave star wheels, China casting ($4-6)(STR)
56. silver-gray body, red base, blue & white interior, white roof & side flash & detailed trim tempa, gold 6 spoke spiral wheels, China casting ($75+)(CHI)
57. metallic blue body, blue base, blue & white interior, white roof & side flash & detailed trim tempa, 5 spoke concave star wheels, China casting ($75+)(CHI)
58. blue body, red base, red & black interior, white roof & side flash & detailed trim tempa, gold 6 spoke spiral wheels, China casting ($75+)(CHI)
59. pale red body, white base, white & black interior, white stripes & "62" on roof tempa, gold 6 spoke spiral wheels, China casting ($75+)(CHI)
60. red body, black base, purple & white interior, white roof & side flash & detailed trim tempa, gold 6 spoke spiral wheels, China casting ($75+)(CHI)
61. gold body & base, gold & white interior, white roof & detailed trim tempa, gold 6 spoke spiral wheels, China casting ($75+)
62. metallic blue body, blue windows, lemon base, blue & white interior, white roof & side flash & detailed trim tempa, China casting ($75+)(CHI)
63. black body, black base, chrome interior, "Matchbox USA 18th Convention & Toy Show" tempa, 5 spoke concave star wheels, China casting ($15-20)(ASAP)
64. black body, black base, chrome interior, "DDCM DuPage Diecast Collectors Meet" tempa, 5 spoke concave star wheels, China casting ($15-20)(ASAP)
65. black body, black base, chrome interior, "BS Auto Seaside Oregon" tempa, 5 spoke concave star wheels, China casting ($15-20)(ASAP)
66. black body, black base, chrome interior, "X Xedia" tempa, 5 spoke concave star wheels, China casting ($75+)(ASAP)
67. black body, black base, chrome interior, no tempa, 5 spoke concave star wheels, China casting ($25-40)(ASAP blank)
68. black body, black base, chrome interior, "Bloomsburg Fair Association/ Millennium 2000" tempa, 5 spoke concave star wheels, China casting ($50+)(ASAP)
69. black body, black base, chrome interior, "Kitchen Aid" tempa, 5 spoke concave star wheels, China casting ($50+)(ASAP)
70. blue body & base, chrome interior, white & red design (sides only) tempa, gold 6 spoke spiral wheels, China casting ($50+)(CHI)
71. metallic red body & base, chrome interior, "Corvette 62" tempa, gold 6 spoke spiral wheels, China casting ($50+)(CHI)
72. blue body, red base, black & white interior, white roof & side flash & detailed trim tempa, gold 6 spoke spiral wheels, China casting ($50+)(CHI)
73. candy red body & base, red chrome & white interior, white roof & detailed trim tempa, gold 6 spoke spiral wheels, China casting ($50+)(CHI)
74. silver-gray body, black base, black & white interior, white roof & side flash & detailed trim tempa, gold 6 spoke spiral wheels, China casting ($50+)(CHI)
75. black body, black base, chrome interior, "Scorchin' Promo Models/ CCI 2004" with yellow & orange flames tempa, 5 spoke concave star wheels, China casting ($18-25)(CCI)
76. black body, black base, chrome interior, "Scorchin' Promo Models/ CCI 2004" with silver & blue flames tempa, 5 spoke concave star wheels, China casting ($18-25)(CCI)

MB71-E SCANIA T142 *see MB8-F*

MB71-F GMC WRECKER *see MB21-F*

MB71-G PORSCHE 944 TURBO, issued 1989 (USA) (MB191)
MB59-E PORSCHE 944 TURBO, issued 1989 (ROW)

1. red body, black base, tan interior, clear windows, 8 dot wheels, doors open, "944 Turbo" & logo tempa, Macau casting ($1-2)
2. black body, black base, no interior, chrome windows, gray disc wheels with rubber tires, doors cast, "944 Turbo" & detailed trim tempa, Macau casting ($5-8)(WC)
3. red body, black base, tan interior, clear windows, 8 dot wheels, doors open, "944 Turbo/Credit Charge" tempa, Macau casting ($7-10)(UK)
4. black body, black base, tan interior, clear windows, 8 dot wheels, doors open, "944 Turbo" & logo tempa, Macau casting ($2-3)(KS)(UK)
5. white body, black base, tan interior, clear windows, 8 dot wheels, doors open, dark blue "Duckhams" tempa, Macau casting ($15-20)(UK)(OP)
6. white body, black base, tan interior, clear windows, 8 dot wheels, doors open, purple "Duckhams" tempa, Thailand casting ($15-20)(UK)(OP)
7. black body, black base, no interior, chrome windows, gray disc wheels with rubber tires, doors cast, "944 Turbo" & detailed trim tempa, Thailand casting ($5-8)(WC)
8. metallic green body, black base, tan interior, clear windows, 8 dot wheels, doors open, "944 Turbo" & logo tempa, Thailand casting ($1-2)
9. yellow body, black base, black interior, clear windows, doors open, "944 Turbo" tempa, 8 dot wheels, Thailand casting ($2-4)(CC)
10. red body, black base, black & red interior, clear windows, doors open, "944 Turbo" & detailed trim tempa, chrome disc wheels with rubber tires, Thailand casting ($3-5)(PC2-ROW)
11. candy red body, black base, tan & black interior, clear windows, doors open, detailed trim tempa, chrome disc wheels with rubber tires, Thailand casting ($15-20)(GC)
12. iridescent white body, black base, brown & black interior, clear windows, doors open, "944 Turbo" & detailed trim tempa, chrome disc wheels with rubber tires, Thailand casting ($3-5)(PC19)
13. metallic green body, black base, clear windows, door open, "944 Turbo" & "American International Recovery" tempa, 8 dot wheels, Thailand casting ($100+)(ASAP promo)

MB71-H MUSTANG COBRA, issued 1995 (USA) (MB277)
MB43-J MUSTANG COBRA, issued 1995 (ROW)

1. red body, smoke windows, gray interior, cobra on black hood tempa, 6 spoke spiral wheels, Thailand casting ($1-2)

2. white body, smoke windows, green interior, cobra on black hood tempa, 6 spoke spiral wheels, Thailand casting ($1-2)(5pk)
3. red body, clear windows, red/ivory interior, detailed trim tempa, chrome disc wheels with rubber tires, Thailand casting ($3-5)(PC2)
4. dark purple body, clear windows, white & black interior, detailed trim tempa, chrome disc wheels with rubber tires, Thailand casting ($3-5)(PC1-JC)
5. black body, smoke windows, orange-brown interior, cobra on gray hood tempa, 6 spoke spiral wheels, Thailand casting ($2-4)
6. white body, clear windows, ivory & red interior, detailed trim tempa, chrome disc wheels with rubber tires, Thailand casting ($3-5)(PC5)
7. black body, clear windows, black & tan interior, detailed trim tempa, chrome disc wheels with rubber tires, Thailand casting ($3-5)(SC2)
8. white body, clear windows, light blue interior, "Ford Pace Car" & black design tempa, 5 spoke concave star wheels, Thailand casting ($1-2)(5pk)
9. pumpkin body, clear windows, white & gray interior, detailed trim tempa, chrome disc wheels with rubber tires, Thailand casting ($15-20)(GC)
10. metallic blue body, clear windows, translucent yellow interior, lime horse design tempa, 5 spoke concave star wheels, Thailand casting ($1-2)
11. metallic gold body, clear windows, gray interior, no tempa, 6 spoke spiral wheels, Thailand casting ($5-10)(CH)
12. metallic blue body, clear windows, white & gray interior, detailed trim tempa, chrome disc wheels with rubber tires, Thailand casting ($3-5)(SC4)
13. gold body, clear windows, white & gray interior, detailed trim tempa, chrome disc wheels with rubber tires, Thailand casting ($3-5)(PC14)
14. slate blue body, clear windows, brown & tan interior, detailed trim tempa, chrome disc wheels with rubber tires, Thailand casting ($3-5)(PC16)
15. dark green body, clear windows, white & gray interior, detailed trim tempa, chrome disc wheels with rubber tires, Thailand casting ($3-5)(SC5)
16. metallic red body, clear windows, gray interior, lime horse design tempa, 5 spoke concave star wheels, Thailand casting ($1-2)(MW73/1998 US)
17. pink body, smoke windows, white interior, "71st Shenandoah Apple Blossom Festival 1998" tempa, 5 spoke concave star wheels, Thailand casting ($8-12)(US)
18. metallic red body, clear windows, mid gray interior, lime horse design tempa, 5 spoke concave star wheels with black hubs, Thailand casting ($15-20)(MW73/1998 US)
19. metallic red body, clear windows, mid gray interior, lime horse design tempa, 5 spoke concave star wheels with black hubs, China casting ($15-20)(MW73/1998 US)
20. metallic red body, clear windows, mid gray interior, lime horse design tempa, 5 spoke concave star wheels, China casting ($1-2)(MW73/1998 US)
21. metallic rose body, clear windows, white interior, lime horse design tempa, 5 spoke concave star wheels, China casting ($1-2)(MW73/1998 US)
22. light rose red body, clear windows, white interior, lime horse design tempa, 5 spoke concave star wheels, China casting ($1-2)(MW73/1998 US)

NOTE: There are numerous intermediate shades of body & tempa color on versions 16 & 18-22.

23. white body, clear windows, light blue interior, "Ford Pace Car" & black design tempa, 5 spoke concave star wheels, China casting ($1-2)(5pk)
24. red body, smoke windows, tan interior, no tempa, 5 spoke concave star wheels, China casting ($1-2)(5pk)
25. bright blue body, smoke windows, gray interior, no tempa, 5 spoke concave star wheels, China casting ($1-2)(5pk)
26. bronze body, clear windows, tan & brown interior, detailed trim tempa, chrome disc wheels with rubber tires, China casting ($4-6)(GS)
27. bright blue body, smoke windows, gray interior, "District 16 Convention Lion's Club" tempa, 5 spoke concave star wheels, China casting ($15-20)(CCI)
28. red body, smoke windows with black trim, black interior, "Coca Cola Play Refreshed" tempa, chrome disc wheels with rubber wheels, chrome base, China casting ($3-5)(Coke PC)
29. lemon body, clear windows with yellow trim, black interior, detailed trim tempa, chrome disc wheels with rubber tires, China casting ($3-5)(TN)
30. pink body, smoke windows, white interior, "Sweet 16th Birthday Shanta" tempa, 5 spoke concave star wheels, China casting ($18-25)(CCI)
31. metallic silver body, clear windows, red interior, "Coca Cola" tempa, lace wheels, Mattel China casting ($2-4)(CK)
32. pink body, smoke windows, white interior, "Marissa Tyler Elliot Christening" tempa, 5 spoke concave star wheels, China casting ($12-18)(CCI)
33. pink body, smoke windows, white interior, "Ad-Ventures Inc. 1st Annual Picnic" tempa, 5 spoke concave star wheels, China casting ($18-25)(CCI)

MB71-I JAGUAR XK8, issued 1998 (MB332)

NOTE: Below models with clear windows, black plastic base & China casting unless otherwise noted.

1. metallic red body, pale tan & black interior, chrome disc wheels with rubber tires, detailed trim tempa ($4-6)(FE)
2. unpainted body, pale tan interior, chrome disc wheels with rubber tires, no tempa ($4-6)(FE)
3. metallic blue body, silver-gray interior, 5 spoke concave star wheels, silver band & "Jaguar XK8" tempa ($1-2)(MW71/1998)
4. green body, silver-gray interior, 5 spoke concave star wheels, white Jaguar design tempa ($1-2)(MW48/1999 US)(MW43/1999 ROW)
5. green body, tan interior, 5 spoke concave star wheels, head & taillights tempa ($3-5)(MW53/1999 GR)
6. green body, silver-gray interior, small 5 spoke concave star wheels, white Jaguar design tempa ($3-5)(MW48/1999 US)(MW43/1999 ROW)
7. green body, gray interior, small 5 spoke concave star wheels, head & tail lights with black lettered license plate tempa ($2-4)(MW2/2000 ROW)
8. green body, gray interior, 5 spoke concave star wheels, head & tail lights tempa with black lettered license plate tempa ($2-3)(MW2/2000 ROW)
9. green body, gray interior, 10 spoke flower wheels, head & tail lights tempa with black lettered license plate tempa ($8-12)(EG)
10. silver blue body, black interior, 5 spoke concave star wheels, head & taillights tempa ($1-2)(5pk)
11. silver blue body, black interior, star with 5 spokes wheels, head & taillights tempa ($1-2)(5pk)
12. silver blue body, black interior, 10 spoke flower wheels, head & taillights tempa ($1-2)(5pk)

13. metallic red body, silver-gray interior, smoke windows, 10 spoke flower wheels, head lights tempa ($2-3)(MW47/2001 ROW)
14. green body, gray interior, clear windows, star with 5 spoke wheels, head & tail lights with white lettered rear license plate tempa ($1-2)(EG)
15. silver-gray body, red interior, smoke windows, lace wheels, small "Matchbox" tempa ($1-2)(LP)
16. metallic blue body, black interior, smoke windows, lace wheels, small "Matchbox" tempa, Mattel casting ($1-2)(LP)
17. lemon body, orange interior, dark smoke windows, lace wheels "Road Runner/ Beep" tempa , Mattel casting ($1-2)(5pk)

MB71-J FOUR WHEELER *see MB91-A*

MB71-K MERCEDES BENZ CLK CONVERTIBLE *see MB1-H*

MB71-L FORD DUMP/ UTILITY TRUCK *see MB91-B*

MB71-M JEEP LIBERTY, issued 2001 (MB504)

NOTE: Below models with clear windows, 10 spoke flower wheels, black base & China casting unless otherwise noted.

1. silver-gray body, black interior, small "Jeep" & "4X4" tempa ($35-50)(US)
2. silver-gray body, black interior, smoke windows, "Police" shield & stripes tempa ($8-12)(MP)
3. red body, blue interior, "Police" shield & stripes tempa ($1-2)(MW71/2001)
4. red body, blue interior, "50th Happy Birthday Matchbox/ Mom Me & Matchbox" tempa ($50+)(CCI)
5. silver-gray body, black interior, smoke windows, "50th Happy Birthday Matchbox/ Mom Me & Matchbox" tempa ($75+)(CCI)
6. metallic gold body, red interior, monkey & wrench tempa ($1-2)(5pk)
7. pale pumpkin body, white interior, smoke windows, "Back In Action" tempa ($1-2)(5pk)
8. pearly white body, brown interior, smoke windows, "Mt. Rushmore"" tempa ($1-2)AW)
9. red body, blue interior, "Police" shield & stripes with "Matchbox Toy Show/ 35 Superfast" tempa ($25-40)(CCI)

MB71-N JEEP WILLYS CONCEPT, issued 2003 (MB575)

NOTE: Below models with 5 spoke oval wheels & China casting.

1. silver blue body, gray interior, blue-gray rollbar, black base, "71" tempa ($1-2)(MW71/2003 ROW)
2. silver blue body, gray interior, blue-gray rollbar, black base, "71" & "Hero City" tempa ($2-4)(MW71/2003)
3. lime body, red interior, blue-green rollbar, blue base, "Martian Manhunter" tempa ($1-2)(5pk)
4. metallic red body, black interior, gray roll bar, black base, small "Matchbox" logo tempa ($1-2)(MW53/2004)
5. red body, black interior, black roll bar, black base, "Coca-Cola Football Town/ Total Tailgate" tempa ($2-4)(CK)
6. metallic lime body, orange-yellow interior, gray roll bar, black base, "Tiki of Hawaii" tempa ($1-2)(AW)
7. metallic purple body, lime interior, yellow roll bar, yellow base, "Patrick- The Spongebob Squarepants Movie" tempa ($1-2)(5pk)

MB72-A JEEP, issued 1970

NOTE: Below models with spiro wheels, black metal base & England casting.

1. yellow body, red interior, red axle covers ($25-40)
2. yellow body, red interior, black axle covers ($25-40)
3. yellow-orange body, red interior, black axle covers ($25-40)
4. bright yellow body, red interior, black axle covers ($25-40)

MB72-B HOVERCRAFT SRN6, issued 1972

NOTE: Below models with England casting.

1. white body, black hull, blue windows, "SRN6" labels, solid black wheels ($5-7)
2. white body, black hull, no windows, "SRN6" labels, solid black wheels ($5-7)
3. white body, black hull, no windows, without labels, solid black wheels ($5-7)
4. white body, black hull, blue windows, "SRN6" labels, 5 spoke wheels with chrome hubs ($12-15)
5. white body, black hull, blue windows, "SRN6" labels, 5 spoke wheels with black hubs ($12-15)
6. white body, black hull with Manaus tab, blue windows, "SRN6" labels, solid black wheels ($35-50)(BR)

MB72-C BOMAG ROAD ROLLER, issued 1979

NOTE: Below models with black front roller, 5 crown rear wheels & England casting.

1. yellow body & base, red interior, yellow hubs ($4-6)
2. yellow body & base, red interior, silver hubs ($3-5)

MB72-D MAXI TAXI, issued 1981 (USA) (MB088)

NOTE: Below models with clear windows, tan interior & 5 spoke wheels.

1. yellow body, black base, "M" towards upper left on roof, Hong Kong casting ($7-10)
2. yellow body, black base, "I" towards upper right on roof, Hong Kong casting ($2-4)
3. yellow body, black base, no roof tempa, Hong Kong casting ($3-5)
4. yellow body, black base, "M" towards upper left on roof, Macau casting ($3-5)

MB72-E DODGE DELIVERY TRUCK, issued 1982 (ROW) (MB072)

NOTE: Below models with blue windows, 5 arch wheels & black plastic base unless otherwise noted.

1. red body, white container, silver hubs, "Pepsi" labels, England casting ($4-6)
2. red body, white container, gold hubs, "Pepsi" labels, England casting ($4-6)
3. red body, white container, silver hubs, "Smith's" labels, England casting ($4-6)(UK)(OP)
4. red body, white container, gold hubs, "Smith's" labels, England casting ($4-6)(UK)(OP)
5. red body, white container, silver hubs, "Kellogg's" labels, England casting ($4-6)
6. red body, white container, gold hubs, "Kellogg's" labels, England casting ($4-6)

NOTE: Below models with silver hubs unless otherwise noted.

7. red body, white container, "Kellogg's" tempa, Macau casting ($4-6)
8. white body, white container, "Street's Ice Cream" tempa, Macau casting ($6-8)(AU)
9. yellow body, yellow container, "Hertz" tempa, Macau casting ($2-4)
10. orange-yellow body & container, "Hertz" tempa, Macau casting ($2-4)
11. red body, red container, "Royal Mail Parcels" tempa , Macau casting ($5-7)(MP)
12. red body, white container, "Kellogg's/Milch-Lait-Latte" tempa, Macau casting ($35-50)(GR)(SW)
13. white body, white container, "Jetspress Road Express" tempa, Macau casting ($6-8)(AU)

14. green body, white container, "Minties" tempa, Macau casting ($6-8)(AU)
15. orange-yellow body, yellow container, "Risi" tempa, Macau casting ($15-25)(SP)
16. blue body, blue container, "Mitre 10" tempa, Macau casting ($6-8)(AU)
17. red body, dark yellow container, "Nestle Chokito" tempa, Macau casting ($6-8)(AU)
18. red body, container & base, red windows, "Kit Kat" tempa, Macau casting ($7-10)(UK)(OP)
19. blue body & base, blue container, "Yorkie" tempa, Macau casting ($7-10)(UK)(OP)
20. white body, white container, "Pirelli Gripping Stuff" tempa, Macau casting ($3-5)(TC)
21. red body, white container, "Matchbox U.S.A. Sheraton Inc. 1989" tempa, Macau casting ($8-12)(US)
22. white body, white container, "XP Express Parcels Systems" tempa, Macau casting ($3-5)(TC)
23. dark green body, orange container, "C Plus Orange" tempa, Macau casting ($10-15)(CN)
24. light gray & dark navy body, light gray container, "British Airways Cargo" tempa, Thailand casting ($3-5)(MC)
25. white body, white container, "Wigwam" tempa, Thailand casting ($7-10)(CY)(DU)
26. white body, white container, "XP Express Parcels Systems" tempa, Thailand casting ($3-5)(TC)
27. red body, white container, "Big Top Circus" tempa, 5 crown wheels, Thailand casting ($3-5)(TP)
28. blue body, container & base, "St. Ivel Gold" tempa, Thailand casting ($10-15)(UK)(OP)
29. dark blue body & container, "Stena Line Freight" tempa, Thailand casting ($12-15)(UK)(LD)
30. white body & container, "MD" tempa, Thailand casting ($12-15)(UK)(LD)
31. red body & container, "H & B Harris & Bailey Ltd." Tempa, Thailand casting ($12-15)(UK)(LD)
32. dark blue body & container, no tempa, Thailand casting ($12-15)(LD blank)
33. white body & container, no tempa, Thailand casting ($12-15)(LD blank)
34. red body & container, no tempa, Thailand casting ($12-15)(LD blank)
35. white body & container, "British Gas" tempa, Thailand casting ($50+)(UK)(LD)
36. white body & container, "CRI Catalysts" tempa, Thailand casting ($50+)(UK)(LD)
37. white body & container, "Mechanix Choice" tempa, Thailand casting ($50+)(UK)(LD)
38. red body & container, "Don" tempa, Thailand casting ($50+)(UK)(LD)
39. red body & container, "Manrose Extractor Fans" tempa, Thailand casting ($50+)(UK)(LD)
40. red body & container, "Personal Post" tempa, Thailand casting ($50+)(UK)(LD)

MB72-F SAND RACER, issued 1984 (USA) (MB146)

1. white body, pearly silver metal base, black interior & roll bar, "Goodyear 211" tempa, 5 crown front & racing special rear wheels, Macau casting ($18-25)

MB72-G AIRPLANE TRANSPORTER, issued 1985 (USA) (MB146)
MB65-E AIRPLANE TRANSPORTER, issued 1985 (ROW)

NOTE: Below models with black plastic base & 8 spoke wheels unless otherwise noted. Versions 5, 8, 10-12 with black hubs; all others with chrome hubs.

1. yellow body, blue windows, "Rescue" & checkers tempa, plastic plane with red wings & white undercarriage, Macau casting ($6-8)
2. yellow body, blue windows, "Rescue" & checkers tempa, plastic plane with white wings & red undercarriage, Macau casting ($6-8)
3. yellow body, blue windows, "Rescue" & checkers tempa, plastic plane with white wings & red undercarriage, China casting ($6-8)
4. white body, blue windows, "NASA" tempa, plastic plane with white wings & undercarriage, Macau casting ($3-5)(MP)
5. olive body, blue windows, black & tan camouflage tempa, black hubs, plastic plane with olive wings & undercarriage, China casting ($35-50)(CM)
6. yellow body, blue windows, "Rescue" & checkers tempa, plastic plane with red wings & white undercarriage, China casting ($6-8)
7. white body, smoke windows, gray & olive camouflage tempa, black hubs, plastic plane with white wings & gray undercarriage, Thailand casting ($3-5)(5pk)
8. white body, smoke windows, "Rescue" with red checkers tempa, plastic plane with black wings & red undercarriage, Thailand casting ($2-4)(MP)
9. silver-gray body, dark smoke windows, red dashes & plane silhouette tempa, plastic plane with yellow wings & black undercarriage, China casting ($1-2)(MW10/1999)
10. black body, red windows, yellow dashes & plane silhouette tempa, plastic plane with silver-gray wings & blue undercarriage, gray base, China casting ($1-2)(MW69/2000 US)(MW49/2000 ROW)
11. black body, red windows, yellow dashes & plane silhouette tempa, plastic plane with blue wings & silver-gray undercarriage, gray base, China casting ($1-2)(MW69/2000 US)(MW49/2000 ROW)
12. black body, red windows, yellow dashes, plane silhouette & "Matchbox 2000" tempa, plastic plane with blue wings & silver-gray undercarriage, gray base, China casting ($3-5)(MW69/2000 US)
13. black body, red windows, yellow dashes, plane silhouette & "Matchbox 2000" tempa, plastic plane with silver-gray wings & blue undercarriage, China casting ($2-4)(MW69/2000 US)
14. olive body, blue windows, black & tan camouflage, 5 crown wheels with black hubs, plastic plane with olive wings & undercarriage (without camouflage), China castings ($35-50)(CM)(CHI)(MP)
15. dark green body, red windows, "M-Force Airshow" tempa, plastic plane with white wings & undercarriage with designs tempa, 7 spoke sawblade wheels, gray base, China casting ($1-2)(5pk)
16. black body, amber windows, globe & grid tempa, plastic plane with yellow wings & undercarriage, 7 spoke sawblade wheels, Mattel China casting ($1-2)(5pk)

MB72-H FORD SUPERVAN *see MB 6-E*

MB72-I CADILLAC ALLANTE, issued 1987 (USA) (MB189)
MB65-F CADILLAC ALLANTE, issued 1987 (ROW)

NOTE: Below models with black plastic base.

1. silver-gray body, red interior, clear windshield, 8 dot wheels, no tempa, Macau casting ($1-2)
2. black body, red interior, clear windshield, laser wheels, red & silver stripes tempa, Macau casting ($3-5)(LW)
3. pink body, gray interior, clear windshield, 8 dot wheels, "Cadillac" tempa, Macau casting ($1-2)
4. light pink body, gray interior, clear windshield, 8 dot wheels, "Cadillac" tempa, China casting ($1-2)

5. silver-gray body, red interior, clear windshield, 8 dot wheels, no tempa, China casting ($1-2)
6. charcoal body, red interior, chrome windshield, gray disc wheels with rubber tires, detailed trim tempa, Macau casting ($5-8)(WC)
7. white body, red interior, clear windshield, gray disc wheels with rubber tires, detailed trim tempa, China casting ($100-150)(US)
8. bright pink body, gray interior, clear windshield, 8 dot wheels, "Cadillac" tempa, Thailand casting ($1-2)
9. pink body, white interior, clear windshield, 8 dot wheels, green zig zags & blue stripes tempa, Thailand casting ($1-2)
10. metallic red body, gray interior, clear windshield, 8 dot wheels, "Official Pace Car 76th Indy" tempa, Thailand casting ($7-10)(IN)
11. metallic red body, dark gray interior, chrome windows, gray disc wheels with rubber tires, detailed trim tempa, Thailand casting ($3-4)(WC)
12. pink body, white interior, clear windshield, 8 dot wheels, green zig zags & blue stripes tempa, China casting ($1-2)
13. white body, red & black interior, clear windshield, chrome disc with rubber tires, detailed trim tempa, Thailand casting ($8-12)(UC)
14. cream body, black & tan interior, clear windshield, chrome disc with rubber tires, detailed trim tempa, Thailand casting ($3-5)(PC2-JC)

MB72-J SPRINT RACER *see MB34-E*

MB72-K DODGE ZOO TRUCK, issued 1992 (ROW) (MB223)
1. white body, blue windows, silver-gray cage with brown lions red/orange/yellow stripes tempa, 5 arch wheels, black base, Thailand casting ($3-5)(MC)

MB72-L 1962 CORVETTE *see MB71-D*

MB72-M PEUGEOT QUASAR *see MB49-E*

MB72-N STRRET STREAK *see MB62-J*

MB72-O CHEVY K-1500 PICKUP, issued 1996 (USA) (MB249)
MB54-M CHEVY K-1500 PICKUP, issued 1998 (ROW)

NOTE: Below models with clear windows, chrome rollbar & plastic base, maltese cross wheels & China casting unless otherwise noted.

1. black body, gray interior, yellow & pink tempa ($1-2)
2. florescent orange body, black interior, blue mountain design tempa ($1-2)(5pk)
3. metallic gold body, black interior, no tempa ($10-15)(CH)
4. florescent lime body, black interior, neon orange/black/white & "454" tempa ($1-2)(5pk)
5. yellow body, black interior, red & white tempa ($1-2)(5pk)
6. red body, gray interior, yellow/black/white "454" tempa ($1-2)(5pk)
7. white body, blue interior, "World Cup Field Maintenance/ France 98" tempa ($1-2)(5pk)
8. metallic blue body, gray interior, green & white tempa ($1-2)(MW54/1998)
9. metallic blue body, gray interior, red & white tempa ($1-2)(5pk)
10. black body, gray interior, yellow & pink with "Farm Credit Services" tempa ($100+)(ASAP)
11. dark blue body, turquoise interior, "Evergreen Landscaping/ Keeping Lawns Beautiful" tempa ($1-2)(MW100/1999 US)
12. lime body, dark blue interior, "01 MTN" & snowflakes tempa, 5 spoke oval wheels, dark blue rollbar ($1-2)(5pk)

NOTE: Above model with Matchbox International or Mattel casting. Below models with China casting.

13. bright blue body, neon orange interior, "Hero City" & shovel design tempa, 5 spoke oval wheels, neon orange rollbar, green base ($1-2)(5pk)
14. dark green body, white interior, "River Outfitters" tempa, 5 spoke oval wheels, black roll bar & base ($1-2)(MW23/2002 US)
15. dark green body, white interior, "River Outfitters" & "Matchbox 50" tempa, 5 spoke oval wheels, black roll bar & base ($2-4)(MW23/2002 US)

MB72-P 1965 FORD MUSTANG, issued 1999 (USA) (MB342)

NOTE: Below models with clear windows, black metal base & China casting.

1. red body, black interior, chrome disc wheels with rubber tires, "Matchbox Toy Show/ Toy Show 99" tempa ($8-12)(US)
2. red body, black & white interior, chrome disc wheels with rubber tires, white stripes tempa ($4-6)(GS)
3. white body, black interior, 5 spoke concave star wheels, blue stripes tempa ($1-2)(MW72/1999 US)
4. white body, black interior, small 5 spoke concave star wheels, blue stripes tempa ($5-8)(MW72/1999 US)
5. white body, black interior, 5 spoke concave star wheels, blue stripes & "Cruisin New England Magazine All Wheels Festival 2001" tempa ($50+)(CCI)

NOTE: Below models with Mattel China casting.

6. dark green body, black interior, chrome disc wheels with rubber tires, detailed trim tempa ($3-5)(MCC)
7. metallic blue body, black interior, chrome disc wheels with rubber tires, white stripes & "100" tempa ($3-5)(CL)
8. red body, black interior, chrome disc wheels with rubber tires, detailed trim tempa ($3-5)(MCC)
9. orange-red body, red interior, 5 spoke wheels, head & tail lights tempa ($3-5)(SF8/2004)
10. black body, red interior, 5 spoke wheels, head & tail lights tempa ($40-60)(SF8/ US promo)

MB72-Q DUNE BUGGY *see MB92-A*

MB72-R PORSCHE 911 CARRARA CABRIOLET, issued 1999 (GR) (MB423)
MB50-M PORSCHE 911 CARRARA CABRIOLET, issued 2001 (ROW)

NOTE: Below models with clear windshield, head & tail lights tempa, black plastic base & China casting.

1. light yellow body, black interior, 5 spoke concave star wheels ($4-6)(MW72/1999GR)
2. red body, black interior, 5 spoke concave star wheels ($4-6)(MW36/2000 GR)
3. red body, black interior, star with 5 spokes wheels ($4-6)(MW36/2000 GR)
4. metallic charcoal body, gray interior, 5 spoke concave star wheels ($1-2)(5pk)
5. metallic charcoal body, gray interior, star with 5 spokes wheels ($1-2)(5pk)
6. metallic charcoal body, gray interior, 10 spoke flower wheels ($1-2)(5pk)
7. red body, black interior, 10 spoke flower wheels ($4-6)(EG)
8. bright blue body, light tan interior, 10 spoke flower windows, blue trim on windshield ($2-4)(MW50/2001 ROW)
9. red body, black interior, lace wheels, head lights & small "Matchbox" tempa ($1-2)(LP)

10. silver-gray body, red interior, dark smoke windows, lace wheels, small "Matchbox" tempa ($1-2)(LP)
11. dark metallic blue body, black interior, lace wheels, none tempa ($3-5)(SG)
12. metallic red body, tan interior, lace wheels, none tempa ($2-4)(MW16/ROW 2004)
13. dark metallic maroon body, very dark gray interior, 5 spoke slotted wheels, detailed trim tempa, gray base ($2-4)(SF36/2004)

MB72-S VW DELIVERY VAN, issued 2000 (USA) (MB405)
MB52-H VW DELIVERY VAN, issued 2000 (ROW)

NOTE: Below models with smoke windows, black interior, 5 spoke concave star wheels & China casting unless otherwise noted.

1. silver-blue body, smoke green windows, white interior, white base, "TNT Tours" & motorcycle design tempa ($1-2)(MW72/2000 US)(MW52/2000 ROW)
2. silver-blue body, smoke green windows, white interior, white base, "TNT" Tours", motorcycle design & "Matchbox 2000" tempa ($2-4)(MW72/2000 USA)

NOTE: Below models with chrome base unless otherwise noted.:

3. white body, no tempa ($25-40)(ASAP/CCI blank)
4. white body, "Tyler James Elliot Memoriam Model 1" & monarch butterfly/ sky design tempa ($25-40)(CCI)
5. white body, "RCA" tempa ($20-30)(ASAP)
6. white body, "Farewell Vaarwell Wiedersehen 2000/ Welcome Welkom Willkommen 2001/ Matchbox Forum 2000-2001" tempa ($20-25)(CCI)
7. white body, "Flashback Toys & Collectibles" tempa ($25-40)(CCI)
8. white body, "Manawatu Model Diecast Collectors New Zealand 2001" tempa ($20-25)(CCI)
9. white body, "Iron City Beer" tempa ($25-40)(CCI)
10. white body, "Scooby-Doo Christmas" tempa ($75+)(CCI)
11. white body, "We've Scored 20th Anniversary Matchbox USA Convention" tempa ($10-15)(CCI)
12. white body, "All You Need To Know About Matchbox..../ Shabbir's Matchbox Website 5th Anniversary" tempa ($20-30)(CCI)
13. metallic blue body, 10 spoke flower wheels, blue/yellow/black fish design tempa ($1-2)(5pk)
14. white body with red roof, black base, 10 spoke flower wheels, Coca Cola Sign of Good Taste" tempa ($5-6)(Avon)(TP)
15. white body, "MICA Goes to Hershey 2001/ Friday June 22 2001" tempa ($15-25)(CCI)
16. white body "MICA Goes to Hershey 2001/ Saturday June 23 2001" tempa ($15-25)(CCI)
17. white body, "MICA Goes to Hershey 2001/ Sunday June 24 2001" tempa ($15-25)(CCI)
18. white body, "On the Way to Woodstock/ Hershey 2001" tempa ($15-25)(CCI)
19. white body, "Model Diecast Toy Display/ Dave's Den" tempa ($12-18)(CCI)
20. white body, "Front Royal- Warren County" tempa ($12-18)(CCI)
21. white body, "American Cancer Society" tempa ($12-18)(CCI)
22. white body, "Hot August Nights 2001" tempa ($12-18)(CCI)
23. white body, "There Are No Matchbox Treasure Hunts" tempa ($18-25)(CCI)
24. white body, "Dukes of Hazzard Fan Club" tempa ($12-18)(CCI)
25. white body, "Napanee Fire Rescue Service/ Bill Cairns Realtor" tempa ($12-18)(CCI)
26. white body, "Indian Automotive/ VW Specialists" tempa ($12-18)(CCI)
27. white body, "Dr. SDK/ Citrix Developer Network" tempa ($18-25)(CCI)
28. white body, "D&S Racing Collectibles 10th Anniversary 2001" tempa ($10-15)(CCI)
29. white body, "The Burger Bus- Snow White Grille/ God Bless America" tempa ($18-25)(CCI)
30. white body, "Melissa & Jerry Jess- Bessie" tempa ($12-18)(CCI)
31. white body, "Toy Literature Memorabilia/ Melissa & Jerry Jess" tempa ($18-25)(CCI)
32. white body, "In Memory of Our Noble Fire & Rescue Crews/ NYC Fire & EMS" tempa ($18-25)(CCI)
33. silver blue body, white base, smoke green windows, "TNT Tours" & motorcycle design tempa, 10 spoke flower wheels ($40-65)(MW52/2000 ROW)
34. lime body, black base, blue windows, "Kellogg's Rice Krispies/ Snap Crackle Pop" tempa, 10 spoke flower wheels ($3-5)(TP)(Avon)
35. metallic burgundy body, black base, clear windows, cream interior, silver stripe & "50th" logo tempa, chrome disc with rubber tires ($3-5)(CL)
36. white body, "Sheriff's Mini Cars Parramatta" tempa ($12-18)(CCI)
37. white body, "20th Century Antique & Collectables Market" tempa ($12-18)(CCI)
38. white & red body, black base, clear windows, red interior, "Coca Cola" with splashes tempa, chrome disc with rubber tires ($3-5)(Coke PC)
39. silver blue body, white base, white interior, "Mom Me & Matchbox" tempa ($25-40)(CCI)
40. white body, "Tyler James Elliot Memorial Model #4" tempa ($12-18)(CCI)
41. white body, "Franklin Pierce College/ Graduation Day 19 May 2002" tempa ($12-18)(CCI)
42. white body, "MAMBO Life Style Service" tempa ($12-18)(CCI)
43. white body, "N.S.V.A." tempa ($12-18)(CCI)
44. white body, "N.S.V.A./ 28th Van Nationals 2002" tempa ($12-18)(CCI)
45. white body, "JMB/ 10. Vyocre Nasej Spolocnosti" tempa ($12-18)(CCI)
46. white body, "It's the Parts that Counts" with blue roof tempa ($18-25)(CCI)
47. white body, "Buggies-N-Blues" tempa, 10 spoke flower wheels ($12-18)(CCI)
48. lime body, gray base, "The Georgia Peach Mobile 4" tempa, 10 spoke flower wheels ($1-2)(AM)
49. white body, "Happy 50th Birthday- Matchbox Collector on Board" tempa ($10-15)(CCI)
50. white body, "Happy 50th Birthday- Matchbox Collector on Board" tempa, 10 spoke flower wheels ($12-18)(CCI)
51. white body, "Parts Express Service" with red roof tempa ($12-18)(CCI)
52. silver blue body, white base, white interior, "TNT" & motorcycle design/ "Reading, PA" & pagoda tempa ($18-25)(CCI)
53. silver-gray body, black base, cream interior, "Matchbox Forum 5 Years/www.mbxforum.com" tempa ($12-18)(CCI)
54. silver-gray body, black base, cream interior, "Messe Nurnberg 2002" tempa ($18-25)(GR)
55. blue painted body, white interior, "MICA Goes to New York" tempa ($18-25)(CCI)

NOTE: Below models with 10 spoke flower wheels unless otherwise noted.

56. white body, "MICA Goes to New York" (blue roof letters) tempa ($12-18)(CCI)
57. white body, "MICA Goes to New York" (red roof letters) tempa ($12-18)(CCI)
58. white body, "Van Toy's R Us" tempa ($12-18)(CCI)
59. white body, "Happy 50th Birthday Poorman/ Long Time" tempa ($12-18)(CCI)
60. white body, "30th National Truck-In" tempa ($12-18)(CCI)
61. white body, "Waterman's/ Tara & Will" tempa, 5 spoke concave star wheels ($18-25)(CCI)
62. metallic blue painted body, "Works of Art with Wheels/ CCI" tempa, 5 spoke concave star wheels ($18-25)(CCI)
63. iridescent white body, black base, clear windows, "Matchbox Series" tempa ($3-5)(SG)
64. white body, "D&S Racing Collectibles Merry Christmas 2002" tempa ($12-18)(CCI)
65. white body, "1st Annual MAMBO Memorial" (all black print) ($12-18)(CCI)
66. white body, "1st Annual MAMBO Memorial" tempa (green & black print)($25-40)(CCI)
67. white body, "1st Annual MAMBO Memorial" tempa (black & gold print)($75+)(CCI)
68. silver blue body, blue base, amber windows, green interior, "Spongebob" tempa ($1-2)(5pk)
69. blue body, yellow base, amber windows, green interior, "Spongebob" tempa ($1-2)(5pk)
70. unpainted body, black base, pop art decals ($75+)(FA)
71. white body, "Happy New Year 2003" tempa ($10-15)(CCI)
72. white body, "People Kars Season's Greeting" with green roof stripes tempa ($18-25)(CCI)
73. white body, "People Kars Season's Greetings" with red roof stripes tempa ($18-25)(CCI)
74. iridescent white body, black base, clear windows, "Matchbox Series- the Real Birthday" with red roof tempa ($18-25)(CCI)
75. iridescent white body, black base, clear windows, "Matchbox Series- the Real Birthday" with green roof tempa ($25-40)(CCI)
76. iridescent white body, black base, clear windows, "Matchbox Series- the Real Birthday" with gold roof tempa ($75+)(CCI)
77. white body, "Parts Express Service" with black roof tempa ($12-18)(CCI)
78. white body, "N.S.V.A./ 30th Anniversary Van" tempa ($12-18)(CCI)
79. white body, "N.S.V.A./ 2003 N.S.V.A. Club Van" tempa ($18-25)(CCI)
80. white body, "N.S.V.A./ 2003 Committee Van" tempa ($75+)(CCI)
81. white body, "Volkswagen Model Club 25 Years" with green roof & print tempa ($12-18)(CCI)
82. white body, "Volkswagen Model Club 25 Years" with blue roof & print tempa ($12-18)(CCI)
83. white body, "Lisa's Baby Delivery" tempa ($18-25)(CCI)
84. white body, "In Memory of Turkey" tempa ($12-18)(CCI)
85. white body, "Fayetteville Dogwood Festival 2003" tempa ($10-15)(CCI)
86. metallic silver body, black base, clear windows, "Model & Hobby 2002/11.10.2002" tempa ($18-25)(C2)
87. metallic silver body, black base, clear windows, "Model & Hobby 2002/12.10.2002" tempa ($18-25)(C2)
88. metallic silver body, black base, clear windows, "Model & Hobby 2002/13.10.2002" tempa ($18-25)(CCI)
89. white body, "75th Annual Jubilee Day/ Mechanicsburg Chamber of Commerce" tempa ($12-18)(CCI)
90. white body, "DBG Der Busbesitzer Gruppe" tempa ($12-18)(CCI)
91. white body, "MBUSA Convention" tempa ($10-15)(CCI)
92. white body, "MBUSA Convention" tempa, 5 spoke concave star wheels ($18-25)(CCI)
93. white & yellow body, white base, clear windows, brown interior, "Drink Coca Cola" tempa, chrome disc with rubber tires ($10-15)(Coke diorama)
94. white body, "Caldwell Medical Center/ Drs. Edwin & Lynette Suarez" tempa ($12-18)(CCI)
95. white body, "Super Bowl XX 1985/ Marion & Joe DiNovo 52 Years" tempa ($18-25)(CCI)
96. white body, "49th Annual Black Walnut Festival" tempa ($10-15)(CCI)
97. white body, "USA" with flag, Uncle Sam & firecrackers design tempa ($12-18)(CCI)
98. white body, "It's A Boy! Michael Anthony Hamm" tempa ($12-18)(CCI)
99. white body, "Matchbox Albuquerque/ 1st Annual Matchbox Community Gathering" tempa ($12-18)(CCI)
100. silver blue body, lime base, red windows & interior, Clifford & flowery design tempa ($1-2)(5pk)
101. iridescent white body, black base, "Matchbox Series-3.10.2003 Matchbox Hero City" tempa ($18-25)(C2)(GR)
102. metallic lime body, yellow base, amber windows, blue interior, "Spongebob" tempa ($1-2)(CA)
103. white body, "Church On The Rock" tempa ($12-18)(CCI)

NOTE: Below models with 5 spoke concave star wheels unless otherwise noted.

104. white body, "Merry Christmas 2003" with reindeer & cardinals tempa ($12-18)(CCI)
105. white body, "Amelia Barbara Cupal" tempa ($12-18)(CCI)
106. white body, "God Bless Our Land/ Happy New Year/ 2004" tempa ($12-18)(CCI)
107. white body, "Vintage Volkswagen Club of America 2004" tempa ($18-25)(CCI)
108. white body, "30th Van Nationals/ National Street Van Association" tempa ($18-25)(CCI)
109. white body, "Kiss A Kollector/ Matchbox Toy Show" with red lettering, 10 spoke flower wheels ($12-18)(CCI)
110. white body, "Kiss A Kollector/ Matchbox Toy Show" with brown lettering, 10 spoke flower wheels ($12-18)(CCI)
111. lime body, "Hershey, PA A Peach of A Place/ Matchbox Toy Show- Hershey Welcome Back 2004" tempa, 10 spoke flower wheels, gray base ($18-25)(CCI)
112. white body, green doors with "Polizei" & "2. BPA Leipzig" tempa ($25-40)(C2)(GR)
113. white body, no tempa, 10 spoke flower wheels ($10-15)(CCI blank)
114. lime body, "Coca-Cola Football Town/ Total Tailgate" tempa, 10 spoke flower wheels, black base ($2-4)(CK)
115. white body, "5th Annual Salmon River Festival 2004" tempa, 5 spoke concave star wheels ($18-25)(CCI)
116. white body, "Apple-Arts-Crafts/ 30th Annual Apple Harvest Arts & Crafts Festival", 5 spoke concave star wheels ($18-25)(CCI)
117. white body, "Antiques on the Mall- Halloween 2004/ Happy Halloween 2004", 5 spoke concave star wheels ($18-25)(CCI)
118. white body, "Creanies Ice Cream" tempa, 5 spoke concave star wheels ($18-25)(CCI)
119. white body, amber windows, yellow interior, "Magenta" tempa, purple base, 10 spoke flower wheels ($1-2)(5pk)
120. white & lime body, gray interior, silver stripe & detailed trim tempa, white base, 5 spoke slotted wheels ($1-2)(SF54/2004)

MB72-T RESCUE CRANE, issued 2001 (MB527)

NOTE: Below models with 4 spoke domed wheels & China casting.

1. red body, orange crane cab, gray boom, amber windows, "X-Treme Action", cross & stripes tempa, black base ($1-2)(MW72/2001)
2. white body, red crane cab, yellow boom, gray base, blue windows, "42" & steer head tempa, gray base ($1-2)(5pk)
3. lemon body, green crane cab, red boom, smoke windows, "24 Alarm" tempa, gray base ($1-2)(MW24/2003)
4. lemon body, green crane cab, red boom, smoke windows, "24 Alarm" & "Hero City" tempa, gray base ($2-4)(MW24/2003)
5. metallic yellow body, green crane cab, red boom, smoke windows, "24 Alarm" tempa, gray base, gold hubs ($3-4)(20pk)
6. red body, neon orange cab, yellow boom, black windows, "Team" tempa, gray base, 5 crown dot wheels ($1-2)(5pk)

MB72-U VW MICROBUS, issued 2002 (MB552)

NOTE: Below models with China casting.

1. silver blue & blue body, smoke windows, gray interior, black base, lace wheels, no tempa ($1-2)(MW72/2002)
2. silver blue & blue body, smoke windows, gray interior, black base, lace wheels, "Matchbox 50" tempa ($3-5)(MW72/2002)

NOTE: Versions 3-10 were a set of 8 individual models distributed to dealers at the Mattel Toy Show in 2002.

3. silver blue & blue body, smoke windows, gray interior, black base, chrome disc wheels with rubber tires, "Matchbox 50" tempa ($10-15)(US)
4. silver blue body & blue body, smoke windows, tan interior, black base, chrome disc wheels with rubber tires, "Matchbox 50" tempa ($10-15)(US)
5. silver blue & blue body, clear windows, tan interior, black base, chrome disc wheels with rubber tires, "Matchbox 50" tempa ($10-15)(US)
6. silver blue & blue body, clear windows, gray interior, black base, chrome disc wheels with rubber tires, "Matchbox 50" tempa ($10-15)(US)
7. silver blue & blue body, clear windows, gray interior, gray base, chrome disc wheels with rubber tires, "Matchbox 50" tempa ($10-15)(US)
8. silver blue & blue body, clear windows, tan interior, gray base, chrome disc wheels with rubber tires, "Matchbox 50" tempa ($10-15)(US)
9. silver blue & blue body, smoke windows, tan interior, gray base, chrome disc wheels with rubber tires, "Matchbox 50" tempa ($10-15)(US)
10. silver blue & blue body, smoke windows, gray interior, gray base, chrome disc wheels with rubber tires, "Matchbox 50" tempa ($10-15)(US)
11. iridescent cream & bronze body, chrome windows, black interior, chrome base, lace wheels, "Matchbox Hero City 2004 Pre-Toy Fair" tempa ($18-25)(US)
12. metallic blue body, blue windows, white interior, black base, lace wheels, "Hero City Elementary" tempa ($1-2)(MW54/2003 US)
13. metallic blue body, blue windows, white interior, black base, lace wheels, "Hero City Elementary" & "Hero City" tempa ($3-5)(MW54/2003 US)
14. iridescent white body, blue windows, black interior, black base, lace wheels, two tone blue design tempa ($1-2)(5pk)
15. iridescent white body, chrome windows, black interior, chrome base, lace wheels, "Matchbox Hero City/ Ready to Play Spielsets" tempa, issued in plexibox ($25-40)(GR)
16. metallic blue body, black windows, yellow interior, black base, lace wheels, "X-Treme Park" & yellow design tempa ($1-2)(MW57/2004)
17. blue body, yellow windows, white interior, light blue base, lace wheels, "The Jetsons" tempa ($1-2)(5pk)
18. metallic silver & metallic red body, smoke windows, black interior, dark gray base, 5 spoke slotted wheels, detailed trim tempa ($2-4)(SF31/2004)
19. charcoal body, smoke windows, red interior, black base, lace wheels, head & tail lights tempa ($3-5)(SoC)
20. yellow body, blue windows, blue interior, green base, 10 spoke flower wheels, "Blue" tempa ($1-2)(5pk)

MB72-V PT CRUISER CONVERTIBLE, issued 2003 (MB580)

NOTE: Below models with black plastic base & China casting.

1. metallic red body, smoke windshield, black interior, 10 spoke flower wheels, "72" tempa ($1-2)(MW72/2003)
2. metallic red body, smoke windshield, black interior, 10 spoke flower wheels, "72" & "Hero City" tempa ($2-4)(MW72/2003)
3. dark purple body, clear windshield with trim, cream interior, chrome disc wheels with rubber tires, detailed trim tempa ($3-5)(SH)
4. lemon body, clear windshield, brown interior, 5 spoke slotted wheels, black tonneau with head & tail lights tempa ($3-5)(SF10/2004)
5. metallic blue body, amber windshield, red interior, 10 spoke flower wheels, "Wonder Woman" tempa ($1-2)(5pk)
6. metallic blue body, red windshield, cream interior, lace wheels, "Nick" tempa, dark blue base ($1-2)(5pk)

MB72-W BULLDOZER, issued 2004 (MB601)

1. orange body, gray interior & motor, neon orange blade, dark blue base, black wheels, "Hero City" & bulldozer tempa, China casting ($1-2)(5pk)
2. dark yellow body, red interior & motor, yellow blade, gray base, black wheels, "Hero City" & bulldozer tempa, China casting ($1-2)(MW72/2004)

MB73-A MERCURY COMMUTER, issued 1970

NOTE: Below models with clear windows, ivory interior, 5 spoke wheels & England casting. Earliest versions with narrow wheels with later versions having wide wheels.

1. lime body, unpainted base, no labels ($20-25)
2. red body, unpainted base, cow head label ($20-25)
3. red body, unpainted base, cat head label (from MB1-B) ($150-175)
4. red body, silver-gray base, cat head label (from MB1-B) ($150-175)

MB73-B WEASEL, issued 1974 (MB773)
MB70-G WEASEL, reissued 1993 (USA)
MB77-B WEASEL, reissued 1996 (USA)

NOTE: Versions 1 to 9 with black turret. Below models with metal base with plastic base insert & 5 spoke wheels.

1. metallic green body & base, green base insert, silver hubs, no tempa, England casting ($4-6)
2. olive drab body, metallic green base, green base insert, black hubs, no tempa, England casting ($65-80)(TP)
3. olive green body, metallic green base, green base insert, black hubs, no tempa, England casting ($6-8)(TP)
4. olive green body & base, green base insert, black hubs, no tempa, England casting ($6-8)(TP)
5. olive green body & base, green base insert, silver hubs, no tempa, England casting ($6-8)(TP)

6. bright olive body & base, black base insert, silver hubs, no tempa, England casting ($6-8)(TP)
7. bright olive body & base, black base insert, black hubs, no tempa, England casting ($6-8)(TP)
8. olive green body & base, black base insert, black hubs, tan & black camouflage tempa, Macau casting ($4-5)(CM)
9. black body & base, black base insert, black hubs, yellow & gray camouflage tempa, Macau casting ($4-5)(CM)
10.beige body, black base, black base insert, black hubs, brown/black/white camouflage tempa, beige turret, China casting ($1-2)
11.beige body, black base, black base insert, black hubs, brown/black/white camouflage tempa, beige turret, Thailand casting ($1-2)
12. pink-tan body, black base, black base insert, black hubs, green & brown camouflage tempa, light tan turret, Thailand casting ($1-2)(5pk)
13. olive body, black base, black base insert, black hubs, star & "M-3173" tempa, olive turret, Thailand casting ($2-3)
NOTE: Some of this version model was packaged in blisterpacks as #77 in error ($2-3)
14. green body & turret, black base, black base insert, black hubs, black & brown camouflage tempa, Thailand casting ($1-2)(5pk)
15. dull olive body, dull olive base with Manaus tab, green base insert, black hubs, green painted turret ($35-50)(BR)
16. black body & base, black base insert, yellow & gray camouflage with no gray at front or rear tempa, China casting ($18-25)(CM)(CHI)(MP)

MB73-C MODEL A FORD, issued 1979 (MB073)
MB55-I MODEL A FORD, reissued 1991 (USA)
MB25-H MODEL A FORD, reissued 1993 (ROW)

NOTE: Some variations may be found with 5 crown front wheels used on the rear axles or dot dash rear wheels used on the front axles. Below models with black plastic base.

1. cream body, dark green chassis with spare tire cast, green windows, no tempa, 5 crown front & dot dash rear wheels, England casting ($6-8)
2. cream body, dark green chassis with spare tire cast, no windows, no tempa, 5 crown front & dot dash rear wheels, England casting ($6-8)
3. cream body, dark green chassis, green windows, no tempa, 5 crown front & dot dash rear wheels, England casting ($4-6)
4. cream body, dark green chassis, no windows, no tempa, 5 crown front & dot dash rear wheels, England casting ($4-6)
5. metallic green body, dark green chassis, green windows, no tempa, 5 crown front & dot dash rear wheels, England casting ($4-6)
6. metallic green body, dark green chassis, no windows, no tempa, 5 crown front & dot dash rear wheels, England casting ($4-6)
7. metallic green body, dark green chassis, green windows, "Climat" label on trunk, 5 crown front & dot dash rear wheels, England casting ($125-175)(FR)
8. beige body, brown chassis, amber windows, no tempa, 5 crown front & dot dash rear wheels, England casting ($4-6)
9. beige body, brown chassis, clear windows, no tempa, 5 crown front & dot dash rear wheels, England casting ($4-6)
10. beige body, brown chassis, clear windows, no tempa, 5 crown front & dot dash rear wheels, Macau casting ($2-4)
11 red body, black chassis, clear windows, no tempa, 5 crown front & dot dash rear wheels, Macau casting ($2-4)
12. black body & chassis, clear windows, flames tempa, 5 arch front & racing special rear wheels, Macau casting ($2-4)
13. purple body, yellow chassis, clear windows, stripes tempa, 5 arch front & racing special rear wheels, Macau casting ($3-5)
14. yellow body, red chassis, clear windows, "Pava" tempa, 5 arch front & racing special rear wheels, Macau casting ($8-12)(DK)
15. red body, dark green chassis, clear windows, no tempa, 5 crown front & dot dash wheels, Macau casting ($15-20)(UK)(OP)
16. red body, dark green chassis, clear windows, no tempa, 5 crown front & dot dash rear wheels, Thailand casting ($15-20)(UK)(OP)
17. red body, dark green chassis, clear windows, no tempa, 5 crown front & dot dash rear wheels, China casting ($15-20)(UK)(OP)
18. purple body, yellow chassis, clear windows, stripes tempa, 5 arch front & racing special rear wheels, Thailand casting ($2-4)
19. orange-yellow body, white chassis, clear windows, "GT" & yellow jacket tempa, 5 crown front & dot dash rear wheels, Thailand casting ($6-8)(WR)
20. powder blue body, red chassis, clear windows, clown tempa, yellow 5 arch front & racing special rear wheels, Thailand casting ($7-10)(MC)
21. white body, pink chassis, clear windows, zigzag design tempa, 5 arch front & racing special rear wheels, Thailand casting ($2-3)
22. dark blue body & chassis, clear windows, green & pink grid tempa, 5 arch front & racing special rear wheels, Thailand casting ($1-2)(MP)
23. metallic red body & chassis, clear windows, black roof & detailed trim tempa, 5 arch front & gray disc insert racing special rear wheels, Thailand casting ($2-4)(CC)
24. red body & chassis, clear windows, blue & yellow tempa, 5 arch front & racing special rear wheels, Thailand casting ($1-2)(5pk)
25. metallic gold body, black chassis, clear windows, "Matchbox Collectors Club" tempa, 5 crown front & dot dash rear wheels, Thailand casting ($10-15)(US)
26. white body, dark purple chassis, clear windows, "Temecula Rod Run 1996" tempa, 5 arch front & racing special rear wheels, Thailand casting ($8-12)(WR)
27. metallic gold body, black chassis, clear windows, "American Iron Cruise 96/Memory Lane" tempa, 5 crown front & dot dash rear wheels, Thailand casting ($15-25)(C2)
28. dark gray body, black chassis, clear windows, "The Untouchables" & bullet marks tempa, 5 crown front & 5 crown rear wheels, China casting ($4-6)(STR)
29. cream body, dark green chassis, green windows, "Hershey 2000" & "Matchbox USA" logo tempa, 5 crown front & dot dash rear wheels, England casting ($75+)(CCI)
30. black body, light gray chassis, clear windows, "The New Crawford" tempa, 5 crown front & dot dash rear wheels, China casting ($75+)(ASAP)
31. black body, light gray chassis, clear windows, no tempa, 5 crown front & dot dash rear wheels, China casting ($25-40)(ASAP blank)
32. black body, light gray chassis, clear windows, "K" in circle tempa, 5 crown front & dot dash rear wheels, China casting ($50+)(ASAP)
33. metallic gold body, black chassis, clear windows, "Hans Irmer/Cottbus 2000" tempa, 5 crown front & dot dash rear wheels, China casting ($18-25)(C2)(GR)
34. black body, light gray chassis, clear windows, "Rental Industry Services" tempa, 5 crown front & dot dash rear wheels, China casting ($50+)(ASAP)

MB73-D TV NEWS TRUCK *see MB68-G*

MB73-E MERCEDES TRACTOR, issued 1990 (USA) (MB218)
MB27-E MERCEDES TRACTOR, issued 1990 (ROW)

NOTE: Below models with black plastic base.

1. pea green upper body, olive chassis & interior, pea green wheels, no tempa, Macau casting ($1-2)
2. pea green upper body, olive chassis & interior, pea green wheels, no tempa, Thailand casting ($1-2)
3. green upper body, pale yellow chassis & interior, green wheels, no tempa, Thailand casting ($2-4)(TP)(TC)
4. pea green upper body, olive chassis & interior, pea green wheels, "MB Trac" tempa, Thailand casting ($1-2)
5. dark green upper body, black plastic chassis, olive interior, pea green wheels, no tempa, Thailand casting ($2-4)(FM)
6. blue upper body, red chassis & interior, blue wheels, "Chieftan Power" tempa, China casting ($1-2)(MW90/1999 US)(MW5/1999 ROW)
7. green upper body, black chassis & interior, red wheels, white roof & "FA2318" tempa, China casting ($4-5)(MW5/1999 GR)
8. mustard upper body, light brown chassis & interior, yellow wheels, "Power" & "Matchbox 2000" tempa, China casting ($2-4)(MW46/2000 US)
9. mustard upper body, light brown chassis & interior, yellow wheels, "Power" tempa, China casting ($1-2)(MW46/2000 US/MW26/2000 ROW)
10. green upper body, yellow chassis & interior, green wheels, "Iowa/ 29 Best Farms" tempa, China casting ($1-2)(AM)

MB73-F JEEP CHEROKEE *see MB27-D*

MB73-G ROLLS ROYCE SILVER SPIRIT *see MB66-F*

MB73-H ROTWHEELER, issued 1995 (USA) (MB275)
MB47-F ROTWHEELER, issued 1995 (ROW)

NOTE: Below models with chrome eyes & engine and Goodyear slicks wheels

1. brown body, brown base, red upper & lower gums with black collar tempa, Thailand casting ($1-2)
2. brown body, brown base, brown upper & red lower gums with black collar tempa, Thailand casting ($1-2)
3. black body, black base, black upper & red lower gums with red collar tempa, Thailand casting ($1-2)
4. metallic gold body, black base, red upper & lower gums with plain collar tempa, Thailand casting ($5-10)(CH)
5. red body, red base, red upper & lower gums with black collar tempa, Thailand casting ($1-2)(MW42/1998 US)
6. red body, dark red base, red upper & lower gums with black collar tempa, Thailand casting ($1-2)(MW42/1998 US)
7. red body, dark red base, red upper & lower gums with black collar tempa, China casting ($1-2)(MW42/1998 US)

MB73-I DIRT BIKE *see MB93-A*

MB73-J 1955 CHEVY BEL AIR, issued 1999 (USA) (MB358)

NOTE: Below models with clear windows & China casting.

1. dark green & cream body, cream roof, green interior, chrome disc wheels with rubber tires, black painted base, silver stripes tempa ($5-8)(FE)
2. unpainted body, cream roof, green interior, chrome disc wheels with rubber tires, chrome base, none tempa ($5-8)(FE)
3. bright blue body, white roof, black interior, 5 spoke concave star wheels, chrome base, white stripes & "Bel Air" tempa ($1-2)(MW73/1999 US)
4. lemon body, white roof, black interior, chrome wire disc wheels with rubber tires, chrome base, "Coca Cola" tempa ($4-6)(Coke PC)
5. lemon body, white roof, black interior, chrome mag disc wheels with rubber tires, chrome base, "Coca Cola" tempa ($4-6)(Coke PC)
6. lemon body, white roof, red interior, 5 spoke concave star wheels, chrome base, "Coca Cola" tempa ($3-5)(TP-Avon)
7. red body, white roof, white interior, 5 spoke concave star wheels, chrome base, "Midwest Collector's/ Dinner Model" tempa ($20-30)(ASAP)
8. bright blue body, white roof, black interior, 5 spoke concave star wheels, chrome base, "Class of 1950/ Westfield NJ Reunion 2000/ W.H.S." tempa ($15-20)(CCI)
9. bright blue body, white roof, black interior, 5 spoke concave star wheels, chrome base, "Cruisin' New England Magazine" tempa ($25-50)(CCI)
10. red body, white roof, white interior, 5 spoke concave star wheels, chrome base, "RCA" tempa ($20-30)(ASAP)
11. red body, white roof, white interior, 5 spoke concave star wheels, chrome base, none tempa ($25-40)(ASAP blank)
12. bright blue body, white roof, white interior, 5 spoke concave star wheels, chrome base, "Matchbox USA Road Race Participant" tempa ($75+)(CCI)
13. baby blue & dark cream body, dark cream roof, blue & white interior, chrome disc with rubber tires, chrome base, detailed trim tempa ($3-5)(BJ)
14. red body, white roof, white interior, 5 spoke concave star wheels, chrome base, "The New Crawford" tempa ($50+)(ASAP)
15. red body, white roof, white interior, 5 spoke concave star wheels, chrome base, "CNBC" tempa ($50+)(ASAP)
16. red body, white roof, white interior, 5 spoke concave star wheels, chrome base, no tempa ($25-40)(ASAP blank)
17. red body, white roof, white interior, lace wheels, chrome base, no tempa ($25-40)(ASAP blank)
18. red body, white roof, white interior, lace wheels, chrome base, "Black Walnut Festival 50th Anniversary" tempa ($18-25)(CCI)
19. red & cream body, cream roof, red interior, 5 spoke slotted wheels, chrome base, silver pinstriping & detailed trim tempa ($1-2)(SF49/2004)

MB73-K CONCEPT I BEETLE CABRIOLET *see MB81-A*

MB73-L PONTIAC PIRANHA, issued 2002 (USA) (MB556)
MB59-N PONTIAC PIRANHA, issued 2003 (ROW)

NOTE: Below models with dark smoke window & roof, 10 spoke flower wheels, black plastic base & China casting.

1. purple body, silver-gray interior, silver-gray doors & "Piranha" tempa ($1-2)(MW73/2002 US)
2. purple body, silver-gray interior, silver-gray doors, "Piranha" & "Matchbox 50" tempa ($75+)(MW73/2002 US)
3. orange-yellow body, purple interior, "000-321-7879" & pet design tempa ($1-2)(MW59/2003)
4. orange-yellow body, purple interior, "000-321-7879" & pet design with "Hero City" tempa ($3-5)(MW59/2003)
5. bright blue body, black interior, "Wonder Woman" tempa ($1-2)(5pk)
6. metallic gold body, black interior, "Wonder Woman" tempa ($1-2)(CA)
7. black body, neon yellow interior, clear windows & roof, scorpion design tempa ($1-2)(5pk)

MB73-M SMART CABRIO, issued 2002 (ROW) (MB561)

NOTE: Below models with lace wheels & China casting.

1. metallic silver body, smoke windows, black interior, small "Matchbox" logo tempa, black base ($2-4)(MW73/2002 ROW)
2. metallic silver body, smoke windows, black interior, small "Matchbox" logo & "Matchbox 50" tempa, black base ($3-5)(MW73/2002 ROW)
3. metallic lime body, smoke windows, blue interior, "Smart" with triangles on blue door tempa, black base ($1-2)(5pk)
4. metallic blue body, smoke windows, black interior, black design tempa, black base ($1-2)(SG)
5. lemon body, clear windows, black interior, "BVB09 Borussia Dortmund" tempa, black base ($6-8)(GR)
6. light blue body, amber windows, bright blue interior, Easter bunny tempa, bright blue base ($1-2)(MP)
7. white body, dark smoke windows, black interior, "Eiffel Tower" with red & blue bands & black tonneau tempa, black base ($1-2)(AW)
8. light blue body, dark smoke windows, black interior, hockey player tempa, black base ($1-2)(5pk)

MB73-N HUMMER H2 SUV CONCEPT, issued 2003 (MB526)

NOTE: Below models with smoke windows, black roof insert & China casting.

1. lemon body, "Matchbox 73" tempa, 4 spoke domed wheels, gray plastic base ($1-2)(MW73/2003)
2. lemon body, "Matchbox 73" & "Hero City" tempa, 4 spoke domed wheels, gray plastic base ($3-5)(MW73/2003)
3. orange body, "The Flintstones" tempa, 5 crown dot wheels, light blue base ($1-2)(5pk)
4. black body, black windows, silver hood louvers & detailed trim tempa, 5 spoke slotted wheels, chrome base ($1-2)(SF43/2004)

MB74-A DAIMLER BUS, issued 1970

NOTE: All versions can be found with red or black axle covers. Below models with white interior, 5 spoke wheels & England casting.

1. red body & base, "Esso Extra Petrol" labels ($18-25)
2. red body, pink-red base, "Esso Extra Petrol" labels ($18-25)
3. pink-red body, red base, "Esso Extra Petrol" labels ($18-25)
4. pink-red body & base, "Esso Extra Petrol" labels ($18-25)
5. red body & base, "The Baron of Beef" labels ($175-225)(LE)
6. red body & base, "Inn On The Park" labels ($200-275)(LE)
7. red body & base, "The Miniature Vehicle/N.A.M.C." labels ($200-275)(US)
8. red body & base, "Beefeater Gin" labels ($300-450)(LE)
9. red body & base, "Fly Cyprus Airways/ London Frankfurt Athens Nicosia" labels ($250-400)(LE)
10. red body & base, "ICP Interchemicals & Plastics" labels ($750+)(LE)
11. red body & base, "Cyprus the Perfect Island" labels ($250-400)(LE)

NOTE: Superfast models in green can not be verified to exist.

MB74-B TOE JOE, issued 1972

NOTE: Below models with yellow-orange interior, amber windows & England casting unless otherwise noted.

1. metallic lime body, unpainted base, green booms, red hooks, 5 spoke wheels ($4-6)
2. metallic lime body, silver-gray base, green booms, red hooks, 5 spoke wheels ($4-6)
3. metallic lime body, unpainted base, green booms, red hooks, maltese cross wheels ($4-6)
4. metallic lime body, black base, green booms, red hooks, 5 arch wheels ($4-6)
5. metallic lime body, unpainted base, green booms, black hooks, 5 arch wheels ($4-6)
6. metallic lime body, unpainted base, green booms, red hooks, 5 arch wheels ($4-6)
7. metallic lime body, unpainted base, red booms, black hooks, 5 spoke wheels ($4-6)
8. dark metallic lime body, black base, green booms, red hooks, 5 arch wheels ($4-6)
9. dark metallic lime body, black base, red booms, black hooks, 5 arch wheels ($15-18)(TP)
10. dark metallic lime body, unpainted base, red booms, black hooks, dot dash wheels ($15-18)(TP)
11. dark metallic lime body, unpainted base, white booms, black hooks, 5 arch wheels ($125-175)(TP)
12. dark metallic lime body, black base, white booms, black hooks, 5 arch wheels ($125-175)(TP)
13. yellow body, unpainted base, green booms, black hooks, 5 arch wheels ($15-18)(TP)
14. yellow body, black base, green booms, red hooks, 5 arch wheels ($15-18)(TP)
15. yellow body, unpainted base, red booms, black hooks, 5 arch wheels ($3-5)(TP)
16. yellow body, black base, red booms, black hooks, 5 arch wheels ($3-5)(TP)
17. yellow body, black base, red booms, black hooks, 5 spoke wheels ($3-5)(TP)
18. yellow body, black base, red booms, black hooks, dot dash wheels ($4-6)(TP)
19. yellow body, black base, white booms, black hooks, 5 arch wheels ($150-175)(TP)
20. yellow-orange body, unpainted base, red booms, black hooks, 5 arch wheels ($3-5)(TP)
21. yellow body, unpainted base, red booms, black hooks, 5 arch wheels, Hitchhiker" labels ($125-175)(TP)
22. yellow-orange body, unpainted base, red booms, black hooks, 5 arch wheels, "Hitchhiker" labels ($125-175)(TP)
23. yellow-orange body, unpainted base, white booms, red hooks, 5 arch wheels ($150-175)(P)
24. red body, black base, green booms, black hooks, 5 arch wheels ($175-250)(TP)
25. red body, black base, red booms, black hooks, 5 arch wheels ($175-250)(TP)
26. red body, black base, red booms, red hooks, 5 arch wheels ($175-250)(TP)
27. bright lime body, black (Manaus inscription) base, green booms, red hooks, 5 arch wheels ($250+)(BR)

MB74-C COUGAR VILLAGER, issued 1978

NOTE: Below models with clear windows, dot dash wheels & England casting unless otherwise noted.

1. light green body, green tailgate, yellow interior, unpainted base ($2-4)
2. light green body, green tailgate, yellow-orange interior, unpainted base ($2-4)
3. dark green body, green tailgate, yellow interior, unpainted base ($2-4)
4. dark green body, green tailgate, yellow-orange interior, unpainted base ($2-4)
5. very dark green body, green tailgate, yellow interior, unpainted base ($2-4)
6. very dark green body, green tailgate, yellow-orange interior, unpainted base ($2-4)

7. dark blue body, blue tailgate, yellow interior, unpainted base ($2-4)
8. dark blue body, blue tailgate, yellow-orange interior, unpainted base ($2-4)
9. olive green body, green tailgate, yellow interior, unpainted with Manaus tab base ($250+)(BR)
   NOTE: Available as a Bulgarian casting. Assorted colors available ($15-25)

MB74-D ORANGE PEEL, issued 1981 (USA)
   NOTE: Hong Kong castings can be "Lesney" or "Matchbox International" castings. Macau and China castings are "Matchbox International". Below models with chrome interior..
1. white body, amber windows, black base, dark orange "Orange Peel" tempa, 5 arch front & maltese cross rear wheels, Hong Kong casting ($3-5)
2. white body, amber windows, black base, light orange "Orange Peel" tempa, 5 arch front & maltese cross rear wheels, Macau casting ($3-5)
3. white body, amber windows, black base, light orange "Orange Peel" tempa, 5 arch front & maltese cross rear wheels, Hong Kong casting ($3-5)
4. white body, amber windows, black base, light orange "Orange Peel" tempa, maltese cross front & rear wheels, Macau casting ($3-5)
5. purple body, clear windows, black base, white/yellow/green flames tempa, 5 arch front & 5 crown rear wheels, China casting ($1-2)(AV)
6. pink body, clear windows, black base, dark green with snake tempa, 5 arch front & 5 crown rear wheels, China casting ($3-5)(PC13)
   NOTE: Rear bumper can be found painted or unpainted & interior seat can be painted blue or not at all- found in MW20 singles in Canada.

MB74-E FIAT ABARTH *see MB9-D*

MB74-F MUSTANG GT, issued 1984 (USA) (MB132)
   NOTE: Below models with black plastic base, clear windows & 5 arch front wheels
1. light orange body, racing special rear wheels, yellow & blue stripes tempa, Macau casting ($2-4)
2. dark orange body, racing special rear wheels, yellow & blue stripes tempa, Macau casting ($2-4)
3. dark orange body, racing special rear wheels, orange & blue stripes tempa, Macau casting ($2-4)
4. dark orange body, dot dash rear wheels, yellow & blue stripes tempa, China casting ($2-4)
5. dull orange body, dot dash rear wheels, yellow & blue stripes tempa, China casting ($2-4)
6. pearly silver body, racing special rear wheels, purple & yellow stripes tempa, China casting ($2-4)
7. white body, racing special rear wheels, red squiggly lines tempa, Thailand casting ($1-2)(5pk)
8. red body, racing special rear wheels, black stripes tempa, China casting ($1-2)(5pk)

MB74-H GRAND PRIX RACING CAR, issued 1987 (USA) (MB203/228/247)
MB14-H GRAND PRIX RACING CAR, issued 1987 (ROW)
   NOTE: Below models with metal base & Goodyear slicks wheels unless otherwise noted.
1. white & powder blue body, dark blue base, red driver, black airfoil, "15/Goodyear/Shell" tempa, Macau casting ($3-4)
2. red body, black base, white driver, black airfoil, "27 Fiat" tempa, Macau casting ($1-2)
3. red body, black base, white driver, black airfoil, "27 Fiat" tempa, Thailand casting ($1-2)
4. yellow body & base, red driver, dark yellow airfoil, "Pennzoil 2" tempa, China casting ($3-4)(IN)
5. dark orange & white body, white base, red driver, orange airfoil, "Indy 4" tempa, China casting ($3-4)(IN)
6. dark yellow body & base, red driver, orange-yellow airfoil, "Squirt" tempa, Thailand casting ($18-25)(US)(OP)
7. chrome plated body, black base, white driver, black airfoil, no tempa, Thailand casting ($12-18)(C2)
8. red body, black base, white driver, black airfoil, "27 Fiat" tempa, China casting ($1-2)
9. red body, black (plastic) base, white driver, black airfoil, "27 Fiat" tempa, China casting ($15-20)
10. red body, black base, white driver, black airfoil, "Scotch/Target" tempa, Thailand casting ($3-4)(IN)
    NOTE: Versions 11, 13-15 cast with small or large airfoil.
11. blue body & base, yellow driver, blue airfoil, "Panasonic 7" tempa, Thailand casting ($3-4)(IN)
12. white & blue body, blue base, red driver, blue airfoil, "Indy 76" tempa, Thailand casting ($3-4)(IN)
13. white & black body, black metal base, red driver, black airfoil, "Havoline/K-Mart 6" tempa, Thailand casting ($3-4)(IN)
14. white & black body, black metal base, red driver, black airfoil, "Havoline/ K-Mart 5" tempa, Thailand casting ($3-4)(IN)
15. yellow body & base, red driver, yellow airfoil, "Pennzoil 4" tempa, Thailand casting ($3-4)(IN)
16. orange/lavender/white body, lavender base, white driver, white airfoil, "Indy 1" tempa, Thailand casting ($4-6)(IN)
17. white & black body, black metal base, red driver, black airfoil, "Texaco/K-Mart 1" tempa, Thailand casting ($3-4)(IN)
18. black body, black metal base, pink driver, black airfoil, "Indy 5" & green/pink spatter tempa, Thailand casting ($3-4)(IN)
19. yellow body, yellow metal base, red driver, yellow airfoil, "Pennzoil 8" tempa, Thailand casting ($3-4)(IN)
20. red body, red metal base, white driver, black airfoil, "Scotch 9" tempa, Thailand casting ($3-4)(IN)
21. blue body, blue metal base, silver-gray driver, blue airfoil, "Mackenzie 15" tempa, Thailand casting ($3-4)(IN)
22. blue & yellow body, blue metal base, yellow driver, blue airfoil, "Panasonic 11" tempa, Thailand casting ($3-4)(IN)
23. blue & white body, blue metal base, red driver, blue airfoil, "Valvoline/Kraco 3" tempa, Thailand casting ($3-4)(IN)
24. white body, blue metal base, red driver, white airfoil, "Indy 500" & "77" tempa, Thailand casting ($3-4)(IN)(KS)
25. white body, white metal base, green driver, white airfoil, "XP 6" tempa, all black slicks, Thailand casting ($8-12)(DU)
26. white body, pink metal base, blue driver, white airfoil, "7" & blue dots tempa, Thailand casting ($1-2)
27. fluorescent orange & yellow body, yellow metal base, white driver, yellow airfoil, "Matchbox Get in the Fast Lane 7" tempa, Thailand casting ($2-4)(CC)
28. green & white body, green metal base, black driver, white airfoil, "4" & black lines tempa, Thailand casting ($1-2)(5pk)
29. white & orange body, black metal base, black driver, white airfoil, "4" & black lines tempa, Thailand casting ($1-2)(5pk)
30. dark purple body, black metal base, white driver, neon yellow airfoil, "Matchbox 20" tempa, China casting ($1-2)(5pk)
31. metallic tan body, metallic tan metal base, white driver, tan airfoil, "Peugeot/ Special 11" tempa, China casting ($2-3)(ROW)
32. red body, black metal base, white driver, black airfoil, "Kids World/ Fiat" tempa, China casting ($35-50)(AU)

33. red body, black metal base, white driver, black airfoil, "Fiat 27" tempa, China casting ($2-4)

MB74-I UTILTY TRUCK *see MB33-G*

MB74-J FORMULA ONE RACER, issued 1996 (USA)(MB246), issued 1994 (MN/F1)
MB61-I FORMULA ONE RACER, issued 1997 (ROW)

NOTE: Below models with metal base & yellow wheel lettering unless otherwise noted.

1. blue & white body, blue driver, white airfoil, black base (cast "Williams Renault"), white wheel lettering, "Canon Williams 5" tempa, Thailand casting ($4-6)(MN)
2. blue & white body, blue driver, white airfoil, black base, "Canon Williams 0" tempa, Thailand casting ($3-5)(Fl)
3. white body, white driver, white airfoil, black base, "Footwork 9" tempa, Thailand casting ($3-5)(Fl)
4. red body, white driver, red airfoil, black base, "Fiat 27" tempa, Thailand casting ($3-5)(Fl)
5. black body, white driver, black airfoil, black base, "Liqui Moly 30" tempa, Thailand casting ($3-5)(Fl)
6. red body, white driver, black airfoil, black base, "Fiat 27" without white band around top tempa, Thailand casting ($3-5)(F1)
7. blue & white body, blue driver, black airfoil, black base, "Elf/Renault 0" with red, white & gold trim tempa, Thailand casting ($3-5)(F1)
8. white body, white driver, white airfoil, black base, "Uliveto/ Lee Cooper, Ford 9" tempa, Thailand casting ($3-5)(F1)
9. white body, white driver, white airfoil, black base, "Mobil 1/ Loctite/Hitachi 72" tempa, Thailand casting ($3-5)(F1)
10. blue body, white driver, blue airfoil, black base, "Sasol 14" tempa, Thailand casting ($3-5)(F1)
11. white body, dark blue driver, orange airfoil, black base, "MB Racing 1" tempa, white wheel lettering, Thailand casting ($1-2)
12. white body, white driver, white airfoil, black base, "BP/ Footwork 9" tempa, Thailand casting ($3-5)(F1)
13. red body, black driver, black airfoil, black base, "Ferrari 27 Pioneer" without white band tempa, China casting ($3-5)(F1)
14. blue & white body, white driver, white airfoil, black base, "Renault Elf 0" tempa, China casting ($3-5)(F1)
15. white body, white driver, white airfoil, black base, "Uliveto/ Lee Cooper 9" tempa, China casting ($3-5)(F1)
16. blue body, white driver, black airfoil, black base, "Sasol 14" tempa, China casting ($3-5)(F1)

NOTE: Below models with white lettered wheels unless otherwise noted.

17. metallic gold body, white driver, black airfoil, metallic gold base, no tempa, China casting ($5-10)(CH)
18. orange body, dark blue driver, dark blue airfoil, black base, "MB Racing 1" tempa, China casting ($1-2)
19. white body, dark blue driver, orange airfoil, black base, "MB Racing 1" tempa, China casting ($1-2)
20. lemon body, black driver, red airfoil, red base, "MB Racing 1" tempa, China casting ($1-2)(MW61/1998)

NOTE: Below models with black driver, airfoil & base.

21. white body, no tempa, China casting ($25-40)(ASAP blank)
22. white body, "STB" tempa, China casting ($50+)(ASAP)
23. white body, "IFS" tempa, China casting ($50+)(ASAP)
24. white body, "White's Guide Car of the Month" (black print) tempa, China casting ($5-8)(ASAP)
25. white body, "White's Guide Car of the Month" (red print) tempa, China casting ($5-8)(ASAP)
26. white body, "IBM Netfinity" tempa, China casting ($75+)(ASAP)
27. white body, "Indy 98 Rotary" tempa, China casting ($75+)(ASAP)
28. white body, "RCA" tempa, China casting ($20-30)(ASAP)
29. white body, "Comp USA/ SAP, $" tempa, China casting ($10-15)(ASAP)
30. white body, "Site Smith" tempa, China casting ($25-30)(ASAP)
31. white body, "Sun Microsystems/ Java" tempa, China casting ($75+)(ASAP)
32. white body, "Hewlett Packard/ HP 2000C/ From Fast to 4X Faster" tempa, China casting ($75+)(ASAP)
33. white body, "Citrix CDN" tempa, China casting ($50+)(ASAP)
34. white body, "Network Associates" tempa, China casting ($50+)(ASAP)
35. white body, "Belterra" tempa, China casting ($50+)(ASAP)
36. white body, "Protective" tempa, China casting ($50+)(ASAP)
37. white body, "IBM" tempa, China casting ($50+)(ASAP)
38. white body, 4 grasped hands logo tempa, China casting ($50+)(ASAP)
39. white body, "UR #1/ Sealed Air" tempa, China casting ($50+)(ASAP)
40. white body, "Net ASPX" tempa, China casting ($50+)(ASAP)
41. white body, "Raytheon/ Indy" tempa, China casting ($50+)(ASAP)
42. white body, "Delta Electrical", China casting ($50+)(ASAP)
43. white body, "Ernst & Young" tempa, China casting ($50+)(ASAP)
44. white body, "Boomtown/ Bossier City" tempa ($50+)(ASAP)
45. white body, "Compaq" tempa ($50+)(ASAP)
46. white body, "AMD" tempa ($50+)(ASAP)
47. white body, "MOCA" tempa ($50+)(ASAP)
48. white body, "CompUSA/ Microsoft" tempa ($50+)(ASAP)
49. white body, "International" tempa ($50+)(ASAP)
50. white body, "Express Personnel Supplies" ($50+)(ASAP)
51. bright blue body, red metal base, white driver, black airfoil, "Fosters" tempa ($75+)(CHI)

MB74-K SNOWMOBILE *see MB94-A*

MB74-L AUDI TT *see MB44-K*

MB74-M BMW Z3, issued 2002 (MB538)

NOTE: Below models with smoke windshield, lace wheels, black plastic base & China casting.

1. metallic red body, black interior, small "Matchbox" & head lights tempa ($1-2)(MW74/2002)
2. metallic red body, black interior, small "Matchbox", head lights & "Matchbox 50" tempa ($8-12)(MW74/2002)
3. charcoal body, red interior, red band & "Z3" tempa ($2-4)(MW39/2003 ROW)
4. charcoal body, red interior, red band, "Z3" & "Hero City" tempa ($3-5)(MW39/2003 ROW)

MB74-N OPEL FROGSTER, issued 2003 (MB573)

NOTE: Below models with red interior, smoke windshield, lace wheels & China casting.

1. metallic green body, gray hatch, gray base, "Frogster 74" tempa ($1-2)(MW74/2003)
2. metallic green body, gray hatch, gray base, "Frogster 74" & "Hero City" tempa ($2-4)(MW74/2003)
3. orange body, yellow hatch, yellow base, "Wile E." tempa ($1-2)(5pk)
4. metallic blue body, gray hatch, gray base, "Frogster" tempa ($2-3)(MW19/2004 ROW)

5. dark yellow body, blue windshield, gray hatch, gray base, "48 Team" & baseball design tempa ($1-2)(5pk)
6. metallic blue body, dark smoke windshield, gray hatch, gray base, "Frogster" tempa ($2-3)(MW19/ 2004 ROW)
7. bright green body, amber windshield, orange hatch, yellow interior, orange base, "Carl" tempa ($1-2)(5pk)

MB75-A FERRARI BERLINETTA, issued 1970

NOTE: All models with unpainted metal base, ivory interior, clear windows & 5 spoke wheels.

1. light metallic green body, plain grille ($75-90)
2. dark metallic green body, plain grille ($75-90)
3. red body, plain grille ($25-35)
4. red body, silver grille ($25-35)

MB75-B ALFA CARABO, issued 1971

NOTE: Below models with clear windows, ivory interior & England casting. 5 spoke wheels are found in two different diameters.

1. light purple body, unpainted base, no tempa, 5 spoke wheels ($15-18)
2. light purple body, yellow base, no tempa, 5 spoke wheels ($15-18)
3. pink body, yellow base, no tempa, 5 spoke wheels ($75-100)
4. pink body, unpainted base, no tempa, 5 spoke wheels ($75-100)
5. pink body, yellow base, with tempa, 5 spoke wheels ($18-25)
6. red body, yellow base, with tempa, 5 spoke wheels ($8-12)
7. red body, yellow base, with tempa, 5 arch wheels ($8-12)(JP)

MB75-C SEASPRITE HELICOPTER, issued 1977

NOTE: Below models with solid black plastic wheels, black blades & England casting unless otherwise noted.:

1. white body, red base, blue windows, "Rescue" labels ($4-6)
2. white body, red base, green windows, "Rescue" labels ($4-6)
3. white body, red base, purple windows, "Rescue" labels ($4-6)
4. white body, red base, red windows, "Rescue" labels ($4-6)
5. white body, red base, no windows, "Rescue" labels ($8-12)
6. dark cream body, red (etched) base, blue windows, "Rescue" labels ($250-350)(BR)
7. dark green body, red (etched) base, blue windows, "Rescue" labels ($350-500)(BR)

NOTE: Available as a Bulgarian casting. Assorted colors available ($10-25)

MB75-D HELICOPTER, issued 1982 (MB075)
MB60-J HELICOPTER, issued 1997 (USA release)
MB30-H HELICOPTER, issued 1997 (ROW reissue)

NOTE: Below models with black blades unless otherwise noted.

1. white body, orange base, black interior & skis, amber windows, "MB TV News" tempa, England casting ($3-5)
2. white body, black base, black interior & skis, clear windows, "MB TV News" tempa, England casting ($8-12)
3. white body, black base, gray interior & skis, clear windows, "MB TV News" tempa, England casting ($8-12)
4. white body, black base, gray interior & skis, clear windows, "36 Police" tempa, England casting ($4-6)
5. white body, black base, gray interior & skis, amber windows, "36 Police" tempa, England casting ($4-6)
6. white body, black base, black interior & skis, clear windows, "36 Police" tempa, England casting ($4-6)
7. white body, black base, black interior & skis, amber windows, "36 Police" tempa, England casting ($4-6)
8. silver-gray body, orange base, gray interior & skis, amber windows, "-600-" tempa, England casting ($2-4)(CY)
9. silver-gray body, orange base, gray interior & skis, clear windows, "-600-" tempa, England casting ($2-4)(CY)
10. silver-gray body, orange base, black interior & skis, amber windows, "-600-" tempa, England casting ($2-4)(CY)
11. silver-gray body, orange base, black interior & skis, clear windows, "-600-" tempa, England casting ($2-4)(CY)
12. silver-gray body, black base, gray interior & skis, amber windows, "-600-" tempa, England casting ($2-4)(CY)
13. silver-gray body, black base, black interior & skis, amber windows, "-600-" tempa, England casting ($2-4)(CY)
14. white body, orange base, gray interior & skis, amber windows, "Police 36" tempa, England casting ($15-20)
15. white body, black base, gray interior & skis, amber windows, "Rescue" tempa, England casting ($2-4)
16. white body, black base, black interior & skis, amber windows, "Rescue" tempa, England casting ($2-4)
17. pearly gray body, orange base, gray interior & skis, amber windows, "-600-" tempa, Macau casting ($2-4)(CY)
18. white body, orange base, black interior & skis, amber windows, blue "Rescue" tempa, Macau casting ($2-4)
19. white body, black base, gray interior & skis, amber windows, blue "Rescue" tempa, Macau casting ($2-4)
20. black body, black base, gray interior & skis, amber windows, "Air Car" tempa, Macau casting ($2-4)(CY)
21. red body, white base, gray interior & skis, amber windows, "Fire Dept." tempa, Macau casting ($2-4)(5pk)
22. white body, red base, gray interior & skis, amber windows, "NASA" tempa, Macau casting ($2-4)(MP)
23. white body, red base, black interior & skis, amber windows, "Virgin Atlantic" tempa, Macau casting ($2-4)(GS)
24. white body, yellow base, red interior & skis, amber windows, "JCB" tempa, white blades, Macau casting ($4-6)(GS)
25. white body, lemon base, gray interior & skis, amber windows, "Fire Dept." tempa, Macau casting ($2-4)(MP)
26. white body, dull orange base, gray interior & skis, amber windows, black "Rescue" tempa, Macau casting ($2-4)
27. red body, white base, gray interior & skis, amber windows, "Red Rebels" tempa, white blades, Macau casting ($2-4)(MC)
28. white body, black base, gray interior & skis, amber windows, Japanese lettered tempa, Macau casting ($8-12)(JP)(GS)
29. red body, white base, gray interior & skis, amber windows, "Fire Dept." tempa, white blades, Macau casting ($2-4)(TC)
30. white body, lemon base, gray interior & skis, amber windows, "Fire Dept." tempa, Thailand casting ($2-3)(MP)
31. black body, black base, gray interior & skis, amber windows, "Air Car" tempa, Thailand casting ($2-3)(CY)
32. white body, black base, gray interior & skis, amber windows, "Rescue" tempa, Thailand casting ($2-3)(MC)
33. white body, yellow base, lime interior & skis, amber windows, "123456" tempa, blue & yellow blades, Macau casting ($6-8)(LL)
34. white body, yellow base, lime interior & skis, amber windows, "123456" tempa, blue & yellow blades, Thailand casting ($6-8)(LL)
35. red body, white base, gray interior & skis, amber windows, "Red Rebels" tempa, white blades, Thailand casting ($1-2)(MC)
36. red body, white base, gray interior & skis, clear windows, "Royal Air Force" tempa, Thailand casting ($2-3)(MC)
37. red body, white base, gray interior & skis, amber windows, "Fire Dept." tempa, white blades, Thailand casting ($1-2)(MP)
38. white body, florescent orange base, gray interior & skis, amber windows, "Air Rescue 10" & "IC" logo tempa, Thailand casting ($10-15)(IC)

39. red body, white base, white interior & skis, blue windows, "Fire Dept." tempa, white blades, Thailand casting ($1-2)(MP)
40. white body, fluorescent orange base, silver-gray interior & skis, blue windows, blue checkers tempa, Thailand casting ($1-2)(EM)
41. white body, red base, silver-gray interior & skis, blue windows, "Aerobatic Team" tempa, Thailand casting ($2-4)(MP)
42. white body, red base, silver-gray interior & skis, blue windows, "Fire Rescue" tempa, China casting ($1-2)(AV)(AP)
43. red body, white base, white interior & skis, blue windows, gray blades, "Fire Dept." tempa, China casting ($1-2)
44. white body, red base, black interior & skis, amber windows, "Fire Dept." tempa, China casting ($1-2)(MW29/1998)
45. red body, white base, white interior & skis, blue windows, gray blades, "Airways Tours" tempa, China casting ($1-2)(5pk)
46. metallic gold body, white base, white interior & skis, blue windows, no tempa, China casting ($5-10)(CH)
47. white body, black base, black interior & skis, amber windows, "Newscam/ News 8" tempa, China casting ($2-4)(RT)
48. red body, red base, black interior & skis, amber windows, "Fire Dept." tempa, China casting ($1-2)(MP)
49. white body, orange base, silver-gray interior & skis, blue windows, "Police" tempa, white blades, China casting, includes orange base attachment ($2-4)(AP)
50. white body, dark red base, silver-gray interior & skis, blue windows, yellow design & "87" tempa, red blades, China casting ($1-2)(MW6/1999) (MW11/1999 GR)
51. orange body, brown base, brown interior & skis, blue windows, yellow & brown stripes & "Magnum P.I." tempa, silver-gray blades, China casting ($8-12)(STR-Avon)
52. white body, red base, silver-gray interior & skis, blue windows, "35-2" with medic logo & red stripes tempa, black blades, China casting ($2-4)(MW13/2000 ROW)
53. lemon body, black base, black interior & skis, blue windows, black stripes & "702" tempa, black blades, China casting ($3-4)(MW13/2000 GR)
54. bright blue body, white base, black interior & skis, blue windows, "Police" & white dashes tempa, silver-gray blades, China casting ($1-2)(MW64/2001 ROW)(MW55/2001 AU)

MB75-E FERRARI TESTAROSSA, issued 1986 (MB172)
MB78-B FERRARI TESTAROSSA, reissued 1996 (USA)

NOTE: Below models with metal base unless otherwise noted.

1. red body & base, black interior, clear windows, 8 dot wheels, "Ferrari" logo tempa, Macau casting ($1-2)
2. black body & base, black interior, clear windows, starburst wheels, silver with logo tempa, Macau casting ($3-5)(SF)
3. metallic pearly silver body & base, black interior, clear windows, laser wheels, gold with logos tempa, Macau casting ($3-5)(LW)
4. yellow body, black base, no interior, dark blue modified windows, starburst wheels, red/blue/yellow tempa, Macau casting, includes plastic armament ($5-8)(RB)
5. yellow body & base, black interior, clear windows, 8 dot wheels, "9 Rabbit Racing Team" tempa, Macau casting ($8-12)(HK)
6. metallic red body & base, black interior, clear windows, laser wheels, silver with logos tempa, Macau casting ($3-5)(LW)
7. orange-red body, black base, black interior, clear windows, 8 dot wheels, "Ferrari" logo tempa, Macau casting ($3-4)(SC)
8. dark red body, black base, black interior, clear windows, 8 dot wheels, "Ferrari" logo tempa, Macau casting ($3-4)(SC)
9. orange body, black base, black interior, clear windows, 8 dot wheels, "Ferrari" logo tempa, Macau casting ($3-4)(SC)
10. rose red body, black base, black interior, clear windows, 8 dot wheels, "Ferrari" logo tempa, Macau casting ($3-4)(SC)
11. red body & base, black interior, clear windows, 8 dot wheels, "Redoxon" tempa, Macau casting ($20-35)(HK)
12. red body & base, black interior, chrome windows, gray disc wheels with rubber tires, detailed trim tempa, Macau casting ($5-8)(WC)
13. red body, lime base, lime interior, clear windows, 8 dot yellow wheels with blue hubs, "1" with face & checkered flag tempa, Macau casting ($6-8)(LL)
14. red body & base, black interior, clear windows, 8 dot wheels, "Ferrari" logo tempa, Thailand casting ($1-2)
15. red body & base, black interior, chrome windows, gray disc wheels with rubber tires, detailed trim tempa, Thailand casting ($5-8)(WC)
16. white body & base, black interior, chrome windows, gray disc wheels with rubber tires, detailed trim tempa, Thailand casting ($5-8)(WC)
17. red body & base, black interior, clear windows, starburst wheels, silver with logos tempa, Macau casting ($8-12)(SF)
18. red body & base, black interior, clear windows, 8 dot wheels, "Ferrari" logo tempa, China casting ($1-2)
19. white body & base, black interior, clear windows, 8 dot wheels, no tempa, China casting ($10-15)(GF)
20. red body & base, black interior, clear windows, 8 dot wheels, "Lloyds/Ferrari" tempa, China casting ($7-10)(UK)
21. red body & base, black interior, clear windows, 8 dot wheels, "Ferrari" logo (all yellow background) tempa, China casting ($1-2)
22. red body & base, black interior, clear windows, 8 dot wheels, small "Ferrari" logo & painted tail lights tempa, Thailand casting ($2-3)(SS)
23. fluorescent yellow body & base, black interior, clear windows, gold 6 spoke spiral wheels, black stripes & pink flash tempa, Thailand casting ($1-2)
24. red body & base, black interior, clear windows, gold 6 spoke spiral wheels, all yellow background "Ferrari" logo tempa, Thailand casting ($2-3)
25. metallic blue body & base, black interior, clear windows, silver 6 spoke spiral wheels, small "Ferrari" logo tempa, Thailand casting ($2-4)(CC)
26. metallic red body & base, black interior, clear windows, silver 6 spoke spiral wheels, no tempa, Thailand casting ($1-2)(5pk)
27. florescent yellow body & base, black interior, clear windows, silver 6 spoke spiral wheels, black stripes & pink flash tempa, Thailand casting ($1-2)
NOTE: Some versions of this model are packaged in blisterpacks as #78 in error ($1-2)
28. red body & base, black interior, clear windows, silver 6 spoke spiral wheels, all yellow background "Ferrari" logo tempa, Thailand casting ($3-5)
29. silver-gray body & base, black & red interior, clear windows, chrome disc wheels with rubber tires, detailed trim tempa, Thailand casting ($18-25)(GC)
30. black body & base, black & red interior, clear windows, chrome disc wheels with rubber tires, detailed trim tempa, Thailand casting ($3-5)(PC10)
31. yellow body & base, black & red interior, clear windows, chrome disc wheels with rubber tires, detailed trim tempa, Thailand casting ($3-5)(PC2-ROW)
32. red body & base, black & red interior, clear windows, chrome disc wheels with rubber tires, detailed trim tempa, Thailand casting ($3-5)(PC19)

33. white body, white plastic base, brown & black interior, clear windows, 5 spoke concave star wheels, "Miami Vice" tempa, China casting ($4-6)(STR)
34. yellow body, yellow plastic base, black interior, clear windows, 5 spoke concave star wheels, small logos tempa, China casting ($4-5)(MW27/1999 GR)
35. black body, black plastic base, black interior, clear windows, 5 spoke concave star wheels, small logos tempa, China casting ($1-2)(MW25/2000 US)(MW20/ ROW)
36. black body, black plastic base, black interior, clear windows, 5 spoke concave star wheels, small logos & "Matchbox 2000" tempa, China casting ($2-4)(MW25/2000 US)

MB75-F AMG MERCEDES C CLASS *see MB35-J*

MB75-G FERRARI F50, issued 1996 (USA) (MB291)
MB21-H FERRARI F50, issued 1996 (ROW)

NOTE: Below models with smoke windows, black plastic base & China casting unless otherwise noted.

1. red body, black interior, 6 spoke spiral wheels, "Ferrari" logo tempa ($1-2)
2. metallic gold body, black interior, 6 spoke spiral wheels, no tempa ($10-15)(CH)
3. red body, black interior, 5 spoke concave star wheels, "Ferrari 50" & yellow/ white stripes tempa ($1-2)(5pk)
4. red body, black interior, 5 spoke concave star wheels, "Ferrari" logo tempa ($2-3)
5. red body, black interior, chrome disc wheels with rubber tires, detailed trim tempa ($8-12)(UC)
6. rose red body, gray interior, 5 spoke concave star wheels, "Go Swans! 1997" tempa ($3-5)(AU)
7. lemon body, black interior, 5 spoke concave star wheels, small "Ferrari" logo tempa ($1-2)
8. black body, dark red interior, 5 spoke concave star wheels, small "Ferrari" logo tempa ($1-2)(MW59/1998)
9. silver-gray body, black & red interior, chrome disc wheels with rubber tires, detailed trim tempa ($3-5)(PC15)
10. yellow body, black & red interior, chrome disc wheels with rubber tires, detailed trim tempa ($3-5)GS-TRU)
11. yellow body, black interior, 5 spoke concave star wheels, "Ferrari" logo tempa ($1-2)(MW35/1999 ROW)
12. black body, brown interior, 5 spoke concave star wheels, small logo tempa ($1-2)(MW30/1999 GR)
13. silver-gray body, red interior, 5 spoke concave star wheels, "Ferrari" & logo tempa ($1-2)(5pk)
14. silver-gray body, red interior, star with 5 spokes wheels, "Ferrari" & logo tempa ($1-2)(5pk)
15. silver-gray body, black interior, dark smoke windows, 5 spoke concave star wheels, small logo, painted lights & "Matchbox 2000" tempa ($5-8)(MW21/2000 US)
16. silver-gray body, black interior, dark smoke windows, star with 5 spokes wheels, small logo, painted lights & "Matchbox 2000" tempa ($2-4)(MW21/2000 US)
17. silver-gray body, black interior, dark smoke windows, 5 spoke concave star wheels, small logo & painted lights tempa ($1-2)(MW21/2000 US)(MW16/2000 ROW)
18. silver-gray body, black interior, dark smoke windows, star with 5 spokes wheels, small logo & painted lights tempa ($1-2)(MW21/2000 US)(MW16/2000 ROW)
19. red body, black interior, smoke windows, 5 spoke concave star wheels, none tempa, China casting ($20-35)(ASAP blank)
20. red body, black interior, smoke windows, 5 spoke concave star wheels, "Citrix/ SD2000" tempa, China casting ($75+)(ASAP)
21. yellow body, black interior, smoke windows, 5 spoke concave star wheels, small logo tempa, China casting ($1-2)(LP)
22. lemon body, black interior, clear windows, 5 spoke concave star wheels, small logo & "Ferrari" tempa, China casting ($1-2)(5pk)
23. lemon body, black interior, clear windows, star with 5 spokes wheels, small logo & "Ferrari" tempa, China casting ($1-2)(5pk)
24. lemon body, black interior, clear windows, 10 spoke flower wheels, small logo & "Ferrari" tempa, China casting ($6-8)(5pk)
25. lemon body, black interior, clear windows, star with 5 spokes wheels, small logo & "Ferrari" tempa, metal base, China casting ($1-2)(5pk)
26. lemon body, black interior, clear windows, 10 spoke flower wheels, small logo & "Ferrari" tempa, metal base, China casting ($1-2)(5pk)
27. red body, black interior, clear windows, 5 spoke concave star wheels, "Novell 6" tempa, China casting ($18-25)(ASAP)
28. red body, black interior, smoke windows, 5 spoke concave star wheels, "Novell 6" tempa, China casting ($18-25)(ASAP)
29. dark green body, black interior, clear windows, lace wheels, small "Ferrari" logo tempa, metal base, Mattel China casting ($2-4)(MW54/2001 ROW)(MW52/2001 UK)
30. dark charcoal body, white interior, clear windows, lace wheels, small "Ferrari" logo tempa, metal base, Mattel China casting ($2-4)(MW52/2001 GR)
31. red body, black interior, amber windows, 5 spoke concave star wheels, "Logitech" tempa, metal base, Mattel China casting ($50+)(ASAP)
32. red body, black interior, smoke windows, 5 spoke concave star wheels, "RPI" tempa, China casting ($12-18)(ASAP)
33. red body, black interior, smoke windows, 6 spoke spiral wheels, "GS Gerber Systems" tempa, China casting ($50+)(ASAP)
34. yellow body, black & red interior, smoke windows, chrome disc wheels with rubber tires, "Shaun 2003/ Albuquerque Academy" tempa, China casting ($25-40)(CCI)
35. lemon body, black interior, smoke windows, lace wheels, silver & black design tempa, Mattel China casting ($2-4)(MW69/2003 ROW)
36. lemon body, black interior, smoke windows, lace wheels, silver & black design with "Hero City" tempa, Mattel China casting ($3-5)(MW69/2003 ROW)
37. red body, black interior, 6 spoke spiral wheels, "Ferrari" logo & "Microsoft/ Intel" tempa, China casting ($50+)(ASAP)
38. red body, black interior, 5 spoke concave star wheels, "Compaq" tempa, China casting ($50+)(ASAP)
39. red body, black interior, 5 spoke concave star wheels, "invitrogen/ Expressway" tempa, China casting ($50+)(ASAP)
40. red body, black interior, 5 spoke concave star wheels, "Huskers" tempa, China casting ($12-18)(ASAP)
41. red body, black interior, 10 spoke flower wheels, no tempa, metal base, Mattel China casting ($18-25)(ASAP blank)
42. orange body, red interior, 5 spoke concave star wheels, "Enjoy Fanta" tempa, China casting ($75+)(CHI)
43. bright blue body, black interior, lace wheels, silver & yellow design tempa, Mattel China casting ($2-3)(MW25/2004)
44. red body, black interior, 10 spoke flower wheels, small "Ferrari" logos tempa, Mattel China casting)($3-5)(SoC)

MB75-H AERO JUNIOR *see MB95-A*

MB75-I 1957 CORVETTE, issued 1999 (USA) (MB361)

NOTE: Below models with clear windows & China casting.

1. red body, white roof, white interior, chrome base, 5 spoke concave star wheels, white flash tempa ($1-2)(MW75/1999 US)

2. red body, white roof, white interior, chrome base, small 5 spoke concave star wheels, white flash tempa ($2-4)(MW75/1999 US
3. black body, black roof, white interior, black base, chrome disc with rubber tires, white flash tempa ($5-8)(PC)
4. red body, white roof, white interior, chrome base, 5 spoke concave star wheels, "Vettes in Glasstown XXI/ Corvettes Unlimited" & white flash tempa ($15-20)(CCI)
5. red body, white roof, white interior, chrome base, 5 spoke concave star wheels, "Cruisin New England Magazine All Wheels Festival 2001" & white flash tempa ($50+)(CCI)
6. red body, white roof, white interior, chrome base, 5 spoke concave star wheels, "Steeltown Corvettes" & white flash ($25-40)(CCI)
7. red body, red roof, gray interior, gray base, lace wheels, "Trix" tempa ($1-2)(5pk)

MB75-J GOLF CART, issued 2000 (USA) (MB449)
MB55-O GOLF CART, issued 2000 (ROW)

NOTE: Below models with white roof, black roof supports, white interior, black golf bags, 8 dot wheels & China casting unless otherwise noted.

1. gray body, silver-gray base, "Canyon Golf 232" tempa ($1-2)(MW75/2000 US)(MW55/2000 ROW)
2. gray body, silver-gray base, "Canyon Golf 232/ Matchbox 2000" tempa ($2-4)(MW75/2000 US)
3. white body, white base, no tempa ($25-40)(ASAP/CCI blank)
4. white body, white base, "RCA" tempa ($20-30)(ASAP)
5. white body, white base, "EMC2 Where Information Lives/ Global Financial Services" tempa ($25-40)(CCI)
6. gray body, silver-gray base, "PMCC Christmas Dinner/ Canyon Golf 232" tempa ($18-25)(CCI)

NOTE: Below models with white base unless otherwise noted.

7. white body, "3rd Annual Mattel Open" label ($18-25)(CCI)
8. white body, "Together For Tyler/ Memorial Golf Tournament" label ($18-25)(CCI)
9. white body, "First Bank 5th Annual Golf Classic 2001" label ($12-18)(CCI)
10. white body, "5th Annual Fore Kids Classic" label ($12-18)(CCI)
11. white body, "MPC Electromechanical Systems & Components" labels ($12-18)(CCI)
12. white body, "9th Annual Hackers International" label ($12-18)(CCI)
13. white body, "Camp Sunshine" labels ($12-18)(CCI)
14. white body, "Intermatic 110 Years 1891-2001" labels ($12-18)(CCI)
15. light blue, silver-gray base, green roof supports & golf bags, ""8SC/ Golf South Carolina" tempa ($1-2)(AM)
16. white body, "Happy Birthday 78 Kerry Pacifico" label ($18-25)(CCI)
17. white body, "Julie & Rhett- Just Married" label ($12-18)(CCI)
18. white body, "2nd Annual Together for Tyler" label ($12-18)(CCI)
19. white body, "9th Annual Dusty Lobb Memorial Golf Tournament" label ($12-18)(CCI)
20. white body, "Alex's 7th Birthday" label ($18-25)
21. white body, "Your Golf Course Name Here! Your Location Here! label ($10-15)(CCI)
22. white body, "4th Annual Mattel Open" label ($12-18)
23. white body, "White Oaks Country Club Newfield NJ" label ($12-18)
24. white body, "MJ/ MJ Engineering & Land Surveying, PC" label ($18-25)(CCI)
25. white body, "Together for Tyler 3rd Annual 2003" label ($12-18)(CCI)
26. white body, "Save the Date! Celebrity Golf Classic" label ($12-18)(CCI)
27. white body, "Glen & Eileen" label ($18-25)(CCI)
28. white body, "Tee Off with Hope" label ($18-25)(CCI)
29. white body, "5th Annual Mattel Open" label ($12-18)(CCI)
30. white body, "6th Mattel Open/ Closed" label ($12-18)(CCI)
31. white body, "Inaugural Jay Taylor Golf Invitational" label ($12-18)(CCI)
32. white body, "4th Annual Together For Tyler/ Make A Wish" label ($12-18)(CCI)
33. white body, "Ferndale Educational Foundation" label ($18-25)(CCI)
34. white body, "Happy Birthday Saggie" label ($18-25)(CCI)
35. white body, "Epilepsy Foundation" tempa ($50+)(ASAP)
36. white body, "Hill-Rom" tempa ($50+)(ASAP)
37. white body, "Buffalo Grove Days" label ($18-25)(CCI)
38. white body, "8th Annual Lt. Cmdr Bill Braker Jr. Memorial Golf Tournament" label ($18-25)(CCI)

MB75-K WATER PUMPER, issued 2002 (MB563)

NOTE: Below models with amber windows, 7 spoke sawblade wheels & China casting.

1. red body, gray base, "Eng. 922" with helmet & hose tempa ($1-2)(MW75/2002)
2. red body, gray base, "Eng. 922", helmet & hose with "Matchbox 50" tempa ($8-12)(MW75/2002)
3. metallic red body, chrome base, "Toy Fair Fire Co. 2003 Matchbox- Hero City" tempa ($18-25)(US)
4. red body, gray base, "Rescue Heroes" tempa ($1-2)(5pk)
5. red body, black base, "Eng. 19 Fire Rescue/2003 Limited Edition" tempa ($1-2)(Duracell in pack)
6. red body, gray base, "Hero City 62" tempa ($1-2)(MW62/2003)
7. red body, gray base, "Hero City 62" & "Hero City" tempa ($3-5)(MW62/2003)
8. metallic red body, gray base, "Hero City 62" tempa, gold hubs ($3-4)(20pk)
9. red body, black base, "Eng. 19 Fire Rescue/2004 Limited Edition" tempa ($8-10)(Duracell in pack)(CN)

MB75-L MINI COOPER S, issued 2003 (MB579)

NOTE: Below models with black plastic base & China casting.

1. dark red body, dark smoke windows, black interior, lace wheels, small "Matchbox", "75" & British flag on roof tempa ($1-2)(MW75/2003)
2. dark red body, dark smoke windows, black interior, lace wheels, small "Matchbox", "75" & British flag on roof with "Hero City" tempa ($5-8)(MW75/2003)
3. lemon body, clear windows, black interior, chrome disc wheels with rubber tires, white roof & detailed trim tempa ($3-5)(SH)
4. lemon body, black windows, black interior, 10 spoke flower wheels, black stripes & black roof tempa ($1-2)(MW65/2004)
5. red body, clear windows, black interior, 5 spoke slotted wheels, black roof & detailed trim tempa ($3-5)(SF12/2004)
6. metallic orange body, chrome windows, black interior, chrome disc wheels with rubber tires, "Matchbox Pre-Toy Fair 2005" & black stripes tempa, plexibox ($20-35)(US)(ROW)
7. light metallic blue body, smoke windows, black interior, 10 spoke flower wheels, white roof & hood stripes tempa ($1-2)(MW7/2005)

MB76-A SAVANNA RX7, issued 1981 (USA)(AU) (MB091)

NOTE: Below models with ivory interior, clear windows, 5 spoke star wheels, black metal base & Hong Kong casting.

1. light green body, no tempa ($15-20)(AU)
2. blue body, no tempa ($2-4)(US-Speedsticks)
3. blue body, black stripe "RX7" tempa ($20-30)(US)

4. blue body, red & white stripes tempa ($4-8)(US)(LE) (issued as "Boulevard Blaster")

MB76-B 4 X 4 OPEN BACK TRUCK *see MB13-D*

MB76-C MODEL A FORD VAN *see MB38-E*

MB76-D INTERNATIONAL FIRE PUMPER, issued 1999 (USA) (MB379)
MB66-K INTERNATIONAL FIRE PUMPER, issued 1999 (ROW)

NOTE: Below models with chrome plastic base & China casting unless otherwise noted.

1. red body, smoke windows, gray interior, blue dome lights, white roof & rear with stripes & door crest tempa, 8 spoke wheels ($2-3)(MW66/1999 ROW)
2. red body, clear windows, black interior, red dome lights, "Fort Wayne Fire Dept." tempa, chrome disc wheels with rubber tires ($15-20)(PC)
3. red body, smoke windows, gray interior, red dome lights, "MB Fire Dept. No. 7" with stripes & door crest tempa, 8 spoke wheels ($1-2)(MW76/1999 US)
4. white body, blue windows, white interior, red dome lights, gray base, "Engine Co. 77" tempa, 8 spoke wheels ($1-2)(5pk)
5. white body, blue windows, white interior, blue dome lights, gray base, "Engine Co. 34" tempa, 8 spoke wheels($2-4)(5pk)
6. orange-yellow body, smoke windows, black interior, red dome lights, black bands, "6532/54" & "Matchbox" in a circular logo tempa, 8 spoke wheels ($1-2)(5pk)
7. metallic gold body, red windows, black interior, red dome lights, "MB Fire Dept. No. 7" & "Matchbox 2000" tempa, 8 spoke wheels ($2-4)(MW30/2000 US)
8. metallic gold body, red windows, black interior, red dome lights, "MB Fire Dept. No. 7" tempa, 8 spoke wheels ($1-2)(MW30/2000 US)
9. red body, smoke windows, gray interior, red dome lights, "73rd Apple Blossom Festival" tempa, 8 spoke wheels ($8-12)(US)
10. white & red body, black windows, black interior & base, red dome lights, "Radio E-75" tempa, 8 spoke wheels ($8-10)(PS)
11. red body, clear windows, blue interior, blue dome lights, "Metro Alarm" & black stripe tempa, 8 spoke wheels ($1-2)(5pk)
12. red body, smoke windows, gray interior, red dome lights, "Hot Springs Vol. Fire Dept." tempa, 8 spoke wheels ($12-18)(CCI)
13. red body, smoke windows, gray interior, red dome lights, "Middlebrook Volunteer Fire Department" tempa, 8 spoke wheels ($12-18)(CCI)
14. red body, smoke windows, gray interior, red dome lights, "Squantz Engine Company" with black roof & hoses tempa, 8 spoke wheels ($12-18)(CCI)
15. maroon body, amber windows, black interior, amber dome lights, silver dashes tempa, 7 spoke sawblade wheels ($2-4)(MW63/2001 ROW)(MW53/2001 AU)
16. red body, amber windows, white interior, amber dome lights, "FD USA" white sides & flag tempa, 7 spoke sawblade wheels, gray base ($1-2)(HR)
17. red body, smoke windows, gray interior, red dome lights, "Reynold's Store Vol. Fire & Rescue Co." tempa, 8 spoke wheels ($12-18)(CCI)
18. white body, clear windows, red interior, red dome lights, "Feuerwehr" tempa, 7 spoke sawblade wheels ($1-2)(MW15/2002 ROW)
19. white body, clear windows, red interior, red dome lights, "Feuerwehr" & "Matchbox 50" tempa, 7 spoke sawblade wheels ($3-5)(MW15/2002 ROW)
20. metallic red body, smoke windows, black interior, blue windows, "Fire Hunter" tempa, 7 spoke sawblade wheels, gray base ($1-2)(MW27/2002 US)
21. metallic red body, smoke windows, black interior, blue windows, "Fire Hunter" & "Matchbox 50" tempa, 7 spoke sawblade wheels, gray base ($2-4)(MW27/2002 US)
22. lemon body, blue windows, white interior, blue dome lights, "Alarm" tempa, 7 spoke sawblade wheels, gray base ($1-2)(5pk)
23. red body, smoke windows, gray interior, red dome light. "Libertytown VFD" tempa, 8 spoke wheels ($12-18)(CCI)
24. red body, smoke windows, gray interior, red dome light, "New York City" tempa, 8 spoke wheels ($12-18)(CCI)
25. red body, smoke windows, gray interior, red dome light, "Dover Delaware" tempa, 8 spoke wheels ($12-18)(CCI)
26. neon yellow body, red windows, white interior, red dome light, "Illinois 27" tempa, 7 spoke sawblade wheels ($8-12)(AM)
27. maroon body, amber windows, white interior, amber dome light, "Station 5" tempa, 7 spoke sawblade wheels, gray base ($1-2)(5pk)
28. red body, smoke windows, gray interior, red dome light, "In Loving Memory Robert J. Minara Sept. 11, 2001" tempa, 8 spoke wheels ($18-25)(CCI)
29. lemon & white body, black windows, black interior, red dome light, "E-75" with red stripes & logo tempa,7 spoke sawblade wheels black base ($3-5)(PS)
30. red body, smoke windows, gray interior, red dome light, "Hancock MD Vol. Fire Co. 75" tempa, 8 spoke wheels ($12-18)(CCI)
31. yellow body, blue windows, white interior, blue dome light, "Metro Alarm" tempa, 7 spoke sawblade wheels, gray base ($1-2)(5pk)
32. neon yellow body, blue windows, white interior, red dome light, "HCFD Alarm 4 Unit" tempa, 7 spoke sawblade wheels, gray base ($1-2)(5pk)
33. red body, smoke windows, gray interior, red dome light, "Maryland State" tempa, 8 spoke wheels, chrome base ($12-18)(CCI)
34. red body, smoke windows, gray interior, red dome light, "Syracuse, NY" tempa, 8 spoke wheels, chrome base ($12-18)(CCI)
35. red body, smoke windows, gray interior, red dome light, "Baltimore, MD 2004" tempa, 8 spoke wheels, chrome base ($12-18)(CCI)
36. red body, smoke windows, gray interior, red dome light, "Cincinnatus Volunteer Fire Department" tempa, 8 spoke wheels, chrome base ($12-18)(CCI)
37. red body, smoke windows, gray interior, red dome light, "Ad-Ventures at Hershey, PA 2004" tempa, 8 spoke wheels, chrome base ($12-18)(CCI)
38. red body, smoke windows, gray interior, red dome light, "C.D.V.F.A. 2000" tempa, 8 spoke wheels, chrome base ($18-25)(CCI)
39. red body, smoke windows, gray interior, red dome light, "Founders Day" tempa, 8 spoke wheels, chrome base ($18-25)(CCI)
40. red body, smoke windows, gray interior, red dome light, "North Mountain Fire Co." tempa, 8 spoke wheels, chrome base ($18-25)(CCI)
41. red body, smoke windows, gray interior, red dome lights, Napanee Fire Rescue" tempa, 8 spoke wheels, chrome base ($18-25)(CCI)

MB77-A TOYOTA CELICA XX, issued 1981 (USA)(AU) (MB092)

NOTE: Below models with ivory interior, clear windows, 5 spoke star wheels, black metal base & Hong Kong casting.

1. red body, no tempa ($3-5)(AU) & (US-Speedsticks)

2. red body, "Sunburner" tempa ($4-8)(US)(LE) (issued as "Sunburner Celica")

MB77-B WEASEL *see MB73-D*

MB77-C MERCEDES BENZ ML430, issued 2000 (USA) (MB427)
MB57-J MERCEDES BENZ ML430, issued 2000 (ROW)
MB63-L MERCEDES BENZ ML430, issued 1999 (GR)

NOTE: Below models with black interior, smoke green windows, plastic base & China casting.

1. metallic maroon body, maroon base, 5 spoke concave star wheels, headlights tempa ($4-6)(MW63/1999 GR)
2. dark green body, dark green base, 5 spoke concave star wheels, headlights tempa ($1-2)(5pk)
3. dark green body, dark green base, star with 5 spokes wheels, headlights tempa ($1-2)(5pk)
4. dark blue body, black base, star with 5 spokes wheels, headlights tempa ($1-2)(MW77/2000 US/MW57/2000 ROW)
5. dark blue body, black base, star with 5 spokes wheels, headlights & "Matchbox 2000" tempa ($2-4)(MW77/2000 US)
6. metallic maroon, maroon base, 10 spoke flower wheels, headlights tempa ($15-18)(EG)
7. metallic maroon, maroon base, star with 5 spokes wheels, "Matchbox/ Midwest Diecast Miniatures Customer Appreciation" tempa ($15-20)(C2)
8. dark blue body, black base, star with 5 spokes wheels, "If you don't Collect Matchbox... Get Out of The Way" tempa ($15-20)(C2)
9. silver-gray body, black base, green interior, clear windows, 10 spoke flower wheels, "MTN01", snowflakes & mountains tempa ($1-2)(5pk)

NOTE: Below models with clear windows & lace wheels unless otherwise noted.

10. silver-gray body, black base, black interior, "Connecticut Constitution News 5" tempa ($2-4)(AM)
11. white body, purple base, purple interior, "ML Series" tempa ($1-2)(MW29/2002)
12. white body, purple base, purple interior, "ML Series" & "Matchbox 50" tempa ($2-4)(MW29/2002)
13. bright blue body, blue base, black interior, tail lights tempa ($4-6)(SG)
14. unpainted body, blue base, black interior, pop art decals ($75+)(FA)
15. silver blue body, black base, black interior, smoke windows, "Polar Bear Watch- Canada" tempa ($1-2)(MP)(AM)
16. metallic lime body, lavender base, white interior, amber windows, "Rugrats" tempa ($1-2)(5pk)
17. metallic blue body, blue base, tan interior, chrome wheels disc with rubber tires, "The Osbournes" tempa ($3-5)(OS)
18. white body, light yellow base, green interior, "Coca Cola the Pause that Refreshes" tempa, chrome disc with rubber tires ($3-5)(Coke PC)
19. red body, black base, black interior, "Feuerwehr 112/ Einsatzelettung" & white stripes tempa ($4-6)(SG)
20. black body, purple base, red interior, red windows, "Broadway- New York" tempa ($1-2)(AW)

MB78-A FAIRLADY Z, issued 1981 (USA)(AU) (MB093)

NOTE: Below models with ivory interior, clear windows, 5 spoke star wheels, black metal base & Hong Kong casting.

1. black body, no tempa ($2-4)(AU)(US-Speedsticks)
2. black body, "Z" tempa ($4-8)(US)(LE) (issued as "Phantom Z")
3. pearly white body, no tempa ($15-20)(AU)

MB78-B FERRARI TESTAROSSA *see MB75-E*

MB79-A GALANT ETERNA, issued 1981 (USA)(AU) (MB090)

NOTE: Below models with ivory interior, clear windows, 5 spoke star wheels, black metal base & Hong Kong casting.

1. light green body, no tempa ($2-4) (AU)(US-Speedsticks)
2. dark green body, no tempa ($2-4) (AU)(US-Speedsticks)
3. light green body, cream & red "Hot Points" tempa ($4-8)(US)(LE) (issued as "Hot Points Challenger")
4. light green body, white & red "Hot Points" tempa ($4-8)(US)(LE) (issued as "Hot Points Challenger")

MB80-A CHEVROLET SUBURBAN, issued 2000 (USA) (MB436)
MB60-L CHEVROLET SUBURBAN, issued 2000 (ROW)

NOTE: Below models with China casting.

1. white body, smoke windows, black interior, "Zero Test Base" & black & red design tempa, 5 spoke concave star wheels, gray base ($1-2)(MW80/2000 US) (MW60/2000 ROW)
2. white body, smoke windows, black interior, "Zero Test Base", black & red design & "Matchbox 2000" tempa, 5 spoke concave star wheels, gray base ($2-4)(MW80/ 2000 US)
3. white body, smoke windows, black interior, blue logo decal, 5 spoke concave star wheels, gray base ($50+)(ASAP)
4. white body, amber windows, gray interior, "911 Emergency" with blue stripes tempa, 10 spoke flower wheels, chrome base ($1-2)(MW74/2001)
5. pink-red body, amber windows, orange-yellow interior, "Stop Drop Roll" tempa, lace wheels, chrome base ($1-2)(MW8/2002 US)
6. pink-red body, amber windows, orange-yellow interior, "Stop Drop Roll" & "Matchbox 50" tempa, lace wheels, chrome base ($2-4)(MW8/2002 US)
7. red body, amber windows, white interior, "4 Alarm" tempa, 10 spoke flower wheels, chrome base ($1-2)(5pk)
8. white body, smoke windows, black interior, "USAF" logo decals, 5 spoke concave star wheels, gray base ($50+)(ASAP)
9. dark red body, smoke windows, white interior, "43rd Annual Spud Day Parade Car- Idaho" tempa, 10 spoke flower wheels, gray base ($2-4)(AM)
10. white body, blue windows, blue interior, "Emergency Rescue/ Limited Edition 2003" with stripes & cross tempa, lace wheels ($2-4)(Duracell in pack)
11. white body, blue windows, blue interior, "Emergency Rescue/Limited Edition 2004" with stripes & cross tempa, lace wheels ($8-10)(Duracell in pack)(CN)

MB81-A CONCEPT 1 BEETLE CABRIOLET, issued 2000 (USA) (MB438)
MB61-L CONCEPT 1 BEETLE CABRIOLET, issued 2000 (ROW)
MB73-K CONCEPT 1 BEETLE CABRIOLET, issued 1999 (GR)

NOTE: Below models with clear windshield, black plastic base & China casting unless otherwise noted.

1. white body, gray interior, white trim on windshield, "Coca Cola" tempa, 5 spoke concave star wheels ($1-2)(5pk)
2. blue body, light tan interior, no trim on windshield, small logos & red tail lights tempa, 5 spoke concave star wheels ($8-12)(MW73/1999 GR)
3. blue body, light tan interior, blue trim on windshield, small logos & red tail lights tempa, 5 spoke concave star wheels ($4-6)(MW73/ 1999 GR)
4. white body, tan interior, white trim on windshield, small logos & red tail lights tempa, 5 spoke concave star wheels ($1-2)(MW81/2000 US)(MW61/2000 ROW)
5. white body, tan interior, white trim on windshield, small logos & red tail lights & "Matchbox 2000" tempa, 5 spoke concave star wheels ($2-4)(MW81/2000 US)

6. red body, black interior, red trim on windshield, small logos tempa, chrome disc with rubber tires ($6-8)(GS-FAO)
7. silver-gray body, black interior, silver trim on windshield, "Beetle" & elliptical design tempa, 10 spoke flower wheels ($1-2)(MW1/2001)
8. silver-gray body, black interior, silver trim on windshield, "Beetle" & elliptical design tempa, 5 spoke concave star wheels ($1-2)(MW1/2001)
9. white body, tan interior, white trim on windshield, small logos & red tail lights tempa, 10 spoke flower wheels ($1-2)(MW81/2000 US)
10. white body, tan interior, white trim on windshield, small logos & red tail lights tempa, 10 spoke flower wheels, metal base ($1-2)(MW81/2000 US)
11. silver-gray body, black interior, silver trim on windshield, "Beetle" & elliptical design tempa, 10 spoke flower wheels, metal base ($2-4)(MW1/2001)
12. red body, tan & brown interior, red trim on windshield, detailed trim tempa, chrome disc wheels with rubber tires, metal base ($3-5)(TN)
13. lime body, orange interior, lime trim on windshield, "Nickelodeon" tempa, 10 spoke flower wheels, metal base ($1-2)(5pk)
14. white body, red interior, white trim on windshield, "Coca Cola" tempa, chrome disc wheels with rubber tires, metal base ($3-5)(Coke PC)
15. white body, gray interior, white trim on windshield, "Coca Cola" tempa, 5 spoke concave star wheels, metal base ($2-4)(5pk)(CK)
16. red body, white interior, red trim on windshield, "Coca Cola Catch the Waves/ Coke Adds Life" tempa, metal base ($3-5)(Coke PC)
17. silver-gray body, red interior, "Coca Cola" tempa, 10 spoke flower wheels, metal base ($2-3)(CK)
18. metallic blue body, tan interior, blue trim on windshield, "22/ Matchbox USA Toy Show" tempa, 5 spoke concave star wheels ($10-15)(CCI)
19. lime body, blue interior, smoke windshield, "Puerto Rico" tempa, 10 spoke flower wheels ($8-12)(AM)
20. metallic lime body, brown interior, smoke windshield, tail lights tempa, lace wheels ($2-4)(MW70/2003 ROW)
21. metallic lime body, brown interior, smoke windshield, tail lights & "Hero City" tempa, lace wheels ($4-5)(MW70/2003 ROW)
22. metallic gold body, white interior, smoke windshield, tiny logos tempa, lace wheels ($2-4)(MW17/ROW 2004)
23. dark orange body, black interior, orange trim smoke windshield, tiny logos & red tail lights tempa, slotted 5 spoke wheels ($3-5)(SF22/2004)
24. metallic blue body, black interior, smoke windshield, tiny logos & red tail lights tempa, lace wheels ($3-5)(SoC)
25. lemon body, blue interior, blue windshield, "Mindy- The Spongebob Squarepants Movie" tempa ($1-2)(5pk)

MB82-A MISSILE LAUNCHER, issued 1999 (USA) (MB384)

NOTE: Below models with black plastic base & China casting.

1. light olive body, dull olive rear section, "476-Unit 61" tempa ($1-2)(MW82/1999 US)
2. beige body & rear section, "United States/ MLS 62/ 314 6985/ 10" & brown dirt tempa ($1-2)(MW52/2000 US)
3. beige body & rear section, "United States/ MLS 62/ 314 6985/ 10", brown dirt & "Matchbox 2000" tempa ($2-4)(MW52/2000 US)
4. beige body & rear section, "Support Our Troops" & USA flag tempa ($50+)(CCI)
5. light olive body, dull olive rear section, "Support Our Troops" & USA flag tempa ($50+)(CCI)
6. green body, brown rear section, metallic blue base, "Man At Arms" tempa ($3-5)(MU)

MB83-A BMW 3 SERIES COUPE, issued 2000 (USA) (MB451)
MB63-M BMW 3 SERIES COUPE, issued 2000 (ROW)

NOTE: Below models with smoke windows, black base & China casting.

1. silver-gray body, black interior, head & tail lights with "Matchbox 2000" tempa, 5 spoke concave star wheels ($2-4)(MW83/2000 US)
2. silver-gray body, black interior, head & tail lights tempa, 5 spoke concave star wheels ($1-2)(MW83/2000 US)(MW63/2000 ROW)
3. silver-gray body, black interior, head & tail lights tempa, 10 spoke flower wheels ($1-2)(MW83/2000 US)(MW63/2000 ROW)
4. metallic blue body, gray interior, black to gray stripe & "3 Series" tempa, 5 spoke concave star wheels ($1-2)(5pk)
5. metallic blue body, gray interior, black to gray stripe & "3 Series" tempa, 10 spoke flower wheels ($1-2)(5pk)
6. metallic maroon body, gray interior, small "Matchbox" tempa, lace wheels ($2-4)(MW7/2002 ROW)
7. metallic maroon body, gray interior, small "Matchbox" & "Matchbox 50" tempa, lace wheels ($3-5)(MW7/2002 ROW)
8. dark blue body, gray interior, clear windows, small "BMW" logo with head & tail lights tempa, lace wheels ($4-6)(ROW BMW promo)
9. metallic gold, black interior, clear windows, small "Matchbox" & head lights tempa, lace wheels ($1-2)(LP)
10. dark green body, gray interior, clear windows, no tempa, lace wheels ($4-6)(SG)
11. unpainted body, gray interior, clear windows, pop art decals, lace wheels ($75+)(FA)
12. white body, black interior, smoke windows, small "Matchbox" tempa, lace wheels ($1-2)(LP)

MB84-A FORD FOCUS, issued 2000 (USA) (MB463)
MB64-K FORD FOCUS, issued 2000 (ROW)

NOTE: Below models with gray interior, black side stripe tempa, black plastic base & China casting unless otherwise noted.

1. bronze body, smoke windows, 5 spoke concave star wheels, "Matchbox 2000" tempa ($2-4)(MW84/2000 US)
2. bronze body, smoke windows, 5 spoke concave star wheels ($1-2)(MW84/2000 US)(MW64/2000 ROW)
3. light bronze body, smoke windows, 5 spoke concave star wheels ($1-2)(MW84/2000 US)(MW64/2000 ROW)
4. bronze body, smoke windows, 10 spoke flower wheels ($1-2)(MW84/2000 US)(MW64/2000 ROW)
5. metallic blue body, smoke green windows, 10 spoke flower wheels ($1-2)(5pk)
6. metallic blue body, smoke green windows, 5 spoke concave star wheels ($1-2)(5pk)
7. dark purple body, black interior, smoke windows, 5 spoke concave star wheels, multiple "Focus" tempa ($1-2)(5pk)
8. dark purple body, black interior, smoke windows, 10 spoke flower wheels, multiple "Focus" tempa ($1-2)(5pk)
9. red body, smoke windows, 10 spoke flower wheels, "Kellogg's Froot Loops/ Toucan Sam" tempa ($1-2)(5pk)
10. orange-yellow body, blue interior, clear windows, 10 spoke flower wheels, "Rugrats/ Dil" tempa ($1-2)(5pk)
11. black body, clear windows, lace wheels, "Focus Focus" tempa ($2-4)(MW6/2002 ROW)

12. black body, clear windows, lace wheels, "Focus Focus" & "Matchbox 50" tempa ($3-5)(MW6/2002 ROW)
13. red body, clear windows, 10 spoke flower wheels, "Rugrats/ Dil" tempa ($1-2)(5pk)
14. lemon body, black interior, clear windows, lace wheels, black stripe & small "Matchbox" tempa ($1-2)(5pk)
15. greenish white & green body, brown interior, clear windows, chrome disc wheels with rubber tires, "Coca Cola Home Refreshment" tempa ($3-5)(Coke PC)
16. metallic blue body, blue & black interior, clear windows, chrome disc wheels with rubber tires, "100" tempa ($3-5)(CL)
17. black body, tan-gray interior, clear windows, chrome disc wheels with rubber tires, "100" tempa ($3-5)(MP)(CL)
18. bronze body, smoke windows, 5 spoke concave star wheels, "Matchbox USA Convention/ 22" tempa ($10-15)(CCI)
19. white body, red interior, smoke windows, 10 spoke flower wheels, "Bears 55" with soccer ball tempa ($1-2)(MW55/2003 US)
20. white body, red interior, smoke windows, 10 spoke flower wheels, "Bears 55" with soccer ball & "Hero City" tempa ($50+)(MW55/2003 US)
21. metallic gold, black interior, smoke windows, 10 spoke flower wheels, "Focus 52" with black & green design tempa ($2-4)(MW52/2003 ROW)
22. metallic gold body, black interior, smoke windows, 10 spoke flower wheels, "Focus 52" with black & green design & "Hero City" tempa ($3-5)(MW52/2003 ROW)
23. light blue body, red interior, amber windows, 10 spoke flower wheels, "San Francisco Cable Car" tempa, red base ($1-2)(AW)
24. salmon body, gray interior, smoke windows, 5 spoke slotted wheels, detailed trim tempa, gray base ($1-2)(SF63/2004)

MB85-A SHERMAN TANK, issued 1999 (USA) (MB397)

NOTE: Below models with black treads & plastic base, China casting.

1. olive body & turret, olive gun, tan camouflage & white star tempa ($1-2)(MW85/1999 US))
2. light olive body & turret, light olive gun, "476"/ No.33857 Power Striker" tempa ($3-5)(PC)
3. olive body & turret, olive gun, mud spatter & "Matchbox 2000" tempa ($2-4)(MW51/2000 US)
4. olive body & turret, olive gun, mud spatter tempa ($1-2)(MW51/ 2000 US)

MB86-A 1999 CHEVY SILVERADO PICKUP, issued 1999 (USA) (MB398)

NOTE: Below models with 5 spoke concave star wheels, chrome base & China casting.

1. white body, dark blue interior, smoke windows, "Fresh Eggs/ Farm Fresh Dairy" tempa ($1-2)(MW86/1999 US)
2. red body, white interior, smoke windows, "Classic Home Builders" tempa ($1-2)(5pk)
3. red body, white interior, smoke windows, tool designs tempa ($1-2)(5pk)
4. yellow body, dark blue interior, clear windows, "Aqua Test Centre" tempa ($1-2)(5pk)
5. white body, black interior, smoke windows, "5 Alarm/ Hangar 34/67" tempa ($1-2)(LP)
6. white body, gray interior, clear windows, "Action Radar/ Xtreme Mission" tempa, red base ($1-2)(5pk)

NOTE: Below models with 10 spoke flower wheels unless otherwise noted.

7. metallic silver body, gray interior, smoke windows, helmet & hose tempa ($1-2)(5pk)
8. red body, gray interior, clear windows, black stripe & bed liner tempa, chrome disc with rubber tires ($3-5)(TN)
9. white body, black interior, smoke windows, "HQ Chief 778" tempa ($1-2)(5pk)
10. black body, dark gray interior, clear windows, "Texaco" logo tempa, chrome disc with rubber tires ($3-5)(Texaco PC)
11. orange-yellow body, black interior, smoke windows, "Hammer & Nails" tempa ($1-2)(MW49/2002 US)
12. orange-yellow body, black interior, smoke windows, "Hammer & Nails" & "Matchbox 50" tempa ($2-4)(MW49/2002 US)
13. white body, black interior, clear windows, "Timberwolves/ Select Heartland Chevy Dealers" tempa ($35-50)(US)
14. bright blue body, black interior, smoke windows, "HQ Chief 7787" tempa ($1-2)(5pk)
15. dark orange body, black interior, black windows, "The Home Depot" tempa, 10 spoke flower wheels ($8-12)(US in pack)

MB90-A BATTERING RAM, issued 2000 (USA) (MB468/603)

NOTE: Below models with separate cast ram, metal base & China casting

1. blue body, amber windows, white turret, yellow ram, "Police" with white & silver stripes tempa, maltese cross wheels, black base ($1-2)(MW90/2000 US)
2. blue body, amber windows, white turret, yellow ram, "Police" with white & silver stripes & "Matchbox 2000" tempa, maltese cross wheels, black base ($2-4)(MW90/2000 US)
3. white body, red windows, gray turret, dark blue ram, "Metro Police 3" tempa, black base ($1-2)(5pk)
4. orange-yellow body, red windows, dark blue turret, red ram, "Police B-12" tempa, 5 spoke oval wheels, black base ($1-2)(MW54/2001 US)
5. silver-gray body, amber windows, red turret, red ram, "Police Ram-1" tempa, 5 spoke oval wheels, metallic blue base ($1-2)(5pk)
6. bright blue body, red windows, yellow turret, yellow ram, "Police Ram-1" tempa, 5 spoke oval wheels, silver-gray base ($1-2)(5pk)
7. bright blue body, red windows, yellow turret, yellow ram, "Police Ram-1" tempa, 5 spoke oval wheels, metallic silver base ($1-2)(5pk)

NOTE: Below models have ram cast to plastic base.

8. blue body, red windows, red turret, cast ram, "Police" tempa, 5 spoke oval wheels, gray plastic base ($1-2)(5pk)

MB91-A FOUR WHEELER, issued 1999 (USA) (MB421)
MB71-J FOUR WHEELER, issued 1999 (ROW)

NOTE: Below models with silver-gray plastic base, silver-gray engine & handlebars, 8 spoke wheels, China casting unless otherwise noted.

1. olive body, tan & blue driver, silver hubs, no tempa ($1-2)(MW91/1999 US)(MW71/1999 ROW)(MW46/1999 GR)
2. green body, brown & black driver, black hubs, brown mud tempa ($1-2)(5pk)
3. red body, yellow & black driver, silver hubs, "400" & blue stripes tempa, gray base ($1-2)(5pk)
4. light red body, two tone gray driver, silver hubs, white & black tempa ($1-2)(MW63/2000 US)(MW43/2000 ROW)
5. light red body, two tone gray driver, silver hubs, white & black with "Matchbox 2000" tempa ($2-4)(MW63/2000 US)
6. red body, yellow & black driver, silver hubs on 7 spoke sawblade wheels, "5" & mud spray tempa ($1-2)(MW34/2001 US)
7. red body, black handlebars & base, yellow with "Beach Patrol" driver, silver hubs on 7 spoke sawblade wheels, white crosses tempa ($1-2)(5pk)

8. dark green body, gray handlebars & base, yellow & black with "Forest Rescue" driver, silver hubs on 7 spoke sawblade wheels, "Ranger" tempa ($3-5)(PS)
9. metallic gold body, blue handlebars & base, white driver, silver hubs on 7 spoke sawblade wheels, "Bat" tempa ($1-2)(LP)
10. red body, blue handlebars & base, orange driver with "Beach Patrol", silver hubs on 7 spoke sawblade wheels, cross tempa ($1-2)(5pk)

MB91-B FORD DUMP/UTILITY TRUCK, issued 2000 (USA) (MB450/590)
MB71-L FORD DUMP/ UTILTY TRUCK, issued 2000 (ROW)

NOTE: Below models with smoke windows, gray plastic base & China casting unless otherwise noted. Early models have "Ford Dump/ Utility Truck" on base. Later issues have "Ford F-Series Truck" base & can be intermixed between versions.

1. red body & plastic dump, smoke windows, gray interior, "Matchbox Bilt", white stripes & "CM-3527" tempa, 8 spoke wheels ($1-2)(MW91/2000 US)(MW71/2000 ROW)
2. red body & plastic dump, smoke windows, gray interior, "Matchbox Bilt", white stripes & "CM-3527" & "Matchbox 2000" tempa, 8 spoke wheels ($2-4)(MW91/2000 US)
3. red body & plastic dump, smoke windows, gray interior, "Matchbox Bilt", white stripes & "CM-3527" tempa, 7 spoke sawblade wheels ($10-15)(5pk)
4. black body, red plastic dump, clear windows, dark red interior, checkers & winged logo tempa, 8 spoke wheels ($4-6)(MW13/2001)
5. black body, red plastic dump, clear windows, dark red interior, checkers & winged logo tempa, 7 spoke sawblade wheels ($1-2)(MW13/2001)
6. maroon body, orange-yellow dump, clear windows, orange-yellow interior, "Nebraska Cornhuskers Local 37" tempa, 7 spoke sawblade wheels ($2-4)(AM)
7. orange body, black dump, dark smoke windows, black interior, "Emergency Road Repair/ MB DOT" tempa, 7 spoke sawblade wheels, chrome base ($3-5)(PS)
8. metallic orange body, orange-yellow dump. light purple windows, orange-yellow interior, "Rescue Heroes" tempa ($1-2)(5pk)
9. red body, red plastic dump, smoke windows, gray interior, "Lawns Plus" tempa ($25-40)(CCI)

MB92-A DUNE BUGGY, issued 1999 (USA) (MB429)
MB72-Q DUNE BUGGY, issued 1999 (ROW)

NOTE: Below models with plastic body & China casting.

1. light blue body & base, black roll cage, silver-gray interior & antenna, white band tempa, 8 spoke wheels ($1-2)(MW92/1999 US)(MW72/1999 ROW)(MW47/1999 GR)
2. red body & base, black roll cage, black interior & antenna, "Beach Patrol/ Matchbox 2000" tempa, 8 spoke wheels ($2-4)(MW15/2000 US)
3. red body & base, black roll cage, black interior & antenna, "Beach Patrol" tempa, 8 spoke wheels ($1-2)(MW15/2000 US)
4. turquoise body, yellow base, silver-gray roll cage, black interior & antenna, "RT450" & mountain scene tempa, 8 spoke wheels ($1-2)(5pk)
5. black body, orange base, lemon roll cage, orange interior & antenna, "88 Rugged Adventure" tempa, 8 spoke wheels ($2-3)(MW39/2000 AU)
6. purple body, yellow base, black roll cage, black interior & antenna, "Sand Blaster" tempa, 7 spoke sawblade wheels ($1-2)(MW35/2001 US)
7. black body, metallic red base, black roll cage & antenna, purple & blue stingrays tempa, 7 spoke sawblade wheels ($1-2)(5pk)
8. red body, red base, red roll cage, blue interior & antenna, "Beach Patrol" tempa, 7 spoke sawblade wheels ($1-2)(5pk)
9. yellow body, yellow base, blue roll cage, maroon interior & antenna, "4X4 Canyon" tempa, 7 spoke sawblade wheels ($1-2)(MW46/2002)
10. yellow body, yellow base, blue roll cage, maroon interior & antenna, "4X4 Canyon" & "Matchbox 50" tempa, 7 spoke sawblade wheels ($8-12)(MW46/2002)
11. blue body, green base, red roll cage, blue interior & antenna, "Mbox AR0004" & turtle tempa, 7 spoke sawblade wheels ($1-2)(LP)
12. light blue body, red base, red roll cage, orange interior & antenna, "Beach Patrol" & turtle tempa, 7 spoke sawblade wheels ($1-2)(5pk)
13. lemon body, white base, black roll cage, interior & antenna, "Unit 3" tempa, 7 spoke sawblade wheels ($1-2)(LP)
14. orange body, orange base, neon yellow roll cage, blue interior & antenna, compass design tempa, 7 spoke sawblade wheels ($1-2)(MP)

MB93-A DIRT BIKE, issued 1999 (USA) (MB430)
MB73-I DIRT BIKE, issued 1999 (ROW)

NOTE: Below models with gray engine, gray wheels, no tempa & China casting unless otherwise noted.

1. red body & handlebars, black seat, blue-gray & brown driver ($1-2)(MW93/1999 US)(MW73/1999 ROW)(MW48/1999 GR)
2. dark red body, red handlebars, black seat, blue-gray & shiny brown driver ($1-2)(MW93/1999 US)(MW73/1999 ROW)(MW48/1999 GR)
3. orange-yellow body, yellow handlebars, blue seat, red & black driver ($1-2)((MW38/2000 AU)(5pk)
4. red body & handlebars, red & black driver, black seat, "Matchbox 2000" tempa ($2-4)(MW13/2000 US)
5. red body & handlebars, red & black driver, black seat ($1-2)(MW13/2000 US)
6. lemon body & handlebars, blue & orange driver ($1-2)(5pk)
7. orange body & handlebars, white & red driver, purple seat ($1-2)(MW33/2001 US)
8. mud brown body, black handlebars, pea green & yellow driver, dark green seat ($1-2)(5pk)

MB94-A SNOWMOBILE, issued 1999 (USA) (MB418)
MB74-K SNOWMOBILE, issued 1999 (ROW)

NOTE: Below models with China casting.

1. red body, black seat & skis, yellow & black driver, smoke windshield, white design tempa, black wheels ($1-2)(MW94/1999 US)(MW74/1999 ROW)(MW49/1999 GR)
2. yellow body, blue seat & skis, dark gray driver, clear windshield, "8" & blue hash marks tempa, gray wheels ($1-2)(5pk)
3. yellow body, blue seat & skis, dark gray driver, clear windshield, "8" & blue hash marks tempa, white wheels ($1-2)(5pk)
4. black body, red seat & skis, dark blue & neon green driver, smoke windshield, neon yellow flash tempa, black wheels ($1-2)(MW76/2000 US)(MW56/2000 ROW)
5. black body, red seat & skis, dark blue & neon green driver, smoke windshield, neon yellow flash & "Matchbox 2000" tempa, black wheels ($2-4)(MW76/2000 US)
6. white & orange body, black seat & skis, orange & blue driver, blue windshield, "TC-3/ Test Centre" & hash marks tempa, black wheels ($1-2)(LP)

7. yellow body, black seat & skis, purple & black driver, smoke windshield, black & red design tempa, black wheels ($1-2)(MW8/2001)
8. lavender body, neon yellow seat & skis, powder blue driver, smoke windshield, "38 Colorado" tempa, black wheels ($2-4)(AM)
9. white & red body, black seat & skis, red driver, smoke windshield, snowflake & "Alarm" tempa, black wheels ($1-2)(5pk)
10. white body, light blue seat & skis, yellow driver, smoke windshield, snowflake & "Alarm" tempa, black wheels ($1-2)(5pk)

MB95-A AERO JUNIOR, issued 1999 (USA) (MB428)
MB75-H AERO JUNIOR, issued 1999 (ROW)

NOTE: Below models with China casting.

1. red body, yellow base & wings, dark blue driver, gray engine, black prop, none tempa ($1-2)(MW95/1999 US)(MW75/1999 ROW)(MW50/1999 GR)
2. metallic blue body, white base & wings, red driver, silver-gray engine, white prop, "NP-20035" tempa ($1-2)(MW70/2000 US)(MW50/2000 ROW)
3. metallic blue body, white base & wings, red driver, silver-gray engine, white prop, "NP-20035" & "Matchbox 2000" tempa ($2-4)(MW70/2000 US)
4. orange-yellow body, blue base, orange-yellow wings, red driver, gray engine, orange-yellow prop, blue & red design tempa ($1-2)(5pk)

MB96-A STREET CLEANER, issued 2000 (USA) (MB469)
MB 3-F STREET CLEANER, issued 2002 (ROW)

NOTE: Below models with smoke windows, black arms, black sweeper, 5 spoke center cut rear wheels & China casting.

1. dark cream body, red interior & bucket, silver-gray base, "Metro Disposal" tempa, 8 spoke front wheels ($1-2)(MW96/2000 US)
2. dark cream body, red interior & bucket, silver-gray base, "Metro Disposal" & "Matchbox 2000" tempa, 8 spoke front wheels ($2-4)(MW96/2000 US)
3. dark green body, neon yellow interior & bucket, black base, "City Service DOT 042076" tempa, 8 spoke front wheels ($4-6)(MW20/2001 US)
4. dark green body, neon yellow interior & bucket, black base, "City Service DOT 042076" tempa, 7 spoke sawblade front wheels ($1-2)(MW20/2001 US)
5. orange-yellow body, clear windows, dark blue interior & bucket, black base, "City Streets Department" tempa, 8 spoke front wheels ($4-6)(PB)
6. purple body, green interior & bucket, gray base, "Big Apple" tempa, 7 spoke sawblade wheels ($1-2)(MW3/2002)
7. purple body, green interior & bucket, gray base, "Big Apple" & "Matchbox 50" tempa, 7 spoke sawblade wheels ($2-4)(MW3/2002)
8. orange-yellow body, clear windows, dark blue interior & bucket, black base, "City Streets Department" tempa, 7 spoke sawblade wheels ($4-6)(PB)
9. lime body, clear windows, red interior & bucket, black base, "Hey! Arnold" tempa, 7 spoke sawblade wheels ($1-2)(5pk)
10. white body, red interior, dark red bucket, orange base, "Turbo Jets 18" tempa ($1-2)(MW18/2003)
11. white body, red interior, dark red bucket, orange base, "Turbo Jets 18" & "Hero City" tempa ($2-4)(MW18/2003)

MB97-A POSTAL SERVICE DELIVERY TRUCK, issued 2000 (USA) (MB370)

NOTE: Below models with black interior, smoke windows, black hubs, black plastic base & China casting.

1. white body, "United States Postal Service" tempa, 5 spoke concave star wheels ($1-2)(MW97/2000 US)
2. white body, "United States Postal Service" & "Matchbox 2000" tempa, 5 spoke concave star wheels ($2-4)(MW97/200 US)
3. white body, "United States Postal Service" & small "Matchbox" tempa, 10 spoke flower wheels ($1-2)(MW18/2001 US)
4. white body, "United States Postal Service" tempa & "Skillman, NJ 08558" decals, 5 spoke concave star wheels ($15-25)(CCI)
5. white body, "United States Postal Service" & small "Matchbox" tempa, 5 spoke concave star wheels ($25-40)
6. white body, "Mailbox" tempa, blue interior & base, 10 spoke flower wheels ($1-2)(5pk)

MB99-A GMC BUCKET TRUCK, issued 2000 (USA) (MB470)

NOTE: Below models with amber windows, 8 spoke wheels, gray base & China casting.

1. dark blue body, white boom & bucket, "Power Inc." tempa ($1-2)(MW99/2000 US)
2. dark blue body, white boom & bucket, "Power Inc." & "Matchbox 2000" tempa ($2-4)(MW99/2000 US)

MB-2 SAVANNA RX-7, issued 1979 (JP) (MB091)

NOTE: Below models with black metal base, ivory interior & 5 spoke star wheels.

1. green body, stripe & "RX7" tempa, Japan casting ($15-20)(JP)
2. yellow body, stripe & "RX7" tempa, Japan casting ($15-20)(JP)

MB-5 FAIRLADY Z, issued 1979 (JP) (MB093)

NOTE: Below models with black metal base, ivory interior & no tempa

1. red body, dot dash wheels, Japan casting ($15-20)(JP)
2. pearly silver body, dot dash wheels, Japan casting ($15-20)(JP)

MB J-21 TOYOTA CELICA XX, issued 1979 (JP) (MB092)

NOTE: Below models with black metal base, ivory interior, 5 spoke star wheels & no tempa.

1. cream body, Japan casting, "J-21" cast on base ($15-20)(JP)
2. red body, Japan casting, "J-21" cast on base ($15-20)(JP)

MB J-22 GALANT ETERNA, issued 1979 (JP) (MB090)

NOTE: Below models with black metal base, ivory interior, 5 spoke star wheels & no tempa.

1. red body, Japan casting, "J-22" cast on base ($15-20)(JP)
2. yellow body, Japan casting, "J-22" cast on base ($15-20)(JP)

NOTE: As of the end of 2004, the following models were not included in the normal 1-75 range. Some of these were promotional castings offered through White Rose Collectibles. These are identified with MB or WR frame numbers, while others were offered through the Farming series and Two Packs.

MB214 FORD AEROMAX, issued 1992 (CY) (MB214/308)

NOTE: This casting was issued exclusively as a part of the Convoy series models. There were no single issues released. The model shown in the photo section is an ASAP blank cab of the CY-39 Box Truck.

MB215 CHEVY PANEL VAN, issued 1995 (USA) (MB215)

NOTE: This is a smaller size than the MB58-H/MB245 Chevy Panel Van, notably marked by a rear bumper that is omitted on the larger casting. Below models with clear windows, 8 dot wheels, black plastic base & China casting unless otherwise noted.

1. metallic red body & chassis, "American Iron Cruise 95" tempa, Thailand casting ($12-18)(US)
2. metallic green body, black chassis, "Seasons Greetings-Matchbox Collectors Club 1995" tempa, Thailand casting ($8-12)(US)
3. florescent orange body & chassis, "Matchbox Get In The Fast Lane-Hershey Convention 1996" tempa, Thailand casting ($8-12)(US)
4. purple body, black chassis, "Continental Aero" tempa, Thailand casting ($10-15)(US)
5. metallic green body, black chassis, "American Iron Cruise 1998" tempa, Thailand casting ($15-20)(C2)
6. silver-gray body, black chassis, "Hot August Nights" tempa, 5 arch wheels ($15-20)(CCI)
7. silver-gray body, black chassis, "Penn State" tempa, 5 arch wheels ($15-20)(ASAP)
8. silver-gray body, black chassis, no tempa, 5 arch wheels ($25-40)(ASAP blank)
9. metallic green body, black chassis, "25th Anniversary S.J.S.R.A. South Jersey Shore Rod Run" tempa ($15-20)(CCI)

NOTE: Below models with Mattel China casting unless otherwise noted.

10. white body, black chassis, no tempa, chrome disc wheels with rubber tires ($25-40)(CCI blank)
11. white body, black chassis, "Omps Funeral Home" tempa, chrome disc wheels with rubber tires ($12-18)(CCI)
12. white body, black chassis, "1st Annual Salmon River Festival" tempa, chrome disc wheels with rubber tires, ($12-18)(CCI)
13. white body, black chassis, FAO Schwarz World of Wheels" tempa, chrome disc wheels with rubber tires, (50+)(CCI)
14. silver-gray body, black chassis, "Andale- www.andale.com" tempa, 5 arch wheels ($50+)(ASAP)
15. red body, black chassis, chrome base, "Texaco" tempa, chrome disc wheels with rubber tires ($3-5)(PC)

NOTE: Below models with black chassis & chrome disc wheels with rubber tires & Mattel China casting unless otherwise noted.

16. white body, "Mac's Roller Rink, Inc." tempa ($18-25)(CCI)
17. white body, "Alpenglow/ Apple House" tempa ($18-25)(CCI)
18. white body, "Caldwell Medical Center" tempa ($12-18)(CCI)
19. white body, "The Grapevine/ Fine Wines- Gift Baskets Since 1987 tempa ($12-18)(CCI)
20. white body, "My Sons-N-Me/ Toy Car Collectibles" tempa ($12-18)(CCI)
21. white body, "Diecast Illustrated" tempa ($12-18)(CCI)
22. white body, "Bill Cairns Realtor/ Ambulance" tempa ($12-18)(CCI)
23. white body, "Bosal- Mark of Excellence" tempa ($12-18)(CCI)
24. white body, "Bill's Classic Toys & Collectibles" tempa ($12-18)(CCI)
25. metallic lilac white, pearly white chassis, "Misse- Billy- Our Wedding Day" tempa ($35-50)(CCI)
26. white body, "G&M Metal Fabricators Inc" tempa ($18-25)(CCI)
27. white body, "The Purple Penguin- Summer Delivery Cruise 2002" tempa ($12-18)(CCI)
28. white body, "20th Century Antique & Collectables Market" tempa ($12-18)(CCI)
29. white body, "10/n- Jordan's Bar Mitzvah" tempa ($12-18)(CCI)
30. white body, "48th West Virginia Black Walnut Festival" tempa ($12-18)(CCI)
31. white body, "United Way- GE" tempa ($12-18)(CCI)
32. white body- "United Way- Rubbermaid" tempa ($12-18)(CCI)
33. white body, "Merry Christmas 2002" tempa ($12-18)(CCI)
34. white body, "Blue Ridge Antique Power Association Inc." tempa ($12-18)(CCI)
35. white body, "February 2003 Matchbox/ CCI" with Mt. Rushmore tempa ($12-18)(CCI)
36. white body, "Happy Birthday- Shahan Turns 40" tempa ($12-18)(CCI)
37. white body, "Cooper" with blue grid tempa ($12-18)(CCI)
38. white body, "Credit Union Direct Lending" tempa ($12-18)(CCI)
39. white body, "Racing for Patrick Wells- Dan Vader" tempa ($12-18)(CCI)
40. white body, "MJ Engineering & Land Surveying, PC" ($18-25)(CCI)
41. white body, "Jennifer/ Michael- Our Wedding Day" tempa ($12-18)(CCI)
42. white body, "Crossroad Ft. Wayne Children's Home/ Car Show & Quilt Auction" tempa ($12-18)(CCI)
43. metallic pea green body, purple chassis, gray base, smoke windows, 10 spoke flower wheels, "Daffy Duck" tempa ($1-2)((5pk)
44. white body, "22nd Annual Fayetteville Dogwood Festival" tempa ($12-18)(CCI)
45. silver-gray body, "Compaq" tempa, 5 arch wheels, Matchbox International casting ($50+)(ASAP)
46. white body, "43rd Annual Sycamore Pumpkin Festival 2004" tempa ($12-18)(CCI)
47. white body, "Snow White Grill" tempa ($12-18)(CCI)
48. white body, "Creanies Ice Cream" tempa ($12-18)(CCI)
49. metallic purple body, black chassis, 10 spoke flower wheels, "Dracula's Castle/ Romania" tempa ($1-2)(AW)
50. metallic silver body, black chassis, 5 arch wheels, "41st Annual Barnesville Pumpkin Festival" tempa ($18-25)(CCI)

NOTE: A series of models with NBA liveries using this casting are not listed here as they are classified as "Models of Yesteryear" on the base.

MB217 D.I.R.T. MODIFIED, issued 1992 (WR) (MB217)

NOTE: Below models with slicks wheels.

1. powder blue body, red interior, chrome base, "White Rose Collectibles 1" tempa, Thailand casting ($60-75)(WR)
2. orange-yellow body, red interior, chrome base, "7X Turbo Blue" tempa, Thailand casting ($5-7)(WR)
3. orange-yellow body, blue interior, blue base, "91 Wheels" tempa, Thailand casting ($5-7)(WR)
4. orange & white body, red interior, chrome base, "9 Kinney" tempa, Thailand casting ($5-7)(WR)
5. red body, red interior, chrome base, "72 Auto Palace" tempa, Thailand casting ($5-7)(WR)
6. brown body, black interior, chrome base, "1 Phil's Chevrolet" tempa, Thailand casting ($5-7)(WR)
7. white body, red interior, chrome base, "6 Freightliner" tempa, Thailand casting ($5-7)(WR)
8. white body, red interior, chrome base, "1 Steak Out Restaurants" tempa, Thailand casting ($6-8)(WR)
9. blue body, red interior, chrome base, "35" tempa, Thailand casting ($6-8)(WR)
10. orange & yellow body, orange interior, chrome base, "12 BR DeWitt" tempa, Thailand casting ($6-8)(WR)
11. dark blue & white body, red interior, chrome base, "74 Smith Brothers" tempa, Thailand casting ($6-8)(WR)
12. white body, black interior, chrome base, "14 R.P. LeFrois" tempa, Thailand casting ($6-8)(WR)
13. white & black body, red interior, chrome base, "115 Doherty Bros." tempa, Thailand casting ($6-8)(WR)
14. red, white & black body, black interior, chrome base, "21 Alfair Studio" tempa, Thailand casting ($6-8)(WR)

15. white & orange body, blue interior, chrome base, "44 Pontiac/ Kneisel Race Cars" tempa, Thailand casting ($6-8)(WR)

MB236 FORD TRACTOR, issued 1993 (FM) (MB236)
1. blue body, red scoop, light yellow interior, pearly silver base, gray hubs with black tires, Thailand casting, no harrow ($3-5)(FM)
2. dark blue body, red scoop, ivory interior, pearly silver base, red hubs with black tires, China casting, yellow harrow ($3-5)(AP)

MB237 TRACTOR SHOVEL, issued 1993 (FM) (MB237)
NOTE: Although cast No.29 on the base, the frame number "MB237" is cast on the forks, which makes this a new model.
1. red body, red scoop, gray arms, black plastic base, black interior/motor, no tempa, Thailand casting ($3-5)(FM)

MB262 CHRYSLER VOYAGER, issued 1994 (BE) (MB262)
NOTE: This is a modified casting of the MB68E/64E Dodge Caravan.
1. blue body & side door, chrome base, 8 spoke wheels, detailed trim tempa, Thailand casting ($15-18)(BE)
NOTE: Roof label lettering can read in either direction
2. blue body & side door, chrome base, detailed trim tempa & "Kipling" roof label, 8 spoke wheels, Thailand casting ($15-18)(BE)

NOTE: MB267, MB268 & MB269 are newer castings and are much larger than their previous counterparts at MB54H, MB7G and MB35I respectively

.

MB267 CHEVY LUMINA, issued 1994 (WR) (MB267)
NOTE: Below models with clear windows, black disc wheels with rubber tires (Goodyear unless noted), black plastic base & China casting.
1. white & dark blue body, black interior, "White Rose Series II in '94" tempa ($4-6)(WR)
2. white/powder blue/dark blue body, black interior, "White Rose Collectibles 94" tempa ($25-35)(WR)
3. metallic blue & orange body, silver-gray interior, "Du Pont 24/ 1993 Rookie of the Year" tempa ($3-5)(WR)
4. orange & white body, gray interior, "Kodak Funsaver 4" tempa ($3-5)(WR)
5. dark blue & yellow body, black interior, Hoosier tires, "Matchbox-White Rose Collectibles 29" tempa ($3-5)(WR)
6. fluorescent lime body, black interior, white lettered "Manheim Auctions 7" tempa ($3-5)(WR)
7. red & yellow body, black interior, "Kellogg's Corn Flakes 5" tempa ($3-5)(WR)
8. white body, black interior, Hoosier tires, "Baltimore Colts 29" tempa ($18-25)(WR)
9. yellow body, gray interior, "Pic N Pay/Shoe World 32" tempa ($8-12)(WR)
10. yellow-orange body, black interior, "Kodak 4" tempa ($3-5)(WR)
11. red body, gray interior, "Fiddle Faddle 34" tempa ($3-5)(WR)
12. white/gray/black body, gray interior, Hoosier tires, "Western Auto 17" tempa ($3-5)(WR)
13. gold plated body, red interior, "Six Time Champion 3 Dale Earnhardt" tempa ($18-25)(WR)
14. red & yellow body, black interior, yellow disc wheels, "Kellogg's Corn Flakes 5" tempa ($4-6)(WR)(TC)
15. gray body, red interior, "Kellogg's 5" tempa ($4-6)(WR)(TC)
16. fluorescent lime body, black interior, Hoosier tires, "Manheim Auctions 7" (black letters) tempa ($4-6)(WR)(TC)
17. fluorescent lime body, black interior, lime disc wheels, "Manheim Auctions 7" (white letters) tempa ($4-6)(WR)(TC)
18. orange body, gray interior, "Polaroid 46" tempa ($18-25)(WR)
19. white & blue body, gray interior, "AC-Delco 52" tempa ($3-5)(WR)
20. black & yellow body, red interior, "Meineke 41" tempa ($4-5)(WR)
21. black body, gray interior, "Stanley 92" tempa ($4-5)(WR)
22. gold plated body, gray interior, "Lifetime Achievement Award 33-Harry Gant" tempa ($20-25)(WR)
23. yellow body, gray interior, "DeWalt 08" tempa ($4-5)(WR)(TM)
24. metallic blue body, gray interior, "Du Pont Automotive Finishes 2" tempa ($3-5)(WR)
25. red body, gray interior, "Detroit Gasket/MGM Brakes 72" tempa ($3-5)(WR)
26. black & orange-yellow body, red interior, "Caterpillar 95" tempa ($3-5)(WR)
27. pink-red & yellow body, gray interior, "Lipton Tea 74" tempa ($3-5)(WR)
28. blue-green & purple body, gray interior, "Vermont Teddy Bear 71" tempa ($3-5)(WR)
29. orange-red & white body, gray interior, "Tracey Lawrence/ Yamaha 1" tempa ($8-12)(WR)
30. white body, gray interior, "Luxaire 99" tempa ($3-5)(WR)
31. gold plated body, red interior, "7 Time Champion 3" tempa ($20-25)(WR)
32. purple body, black interior, "Kandi & Steve/ October 1, 1994" tempa ($250-500)(WR)
33. white body, black interior, "Diecast Digest 01" tempa ($3-5)(WR)
34. cream body, gray interior, "December 10, 1994/ Steph & Mike/ The Desenberg's" ($250-500)(WR)

MB268 FORD THUNDERBIRD, issued 1994 (WR) (MB268)
NOTE: Below models with clear windows, black disc wheels with Goodyear rubber tires, black plastic base & China casting unless noted otherwise
1. blue body, gray interior, "Factory Stores of America 75" tempa ($3-5)(WR)
2. black body, gray interior, "Winn Dixie 60" tempa ($3-5)(WR)
3. white/red/dark blue body, gray interior, "Valvoline 6/Reese's" tempa ($3-5)(WR)
4. black body, gray interior, "Ford Motorsports 2" tempa ($3-5)(WR)
5. metallic blue & white body, gray interior, "Family Channel 16" tempa ($3-5)(WR)
6. green body, gray interior, "Quaker State 26" tempa ($3-5)(WR)
7. black body, gray interior, "Petron Plus 55" tempa ($15-20)(WR)
8. black body, gray interior, "Exide Batteries 7" with "Exide Batteries" on trunk tempa ($3-5)(WR)
9. metallic blue & powder blue body, gray interior, "Quality Care 15" tempa ($3-5)(WR)
10. black body, gray interior, "Fingerhut 98" tempa ($3-5)(WR)
11. white body, gray interior, Hoosier tires, "Hooters 19" tempa ($3-5)(WR)
12. metallic blue body, gray interior, Hoosier tires, "Raybestos 8" tempa ($3-5)(WR)
13. yellow & purple body, gray interior, "Smokin' Joe 23" tempa, sealed in plexibox with yellow base stand ($20-25)(WR)
14. yellow & purple body, black interior, "Smokin' Joe 23" tempa, sealed in plexibox with purple base stand ($20-25)(WR)
15. red body, red interior, "McDonald's 94" tempa ($3-5)(WR)
16. black body, black interior, "McDonald's/Batman Forever 94" tempa ($10-15)(WR)

17. gold plated body, red interior, "1994 Rookie of The Year-8 Jeff Burton" tempa ($20-25)(WR)
18. bright blue & yellow body, gray interior, "Lowe's 11" tempa ($3-5)(WR)
19. turquoise & black body, gray interior, "Heilig-Meyers 90" tempa ($3-5)(WR)
20. black body, gray interior, "Exide Batteries 7" tempa ($3-5)(WR)
21. gold plated body, red interior, "1994 Most Popular Driver-Bill Elliot" tempa ($20-25)(WR)
22. blue & white body, gray interior, "Raybestos 8" tempa ($3-5)(WR)
23. white & dark blue body, gray interior, "Valvoline/Cummins 6" tempa ($3-5)(WR)
24. multi-color body, black interior, "Mane N Tail/Straight Arrow 12" tempa ($3-5)(WR)
25. black body, red interior, "Havoline 28" tempa ($3-5)(WR)
26. blue & orange body, gray interior, "Purex Dial 40" tempa ($3-5)(WR)
27. black body, black interior, "Burnfoundation/Motorsports 96" tempa ($7-10)(US)
28. blue body, black interior, "Kleenex 40" tempa ($3-5)(WR)
29. blue body, gray interior, slicks, "Kleenex 40" tempa ($10-15)(WR)
30. red & orange body, gray interior, "Citgo 21" tempa ($3-5)(WR)
31. purple body, red interior, "K-Mart/Little Caesars 37" tempa ($3-5)(WR)
32. orange body, black interior, Hoosier tires, "White Rose Collectibles 00" tempa ($10-15)(WR)
33. blue body, gray interior, "New Holland 94" tempa ($3-5)(WR)
34. black body, gray interior, "Exide 99" tempa ($3-5)(WR)
35. white & blue body, gray interior, "White Rose Collectibles 95" tempa ($3-5)(WR)
36. blue body, red interior, "Straight Arrow 12" tempa ($3-5)(WR)

MB269 GRAND PRIX PONTIAC, issued 1994 (WR) (MB269)

NOTE: Below models with clear windows, black disc wheels with Goodyear rubber tires, black plastic base & China casting unless noted otherwise

1. yellow/black & red/blue body, black interior, "Black Flag 43/ French's 43" tempa ($35-40)(WR)
2. black body, black interior, "Black Flag 43" tempa ($3-5)(WR)
3. black body, gray interior, "Kendall 40" tempa ($3-5)(WR)
4. yellow body, black interior, "French's 43" tempa ($3-5)(WR)
5. yellow body, yellow interior & wheels, "Pennzoil 30" tempa ($3-5)(WR)
6. blue body, black interior, "Richard Petty Pit Tour 43" tempa ($10-15)(WR)
7. dark blue & white body, black interior, "Cobra 24" tempa ($10-15)(WR)
8. metallic blue & pink body, black interior, "Coors Light 42" tempa, sealed in plexibox with silver-gray stand ($20-25)(WR)
9. light blue body, gray interior, "USA Bobsled Team 43" tempa ($10-15)(WR)
10. silver-gray, metallic blue & pink body, black interior, "Coors Light 42" tempa, sealed in plexibox with white stand ($20-25)(WR)
11. red body, gray interior, "Hulkster 43" tempa ($6-8)(WR)(TC)

MB283 CHEVY MONTE CARLO, issued 1995 (WR) (MB283)

NOTE: Below models with black base, clear windows, black disc wheels with Goodyear rubber tires, black plastic base & China casting unless noted.

1. florescent pink body, black interior, "Matchbox 1995/1" tempa ($85-125)(US)
2. florescent yellow body, black interior, "Matchbox 1995/1" tempa ($85-125)(US)

NOTE: Above two models used as raffle prizes at the 1995 Hershey, PA convention

3. yellow & red body, black interior, "Kellogg's 5" with "Pop Tarts" on trunk tempa ($3-5)(WR)
4. red body, gray interior, "Lipton Tea 74" tempa ($3-5)(WR)
5. orange-yellow body, black interior, "DeWalt 1" tempa ($3-5)(WR)
6. black body, black interior, "Goodwrench 3" tempa ($3-5)(WR)
7. blue & white body, black interior, "Hyde Tools 08" tempa ($3-5)(WR)
8. purplish & yellow body, black interior, "Burger King 87" tempa ($3-5)(WR)
9. blue & white body, black interior, "Bell South Mobility 87" tempa ($10-15)(WR)
10. white body, black interior, "The Budget Gourmet 57" tempa ($3-5)(WR)
11. red body, black interior, "Budweiser 25" tempa, sealed in plexibox ($20-25)(WR)
12. green & black body, gray interior, "Interstate Batteries 18" tempa ($3-5)(WR)
13. metallic blue & florescent orange body, gray interior, "Du Pont 24" tempa ($3-5)(WR)
14. black body, red interior, yellow wheel hubs, "Caterpillar/Cat 95" tempa ($6-8)(WR)(TC)
15. blue/white/red body, red interior, "Lance Snacks 43" tempa ($3-5)(WR)
16. gold plated body, black interior, "1995 Rookie of The Year-Ricky Craven 41" tempa ($20-25)(WR)
17. gold plated body, gray interior, "1995 Champion-Lipton Tea 74" tempa ($20-25)(WR)
18. orange-yellow body, black interior, "Kodak Film 4" tempa ($3-5)(WR)
19. red & yellow body, gray interior, "Royal Oak Charcoal 34" tempa ($3-5)(WR)
20. mid blue body, black interior, "Channellock 10" tempa ($3-5)(WR)
21. gold plated body, gray interior, "Du Pont 95 Points Champion" tempa ($20-25)(WR)
22. orange-yellow body, black interior, "Caterpillar/Cat 96" tempa ($3-5)(WR)
23. white & green body, gray interior, "Kodiak 41" tempa, sealed in plexibox ($20-25)(WR)
24. black & orange-yellow body, black interior, "Burger King 87" tempa ($7-10)(WR)
25. black body, red interior, "Hype 88" tempa ($3-5)(WR)
26. red body, black interior, "Budweiser 25" tempa, sealed in glass bottle ($25-35)(WR)
27. blue/ white/ dark rose body, black interior, "White Rose Collectibles 96" tempa ($8-12)(WR)
28. lemon & red body, black interior, "Kellogg's Corn Flakes 5" with "Starburst" on trunk tempa ($3-5)(WR)
29. lemon & red body, black interior, "Kellogg's Corn Flakes" with 2 logos on trunk tempa ($3-5)(WR)
30. gold plated body, black interior, "Kellogg's Corn Flakes 5/ 1996 Champion" tempa ($20-25)(WR)
31. blue body, gray interior, "Fina 74" tempa ($3-5)(WR)
32. gold plated body, gray interior, "Fina 74- 1996 Champion" tempa ($20-25)(WR)
33. green & white body, gray interior, "Skoal 33" tempa, sealed in plexibox with Convoy ($25-35)(WR)
34. blue & light yellow body, gray interior, "Coors light 40" tempa, sealed in glass bottle ($25-35)(WR)

MB284 CHEVY SUPER TRUCK, issued 1995 (WR) (MB284)

NOTE: Below models with clear windows, disc wheels with Goodyear rubber tires, black plastic base & China casting unless noted otherwise.

1. black body, black interior, "Goodwrench 3" tempa ($3-5)(WR)
2. black body, black interior, "Sears Diehard 1" tempa ($3-5)(WR)
3. white, blue & red body, red interior, "Total 6" tempa ($3-5)(WR)
4. gold plated body, red interior, "3-1995 Super Truck Champion" tempa ($20-25)(WR)
5. black body, blue-green interior, "The Magic Mile 96" tempa ($7-10)(WR)
6. grape body, gray interior, "Westview Capital 33" tempa ($3-5)(WR)
7. grape body, gray interior, "Manheim Auctions 33" tempa ($3-5)(WR)
8. blue/ white/ red body, red interior, "Lance Snacks 43" tempa ($3-5)(WR)
9. metallic blue & orange body, red interior, "Du Pont 24" tempa ($3-5)(WR)
10. white & green body, white interior, "Quaker State 24" tempa ($3-5)(WR)

MB285 ICE MAKER, issued 1995 (WR) (MB285)

1. red lower body, white upper body, chrome wheels, black groomer, blue driver, "White Rose collectibles-No. 1 In Sports 1995" tempa, China casting ($75-100)(WR)

NOTE: The 1995 Hockey series models had bases altered from "Matchbox" to "White Rose Collectibles," however a small quantity (1-5) of each were found with "Matchbox" still cast on the base. Because of this rarity there is no firm $ value on these as most belong in private collections and none have been offered on the market. Those teams reported include Hartford Whalers, Chicago Blackhawks, New York Rangers, Philadelphia Flyers, Toronto Mapleleafs, Ottawa Senators, Detroit Redwings, San Jose Sharks, Washington Capitals & Tampa Bay Lightning. Others may exist but have not been reported.

MB315 VOLVO TRUCK, issued 1997 (AP) (MB315)

NOTE: Below models with amber windows, 5 arch wheels & China casting.

1. blue body, black stakes, tan load of four frames, "MB Builders" tempa, black base ($3-4)(AS)
2. blue body, brown stakes, two bales of straw load, no tempa, silver-gray base ($3-5)(AP)

MB317 FORD CARGO SKIP TRUCK, issued 1999 (AP) (MB317)

NOTE: Below models with 8 spoke wheels, black plastic base & China casting.

1. bright green body, smoke windows, black hubs, orange cage, orange arms with lever, dark green camouflage & "The Lost World" tempa ($3-5)(JR)
2. light beige body, blue windows, silver hubs, black cage, black arms with lever, green stripes tempa ($2-4)(AS)
3. red body, blue windows, silver hubs, silver-gray cage, silver-gray arms with lever, "Big Top Circus" tempa ($3-5)(AP)

MB319 MERCEDES AAV, issued 1997 (JR) (MB319)

1. light green body, light plastic gray base (without base name), black painted windows, turret with arms on roof, "The Lost World" & green camouflage tempa, China casting ($5-8)(JR)

MB337 MERCEDES AAV, issued 1997 (JR) (MB337)

1. light green body, light gray plastic base (with base name), black painted windows, luggage rack on roof, "The Lost World" & green camouflage tempa, China casting ($5-8)(JR)

MB338 1938 DODGE AIRFLOW VAN, issued 1998 (CL) (MB338)

NOTE: Below models have no origin cast on metal base & rubber tires unless otherwise noted.

1. mustard body, black roof, chassis & base, gold wheels & grille, "Catamount Porter" tempa ($8-12)(MB)
2. red body & roof, green-gold chassis, black base, gold wheels & grille, "Penn Brewery St. Nikolaus Bock Bier" tempa ($8-12)(MB)
3. lemon body & roof, pale green chassis, black base, gold wheels & grille, "Zephyr Golden Ale" tempa ($8-12)(MB)
4. purple body & roof, black chassis, black base, chrome wheels & grille, "Continental Aero/ Purple Plastic Inserts..." tempa ($8-12)(US)
5. red body & roof, green-gold chassis, black base, gold wheels & grille, "Australian Matchbox News 2002" ($18-25)(C2)(AU)
6. lemon body & roof, pale green chassis, black base, gold wheels & grille, "Australian Matchbox News 2002" ($18-25)(C2)(AU)
7. white body, black roof & chassis, black base, chrome wheels & grille, "Drink Coca Cola Bottles" tempa ($10-15)(Coke diorama)

NOTE: A series of models with NBA liveries using this casting are not listed here as they are classified as "Models of Yesteryear" on the base.

MB339 1937 MACK JUNIOR VAN, issued 1998 (CL) (MB339)

NOTE: Below models with rubber tires & metal base.

1. dark green body, light lime chassis, black base, silver wheels & grille, "Arapahoe Amber Ale" tempa ($8-12)(MB)
2. black body, salmon pink chassis, black base, silver wheels & grille, "Dixie Jazz Beer" tempa ($8-12)(MB)
3. lemon body, red chassis, black base, gold wheels & grille, "Pony Express" tempa ($8-12)(MB)
4. purple body, black chassis, black base, chrome wheels & grille, "Continental Aero/ Purple Plastic Inserts..." tempa ($8-12)(US)
5. black body, salmon pink chassis, black base, silver wheels & grille, "Bendigo National Swap Meet 2002" tempa ($18-25)(C2)(AU)
6. lemon body, red chassis, black base, gold wheels & grille, "Bendigo National Swap Meet 2002" tempa ($18-25)(C2)(AU)

NOTE: A series of models with NBA liveries using this casting are not listed here as they are classified as "Models of Yesteryear" on the base.

NOTE: Models MB343 through MB350 were originally Hot Wheel castings and were retooled into Matchbox castings. MB349 was to have been the retooled Hot Wheel Peterbilt Dump Truck but this was changed to include the MB30-E Peterbilt Quarry Truck in the Caterpillar series instead.

MB343 EXCAVATOR, issued 1998 (MB343)

1. orange-yellow body & plastic arm, black treads, yellow base, "CAT" tempa ($3-4)(CT)

MB344 DUMP TRUCK, issued 1998 (MB344)

1. orange-yellow cab, dump & base, "Caterpillar" tempa, yellow hubs ($3-4)(CT)

MB345 BULLDOZER, issued 1998 (MB345)

1. orange-yellow body, blade & arms, yellow plastic base, black treads, "CAT" tempa ($3-4)(CT)

MB346 WHEEL LOADER, issued 1998 (MB346)

1. orange-yellow body & base, yellow plastic bucket, yellow hubs, "CAT" tempa ($3-4)(CT)

MB347 ROAD ROLLER, issued 1998 (MB347)

1. orange-yellow body, black rollers & base, "Caterpillar" tempa ($3-4)(CT)
2. chrome plated body, black rollers & base, "Caterpillar" tempa ($3-4)(CT)

MB348 SCRAPER, issued 1998 (MB348)

1. orange-yellow plastic cab & rear, orange-yellow metal mid section, yellow hubs, "CAT" tempa ($3-4)(CT)
2. black plastic cab & rear , chrome plated metal mid section, black hubs, "CAT" tempa ($3-4)(CT)

MB350 MOTOR GRADER, issued 1998 (MB350)

1. orange-yellow plastic body, orange-yellow metal base, 8 spoke wheels, "Caterpillar" tempa ($3-4)(CT)
2. olive green plastic body, black metal base, 8 spoke wheels, "Caterpillar" tempa ($3-4)(CT)

MB351 CHALLENGER AG TRACTOR, issued 1998 (MB351)

1. orange-yellow body, yellow plastic roof, smoke green windows, black base, wheels & treads, "CAT" tempa ($3-4)(CT)
2. orange-yellow body, yellow plastic roof, clear windows, black base, wheels & treads, "CAT" tempa ($5-8)(PC)

MB352 TRAILER, issued 1998 (MB352)

1. orange-yellow plastic body, orange-yellow metal chassis, yellow wheels, black treads ($3-4)(CT)

MB353 BACKHOE/ LOADER, issued 1998 (MB353)

1. orange-yellow body, smoke windows, yellow-orange plastic shovel, arms, backhoe & wheels, "CAT" tempa ($3-4)(CT)
2. orange-yellow body, smoke windows, black plastic shovel, arms & backhoe, yellow-orange wheels, "CAT" tempa ($3-4)(CAT)
3. orange-yellow body, clear windows with black trim, black plastic shovel, arms & backhoe, yellow-orange wheels, "CAT" tempa ($5-8)(PC)

MB354 SOIL COMPACTOR, issued 1998 (MB354)

1. orange-yellow body, orange-yellow plastic grader & base, smoke green windows, yellow studded wheels, "CAT" tempa ($3-4)(CT)
2. orange-yellow body, orange-yellow plastic grader & base, clear windows with black trim, yellow studded wheels, "CAT" tempa ($5-8)(PC)
3. olive green body, black plastic grader & base, clear windows, black studded tires, "CAT" tempa ($3-4)(CT)

NOTE: An independent company Strottman International Inc. through a license agreement has retooled the following four vehicles with Mattel Toys using Matchbox's pattern molds. Strottman International Inc. (S.I.I.) is a manufacturing company that supplies Taco Bell with their toy give-aways. This is why they are not listed under the original casting number. The baseplates are cast "Made in China by S.I.I.". A further four models were made in 1999 but as these had no frame number for identification, these are listed at the end of the listing for miniatures with "TB" numbers for identification purposes only.

MB374 '62 CORVETTE, issued 1998 (MB374)

1. black body, windows & plastic base, dual white stripes, Taco Bell logo & red side band tempa, 5 spoke concave star wheels ($3-5)(TB)

MB375 HUMVEE, issued 1998 (MB375)

1. black body & plastic base, silver painted windows, white & red swirls tempa, 8 spoke wheels with black hubs ($3-5)(TB)

MB376 VW CONCEPT, issued 1998 (MB376)

1. red body with black fenders & plastic base, silver painted windows, swirl & lines design, 6 spoke spiral wheels ($3-5)(TB)
2. green body, black plastic base, silver painted windows, no tempa, 5 spoke concave star wheels, Mattel casting ($8-12)(PS)

MB377 FIREBIRD FORMULA, issued 1998 (MB377)

1. black body with silver painted windows, black plastic base, "Taco Bell" with red & white flames tempa, 6 spoke spiral wheels ($3-5)(TB)

MB381 MATERIAL HANDLER, issued 1999 (MB381)

NOTE: Below models with yellow arm, black base, "CAT" tempa, China casting

1. yellow-orange body, smoke windows ($3-5)(CT)
2. yellow-orange body, clear windows with black trim ($8-12)(PC)

MB382 TOOL CARRIER, issued 1999 (MB382)

1. orange-yellow body & roof, black forks & arms, orange-yellow hubs, smoke windows, China casting ($3-5)(CT)

MB383 TRACTOR SHOVEL, issued 1999

NOTE: Below models with orange-yellow roof, black arms & forks, China casting.

1. orange-yellow body, smoke windows, black wheels with orange-yellow hubs ($3-5)(CT)
2. orange-yellow body, clear windows with black trim, orange-yellow wheels with black tires ($15-20)(PC)

MB388 PETERBILT DUMP TRUCK W/PLOW, issued 1998 (MB388)

1. orange-yellow body, orange-yellow dump, chrome plated plastic base & plow, "CAT" tempa, clear windows, 8 spoke wheels, China casting ($3-5)(PS)

MB389 VOLVO CONTAINER TRUCK, issued 1998 (MB389)

1. blue-green body, clear aquarium load, smoke windows, 5 arch wheels, silver-gray plastic base, dolphin & waves tempa, China casting ($3-4)(AP)

MB393 HARLEY DAVIDSON H-D FXSTS SPRINGER SOFTAIL, issued 1995 (HD) (MB393)

NOTE: Below models with chrome handlebars & engine, spoked wheels with black tires, "Harley Davidson" tempa, black seat & China casting.

1. metallic blue body ($3-5)
2. metallic turquoise body ($3-5)
3. metallic purple body ($3-5)
4. metallic red body ($3-5)
5. black body ($3-5)

MB394 1939 HARLEY DAVIDSON H-D KNUCKLEHEAD, issued 1995 (HD) (MB394)

NOTE: Below models with chrome handlebars & engine, black seat, spoked wheels with black tires, "Harley Davidson" tempa & China casting.

1. powder blue body & gas tank ($3-5)
2. black body, white gas tank ($3-5)

MB403 ARTICULATED DUMP TRUCK, issued 1999 (MB403)

1. orange-yellow cab & body, orange-yellow plastic dump, orange-yellow hubs, "CAT" tempa, China casting ($3-5)(CT)

MB404 CATERILLAR SKIDDER, issued 1999 (MB404)

1. orange-yellow body & base, orange-yellow plow, arm & rear claw, black roof, "CAT" tempa, China casting ($3-5)(CT)

MB443 TRAILER, issued 1999 (MB443)

1. orange-yellow body with gray bed, yellow rollers, black treads ($2-4)(CT)

MB455 BLIMP, issued 1999 (MB455)

NOTE: Below models with China casting.

1. red body, dark blue cab unit, "Coca Cola" tempa ($6-8)(Coke PC)
2. red body, dark blue cab unit, "Coca Cola" with "www.cocacolastore.com" tempa ($75+)(CCI)
3. light blue body, yellow cab unit, "Peanuts" & Snoopy tempa ($1-2)(5pk)
4. black body, yellow cab unit, "Nickelodeon" tempa ($1-2)(5pk)
5. light blue body, red cab unit, "Mrs. Puff/ Rules of the Road" ($1-2)(5pk)

MB456 PONTIAC FIREBIRD SE POLICE, issued 2000 (MB456)

NOTE: Below models with clear windows, gray interior, 8 dot wheels & China casting unless otherwise noted.

1. red body, black dome lights, "DARE/ Police" tempa, red base ($3-5)(DR)
2. black & white body, triangular dome lights, "DARE To Resist Drugs & Violence" tempa, black base ($3-5)(DR)

MB457 CAMARO IROC Z-28 POLICE, issued 2000 (MB457)

NOTE: Below models with 8 dot wheels, black plastic base & China casting

1. white body, smoke windows, red dome lights, gray interior, "Medford Police/ DARE- No Drugs" & stripes design tempa ($3-5)(DR)
2. black body, clear windows, red & blue dome lights, black interior, "DARE" with yellow & red stripes tempa ($3-5)(DR)

MB460 1999 MUSTANG POLICE, issued 2000 (MB460/509)

NOTE: Below models with black base & China casting.

1. black body, clear windows, blue & red dome lights, red interior, 5 spoke concave star wheels, "DARE Police" tempa ($3-5)(DR)
2. metallic red body, clear windows, amber dome lights, black interior, gold lace wheels, "DARE" with white & black design tempa ($1-2)(5pk)
3. yellow & red body, smoke windows, blue dome light, gray interior, lace wheels, hose & helmet tempa ($1-2)(LP)
4. black body, clear windows, amber dome lights, orange interior, lace wheels, "Mission H2O" tempa ($1-2)(LP)
5. blue body, clear windows, red dome lights, black interior, chrome disc wheels with rubber tires, "MBPD" tempa ($3-5)(MP)(HR)
6. white body, clear windows, red dome lights, black interior, lace wheels, "Mission H2O" tempa ($1-2)(LP)
7. white body, red windows, red dome light, black interior, lace wheels, "Mission H2O" tempa ($2-3)(LP)

MB462 CAT QUARRY DUMP TRUCK, issued 2000 (MB462)

NOTE: Below model was issued with a CD-ROM entitled "Adventures in Time"

1. orange-yellow body, orange-yellow plastic dump & base, yellow hubs, black cab grille with "CAT" & "Caterpillar" tempa, China casting ($5-8)

MB464 CHEVROLET CORVETTE POLICE, issued 2000 (MB464/473)

1. white body, clear windows, black interior, black, red & gray triangular dome lights, 5 spoke concave star wheels, "DARE America/ Moorehead Police" & stars tempa, black base, China casting ($3-5)(DR).
2. yellow body, clear windows, black interior, red bar dome lights, 5 spoke concave star wheels, "DARE Suffern Police" & purple flames tempa, black base, China casting ($3-5)(DR)

MB465 VOLKSWAGEN CONCEPT 1 POLICE, issued 2000 (MB465)

1. white & black body, clear windows, gray interior, red & blue dome lights, 5 spoke concave star wheels, "DARE Bellevue Police" tempa, black plastic base, China casting ($3-5)(DR)
2. yellow body, smoke windows, black interior, blue dome lights, 10 spoke flower wheels, "DARE" with black hood & doors tempa, black metal base, China casting ($1-2)(5pk)
3. white & blue body, clear windows, black interior, red dome lights, 10 spoke flower wheels, "Police 24" tempa, black metal base, China casting ($10-15)(PS)

MB474 FORD PANEL VAN, issued 2000 (MB474)

1. black body, smoke windows, red & blue dome light, 5 spoke concave star wheels, black base, "DARE Dover Police" tempa, China casting ($3-5)(DR)
2. dark green body, blue windows, amber dome light, 10 spoke flower wheels, gray base, "M-Force Airshow" tempa, China casting ($1-2)(5pk)
3. iridescent white body, blue windows, blue dome light, 10 spoke flower wheels, bright blue base, "USA Police" tempa, China casting ($1-2)(MP)(HR)
4. bright blue body, smoke windows, amber dome light, 10 spoke flower wheels, gray base, "Metro 7" tempa ($1-2)(LP)

MB477 CHEVY SUBURBAN, issued 2000 (MB477/615)

NOTE: Below models with China casting.

1. black body, smoke windows, triangular dome light, 5 spoke concave star wheels, black base, "DARE America/ Pima County Sheriff" tempa ($3-5)(DR)
2. blue body, smoke windows, triangular dome light, lace wheels, gray base, "Police" with white/yellow/blue design ($1-2)(5pk)
3. metallic red body, smoke windows, triangular dome light, 10 spoke flower wheels, gray base, "Team 04" tempa ($1-2)(LP)

MB502 1960 MGA, issued 2001 (EL)(MB502)

NOTE: Below models with clear windshield, chrome plastic base & China casting.

1. maroon body, black interior, chrome disc wheels with rubber tires, detailed trim tempa, with diorama ($10-15)(EL)
2. maroon body, black interior, lace wheels, detailed trim tempa ($2-4)(MP)(Avon)

3. black body, white interior, chrome disc wheels with rubber tires, "Coca Cola Ice Cold" tempa ($3-5)(Coke PC)

MB507 1955 CHEVY BEL AIR POLICE CAR, issued 2001 (MB507)
1. metallic blue body, gray interior, clear windows, red bar dome light, 10 spoke flower wheels, chrome plastic base, "DARE" & white sides tempa, China casting ($1-2)(5pk)

MB508 '33 FORD COUPE POLICE CAR, issued 2001 (MB508)
NOTE: Below models with smoke windows, gold lace wheels, black plastic base & China casting.
1. metallic purple body, amber bar dome light, "DARE" with black & orange design tempa ($1-2)(5pk)
2. metallic purple body, amber triangular dome light, "DARE" with black & orange design tempa ($10-15)(5pk)

MB533 BMW Z3, issued 2002 (BMW) (MB533)
NOTE: This model differs from the MB74-M in that the doors open. Below models with clear windshield, black interior, lace wheels, black plastic base & China casting.
1. silver-gray body, grille & tail lights tempa ($6-8)(ROW BMW promo)
2. silver-gray body, "7. Treffen MCCD" tempa ($15-20)(C2)

MB534 BMW 3 SERIES CABRIO, issued 2002 (BMW) (MB534)
NOTE: Below models with gray interior, lace wheels, black plastic base & China casting.
1. metallic blue body, clear windshield, head & tail lights tempa ($6-8)(ROW BMW promo)
2. metallic green body, smoke windshield, head & tail lights tempa ($6-8)(SG)
3. unpainted body, smoke windshield, pop art decals ($75+)(FA)

MB535 BMW X5, issued 2002 (BMW) (MB535)
NOTE: This models differs from MB31-O in that the doors open.
1. light gray body, clear windows, black interior, lace wheels, grille & tail lights tempa, black base, China casting ($6-8)(ROW BMW promo)

MB560 '56 FORD FAIRLANE SUNLINER, issued 2002 (MB560)
NOTE: Below models with chrome disc wheels with rubber tires, chrome base & China casting.
1. white body, white & red interior, red flames tempa ($10-15)(EL)
2. white & lemon body, black & white interior, silver stripe & detailed trim tempa ($3-5)(BJ)
3. black & white body, black & white interior, silver stripe & detailed trim tempa ($3-5)(BJ)

MB570 1960 JEEP, issued 2003 (CL) (MB570)
1. olive body, black interior & roll bar, olive disc wheels with rubber tires, "The Osbournes" tempa, black base, black base ($3-5)(OS)

MB596 BMW X5 POLICE CAR, issued 2003 (GR)(MB596)
1. white body, black interior, clear windows, orange & blue dome light, lace wheels, "Notarzt" & orange band tempa, black base, China casting ($6-8)(SG)
2. red body, black interior, clear windows, blue dome light, 10 spoke flower wheels, "Feuerwehr 112" tempa, black base, China casting ($3-5)(SoC)

MB710 TIPPING TRAILER, issued 1993 (FM) (MB710)
1. red plastic bed, silver-gray chassis, black tailgate, gray wheels with black plastic tires, Thailand casting ($2-4)(FM)

MB711 FARM TRAILER, issued 1993 (FM) (MB711)
1. yellow stake body, silver-gray base, gray wheels with black plastic tires, Thailand casting ($2-4)(FM)

MB712 SEEDER, issued 1993 (FM) (MB712)
1. green body, yellow wheels, silver-gray spreader, black tires, no origin cast ($2-4)(FM)

MB713 ROTOVATOR, issued 1993 (FM) (MB713)
1. blue body, gray rotors, no origin cast ($2-4)(FM)

MB720 SIDE TIPPER, issued 1977 (TP) (MB720)
NOTE: Base lettering reads front to rear or rear to front on all variations.
1. yellow body, black base, red tipper, black wheels, no tempa, England casting ($2-4)(TP)
2. yellow body, black base, black tipper, black wheels, no tempa, England casting ($3-5)(TP)
3. yellow body, black base, red tipper, black wheels, no tempa, Macau casting ($2-4)(TP)
4. blue body, red base, yellow tipper, blue wheels, "4567/ABCD" tempa, Macau casting ($6-8)(LL)
5. yellow body, black base, red tipper, black wheels, no tempa, China casting ($2-4)(TP)
6. light yellow body, black base, red tipper, black wheels, no tempa, China casting ($2-4)(TP)

MB724 PETERBILT TRACTOR, issued 1984 (CY)(MB724)
NOTE: This casting was used exclusively as a part of the Convoy series models. There were no single issues released.

MB791 MOTORCYCLE TRAILER, issued 1979 (MB791)
NOTE: Below models with black plastic base.
1. blue body, lemon cycles, 5 spoke center cut wheels, England casting ($2-4)(TP)
2. blue body, yellow cycles, 5 spoke center cut wheels, England casting ($2-4)(TP)
3. red body, yellow cycles, 5 spoke center cut wheels, England casting ($2-4)(TP)
4. yellow body, black cycles, 5 spoke center cut wheels, England casting ($2-4)(TP)
5. yellow body, dark green cycles, 5 spoke center cut wheels, England casting ($15-20)(TP)
6. yellow body, yellow cycles, dot dash wheels, England casting ($7-10)
NOTE: Versions 5 & 6 found as single boxed releases in the US.
7. yellow body, red cycles, dot dash wheels, England casting ($2-4)(TP)
8. yellow body, red cycles, dot dash wheels, Macau casting ($2-4)(TP)
9. yellow body, red cycles, dot dash wheels, no origin cast ($2-4)(TP)
10. beige body, black cycles, dot dash wheels, no origin cast ($2-4)(MP)
11. pearly silver body, black cycles, dot dash wheels, no origin cast ($2-4)(TP)
12. black body, dark red cycles, dot dash wheels, no origin cast ($1-2)(5pk)
13. black body, dark red cycles, dot dash wheels, China casting ($1-2)(5pk)

MB792 CATTLE TRAILER, issued 1979 (TP) (MB792)
NOTE: Below models with black wheels and silver hubs unless otherwise noted.
1. red body, light beige stakes, black cows, England casting ($2-4)(TP)

2. red body, dark beige stakes, black cows, England casting ($2-4)(TP)
3. red body, dark beige stakes, brown cows, England casting ($2-4)(TP)
4. yellow body, chocolate stakes, coffee cows, England casting ($2-4)(TP)
5. red body, orange-yellow stakes, black cows, England casting ($2-4)(TP)
6. yellow body, chocolate stakes, red-brown cows, England casting ($2-4)(TP)
7. yellow body, chocolate stakes, coffee cows, Macau casting ($2-4)(TP)
8. powder blue body, chocolate stakes, black cows, no origin cast ($2-4)(TP)
9. yellow body, chocolate stakes, coffee cows, no origin cast ($2-4)(TP)
10. green body, yellow stakes, black cows, no origin cast ($2-4)(TP)
11. red body, yellow stakes, blue wheels with yellow hubs, no cows, no origin cast ($6-8)(LL)

MB793 INFLATABLE, issued 1984 (TP) (MB793)
1. orange deck, white hull & seats, black motor, no tempa, England casting; black trailer with no tempa, England casting ($2-4)(TP)
2. orange deck, white hull & seats, black motor, blue "SR" tempa, England casting; black trailer with no tempa, England casting. ($2-4)(TP)
3. orange body, white hull & seats, black motor, red "SR" tempa, England casting; black trailer with no tempa, England casting ($2-4)(TP)
4. lemon deck, white hull & seats, black motor, blue "SR" tempa, England casting; black trailer with no tempa, England casting ($5-8)(TP)
5. red deck, white hull & seats, black motor, blue "SR" tempa, England casting; black trailer with no tempa, England casting ($5-8)(TP)
6. orange deck, white hull & seats, black motor, blue "SR" tempa, Macau casting; black trailer with no tempa, Macau casting ($2-4)(TP)
7. black deck, orange hull & seats, white motor, no tempa, no origin cast; black trailer with "2" tempa, no origin cast ($2-4)(TP)
8. orange deck, black hull & seats, black motor, blue "SR" tempa, no origin cast; black trailer with no tempa, no origin cast ($2-4)(TP)
9. orange deck, black hull & seats, white motor, no tempa, no origin cast; white trailer with dark blue & red stripes tempa, no origin cast ($2-4)(TP)
10. dark blue deck, gray hull & seats, white motor, no tempa, no origin cast; white trailer with blue & red stripes tempa, no origin cast ($2-4)(TP)
11. orange deck, silver-gray hull & seats, white motor, "Rescue" tempa, no origin cast; white trailer with blue anchor tempa, no origin cast ($2-4)(TP)
12. orange deck, black hull & seats, white motor, "R1" tempa, no origin cast; white trailer with "Rescue" & stripes tempa, no origin cast ($2-4)(EM)
13. orange deck, black hull & seats, white motor, anchor emblem tempa, no origin cast; white trailer with blue & orange stripe tempa, no origin cast ($2-4)(EM)
14. red deck, yellow hull & seats, black motor, "Red Valley Camp" tempa, no origin cast; black trailer with no tempa, no origin cast ($1-2)(5pk)
15. red deck, yellow hull & seats, black motor, "Red Valley Camp" tempa, no origin cast; black trailer with no tempa, China casting ($1-2)(5pk)

MB794 GLIDER TRANSPORTER, issued 1977 (TP) (MB794)

NOTE: Below models with white glider & wings, dot dash wheels & black plastic base.
1. yellow body, light amber canopy, "Gliding Club" labels, England casting ($2-4)(TP)
2. yellow body, dark amber canopy, "Gliding Club" labels, England casting ($2-4)(TP)
3. yellow body, dark amber canopy, no labels, England casting ($2-4)(TP)
4. metallic green body, clear canopy, no labels, England casting ($2-4)(TP)
5. metallic green body, clear canopy, "Seagull Gliding Club" labels, England casting ($2-4)(TP)
6. red body, dark amber canopy, "Gliding Club" labels, England casting ($500-750)(TP)
7. dark green body, dark amber canopy, "Seagull Gliding Club" labels, England casting ($2-4)(TP)
8. dark green body, light amber canopy, "Seagull Gliding Club" labels, England casting ($2-4)(TP)
9. red body, clear canopy, "Auto Glide" tempa, no origin cast ($2-4)(TP)
10. dark blue body, clear canopy, yellow stripes tempa, no origin cast ($2-4)(TP)
11. lemon body, clear canopy, purple & pink spatter tempa, no origin cast ($2-4)(TP)

NOTE: In 1996, most of the White Rose castings were no longer issued with "MB" frame numbers. Each had its own type of identification number.

FS001/WR002 FORD F800 DELIVERY VAN, issued 1995 (WR)

NOTE: Below models with clear windows, chrome disc wheels with rubber tires unless otherwise noted.
1. green body & base, orange-yellow container, "York Fair 1995" tempa ($7-10)(WR)
2. red body, black base, orange-yellow container, "Hulkster/ Hogan 43" tempa ($7-10)(WR)(TC)
3. dark blue body, silver-gray base, white container with blue roof, "We Are Penn State 95" tempa ($7-10)(WR)
4. white body, base & container, "UGI Gas Service" tempa ($8-12)(WR)
5. red body & base, white container, "World Series 1995-Atlanta Braves Champs" tempa ($8-12)(WR)
6. blue body & base, white container, "World Series 1995-Atlanta Braves Champs" tempa ($8-12)(WR)
7. red body, gold base & wheels, white container, "All Star Game 1996" tempa ($8-12)(WR)
8. blue body & base, white container, "KC Royals 1996" tempa ($6-8)(WR)
9. blue body & base, white container, "Chicago Cubs 1996" tempa ($6-8)(WR)
10. blue body & base, red container, "Philadelphia Phillies 1996" tempa ($6-8)(WR)
11. dark blue body & base, red container, "Boston Red Sox 1996" tempa ($6-8)(WR)
12. dark blue body & base, red container, "St. Louis Cardinals 1996" tempa ($6-8)(WR)
13. dark blue body & base, orange container, "Detroit Tigers 1996" tempa ($6-8)(WR)
14. dark blue body & base, orange container, "San Diego Padres 1996" tempa ($6-8)(WR)

15. dark blue body & base, gold container, "Milwaukee Brewers 1996" tempa ($6-8)(WR)
16. mid blue body & base, dark blue container, "Toronto Blue Jays 1996" tempa ($6-8)(WR)
17. purple body & base, silver-gray container, "Colorado Rockies 1996" tempa ($6-8)(WR)
18. blue-green body & base, dark blue container, "Seattle Mariners 1996" tempa ($6-8)(WR)
19. black body & base, turquoise container, "Florida Marlins 1996" tempa ($6-8)(WR)
20. black body & base, orange container, "San Francisco Giants 1996" tempa ($6-8)(WR)
21. black body & base, white container, "Chicago White Sox 1996" tempa ($6-8)(WR)
22. orange body & base, blue container, "New York Mets 1996" tempa ($6-8)(WR)
23. orange body & base, black container, "Baltimore Orioles 1996" tempa ($6-8)(WR)
24. red body & base, blue container, "Montreal Expos 1996" tempa ($6-8)(WR)
25. red body & base, blue container, "Atlanta Braves 1996" tempa ($6-8)(WR)
26. red body & base, dark blue container, "Minnesota Twins 1996" tempa ($6-8)(WR)
27. pink-red body & base, dark blue container, "Cleveland Indians 1996" tempa ($6-8)(WR)
28. yellow body & base, black container, "Pittsburgh Pirates 1996" tempa ($6-8)(WR)
29. yellow body & base, green container, "Oakland Athletics 1996" tempa ($6-8)(WR)
30. gold body & base, dark blue container, "Houston Astros 1996" tempa ($6-8)(WR)
31. silver-gray body & base, dark blue container, "California Angels 1996" tempa ($6-8)(WR)
32. light gray body & base, red container, "Texas Rangers 1996" tempa ($6-8)(WR)
33. white body & base, pink-red container, "Cincinnati Reds 1996" tempa ($6-8)(WR)
34. white body & base, blue container, "New York Yankees 1996" tempa ($6-8)(WR)
35. white body & base, blue container, "Los Angeles Dodgers 1996" tempa ($6-8)(WR)
36. green body & base, white container, "Rutters Dairy Celebrates 75 Years" tempa ($15-20)(WR)
37. orange body, black base, white container, "Preston-The 151 Line" tempa ($15-20)(WR)
38. white body, black base, white container, "Cat Racing" tempa ($6-8)(WR)(TC)
39. red body & base, white container, "Bill Elliot/M/10" tempa ($6-8)(WR)(TC)
40. white body, dark gray base, white container, "ABC Sports" tempa ($10-15)(WR)
41. white body, white base, white container, "Quality You Can See-Maple Donuts" tempa ($7-10)(WR)
42. white body, dark blue base, white container, "NY Yankees World Series 1996" tempa ($7-10)(WR)
43. white body, base & container, "All Star Game 1997- Indians" tempa ($6-8)(WR)
44. white body, base & container, "York Daily Record" tempa ($6-8)(WR)
45. blue body, white base & container, "Dutch Valley" tempa ($6-8)(WR)
46. white body, blue base, white container, "American Lung Association" tempa ($7-10)(WR)
47. white body, white base, white container, "Pifer Office Supply Inc." ($25-40)(CCI)

FS002 FORD F800 DELIVERY VAN, issued 1996 (WR)

NOTE: This model differs from the FS001/WR002 in that the container overhangs the cab. Below models with clear windows, chrome disc wheels with rubber tires & China casting unless noted otherwise.

1. beige body, dark brown base, beige container, "York Fair 1996" tempa ($7-10)(WR)
2. metallic silver body, dark blue base, metallic silver container, "Nittany Lions/PSU 1996" tempa ($7-10)(WR)
3. white body, dark blue base, white container with dark blue roof, "Penn State 1996" tempa, blue wheels ($7-10)(WR)

FST FORD SUPER TRUCK, issued 1996 (WR)

NOTE: Below models with clear windows, disc wheels with Goodyear rubber tires, black plastic base & China casting unless otherwise noted.

1. black body, black interior, "Exide 7" tempa ($3-5)(WR)
2. yellow body, yellow interior, "Ortho 21" tempa ($3-5)(WR)
3. blue & white body, red interior, "Team ASE 2" tempa ($3-5)(WR)
4. white body, white interior, "Larry's Heavenly/Petron Plus 78" tempa ($5-7)(WR)
5. white & red body, red interior, "Remax 6" tempa ($5-7)(WR)

MLB97 PLYMOUTH PROWLER, issued 1997 (WR)

NOTE: Although this model looks exactly like the MB34-G Plymouth Prowler, this is a new casting produced by White Rose Collectibles and the notable difference between the two castings is that the MB34-G has a PLASTIC base whereas this casting has a METAL base. There is no notation cast inside this model to identify this casting with any frame number like standard models. The only discernable catalog reference number is an "MLB97" cast inside box flaps so this will be used to identify this particular model.

NOTE: Below models with dark gray interiors with painted dashboards on some versions, 5 spoke concave star wheels, clear windshield, & silver-gray metal base.

1. iridescent white body, "Houston Astros 1997" tempa ($4-6)(WR)
2. iridescent white body, "Anaheim Angels 1997" tempa ($4-6)(WR)
3. iridescent white body, "Montreal Expos 1997" tempa ($4-6)(WR)
4. silver-gray body, "Florida Marlins 1997" tempa ($4-6)(WR)
5. silver-gray body, "Seattle Mariners 1997" tempa ($4-6)(WR)
6. silver-gray body, "San Diego Padres 1997" tempa ($4-6)(WR)
7. silver-gray body, New York Yankees 1997" tempa ($4-6)(WR)
8. silver-gray body, "Cleveland Indians 1997" tempa ($4-6)(WR)
9. metallic tan body, "St. Louis Cardinals 1997" tempa ($4-6)(WR)
10. metallic tan body, "Atlanta Braves 1997" tempa ($4-6)(WR)
11. metallic tan body, "Kansas City Royals 1997" tempa ($4-6)(WR)
12. metallic orange body, "Detroit Tigers 1997" tempa ($4-6)(WR)
13. metallic orange body, "New York Mets 1997" tempa ($4-6)(WR)
14. black body, "Baltimore Orioles 1997" tempa ($4-6)(WR)
15. black body, "Chicago White Sox 1997" tempa ($4-6)(WR)
16. black body, "Pittsburgh Pirates 1997" tempa ($4-6)(WR)
17. black body, "San Francisco Giants 1997" tempa ($4-6)(WR)
18. metallic green body, "Oakland A's 1997" tempa ($4-6)(WR)
19. metallic green body, "Milwaukee Brewers 1997" tempa ($4-6)(WR)

20. metallic blue body, "Minnesota Twins 1997" tempa ($4-6)(WR)
21. metallic blue body, "Chicago Cubs 1997" tempa ($4-6)(WR)
22. metallic blue body, "Los Angeles Dodgers 1997" tempa ($4-6)(WR)
23. metallic blue body, "Toronto Blue Jays 1997" tempa ($4-6)(WR)
24. metallic red body, "Boston Red Sox 1997" tempa ($4-6)(WR)
25. metallic red body, "Texas Rangers 1997" tempa ($4-6)(WR)
26. metallic red body, "Philadelphia Phillies 1997" tempa ($4-6)(WR)
27. metallic red body, "Cincinnati Reds 1997" tempa ($4-6)(WR)
28. dark met. purple body, "Colorado Rockies 1997" tempa ($4-6)(WR)
29. metallic purple body, "Tampa Bay Devil Rays Inaugural Season 1998" tempa ($4-6)(WR)
30. metallic purple body, "Arizona Diamondbacks Inaugural Season 1998" tempa ($4-6)(WR)
31. turquoise body, "World Series 1997 Champions Marlins" tempa ($4-6)(WR)
32. turquoise body, "World Series 1997 Champions Marlins" tempa, sealed in bat-shaped glass bottle ($30-45)(WR)

WRP01 1996 PONTIAC GRAND PRIX, issued 1996 (WR)

NOTE: Below models with black plastic base & disc wheels with Goodyear rubber tires.

1. dark green body, clear windows, gray interior, "White Rose Collectibles/December 25" tempa, China casting ($50-75)(WR)
2. black body, clear windows, gray interior, "MBNA America 72" tempa, China casting ($4-6)(WR)
3. red & blue body, clear windows, gray interior, "Skittles 36/ Starburst" tempa, China casting ($4-6)(WR)
4. red body, clear windows, gray interior, "White Rose Collectibles/ Merry Christmas 1997" tempa, China casting ($35-50)(WR)

WRP02 1996 FORD THUNDERBIRD, issued 1996 (WR)

NOTE: This model is modified from the MB268, notably the grille & new base casting. Below models with clear windows, black plastic base, disc wheels Goodyear rubber tires & China casting unless noted otherwise.

1. white & blue body, red interior, "Valvoline 6" tempa ($3-5)(WR)
2. red & white body, red interior, "McDonald's 94" tempa ($3-5)(WR)
3. metallic blue & white body, gray interior, "Family Channel/ Primestar 16" tempa ($3-5)(WR)
4. black body, gray interior, "Miller Racing 2" tempa, encased in glass bottle on wooden stand ($50-75)(WR)
5. white body, gray interior, "Jasper/Federal Mogul 77" tempa ($3-5)(WR)
6. blue body, black interior, "Spam 9" tempa ($3-5)(WR)
7. blue body, red interior, "QC Quality Care/Red Carpet Lease 88" tempa ($3-5)(WR)
8. red & white body, red interior & wheels, "McDonald's 94" tempa ($6-8)(WR)(TC)
9. red body, red interior, "McDonald's/Monopoly 94" tempa ($8-12)(WR)
10. orange & blue body, black interior, "Badcock 12" tempa ($8-12)(WR)
11. purple & turquoise body, gray interior, "Hayes Modems 15" tempa ($8-12)(WR)
12. red body, red interior, "McDonald's 94" tempa ($3-5)(WR)
13. blue body, gray interior, "New Holland 94" tempa ($3-5)(WR)
14. orange-yellow body, red interior, "Caterpillar 97" tempa ($3-5)(WR)
15. metallic green body, gray interior, "Remington 75" tempa, sealed in glass bottle ($25-35)(WR)
16. blue body, black interior, "Mac Tonight" tempa ($18-25)(WR)
17. dark blue & white body, black interior, "Miller Lite" tempa, sealed in plexibox with Convoy ($20-30)(WR)
18. brown-gold body, gray interior, "QVC 7" tempa ($3-5)(WR)
19. dark red body, gray interior, "Circuit City 8" tempa ($3-5)(WR)
20. grape body, black interior, "Remington Stren 75" tempa, sealed in glass bottle ($25-35)(WR)
21. olive, tan & black camouflage body, gray interior, "Remington 75" tempa, sealed in glass bottle ($25-35)(WR)
22. dark metallic green body, gray interior, "Remington 75" tempa, sealed in glass bottle ($25-35)(WR)

SUBMERSIBLE, issued 1998 (PS)

NOTE: Model has no casting markings identifying this piece as a "Matchbox".

1. yellow upper body, gray plastic lower body, orange arms, blue window, black stripe tempa ($10-15)(PS)

LV-1 DODGE DAYTONA, issued 1983 (VEGAS)

1. burgundy body, black interior, clear windows, silver-gray metal base with black plastic insert, casting closed, base cast "Expressly For Dodge Las Vegas", England casting ($75-100)(VG)

LV-2 DODGE CARAVAN, issued 1983 (VEGAS)

1. burgundy body, maroon interior, clear windows, chrome plastic base, casting closed, base cast "Expressly for Dodge Las Vegas", 8 spoke wheels, England casting ($75-100)(VG)

NOTE: If above two models are mounted by Velcro to a wooden plinth with gold plate denoting models made for Las Vegas with Lee Iacocca signature ($500-750)(VG). The LV numbers are used for identification purposes only.

UN-NUMBERED PROMOTIONAL MODELS

The following model castings were un-numbered by the factory. The numbers listed below are for identification purposes only.

NOTE: The following models have "Made in China by S.I.I." cast on the baseplates and are modified versions of existing castings.

TB-005 '97 CHEVY TAHOE, issued 1999 (TB)

1. white body, green/blue/black tempa, black painted windows, 8 spoke wheels with black hubs, black plastic base, China casting ($3-5)(TB)

TB-006 '97 CHEVROLET CORVETTE, issued 1999 (TB)

1. green body, blue & white tempa, black painted windows, black plastic base, 5 spoke concave star wheels, China casting ($3-5)(TB)

TB-007 '80 CHEVY K-1500 PICKUP, issued 1999 (TB)

1. blue body, white wavy tempa, black painted windows, 8 spoke wheels with black hubs, black plastic base, China casting ($3-5)(TB)

TB-008 '57 CHEVROLET BEL AIR, issued 1999 (TB)

1. white body, green & blue bands tempa, black painted windows, black plastic base, 5 spoke concave star wheels, China casting ($3-5)(TB)

SW-001 TRACTOR SHOVEL, issued 2000

NOTE: The following model has been retooled & is slightly larger than the MB29-C casting. The baseplate reads "Mfg. By b. little". This was released only at Subway restaurants. The companion model is listed at MB36-F.

1. pumpkin body, black scoop, engine & plastic base, black hubs ($2-4)

NOTE: The following models were marketed in Europe exclusively by Burger King and are designated as such on the base.

BK-001 BEACH 4X4, issued 2002

1. metallic orange body, purple windows, gray rear compartment, black plastic base, 5 spoke oval wheels with black hubs ($8-12)

BK-002 DESERT 4X4, issued 2002

1. metallic silver green body, orange windows, black plastic base, 5 spoke oval wheels with black hubs ($8-12)

BK-003 JUNGLE 4X4, issued 2002

1. metallic olive body, blue windows, black plastic base, 5 spoke oval wheels with black hubs ($8-12)

BK-004 WATER PUMPER, issued 2003 (BK)

1. red body, translucent yellow windows, 7 spoke sawblade wheels, gray plastic base ($8-12)(BK)

BK-005 RESCUE HELICOPTER, issued 2003 (BK)

1. blue body, translucent orange windows, gray blades, neon orange tail, gray plastic base ($8-12)(BK)

BK-006 TROOP CARRIER, issued 2003 (BK)

1. lime body, translucent milk white windows, gray bed, 4 spoke domed wheels, gray plastic base ($8-12)(BK)

NOTE: The following models were issued either in the U.S. or Canada exclusively by McDonald's and are designated as such on the base. Bilingual text baseplates were exclusive to Canada as are the generic labels supplied.

MD-001 SNORKEL FIRE TRUCK, issued 2002 (MD)

NOTE: Below models with translucent red windows, lace wheels, black interior, blue boom & black plastic base.

1. baby blue boom, "North Carolina" labels supplied, model name on base in English ($2-4)
2. baby blue body, generic labels supplied, model name on base in English & French ($5-8)

MD-002 DODGE DAKOTA, issued 2002 (MD)

NOTE: Below models with dark smoke windows, yellowish roof light, lace wheels

1. blue body, "Texas" labels supplied ($2-4)
2. blue body, generic labels supplied ($5-8)

MD-003 FORD CROWN VICTORIA, issued 2002 (MD)

NOTE: Below models with dark smoke windows, yellowish roof lights, lace wheels

1. white body, "Ohio" labels supplied ($2-4)
2. white body, generic labels supplied ($5-8)

MD-004 INTERNATIONAL PUMPER, issued 2002 (MD)

NOTE: Below models with 5 spoke wheels, yellowish dome lights, black windows & base

1. red body, "Illinois" labels supplied, model name on base in English ($2-4)
2. red body, generic labels supplied, model name on base in English & French ($5-8)

MD-005 WRECKER TRUCK, issued 2002 (MD)

NOTE: Below models with dark smoke windows, red opaque dome lights, dark blue boom, 5 spoke wheels

1. yellow body, "New York" supplied labels, model name on base in English ($2-4)
2. yellow body, generic labels supplied, model name on base in English & French ($5-8)

MD-006 AMBULANCE, issued 2002 (MD)

NOTE: Below models with opaque red windows, 5 spoke wheels, blue plastic base.

1. white body, "Washington" labels supplied ($2-4)
2. white body, generic labels supplied ($5-8)

ROMAN NUMERAL EDITIONS

The following models have Roman numeral designations on their bases. Although some look like their original counterparts, these are listed here because of the base number!

MB I SILVER STREAK, issued 1978 (USA)

NOTE: Below models with orange interior, 5 spoke front & 4 spoke rear wheels & England casting.

1. yellow body, amber windows, cat head label, chrome motor ($35-50)
2. yellow body, amber windows, cat head label, black motor ($75-100)
3. chrome plated body, black windows, stripes tempa, black motor ($10-15)

MB II SLEET-N-SNOW, issued 1978 (USA)

NOTE: Below models with black interior, 5 crown wheels & England casting.

1. blue body, white base, white canopy, silver hubs, "U.S. Mail" tempa ($8-12)
2. dull blue body, white base, white canopy, silver hubs, "U.S. Mail" tempa ($8-12)
3. powder blue body, white base, white canopy, silver hubs, "U.S. Mail" tempa ($8-12)
4. olive body, black base, gun cast, black hubs, "21 * 11" labels ($15-20)
5. yellow body, black base, no canopy or gun, black hubs, "Gliding Club" labels ($15-20)(TP)
6. yellow body, black base, no canopy or gun, silver hubs, "Gliding Club" labels ($15-20)(TP)

MB III WHITE LIGHTNING, issued 1978 (USA)

NOTE: Below models with black windows, chrome engine, red & yellow tempa, maltese cross wheels, black metal base & England casting.

1. cream body, black engine stacks ($10-15)
2. white body, black engine stacks ($10-15)
3. white body, dark gray engine stacks ($10-15)

MB IV FLYING BEETLE, issued 1978 (USA)

1. orange body, black windows, flesh colored driver with chrome helmet, black & white insect tempa, 5 spoke wheels & England casting ($10-15)

MB V HOT SMOKER, issued 1978 (USA)

NOTE: Below models with chrome interior, red windows, "Hot Smoker" tempa & England casting.

1. yellow body, black base, 5 spoke front & 4 spoke rear wheels ($10-15)
2. yellow body, black base, 5 spoke front & rear wheels ($10-15)
3. yellow body, black base, 5 spoke front & maltese cross rear wheels ($10-15)
4. yellow body, charcoal base, 5 spoke front & 4 spoke rear wheels ($10-15)
5. yellow body, black base, dot dash front & rear wheels ($10-15)
6. yellow body, black base, dot dash front & 5 crown rear wheels ($10-15)
7. yellow body, black base, 5 spoke front & 5 crown rear wheels ($10-15)

MB VI LADY BUG, issued 1978 (USA)

NOTE: Below models with chrome engine, 5 spoke wheels, unpainted metal base & England casting.

1. red body, purple windows, yellow interior, eyes labels ($15-20)
2. black body, purple windows, yellow interior, flames & beetle tempa ($10-15)

MB VII BROWN SUGAR, issued 1978 (USA)

NOTE: Below models with chrome engine, maltese cross wheels, white metal base & England casting.

1. brown body, white base, black windows, brown background & outlined cherries labels ($10-15)
2. brown body, white base, black windows, brown background & solid cherries labels ($10-15)
3. dark brown body, white base, blue windows, brown background & outlined cherries labels ($10-15)
4. brown body, white base, blue windows, brown background & outlined cherries labels ($10-15)
5. brown body, white base, blue windows, brown background & solid cherries labels ($10-15)
6. brown body, white base, blue windows, tan background & solid cherries labels ($10-15)
7. brown body, white base, amber windows, brown background & solid cherries labels ($10-15)
8. brown body, white base, amber windows, tan background & solid cherries labels ($10-15)
9. red-brown body, white base, amber windows, tan background & solid cherries labels ($10-15)
10. dark brown body, white base, amber windows, brown background & solid cherries labels ($10-15)

MB VIII BLACK WIDOW, issued 1978 (USA)

NOTE: Below models with ivory interior, 5 spoke wheels, black spider & web tempa, unpainted metal base & England casting.

1. powder blue body, clear windows ($15-20)
2. powder blue body, black windows ($10-15)

MB IX FLAMIN MANTA, issued 1978 (USA)

NOTE: Below models with 5 spoke front & maltese cross rear wheels, black metal base & England casting.

1. yellow body, chrome interior, amber windows, flames tempa ($10-15)
2. dark yellow body, chrome interior, amber windows, flames tempa ($10-15)

Available as a Bulgarian casting. Assorted colors available ($35-50)

MB X GOLDEN X, issued 1978 (USA)

NOTE: Below models with chrome interior & engine, 5 spoke wheels & England casting.

1. yellow body, black base, amber windows, red & black flames tempa ($35-50)
2. gold plated body, black base, black windows, light green tempa ($10-15)
3. gold plated body, black base, black windows, dark green tempa ($10-15)

FEATURE CARS

Feature cars were introduced in 2000 to replace the popular Premiere series. The main feature to the line-up was the addition of opening features, be it doors, hood or trunk compartments. Regrettably, these were not given "frame numbers" for identification, although the few here with frame numbers noted are when the model was actually intended to be part of the basic lineup. The numbers given here are for identification purposes only.

FC-01 CHEVY SUBURBAN, issued 2000

1. white body, gray interior, "NYPD" tempa ($8-10)
2. red body, gray interior, "DC1/ City of Miami/ Fire Rescue" tempa ($8-10)
3. white body, gray interior, "FDMB/ TR3" tempa ($8-10)(KB)
4. white body, gray interior, "Chevrolet Police Vehicle" tempa ($8-10)
5. red & white body, gray interior, "Fire MBFD 45" tempa ($8-10)
6. olive body, gray interior, "MP- Military Police" tempa ($8-10)
7. burgundy body, black interior, "Matchbox 50" tempa ($8-10)

FC-02 CHEVROLET IMPALA POLICE CAR, issued 2000

1. white body, gray interior, "NYPD 2419" tempa ($8-10)
2. white body, gray interior, red band with "Twp of Franklin/ 43-5" tempa ($8-10)
3. white body, gray interior, "Chevrolet Police Vehicle" tempa ($8-10)
4. charcoal body, gray interior, "State Highway Patrol Ohio" tempa ($8-10)
5. white body, gray interior, "FDMB R32" tempa ($8-10)(KB)
6. burgundy body, gray interior, "Matchbox 50" tempa ($8-10)

FC-03 1998 CHEVROLET CORVETTE , issued 2000

1. dark blue body, gray interior ($8-10)

FC-04 1957 CHEVY BEL AIR HARDTOP, issued 2000

1. red body, white roof, red & white interior ($8-10)
2. baby blue body, white roof, blue & white interior ($20-35)

FC-05 T-BIRD CONCEPT, issued 2000 (MB435)

1. pale yellow body & roof, black interior ($8-10)
2. red body & roof, black interior ($8-10)

FC-06 FORD F350 PICKUP, issued 2000

1. silver-gray body, gray interior ($8-10)
2. metallic sand body, tan interior ($8-10)
3. burgundy body, black interior, "Matchbox 50" tempa ($8-10)

FC-07 JEEP GRAND CHEROKEE, issued 2000

1. silver-gray body, gray interior ($8-10)
2. maroon body, tan interior ($8-10)
3. red body, black interior, "FDMB/ EMT" tempa ($8-10)(KB)

FC-08 FORD F350 KME PUMPER, issued 2000
1. white & red body, "Trucksville" tempa ($10-12)
2. white & red body, "Elizaville" tempa ($12-15)
3. neon yellow body, "Base 24" tempa ($8-10)
4. burgundy body, "MBFD 50" tempa ($8-10)

FC-09 1965-1/2 MUSTANG CONVERTIBLE, issued 2000
1. black body, red interior ($8-10)

FC-10 1957 CHEVY BEL AIR CONVERTIBLE, issued 2000
1. light yellow body, cream & black interior ($8-10)

FC-11 T-BIRD CONCEPT CONVERTIBLE, issued 2000
1. pale yellow body, black interior ($8-10)

FC-12 1998 CORVETTE CONVERTIBLE, issued 2000
1. red body, tan & black interior ($8-10)

FC-13 1965-1/2 MUSTANG SOFT TOP, issued 2000
1. dark green body, white roof, tan interior ($75-100)

FC-14 BRADLEY FIGHTING VEHICLE, issued 2001
1. dark tan body, green, black & white camouflage tempa ($8-10)

FC-15 2-1/2 TON TRUCK, issued 2001 (MB414)
1. dark tan body, green, black & white camouflage tempa, dark olive canopy ($8-10)
2. tan body, detailed trim tempa, tan canopy ($8-10)

FC-16 LP7 LANDING CRAFT, issued 2001
1. beige body, black painted treads ($8-10)

FC-17 M-4 SHERMAN TANK, issued 2001
1. olive body, light blue camouflage & star tempa ($8-10)

FC-18 M3 A2 HALFTRACK, issued 2001 (MB415)
1. olive body, star & black treads tempa ($8-10)

FC-19 M1A1 ABRAMS TANK, issued 2001
1. beige body, black painted treads ($8-10)

FC-20 4X4 JEEP WILLYS & TRAILER, issued 2002
1. olive green jeep & trailer ($8-10)

FC-21 M 60-A TANK, issued 2002
1. tan body, detailed trim tempa ($8-10)

FC-22 SEAGRAVE MEANSTICK FIRE TRUCK, issued 2002

NOTE: Below models with chrome disc wheels with rubber tires.
1. gold body, chrome ladder & base, "50th/ logo & "M.B.F.D." tempa ($8-12)(CL)
2. burgundy body, chrome ladder & base, "50th" logo & "M.B.F.D." tempa ($8-12)(CL)
3. burgundy body, chrome ladder & base, "Vincentown" tempa ($50+)(CCI)
4. gold body, chrome ladder & base, "Vincentown" tempa ($50+)(CCI)
5. gold body, chrome ladder & base, "Montgomery County" tempa ($50+)(CCI)
6. burgundy body, chrome ladder & base, "Montgomery County" tempa ($50+)(CCI)

REAL TALKERS

Although not part of the miniatures range as a Real Talker, some of the castings were issued into the range without the talking mechanism later on. Several others were scheduled to be issued into the range but due to too high of a cost to produce were not chosen for the range. Like the feature car series, no identification numbers were issued, so numbers listed here are for identification purposes only. All single issue versions were issued with both English and Spanish speaking voice mechanisms. The frame number listed after year of issue was its proposed number into the range.

RT-01 POLICE CAR, issued 1998

NOTE: Below models with black windows, red bar dome light, 5 spoke concave star wheels & China casting.
1. white & blue body, "C-51", "Sheriff" & gold badge logo tempa, black base ($3-5)
2. white body, "Metro Police 8" & black lower body edge tempa, black base ($3-5)
3. white body, "Police 34" & "state Trooper" tempa, white base ($3-5)(TP)

RT-02 FIRE TRUCK, issued 1998 (MB396)

NOTE: Below models with black windows, red bar light, 8 spoke wheels, red bar light, gray base & China casting.
1. red body, white painted cab with "Fire Department 14" tempa ($3-5)
2. neon yellow body, "Fire Fighter 14" tempa ($3-5)

RT-03 SNACK TRUCK, issued 1998 (MB385)

NOTE: Below models with translucent windows, 8 spoke wheels & China casting.
1. salmon body, gray base, yellow splats & design tempa ($3-5)
2. white body, blue base, "Mister Softee" tempa ($3-5)

RT-04 GARBAGE TRUCK, issued 1998 (MB387)

NOTE: Below models with black windows, 8 spoke wheels & China casting.
1. red cab, silver-gray container, gray arms, "Recycler" tempa, gray base ($3-5)
2. dark blue body, dirty brown container, light gray arms, "City Garbage" tempa, black base ($3-5)

RT-05 RESCUE TRUCK, issued 1998 (MB386)

NOTE: Below models with black windows, red bar light, 8 spoke wheels & China casting.
1. green body, yellow base, yellow painted rear area, "Bear Patrol Forest Service/ Ranger Unit 217" tempa ($3-5)
2. orange & white body, black base, silver painted rear area, "Beach Patrol/ B-1" tempa ($3-5)
3. lemon body, black base, "Lifeguard T-2" & white sides with red stripes tempa ($3-5)(TP)

RT-06 TOW TRUCK, issued 1998

NOTE: Below models with 8 spoke wheels & China casting.
1. black body, gray windows & boom,. gray base, "Z Towing/ Zaks" tempa ($3-5)
2. white body, black windows & boom, black base, "Police" & eagle head tempa ($3-5)

RT-07 ROCKET LAUNCHER, issued 1998 (MB384)

NOTE: Below models with amber dome lights, black wheels, black base & China casting.(See also MB82-A)
1. olive body, tan and dark green camouflage tempa ($3-5)

2. beige body, brown spotted camouflage tempa ($3-5)
3. dull olive body, "Unit 5 Stand Clear" & star tempa ($3-5)(TP)

RT-08 UFO, issued 1998 (MB378)

NOTE: Below models with clear window & China casting. (See also MB61-K/56-L)

1. light brown body with silver brushed effect, blue dot lights ($3-5)
2. gray body with green & gold brushed effect, orange dot lights ($3-5)
3. black body with gold brushed effect, green dot lights ($3-5)(TP)

THUNDERBIRDS

Although not technically a miniature, this model could fall into the miniature category. It's the only model from the Thunderbirds series that could fall into the category.

TB-5 PENELOPE'S FAB 1, issued 1992

1. pink body, clear windows, cream interior, chrome base, dot dash wheels with chrome hubs ($10-15)(TB)
2. gold plated body, chrome windows & interior, chrome base, dot dash wheels with gold hubs ($50-75)(TB)

SUPER GTs

Super GTs are a type of miniature. These models are based on older 1970s castings in which interiors are no longer fitted, the windows are solid in color (opaque) and opening features are cast shut. All baseplates are black plastic. The original name for the line was to be the "Budget Range" and models were designated with "BR" numbers. All models are in paired numbers i.e. BR1/2, BR3/4, etc. The line was introduced in 1985 and ran through 1988. This line consists of varied tempa and wheel variations. Model names do not appear on the castings. Model names are taken from the original name in the 1970s. The first Chinese made Super GT range in 1987 contained all the basic color variations previously made in England. The only exceptions being the gold Monteverdi and the green Hairy Hustler. For 1988, they were all recolored. In 1990, some models were reissued in neon colors called "Neon Racers" and these are denoted with "NR"

BR1/2 Iso Grifo	BR21/22 Alfa Carabo
BR3/4 Gruesome Twosome	BR23/24 Vantastic
BR5/6 Datsun 126X	BR25/26 Ford Escort
BR7/8 Siva Spyder	BR27/28 Lamborghini Marzal
BR9/10 Lotus Europa	BR29/30 Maserati Bora
BR11/12 Saab Sonnet	BR31/32 Fandango
BR13/14 Hairy Hustler	BR33/34 Hi-Tailer
BR15/16 Monteverdi Hai	BR35/36 Porsche 910
BR17/18 Fire Chief	BR37/38 Ford Capri
BR19/20 Ford Group 6	BR39/40 DeTomaso Pantera

BR 1/2 ISO GRIFO, issued 1985

1. cream body, 8 dot wheels, black windows, red & black tempa, England casting ($3-5)
2. cream body, 8 dot wheels, white glow windows, red & black tempa, England casting ($12-15)
3. pale yellow body, 8 dot wheels, black windows, red & black tempa, England casting ($7-10)
4. pale yellow body, dot dash wheels, black windows, red & black tempa, England casting ($7-10)
5. yellow body, 8 dot wheels, black windows, red & black tempa, England casting ($7-10)
6. yellow body, dot dash wheels, black windows, red & black tempa, England casting ($7-10)
7. light blue body, 8 dot wheels, black windows, black & purple tempa, England casting ($4-6)
8. light blue body, dot dash wheels, black windows, black & purple tempa, England casting ($4-6)
9. metallic blue body, 8 dot wheels, black windows, lime & maroon with "57" tempa, England casting ($3-5)
10. metallic blue body, 8 dot wheels, white glow windows, lime & red with "57" tempa, England casting ($12-15)
11. metallic blue body, 8 dot wheels, black windows, lemon & brown with "57" tempa, England casting ($4-6)
12. metallic blue body, 8 dot wheels, black windows, yellow & red with "57" tempa, England casting ($4-6)
13. metallic blue body, 8 dot wheels, black windows, red & black tempa, England casting ($7-10)
14. metallic blue body, 8 dot wheels, black windows, purple & back tempa, England casting ($7-10)
15. metallic blue body, dot dash wheels, black windows, purple & black tempa, England casting ($7-10)
16. metallic blue body, 8 dot wheels, black windows, maroon & black tempa, England casting ($7-10)
17. metallic blue body, 8 dot wheels, black windows, lime & red with "57" tempa, China casting ($7-10)
18. bright green body, 8 dot wheels, black windows, white & black with "57" tempa, China casting ($3-5)
19. cream body, 8 dot wheels, black windows, red & black tempa, China casting ($6-8)
20. yellow body, 8 dot wheels, black windows, red & black tempa, China casting ($3-5)

BR3/4 GRUESOME TWOSOME, issued 1985

NOTE: Below models with black windows & 8 dot wheels unless otherwise noted. Base lettering reads front to rear or rear to front on all variations.

1. yellow body, blue & orange with "Gruesome" tempa, England casting ($4-6)
2. yellow body, green & orange with "Gruesome" tempa, England casting ($4-6)
3. powder blue body, white arrow design tempa, England casting ($4-6)
4. powder blue body, white arrow design with no tempa on tail, England casting ($4-6)
5. dark blue body, white arrow design tempa, England casting ($5-8)
6. yellow body, blue & orange with "Gruesome" tempa, China casting ($7-10)
7. white body, red & black with "Gruesome" tempa, China casting ($3-5)
8. white body, red & black with "Gruesome" tempa, white glow windows, China casting ($20-25)
9. gray body, dark blue arrow design tempa, China casting ($3-5)
10. florescent orange body, yellow & black tempa, China casting ($4-6)(NR)
11. powder blue body, white arrow design with no tempa on tail, China casting ($4-6)

BR5/6 DATSUN 126X, issued 1985

1. dark blue body, 5 arch wheels, black windows, gold & white tempa, England casting ($4-6)
2. dark blue body, 8 dot wheels, black windows, gold & white tempa, England casting ($4-6)
3. silver body, 5 arch wheels, black windows, green & red stripes tempa, England casting ($4-6)

4. silver body, 8 dot wheels, black windows, green & red stripes tempa, England casting ($4-6)
5. silver-gray body, 5 arch wheels, black windows, green & red stripes tempa, England casting ($4-6)
6. pearly silver body, 5 arch wheels, black windows, green & red stripes tempa, China casting ($7-10)
7. powder blue body, 5 arch wheels, black windows, white & blue stripes tempa, China casting ($3-5)
8. beige body, 5 arch wheels, black windows, 2 tone blue tempa, China casting ($3-5)
9. beige body, 5 arch wheels, white glow windows, 2 tone blue tempa, China casting ($20-25)
10. dark blue body, 5 arch wheels, black windows, gold & white tempa, China casting ($4-6)

BR7/8 SIVA SPYDER, issued 1985

NOTE: Below models fitted with black windows.

1. orange-yellow body, 8 dot wheels, black & white "Turbo" tempa, England casting ($4-6)
2. orange-yellow body, dot dash wheels, black & white "Turbo" tempa, England casting ($7-10)
3. yellow body, 8 dot wheels, black & red "Turbo" tempa, England casting ($7-10)
4. yellow body, 8 dot wheels, black & white "Turbo" tempa, England casting ($7-10)
5. white body, 8 dot wheels, blue & lemon tempa, England casting ($4-6)
6. white body, 8 dot wheels, blue & yellow tempa, England casting ($4-6)
7. white body, dot dash wheels, blue & yellow tempa, England casting ($4-6)
8. blue body, 8 dot wheels, white & black tempa, England casting ($7-10)
9. gray body, 8 dot wheels, white & black tempa, England casting ($7-10)
10. gray body, 8 dot wheels, gray & black tempa, England casting ($7-10)
11. white body, 8 dot wheels, blue & yellow tempa, China casting ($7-10)
12. dark red body, 8 dot wheels, white & gold tempa, China casting ($3-5)
13. orange-yellow body, 8 dot wheels, black & white "Turbo" tempa, China casting ($7-10)
14. yellow body, 8 dot wheels, black & red "Turbo" tempa, China casting ($3-5)

BR9/10 LOTUS EUROPA, issued 1985

NOTE: Below models with black windows & 8 dot wheels. Base lettering reads front to rear or rear to front on all variations.

1. white body, red & black with "1" tempa, England casting ($4-6)
2. metallic blue body, lemon leaf pattern tempa, England casting ($4-6)
3. metallic blue body, cream leaf pattern tempa, England casting ($4-6)
4. metallic blue body, yellow leaf pattern tempa, England casting ($4-6)
5. purple body, gold leaf pattern tempa, China casting ($3-5)
6. white body, red & black with "1" tempa, China casting ($7-10)
7. blue body, yellow & black with "1" tempa, China casting ($3-5)
8. metallic blue body, lemon leaf pattern tempa, China casting ($3-5)

BR11/12 SAAB SONNET, issued 1985

NOTE: Below models fitted with black windows.

1. orange body, 8 dot wheels, white & red with "5" tempa, England casting ($4-6)
2. light tan body, 8 dot wheels, white & red triangle tempa, England casting ($4-6)
3. dark tan body, 8 dot wheels, white & red triangle tempa, England casting ($4-6)
4. light tan body, dot dash wheels, white & red triangle tempa, England casting ($4-6)
5. light tan body, 8 dot wheels, white & red with "5" tempa, England casting ($7-10)
6. blue body, 8 dot wheels, white & red triangle tempa, England casting ($7-10)
7. light tan body, dot dash wheels, white & red with "5" tempa, England casting ($3-5)
8. light tan body, 8 dot wheels, white & red triangle tempa, China casting ($7-10)
9. powder blue body, 8 dot wheels, yellow & black triangle tempa, China casting ($3-5)
10. orange body, 8 dot wheels, white & red with "5" tempa, China casting ($7-10)
11. green body, 8 dot wheels, white & gold with "5" tempa, China casting ($3-5)
12. orange body, 8 dot wheels, no tempa, England casting ($18-25)

BR13/14 HAIRY HUSTLER, issued 1985

NOTE: Below models fitted with black windows

1. lemon body, 5 arch front & 5 crown rear wheels, black & red "L" & reverse "F" with "7" on roof with tail stripes tempa, England casting ($4-6)
2. yellow body, 5 crown wheels, black & red "L" & reverse "F" with "7" on roof with tail stripes tempa, England casting ($4-6)
3. yellow body, 5 arch front & crown rear wheels, black & red "L" & reverse "F" tempa only, England casting ($7-10)
4. yellow body, 5 arch front & 5 crown rear wheels, black & red "L" & reverse "F" with "7" on roof with tail stripes tempa, England casting ($4-6)
5. yellow body, 5 arch wheels, black & red "L" & reverse "F" with "7" on roof with tail stripes tempa, England casting ($4-6)
6. yellow body, 5 crown front & 5 arch rear wheels, black & red "L" & reverse "F" tempa with "7" on roof with tail stripes tempa, England casting ($4-6)
7. yellow body, 8 dot wheels, black & red "L" & reverse "F" with "7" on roof with tail stripes tempa, England casting ($4-6)
8. green body, 5 crown wheels, yellow & black with "2" tempa, England casting ($4-6)
9. green body, 5 arch front & 5 crown rear wheels, yellow & black with "2" tempa, England casting ($4-6)
10. dark green body, 5 arch front & 5 crown rear wheels, yellow & black with "2" tempa, England casting ($7-10)
11. gray body, 5 arch front & 5 crown rear wheels, red & black with "2" tempa, China casting ($3-5)
12. yellow body, 5 arch front & 5crown rear wheels, black & red "L" & reverse "F" with "7" on roof with tail stripes tempa, China casting ($7-10)
13. red body, 5 arch front & 5crown rear wheels, white & yellow "L" & reverse "F" with "7" on roof with tail stripes tempa, China casting ($3-5)

BR15/16 MONTEVERDI HAI, issued 1985

1. green body, 8 dot wheels, black windows, no tempa, England casting ($12-15)

2. green body, 8 dot wheels, black windows, black windows, white & gold tempa, England casting ($4-6)
3. green body, dot dash wheels, black windows, white & gold tempa, England casting ($6-8)
4. green body, 8 dot wheels, white glow windows, white & gold tempa, England casting ($12-15)
5. black body, 8 dot wheels, white glow windows, white & gold tempa, England casting ($15-20)
6. yellow body, 8 dot wheels, black windows, white & gold tempa, England casting ($50-65)
7. light tan body, 8 dot wheels, black windows, blue & white with "28" tempa, England casting ($4-6)
8. light tan body, 8 dot wheels, black windows, green & white with "28" tempa, England casting ($6-8)
9. mid tan body, 8 dot wheels, black windows, black & white with "28" tempa, England casting ($6-8)
10. dark tan body, 8 dot wheels, black windows, green & white with "28" tempa, England casting ($6-8)
11. gold body, 8 dot wheels, black windows, blue & white with "28" tempa, England casting ($7-10)
12. white body, 8 dot wheels, black windows, orange & black with "28" tempa, China casting ($30-45)
13. orange body, 8 dot wheels, black windows, red & blue with "28" tempa, China casting ($3-5)
14. green body, 8 dot wheels, black windows, white & gold tempa, China casting ($7-10)
15. blue body, 8 dot wheels, black windows, red & lime tempa, China casting ($3-5)
16. florescent pink body, 8 dot wheels, black windows, black & yellow tempa, China casting ($4-6)(NR)
17. tan body, dot dash wheels, black windows, blue & white with "28" tempa, China casting ($8-12)

BR17/18 FIRE CHIEF

NOTE: Below models fitted with black window unless otherwise noted. There can be other combinations of front & rear wheels to make other permutations.

1. white body, 5 crown wheels, "Police" tempa, England casting ($4-6)
2. white body, 5 arch front & 5 crown rear wheels, "Police" tempa, England casting (4-6)
3. white body, 5 arch wheels, "Police" tempa, England casting ($4-6)
4. red body, 5 crown wheels, white "Rescue" tempa, England casting ($4-6)
5. red body, 5 arch front & 5 crown rear wheels, white "Rescue" tempa, England casting ($4-6)
6. red body, 5 arch wheels, white "Rescue" tempa, England casting ($4-6)
7. red body, 8 dot wheels, white "Rescue" tempa, England casting ($4-6)
8. orange body, 5 arch front & 5 crown rear wheels, black "Rescue" tempa, China casting ($3-5)
9. white body, 5 arch front & 5 crown rear wheels, "Police" tempa, China casting ($7-10)
10. blue body, 5 arch front & 5 crown rear wheels, "Police" tempa, China casting ($3-5)
11. white body, 8 dot wheels, "Police" tempa, England casting ($7-10)
12. red body, 5 arch front & 5 crown rear wheels, "Rescue" tempa, China casting ($3-5)
13. olive body, blue windows, 5 arch front & 5 crown rear wheels with black hubs, white "Police" tempa, China casting ($75-100)(CM)(CHI)
14. black body, blue windows, 5 arch front & 5 crown rear wheels with black hubs, yellow "Rescue" tempa, China casting ($75-100)(CM)(CHI)

BR19/20 FORD GROUP 6, issued 1985

NOTE: Below models with black windows.

1. white body, 8 dot wheels, red & black "18" tempa, England casting ($4-6)
2. white body, dot dash wheels, pink & black "18" tempa, England casting ($4-6)
3. yellow body, 8 dot wheels, red & black "18" tempa, England casting ($7-10)
4. red body, 8 dot wheels, white & yellow "2" tempa, England casting ($4-6)
5. red body, dot dash wheels, white & yellow "2" tempa, England casting ($4-6)
6. red body, 8 dot wheels, white & yellow "2" tempa, China casting ($7-10)
7. gray body, 8 dot wheels, purple & white "2" tempa, China casting ($3-5)
8. white body, 8 dot wheels, red & black "18" tempa, China casting ($7-10)
9. dark red body, 8 dot wheels, blue & black "18" tempa, China casting ($3-5)
10. florescent lime body, 8 dot wheels, yellow & black "18" tempa, China casting ($4-6)(NR)

BR21/22 ALFA CARABO, issued 1985

NOTE: Below models fitted with black windows & 8 dot wheels. Various shades of the panel tempa exist on the silver model. England castings exist with the Matchbox logo omitted from the baseplate.

1. silver body, light & dark blue panels tempa, England casting ($4-6)
2. silver body, light blue & dark green panels tempa, England casting ($4-6)
3. silver body, no tempa, England casting ($12-15)
4. green body, dark blue & white panels tempa, England casting ($12-15)
5. beige body, light & dark blue panels tempa, England casting ($35-50)
6. yellow body, blue & green panels tempa, England casting ($35-50)
7. yellow body, light & dark blue panels tempa, England casting ($35-50)
8. silver body, white & blue panels tempa, England casting ($7-10)
9. orange body, blue & white with "6" tempa, England casting ($4-6)
10. orange body, blue & white with "6" tempa, 5 crown wheels, England casting ($7-10)
11. orange body, no tempa, England casting ($12-15)
12. orange body, dark & light blue panels tempa, England casting ($12-15)
13. orange body, green & light blue panels tempa, England casting ($12-15)
14. silver body, black & blue panels tempa, 5 arch wheels, England casting ($7-10)
15. green body, black & blue panels tempa, England casting ($7-10)
16. orange body, blue & white with "6" tempa, 5 arch wheels, England casting ($4-6)
17. pearly silver body, black & dark blue panels tempa, China casting ($7-10)

18. powder blue body, yellow & white panels tempa, China casting ($3-5)
19. green body, gold & white with "6" tempa, China casting ($3-5)
20. orange body, blue & white with "6" tempa, China casting ($3-5)

BR23/24 VANTASTIC, issued 1986

NOTE: Below models with 5 arch front & 5 crown rear wheels.
1. beige body, blue & red "Starfire" tempa, black windows, China casting ($3-5)
2. blue body, red & yellow with "51" tempa, black windows, China casting ($3-5)

BR25/26 FORD ESCORT, issued 1985

NOTE: Below models with black windows and 8 dot wheels.
1. red body, gold & white with "10" tempa, England casting ($4-6)
2. red body, blue & white with "10" tempa, England casting ($4-6)
3. blue body, blue & white with "10" tempa, England casting ($5-8)
4. beige body, light & mid blue with "9" tempa, England casting ($4-6)
5. beige body, light blue & green with "9" tempa, England casting ($4-6)
6. yellow body, light & dark blue with "9" tempa, England casting ($15-18)
7. blue body, yellow & dark blue with "9" tempa, China casting ($3-5)
8. purple body, white & black with "10" tempa, China casting ($3-5)
9. red body, gold & white with "10" tempa, China casting ($3-5)
10. beige body, light & dark blue with "9" tempa, China casting ($3-5)

BR27/28 LAMBORGHINI MARZAL, issued 1985

NOTE: Below models with black windows & 8 dot wheels unless otherwise noted. White & yellow tempa exists with white & yellow parts reversed.
1. green body, white & yellow with "8" tempa, dot dash wheels, England casting ($7-10)
2. green body, white & yellow with "8" tempa, England casting ($4-6)
3. green body, black & gray with "16" tempa, England casting ($12-15)
4. blue body, white & yellow with "8" tempa, England casting ($7-10)
5. cream body, black & gray with "16" tempa, England casting ($4-6)
6. white body, black & gray with "16" tempa, England casting ($12-15)
7. green body, white & yellow with "8" tempa, 5 arch wheels, England casting ($5-8)
8. cream body, black & gray with "16" tempa, 5 arch wheels, England casting ($5-8)
9. cream body, black & gray with "16" tempa, China casting ($7-10)
10. yellow body, blue & gold with "16" tempa, China casting ($3-5)
11. yellow body, black & red with "16" tempa, China casting ($7-10)
12. green body, white & yellow with "8" tempa, China casting ($7-10)
13. red body, black & red with "8" tempa, China casting ($3-5)

BR29/30 MASERATI BORA, issued 1985

NOTE: Below models with black windows & 8 dot wheels unless otherwise noted. The tempa on the yellow model exists in varying shades.
1. yellow body, blue & orange tempa, England casting ($4-6)
2. yellow body, green & orange tempa, England casting ($4-6)
3. yellow body, green & orange tempa, dot dash wheels, England casting ($7-10)
4. yellow body, purple & orange tempa, England casting ($4-6)
5. yellow body, blue & brown tempa, England casting ($4-6)
6. light blue body, dark blue & white with "70" tempa, England casting ($4-6)
7. light blue body, black & white with "70" tempa, England casting ($4-6)
8. light blue body, black & white with "70" tempa, dot dash wheels, England casting ($7-10)
9. dark blue body, black & white with "70" tempa, England casting ($6-8)
10. dark blue body, black & white with "70" tempa, dot dash wheels, England casting ($7-10)
11. light blue body, black & white with "70" tempa, China casting ($7-10)
12. beige body, 2 tone blue with "70" tempa, China casting ($3-5)
13. yellow body, blue & orange tempa, China casting ($7-10)
14. powder blue body, purple & black tempa, China casting ($3-5)
15. florescent lime body, black & white with "70" tempa, China casting ($4-6)(NR)

BR31/32 FANDANGO, issued 1985

NOTE: Below models fitted with black windows.
1. yellow body, 5 crown wheels, blue & red with "19" tempa, England casting ($4-6)
2. yellow body, 5 arch front & 5 crown rear wheels, blue & red with "19" tempa, England casting ($4-6)
3. maroon body, 5 crown wheels, white & yellow with "217" & white prop tempa, England casting ($4-6)
4. maroon body, 5 crown wheels, white & yellow with "217" & unpainted prop tempa, England casting ($4-6)
5. maroon body, 5 arch front & 5 crown rear wheels, white & yellow with "217" & white prop tempa, England casting ($4-6)
6. maroon body, 5 arch front & 5 crown rear wheels, white & yellow with "217" & white prop tempa, China casting ($7-10)
7. yellow body, 5 arch front & 5 crown rear wheels, red & black with "217" & red prop tempa, China casting ($3-5)
8. lemon body, 5 arch front & 5 crown rear wheels, blue & red with "19" tempa, China casting ($7-10)
9. gray body, 5 arch front & 5 crown rear wheels, gray & red with "19" tempa, China casting ($3-5)

BR33/34 HI-TAILER, issued 1986

NOTE: Below models with black driver & engine & 5 arch front & 5 crown rear wheels.
1. lemon body, black & red with "Super 61" tempa, China casting ($3-5)
2. yellow body, black & red with "Super 61" tempa, China casting ($3-5)
3. white body, black & red with "45" tempa, China casting ($3-5)

BR35/36 PORSCHE 910, issued 1985

NOTE: Below models fitted with black windows.

1. dark blue body, 8 dot wheels, blue & white with "49" tempa, England casting ($4-6)
2. light blue body, 8 dot wheels, blue & white with "49" tempa, England casting ($4-6)
3. light blue body, dot dash wheels, blue & white with "49" tempa, England casting ($4-6)
4. light blue body, dot dash wheels, black "3" & "Drive" tempa, England casting ($7-10)
5. light blue body, 8 dot wheels, black "3" & "Drive" tempa, England casting ($7-10)
6. silver body, 8 dot wheels, black "3" & "Drive" tempa, England casting ($4-6)
7. silver-gray body, 8 dot wheels, black "3" & "Drive" tempa, England casting ($4-6)
8. silver body, 8 dot wheels, black & white with "49" tempa, England casting ($7-10)
9. silver body, dot dash wheels, black & white with "49" tempa, England casting ($7-10)
10. pearly silver body, dot dash wheels, black "3" & "Drive" tempa, China casting ($7-10)
11. white body, 5 arch wheels, red "3" & "Drive" tempa, China casting ($3-5)
12. light blue body, 5 arch wheels, black with "49" tempa, China casting ($7-10)
13. lime body, 5 arch wheels, gold & white with "49" tempa, China casting ($3-5)
14. florescent orange body, 5 arch wheels, dark blue & yellow with "49" tempa, China casting ($4-6)(NR)

BR37/38 FORD CAPRI, issued 1986

NOTE: Below models with black windows & 5 arch wheels.

1. cream body, red-brown & green with "48" tempa, China casting ($3-5)
2. blue body, red & white with "8" tempa, China casting ($3-5)

BR39/40 DE TOMASO PANTERA, issued 1986

NOTE: Below models with black windows, 5 arch front & 5 crown rear wheels.

1. maroon body, orange & white with "4X4" tempa, China casting ($3-5)
2. orange body, blue & brown with "Ace" tempa, China casting ($3-5)
3. florescent yellow body, blue-green & orange with "4X4" tempa, China casting ($4-6)(NR)

Matchbox®
Superfast Illustrated

Start here pics

WHEEL TYPES

5-Spoke

4-Spoke

Maltese Cross

Spiro

5-Arch

5-Crown

Dot Dash

5-Spoke Center Cut

5-Spoke Star

8-Spoke

8-Dot

Racing Special

Starburst

Laser

Chrome Disc with Rubber Tires

Chrome Disc with Rubber Tires & White Walls

6-Spoke

Goodyear Slicks

9-Spoke Goodyear Slicks

6-Spoke Ringed

Lightning

Goodyear Rubber

Hoosier Rubber

4-Arch

6-Spoke Spiral

Solid Disc

4-Dot Ringed

5-Spoke Concave Star

Star With 5 Spokes

10-Spoke Flower

4-Dot Domed

7-Spoke Sawblade

5-Spoke Oval

Lace

5-CrownDot

5-Spoke Slotted

BASIC MODELS

MB 1-A2 Mercedes Truck

MB 1-A3 Mercedes truck

MB 1-B1 Mod Rod

MB 1-B2 Mod Rod

MB 1-B3 Mod Rod

MB 1-B8 Mod Rod

MB 1-C4 Dodge Challenger

MB 1-C5 Dodge Challenger

MB 1-D2 Dodge Challenger

MB 1-D3 Dodge Challenger

MB 1-D6 Dodge Challenger

MB 1-D14 Dodge Challenger

MB 1-D17 Dodge Challenger

MB 1-D19 Dodge Challenger

MB 1-F1 Jaguar XJ6 Police Car

MB 1-F2 Jaguar XJ6 Police Car

MB 1-G/35-K3 Dodge Viper GTS

MB 1-G/35-K7 Dodge Viper GTS

MB 1-G/35-K33 Dodge Viper GTS

MB 1-G/35-K39 Dodge Viper GTS

MB 1-H/71-K2 Mercedes Benz CLK

MB 1-H/71-K4 Mercedes Benz CLK

MB 1-I1 Highway Pumper

MB 1-J1 Whistle Car

MB 2-A1 Mercedes Trailer

MB 2-A2 Mercedes Trailer

MB 2-B4 Jeep Hot Rod

MB 2-B12 Jeep Hot Rod

MB 2-C1 Hovercraft

MB 2-C7 Hovercraft

MB 2-C10 Hovercraft

MB 2-C11 Hovercraft

MB 2-C16 Hovercraft

MB 2-C17 Hovercraft

MB 2-D1 S.2 Jet

MB 2-D5 S.2 Jet

MB 2-D7 S.2 Jet

MB 2-E2 Pontiac Fiero

MB 2-E6 Pontiac Fiero

MB 2-G/15-G8
Corvette Grand Sport

MB 2-G/15-G10
Corvette Grand Sport

MB 2-G/15-G13
Corvette Grand Sport

MB 2-G/15G17
Corvette Grand Sport

MB 2-G/15-G28
Corvette Grand Sport

MB 2-G/15-G35
Corvette Grand Sport

MB 2-I1 '98 Chevrolet
Camaro SS Convertible

MB 2-J1 Badge Car

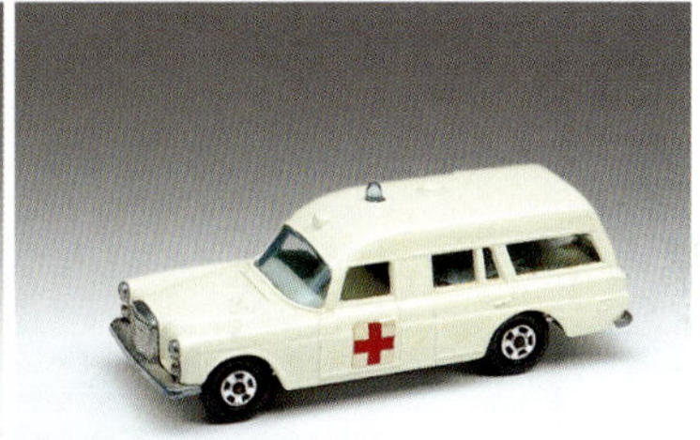

MB 3-A1 Mercedes Benz
'Binz' Ambulance

MB 3-B1 Monteverdi Hai

MB 3-B6 Monteverdi Hai

MB 3-B9 Monteverdi Hai

MB 3-C1 Porsche Turbo

MB 3-C5 Porsche Turbo

MB 3-C16 Porsche Turbo

MB 3-C20 Porsche Turbo

MB 3-C29 Porsche Turbo

MB 3-C33 Porsche Turbo

MB 3-C40 Porsche Turbo

MB 3-C41 Porsche Turbo

MB 3-C54 Porsche Turbo

MB 3-D1 Hummer

MB 3-D3 Hummer

MB 3-D4 Hummer

MB 3-D19 Hummer

MB 3-E3 Alfa Romeo 155

MB 3-E5 Alfa Romeo 155

MB 3-G/1-K1 Squawkie Talkie

MB 4-A1 Cattle Truck

MB 4-A4 Cattle Truck

MB 4-B1 Gruesome Twosome

MB 4-B2 Gruesome Twosome

MB 4-B8 Gruesome Twosome

MB 4-C4 Pontiac Firebird

MB 4-D1 '57 Chevy

MB 4-D2 '57 Chevy

MB 4-D6 '57 Chevy

MB 4-D21 '57 Chevy

MB 4-D27 '57 Chevy

MB 4-E1 Taxi FX4R

MB 4-E9 Taxi FX4R

MB 4-E10 Taxi FX4R

MB 4-F4 1997 Corvette

MB 4-F13 1997 Corvette

MB 4-F29 1997 Corvette

MB 4-F56 1997 Corvette

MB 4-G/37-K1
Audi TT Roadster

MB 4-G/37-K2
Audi TT Roadster

MB 4-I/3-H1 Fire Extinguisher

MB 5-A2 Lotus Europa

MB 5-A3 Lotus Europa

MB 5-A4 Lotus Europa

MB 5-A5 Lotus Europa

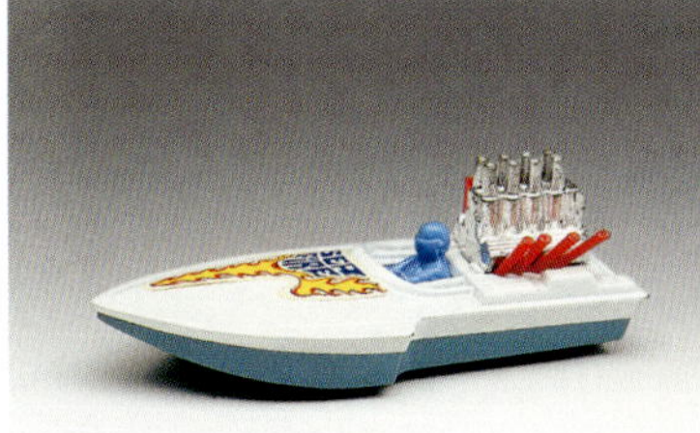

MB 5-B2 Seafire

MB 5-B4 Seafire

MB 5-B10 Seafire

MB 5-C2 U.S. Mail Truck

MB 5-C7 U.S. Mail Truck

MB 5-D/56-F1 4 X 4 Jeep

MB 5-D/56-F4 4 X 4 Jeep

MB 5-D/56-F10 4 X 4 Jeep

MB 5-D/56-F18 4 X 4 Jeep

MB 5-D/56-F20 4 X 4 Jeep

MB 5-D/56-F22 4 X 4 Jeep

MB 5-G/4-J1 Flame Chopper

MB 6-A4 Ford Pickup

MB 6-A7 Ford Pickup

MB 6-B3 Mercedes Tourer

MB 6-B6 Mercedes Tourer

MB 6-B 8 Mercedes Tourer

MB 6-B10 Mercedes Tourer

MB 6-B11 Mercedes Tourer

MB 6-B14 Mercedes Tourer

MB 6-B20 Mercedes Tourer

MB 6-B25 Mercedes Tourer

MB 6-C/7-E1 IMSA Mazda

MB 6-E/72-H2
Ford Supervan II

MB 6-E/72-H18
Ford Supervan II

MB 6-I1 Arctic Track Truck

MB 6-I4 Arctic Track Truck

MB 6-J1 Opel Speedster

MB 6-K1 Max Tractor

MB 7-A2 Ford Refuse Truck

MB 7-B1 Hairy Hustler

MB 7-B6 Hairy Hustler

MB 7-B11 Hairy Hustler

MB 7-B13 Hairy Hustler

MB 7-B17 Hairy Hustler

MB 7-B19 Hairy Hustler

MB 7-C1 VW Golf

MB 7-C8 VW Golf

MB 7-C11 VW Golf

MB 7-C17 VW Golf

MB 7-C22 VW Golf

MB 7-D3 Rompin' Rabbit

MB 7-D4 Rompin' Rabbit

MB 7-D5 Rompin' Rabbit

MB 7-F/51-I2 Porsche 959

MB 7-F/51-I5 Porsche 959

MB 7-F/51-I10 Porsche 959

MB 7-F/51-I22 Porsche 959

MB 7-F/51-I29 Porsche 959

MB 7-F/51-I34 Porsche 959

MB 7-F/51-I40 Porsche 959

MB 7-F/51-I47 Porsche 959

MB 7-F/51-I49 Porsche 959

MB 7-F/51-I50 Porsche 959

MB 7-F/51-I51 Porsche 959

MB 7-F/51-I52 Porsche 959

MB 7-F/51-I53 Porsche 959

MB 7-G/39-H25 Ford Thunderbird Stock Car

MB 7-G/39-H54 Ford Thunderbird Stock Car

MB 7-G/39-H58 Ford Thunderbird Stock Car

MB 7-G/39-H62 Ford Thunderbird Stock Car

MB 7-G/39-H63 Ford Thunderbird Stock Car

MB 7-G/39-H69 Ford Thunderbird Stock Car

MB 7-H1 Scissors Truck

MB 7-H3 Scissors Truck

MB 7-H7 Scissors Truck

MB 7-J1 Milk Moo-ver

MB 8-A1 Ford Mustang

MB 8-A4 Ford Mustang

MB 8-B1 Wildcat Dragster

MB 8-B10 Wildcat Dragster

MB 8-B13 Wildcat Dragster

MB 8-B14 Wildcat Dragster

MB 8-C1 DeTomasso Pantera

MB 8-C8 DeTomasso Pantera

MB 8-C9 DeTomasso Pantera

MB 8-C13 DeTomasso Pantera

MB 8-D1 Rover 3500

MB 8-D7 Rover 3500

MB 8-D15 Rover 3500

MB 8-E1 Greased Lightning

MB 8-F/71-E1 Scania T142

MB 8-F/71-E2 Scania T142

MB 8-F/71-E4 Scania T142

MB 8-G1 Vauxhall Astra Police Car

MB 8-G3 Vauxhall Astra Police Car

MB 8-G10 Vauxhall Astra Police Car

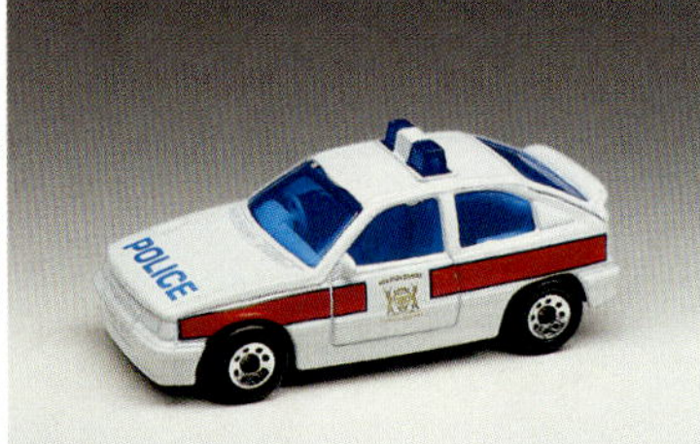

MB 8-G14 Vauxhall Astra Police Car

MB 8-G18 Vauxhall Astra Police Car

MB 8-H/39-F1 Mack CH600

MB 8-I/24-I1 Airport Fire Tender

MB 8-I/24-I9 Airport Fire Tender

MB 8-I/24-I10 Airport Fire Tender

MB 8-I/24-I11 Airport Fire Tender

MB 8-I/24-I14 Airport Fire Tender

MB 8-I/24-I21 Airport Fire Tender

MB 8-J/54-I2 Mazda RX7

MB 8-J/54-I6 Mazda RX7

MB 8-J/54-I9 Mazda RX7

MB 8-J/54-I20 Mazda RX7

MB 8-J/54-I25 Mazda RX7

MB 8-J/54-I28 Mazda RX7

MB 8-K1 Q.B. Roller

MB 9-A1 Boat & Trailer

MB 9-B1 AMX Javelin

MB 9-B4 AMX Javelin

MB 9-B9 AMX Javelin

MB 9-B18 AMX Javelin

MB 9-B20 AMX Javelin

MB 9-C1 Ford Escort

MB 9-C5 Ford Escort

MB 9-D/74-E2 Fiat Abarth

MB 9-D/74-E5 Fiat Abarth

MB 9-D/74-E13 Fiat Abarth

MB 9-F/74-G1 Toyota MR2

MB 9-H/53-E1 Faun Dump Truck

MB 9-H/53-E5
Faun Dump Truck

MB 9-H/53-E8 Faun
Dump Truck

MB 9-H/53-E12
Faun Dump Truck

MB 9-H/53-E14 Faun
Dump Truck

MB 9-H/53-E19
Faun Dump Truck

MB 9-H/53-E21
Faun Dump Truck

MB 9-I1 BMW Z8

MB 9-I4 BMW Z8

MB 9-H8 BMW Z8

MB 9-H13 BMW Z8

MB 9-K1 Bass Bus

MB10-A1 Pipe Truck

MB10-A3 Pipe Truck

MB10-A5 Pipe Truck

MB10-B2 Piston Popper

MB10-B6 Piston Popper

MB10-C1 Plymouth
Gran Fury Police Car

MB10-C4 Plymouth
Gran Fury Police Car

MB10-C10 Plymouth
Gran Fury Police Car

MB10-C13 Plymouth
Gran Fury Police Car

MB10-D1 Buick LeSabre

MB10-D9 Buick LeSabre

MB10-D10 Buick LeSabre

MB10-F/12-J1
Dodge Viper RT/10

MB10-F/12-J18
Dodge Viper RT/10

MB10-F/12-J30
Dodge Viper RT/10

MB10-F/12-J60
Dodge Viper RT/10

MB10-F/12-J88
Dodge Viper RT/10

MB10-F/12-J94
Dodge Viper RT/10

MB10-G1 J.R. Bumper

MB11-A1 Scaffold Truck

MB11-B2 Flying Bug

MB11-B5 Flying Bug

MB11-C1 Car Transporter

MB11-C4 Car Transporter

MB11-C11 Car Transporter

MB11-C33 Car Transporter

MB11-C36 Car Transporter

MB11-C41 Car Transporter

MB11-C42 Car Transporter

MB11-D2 Boss Mustang

MB11-D3 Boss Mustang

MB11-D5 Boss Mustang

MB11-E/67-E2 IMSA Mustang

MB11-E/67-E3 IMSA Mustang

MB11-E/67-E9 IMSA Mustang

MB11-E/67-E10 IMSA Mustang

MB11-G/34-I1 Chrysler Atlantic

MB11-H/29-D1 BMW 328i Police Car

MB11-H/29-D2 BMW 328i Police Car

MB11-H/29-D3 BMW 328i Police Car

MB11-H/29-D8 BMW 328i Police Car

MB11-H/29-D11 BMW 328i Police Car

MB11-I1 Wrecker Truck

MB11-I4 Wrecker Truck

MB11-I8 Wrecker Truck

MB11-J1 Emergency Response 4X4

MB11-K1 Dragonfly Helicopter

MB12-A1 Land Rover Safari

MB12-B1 Setra Coach

MB12-B2 Setra Coach

MB12-B3 Setra Coach

MB12-B4 Setra Coach

MB12-B5 Setra Coach

MB12-B7 Setra Coach

MB12-C1 Big Bull

MB12-C2 Big Bull

MB12-D1 Citroen CX

MB12-D23 Citroen CX

MB12-E/51-E1
Pontiac Firebird SE

MB12-E/51-E6
Pontiac Firebird SE

MB12-E/51-E8
Pontiac Firebird SE

MB12-E/51-E13
Pontiac Firebird SE

MB12-H/33-H1
Mercedes Benz 500SL

MB12-H/33-H4
Mercedes Benz 500SL

MB12-H/33-H15
Mercedes Benz 500SL

MB12-K/31-K1
Audi Avus Quattro

MB12-K/31-K7
Audi Avus Quattro

MB12-K/31-K12
Audi Avus Quattro

MB12-K/31-K13
Audi Avus Quattro

MB12K/31-K14
Audi Avus Quattro

MB12-M1 Grasshopper
Tow Truck

MB13-A2 Dodge Wreck Truck

MB13-B6 Baja Buggy

MB13-B12 Baja Buggy

MB13-B13 Baja Buggy

MB13-C3 Snorkel

MB13-C6 Snorkel

MB13-C8 Snorkel

MB13-D/63-F/76-B1 4 X 4
Open Back Truck

MB13-D/63-F/76-B4 4 X 4
Open Back Truck

MB13-D/63-F/76-B5 4 X 4
Open Back Truck

MB13-D/63-F/76-B-11 4 X 4 Open Back Truck

MB13-D/63-F/76-B16 4 X 4 Open Back Truck

MB13-F/28M1 The Buster

MB13-F/28-M5 The Buster

MB13-F/28-M6 The Buster

MB13-G3 Kenworth T2000

MB13-H1 Snail Truck

MB14-A2 Iso Grifo

MB14-A5 Iso Grifo

MB14-A8 Iso Grifo

MB14-B1 Mini Ha Ha

MB14-B2 Mini Ha Ha

MB14-B7 Mini Ha Ha

MB14-C1 Rallye Royale

MB14-C2 Rallye Royale

MB14-D2 Leyland Articulated Tanker

MB14-D5 Leyland Articulated Tanker

MB14-D6 Leyland Articulated Tanker

MB14-E/69-E1 1984 Corvette

MB14-E/69-E3 1984 Corvette

MB14-G/28-G1 1987 Corvette

MB14-G/28-G13 1987 Corvette

MB14-G/28-G17 1987 Corvette

MB14-G/28-G21 1987 Corvette

MB14-G/28-G22 1987 Corvette

MB14-K1 Web Wheeler

MB15-A1 Volkswagen 1500 Saloon

MB15-A6 Volkswagen 1500 Saloon

MB15-B1 Fork Lift Truck

MB15-B12 Fork Lift Truck

MB15-B14 Fork Lift Truck

MB15-B17 Fork Lift Truck

MB15-B18 Fork Lift Truck

MB15-B21 Fork Lift Truck

MB15-C1 Hi Ho Silver

MB15-E/25-G3
Peugeot 205 Turbo 16

MB15-E/25-G7
Peugot 205 Turbo 16

MB15-E/25-G9
Peugeot 205 Turbo 16

MB15-F/22-F1
Saab 9000 Turbo

MB15-F/22-F5
Saab 9000 Turbo

MB15-H/6-G1 Alfa Romeo SZ

MB15-H/6-G5 Alfa Romeo SZ

MB15-I/41-I1 Sunburner

MB15-I/41-I3 Sunburner

MB15-J/28-K1
Mustang Mach III

MB15-J/28-K9
Mustang Mach III

MB15-J/28-K16
Mustang Mach III

MB15-J/28-K17
Mustang Mach III

MB15-K/50-N2
Ford Transit Van

MB15-K/50-N53
Ford Transit Van

MB15-K/50-N63
Ford Transit Van

MB15-K/50-N71
Ford Transit Van

MB15-K/50-N101
Ford Transit Van

MB15-K/50-N112
Ford Transit Van

MB15-K/50-N120
Ford Transit Van

MB15-L1 DAF 3300 Space Cab

MB15-M1 Litter Bug

MB16-A1 Badger

MB16-A5 Badger

MB16-A14 Badger

MB16-B1 Pontiac Firebird

MB16-B15 Pontiac Firebird

MB16-B16 Pontiac Firebird

MB16-D/6-D1 F.1 Racer

MB16-E/51-H1 Ford
LTD Police Car

MB16-E/51-H20 Ford
LTD Police Car

MB16-E/51-H26 Ford
LTD Police Car

MB16-E/51-H29 Ford
LTD Police Car

MB16-E/51-H32 Ford
LTD Police Car

MB16-E/51-H34 Ford
LTD Police Car

MB16-E/51-H35 Ford
LTD Police Car

MB16-G1 School Bus

MB16-G4 School Bus

MB16-G7 School Bus

MB16-H1 Car Carrier

MB16-H3 Car Carrier

MB16-I1 Dump Truck 2004

MB17-A1 Horse Box

MB17-A3 Horse Box

MB17-A4 Horse Box

MB17-B2 The Londoner

MB17-B18 The Londoner

MB17-B28 The Londoner

MB17-B64 The Londoner

MB17-B70 The Londoner

MB17-B71 The Londoner

MB17-B72 The Londoner

MB17-C/51-F/28-F1
Leyland Titan

MB17-C/51-F/28-F2
Leyland Titan

MB17-C/51-F/28-F
Leyland Titan

MB17-C/51-F/28-F23
Leyland Titan

MB17-C/51-F/28-F32
Leyland Titan

MB17-C/51-F/28-F49
Leyland Titan

MB17-C/51-F/28-F63
Leyland Titan

MB17-C/51-F/28-F64
Leyland Titan

MB17-D/9-E1 AMX Prostocker

MB17-D/9-E3 AMX Prostocker

MB17-D/9-E5 AMX Prostocker

MB17-E/37-G4 Ford Escort Cabriolet

MB17-E/37-G5 Ford Escort Cabriolet

MB17-E/37-G8 Ford Escort Cabriolet

MB17-F/50-F1 Dodge Dakota

MB17-G/41-J1 Ferrari 456 GT

MB17-G/41-J2 Ferrari 456 GT

MB17-G/41-J3 Ferrari 456 GT

MB17-G/41-J4 Ferrari 456 GT

MB17-G/41-J7 Ferrari 456 GT

MB17-G/41-J9 Ferrari 456 GT

MB17-G/41-J11 Ferrari 456 GT

MB17-G/41-J12 Ferrari 456 GT

MB17-G/41-J15 Ferrari 456 GT

MB17-I/68-P5 '99 Ford Mustang

MB17-I/68-P17 '99 Ford Mustang

MB17-I/68-P18 '99 Ford Mustang

MB17-I/68-P33 '99 Ford Mustang

MB17-J/7-K1 Bulldozer '04

MB18-A1 Field Car

MB18-A28 Field Car

MB18-B1 Hondarora

MB18-B4 Hondarora

MB18-B5 Hondarora

MB18-B10 Hondarora

MB18-B12 Hondarora

MB18-B15 Hondarora

MB18-C2 Fire Engine

MB18-C4 Fire Engine

MB18-C17 Fire Engine

MB18-C24 Fire Engine

MB18-C26 Fire Engine

MB18-C34 Fire Engine

MB18-C38 Fire Engine

MB18-C39 Fire Engine

MB18-C41 Fire Engine

MB18-C48 Fire Engine

MB18-C51 Fire Engine

MB18-D1 Mixopotamus

MB19-A1 Lotus Racer

MB19-B1 Road Dragster

MB19-B5 Road Dragster

MB19-B11 Road Dragster

MB19-B12 Road Dragster

MB19-B13 Road Dragster

MB19-C1 Cement Truck

MB19-C2 Cement Truck

MB19-C4 Cement Truck

MB19-C8 Cement Truck

MB19-C13 Cement Truck

MB19-D1 Peterbilit Cement Truck

MB19-D11 Peterbilt Cement Truck

MB19-D9 Peterbilt Cement Truck

MB19-D12 Peterbilt Cement Truck

MB19-D25 Peterbilt Cement Truck

MB19-D26 Peterbilt Cement Truck

MB19-D29 Peterbilt Cement Truck

MB19-D30 Peterbilt Cement Truck

MB19-D32 Peterbilut Cement Truck

MB19-D33 Peterbilt Cement Truck

MB19-D34 Peterbilt Cement Truck

MB19-D36 Peterbilt Cement Truck

MB20-A1 Lamborghini Marzal

MB20-A2 Lamborghini Marzal

MB20-A7 Lamborghini Marzal

MB20-A9 Lamborghini Marzal

MB20-B22 Police Patrol

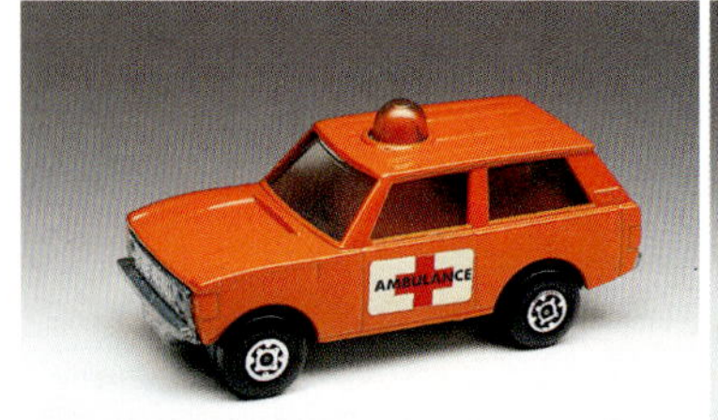
MB20-B23 Police Patrol

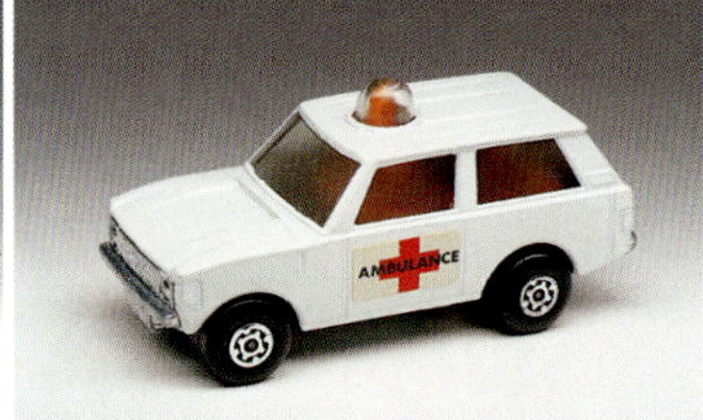
MB20-B24 Police Patrol

MB20-B25 Police Patrol

MB20-B29 Police Patrol

MB20-B32 Police Patrol

MB20-B40 Police Patrol

MB20-B43 Police Patrol

MB20-B47 Police Patrol

MB20-C/14-F1 4 X 4 Jeep

MB20-C/14-F2 4 X 4 Jeep

MB20-C/14-F4 4 X 4 Jeep

MB20-C/14-F5 4 X 4 Jeep

MB20-C/14-F13 4 X 4 Jeep

MB20-C/14-F17 4 X 4 Jeep

MB20-C/14-F 4 X 4 Jeep

MB20-C/14-F19 4 X 4 Jeep

MB20-C/14-F23 4 X 4 Jeep

MB20-D/23-G/62-I1
Volvo Container Truck

MB20-D/23-G/62-I7
Volvo Container Truck

MB20-D/23-G/62-I26
Volvo Container Truck

MB20-D/23-G/62-I30
Volvo Container Truck

MB20-D/23-G/62-I33
Volvo Container Truck

MB20-D/23-G/62-I37
Volvo Container Truck

MB20-D/23-G/62-I47
Volvo Container Truck

MB20-D/23-G/62-I48
Volvo Container Truck

MB20-D/23-G/62-I57
Volvo Container Truck

MB20-D/23-G/62-I58
Volvo Container Truck

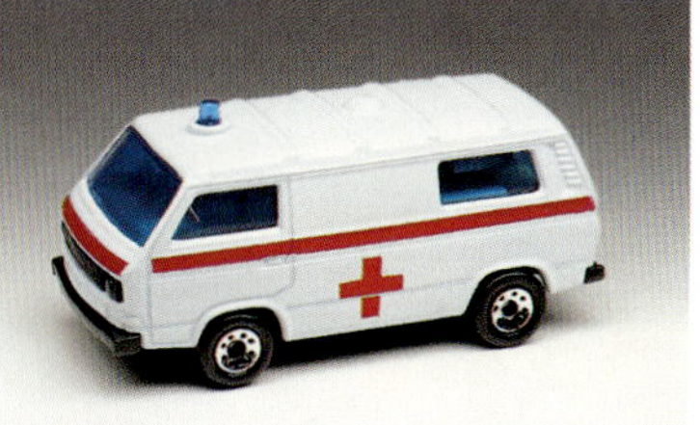

MB20-E1 Volkswagen
Transporter

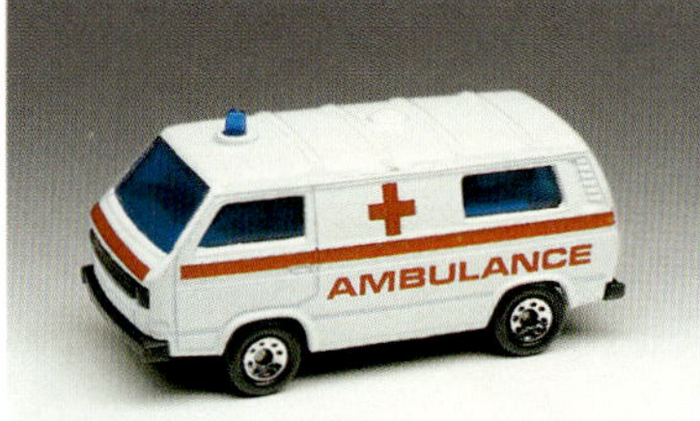

MB20-E7 Volkswagen Transporter

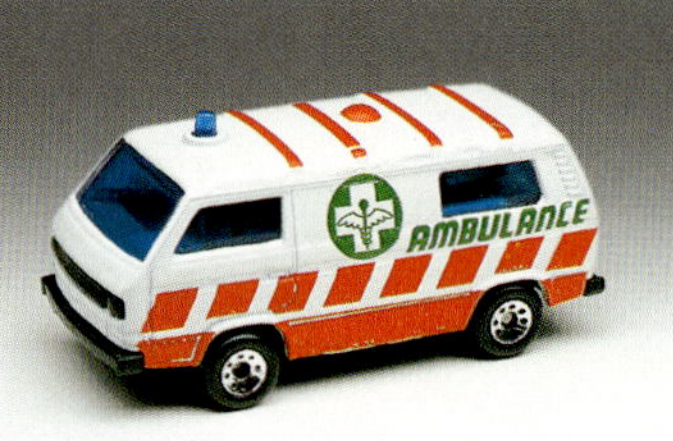

MB20-E8 Volkswagen Transporter

MB20-F/66-H1 Pontiac Firebird Ram Air

MB20-F/66-H3 Pontiac Firebird Ram Air

MB20-H1 Jumbo Sweeper

MB21-A Foden Concrete Truck

MB21-B1 Rod Roller

MB21-B2 Rod Roller

MB21-B3 Rod Roller

MB21-C4 Renault 5TL

MB21-C17 Renault 5TL

MB21-C18 Renault 5TL

MB21-C21 Renault 5TL

MB21-C23 Renault 5TL

MB21-C33 Renault 5TL

MB21-C44 Renault 5TL

MB21-D1 Corvette Pace Car

MB21-E/53-F1 Chevy Breakdown Van

MB21-E/53-F3 Chevy Breakdown Van

MB21-E/53-F4 Chevy Breakdown Van

MB21-E/53-F9 Chevy Breakdown Van

MB21-F/71-F1 GMC Wrecker

MB21-F/71/F15 GMC Wrecker

MB21-F/71-F21 GMC Wrecker

MB21-F/71-F27 GMC Wrecker

MB21-F/71-F28 GMC Wrecker

MB21-F/71-F32 GMC Wrecker

MB21-F/71-F33 GMC Wrecker

MB21-F/71-F43 GMC Wrecker

MB21-I/14-J/31-N1
Ford Transit Van

MB21-I/14-J/31-N2
Ford Transit Van

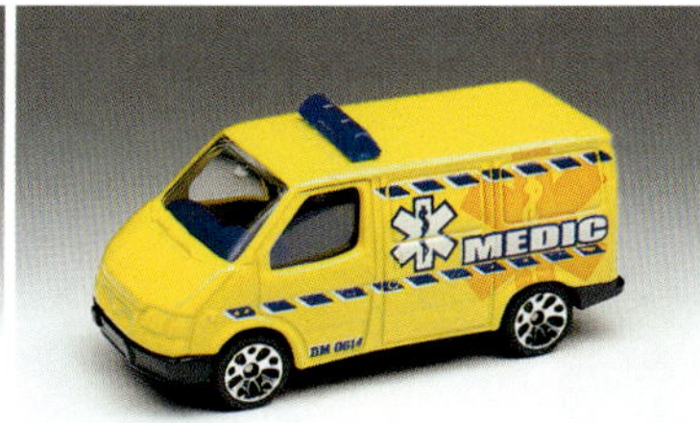

MB21-I/14-J/31-N3
Ford Transit Van

MB21-I/14-J/31-N7
Ford Transit Van

MB21-I/14-J/31-N10
Ford Transit Van

MB21-K1 Tower Boat

MB21-K4 Tower Boat

MB21-L1 Cadillac Escalade

MB21-M/9-L1 Mush Puppy

MB22-A2 Pontiac
GP Sports Coupe

MB22-A3 Pontiac
GP Sports Coupe

MB22-B1 Freeman
Intercity Commuter

MB22-B3 Freeman
Intercity Commuter

MB22-B5 Freeman
Intercity Commuter

MB22-C2 Blaze Buster

MB22-C3 Blaze Buster

MB22C15 Blaze Buster

MB22-D/35-E1 4 X 4
Mini Pickup

MB22-D/35-E7 4 X 4
Mini Pickup

MB22-D/35-E11 4 X 4 Mini Pickup

MB22-E4 Jaguar XK120

MB22-E8 Jaguar XK120

MB22-G/41-G1 Vectra Cavalier Gsi2000

MB22-H/49-F1 Lamborghini Diablo

MB22-H/49-F8 Lamborghini Diablo

MB22-H/49-F10 Lamborghini Diablo

MB22-H/49-F14 Lamborghini Diablo

MB22-H/49-F18 Lamborghini Diablo

MB22-H/49-F23 Lamborghini Diablo

MB22-H/49-F30 Lamborghini Diablo

MB22-H/49-F32 Lamborghini Diablo

MB22-H/49-F34 Lamborghini Diablo

MB22-H/49-F35 Lamborghini Diablo

MB22-H/49-F36 Lamborghini Diablo

MB22-K/5-H1 Pound Hound

MB23-A1 Volkswagen Dormobile

MB23-A3 Volkswagen Dormobile

MB23-A6 Volkswagen Dormobile

MB23-A11 Volkswagen Dormobile

MB23-B1 Atlas

MB23-B8 Atlas

MB23-B9 Atlas

MB23-B11 Atlas

MB23-C1 Mustang GT 350

MB23-D/25-F1 Audi Quattro

MB23-D/25-F3 Audi Quattro

MB23-D/25-F6 Audi Quattro

MB23-D/25-F10 Audi Quattro

MB23-D/25-F13 Audi Quattro

MB23-D/25-F15 Audi Quattro

MB23-F1 Honda ATC 250R

MB23-F3 Honda ATC 250R

MB23-H1 Ford Box Van

MB23-J1 Ford
Explorer Sport Trac

MB23-J6 Ford
Explorer Sport Trac

MB23-J10 Ford
Explorer Sport Trac

MB23-J12 Ford
Explorer Sport Trac

MB23-K1 Lock Boxer

MB24-A1 Rolls Royce
Silver Shadow

MB24-A9 Rolls Royce
Silver Shadow

MB24-B7 Team Matchbox

MB24-B9 Team Matchbox

MB24-C2 Shunter

MB24-C6 Shunter

MB24-D3 Datsun 280ZX

MB24-D4 Datsun 280ZX

MB24-E1 Datsun 280ZX 2 + 2

MB24-E2 Datsun 280ZX 2 + 2

MB24-E3 Datsun 280 ZX 2 + 2

MB24-F1 Nissan 300ZX Turbo

MB24-H/70-F1 Ferrari F40

MB24-H/70-F20 Ferrari F40

MB24-H/70-F27 Ferrari F40

MB24-H/70-F35 Ferrari F40

MB24-H/70-F39 Ferrari F40

MB24-H/70-F45 Ferrari F40

MB24-H/70-F48 Ferrari F40

MB24-H/70-F49 Ferrari F40

MB24-K1 Chevy Transport Bus

MB24-K3 Chevy Transport Bus

MB24-K5 Chevy Transport Bus

MB24-L1 Huski-Patrol

MB25-A2 Ford Cortina

MB25-B1 Mod Tractor

MB25-B4 Mod Tractor

MB25-C1 Flat Car
with Container

MB25-C2 Flat Car
with Container

MB25-C3 Flat Car
with Container

MB25-C4 Flat Car
with Container

MB25-C5 Flat Car
with Container

MB25-D2 Toyota Celica GT

MB25-D6 Toyota Celica GT

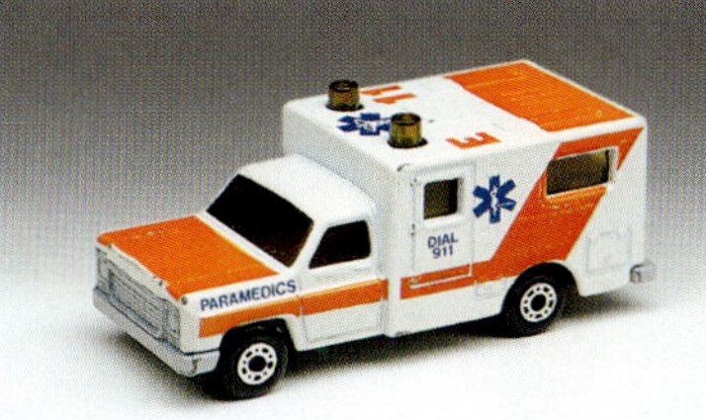

MB25-E6 Ambulance

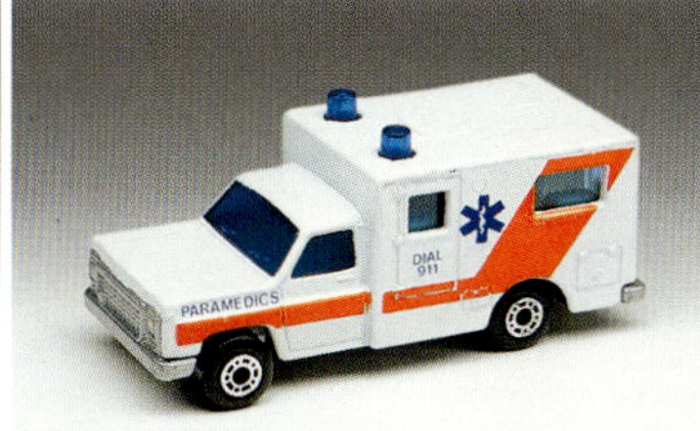

MB25-E13 Ambulance

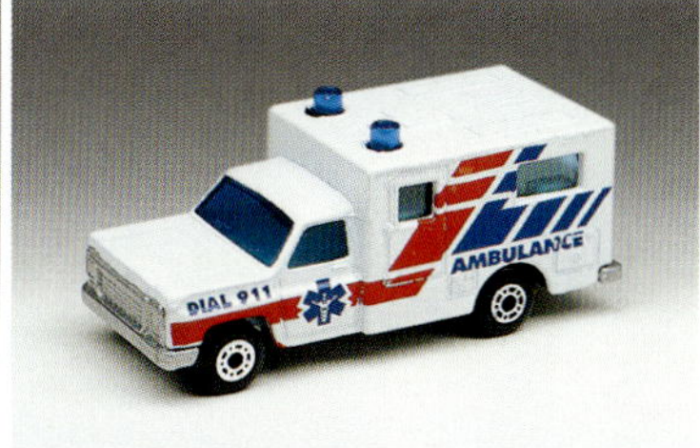

MB25-E16 Ambulance

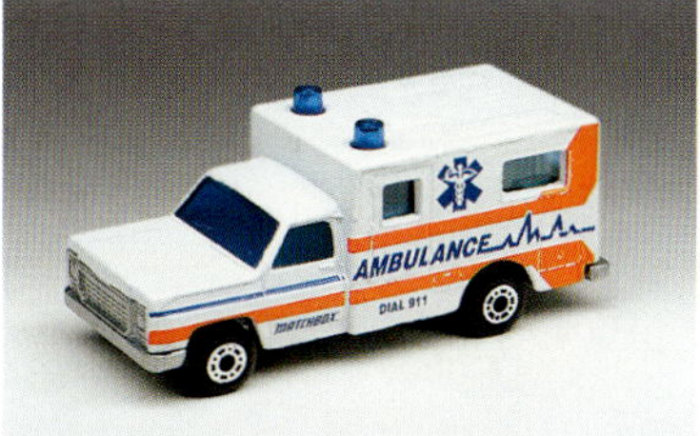

MB25-E18 Ambulance

MB25-E21 Ambulance

MB25-J/61-H3 BMW Z3

MB25-J/61-H8 BMW Z3

MB25-J/61-H13 BMW Z3

MB25-J/61-H16 BMW Z3

MB25-J/61-H25 BMW Z3

MB25-J/61-H28 BMW Z3

MB25-K2 ’98 Jeep Wrangler

MB25-K4 ’98 Jeep Wrangler

MB25-L1 Space Buggy

MB26A1 GMC Tipper Truck

MB26-B1 Big Banger

MB26-B2 Big Banger

MB26-C2 Site Dumper

MB26-C Site Dumper

MB26-C11 Site Dumper

MB26-D/41-H2 Cosmic Blues

MB26-D/41-H6Cosmic Blues

MB26-D/41-H8 Cosmic Blues

MB26-D/41-H10 Cosmic Blues

MB26-D/41-H13 Cosmic Blues

MB26-E8 Volvo Cable Truck

MB26-E12 Volvo Cable Truck

MB26-E14 Volvo Cable Truck

MB26-F/49-G1
Volvo Tilt Truck

MB26-F/49-G2
Volvo Tilt Truck

MB26-F/49-G4
Volvo Tilt Truck

MB26-F/49-G6
Volvo Tilt Truck

MB26-F/49-G7
Volvo Tilt Truck

MB26-F/49-G14
Volvo Tilt Truck

MB26-F/49-G18
Volvo Tilt Truck

MB26-H/31-H1 BMW 5 Series

MB26-G/31-H3 BMW 5 Series

MB26-J1 Airport Fire Pumper

MB26-J5 Airport Fire Pumper

MB26-J7 Airport Fire Pumper

MB26-K1 Sport SUV

MB26-L/11-L1 Police Hat

MB26-M1 GMC Bucket Truck

MB27-A1 Mercedes 230SL

MB27-A2 Mercedes 230SL

MB27-A3 Mercedes 230SL

MB27-A4 Mercedes 230SL

MB27-B1 Lamorghini Countach

MB27-B8 Lamborghini Countach

MB27-B11 Lamborghini Countach

MB27-B16 Lamborghini Countach

MB27-C2 Swept Wing Jet

MB27-C4 Swept Wing Jet

MB27-C5 Swept Wing Jet

MB27-D/73-F/51-J1 Jeep Cherokee

MB27-D/73-F/51-J3 Jeep Cherokee

MB27-D/73-F/51-J4 Jeep Cherokee

MB27-D/73-F/51-J14 Jeep Cherokee

MB27-D/73-F/51-J17 Jeep Cherokee

MB27-D/73-F/51-J18 Jeep Cherokee

MB27-D/73-F/51-J26 Jeep Cherokee

MB27-D/73-F/51-J32 Jeep Cherokee

MB27-F2 Tailgator

MB27-F3 Tailgator

MB27-F6 Tailgator

MB27-F7 Tailgator

MB27-G1 Ladder Truck

MB27-G3 Ladder Truck

MB27-G7 Ladder Truck

MB27-H/49-J1 Ford Falcon Police Car

MB27-H/49-J2 Ford Falcon Police Car

MB27-H/49-J5 Ford Falcon Police Car

MB27-H/49-J6 Ford Falcon Police Car

MB27-I/12-N1 Military Helmet

MB28-A1 Mack Dump Truck

MB28-B2 Stoat

MB28-C2 Lincoln Continental Mk V

MB28-D1 Formula 5000

MB28-E1 Dodge Daytona

MB28-E6 Dodge Daytona

MB28-E13 Dodge Daytona

MB28-H/61-F1 Fork Lift Truck

MB28-H/61-F2 Fork Lift Truck

MB28-H/61-F3 Fork Lift Truck

MB28-H/61-F4 Fork Lift Truck

MB28-H/61-F5 Fork Lift Truck

MB28-L/22-J1 Mitsubishi Spyder

MB28-L/22-J2 Mitsubishi Spyder

MB28-L/22-J3 Mitsubishi Spyder

MB28-L/22-J10 Mitsubishi Spyder

MB28-L/22-J18 Mitsubishi Spyder

MB28-L/22-J24 Mitsubishi Spyder

MB28-O1 Hot Head

MB29-A1 Fire Pumper

MB29-B1 Racing Mini

MB29-B2 Racing Mini

MB29-B5 Racing Mini

MB29-C1 Tractor Shovel

MB29-C5 Tractor Shovel

MB29-C17 Tractor Shovel

MB29-C31 Tractor Shovel

MB29-C39 Tractor Shovel

MB29-C51 Tractor Shovel

MB29-C52 Tractor Shovel

MB29-C53 Tractor Shovel

MB29-C64 Tractor Shovel

MB29-C65 Tractor Shovel

MB29-E/14-L1 Rig Digger

MB30-A1 Eight Wheel Crane

MB30-B1 Beach Buggy

MB30-B2 Beach Buggy

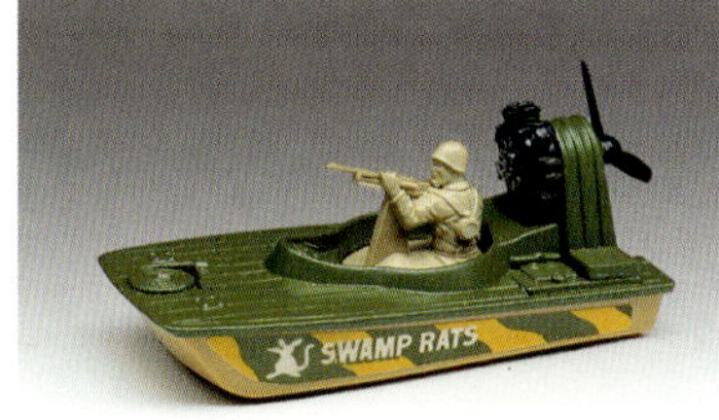

MB30-C1 Swamp Rat

MB30-D2 Articulated Truck

MB30-D4 Articulated Truck

MB30-D6 Articulated Truck

MB30-D7 Articulated Truck

MB30-D9 Articulated Truck

MB30-E/23-E2
Peterbilt Quarry Truck

MB30-E/23-E10
Peterbilt Quarry Truck

MB30-E/23E13
Peterbilt Quarry Truck

MB30-E/23-E22
Peterbilt Quarry Truck

MB30-E/23-E25
Peterbilt Quarry Truck

MB30-F/40-L1
Mercedes G Wagon

MB30-F/40-L4
Mercedes G Wagon

MB30-F/40-L15
Mercedes G Wagon

MB30-F/40-L25
Mercedes G Wagon

MB30-F/40-L29
Mercedes G Wagon

MB30-F/40-L34
Mercedes G Wagon

MB30-F/40-L38
Mercedes G Wagon

MB30-G/60-I1 Toyota Supra

MB30-G/60-I9 Toyota Supra

MB30-G/60-I11 Toyota Supra

MB30-G/60-I21 Toyota Supra

MB30-G/60-I24 Toyota Supra

MB30-I1 Chevy Tahoe Police

MB30-I8 Chevy Tahoe Police

MB30-I9 Chevy Tahoe Police

MB30-I19 Chevy Tahoe Police

MB30-K/15-N1 Cap'n Cop

MB31-A1 Lincoln Continental

MB31-B1 Volksdragon

MB31-B6 Volksdragon

MB31-C1 Caravan

MB31-C6 Caravan

MB31-C 11 Caravan

MB31-C27 Caravan

MB31-D4 Mazda RX7

MB31-D6 Mazda RX7

MB31-E1 Mazda RX7

MB31-E2 Mazda RX7

MB31-G/2-F1 Sterling

MB31-G/2-F8 Sterling

MB31-I/21-G1 Nissan Prairie

MB31-I/21-G2 Nissan Prairie

MB31-I/21-G5 Nissan Prairie

MB31-I/21-G6 Nissan Prairie

MB31-J/26-K5 Jaguar XJ220

MB31-J/26-K9 Jaguar XJ220

MB31-J/26-K10 Jaguar XJ220

MB31-J/26-K15 Jaguar XJ220

MB31-J/26-K20 Jaguar XJ220

MB31-J/26-K24 Jaguar XJ220

MB31-J/26-K25 Jaguar XJ220

MB31-J/26-K27 Jaguar XJ220

MB31-L3 1957 Chevy
Bel Air Hard Top

MB31-M/45-H1 Beetle 4 X 4

MB31-M/45-H2 Beetle 4 X 4

MB31-M/45-H4 Beetle 4 X 4

MB31-M/45-H7 Beetle 4 X 4

MB31-M/45-11 Beetle 4 X 4

MB31-O2 BMW X5

MB31-O9 BMW X5

MB31-P1 Volkswagen Beetle Taxi

MB31-P3 Volkswagen Beetle Taxi

MB31-Q1 Airport Fire Tanker

MB32-A3 Leyland Petrol Tanker

MB32-B1 Maserati Bora

MB32-B6 Maserati Bora

MB32-C2 Field Gun

MB32-D/6-F1 Atlas Excavator

MB32-D/6-F8 Atlas Excavator

MB32-D/6-F12 Atlas Excavator

MB32-D/6-F15 Atlas Excavator

MB32-D/6-F17 Atlas Excavator

MB32-D/6-F19 Atlas Excavator

MB32-D/6-F21 Atlas Excavator

MB32-D/6-F23 Atlas Excavator

MB32-E/12-G4 Modified Racer

MB32-G3 1970 El Camino

MB32-G6 1970 El Camino

MB32-G9 1970 El Camino

MB32-I1 Nissan X-terra

MB32-I2 Nissan X-terra

MB32-I3 Nissan X-terra

MB32-J1 4 X 4 Fire Truck

MB33-A3 Lamborghini Miura

MB33-A7 Lamborghini Miura

MB33-B1 Datsun 126X

MB33-B3 Datsun 126X

MB33-B4 Datsun 126X

MB33-C1 Police Motorcycle

MB33-C2 Police Motorcycle

MB33C4 Police Motorcycle

MB33-C5 Police Motorcycle

MB33-C14 Police Motorcycle

MB33-C16 Police Motorcycle

MB33-C23 Police Motorcycle

MB33-D/56-E/63-G1
Volkswagen Golf GTi

MB33-D/56-E/63-G2
Volkswagen Golf GTi

MB33-D/56-E/63-G7
Volkswagen Golf GTi

MB33-D/56-E/63-G10
Volkswagen Golf GTi

MB33-E/43-F2 Renault 11

MB33-G/74-I1 Utility Truck

MB33-G/74-I8 Utility Truck

MB33-G/74-I10 Utility Truck

MB33-G/74-I13 Utility Truck

MB33-G/74-I18 Utility Truck

MB33-G/74-I20 Utility Truck

MB33-G/74-I25 Utility Truck

MB33-K1 Boom Fire Truck

MB34-A1 Formula 1

MB34-A4 Formula 1

MB34-A10 Formula 1

MB34-A18 Formula 1

MB34-B2 Vantastic

MB34-B8 Vantastic

MB34-B9 Vantastic

MB34-C12 Chevy Prostocker

MB34-C14 Chevy Prostocker

MB34-C20 Chevy Prostocker

MB34-D1 Ford RS200

MB34-D3 Ford RS200

MB34-D5 Ford RS200

MB34-E/72-J1 Sprint Racer

MB34-G/6-H1
Plymouth Prowler

MB34-G/6-H31
Plymouth Prowler

MB34-G/6-H39
Plymouth Prowler

MB34-G/6-H45
Plymouth Prowler

MB34-I3 '33 Ford Coupe

MB34-I12 '33 Ford Coupe

MB34-I14 '33 Ford Coupe

MB34-J1 Chevy Impala Police Car

MB34-J8 Chevy Impala Police Car

MB34-J10 Chevy Impala Police Car

MB34-J19 Chevy Impala Police Car

MB34-K1 Mercedes Benz E430 Police Car

MB34-K2 Mercedes Benz E430 Police Car

MB35-A1 Merryweather Fire Engine

MB35-A6 Merryweather Fire Engine

MB35-B1 Fandango

MB35-B2 Fandango

MB35-B13 Fandango

MB35-B17 Fandango

MB35-B18 Fandango

MB35-C/16-C1 Pontiac T-Roof

MB35-C/16-C4 Pontiac T-Roof

MB35-C/16-C6 Pontiac T-Roof

MB35-D1 Zoo Truck

MB35-D7 Zoo Truck

MB35-D14 Zoo Truck

MB35-D15 Zoo Truck

MB35-F/16-F1 Land Rover Ninety

MB35-F/16-F2 Land Rover Ninety

MB35-F/16-F4
Land Rover Ninety

MB35-F/16-F17
Land Rover Ninety

MB35-F/16-F26
Land Rover Ninety

MB35-F/16-F29
Land Rover Ninety

MB35-F/16-F30
Land Rover Ninety

MB35-F/16-F33 Land
Rover Ninety

MB35-F/16-F34
Land Rover Ninety

MB35-F/16-F35
Land Rover Ninety

MB35-F/16-F36
Land Rover Ninety

MB35-F/16-F41
Land Rover Ninety

MB35-H/22-I22 Pontiac
Gran Prix Stock Car

MB35-H/22-I23 Pontiac
Gran Prix Stock Car

MB35-I2 Pontiac
Gran Prix Stock Car

MB35-J/75-F2 AMG
Mercedes C-Class

MB35-J/75-F5 AMG
Mercedes C-Class

MB35-L/65-J1 Police Motorcycle

MB35-L/65-J3
Police Motorcycle

MB35-L/65-J4
Police Motorcycle

MB35-M1 Holden
Commodore Police Car

MB36-A1 Opel Diplomat

MB36-A3 Opel Diplomat

MB36-B3 Draguar

MB36-B15 Draguar

MB36-C2 Formula 5000

MB36-C4 Formula 5000

MB36-C5 Formula 5000

MB36-D2 Refuse Truck

MB36-D6 Refuse Truck

MB36-D10 Refuse Truck

MB36-D13 Refuse Truck

MB36-D17 Refuse Truck

MB36-D19 Refuse Truck

MB36-D22 Refuse Truck

MB36-D24 Refuse Truck

MB36-D27 Refuse Truck

MB36-D32 Refuse Truck

MB36-D34 Refuse Truck

MB36-D35 Refuse Truck

MB36-D36 Refuse Truck

MB36-D40 Refuse Truck

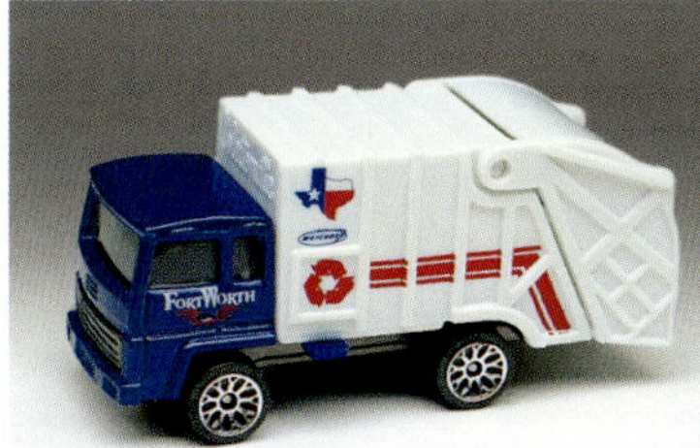
MB36-D43 Refuse Truck

MB36-E4 1957 Chevy
Bel Air Convertible

MB36-E7 1957 Chevy
Bel Air Convertible

MB36-F/12-L2 '99
Mustang Convertible

MB36-F/12-L7 '99
Mustang Convertible

MB36-F/12-L15 '99
Mustang Convertible

MB36-F/12-L16 '99
Mustang Convertible

MB36-H/21-J1 X-33 RLV

MB36-I1 Road Roller

MB36-I2 Road Roller

MB36-I6 Road Roller

MB36-I11 Road Roller

MB36-K1 Taxi Cab

MB36-K4 Taxi Cab

MB36-L1 Honda Element

MB37A1 Cattle Truck

MB37-A3 Cattle Truck

MB37-B1 Soopa Coopa

MB37-B8 Soopa Coopa

MB37-C1 Skip Truck

MB37-C16 Skip Truck

MB37-D1 Sunburner

MB37-E2 Matra Rancho

MB37-E4 Matra Rancho

MB37-F/25-I1 4 X 4 Jeep

MB37-F/25-I3 4 X 4 Jeep

MB37-F/25-I8 4 X 4 Jeep

MB37-F/25-I11 4 X 4 Jeep

MB37-F/25-I16 4 X 4 Jeep

MB37-F/25-I18 4 X 4 Jeep

MB37-F/25-I19 4 X 4 Jeep

MB37-I3 1970 Boss Mustang

MB39-I1 1971 Camaro Z28

MB39-I4 1971 Camaro Z28

MB40-A1 Vauxhall Guildsman

MB40-A3 Vauxhall Guildsman

MB40-A6 Vauxhall Guildsman

MB40-A9 Vauxhall Guildsman

MB40-A10 Vauxhall Guildsman

MB40-B7 Horse Box

MB40-B11 Horse Box

MB40-B21 Horse Box

MB40-B31 Horse Box

MB40-B38 Horse Box

MB40-B49 Horse Box

MB40-B50 Horse Box

MB40-C/62-E/58-F1
Corvette T-Roof

MB40-C/62-E/58-F10
Corvette T-Roof

MB40-C/62-E/58-F12
Corvette T-Roof

MB40-C/62-E/58-F18
Corvette T-Roof

MB40-C/62-E/58-F24
Corvette T-Roof

MB40-C/62-E/58-F27
Corvette T-Roof

MB40-C/62-E/58-F29
Corvette T-Roof

MB40-C/62-E/58-F30
Corvette T-Roof

MB40-C/62-E/58-F35
Corvette T-Roof

MB40-C/62-E/58-F41
Corvette T-Roof

MB40-D/60-H1
Rocket Transporter

MB40-D/60-H9
Rocket Transporter

MB40-D/60-H17
Rocket Transporter

MB40-D/60-H20
Rocket Transporter

MB40-F/68-H1 Road Roller

MB40-F/68-H2 Road Roller

MB40-F/68-H3 Road Roller

MB40-F/68-H4 Road Roller

MB40-F/68-H5 Road Roller

MB40-G/33-I1 Ford Mondeo

MB40-G/33-I3 Ford Mondeo

MB40-H1 1969 Camaro SS

MB40-H5 1969 Camaro SS

MB40-I29 FJ Holden Van

MB40-I31 FJ Holden Van

MB40-I32 FJ Holden Van

MB40-I34 FJ Holden Van

MB40-K3 Dodge
Concept Vehicle

MB40-M1 Cement Mixer

MB40-M2 Cement Mixer

MB40-M7 Cement Mixer

MB41-A1 Ford GT

MB41-A4 Ford GT

MB41-A11 Ford GT

MB41-A12 Ford GT

MB41-B1 Siva Spyder

MB41-B2 Siva Spyder

MB41-B8 Siva Spyder

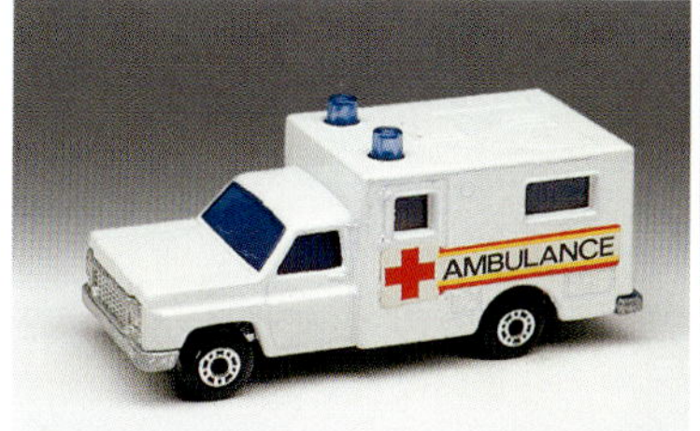

MB41-C1 Ambulance

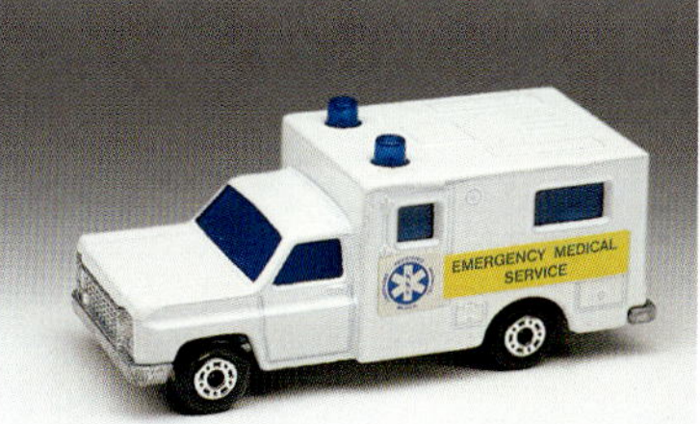

MB41C7 Ambulance

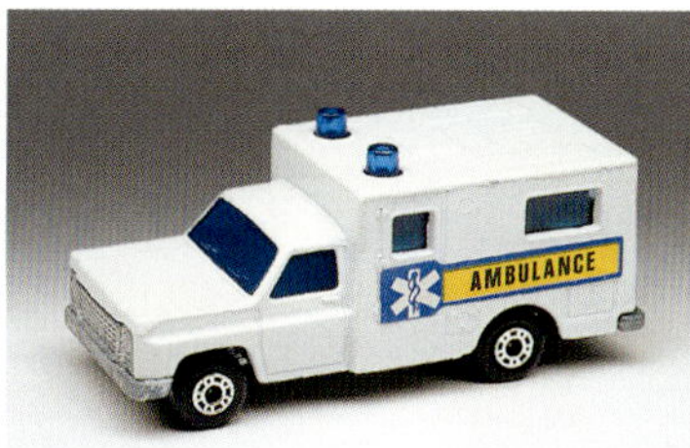

MB41-C12 Ambulance

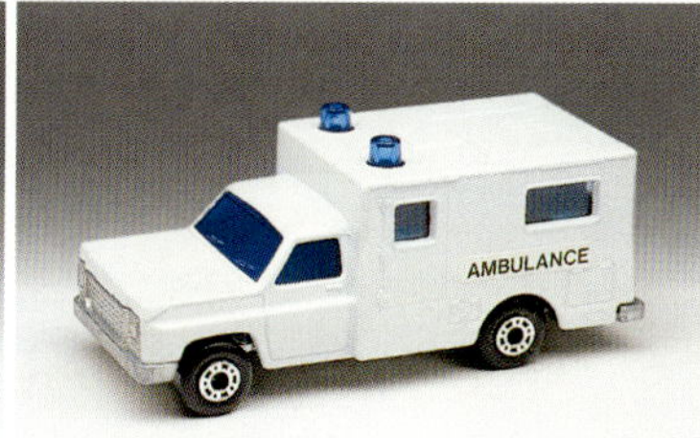

MB41-C15 Ambulance

MB41-D2 Kenworth Aerodyne

MB41-D4 Kenworth Aerodyne

MB41-D5 Kenworth Aerodyne

MB41-D6 Kenworth Aerodyne

MB41-D7 Kenworth Aerodyne

MB41-F/1-E1 Jaguar XJ6

MB41-F/1-E4 Jaguar XJ6

MB41-F/1-E7 Jaguar XJ6

MB41-F/1-E14 Jaguar XJ6

MB41-F/1-E15 Jaguar XJ6

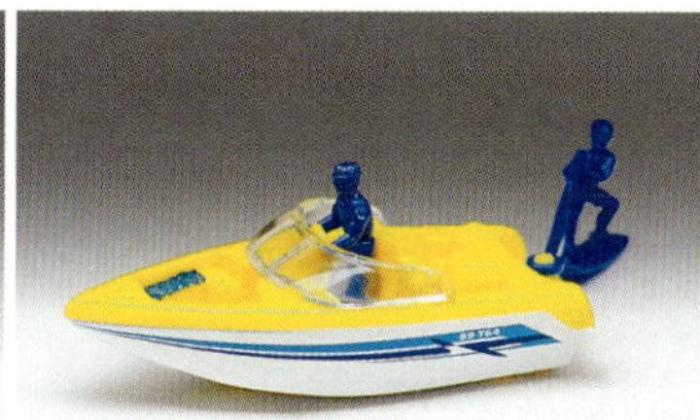

MB41-K/36-G1 Ski Boat

MB41-K/36-G3 Ski Boat

MB41-L/14-I1 Flatbed Truck

MB41-L/14-I3 Flatbed Truck

MB41-M1 Radar Plane

MB41-M4 Radar Plane

MB41-M7 Radar Plane

MB41-N1Sea Rescue Helicopter

MB41-N4 Sea Rescue Helicopter

MB41-O1 Checker Cab

MB42-A1 Iron Fairy Crane

MB42-A3 Iron Fairy Crane

MB42-A4 Iron Fairy Crane

MB42-B6 Tyre Fryer

MB42-C3 Mercedes Container Truck

MB42-C5 Mercedes Container Truck

MB42-C7 Mercedes Container Truck

MB42-C12 Mercedes Container Truck

MB42-C13 Mercedes Container Truck

MB42-C18 Mercedes Container Truck

MB42-D2 1957 Ford Thunderbird

MB42-D6 1957 Ford Thunderbird

MB42-D8 1957 Ford Thunderbird

MB42-D24 1957 Ford Thunderbird

MB42-E1 Mobile Crane

MB42-E6 Mobile Crane

MB42-E7 Mobile Crane

MB42-E10 Mobile Crane

MB42-E13 Mobile Crane

MB42-E14 Mobile Crane

MB42-E17 Mobile Crane Truck

MB42-E18 Mobile Crane

MB42-F/37-J1 Seaplane

MB42-F/37-J6 Seaplane

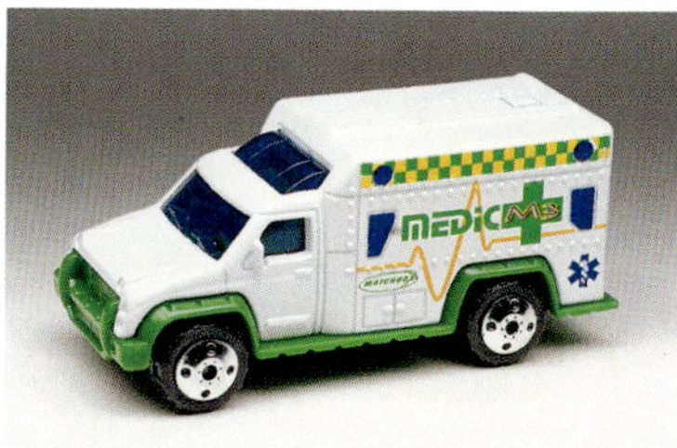
MB42-H1 Ambulance

MB42-H4 Ambulance

MB42-H11Ambulance

MB42-H15 Ambulance

MB42-I1 2004 School Bus

MB43-A2 Pony Trailer

MB43-B2 Dragon Wheels

MB43-C1 0-4-0 Loco

MB43-C6 0-4-0 Loco

MB43-C10 0-4-0 Loco

MB43-C22 0-4-0 Loco

MB43-D2 Peterbilt Conventional

MB43-D5 Peterbilt Conventional

MB43-D7 Peterbilt Conventional

MB43-D12 Peterbilt Conventional

MB43-E2 Mercedes 500 SEC

MB43-E4 Mercedes 500 SEC

MB43-E7 Mercedes 500 SEC

MB43-E8 Mercedes 500 SEC

MB43-G/24-G1 Lincoln Town Car

MB43-G/24-G6
Lincoln Town Car

MB43-G/24-G7
Lincoln Town Car

MB43-I/56-H1 Camaro Z28

MB43-I/56-H15 Camaro Z28

MB43-I/56-H19 Camaro Z28

MB43-I/56-H26 Camaro Z28

MB43-K/38-K1
Sea Rescue Boat

MB43-K/38-K2
Sea Rescue Boat

MB43-K/38-K7
Sea Rescue Boat

MB43-K/38-K13
Sea Rescue Boat

MB43-L1 Ford F Series Truck

MB43-L4 Ford F Series Truck

MB43-L10 Ford F Series Truck

MB44A1 Refrigerator Truck

MB44A2 Refrigerator Truck

MB44-B1 Boss Mustang

MB44-B2 Boss Mustang

MB44-B6 Boss Mustang

MB44-C1 Passenger Coach

MB44-C11 Passenger Coach

MB44-C12 Passenger Coach

MB44-C19 Passenger Coach

MB44-C21 Passenger Coach

MB44-C22 Passenger Coach

MB44-C23 Passenger Coach

MB44-C27 Passenger Coach

MB44-D/68-D/26-H/10-E1
4 X 4 Chevy Van

MB44-D/68-D/26-H/10-E5
4 X 4 Chevy Van

MB44-D/68-D/26-H/10-E6
4 X 4 Chevy Van

MB44-D/68-D/26-H/10-E20
4 X 4 Chevy Van

MB44-D/68-D/26-H/10-E25
4 X 4 Chevy Van

MB44-D/68-D/26-H/10-E26
4 X 4 Chevy Van

MB44-D/68-D/26-H/10-E32
4 X 4 Chevy Van

MB44-E1 Citroen 15 CV

MB44-E7 Citroen 15 CV

MB44-F1 Datsun
280ZX Police Car

MB44-G1 Skoda 130 LR

MB44-H1 1921
Ford Model T Van

MB44-H19 1921
Ford Model TT Van

MB44-I1 Ford Probe

MB44-I3 Ford Probe

MB44-I4 Ford Probe

MB44-I8 Ford Probe

MB44-I10 Ford Probe

MB44-J/39-J1 Hydroplane

MB44-J/39-J5 Hydroplane

MB44-K/74-K/67-I1
Audi TT Coupe

MB44-K/74-K/67-I2
Audi TT Coupe

MB44-K/74-K/67-I9
Audi TT Coupe

MB44-K/74-K/67-I12
Audi TT Coupe

MB44-K/74-K/67-I16
Audi TT Coupe

MB44-L1 Truck
Camper Ambulance

MB44-L2 Truck
Camper Ambulance

MB45-A2 Ford Group 6

MB45-A5 Ford Group 6

MB45-A6 Ford Group 6

MB45-A17 Ford Group 6

MB45-A24 Ford Group 6

MB45-A30 Ford Group 6

MB45-A32 Ford Group 6

MB45-B5 BMW 3.0 CSL

MB45-B8 BMW 3.0 CSL

MB45-B10 BMW 3.0 CSL

MB45-C1 Kenworth Aerodyne

MB45-C3 Kenworth Aerodyne

MB45-C6 Kenworth Aerodyne

MB45-E/69-G1 Highway
Maintenance Vehicle

MB45-E/69-G3 Highway
Maintenance Vehicle

MB45-E/69-G8 Highway
Maintenance Vehicle

MB45-E/69-G11 Highway
Maintenance Vehicle

MB45-E/69-G13 Highway
Maintenance Vehicle

MB45-E/69-G15 Highway
Maintenance Vehicle

MB45-E/69-G18 Highway Maintenance Vehicle

MB45-E/69-G26 Highway Maintenance Vehicle

MB45-F/40-J1 Submersible

MB45-F/40-J2 Submersible

MB45-F/40-J3 Submersible

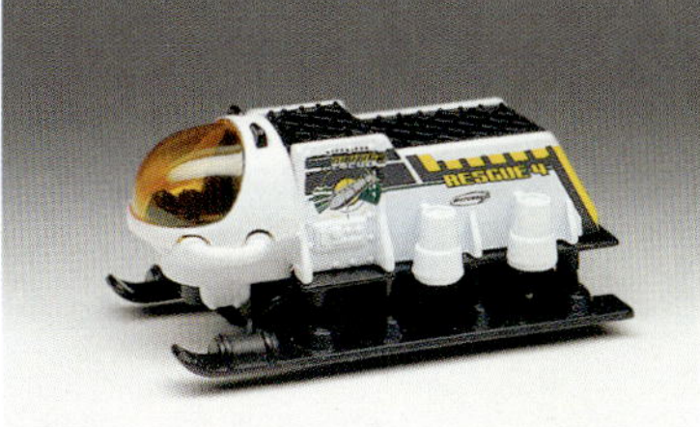
MB45-F/40-J8 Submersible

MB46-A1 Mercedes 300SE

MB46-A2 Mercedes 300SE

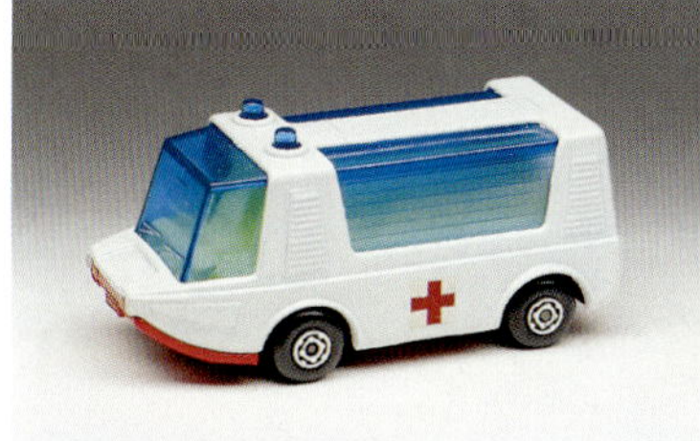
MB46-B4 Stretcha Fetcha

MB46-B9 Stretcha Fetcha

MB46-B12 Stretcha Fetcha

MB46-C1 Ford Tractor

MB46-C8 Ford Tractor

MB46-C17 Ford Tractor

MB46-D1 Hot Chocolate/ Beetle Streaker

MB46-D3 Hot Chocolate/ Beetle Streaker

MB46-F/57-F1 Mission Helicopter

MB46-F/57-F2 Mission Helicopter

MB46-H/57-F3 Mission Helicopter

MB46-H/57-H13 Mission Helicopter

MB46-H/57-H17 Mission Helicopter

MB46-H/57-H27 Mission Helicopter

MB46-H/57-H33 Mission Helicopter

MB46-F/57-F39 Mission Helicopter

MB46-F/57-F43
Mission Helicopter

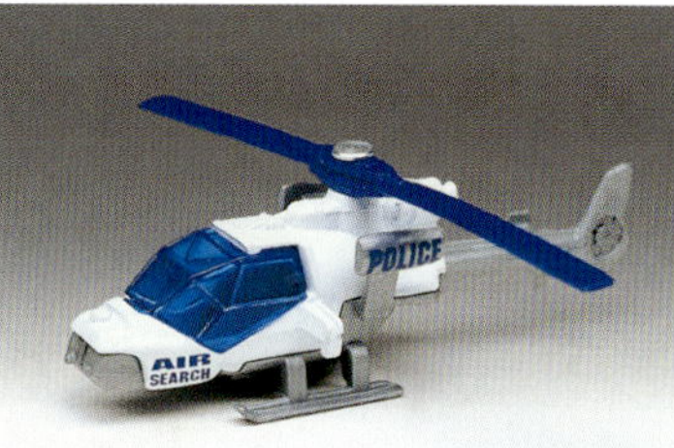

MB46-F/57-F47
Mission Helicopter

MB46-F/57-H48
Mission Helicopter

MB46-H3 Chevy Tahoe

MB46-H9 Chevy Tahoe

MB46-H10 Chevy Tahoe

MB46-H20 Chevy Tahoe

MB46-J2 1955 Chevy
Bel Air Convertible

MB46-K1 4 X 4 Buggy

MB46-K4 4 X 4 Buggy

MB46-L1 Ambulance

MB47-A1 DAF Container Truck

MB47-A2 DAF Container Truck

MB47-B2 Beach Hopper

MB47-B5 Beach Hopper

MB47-B10 Beach Hopper

MB47-C1 Pannier Loco

MB47-D1 Jaguar SS100

MB47-D3 Jaguar SS100

MB47-D6 Jaguar SS100

MB47-E1 School Bus

MB47-E19 School Bus

MB47-E24 School Bus

MB47-E31 School Bus

MB47-E42 School Bus

MB47-E64 School Bus

MB47-G1 Bradley M1 Fighting Vehicle

MB47-G2 Bradley M1 Fighting Vehicle

MB47-H/39-K1 Armored Response Vehicle

MB47-H/39-K2 Armored Response Vehicle

MB47-H/39-K8 Armored Response Vehicle

MB47-I4 Nissan X-terra

MB47-I7 Nissan X-terra

MB48-A4 Dodge Dump Truck

MB48-B1 Pi-Eyed Piper

MB48-C1 Sambron Jack Lift

MB48-D3 Red Rider

MB48-E1 Unimog with Plow

MB48-E2 Unimog with Plow

MB48-F2 Vauxhall Astra/ Opel Kadette

MB48-F4 Vauxhall Astra/ Opel Kadette

MB48-F8 Vauxhall Astra/ Opel Kadette

MB48-H3 1956 Ford Pickup

MB48-H6 1956 Ford Pickup

MB48-H13 1956 Ford Pickup

MB48-H17 1956 Ford Pickup

MB48-H19 1956 Ford Pickup

MB48-H27 1956 Ford Pickup

MB48-H46 1956 Ford Pickup

MB48-J/28N1 Delivery Truck

MB48-L/33-J1 Hummer Police

MB48-L/33-J2 Hummer Police

MB48-L/33-J3 Hummer Police

MB48-L/33-J7 Hummer Police

MB49-A1 Unimog

MB49-A6 Unimog

MB49-B3 Chop Suey

MB49-B4 Chop Suey

MB49-C2 Crane Truck

MB49-C5 Crane Truck

MB49-C9 Crane Truck

MB49-D1 Sand Digger

MB49-D2 Sand Digger

MB49-E/72-M1 Peugeot Quasar

MB49-E/72-M6 Peugeot Quasar

MB49-H/2-H5 BMW 850i

MB49-H/2-H7 BMW 850i

MB49-H/2-H9 BMW 850i

MB49-H/2-H11 BMW 850i

MB49-H/2-H16 BMW 850i

MB49-H/2-H19 BMW 850i

MB49-H/2-H22 BMW 850i

MB49-H/2-H25 BMW 850i

MB49-I/58-G1
Volkswagen Concept I

MB49-I/58-G7
Volkswagen Concept I

MB49-I/58-G8
Volkswagen Concept I

MB49-I/58-G20
Volkswagen Concept I

MB49-I/58-G21
Volkswagen Concept I

MB49-I/58-G31
Volkswagen Concept I

MB49-I/58-G35
Volkswagen Concept I

MB49-I/58-G48
Volkswagen Concept I

MB49-I/58-G79
Volkswagen Concept I

MB50-A2 Kennel Truck

MB50-A7 Kennel Truck

MB50-B1 Articulated Truck

MB50-B2 Articulated Truck

MB50-B13 Articulated Truck

MB50-D1 Harley
Davidson Motorcycle

MB50-D7 Harley
Davidson Motorcycle

MB50-E1 Chevy Blazer

MB50-E14 Chevy Blazer

MB50-E16 Chevy Blazer

MB50-E19 Chevy Blazer

MB50-E23 Chevy Blazer

MB50-E27 Chevy Blazer

MB50-E28 Chevy Blazer

MB50-E31 Chevy Blazer

MB50-E35 Chevy Blazer

MB50-J4 Ford F150 Pickup

MB50-J9 Ford F150 Pickup

MB50-J10 Ford F150 Pickup

MB50-J13 Ford F150 Pickup

MB50-J19 Ford F150 Pickup

MB50-L/5-F5 Ford Expedition Police

MB50-L/5-F14 Ford Expedition Police

MB51A3 Eight Wheel Tipper

MB51-B1 Citroen SM

MB51-B9 Citroen SM

MB51-C1 Combine Harvester

MB51-C13 Combine Harvester

MB51-C14 Combine Harvester

MB51-C15 Combine Harvester

MB51-D1 Midnight Magic

MB51-G/68-F2 Camaro IROC Z28

MB51-G/68-F4 Camaro IROC Z28

MB51-G/68-F9 Camaro IROC Z28

MB51-G/68-F15 Camaro IROC Z28

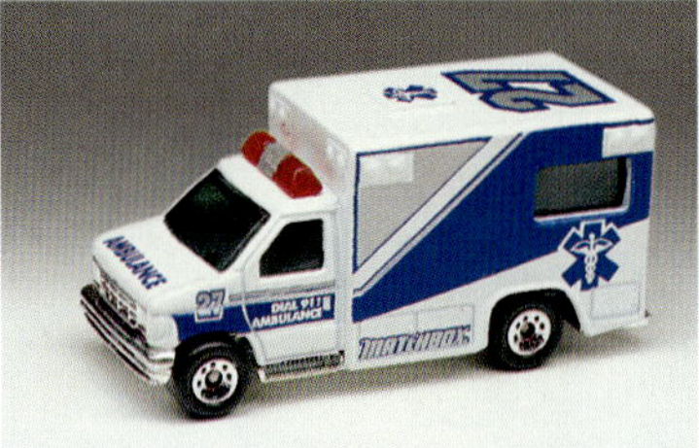
MB51-K/17-H3 Ford Ambulance

MB51-K/17-H5 Ford Ambulance

MB51-K/17-H12 Ford Ambulance

MB51-K/17-H24
Ford Ambulance

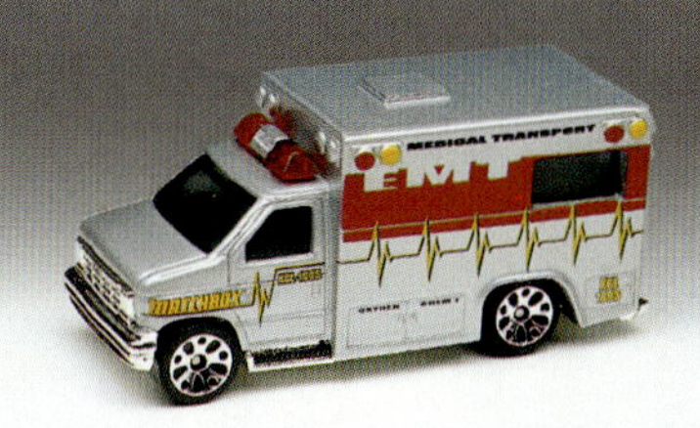

MB51-K/17-H33
Ford Ambulance

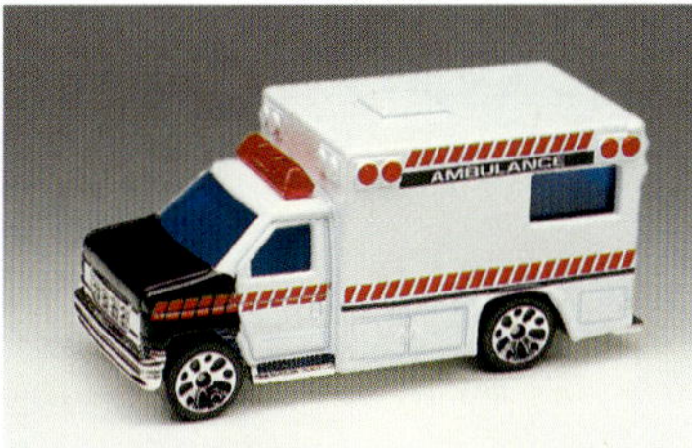

MB51-K/17-H39
Ford Ambulance

MB51-L/46-I1
Watercraft & Trailer

MB51-L/46-I4
Watercraft & Trailer

MB51-L/46-I8
Watercraft & Trailer

MB51-L/46-I11
Watercraft & Trailer

MB51-N/37-M1 Robot Truck

MB51-N/37-M4 Robot Truck

MB51-O1 Ford
Falcon Police Car

MB51-P1 Pontiac Vibe

MB51-Q1 Jeep Compass

MB52-A2 Dodge
Charger MKIII

MB52-A4 Dodge
Charger MKIII

MB52-A6 Dodge
Charger MKIII

MB52-A8 Dodge
Charger MKIII

MB52-A15 Dodge
Charger MKIII

MB52-B1 Police Launch

MB52-B16 Police Launch

MB52-C1 BMW M1

MB52-C5 BMW M1

MB52-D1 BMW M1

MB52-D2 BMW M1

MB52-D3 BMW M1

MB52-D6 BMW M1

MB52-E1 Isuzu Amigo

MB52-E3 Isuzu Amigo

MB52-E9 Isuzu Amigo

MB52-F1 Ford
Escort RS Cosworth

MB52-F5 Ford
Escort RS Cosworth

MB52-F13 Ford
Escort RS Cosworth

MB52-F14 Ford
Escort RS Cosworth

MB52-I/36-J1 Troop Carrier

MB52-I/36-J5 Troop Carrier

MB52-J1 Land Rover SVX

MB53-A2 Ford Zodiac MK IV

MB53-A4 Ford Zodiac MK IV

MB53-A6 Ford Zodiac MK IV

MB53-B1 Tanzara

MB53-B2 Tanzara

MB53-B7 Tanzara

MB53-B8 Tanzara

MB53-C3 Jeep CJ6

MB53-C8 Jeep CJ6

MB53-C9 Jeep CJ6

MB53-C14 Jeep CJ6

MB53-D/55-J1 Flareside Pickup

MB53-D/55-J6 Flareside Pickup

MB53-D/55-J7
Flareside Pickup

MB53-D/55-J9
Flareside Pickup

MB53-D/55-J18
Flareside Pickup

MB53-D/55-J22
Flareside Pickup

MB53-D/55-J26
Flareside Pickup

MB53-G/55-J30
Flareside Pickup

MB53-G/56-G1 Ford LTD Taxi

MB53-G/56-G3 Ford LTD Taxi

MB53-H/24-J1 Rhino Rod

MB53-H/24-J4 Rhino Rod

MB53-H/24-J6 Rhino Rod

MB53-H/24-J8 Rhino Rod

MB53-I/48-J1 1962 VW Beetle

MB53-I/48-J5 1962 VW Beetle

MB53-K1 Police Car

MB53-K7 Police Car

MB53-K9 Police Car

MB53-K14 Police Car

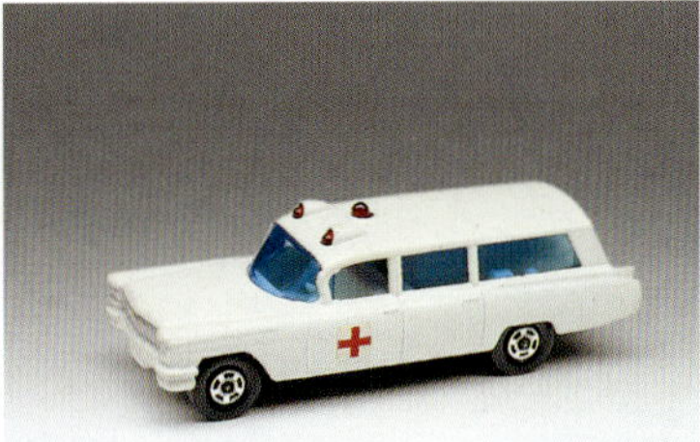

MB54A2 Cadillac Ambulance

MB54-B1 Ford Capri

MB54-B3 Ford Capri

MB54-C1 Personnel Carrier

MB54-C4 Personnel Carrier

MB54-D3 Mobile Home

MB54-D12 Mobile Home

MB54-E1 NASA Tracking Vehicle

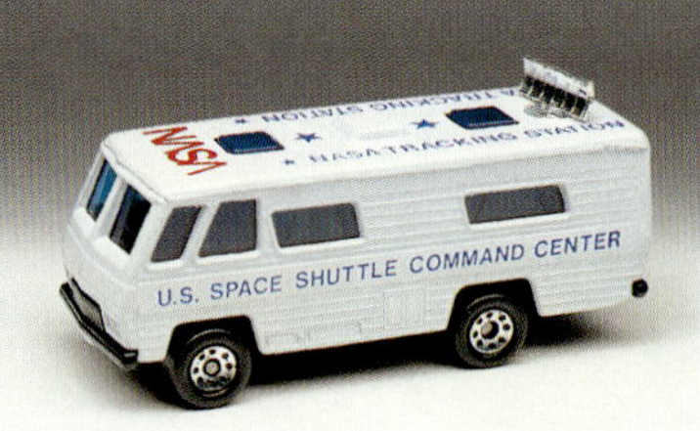
MB54-E4 NASA Tracking Vehicle

MB54-E7 NASA Tracking Vehicle

MB54-F1 Command Vehicle

MB54-F3 Command Vehicle

MB54-F14 Command Vehicle

MB54-F16 Command Vehicle

MB54-H8 Chevy Lumina

MB54-H35 Chevy Lumina

MB54-H61 Chevy Lumina

MB54-J/61-G1 Abrams Battle Tank

MB54-J/61-G2 Abrams Battle Tank

MB54-J/61-G6 Abrams Battle Tank

MB54-J/61-G12 Abrams Battle Tank

MB54-K/38-J1 Ford Crown Victoria Police Car

MB54-K/38-J2 Ford Crown Victoria Police Car

MB54-K/38-J19 Ford Crown Victoria Police Car

MB54-K/38-J26 Ford Crown Victoria Police Car

MB54-K/38-J41 Ford Crown Victoria Police Car

MB54-K/38-J46 Ford Crown Victoria Police Car

MB54-K/38-J54 Ford Crown Victoria Police Car

MB54-K/38-J58 Ford Crown Victoria Police Car

MB54-K/38-J91 Ford Crown Victoria Police Car

MB54-L/64-H13 Holden Commodore

MB54-L/64-H14 Holden Commodore

MB54-O1 Tanker Truck

MB54-O7 Tanker Truck

MB55-A1 Mercury Police Car

MB55-A2 Mercury Police Car

MB55-B1 Mercury Police Commuter

MB55-B2 Mercury Police Commuter

MB55-C1 Hellraiser

MB55-C5 Hellraiser

MB55-C8 Hellraiser

MB55-C11 Hellraiser

MB55-D1 Ford Cortina

MB55-D3 Ford Cortina

MB55-D4 Ford Cortina

MB55-D5 Ford Cortina

MB55-D12 Ford Cortina

MB55-D18 Ford Cortina

MB55-D20 Ford Cortina

MB55-E/15-D/40-E2 Ford Sierra XR4i

MB55-E/15-D/40-E6 Ford Sierra XR4i

MB55-E/15-D/40-E11 Ford Sierra XR4i

MB55-E/15-D/40-E17 Ford Sierra XR4i

MB55-E/15-D/40-E23 Ford Sierra XR4i

MB55-E/15-D/40-E40 Ford Sierra XR4i

MB55-F/41-E1 Racing Porsche 935

MB55-F/41-E6 Racing Porsche 935

MB55-F/41-E10 Racing Porsche 935

MB55-G/33F1 Mercury Sable Wagon

MB55-L/50K7 Porsche Boxster

MB55-L/50-K8 Porsche Boxster

MB55-L/50-K14 Porsche Boxster

MB55-L/50-K16 Porsche Boxster

MB55-N1 Amphibious Personnel Carrier

MB55-P1 Dump Truck

MB55-P5 Dump Truck

MB55-P7 Dump Truck

MB56-A1 BMC Pininfarina

MB56-A3 BMC Pininfarina

MB56-A4 BMC Pininfarina

MB56-A6 BMC Pininfarina

MB56-A7 BMC Pininfarina

MB56-B1 Hi Tailer

MB56-B4 Hi Tailer

MB56-B7 Hi Tailer

MB56-C1 Mercedes 450SEL

MB56-C2 Mercedes 450SEL

MB56-C3 Mercedes 450SEL

MB56-C7 Mercedes 450SEL

MB56-C8 Mercedes 450SEL

MB56-C10 Mercedes 450SEL

MB56-C12 Mercedes 450SEL

MB56-D/5-E1 Peterbilt Tanker

MB56-D/5-E6 Peterbilt Tanker

MB56-D/5-E8 Peterbilt Tanker

MB56-D/5-E9 Peterbilt Tanker

MB56-D/5-E10 Peterbilt Tanker

MB56-D/5-E13 Peterbilt Tanker

MB56-D/5-E14 Peterbilt Tanker

MB56-D/5-E16 Peterbilt Tanker

MB56-D/5-E17 Peterbilt Tanker

MB56-D/5-E19 Peterbilt Tanker

MB56-D/5-E21 Peterbilt Tanker

MB56-D/5-E38 Peterbilt Tanker

MB56-D/5-E42 Peterbilt Tanker

MB56-D/5-E43 Peterbilt Tanker

MB56-I/59-I1 Isuzu Rodeo

MB56-I/59-I2 Isuzu Rodeo

MB56-I/59-I3 Isuzu Rodeo

MB56-I/59-I5 Isuzu Rodeo

MB56-I/59-I7 Isuzu Rodeo

MB56-I/59-I8 Isuzu Rodeo

MB56-I/59-I10 Isuzu Rodeo

MB56-I/59-I15 Isuzu Rodeo

MB56-I/59-I19 Isuzu Rodeo

MB56-I/59-I20 Isuzu Rodeo

MB56-I/59-I23 Isuzu Rodeo

MB56-K/51-M1
Mercedes A Class

MB56-K/51-M2
Mercedes A Class

MB56-K/51-M3
Mercedes A Class

MB56-K/51-M7
Mercedes A Class

MB56-M2 Dodge Viper GTSR

MB56-M2 Dodge Viper GTSR

MB56-N1 Bucket Fire Truck

MB56-N3 Bucket Fire Truck

MB56-N6 Bucket Fire Truck

MB56-N8 Bucket Fire Truck

MB56-N9 Bucket Fire Truck

MB56-02 Buildboard Truck

MB57-A1 Land Rover Fire Truck

MB57-B1 Eccles Caravan

MB57-B5 Eccles Caravan

MB57-C1 Wildlife Truck

MB57-C13 Wildlife Truck

MB57-D1 4 X 4 Mini Pickup

MB57-D3 4 X 4 Mini Pickup

MB57-D4 4 X 4 Mini Pickup

MB57-D6 4 X 4 Mini Pickup

MB57-E1 Carmichael Commando

MB57-E3 Carmichael Commando

MB57-H/50-G1 Mack Auxiliary Power Truck

MB57-H/50-G4 Mack Auxiliary Power Truck

MB57H/50-G9 Mack Auxiliary Power Truck

MB57-H/50-G14 Mack Auxiliary Power Truck

MB57-H/50-G17 Mack Auxiliary Power Truck

MB57-H/50-G23 Mack Auxiliary Power Truck

MB57-H/50-G31 Mack Auxiliary Power Truck

MB57-H/50-G32 Mack Auxiliary Power Truck

MB57-H/50-G40 Mack Auxiliary Power Truck

MB57-I/52-G1 Snow Groomer

MB57-I/52-G2 Snow Groomer

MB57-I/52-G5 Snow Groomer

MB57-K1 2000 Chevrolet Corvette

MB57-K2 2000 Chevrolet Corvette

MB57-K4 2000 Chevrolet Corvette

MB57-L1 Trash Truck

MB57-L3 Trash Truck

MB57-L5 Trash Truck

MB58-A1 DAF Girder Truck

MB58-A2 DAF Girder Truck

MB58-B1 Woosh-N-Push

MB58-B3 Woosh-N-Push

MB58-B5 Woosh-N-Push

MB58-B8 Woosh-N-Push

MB58-B9 Woosh-N-Push

MB58-C3 Faun Dump Truck

MB58-C4 Faun Dump Truck

MB58-D1 Ruff Trek

MB58-D2 Ruff Trek

MB58-E1 Mercedes Benz 300E

MB58-E3 Mercedes Benz 300E

MB58-E4 Mercedes Benz 300E

MB58-J/53-J1 Truck Camper

MB58-J/53-J2 Truck Camper

MB58-J/53-J5 Truck Camper

MB58-K1 International Armored Car

MB58-K8 International Armored Car

MB58-K18 International Armored Car

MB58-L1 Chevy Avalanche

MB58-L5 Chevy Avalanche

MB59-A2 Ford Galaxie Fire Chief

MB59-B1 Mercury Fire Chief Car

MB59-B6 Mercury Fire Chief Car

MB59-B8 Mercury Fire Chief Car

MB59-B24 Mercury
Fire Chief Car

MB59-B25 Mercury
Fire Chief Car

MB59-B32 Mercury
Fire Chief Car

MB59-C2 Planet Scout

MB59-C3 Planet Scout

MB59-C4 Planet Scout

MB59-C5 Planet Scout

MB59-C6 Planet Scout

MB59-D1 Porsche 959

MB59-D20 Porsche 959

MB59-D28 Porsche 959

MB59-D32 Porsche 959

MB59-D33 Porsche 959

MB59-F/61-D/28-J1 Ford
T-Bird Turbo Coupe

MB59-F/61-D/28-J11 Ford
T-Bird Turbo Coupe

MB59-G/63-I1
Aston Martin DB7

MB59-G/63-I2 Aston Martin DB7

MB59-G/63-I8 Aston Martin DB7

MB59-H/56-J2 Chevrolet
Camaro Police Car

MB59-H/56-J8 Chevrolet
Camaro Police Car

MB59-H/56-J10 Chevrolet
Camaro Police Car

MB59-H/56-J20 Chevrolet
Camaro Police Car

MB59-H/56-J27 Chevrolet
Camaro Police Car

MB59-H/56-J34 Chevrolet
Camaro Police Car

MB59-H/56-J37 Chevrolet Camaro Police Car

MB59-J/54-N1 White Water Raft Boat

MB59-J/54-N2 White Water Raft Boat

MB59-J/54-N3 White Water Raft Boat

MB59-J/54-N4 White Water Raft Boat

MB59-J/54-N5 White Water Raft Boat

MB59-L1 Chrysler Panel Cruiser

MB59-L6 Chrysler Panel Cruiser

MB59-L14 Chrysler Panel Cruiser

MB59-M1 Cycle with Sidecar

MB59-M5 Cycle with Sidecar

MB59-M12 Cycle with Sidecar

MB60-A1 Site Hut Truck

MB60-B1 Lotus Super Seven

MB60-B3 Lotus Super Seven

MB60-C1 Holden Pickup

MB60-C8 Holden Pickup

MB60-C10 Holden Pickup

MB60-C13 Holden Pickup

MB60-C14 Holden Pickup

MB60-C19 Holden Pickup

MB60-D2 Piston Popper

MB60-D9 Piston Popper

MB60-F/12-G/48-G1 Pontiac Firebird Racer

MB60-F/12-G/48-G7
Pontiac Firebird Racer

MB60-F/12-G/48-G11
Pontiac Firebird Racer

MB60-F/12-G/48-G21
Pontiac Firebird Racer

MB60-F/12-G/48-G24
Pontiac Firebird Racer

MB60-F/12-G/48-G25
Pontiac Firebird Racer

MB60-F/12-G/48-G26
Pontiac Firebird Racer

MB60-G/57-G1 Ford Transit Van

MB60-G/57-G4 Ford Transit Van

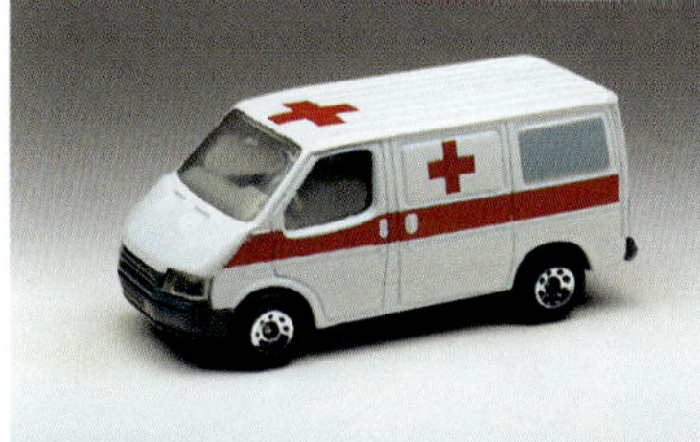

MB60-G/57-G5
Ford Transit Van

MB60-G/57-G30
Ford Transit Van

MB60-G/57-G36
Ford Transit Van

MB60-K/55M-1
Rescue Chopper

MB60-K/55-M5
Rescue Chopper

MB60-K/55-M9
Rescue Chopper

MB60-M1 Mobile Light Truck

MB60-M3 Mobile Light Truck

MB61-A2 Blue Shark

MB61-A6 Blue Shark

MB61-A9 Blue Shark

MB61-B1 Wreck Truck

MB61-B2 Wreck Truck

MB61-B5 Wreck Truck

MB61-B10 Wreck Truck

MB61-B16 Wreck Truck

MB61-B24 Wreck Truck

MB61-B28 Wreck Truck

MB61-C2 Peterbilt Wrecker

MB61-C4 Peterbilt Wrecker

MB61-C5 Peterbilt Wrecker

MB61-C8 Peterbilt Wreck Truck

MB61-C10 Peterbilt Wrecker

MB61-C24 Peterbilt Wrecker

MB61-E/37-H1 Nissan 300ZX

MB61-E/37-H20 Nissan 300ZX

MB61-E/37-H22 Nissan 300ZX

MB61-E/37-H23 Nissan 300ZX

MB61-E/37-H28 Nissan 300ZX

MB61-E/37-H29 Nissan 300ZX

MB61-E/37-H31 Nissan 300ZX

MB61-K/56-L1 UFO

MB61-M/38-N1 Rescue Boat

MB61-M/38-N3 Rescue Boat

MB61-M/38-N5 Rescue Boat

MB61-N1 Ford Falcon

MB61-O1 Ice Breaker

MB61-O6 Ice Breaker

MB61-P1 Dennis Sabre

MB61-P3 Dennis Sabre

MB61-Q1 BMW Z4

MB62-A1 Mercury Cougar

MB62-A2 Mercury Cougar

MB62-B1 Cougar Dragster

MB62-B3 Cougar Dragster

MB62-B5 Cougar Dragster

MB62-C1 Renault 17TL

MB62-C4 Renault 17TL

MB62-C4 Renault 17TL

MB62-D2 Chevrolet Corvette

MB62-D7 Chevrolet Corvette

MB62-D12 Chevrolet Corvette

MB62-F/31-F2 Rolls Royce Silver Cloud

MB62-G1 Volvo 760

MB62-G3 Volvo 760

MB62-H/64-F1 Oldsmobile Aerotech

MB62-H/64-F3 Oldsmobile Aerotech

MB62-H/64-F4 Oldsmobile Aerotech

MB62-J/72-N1 Street Streak

MB62-J/72-N3 Street Streak

MB62-J/72-N6 Street Streak

MB62-L/42-G2 Pop Up Camper

MB62-M/35-N1 Hovercraft

MB62-N/35-N2 Hovercraft

MB62-M/35-N4 Hovercraft

MB62-N1 GMC Terradyne

MB62-N3 GMC Terradyne

MB62-O1 Nissan Z

MB63-A1 Dodge Crane Truck

MB63-B1 Freeway Gas Tanker

MB63-B2 Freeway Gas Tanker

MB63-B8 Freeway Gas Tanker

MB63-B9 Freeway Gas Tanker

MB63-B12 Freeway Gas Tanker

MB63-B18 Freeway Gas Tanker

MB63-B19 Freeway Gas Tanker

MB63-B20 Freeway Gas Tanker

MB63-B23 Freeway Gas Tanker

MB63-B25 Freeway Gas Tanker

MB63-D3 Dodge Challenger

MB63-D4 Dodge Challenger

MB63-E/13-E4 Snorkel

MB63-E/13-E6 Snorkel

MB63-E/13-E9 Snorkel

MB63-E/13-E13 Snorkel

MB63-E/13-E17 Snorkel

MB63-E/13-E20 Snorkel

MB63-E/13-E24 Snorkel

MB63-E/13-E25 Snorkel

MB63-E/13-E32 Snorkel

MB63-J/68-K/4-H16 Ford Falcon

MB63-J/68-K/4-H17 Ford Falcon

MB63-J/68-K/4-H24 Ford Falcon

MB63-J/68-K/4-H25 Ford Falcon

MB63-N1 Airboat

MB63-01 Rescue Helicopter

MB63-03 Rescue Helicopter

MB63-07 Rescue Helicopter

MB63-P2 Chevrolet Corvette C6

MB64-A2 M.G. 1100

MB64-B1 Slingshot Dragster

MB64-B4 Slingshot Dragster

MB64-B6 Slingshot Dragster

MB64-B8 Slingshot Dragster

MB64-C3 Fire Chief

MB64-D/9-G2
Caterpillar Bulldozer

MB64-D/9-G5
Caterpillar Bulldozer

MB64-D/9-G8
Caterpillar Bulldozer

MB64-D/9-G24
Caterpillar Bulldozer

MB64-D/9-G28
Caterpillar Bulldozer

MB64-D/9-G29
Caterpillar Bulldozer

MB64-D/9-G34
Caterpillar Bulldozer

MB64-D/9-G36
Caterpillar Bulldozer

MB64-D/9-G38
Caterpillar Bulldozer

MB64-I/59-K1 VW Transporter

MB64-I/59-K2 VW Transporter

MB64-I/59-K7 VW Transporter

MB64-I/59-K11 VW Transporter

MB64-I/59-K32 VW Transporter

MB64-J1 Mercedes
Benz Actross 1857

MB64-L1 Fork Lift Truck

MB64-L3 Fork Lift Truck

MB64-L8 Fork Lift Truck

MB64-M1 Pontiac Solstice

MB65-A1 Saab Sonnett III

MB65-B2 Airport Coach

MB65-B7 Airport Coach

MB65-B12 Airport Coach

MB65-B17 Airport Coach

MB65-B20 Airport Coach

MB65-B24 Airport Coach

MB65-B27 Airport Coach

MB65-B28 Airport Coach

MB65-C9 Bandag Bandit

MB65-D1 F.1 Racer

MB65-D6 F.1 Racer

MB65-D30 F.1 Racer

MB65-G1 Ford F150 Pickup

MB65-G5 Ford F150 Pickup

MB65-G7 Ford F150 Pickup

MB65-G10 Ford F150 Pickup

MB65-G14 Ford F150 Pickup

MB65-I/45-G1 Jeep Grand Cherokee

MB65-I/45-G4 Jeep Grand Cherokee

MB65-I/45-G10 Jeep Grand Cherokee

MB65-K/60-N1 Ice Cream Truck

MB65-K/60-N3 Ice Cream Truck

MB65-K/60-N5 Ice Cream Truck

MB65-K/60-N6 Ice Cream Truck

MB65-L/7-F2 Ferrari 360 Spider

MB65-L/7-F3 Ferrari 360 Spider

MB65-L/7-F5 Ferrari 360 Spider

MB66-A4 Greyhound Bus

MB66-B2 Mazda RX500

MB66-B3 Mazda RX500

MB66-B8 Mazda RX500

MB66-B10 Mazda RX500

MB66-B13 Mazda RX500

MB66-C15 Ford Transit

MB66-C15 Ford Transit

MB66-D1 Super Boss

MB66-E/46-E2 Sauber Group C Racer

MB66-E/46-E4 Sauber Group C Racer

MB66-E/46-E12 Sauber Group C Racer

MB66-E/46-E13 Sauber Group C Racer

MB66-E/46-E22 Sauber Group C Racer

MB66-E/46-E24 Sauber Group C Racer

MB66-F/55-H/73-G1 Rolls Royce Silver Spirit

MB66-F/55-H/73-G2 Rolls Royce Silver Spirit

MB66-F/55-H/73-G4 Rolls Royce Silver Spirit

MB66-F/55-H/73-G5 Rolls Royce Silver Spirit

MB66-G/46-G1 Opel Calibra

MB66-I1 MGF

MB66-I2 MGF

MB66-I3 MGF

MB66-I6 MGF

MB66-J/61-J4 Land Rover Freelander

MB66-J/61-J7 Land Rover Freelander

MB66-J/61-J13 Land Rover Freelander

MB66-L/32-H1 Mercedes Benz S500

MB66-L/32-H2 Mercedes Benz S500

MB66-L/32-H10 Mercedes Benz S500

MB66-M2 Radar Truck

MB66-M4 Radar Truck

MB66-M7 Radar Truck

MB66-M11 Radar Truck

MB66-N1 Limousine

MB66-N11 Limousine

MB66-O1 Dodge Ram SRT-10

MB66-O3 Dodge Ram SRT-10

MB66-P1 City Police Car

MB67-A2 Volkswagen 1600TL

MB67-A6 Volkswagen 1600TL

MB67-B3 Hot Rocker

MB67-B6 Hot Rocker

MB67-C1 Datsun 260Z 2 + 2

MB67-C15 Datsun 260Z 2 + 2

MB67-C19 Datsun 260Z 2 + 2

MB67-C31 Datsun 260Z 2 + 2

MB67-D2 Flame Out

MB67-F/11-F3
Lamborghini Countach

MB67-F/11-F5
Lamborghini Countach

MB67-F/11-F10
Lamborghini Countach

MB67-F/11-F21
Lamborghini Countach

MB67-F/11-F22
Lamborghini Countach

MB67-F/11-F29
Lamborghini Countach

MB67-F/11-F39
Lamborghini Countach

MB67-F/11-F40
Lamborghini Countach

MB67-F/11-F43 Lamborghini Countach

MB67-F/11-F46 Lamborghini Countach

MB67-G1 Ikarus Coach

MB67-G4 Ikarus Coach

MB67-G5 Ikarus Coach

MB67-G6 Ikarus Coach

MB67-G13 Ikarus Coach

MB67-G16 Ikarus Coach

MB67-H/62-K3 Ford Expedition

MB67-H/62-K5 Ford Expedition

MB67-H/62-K10 Ford Expedition

MB67-H/62-K11 Ford Expedition

MB67-H/62-K22 Ford Expedition

MB67-J1 Land Rover Discovery

MB67-J4 Land Rover Discovery

MB67-J6 Land Rover Discovery

MB67-K2 Foam Fire Truck

MB67-K4 Foam Fire Truck

MB67-K7 Foam Fire Truck

MB68-A3 Porsche 910

MB68-A4 Porsche 910

MB68-A6 Porsche 910

MB68-A9 Porsche 910

MB68-B1Cosmobile

MB68-B3 Cosmobile

MB68-C6 Cosmobile

MB68-C8 Cosmobile

MB68-C9 Cosmobile

MB68-C1 Chevy Van

MB68-C3 Chevy Van

MB68-C4 Chevy Van

MB68-C8 Chevy Van

MB68-C9 Chevy Van

MB68-C11 Chevy Van

MB68-C13 Chevy Van

MB68-C14 Chevy Van

MB68-C15 Chevy Van

MB68-C16 Chevy Van

MB68-C19 Chevy Van

MB68-E/64-E1 Dodge Caravan

MB68-E/64-E2 Dodge Caravan

MB68-E/64-E6 Dodge Caravan

MB68-E/64-E7 Dodge Caravan

MB68-E/64-E9 Dodge Caravan

MB68-G/73-D1
TV News Truck

MB68-G/73-D7
TV News Truck

MB68-G/73-D10
TV News Truck

MB68-G/73-D
TV News Truck

MB68-G/73-D20
TV News Truck

MB68-G/73-D21
TV News Truck

MB68-G/73-D26
TV News Truck

MB68-G/73-D29
TV News Truck

MB68-G/73-D33
TV News Truck

MB68-I1 Stinger

MB68-I3 Stinger

MB68-I4 Stinger

MB68-J/58-I1 Porsche 911 GT1

MB68-J/58-I2 Porsche 911 GT1

MB68-J/58-I3 Porsche 911 GT1

MB68-J/58-I5 Porsche 911 GT1

MB68-J/58-I6 Porsche 911 GT1

MB68-J/58-I13 Porsche 911 GT1

MB68-J/58-I16 Porsche 911 GT1

MB68-J/58-I18 Porsche 911 GT1

MB68-L/30-J1 Dennis Sabre

MB68-L/30-J3 Dennis Sabre

MB68-L/30-J4 Dennis Sabre

MB68-L/30-J6 Dennis Sabre

MB68-I/30-J11 Dennis Sabre

MB68-M/63-K1 '98
Jeep Wrangler

MB68-M/63-K2 '98
Jeep Wrangler

MB68-M/63-K4 '98
Jeep Wrangler

MB68-N/55-Q1 Mercedes Benz E430 Wagon

MB68-N/55-Q2 Mercedes Benz 430E Wagon

MB68-N/55-Q3 Mercedes Benz E430 Wagon

MB68-N/55-Q5 Mercedes Benz E430 Wagon

MB68-O/48-K1 Air Lift

MB68-O/48-K4 Air Lift

MB68-O/48-K5 Air Lift

MB68-O/48-K8 Air Lift

MB68-Q1 Speedboat

MB68-Q2 Speedboat

MB68-Q5 Speedboat

MB69-A1 Rolls Royce Silver Shadow Coupe

MB69-A7 Rolls Royce Silver Shadow Coupe

MB69-A13 Rolls Royce Silver Shadow Coupe

MB69-A21 Rolls Royce Silver Shadow Coupe

MB69-B1 Turbo Fury

MB69-B3 Turbo Fury

MB69-B6 Turbo Fury

MB69-C2 Armored Truck

MB69-C3 Armored Truck

MB69-D2 '33 Willys Street Rod

MB69-D6 '33 Willys Street Rod

Mb69-D13 '33 Willys Street Rod

MB69-D15 '33 Willys Street Rod

MB69-F2 Volvo 480ES

MB69-H/20-G3 '68 Ford Mustang Cobra Jet

MB69-H/20-G6 '68 Ford Mustang Cobra Jet

MB69-I/19-E1 BMW 328i

MB69-I/19-E4 BMW 328i

MB69-I/19-E6 BMW 328i

MB69-I/19-E8 BMW 328i

MB69-J/8-M1 Lotus Elise

MB69-J/8-M2 Lotus Elise

MB69-J/8-M3 Lotus Elise

MB69-J/8-M7 Lotus Elise

MB69-J8 Lotus Elise

MB69-K4 Humvee

MB69-K5 Humvee

MB69-L/9-J1
Porsche 911 Turbo

MB69-L/9-J5
Porsche 911 Turbo

MB70-A Ford Grit Spreader

MB70-B11 Dodge Dragster

MB70-B12 Dodge Dragster

MB70-B13 Dodge Dragster

MB70-B14 Dodge Dragster

MB70-C2 S.P. Gun

MB70-D1 Ferrari 308 GTB

MB70-D6 Ferrari 308 GTB

MB70-D10 Ferrari 308 GTB

MB70-D16 Ferrari 308 GTB

MB70-E/45-D3 Ford Cargo Skip Truck

MB70-E/45-D6 Ford Cargo Skip Truck

MB70-E/45-D7 Ford Cargo Skip Truck

MB70-H/64-G1 '70 Pontiac GTO

MB70-H/64-G10 '70 Pontiac GTO

MB70-H/64-G13 '70 Pontiac GTO

MB70-H/64-G20 '70 Pontiac GTO

MB70-I1 Mercedes E Class

MB70-I2 Mercedes E Class

MB70-I3 Mercedes E Class

MB70-I5 Mercedes E Class

MB70-I8 Mercedes E Class

MB70-J/65-H1 '99 Chevrolet Silverado 4 X 4

MB70-J/65-H2 '99 Chevrolet Silverado 4 X 4

MB70-J/65-H3 '99 Chevrolet Silverado 4 X 4

MB70-J/65-H6 '99 Chevrolet Silverado 4 X 4

MB70-J/65-H7 '99 Chevrolet Silverado 4 X 4

MB70-K/57-M1 Chevy SSR

MB70-K/57-M5 Chevy SSR

MB70-L1 VW W12 Concept

MB70-L7 VW W12 Concept

MB70-L9 VW W12 Concept

MB71-A1 Ford Heavy Wreck Truck

MB71-B1 Jumbo Jet

MB71-C/12-I1 Cattle Truck

MB71-C/12-I8 Cattle Truck

MB71-C/12-I12 Cattle Truck

MB71-C/12-I20 Cattle Truck

MB71-C/12-I21 Cattle Truck

MB71-C/12-I25 Cattle Truck

MB71-C/12-I29 Cattle Truck

MB71-C/12-I52 Cattle Truck

MB71-C/12-I70 Cattle Truck

MB71-C/12-I75 Cattle Truck

MB71-C/12-I79 Cattle Truck

MB71-C/12-I80 Cattle Truck

MB71-C/12-I81 Cattle Truck

MB71-D/32-F/72-L1 '62 Corvette

MB71-D/32-F/72-L5 '62 Corvette

MB71-D/32-F/72-L8 '62 Corvette

MB71-D/32-F/72-L12 '62 Corvette

MB71-D/32-F/72-L15 '62 Corvette

MB71-D/32-F/72-L25 '62 Corvette

MB71-D/32-F/72-L30 '62 Corvette

MB71-D/32-F/72-L36 '62 Corvette

MB71-D/32-F/72-L46 '62 Corvette

MB71-G/59-E1
Porsche 944 Turbo

MB71-G/59-E4
Porsche 944 Turbo

MB71-G/59-E8
Porsche 944 Turbo

MB71-H/43-J1 Ford
Mustang Cobra

MB71-H/43-J5 Ford
Mustang Cobra

MB71-H/43-J10 Ford
Mustang Cobra

MB71-H/43-J16 Ford
Mustang Cobra

MB71-I3 Jaguar
XK8 Convertible

MB71-I4 Jaguar
XK8 Convertible

MB71-I5 Jaguar
XK8 Convertible

MB71-I13 Jaguar
XK8 Convertible

MB71-M2 Jeep Liberty

MB71-M3 Jeep Liberty

MB71-N1 Jeep Willys Concept

MB71-N4 Jeep Willys Concept

MB72-A1 Jeep

MB72-A3 Jeep

MB72-B2 Hovercraft SRN6

MB72-C1 Bomag Road Roller

MB72-D1 Maxi Taxi

MB72-E1 Dodge Commando

MB72-E6 Dodge Commando

MB72-E9 Dodge Commando

MB72-E10 Dodge Commando

MB72-F1 Sand Racer

MB72-G/65-E1 Plane Transporter

MB72-G/65-E3 Plane Transporter

MB72-G/65-E9 Plane Transporter

MB72-G/65-E10 Plane Transporter

MB72-G/65-E10 Plane Transporter

MB72-I/65-F1 Cadillac Allante

MB72-I/65-F3 Cadillac Allante

MB72-I/65-F9 Cadillac Allante

MB72-O/54-M1 Chevy K1500 Pickup

MB72-O/54-M8 Chevy K1500 Pickup

MB72-O/54-M91 Chevy K1500 Pickup

MB72-O/54-M11 Chevy K1500 Pickup

MB72-O/54-M14 Chevy K1500 Pickup

MB72-P1 '65 Ford Mustang Fastback

MB72-K/50-M1 Porsche 911 Carrera Convertible

MB72-K/50-M2 Porsche 911 Carrera Convertible

MB72-R8 Porsche 911 Carrera Convertible

MB72-R12 Porsche 911 Carrera Convertible

MB72-S/52-H1 VW Delivery Van

MB72-T1 Rescue Crane

MB72-T3 Rescue Crane

MB72-U1 Volkswagen Microbus

MB72-U12 Volkswagen Microbus

MB72-U16 Volkswagen Microbus

MB72-V1 Chrysler PT Cruiser Convertible

MB72-W1 Bulldozer

MB73-A1 Mercury Commuter

MB73-A2 Mercury Commuter

MB73-A3 Mercury Commuter

MB73-B/70-G/77B-1 Weasel

MB73-B/70-G/77-B10 Weasel

MB73-B/70-G/77-B13 Weasel

MB73-C/55-I/25-H1 Model A Ford

MB73-C/55-I/25-H4 Model A Ford

MB73-C/55-I/25-H5 Model A Ford

MB73-C/55-I/25-H8 Model A Ford

MB73-C/55-I/25-H11 Model A Ford

MB73-C/55-I/25-H12 Model A Ford

MB73-C/55-I/25-H18 Model A Ford

MB73-C/55-I/25-H21 Model A Ford

MB73-E/27-E1 Mercedes Tractor

MB73-E/27-E5 Mercedes Tractor

MB73-E/27-E6 Mercedes Tractor

MB73-E/27-E7 Mercedes Tractor

MB73-E/27-E9 Mercedes Tractor

MB73-H/47-F1 Rotwheeler

MB73-H/47-F3 Rotwheeler

MB73-H/47-F7 Rotwheeler

MB73-J3 1955 Chevy Bel Air Hard Top

MB73-L/59-N1 Pontiac Piranha

MB73-L/59-N3 Pontiac Piranha

MB73-M2 Smart Cabrio

MB73-N1 Hummer H2 SUV Concept

MB74-A1 Daimler Bus

MB74-A3 Daimler Bus

MB74-A5 Daimler Bus

MB74-B3 Toe Joe

MB74-B7 Toe Joe

MB74-B13 Toe Joe

MB74-B15 Toe Joe

MB74-B22 Toe Joe

MB74-C1 Cougar Villager

MB74-C7 Cougar Villager

MB74-D1 Orange Peel

MB74-F1 Ford Mustang GT

MB74-F5 Ford Mustang GT

MB74-F6 Ford Mustang GT

MB74-H/14-H1 Grand Prix Racing Car

MB74-H/14-H2 Grand Prix Racing Car

MB74-H/14-H26 Grand Prix Racing Car

MB74-H/14-H31 Grand Prix Racing Car

MB74-J/61-I11 Formula 1

MB74-J/61-I18 Formula 1

MB74-J/61-I20 Formula 1

MB74-M1 BMW Z3

MD74 M1 BMW Z3

MB74-N1 Opel Frogster

MB74-N5 Opel Frogster

MB75-A1 Ferrari Berlinetta

MB75-A4 Ferrari Berlinetta

MB75-B1 Alfa Carabo

MB75-B5 Alfa Carabo

MB75-B6 Alfa Carabo

MB75-C2 Seasprite Helicopter

MB75-D/60-J/30-H1 Helicopter

MB75-D/60-J/30-H5 Helicopter

MB75-D/60-J/30-H14 Helicopter

MB75-D/60-J/30-H15 Helicopter

MB75-D/60-J/30-H28 Helicopter

MB75-D/60-J/30-H44 Helicopter

MB75-D/60-J/30-H50 Helicopter

MB75-D/60-J/30-H52 Helicopter

MB75-D/60-J/30-H53 Helicopter

MB75-D/60-J/30-H54 Helicopter

MB75-E/78-B1 Ferrari Testarossa

MB75-E/78-B27
Ferrari Testarossa

MB75-E/78-B34
Ferrari Testarossa

MB75-E/78-B35
Ferrari Testarossa

MB75-G/21-H1 Ferrari F50

MB75-G/21-H7 Ferrari F50

MB75-G/21-H8 Ferrari F50

MB75-G/21-H29 Ferrari F50

MB75-G/21-H30 Ferrari F50

MB75-G/21-H36 Ferrari F50

MB75-G/21-H41 Ferrari F50

MB75-G/21-H44 Ferrari F50

MB75-I1 '57 Chevy
Corvette Hard Top

MB75-J/55-O1 Golf Cart

MB75-K1 Water Pumper

MB75-K6 Water Pumper

MB75-L1 Mini Cooper S

MB75-L4 Mini Cooper S

MB76-A1 Savanna RX-7

MB76-A2 Savanna RX-7

MB76-A3 Savanna RX-7

MB76-A4 Savanna RX-7

MB76-D/66-K1
International Pumper

MB76-D/66-K5
International Pumper

MB76-D/66-K8
International Pumper

MB76-D/66-K15
International Pumper

MB76-D/66-K18
International Pumper

MB76-D/66-K20
International Pumper

MB77-A1 Toyota Celica XX

MB77-A2 Toyota Celica XX

MB77-C/57-J/63-L1
Mercedes ML 430

MB77-C/57-J/63-L2
Mercedes ML430

MB77-C/57-J/63-L4
Mercedes ML 430

MB77-C//57-J/63-L11
Mercedes ML 430

MB78-A1 Fairlady Z

MB78-A2 Fairlady Z

MB78-A3 Fairlady Z

MB79-A1 Galant Eterna

MB79-A3 Galant Eterna

MB80-A/60-L1
Chevy Suburban

MB80-A/60-L4
Chevy Suburban

MB80-A/60-L5 Chevy Suburban

MB81-A/61-L/73-K3 Concept I
Beetle Convertible

MB81-A/61-L/73-K4 Concept
I Beetle Convertible

MB81-A/61-L/73-K11 Concept
1 Beetle Convertible

MB81-A/61-L/73-K20 Concept
1 Beetle Convertible

MB81-A/61-L/73-K22 Concept
1 Beetle Convertible

MB82-A1 Missile Launcher

MB82-A2 Missile Launcher

MB83-A/63-M3 BMW
3 Series Coupe

MB83-A/63-M6 BMW
3 Series Coupe

MB83-A/63-M8 BMW
3 Series Coupe

MB84-A/64-K2 Ford Focus

MB84-A/64-K11 Ford Focus

MB84-A/64-K19 Ford Focus

MB84-A/64-K21 Ford Focus

MB85-A1 M4 Sherman Tank

MB85-A4 M4 Sherman Tank

MB86-A1 1999
Chevrolet Silverado

MB86-A11 1999
Chevrolet Silverado

MB90-A1 Battering Ram

MB90-A4 Battering Ram

MB91-A/71-J1 4-Wheeler

MB91-A/71-J4 4-Wheeler

MB91-A/71-J7 4-Wheeler

MB91-B/71-L3 Ford
Dump/ Utility Truck

MB91-B/71-L5 Ford
Dump/ Utility Truck

MB92-A/72-Q1 Dune Buggy

MB92-A/72-Q3 Dune Buggy

MB92-A/72-Q5 Dune Buggy

MB92-A/72-Q6 Dune Buggy

MB92-A/72-Q9 Dune Buggy

MB93-A/73-I1 Dirt Bike

MB93-A/73-I3 Dirt Bike

MB93-A/73-I5 Dirt Bike

MB93-A/73-I7 Dirt Bike

MB94-A/74-K1 Snowmobile

MB94-A/74-K4 Snowmobile

MB94-A/74-K7 Snowmobile

MB95-A/75-H1 Aero Junior

MB95-A/75-H2 Aero Junior

MB96-A/3-F1 Street Cleaner

MB96-A/3-F3 Street Cleaner

MB96-A/3-F6 Street Cleaner

MB96-A/3-F10 Street Cleaner

MB97-A1 Postal
Service Delivery Truck

MB99-A1 GMC Bucket Truck

MB236-A2 Ford
Tractor with Shovel

MB237-A1 Tractor Shovel

MB533-A1 BMW Z3

MB534-A1 BMW 3 Series Cabrio

MB535-A1 BMW X5

MB710-A1 Tipping Farm Trailer

MB711-A1 Hay Farm Trailer

MB712-A1 Seeder

MB713-A1 Rotovator

MB 2-1 Savanna RX7

MB 2-2 Savanna RX7

MB 5-1 Fairlady Z

MB 5-2 Fairlady Z

J-21-A1 Toyota Celica XX

J-21-A2 Toyota Celica XX

J-22-A1 Galant Eterna

J-22-A2 Galant Eterna

LV-1 Dodge Daytona
(Las Vegas)

LV-2 Dodge Caravan
(Las Vegas)